119.00

FOR REFERENCE
Do Not Take
From This Room

Contemporary
Literary Criticism

Guide to Gale Literary Criticism Series

For criticism on	Consult these Gale series
Authors now living or who died after December 31, 1959	*CONTEMPORARY LITERARY CRITICISM (CLC)*
Authors who died between 1900 and 1959	*TWENTIETH-CENTURY LITERARY CRITICISM (TCLC)*
Authors who died between 1800 and 1899	*NINETEENTH-CENTURY LITERATURE CRITICISM (NCLC)*
Authors who died between 1400 and 1799	*LITERATURE CRITICISM FROM 1400 TO 1800 (LC)* *SHAKESPEAREAN CRITICISM (SC)*
Authors who died before 1400	*CLASSICAL AND MEDIEVAL LITERATURE CRITICISM (CMLC)*
Black writers of the past two hundred years	*BLACK LITERATURE CRITICISM (BLC)*
Authors of books for children and young adults	*CHILDREN'S LITERATURE REVIEW (CLR)*
Dramatists	*DRAMA CRITICISM (DC)*
Hispanic writers of the late nineteenth and twentieth centuries	*HISPANIC LITERATURE CRITICISM (HLC)*
Native North American writers and orators of the eighteenth, nineteenth, and twentieth centuries	*NATIVE NORTH AMERICAN LITERATURE (NNAL)*
Poets	*POETRY CRITICISM (PC)*
Short story writers	*SHORT STORY CRITICISM (SSC)*
Major authors from the Renaissance to the present	*WORLD LITERATURE CRITICISM, 1500 TO THE PRESENT (WLC)*

ISSN 0091-3421

Volume 84

Contemporary Literary Criticism

Excerpts from Criticism of the Works
of Today's Novelists, Poets, Playwrights,
Short Story Writers, Scriptwriters, and
Other Creative Writers

James P. Draper
EDITOR

Christopher Giroux
Brigham Narins
Lynn M. Spampinato
ASSOCIATE EDITORS, *CLC*

Jennifer Brostrom
Jeff Chapman
Pamela S. Dear
Jennifer Gariepy
Margaret Haerens
Drew Kalasky
Thomas Ligotti
Sean René Pollock
David Segal
Deborah A. Stanley
Janet Witalec
ASSOCIATE EDITORS

 Gale Research Inc.

An International Thomson Publishing Company

I(T)P
NEW YORK • LONDON • BONN • BOSTON • DETROIT • MADRID
MELBOURNE • MEXICO CITY • PARIS • SINGAPORE • TOKYO
TORONTO • WASHINGTON • ALBANY NY • BELMONT CA • CINCINNATI OH

STAFF

James P. Draper, *Editor*

Jennifer Brostrom, Jeff Chapman, Pamela S. Dear, Jennifer Gariepy, Christopher Giroux, Margaret Haerens, Drew Kalasky, Thomas Ligotti, Brigham Narins, Sean René Pollock, David Segal, Lynn M. Spampinato, Deborah A. Stanley, Aarti D. Stephens, Janet Witalec, *Associate Editors*

Christine Bichler, George H. Blair, Matt McDonough, *Assistant Editors*

Marlene H. Lasky, *Permissions Manager*
Margaret A. Chamberlain, Linda M. Pugliese, *Permissions Specialists*
Susan Brohman, Diane Cooper, Maria Franklin, Pamela A. Hayes, Arlene Johnson, Josephine M. Keene, Michele Lonoconus, Maureen Puhl, Shalice Shah, Kimberly F. Smilay, Barbara A. Wallace, *Permissions Associates*
Brandy C. Merritt, Tyra Y. Phillips, *Permissions Assistants*

Victoria B. Cariappa, *Research Manager*
Frank Vincent Castronova, Mary Beth McElmeel, Donna Melnychenko, Tamara C. Nott, Tracie A. Richardson, Norma Sawaya, *Research Associates*
Eva M. Felts, Shirley Gates, Michele McRobert, Michele P. Pica, Amy T. Roy, Laurel D. Sprague, *Research Assistants*

Mary Beth Trimper, *Production Director*
Catherine Kemp, *Production Assistant*

Cynthia Baldwin, *Product Design Manager*
Barbara J. Yarrow, *Graphic Services Supervisor*
Sherrell Hobbs, *Macintosh Artist*
Willie F. Mathis, *Camera Operator*

Library of Congress Catalog Card Number 76-38938
ISBN 0-8103-4993-0
ISSN 0091-3421

Printed in the United States of America
Published simultaneously in the United Kingdom
by Gale Research International Limited
(An affiliated company of Gale Research Inc.)
10 9 8 7 6 5 4 3 2 1

 Gale Research Inc., an International Thomson Publishing Company.
ITP logo is a trademark under license.

Contents

Preface vii

Acknowledgments xi

Preface

A Comprehensive Information Source
on Contemporary Literature

Named "one of the twenty-five most distinguished reference titles published during the past twenty-five years" by *Reference Quarterly*, the *Contemporary Literary Criticism (CLC)* series provides readers with critical commentary and general information on more than 2,000 authors now living or who died after December 31, 1959. Previous to the publication of the first volume of *CLC* in 1973, there was no ongoing digest monitoring scholarly and popular sources of critical opinion and explication of modern literature. *CLC*, therefore, has fulfilled an essential need, particularly since the complexity and variety of contemporary literature makes the function of criticism especially important to today's reader.

Scope of the Series

CLC presents significant passages from published criticism of works by creative writers. Since many of the authors covered by *CLC* inspire continual critical commentary, writers are often represented in more than one volume. There is, of course, no duplication of reprinted criticism.

Authors are selected for inclusion for a variety of reasons, among them the publication or dramatic production of a critically acclaimed new work, the reception of a major literary award, revival of interest in past writings, or the adaptation of a literary work to film or television.

Attention is also given to several other groups of writers—authors of considerable public interest—about whose work criticism is often difficult to locate. These include mystery and science fiction writers, literary and social critics, foreign writers, and authors who represent particular ethnic groups within the United States.

Format of the Book

Each *CLC* volume contains about 500 individual excerpts taken from hundreds of book review periodicals, general magazines, scholarly journals, monographs, and books. Entries include critical evaluations spanning from the beginning of an author's career to the most current commentary. Interviews, feature articles, and other published writings that offer insight into the author's works are also presented. Students, teachers, librarians, and researchers will find that the generous excerpts and supplementary material in *CLC* provide them with vital information required to write a term paper, analyze a poem, or lead a book discussion group. In addition, complete bibliographical citations note the original source and all of the information necessary for a term paper footnote or bibliography.

Features

A *CLC* author entry consists of the following elements:

■ The **Author Heading** cites the author's name in the form under which the author has most commonly published, followed by birth date, and death date when applicable. Uncertainty as to a birth or death date is indicated by a question mark.

■ A **Portrait** of the author is included when available.

■ A brief **Biographical and Critical Introduction** to the author and his or her work precedes the excerpted criticism. The first line of the introduction provides the author's full name, pseudonyms (if applicable), nationality, and a listing of genres in which the author has written. To provide users with easier access to information, the biographical and critical essay included in each author entry is divided into four categories: "Introduction," "Biographical Information," "Major Works," and "Critical Reception." The introductions to single-work entries—entries that focus on well-known and frequently studied books, short stories, and poems—are similarly organized to quickly provide readers with information on the plot and major characters of the work being discussed, its major themes, and its critical reception. Previous volumes of *CLC* in which the author has been featured are also listed in the introduction.

■ A list of **Principal Works** notes the most important writings by the author. When foreign-language works have been translated into English, the most common English-language version of the title follows in brackets.

■ The **Excerpted Criticism** represents various kinds of critical writing, ranging in form from the brief review to the scholarly exegesis. Essays are selected by the editors to reflect the spectrum of opinion about a specific work or about an author's literary career in general. The excerpts are presented chronologically, adding a useful perspective to the entry. All titles by the author featured in the entry are printed in boldface type, which enables the reader to easily identify the works being discussed. Publication information (such as publisher names and book prices) and parenthetical numerical references (such as footnotes or page and line references to specific editions of a work) have been deleted at the editor's discretion to provide smoother reading of the text.

■ Critical essays are prefaced by **Explanatory Notes** as an additional aid to readers. These notes may provide several types of valuable information, including: the reputation of the critic, the importance of the work of criticism, the commentator's approach to the author's work, the purpose of the criticism, and changes in critical trends regarding the author.

■ A complete **Bibliographical Citation** designed to help the user find the original essay or book precedes each excerpt.

■ Whenever possible, a recent, previously unpublished **Author Interview** accompanies each entry.

■ A concise **Further Reading** section appears at the end of entries on authors for whom a significant amount of criticism exists in addition to the pieces reprinted in *CLC*. Each citation in this section is accompanied by a descriptive annotation describing the content of that article. Materials included in this section are grouped under various headings (e.g., Biography, Bibliography, Criticism, and Interviews) to aid users in their search for additional information. Cross-references to other useful sources published by Gale Research in which the author has appeared are also included: *Children's Literature Review, Contemporary Authors, Dictionary of Literary Biography, DISCovering Authors, Drama Criticism, Hispanic Literature Criticism, Native North American Literature, Poetry Criticism, Something about the Author, Short Story Criticism, Contemporary Authors Autobiography Series,* and *Something about the Author Autobiography Series.*

Other Features

CLC also includes the following features:

- An **Acknowledgments** section lists the copyright holders who have granted permission to reprint material in this volume of *CLC*. It does not, however, list every book or periodical reprinted or consulted during the preparation of the volume.

- Each new volume of *CLC* includes a **Cumulative Topic Index,** which lists all literary topics treated in *CLC, NCLC, TCLC,* and *LC 1400-1800.*

- A **Cumulative Author Index** lists all the authors who have appeared in the various literary criticism series published by Gale Research, with cross-references to Gale's biographical and autobiographical series. A full listing of the series referenced there appears on the first page of the indexes of this volume. Readers will welcome this cumulated author index as a useful tool for locating an author within the various series. The index, which lists birth and death dates when available, will be particularly valuable for those authors who are identified with a certain period but whose death dates cause them to be placed in another, or for those authors whose careers span two periods. For example, Ernest Hemingway is found in *CLC,* yet a writer often associated with him, F. Scott Fitzgerald, is found in *Twentieth-Century Literary Criticism.*

- A **Cumulative Nationality Index** alphabetically lists all authors featured in *CLC* by nationality, followed by numbers corresponding to the volumes in which the authors appear.

- A **Title Index** alphabetically lists all titles reviewed in the current volume of *CLC*. Listings are followed by the author's name and the corresponding page numbers where the titles are discussed. English translations of foreign titles and variations of titles are cross-referenced to the title under which a work was originally published. Titles of novels, novellas, dramas, films, record albums, and poetry, short story, and essay collections are printed in italics, while all individual poems, short stories, essays, and songs are printed in roman type within quotation marks; when published separately (e.g., T. S. Eliot's poem *The Waste Land*), the titles of long poems are printed in italics.

- In response to numerous suggestions from librarians, Gale has also produced a **Special Paperbound Edition** of the *CLC* title index. This annual cumulation, which alphabetically lists all titles reviewed in the series, is available to all customers and is published with the first volume of *CLC* issued in each calendar year. Additional copies of the index are available upon request. Librarians and patrons will welcome this separate index: it saves shelf space, is easy to use, and is recyclable upon receipt of the following year's cumulation.

Citing *Contemporary Literary Criticism*

When writing papers, students who quote directly from any volume in the Literary Criticism Series may use the following general forms to footnote reprinted criticism. The first example pertains to material drawn from periodicals, the second to material reprinted in books:

[1]Anne Tyler, "Manic Monologue," *The New Republic* 200 (April 17, 1989), 44-6; excerpted and reprinted in *Contemporary Literary Criticism,* Vol. 58, ed. Roger Matuz (Detroit: Gale Research Inc., 1990), p. 325.

[2]Patrick Reilly, *The Literature of Guilt: From 'Gulliver' to Golding* (University of Iowa Press, 1988); excerpted and reprinted in *Contemporary Literary Criticism,* Vol. 58, ed. Roger Matuz (Detroit: Gale Research Inc., 1990), pp. 206-12.

Suggestions Are Welcome

The editor hopes that readers will find *CLC* a useful reference tool and welcomes comments about the work. Send comments and suggestions to: Editor, *Contemporary Literary Criticism,* Gale Research Inc., Penobscot Building, Detroit, MI 48226-4094.

Acknowledgments

The editors wish to thank the copyright holders of the excerpted criticism included in this volume and the permissions managers of the many book and magazine publishing companies who assisted us in securing reprint rights. We are also grateful to the staffs of the Detroit Public Library, the Library of Congress, the University of Detroit Mercy Library, Wayne State University Purdy/Kresge Library Complex, and the University of Michigan Libraries for making their resources available to us. Following is a list of the copyright holders who have granted us permission to reprint material in this volume of *CLC*. Every effort has been made to trace copyright, but if omissions have been made, please let us know.

COPYRIGHTED EXCERPTS IN *CLC*, VOLUME 84, WERE REPRINTED FROM THE FOLLOWING PERIODICALS:

Africa Today, v. 14, December, 1967. © Africa Today Associates. Reprinted by permission of *Africa Today,* Graduate School of International Studies, University of Denver, CO 80208.—*African Arts,* v. 3, 1970. © 1970 by the Regents of the University of California. Reprinted by permission of the publisher.—*African Literature Today,* n. 6, 1973. Copyright 1973 by Heinemann Educational Books Ltd. All rights reserved.—*The American Book Review,* v. 8, November-December, 1985; v. 14, December 1992-January 1993. © 1985, 1993 by *The American Book Review.* Both reprinted by permission of the publisher.—*American Indian Quarterly,* v. 5, November, 1979; v. 6, Fall-Winter, 1982; v. 7, Spring, 1983. Copyright © Society for American Indian Studies & Research 1979, 1982, 1983. All reprinted by permission of the publisher.—*Ariel: A Review of International English Literature,* v. 22, October, 1991 for "Margaret Atwood's 'Cat's Eye': Re-Viewing Women in a Postmodern World" by Earl G. Ingersoll; v. 22, October,1991 for "'Lady Oracle': The Politics of the Body" by Marilyn Patton. Copyright © 1991 The Board of Governors, The University of Calgary. Both reprinted by permission of the publisher and the respective authors.—*Belles Lettres: A Review of Books by Women,* v. 5, Summer, 1990; v. 6, Winter, 1991. Both reprinted by permission of the publisher.—*Black Images,* v. 2, Spring, 1973 for "New Perspectives on Leon Damas" by Keith Q. Warner; v. 3, 1974 for "'Pigments'—A Dialogue with Self" by E. A. Hurley. Both reprinted by permission of the respective authors.—*Book World—The Washington Post,* January 10, 1993. © 1993, *The Washington Post.* Reprinted with permission of the publisher.—*Booklist,* v. 90, February 1, 1994. Copyright © 1994 by the American Library Association. Reprinted by permission of the publisher.—*Chicago Tribune—Books,* February 28, 1993. © copyrighted 1993, Chicago Tribune Company. All rights reserved./ February 24, 1991 for "Corporate Lawyers who Lead Wild Lives" by Bill Brashler; February 23, 1992 for "Still More Lawyer-Bashing from Novelist John Grisham" by Jeffrey Toobin. © copyrighted 1991, 1992, Chicago Tribune Company. All rights reserved. Both reprinted by permission of the respective authors.—*The Christian Science Monitor,* December 27, 1991 for "Time Telescoping Tales" by Merle Rubin. © 1991 by the author. All rights reserved. Reprinted by permission of the author./ March 19, 1987; March 5, 1993. © 1987, 1993 The Christian Science Publishing Society. All rights reserved. Both reprinted by permission from *The Christian Science Monitor.*—*Commentary,* v. 83, March, 1987 for "The Schlesinger Thesis" by Kenneth S. Lynn; v. 93, June, 1992 for "Toward Yugoslavia?" by Heather MacDonald. Copyright © 1987, 1992 by the American Jewish Committee. All rights reserved. Both reprinted by permission of the publisher and the respective authors./ v. 36, July, 1963 for "New Frontiers" by Lewis A. Coser. Copyright © 1963, renewed 1991 by the American Jewish Committee. All rights reserved. Reprinted by permission of the publisher and the author.—*Commonweal,* v. 110, April 8, 1983. Copyright © 1983 Commonweal Publishing Co., Inc. Reprinted by permission of Commonweal Foundation.—*The Detroit News,* May 25, 1994. Copyright 1994, *The Detroit News,* a Gannett newspaper. Reprinted with permission of the publisher.—*Esquire,* January, 1960. Copyright © 1960, Esquire Associates. Used by courtesy of the magazine.—*French Literature Series,* v. XIX, 1992. Copyright © 1992 University of South Carolina. Reprinted by permission of the publisher.—*Harper's Bazaar,* n. 3388, March, 1994. © 1994 by The Hearst Corporation. All rights reserved. Reprinted by permission of the publisher.—*Ideologies and Literature,* v. 3, January-March, 1981. Reprinted by permission of the publisher.—*Journal of American Folklore,* v.103, April-June, 1990 for a review

PHOTOGRAPHS AND ILLUSTRATIONS APPEARING IN *CLC*, VOLUME 84, WERE RECEIVED FROM THE FOLLOWING SOURCES:

Paula Gunn Allen

1939-

American poet, critic, essayist, novelist, educator, and editor.

The following provides an overview of Allen's career through 1993.

INTRODUCTION

A renowned literary figure, an eminent scholar, and dedicated feminist, Allen attempts to educate mainstream audiences about Native American themes, issues, and concerns by promoting Native American literature as a viable and rich source of study. Her fiction and poetry frequently refer to her identity as a mixed blood and, like her critical essays and the numerous anthologies she has edited, emphasize the status of Amerindian women in various Native cultures.

Biographical Information

A registered member of the Laguna Pueblo tribe, Allen was born in Cubero, New Mexico, a rural land grant situated next to the Laguna Pueblo reservation, the Acoma reservation, and Cibola National Forest. Her mother was of Laguna Pueblo, Sioux, and Scottish descent, and her father, who grew up on a Mexican land grant in the American Southwest and once served as lieutenant-governor of New Mexico, was of Lebanese ancestry. Allen credits these mixed origins as a major influence on her writing as well as a source of hope and inspiration: "I think in some respects the whole world is a multicultural event, and it's possible, if it's possible for me to stay alive, then it's possible for the whole world to stay alive. If I can communicate, then all the different people in the world can communicate with one another." Spending her early years in Cubero, Allen was sent to a Catholic boarding school in Albuquerque at age six, and her Christian upbringing is often reflected in her writings. An avid reader, Allen encountered the works of Gertrude Stein in high school, and she notes that her early attempts at writing were highly influenced by the American novelist and poet. Allen also cites American poet Robert Creeley, under whose direction she once studied writing, and Kiowa novelist N. Scott Momaday as individuals who have had a strong impact on her work. Initially intending to become an actress, Allen attended various schools before earning a B.A. in English in 1966 and an M.F.A. in creative writing in 1968 from the University of Oregon. She received her Ph.D. in American Studies and American Indian Studies from the University of New Mexico in 1975. Since then she has taught there and at the University of California-Berkeley, the University of California-Los Angeles, and San Francisco State University. Allen has also been the recipient of numerous prizes: she has received a National Endowment for the Arts Fellowship and was awarded the 1990 Before

Columbus Foundation American Book Award for *Spider Woman's Granddaughters* (1989).

Major Works

Much of Allen's work is preoccupied with her identity as a woman, mixed blood, and lesbian in Laguna and white society. Focusing on the themes of assimilation, self-identity, and remembrance, she frequently examines the quest for spiritual wholeness. For example, her poetry collections, which include *The Blind Lion* (1974), *Shadow Country* (1982), and *Skins and Bones* (1988), often emphasize the female journey to spiritual transcendence. The search for self-actualization and an integrated self are also central to her 1983 novel, *The Woman Who Owned the Shadows,* in which the protagonist, a lesbian half blood, eventually learns to accept her sexual orientation and cultural identity rather than conform to social stereotypes. This work, which is dedicated to the Native American deity Thought Woman, additionally emphasizes the importance of storytelling in Native American culture, incorporating such diverse narrative modes as folk tales, letters, legends, dreams, and Pueblo "thought singing." Allen's scholarly works, including her popular essay collection *The Sacred Hoop* (1986), deal with women's issues, the oral tradition, lesbianism, and female deities. In *Spider Woman's Granddaughters,* an anthology of tales by Leslie Marmon Silko, Linda Hogan, Louise Erdrich, Anna Lee Waters, Pretty Shield, and other Native American women, Allen attempts to introduce "tribal women's literature" to non-Native readers. She similarly collects creation myths concerning Native American goddesses in *Grandmothers of the Light* (1991), projecting historical fact and her own insights onto these tales.

Critical Reception

Allen's works have generally received positive acclaim. Her poetry is recognized for its musical qualities and her novel, though faulted at times for its broad focus, has been praised for its examination of racism and sexism. While occasionally criticized for their lack of documentation, her nonfiction works have been lauded as attempts to preserve Native American culture for all individuals regardless of their ethnic heritage. Elizabeth I. Hanson has asserted: "Where Allen registers her strongest Western literary key is in the shade and movement of her hymns to the sacred in Native American experience. By discovering her own mode of American sacred, Allen creates her own myths; she reinvokes primordial sacred time with a contemporary profane time in order to recover and remake her self. That restored, renewed self suggests in symbolic terms a revival within Native American experience as a whole. Like Allen's own vision of self, contemporary Native Americans exist not in a romantic past but instead in a community which extends through the whole of American experience."

PRINCIPAL WORKS

The Blind Lion (poetry) 1974
Coyote's Daylight Trip (poetry) 1978
A Cannon between My Knees (poetry) 1981
Star Child (poetry) 1981
Shadow Country (poetry) 1982
Studies in American Indian Literature: Critical Essays and Course Designs [editor] (essays and nonfiction) 1983
The Woman Who Owned the Shadows (novel) 1983
The Sacred Hoop: Recovering the Feminine in American Indian Traditions (essays) 1986
Wyrds (poetry) 1987
Skins and Bones (poetry) 1988
Spider Woman's Granddaughters: Traditional Tales and Contemporary Writing by Native American Women [editor] (short stories) 1989
Grandmothers of the Light: A Medicine Woman's Sourcebook (stories and essays) 1991

CRITICISM

Kenneth Lincoln   (essay date 1982)

SOURCE: "The Now Day Indi'ns," in his *Native American Renaissance,* University of California Press, 1983, pp. 183-221.

[*An American educator and critic, Lincoln is the author of several books on Native American literature and culture. In the excerpt below, which appeared in 1982 as the foreword to* Shadow Country *and which appeared in slightly different form in the Summer 1982 issue of* Four Winds: The International Forum for Native American Art, Literature, and History, *he offers a thematic and stylistic analysis of* Shadow Country.]

Laguna mother, Lakota grandfather, Lebanese father, life on the margins of mainstream and Indian: Paula Gunn Allen lives somewhere between American norms and Native American closures. She writes in the shadows of visions, "fingering silence and sound" with a poet's touching measure. She sings of desire and grief, confusion and rage over a horizon note of loss. *Shadow Country:* that marginal zone of interfusions, neither the shadower, nor the shadowed, both and neither, in liminal transition. "I looked about me and could see that what we then were doing was like a shadow cast upon the earth from yonder vision in the heavens, so bright it was and clear," Black Elk remembered [in *Black Elk Speaks; Being the Life Story of a Holy Man of the Oglala Sioux,* 1932]. "I knew the real was yonder and the darkened dream of it was here."

Paula Allen grew up in the halfway house of mixed ancestry. This woman lives not so much in a given tribe as working to articulate her sense of the tribal, without rhetorical claims. She chooses Native American definitions, defining Native American *in* her life. Her Laguna origins come mixed. Ruth Underhill sees the Laguna Pueblo in *First Penthouse Dwellers of America* as "a refugee town of Spanish days" back many centuries, a mixture of Keresan, Shoshonean, Tanoan, and Zuñian influx with Navajo, Spanish, and immigrant Anglo settlers. Edgar Hewett elsewhere describes this settlement as "an old aggregate of tribes and clans brought more or less together by acculturation and intermixes" (*Indians of the Rio Grande Valley*).

Both part of and apart from Laguna, Allen knows only too well the tribal sense of alienation, the corresponding necessity for mutual assimilation. She lives America *and* Native America. And fall is always back of the country, under dreams of spring. Allen sees a changed America, unknown to her now, remembered lyrically as "native" for indigenous peoples. In **"Tucson: First Night"** she recalls,

> "the Road," we said,
> implying that time had no changing.
> (Like Plato in our innocence)
> clouds that were there
> are here. Now. My mind and the sky,
> one thing on the edge of surmise (sunrise).

Paula Allen rediscovers old traditions and records new Indian adaptations. Her poems shatter stereotypes of blood warriors and demure squaws. *Shadow Country* gives voice to the polychromatic shock of Indian modernism as, for example, visualized in Fritz Scholder's paintings: cowboy Indians slouch with cigarettes and dark glasses, Coors beer cans and American flag shawls, ice cream cones and flared umbrellas on horses. Scholder's *Portrait of a Massacred Indian* portrays an image of bow and plains buckskin, the warrior's head a blurred acrylic palette. *Indian Power* silhouettes a naked red torso on a lunging purple pony, Kafka not far away.

Paula Allen experiments with personal quests through poetic forms and subjects. A mood or technique carries her an uncharted distance through open forms; on the way she sets her own standards of honesty and love. The poet's body is her receptor, mind her tool, spirit her courage. Allen's *impress*ion leads toward thought; she follows a sentiment diversely, wherever it goes, without compulsion to answer or solve the problems encountered. Her poetry accepts a common "negative capability": the aloneness, irresolution, even tragedy a person lives out honestly and struggles to voice.

Allen explores a woman's self-images and self-esteems, with a girl-child's sensitivity to pain. Men stand in the distances, women foregrounded. In **"Off Reservation Blues"** she dreams the Lady of Laguna, locked in a tower of defeated fantasy, earth-fearing, behind glass and above a white-skinned figure who waves but cannot hear:

> night was coming
> and I had to speak
> raise my hand and hit the glass
> I groaned
> sound too soft to hear

The grief language of her body registers in mute acts. She braves see-through barriers of sex, race, class, education, language, "civilization," even consciousness itself in its many definitions—out of that breed no (wo)man's land of pained articulation, potentially revolutionary on the poet's tongue. Existing wholly neither Indian nor non-Indian, Allen assimilates both as best she can, through the racist fractures of native history.

Euro-Americans pull back from a dark-light otherness in mixed bloods, who are left peoples without a people when dark skins reject them too. In [**"A Stranger in My Own Life: Alienation in American Indian Prose and Poetry,"** *MELUS* 7 (Summer 1980)] Paula Allen states simply, "The breed is an Indian who is not an Indian." "That is, breeds are a bit of both worlds, and the consciousness of this makes them seem alien to Indians while making them feel alien among whites." Realistically, more than half the native peoples in America today are neither Red nor white; the majority of Indians are mixed bloods living off the reservation. Fuller bloods reject these breeds on paling racial lines and broken cultural origins.

Artist of this crossed setting, Allen uses what-is to push toward her own self-definition, however painful and complex:

> If my language is oblique
> misunderstandable—
> if I confine myself
> within demands of imaged time—

> I saw true one night:
> the keeper and the kept,
> saw myself,
> how I must
> be—not in the forests of *should*—
> but actually:
> this narrow pass,
> this sharpness of tongue,
> this blade to cut your heart out
> and offer it to the sun
> must stay quiet awhile.

She will wait, meditate, assimilate her own life, another day to speak.

On the diagonal, such a poet can write of **"Relations"** from the underside: Trickster's contrary perceptions, knowing the world from bottom up, inside out, as Peter Blue Cloud says, asshole to grin-hole. Cast out and down, Trickster knows a ground sense *in* things, as poets plead and cajole, a study of thought in its origins, and felt thought

> of dead poets, dead buffalo, dead coyotes, dead
>   waters, dead ground
> where understanding hangs in the balance,
> precariously.

Not-knowing, knowing forbidden or dangerous things, knowing obliquely, keeps this woman desperately alive, a chill in her courage to look down under words.

> cántas encantadas, wondering, de la luna, del
>   sol, del muerte,
> de la vida
> (forgotten and lost) where song is a one-time
>   shot, where
> pain and bearing in blood make the herbs of understanding bloom
> on this once new earth that is dying once again:

Dying also wakens the poet, her agony a birthing resurrection, her loss a new awareness. She knows by the shadows where we are: like memory in an afterimage, but more presently tense, absently and darkly with us.

> There are no shadows
> to tell us where we are,
> but memory of yesterday's
> perfect songs, when tomorrow was sure,
> a time of met images and kept fires:
> winter dreams that almost disappeared
> in scattered light.

Here, in canceled lines from **"The Return,"** the price of knowledge is shaded by loss, the gap between being and knowing-of-being.

Allen's clarity, within confusions openly embraced, comes by way of her need to regain that still place of earth-integrated acceptance.

> This winter or next
> we will go home again
> back to our own time and earth
> and know the silence of change and bone,
> of easy disappearance and of flight.

"The Trick is Consciousness," she says in the chapbook, *Coyote's Daylight Trip,* but an inverting trick at times, unpredictable. Backtracking romantic and traveler of memory, betrayal, secret love, the night that covers and forgives all in mystery, Coyote reminisces dreams of truths in all lights, day or night. To know is painful too often, not to know can be innocent wonder.

> The key is in remembering, in what is chosen for
>   the dream.
> In the silence of recovery we hold
> the rituals of the dawn,
> now as then.
>
> Watch

The "silence of recovery" reconciles: that looking back to witness, without questioning, without pain, momentarily.

This poet asks questions of human beings needing one another. Her poems speak of desiring out of the passion to touch and bridge distances; yet she realistically accepts this love as longing, bred out of failures and infrequencies of romance. Allen's true peace comes in accepting our common losses. She writes in **"Moonshot: 1969"** of a

> heart, a quiet cool house;
> children breathing dreams,
> whimpering sometimes to their visions;
> moon: a light softly centering inside my eyes:

But the moon's light illuminates a pale distance *between* people and things. Even light absorbs a time of loss traveling, the stars tell us; recollection falls away from immediate sensation. "The moon is still more imagination than rock," Allen argues a vision *of* reality, perceiver and consciously interpenetrant.

>   the moon reaches of the mind,
> searching with careful fingers of sense-memory,
> listening inside the ear for lost songs,
> almost forgotten footfalls,
> feeling gingerly with the tongue-tip of the
>   heart—
> this gazing, steady, frightened, is the scape of
>   moon madness,
> the certain consequence of remembering
> what is best forgot.

At cost, there is clarity in looking back, by way of an inner moon of remembrance. This is not the "real" world of things imposed on the poet, but a lyric counterstressing of freedom and will, the mind re-imagining its own world.

Paula Allen admits and accepts places/things/peoples *un*-known. She writes in the shadows between "here" and "there," crystalline in **"Snowgoose":**

> North of here where
> water marries ice,
> meaning is other than what
> I understand.

Love recedes and proves abstract for the dislocated poet, unfulfilled on Indian relocation, a dreamed need more than a comfort. Surreal ache slaps her conscious in **"Paradigm":**

> I dreamed
> of making love, of needing
> to make love, of
> not being able to. Of touching your face

in awe, of seeing the rose of life on it,
your skin a matin in a moister place.
I dreamed of a dead cat they skinned for the
   party,
a striped-grey cat that decided not to die
but got up from its skinning and began to eat.

The losses of love reflect dreams and disappointments back on this woman's desire, tensing her to search herself.

Paula Allen writes with the complete and myriad sensitivities of a woman with children, with a husband, in love, out of love, marriage, divorce, redefinition: old women with weavings and potteries, new women with separations and self-definitions, **"He na Tye Woman"** chants the waters of the ever fertile earth mother, in "recognition and remembering," through the "Long shadows of afternoon" now in the poet's life:

> (Lady, why does your love so touch me?
> (Lady, why do my hands have strength for you?
> (Lady, how could I wander so long without you?

Often, a woman's opaque teasing tints the poems, refusing linear logics and singular openings of meaning. Shared American questions place the poet, many-minded and multiplexly emotional, among her true "native" shadows, with echoes of Whitman, not to mention his descendants Pound, Williams, Olson, Creeley, and Snyder. "No you can't use me," an Indian mother defies abuse,

> but you can share
> me with me as though
> I were a two-necked wedding jar
> they make, over in Santa Clara—
> some for each of us
> enough

The poetry is feminist in an older sense. A woman's work lies at the heart of this poet's living, food and water, clothing and shelter, birthing and continuation:

> some make potteries
> some weave and spin
> remember
> the Woman/celebrate
> webs and making
> out of own flesh
> earth

In a land of sacred rain, where the Laguna *kashare* priests merge with storm clouds, often the only lasting reservoirs have been women's bowls. Pueblo potteries catch the spirits of the dead coming back in rainfall. Over centuries Pueblo women re*member* the old pots that cradle and carry water. These forms prove reusable with a sense of continuous ancestry, answering the people's daily needs:

> brown hands shaping
> earth into earth
> food for bodies
> water for fields
> they use
> old pots
> broken
> fragments
> castaway
> bits

to make new
mixed with clay
it makes strong
bowls, jars
new
she
brought
light
we remember this
as we make
the water bowl

Allen on publishing in white society:

Lynn Andrews, a white woman writer who publishes
with Harper and Row, read my novel. So she says, "I'm
going to take it to my editor." She did, and some time
went by. And apparently the editorial staff loved it; in
fact, she thought they were going to accept it. So she
called me, all excited, and says, "Where will you be if
they try to reach you" (as usual I was out of touch). So
I told her how they could reach me, and it turned out
they didn't want it. OK. And they sent me the reader's
comments, and the reader's comments were simply bizarre, on any number of levels. The point is, that if I
write a book that's about a media Indian—not a human
being, but a media Indian—I can get it published. If my
heroine walks around and says "Ugh" a lot and beats the
drums and is terribly romantic and wise and noble, I'll
get it published. Or if she talks funny and she's very poor
and browbeaten and persecuted and oppressed, I'll get
that published. But if she's a person with a mixed bag of
experiences, some good, some bad, some brutal, some en-
nobling, sometimes she's smart and sometimes she's
really dumb—if she is that kind of person, I'm not going
to get it published in any major kind of press.

Paula Gunn Allen, in an interview with Franchot
Ballinger and Brian Swann, in MELUS, *Summer,*
1983.

Jim Ruppert (essay date Spring 1983)

SOURCE: "Paula Gunn Allen and Joy Harjo: Closing the
Distance between Personal and Mythic Space," in *American Indian Quarterly,* Vol. 7, No. 1, Spring, 1983, pp. 27-
40.

[*In the following excerpt, Ruppert discusses Allen's use of
personal and mythic space in her poetry.*]

Much of Allen's work is a search for meaning, an attempt
to understand natural harmony and to place the individual in that fusion of person, land, and spirit. Each moment
is placed on a web of history, natural harmony and traditional understanding. Through this perceptive act, the
moment is given significance such as in the poem **"Jet
Plane/Dhla-nuwa,"** where the flight on the plane is seen
in scientific historical terms, personal historic terms and
in mythological terms or, as in **"Affirmation,"** where
Grandmother Spider's webs and thoughts are seen

throughout the world and the narrator sees "each journey
retracing some ancient myth."

Allen's stance is a highly meditative one wherein she
forges connections between mundane and mythic space.
Making these connections is frequently referred to as
"going home," for we see the physical journey often combined with the mythic journey and the personal search.
However, as in the poem **"Displacement,"** we see a world
today where "nothing stays in the any sense where it belongs" and home is, consequently, hard to find.

Allen's work is personal in the sense that it often is initiated by her emotional reactions to the mundane world's lack
of mythic space. This barren world is America today, but
it is where most of America places its values. In poems like
"Surfacing in Private Spaces," "The Last Fantasy," and
"The Kerner Report on Camp Creek Road," we see the average American reader lost as he/she searches for control,
for certainty, for meaning where he/she can find none. All
that remains are the tentative solutions on the mundane
plane and the despair and dissatisfaction which must follow. Perhaps Allen has followed some of these paths herself: "Our private search for meaning, / for certainty, for
a silver peg / to hang ideals on." Because of her understanding of herself and modern America, she can perceive
the significance imparted by a vision of the mythic space;
she can penetrate the illusions. Frequently, as in the poem
"Hanging Out in America," the narrator seems like a
ghost, a shade wandering the paths of America, outside
the process but watching the "alien ways empty." She
knows Americans are "dead to the visions / that could
give us life."

Allen's initial perceptual impulse is to look inward first,
to follow her emotions and perceptions, to seek truth
there, then to move out. "I play it close to my chest, look
down / and out, look inside, in city, in street, in body, both
/ ways before I move." She may act physically or write
poetry to create an image to aid perception of mythic
space. She will make the connections for herself first, then
write so as to help others make them. A good example of
this process is in the poem **"The Turning Point."** In this
poem, another person's desire to find the origin of mankind in another time—millions of years ago and on another continent—is internalized by Allen as a personal journey into herself and there to find a personal/mythic understanding.

iii

I have never dreamed of Africa
A man I knew, I married, had that vision, he
wanted the origin, hoped to find in the mud
what I now find in a bed, in a forest place on
the edge
of North America.
Origin. Primal. Emergence. Begin.
The new direction, completely unsought, with-
    out guile,
grows in me: all the directions of this time, this
place, converge and focus in these shadows, this
half-light. I am a child of water, daughter of the
    dawn.
I enter the sea, begin the long journey at last
toward, home, hardly knowing I have begun.

iv

I have always thought that *new* meant *bright:*
like water tumbling downhill on a sun-stricken
    day
pepsi images of the great commercial state.
America, the hopeless, your images have broken
    my heart.
The gods are wakening here
and the storm breaks above our heads:
oppression, this heavy air on our spirit,
oppression is at its peak.
There is new life already born
elsewhere. In the dark, the hidden moon.
I turn from you at last alien country
superimposed over my home.
I return to letting be:
all I know
goes down the earth-thick stream
into undreamed space, absorbed by heat
and crocodiles. There is no sense
of movement in this time,
as I thought *new* would be.
This is one thing.
Where humankind is born
and the ancient being of our Mother waits
I lie, across a bed,
tied by bonds I neither comprehend nor want to
no strangeness in it
no bright; but somewhere inside me
she moves.

The narrator must relinquish the things she has learned
of America: she must seek inside herself the ancient
power, the origin, the source of life. The poem ends with
the narrator—unafraid, knowing the steps, the chain of
spirit—asking for the ancient power of life to be restored
to her. Only through this personal completion can any action on the human plane with other beings be meaningful
and effective.

The poet may recoil from this formidable task, but as in
the poem **"Nos Vemos,"** there is always the sense in
Allen's work that the earth and spirit are working to re-
unite their harmony and that the mythic and mundane
space will be inevitably reunited at some point in the future. Mythic space has always been here and always will
be. It is what gives meaning to life. The holistic fabric of
meaning is like an old rug; the poet merely mends the
holes in the ancient creation. If the poet doesn't then
someone else will because the rug—the fusion of person,
spirit, and land which creates mythic space—is valuable.
It is all we have. In the poem **"Grandmother,"** Allen
speaks of Grandmother Spider's efforts in creating bright,
complete life, and of the poet's task.

    after her,
    the women and men weave blankets into tales of
        life,

    memories of light and ladders,
    infinity-eyes, and rain.
    After her I sit on my laddered rain-bearing rug
    and mend the tear with the string.

It is this fusion, this blending of mythic and personal, that
creates the perfect harmony. The old informs, strengthens
the new, as in the poem **"Womanwork,"** where present-
day women remember "The Mythic Woman" and use that

understanding to strengthen themselves much as old pottery fragments are used to strengthen new pieces. The
women's lives are informed by the mythic space and they
celebrate it.

Allen on thematic aspects of her work:

I've been entirely preoccupied with colonization for
probably all my writing life, and that would be twenty-
five years. And metaphorically light and dark, shadows
and sun, death and life, and transformation. And now
I'm moving much more toward transformation and
magic. And not colonization as it's going on so much,
but what it brings about, what arises from this phenomenon. I've always been interested in what Elaine Jahner
calls mythologizing the cities and finding out where the
non-human, the wilderness, dimensions are in the city.
Instead of seeing it as a dead thing, seeing it as a live
thing. And I'll continue with that, so some of my earlier
preoccupations will hang on. I am much more concerned
with women, especially with women's ritual and
women's spirituality. . . . Finding whatever's left of
women's rituals and women's magic and women's religions and women's politics and women's whatever.
That's what I probably will be doing for the next twenty
years or so.

Paula Gunn Allen, in an interview in Winged Words:
American Indian Writers Speak, *edited by Laura
Coltelli, University of Nebraska Press, 1990.*

Paula Gunn Allen with Joseph Bruchac   (interview date 1983)

SOURCE: An interview in *Survival This Way: Interviews
with American Indian Poets* by Joseph Bruchac, Sun
Tracks and the University of Arizona Press, 1987, pp.
1-21.

[*A member of the Abenaki tribe, Bruchac is an American
short story writer, poet, editor, novelist, translator, and critic whose works are informed by his experiences as a Native
American. In the following interview, originally conducted
in 1983, Allen discusses Laguna society and culture, her upbringing, her influences, and thematic and stylistic aspects
of her work.*]

[*Bruchac*]: *In [your poem]* **"Recuerdo,"** *there are images
of movement, of loss, and of searching, images I see in
many of your poems. What is it that is lost or looked for?*

[Allen]: A sense of being securely planted. A therapist
once said to me, "You're balanced but not grounded." I'm
balanced but, the thing is, I float. It's fairly easy to shove
me by the shoulders and knock me over. It's not because
I'm off balance; it's because I'm not grounded. That's my
body's way of expressing what my poems also express.
One of my most important, basic images is the road outside the house where I grew up, in Cubero. That tiny part
of western Valencia Country, New Mexico, where I grew
up is absolutely primary to me. In moments of stress or

when I'm dreaming, at a time when important changes are going on, or in visions, the first thing I'll get is the road, and then other things will be superimposed on it. The road is—do you go up to the hills and the mountains or do you go out to the highway, to the urban Western World?

Mountains and the landscape of the Southwest appear often in your poetry. What do those mountains mean to you?

To me, they are the gods, just as it is saying in **"Recuerdo."** It's the mountains to the north and it's Mount Taylor. It just *sits there.* Of course, we're quite high in Cubero, we're at sixty-five hundred feet. But the mountain rises another eight thousand. So it's just there. It doesn't loom. It's there. It's a soft and lovely mountain, but when you get to that mountain it becomes a very frightening place. It is so powerful. It's not scary like "I'm going to get lost and never come back." It's scary like "Who lives here that I don't know?" It's not a sense of personal danger; it's a sense of overwhelming wilderness. My home is in that exact hollow which the poem talks about. I lived literally in a hollow. Most of the village was above us, and we lived in a little hollow. So the wind went over us rather than being on us all the time. To me it's like the hollow of a hand—and that's a Christian metaphor.

There's a moving back and forth in some of your work between that Christian awareness and a more Indian sense of land and place. Is that a balance you're conscious of in your poems?

I seldom do it on purpose. It's implicit in my life, so it's implicit in my work. Sometimes I get in a dialogue between what the Church taught me, the nuns taught me, and what my mother taught me, what my experience growing up where I grew up taught me. Often you can't reconcile them. I can't reconcile them.

What did your mother teach you?

My mother taught me several things. One is that reality is all important and reality meant paying attention to what was going on—the sunset, the birds. There's a bullsnake that lives under the house and that's my snake and we don't kill her. You take care of people and you take care of creatures because that's what you do and you don't do anything else. You don't lie because, if you lie, you'll get lost. You treat people as though they are real, even little tiny people. You don't trivialize them and act like they're idiots. Instead, you treat them as though they are perfectly intelligent beings. You remember that your mind is inviolably yours, that no one can have it, ever. So you act this way or that way, depending on what they want from you because that's not what is important. What's important is that they can't change your mind, which is a very Laguna thing. They're very stubborn people. She's got that stubbornness of, It's my mind and that's that!

Laguna is important to you . . .

Laguna to me is where you go when you're going home. Laguna to me is where people are grounded. Laguna is Feast Day. What I remember about that, one of the first things I ever remember, is leaving Feast with my grandparents and looking out the back window of the car. It was dark and there were fires. Laguna is on a hill and you could see campfires on all the hills around it. Of course you can't see that anymore, but when I was little a lot of people traveled by wagon and that's what you could see. To me, that was the absolute essence of a perfect place to be. That was *it.*

It's interesting that such a small pueblo as Laguna has produced so many writers: you, your sister Carol Lee Sanchez, Leslie Silko, Harold Littlebird, and others not yet as well known.

It's a crossroads. One of its fundamental values from the time of its founding has been progressivism. They acted from between 1945 and 1979 or '80 as if they were going to be very conservative. But as the Pueblos go, they are the most "liberal." They've always been. That's because they weren't "Lagunas" to begin with. They were a polyglot people. They had to be liberal. So, when they started getting very rigid elements in the village, they threw them out. Ceremonially, that is—through a ceremonial "fight" they threw them out. The Lagunas have always valued learning Most of the young people today hold college degrees. There's not a lot of illiteracy there. There's a very high standard of living, or at least there was until the mines closed last year or the year before. I understand the income dropped to some abysmal level and there's growing unemployment where there was full employment two years ago. *Full* and at very good wages. Anyway, they've always been like that. When the Bookmobile comes out to the Laguna villages, it doesn't get to half of them before it's empty. That's just how they are. Whether they're very traditional or very peripheral, it doesn't make any difference. They value knowledge and they value learning. It isn't that they value hustling and making it in the white man's world—they just value learning. I think that's what happened. I think that's why we get writers and artists who, in our own way, just value it. We just like to do, it, so we do it.

Certain anthropologists, such as Elsie Clew Parsons, have "written off" Laguna, saying it no longer has a kiva, it's no longer really a Pueblo. Parsons comes close to saying it's not even Indian. How do you respond to that point of view?

I usually laugh because it's such a limited point of view. But then I say, "Okay, why are people always looking *further back?*" They've got to find a utopia—the perfect place—and Indians always fail them. Indians are always *not quite* something or other, whatever the something or other is that they want. People will come up to you and say, "There aren't any Indians anymore. You know, Indians put Pampers on their babies! They watch T.V.!" And all of this means that Indians are not Indian to the white world which loves Indians and is looking for the lost noble savage or savage or something like that. I will say that Laguna has never been very good at noble savagery. But Parsons's work in itself indicates that they were so thoroughly primitive, so thoroughly wilderness people, that how she could write them off simply astonishes me.

My mountain is wilderness. Where Cubero is, is between civilization and wilderness; and the choice for me is: Which way do I go? The resolution for me is that I don't take either choice. I stay in the middle of both. I tend to value wilderness as an aesthetic and moral and personal value over civilization, though I can see civilization being useful for me personally. Nevertheless, I always judge the civilization in terms of the wilderness, rather than the other way around.

And "primitive"?

Primitive means several things. Savage is a better word and I'd rather use savage. I censored myself when I started to say "savage" and thought, "I can't say *that.*" So I said "primitive," meaning uncluttered with alienating concepts such as secularized or industrialized or urbanized people are fraught with.

Going back to that duality you mentioned between the lessons of your mother and the lessons of the Church—what were the lessons of the Church?

Do you know that poem of mine called **"Resurrection: Easter Sunday"**? Those are the lessons of the Church. The lessons of the Church are that everybody I love is a murderous, vicious, guilty creature, including myself. The only good person was killed and we killed him. What I'm supposed to do about that is be abjectly sorry and I'm supposed to worship a corpse. A very frightening reality to be raised in and I *was* raised in it.

A lot of Indians were.

It's just overwhelming. It took me until I wrote that poem to make some kind of peace between the crucifixion and my own sense of innocence and my sense of my people's innocence. None of the people I know are going to crucify anybody, never mind Jesus Christ! But the Church, the nuns, and the images around you keep saying, "You're a murderer, you're a murderer, you're a murderer. You ought to be dead, you ought to be dead, you ought to be dead." And you ought to want to kill yourself.

What have been the influences on your writing, both when you were beginning to write and at present?

I really wish I could tell you a lot about this, but I'm not really clear on them. I've always had an affinity for literacy, always. My aunts, my father's sisters, were just delighted by that. I would learn anything. They taught me "Mary had a little lamb," and "There was a little girl who had a little curl," and all those nursery rhymes. I would say anything. By the time I was two and a half they had me saying "The Gettysburg Address." In public. I was taken around here and there and shown to eighth graders who couldn't learn it. They'd put me up on the desk and have me recite it and say, "She can learn it. Why can't you?" So that's very early. That's an early influence. I read. From the day I could read, I read and read and read. I read anything and everything. I read the Hardy Boys and the Bobbsey Twins and *Anne of Green Gables* and Shakespeare, whatever there was to read. My mother had quite a collection of books—you've seen it—and I read my way through it. At school, whatever was in the library I read. I didn't like school. It was an uncomfortable place for me. So I would do my work real quick and then I'd hide a book in my notebook and I'd read. So, who knows what influences are working here?

> **Laguna to me is where you go when you're going home. Laguna to me is where people are grounded. Laguna is Feast Day.**
>
> —*Paula Gunn Allen*

More consciously, I fell in love with Gertrude Stein when I was in high school—ninth or tenth grade. My mother bought me everything she could find, everything that was available, and I read Stein and tried to copy her, tried to write like her. Then I gave up for a while. But the earliest work I ever wrote, which no one will ever see because I lost it, is noticeably Stein.

The other people that I was simply made for were the Romantic poets. Shelley, in particular, and Keats. If you look at my poem **"Moonshot,"** it's Keats. It came to me as quite a shock last summer. I was listening to some dramatic readings and this man up on stage happened to be reading "Ode to a Nightingale." I had come in halfway through the performance, so I heard just the last half. I realized then that I had written **"Moonshot"** like a tangent to "Ode to a Nightingale." Even some of the images are the same except that they're skewed slightly. I was just stunned. I wasn't conscious of doing that, but that's what I did.

What about current influences?

Among them the most important single influence on my work at present—and for the last couple of years—has been Judy Grahn. In her poetry she works for clarity and she works for ease of comprehensibility so that anybody walking into your reading can understand what you're saying and anybody who picks up the book can understand what you're saying. She's taught me a great deal about doing that and simplifying the structures that are so ridiculously obscure. Some of the changes you've noticed in my work come directly from studying her work as well as living with her. I wrote **"Recuerdo,"** and **"Los Angeles 1980"** and **"Laguna Ladies Luncheon"** before I met her, so I was moving in that direction. But it's like she jumped it up. Adrienne Rich has also had a real influence on me and more recently Audre Lorde.

When did you return again to writing after that earliest work influenced by Stein?

In college I happened to get into creative writing as a direct result of Bob Creeley's *For Love.* By accident I read the book, and I was absolutely thunderstruck. I thought he was a genius. I had fallen for this man Creeley hook, line, and sinker. The man who had loaned me the book told me, "Well, he's teaching here." This was in Albuquerque. He also told me I ought to get into Creeley's class. I said, "Who, me?" I had, by then, written five poems in my whole life and I was going to be a fiction writer or a nonfiction writer. I never thought about being a poet.

Well, I went to see Bob and, of course, he let me in his class. I think I worked with him for about two years. He introduced me to Charles Olson, Allen Ginsberg—and Ginsberg has been a major model. of mine. Olson has been a major model. Robert Duncan, Denise Levertov. Levertov was the first poet I ever saw read, and that was actually over twenty years ago. She was very important to me. Partly as a model, as a woman up there reading, partly because she knows how to end the poem more effectively than anybody I know. I could not end poems. I'm not good at ending things. So I studied her intensively to learn that. So, those are really the primary shaping people until 1965. About then I began to take it over for myself—and it took a long time to take it over for myself.

There is often a certain kind of density, a layering of meaning in your poems. That reminds me very much of the Black Mountain School.

Well, they were really really important to me for the first two or three years I was trying to learn how to be a writer. It was Black Mountain all the way. I didn't pay attention to anyone else.

But then in 1965 there was a change?

Yes, when I went up to Oregon. I finished my last year there and I took a lot of writing classes. Then I did an M.F.A. there. By that point I knew that I knew enough from other poets and that what I had to do now was find Paula. I didn't find Paula, although I did write several poems in that period where you can hear me. There are several in my book **The Blind Lion. The Blind Lion** covers that whole period, and here and there you can hear what's eventually going to be Paula. A transitional voice begins to show up. I was working with Ralph Salisbury who, at the time, was just as "white" as white could be as far as I knew. Now it turns out he's an Indian.

Cherokee.

I'm really sorry I didn't know that at the time because I was dreadfully alone and dreadfully suicidal. There was absolutely nobody there. Luckily for me, Dick Wilson came up. He's an old friend, not the Dick Wilson of infamy, but another one from home, a Santee Sioux whom I'd known since my hippy days in Albuquerque. This was before there were hippies, but he and I and a number of other weirdos from Grants and Pruitt, New Mexico, were hippy types. He came up to Oregon to teach and probably saved my life. Dick's presence and Momaday's novel are probably what saved my life.

House Made of Dawn *has been very important to innumerable Indian writers, hasn't it?*

I wouldn't be writing now if Momaday hadn't done that book. I would have died.

What did it do for you?

It told me that I was sane—or if I was crazy at least fifty thousand people out there were just as nutty in exactly the same way I was, so it was okay. I was not all alone. It did that and it brought *my land* back to me. Eugene, Oregon is nothing like *Cubero*. Part of what I was going through was land sickness—loss of land. It brings great grief to you

not to be at home, and he brought it back because he's such a careful writer. I could read the passages and I had been there to the places that he describes. I knew every inch of what he was saying. It was that and the fact that he could write a novel about an "Abel." An Abel with the same sickness that I had—or something like it—but Momaday had enough control over that sickness to write a book about it. That said to me, "You're okay. This is nothing to get all excited about." (laughs) This goes back to my mother: "Just be calm, stay cool, and everything will work out. You're not nuts, you're just different, but that doesn't make you nuts." It's taken me years and years to get over all of that, but if that line hadn't been thrown in my direction, I wouldn't be here now.

There's a clear, storytelling quality to some of your recent poems, which I like very much. Do you think your work is now tending in that direction?

Yes, yes. As I get more control over what I do, as I'm less concerned about whether or not anybody understands me—and, more importantly, as I'm less concerned about whether or not anybody misunderstands me. Misunderstanding doesn't mean they're going to kill me. That's what it always meant to me, but I've begun to learn that they're not going to kill me. Laugh at me perhaps, but not kill me. So it's okay to take chances and you've noticed that. The work gets calmer and less dense and less obscure. It becomes easier and easier to say what it is I want to say.

You know, part of it was getting to be forty. Now you're forty you can say what's on your mind. Until then you weren't allowed to because you were just a child. Don't ask me where I got that, but I've known it all my life. I've always known that, once you were forty, then you got to speak up clearly.

Isn't there generally a different idea about women aging, though, among American Indian people?

Sure. The young girls are the ones who are in a very, I don't know, *backwards* kind of position. You're supposed to be shy and gentle and careful—if you're a Laguna, anyway. But the older you get the more you come into your own and the more your stability increases and your knowledge and your sense of who you are and how things ought to go. Your sense of properness becomes more and more useful, not only to yourself but to the people around you. They're supposed to listen to you. It's like I knew all that. My mother has always made fun of people who dye their hair or who try to hide their wrinkles or in any way try to alter the fact of how old they are. To her, the older you get the better you are—and the better life is supposed to go for you. You're more valuable. And so, of course, I'm the same way. The first few white hairs I got, I was just so proud of them. I was scared to death somebody was going to take them away from me. I like having all this white hair. It makes my life easier. It's easy for me to go out now and talk, and it used to be excruciating. I attribute it to my white hair.

That probably explains why some of the strongest people I know are Indian women over the age of forty.

Aren't they, though? In fact, some of them are downright terrifying.

Yet within majority white culture, once you're over forty you either have to think of a facelift or doing something . . .

You think of ways to placate people so they won't punish you and they won't ignore you and they won't abandon you. That's what women in the dominant culture between the ages of about thirty-five and seventy-five do. Then they reach a point where it finally dawns on them that they're *old*. There's nothing they can do about it, they're still here and the hell with it.

Why has majority white culture perpetrated this on women?

Old women are powerful. They really are powerful. That's not a culture perception, that's a fact. So, what you do with powerful people whom you don't wish to have powerful is you put a mind trick on the whole society. You convince them that those who have power do not have power. You do that by degrading them, trivializing them, disappearing them, and murdering them. They were murdered in great numbers toward the end of the Middle Ages. And that thing is kept up by talking about "old bags" and "old witches" and "old crones" and making fun of them, laughing, and saying, "Don't go near her—she's got the Evil Eye," which is what immigrant populations do. All those sorts of things instill in the minds of all people that old women are not powerful because, of course, they are. If they weren't really powerful, would it be necessary to do all we do to them? It wouldn't be.

Isn't this one of the lessons now being learned by many women in the United States?

Finally.

A lesson that American Indian women could have taught . . .

If non-Indians had bothered to pay attention. Yes. I think of old women not as grotesque and ugly, but as singular with vibrancy, alive just as the leaves get before they fall. That total brilliance of them. I wish that white women could see that in themselves and in their mothers and grandmothers and in aging women, in general. I wish they could see that incredible brilliance and fire that's so magnificent. Then they would think, "Well, these are the most beautiful of all." Of course—because old women are, they are so beautiful.

Could you talk a bit about **Shadow Country?** *I'm curious about the name.*

It's "Shadow Country" because shadows are important. My novel explains a lot of this, by the way, because to me shadows are good, good places. Hollows, you know, have shadows in them.

As in the hollow where your house was located in Cubero?

That's right. You see, it's cool there and, where I come from, the sun can get so hot you can get sick from it. So the people who are always running around with their images of bright daylight give me a headache because bright daylight gives me a headache. I like the sun to shine, I like to be in the shade watching the sun shine, you see. A tree is so valuable out there in New Mexico because the tree gives shade. The mesas are valuable because the rocks give shade. So, shadow means that. Shadow also means the land of the dead. Where I come from the land of the dead isn't a terrible place, it's where the rain comes from. Rain clouds, oh the shadows they make are not to be believed. And they are the people coming back to bring the rain.

And shadow means it's not dark and it's not light. It's Cubero, as I said earlier in this interview, the wilderness on one hand and civilization on the other. That's where shadow land, the shadow country, is. It also means half-breed. Quite simple—neither dark nor light. It also means not really in focus, blurred. It has a whole bunch of meanings. So, when you look at **"Que Cante Quetzal,"** which means "what do you sing, god?" because the quetzal bird is the god (actually the goddess, not the god), that's all the traditional, that's the wilderness and what's happened to the wilderness. It's both things. How I relate to wilderness and where the wilderness is—that's the first part. The second part, which is "Shadow Country," is going back and forth. It's really being in shadow country. Back and forth and back and forth. So you have such poems as **"Los Angeles 1980"** and **"Words for a Bike-Riding, Osprey-Chasing, Wine-Drunk Squaw Man."** I like that title better than the poem. (laughs) And you've got the poem **"Shadow Country"** itself which ends dark and light, side by side—and it's set in a bar. Bars are notorious for the fact that they're shadowy and dark, intimate and sexy and full of deviant kinds of folks. Nice people don't go there. They are the city's interface between wilderness and civilization, between fertile chaos and focusing structure. Everybody goes there to meet who they really want to meet. Everybody parties there and everybody puts on all their trips there and everybody lays all their crap on you there—and so on. Another section of the book, "Recuerdo," means recovering. Going back, putting back together, assembling in another way. That section is really about the hollow where things meet, which side is which. The last section, "Medicine Song," is simply about women and about women as healing agents and happy-making agents. Just women. The way the book is made up I see "Medicine Song" as something akin to a resolution. It's really moving the whole song to another key, it's really the section that does the transposing. The next book, presumably, will actually be in the new key. I don't see "Medicine Song" as the solution but as a modulation.

Song and singing seem very important to you and to your poetry.

Song structures are my favorite structures to work with. My sister Kathy is a musician. My mother and father are musicians. We had a lot of music in our house. When I was young, Kathy was studying at the Conservatory of Music in Cincinnati. We had this big upright piano that Pop had bought for Mother when they were first married, you know. It cost $15. Kathy used to sit at that thing and she'd play Chopin and Mozart and Rachmaninoff. Mozart, particularly I loved. I was determined to write poetry that had as a structure what classical music, particularly Mozart, has as a structure. When I wrote **"Los Angeles, 1980,"** I showed it to Kathy and she analyzed it musically.

I was very astonished. I actually succeeded in doing what I had set out years and years and years before to do. That's the basic structure of what I write, that's really my . . . it's my notion. You set out a theme and then you do variations on the theme. You set out a tempo and you vary the tempo. In the end you bring them together like a watershed—not like an answer to the question, because there's never an answer to the question.

I sometimes sense another music, an Indian sound.

I just noticed it. Yesterday I was reading a poem of Simon's in that article "First Languages: Perception and Expression." Well, he's got a little hunting song in there, and I'm saying the hunting song and I come to the refrain which is exactly Pueblo! The beat in it is exactly Pueblo. Particularly in my earlier work I would do that. I would wind up the ending so it would keep going and keep going and keep going—which is what they do. My poetry professors kept telling me to stop doing that. So now I write a truncated last line which is the exact opposite of what I want to write. My last line should be going, spread out like a fan. Left to myself, that's what they'd be.

For me, music always ties in strongly to the world of the spirit. I find that world of the spirit very strongly present in your work as well. Could you talk a bit about your involvement with psychic phenomena in your personal life and your poetry?

Let me talk about my own personal involvement and then go on to the poetry. My own personal involvement, is of course, all my life. More specifically, as I've gotten older and older, I've become more centered in that particular world. It actually began as a conscious thing when I lived in Oregon. That was during the drug revolution, if you remember. I took some TCP one night and I was sitting out in the back yard. I was living on the MacKenzie River. God, it was beautiful! And I looked up and there were the trees—and I could see that the trees were people. So I started talking to the trees. Well, I knew that I could do that and I've always done it subliminally, but I had never before done it out loud, consciously. That was the first time and, of course, I didn't lose that sense ever. I don't do any drugs except nicotine and caffeine now. I can't take them. What they do is they put me to sleep. (laughs) It's an overload to my system. I'm naturally stoned a lot of the time and apparently I always have been. My youngest brother once commented that it wasn't until he started smoking dope that he understood what I was laughing at all the time. (laughs) Then he went, *"That's* why she acts like that." I always see the world from a corner, from a slant, so to speak. I think that's what it is. I know a lot about Western occult traditions and about Tibetan traditions and about Egyptian traditions. In other words, I've made it a real study, and I've devoted years to learning all these different traditions. I see the American Indian traditions as fitting quite easily into the worldwide traditions. I'm a very religious person. I always have been. Catholicism is terribly important to me because I'm a religious person. It was the politics of the Church that I couldn't abide . . . and their incredible stupidity about human beings . . . and what they would do. The viciousness! I knew perfectly well they knew what they were doing.

Racism, sexism . . .

Colonialism—all of it. They had no excuse. If they paid any attention to Jesus, to the Master, they could never have done those things. I've read The New Testament. Even as it stands—and it's a flawed document—even as it stands there is no excuse for their behavior, absolutely none in the New Testament. So, that's just simply a part of my mind. I learned it from my grandparents, all of them. By the way, the Lebanese people are the same way. My Lebanese ancestors are the same way. My father is enormously psychic. His grandmother was a fortune-teller in the sense that she could predict the future. She was clairvoyant. His grandfather just loved that sort of thing. He used to charm snakes and do that kind of thing. So it comes at me from both sides. It has its very bad side. I haven't worked . . . it's in *Coyote's Daylight Trip,* but its hovering around the edges. I haven't yet learned how to talk out loud, on purpose, about the terrible evilness of it. And it can be very evil. There is so much evil about it—I mean in the Indian systems as much as I mean in the white system. That's why it's called the occult, of course, because it can be devastatingly vicious when misused.

Adrienne Rich wrote me a letter recently, and what she said about **Shadow Country** is that what astonished her was that this poetry could have a clear spiritual presence without ever going into Romanticism and that idealistic sentimental crap that goddess-worship people tend to get into . . . and it never has to deny political realities, either. That she liked, and she kept reading it over and over because she hadn't seen anything like that before. Of course, it's common for Indian poets to do that. I think some white poets do it, but not the way Indians do. I've never seen anything which so clearly showed that as the Third World Writers Conference in May 1982 in Sacramento. It was so clear it was almost funny. You could count on the Indians to get up there and do it every time. The more political and biased and radical the rhetoric of the other poets got, the more likely the Indians would choose not their most political poems but their most spirit-directed poems. And they kept doing it. It just cracked me up. Toward the end I was just walking around laughing. That's why I wrote that paper called, **"This Wilderness in My Blood: The Spiritual Foundations of the Poetry of American Indian Women,"** because I saw so clearly that spring what the difference was between us. That's the paper Bo Schöler published in *Coyote Was Here.* I went through Wendy Rose's work and Linda Hogan's work, Joy Harjo's work, and my work and Carol Lee Sanchez's work and Mary Tall Mountains's work and we all do it differently. We all have a different approach to it, but we all do it. It is always there in the poetry. My poetry addresses it as I address anything that's going on in my life. It's not something I'm doing deliberately. It's just common mind work, and to me a poem is a recording of an event in the mind.

How has your mixed-blood heritage affected your worldview or your poetry?

My poetry has a haunted sense to it and it has a sorrow and a grievingness in it that comes directly from being split, not in two but in twenty, and never being able to reconcile all the places that I am. I think of it as Wordsworth did when he said we come into this world "trailing clouds of glory," when he said nothing can bring back the hour when we saw "splendor in the grass and glory in the flower." We shall not weep but find strength in what remains behind. That poem—I was in college, I was a sophomore when I read it, and I just wept. I was completely, absolutely desolate because I thought he understood. He understood, of course, in his own way exactly what happens when your reality is so disordered that you can't ever make it whole, but you have the knowledge of what has happened, what has been done. There's a song that goes, "what have they done to my song?" For the longest time, I thought that song said "what have they done to my *soul?*" That's the experience of the half-breed.

My poetry has a haunted sense to it and it has a sorrow and a grievingness in it that comes directly from being split, not in two but in twenty, and never being able to reconcile all the places that I am.

—*Paula Gunn Allen*

The other experience is that we have a mediational capacity that is not possessed by either of the sides. What we are able to do is bridge variant realities because everybody is pissed off at us and we are pissed off at ourselves. What we are able to do is move from flower to flower, so to speak, and get the pollen moved around among each of our traditions. Then we can plant back into them. You find that the writers from Laguna are all breeds and you find that Laguna is a breed Pueblo. It always has been, culturally speaking, not necessarily blood speaking. But even blood speaking, the people who formed the Laguna settlement were from several different Pueblos and they included some Navajo. They were mediational people. They were people who chose to live together and then to work out their differences. I think you can look at the Laguna people as a culture that has worked out this capacity to be a breed. Then we ourselves are not as estranged as we might be if we were, say, Hopi and having to deal with it or if we were Iroquois and had to deal with it, because our whole Pueblo is that way—whether they want to admit it or not. Most often, they do want to admit it.

So this ties in to why there are so many American Indian writers of mixed blood? That dual vision leads them to mediate?

That's right and that, of course, is what a writer does. Ideally, what a writer does is talk to two perspectives. I don't know a writer who doesn't feel essentially alienated and that's what a breed is. It's fundamentally, "I'm not this and I'm not that and I am two of everything."

If there is such a thing as a "Pan-Indian Consciousness," it seems it is being expressed by contemporary American Indian poets.

And artists and painters.

Do you think that American Indian poets are too aware of each other these day? Our names keep turning up in each other's poems.

Not aware enough. We need a school and we need to have a very clearly developed sense of what that school is. We *are* a school. We really are a very special group of poets.

That makes me think of the American Writers' Congress. I remember, after the American Indian writers session, people kept saying "You Indians all seem to know each other and to work so well together." Why is that?

We're strangers in a strange land, that's why. (laughs) We need each other. Our work is very unique and we need to recognize that. So that our names keep cropping up in each other's poems, our images keep cropping up in each other's poems, our understandings keep cropping up in each other's poems and articles and reviews and so forth is all to the good. What do you think the Imagists were doing? If we are to have the impact that I believe we all want to have, this is how you do it.

What is it that is unique and important?

Our spiritual vision, our ability to be fundamentally practical *and* spiritual because Indian people *are* practical and spiritual. We don't horseshit around. We're not coy and cute. Occasionally we're difficult, but that's different. We don't believe in metaphor. Very few of us even understand what that term means in terms of what it means to the greater poetry community around us or to the critical establishment.

Or surrealism?

Or surrealism, which is silly. We really have a *vision* that the Imagists attempted to get at, that they lied about where they got it. You know that. They got it from Native American tribal literature and then they pretended that they got if from the Chinese, and that is so much horse hockey. Pisses me off. But that's fine because we were the only ones who could do it. They couldn't do it, so I suppose it works out pretty well. Yeah. You know, we can transform American culture because that's what writers do.

Paula, you've developed a reputation as critic, as poet, as prose writer. Are any of those genres more important to you or is this just an artificial division?

They're artificial divisions. I do each in itself, of course, but I suit the form to what it is I'm trying to do—to the purpose. So the novel—I couldn't do that in poems. What the novel does is what novels do and what the critical articles do is what criticism can do and what the poems do is what poems can do. My form is determined by my purpose, my point. They're all writing and that's what I'm doing. I'm a writer. It's like asking a seamstress if making dresses is somehow separate from making skirts and blouses. Sure, one has a waistband that's separate and in the others one part is connected to the other, but it's all sewing.

Alice Hoffman   (review date 3 June 1984)

SOURCE: "Ephanie's Ghosts," in *The New York Times Book Review,* June 3, 1984, p. 18.

[*Hoffman is an American novelist, scriptwriter, and short story writer. In the following mixed review, she faults* The Woman Who Owned the Shadows *for its sentimentality, didacticism, and broad focus, but praises it as an "exploration of racism . . . [and] a powerful and moving testament to feminism."*]

In one of the many legends told in this ambitious first novel [**The Woman Who Owned the Shadows**], a father forces his daughter to marry a sorcerer. Each time the young woman's courage is tested by impossible deeds, she manages to succeed. But her powers are mistrusted by her ailing husband and the other sorcerers. They advise him to uproot the tree of light and persuade his wife to jump into the hole. Arrogant, tricked into believing that she can float like a petal, the wife jumps. They replace the tree so she can never return, and the world as we know it is begun on the shining blue globe below.

A Guadalupe Indian girl—Ephanie—makes a similar leap. Challenged by a jealous boy, she tests her daring in a catastrophic jump from an apple tree. Ephanie breaks two ribs and punctures a lung, but the scars go much deeper—this moment of weakness changes Ephanie's vision of herself, and even when the incident is forgotten, it continues to haunt her. She abandons bravery and becomes a good girl, one who yearns for "high heels and lipstick"; she leaves the mesas and arroyos behind, and replaces a beloved Chicana friend with a cruel husband.

Ephanie is an outcast, shunned by the Indian community for her mixed blood (her grandmother and mother having "married out"), exploited as an "exotic" by whites in San Francisco where she flees with her children to start a new life. **The Woman Who Owned the Shadows** charts the progress of Ephanie's recovery from self-doubt to wholeness. Her interior journey is guided by the traditional tales of spirit women: Gato Kepe, the murdered healer; the betrayed Yellow Woman; the mythic grandmother, the Spider.

Miss Allen, who was raised on a Spanish land grant in New Mexico and is the author of five books of poetry teaches Native American studies at the University of California, Berkeley. She uses many voices to tell her story—folk tales and legends, letters written home, transcripts of therapy sessions, dream sequences. But it is a stylistic mixture that fails to illuminate.

Within the shifting narrative, experiences are compartmentalized; emotions seem dull, political insight becomes preachy. The brilliant meshing of legend and American reality found in Maxine Hong Kingston's nonfiction book, *The Woman Warrior,* is sadly absent here. Like Mrs. Kingston, Miss Allen has written a memoir of a girlhood among ghosts, but she fails to give her ghosts life on the page. The motivations of her characters seem hazy, their epiphanies forced and—oddly enough—we know both too little and too much about them.

In those sections where the author forsakes the artifice of

her style, an absorbing, often fascinating world is created. A scene in Oakland, Calif., where "we go to powwows and they dance" reveals not only Ephanie's fears, but her charms in dealing with some individuals. The death of one of Ephanie's newborn twin sons (on the night his exhausted parents refuse to answer his cries) is, in its simplicity and depth of emotion, beautifully told. And when Ephanie's grandmother, Sylvia (whose Indian name, Shimanna, means nightshade), decides that her time has come, Miss Allen's prose is understated and affecting, a true accompaniment to the legends of the spirit women:

> The children grew worried, "Come on, Mama," they said. "We're going to take you to Albuquerque to the doctor." And they took her, and she was admitted to the hospital. There was nothing wrong with her. She wasn't sick. Maybe a sniffle, a small cold, but nothing fatal. Still, she was clearly dying. And in a few days, curled within herself in her bed, covered with her shawl, she did. She stepped over to some other world . . . When Shimanna was through living, being too worn out to live her life for herself in her earthly form, she died. That's what she did.

The Woman Who Owned The Shadows feels more like an exorcism than like fiction, and the author's compulsion to put everything into one book has nearly obscured her talents. But in spite of its excesses, the effort it takes to read this novel is worthwhile. Not only is it an exploration of racism, it is often a powerful and moving testament to feminism. For those willing to look, there are the bare outlines of those ghosts which can either haunt a girl forever or guide her to womanhood.

Tom King   (review date Summer 1984)

SOURCE: A review of *Studies in American Indian Literature,* in *Western American Literature,* Vol. XIX, No. 2, Summer, 1984, pp. 170-71.

[*In the excerpt below, King discusses the strengths and weaknesses of* Studies in American Indian Literature.]

Studies in American Indian Literature is a collection of essays on Indian oral literature, autobiography, and Indian women's literature. There is a section on modern and contemporary Indian literature, a section on the Indian in American literature, and a section on available resources in the field such as anthologies, texts, and scholarly articles. Each of the major sections in the book is followed by suggested course outlines and suggested reading lists. It is a text that is designed for the teacher who wishes to teach a course in this area rather than for the student.

As a secondary source book, **Studies in American Indian Literature** has much to recommend it. Many of the articles such as Patricia Clark Smith's "Coyote Ortiz," LaVonne Ruoff's "American Indian Literatures," and James Ruppert's "Discovering America" are first rate. While the level of the other articles tends to vary, the majority are competent.

The most obvious problem is that several of the articles are out of date and should have been revised prior to publication. Paula Gunn Allen's **"The Sacred Hoop,"** which discusses oral literature, is one such example. Originally written in 1975, the article has received no additional attention even though the discussion of Indian oral literature has produced new ideas and directions. A second problem lies in the suggested reading lists. For whatever reason, the lists are highly selective. Normally this would not be a particular concern, but the additions and the omissions tend to suggest that the lists were developed along the lines of personal taste rather than as a result of a scholarly stance.

Nonetheless, *Studies in American Indian Literature* is a book that should be recommended and read. At the same time, the Modern Language Association should seriously consider publishing a second edition, updating several of the articles that need revision, adding a number of newer articles, and correcting the deficiencies in the reading lists.

Allen on her life:

The events of my own life (as distinct from my community and family life, if such distinctions are possible) are fairly simple. Some of their connections are elegant, like a good mathematical proof; others are not yet jointed, joined. Throughout, the social and personal events are mirrored or reinforced by those that are more properly literary, that have a definite effect on my work.

Essentially, my life, like my work, is a journey-in-between, a road. The forty years since I left Cubero for convent school have been filled with events—adventures on the road—all of which find their way into my work, one way or another. In my mind, as in my dreams, every road I have traveled, every street I have lived on, has been connected in some primal way to The Road, as we called it, like Plato in our innocence. That Road has many dimensions; it exists on many planes; and on every plane it leads to the wilderness, the mountain, as on every plane it leads to the city, to the village, and to the place beneath where Iyatiku waits, where the four rivers meet, where I am going, where I am from.

Paula Gunn Allen, in her "The Autobiography of a Confluence," in I Tell You Now: Autobiographical Essays by Native American Writers, *edited by Brian Swann and Arnold Krupat, University of Nebraska Press, 1987.*

Elaine Jahner   (review date November 1986)

SOURCE: A review of *The Sacred Hoop: Recovering the Feminine in American Indian Traditions,* in *Parabola,* Vol. XI, No. 4, November, 1986, pp. 102, 104.

[*An educator, editor, and critic, Jahner teaches English and Native American Studies. In the review below, she offers a thematic discussion of* The Sacred Hoop, *praising Allen's incorporation of personal experiences and beliefs.*]

Paula Gunn Allen is a leading American Indian poet, novelist, and essayist. The current collection, *The Sacred Hoop: Recovering the Feminine in American Indian Tra-*

ditions, reprints the best of her earlier essays and adds several new ones. The twenty pieces that make up the new book represent attempts to measure her distance from any sensibility or historical paradigm imposed by cultural outsiders, and through that measuring to situate events and texts within alternative historical codes. In such a project, the writer's own position is basic. Her background is certainly not one that belongs to any "dominant culture" in America or the western world in general. She comes from New Mexico where she grew up participating in the Laguna Pueblo traditions of her mother's people and in the Lebanese ways of her father's side of the family. Her formal education, which includes a Ph.D. and an M.F.A., gave her access to the analytic perspectives of mainstream culture, but the necessity to enter these alternative histories as acting subject rather than as uncomprehending victim meant years of thought and work, which gradually allowed an understanding of how her own peoples' histories can help shape a future shared by people of widely divergent pasts.

Allen grounds her entire project in religious assumptions as they are enacted ceremonially and transmitted through the myths of various tribes. Having established the foundations for her arguments, she is free to employ the combination of descriptive explication, personal meditation, and informed academic commentary that is the source of the essays' strengths and vulnerabilities. In her introductory comments she lists seven major themes that recur throughout the essays. The first and last of these establish the place of the sacred in her endeavor, and many of her other themes refer to what she sees as a source of fundamental distortions in mainstream approaches to American Indian thought and history—namely, the inability to recognize the place of the feminine in Indian cultures. But while she firmly defines herself a feminist, she also asserts her sense that mainstream feminists, unaware of the ceremonial foundations for tribal ideas of sexuality, miss the significance of their stance for tribal peoples.

Although Allen faces problems that others choose to ignore, her approach remains unabashedly idealistic, even didactic. For her, thinking and remembering is a mission; it is the means whereby she lives as witness to values that she sees as endangered. She speaks of America's "amazing loss of memory concerning its origins in the matrix and context of Native America," and in the face of such amnesia she speaks directly and personally. . . .

All of Allen's essays have a graceful complexity that charts her responses to the pressures of insights and ideas that seem elusive, not because they are so difficult, but because of their oblique relationship to the accepted and expected. To give her prose writing its required coherence, she has sought analogies among various systems of order; the model that I found most illuminating is found in the [essay] entitled **"The Ceremonial Motion of Indian Time: Long Ago, So Far"**; here Allen describes how her conversations with the Navajo mathematician and physicist Fred Young gave her a way of visualizing the tribal sense of self "as a moving event within a moving universe," a view that corresponds to physicists' understandings about space and time. She then comments on various works of American

Indian literature, including one of her own poems and her novel, showing how their structure "emphasizes the motion inherent in the interplay of person and event." She makes the point that structural innovations in American Indian literature are efforts to allow literature to reflect a mode of consciousness that belongs to ceremony as well as to the advanced frontiers of scientific inquiry.

Change and transformation preoccupy Allen. All of her writing is an attempt to work out what it means to retain a traditional identity in spite of change. In **"Answering the Deer,"** a discussion of American Indian women's poetry, she writes of her own search for "the ideal metaphor" that can "harmonize the contradictions and balance them so that internal equilibrium can be achieved, so that each perspective is meaningful and that in their joining, psychic unity rather than fragmentation occurs." Through such metaphors, the poet and writer does more than merely record continuity; she establishes the means of achieving it, and her language engenders hope—the kind of hope "that comes about when one has faced ultimate disaster time and time again over the ages."

What Allen attempts in her essays is a staggeringly difficult task. Recasting basic cultural assumptions about time, space, sexuality, and history and establishing that recasting within discourses like that of feminism, which is itself a mark and force of change, render all language more than usually vulnerable. Because of her maturity and breadth of experience, Allen succeeds in giving us what no one else has, a highly intelligent yet personal critique of basic cultural assumptions from a Native American feminist perspective.

Quannah Karvar (review date 25 January 1987)

SOURCE: A review of *The Sacred Hoop: Recovering the Feminine in American Indian Traditions,* in *Los Angeles Times Book Review,* January 25, 1987, p. 11.

[*Karvar is known for her English translations of Ponca and Lakota histories and myths. In the review below, she favorably assesses* The Sacred Hoop.]

> My great-grandmother told my mother: Never forget you are Indian. And my mother told me the same thing. This, then, is how I have gone about remembering, so that my children will remember too.

In [*The Sacred Hoop: Recovering the Feminine in American Indian Traditions*], a collection of 17 essays representing more than a decade of cultural research, Native American author and scholar Paula Gunn Allen challenges five centuries of misconceptions surrounding the role of Native American women in many "pre-contact" tribal societies; misconceptions the author contends have ". . . transformed and obscured what were once woman-centered cultures. . . . "

In her first section, "The Ways of Our Grandmothers," Allen explores the relationship between female creation deities and their teachings and the pre-eminent status of women as creators and teachers of the rituals and laws

that defined tribal consciousness, and the significance of mother and grandmother in Native American culture.

Allen also probes the effects of "colonization" by Western society and suggests that the degradation of female tribal status, indeed, the dehumanization of native people as a whole in American history, was not coincidental but imperative to the dissolution of tribal unity and identity. That ". . . fragile web of identity . . . has gradually been weakened and torn. But the oral tradition . . . has prevented the complete destruction of the web . . . it heals itself and the tribal web by adapting to the flow of the present while never relinquishing its connection to the past."

Through "The Word Warriors," Allen reveals the influence of the oral tradition on contemporary Native American literature including selection from the works of N. Scott Momaday, James Welch, Leslie Marmon Silko, and other novelists and poets. A particular essay, **"The Wilderness in My Blood: Spiritual Foundations of the Poetry of Five American Indian Women,"** expresses with stunning clarity the conflict between a culture that professes a universal sense of belonging and "enwholement," often symbolized by the sacred circle or, as Allen has entitled her work, the sacred hoop, and more recent Indian history in which a profound sense of alienation and loss are the common experience.

Six final essays examine the lives of Native American women in "a contemporary setting" covering a broad range of topics, including traditions, politics, lesbianism in tribal culture, tribal women's social status and the emergence of feminism in America, and the struggle for cultural and biological survival.

"Our number grows," the author states, ". . . our determination to define ourselves grows, and our consciousness of our situation, of the forces affecting it, and of the steps we can take to turn our situation around grows."

Allen's life experiences as a Ph.D. in the field of Native American studies and professor at the University of California, Berkeley, and more important, as a Laguna Pueblo/Sioux woman who believes that personal and cultural truth are inseparable and vital to survival, form the bias of this book. It is precisely this bias that gives *The Sacred Hoop* its power and insight as a commentary on the perceptions and priorities of contemporary Native American women and as a source of information for those who continue to seek more than sociological and bureaucratic definition.

Paula Gunn Allen with Annie O. Eysturoy (interview date March 1987)

SOURCE: An interview in *This Is about Vision: Interviews with Southwestern Writers,* William Balassi, John F. Crawford, and Annie O. Eysturoy, eds., University of New Mexico Press, 1990, pp. 95-107.

[*Eysturoy specializes in American Studies. In the following interview which took place in March, 1987, after a poetry reading held in Albuquerque, New Mexico, Allen discusses the impact of the American Southwest on her work, her lit-*

erary beginnings and aims, her cultural identity, the writing process, and feminist issues.]

[*Eysturoy*]: *You were born and raised here [in Albuquerque.] How has that influenced you and your work?*

[Allen]: My work is all tangled up with landscape around here. But landscape for me does not mean "the landscape"; it does not mean something that great dramas are enacted upon. Maybe that's because so much of the drama in the Southwest *is* the land, not the people. We are, to me, the background against which the land enacts *her* drama, and by landscape I don't mean only the mountains and those vast plains, but the weather, the climatic conditions and rainstorms, the overpowering thunderstorms.

So it is the power of the landscape, more than anythig else, that has left an impression on you?

Right. It has given me an entirely different notion of how women are supposed to be. Other people in America keep thinking that women are supposed to be sort of helpless, cute, and that's femininity. But to me femininity means these great craggy mountains and these deep arroyos and tremendous storms, because mother nature after all is feminine, right? This is all mother nature happening, so I cannot think of her as something that is so terrifying that I have to control her, because storms are exciting, terribly exciting.

You see, you have to live with her, in her, and there is no escape from it. Maybe in England—I have never been there—everything is gentler, more controlled, so that creates the belief that people should be either weak and helpless or power mad, one or the other; maybe that's what creates all those truly bizarre images descending from the English literary tradition. Certainly all the rhetorical forms and especially the artistic forms, those that are about nature, tend to be about a tidy little gentle place.

So this very powerful natural setting of the Southwest does not invite images of a conquering and controlling of nature?

Right, and those images we do have are going to have an effect. Certainly my own writing comes out of the consciousness of my own landscape, where I come from, the trees and mesas I climbed, my physical interaction with where I was. To me that is the real world. American writers tend to think of the real world as ugly, social stuff. They focus on reality as being the yucky things that people do. To me reality is the natural world, and the yucky social stuff, like ugly cities or dreadful political conditions, is the artificiality.

You see this as a balance in nature?

That's right. She gives us our life, so she has a right to take it. What I notice the most when I look at my work is that the land is always there.

The landscape, then, has been important in shaping your perception of the world?

Right. I look at the natural world to see what something in the human world means, because I have no other way of knowing. The natural world might mean inside my body, but even then I will check with the world out there,

the planet, the climate, the seasons, how plants function, how the earthy people function. Then I know how I am functioning, because I am an earthy person.

What about the people of the Southwest, your family and the people you grew up with?

My dad mentioned this morning that most of the poems I read last night were either about my family or they were somehow connected to it, and we talked about that. I think that Indian writers, Chicano writers and black and Asian American writers do a lot of family stuff, because we don't distinguish ourselves from the family base. We exist within the matrix of the people who are our relatives or family friends, or our tribe. I'm raised that way, and I can't write any other way. It may seem this is too peculiar, too local, too personal and not universal. But that's not true, because everybody has a human part that is about their connections, their blood-ties. To me, my work has to speak back to the people from whom it comes, if it comes through my voice, my mind, and my art.

Does your spiritual view of life also originate in your family?

It was just something you knew, I guess we all knew. There were always the dances, those things going on at the pueblo. There was Mass, there was church, but this is something more than that. I knew about magic. My mother used to read me European fairytales, Greek mythology, Indian stories, and the Bible, and she did not make any distinction among them. They were all literature. So I grew up thinking that these were all analogues of one another, because she said they were. It must be where I got the whole thing about spirituality, the metaphysics.

I also think that nature herself is metaphysical. I think that if you are really connecting with the land then you are going to have to connect with the spirits. So probably as a consequence of being with the land, I developed a spiritual dimension, because there is no way not to. I think you have to get away from the land and think of it as something you take pictures of before you can lose your spiritual connections. But if you talk to the tree periodically, which I do, you cannot lose your spiritual connection, because the tree talks back and so you know that there is a person in there.

How did you realize that you wanted to become a writer?

I think it was an accident! When I was younger I wanted to become an actress. My first two years in college I majored in drama, and I was pretty good at it; I liked it. I wrote some poems that looked like prose poems, but it wasn't what I focused on. Then I got married, and I wrote some essays just because I needed to say some things. I was reading Ayn Rand and wrote two or three essays in response to what she was saying.

Then I got divorced, moved to Albuquerque, and decided to sign up for something called "The Famous Writers School." At that point I thought I would be a fiction writer. At the time, I had two babies and a job making seventy-five cents an hour. I don't know how I lived through those years, I really don't. But I did. . . . Then I decided to go back to the university.

I had met a young man from Kenya, and as I was sitting in his house one day there was a book of poems by Robert Creeley on the table. Poetry was not going to be my thing, but I really liked that poetry, so I took the book home, read it from cover to cover, and took it back to my friend who said, "Well, you know, Creeley is teaching on campus. Why don't you see if you can get into his class?" So I went. It was sort of intentional and sort of not.

Meanwhile I had decided that I could not become an actress. For one thing I had two babies; I couldn't get on a bus and go to New York City and live on the streets. So to some extent I became a writer because I had these babies and couldn't just go and do anything I wanted.

In Creeley's class I got an A. He really liked my work, but every time he looked at me he could not believe I had done it, because I looked like a housewife from Grants. This was the early sixties when a person was supposed to look cool, you know. And in fiction I got A's, so it was sort of easy. So, to some extent it was a forced choice. I couldn't do what I wanted to do and there didn't seem to be any way out, so that must be fate. . . .

I don't like to write. I do once I get going, but it is difficult. I'll clean house, I'll do anything other than sit down and write; it is very difficult. In Oregon, once, I had to write a little thing about writing, and I remember writing that as far as I could see writing was a series of small suicides, some of which are fatal. And I still believe that; it is amazing how many delusions and illusions you have to blow to smithereens just to write a paragraph, a good paragraph.

In a way writing is more painful than birthing, and birthing hurts. That was also something I said I was never going to do again after the first time. I did it again, but very, very unhappily, because I knew what it was going to cost. I wanted the kids, but I did not want the anguish. It is the same thing with writing: I want the book, but, oh, I don't want the agony.

How long did it take you to write **The Woman Who Owned the Shadows?**

Thirteen years! I wrote parts in Albuquerque, then I moved to California and wrote parts in San Francisco. I moved back to Albuquerque, wrote a little more, moved back to San Francisco and finished it there. Later I revised it in L.A. and added a number of new passages in El Cerrito.

Is writing like a vision quest for you?

I like that question, because that's exactly right. That's what I am searching for, to pull the vision out of me, because it is here, I know it is. It is a path, a road, and it is *how* I am that molecule that does that dance that makes up her being. Our job is to be conscious of our dance, because that's the way we play for our mother. And that is what I do and, I think, that's what writers must do. That's why writers are important, as long as they are working toward consciousness.

I don't mean evolution. I mean noticing what we already know; we were born knowing it; maybe it is in our genes, or maybe it is in our soul. I don't know where it is, but

I know that it is. So the trick is to get back to our origin, to know what it knows or what she knows.

That's what a vision quest is for, you know. You go out in the wilderness—or men do—and you find out who you are. Well, a writer goes into the wilderness and finds out who she is. And it is awful! But I love it once I get past the garbage, the fear, all the walls and resistance, and I finally am working; when the voice begins to come and the work starts doing me—because I am not doing it by then—then it is great rejoicing and I won't leave the word processor.

But it might take me four days of work to get to that point; in that sense it is sacred.

Do you think the vision quest of women is different from that of men?

As far as I understand, it *was* different for women. A person with the female anatomy might go on a mountaintop vision quest; but by and large she stayed very near the village. There are reasons for that. For one thing, how far do you have to go when you have so much happening in your own body?

Certainly, the cultures that do vision quests also do menstrual huts, and that's a vision quest all by itself and very frightening.

It is not as though we are not allowed to do vision quests, but rather that the male impulse requires one set of circumstances and the female impulse requires another. Our anatomies are different and so we have to have different methods suited to our anatomies, to our hormonal system that will work for that entity.

The forms are different and their way of sharing is different, but the fact of sharing is always the same; you don't get to keep it. You have to put it to use in the community or you didn't do anything.

Is your writing, then, an act of sharing with others what you are envisioning on your quest?

That's right. It's like cooking; you'll try to make something that will feed and nourish your guests.

Is putting the past together, remembering, or as you say, re-membering the past a form of providing nourishment for others?

Right—re-membering the past, putting it back together, recovering; knowing who we are and who we have been. How are we going to know who we are going to be, if we don't know where we have been?

The Indian potters, the women, take old pottery and grind it up and put it into the clay-mix with the new pot. The reason why they do it that way is that the clay will bond more securely all around so it will not fall apart easily. If you don't do it right, the pot will blow up when you are cooking it; it doesn't have the right consistency. But if you don't do it at all, the pot will crumble; it won't hold up over time and you won't be able to put water in it.

So you see yourself as creating a fabric that will strengthen

and nurture others, and give them a sense of who they are and where they came from?

That's right.

In **The Sacred Hoop** *you talk about alienation as a predominant theme in American Indian fiction. . . . Most of those writers are male. Do you think that that in itself could have been a reason for the predominance of the alienation theme?*

You know, I don't know yet; it very well might be. For one thing, there are not that many women writing novels yet, so it is hard to tell. But thinking of Anna Lee Walters's stories, for example, then she is certainly telling a different story entirely.

I wrote that essay, **"Stranger in My Own Land,"** in 1977. At that time there were a lot of urban, marginal Indians writing, who really did not have any connections back to a homeland. But on the other hand, those same men writing in the eighties do write differently. There are a lot more people from the reservations or from intact communities who are in print now, you know, and we don't find the alienation theme, the degree of it, with nearly the kind of intensity that you did in the seventies.

Once, I had to write a little thing about writing, and I remember writing that as far as I could see writing was a series of small suicides, some of which are fatal. And I still believe that; it is amazing how many delusions and illusions you have to blow to smithereens just to write a paragraph, a good paragraph.

—*Paula Gunn Allen*

I am thinking about James Welch. There is a real progression in his three novels to where his new novel, *Fools Crow,* explains the alienation. He goes back to the conquest of that particular band, the Blackfeet, to which tribe he belongs. In a way it is a healing process, because I am sure it has healed something, not only his consciousness, but also in the consciousness of his people. And I think that is true for Indians across the country. So the alienation of the seventies has moved to the spiritual, powerful voice of the eighties.

Do you see it as a process of exorcising the alienation and then coming back to the original center?

Right. Now where are we? That's where **The Sacred Hoop** comes in, and that's right where **The Woman Who Owned the Shadows** ends. It stops where the healing process begins, and **The Sacred Hoop** is about recovery, recovery of our selves.

A lot of people will probably say, after having read **The Sacred Hoop,** *that the theories presented there of a gynocratic*

Indian past are mostly conjecture. If we can generalize, how gynocratic were the tribes in the past?

Well, we can generalize, in fact, I can make better generalizations as each year goes by. **The Sacred Hoop** was published in 1985, was at the press in '83, so almost everything in it was written by '82–'83, except for the introduction, so we are dealing with a time-lag here.

By '77 social anthropologists could say that if you drew a line from Maine through San Diego, everything south of that line would be gynocratic, and the way you could tell was that they were corn-based cultures. Where you found corn, squash, and beans, you found predominantly female deities and powerful female beings, and you would always have a matrilocality, matrifocality, and matrilineality. What is that if not a gynarchy? Some are still arguing about this, but if you descend from a woman, and if the culture is centered on female deities, I am willing to call that a gynarchy or a gynocentric civilization.

I have never found a patriarchal culture in Native America, North or South. Never. I have found cultures where women appeared to be under the dominance of clan head men, but I have never found a culture where that meant that the men told the women what to do. In a lot of these cultures the older women told the younger women what to do, and the older men told the younger men what to do. But if the young woman or the young man did not want to do it, there were not a lot of mechanisms of enforcement. So in the sense of a nonauthoritarianism, in the sense of equal distribution of goods—or equal distribution of starvation—and in the sense of sharing of tasks and responsibilities between genders, I don't think you are going to find a Native American culture where that is not going on.

You are never going to find a patriarchy, is what I am saying. Absolutely never. There isn't any.

Do they then fulfill the Jungian androgynous ideal of balance?

They might. . . . Certainly, that's why I used the term gynocratic or gynocentric, because I am not talking about matriarchy, and I won't use that word. It tends to mean that women dominate, because patriarchy means that the men dominate. So to avoid triggering that idea in people's minds, I use the term gynarchy or gynocentrism, meaning that femaleness or femininity is the central cultural value.

This is reflected in the female deities. The status of individual women ranges from abject dependency to complete and absolute autonomy, just as it does with men, and you can find anything in between, but you find significant female deities and you find significant female rituals that are necessary to the ongoing life of the tribe. You find women significantly present in one way or another in every ceremony, whether it be male or female. Now, that's saying something about all of Native America, and that is not really all that conjectural.

You mention in **The Sacred Hoop** *that deities who were perceived as only feminine in the past have recently emerged as male after having gone through an androgynous process. Is it your contention, then, that that process* *in itself says something about the social structures they must have reflected in the past?*

Right, that's my point. The female deities reflected the social system and the understandings of the people within that system. Metaphysically I would argue that the people were reflecting the gods. But in a sociological, scholarly framework I am perfectly willing to argue in the other direction, that the gods reflected the people.

It works both ways . . .

Yes, they go both ways; you cannot have one without the other.

So when you are talking about the centrality of the role of women, you are talking about a value rather than a position of power or control?

Absolutely. That was never going on—not as far as I can tell—in any Native American system.

It seems to me that in **The Woman Who Owned the Shadows,** *Ephanie, the central character, is on a vision quest. On that quest she moves further and further into a female universe, while the male characters are basically negative characters. How do you achieve the balance there that—as we have talked about—is so important in American Indian philosophy, the balance of male and female? How does Ephanie reach that balance?*

She reaches it because in a woman's life femininity is central; in a man's life masculinity is central. You don't get egalitarianism by women relating to men and you don't get it by men relating to women. What I am saying is that gender norms are for the gender to which they apply; they are not for the other gender. For Ephanie to locate who she is, she has to move from thinking of her reference group as male to thinking of her reference group as female. That says nothing about the men. Ephanie herself is pretty crazy—out of touch with herself—until she understands that she is female.

So she has to move into a female universe in order to explore herself?

A truly female universe.

. . . from which she can emerge and be her true self, and then unite with her male counterpart?

Or not. Uniting is one of the things white people do. There is a male and there is a female. There is not a "unite" in there anywhere, and there never is in the tribes. And why should they unite? They are different.

So they should operate in their separate spheres with balance between those spheres?

That's right. Yes, and with mutual respect. You know, if you look at the plain we are on, you see the Sandias, which I have always thought of as male, and across, way across, is Mt. Taylor, whom I always have thought of as female. She stays there, and he stays here and they converse. They don't get mixed up in thinking that one has to be the other one, and they don't think they have to merge. If they ever do think that, we are in trouble, all of us who live in between. And that's why the mountains are that way, and

that's how I see the appropriate balance of genders. I think that we live in separate spheres. We have different consciousnesses, because we have different bodies. We need each other; but only if we recognize the validity of our own way, and therefore the validity of the other person's way, are we ever going to be able to actually function together.

We should accept the differences?

Absolutely, and use them; it is essential. You know, patriarchy is about monogamy, it is about monotony, it is about monotheism, it is about unity, and it is about uniformity. No Indian system is like that, in any sense. They never wanted other people to be like them. That's why they don't recruit members. They don't only respect difference and acknowledge it; they expect it, and they always have. That's why they got conquered, as a matter of fact. They did not understand that there were people who thought that there was only one way of doing things and that was their way, and if you did not do it their way they would kill you.

Ephanie, in *The Woman Who Owned the Shadows,* is not supposed to unite with the men. She keeps expecting men to do her life for her, because she got feminized in the western way instead of the tribal way. She made a terrible mistake and she paid for it until she understood that she had power in her own right.

And the healing process is the recovering of her past?

Her past and her place in the world, yes; her past, her place, and therefore her identity.

How has all this helped you resolve your own sense of who you are, your own sense of identity?

I had a lot of questions about that when I was quite a bit younger. It was really important in my twenties. By the time I was in my early thirties, I had pretty much resolved it for myself. I am Lebanese-American, I am Indian, I am a breed, and I am New Mexican and they have a lot to do with how I act and what I think and how I interpret things. I was raised in a family and in a world that was multicultural, multiethnic, multireligious, and multilinguistic, with a number of social classes involved. All of those people were my relatives, and all of those people were part of me, because they had an impact on me.

You mention in **The Sacred Hoop** *that there is an unconscious assumption that these identities must be in conflict, and a choice therefore has to be made, but that you don't see that this necessarily has to be.*

No, it does not have to be. Though, certainly, there are times where the Lebanese Paula and the Indian Paula come into awful conflict, because they are different. So certainly, there is intra-psychic conflict and stress that arises. And then I have a kind of overlaying or underlaying American or Anglo culture that I mostly picked up in school. It is all me. It sometimes comes into conflict with itself, but it is all me.

Does incorporating all parts of your origins, rather than making a choice, become a means of survival?

You have to incorporate them all. I think that's where you

get into alienation, thinking that you cannot have the whole bulk, that you *have* to choose.

Do you think the philosophy or ideology that you have to be either one or the other is part of the colonization process?

Yes, I do, absolutely. It is very clear in the case of the Native Americans. They have been propagandized for anywhere from one hundred to four hundred years—depending on the region of the country—that they have to choose. Then all the stories that were written about the Indian between two chairs—all of La Farge and Frank Waters—and of course the Indian between two chairs has to choose, cannot choose, and therefore dies. This tells all the youngsters growing up that they are going to die. It is a genocidal myth. I know all kinds of people, Indian people, full bloods, traditionals, half-bloods, whatever, who can manage to do both quite nicely. But they are not the ones that show up in literature, and there is a reason for that. If it is white writers, it is because they really want all the Indians dead. They are not going to admit that; they really think they pity the Indian. But why are they killing them all in their books, if they really want them to live? How come they are always dying? Good question!

You see these writers creating a myth they would like to see realized?

That's right. What is it? The self-fulfilling tendency of expectation? And it works very insidiously, but it works. So I have been teaching for a long, long time that you must accept all your identities; they are yours, and nobody has the right to take them away from you. You have to be a lot smarter to manage two cultures or five cultures than you do to manage one. Americans—white Americans, I mean, because nobody else in America has this luxury but white Americans—think they are smarter because they have only one culture, and they don't understand that the more cultures you have, the greater your range; your personal range, your intellectual range, and your emotional range is much greater. It is like assuming that if you only eat potatoes, that somehow you are better than the people who eat rice, corn, wheat, potatoes, and pasta.

And I think that of the western nations the United States is very peculiar in that way. It tends to think that there is only the Anglo-Protestant capitalist way of doing things.

You know how white folks like to go out to the reservation to see Indians? Well, I love to watch TV and watch white folks; it's great fun. But I didn't know why I liked it so much. I used to get mad, because they said the dumbest things, until it finally dawned on me that they are talking to each other, and to them American means this very narrow group of middle- to upper-class Anglo-European people who go to Protestant church—not fundamentalist Protestant, but respectable Protestant—and they have homes and cars, and they all look the same way, eat the same food, and do the same things. They are only these people on TV, and that leaves out at least 40 percent of the people in the United States, a lot of whom are white, a lot of whom are European, but they don't happen to live in that little tiny culture box, so they don't show up on TV as being Americans.

I finally realized that that's because we are *not* Americans. Americans are a very specifically defined cultural entity to which a lot of citizens of the United States do not belong. We are citizens of the United States, but we are not Americans. And that's definitely very weird! It doesn't make me mad anymore; it strikes me as hilarious and stupid and short sighted, and possibly dangerous. But it is pretty funny. How can you live in Washington, DC, surrounded by black people and think that way?

You say that you have incorporated your different ethnic backgrounds. How does Ephanie, in **The Woman Who Owned the Shadows,** *incorporate the white world? She seems to go further and further into her Indianness.*

And then she goes back to teach white people. So her resolution is that this is not about race; this is about vision. The people who live on this continent are Indians, that is to say, they live on the Indian continent, and what we must do is teach them how to live here. We tried and they kept killing us. That was then; but now maybe there are people here, lots of them, who are ready. . . . Ephanie goes back to the world as a teacher and she knows who she is.

Is that why she says "I mix my metaphors with care"?

That's right. You have to do it, and she learns very carefully. She has to have that whole period of isolation and relearning herself before she is in any position to be able to do that. Then she is going as herself back into the white world; it is different from the way she originally did it. First she went into the white world to find herself, and that did not work; it made her crazy, literally crazy and suicidal. You can't do that, you can't borrow an identity, you have to go out from your own identity.

Ephanie goes into the mythical past and recovers the myth. As a writer, do you see yourself as a recoverer of myths or as a creator of myths?

As a writer I am not a creator of myths. As a channel I am.

How do you distinguish between being a writer and being a channel?

Well, writers invent and I do it, too. But there are passages where, frankly, somebody else takes over. It is not me, and the reason I know it is not me is because they say stuff I wouldn't have said, and in fact, some of it I disagree with.

There is a passage in **The Woman Who Owned the Shadows** about the Grandmothers, "And then for long eons they slept." I love that passage, and I wrote it in the physical sense of writing down the words, but, frankly, somebody took hold of my pencil and they wrote it. I was just the typewriter, so to speak. And it wasn't as though I was in a trance or unconscious; I don't mean that. It was conscious, but I would not have thought of writing that. So I am talking about another order. I think you touch into the mythstream that is always there; it is part of the world; it is part of the universe.

Is that what you are getting at when you mention that rather than say "I wrote it," you say "I listened"?

Yes, and a writer's job is to be as accurate a receiver as you can be. It is hard work. For one thing you have to read a lot, talk a lot, and think a lot, and take a lot of time for yourself. You have to know a lot of people, and you have to have a good ear. Otherwise, when the stuff comes through, you are going to try to change it, because you are not going to recognize it. So you have to be a very knowledgeable, experimental instrument; you have to have a range of knowledge and adaptability and physical experience, because only then can you become a good instrument.

And you have to learn how to listen.

That's it; you have to learn how, especially if you were raised in America. I don't mean rural America, though, because I was raised on those mesas, with a great deal of freedom to listen to myself. My mother was very verbal about it. She would complain about people who would not let their children just daydream. I spent weeks up on the mesa. I didn't talk a lot to people; I did not learn to talk to people until I was well into my twenties. I was an introverted person and I needed to be, so I would have the ability to listen.

What new directions are you taking in your new novel, Raven's Road?

That's such a hard book, another thirteen-year book, and I really would like to get it done soon instead of thirteen years from now. But I have a cast of characters that is huge, and an outline that is seventeen pages long and I can't make head or tails of it. I started out to write a very simple lesbian novel just for fun. But I got involved. So I have a story about Indian people in Albuquerque, an urban group; some folks out in Isleta; a lesbian community in Albuquerque; the national lesbian community; alcoholism and battering; the bomb; and the antipornography movement, and I am trying to work this out over a time frame of about forty years, from '45 to '85. Meanwhile I want to write a thousand-page novel, and I don't want to write a trilogy; so I am stuck.

The excerpt that was published in The New Native American Novel, *where Allie and Raven watch a nuclear explosion at Yucca Flats, Nevada, seems to suggest that you are dealing with the geopolitical aspect of the nuclear bomb, and also that you see a deeper meaning behind nuclear power.*

That excerpt is the sacred heart of the novel.

As I see it at this point, the bomb is seen because of the Grandmothers, and because Allie and Raven are both medicine-women, for lack of a better word. They are who they are because of what another Indian woman had said to Raven years before.

The bomb is about cleansing the planet; it is about the voice of another power. There are reasons why I see it that way, some of which are metaphysical. Well, for heaven's sake, all the Buddhists have always been praying for enlightenment, so why are they not thrilled about this bomb? It would be very enlightening. You get more light from those things than you could possibly get in any other way. . . .

Uranium was first mined at Laguna, and the form it comes in is called yellowcake. The color of femaleness is yellow, and at Laguna a woman's face is painted yellow with some red spots when she dies, so that when she comes to Shipap, the Mother will know who she is and that she is respectful and respectable. So that is sitting in my head. Then the bomb is all of this light, and for me light means two things: it means colonization and genocide, and it also means "Turn on the light so I can see in the dark."

> A writer's job is to be as accurate a receiver as you can be. It is hard work. For one thing you have to read a lot, talk a lot, and think a lot, and take a lot of time for yourself. You have to know a lot of people, and you have to have a good ear. Otherwise, when the stuff comes through, you are going to try to change it, because you are not going to recognize it.
>
> *—Paula Gunn Allen*

Since I think the planet is the Mother and the galaxy is the Grandmother, and since I think that nothing goes on here that She did not think of to begin with, then I am left with the question of why She would think of this. That's the question I am working on in those segments. I don't know what the answer is going to be, and neither do Allie and Raven. All they know is that they are supposed to be watching this thing. But certainly, one of the things I can see right now is that a bunch of complacent colonizers are threatened with the extinction that they have visited upon everyone else. And, I don't know—I have a tacky sense of humor—I enjoy it. I think it is very funny watching them racing around trying to stop their own ultimate extinction.

They haven't cared about ultimate extinction before. They have extinguished race after race after race, and all the species of animals who ever lived—right now 99 percent are extinct—and nobody cared. Now all of a sudden . . .

But were they not created by the Mother, too?

Yes, they were created, and they have to leave. I mean, I figure that even privilege was created to create exactly *this* situation, but I am not really sure if we have to blow up. Sometimes I think, great, I can't think of a better way to get to Nirvana. I mean—think of it—instant vaporization; there couldn't be a more pleasant way to die. Fifteen minutes is all you've got; you don't have six months or three years, you know. Not only that, but you're instantly vaporized, turned into spirit. That's really something to think about. So maybe that's what She is doing; that's a neat way to do it . . .

So you think there is a meaning behind it all, a pattern that we are just enacting?

We might find it very uncomfortable; I am sure that we

don't want to go. But people don't like it too much when a mountain blows up and there is a volcano; they will have to get out of the way or perish. The Mother cares for us greatly, but not for us more than for herself. And the thing is, we don't know what time it is.

You have talked a lot about the Mother, the Mother Earth, Grandmother Universe. What has being a mother meant to you?

I always thought that I would go on to the beach, become a beatnik and have a good time. But I had to feed the kids, and more importantly, I lived in a world that to my eyes was a real mess, and here I had brought these innocent people into it—it was my idea, after all, it wasn't their idea—so I was responsible. That meant I had to work, I had to write, and I had to teach, because I had to have some input into the situation that they would grow up in, and I think that their existence impelled me. They are also very bright and interesting people, so they themselves push me in all kinds of directions. And then there is the simple fact of knowing what being a mother means. Sometimes it means not being nice; sometimes it is not smelling sweet and baking cookies, and doing everything baby wants just because that's what baby wants.

It is like that in nature, and you have to think about the larger picture, the whole, and what's going on around you. It has allowed me to notice parts of Mother Earth that I didn't understand before, because I could just have said that mothers are terrible people, which people in America love to say, if-my-mother-hadn't-been-so-rotten-I-would-have-been-wonderful, you know. Some mothers really are dreadful, and that's part of it. Have you even seen birds function with babies? They are not nice. In a patriarchy, of course, we are supposed to think that we are better than the animals, but I don't think so; they seem to be pretty smart. But I had to notice all that, because I had to reconcile conflicts within myself; I wanted to be a good mother, but then I had to bring out what that means, had to think about it.

So being a mother led you back to the earth and its mothering cycle?

Yes. And then, in fact, you become immortal; not because you have kids, but because you reclaim yourself for being. You close the circle.

Ursula K. Le Guin   (review date 14 May 1989)

SOURCE: "Above All, Keep the Tale Going," in *The New York Times Book Review,* May 14, 1989, p. 15.

[*Le Guin is an American novelist, short story writer, nonfiction writer, critic, editor, poet, playwright, and author of children's books. In the following, she discusses the arrangement and focus of the stories collected in* Spider Woman's Granddaughters.]

Louise Erdrich has become a best seller, and Leslie Marmon Silko, Linda Hogan and other Native American women rank high among modern writers. First with her critical essays in *The Sacred Hoop,* and now with this fine collection of stories [entitled *Spider Woman's Grand-*

daughters: Traditional Tales and Contemporary Writing by Native American Women], Paula Gunn Allen gives us a much needed context for their work. In her introduction and in notes to the stories, Ms. Allen, a professor of Native American studies at the University of California, Berkeley, discusses who these writers are, why they write as they do and how they are linked by tradition, by experience as women and as Indians, and above all by an understanding of what a story *does.*

For underlying these narratives, conventional as some of them appear, is a very different idea of the function of art than the Euro-American one. The difference is exhilarating. Ms. Allen helps us to appreciate it and to use it to get past the merely ethnic to the value of the stories as works of art.

And every story in the book, which covers nearly a century of tradition, is interesting, written with intelligent passion; several are real treasures. Impressive, too, is Ms. Allen's arrangement of them, so that they interact to form larger patterns, giving the book an esthetic wholeness rare in anthologies. That wholeness may itself be seen as a demonstration of a Native American esthetic principle: "Tribal art of all kinds," Ms. Allen writes in the introduction, "embodies the principle of kinship, rendering the beautiful in terms of connectedness of elements in harmonious, balanced, respectful proportion of each and any to all-in-All." So, despite its richness, the book may be read right through without surfeit. But one will want also to dwell on individual pieces, as one's gaze returns to the bluest turquoises in a fine bracelet.

Grouping the stories in three sections, "The Warriors," "The Casualties" and "The Resistance," Ms. Allen explains a guiding theme: "In the tribal way, war means a ritual path, a kind of tao or spiritual discipline that can test honor, selflessness, and devotion, and put the warrior in closer, more powerful harmony with the supernaturals and the earth."

Such a use of the war-warrior metaphor is familiar from the works of Carlos Castaneda, Maxine Hong Kingston and others. But I find myself asking if, in a world where war in fact means genocide in the service of institutionalized power, the word can be reclaimed as spiritually meaningful. Does it appropriately describe these stories? Are they war stories? There is indeed violence in them, underlying every one of them, though some don't show it directly. There is anger and determined courage in them. And the Native Americans' perception of themselves as being in an invaded country, at war, is neither metaphor nor exaggeration. But still I have to force myself to read these stories as hero tales about warriors. Ms. Allen's title, *Spider Woman's Granddaughters,* points to another central image in these stories—the family, a deeper, richer idea than that of war.

The characters in these stories are seen not only *against,* but *with.* They are members of a great family, honoring the propriety of kinship, grieving when relationship is dishonored or betrayed, celebrating familiarity with people, animals, places, suffering when isolated, striving to maintain connection under the indifferent, dispersing pressure of an alien power. These are sisters and brothers, parents and babies, uncles and nieces, grandsons and grandmothers, wives and husbands, cousins, orphans, lost children, adopted children, children of the People, of the earth. They are all related.

Pointedly and charmingly, Ms. Allen distinguishes the oral and the written as "told to people" and "told to the page." She shows how the two narrative modes work together in contemporary Indian literature. Leslie Marmon Silko's haunting story "Yellow Woman" gathers new echoes and depths by being placed after three traditional tales of Yellow Woman, Corn Woman of the Pueblos.

Reading an oral piece translated from its original language to English, and from voice to print, is like reading a musical score: you have to know a lot before you can hear what's happening. On the page, oral literature seems stiff and "primitive," because it's less than half there; it's only the notation of a performance. Dell Hymes, Dennis Tedlock and other scholars have solved some of the problems; I wish Ms. Allen had used examples of more readable oral transcription. But though we miss the music, we can pick up the story line; we can begin to get some sense of the world in which Yellow Woman has her multiple and immortal being.

One of the pieces in the anthology is a "told to the whiteman" story, an excerpt from the extraordinary autobiography narrated to an ethnographer by a Crow, Pretty Shield. "Pretty Shield makes it clear," Ms. Allen notes, that "the one who tells the stories rules the world." Rather than ruling the world, perhaps, for Crow women had little political power, the storyteller *runs* it—she keeps it going, holds things together, weaves and reweaves the thought-web. That is what the women in these stories and the women who wrote them are doing.

Old-fashioned and melodramatic in style, "As It Was in the Beginning," published in 1913 by E. Pauline Johnson, tells of the betrayal of one way of life by another, the betrayal of a woman by a man, the vengeance she exacts and the loss she suffers. The loss is total. Nothing is palliated. The missionaries "teach me of [hell], only to fling me into it." The fierce clarity of this story is transmuted, three quarters of a century later, in Vickie L. Sears's "Grace." The tone now is quiet; the subject is an interlude of grace in a child's short lifetime of abuse and endurance. It is unforgettable. As in Chekhov, the voice of the child narrator gives pain a luminous edge almost too bright to bear.

"The Warriors" of Anna Lee Walters's story are Uncle Ralph, a drunk and a bum, and his sister and her children, who watch their warrior lose his war and do not cease to love and respect him. "He knew that we must live beautifully or not live at all." In this, as in so many of the stories, it is very important that the women talk together, stay together, keep the tale going.

The enchanting tale "The Clearing in the Valley" by Soge Track is a kind of many-leveled dream, like a pueblo dwelling where you climb up the ladder to come out into the light. That a girl child could actually take over the sacred duty of the *hochin,* the "watcher," as a character does in the story, is unlikely, Ms. Allen says in a note; but the

passionately vivid detail of the telling compels belief. After his death, an Old Man talks to the child by the water, under the trees. He tells her a story; the story is true. Its truth is her obedience to it. "In beauty shall you sing for your people."

Humishima, or Cristal Galler, wrote her novel *Cogewea, the Half-Blood* while working as field laborer in the 1920's. Terms like "squaws," "papooses," "many snows"—the stock lingo of prejudice—impede appreciation of the real purity of the language and vision in the excerpt here presented, but soon one is caught, and longs to read the whole book. Linda Hogan, a fine poet, writes with great control and art, but her story "Making Do," about a woman who loses her children, has that same purity as Humishima's, and the same aching sense of betrayal and loss. "She looked at his small roughbox and said, 'He died of life and I know how that can happen.'" Every word of her story weighs heavy, like gold. "We make do," she says. "We make art out of our loss."

Indian humor is probably the quietest and driest in the world. The title of LeAnne Howe's 1987 story "An American in New York" is a good example. Her narrator goes on "high-stakes bond business" to the Big Apple; it doesn't take long for the worm to turn. "No wonder we sold the whole place for twenty-six bucks and some beads," she remarks. She talks to immigrants—an Irishman after the good life, a Nigerian cab driver who wants to "do something" about the plight of Native Americans. When she gets to the Statue of Liberty, she decides that Emma Lazarus was really an Indian.

"Give me your tired, your poor, your huddled masses yearning to breathe free."

"You did," says the narrator. "Now where do we go from here?"

Margaret Randall   (review date September 1989)

SOURCE: "Many-Colored Poets," in *The Women's Review of Books,* Vol. VI, No. 12, September, 1989, pp. 29-31.

[*An American poet, short story writer, and editor, Randall frequently writes on Hispanic themes. In the excerpt below, she offers a positive assessment of* Skins and Bones, *asserting that these are "poems of identity: moving back in time, conjuring, inventing, reclaiming memory and using it powerfully."*]

Paula Gunn Allen, recently 50, is a Laguna Pueblo/Sioux/Lebanese woman whose critical work as well as her poetry and fiction have reached a powerful maturity. Born in 1939, she was raised on a Spanish land grant in New Mexico. Her life and work move back and forth between the landscapes of her growing, her culture in its traditions, and the scholarship that has made that heritage a documented resource for us all.

Allen is best known for ***The Sacred Hoop: Recovering the Feminine in American Indian Traditions.*** Before that there was the volume of critical essays and course designs she edited, ***Studies in American Indian Literature,*** published in 1983. Her novel, *The Woman Who Owned the Shadows* reminds us of her great richness with words. *Skins and Bones* is her sixth book of poems; previous volumes go back to 1975. Allen teaches Native American Studies at the University of California in Berkeley. . . .

In her moving effort to retrieve a spurned history, Paula Gunn Allen begins her [*Skin and Bones*] with "Songs of Tradition" and moves through "Songs of Colonization" and "Songs of Generation." We have learned to expect such attention to history from this author of *The Sacred Hoop.* I found the poems in the first section, "C'koy'u, Old Woman," the most provocative and exciting. They comprise a deeply female journey in the tradition of Muriel Rukeyser, Jane Cooper and Adrienne Rich, whose work has brought so many of our foremothers to life. Allen's sense of history also moves along a road cleared by the likes of Uruguayan Eduardo Galeano in his trilogy *Genesis of Fire.*

And Allen takes on difficult foremothers. She explores complex figures like La Malinche, Pocahontas and Sacagawea, by beginning with images of their lives prefaced by short passages from more often heard male voices. Then her renditions take off on their own, free of sweetened metaphor or an urge to turn it all to right. Listen to these lines, from **"Molly Brant, Iroquois Matron, Speaks":**

> . . . But
> we had forgotten the Elder's Plan.
> So it was we could not know
> a Council Fire would be out,
> . . . We had not counted on fate—
> so far from the Roots of our being
> had we flown . . .
> That's how it is with revolutions.
> Wheels turn. So do planets.
> Stars turn. So do galaxies.
> Mortals see only this lifetime
> or that. How could we know,
> bound to the borders we called home,
> the Revolution we conspired for
> would turn us under
> like last year's crop? . . .
> I speak now because I know
> the Revolution has not let up.
> Others like my brother and like me
> conspire with other dreams,
> argue whether or not
> to blow earth up, or poison it mortally
> or settle for alteration . . .
> Still, let them obliterate it, I say.
> What do I care?
> What have I to lose,
> having lost all I loved so long ago?
> Aliens, aliens everywhere,
> and so few of the People
> left to dream. All that is left
> is not so precious after all—
> great cities, piling drifting clouds
> of burning death, waters that last drew
> breath
> decades, perhaps centuries ago,
> fourleggeds, wingeds, reptiles all
> drowned in bloodred rivers of an alien
> dream
> of progress. Progress is what

> they call it. I call it cemetery,
> charnel house, soul sickness,
> artificial mockery
> of what we called life.

Skins and Bones is filled with lost history, wisdom and humor. Poems like **"Eve the Fox," "Taking a Visitor to See the Ruins"** and **"Teaching Poetry at Votech High, Santa Fe, the Week John Lennon Was Shot"** offer a particular mix of American Indian humor with the raw context from which it emerges; and the joke only superficially provides a cover for the serious statement even as it salts our lips for more.

The ruins of the second poem are not ancient Indian dwellings but Allen's family:

> Joe, I said when we'd gotten inside the chic
>   apartment,
> I'd like you to meet the old Indian ruins
> I promised.
> My mother, Mrs. Francis, and my
> grandmother, Mrs. Gottlieb.
> His eyes grew large, and then he
> laughed . . .

Allen on the exploitation of Native Americans:

There is no America without the death of an Indian. And there can *be* no America without acknowledgement of one of its major sources. Every time you flush the toilet, some Navajo goes without water. You understand that. Staying in this hotel in LA means that those folks out on the res are in trouble because we have all these goodies. And that's true across the board, for every aspect of American life. There *is* no America that is not deeply wedded to the Indian. So, you know, exploitation, what does that mean? We've been exploited right out of house and home.

> *Paula Gunn Allen, in an interview with Franchot Ballinger and Brian Swann, in* MELUS, *Summer, 1983.*

Carol Bruchac   (review date November 1989)

SOURCE: A review of *Spider Woman's Granddaughters: Traditional Tales and Contemporary Writing by Native American Women,* in *Parabola,* Vol. XIV, No. 4, November, 1989, pp. 98, 102.

[*An editor and critic, Bruchac helped establish the* Greenfield Review Magazine and Press, *which frequently promotes and publishes Native American literature. In the review below, she praises* Spider Woman's Granddaughters *as "unique historically, culturally, and creatively."*]

Paula Gunn Allen's anthology, *Spider Woman's Granddaughters,* combines traditional Native American tales with compelling contemporary writings from a variety of native voices and, most importantly, all told by tribal women. As Allen puts it in her extensive introduction, "One of my major concerns has been that these stories not be read as 'women's literature' as that term has come to be applied in contemporary feminist writing. Rather, it is of great importance that they be read as 'tribal women's literature.'"

This collection is unique historically, culturally, and creatively. It brings together and brings to life a special group of women. Some of them are long dead—for example, the Crow wise-woman Pretty Shield, who told her life to Frank Linderman, and Zitkala-Sa, whose stories were first published in *The Atlantic Monthly* at the turn of this century—yet their voices remain immediate and alive. Some have acquired respect and attention as writers, such as Louise Erdrich, Leslie Silko, Linda Hogan, and Anna Lee Walters. Others, such as Misha Gallagher and LeAnne Howe, are just beginning to see their work in print. What all of them have in common, though, is that their work teaches us, making us more aware of what being female and being Native American means. We begin to understand this in Allen's introduction, as she tells us why and how she went about collecting the stories for this book, giving us a history of Native American literature and the difficulties faced by native women in finding publishers.

Most helpful to the reader is the concise, chilling history she provides of the destruction and dislocation of Native American cultures. She truly gives, in her own words, "a sense of the cultural values that informed Anglo-European culture at the time of conquest and throughout the conquest and colonization periods" which succeeds in aiding one to understand "some of the differences between Native and non-Native understanding of both aesthetics and history." In the face of the white male domination of Anglo-European aesthetics, it is a tribute to the strength of female-centered, non-materialistic Native American cultures that they were able to survive at all, much less produce powerful writers less than a century after full-scale genocide was attempted against them.

The anthology is divided into three parts: "The Warriors," "The Casualties," and "The Resistance," further evidence of Allen's awareness of the sort of victory this volume symbolizes. In the first section, "Oshkikwe's Baby," a traditional Chippewa tale of supernatural baby-stealing, precedes and is set against Louise Erdrich's superb "American Horse," on the same subject. (The separation of children from parents is only one of the important themes running through this anthology.) Ella Cara Deloria's "Blue Bird's Offering" (which comes from Deloria's novel *Waterlily,* completed in 1944 but not published until 1988) tells of a young woman's discovery of the power of prayer as she saves her baby and finds her own "camp circle." The eleven stories in this section, arranged in such a way as to form a coherent whole, are all memorable. None, however, is more meaningful than the story which lends this section its title. In Anna Lee Walters' "The Warriors," two young sisters learn pride in their Pawnee heritage from their Uncle, a disillusioned homeless alcoholic.

The second section of the book includes only five tales, closing with "Grace" by Vicki Sears and "Making Do" by Linda Hogan. The power of the Sears story is not in its depiction of the physical and sexual abuse of two small Indi-

an children, but rather in the short respite from that abuse. The sweetness of the children's time with kind foster parents makes their forced return to the orphanage that much more horrifying. "Making Do" is yet another example of Hogan's special ability to capture moments of bleakness and despair and fill them with rich spiritual and physical beauty.

The final section of the anthology, "The Resistance," continues to match traditional narratives with powerful contemporary stories. It links, for example, Leslie Silko's often anthologized "Yellow Woman" with the Laguna Pueblo traditional tale of how Whirlwind stole Yellow Woman (a powerful being who represents not only "concerns of loss, persecution, rescue, and the relation of these to the sacred," but also the sacred ears of corn which sustain human life).

Upon finishing this anthology, I found myself in complete agreement with Allen's introduction which said, "The stories are informed with humor and rich in insight. They sing the songs of the tribes as we make our way from near extinction at the beginning of the century to increased health and vitality as we near its end." This book is a treasure which informs, inspires, and leaves one wanting to hear more from these "tribal voices."

Robert L. Berner   (review date Spring 1990)

SOURCE: A review of *Spider Woman's Granddaughters: Traditional Tales and Contemporary Writing by Native American Women,* in *World Literature Today,* Vol. 64, No. 2, Spring, 1990, pp. 344-45.

[*In the following negative review of* Spider Woman's Granddaughters, *Berner claims that the book is at times historically inaccurate and that Allen's editorializing and rhetoric have the potential to mislead readers and reinforce stereotypes.*]

[In *Spider Woman's Granddaughters: Traditional Tales and Contemporary Writing by Native American Women*] Paula Gunn Allen has combined several traditional stories with short works by seventeen writers, eleven of them contemporary. One can only hope that anyone who buys her book will read the stories and ignore her introduction and notes, which are marred by extraordinary historical errors. Some of them, such as referring to the Dawnes Severalty Act (Dawes) and John Rolling Ridge (Rollin) and implying that Calhoun was Jefferson's secretary of state, may be due in part to careless editing; but others, such as saying that "the Allies liberated . . . Greece or Lebanon earlier in this century," can only be blamed on her faulty grasp of historical fact. These lapses are nothing compared to her claim that in the twenty-five years after the Civil War "the Anglo-Americans" slaughtered "millions" of Indians, a process of which she says later, "No holocaust in this millennium has been more destructive." One can only wonder what she expects any reader who knows anything at all about Hitler or Pol Pot or the demography of the Great Plains in the nineteenth century to make of such a hysterical statement.

Not that this would matter if Allen's editorial rationale

derived not from this preposterous premise but from a real concern for the literature that has been produced by American Indian women. Certainly the thrust of this review would be toward the selections themselves rather than what Allen says about them, if she were able to say anything at all about her texts that is not merely political. Beginning with her wild genocidal charge—which actually belittles the real victims of Sand Creek and Wounded Knee by submerging them in her fictitious "millions"—she develops the premise that American Indian women are "women at war" and then selects works which reveal women who are warriors or whose exploits she can interpret as warriorlike. She reveals little interest in the great variety of roles played by American Indian women either before or since their conquest. Her rhetoric, in other words, is that of radical feminism; and because she has chosen to define the enemy of American Indian women as both male and white, it is that of the reverse sexism and reverse racism of the fashionably "progressive."

One can only wonder for what audience Allen intended her commentaries. Why would any male—white or Indian—be pleased to have read them? Why would any Jew or Cambodian? Why would any white woman? Why would any Indian woman who does not share Allen's political premises? Anyone really interested in the subject can find almost all of Allen's texts in other editions and can leave **Spider Woman's Granddaughters** to those who read only to reinforce their prejudices.

Yvonne J. Milspaw (review date April-June 1990)

SOURCE: A review of *The Sacred Hoop: Recovering the Feminine in American Indian Traditions,* in *Journal of American Folklore,* Vol. 103, No. 408, April-June, 1990, pp. 245-47.

[*In the following, Milspaw faults the uneven quality of the essays included in* The Sacred Hoop, *but argues that the collection "is enormously important to our understanding of the growing body of superb Native American Literature."*]

Paula Gunn Allen's collection of essays on contemporary American Indian literature [**The Sacred Hoop: Recovering the Feminine in American Indian Traditions**] focuses on her conviction that Native American cultures were essentially gynocentric, and, as a result, Native American literature is inherently feminist. Arguing from her position as a feminist, an American Indian, a poet, a novelist, a critic, and a scholar (she teaches Native American Studies at Berkeley), she presents her material forcefully, gracefully, and at times, quite convincingly.

Her major argument is built around the centrality of Woman (in her guises as Mother, Grandmother, Old Woman Spider, Thought Woman, or Kochinnenaka, Yellow Woman), in her own Keresian Pueblo/Sioux tradition. She extends her argument to include much of Native American literature. But a second theme, that of the interchangeability of the spirit world and the natural world, of "real" time and ceremonial time, quickly emerges as the more important focus of her essays. That the spirit beings who cluster around these ceremonies are female is impor-

tant to the reader's understanding of the literature; however, it quickly appears less important to the literature than does the reader's emergent understanding of the underlying nature of the ritual/ceremony itself. Allen's feminist argument is discouragingly strained and overextended at points, though it is largely convincing. On the other hand, her discussion of time, myth, ritual, and ceremony in American Indian literature is nothing short of stunning. It is in this area that Allen's book is enormously important to our understanding of the growing body of superb Native American literature.

Allen's work introduces us to the common world of Native American experience, a world deeply and fundamentally different from the Anglo common world. As Hannah Arendt articulated it in *The Human Condition:*

> The common world is what we enter when we are born and what we leave behind when we die. It transcends our life-span into past and future alike; it was there before we came and will outlast our brief sojourn into it. It is what we have in common not only with those who live with us, but also with those who were here before and with those who will come after us. But such a common world can survive the coming and going of the generations only to the extent that it appears in public. It is the publicity of the public realm which can absorb and make shine through the centuries whatever men [sic] may want to save from the natural ruin of time.

The "common world" of Native American experience is one not open to most of us, just as the Anglo world mystifies many Native Americans; furthermore, the public presentation of the Native "common world" has been variously misinterpreted, misunderstood, misrepresented, and homogenized (usually, but not always inadvertently) by Anglicized scholars whose world of common experience is far different from the tradition they hope to represent faithfully. In attempting to make public a "common world" that departs so radically and fundamentally from the public Anglo norm (matriarchal versus patriarchal, synchronic versus diachronic), both Native American and feminist scholars have found a common ground. Allen's work attempts to bridge the gap between both the Native and Anglo worlds of common experience, and by extension between the feminist/other world. It is a tall order.

It is, however, also an essential order. If Arendt is correct that without "the publicity of the public realm" the common world will not survive, then works like Allen's are crucial to our proper understanding of the literature and culture of Native Americans. Feminist scholars have happily interpreted Arendt's words as a plea to rescue and make public women's history. But the survivalist approach, implied in Arendt's explanation, is especially problematic in folklore. Most cultures seem to muddle along quite nicely whether we (Anglo scholars) know about them or not. On the other hand, knowing about them, making other ideas and other worlds public, enriches our own common world. And of course that is what folklorists try to do. It is also what Paula Gunn Allen attempts to do. And to a large extent she succeeds.

Allen bases most of her material and her understanding

of it in her own experience as a Keresian Pueblo woman. Her analysis of gynocentricity, myth, ritual, ceremony, and of literature depends heavily on her careful articulation of her own "common world." This is essential to her argument. But it also creates a limit to her best literary criticism. Though she concludes that her analyses apply to Native American literature in general, her very best critiques are predictably those of other Southwestern Native American writers, particularly Leslie Marmon Silko. Allen's critiques of James Welch's fine novel, *Winter in the Blood,* and N. Scott Momaday's prize-winning *House Made of Dawn* are cases in point. Her comments on the books, especially on the use of time, are quite good, but neither review has the depth or insight she is able to lavish on writers from her own cultural background, particularly on Silko's extraordinary work, *Ceremony.* It is difficult to determine whether it is the differences of gender or culture (Momaday is Kiowa, Welch is Blackfeet/Gros Ventre) which might account for the differences, or simply that those reviews suffer by comparison. Allen is so close to Silko by culture, gender, and, one suspects, sympathy that Allen's critique of her work is unsurpassed.

The essays in *The Sacred Hoop,* compiled from many earlier sources, are uneven. They range from the merely rhetorical and uninspired to the absolutely wonderful. Her arguments on "cultural fears" resound hollowly; her feminist arguments are sometimes angry rather than compelling; her extraordinary argument for a lesbian tradition in Native American women's culture, though engaging, seems based on flimsy evidence. On the other hand, much of what is offered in *The Sacred Hoop* is extremely good. In spite of its unevenness, Allen never loses sight of her central thesis. Throughout her analyses she strives to reveal the feminine forces at the center of the world. She herself becomes Kochinnenaka, Yellow Woman, who leads the way from winter to summer, from myth to reality, from darkness to understanding in Keresian myth and ceremony. She is at the center of the world, of the sacred hoop. She is able to bring the willing reader to a deeper understanding of the common world of American Indian tradition. Unfortunately those who stand to benefit most from this book—literary scholars in the Anglo tradition—may be the very ones who will focus most sharply on its shortcomings, and thereby deprive themselves of the cultural insights so necessary to understanding the very literature they love. Let us hope, perhaps naïvely, that it will not happen.

Charlotte Tsoi Goodluck   (review date Summer 1990)

SOURCE: A review of *Spider Woman's Granddaughters: Traditional Tales and Contemporary Writing by Native American Women,* in *Belles Lettres: A Review of Books by Women,* Vol. 5, No. 4, Summer, 1990, pp. 40, 42.

[*In the review below, Goodluck positively assesses* Spider Woman's Granddaughters *and praises the collection's focus and organization.*]

Paula Gunn Allen, the editor of *Spider Woman's Granddaughter,* is a Laguna Pueblo/Sioux scholar, feminist, and professor of Native American studies. In *The Sacred Hoop,* she gave her audience a vision of the feminine in traditional native thought and literature. In this book [*Spider Woman's Granddaughters*] she has gathered views, ideas, and wisdom about surviving personal and social conflict, written by women from a number of different tribes. Stories about women warriors and their resistance to white encroachment accompany prose, by traditional and contemporary Native American women, concerning stress, conflict, loss, separation, relocation, death, rebirth, and revitalization.

Allen's review of historical events in her excellent introductory chapter is important in understanding the Native American struggle, as is her discussion of pertinent values and belief systems, such as community versus individuality. Her analysis of the philosophical and political differences between Western and Native American canons of thought, and her references to other Native American women's literature beyond this collection, set the mood.

The book is divided into three main sections: warriors, causalties, and resistance. This war theme serves as a metaphor upon which selected Native American women authors build throughout the book, and it is seen from several points of view (historical, contemporary, contextual, personal, familial, social, and political), all captured with rich, reflective prose.

External war between the Native American nations and the U.S. government has existed for more than two hundred years, accompanied by internal symptoms such as depression, alcoholism, suicide, and alienation. The women's stories, however, exhibit hope, personal and tribal empowerment, and examples of surviving oppression and racism as nations within nations. For example, LeAnne Howe, in "An American in New York," presents a Native American's take on the Big Apple and her struggle to integrate Indian and white cultures. She shares her "urban vision quest" with irony, joy, and witty cross-cultural observation.

Besides being an entertaining and informative book of general interest, *Spider Woman's Granddaughters* is an excellent educational resource. It includes twenty-one tribal women's voices, spanning time from the 1850s to the 1990s. Included are the works of well-known authors such as Louise Erdrich, Ella Cara Deloria, Linda Hogan, and Leslie Marmon Silko, but also offers an opportunity for readers to acquaint themselves with authors such as Zitkala-Sa and Mary TallMountain. The book also includes a selected biography and a glossary of Native American-related terms.

Spider Woman's Granddaughters weaves a web of interlocking suspension bridges made up of thoughts and visions for our contemporary world. Allen's insight and wisdom are gifts for others to savor and appreciate—much like the Cherokee legend about the Spider Woman referred to in creation stories and oral traditions of several tribes. Spider Woman is a powerful metaphor of strength, resilience, and re-construction of tribal ideologies and value systems. Allen is a quintessential Spider Woman, weaving her works for many grandchildren.

Annette Van Dyke   (essay date 1990)

SOURCE: "The Journey Back to Female Roots: A Laguna Pueblo Model," in *Lesbian Texts and Contexts: Radical Revisions,* edited by Karla Jay and Joanne Glasgow, New York University Press, 1990, pp. 339-54.

[*In the essay below, Van Dyke offers a thematic analysis of* The Woman Who Owned the Shadows, *arguing that Allen employs tribal concerns to discuss alienation, sexual identity, lesbianism, and, more specifically, "a journey to healing—a journey to the female center."*]

Paula Gunn Allen is a mixed-blood Native American lesbian who says she is Laguna Pueblo/Sioux/Lebanese-American and that she "writes out of a Laguna Indian woman's perspective" (*Sacred Hoop*). Allen continues her cultural traditional in her novel by using it in the same way in which the traditional arts have always functioned for the Laguna Pueblo. She has extended traditional storytelling into the modern form of the novel by weaving in the tribal history, cultural traditions, and mythology of the Laguna Pueblo to create a form of curing ceremony for her readers.

Allen published her novel *The Woman Who Owned the Shadows,* in 1983. She has many scholarly articles and chapbooks of poetry, and she has edited *Studies in American Indian Literature* (1983). A major book of poetry, *Shadow Country,* was published in 1982; her new book of poetry is entitled *Wyrds,* and a novel, *Raven's Road,* [portions of which have appeared as **"From *Raven's Road"*** in *The New Native American Novel, Works in Progress,* edited by Mary Dougherty Bartlett, 1986], is in progress.

Underlying American Indian literature are cultural assumptions and a worldview which contrast sharply with those underlying most non-Indian literature. To understand how Allen uses her cultural tradition in her novel, it is best to know something about the culture from which she comes. The Pueblo worldview, like that of other tribal cultures, is based on the concept that all things inanimate and animate are related and are part of the whole. Plants, animals, rocks, and people are in a reciprocal relationship, and people must carry on rituals, prayers, and offerings to keep things in balance in that reciprocal relationship. To the Pueblo, who have kept their worldview essentially intact, life is sacred and everything including the arts contributes to "light, life, well-being" [Elsie Clews Parsons, *Pueblo Indian Religion,* 1939]. The task of the individual is to contribute to the well-being of the group and keep the shifting balances in harmony.

Since the invasion of white men bringing a worldview which separates spirit and body, inanimate and animate, ceremonies are even more important to keep the relationships between all things in balance. The ultimate expression of this lack of balance is the development and use of the atomic bomb which another Laguna writer, Leslie Marmon Silko, documents in her novel, *Ceremony.* In this sense, lack of balance affects not only the individual but the whole of civilization. A worldview which separates spirit and body, inanimate from animate lacks respect for other parts of creation and fails to see the interrelatedness of all things—one's place in the web of being. The Euro-American worldview elevates one part of creation above others: humans over plants, animals, and earth; and mind/spirit over the physical. This leads ultimately to a lack of balance.

For the Laguna, geographic place is intricately tied into understanding one's place in the web of being, a special tie to the land. Balance cannot be achieved without a "knowing" related to continuity in a certain place. That place is important in Laguna culture is not surprising because the Pueblo are part of a continuum of inhabitation of the area from southern Utah and Colorado to northern Mexico since 10,000 B.C. The ancestors of the Pueblo occupied the four corners area, the spot where the states of Colorado, Utah, Arizona, and New Mexico intersect, and the Lagunas themselves have occupied their present area since about the thirteenth century.

In contrast to the Laguna way of harmony with the environment, critic Reyes Garcia points out [in "Senses of Place in *Ceremony," MELUS* 10, No. 4 (1983)] that the Euro-American way of shaping and controlling the environment "deprive[s] all lives, most of all their own, of substance." He feels that without our being able to "respond to the fertile meaning places hold, . . . our pulsing lives here will stop and Earth will come to an end, its radioactive memory locked in 'witchery's final ceremonial sand painting.' " Allen explores this theme in her novel *Raven's Road,* when she refers to the possible rebirth of Sun Woman as part of the atomic testing going on in the desert. As the main character watches the rising mushroom cloud, she saw "the old woman or great white bear or sun maiden or sun shield. . . . In her memory's eye she could see that the visual was of an old woman's face huge as the sky. . . ." Allen points out that Euro-Americans have no respect for the forces of the environment with which they tamper because they believe that they control everything. The delicate balances have been disrupted, and we must work to recover them. One way of righting the balance is by storytelling.

For the Lagunas, storytelling often functions as a ceremony for curing. Allen continues in this tradition—her novel is an offering to balance the world and enact healing rituals for herself and others. In an essay Allen says: "As base, every story, every song, every ceremony, tells the Indian he [*sic*] is part of a living whole, and that all parts of the whole are related to one another by virtue of their participation in the whole of being" [**"Sacred Hoop: A Contemporary Indian Perspective on Native American Literature,"** in *Literature of the American Indians: Views and Interpretation,* edited by Abraham Chapman, 1975]. She says that when the Europeans came in the fifteenth century. "the fragile web of identity that long held tribal people secure has gradually been weakened and torn. But the oral tradition has prevented the complete destruction of the web, the ultimate disruption of tribal ways" (*Sacred Hoop*). Through "the women who speak and work and write," the oral tradition continues now in English and helps to mend the web (*Sacred Hoop*). In an interview, Allen has said that her novel is a "medicine novel" or a "ritual handbook" meant to "get inside" the reader's head.

Allen's novel, then, can be seen as a kind of curing ceremony—a ceremony to insure survival and create new life. In [**"Who Is Your Mother? Red Roots of White Feminism,"** a recent essay in *Sinister Wisdom* 25 (1987)], Allen argues that feminists need to know about American Indian societies which are "recent social models from which its [feminism's] dream descends and to which its adherents can look for models" to reclaim the lost heritage of what she calls "gynarchial societies." Allen continues:

> We as feminists must be aware of our history on this continent. We need to recognize the same forces that devastated the gynarchies of Britain and the Continent also devastated the ancient African civilizations. . . . I am convinced that those wars have always been about the imposition of uncontested patriarchal civilization over the wholistic, pacifistic and spirit-based gynarchies they supplant, and to this end the wars . . . have not been . . . waged over the land and its resources, but more, they have been fought within the bodies, minds, and hearts of the people of the earth. This is, I think, the reason traditionalists say we must remember our origins, our cultures, our histories and our mothers and grandmother, for without that

memory, which implies continuance . . . we are doomed to extinction.

Because Indian values and culture have informed generations of Euro-Americans from the beginning of their emigration to America, and the Indian vision of a free and equal society has been the same as that of radical thinkers throughout history to recover the Indian values is to recover our own most radical values. Therefore, as we trace the journey of the main character in Allen's novel, we trace a model for our own.

Allen's novel, *The Woman Who Owned the Shadows,* is about a journey to healing—a journey back to the female center. At the beginning of the novel, the central character, Ephanie Atencio, is a half-breed who has lost the sense of who she is; she is isolated and fragmented as a human being, belonging neither to the Pueblo community nor to the non-Indian community. Ephanie has a fragmented self from an inner war. As a half-breed Guadalupe woman, Ephanie is caught in the erosion of the traditional place of honor and respect in which a Guadalupe woman is held by her tribe and in the stereotyped and patriarchal view from which she is viewed by non-Indians. She is surrounded by forces which work to destroy whatever link she has to the traditional culture in which the women were central figures. The reader follows her struggle to regain her sanity as she sorts out her childhood and her tribal beliefs and connections, marries a second-generation Japanese-American man, and deals with the death of one of their twins. She joins a consciousness-raising group, goes to a psychiatrist, studies the old traditions, and tries to commit suicide, but it is only when she is able to synthesize what she has learned from all of this, see its connection to her tribal traditions, and reaffirm the importance of the female, especially the importance of the "amazon tradition," that she is healed.

The Laguna society to which Allen's mother and maternal grandmother belonged and in which she places her character was matrilineal (descent recognized through the female line) and matrilocal (ownership of houses held by women). Allen says her "mother's Laguna people are Keres Indian, reputed to be the last extreme mother-right people on earth" (*Sacred Hoop*). Women also controlled and cared for the ceremonial objects and the power to conduct ceremonies came from both men and women. According to Allen, one of the problems with Christianity is that it attempts to use "male power" only. Women also owned the crops while men did the farming. The primary deities were Thought Woman (Tsitstinako) and her sisters, Corn Woman (Iyatiku), and Sun Woman (Nautsityi). For Allen, "womanness . . . is preponderant; it is the source of human male and human female, the giver and bestower of life, ritual, afterlife, social power, and all that is sacred" [**"Where I Come From God Is a Grandmother,"** *Sojourner: The Women's Forum* (August 1988)]. Because the Laguna society in which Allen places her characters has lost this central importance of the female, both the Laguna and Euro-American society need balancing. The old stories are not effective in acting as curing ceremonies because they do not account for the influence of Euro-American culture.

Allen's main character in *The Woman Who Owned the Shadows* illustrates the isolation and fragmentation which occur if individuals pull away or are left out of the community and their experience or "story" cannot be seen as part of the whole. As a mixed-breed person who lives apart, Ephanie is unable to fit into the old ways; there are no stories for her experiences. Only when she makes sense of the old stories by seeing the continuities in them and how she fits into those continuities can she be healed, for the Laguna believe that everything that has happened will happen again only in a different form. Her journey to healing is primarily an isolated one, an interior journey. She puzzles over the old stories, searching for answers, looking for the patterns until, one day, she understands their continuity—how they fit together:

> She understood the combinations and recombinations that had so puzzled her. . . . First there was Sussinstinaku, Thinking Woman, then there was She and two more: Uretsete and Naotsete. Then Uretsete became known as the father, Utset, because Naotsete had become pregnant and a mother, because the Christians would not understand and killed what they did not know. And Iyatiku was the name Uretsete was known by . . . and so the combinations went on, forming, dissolving, doubling, splitting. . . . All of the stories informed those patterns, laid down long before time, so far.

An important role of the storyteller, then, is to tell the story according to the requirements of the listeners. Therefore, the story must be adapted to the particular audience. Leslie Marmon Silko, another Laguna writer, reminds us in an essay that "Storytelling always includes the audience and the listeners, and in fact, a great deal of the story is believed to be inside the listener and the storyteller's role is to draw the story out of the listeners" ["Language and Literature from a Pueblo Perspective," in *English Literature: Opening Up the Canon,* edited by Leslie A. Fiedler and Houston A. Baker, Jr., 1981].

Having identified her readers as needing stories to make sense out of today's complicated world and yet connect to the important "stories" or values of the past, Allen tells a modern story calculated to do this. She begins with the Laguna creation myth which opens with a female creator spirit, Tsitstinako or Thought Woman. She is also identified as Spider Woman in some versions of the myth. She creates two sisters, Iyatiku and Nautsityi, who with various animal helpers bring the people from the four worlds of the underworld. They emerge at Shipap. Iyatiku or Corn Woman becomes the mother of the Indians while Nautsityi or Sun Woman becomes the mother of the others. In her function as a storyteller in the Laguna tradition, then, Allen evokes Thought Woman at the beginning of her novel. Allen's prologue recounts the creation story, and she dedicates the novel to her "great grandmother, Meta Atseye Gunn. / To Naiya Iyatiku. / And to Spider Grandmother, Thought Woman, / who thinks the stories I write down."

By dedicating her novel to Thought Woman, from whose intelligence all life comes, Allen celebrates and honors her as the supreme storyteller. Through the novel, Allen shows Thought Woman/Spider Woman the love and respect she deserves, and in turn she will give her blessing. "After her," as a line in one of Allen's poems goes, the poet "mend[s] the tear with string"—the poet, following the Creator's example, attempts to weave together the stories to affect healing for the people ["**Grandmother,**" in *The Third Woman: Minority Women Writers of the United States,* edited by Dexter Fisher, 1980]. Allen places her novel in the context of the Laguna tradition and signifies that she is honoring Spider Grandmother while taking part in the Grandmother's thinking by telling a story for the people which will bring old and new experiences together in a coherent whole. In an essay, Allen says such activity attempts "to bring the isolated self into harmony and balance" with the reality celebrated in legends, sacred stories, songs, and ceremonies and "to actualize in language, those truths of being and experience that give to humanity its greatest significance and dignity" ("**Sacred Hoop**").

In Laguna mythology, there is a story about how Thought Woman's sisters, who have been given the task of naming and giving "human form to the spirit which was the people," quarrel and separate. The quarrel and subsequent separation seem to be the prototype for much of the evil in the world. The result in the modern stories is that the children of the two sisters (whites, Asians, Indians, Africans, etc.) have forgotten that they are related and have forgotten as well that they are related to things inanimate and animate. Most of the descendants of the two sisters have forgotten that people must carry on rituals to keep things in balance. This forgetting leads to separation from the land, to drought, to war, to division of the self.

This is what happens to Allen's main character, Ephanie. In Allen's novel, the quarrel and subsequent separation of Corn Woman and Sun Woman form the central mythic antagonism. In the novel, the sisters are called "double women," and the modern conflict is that Ephanie is separated from herself—she is herself a double woman comprised of warring parts: "She wished she could tear out the monstrous other in her, reveal or find the one within that matched her, loving, passionate, wild and throbbing. . . ."

Ephanie has lost her connection to the Guadalupe community and the traditions which sustain them. As a mixed-breed, Ephanie is caught between cultures—accepted neither as Guadalupe nor as white. In her torment to discover who she is, Ephanie says:

> One thing she could not go back to, though she had tried symbolically, in dreams, in books, was the old heathen tradition. She had never been to a masked dance. She had not been allowed. Even her mother had not been there since she was a small child, taken by Grandma Sylvia, Shimanna, across the spaces between one village and the next, around the lake that was no longer there, to the square to see the katsinas, the gods, enter and bowing, stepping, dance, the spruce collars dipping and swaying gravely with their steps.

> "I never saw them," she said quiet, wistful, "because they left, and left me out."

When Sylvia left, when Ephanie's mother grew up and married out as well, those doors had closed.

Besides her difficulties with her Guadalupe heritage, Ephanie also has difficulty meeting the non-Indians' stereotyped expectations of her. They expected her to be an "Indian maiden" who was "noble, . . . wise, . . . and exotic," when, in fact, she was just like other women who had gone to college and had been involved in political activities. They just made her feel as if she didn't belong.

In the novel, the division of the self in the main character has to do with her separation from the earth which is seen as the Mother. Allen says in an essay that the essential nature of femininity is associated "with the creative power of thought," thought of the kind which produces "mountains, lakes, creatures and philosophical/sociological systems." She warns, however, that "it is not in the mind of the Pueblo to simply equate in primitive modes earth-bearing-grain with woman-bearing-child" [**"The Feminine Landscape in Leslie Marmon Silko's *Ceremony*,"** in *Studies in American Indian Literature: Critical Essays and Course Designs,* 1984]. Allen's use of the Laguna view toward the land, its femaleness, and its spirituality underlies her work:

> The land: a vast, intense, spirit woman, whose craggy vastnesses, deep dry waterways, miles and miles of forest and wilderness, reaches upon reaches of mesas, 40,000 deep skies where thunderheads of frightening force and awesome majesty sail ponderously, give me my primary understanding of womanness, of gender in its female sensibility. (**"Where I Come From"**)

Ephanie experiences this division from self, from the land, the Mother, as her cutting "herself off from the sweet spring of her own being" [*The Woman Who Owned the Shadows*] because she is a woman from a traditionally female-centered culture. Like the Creator sisters of the ancient story who compliment one another as they go about their tasks, Ephanie has a best friend as she grows up in Guadalupe—a Chicanà named Elena. "They were so close they were like twins: Because Elena's gold-tinged hair looked dark in the photograph's light, no one could say which was Elena, which Ephanie. With each other they were each one doubled. They were thus complete."

However, when they are nine, the nuns find out they have been "playing . . . between each other's legs" and warn them of the seriousness of their offense. When the nuns tell Elena's mother, Elena has to tell Ephanie that they cannot see each other anymore:

> Ephanie sat. Stunned. Mind empty. Stomach a cold cold stone. The hot sun blazed on her head. She felt sick. She felt herself shrinking within. Understood, wordlessly, exactly what Elena was saying. How she could understand what Ephanie had not understood. That they were becoming lovers. That they were in love. That their loving had to stop. To end. That she was falling. Had fallen. Would not recover from the fall, smashing the rocks. That they were in her, not on the ground.

Later at the convent school, Ephanie watches as two nuns fall in love and are joyous in each other's presence in an otherwise joyless and somber place. However, when one of the nuns is sent away, the somberness returns and the girls lament the loss of love and happiness. Step by step, Ephanie learns to distrust herself and her love for other women.

When she is twelve, Ephanie falls from a tree when she is challenged by her cousin Stephen to jump from a rope. She slips and ends up with two broken ribs and a punctured lung which collapses. She feels she has been tricked and betrayed by Stephen and like the loss of her relationship with Elena, this "fall" causes her much pain, both psychically and physically. "After she fell the sun went out. . . . [She] learned to prance and priss, and did not notice the change, the fear behind it. The rage. And did not ever say aloud, not even in her own mind, what it was all about." The tree from which she falls becomes the symbol of her "drought of the spirit." It was "lying, against the ground, split in two"—"dying, all filthy and rotting and dying."

Ephanie begins to put all of her energy into becoming a "lady." Here the Catholicism combines with other pressures to force her to be "alien" to herself. Her Catholic school experience tries to train her to be the Euro-American ideal of womanhood:

> Long, empty, polished corridors. Silent white faces of women whose whole heads and bodies were encased in black heavy fabric. Whose rosaries hanging dark and heavy down their legs clinked with every quiet step they took. Of those white faces, almost always unsmiling. Of those white hands that never touched a child. Of those white faces smiling, tight and stiff, as though that simple expression caused great pain. Who said she must pray. Must ask to be forgiven. . . . Must remember to sit quietly at the table. And never ask for more. Who must eat when told, sleep when told, wake when told, play when told, work when told, study when told, piss when told, shit when told, and must never never use too much paper to wipe her butt. Her tiny child's butt.

Part of herself is at war with the other, trying to kill that loving part which had transgressed in Euro-American culture: "She felt rise within her words and pictures, understandings and interpretations that were not hers, not her, alien, monstrous, other than her, in her, that wanted her dead, wanted her to kill, to destroy whatever was of meaning or comfort to her. . . ."

Ephanie has learned to doubt herself and her love for other women. She "abandons" herself—she never again believes in herself: "I was going to be a hero, before I got sidetracked, she thought. I was going to be full of life and action. I wasn't going to be the one who lived alone, afraid of the world. Elena and I, we were going to do brave things in our lives. And we were going to do them together."

Of lesbianism in traditional Indian cultures, Allen says that because young men and women were often separated from the large group for extended periods, same-sex relationships "were probably common" (*Sacred Hoop*). However, besides this opportunity, there were also those women whose orientation toward other women was a matter of "Spirit direction." In the case of the Lakota (Sioux—part of Allen's heritage), such a woman would have dreamed of "Double Woman," and from then on, she would be a skilled craftsperson, doing both women's and men's work. According to a Lakota account, a "Double Woman dreamer" could act "like a crazy woman"— "deceptively," promiscuously, and such women are known to "cause all men who stand near them to become possessed" ["Double Woman," in *Living the Spirit: A Gay American Indian Anthology*, edited by Will Roscoe, 1988]. This account points out the power and special burden that was considered to accompany this kind of dream—a power that was highly respected by the Lakota—and it also mentions a ritual that two women who were "Double Woman Dreamers" might carry out to "become united by the power of the Deity" (*Sacred Hoop*). The Lakotas would have considered a woman who dreamed of the moon spirit, Double Woman, to be a sacred person or *wakan*. According to Allen, such a woman would have been a "medicine woman in a special sense. She probably was a participant in the Spirit . . . of an Entity or a Deity who was particularly close to earth during the Goddess period. . . ." Allen goes on to say that "essentially a woman's spiritual way is dependent on the kind of power she possesses, the kind of Spirit to whom she is attached, and the tribe to which she belongs. She is required to follow the lead of Spirits and to carry out the tasks they assign her." However, as Walter Williams notes [in *The Spirit and the Flesh: Sexual Diversity in American Indian Culture*, 1986], "It is common for people to claim reluctance to fulfill their spiritual duty no matter what vision appears to them. Becoming any kind of sacred person involves taking on various social responsibilities and burdens."

It is also true [as Williams notes] that by "interpreting the result of the vision as being the work of a spirit, the vision quest frees the person from feeling responsibility for his [or her] transformation." Allen describes this belief in a transforming spirit in *Raven's Road*. The protagonist, Allie Hawker, recalls her initiation into lesbian sex by her female army captain:

> She stood, drawing Allie to her until their breasts touched, until their breasts fell into the softness of each other. Then slowly, deliberately, the captain kissed Allie, and that was all there was to it, and just like, swiftly and silently as a deer pauses a moment then vanishes into the bush, Allie was taken by that twilight world, made a citizen of it, an outcast who forever would belong to wilderness, and there would be at home.

> They had stories about it, the Indian people. Some of them, not her tribe, but her friends, had told her about Deer Woman, how she would come to a dance, so beautiful, so enchanting. She would choose you to dance with, circling the drum slowly, circling, circling, in the light that blazed darkly from the tall fires that ringed the dance ground; she would dance with you, her elbow just touching yours, her shawl spread

carefully around her shoulders and arms, held with breathtaking perfect precision over her cocked right arm, torso making just the right sideward bow, tiny steps perfect in their knowing of the drum. She would dance you, dance into you, holding your gaze with her eyes, for if your eyes looked down at her feet you would see her hooves and the spell would be broken. And after a time she would incline her head, say, perhaps, come, and you would follow. Away from the fire and the dancing, into the brush, into the night. And you would not return, or if you did, it would be as somebody else.

In *The Woman Who Owned the Shadows,* Ephanie has not followed her spiritual way. As a child she had had a strong sense of herself as brave and free, which she had given up as an adolescent. However, the spirits did not give up on her that easily and later, when she is an adult, her friend Teresa tells her that "the spirits" are trying to tell her "something important." Again she tries to avoid hearing their message. Finally, they tell her to investigate "some trouble that has been going on for a long time." It is the vision of herself rejecting the role which the spirits had given her that she finally remembers. However, before she begins to understand what has happened, she listens to her warring self and tries to hang herself. According to Williams, for one who resisted her spiritual duty, this action is not particularly unusual. Williams tells a story of a Lakota boy in the 1880s "who tried to resist following his vision from Double Woman." After his rebellion, the boy committed suicide.

Ephanie, however, hanging from a ceiling pipe, is able to cut herself loose, and this subsequent third fall jars her from her death wish into an understanding and an appreciation of life:

> After she had begun to weep, quietly, with relief, with sorrow, with comprehension. Of what had driven her. The grief, the unbearable anguish, the loneliness. The rage. She realized how grateful she was. For air. For life. For pain. Even for the throbbing pain in her throat.

This fall duplicates the fall of Sky Woman (a Seneca-origin myth and the title of a section in Allen's book), who with the help of some animals turned what should have been a fall to her death into life, populating a new world. In Ephanie's case, the fall begins a process of healing and reclaiming what is hers. She must separate the truth from the lies—see how her life could be made one again. Ephanie must see how the Catholicism had acted to reinforce the Euro-American values about gender and sexuality. Euro-American society holds that there are only two genders—male and female; however, many traditional Native American societies offered another alternative for both men and women—a position [Williams notes] with "a clearly recognized and accepted social status, often based on a secure place in the tribal mythology." In the Lakota tradition, for example, one of the Creator sisters was changed to a male so that the Christians could understand how the Creators could give birth to the people. Ephanie must see that her traditional culture would have seen her desire to live with and love women as a spiritual calling. They would have urged her to use the special powers she would have been given by her acceptance of her spiritual duty for the good of the tribe and her clan.

Allen's *The Woman Who Owned the Shadows* is patterned into sections in which the contemporary story parallels the mythic accounts at the beginning of each section. Part II, for instance, begins with a Prologue entitled, "Rite of Exorcism: (The Spruce Dress)" which promises that Ephanie will recover. In the Prologue, the spirits join the patient, aiding her with their power: "She dwells with me." The patient with their help becomes "one who slays alien gods," thereby "sweeping away the sickness" until she can accept the gifts of the gods. In the contemporary story, part of Ephanie's healing comes when she recovers her own vision of herself, accepting her strong connection to the ancient tribal power of the sisterhood of the medicine women:

> And she understood. For those women, so long lost to her, who she had longed and wept for, unknowing, were the double women, the women who never married, who held power like the Clanuncle, like the power of the priests, the medicine men. Who were not mothers, but who were sisters, born of the same mind, the same spirit. They called each other sister. They were called Grandmother by those who called on them for aid, for knowledge, for comfort, for care.

Ephanie comes to understand how "spirit, creatures and land can occupy a unified whole" (*Sacred Hoop*). According to Williams, the role of the man or woman who took on qualities of the other sex, was to act as a mediator not only "between the sexes but between the psychic and the physical—between the spirit and the flesh. . . . They have double vision, with the ability to see more clearly than a single gender perspective can provide." But this gift of the spirits was also a burden as Ephanie comes to realize. If her understanding is doubled, in times of trouble there is also double pain and the task of healing:

> The curse laid upon her flesh was her gift as well. She knew that with certainty. That she was always, unendingly, aware of the pain. Of the people. Of the air. Of the water. Of the beasts and the birds. She could not escape that knowledge. In every eye, in every mind, the pain lay, blossoming in bewilderment, in blood. They never knew why they suffered. Nor did she. . . . And they also understood the gift, the curse, some of them. . . . They thought she could make them well.

As her room fills with the spirits of the Grandmothers, she is able to join them in their dance and listen to their message. They tell her that "there are no curses. There are only descriptions of what creations there will be." A spirit woman shows Ephanie her destiny—how she fits into the Double Woman pattern:

> "It is the sign and the order of the power that informs this life and leads back to Shipap. Two face outward, two inward, the sign of doubling, of order and balance, of the two, the twins, the doubleminded world in which you have lived," she chanted.

Ephanie is told to pass the story—the information—on to the Euro-American woman, Teresa, "the one who waits," and presumably on to us, the readers. By accepting her spiritual duty, Ephanie is healed and the story is complete.

By allowing the reader to participate in the curing ceremony of the novel by following the main character in her own restoration of balance, Allen seeks to restore balance to the community-at-large. Through this the reader is reminded of the power of storytelling and the responsibility of each human to the community. Further, if, as Judy Grahn says in her comment on the back cover, "you come with an honest heart," the novel enables the non-Indian reader to begin to see from a non-Euro-American perspective. To begin to change the Euro-American vision of disconnectedness to one of connectedness would be a "curing" indeed. As Williams notes, a most important function of a curing is a "healing of the mind." Although the novel

---

Allen on her influences:

My life is history, politics, geography. It is religion and metaphysics. It is music and language. For me the language is an odd brand of English, mostly local, mostly half-breed spoken by the people around me, filled with elegance and vulgarity side by side, small jokes that are language jokes and family jokes and area jokes, certain expressions that are peculiar to that meeting of peoples who speak a familiar (to me) laconic language filled with question and comment embedded in a turn of phrase, a skewing of diction, a punning, cunning language that implies connections in diversity of syntax and perception, the oddness of how each of us seems and sees. It is the Southwest, the confluence of cultures, the headwaters of Mexico. . . .

The triculture state, as New Mexico is often called, is more than three-cultured, as it works itself out in my life. It is Pueblo, Navajo and Apache, Chicano, Spanish, Spanish-American, Mexican-American; it is Anglo, and that includes everything that is not Indian or Hispanic-in my case, Lebanese and Lebanese-American, German-Jewish, Italian-Catholic, German-Lutheran, Scotch-Irish-American Presbyterian, halfbreed (that is, people raised white-and-Indian), and Irish-Catholic; there are more, though these are the main ones that influenced me in childhood, and their influence was literary and aesthetic as well as social and personal. The land, the family, the road-three themes that haunt my mind and form my muse, these and the music: popular, country and western, Native American, Arabic, Mexican, classical like operas and symphonies, especially Mozart, the Mass. The sounds I grew up with, the sounds of the voices, the instruments, the rhythms, the sounds of the land and the creatures. These are my sources, and these are my home.

Paula Gunn Allen, in her "The Autobiography of a Confluence," in I Tell You Now: Autobiographical Essays by Native American Writers, *edited by Brian Swann and Arnold Krupat, University of Nebraska Press, 1987.*

ends with Ephanie's understanding of her connection to her heritage and although the reader does not see how it will affect her life, Allen's novel is also an important offering to Native American lesbians. She has shown a connection that present-day lesbians might make to a special spiritual heritage and role which such women played in Native American cultures. As Allen says, "It all has to do with spirit, with restoring an awareness of our spirituality as gay people."

More generally in the novel, the healing of the main character occurs when she is able to reconnect with the female principle which is exemplified in thought Woman and her sisters and consists particularly of life and strength—she recovers the ancient qualities of woman who was seen as "strong and powerful," balancing the ancient qualities of man who was seen as having "transient or transitory" qualities (**"Where I Come From"**). This balancing of qualities where "woman-ness is not of less value than man-ness" allows both the individual and tribe to continue and prosper. The telling of the story allows the listeners/readers to visualize how their experiences fit into the great web of being, the patterns of life. The story and the experiences become one, leading to harmony and healing. By using this journey as a model, we can begin to see how to reclaim our female deities and "the wholistic, pacifistic and spirit-based" (**"Who Is Your Mother?"**) principles of our grandmothers in order to bring together mind/spirit and body, inanimate and animate, to insure continuance of the earth as well as the individual.

Elizabeth I. Hanson   (essay date 1990)

SOURCE: *Paula Gunn Allen,* Boise State University, 1990, 50 p.

[*In the excerpt below, Hanson provides an overview of Allen's literary career through 1983.*]

At the center of Paula Gunn Allen's vision of self and art is an individual alienated within. For Allen the idea of the "breed" reflects a preoccupation with alienation as a personal and as an aesthetic experience. Allen's biography, her understanding of Native American literature, and her works of art and criticism are informed by the consciousness that "breeds" are aliens to traditional Native Americans and yet also aliens among whites. To know Allen's life and work is to reflect deeply on the meaning of "breed" in Native American experience. Also, to know her life and work is to gain peculiar insight into the transformative art concealed within the alien's exceptionally acute visionary power. To stand outside, to be and yet not to be, becomes, at least in Allen's case, a source of subtle self-exploration as well as extraordinary art. . . .

. . . . .

Allen turns to the images of ancient Keres traditions to determine her principles of literary criticism. Ancient Native American aesthetics and her own self-divided sense of the "breed" experience shape her most important critical ideas. For Allen, her criticism of Native American texts and cultures emerges so that readers may learn to view themselves and Native American experience "so as to approach both rightly." Her literary criticism is a further extension of the alienation inherent in her self-portrait; both race and gender create dilemmas she seeks to explain to herself and her readers. The "breed" experience becomes a mediative, revealing means of adding "breath" to "breath" and thereby extending the life of Native American literature in a white American literary context.

Always Allen is concerned with illuminating Native American experience without trivializing or invalidating its meaning. To approach that experience "rightly" demands much of the reader, whatever that reader's training or tradition, and to Allen's credit, she offers tools and strategies for the teacher and the reader of Native American materials, tools and strategies which are clear and sensitive despite the complexity of the task. In her *Studies in American Indian Literature: Critical Essays and Course Designs* (1983), Allen fulfills in practical terms her commitment to extend the creative life of the Native American within white America. Here the "breed" speaks not of alienation of the Indian without a tribe, but of linkages of human beings within an American landscape. This larger community is made up not only of members of a single tribe but also includes all who inhabit the Native American's universe.

It is only within the contexts of community and ceremony—these institutions each reinforce the meaning of the other—that Native American experience can be understood. In Allen's critical vision "all ceremonies, whether for war or healing, create and support a sense of community that is the bedrock of tribal life" and they are also the clearest and most sensitive means of exploring Native American literature. Allen's "Introduction," the selection of critical essays, and the structure of the course designs in *Studies in American Indian Literature* are each formulated to shape the response of the reader and teacher of Native American materials by suggesting historical and traditional information as well as interpretive insight.

Allen's own critical methodology and editorial policy is eclectic and rigorous in *Studies in American Indian Literature.* The selection of critical essays represents the range of critical perspective—from oral literature and personal narrative to feminist writings and the Indian theme in standard American literature courses—and the gathering of course designs reveals introductory, survey, and alternative book lists and teaching strategies for American academic study of the Native American. The result is pragmatic and creative. Many teaching approaches and research possibilities are tendered to readers and students. What the approaches and possibilities all have in common is that they prepare the teacher/critic/student to explore multiple factors and associations relating to the experience of the Native American in a dominantly white cultural system.

In the "Introduction" to *Studies in American Indian Literature,* Allen articulates the essential dilemma of the literate and even sophisticated white reader who is not very knowledgeable about the Native American, but who nonetheless wishes to learn more and communicate that knowledge through scholarship and teaching. By using only the technique of close reading, or by searching merely for symbolic patterns of European and American traditions, or by simply ignoring historical and anthropological evidence, the teacher or critic might well assume that a character such as Ts'its'tsi'nako (in Leslie Marmon Silko's frequently taught novel *Ceremony*) is a persona of Silko herself, or might not grasp materials of Kiowa oral traditions when writing about N. Scott Momaday's first novel, *House Made of Dawn* (1968). But as Allen explains, such failures and confusions reflect the inadequacies of even careful readers when confronted with another highly complex cultural system. And imposing white cultural and academic strictures on texts of other cultural experiences increases the chances for distortion. It is as if the losses Native Americans have sustained for centuries are not enough; now these peoples must face further diminishment as their English-composed documents of that loss are interpreted by white scholars and critics. Always, the Native American is the "white man's Indian," even in the white man's classroom.

By turning the complexities of Native American experience into the simple shapes of the white man's imagination of the Indian, the literary critic may well express sympathy for the "Indians' plight" and may even defend them somewhat militantly against the evil of a greedy white world, but still the critic is denying Native Americans their realness and their humanness. As Allen reminds the readers of *Studies in American Indian Literature,* such distortions negate "the dignity that people in difficult circumstances most need." Despite the perhaps inevitable failures of white readers to grasp the real experience of Native Americans, honest and sensitive critical appraisals and teaching approaches do exist. The course designs and critical essays Allen includes are solid evidence of success; the more than forty closely printed pages of the bibliography in *Studies in American Indian Literature* represent a triumph of selectivity and strength in literary scholarship concerning the Native American.

Stridency and divisiveness are not in Allen's critical vocabulary. As she writes, "the present political and social climate encourages an overly romantic response to Indians, their values, and their traditions, and teachers or critics must not allow natural sympathies or political biases to color their presentation of the materials." Prejudice based on emotional or political efforts to control readers' responses is fundamentally an example of "literary colonialism." Its effect, whatever the motives of the teacher or critic, is intellectual confusion, contempt for Native Americans, or rejection of the education such study is designed to foster. Allen's critical methodology is designed to stimulate neither prejudice nor overromanticization, but rather clarity and insight. By providing compelling evidence of the range and variety of possible approaches to Native American literature, she demonstrates how teachers can present this literature so that students and readers "can enter into the universe in which the material belongs." Native American peoples have created a body of history, culture, literature, and philosophy worthy of study, and their treatment as citizens in a dominant white culture has been destructive and unfair in many instances. *Both* of these elements of Native American experience demand dispassionate study and remedy. And both of these

elements are sensitively reflected in contemporary Native American literature; reading and evaluating that literature's depiction of past mistreatment of Native American people may lead to greater consideration, even if correction is improbable. Still, Allen's effort is to enhance such considerations. Dispassionate observation of Native American experience holds the promise that readers will see Native Americans as human beings of diverse and sophisticated cultures—not as noble stereotypes or degraded, ignored nonentities, but as individuals who offer much to those who know and study their literature.

In addition to Allen's role as spokesperson within the scholarly community, she has also published numerous critical essays, particularly relating to Native American Women's Studies, and these essays have been collected in a volume entitled *The Sacred Hoop: Recovering the Feminine in American Indian Traditions* (1986). This important text and testimony to Native American feminism is addressed "to my Rainbow Warrior Women," that is, to women of color and women of aggressively feminist sources, purposes, and obsessions. In several senses, *The Sacred Hoop* represents a shift in Allen's "breed" persona; interestingly, she articulates this reshaping of self in the "Introduction" to the book, almost as if explaining it to herself. Allen's self-design is subtly altered here, and her voice is concerned with the justification of a gynocratic, lesbian experience within the context of Native American cultures.

What is so striking about Allen's departure into new critical territory is how she seeks to interpenetrate her earlier self-formulations with this changed portrait. For example, she writes the "Introduction" with a tone of intimacy and self-speculation: "Whenever I read about Indians I check out with my inner self. Most of what I have read—and some things I have said based on that reading—is upside-down and backward." Here she suggests that the reader might well deprecate earlier writings by Allen; after all, *now* Allen does herself. Amid this view of self and even her view of other writers emerges Allen's idea of an internal early warning system which now protects her from self-deceptions, whether within or without: "With that warning, I am moved to do a great deal of reflecting, some more reading, and a lot of questioning and observing of real live human beings who are Indian in order to discover the source of my unease." Allen remains for herself and for us (at least as she wishes us to know her) the quintessential "breed." "So you see," she explains, "my method is somewhat western and somewhat Indian; I draw from each"; but in *The Sacred Hoop* the mediative interchange within Allen's self-drama is complicated further by the dilemmas posed by gender and sexuality.

In *The Sacred Hoop* Allen notes, for the first time in her critical writings, that "the major difference between most activist movements and tribal societies is that for millennia American Indians have based their social systems, however diverse, on ritual, spirit-centered, woman-focused world views." This definition marks a deviation from the critical perspective she articulated in the "Introduction" to *Studies in American Indian Literature* and in her essay **"The Sacred Hoop: Contemporary Perspective"** (reprinted in both *Studies in American Indian Literature* and in *The Sacred Hoop,* but appearing first in Abraham Chapman's work, *Literature of the American Indians: Views and Interpretations*). Allen did not express any ideas or suggestions concerning a "woman-focused world view" in each of those earlier texts where she repeats and reprints her contention that "American Indian thought is essentially mystical and psychic in nature." Also, in the "Introduction" to the feminist book *The Sacred Hoop,* Allen adds another new dimension to her definition of Native American culture: "some distinguishing features of a woman-centered social system include free and easy sexuality and wide latitude in personal style. This latitude means that a diversity of people, including gay males and lesbians, are not denied and are in fact likely to be accorded honor."

Allen's vision of tribal life as gynocratic in nature, rather than simply mystical or psychic, reveals a remarkable contention, one that Allen herself recognizes as supported by limited verifiable evidence. She explains this lack of supporting evidence by speculating that the "invaders have exerted every effort to remove Indian women from every position of authority, to obliterate all records pertaining to gynocratic social systems and to ensure that no American and few American Indians would remember that gynocracy was the primary social order of Indian America." The difficulty with Allen's position here is that it is at variance with her own earlier and highly sophisticated definitions of Native American cultural dimensions. It is also at variance with the definitions of gifted and sensitive historians of the Native Americans such as Robert Berkhofer and Francis Paul Procha. Even if Allen's hypothesis were entirely correct, it would be impossible to determine, because there *is* little evidence available. In fact, *The Sacred Hoop* itself offers limited supporting evidence for the contentions which are raised by Allen in her own "Introduction."

What *The Sacred Hoop* does contain is the reprinting of a number of Allen's excellent earlier critical essays—the very essays which counter the arguments offered in the "Introduction." The most important of these is **"Whose Dream Is This Anyway? Remythologizing and Self-Definition in Contemporary American Indian Fiction."** In this remarkable essay Allen—with particular acuity and insight—succeeds in exploring a range of novels about Native American experience. For example, she observes,

> American Indian novelists use cultural conflict as [a] major theme, but their work shows an increasing tendency to bind them to its analogues in whatever tribal oral tradition they write from. So while the protagonists in Native American novels are in some sense bicultural and must deal with the effects of colonization and an attendant sense of loss of self, each is also a participant in a ritual tradition that gives their individual lives shape and significance.

The rituals of sacred ceremonial forms become, in Allen's view, the aesthetic process through which these novels cohere and must be understood. In this carefully wrought and recently published essay, Allen's critical understanding of Native American fiction focuses once more on the artistic possibilities of oral traditions and rituals for the Native American literary artist. Neither politics nor language informs the making of these works of art. Here, it is not gynocratic activism, nor the use of English, nor any other external factor that forms the center of Allen's vision of Native American visionary consciousness. Rather, the transformative, even transcendent meaning of ceremony within the tribal community signifies the essential unity inherent in Allen's vision of Native American and, indeed, all human experience.

> **What Allen proposes to accomplish in her criticism is nothing less than the revelation of Native American culture in which the mutual relationships between whites and Native Americans are perceived in all their varying degrees of intensity and significance.**
>
> —*Elizabeth I. Hanson*

In essays such as **"Whose Dream Is This Anyway?"** and others including **"A Stranger in My Own Life: Alienation in American Indian Poetry and Prose," "The Ceremonial Motion of Indian Time: Long Ago, So Far," "Answering the Deer: Genocide and Continuance in the Poetry of American Indian Women,"** and **"This Wilderness in My Blood: Spiritual Foundations of the Poetry of Five American Indian Women,"** Allen locates her vision of a spirit-infused experience in the texts of her contemporaries and her predecessors. Her critical journey through the writings of Native American literary artists becomes a guide, like her *Studies in American Indian Literature,* although now enriched and developed further for scholars and students of Native American culture. She plunges within these texts to provide the information and the patterns for continuance so that "we will accept them for what they can signify and use them to lend vitality and form to our life." A text which gathers together the materials of her efforts in the field of Native American literature over a long period, *The Sacred Hoop* reveals her immersion in the particulars of Native American place and time. Subjective at points, reflective of a chosen audience at others, Allen's criticism is ambitiously large-scale, enthusiastic, mythic, prolix, and uneven in its tone. By turns sensuous, transcendental, argumentative, and charming, Allen's critical persona is as divided and stimulating as her poetic persona.

Allen sees herself as a member of a community composed of Native American women writers—in contradistinction to other American women writers—which has as its first and most significant perceptual characteristic, "a solid, impregnable, and ineradicable orientation toward a spirit-informed view of the universe." Calling herself a "Kochinnenako in Academe," Allen defines a further element of her "breed"-made self; the internal divisions so central to that self-portrait are articulated in Allen's sense of "tribal-feminism." She determines this intellectual bifurcation as a critical approach rather than a fully formed methodology: "if I am dealing with feminism," she writes, "I approach it from a strongly tribal posture, and when I am dealing with American Indian literature, history, culture, or philosophy I approach it from a strongly feminist one." As Allen herself acknowledges, "how one teaches or writes about one perspective in terms of the other is problematic." Inevitably, the separations she attempts to draw in her own perspectives, and the critical interpenetrations she seeks to suggest, at times may appear ambiguous and even confusing, given the wide range of texts and subjects she addresses. But like one playing the role of a "Kochinnenako in Academe," Allen is concerned with "agency," with the transference of meaning. As a particularly sensitive messenger with an astoundingly complex message, she does not create a simple task for her readers. What she proposes to accomplish is nothing less than the revelation of Native American culture in which the mutual relationships between whites and Native Americans are perceived in all their varying degrees of intensity and significance.

Allen's continuing effort to enhance the teaching of Native American literature can be seen in her anthology, *Spider Woman's Granddaughters: Traditional Tales and Contemporary Writing by Native American Women* (1989). Allen presents only works by Native American women writers because she believes that their texts have been neglected in favor of male authors such as N. Scott Momaday and James Welch. The volume is designed around the theme of war as a ritualized experience that leads to spiritual enlightenment, and the tales, short stories, and oral transcriptions are divided into three categories: "The Warriors," "The Casualties," and "The Resistance." One difficulty for the reader and teacher of the anthology is that the war theme is not coherently integrated with Allen's idea of Spider Woman as storyteller of transcendent wholeness. In her verse Allen has explored both tribal notions of war, and in her novel, *The Woman Who Owned the Shadows,* she explores the aesthetic possibilities of Spider Woman, but here she fails to interpenetrate with real precision these paradoxical yet linked ideas. Especially for the new reader of Native American literature—exactly the audience Allen is seeking here! —the complex, even confusing interconnection may be nearly impenetrable. What is abundantly clear is that Allen will continue her journey toward renewing the conscience and the consciousness of Native American feminism in American literary criticism. Both for herself and for the audience she seeks to influence, that journey remains fascinating to explore.

Presciently, Allen herself recognizes her own future role in Native American Studies in American academe; she writes that as "we move into the nineties and my lone voice is joined by a growing multitude of women's voices across the country and within the profession of writing and literary scholarship," artists and scholars will design new presentations of the Native American experience within a white America. The critical reception of Allen's works of art has been limited. Her work as an editor and lecturer on Native American topics is highly respected, yet few scholars have examined her poetry or her novel,

partly because these works are extremely difficult to obtain in libraries or bookstores. The Smithsonian American Indian collection can make these scarce resources available through interlibrary loan. One fine exception to the paucity of critical attention devoted to Allen is Elaine Jahner's essay "A Laddered, Rain-Bearing Rug: Paula Gunn Allen's Poetry" [*Women and Western Literature,* edited by Susan Rosowski and Helen Stauffer, 1982]. Jahner's article is the standard study on Allen's poetic themes and ideas. Much critical work remains to be done, however. New quests for selfhood, new means of intercession, will be explored by Allen herself in her criticism. Her "lone voice"—she defines it herself even now as a "breed" who is separated and alone—will continue to be heard in her literary criticism and in her poetry as well. . . .

· · · · ·

At the same time as Allen sought to develop her skills as a literary critic of Native American literature, she also came to discover her voice as a Native American poet. Her first published poems contain the special characteristics that mark all her work—ambition, originality, and subtle force—and it is via these particular means that Allen determines and defines her recurrent themes and strategies. She seeks to confront the "shadows [that] cannot speak except through the poet." *She* can make the shadows speak through her own words. Within her early poems can be discerned an enterprise of healing; she seeks to restore the "blind" by seeking a curative truth that lies beneath the surface of accepted, stereotypical beliefs.

In the first and title poem of *The Blind Lion,* Allen insists, "Look at me and / draw close to me. / I have care to bring you." Her poems in this volume adumbrate the interior journey pursued within the shadows of the searching self:

> The silence I have grown carefully through the
>   day
> slides away from me
> leaving me in shadows exposed—
> as if the network of my silence
> opened me to the soft force of lamplight. I
> fall into noisy abstraction,
> cling to sound as if it were the last protection
> against what I cannot name.
>
>   **("Shadows")**

The questions: "What is the secret?" "Why is the promise never kept?" "What letters should be written?" and, finally, "What form can the as yet unknown emblem take to make me less a stranger?" form the center of the poem's movement. But the answer is partial: "The shadows cannot speak, even in a whisper. What did I think I heard them tell me?" the poet continues to demand.

Allen designs one exquisite response to the questions pondered in **"Shadows"** by ending *The Blind Lion* with her fine sonnet **"Coda"**:

> If I had emptied all your words of tears and
>   caught
> your shadow dreams in yellow glaze and used
>   your
> blistered thought for silk displays would you
>   have

offered caution, banked my fear? Or if I'd had
the
flame of melted streets and lived in laughter
sharp
as August grass, if I had woven rainbows smooth
as
glass would you have stood and let me salve your
feet? Love is empty fire that voids the eyes of
fluted shadows, fused and melted tears: lover,
drenched in darkness as my sight grew open in
the
silence of surprise should I have fashioned futile
words to clear the cinders from your eyes and
give
you sight?

Here the poet answers the questions of the past voice of **"Shadows"** by raising more questions, but now in the past perfect or a remote, lost time: "If I had emptied . . . and caught the teary words and dreamy shadows, would healing be possible, would fear be removed?" asks the poet. The only answer is derived from the writing (and reading) of the poem itself. The fashioning of "futile words" to give sight is exactly the poetic enterprise; inevitably, no language can heal literal blindness or raise the actual dead—and so in that sense it is futile. What the experience can induce is an interior journey. Such an exploration toward vision brings consolation and healing not only for the poet, but for all in need of (in)sight; within the self, the blind "may no longer weep," for they are hearing you (the poet) "sing" of a new world of aesthetic meaning.

Such a world is explicitly articulated in Allen's second volume of verse, *Coyote's Daylight Trip* (1978). In **"The Kerner Report on Camp Creek Road,"** Allen explores the aesthetic possibilities within the world of disaster and defeat that surrounds America's racial minorities:

Take the full length of a club
And a street full of people crying
tie them together to make
a journey as long as a night of rot.

But Allen deliberately shifts the focus of the poem from the analysis of racial malaise, something she knows at first hand, to an examination of the poet's visionary role in light of the American calamity the Kerner Report addresses. Later in the poem the poet's voice conceives:

If I had a metaphorical knife
And a metaphorically thick cutting board
and a whole pile of translucent metaphors
I would cut them finely and watch
them quiver in the light.

Again, the light of metaphorical imagination portends insight in a "night of rot."

For Allen, through the imagination the poet holds power over catastrophe. In **"Locus"** the voice of the poet learns: "the image is where the action is begotten." Through the Trickster, Coyote (a master at designing illusions and distinguishing realities), Allen explores her Native American past as it is interpenetrated with the need for image-begotten actions in the coyote's daylight journey through streets "of people crying" in America. In **"Affirmation"** the voice of the poet speaks to Grandmother Spider of the gift that this Native American matriarchal spirit-giver and

Creator of the Laguna Pueblo offers to all her children:

So grandmother,
Your gifts still go with me
Unseen.
To reach,
Slowly
To go.

Grandmother Spider, who makes an important reappearance in Allen's first novel, *The Woman Who Owned the Shadows* (1983), provides a spiritual affirmation amid Allen's vision of the nearly defeated "breeds" of all kinds in white contemporary America. Through the aesthetic process, as it is recapitulated in the poem,

Small things count after all:
each leaf a tale,
each journey retracing some ancient myth
told in shadows and whispers.

The "daylight trip" is a means of art; the "shadows and whispers" of Allen's poems trace once more through the figures of trickster and grandmother a tale of small things, metaphorical meanings which signify affirmation. . . .

. . . . .

Allen writes the history of the self as the history of a particular time, and for her that "breed" self is challenged and re-empowered by her experience of feminism in late twentieth-century American culture. American feminism as a political and literary construct ebbs and flows in its power to effect change in American life and has done so for nearly two centuries. At its essence, feminist American literature, from Kate Chopin to Joyce Carol Oates, has insisted that women look at their lives to discern their own powerlessness and ultimately confront their own passivity and attempt to understand what it means. As Allen writes in her poem **"Shipapu Iyetico,"** "They don't tell how they put women out of the center," and therefore, Allen herself must examine women's lives on the periphery and design her own aesthetic versions of the inner reality of women's experience. She puts women back into the center of consciousness.

Allen's explorations of the meaning of modern feminism must always be seen within the context of her sense of herself as "breed," as being apart twice removed because she is alienated by race and by gender. Experiences of betrayal, victimization, and loss—the familiar ingredients of women's literature—are employed in Allen's poetry as means of ultimate grace and power. In the poem, **"Shadow Path (the encounter group),"** Allen's vision takes the reader

In this room where voices spin the light
making webs to catch forbidden visions
(center that cannot be grasped) climb
ladders that do not reach the sky.

The fragile creatures, Allen's portraits of a group of women intent on encountering their own "forbidden visions" and unclimbed ladders, "hold the song inside." As their "helpless voices climb," they form the "night's entertainment," but the voice of the poet sees more than entertainment in women communicating with one another. The "Shadow Path" which women follow if they will understand themselves leads toward vision; it begins with the sounds of the alienated "helpless voice" that does not give up its deliberate search for the sacred:

> voices climb,
> circle, spin toward finity,
> sing obstinately.

For this obstinate searcher is engaged in the act of creating a "medicine song," a means of healing whereby "I add my breath to your breath / That our days may be long on the Earth." This voice is that of a woman seeking the way out of helplessness by seeing the musings of an encounter as trustworthy evidence of women's pain and of women's significance.

The poet seeks also to create a new set of values and images of sacred wholeness through her songs:

> . . . I might make of wandering a reason
> an image of sacred ladder I might climb
> as earth and water climb to help
> the wingless fish upstream.

Here women's authentic experience of victimization is transformed into a vision of a "wingless fish" supported by a gently flowing stream of consciousness upward toward reason in a "sacred ladder" of newfound help and understanding. Yet this subtle, healing moment in the poem is in conflict with women's lived experience, "where shame is emblem / and fear its hopeless twin." They may be "too blind to dream," but Allen's whole body of feminist verse is never too blind not to discover new symbologies and news forms of celebration.

The feminist literary artist hopes that other women, and men as well, will recognize themselves and their relations with one another in the story/poem and will join the artist in seeking to transform their shared culture. For Allen, that shared culture is itself ambiguous; feminism is interpenetrated in her vision of self with her point of view as a "breed." The two co-mingle—feminist and "breed"—as Allen creates art which reveals, criticizes, and examines the margins between race and gender in American literature. In the fourth section of **"Medicine Song"** Allen transmutes her image of woman as "wingless fish" whose "blank utterance" is unheard in a world of androcentric literary and cultural traditions and patriarchal social and personal circumstance. Allen reexplores the inner being of her "child of water . . . webbed and broken / on the surface of the lake," dead, but not dead, because the image or shadow of its being does not die. That image is transfigured from being "too blind to dream" in its lament to being a shadow source of meaning for the imagining voice of the poet. In the final section, called "The Dead Spider (the judgment)," the poet intervenes to adjudicate the possibilities as well as the losses women sustain. Like an old medicine woman, Allen concludes the poem with a healing blessing: "dream in your silent shadow / celebrate." Allen opens the space of women's writing by moving beyond a patriarchal system as an enemy or as a symptom of a malignant condition; in the process, she seeks to articulate not a battleground, but a sacred terrain, a center of being where "silent shadows celebrate." . . .

. . . . .

Allen explores "the prancing black stallion of I" in her master volume of verse, **Shadow Country** (1982), in order to control and reconcile the "I" within the white/Native American experience. The poems of **Shadow Country** are marked by precisely the control and certainty that Allen calls for in her essay on contemporary Native American poetry, **"Answering the Deer"**; there she writes, "Divergent realities must meet and form comprehensible patterns" for the Native American artist, and so that artist "must develop metaphors that not only will reflect the dual perceptions" of whites and Native Americans, but "also will reconcile them." Like that "prancing black stallion" within the self, the "ideal metaphor will harmonize the contradictions and balance them so that internal equilibrium can be achieved" as an external vital chaos is revealed. The "I" prances and yet is fixed within the mind's eye; order within the poem devises disorder within the perceiver. Again and again, Allen locates an aesthetic of equilibrium in the poems of **Shadow Country** as she paces with "strong, sure steps" toward her own country, her own time, and her own earth (**Sacred Hoop.**)

For Allen, the "breed," a sense of self divided, demands that both aspects of her experience be comprehended and retrieved within the larger unity of her poetic vision. In a master poem called **"Hoop Dancer,"** Allen examines the forces that beset the "breed," who may be seen as a dancing, prancing "I" in search of some reconciling meaning to the disparate elements of time, race, and sorrow inside the alienated self:

> It's hard to enter
> circling clockwise and counter
> clockwise moving no
> regard for time, metrics
> irrelevant to the dance
> where pain is the prime number
> and soft stepping feet
> praise water from the skies:
>
> I have seen the face of triumph
> the winding line stare down all moves
> to desecration: guts not cut from arms,
> finger joined to minds,
> together Sky and Water
> one dancing one
> circle of a thousand turning lines
> beyond the march of gears—
> out of time, out of
> time, out
> of time.

If it is difficult "to enter" the interface which is the "breed's" particular terrain, nonetheless that space must be sought, for it contains the "one dancing one / circle" of wholeness within. The dance toward reconciliation requires pain as its "prime number," but its "soft" steps lead toward celebratory, life-giving water flowing "from the skies." A "winding line," like a flowing rain, restores those it touches by destroying "all moves / to desecration" and joining dancing fingers "to minds" now consecrated. "[T]ogether Sky and Water" coalesce; their fusion reflects the merging space within which the poet's voice dances and discovers transcendence.

In this important poem, one of the most revealing and

meaningful within the body of Native American contemporary poetry, Allen displays her "sure strong steps home" to poetic control. The "breed," a self divided against its self, is here shown a way "beyond the march of gears" of mechanized, materialistic white society. Now the alienated "breed" is enabled to join the "one circle" of "one dancing" in which there are "a thousand turning lines" representing the myriad possibilities of individuality within the singleness of purpose in Allen's vision. For the Hoop Dancer is a poet in search of a life transfigured, a life "out of time, out of / time, out / of time" in an aesthetic realm remote from transitory experience and attached to the qualities of consciousness.

Other poems in the volume *Shadow Country* reiterate the problems posed and the solutions tendered in **"Hoop Dancer,"** but not always with its subtle density. **"Peace Is a Stratified Concept"** reveals Allen seeking herself in relation to others. Here the poet immerses herself in the stratigraphy of self-discovery:

> At this late date
> I have come
> to understand
> the outcropping
> from which you strike:
>
> it is the same
> ancient bed
> from which I dip—
> the angle of vision
> determines
> both prominence
> and the direction
> of the stream's flow.

On the "ancient bed[rock]" ebb and flow the streams of consciousness—calm, changeable yet constant, wild, yet always powerful. The poet has come "to understand" that the "ancient bed" sustains us all—those of the "outcroppings" and those within. The versions of peace, the poet defines, are stratified but form "the same" foundation of insight. What matters is "the angle of vision," for it is that which "determines" the "prominence" and the "direction" of consciousness itself.

Shadow Country contains additional poems that center on the poet's quest for versions of peace with and without her divided self. Allen's creation of self as mediator, as peacemaker, becomes a means whereby she may transform herself from a "breed" into a being of universal meaning. Allen looks back to Native American myth and to her own memories for examples of common feeling between men and women, between whites and Native Americans, between the included and the excluded, in order to discover a fully shared and valued experience. Her poem, **"Recuerdo"** (memories), proffers a record of her quest:

> I have climbed into silence trying for clear air
> and saw the peaks rising above me like the gods.
> This is where they live, the old people say.
> I used to hear them speak when I was a child.

Allen's ascent "into silence" is a movement through the space of the "breed," where the "old people's" voices and gods are seen as far above the needy alienated self. But the vision, however remotely held by the past, is still with the poet,

> Lately I write, trying to combine sound and
> memory,
> searching for that significance once heard and
> nearly lost.
> It was within the tall pines, speaking.

"Once heard," the significance of being within the Native American experience must be searched for; it may even be "nearly lost" to the "breed." Even though it appears as a form of silence to those estranged from its voice, "it [is] within the tall pines, speaking" to the poet.

Here the poet's *donnée* is that of a strained relationship within the self that possesses meaning and the self that does not possess meaning. Meaning exists—"it was within"—and yet where is it? By combining "sound and memory" the poet writes and searches and listens to the past. No longer warmed by family campfires, the poet tells us that "now I climb the mesas in my dreams" because I am "obsessed with a memory that will not die." This narrative of inner divisions and "breed"-bred obsessions is remembered from a perspective that suggests an ironic glint: "I stir wild honey into my carefully prepared cedar tea and wait for meaning to greet and comfort me." Amid revelations of self-estrangement, there is meaning even in a cup of tea. Yet, devoid of solace, the poet's voice is exposed—to Allen and to her readers—within such gestures; and in the nearly archaeological reading, the poet's voice reveals a breed's memory and a breed's hope:

> Maybe this time I will not turn away.
> Maybe I will ask instead what that sounding
> means
> Maybe I will find that exact hollow
> where terror and comfort meet.
> Tomorrow I will go back and climb the endless
> mesas
> of my home. I will seek thistles drying in the
> wind,
> pocket bright bits of obsidian and fragments
> old potters left behind.

So little remains among the possibilities and the "maybes"—only "bits" and "fragments" of a Native American being. The narrator, who is identified explicitly with the act of writing, may be able to face the reality of a divided self without turning away and may be able to ask what the sounds of deracination actually mean. Yet the aspirations of the divided heart, a heart that demands an "exact" space of wholeness within, may never be fully met. The climb toward this aspiration is to "endless mesas" of a home that is itself bereft of vitality. What the poet will seek there are "thistles drying in the wind" and other pathetic remains "left behind" by an "old" lost culture of the past.

Memories of a version of an old Native American peace within the self are an obsession "that will not die" for Allen. She uses demotic diction, shifts in sequential organization, rejection of received structures and strict meters, and personal subject matters (often with only the barest mediation via personae) to signify the fractured meanings within the self. But that is not to say that her verse is without an intellectual order or aesthetic principle. Allen's poetry is without precedents or antecedents; the American "breed," as Allen is careful to remind readers of her criticism, is "particularly bereft of readers" from the Native American audience and so must seek to reserve the nearly deracinated elements of culture that remain, like fragments from the hands of old potters, while accommodating those elements to the larger white society (**"Answering the Deer"**). Because the Native American literary renaissance is a recent phenomenon and because these writers are forced to write in English in order to have a wide audience, the problem of alienation for the "breed" is intensified beyond measure and, perhaps, beyond communication. But that does not stop Allen from bearing witness.

Hers is a voice that will not die; nor will it speak solely of aloneness. Requiring that someone listen and comprehend, she writes one of her most important poems, entitled **"Two,"** about Vine Deloria, Jr., the distinguished critic of the Native American experience in contemporary America. **"Two"** is a poem of affirmation, of triumph over the exigencies inevitable to the "breed"—loneliness, distorted identities, depression, alienation. The poem begins subtly:

> In the winter everything disappears,
> leaving a lonely bird or two
> and some dry stalks of last year's grass.

The words "lonely bird or two" repeat and deepen the significance of the poem's title, **"Two,"** and convey the alienated atmosphere of the contemporary "breed" who witnesses Native American cultural genocide as the "winter [when] everything disappears." Only loneliness is left behind for the one or two who remain. Yet "two" are enough, if those "two" are "lords who could still display themselves to fire" as an old sachem might. Allen personalizes the poem to Deloria's own passionate fire for justice and his long legal struggles on behalf of all Native Americans, "breeds" included. The poem records Deloria's public triumph of memory and compassion:

> remembering somehow in that celebration the
> Law, the
> Winter, the
> long flight of moon in the dry sky.

This is a poem of celebratory intent; Allen seeks to reconcile the opposites of life and death, of loneliness and mutuality, of disappearance (even extinction) and changeless restoration. However painful the winter of celebration and fire and certainty, at least

> In tribal dreams
> image and sound together make complicated
>   song.

That song which traces "our spiraling path," the narrator reminds her listeners, is not lost completely. For Allen, there is always a transformative vision lurking within the "winter" self of alienation:

> We

> simply follow disappearance over
> each next rise, but
> this winter, or that, we shall go home again,
> back to our own time and earth,

> and know again the changelessness,
> the silence, the
> strong
> sure steps of home.

Here the persona called "I"—the voice of so much of Allen's poetry—is remade to a shared voice, "We," in the same manner that the poet affirms a transfiguring poetic unity: "we shall go home again, / back to our own time." For the "breed," this "changeless" time of "sure" strength signifies a vision of wholeness, of "homeness," where heretofore no home was more than imagined.

Deracination, singing, shadows, silence: these are the figures of Allen's vision. The tribal ties within the self form the center of consciousness and shape the range of meaning in her poems. Through her transfigurative images, at least, the "breed" belongs. The voice that Allen articulates may be obsessed with the alienation it so resolutely explores in verse and in her only novel, *The Woman Who Owned the Shadows.* But in singing her songs of the "breed's" experience, Allen discovers a palpable presence of "home" in America that assuages isolation and leavens despair both for herself and for her reader. . . .

. . . . .

Allen's first and only novel, *The Woman Who Owned the Shadows* is most successful when it explores women's traditions within the Keres Pueblo for their ritual significance. Elements of pueblo "thought-singing" form the novel's theme, imagery, narrative method, and whatever its unity of design. Interpenetrated within this rich, complex recreation of Native of American aesthetic experience is the quasi-autobiographical tale of a "halfblood breed," Ephanie. "Too strange," even deranged by her own alienation, Ephanie attempts to find some version of selfhood within the "empty paces" and "long shadows" of her divided Native American/white past.

The "Prologue" to the novel contains its essence. Here Allen redesigns her own creation myth and, in the process, she feminizes and personalizes the myth of Spider Woman and her twin so that it becomes a means of viewing and revealing the events of the narrative to come. Allen writes, "In the beginning was the Spider. She divided the world. She made it . . . In the center of the universe she sang . . . Her singing made all the worlds." Like the novelist Allen herself, Spider "places her will" on the world through art and weaves "her design" through the novel.

In this novel about novel-making, or more proximately the difficulties of creative work, Allen evokes a symbolic women's universe created by women. The novel is about how a woman artist heals herself through the act of aesthetic creation; and its setting, time, plot, and characters are derived largely from Allen's own contemporary time and experience in the post-war American Southwest. The episodic, uneven, seemingly unedited novel that results is of unfulfilled promise and momentary brilliance. (The closest literary analogue to Allen's novel is Sylvia Plath's *The Bell Jar* [1963], also a quasi-autobiographical and only novel of uneven quality by a woman who is primarily a poet). *The Woman Who Owned the Shadows* demands critical attention, despite its deficiencies, because of its subtle use of Native American aesthetic materials and because of its revelations concerning gender-related restrictions and the critical evaluation of writing women, whether Native American or white or whatever their experience.

Allen's fiction is a "melodrama of beset womanhood"—to revise Nina Baym's cogent analysis of American literature ["Melodramas of Beset Manhood: How Theories of American Fiction Exclude Women Authors," *American Quarterly* 33 (1981)] as an exclusively male canon from which the writing woman is pushed to the margins. The male convention followed by Melville, Twain, Faulkner, and the Native American N. Scott Momaday consists of the quest of a young, male dreamer in search of freedom. In the "Prologue" to her own melodrama, Allen turns the convention on its head. For Allen the role of the dreamer beset by a world of horror is that of a magical woman who breaks the boundaries within which her society restricts her and, in the process of unmasking the reflections of sexist ideology, discovers in them the empowering myth of Spider Woman, a creative being of her own devising.

However celebratory Allen's creation, at least at the outset of the text, the novel itself slips into a personal narrative of melodramatic victimization. Allen documents her sense of deception and suffering; she prints a "Divorce Settlement" and a copy of "Therapist's Notes." The concrete details of victimization do not revivify the soap-opera elements in the narrative; Ephanie is still "seduced and abandoned" in the conventional mode. Even though one of those lovers abandoning her is a woman, many others are men. The effect of powerlessness and betrayal is hopelessness, whether the relationship is heterosexual or lesbian. The Native American imagination of Spider Woman—of woman as creator, not victim—acts as a gloss on the actual experience of Ephanie; Spider Woman reveals how limited are the lives of women and how vulnerable, in Allen's vision.

For Ephanie is a character caught within the tension between positive and negative interpretations: a negative interpretation that discloses her complicity within a patriarchal, white ideology (she marries and she seeks male approval for her writing) and a positive interpretation that triumphs through the imagination of a woman creating for herself and other women, especially Native American women. To reveal the tension inherent in Ephanie and her experience, Allen uses an image of a "dream of years. Of her whole life." Ephanie's dream is of Elena, the girl who will abandon her. But in the dream Ephanie and Elena are "tiny girls running in frantic circles" because they are being "chased by a long circle of animals" and "running forever with no way to escape while the others—mother and aunts, sisters and grandmother stood, watched, slouching familiarly with each other, laughing and pointing. Unconcerned." In the dream Ephanie recapitulates her sense of fear and victimization in an imaginative world in which even those she trusts, those within her own matriarchal universe, are unable to halt the violence. They, too, are victims; no wonder they are "unconcerned," for they can do nothing but watch since they also share the vulnerable status of woman. What is interesting about the image here is how fully it transforms and denies the vision

of the first "Prologue"; in that image Spider Woman shapes and names the animals of the earth. They are in her control, as they are made "ready for their children." But in Ephanie's dream "of her whole life" nothing is in control, nothing is made ready, and all that remains for women is to run "forever with no way of escape."

The tension between these two visions of women's experience is what, paradoxically, holds the novel together. The narrative of Ephanie's fear is made visible through the minutiae of her life; the details of her private rituals of daily experience—what she wears, what she eats, how she deals with the "simple dust of her house"—are juxtaposed to a Native American belief system that might explain the workings of the world. Allen's drive to create a new world, at least in symbols, does not prevent her from the recording of the quotidian. Rather, she seeks to work within the minute-to-minute record of everyday experience, looking there for clues to a new way of seeing and interpreting women's writing, her own included.

If the effect of recording minute strands of dailyness is repetitious, even boring, then Allen's insistence on looking at the ordinary life in ordinary spoken rhythms may numb and confuse. The urge to repeat the data of habitual experience may also seem to conflict with Allen's desire to create a vision of authentic and nurturing emotional relations and Native American beliefs that will develop the force of mythic experience. Among "the litter of things," for example, Ephanie sees "a prayer, a ritual, a rite. Among. Pick up the robe. The litter. Walk with it. Of my. Put it down." Again and again in the text, language moves via synonyms and repetitions rather than new thinking or feeling. Only momentarily is Allen able to discover the vision embedded in the immediate, untransmuted minutiae.

When Allen succeeds in pointing to the existence of an alternative world view in Native American matriarchal belief systems, the language of the novel becomes clearer, less arbitrarily repetitive. The character Ephanie is shaped as a victim to a structure of white values; as Ephanie abandons those values, she clings to felt reality—the things of dailyness—even if this reality is perceived as mad. Ephanie writes of herself, "Which is I. Which them. And wondered how she had come to believe herself possessed . . . I must be mad." In the moments of "craziness building, building" within her, Ephanie is made to focus on clues to a new interpretive paradigm for describing Native American experience: "Everybody thinks it's the other guy who's responsible for what happens to Indians and never themselves." First, her questions are more disturbances in orthodox theory, but gradually, Ephanie comes to know that "no matter which side of this stupid discussion wins, it's Indians who suffer and it's Indians who die." For Ephanie, nothing is simple: "What do you do," she asks, "when you love everybody on every side of the war?" Her response is to attempt suicide. Yet she saves herself by cutting the rope she had prepared so carefully for her death. And she finds her own essential identity by choosing her own side of the war in her own self.

By re-possessing her own version of selfhood and her own void with all its shadows, Ephanie searches for the means

> **At the center of Paula Gunn Allen's vision
> of self and art is an individual alienated
> within. For Allen the idea of the "breed"
> reflects a preoccupation with alienation as
> a personal and as an aesthetic experience.**
>
> —*Elizabeth I. Hanson*

"to knit in" herself by an "invisible seam." As a counterpoint to Ephanie's struggle for self, Allen tells the story of Kochinnenako who bears twin sons after a visitation by the sun god. Later the boys wish to find their father and so Kochinnenako agrees to take them on the long journey. Grandmother Spider Woman helps them on their way, and the boys are able to prove their paternity and go on to "become the helpers of the people for a long, long time."

In this simple retelling of a tale of guardianship and protections, Allen explores the nurturing relationship human beings may discover in the new yet ancient symbology of Native American experience. In those symbolic tales "all the fragments of all the shattered hearts gathered carefully in one place" would create a new wholeness. In the "empty spaces" of Ephanie's "room of long shadows" Allen devises the alternative world view which she believes may be a future not yet invented, but still felt and dreamed about. It is a view of woman stronger than man; she arouses man's fear and jealousy, and she falls "beneath the shining boughs of the tree almost forever" but not quite. In her falling, she enters "a new world and upon it [plants] her seed." It is she "who gave the sun and moon their light. Who from death made life. Who knew nothing was ever ended. Who just went on." This female explorer comes to see that "everything [is] related," that falling into the void occurs not just for her as "herself, but as a being upon a world, the world we knew. The world we guide and protect. We have ever guarded it. We ever will protect it." By this fortunate fall, Allen's Ephanie finds and repossesses her own shadows. This character—confused, obsessed, repetitive, on the verge of slipping into madness—rages through her victimization in a manner that redeems it: "the room filled with shadows. And the shadows became shapes. And the shapes became women singing . . . and she began to sing with them."

Allen's visionary novel is made from women singing. Against the pessimism inherent in Native American experience in white America, Allen asserts the value of life in art. She does not provide us with a positive answer about the future of Native Americans, but she does show us a Native American mythic universe where we may find new ways of illuminating its shadows and understanding its meaning. Her characters look for answers, desperate to find a world with a coherent structure where human beings can live with dignity. This quest of humankind is not unique to Allen's vision; visionary artists from Cooper and Melville to Momaday and Silko have sought to comprehend the Native American's and the American's dilemma

in a white man's land. What Allen offers is her unique testimony. She communicates in order to heal wounds caused by the shadowed divisions of Native American experience.

. . . . .

Paula Gunn Allen always shapes her aesthetic and critical work to mediate between Native American and white experience. For example, in the poem **"Hoop Dancer"** Allen begins by empathizing with the white reader's difficulty in ever understanding the mental space of the Native American:

> It's hard to enter
> circling clockwise and counter
> clockwise moving no
> regard for time, metrics
> irrelevant to this place
> where pain is the prime number
> and soft stepping feet
> praise water from the skies

The difficulty, however, goes beyond confrontations between cultures; in "this place" of ceremonial time and significance, even metrics are "irrelevant" as even the white man's aesthetic formulae fail to encompass the integrating and empowering vision of the Native American. For the Native American's space, in Allen's vision, is one of balance and timelessness, always sought, rarely recovered.

Allen devises mediative metamorphoses of self because she intends to explore and clarify the roles and meaning of Native American literature within the whole body of American literature. For example, in an introductory work, **"Whose Dream Is This Anyway: Remythologizing and Self-Redefinition in Contemporary American Indian Fiction,"** Allen succeeds in summarizing with a good deal of sensitivity and good sense the various kinds of novels about American Indians, including those by James Fenimore Cooper, Frank Waters, and Oliver La Farge, as well as those by N. Scott Momaday, James Welch, and Leslie Marmon Silko. In succinct terms and careful arguments, Allen succeeds in eight pages in explaining a number of useful perspectives on American fiction as a whole and especially on contemporary writings by Native Americans and by white writers also.

Allen argues that "the most favored theme in novels about Indians by non-Indians is the plight of the noble Indian who is the hapless victim of civilized forces beyond his control," and that this theme simply reinforces the view common to both Indians and whites that Indians who attempt to adapt to white ways in any manner are doomed to death. In these novels, the emphasis is on white guilt, anger, and grief, at times, but the effect is always the same: the "supposed disappearance (always about to happen) of the American Indian." Allen suggests that writers used this dying Indian theme—the most popular examples were Cooper's *Leatherstocking Tales,* Longfellow's *Hiawatha,* and Mark Twain's *The Adventures of Tom Sawyer*—because it was so appealing to American readers. Indeed, works such as Thomas Berger's *Little Big Man* and Ken Kesey's *One Flew Over the Cuckoo's Nest* and others indicate the continuing potential for a theme which allows white writers to cast the Native American into roles which serve to fill the needs of white American dramas of self-hood.

Allen's *oeuvre* is designed quite deliberately with knowledge of and in relation to white portraits of the Indian, particularly the "essentially pastoral" creations by Willa Cather, Frank Waters, and John Neihardt. As John R. Milton suggests in his *The Novel of the American West* (1980), Western American writers of high literary aspirations discover within an American Western pastoral setting elements of the sacred; in these liminal experiences the Native American is imagined as a being of transformative, visionary power. Milton is a revealing interpreter of contemporary Native American and Western American literature, and he was a significant influence on Allen's early career when he chose her work to be included in his *Four Indian Poets* (1974). As always, Allen is conscious of her own revealing role within white American ideas of self-exploration and self-justification. She evokes the themes and images of the Western pastoral in her poems and in her novel, **The Woman Who Owned the Shadows,** but she also seeks to negotiate her own visionary detour into her own transformative terrain.

While Allen's imaginative landscape is rich in authentic detail of the American West within and without the reservations, she is far more concerned with the effects of translocation and dislocation than with the meanings of actual lands and creatures. Where Allen registers her strongest Western literary key is in the shade and movement of her hymns to the sacred in Native American experience. By discovering her own mode of American sacred, Allen creates her own myths; she reinvokes primordial sacred time with a contemporary profane time in order to recover and remake her self. That restored, renewed self suggests in symbolic terms a revival within Native American experience as a whole. Like Allen's own vision of self, contemporary Native Americans exist not in a romantic past but instead in a community which extends through the whole of American experience.

Yet the revival Allen addresses in her works of art and criticism also creates inextricable tensions and paradoxes. Like the "breeds" of American literature—Thoreau's Joe Polis, Melville's Queequeg, Hemingway's Prudie/Trudie, and Faulkner's Sam Fathers—the perspective of the figure on the margin is acutely responsive and must respond to sensitive, even radically conscious circumstances. But it is within these lightning rod beings between two worlds that the essential paradoxes within American's heterogeneity are most clearly faced and understood. It is the "breed" who is compelled to deal with two cultures as his or her daily bread. It is the "breed" who may understand two cultures, quite diverse in themselves, and may live to tell the tale. It is the "breed" who knows that Native Americans may learn something of the world view of whites and whites may learn something of the cultures of Native Americans, but neither can be fully judged by the norms of the other. In her criticism and in her creative writings Allen provides a gloss on Native American experience and literature, but more even than that, she offers a particular telescope through which we may explore the whole range of classic American fiction. In her vision and art she stimulates scholars and students of American literature to see the canon through new eyes.

The Indian stereotypes, even the inverted Indian stereotypes of Berger and Kesey, reveal more about the experience and traditions of white American life than they do of the complex and diverse cultures of Native Americans. Yet both experiences, that of the Main Street mainstream and that of the Native American, require clarification. For example, Allen notes that Native Americans "in general have more often than not refused to engage in protest in their politics as in their fiction and poetry." By choosing to focus on their own traditions and to merge European and American literary forms with tribal ones, writers such as Momaday, Welch, Silko, Gerald Vizenor, Louise Erdrich, and Allen herself, have created "more positive (because more actual) images of Indians." In the process, Allen shows how such adaptive traditions have enabled contemporary Native American writers "to resist effectively both colonization and genocide" of the imagination. Just as Native Americans have resisted the early predictions of their total dissolution, so also do their literary imaginers shape the images of a "nativistic renewal" which characterizes Native American public life in the last quarter of the twentieth century, Allen believes.

The mediative role Allen assumes in her criticism of Native American literature is meant to act as a catalyst to new inquiries into perhaps the most crucial of all questions in American Studies: what is an American? The complex

---

Allen on critics:

Sometimes critics are very good; sometimes the lack of information is depressing. Everybody, or almost everybody, is well intentioned, sympathetic. They want to understand and they don't understand the degree to which they've been conditioned to think certain thoughts and to not think others. But I long for the day when we have critics who are very knowledgeable, because we need that. We, the writers, need that. We need critics who can address specifically what we're doing and not what they wish we had done and not what they imagine we did, but who know what's going on and therefore can make distinctions and illuminations about the literature. But we're developing people like that and there are probably twenty critics in the country who are really good. And they're training new ones. So I don't think it will be too long before I can send out a book and I can trust the reviewers to tell me what I need to know. And I have already got two or three critics that I know I can trust, because they know what I am doing and they know when I fail to do it. And that's what a writer needs; we've got to have that before we can really be a literary movement. We're beginning a literary movement, but we don't quite have all the parts of it yet. We're getting there.

Paula Gunn Allen, in an interview in Winged Words: American Indian Writers Speak, *edited by Laura Coltelli, University of Nebraska Press, 1990.*

dialogue among white Americans engaged in struggle with the American continent, a dialogue so fully explored by Melville, Thoreau, Hawthorne, Mark Twain, and Faulkner, is illuminated and complicated by the voices of Native Americans such as Allen's. Main Street American literature leads to Indian territory, after all, but now the white man's Indians can speak for themselves.

Suzanne Ruta   (review date November 1991)

SOURCE: "Myth America," in *VLS,* No. 100, November, 1991, p. 26.

[*Ruta is an American short story writer. In the following, she praises Allen's storytelling skills, focus on Native American myth, and incorporation of historical fact in* Grandmothers of the Light.]

Paula Gunn Allen is a lesbian feminist scholar of Native American literature, a critic (*The Sacred Hoop*), an anthologist (*Spider Woman's Granddaughters*), a mother, a grandmother, Laguna Pueblo and Lakota Sioux by birth, Cherokee by marriage. *Grandmothers of the Light* is a collection of Native American creation myths in which goddesses do all the work and even get the credit. But *goddesses* is probably the wrong word for these divinities, who don't dazzle or attack from distant thrones. Like the cultures that nourished them, they're down to earth, egalitarian, democratic, and resourceful, plunging their arms into the clay, the corn dough, the ashes, to come up with what's needed to create or sustain life. The Quiché Maya grandmother Xmucané grinds corn and mixes it with water to create the first men and women, after her previous attempts with mud and wood were comic failures. Spider Woman, another grandmother, is the Cherokee Prometheus. Old, slow, and weak in the joints, she invents pottery to carry a spark of fire back to her people from a neighbor country.

Unlike your run-of-the-mill tape-recorder anthropologist, transmitting tales verbatim down to the last grunt, Allen feels free to retell these stories in her own voice, conflating earlier versions, adding snippets of psychology, jokes, historical asides, and plenty of built-in interpretation. It's her tradition. She learned some of the stories from her great-grandmother, a Laguna Pueblo, and others from her uncle, who published collections of them, and still others from friends, swapping tales around the country. It's a live tradition and she's helping it grow, clearing away patriarchal accretions and restoring women's roles that were downplayed or cut out when male informants spoke to Jesuit priests or male anthropologists. Telling how White Buffalo Woman brought the sacred pipe to the Lakota Sioux, she's careful to note in passing that it was the woman of the tribe who put up the great lodge of four conjoined tipis, where the bestowal took place. And to shake up our preconceptions about the fierce warrior Sioux, she paints a slow, poignant portrait of the tribe at peace among themselves, during a time of plenty, before the Europeans came.

In the best stories, the gods are as close as family, only a bit older. Allen isn't afraid to fuse chant, landscape, and

some fairly didactic bits of explanation to tell how Spider Woman thought the cosmos into being.

> So she thought to the power once and knew a rippling, a wrinkling within. Then she knew she was old, and wrinkled, and that the power's first song was a song of great age. The wrinkling became tighter, more spidery, stronger. It became in one place. She named that place Northwest. . . . Later the earth would be ripples and wrinkles, spidery lines of power folded and enfolded into a tight moving shape, and it would also hold the great power within, like a mother holds new life. Others would also imitate this time: walnuts and acorns, apples and pineapples, cactuses and mountains, even the oceans would be like that. And humans, five-fingered beings, would grow wrinkled in their skin and brains, in honor of this time when she and the power made a song to form new life, new beings.

Some stories lack the personal touch. Allen's hushed, solemn account of the Aztec goddess Tonantzin's transformation under Catholicism doesn't begin to suggest the enormous vitality of her cult—as Our Lady of Guadalupe—in Mexico today. When she writes about the Maya it sounds worked up from books, and out-of-date books at that. At other times, her personality gets in the way of her message, as when she claims she has channeled communications from a crystallized human skull found in Belize some years ago. The last of the book's 21 myths is simply what the skull told her: a coy account of its genesis, discovery, and journey to Canada, where it now reposes. The channeled message ends with a prophecy of a new age of peace and harmony in the 21st century.

Goddess knows it's time for such a change. Allen's own pueblo, Laguna, lies just west of Albuquerque, where Sandia Laboratories, Los Alamos's evil twin, has engineered nuclear weapons since the 1950s, and just east of the New Mexico uranium mines that poisoned the Navajo water sources. The old stories foresaw these modern developments. The Quiché grandmother Xmucané made a race of people carved from wood who were too stiff and stubborn to bow down and worship. Because of their arrogance,

---

Allen on her identity:

Of course, I always knew I was Indian. I was never told to forget it, to deny it. Indians were common in the family, at least on my mother's side. In fact, unlike many people I meet who are claiming they're "Indian" or reluctantly revealing it, far from being denied, my relationship to the pueblo down the line was reinforced in a number of ways. I was told over and over, "Never forget that you're Indian." My mother said it. Nor did she say, "Remember you are part Indian."

Paula Gunn Allen, in her "The Autobiography of a Confluence," in I Tell You Now: Autobiographical Essays by Native American Writers, *edited by Brian Swann and Arnold Krupat, University of Nebraska Press, 1987.*

---

their own inventions rose up and destroyed them in the end. The Navajo goddess Changing Woman wouldn't allow her son, Monster Slayer, to banish death from the world. "Some things are better left as they are," she told him, which could stand as a motto for the whole environmental movement. We need more of these wonderful myths. What we don't need is facile New Age optimism. Allen's power as a medicine woman derives not from talking skulls but from her own gift as a teller of unkillable tales.

Gretchen Ronnow   (review date December 1992-January 1993)

SOURCE: "Sorcery of Her Own," in *American Book Review*, Vol. 14, No. 5, December, 1992-January, 1993, p. 12.

[*Author of various critical essays on such Native American writers as John Milton Oskison and Leslie Marmon Silko, Ronnow has served as vice-president of the Association for the Study of Native American Literatures. In the following, she offers a mixed assessment of* Grandmothers of the Light.]

Paula Gunn Allen's *Grandmothers of the Light—A Medicine Woman's Sourcebook* is divided into three main parts—"Cosmogyny: the Goddesses," "Ritual Magic and Aspects of the Goddesses," and "Myth, Magic, and Medicine in the Modern World"—plus an introductory essay, a postscript that explains the tribes involved, a glossary, and a bibliography. Allen writes in the preface that she has "gleaned from the vast oral tradition of Native American" twenty-one stories that have served as her own "guides and sourcebook [to] navigate the perilous journey along the path that marks the boundary between the mundane world and the world of the spirit." She asserts that "each of the stories in this collection contains information central to a woman's spiritual tradition" since each speaks of the creative power of the goddesses of myth and ritual. She draws from a variety of "ethnographic and literary sources, from the oral tradition, and from direct communication from her own spirit guides."

In the introductory essay, **"The Living Reality of the Medicine World,"** Allen assures us that "an apprentice medicine person becomes familiar with a number of these stories because they act as general guides" to the universe of power, hence she implicitly identifies her audience as those would-be apprentice medicine women. These stories, according to Allen, "enable practitioners of the sacred to recognize where they are and how to function, the entities they might encounter, their names, personalities, and likely disposition toward them, the kinds of instruction they might gain from them, and how to explore the universe of power to gain greater paranormal knowledge and ability." Allen is convinced that walking the path of power is "not the same as therapy, university studies, or activities such as drumming, chanting, dancing, or pointing magic wands. To walk the medicine path is to live and think in ways that are almost but not quite entirely unlike our usual ways of living and thinking, and the stories show the right and wrong ways to proceed."

Allen performs a kind of sorcery of her own upon certain key etymologies. For "myth" she branches from the Indo-Germanic root MU to produce derivatives meaning "a mystery, a secret, a thing muttered," or "ritual verbalization," or "a slight sound," or "a mother"—although she does admit that muttering "is an activity presently ascribed to the mad, the elderly, the female, and the powerless." MA can be "discerned in words such as mother, mom, mammary, mutter, *immic,* and *om*" and in related concepts such as sea (French *mer*), evil (Spanish *mal*), and lord (Arabic *mar*). She likes the fragment GE in "geology, geomancy, geas, geometry, geophysics, and geopolitics"— all from GAIA, "the Great Goddesses' powers that emanate from her [*sic*] planetary body [*sic*]." Allen's discussion of etymological fragments eventually produces the shaman's ma-ge-[c] which has been her point all along.

In the same way that she likes language sources to run together, she likes to find affinities in objects: "the ritual dancer with the power to transform dry air into rain bearing clouds is similar to the card called 'the World' in the Tarot deck, to Shiva of the Hindu Way, to the Dancer of the African mysteries. Rain Dancer is a key, a point of entry into the mystery, the myth-matter-mother of arcane reality." And she delineates seven ways one is/becomes a medicine woman: the ways of the daughter, the Householder, the Mother, the Gatherer, the Ritualist, the Teacher, and the Wise Woman. Allen discourses at length on each of these apparently sequential phases of a woman's life, yet none of her discussion is documented in any way except a reference or two to her dictionary and short, general acknowledgements of the tribal tradition behind each story. We must take only her word for the validity of her research and self-confident conclusions. For example, Allen proclaims that during the "Gatherer" stage the woman/shaman goes forth to harvest from the earth, "armed only with a digging stick (which is the mother of tools), knowledge, intuition (inner knowledge), and prayer." Yet unanswered is the obvious question, why is the digging stick the "mother of tools"? Why not a basket or other similar vessel, which seems more appropriately female and also much more practical for gathering? Actually Allen never mentions baskets or containers at all in her discussion of gatherers. Finally, she advises the apprentice shaman that "travel to and in the universe of power thus is more a matter of psychic travel than of physical movement." Although she uses the word "advisedly," she proposes " 'dialing' different gestalts" (a procedure "analogous to selecting a television channel") to become conscious in other worlds.

She writes that she is devoting her volume to "an investigation of myths from the women's shamanic tradition" in order to introduce a number of female entities ranging in order of being from goddess to medicine woman. It is obvious that this book will appeal mainly to a naive or popular audience, especially to readers interested in the romanticization of Native American spirituality and easy access to it, and to readers who do not care about documentation of sources, differentiation between tribes, or original texts and original languages. Questions of translation, transmission, privacy (even secrecy), appropriation by outsiders, or appropriateness of place and time of the telling/retelling are not raised, and by implication are not expected to be asked.

The best parts of Allen's volume are the stories themselves, thanks to Allen's literary and imaginative skills. The very flaw mentioned above—the lack of any sense of the presence of the myth's original time and place—becomes here an advantage to the reader who wants a lovely, graceful, easy-to-read story in English. Allen writes that she presents the myths "not necessarily as recorded or told, but as [she] understands them. Rendering works from the tribal ritual tradition aims to enable readers unfamiliar with those traditions to comprehend implicit as well as explicit meanings of the myth." Allen insists that a "story must remain a story and such apparatus as glossaries, cultural notes, and alternate texts can become so cumbersome that readers may well find themselves lost in an intellectual wilderness, unable to discover the central point." In this book, the central issue as defined by Allen is "to enable women to recover our path to the gynocosmos that is our spiritual home." Thus Allen's serious readers are, tacitly, her acolytes.

Allen does include myths from a variety of tribal traditions: the Navajo, the Pueblo, the Cherokee, the Haudinashone, the Chippewa, the Lakota, and the Mayan. She asks us to notice the "complexity of the weave of the goddesses in these stories"; certainly what we notice is the complexity that Allen has found in her own project and that she writes into the stories for us. Allen's versions of the myths have much philosophical explanation. For instance, in one of the creation stories of the Pueblo we find this explanation, unusual for a myth: Spider is

> a great wise woman, whose powers are beyond imagining. No medicine person, no conjurer or shaman, no witch or sorcerer, no scientist or inventor can imagine how great her power is. Her power is complete and total. It is pure, and cleaner than the void. It is the power of thought. . . . It's like the power of dream, but more pure. Like the spirit of vision, but more clear. It has no shape or movement, because it just is. It is the power that creates all that is, and it is the power of all that is.

This kind of lengthy explanation is common in Allen's texts. She also embellishes the stories with modern phrasing and philosophy. In an origin story from the Haudinashone Allen writes:

> Seven Waterfowl moved through the emptiness and came together, forming a firm nexus of energy, a tidal whorl, a security. So arranged, they moved their thought wings, their intelligence-

net beneath her, and her fall came to rest in their arms. Not that her motion ended; they all moved together in harmony. The directionless movement, the endless drift through the nothing she had entered when the other world ended and she fell beneath the tree of light took on a coherence, a form, that connected her within the order of all that is. . . . They knew as they contemplated a time that she should enter another kind of motion, one that spun slowly, slowly, one as ordered and serene as the dancing of human women as it would arise out of the same pattern, the same knowing in another loop of the endless coil of creation.

Yet this writing is also beautiful, embellished with Allen's poetic rhythms and sense of language. Perhaps for some readers Allen's beautiful, heartfelt writing is reason enough to read.

FURTHER READING

Criticism

Gomez, Jewelle. "Who Tells the Stories Rules the World." *The Women's Review of Books* VI, Nos. 10-11 (July 1989): 8.

> Favorable assessment of *Spider Woman's Granddaughters*.

Karvar, Quannah. "Tribal Women Speak." *Los Angeles Times Book Review* (9 July 1989): 10.

> Praiseworthy review of *Spider Woman's Granddaughters*. Karvar notes: "These remarkable narratives represent the oral tradition as it journeys into its contemporary form, bringing with it all that is sacred and significant to tribal women and tribal people as a whole."

McEwen, Christian. "Tribes That Bind." *The Village Voice* XXXIV, No. 38 (19 September 1989): 57.

> Offers praise for *Spider Woman's Granddaughters*. The critic argues that the stories in this volume are "war stories" in that they present "a means of making order in the universe, of maintaining harmony and balance, of strengthening personal and cultural identity."

Njeri, Itabari. "The Compelling Stories of a Conquered Nation." *Los Angeles Times* (19 October 1990): E1, E7.

> Feature essay relating biographical information about Allen and critical reception of *Spider Woman's Granddaughters*.

Additional coverage of Allen's life and career is contained in the following sources published by Gale Research: *Contemporary Authors*, Vol. 112, and *Native North American Literature*.

Margaret Atwood

1939-

(Full name Margaret Eleanor Atwood) Canadian poet, novelist, short story writer, critic, and author of children's books.

The following entry provides an overview of Atwood's career through 1994. For further information on her career and works, see *CLC,* Volumes 2, 3, 4, 8, 13, 15, 25, and 44.

INTRODUCTION

Internationally acclaimed as a poet, novelist and short story writer, Margaret Atwood has emerged as a major figure in Canadian letters. Using such devices as irony, symbolism, and self-conscious narrators, she explores the relationship between humanity and nature, the dark side of human behavior, and power as it pertains to gender and politics. Popular with both literary scholars and the reading public, Atwood has helped to define and identify the goals of contemporary Canadian literature and has earned a distinguished reputation among feminist writers for her exploration of women's issues.

Biographical Information

Atwood was born in Ottawa and grew up in suburban Toronto. As a child she spent her summers at her family's cottage in the wilderness of northern Quebec, where her father, a forest entomologist, conducted research. She first began to write while in high school, contributing poetry, short stories, and cartoons to the school newspaper. As an undergraduate at the University of Toronto, Atwood was influenced by critic Northrop Frye, who introduced her to the poetry of William Blake. Impressed with Blake's use of mythological imagery, Atwood published her first volume of poetry, *Double Persephone,* in 1961. In 1962 Atwood completed her A.M. degree at Radcliffe College of Harvard University. She returned to Toronto in 1963, where she began collaborating with artist Charles Pachter, who designed and illustrated several volumes of her poetry. In 1964 Atwood moved to Vancouver, where she taught English at the University of British Columbia for a year and completed her first novel, *The Edible Woman* (1969). After a year of teaching Victorian and American literature at Sir George Williams University in Montreal in 1967, Atwood began teaching creative writing at the University of Alberta while continuing to write and publish poetry. Her poetry collection *The Circle Game* (1966) won the 1967 Governor General's Award, Canada's highest literary honor. Atwood's public visibility increased significantly with the publication of *Power Politics* in 1971. Requiring an escape from increasing media attention, Atwood left a teaching position at the University of Toronto to move to a farm near Alliston, Ontario, with her husband, Graeme Gibson. Atwood received the Governor

General's Award in 1986 for her novel *The Handmaid's Tale,* which was published that same year. She continues to be a prominent voice in Canada's cultural and political life.

Major Works

Since 1961 Atwood has produced a highly acclaimed body of work that includes fiction, poetry, and literary criticism. *The Circle Game* established the major themes of Atwood's writing: inconsistencies of self-perception, the paradoxical nature of language, the issue of Canadian identity, and conflicts between humankind and nature. In the same year that she published her second novel, *Surfacing* (1972), Atwood also earned widespread attention for *Survival* (1972), a seminal critical analysis of Canadian literature that served as a rallying point for the country's cultural nationalists. In the poetry collection *The Journals of Susanna Moodie* (1970), Atwood devoted her attention to what she calls the schizoid, or double, nature of Canada. Based on the autobiographies of a Canadian pioneer woman, *The Journals of Susanna Moodie* examines why Canadians came to develop ambivalent feelings toward their country. Atwood further developed this dichotomy in *Power Politics,* in which she explores the relationship between sexual roles and power structures by focusing on personal relationships. Atwood's novels explore the relationship between personal behavior and political issues as well. These include *Lady Oracle* (1976), about a protagonist who fakes her own death and thereby creates a new life for herself; *The Handmaid's Tale,* a dystopian novel concerning an oppressive future society; *Cat's Eye* (1990), a coming-of-age novel that contains autobiographical elements; and *The Robber Bride* (1993), a contemporary recasting of a folktale, which explores jealousy and sexual manipulation.

Critical Reception

Criticism of Atwood's work has tended to emphasize her political and social views. Many critics identify her use of grotesque, shocking imagery and heavy irony as hallmarks of her style. Because her poetry and fiction often portray physical and psychological violence in relationships between men and women, some commentators have labeled Atwood pessimistic and dismissed her as little more than an ideologue, but other critics have found her a visionary interpreter of feminist thought. *The Handmaid's Tale,* for example, has been favorably compared with George Orwell's *Nineteen Eighty-Four* (1949) and other distinguished dystopian novels for its disturbing extension of contemporary trends and its allegorical portrait of political extremism. The many critics who praise Atwood's work admire her spareness of language, emotional restraint, and willingness to examine the harsh realities of both society and the natural world.

PRINCIPAL WORKS

CRITICISM

Barbara Hill Rigney   (essay date 1978)

SOURCE: " 'After the Failure of Logic': Descent and Return in *Surfacing*," in her *Madness and Sexual Politics in the Feminist Novel,* The University of Wisconsin Press, 1978, pp. 91-115.

[*In the following excerpt, Rigney discusses the theme of discovering the self through descent and return in Atwood's* Surfacing.]

It is inevitable for Margaret Atwood's nameless protagonist of **Surfacing** that there should occur a "failure of logic," for her journey "home" is an exploration of a world beyond logic. Her quest, like that of Jane Eyre, Clarissa Dalloway, and Martha Quest Hesse, is for an identity, a vision of self. She must find that self—not only through the father for whom she searches the Canadian backwoods, but also through the mother for whom she must search in the depths of her own psyche.

Atwood, much like Virginia Woolf, juxtaposes and compares two internal worlds: the world of the male principle, characterized by rationality and logic but often also by cruelty and destruction, and the world of the female principle, which for Atwood implies an existence beyond reason, a realm of primitive nature where there are connections between life and death, suffering and joy, madness and true sanity, where opposites are resolved into wholes. A failure to recognize these connections is a failure to perceive the "female" part of one's self, and this results, for Atwood, in a catastrophic splitting of the self. Like R. D. Laing's patients in *The Divided Self,* alienated from the self and from society, Atwood's protagonist perceives herself as rent, torn asunder:

> I'd allowed myself to be cut in two. Woman sawn apart in a wooden crate, wearing a bathing suit, smiling, a trick done with mirrors, I read it in a comic book; only with me there had been an accident and I came apart. The other half, the one locked away, was the only one that could live; I was the wrong half, detached, terminal. I was nothing but a head, or, no, something minor like a severed thumb; numb.

The protagonist has separated her body from her head, divided the parts of her self, and thus committed psychological suicide: "If the head is detached from the body, both of them will die." "At some point," she says, "my neck must have closed over, pond freezing or a wound, shutting me into my head. . . ."

The division of the self is, at least partly, "a trick done with mirrors." In Atwood's novel and in much of her poetry, the mirror becomes a symbol of the split self, and one's own reflection functions like a kind of negative doppelgänger. Presumably, the mirror provides a distorted image of the self, thus stealing one's sense of a real or complete self, robbing one of an identity. Anna, that character in *Surfacing* who has no self left to lose, whose identity has been lost in her preoccupation with the false, made-up self in the mirror, has become "closed in the gold compact." In order to see herself as whole, the protagonist ultimately realizes, she must "stop being in the mirror." The mirror must be turned to the wall so that its reflection will not intrude between "my eyes and vision." She wishes, finally, "not to see myself but to see." In the poem **"Tricks with Mirrors"** Atwood considers the dangers of perceiving reflection rather than whatever reality might exist, and concludes: "It is not a trick either, / It is a craft: / mirrors are crafty." It is interesting at this point to recall that in Brontë's *Jane Eyre,* Jane's first visual contact with the mad Bertha, her doppelgänger, is a reflection in a mirror.

The camera is another device which Atwood sees as revealing the split self or doppelgänger, the "not me but the missing part of me." Cameras, like mirrors, according to Atwood's protagonist, can also steal the soul, as the Indians believed. Like "toilets and vacuum cleaners," other examples of "logic become visible," cameras might operate to "make people vanish," stealing "not only your soul but your body also." Photographs serve to shut one in "behind the paper."

As products of the world of logic, cameras are always operated by men in Atwood's works. The fiancé in *The Edible Woman,* for example, is a camera enthusiast. When he explodes his flash attachment in the eyes of the protagonist, she runs for her psychological life. In *Surfacing,* David and Joe complete their victimization of Anna by what amounts to a form of rape as they coerce her into revealing her naked body before their intrusive, phallic movie camera, which they use against her "like a bazooka or a strange instrument of torture." The protagonist considers herself reprieved in having evaded the movie camera, and, ultimately, she demonstrates a superior wisdom by emptying the footage of movie film into the lake. But those characters in Atwood's works who victimize others with cameras are themselves victims of faulty vision. David perhaps more than Joe sees reality only through a lens, which clouds and distorts. Perhaps it is also symbolic of a lack of vision that the protagonist's father is associated with cameras; it is the weight of a camera which prevents his drowned body from "surfacing."

Cameras and mirrors thus serve to make the self more vulnerable by emphasizing its division, but the doppelgänger or missing part of the self is also detectable by other means. Anna, employing a perverted version of the magic which is part of Atwood's representation of the female principle, reads the protagonist's palm. She perceives that some of the lines are double and asks, "Do you have a twin?" The protagonist's twin, of course, is that part of herself which is alienated, suppressed, and almost irretrievably lost.

Part of that lost self is an artist who compromised and became an illustrator, acting on the advice that "there has never been any important women artists." All Canadian artists, according to Atwood, suffer a kind of schizophrenia. In *Survival* Atwood's exploration of Canadian literature and the Canadian psyche, she writes:

> We speak of isolated people as being "cut off," but in fact something is cut off from them; as artists, deprived of audience and cultural tradition, they are mutilated. If your arm or leg has been cut off you are a cripple, if your tongue has been cut off you are a mute, if part of your brain has been removed you are an idiot or an amnesiac, if your balls have been cut off you are a eunuch or a *castrato.* . . . Artists have suffered emotional and artistic death at the hands of an indifferent or hostile audience.

The subject of the protagonist's illustrations is, significantly, children's fairy tales. "I can imitate anything," she declares. She does not, however, imitate reality, but rather she creates a fantasy world with her sketches of idealized princesses and unconvincing giants. She also has created a fairy tale for her own history, the facts of which are obscured even in her own mind. Thus, she has lost a part of herself somewhere between memory and lie. She fears the truth, but also fears losing it, as she takes inventory of her memories. "I'll start inventing them and then there will be no way of correcting it, the ones who could help are gone. I run quickly over my version of it, my life, checking it like an alibi."

For example, she has invented the alibi of an unsuccessful marriage and a childbirth to sublimate the more painful fact that she unwillingly underwent an abortion and was then abandoned by a complacent, middle-aged lover. Fragments of memory of the abortion itself—often described in terms of amputation, cutting, splitting—cause such pain that she cannot accept their reality. She considers that her invented son, in reality an aborted fetus, is "sliced off from me like a Siamese twin, my own flesh canceled." But it is an unborn child who represents her twin, a part of her self, and she is haunted by unbidden visions of the abortion which symbolizes her division from herself:

> I knew when it was, it was in a bottle curled up, staring out at me like a cat pickled; it had huge jelly eyes and fins instead of hands, fish gills, I couldn't let it out, it was dead already, it had drowned in air.

The abortion itself, however, is not a cause for but an effect of the protagonist's split psyche. If a complete self had been in control, she is ultimately to realize, the operation would never have occurred. In order to become an autonomous, completed self, however, the protagonist must heal yet another kind of split—that between "good" and "evil." She must come to terms with herself as perpetrator as well as victim, or at least as a correspondent in her own victimization. During an interview, Atwood explained her protagonist's problem in the following way:

> If you define yourself as intrinsically innocent, then you have a lot of problems, because in fact

you aren't. And the thing with her is she wishes not to be human. She wishes to be not human, because being human inevitably involves being guilty, and if you define yourself as innocent, you can't accept that.

Atwood's concern with this delusion of female innocence is also reflected in other of her works. Marian in **The Edible Woman,** for example, maintains her own innocence throughout a destructive sexual relationship until the very end when she realizes that she, too, is guilty of exploitation and destruction. In **Survival,** Atwood groups the subjects of Canadian literature into what she terms "basic Victim Positions." She states that the central question in Canadian literature is: "Who is responsible?" The answer to that question, provided most clearly in **Surfacing,** is that ultimate responsibility lies almost inevitably in the self. Like Lessing's Martha Quest Hesse in *The Four-Gated City* confronting the "self-hater," that part of the self which victimizes both the self and others, Atwood's protagonist must confront her own complicity in such acts as the abortion. Carol P. Christ, in her article "Margaret Atwood: The Surfacing of Women's Spiritual Quest and Vision," upholds a similar contention:

> Her association of power with evil and her dissociation of herself from both reflect a typical female delusion of innocence, which hides her complicity in evil and feeds her fake belief that she can do nothing but witness her victimization. In order to regain her power the protagonist must realize that she does not live in a world where only others have power to do evil.

Even God, or perhaps most especially God, the protagonist comes to realize, incorporates evil: "If the Devil was allowed a tail and horns, God needed them also, they were advantages."

In searching her childhood for the self she has lost and the memories of evil which she has unconsciously suppressed, the protagonist comes across two scrapbooks preserved by her mother. One contains drawings by her brother, all depicting war, bomber planes decorated with swastikas, people under torture—all obvious symbols for what the protagonist sees as male power in its most evil form. Her own drawings, in contrast, are representations of an impossible innocence, a feminine vision of fertility represented by artificial Easter heavens of bunnies and eggs and colored grass. The male and female principles, always in perfect balance in these childish drawings, are represented by a moon in the upper left hand corner and a sun in the right. A more enlightened, adult protagonist recalls:

> I didn't want there to be wars and death, I wanted them not to exist; only rabbits with their colored egg houses, sun and moon orderly above the flat earth, summer always, I wanted everyone to be happy. But his pictures were more accurate, the weapons, the disintegrating soldiers: he was a realist, that protected him.

At another point in her memory gathering, the protagonist recalls her brother's childhood occupation of capturing and imprisoning wild animals and insects, and then allowing them to die. Her own "feminine" role was to free the animals, risking her brother's anger. A memory which

is less congenial to her self-delusion of feminine innocence involves her cooperation with her brother in an act which foreshadows her cooperation in the abortion, the stabbing and dismembering of a doll, left then to float, mutilated, in the lake.

For the protagonist, the brother thus represents male power in general, manifesting itself in war games and in the violation of an essentially feminine nature, the wilderness. His exploitation of animals is repeated in the actions of "the Americans," hunters and fishermen who come to Canada to gratuitously destroy for sport. The Americans represent society's destruction of nature, obvious even in the Canadian backwoods as pollution and land "development" encroach upon the island sanctuary which is the protagonist's home. Americans, she says, "spread themselves like a virus." They represent power: "Straight power, they mainlined it. . . . The innocents get slaughtered because they exist." Finally, the Americans are manifestations of that origin of evil, the Hitler-boogie of the protagonist's childhood. They call to mind the fascist figure as sexual oppressor in the works of Woolf and Lessing.

Atwood's symbolism involving nature as victim is, quite obviously, multilayered. The protagonist, like the exploited wilderness, represents Canada itself and its predicament as a political victim. As Brontë, Woolf, Lessing, and Laing have also maintained, . . . individual schizophrenia is often a reflection of a greater, more pernicious national schizophrenia. Atwood's protagonist is a divided self, as Canada is a country divided and exploited by Americans. Atwood writes in the afterword to **The Journals of Susanna Moodie:** "If the national mental illness of the United States is megalomania, that of Canada is paranoid schizophrenia."

The representative crime of the Americans in **Surfacing** is the killing of a heron, slaughtered not for food but in truth merely because "it exists." The bird, as a trophy of power, is hanged from a tree, wings outspread, in crucifixion position. The protagonist sees the heron as symbolic of her own psychological death, but sees herself as free of responsibility for both the heron's and her own fate. She is to learn, however, that the "Americans" are, in reality, Canadians, like herself, and thus she too is somehow guilty, involved. Through her passivity in refusing to prevent the heron's death, she has cooperated in its execution, very much in the same way that she has cooperated in the perpetration of the abortion. Of the heron's death she says, "I felt a sickening complicity, sticky as glue, blood on my hands, as though I had been there and watched without saying No or doing anything to stop it." Later in the novel, she says of her participation in the abortion: "Instead of granting it sanctuary, I let them catch it. I could have said No but I didn't; that made me one of them, too, a killer."

Thus the exploiter is not "they" but "we"; women too are human and therefore killers—but perhaps with some mitigation. The protagonist kills animals only for food and then only with a kind of religious reverence for the creature she has destroyed. She fantasizes, as she clubs a flailing fish on the back of the head or fastens a squealing frog onto a fish hook, that the animals will their own victimization just as people do and are willing to die to sustain her:

"They had chosen to die and forgiven me in advance."
Later, she thinks:

> The shape of the heron flying above us the first
> evening we fished, legs and neck stretched, wings
> outspread, a blue-gray cross, and the other
> heron or was it the same one, hanging wrecked
> from the tree. Whether it died willingly, con-
> sented, whether Christ died willingly, anything
> that suffers and dies instead of us is Christ; if
> they didn't kill birds and fish they would have
> killed us. The animals die that we may live, they
> are substitute people, hunters in the fall killing
> the deer, that is Christ also. And we eat them out
> of cans or otherwise; we are eaters of death, dead
> Christ-flesh resurrecting inside us, granting us
> life. Canned Spam, canned Jesus. . . .

It is perhaps her delusive claim to innocence, and thus her
lack of reverence, which prevents Marian in **The Edible
Woman** from eating meat and, later in the novel, from eating almost anything at all. Only when she recognizes her
complicity in her own victimization, when she understands that she has allowed men to "eat" or destroy her
and that she has also attempted to destroy them, can Marian overcome her antipathy to food, bake a huge cake
which is an effigy of herself, and gobble it down.

The traditional greeting of the fishermen in **Surfacing,**
"Getting any?", is also a sexual allusion. The violation of
nature by society is, for Atwood's protagonist, paradigmatic of the violation of women by men. Sexual politics,
too, she sees as a battle, with herself as victim. The protagonist recalls her childhood arguments with her brother in
which "after a while I no longer fought back because I
never won. The only defense was flight, invisibility."

More victimized in sexual politics than the protagonist,
who at least intuits something of her complicity in her situation, is Anna, whose "invisibility" is achieved behind
her excessively applied cosmetics and the smoke from her
constant cigarette. Her only reading material is murder
mysteries, though she never realizes the ironic fact that
she herself is a victim of another sort of murder. In Anna's
relationship with David, her body is "her only weapon
and she was fighting for her life, he was her life, her life
was the fight: she was fighting him because if she ever surrendered the balance of power would be broken and he
would go elsewhere. To continue the war." Anna says of
David's tyranny over her: "He's got this little set of rules.
If I break one of them I get punished, except he keeps
changing them so I'm never sure." David, thus, is uncon-
testably the winner as Anna masochistically endures, perhaps even enjoys, his crude and insulting sexual allusions,
his insistence on her stupidity, her own reduction as a
human being.

The protagonist, perhaps, has chosen her mate a bit more
wisely. Joe is more "natural" than civilized, more animal
than man, with his exceptionally hairy body and his inability to communicate verbally: "Everything I value
about him seems to be physical: the rest is either unknown,
disagreeable or ridiculous." "What will preserve him," she
says at another point, "is the absence of words." Joe's ability to manipulate power, too, is limited, as indicated by his
professional failure as a potter whose grotesque vases no

one ever buys. "Perhaps it's not only his body I like," the
protagonist thinks, "perhaps it's his failure; that also has
a kind of purity." Finally, Joe is desirable because "he isn't
anything, he is only half formed, and for that reason I can
trust him."

But even Joe, for a time, insists on commitment, "love"
and marriage. For the protagonist, with the living proof
provided by Anna and David constantly before her, marriage is more a surrender than a commitment; it is, for the
woman, total immersion in the male world and thus a further division of the female self. One ceases, in marriage,
to be a whole self and turns "into part of a couple." The
protagonist thinks of her imagined former marriage as
"like jumping off a cliff. That was the feeling I had all the
time I was married; in the air, going down, waiting for the
smash at the bottom." Married people, she thinks, are like
the wooden man and woman in the barometer she saw
when she was little, balancing each other in a perpetual
kind of opposition.

Marriage and sex, for Atwood much as for Brontë, Woolf,
and Lessing, are linked not only to the psychological death
of the self, but to physical death as well. Atwood's protagonist perhaps confuses childbirth and abortion, but the
process is nonetheless grotesque. "They take the baby out
with a fork like a pickle out of a jar. After that they fill
your veins up with red plastic, I saw it running down
through the tube, I won't let them do that to me ever
again." Contraception in itself poses a very real and practical danger. The protagonist discusses with Anna the ad-
verse and potentially lethal effects of "the pill" on
women's bodies. It is diabolic that pills come in "moon-
shaped" packages, masquerading as feminine creations,
because, like cameras, they are inventions of male logic.
Also, like cameras, they act to obscure vision, covering the
eye with a film like vaseline. The protagonist concludes:

> Love without fear, sex without risk, that's what
> they wanted to be true; and they almost pulled
> it off, but as in magicians' tricks or burglaries
> half-success is failure and we're back to the other
> things. Love is taking precautions. . . . Sex
> used to smell like rubber gloves and now it does
> again, no more handy green plastic packages,
> moon-shaped so that the woman can pretend
> she's still natural, cyclical, instead of a chemical
> slot machine. But soon they'll have the artificial
> womb, I wonder how I feel about that.

Later, as she overhears Anna's strangled cries and inhuman moans through the thin walls of the cabin, the protagonist thinks that sex is "like death." Love and sex as
destructive forces are also themes in Atwood's poetry:
"next time we commit / love, we ought to / choose in advance what to kill." By the conclusion of **Surfacing,** however, the protagonist is able to understand that sex includes life as well as death, that it can, at least theoretically, be natural and positive as well as mechanical and destructive.

In the meantime, however, the protagonist is still divided,
unable to achieve any resolution of such opposites as life
and death, creation and destruction. She fears sexual commitment and so elects the defensive mechanism of refusing

to "feel." A similar technique . . . is used by Woolf's Septimus Warren Smith and Clarissa Dalloway and by Lessing's Martha Quest Hesse. The first indication that Atwood's protagonist has chosen such a procedure is her dispassionate, almost journalistic narrative reporting of events and developments. "Anesthesia," she says, "that's one technique. . . ." Most often, however, she does not accept the responsibility for her inability to feel, classing it as a kind of congenital condition or birth defect: "Perhaps I'd been like that all my life, just as some babies are born deaf or without a sense of touch." But as she observes her companions, hears their "canned laughter," and realizes that they too are incapable of feeling, she thinks "or perhaps we are normal and the ones who can love are freaks, they have an extra organ, like the vestigial eye in the foreheads of amphibians they've never found the use for."

Another protective technique . . . is the depersonalization of sex. Atwood takes the idea to its extreme absurdity: "two people making love with paper bags over their heads, not even any eyeholes. Would that be good or bad?" But, she imagines, if sex and marriage could be relegated to the inconsequential, the trivial, they could not perhaps claim so many victims. Marriage, says the protagonist, is "like playing Monopoly or doing crossword puzzles;" moving in with Joe is "more like buying a gold fish or a potted cactus plant, not because you want one in advance but because you happen to be in the store and you see them lined up on the counter." Even relationships with other women are superficial; the protagonist has known Anna only two months, yet she is "my best woman friend."

Such procedures as refusing to feel and to relate to other people, however, limit and divide the self almost as effectively as the dangers they minimize. The protagonist longs for the ability to feel: "I rehearsed emotions, naming them: joy, peace, guilt, release, love and hate, react, relate; what to feel was like what to wear, you watched others and memorized it." The protagonist has even resorted to pricking herself with pins to experience at least a physical feeling: "They've discovered rats prefer any sensation to none. The insides of my arms were stippled with tiny wounds, like an addict's."

Coincidental with the inability to feel is the protagonist's inability to communicate. The very language, for her, becomes useless and finally undesirable: "Language divides us into fragments." In replying to Joe's proposal of marriage, she finds "the words were coming out of me like the mechanical words from a talking doll, the kind with the pull tape at the back; the whole speech was unwinding, everything in order, a spool." In order to ever communicate again, the protagonist thinks that she must find a language of her own:

> I was seeing poorly, translating badly, a dialect problem. I should have used my own. In the experiments they did with children, shutting them up with deaf-and-dumb nurses, locking them in closets, depriving them of words, they found that after a certain age the mind is incapable of absorbing any language; but how could they tell the child hadn't invented one, unrecognizable to everyone but itself?

Woolf's Septimus Warren Smith can understand the birds; Lessing's Lynda Coldridge communicates with spirits in code. Atwood's protagonist ultimately is to conclude: "The animals have no need for speech, why talk when you are a word. . . ."

If one cannot communicate, cannot feel, has no name, has been so thoroughly divided, one is, like Atwood's protagonist at the beginning of the novel, psychologically dead. Atwood herself has referred to **Surfacing** as "a ghost story." Her protagonist has, in the sense of Laing in *The Divided Self,* been engulfed, "drowned," ceased to exist as a self, just as both her father and her aborted baby have drowned, one in the lake, the other "in air." She speaks also of her brother having drowned as an infant, an event which she has vicariously experienced, or at least somehow observed from what she describes as her mother's transparent womb. Later we learn that the brother was saved by the mother's intervention, but according to the protagonist, he has not regarded his experience with the respect it warrants; it was, the protagonist thinks, a kind of rebirth. "If it had happened to me I would have felt there was something special about me, to be raised from the dead like that; I would have returned with secrets, I would have known things most people didn't."

Drowning thus comes to represent not only death or a loss of self, but also a procedure for finding the self. The protagonist's descent into the lake in search of the Indian cave paintings is symbolic of her descent into her own psyche, from which return, resurrection, "surfacing," is possible. Similarly, Lessing's Martha descends into madness before she can emerge as truly and divinely sane. **Surfacing** is as much an allegory of the quest for psychological rebirth, for life, as it is a search for the theological meaning Carol P. Christ describes.

To be "reborn," just as to be born, the protagonist must have a "gift" from both father and mother. She has carried "death around inside me, layering it over, a cyst, a tumor, black pearl." To be alive, whole, she must recognize that she is a product of both the male and the female principles. She must understand her parentage and her origins before she can understand herself.

Her search for the father ends in the depths of the lake. "Return" for him is impossible; his body, weighed down by the symbolic camera, has never "surfaced." He is reduced to "a dark oval trailing limbs." Like Virgil, who can guide Dante's descent and show him the way through hell but never enter paradise himself, the protagonist's father represents human reason and its limitations. He can point the way with his drawings and maps, "pictographs," to "the place of the gods," the sacred places "where you could learn the truth," but he cannot himself see truth.

In the beginning, the protagonist imagines that her missing father has gone mad and lurks in the wilderness outside their cabin. His madness, she imagines, would be "like stepping through a usual door and finding yourself in a different galaxy, purple trees and red moons and a green sun." Such experiences, she thinks, could lead to revelation: "He had discovered new places, new oracles, they were things he was seeing the way I had seen, true vision; at the end, after the failure of logic." But it is only the protagonist herself and not her father who has such visions. In her dive deep into the lake she discovers not the cave paintings her father has described but the "galaxy" of her own psyche: "pale green pinpricks of light," strange shapes and mysterious fish, "chasm-dwellers."

The father himself is incapable of such visions because, for him, logic has never failed. He represents, however, the best of the male principle—logic without destruction. He has, for himself and his children, reasoned away evil, teaching them that even Hitler, "many-tentacled, ancient and indestructible as the Devil," is not, after all, "the triumph of evil but the failure of reason." The father has attempted to protect his family from evil by secluding them in the Canadian wilderness where World War II is only a subject for children's games. Yet these very games reflect the failure of the father's teaching and indicate the inevitability of evil: the first pages of the novel describe the young brother and sister, their feet wrapped in blankets, pretending that "the Germans shot our feet off."

As the father tries to eclipse evil, so he tries to reason away superstition, fear, religion: "Christianity was something he'd escaped from, he wished to protect us from its distortions." But this too is impossible. The protagonist's childhood is haunted by the idea that "there was a dead man in the sky watching everything I did." Ultimately, she must go beyond the father, beyond the world of logic which he represents. She must confront the presence of evil, in the world and in the self, and she must also confront the gods: "The power from my father's intercession wasn't enough to protect me, it gave only knowledge and there were more gods than his, his were the gods of the head, antlers rooted in the brain."

The father's gift of knowledge, however, cannot be considered inconsequential. He has led the way to self-knowledge and pointed out reality. Even the father's drowned body is "something I knew about," it is, symbolically, also the body of her own aborted fetus, "drowned in air," its fishlike corpse having been flushed through the sewers, "travelling . . . back to the sea." As she recognizes her father's body, the protagonist's past suddenly becomes very clear to her and her fantasy past disintegrates. "I killed it. It wasn't a child but it could have been one, I didn't allow it." "It was all real enough, it was reality enough for ever. . . ." With this recognition the protagonist begins to experience feeling, life: "Feeling was beginning to seep back into me, I tingled like a foot that's been asleep." Shortly afterward she finds that she is even able to cry. But her resurrection is not yet complete: "I wanted to be whole."

The father thus participates in a kind of conception, but the actual birth process is the business of the female. In order to be reborn, to become whole, the protagonist must also find a "gift" from her dead mother:

> It would be right for my mother to have left
> something for me also, a legacy. His was compli-
> cated, tangled, but hers would be simple as a
> hand, it would be final. I was not completed yet;
> there had to be a gift from each of them.

The mother's legacy is the revelation of a drawing from the protagonist's childhood of a woman "with a round moon stomach: the baby was sitting up inside gazing out." Just as the protagonist has earlier envisioned herself as present before her birth, able to see the world through her mother's transparent womb.

The protagonist interprets the message of the drawing as an instruction: in order to be alive and whole she must replace, resurrect, that part of herself which she has killed—the aborted fetus and the fertility aspect of the female principle which it represents. Early in the novel the protagonist has found it "impossible to be like my mother": now she must *become* her mother, "the miraculous double woman," giving birth to herself as well as to new life. The protagonist thus seeks out her lover and takes him to the shore of the lake, carefully arranging their positions so that the moon, representing the female principle as in the childhood drawings, is on her left hand and the absent male sun on her right. According to Carol P. Christ the conception itself is a religious act: "As she conceives, the protagonist resembles the Virgin Mother goddesses of old: at one with her sexual power, she is complete in herself; the male is incidental." The conception is also, however, a psychological rebirth, a healing of the divided self:

> He trembles and then I can feel my lost child
> surfacing within me, forgiving me, rising from
> the lake where it had been prisoned so long, its
> eyes and teeth phosphorescent; the two halves
> clasp, interlocking like fingers, it buds, it sends
> out fronds.

Whereas images of cutting, splitting, division, fragmentation have dominated the novel to this point, now images of unity, joining, completeness begin to supercede. The protagonist has united the two halves of herself, found her parentage, reconciled the male and female principles within the self. Thus the "two halves" of herself also "clasp, interlocking like fingers." The body, which has been for her "even scarier than god," has been integrated with the head: "I'm not against the body or the head either; only the neck which creates the illusion that they are separate," For a second time the protagonist refers to palmistry: "When the heartline and the headline are one . . . you are either a criminal, an idiot or a saint." Now saintlike, in the sense that Woolf's Septimus is a saint, Atwood's protagonist has also resolved within herself the opposites of life and death. Thus she reflects nature itself:

> I lie down on the bottom of the canoe and wait.
> The still water gathers the heat; birds, off in the
> forest a woodpecker, somewhere a thrush.
> Through the trees the sun glances; the swamp
> around me smolders, energy of decay turning to
> growth, green fire. I remember the heron; by
> now it will be insects, frogs, fish, other herons.
> My body sends out filaments in me; I ferry it se-
> cure between death and life, I multiply.

Although the argument for androgynous vision may be made with some relevancy in the case of Virginia Woolf, it is not a meaningful concept when applied to Atwood. For Atwood even more than for Woolf the male principle is ultimately expendable. The female principle alone and in itself incorporates and resolves opposites. Life and death, good and evil, exist within the protagonist, within all women, as they exist in nature. Atwood has described nature in *Survival* as being, not benevolently motherlike or nurselike in the Wordsworthian sense, but rather as a living process "which includes opposites: life and death, 'gentleness' and 'hostility.'" She invariably associates the female principle with nature; she deals, not with nature as a woman, but rather with women as nature. Therefore, although nature is not a mother in Atwood's novel, the protagonist's mother is aligned with nature, at home with it as with an extension of herself. Almost witchlike, with her long hair and wearing her magically powerful leather jacket, the mother feeds wild birds from her hand, charms a bear, and is in tune with the seasons which she carefully records in a special diary. It is she and not the father who represents life as she gives birth, saves her drowning son, prohibits cruelty; yet, dying herself, she also understands the mysteries of death. The protagonist, as a child asking about death, is convinced that her mother "had the answers but wouldn't tell." The protagonist recalls her mother's own death and wishes she might have taken her from the hospital room to die in the forest. There, perhaps, she might have been reborn, like nature itself: "It sprang up from the earth, pure joy, pure death, burning white like snow." It is only the male world of logic which insists on the finality of death. "The reason they invented coffins, to lock the dead in, to preserve them, they put makeup on them; they didn't want them spreading or changing into anything else. The stone with the name and the date was on them to weight them down."

Like her mother, the protagonist, although she hardly realizes it, is also aligned with nature, acting as guide for her companions in the backwoods and insuring their survival. She is instinctively aware of the dangers of the wilderness; she knows how to catch a fish and balance a canoe. She is even immune from the insects which so plague the others.

The protagonist is truly a part of nature, able to incorporate its powers into herself, however, only after she has received her mother's legacy and conceived both herself and her child. Her next act is to reject the world of male logic, the elements of civilization, its canned food and its clothing and its values. "Everything from history must be eliminated," she says, as she burns and tears books, clothing, even her fake wedding ring. The cabin itself is unbearable because it is man-made, and so she enters the forest naked except for a blanket which she will need "until the fur grows."

Here she can experience her own birth:

> My back is on the sand, my head rests against the rock, innocent as plankton; my hair spreads out, moving and fluid in the water. The earth rotates, holding my body down to it as it holds the moon; the sun pounds in the sky, red flames and rays pulsing from it, searing away the wrong form that encases me, dry rain soaking through me, warming the blood egg I carry. I dip my head beneath the water, washing my eyes. . . .
>
> When I am clean I come up out of the lake, leaving my false body floated on the surface. . . .

Now in tune with the powers of nature, the protagonist is granted a series of visions, one of prehistory itself: "The forest leaps upward, enormous, the way it was before they cut it, columns of sunlight frozen; the boulders float, melt, everything is made of water." She also sees her mother, who has always been "ten thousand years behind the rest," and who is also an extension of eternal nature. The protagonist *becomes* her mother, placing her feet in the footprints left by the vision, and finding "that they are my own." Thus she too is synonomous with nature: "I am not an animal or a tree, I am the thing in which the trees and animals move and grow, I am a place."

In this mystical identification with nature and with the female principle it represents, the protagonist surrenders individual human identity. In so doing, she comes face to face with the world beyond logic. "Logic," she says, "is like a wall"; in tearing down this wall she finds "on the other side is terror." Once the wall is destroyed, however, there is no choice: "From any rational point of view I am absurd; but there are no longer any rational points of view." She confronts madness personified, the ultimate mirror:

> It is what my father saw, the thing you meet when you've stayed here too long alone.
>
> I'm not frightened, it's too dangerous for me to be frightened of it; it gazes at me for a time with its yellow eyes, Wolf's eyes, depthless but lambent as the eyes of animals seen at night in the car headlight. Reflectors.

In *Survival,* Atwood discusses the theme of "bushing" in Canadian literature and the fascination of Canadian authors with the madness which occurs when one merges human identity with nature.

But for the protagonist the descent into madness, into the "chasm" of experience, must be temporary and therapeutic, rather than permanent. She desires survival, and she knows, for example, that what society sees as insanity might well serve as an excuse for persecution; she might be victimized, like the heron:

> They can't be trusted. They'll mistake me for a human being, a naked woman wrapped in a blanket: possibly that's what they've come here for, if it's running around loose, ownerless, why not take it. They won't be able to tell what I really am. But if they guess my true form, identity, they will shoot me or bludgeon in my skull and hang me up by the feet from a tree.

Society is incapable of recognizing that what they perceive as a mad woman is, in reality, "only a natural woman, state of nature."

Thus the protagonist, like Lessing's Martha, loses a tenuous identity only to gain a firmer one. She "surfaces" from the illogical to return to a world of logic, but not now, as before, divided, incapable of coping. Their purpose accomplished, father and mother, as principles of nature and as "gods," have reassumed their humanity and the vision has faded. "No total salvation, resurrection. Our father, our mother, I pray, Reach down for me, but it won't work: they dwindle, grow, become what they were, human."

There are "no gods to help me now." Even nature's power is now benign, impersonal: "The lake is quiet, the trees surround me, asking and giving nothing." Like Jane Eyre, Atwood's protagonist has found the mother within herself. Secure in an undivided self, the protagonist no longer needs parents or gods; she recognizes her own power and the fact that she can refuse victimization. "This above all, to refuse to be a victim. Unless I can do that I can do nothing." Now even "the Americans" can be managed and seen in perspective: "They must be dealt with, but possibly they can be watched and predicted and stopped without being copied." As Carol P. Christ says, the protagonist is "awakening from a male-defined world, to the greater terror and risk, and also the great potential healing and joy, of a world defined by the heroine's own feeling and judgment."

Atwood writes in *Survival:* "A reader must face the fact that Canadian literature is undeniably sombre and negative, and that this to a large extent is both a reflection and a chosen definition of the national sensibility." In its ringing affirmation, *Surfacing* is the exception to prove the rule. Withdrawal is no longer possible, says the protagonist, and "the alternative is death." She chooses instead a new life and a new way of seeing. She carries a new child, a new messiah: "It might be the first one, the first true human; it must be born, allowed." To the protagonist belongs the ultimate sanity: the knowledge that woman can descend, and return—sane, whole, victorious.

Carol P. Christ   (essay date 1980)

SOURCE: "Refusing to be a Victim: Margaret Atwood," in her *Diving Deep and Surfacing: Women Writers on Spiritual Quest,* Beacon Press, 1980, pp. 41-53.

[*In the following essay, Christ offers an analysis of* Surfacing, *focusing on the protagonist's quest for self-discovery and Atwood's focus on nature and power in the novel.*]

The spiritual quest of the unnamed protagonist of *Surfacing* begins with her return to the Canadian wilderness, where she had lived as a child. Ostensibly, the protagonist is in search of her missing father, who is presumed dead. But the search is really for her missing parents, her mother having died a few years earlier, and for the power she feels it was their duty to have communicated to her. The external detective story of the protagonist's search for her father is paralleled by an internal search—half obscured by her obsession with her father—to discover how she lost the ability to feel. The scene of the mystery is strewn with false clues from her fictitious memories, which she created to shield herself from the pain of confronting her true past. While the protagonist's interest remains focused on her father's disappearance, the reader struggles to make sense of the inconsistencies in her story about her marriage, husband, and child. Why couldn't she return home after the wedding? Why did she hide the child from her parents? Why is she obsessed with the bizarre image of her brother floating just below the surface of the water, a near drowning that occurred before she was born? The unraveling of her father's mystery awakens her to the powers that enlighten her, but the unraveling of her own mystery is the

key to the redemption she seeks. The two mysteries intersect when she recognizes that "it was no longer his death but my own that concerned me."

Even at the beginning of the journey the protagonist recognizes that she has experienced a death. Like the three friends, Anna, David, and Joe, who accompany her, she is completely cut off from her past: "Any one of us could have amnesia for years and the others wouldn't notice." She has also lost the ability to experience normal feelings. She recalls that her current man-friend, Joe, was impressed by her coolness the first time they made love. She, on the other hand, found her behavior unremarkable because she did not feel anything. She is tortured by Joe's demand that she say she love him because she does not believe the word has any meaning.

The protagonist's alienation from her feelings is reflected in her dispassionate voice. Everything is seen; nothing is felt. The small town, the cabin in the woods where she grew up, her three friends, even her memories are accurately recorded—or so it seems. Occasionally she slips, as when she says, "I keep my outside hand on the [car] door . . . so I can get out quickly if I have to," causing the reader to ask whether she is similarly defensive about her life, perhaps censoring her story. The reader is suspicious when the protagonist reports how she copes with the pain of seeing the town of her childhood changed: "I bite down into the cone and I can't feel anything for a minute but the knife—hard pain up the side of my face. Anesthesia, that's one technique: if it hurts invent a different pain." How much unacknowledged anesthesia, the reader wonders, does the protagonist use? Might her whole story be a shield from a pain she wishes to deny?

The protagonist's inability to feel is paralleled by an inability to act. Her selective vision holds fast to the illusion that she is helpless and "they" do things to her. Hurt and angry that her parents died before endowing her with their power, she accuses them of having hurt her. "They have no right to get old," she complains, remaining blind to the pain her abrupt departure from home doubtless caused them. Always conscious of how she might be hurt, she remains oblivious to her power to hurt others. Moreover, as the reader later discovers, she studiously avoids confronting the center of her pain, the place where she lost the ability to feel and to act—her betrayal by the first man she loved.

Unable to come to terms with his violation of her self and her body she obsessively focuses her attention on the violation of the Canadian wilderness by the men she calls "Americans," some of whom turn out to be Canadians. In *Surfacing,* the image of Canada victimized by Americans is a mirror of the protagonist's victimization by men. The conflict between Americans in powerboats and Canadians in canoes—one apparently stronger but alienated from nature, the other seemingly weaker but in tune with it—becomes a cover for her own pain. She identifies with Canada, the wilderness, innocent, virgin, and violated by nameless American men. Her illusion that the wilderness has no power to recover from American violation prevents her from realizing her own power to overcome her sense of violation. Though the wilderness initially deflects her vision, in the end it will provide the key, the revelation that releases her power.

Though the protagonist continually imagines herself as powerless, she is extraordinarily concerned with power. Anything out of the ordinary—Madame with one hand, a purple bean at the top of a high pole, the cool blue lake, a white mushroom, the toes of saints—all are seen as harboring magical power. To her, religion and magic are one—a view modern Westerners have often associated with children or people they call primitives. Eventually the protagonist's sense of the magic-religious powers resident in things will become a key to revelations that enable her to contact the source of her power.

At first, however, the protagonist seeks her lost power in the wrong places. Realizing that she lost the ability to feel somewhere in the past, she imagines that a simple return to childhood will provide the answer. Searching through old scrapbooks kept by her mother, she discovers that she looked normal in all the pictures—no clues there. There is a clue in the drawings from her childhood—hers of eggs and bunnies, everything peaceful, her brother's of airplanes and bombs—but she cannot quite fathom it. Another clue surfaces from the garden. She remembers that once she thought a certain purple bean on a high pole was a source of power. She says she is glad the bean did not give power to her because "if I'd turned out like the others with power I would have been evil." Her association of power with evil and her dissociation of herself from both reflect a typical female delusion of innocence. Hiding from her complicity in evil feeds a false belief that she can do nothing but witness her victimization. In order to regain her power the protagonist must realize that she does not live in a world where only others have power or do evil. An unexpected thing, the sight of a dead heron strung up on a tree, monument to some "American" victory, mediates revelation.

The reaction of the protagonist and her friends to the dead heron, symbol of purposeless killing, reveals some truth about each of them. Anna's weakness is evident when she holds her nose, not from any real feeling, but simply to make an impression on the men. David's concern to preserve the Canadian wilderness from crass commercialism is revealed as mere rhetoric when he and Joe film the bird, trapping its humiliation while distancing themselves with their "art." Only the protagonist realizes the enormity of the crime as she imagines the heron in its natural habitat killing its appointed food with effortless grace. She identifies herself with the bird, wondering "what part of them the heron was, that they need so much to kill it," but she does nothing to protect the heron from further humiliation.

When they pass the spot again, a day later, the sight of the heron mediates the knowledge the protagonist requires to escape her passive sense of victimization, the delusion of her childhood innocence. For her the heron is sacred object, mediator, like Christ to the Christian. Seeing it again, she realizes that her passivity is not innocence. She does not live in a world of eggs and bunnies; she did not escape the evil others are immersed in. "I felt a sickening complicity, sticky as glue, blood on my hands, as though I had

been there and watched without saying No or doing anything to stop it." Memories of her active participation in acts of cruelty equally senseless surface in her as she remembers how she and her brother used to throw the "bad kind" of leeches into the fire. She realizes there is no innocence in childhood. "To become like a little child again, a barbarian, a vandal: it was in us too, it was innate. A thing closed in my head, hand, synapse, cutting off my escape." Though she feels trapped, recognizing her guilt and responsibility is a step toward claiming her power to refuse to be a victim.

With the path to redemption through childhood closed, the protagonist decides the clue to her redemption lies in deciphering her father's final obsession—a series of unintelligible drawings and marks on maps. At first she fears he had gone mad and wandered off into the woods, but then she discovers he was copying Indian paintings and marking their locations on maps. She goes in search of the paintings to verify his sanity and her own. Deciding that the painting she seeks is submerged underwater, she dives deep into the lake to look for it. Instead of a painting, she discovers an image from her past: "It was there but it wasn't a painting, it wasn't on the rock. It was below me, drifting towards me from the furthest level where there was no life, a dark oval trailing limbs. It was blurred but it had eyes, they were open, it was something I knew about, a dead thing, it was dead." Seeing the body of her father forces her to acknowledge he is dead. The mystery of her father's death solved, his image becomes a clue to her own mystery, her own death. The open eyes of his corpse remind her of the bizarre image of her brother's near drowning, but with a shock she recognizes, "it wasn't ever my brother I'd been remembering." The thing approaching becomes the image of her aborted fetus "drowned in air." This revelation unlocks the mystery of the confusing stories of husband, child, marriage. The childbirth was an abortion; the wedding day—the day of the abortion; the husband—the lover who told her to have the abortion. "It wasn't a wedding, there were no pigeons, the post office and the lawn were in another part of the city," she remembers, finally accepting the truth about her first love affair.

The protagonist sees the fetus as a living thing, not yet a child, but an animal deserving protection like the heron. Wanting to convince her to have the abortion, her lover "said it wasn't a person, only an animal." Now she realizes, "I should have seen that it was no different, it was hiding in me as if in a burrow and instead of granting it sanctuary I let them catch it." She views her abortion as no more or less a crime than the murder of the heron, but her guilt is more direct, because the creature was in her body. As the knowledge of her complicity in a killing comes to her, she realizes why she hid her past in false memories. "It was all real enough, it was enough reality forever, I couldn't accept it, that mutilation, ruin I'd made, I needed a different version." She understands, too, that the anesthesia of false memory is no escape, but rather the beginning of a fatal disease: blocked feelings do not go away; they fester inside. "Since then I'd carried that death around inside me, layering it over, a cyst, a tumor, black pearl." Her ability to accept the painful truth about the past counteracts the anesthesia, abolishes the need for false stories to cover up true pain. By allowing herself to feel pain, she unblocks her feelings and contacts her energy and power. "Feeling was beginning to seep back into me, I tingled like a foot that's been asleep."

The protagonist sees this new self-knowledge for what it is—a revelation from great powers. "These gods, here on the shore or in the water, unacknowledged or forgotten, were the only ones who had ever given me anything I needed . . . The Indians did not own salvation but they had once known where it lived." In the presence of great powers, she feels the need to worship. She leaves her sweatshirt as a thank offering to the gods whose names she does not know but whose power she has felt.

She correctly understands that her redemption comes from facing the truth and accepting the pain, guilt, and responsibility it entails. With this act, the protagonist also divorces herself from the interpretations men use to justify their crimes. She no longer believes killing can be justified as "sport." She rejects her brother's distinction between "good" leeches that deserve to live and "bad" leeches that deserve to die. She rejects her lover's distinction between "good" (legitimate) fetuses that grow up to have birthday parties and "bad" (illegitimate) fetuses that must be killed. The protagonist is allowing her own feeling, not male "morality," to define reality for her.

The revelations that come to the protagonist through the heron and the underwater image of death provide her with the knowledge that unlocks her past, but she finds the revelation incomplete. Her father's "were the gods of the head, antlers rooted in the brain." She believes a gift from her mother must complement her father's gift—"Not only how to see but how to act." Searching again for something out of the ordinary to provide guidance, she senses power in one of the scrapbooks her mother had made. Heavy and warm, the scrapbook opens to a picture the protagonist had drawn as a child of "a woman with a round moon stomach: the baby was sitting up inside her gazing out." Her mother's gift is a reminder of the powers of her body. Though the gifts of the parents reflect a traditional stereotyping of men with the mind, women with the body, the protagonist incorporates both gifts and transcends the limitations of her parents' lives.

That night she conceives a child by Joe with the moon, a Goddess symbol, on her left. In a heightened state of awareness she feels "my lost child surfacing within me, forgiving me, rising from the lake where it has been prisoned for so long . . . it buds, it sends out fronds." As she conceives, the protagonist resembles the Virgin Mother Goddesses of old: at one with nature and her sexual power, in tune with the rhythms of the moon, complete in herself, the male being incidental.

The protagonist's extraordinary insight and sense of her power alienates her from her friends. She realizes that if she wishes to pursue the revelations and experience the powers more deeply, she must choose the isolation of the visionary quest. She can't stay with people because "they'd had their chance but they had turned against the gods, and it was time for me to choose sides." When the

time to leave the island comes, she hides, escaping from her friends. "I am by myself; this is what I wanted, to stay here alone." "The truth is here." The choice of solitude is not so much a rejection of community as a recognition that certain experiences and truths are so alien to ordinary consciousness that the individual must withdraw in order to experience them.

After the others have left, the protagonist has time and space to plumb more deeply the knowledge and experience that has been given her. Lying alone at the bottom of her canoe she has a vision of the great powers of the universe, the gods who have guided her journey: "Through the trees the sun glances; the swamp around me smolders, energy of decay turning to growth, green fire. I remember the heron; by now it will be insects, frogs, fish, other herons." The great powers of the universe transform the swamp; they transform the heron from death to life. The life power rises from death. This is the meaning of the incredible words she had spoken earlier, "nothing has died, everything is alive, everything is waiting to become alive."

The protagonist recognizes her body as both *revelation* and *incarnation* of the great powers of life and death. "My body also changes, the creature in me, plant-animal, sends out filaments in me; I ferry it secure between death and life, I multiply." The female experience of the transformation of parts of her body into plant, animal, and infant is perhaps the most complete human incarnation of the great powers. The protagonist's vision of the universal transformative energy of life into death and death into life is reflected in her characteristic perception of the fluidity of the boundaries between objects, plants, animals, humans. Joe has "fur" like a bear, canoers are "amphibian," the fetus is "plant-animal" sending out "filaments."

After her vision, the protagonist enters the final phase of her visionary journey: transformation itself. She realizes that she can see her dead parents, and perhaps the gods themselves, if she follows the path she is beginning to sense. "The gods, their likenesses: to see them in their true shape is fatal. While you are human; but after the transformation they could be reached." Her transformation is frightening. Though she knows it is beyond "any rational point of view," it is neither mad nor illogical. Whereas before she had abandoned false memories, now she will give up all identity as a human. Before she had experienced the fetus transforming her body, now she will change herself into a different state.

She ritually breaks her connections to the human world— burning or purifying clothing, books, one of everything in the cabin. She is purified and transformed by immersion in the lake. Like the fetus in her womb, she changes in water. "The earth rotates, holding my body down as it holds the moon; the sun pounds in the sky, red flames pulsing from it, searing away the wrong form that encases me." The powers guide her away from the garden, the house, into the woods. She becomes wild. She is animal: "I hollow a lair near the woodpile, dry leaves underneath and dead branches leaned over." Having undergone transformation, she experiences mystical identification with all forms of life: "Leopard frog with green spots and gold-rimmed eyes, ancestor. It includes me, it shines, nothing moves but its throat breathing." She experiences direct union with the great powers of life and death in nature. All boundaries between herself and other forms of life are abolished. She *becomes the transformative energy:* "I lean against a tree, I am a tree leaning . . . I am not an animal or a tree, I am the thing in which the trees and animals move and grow."

Later she sees a vision of her mother feeding the birds; then her mother disappears, the birds remain. She is translated. This vision confirms her sense that her mother's gift is connection to nature. As Barbara Hill Rigney says, "Almost witchlike, with her long hair and wearing her magically powerful leather jacket, the mother feeds wild birds from her hand, charms a bear, and is in tune with the seasons." In a similar vein, Adrienne Rich calls the mother as she appears "Mistress of the Animals."

The next day she sees what her father saw. What he has seen "gazes at me with its yellow eyes, wolf's eyes, depthless but lambent as the eyes of animals seen at night in the car headlights." The eyes of the wolf remind her that her father's gift is the power of seeing, or insight. The protagonist is terrified as she realizes that in the state of transformation individual human identity has no meaning. Her father's vision is impersonal, but it is also strangely comforting because it means that the life power survives a particular identity. With the vision of the parents, the protagonist's circle is complete. Her parents' power has been communicated to her.

The vision granted, the gods then retreat into "the earth, the air, the water, wherever they were when I summoned them." Translated back to human form, the protagonist returns to the cabin and opens a can of beans, symbolizing her return to modern human life. Though she is no longer in direct contact with the powers, she has gained wisdom and consciousness of her own power through her encounter with them. She marks her new power with a declaration: "This above all, to refuse to be a victim . . . give up the old belief that I am powerless." The source of her newly discovered power is twofold. First, she renounces the fictitious memories that held together her delusions of innocence and powerlessness. Letting go and allowing her true past to surface is itself a source of tremendous energy. Second, her grounding in her own past and in the powers of the universe provides her with a sense of authentic selfhood.

Though Atwood has effectively portrayed a woman's spiritual quest, she has left the question of its integration with the social quest open. It seems likely that the protagonist, now pregnant, will return to the city with Joe and attempt to reconstruct their relationship on the basis of her recovered ability to feel. The potential for a deeper relationship with Joe is "a possibility which wasn't there at the outset." But it remains an unexplored possibility. Will Joe understand how she has changed? Will he assume equal responsibility for the care of their child? Will he view her work and personal growth as being as important as his own? Atwood's failure to address such questions makes Marge Piercy skeptical that the protagonist has achieved power at all. Using a social or political definition of power, she objects, "Power exists and some have it." To Piercy, At-

wood's protagonist might reply, "Power exists in many more forms than are usually recognized. I have gained power by experiencing my grounding in the great transformative powers of the universe. I don't know yet how I will translate my power into social and political forms. But you cannot deny that I have gained power." Atwood's protagonist has experienced a spiritual and psychological transformation that will give her the inner strength to change her social and political relationships. She no longer sees herself as inevitably powerless and victimized. And since Atwood's story is set in the 1970s, not the 1890s, the reader has some reason to hope that her quest to integrate the spiritual and the social will be more successful than Edna Pontellier's [as related in Kate Chopin's *The Awakening.*] I am not as uneasy about Atwood's protagonist's future as Piercy. But like her, I recognize the need for stories that describe how the woman who has awakened will live in the social world. Still, I wish Piercy had understood more clearly the contribution novels like **Surfacing** make to women's total quest: by naming anew the great powers and women's grounding in them, such novels provide women with alternatives to patriarchal notions of power that can aid their struggle to change the social world.

The newly named power, the transformative energy of life to death and death to life in **Surfacing** is, of course, not new to the historian of religions. Atwood believes that her protagonist has discovered the great power worshiped by the Canadian Indians. Many tribal and ancient peoples, both men and women, have worshiped similar powers. However, as Ruether has shown, when societies become urbanized, the culture-creating males celebrate their relative freedom from the body and nature in myth, symbol, philosophy, and theology. The traditional values derived from the body and nature then become identified primarily with women, both because women's close relation to the body and nature is evident in their traditional roles of child-bearing and nurture of the young and because the culture-creating males identify the traditional values their culture has transcended with the other, woman. This development produces the paradox that the surfacing of female values in alienated urban cultures may also be a return to *some*—but not all—of the values of traditional tribal or less urbanized cultures. Even the experience of connection to nature as a life and death power may reflect a particularly female viewpoint in modern culture. Western male heroes commonly envision nature as something that must be conquered or as inert matter that can be shaped to their purposes. A woman's experience of the intertwining of life and death processes in pregnancy and childbirth—the fetus might die or its movement toward life might kill her—seems to encourage in her a realistic acceptance of death as an element in all life processes.

Tribal and ancient peoples who worshiped natural powers such as those represented in **Surfacing** knew that the close connection of life and death in the hunting and agricultural cycles and in the birth processes was a reflection of the interpenetration of life and death in all natural processes. They knew the hunted or domesticated animal and the wild plant or crop as sacred sacrifices to human life. But in Christianity, the transformative mysteries of birth and the earth were spiritualized and the notion of sacrifice was limited to Christ's death for the sins of humankind. At-wood's protagonist reverses this spiritualization when she intuits, "the animals die that we may live . . . we are the eaters of death, dead Christ-flesh resurrecting inside us . . . Canned spam, canned Jesus . . . but we refuse to worship." Though speaking irreverently, the protagonist is expressing her sense that the ultimate mystery of life and death is reflected in the process of eating. Indeed the original guilt may be that we must kill to live. By showing how the ancient sense of the mysteries of life and death emerges in the consciousness of a thoroughly modern woman, At-wood has done more than nostalgically recall an ancient world view. She has suggested a direction for the transformation of modern consciousness that would be beneficial for women and all life. Reverence for the human connection to natural processes would create an atmosphere in which the natural functions of women's bodies would be celebrated rather than ignored or treated as sources of shame. Menstruation, childbirth, and menopause might once again be viewed as religiously significant events. And while it would not provide solutions to all the complex problems that arise in modern technological societies, a new naming of humankind's grounding in nature might create an atmosphere, or in Crites's terms, an "orientation," in which solutions to the ecological crisis could be developed.

The issue of abortion raised by the novel provides a crucial test of the viability of the novel's vision for women's quest. The affirmation of a woman's right to control her own body and to choose abortion has been fundamental in the women's movement. And the question naturally arises: Does Atwood's protagonist's vision of her connection to nature mean that women must not have abortions but must give birth over and over again, "naturally"? A careful reading of the novel's vision suggests that this would be the wrong conclusion to draw. The novel compares the fetus in the womb to an animal in a burrow and suggests the comparison of the termination of a pregnancy to the killing of an animal living in one's body. The novel suggests that no killing should be undertaken lightly, but it also recognizes that some must die so that others may live. The protagonist's abortion was wrong for her because she did not choose it herself, but allowed her lover to choose it for his own personal convenience and because she did not allow herself to feel the sense of loss that will naturally be felt when a life is taken. The novel does not suggest that abortion is wrong, but it does suggest that abortion is not a matter of little consequence. The woman who decides that she must have an abortion should recognize, as she does in eating, that some deaths are necessary for other life and that the proper response to the sacrifice of one life for another is worship and gratitude.

The emergence of a powerful vision of women's connection to nature in a novel of women's spiritual quest seems to suggest that women can achieve power through the acceptance of female biological roles. The traditional identification of women and nature that has been a legacy of oppression can also be a potential source of power and vision. As one critic has written, to entirely reject the identification of women with the body and nature might be "to neglect that part of ourselves we have been left to cultivate

and to buy—into that very polarization [of culture and nature] of which we have been the primary victims." More importantly, it may lead to the kind of psychic suicide that the first part of **Surfacing** portrays.

It seems to me that women must positively name the power that resides in their bodies and their sense of closeness to nature and use this new naming to transform the pervasive cultural and religious devaluation of nature and the body. Atwood's novel suggests that the opposition of spirit and body, nature and person, which is endemic in Western culture, is neither necessary nor salutary; that spiritual insight surfaces through attention to the body; and that the achievement of authentic selfhood and power depends on understanding one's grounding in nature and natural energies.

Estella Lauter   (essay date 1984)

SOURCE: "Margaret Atwood: Remythologizing Circe," in her *Women as Mythmakers: Poetry and Visual Art by Twentieth Century Women,* Indiana University Press, 1984, pp. 62-78.

[*In the following essay, Lauter examines Atwood's revision of the myth of Odysseus and Circe in her "Circe/Mud Poems.* "]

In her sequence of poems entitled "Circe/Mud Poems," Margaret Atwood engages in a complex act of remythologizing. That is, she steps back into the mythic realm of Homer's *Odyssey* to recreate and revise the story of the year-long sojourn of Odysseus with Circe from Circe's point of view. Simply by refocusing our attention within the story, Atwood reveals a more essential power in Circe than her infamous ability to seduce and deform men—namely, her highly developed capacity to see, see into, and see beyond her relationships to the persons, things, and events called "reality." Because Atwood shows how Circe exercises her capacity for insight, we are able to penetrate the masks and armor of the "hero with a thousand faces," and understand with her how the myth of the quest has become a disease in whose clutches the hero is helpless. By adopting Circe's perspective within the quest myth, Atwood is able to revalue Circe positively; at the same time, she exposes the limitations of a myth that still dominates Western civilization. Atwood's strategy of participating in mythic thinking, instead of making the usual distinction between myth and truth, allows her to suggest a surprisingly radical revision of the myth itself. She points out that we do not yet know the ending of Circe's story after Odysseus leaves her island, and that in our visions of a new ending lie the possibilities for an alternative myth, in which there is no need to journey. Atwood's work has implications for those of us who are exploring alternative images of women, and for others who believe that mythic structures offer essential knowledge that can be used to free as well as to enslave us.

In order to involve us in her mythmaking process, Atwood has us enter the island landscape of a forest blackened by fire as we would enter a dream, in a boat that glides over land "as if there is water." She explains through Circe's voice that she has not given us a full description of the landscape because she is quite sure that we live there right now and can see for ourselves. Atwood has Circe speak directly to a person who is never named, leaving open the possibility that she is addressing us. Since her awareness of Bronze Age rituals and modern steam-engines transcends ordinary boundaries of time and culture, we begin to believe that she can also transcend other restrictions that operate on our thought. Atwood reinforces this expectation of mythic behavior in her surrealistic images of bodies coming apart and crashing to the ground or trays of food containing "an ear, a finger."

In order to retain the degree of power Homer has assigned to Circe while she relocates its source and meaning, Atwood includes many of the trappings of Greek mythology: Circe has a temple where moon snakes speak of the future, and she wears a withered fist on a chain around her neck. But Circe knows the meaning of such symbols better than Odysseus or Homer did. As for her supposed power to turn her lovers into swine, she denies that she is anything more than a silent accomplice in the metamorphoses: she explains, "they happened / because I did not say anything." Actually, the men came to her in accordance with their own drives. She "decided nothing." They became animals because they allowed their skin to harden into impenetrable, armor-like hide, and because they failed to speak.

Homer was misguided on several other counts. Circe was not superhuman in the sense of being above feeling love, pain, fear, and anxiety; she did not willingly grant Odysseus' request to leave her. Nor was she rendered powerless during his stay. In Atwood's version, the lover unbuckles the fist on Circe's chain; instead of gaining control over her, he frees her from a dehumanizing pattern of action. He frees her, not to be like the totally receptive and unfeeling surrogate woman made out of mud, reported in a story by another traveller, but to penetrate his armor because her caring for him enables her to see who he is, what he intends, and how it will affect her life. The nineteenth poem shows clearly who is in command of reality. In it, Circe says (in prose),

> You think you are safe at last.
>
> . . . . .
>
> I bring you things on trays, food mostly, an ear, a finger. You trust me so you are no longer cautious, you abandon yourself to your memoranda . . . ; in the clutch of your story, your disease, you are helpless.
>
> But it is not finished, that saga. The fresh monsters are already breeding in my head. I try to warn you, though I know you will not listen.
>
> So much for art. So much for prophecy.

Circe's power is not sufficient to transform her lover's story without his consent, but her insight that the story continues to happen partly because she has not revealed how she felt about it, and partly because "fresh monsters" are "breeding" in her head to test his mortal courage with more misadventures, suggests that she may also have some unused ability to alter Odysseus' script.

In Atwood's sequence, Circe does attempt to change her relationship to the quest myth by proclaiming her disinterest in Odysseus' heroic gesticulations. Her attitude toward his infamous arrival on her island is scornful. The merits of his courage, pride and perseverance dissolve as she questions: "Don't you get tired of saying Onward?" With Circe's revelation of her boredom with the masks of heroism and of her disgust for the greedy, deceitful, arrogant, oppressive, vain men who have predictable desires for fame and immortality, Atwood dislodges one of the reasons that the myth of the hero survives: female approval of heroic behavior.

As the poems proceed, it becomes clear that the hero's dissatisfaction with mere material abundance has a deleterious effect not only on his lover, but also on the landscape, which is burned over, worn down, and strewn with skeletons. Since Circe states at the outset her intention to search (without journeying) for the "ones who have escaped from these / mythologies with barely their lives," and since she gives ample proof of her ability to love those who will unmask, clearly she is not the source of the misery on her island.

By the final poem, we are convinced not only that Circe's position outside the framework of the quest allows her to see more than those who remain inside it can, but also that her boundary position is a source of hope. Her capacity for breeding new disasters to appease the hero's desire for action is easily converted into a capacity for creating valid images. In the final poem, she "sees" two islands—one on which things happen pretty much as she has just recounted, over and over again like a bad film running faster and more jerkily each time it goes through the projector. The second island, independent of the first, exists only in her imagination. On the second, "we" walk together in a November landscape and are astonished by the orange hue of the apples "still on the trees." We lick the "melted snow / from each other's mouths" without sexual passion, and we are free to notice the track of a deer in the mud beside the not-yet-frozen stream. On this island, which Circe says "has never happened," our delight in the November landscape does not require any journey; the birds are birds, not omens from the dead whispering "Everything dies;" the gentle, sensuous caress between two people is enough; and mud is mud, not a symbolic woman to be fucked by man.

Circe's story remains unfinished in Atwood's sequence. We still do not know her fate after Odysseus leaves her island. We do know that she is not the seductress we thought she was. As an enchantress, her talents lay in gathering the syllables from the earth into healing words. Even without her magic powers, she is capable of imagining an alternative to the story that has imprisoned her. She emerges from the poem as an independent woman (perhaps a poet) who is capable of turning her considerable talent for seeing through others' stories into a strategy for her own survival—and perhaps the survival of all who are wise enough to trust her. Atwood's revision of Circe's story strikes us as true because it corresponds to centuries of partly-conscious experience of silent complicity in a myth we did not choose. Atwood's work raises important questions: How many other stories remain similarly unfinished? Should we finish them now? Is it really possible to change a myth?

Atwood does not provide us with an ideal goddess so much as with a believable woman, "by turns comic, cynical, haughty, vulnerable and sad," as Sherrill Grace has observed [in *Violent Quality: A Study of Margaret Atwood*]. But for all her realism, Atwood does not "demythologize" Circe. In the context of modern theological debate, that term is reserved for the process of stripping away the fanciful layers of image and story in order to penetrate to the (preferably historical) truth. Since, we have no reason, apart from the say-so of poets like Homer and Hesiod, to believe that Circe ever exsisted (she was never an object of widespread worship, for example), the most likely approach of the demythologizer would be to ignore or discredit her. As scholar or poet, then, the demythologizer might turn to the records of history for information about the lives of Greek women, but she would not bother to retell Homer's story.

In fact, of course, Atwood is sufficiently aware of Homer's conventions to give her poem exactly the same number of parts as Homer's book. She counts on our knowing the appropriate section (book X) so well that she can alter the story without repeating it first (as a daring jazz musician might begin a piece with an improvisation without stating the tune on which it is based). In other words, Atwood assumes that Circe is familiar enough to seem "real" to us before we begin reading her poem. Whether this reality has accrued from aesthetic persuasion (the effectiveness of Homer's text) or from psychological persuasion (our familiarity with women who seem to correspond with Homer's story) matters very little. Atwood does not want to disturb our belief; she wants to restructure it.

The extent of her investment can be measured by comparing her poem to Katherine Anne Porter's brief and charming essay, "A Defense of Circe." Porter not only accepts but repeats Homer's story, presumably in order to earn the right to reinterpret it. Enthralled by the bard's "sunny high comedy," she exclaims, "this is all pure magic, this poem, the most enchanting thing ever dreamed of in the human imagination, how have I dared to touch it?" Indeed, she does touch it lightly, retelling all sorts of details that Atwood omits: about Circe's immortal lineage and sunny disposition, her lovely stone hall in the forest glade, her handmaidens, her loom, her song, the role of Hermes in providing the herb (moly) to disarm her, her oath that she will not harm Odysseus, her restoration of Odysseus' men to forms more beautiful than the ones they had, her advice about how to visit Teiresias in Hades, and so on.

Porter does point out several minor flaws in Homer's logic. She cannot quite believe that the immortal Circe would feel threatened by Odysseus' sword. She finds unfounded the hero's claim that Circe promised to send him and his companions safely on their way. She knows that Circe's "divine amiability and fostering care" could not save Odysseus and his men from their ordained suffering. She also wonders why Circe did not steal the moly to destroy Odysseus' power, or why she did not break her oath and turn him into a fox! She resolves these problems by accepting the text as given ("this is Circe") and by offering

her own non-traditional interpretation of Circe's character: whereas Odysseus and Hermes are foxy by nature, Circe can be trusted completely. Her purity extends to other realms as well; she is a "creatrix," an "aesthetic genius," whose "unique power as goddess was that she could reveal to men the truth about themselves by showing each man himself in his true shape according to his inmost nature. For this she was rightly dreaded and feared; her very name was a word of terror." This assertion of Circe's superior understanding is Porter's "defense" of Circe against those who fasten on her reputation for turning human beings into monsters.

Porter does not accept the theological distinction between myth and truth. She expects us to find her interpretation of Homer's story truthful, and she believes that *The Odyssey* is true in a way that "still hovers glimmering at the farthest edge of consciousness, a nearly remembered dream of glory." For her, the story is a myth only in the sense of being something that was once believed, or in the sense of being an enduring fiction that continues to touch a sensitive nerve. Its truth is limited. Porter's main reason for not altering the fiction is respect for her venerable colleague.

Not so in Atwood's case. Although she shares with Porter the interpretation that the men turned themselves to swine, Atwood knows that no successful "defense" of Circe is possible within the framework of Odysseus' story. I speculate that she also knows how difficult it is to rid the human consciousness of a stereotype that has such a long and venerable history. She *could* have created an historical prototype, from Greece or elsewhere, to counter the myth; indeed, many critics agree that her most successful book of poems to date is *The Journals of Susanna Moodie,* where she shows an uncanny ability to work with historical materials. She chose instead to remythologize the figure of Circe.

If the reader is to believe that women's essential power is not to seduce (or shall we say influence?) men but to see through them and free them from their stories, then the poet must demonstrate this power in the figure who carries the imago of seduction. The image must be transformed from within. Atwood chooses the surest way to convince us that her vision of Circe is true by letting Circe tell her own story in an authentic language. She counts on our natural desire to believe the stories that people tell about themselves—when the stories are good. But such a strategy alone would not suffice. The poet must preserve enough of the character of the original myth to give weight to her story; she must also extend it enough so that it stands on its own in the modern world. The *poet* must perform Circe's feats of penetrating vision with respect to the myth that has entrapped both of them.

Thus, Atwood has Circe describe her setting as the opposite of Homer's lush idyllic island. It is instead a burned forest which nonetheless spawns fireweed that splatters the air, symbolizing both nature's power of regeneration and Circe's verbal power over those who land within range of her voice. The voice, instead of singing seductive songs, asserts that Circe prefers self-effacing men who stand in humble relationship with nature to heroes who, like Icarus, regularly "swoop and thunder" around her island. She denies blame, or even responsibility, for the dismal fate of these "common" heroes; at the same time she admits her complicity. The fact that she "did not say anything" until now has meant that her words were wrecked along with their bodies.

In the fourth poem, Atwood begins to alter our image of Circe's role, presenting her as a healer (perhaps a psychiatrist?) whose people call upon her to soothe their pain, fear, and guilt with words from the earth they have assaulted. She is a hardworking witch who presses her head to the earth faithfully to collect the "few muted syllables left over." So depleted is her island that she can collect only syllables, "a letter at a time." Her wonderfully wry comment that she is a desert island (which she reports having quipped to the arriving hero) works on several levels at once. While she scores a point for clever repartee in the battle of the sexes, she also accepts the ancient identification of woman with earth as her source of power, and admits to the depletion of her own as well as the earth's resources.

In the next eight poems, a curious reversal of our expectations occurs as Circe "loses" the battle she initiates. The poems correspond to and replace about sixty lines of Odysseus' story about his "victory" over Circe which supposedly culminated in her invitation: "Come then, put away your sword into its sheath, and let us / two go up into my bed so that, lying together / in the bed of love, we may then have faith and trust in each other." In Atwood's sequence, the battle between the two is more strenuous. Circe's part in it is largely verbal; she openly berates Odysseus for his lies, his passivity, his greed, and his delusions of power, interjecting that he need only inquire of the moon snakes at her temples in order to know the future. Her magic may be diminished, but she still knows "what is sacred." In the seventh poem, she includes us in the fray, taunting or chiding us to recognize this scene as part of our own landscape, but also revealing that it is a landscape of "ennui" that offers little satisfaction.

What is remarkable about this Circe is her consciousness of what is happening to her and her articulation of that consciousness at the moment of interaction with the "other." She watches Odysseus coldly as he approaches her for her sexual favors clothed in his shell of confident expectation. She anticipates that if she grants him his wish, she will either fear or despise him. Finally, she does capitulate, and she even allows herself some moments of generosity before she notices that he receives her gifts as his due without acknowledging them. Still, she protests his rough approach to her body, calling it "extortion" and pointing out the fine line between love and hate in such gestures. She knows that underneath her own soft masks there is a face of steel to match his own, and she dares the hero to see his reflection in it.

Despite her consciousness and her protests, however, Odysseus "wins." Atwood invents her own symbol for Circe's magic power—a closed fist on a chain around Circe's neck—and presents Odysseus' conquest as a triumph of the hero's armor over the fist's stuttering and muttering in the language of magic. Finding its foe unas-

Dust jacket for Atwood's 1983 short story collection, Bluebeard's Egg.

sailable, the fist gives up—even "renounces" Circe. So, far from graciously offering her body to achieve a fantasy of faith and trust (or to continue the struggle for power in a more "seductive" way), Atwood's Circe is overpowered. The prettiness of Homer's version is stripped away.

The surprising feature of Atwood's poem is that having "lost" the battle of wills, Circe is released from the mentality of battle. Circe "opens" like a hand cut off at the wrist clutching at freedom. The image is grotesque and not entirely successful. It is not clear how a hand can open and clutch at the same time; and the arm that feels the pain of her absence (the goddess who surrenders to patriarchal force?) is not sufficiently defined. Still, the poem clearly asserts that Circe is released into the freedom of guiltless sexual enjoyment. The result is that she is able to see her lover's body for what it is—a scarred and flawed instrument—and to continue to feel desire for him, even though she knows that his body is not the essence of what she wants.

At the same time, she suspects that her body is all he wants. Extreme as the image of the "mud woman" is, in the story "told by another traveller," Circe is vulnerable to it. She has already acknowledged her affinity with the earth, and in her present state of sexual responsiveness, she admits that it would be "simple" for her to give in to his desire, especially if Odysseus allows himself to be transformed into a gentle lover (as it appears he does later in the poem).

Circe's "freedom" is short-lived. The lovers are assailed from all sides. Their pleasure offends "the suicides, returned / in the shapes of birds" to warn or complain that "everything dies," who had not found the fruits of the earth sufficient, and who demand the lovers' death as vengeance for their own unhappiness. Circe still fears the goddess "of the two dimensions" (Hecate), who wants her to resist her lover, wants her to make herself "deaf as an eye, / deaf as a wound, which listens / to nothing but its own pain." Hecate would have Circe kick Odysseus out, and Circe knows that Hecate "gets results."

As for the hero, he becomes preoccupied with his own story, and perhaps too trusting: as Circe becomes more servant than lover, her mind turns to the creation of "fresh monsters" to feed his heroic appetite. Whether these monsters are created to make him afraid to leave, or to keep him from leaving by giving him something more to write about, they have the negative effect of undermining the couple's newly found ability to value each other apart from their stories. That ability is also undermined by Circe's jealousy of Penelope, and her resentment of the fact (which she foresees) that Odysseus will believe Penelope's defense of her wifely honor.

The hero's lack of contentment with the present, the only motive Homer provides for Odysseus' departure, is also an element in the disintegration of the lovers' relationship in Atwood's poem. Odysseus naively wants Circe to tell him the future. She responds caustically,

> That's my job,
> one of them, but I advise you
> don't push your luck.
>
> To know the future
> there must be a death.
> Hand me the axe.
>
> As you can see
> the future is a mess.

Here, as elsewhere in the last eight poems of the sequence, Circe has powers that may be explained as psychological or cognitive rather than magical. Her ability to change the island's summer climate to winter in the twenty-second poem is presumably a correlative for the psychological state of coldness she must develop in order to let her lover go. Her knowledge and insight are more acute in relationship to others, however, than they are in predicting her own fate. She worries that when Odysseus leaves the animals "may transform themselves back into men" and threaten her life. She questions whether her father, Helios, cares about her enough to restore her immortality. She wonders if Odysseus will give her back the facility with words that he released from her fist. In the face of her own fate, she is the vulnerable woman.

The final poem shows, however, that despite her worries Circe the woman retains her goddess-like capacity for envisioning the future. The first island that she sees would maintain the power of the story—revised, of course, so that she "is right." The second island seems more than anything to be a place where *neither story counts*. On it, the deer is not a stag to be killed for Odysseus' men, as it is in *The Odyssey*. The birds are not disguised suicides and the snow is not a symbol of psychological coldness as they are in Circe's story. The landscape is neither idyllic nor burned. The lovers are not surrogates for the traveller and his mud woman. The image of the second island is too open to be quite convincing—but perhaps that is its source of power. Since Circe does not articulate her dream fully, we are encouraged to dream it onward ourselves.

The Circe we see here needs no defense, although she is vulnerable. Certainly she is not pure, although she is no worse than Odysseus. Despite all the fanciful elements in the poem, we believe that Atwood has put her finger on a significant aspect of woman's power that was embodied in the ancient figure of Circe and needed only to be articulated clearly: the ability to see, see into, and see beyond the stories we tell about who we are. This is not exclusively a female power; traditionally it belongs to both Cassandra and Teiresias. But perhaps women have more often been consigned to the islands where such capacities flourish. Specifically, we have long had a different vantage point from which to view the male hero. Perhaps the delight that this poem produces in female audiences has to do with Atwood's success in modelling how to reveal the dark spot on the back of the man's head, without which, Virginia Woolf said, the man's portrait remains incomplete.

Some will say that Atwood's Circe is ungenerous; Homer's Odysseus, after all, was capable of great sorrow and guilt, not to mention aesthetic appreciation. But Atwood knows, as most of us do, how often those capacities have been repressed in favor of rapaciousness. Others will say she is too generous—that men like Odysseus have no reason to change. Atwood presents the many difficulties we would experience in achieving a real partnership, but at the same time she holds out hope for change. Whereas Homer's Circe is a minor goddess whose power to seduce men is overcome by the superior connections of Odysseus with the pantheon of gods, Atwood's is a woman who had certain enduring goddess-like capacities.

Atwood herself might describe Circe as a Venus released from the "Rapunzel Syndrome" the poet described in her book of criticism, *Survival: A Thematic Guide to Canadian Literature,* published two years before *You Are Happy.* This literary pattern "for realistic novels about 'normal' women" includes Rapunzel, "the wicked witch who has imprisoned her," "the tower she's imprisoned in," and the Rescuer "who provides momentary escape." In the literary versions of the fairy tale, however, "the Rescuer is not much help. . . . Rapunzel is in fact stuck in the tower, and the best thing she can do is to learn how to cope with it." Atwood speculates that although the Rapunzel Syndrome transcends national boundaries, it takes a Canadian form: the Rapunzel figures have difficulty in communicating, or even acknowledging, their fears and hatreds; "they walk around with mouths like clenched fists."

Certainly Atwood's Circe symbolizes the release from such difficulties of communication. She has not become her own tower by internalizing the values of Western culture that would consign her to the role of cold seductress, *la belle dame sans merci.* Her enjoyment of sexual pleasure in the center of the poem identifies her as more Venus than Diana or Hecate, in the triple goddess figure from Robert Graves that Atwood uses to describe the possibilities for women in fiction. Circe is perhaps not a perfect Venus, as Atwood understands the figure, both sexual and maternal—unless we think of Circe's healing and serving capacities as products of maternal impulse. She is Venus with a difference: a Venus who finally does not lose her self in expressing her sexuality; one with the capacity to conceive of a new tower (island) in which she will not be imprisoned; one with the potential to be her own muse.

If the potential of this Rapunzel to liberate herself is not yet fully realized, we should not complain. It is up to us to do better. Whatever we might wish for Circe's future, we must admit that Atwood, through her knowledge of the psychology and history of relationships between males and females and through her brilliant use of literary precedents both ancient and modern, has restored her to the realm of living myth where there is no opposition between myth and truth. In this realm, myth is one kind of truth—a kind that retains its power long after philosophers and historians have revealed its impossibility, a kind that continues to glide through our dreams, fantasies, and even our gestures "as if there is water." Atwood gambles here on the possibility that myth can be transformed from within without losing its power.

Clearly the transformation worked for Atwood, as she demonstrates in the poems surrounding "Circe/Mud Poems." The first section of *You Are Happy* is the record of relationships between men and women that are just short of violent in their outcome—where the only moment of "happiness" occurs when the woman, walking alone in sub-freezing weather, feels the images "hitting" her eyes "like needles, crystals." Then, **"Songs of the Transformed,"** a contemporary bestiary, ends with the warning song of the human corpse who hoarded both words and love until it was too late.

The section that follows the Circe poems, however, is markedly different. In these poems, enigmatically called "There Is Only One of Everything," the lovers make an honest attempt to inhabit their bodies instead of abandoning them "in favour of word games or jigsaw puzzles." The woman seeks to express both her anger and her desire. They move from the experience of love based on need to an experience based on ripeness. Together, they transform an ancient ritual of sacrifice into a ritual of love. Coming after the Circe poems and drawing on the same mythic elements, these poems have the effect of confirming Circe's vision of the new island and validating its essential truthfulness.

In turn, the presence of the Circe poems in the volume gives to the final sequence the status of myth. In it two people transcend both the powerful myth of the war between the sexes and its brutal history in order to participate in life organized by the values of Circe's vision. The lovers' responsiveness to each other and to nature, in a moment to be appreciated for its own unique *presence,* is sufficient to overcome all other imperatives—whether of life or of death. "There Is Only One of Everything" does not mean that the lovers submerge their identities to achieve the "oneness" promised in the traditional marriage ceremony, but that in sharing the uniqueness of each moment ("the tree / we saw."), each opens him/herself and becomes whole.

In the poem **"Is/Not,"** from the fourth section of *You Are Happy,* Atwood's female protagonist explains to her lover,

> This is a journey, not a war,
> there is no outcome.
> I renounce predictions
>
> and aspirins, I resign the future
> as I would resign an expired passport:
> . . .
>
> we're stuck here
>
> . . .
>
> where we must walk slowly,
> where we may not get anywhere
>
> or anything, where we keep going,
> fighting our ways, our way
> not out but through.

What kind of a journey has no outcome and goes nowhere? Unlike Circe's flippant dismissal of her powers in a moment of frustration ("So much for art. So much for prophecy,") this paradoxical formulation seems to be serious. But what does Atwood mean?

Furthermore, what should we make of the fact that "Circe/Mud Poems" does not take the form of a journey at all? Indeed, one of its most intriguing features is that it does not propose an alternative form of the quest it criticizes so bitingly—not even the form Annis Pratt describes as the female rebirth journey. Perhaps we could say that Circe's island itself represents a release from societal norms, or that Circe's rejection of Odysseus' story about her represents such a release. But this is more a matter of externalizing her private knowledge (splattering the fireweed) than it is part of an inward exploration—more an assertion of ego in defiance of patriarchal norms than a retreat from its concerns, as in other rebirth journeys by women. It would likewise be difficult to locate a green-world guide or token, unless it is the syllables from the earth that Circe gathers in her role as witch/healer. But that is the substance of her reality, not a deviation from it. Odysseus never really becomes Circe's "green-world lover"; although for a brief period he does reveal his body beneath his armor, he quickly returns to his own concerns. Perhaps we can see him as a catalyst in Circe's life, since he does undo the fist and release her capacity for passion. There is no overt confrontation with parental figures, although Circe does wonder whether her father, the sun, will rescue her. But her immortality is assured by language, not by Helios.

Circe's report of Hecate's desire for her relationship to fail, her jealousy of Penelope, and her spiteful creation of new monsters to inhibit Odysseus might appropriately be described as manifestations of self-destructive potential (or "shadow"). If she gives in to the part of herself that experiences Odysseus' love as an invasion of her privacy, she dooms herself to loneliness. If she derides Penelope's story, she devalues her own capacity for telling a believable story. If she creates new monsters for Odysseus to conquer, she becomes a participant in the quest she criticizes. Presumably she manages to overcome all of these impulses in order to envision the second island. But can we call these acts a "plunge into the unconscious" for purposes of rebirth? This Circe seems to emerge from centuries in the unconscious to complete the cleansing acts of telling off the hero and admitting all sorts of other feelings she did not know she had.

It would be more accurate to see the whole poem sequence as proceeding from the inside out rather than in the usual manner of the spiritual quest. Circe says she "searches" for a certain kind of man. But it is more true to say that she opens herself to the possibility of a relationship that will develop that kind of man—and in turn will allow her to be the loving woman she would like to be. The poem is not so much a rebirth journey (there is no journey) as it is an exploration of what might happen if we *stopped* questing and made the most of the capabilities for relationship that we have "Right now I mean. See for yourself."

This is curious, for elsewhere in her work Atwood seems to be as committed to the idea of the quest as any modernist writer. Certainly ***Surfacing*** fits the pattern Annis Pratt describes, and many of her titles suggest a preoccupation with a psychological journey, usually in the form of a descent. Robert Lecker suggests that Atwood uses such patterns to question their assumptions—even to prove them false. He points out, for example, that Atwood often makes use of the romance pattern without its happy ending, return or ascent. In the case of ***Surfacing,*** he claims, "What Atwood really seems to be saying is that the mythical pattern of separation, initiation and return must itself be seen as a sham in a culture where rituals have lost their potency."

I doubt this explanation. Clearly rituals have not lost their potency for Atwood. In ***Two-Headed Poems,*** she and her sister sew a red shirt for her baby girl with every expectation of passing on to her daughter the heritage or "birthright" of the world's mothers. She says,

> It may not be true
> that one myth cancels another.
> Nevertheless, in a corner
> of the hem, where it will not be seen,
> where you will inherit
> it, I make this tiny
> stitch, my private magic.

And the child, as innocently as Sleeping Beauty once received her fatal prick from the wicked fairy, receives her mother's life-supporting gift with joy. Atwood still hopes that one myth *does* cancel another.

I think that what is finally mythologized in Atwood's

poems is the possibility of altering myths that are so basic that we can scarcely dream of existence without them. Atwood knows that if one myth cancels another, it happens slowly. "Circe/Mud Poems," then, is part of a long process of rearranging the elements of the quest myth into a shape which may finally negate the idea of questing, as we now understand it, in order to embrace an idea of self-acceptance and relationship quite different from the traditional ideal of self-transcendence and attainment perpetuated by the quest. Atwood's vision is not "duplicitous" so much as it is double.

Like Circe, she envisions two possibilities, and she sees that, at least for the moment, "they do not exclude each other." In the first, the quest myth is simply changed from within so that the silent participants have their opportunity to "be right." In the second, the image of the journey itself is transformed, so that it becomes admirable to go through experience without going forward or getting anywhere. It is an image of movement "in place." The challenge of this kind of "journey" is simply to "Be Alive." Eventually, the antinomy between self and other that informed the quest will appear quite different, as it does in a later poem:

> We do not walk on the earth
> but in it, wading
> in that acid sea
> where flesh is etched from
> molten bone and re-forms.
>
> In this massive tide
> warm as liquid
> sun, all waves are one
> wave; there is no *other.*

Atwood's mythic sequence stands in a pivotal position in her work, looking back to the "power politics" of earlier volumes and ahead to her developing sense of fruitful relationship among forms of life she does not regard as totally separate from each other. Thus her title "Circe/Mud Poems," cuts both ways. On the one hand, it protests the vision of woman which reduces her to her sexuality and materiality without recognizing her consciousness. On the other hand, from that same woman's consciousness comes a vision of the satisfaction of material reality. Perhaps Atwood will be the "poet of earth" that Wallace Stevens wanted to be, to match the poets of heaven and hell of the great tradition. As she says,

> So much for the gods and their
> static demands . our demands, former
> demands . . .
>
> History
> is over, we take place
> in a season, an undivided
> space, no necessities
>
> hold us closed, distort
> us.

Change is possible—even at the roots of our lives, in the myths that govern our experience.

John Lanchester   (review date 23 July 1987)

SOURCE: "Dying Falls," in *London Review of Books*, Vol. 9, No. 14, July 23, 1987, pp. 24, 26.

[*In the following excerpt, Lanchester provides a mixed assessment of the short story collection* Bluebeard's Egg.]

[The endings of Margaret Atwood's fiction] tend to leave things slightly in the air, and to present themselves to the reader for interpretation. The dystopian fantasy of *The Handmaid's Tale* was followed by a framing fiction—of the kind that is more usually put in front of a narrative—which pretended that what we had just read had been the material presented at an academic conference, centuries after the events depicted. The academic ended with a question: 'Are there any questions?' Many of the stories in *Bluebeard's Egg* implicitly ask the same thing.

The material treated in *Bluebeard's Egg* is largely conventional, consisting as it does of relationships of one kind or another (parents in the stories which begin and end the collection, elsewhere first boyfriends, ex-lovers, new husbands: the usual). Her narrators are constantly interpreting themselves, their pasts and their relationships—a business that often goes on ruefully and after-the-event. The ideas behind this interest in the act of interpretation have been around for a little while now, and Atwood's focus on the subject is not flame-belchingly original. But the subject is an important one for her for reasons which can be discerned from little asides in the stories. When a boy gives an identification bracelet to his girlfriend, he misnames it an 'identity bracelet': she ponders a possible reason for the error, and then says: 'Another interpretation has since become possible.' The remark is more of a clue to her concerns than the interpretation which follows it: it gives us a sense of the way feminism has empowered Atwood to take familiar material and scrutinise it from a new perspective. The point about **'Significant Moments in the Life of My Mother'**, the first story, is that not so long ago, or to another writer, the moments would not have seemed to signify anything at all. Perhaps it is her Canadianness—the fact of coming from a country where you can say 'Yes, I am a liberal' without feeling ridiculous—which helps her to retain that combination of feminist ideas with an essentially traditional aesthetic which is one of her great strengths. 'If writing novels—and reading them—have any redeeming social value it's probably that they force you to imagine what it's like to be somebody else.' George Eliot might have said the same.

A flexible and thought-out moral and critical position is rare enough: Atwood is also a talented writer. She has a particular gift for aperçus which combine sympathy (for the character), insight (into the character) and a wry, ironic humour (which is often a matter of catching the reader's eye behind the character's back). She is very good at all varieties of rationalisation and minor deceit. Loulou, a sculptor, lives with a whole collective of male poets—very bad poets, too, we soon gather, though are never directly told. The poets use their more developed vocabularies to tease and bully her: when they call her 'marmoreal' she looks it up in the dictionary 'to find out whether she'd been insulted'. (The story's full title is **'Loulou; or, The Domestic Life of the Language'**.) After sleeping with one of the poets for the first time, she had cleaned up his definitively squalid room for him. 'Bob looked on, sullen but appreciative, as she hurled and scoured. Possibly this was why he decided to love her: because she would do this kind of thing. What he said though was, "You complete me.' "

Moments like that provide much of the pleasure of *Bluebeard's Egg;* that kind of insight, and that kind of comedy, come very easily to Atwood. Perhaps too easily. There are times when it seems that characters are being described and events are being evoked rather mechanically, through a few carefully-chosen details and a well-modulated irony or two-giving a feeling that things are being made to happen in order to give the ironic tone of voice a work-out. In **'Scarlet Ibis'**, for instance, a character wheeled on to provide local colour on page 187 ('a trim grey haired woman in a tailored pink summer suit that must have been far too hot') changes her hair colour by her next appearance, two pages and about five minutes of narrative time later ('Christine talked with the pink-suited woman, who had blonde hair elegantly done up in a French roll. She was from Vienna . . .'). It's not a disastrous lapse, but for me it crystallised an unease with the way that what goes on in the stories sometimes comes to seem a consequence of the kind of narratorial voice Atwood has decided in advance to employ.

The title story shows her at her best. Sally is in love with Ed 'because of his stupidity, his monumental and almost energetic stupidity'; he is a heart doctor, 'and the irony of this is not lost on Sally: who could know less about hearts, the kind symbolised by red satin surrounded by lace and topped by pink bows, than Ed.' In plot terms, very little happens. We meet Sally as she stands looking out the kitchen window at Ed: their marriage is described (it's his third); we see that Sally, though brighter than her husband, is not as bright as she thinks she is; we watch the progress of the dinner party Sally was preparing (as in a lot of the stories, the background is filled in while the main character is performing a domestic chore). After the dinner party she walks into her study and sees Ed with his hand on her best friend's bum. Everyone acts as though nothing has happened.

While this has been going on, Atwood has been exploring Sally's attempts to understand Ed, whose wall-like stupidity makes him very enigmatic. Sally has been attending a night class in 'Forms of Narrative Fiction', in which the set text is an old version of the Bluebeard story: the class has been told to write the story from the point of view of any one character. Sally is inside a version of the Bluebeard story herself, of course, though she cannot realise it: the incidental ironies of the narrative all serve this larger structural irony. There is an unsummarisable richness about the thirty-page **'Bluebeard's Egg'**. Many of Atwood's concerns are present in it, vividly dramatised: her interest in adapting and co-opting genre; relationships between women; the nuances of modern marriages and re-marriages; the nature of female experience; what men are like. The climax of the story—as well as being thematically important (it presents Sally with a crisis of interpretation) and funny (in an adult and uncomfortable way)—is a moment of pure, dreamlike awfulness for the heroine, who is seeing happen what is for her the worst possible thing. The personal, for Atwood, is political—but it is personal too. Enjoyable though most of this collection is, **'Bluebeard's Egg'** gives the reader a sense that Atwood has available a whole extra set of gears.

Dave Smith   (review date Summer 1988)

SOURCE: "Formal Allegiances: Selected Poems x 6," in *The Kenyon Review,* n.s. Vol. X, No. 3, Summer, 1988, pp. 127-46.

[*In the excerpt below, Smith offers a mixed review of Atwood's* Selected Poems II.]

Among American readers Margaret Atwood *is* Canadian literature. She has published a book annually for more than two decades, deploying a strong historical consciousness, a rich narrative imagination, and a willingness to use formal literary expression to confront whatever wrongs human dignity and freedom. Her accomplishments have been manifest in best-selling fiction, in literary criticism (the often cited *Survival: A Thematic Guide to Canadian Literature* suggests her range), and in ten books of poetry beginning with *The Circle Game* in 1966. Many readers consider her foremost a poet. The simultaneous republication of her 1978 volume *Selected Poems 1965-1975* with her 1987 *Selected Poems II: Poems Selected and New 1976-1986* may do more than confuse readers with overlapping titles. It may raise questions about how often Margaret Atwood has written successful poetry.

An Atwood poem is an intense sermonic in shortish, spare lines that whip domestic dramas and wilderness imagery down the page. Deliberately unliterary, its righteousness puts a finger in the middle of your chest. The results are predictable: a mixture of exhilaration, irritation, and boredom. A style meant to simulate no-bullshit veracity, this language has studied biology, current affairs, and recent movies. Even the belligerent tone of **"A Woman's Issue"** asserts blunt authenticity: "You'll notice that what they have in common / is between the legs."

Political or issue-centered poetry claims us by shock or argument, while most other poetry works through accumulation of specific image or the clear tug of narrative. Atwood's poems often slacken anecdotally or slide into mission chatter, oddly both the curse of the poetry-writing fictioneer and Emily Dickinson, mechanical lineation being a grid, not form. It's actually a pseudo-poem as in **"The Words Continue Their Journey"**:

> Do poets really suffer more
> than other people? Isn't it only
> that they get their pictures taken
> and are seen to do it?
> The loony bins are full of those
> who never wrote a poem.
> Most suicides are not
> poets: a good statistic.

Margaret Atwood's imagination, which sees the world as plastic, is metaphoric and metamorphic. She is extraordinarily receptive to places and moments resonant with apocalyptic significance, and is equally willing to render words stiffened by moral indignation. As she says, "my passive eyes transmute / everything I look at to the pocked / black and white of a war photo." For Atwood the poem frees the muted voice; it's poetry as liberation, as therapeutic function. Can art make anything happen?

Atwood suggests poetry is *the happening,* its language the public psychiatric process of exposure, rehearsal, correction. Metaphor (poetry = sight / sight = metamorphosis) is enactment. Her preferred form is the lyrical monologue, sincerity and diagnosis at once. It's good form for fiction, but why is the following poetry, if it is?

> :moles dream of darkness and delicate
> mole smells
>
> frogs dream of green and golden
> frogs
> sparkling like wet suns
> among the lilies

"Dreams of the Animals"

Merely personal, perhaps trivial, this world is a papiermâché background. Such writing trots along in the self-absorption of idealism that strains credulity with childish personification, melodramatic effects, and the gimmicks of standup persuaders. Banality replaces profundity:

> though we knew we had never
> been there before
> we knew we had been there before.

"A Morning"

Atwood's discomfort with the demands and resources of lyric form encouraged her to employ her strengths: fictional coherence, dramatic immediacy, the arresting strangeness and authority of tale. In *Procedures for Underground* (1970) she echoed the mythic journey of psychoanalysis (and Dostoyevski) which leads to spiritual rebirth. With *Power Politics* (1971) she dramatized sexual struggles and revelations. Both books searched for large, coherent form in theme. In 1976, with *The Journals of Susanna Moodie* she joined in a segmented long poem a witnessing character, story, and historical veracity to testify to "Those who went ahead / of us in the forest" and thereby evoked the archetypal society and memory which is poetry's trade. Fiction gave her a form of coherence she had been unable to achieve with lyric.

From *The Journals of Susanna Moodie* Atwood moved to poems in sequences of numbered sections or signaling repetitions of place, subject, or title. What might be called "sequentialing form" dominated *Two-Headed Poems* (1978) and *Interlunar* (1981), but Atwood also encountered some old troubles, as evidenced in a stanza about pain and poetry:

> This is the place
> you would rather not know about,
> this is the place that will inhabit you,
> this is the place you cannot imagine,
> this is the place that will finally defeat you
>
> where the word *why* shrivels and empties
> itself. This is famine.

"Notes towards a Poem That Can Never Be Written"

This is less poetry than merely evasive language. Nothing offered necessarily defines *famine* any more than it defines Cleveland.

But with rare energy and an acute eye, Atwood has created passages remarkable for density of particulars and rhythmic prowess. Her preacherly imagination is also pastoral: she celebrates unspoiled worlds, landscapes which now mirror the fouled human enterprise. Her view in **"A Sunday Drive"** reveals "a beach reeking of shit" and a "maze / of condemned flesh without beginning or end." As priestess of the revolutionary spirit, she makes arrowed accusations of poems. While her animistic identity with wild creatures may verge on comic book simplemindedness, as does Ted Hughes's, her wolves, crabs, and vultures leap from inert words to real beasts. Even in **"Mushrooms"** there is the powerful acknowledgment of lives utterly apart from and yet ancestral to one's own: "They taste / of rotten meat or cloves / or cooking steak bruised / lips or new snow." And in **"Marsh, Hawk"** the inward echoing of the scene provides the lyric form her passion has needed:

> Diseased or unwanted
> trees, cut into pieces, thrown
> away here, damp and soft in the run, rotting and
>   half
> covered with sand, burst truck
> tires, abandoned, bottles and cans hit
> with rocks or bullets, a mass grave,
> someone made it, spreads on the
> land like a bruise and we stand on it, vantage
> point, looking out over the marsh.

Atwood's particulars compose a landscape-medallion of ultimate knowledge, while controlled cadence and perspective establish emotional congruity. The voice "feels" with the eye from object to object—as the body would move, with cumulative jarrings—drawing us into the metaphor rather than pressing its grid upon us. Poetry is discovered and released, not commanded. A life of sores—seen instead of explained—leads not to strident opinion but to record and conviction, the voice of human will.

Although certain permutations of form are obvious in Atwood's two selecteds, she remains the same poet early and late. She is a naturalist, a traveler, but a woman ill-suited to the urban world. One finds little humor, less joy in her. Surprisingly, her best poems concern love: tenderness for ancestors, yearning for individual belonging, erotic gratification. To Atwood love defines us all: "those who think they have love / and those who think they are without it." In the fifteen new poems in **Selected Poems II,** Atwood, now a year shy of her fiftieth birthday, seems to try to work beyond characteristic anger, bitter portraits of harmed women, and blunt-tongued raking of those less pure-hearted than herself. She seeks "Some form of cheering. / There is pain but no arrival at anything." Still, she shows greater tolerance, an understanding, is occasionally bemused. Among all that takes the edge off revolutionary fervor, nothing beats age. Atwood's poems, now tighter, are not serene, but they approach the grace of love

through understanding. Maybe she speaks for us all—a little—in a parable of maturing:

> Amazingly young beautiful women poets
> with a lot of hair falling down around
> their faces like a bad ballet,
> their eyes oblique over their cheekbones;
> they write poems like blood in a dead person
> that comes out black, or at least deep
> purple, like smashed grapes.
> Perhaps I was one of them once.
> Too late to remember
> the details, the veils.
> If I were a man I would want to console them,
> and would not succeed.
>   **"Aging Female Reads Little Magazines"**

Helen Yglesias   (review date July 1989)

SOURCE: "Odd Woman Out," in *The Women's Review of Books,* Vol. VI, Nos. 10-11, July 1989, pp. 3-4.

[*Yglesias is an American-born educator and novelist whose works include* How She Died *(1972),* Family Feeling *(1976), and* Sweetsir *(1981). In the following review, Yglesias praises Atwood's style and commitment to issues, but finds the novel* Cat's Eye *an uneven work.*]

The successful publication of ***The Handmaid's Tale*** transformed the distinguished Canadian poet and prose writer Margaret Atwood into a world-class, internationally acclaimed, best-selling writer—to use some of publishing's most favored phrases. Her next novel, ***Cat's Eye,*** inevitably became an occasion for critics to weigh and measure this current work against the brilliant evocation of a repressively anti-woman dystopia depicted in ***The Handmaid's Tale.*** Those looking for a falling off found it. Though ***Cat's Eye*** has been sufficiently well-marketed and praised, placing Atwood once again on the best-seller list, reviewers have also expressed disappointment. (Sharon Thompson in the *Village Voice,* Vivian Gornick in *New York Woman* are only two examples.)

Why this carping? Atwood's oeuvre is astonishingly varied, copious and good. Beginning publication in 1961 with a book of poems, she continued with other works of poetry, a solid body of short fiction, and seven novels, including the stunning ***Surfacing.*** She has written children's books and collections of prose criticism and theory, so rich an outpouring in fact that the usual rumblings have been voiced, the uneasiness that often greets prolific "serious" writers. (Joyce Carol Oates is a prime target for this specious concern of critics.) There is no such thing as too much good and important writing, and Atwood's work is certainly good and important; but there *is* room, within the rejoicing over her accomplishment, to inquire into the force and future direction of her output. Where are Atwood the writer, and her creation. The Atwood Woman, going?

Not directly in response to this question, but to a related one, the title poem of a 1985 collection, ***True Stories,*** reins the reader in. Atwood writes:

> Don't ask for the true story;
> Why do you need it?

> It's not what I set out with
> or what I carry.
>
> What I'm sailing with,
> a knife, blue fire,
>
> luck, a few good words
> that still work, and the tide.

But in *Cat's Eye* it is Atwood herself who is in desperate quest for "the true story" of a childhood experience which has eluded her until now in her fiction. If she has at long last reworked this material to her own satisfaction, she fumbles in passing on gratification to her readers.

The power to pleasure the reader, to gratify, is perhaps the single most important gift a writer possesses, not teachable in creative writing courses, not to be enforced in fact by any of the devices in the critic's arsenal and, conceivably, useless to talk about. If it's a case of the writer either having it, what is left to analyze beyond the harsh sentence of an absence of gift? The overwhelming love the great heroines of literature have called up from readers, those girls and women who step off the page into one's own life and consciousness, imparting an almost physical quality of identification and hope, seems to be, if not entirely lost to contemporary literature, then so diminished as to be effectively gone. It doesn't even seem proper for the reader to request a passionate response any more.

Post-Modernism (a term I use reluctantly as a shortcut definition of a pervasive type of contemporary novel) scoffs at such yearnings, finding them repulsively nostalgic. Understandably, since Romanticism has had its day and its say, and didn't do all that much for us anyway. But must the reader give up altogether the emotional release of gratification? Are dreariness, misery and failure, and the negative joys of satire, the substitutes we must accept as part of the modernist resolve to move beyond romantic realism?

The current Atwood Woman, Elaine Risley, is an accomplished artist who returns to Toronto, where she mostly grew up, to attend a retrospective of her work, heralded by the women's movement. Like Atwood herself, she is nearing 50, and the occasion becomes a memory trip in which her tormented girlhood is relived in the kind of detail Atwood can shape so obsessively. But there is an uneasiness in Atwood's handling of this experience, an uncertainty of direction and, yes, meaning—though, again, in modernist terms stories are not supposed to "mean," or at least no more or less than whatever they may happen to signify to individual readers. But Atwood isn't that kind of writer, or critic either. She means to "mean" something specific when she writes, no matter the disclaimers she supplies at the front of the book. But in *Cat's Eye* her purpose is opaquely veiled.

Much of the matter of *Cat's Eye,* as well as its themes (to borrow an Atwood word from her quite brilliant 1972 survey of Canadian literature, *Survival: A Thematic Guide*), will be recognized from earlier Atwood fictions: the unconventional parents, the challenge of the natural world, the thin quality of men-women relationships, the suppressed horror of the heroine's inner life, and the excitement and nourishment of creativity, in art and in science.

And here, once again, she gives us the ultimate outsider as nail-biting third-world person, a mirror-image of her heroine, echoing the disquieting parallels she has found before between that displaced condition and the heroine's precarious sense of herself in a middle-class corner of a colonized country.

Mr. Banerji is a guest at Christmas dinner,

> a student of my father's a young man from India who's here to study insects and who has never seen snow before. He's polite and ill at ease and he giggles frequently, looking with what I sense is terror at the array of food spread out before him, the mashed potatoes, the gravy, the lurid green and red Jell-O salad, the enormous turkey . . . I know he's miserable underneath his smiles and politeness . . . His spindly wrists extend from his over-large cuffs, his hands are long and thin, ragged around the nails like mine. I think he is very beautiful, with his brown skin and brilliant white teeth and his dark, appalled eyes . . . I can hardly believe he's a man, he seems so unlike one. He's a creature more like myself: alien and apprehensive. He's afraid of us. He has no idea what we will do next, what impossibilities we will expect of him, what we will make him eat. No wonder he bites his fingers.

We have met this creature before in Atwood fictions, most notably in the masterly short story, **"The Man From Mars,"** from *Dancing Girls,* where too-large, unattractive Christine, "statuesque her mother called it when she was straining," is relentlessly pursued by "a person from another culture" because she has been kind to him in a perfunctory fashion, giving him directions to a particular location on campus. He is so small, she mistakes him for a child at first; then she notes his thinning hair and the aging lines on his face. The threaded edges of his jacket sleeves hang down over his thin wrists, his nails and the ends of his fingers are so badly bitten "they seemed almost deformed." His insanely fixed obsession with Christine makes her a laughing-stock. He ends up arrested and deported, and Christine remains an odd-woman-out for the rest of her life.

Atwood's persons "from another culture," dual images for her heroines (in *Cat's Eye* Elaine not only bites her nails and her fingers, she peels the skin of her feet every night until she is barely able to walk), also add complex values to her fiction, deepening the narrow, mean-spirited, middle-class dreariness of her milieus with a more painfully sharp social reality, just as the neat, swiftly executed satirical scenes at which she excels supply a deliciously nasty refreshment.

The core of *Cat's Eye,* the terrors and heartbreak of the realm of "girls" and "best-friends," has already been explored in *Murder in the Dark* and especially in *Lady Oracle,* where the anguish of the innocent youngster victimized by her best-friends is similarly played out, down to the symbolic locale of the sexually threatening ravine, the shaky bridge to safety, and the fall from grace, though without the mesmerizing effect Atwood produces in *Cat's Eye.*

That Atwood can mesmerize to some purpose was amply

proven by *The Handmaid's Tale.* There her strengths and weaknesses came together to produce a classic, and the narrow path of her vision worked perfectly for a story in which every detail was controlled by the artists's imagination. But *Cat's Eye* is about life here and now, the life we all know, the life we live and question daily, not a construct totally bent to the author's will, and it is subject therefore to a set of different reader demands: a stacking up of the work's achievement not only against the author's intent, but against our own concept of what's what in the world.

What Atwood seems to be grappling with in *Cat's Eye* is a fundamental ambivalence about women, which many women share and should not be dismissed out of hand as simple-minded. It is the first, basic disfigurement of the oppressed: being taught, and learning well, to hate oneself. From her first novel, *The Edible Woman.* Atwood has mapped the syndrome eloquently. Among her women co-workers at an office party, this Atwood Woman reflects:

> She examined the women's bodies with interest, critically, as though she had never seen them before . . . she could see the roll of fat pushed up across Mrs. Gundridge's back by the top of her corset, the ham-like bulge of thigh, the creases around the neck, the large porous cheeks; the blotch of varicose veins glimpsed at the back of one plump crossed leg, the way her jowls jellied when she chewed, her sweater a wooly tea cosy over those rounded shoulders; and the others too, similar in structure but with varying proportions and textures of bumpy permanents and dune-like contours of breast and waist and hip . . . What peculiar creatures they were . . . and the continual flux between the outside and the inside, taking things in, giving them out, chewing, words, potato chips, burps, grease, hair, babies, milk, excrement, cookies, vomit, coffee . . . blood, tea, sweat, liquor, tears and garbage . . . she was one of them, her body the same, identical, merged with that other flesh that choked the air in the flowered room with its sweet organic scent; she felt suffocated by this thick sargasso-sea of femininity . . . she wanted something solid, clear: a man; she wanted Peter in the room so that she could put her hand out and hold on to him to keep from being sucked down.

There are similar passages in all Atwood's novels.

In *Cat's Eye,* ambivalence lives at the center of the story. Elaine Risley is pulled towards the rich intellectual and scientific interests of her father, and particularly of her brilliant brother. At the same time, she worries that she is failing at being one of the boys, and longs for the mysteries of best-friends, the unknown world of girls. The vagaries of attitude of her unconventional mother leave her prey to the stupid and cruelly distorting conventions of the middle-class mothers and girls of the neighborhood in Toronto in which her odd family settles down after the Second World War. Torn, and ignorant of feminine lore, she tries to make her way.

Boys are easier in some ways, but girls and their exotic concerns are irresistible. She dissects frogs with aplomb, but the complexities of sweater-sets, girdles, perms, Church-going and Sunday School are unattainable however hard she strives. She never measures up. Among the group of best-friends into which she is initiated, Elaine is chosen as victim to be mocked, teased, mistreated and tortured to the point of real harm. She is buried at one point, and left to freeze or possibly be raped at another. As she grows into adolescence, she finds her relationships with boys "effortless . . . It's girls I feel awkward with. It's girls I feel I have to defend myself against; not boys."

And well she might. Apart from her mother, the women in Elaine Risley's girlhood are very nasty indeed. Cordelia, the particular best-friend who leads the pack in torturing Elaine, seems to be utterly without redeeming characteristics, yet Elaine remains obsessed with her even into her own maturity and success as an artist, though Cordelia has achieved nothing in contrast, and is last seen confined to a mental institution. It isn't Cordelia who is the subject of Elaine's paintings, however, but the mother of one of the other best-friends, a woman who devoted herself to re-molding Elaine into a proper, Church-going, right-thinking, middle-class female—and failed. In the paintings so praised by the women's movement, Elaine exacts the ultimate revenge and Mrs. Smeath is rendered in canvas after canvas as the damaging, monstrous creature she had been to the young girl.

But the women's movement is no haven. Here too ambivalence flourishes. Elaine is between husbands, a single mother, and a beginning artist when she becomes reluctantly involved in a support group:

> Confession is popular, not of your flaws but of your sufferings at the hands of men. Pain is important, but only certain kinds of it: the pain of women, but not the pain of men. Telling about your pain is called sharing. I don't want to share in this way; also I am insufficient in scars. I have lived a privileged life, I've never been beaten up, raped, gone hungry . . . A number of these women are lesbians . . . according to some, it's the only equal relationship possible, for women. You are not genuine otherwise . . . I am ashamed of my own reluctance . . . but I would be terrified to get into bed with a woman. Women collect grievances, hold grudges and change shape. They pass hard, legitimate judgments, unlike the purblind guesses of men, fogged with romanticism and ignorance and bias and wish. Women know too much, they can neither be deceived nor trusted. I can understand why men are afraid of them, as they are frequently accused of being . . . I avoid gatherings of these women, walking as I do in fear of being sanctified, or else burned at the stake. I think they are talking about me behind my back . . . They want to improve me. At times I feel defiant . . . I am not Woman, and I'm damned if I'll be shoved into it. *Bitch,* I think silently. *Don't boss me around* . . . But also I envy their conviction, their optimism, their carelessness, their fearlessness about men, their camaraderie. I am like someone watching from the sidelines, waving a cowardly handkerchief, as the troops go boyishly off to war, singing brave songs.

The most mystifying event in the book is the scene in which Elaine is deserted by her best-friends and left to freeze in the snow at the bottom of a ravine. Rescue comes in the shape of a vision of the Virgin, though it is the down-to-earth concern of her mother that truly leads Elaine to warmth and safety. Oddly, too, in winding up the threads of this long book, Elaine's beloved brother Stephen is killed off suddenly, without a design intrinsic to the book's intent, or at least to the reader's understanding. On a journey to Frankfurt to present a scientific paper "on the subject of the probable composition of the universe," his plane is hijacked, and he is singled out by the terrorists and killed. This act of cruelty summarily ejects the reader from the world of the book, in a state of shock and blame for its senselessness. There is something so wayward and arbitrary in this killing that one's primary emotion is rage at the author: *You killed him and I don't know why and I don't think you do either.*

On the final page, in what was for me a failed attempt to sum up and resolve the book's concerns, Elaine is herself on a plane, returning home from her memory trip. In the two seats beside her are

> two old ladies, old women, each with a knitted cardigan, each with yellow-white hair and thick-lensed glasses with a chain for around the neck, each with a desiccated mouth lipsticked bright red with bravado . . . They have saved up for this trip and they are damn well going to enjoy it, despite the arthritis of one, the swollen legs of the other. They're rambunctious, they're full of beans; they're tough as thirteen, they're innocent and dirty, they don't give a hoot. Responsibilities have fallen away from them, obligations, old hates and grievances; now for a short time they can play again like children, but this time without the pain . . . This is what I miss, Cordelia: not something that's gone but something that will never happen. Two old women giggling over their tea.

Stubbornly, these happenings fail to coalesce or to peak. Does the death of Stephen signify *anything?* Is it divine punishment for being male? (Women and children are allowed to leave the plane.) Does the vision of the Virgin? Woman as a force for good? That notion takes some straining. "Two old women giggling over their tea"——a (condescending) image for the strengthening joys of long-lasting friendships between women. Perhaps Atwood is straining out the essence of her ambivalence, locating the pure liquid of her passionate negation of traditional femininity, seeking its source so as to choke it off; or perhaps she is struggling through to an open acknowledgement and embrace of sisterhood, down to its most repellent characteristics.

A novel is like a single breaking ocean wave, its waters gathered from far-away coasts, diverted by channels and chance winds, yet moving inexorably towards a crashing silvery moment that peaks and breaks on a designated shore. *Cat's Eye* gathers its many streams, sends them flowing forward in wash after wash of rich detail and observation, but disappointingly no wave forms. Fizzling, it disperses its brilliant waters ineffectually, allowing them to be sucked back into the general stream. But water is one of Margaret Atwood's powerful elements, and there is no doubt that her extraordinary gifts will keep her and her readers sailing.

J. Brooks Bouson (essay date 1989)

SOURCE: "Comic Storytelling as Escape and Narcissistic Self-Expression in Atwood's *Lady Oracle*," in his *The Empathic Reader: A Study of the Narcissistic Character and the Drama of the Self,* The University of Massachusetts Press, 1989, pp. 154-168.

[*In the following excerpt, Bouson explores the psychology of the protagonist in* Lady Oracle.]

Margaret Atwood's *Lady Oracle* has tantalized, amused, and baffled critics who are fascinated with its duplicitous, protean narrator-heroine. "The task of fitting the pieces of the puzzle together, the puzzle of Joan Foster," writes one critic, "is left to the reader." As Joan narrates the story of her life and exposes her narcissistic anxieties, hurts, and rage, she is undeniably funny. But even while we laugh at her comic descriptions of her mother-dominated childhood, her childhood obesity, her recurring fat lady fantasies, and her troubled relationships with men, we are aware that her comedic voice "covers a prolonged scream of pain." Like the opera singer, Joan wants to "stand up there in front of everyone and shriek as loud" as possible "about hatred and love and rage and despair," to "scream at the top" of her lungs "and have it come out music." The kind of storyteller we've encountered before, Joan wants to seduce her listeners, compel their attention. Creating a character who amuses and disarms, keeping reader attention riveted on Joan, Atwood enjoins us to become accomplices, an appreciative audience for Joan's secret but nevertheless exhibitionistic exploits. Urging us into a pact with her storyteller-heroine, Atwood takes us into a comic version of a world we've come to know well . . . the solipsistic, hall-of-mirrors world of the narcissistic character.

A text replete with messages and clues for the psychoanalytic inquirer, *Lady Oracle* focuses attention on a troubled mother-daughter relationship. The preestablished plot Joan acts out finds its source in her mother-controlled and tormented childhood, a world in which the "huge but ill-defined figure" of her mother blocks "the foreground" while her father is essentially an "absence." An autobiographer, Joan tells the story of her childhood in an attempt to understand and thus master her memories of the corrosive emotional hurts of her past and also to verbally retaliate against her mother. Cast in the role of sympathetic listener, the reader is encouraged to take Joan's side in the mother-daughter conflict. Part of the text's agenda is to use comic accusation to expose and undercut the lethal powers of the unempathic, and hence dangerous, mother figure.

Her mother is "the manager, the creator, the agent," and she "the product," says Joan as she reconstructs her childhood relationship with her mother. Motherly "concern" in Joan's childhood is equated with "pain," her mother's anger barely camouflaged by her public pose as the concerned mother. "On her hands, in her hair," these are the metaphors Joan's mother uses to describe her, even though she "seldom" touches her. Unconsciously, her mother conspires to deny Joan's healthy childhood assertiveness and curtail her development of feelings of self-worth and authenticity. She wants Joan to "change into someone else," continually berates and finds fault with her, and always tries to teach her "some lesson or other." When Joan becomes an overweight child, she becomes a "reproach" to her mother, the "embodiment" of her mother's "failure and depression, a huge edgeless cloud of inchoate matter which refused to be shaped into anything" for which her mother "could get a prize." Joan's dreams depict her childhood anxieties about her self-absorbed, non-responsive, and angry mother. In one dream, she envisions herself struggling on a collapsing bridge; as she falls into a ravine, her nearby mother remains oblivious of the fact that "anything unusual" is happening. In another dream, Joan's memory of her mother putting on make-up in front of her three-sided mirror surfaces as a nightmare in which her mother metamorphoses into a three-headed monster and only Joan is aware of her "secret" monstrousness. And in her most terrifying dream, Joan, overhearing voices talking about her and realizing that "something very bad" is about to happen, feels utterly "helpless." The persecutory fears that Joan fictionalizes in her Gothic novels and that plague her as an adult in her dreams and real life—like her Gothic heroines, she feels vulnerable, exposed, haunted and hunted down by malevolent, spectral pursuers—find their source in her crippling childhood encounters with her mother. With her childhood contemporaries, her companion Brownies who take special delight in persecuting her since she makes such a good victim and cries so readily, she repeats her troubled relationship with her mother. Later, when she meets Marlene, one of her childhood tormentors, these painful memories erupt. "Like a virus meeting an exhausted throat, my dormant past burst into rank life. . . . I was trapped again in the nightmare of my childhood, where I ran eternally after the others, the oblivious or scornful ones, hands outstretched, begging for a word of praise." What Joan attempts to elicit from others is the confirming attention she never received in childhood. Like Atwood, who plays the "good mother" to Joan by making her the focal point of attention, the reader is encouraged to enact the "good mother" role by becoming an appreciative audience for Joan's comic misadventures. Divulging to us her character's needs and hurts, positioning us as confidants, Atwood invites our active listening and empathic interest.

Joan's early pursuit of audience recognition is dramatized in her childhood experiences as an overweight, would-be ballet dancer. Exposing herself to control her fear of exposure, laughing at herself to disarm those who would laugh at her, Joan describes her childhood fascination with ballet dancers. "I idealized ballet dancers . . . ," she recalls, "and I used to press my short piggy nose up against jewelry store windows and goggle at the china music-box figurines of shiny ladies in brittle pink skirts, with roses on their hard ceramic heads, and imagine myself leaping through the air . . . my hair full of rhinestones and glittering like hope." Enrolled in Miss Flegg's dancing school, Joan eagerly awaits the recital performance of the "But-

terfly Frolic," which is her "favorite" dance and which features her favorite costume: a short pink skirt, a headpiece with insect antennae, and a pair of cellophane wings. In her outfit, as she later reconstructs this incident, she looks "grotesque": "with my jiggly thighs and the bulges of fat where breasts would later be and my plump upper arms and floppy waist, I must have looked obscene, senile almost, indecent. . . ." Provoked to laugh as Joan makes wisecrack after wisecrack about her weight, Atwood forces us to confront, even as we laugh at Joan's jokes about her obesity, our own—and the text's—latent cruelty.

After her embarrassed mother betrays her to Miss Flegg, Joan is given a new role in the dance: that of a mothball. Joan's "humiliation [is] disguised as a privilege," for Miss Flegg tells her it is a special part that she has been selected to dance. "There were no steps to my dance, as I hadn't been taught any, so I made it up as I went along. . . . I threw myself into the part, it was a dance of rage and destruction, tears rolled down my cheeks behind the fur, the butterflies would die. . . . 'This isn't me,' I kept saying to myself, 'they're making me do it'; yet even though I was concealed in the teddy-bear suit . . . I felt naked and exposed, as if this ridiculous dance was the truth about me and everyone could see it." Though thwarted in her desire to have wings, she does provoke both laughter and vigorous applause. Left alone, center stage, she is a special person, a grotesque clown.

At the time, she is filled with "rage, helplessness and [a] sense of betrayal," but she gradually comes to view this episode as "preposterous," most particularly when she thinks about telling others about it. "Instead of denouncing my mother's injustice, they would probably laugh at me. It's hard to feel undiluted sympathy for an overweight seven-year-old stuffed into a mothball suit and forced to dance; the image is simply too ludicrous." While we are invited to laugh at this episode, we also are meant to feel sorry for Joan and disapprove of her mother's unempathic behavior. As one critic observes, "Joan swings back and forth between self-pity and self-mockery. She thinks of herself as a victim and the 'pity the unwanted child' tone is very strong, but she also sees and shows herself to be ridiculous as well as pathetic." Despite Joan's comic dismissal, this incident causes a deep narcissistic wound. It later resurfaces in her recurring fat lady fantasy and gives birth to her identity as the escape artist who fears exposure and thus compulsively assumes a series of identities, each identity becoming a new trap. And here we find the precursor of the writer who achieves narcissistic revenge via her art and the comedian who later learns how to disarmingly throw the cloak of humor over her rage to win the approval of others. This also points to one of the defensive strategies of the narrative: the use of humor to partially contain and diffuse the explosive anger that threatens to erupt from just beneath the surface of the text. "All that screaming with your mouth closed," Joan says, her depiction of an Italian fotoromanzo an apt depiction of her own inner life.

As Joan battles her hostile and intrusive mother during adolescence, she transforms herself into a grotesque monster. Insistently, the text draws attention to Joan's defective body. A physical statement, Joan's obesity is a visible signifier of her thwarted and angry grandiosity, her inner defectiveness and hollowness, and her introjection of her mother's monstrousness. "Eat, eat, that's all you ever do," Joan recalls her mother saying. "You're disgusting, you really are, if I were you I'd be ashamed to show my face outside the house." Using eating as a weapon, Joan eats "steadily, doggedly, stubbornly." "The war between myself and my mother was on in earnest; the disputed territory was my body," as she later analyzes it. "I swelled visibly, relentlessly, before her very eyes, I rose like dough, my body advanced inch by inch towards her across the dining-room table, in this at least I was undefeated." Determined not to be "diminished, neutralized" by the nondescript clothes her mother wants her to wear, she chooses outfits of "a peculiar and offensive hideousness, violently colored, horizontally striped." Her confidence undercut when she recognizes that others view her obesity as an "unfortunate handicap," she comes to derive a "morose pleasure" from her weight "only in relation" to her mother. In particular, she enjoys her ability to clutter up her mother's "gracious-hostess act." Putting on her fashion shows "in reverse," she calls attention to herself by "clomping silently but very visibly" through the rooms where her mother sits. "[I]t was a display, I wanted her to see and recognize what little effect her nagging and pleas were having." Eating to "defy" her mother, Joan also eats from "panic": "Sometimes I was afraid I wasn't really there, I was an accident; I'd heard her call me an accident. Did I want to become solid, solid as a stone so she wouldn't be able to get rid of me?" Conflating her memory of herself as a fat ballerina and her fantasy of the fat lady in the freak show, she envisions herself as a fat lady in a pink ballerina costume walking the high wire, proceeding inch by inch across Canada, the initial jeers of the audience transforming into the roar of applause when she triumphantly completes her death-defying feat. Dramatizing Joan's need to exhibit her grandiose self and gain self-confirming attention, this fantasy also depicts her anxieties about her fragile self-stability, which is expressed as the fear of falling.

When Joan, left two thousand dollars by her Aunt Lou on condition that she lose one hundred pounds, goes on a diet, the mother-daughter battle enters a new phase. "Well, it's about time, but it's probably too late," her mother says at first. But when Joan begins to successfully shed her fat, her mother becomes progressively "distraught and uncertain," for as Joan grows thinner and thinner her mother loses control over her. "About the only explanation I could think of for this behavior of hers was that making me thin was her last available project. She'd finished all the houses, there was nothing left for her to do, and she had counted on me to last her forever." After Joan has stripped away most of her protective covering of fat, her mother's "cutting remarks" are finally literalized: she attacks Joan with a knife, this actual infliction of a narcissistic wound concretizing the verbal wounds Joan has suffered for years. Consequently, Joan leaves home, determined to sever her connection with her mother and to discard her past with all its "acute concealed misery."

Discovering that she is the "right shape" but has "the wrong past," she determines "to get rid of it entirely" and create "a different" and "more agreeable one" for herself. Thus she begins her life-long habit of compulsive lying and storytelling, as she invents, first for her lover Paul and later for Arthur and her adoring public, a "more agreeable" personal history. Consciously, she attempts to divest herself of her past. But she remains haunted by it, and she constantly fears exposure. No matter what she achieves, she feels that she is an impostor, a fraud, and that others will uncover her persisting defectiveness. She is also unable to escape her mother's malevolent presence and her own buried rage. When Joan receives a telegram announcing her mother's death, she thinks it might be a trap, her mother's attempt to bring her "back within striking distance." Subsequently, she imagines that she somehow has killed her mother for unconsciously she perceives her angry thoughts as lethal. Strategically "killed off" and banished from the text, the mother figure resurfaces in a potentially more dangerous form. Twice after her mother's death Joan hallucinates what she thinks is her mother's astral body. Married to Arthur, she remains a partial prisoner of her noxious past. "All this time," she recalls, "I carried my mother around my neck like a rotting albatross. I dreamed about her often, my three-headed mother, menacing and cold." When she looks at herself in the mirror, she does not see what others see. Instead, she imagines the "outline" of her "former body" still surrounding her "like a mist, like a phantom moon, like the image of Dumbo the Flying Elephant superimposed on my own. I wanted to forget the past, but it refused to forget me; it waited for sleep, then cornered me." That the narrative seemingly delivers Joan from her mother's noxious presence and from her own grotesque shape only to sabotage the rescue points to a drama which recurs in the text: the thwarted rescue.

In Joan's relationships with men, we find a repetition of this narrative pattern of thwarted rescues. Desiring magic transformations, wishing to escape from her past, Joan imagines that the men in her life are like the romantic figures populating her Gothic novels. When she meets Paul, the Polish count, and listens to his story, she thinks she has met "a liar as compulsive and romantic" as herself. Arthur, at first, seems a "melancholy fighter for almost-lost causes, idealistic and doomed, sort of like Lord Byron." Similarly, the Royal Porcupine has "something Byronic about him." But when the romance wears off and these men become "gray and multidimensional and complicated like everyone else," the inevitable happens: Joan relives her past in her relationships with men.

Her husband, Arthur, for example, is an amalgam of her father's aloofness and her mother's disapproving behavior. Arthur faults Joan for being obtuse and disorganized, is in the habit of giving expositions on her failures, and, like her mother, is "full of plans" for her. Fearing that Arthur will find her unworthy, she protects her fragile self-esteem by keeping secret her childhood obesity and her identity as Louisa K. Delacourt, the writer of costume Gothics. Both Arthur and Paul, her first lover, seem bent on changing her, transforming her into their own likenesses. While Arthur enjoys her defeats in the kitchen—"[m]y failure was a performance and Arthur was the audience. His applause kept me going"—she also comes to feel that no matter what she does Arthur is "bound to despise" her and that she can never be what he wants.

What Joan seeks from the men in her life is the mirroring attention she never got from her mother. "I'd polished them with my love," as she puts it, "and expected them to shine, brightly enough to return my own reflection, enhanced and sparkling." But the men she loves are also objects of fear. She realizes that all the men she has been involved with have had "two selves": her father, a doctor-savior and wartime killer; the man in the tweed coat, her childhood rescuer but also possibly the daffodil man, a pervert; Paul, an author of innocuous nurse novels and a man she suspects of having a secret sinister life; the Royal Porcupine, her fantasy lover and feared "homicidal maniac"; and Arthur, her loving husband and suspected madman, possibly the unknown tormentor sending her death threats. She splits men into dual identities: the apparently good man is a lurking menace, a hidden pervert, a secret killer. In the text's code, men are an embodiment of Joan's split good/bad mother and her own hidden energies and killing rage. What Arthur doesn't know about her, she tells us, is that behind her "compassionate smile" is "a set of tightly clenched teeth, and behind that a legion of voices, crying, *What about me? What about my own pain? When is it my turn?* But I'd learned to stifle these voices, to be calm and receptive."

Perpetually trapped, Joan perpetually attempts to escape as she assumes a series of identities and becomes a writer of Gothic novels. "Escape literature," Paul tells Joan, "should be an escape for the writer as well as the reader." While Joan uses her writing to escape her daily life, she also persistently dramatizes in her work her amorphous anxieties, her conflicted selfhood, and her need for self-rescue. For while her heroine is perpetually "in peril" and "on the run," she is also, of course, always rescued. In her work-in-progress, *Stalked By Love*, Joan fictionalizes her contrasting selves. Charlotte represents her socially compliant, conventional female self, the role that she assumes with Paul and Arthur, while the possessive, angry, powerful Felicia embodies her camouflaged grandiosity. Publicly, Joan plays the role of Arthur's self-effacing, inept, always-apologizing wife; in secret, she becomes Louisa Delacourt, writer of Gothic novels. As time passes, Joan's desire for public acknowledgment grows. But she also fears that if she brings the two parts of her life together there will be "an explosion." And in a sense there is.

In an episode designed to compel reader attention and provoke the critic's speculative gaze, Atwood describes Joan's discovery of her own "lethal energies" when she experiments with automatic writing. Sitting in the dark in front of her triple mirror and staring at a candle, Joan, in a symbolic act of narcissistic introversion, imagines herself journeying into the world of the mirror. "There was the sense of going along a narrow passage that led downward," she recalls, "the certainty that if I could only turn the next corner or the next—for these journeys became longer—I would find the thing, the truth or word or person that was mine, that was waiting for me." On the trail

of an elusive stranger, she discovers, in the subterranean world of the unconscious, a woman unlike anybody she's "ever imagined," a woman who, she feels, has "nothing to do" with her. "[S]he lived under the earth somewhere, or inside something, a cave or a huge building. . . . She was enormously powerful, almost like a goddess, but it was an unhappy power":

> She sits on the iron throne
> She is one and three
> The dark lady   the redgold lady
> the blank lady   oracle
> of blood, she who must be
> obeyed   forever.

Figured as the mother-goddess Demeter, Lady Oracle—who is potent and blank—is a composite of the internalized mother and Joan's grandiose, empty self. It is the Lady Oracle in Joan that compels her to endlessly construct herself, to create a series of fictional lives for herself, each new creation ultimately becoming a new trap, a new replication of her past. "There was always," she remarks, "that shadowy twin, thin when I was fat, fat when I was thin, myself in silvery negative, with dark teeth and shining white pupils glowing in the black sunlight of that other world."

When Joan publishes her Lady Oracle poems and consequently becomes a cult figure, she achieves the recognition she has always craved. But this only serves to deepen the cracks in her fractured self. Again the narrative pattern of the thwarted rescue is repeated. Joan's celebrity self, which takes on a deadly energy of its own, seems alien. "[I]t was as if someone with my name were out there in the real world, impersonating me . . . doing things for which I had to take the consequences: my dark twin, my fun-house-mirror reflection. She was taller than I was, more beautiful, more threatening. She wanted to kill me and take my place. . . ." At long last Joan acts out her archaic grandiosity only to feel unreal, that she is "hollow, a hoax, a delusion." In a new variation on her recurrent fat lady fantasy, she expresses her growing recognition of her subjective emptiness. Fantasying the fat lady floating up like a helium balloon, she realizes that the fat lady, despite her large size, is "very light" for she is "hollow." *"Why am I doing this? . . . Who's doing this to me?"* Joan asks herself. Unable to "turn off" her "out-of-control fantasies," she is forced to "watch them through to the end." Although we find Joan's apparent lack of control unsettling, we also sense that as a storyteller she is perpetually playing up to her audience, embroidering her preposterous fantasies. "As the teller of a humorous tale," writes Sybil Vincent, "Joan gains a sense of power. She deliberately manipulates her audience and experiences a sense of control lacking in her actual life." Situated as appreciative listeners and suspicious critics, we sense that one of the text's errands is to rivet reader attention on Joan and thus, as it were, to gratify her grandiose-exhibitionistic needs.

When all the convoluted plots of Joan's life converge—her current lover, the Royal Porcupine, wants her to marry him; Paul, her former lover, traces her and wants her back; a blackmailer hounds her; she imagines that Arthur is the persecutor sending her death threats—she determines to escape her life which has become "a snarl, a rat's nest of dangling threads and loose ends." Accordingly, she fakes her death by drowning and lives, incognito she thinks, in Italy. In a symbolic gesture, she buries her clothes, attempting to shed her past identity. But what she can never escape is her inner sense of defectiveness. In one of her more lurid fantasies, she imagines her buried clothes growing a body, which shapes itself into "a creature composed of all the flesh that used to be mine and which must have gone somewhere." Transforming into a featureless monstrous form, it engulfs her. "It was the Fat Lady. She rose into the air and descended on me. . . . For a moment she hovered around me like ectoplasm, like a gelatin shell, my ghost, my angel; then she settled and I was absorbed into her. Within my former body, I gasped for air. Disguised, concealed. . . . Obliterated." When Joan suspects that Mr. Vitroni may be in league with her secret pursuers, she fantasies herself spending the rest of her life "in a cage, as a fat whore, a captive Earth Mother for whom somebody else collected the admission tickets." As her narcissistic anxieties become more and more ungovernable, not only do her Gothic fantasies intrude into her real life, her real life invades her art: Felicia metamorphoses into the bloated, drowned fat lady and is rejected by her husband, Redmond-Arthur.

As the narrative progresses and Atwood carries us deeper and deeper into Joan's fun-house, hall-of-mirrors world, a kind of infinite regression occurs as fantasy and reality coalesce and we gradually come to the realization that Joan's descriptions of others—those in her life and her art—are autorepresentational. Joan's final and terrifying dream encounter with the "dark vacuum" of her mother forces her to recognize that her mother is her own reflection. "She'd never really let go of me because I had never let her go. It had been she standing behind me in the mirror, she was the one who was waiting around each turn, her voice whispered the words. . . . [S]he had been my reflection too long." In her Gothic novel, *Stalked by Love*, Joan's stand-in, Felicia, is compulsively drawn into the labyrinth's "central plot." At the psychocenter of the novel, the "central plot" of the maze depicted in the inset Gothic text provides interpretive clues to the narrative plot of the text we are reading. For at the maze's center, Joan-Felicia encounters her mirror selves. There she finds the ubiquitous fat lady, her defective self; there she also finds an embodiment of her identity as Louisa Delacourt, the middle-aged writer of Gothic novels and her dual red-haired, green-eyed self: Joan, the self-effacing wife and Joan the powerful poet cult figure. And there behind a closed door which she imagines is her pathway to freedom, her escape from the trap of self-entanglement, she discovers yet another alter-ego, fictional self, Redmond, who transforms sequentially into the men in her life—her father, Paul, the Royal Porcupine, Arthur—and then into a death's skull. In the specular world of the maze, Joan encounters, recursively, images of self. As Redmond reaches out to grab her, she experiences, once again, the smothering, self-fragmenting dominance of her childhood mother who unconsciously sought to obliterate Joan's fledgling self. Twice before—first during her Lady Oracle experiments with automatic writing and then in a terrifying nightmare in which she seemed about to be sucked into

the "vortex" of her mother—Joan approached this world of suffocating darkness, the self-annihilating world of the engulfing, destructive mother. Joan's faked drowning, in effect, is stage managed by her dead but potent mother, who remains a menacing presence in Joan's psyche. But Joan's faked death *is* faked. She is the escape artist who uses deception to appease her lethal, interiorized mother-self. Her faked suicide is a signifier of her desire to live, to rescue and repair her self.

To the Italian village women, the resurrected Joan becomes an object of fear. Joan imagines that they see her as a kind of science fiction creature, "[a] female monster, larger than life. . . striding down the hill, her hair standing on end with electrical force, volts of malevolent energy shooting from her fingers. . . ." The monster of her own narcissistic ire possesses her like an alien presence. In her anger, she resembles her mother. No wonder she is bent on escape, on comic diffusion of her deadly rage. In a comic denouement, Joan, fearing that her murderous pursuer is at the door, exposes her wrath when she attacks a reporter who has come to interview her. "I've begun to feel," she comments, "he's the only person who knows anything about me. Maybe because I've never hit anyone else with a bottle, so they never got to see that part of me." As the novel ends, Joan determines to stop writing Gothic novels and to turn, instead, to science fiction, a process she has already begun in her comic, self-parodic depiction of herself as a science fiction monster.

The victim of repeated maternal denials of her self, Joan, as she repeatedly fabricates her life, constructs a series of fictional identities which she disposes of at will. Through this symbolic act of self-creation and self-annihilation, she replicates and replaces her mother and becomes the guarantor of her own identity. The victim of maternal betrayal and control, Joan becomes a dissembler who secretly betrays and controls others. When Joan describes herself as "essentially devious, with a patina of honesty," readers may suspect that they, too, despite their privileged perspective, are being deceived. Again and again, critics have remarked on this. One critic comments that Joan's "absolute honesty in confessing her lies, tricks, and deceptions becomes, in itself, a confidence game which lulls the reader into a misguided trust in Joan's ability to interpret her experiences"; another insists that readers "have more reason to suspect Joan than to believe her"; and yet another says that Atwood's novel leaves readers with "the vague suspicion" that they have been "duped." In their uneasy feeling that they are being gulled and manipulated, critic/readers repeat Joan's childhood and persisting experiences of being deceived and controlled by others, by her mother and the men in her life. Depicted as a confessed liar, Joan escapes reader control and stubbornly resists being made into a stable, literary property.

"Most said soonest mended"—this garbled rendering of one of her Aunt Lou's trite sayings provides a central clue to the impulse behind Joan's autobiographical writing. Admitting, at one point, that she could never say the word "fat" aloud, Joan describes, in a vivid, comic-angry way, her childhood obesity and her persisting fat lady fantasies. Her self-exposure and self-condemnation repeat her mother's cutting remarks and also act as a form of verbal exorcism. Verbally striking back at the mother who verbally abused her as a child, Joan, as a wielder of words, fictively mothers and then obliterates the mother who attempted to annihilate her. In a similar vein, readers of **Lady Oracle** are urged to collude in the narrational plot to fictively "kill off " Joan's mother, who is represented in the text, in the words of one critic, "not as a woman, but as a fetish or witch-doll." Achieving verbal mastery over the men in her life who attempted to master her, Joan secretly attacks her perceived attackers and becomes a hidden menace to those who menace her. She acts this out in the novel's final scene when she assaults the reporter. When she consequently gives a bunch of wilted flowers to the hospitalized reporter as she plays nurse to him, she unconsciously signals her identification not only with the Mavis Quilp nurse heroines, but also with the daffodil man, an exhibitionist. Her artistry springs, in part, from her covert exhibitionism and rage, both expressed in her genesis as an artist—her mothball dance—and in her Lady Oracle manifestation.

In **Lady Oracle** autobiographical creation allows Joan to assert her grandiosity, vent her anger, and express her autonomy. Situated as a witness of Joan's conspiracy against others, the reader revels in her disguises and concocted plots and laughs at her descriptions of political activism, spiritualism, the publishing establishment, artistic creation, and faddish artists. Again and again Joan confesses her inability to control her overactive imagination, describing how her fantasies must play themselves out to their appointed ends. Indeed there are undertones of hysteria in her Gothic imaginings—her fears about being pursued in Italy—and in her fat lady fantasies, which progressively grow more and more ludicrous and elaborate. But just as Joan, as a Gothic storyteller, adroitly manipulates her audience, so she, as a comic character, compels our attention. At the outset of the novel, Joan, newly arrived in Italy, imagines all the people she has left behind. She envisions them grouped on the seashore talking to each other and ignoring her. But one thing the reader cannot do is ignore Joan. Atwood prompts us to give Joan the smiling attention that her mother never gave to her and that Arthur, who is subject to periodic depression—he gives off a "gray aura . . . like a halo in reverse," as she puts it— gives her less and less frequently.

"I longed for happy endings," Joan remarks, "I needed the feeling of release when everything turned out right and I could scatter joy like rice all over my characters and dismiss them into bliss." While some readers of **Lady Oracle** might share Joan's longing and wish to see a conclusive ending to her story and a final rescue, Atwood frustrates such a desire. "[T]here is no way for the reader to be certain that anything has changed by the end of Joan's narration," observes one critic. At the end "the reader suspects that there are more Joans to come," writes another; the reader watches "in helpless recognition," writes yet another, as Joan assumes a new role at the novel's end. Thwarting our desire for happy endings, for artistic coherence, for neat foreclosures, for final rescues, Atwood creates a plot like her character: one that is entangled and full of loose ends.

Installed as appreciative listeners, collaborators, and accomplices, we revel in Joan's zany exploits, her proliferating mirror encounters and angry-comic rhetoric. Joan's confessions are designed to entertain us, to win our smiling approbation of her thwarted grandiosity. But we are also implicitly led to reflect on our own need to escape through and live vicariously in art and to ask ourselves whether we, like Joan the compulsive creator of plots, are compulsive readers of plots. We are also led to ask ourselves to what extent we read ourselves into a fictional text just as Joan writes herself into her art. Coaxed throughout the novel to see the parallels between Joan's fictional and real worlds, we are also urged to consider to what extent we blur fact and fantasy as we construct the plots and texts of our own lives.

"I might as well face it," Joan admits in the novel's conclusion, "I was an artist, an escape artist. . . . [T]he real romance of my life was that between Houdini and his ropes and locked trunk; entering the embrace of bondage, slithering out again." So, too, she escapes our grasp as she multiplies before our eyes. As the realistic surface of her autobiographical account dissolves into a richly complex and redundant subjective fantasy, we gain momentary access to the shape-shifting world of the narcissist. Swerving out of our grasp, Joan lures us into a strange world in and beyond the looking glass: the multiple, mirrored, decertainized world of the narcissistic character.

Margaret Atwood with Earl G. Ingersoll (interview date Spring-Summer 1990)

SOURCE: "Waltzing Again: A Conversation with Margaret Atwood," in *Margaret Atwood: Conversations,* Ontario Review Press, 1990, pp. 234-38.

[*In the following interview, Atwood discusses her relationship to her readers and critics of her works as well as the themes of* Cat's Eye.]

[*Ingersoll*]: *Since as you know I've been working on a collection of your interviews, could we begin by talking about interviews? You have been interviewed very frequently. How do you feel about being interviewed?*

[Atwood]: I don't mind "being interviewed" any more than I mind Viennese waltzing—that is, my response will depend on the agility and grace and attitude and intelligence of the other person. Some do it well, some clumsily, some step on your toes by accident, and some aim for them. I've had interviews that were pleasant and stimulating experiences for me, and I've had others that were hell. And of course you do get tired of being misquoted, quoted out of context, and misunderstood. You yourself may be striving for accuracy (which is always complicated), whereas journalists are striving mainly for hot copy, the more one-dimensional the better. Not all of them of course, but enough.

I think the "Get the Guest" or "David and Goliath" interview tends to become less likely as you age; the interviewer less frequently expects you to prove you're a real writer, or a real woman, or any of the other things they expect you to prove. And you run into a generation of interviewers who studied you in high school and want to help you hobble across the street, rather than wishing to smack you down for being a presumptuous young upstart.

Let's not pretend however that an interview will necessarily result in any absolute and blinding revelations. Interviews too are an art form; that is to say, they indulge in the science of illusion.

You've said that when you began writing you imagined you'd have to starve in an attic without an audience sufficiently large to support your writing. Is there a Margaret Atwood who would have preferred the obscurity of a Herman Melville to whom you refer so frequently, or do you draw upon your readers' responses to your work? How much do you feel involved in a kind of dialogue with your readers?

The alternative, for me, to selling enough books or writing enough scripts and travel articles to keep me independent and to buy my time as a writer would be teaching in a university, or some other job. I've done that, and I've been poor, and I prefer things the way they are. For instance, this way I can say what I want to, because nobody can fire me. Not very many people in our society have that privilege.

I did not expect a large readership when I began writing, but that doesn't mean I'm not pleased to have one. It doesn't mean either that I write for a "mass audience." It means I'm one of the few literary writers who get lucky in their lifetimes.

My readers' responses to my work interest me, but I don't "draw upon" them. The response comes after the book is published; by the time I get responses, I'm thinking about something new. Dialogue with the readers? Not exactly. Dickens could have a dialogue with his readers *that affected the books* when he was publishing his novels in serial form, but we've lost that possibility. Though it does of course cheer me when someone likes, appreciates, or shows me that he or she has read my books intelligently.

Are you worried by self-consciousness as you write? Or is it an asset?

Self-consciousness? Do you mean consciousness of my self? That's what you have to give up when writing—in exchange for consciousness of the work. That's why most of what writers say about how they write—the process—is either imperfect memory or fabrication. If you're paying proper attention to what you're doing, you are so absorbed in it that you *shouldn't* be able to tell anyone afterwards exactly how you did it. In sports they have instant replay. We don't have that for writers.

The Edible Woman, Lady Oracle *and now* **Cat's Eye** *seem in large part jeux d'esprit. You give your readers the impression that you are having a good time writing—it's hard work, but also good fun. How important is "play" to you in writing? Do you have a sense of how much the reader will enjoy what you write, as you're writing it?*

I don't think **Cat's Eye** is a *jeu d'esprit*. (*Oxford Shorter*: "a witty or humorous trifle.") In fact, I don't think my other "comic" novels are *jeux d'esprit*, either. I suspect

that sort of definition is something people fall back on because they can't take women's concerns or life patterns at all seriously; so they see the wit in those books, and that's all they see. Writing is *play* in the same way that playing the piano is "play," or putting on a theatrical "play" is play. Just because something's fun doesn't mean it isn't serious. For instance, some get a kick out of war. Others enjoy falling in love. Yet others get a bang out of a really good funeral. Does that mean war, love, and death are trifles?

Cat's Eye *strikes me as unusual in one especially dramatic way: it builds upon the most detailed and perceptive exploration of young girlhood that I can recall having read. Once we've read that section of the novel, we readers might think, we've had fiction which explores this stage of young boyhood, but why haven't writers, even writers who are women, dealt with this stage of a woman's development before? How did you get interested in this area of girlhood, from roughly eight to twelve?*

I think the answer to this one is fairly simple: writers haven't dealt with girls age eight to twelve because this area of life was not regarded as serious "literary" material. You do get girls this age in *juvenile* fiction—all those English boarding-school books. And there have been some—I'm thinking of *Frost in May*. But it's part of that "Man's love is of man's life a thing apart, / 'Tis woman's whole existence" tendency—that is, the tendency to think that the only relationships of importance to women are their dealings with men (parents, boyfriends, husbands, God) or babies. What *could* be of importance in what young girls do with and to one another? Well, lots, it seems, judging from the mail. . . . I guess that's where "dialogue with the readers" comes in. Cordelia really got around, and she had a profound influence on how the little girls who got run over by her were able to respond to other women when they grew up.

I sometimes get interested in stories because I notice a sort of blank—why hasn't anyone written about this? *Can* it be written about? Do I dare to write it? **Cat's Eye** was risky business, in a way—wouldn't I be trashed for writing about little *girls,* how trivial? Or wouldn't I be trashed for saying they weren't all sugar and spice?

Or I might think about a story form, and see how it could be approached from a different angle—*Cinderella* from the point of view of the ugly sister, for instance. But also I wanted a literary home for all those vanished *things* from my own childhood—the marbles, the Eaton's catalogues, the Watchbird Watching You, the smells, sounds, colors. The textures. Part of fiction writing I think is a celebration of the physical world we know—and when you're writing about the past, it's a physical world that's vanished. So the impulse is partly elegiac. And partly it's an attempt to stop or bring back time.

The reviewer in Time *said that "Elaine's emotional life is effectively over at puberty." Does that seem accurate to you now as a reader of your own work?*

That ain't the book I wrote, and it ain't the one I read when I go back to it; as I'm doing now, since I'm writing the screenplay. I don't think Elaine's emotional life is over at puberty any more than any of our lives are over then. Childhood is very intense, because children can't imagine a future. They can't imagine pain being *over*. Which is why children are nearer to the absolute states of Heaven and Hell than adults are. Purgatory seems to me a more adult concept.

There are loose ends left from Elaine's life at that time, especially her unresolved relationship with Cordelia. These things have been baggage for her for a long time. But that's quite different from saying she stopped dead at twelve.

At the end of **Cat's Eye** *Elaine has lost both her parents and her brother, and said goodby finally to her ex- and to Cordelia. She has a husband and daughters she loves, but she seems very alone. What do you make of her aloneness now as a reader of your own novel?*

Writers can never really read their own books, just as film directors can never really see their own movies—or not in the way that a fresh viewer can. Because THEY KNOW WHAT HAPPENS NEXT.

Elaine "seems" alone at the end of the book because she's on an airplane. Also: because *the story* has been about a certain part of her life, and that part—*that* story—has reached a conclusion. She will of course land, get out of the plane, and carry on with the next part of her life, i.e. her ongoing time-line with some other characters about whom we have not been told very much, because *the story was not about them*.

Why do authors kill off certain characters? Usually for aesthetic, that is, structural reasons. If Elaine's parents etc. had still been around, we would have to have scenes with them, and that wasn't appropriate for this particular story. *Cat's Eye* is partly about being haunted. Why did Dickens kill off Little Nell? Because he was making a statement about the nature of humanity or the cruelty of fate? I don't think so. He just had to polish her off because that was where the story was going.

Related to that question, a reviewer in New Statesman *has written: "The novel is extremely bleak about humanity. . . . Through most of the novel you feel distance, dissection: a cat's eye. It ends on a note of gaiety, forgiveness and hope: but I don't believe it." When you were writing the novel did you have the sense of painting a "bleak" picture of "humanity"?*

One reason I don't like interviews, when I don't like them, is that people tend to come up with these weird quotes from reviewers, assume the quote is true, and then ask you why you did it that way. There are a lot of "when did you stop beating your wife" questions in interviews.

For instance, what is this "gaiety, forgiveness and hope" stuff? I'm thinking of doing a calendar in which each day would contain a quote by a reviewer of which the next day's quote would be a total contradiction by another reviewer. I'll buy the forgiveness, sort of; but gaiety? Eh? Where? The jolly old women on the plane are something she *doesn't* have. You find yourself looking under the sofa for some other book by the same name that might have strayed into the reviewer's hands by mistake. Or maybe they got one with some of the pages left out.

Nor, judging from the mail I received, did readers "feel distance, dissection." Total identification is more like it. Maybe the readers were identifying with the character's *attempt* to achieve distance, etc. She certainly attempts it, but she doesn't get it. As for "bleak," that's a word that tends to be used by people who've never been outside Western Europe or North America, and the middle class in either location. They think *bleak* is not having a two-car garage. If they think I'm bleak, they have no idea of what real bleak is like. Try Kierkegaard. Try Tadeusz Konwicki. Try Russell Banks, for that matter.

Or maybe . . . yes, maybe . . . I'm bleak *for a woman*. Is that the key? Are we getting somewhere now?

David Lucking   (essay date 1990)

SOURCE: "In Pursuit of the Faceless Stranger: Depths and Surfaces in Margaret Atwood's *Bodily Harm*," in *Studies in Canadian Literature,* Vol. 15, No. 1, 1990, pp. 76-93.

[*In the following essay, Lucking discusses the motifs of depth and surface in relation to Atwood's "thematic concern with the quest for authentic selfhood" in* Bodily Harm.]

Margaret Atwood's recurrent use of the descent motif to dramatize her thematic concern with the quest for authentic selfhood makes her work a tempting target for explication in terms of the initiatory archetype as this has been analyzed by such writers as C.G. Jung, Mircea Eliade and Joseph Campbell. This aspect of her writing has come in for considerable attention on the part of critics who, like the novelist herself, experienced the impact of Northrop Frye's theories concerning the relationship between myth and literature in the late fifties and sixties. At the same time, the irony implicit in Atwood's repeated use of what has been described as a "basic romance structure" involving a "symbolic journey to an underground prison" has also not escaped notice, and critics such as Frank Davey put us on our guard against the tendency to "mistake novels which deconstruct archetypes for novels which confirm them." There can be no doubt that there is a complex interplay, amounting at points almost to a formal dialectical tension, between the underlying structure of this author's works and the direction of moral implication in which those same works tend. Whereas the classic romance scenario concludes with the triumphant return to his community of a hero newly possessed of life-giving powers or knowledge, in Atwood's work the question of whether anything positive is ultimately to be gained from her protagonist's revelatory flight from a destructive civilization never receives an unequivocal answer. In **The Edible Woman, Surfacing** and **Lady Oracle** we are not informed whether or on what terms the protagonists will rejoin the social order from which they have severed themselves, while in **The Handmaid's Tale** doubts are raised as to whether the fugitive is destined to survive at all. Though it may well be subjected to ironic qualification or inversion or "deconstruction" in the very course of its fictional embodiment, however, the fact remains that the initiatory archetype is present in Atwood's works, and that no critical discussion of these novels can afford to ignore a pattern whose validity in the contemporary context the author herself is so obviously concerned to examine.

A work in the Atwood canon that illustrates with particular clarity the ambivalence attaching to the initiatory journey is **Bodily Harm** (1981), the thematic and metaphorical structure of which hinges on a paradoxical "rebirth" into the knowledge of death and of the things that death can symbolize. The plot of the novel is not complicated in itself, although some effort must be expended in order to reconstruct the precise chronology of events from the intricately wrought analeptic structure of the work. The protagonist Rennie (Renata) Wilford is a journalist, living in Toronto with an advertising designer named Jake. She is diagnosed as having cancer and undergoes a partial mastectomy which is clinically successful, although she continues to be haunted by the fear of recurrence. She falls in love with Daniel, her physician, but although he partially reciprocates her feelings the affair is more a source of frustration than of fulfillment, and in the meantime the relationship with Jake comes to an end. Shortly afterwards Rennie learns that somebody has broken into her home in her absence and before being frightened away by the police has been waiting for her "as if he was an intimate." The intruder has left a length of rope coiled on the bed, and the police warn Rennie that he will probably return. This sinister incident prompts Rennie's decision to travel to the Caribbean and write a piece about the island of St. Antoine. Among the people she encounters here and on the neighbouring island of Ste. Agathe are Paul, an American involved in contraband activities, and his former mistress Lora, who exploits Rennie to smuggle weapons into the country on Paul's behalf. Despite herself, Rennie becomes embroiled in the turmoil of a local election, a political assassination and an aborted uprising, and together with Lora is arrested and confined to a subterranean cell in an old fort. Here she is forced to witness various scenes of brutality, culminating in the sadistic beating of Lora by their prison guards. The novel ends with the anticipation of Rennie's release through the intervention of Canadian diplomatic authorities, although there is some uncertainty as to whether this will in fact take place or is only a hopeful fantasy on her part.

Atwood has been accused, not without an element of justice, of sacrificing characterization to thematic representation, of making her personages the vehicles of ideas or attitudes that she is intent on exploring rather than endowing them with an autonomous fictional life of their own. The character of Rennie Wilford, too, like that of her predecessors in Atwood's fiction, is somewhat excessively determined by the function she performs in articulating the novel's structure of ideas, and there is much in her portrayal which tends toward the merely schematic. Her personality is not so much dramatized as it is defined for us, with the consequence that she reads on occasion like a textbook on alienation. She is described as being almost neurotically disengaged, striving even in her dress for "neutrality" and "invisibility," deliberately living at the level of "surfaces" and "appearances." She "couldn't stand the idea of anyone doing her a favour," thinks of sex as no more than "a pleasant form of exercise," fears love

Dust jacket for Lady Oracle.

because it "made you visible, soft, penetrable [and] ludicrous," looks upon herself as "off to the side. She preferred it there." As a journalist she has abandoned social and political issues in favour of what she terms "lifestyles," the ephemeral mores of the society she lives in and to a large degree is evidently meant to reflect. Of the celebrities monopolizing the cultural limelight she decides that "she would much rather be the one who wrote things about people like this than be the one they got written about." Rennie's studiously cultivated detachment, her calculated nonparticipation in life, is summed up in the lugubrious pun with which she greets the news that drastic cancer operations are performed only in the case of what Daniel describes as "massive involvement." "Massive involvement," says Rennie: "It's never been my thing."

It is arguable of course that the self-consciousness with which Rennie formulates her own attitude towards life is in itself symptomatic of her estrangement, and that these explicit comments are therefore meant to be obliquely rather than directly revealing. Whether this is indeed the case or not, Atwood does not limit herself to exhibiting Rennie's character exclusively through the filter of her own self-conception, and many readers will doubtless prefer the alternative strategies that the author brings to bear.

When we learn for instance that Rennie has written an article about picking up men in laundromats, although "she never actually picked men up in laundromats, she just went through the preliminaries and then explained that she was doing research," the irony involved is of a different order from that with which Rennie perceives her own situation. A similar irony informs the scene in which Paul initiates a conversation with her at her hotel on St. Antoine, and she decides that his overture "does not have the flavour of a pickup. File it under *attempt at human contact.*" At one point in the hotel restaurant she catches herself compulsively churning out deftly turned phrases concerning the cuisine, and impatiently "wishes she could stop reviewing the food and just eat it." The techniques of thematic exposition and symbolic commentary mesh imperfectly when Rennie takes an excursion on a boat with an observation window set in the bottom, and, although she "looks, which is her function," she manages to see very little because of the murkiness of the marine floor. The strikingly effective image of the observation window, which relates (through Dr. Minnow, whose political sobriquet is "Fish") to Rennie's incapacity to fathom local politics, as well as to the dream in which she surveys her own body "under glass," is somewhat spoiled by the intrusive definition of her function.

The epigraph to **Bodily Harm** is taken from John Berger's *Ways of Seeing,* a work which is centrally concerned with the social and ideological determinants of perception. It is perfectly apparent that Rennie, though she affects a spectator attitude towards life which is emphasized still further when she assumes the role of tourist, is anxious more than anything else to cultivate ways of *not* seeing. Atwood elaborates a dense but highly subtle pattern of imagery to characterize Rennie's tendency to experience the world not at first hand but as filtered through the clichés of a media-ridden civilization. She habitually thinks in terms of films, or photographs, or pictures, or the various other civilized stratagems by which events are framed and neutralized and rendered innocuous. She persists in writing about St. Antoine in tourist brochure terms while an uprising is brewing all around her, and carries a camera slung over her shoulder even while she is transporting an illegal machine gun from one island to another. Dr. Minnow, a native of Ste. Agathe who, after a period of training abroad, chose to return to his birthplace and involve himself in local politics, urges her to modify her perspective. "All I ask you to do is look," he tells her: "We will call you an observer. . . . Look with your eyes open and you will see the truth of the matter." That this is no elementary undertaking becomes apparent to Rennie when she is compelled at the end to witness the raw spectacle of human viciousness, and she "doesn't want to see, she has to 'see, why isn't someone covering her eyes?'"

As the allusion to Berger's work perhaps suggests, Rennie's addiction to the world of surfaces and appearances is not meant to be viewed as a purely individual phenomenon, but rather as characteristic of the culture to which she belongs. At the same time, however, Atwood does furnish a psychological explanation for Rennie's attitude, relating it to specific incidents in her personal past which are recalled through flashback. Much of Rennie's attitude to

life is the direct legacy of her upbringing in a small Ontario town with the gloomily suggestive name of Griswold, which she thinks of as a "subground . . . full of gritty old rocks and buried stumps, worms and bones"—the reverse of a surface. In her adult life she "tries to avoid thinking about Griswold," which is reduced to being "merely something she defines herself against." "Those who'd lately been clamouring for roots had never seen a root up close" is her characteristically ironic comment on her background, the obvious implication being that she is consciously detaching herself as completely as possible from her own roots. To some degree this would seem to represent a purely personal reaction against a claustrophobic environment, a determination not to assume potentially encumbering responsibilities or commitments:

> All I could think of at the time was how to get away from Griswold. I didn't want to be trapped . . . I didn't want to have a family or be anyone's mother, ever; I had none of those ambitions. I didn't want to own any objects or inherit any.

But the spiritual climate of Griswold itself, with its vacant formalisms and grim pieties, seems more than any personal failure of adaptation to have been responsible for this almost pathological detachment. "As a child," recalls Rennie, "I learned three things well: how to be quiet, what not to say, and how to look at things without touching them." One of Rennie's earliest recollections is of her grandmother in Griswold, "prying my hands away finger by finger" in punishment for some unremembered transgression, after which the girl was confined in a cellar which is a "depth" *par excellence,* and which foreshadows the cell in which her older self will be incarcerated on St. Antoine.

This emblematic episode of the severing of hand contact assumes its place in an elaborate pattern of images constructed around hands and what hands represent both as vehicles of human contact and as instruments of manipulation and domination. Rennie's grandmother, who had attempted to eradicate in the girl any impulse towards tactile participation in her environment, succumbs finally to the senile delusion that she has lost her own hands. She insists to Rennie that the hands on the ends of her arms "are no good any more," and wants "my other hands, the ones I had before, the ones I touch things with." Only at the conclusion of the novel do we learn what Rennie's actual response to her grandmother's delusion has been. "Rennie cannot bear to be touched by those groping hands. . . . She puts her own hands behind her and backs away," while it is her mother who saves the situation by "tak[ing] hold of the grandmother's dangling hands, clasping them in her own." Rennie is evidently afflicted by subconscious guilt at having duplicated her grandmother's cold gesture of rejection. This latent sense of guilt, the obscure recognition of her own failure, manifests itself in her dream that her dead grandmother is appearing to her, extending an impossibly remote promise of salvation:

> Rennie puts out her hands but she can't touch her grandmother, her hands go right in, through, it's like touching water or new snow. Her grandmother smiles at her, the humming-

birds are around her head, lighting on her hands.
Life everlasting, she says.

When Rennie wakes from this dream, or thinks she does, she is convinced as her grandmother was years before that "there's something she has to find. . . . It's her hands she's looking for," and a few days later she dreams that "her hands are cold, she lifts them up to look at them, but they elude her. Something's missing." It is clear that Jake's remark to Rennie that "you're cutting yourself off" has a punning significance that extends well beyond her relationship with him.

The event that precipitates the gradual awakening to her own symbolic handlessness which such dreams as these reflect is Rennie's discovery that she has cancer. The disease begins to restore in the most brutal way possible the severed contact between "surface" and "depths," between the individual and her "roots," between Rennie and the body in which she has up to then merely been a tenant. The first stage of this process is the recognition that those elements in her which have been rejected or repressed or simply ignored are in fact inseparable from the self they are now menacing with extinction:

> The body, sinister twin, taking its revenge for whatever crimes the mind was supposed to have committed on it. . . . She'd given her body swimming twice a week, forbidden it junk food and cigarette smoke, allowed it a normal amount of sexual release. She'd trusted it. Why then had it turned against her?

Rennie has been treating her body as a machine to be kept in good repair, as something subordinate to what she considers to be her real self, and has accordingly tended to regard illnesses such as cancer as no more than the outward manifestations of some mental disability. Daniel tells her that while "the mind isn't separate from the body," neither can the body and its ailments be regarded merely as a function of the mind. Cancer, he reminds her, "isn't a symbol, it's a disease." After the operation that makes this only too vivid to her, her literal "opening up" at Daniel's hands, Rennie finds it increasingly difficult to live at the same level as before, and, as she anxiously probes her body for symptoms of recurrence, she reflects that "from the surface you can feel nothing, but she no longer trusts surfaces."

Rennie's evolving view as to the relative importance of surfaces and depths reveals itself among other things in her relation with two men who represent real or potential aspects of herself: her companion Jake and her physician Daniel. Jake, an adept in the field of advertising, inhabits the plane of disembodied appearances alone, manipulating images which bear no relation to the world of substance. "He was a packager" by profession, and Rennie eventually discovers that "she was one of the things Jake was packaging." Prior to her illness, Rennie has resembled Jake in evaluating attitudes and beliefs not according to their intrinsic validity or sincerity but in terms of whether they are fashionable or not, while one of her own favourite games has been "redoing" people, imagining how they would look if they were differently attired or otherwise altered.

In her way, she has also been a "packager," exploiting the media in order to manipulate tastes and inspire fashion trends of almost awesome triviality. The casual, nonbinding relationship she has formed with Jake, a contract of mutual gratification, cannot survive the revelation of depths that Rennie's illness both entails and symbolizes: afterwards "she didn't want him to touch her and she didn't know why, and he didn't really want to touch her either but he wouldn't admit it." On the one hand Rennie's surface is too marred after her operation to lend itself any longer as a convenient screen on which Jake can project his fantasies, while on the other the deeper implications of these same fantasies become increasingly obvious to Rennie herself.

Daniel, by contrast, lives and works at the level of depths rather than surfaces. Rennie attributes the sentiments he arouses in her to the fact that "he knows something about her she doesn't know, he knows what she's like inside." She supposes that he must exert a similar fascination on all of his patients, for "he's the only man in the world who knows the truth, he's looked into each one of us and seen death." At the same time, unlike Jake and Rennie herself, he is virtually unconscious of himself, indifferent to his own surface or public image: "he didn't seem to think of himself much in any way at all. This was the difference between Daniel and the people she knew." When Daniel asks her how she would "redo" him her reply is formulated in terms of the hand imagery that is employed throughout the novel as a kind of symbolic notation: " 'If I could get my hands on you?' said Rennie. 'I wouldn't, you're perfect the way you are.' " In making this disclaimer she is not being altogether sincere, for she does in her way try to "redo" him by manoeuvering him into an affair which is contrary to his principles, an effort that might be a displaced manifestation of her compulsion to control the knowledge of disease and death that he has gained by "looking into" her. She is unsuccessful in this endeavour, however, and her incapacity to relate to Daniel on his own terms indicates her continuing failure to come to grips with the depths at which he both literally and figuratively operates.

At this point Rennie is still suspended between the dimensions of surface and depths, dislodged from the one but not yet able to immerse herself in the other. She thinks of her position with respect to these dimensions in terms of the impossibility of contact with the two men who represent them—"One man I'm not allowed to touch . . . and another I won't allow to touch me"—but it is clear that this incapacity to relate to people in the external world reflects a profound schism within herself. It is above all with her own forgotten self, her "sinister twin," that Rennie must establish contact, as she herself intuits during a dream she has of herself undergoing a surgical operation: "she can see everything, clear and sharp, under glass, her body is down there on the table . . . she wants to rejoin her body but she can't get down." It is thus symbolically appropriate that the actual operation through which Daniel saves Rennie's life and at the same time initiates the process by which she awakens to an understanding of her own real nature should be described in terms of a rebirth. When she recovers from the anaesthetic after her operation her hand is being held by Daniel, who is "telling her that he had saved her life . . . and now he was dragging her back into it, this life that he had saved. By the hand." Later Daniel says of her operation that "it was almost like being given a second life," and Rennie thinks of him that "he knows we've been resurrected."

Although the symbolic significance of the name Renata is reinforced by these images of resurrection from some figurative death, the future projection implied by the name Wilford suggests quite clearly that rebirth is only the first stage in a long journey. For a descent into the "depths" that underlie surfaces cannot cease with the simple acknowledgement that one has a vulnerable and in the end "provisional" body, however important a phase in the process of self-discovery this may be. Shortly before her operation Rennie has been conducting research into the pornographic exploitation of sexual violence, and she been so repelled by the momentary glimpse she has caught into the dark abyss of human depravity that she has abandoned the project, deciding that "there were some things it was better not to know any more about than you had to. Surfaces, in many cases, were preferable to depths." Once having been evicted from the world of surfaces by the consciousness of her own susceptibility to the diseases of the flesh, however, Rennie is obliged to pursue her exploration of the depths still further, learning in the end that the "malignancy" she has encountered in the form of her illness is in fact an attribute of the world at large.

From the symbolic point of view, the discovery that a stranger has been occupying her home while she is away is an external correlative of Rennie's anguished discovery that a tumour has lodged itself within her body. The police warn Rennie that the stranger will return ("That kind always comes back"), just as she fears a recurrence of her illness. The incident therefore objectifies her growing awareness of the destructive forces lurking just below the familiar surface of life, while the rope the intruder leaves with evidently vicious intent betokens a connection which must be established, however undesired it may be. Perhaps significantly, ropes are several times associated with hands and arms in this novel. On St. Antoine Rennie is assisted into a boat by a man who "reaches out a long ropy arm, a hand like a clamp, to help her up," while another boat is later described as having "looped ropes thick as a wrist." Ropes, like hands, can serve as symbols of mediation, and the intruder who breaks into Rennie's Toronto apartment thus assumes the bizarre function of emissary:

> He was an ambassador, from some place she didn't want to know any more about. The piece of rope . . . was . . . a message; it was someone's twisted idea of love. . . . And when you pulled on the rope, which after all reached down into darkness, what would come up? What was at the end, *the end*? A hand, then an arm, a shoulder, and finally a face. At the end of the rope there was someone. Everyone had a face, there was no such thing as a faceless stranger.

After this invasion Rennie can no longer maintain her pose of cool detachment from the world: "She felt implicated, even though she had done nothing and nothing had been done to her." The sense of dissociation from herself which has already been growing in her in consequence of her illness, which expresses itself among other things in the dream in which she witnesses an operation being performed on her own body, is aggravated still further, to the point that she begins to "see herself from the outside, as if she was a moving target in someone else's binoculars."

Rennie's initial reaction to this intrusion and to her consequent sense of having been implicated despite herself (the "massive involvement" which refers both to cancer and to an attitude of mind) is one of refusal and flight, a reversion to the strategy of avoidance which has already prompted her repudiation of Griswold and all it represents. Her decision to travel to St. Antoine is explained in terms of a search for anonymity: "She is away, she is *out*, which is what she wanted. . . . In a way she's invisible. In a way she's safe." After witnessing the exaggerated terror with which she recoils from an innocent attempt at personal contact on the island, Paul tells her that she is suffering from what he terms "alien reaction paranoia," that "because you don't know what's dangerous and what isn't, everything seems dangerous." But her effort to avoid danger by attaining to a personal limbo of perfect neutrality is destined to failure. Not only do the destructive forces she fears reside no less within herself than in the external world, but her desire to insulate herself from that world runs counter to an even more powerful impulse operating within her, the instinctive craving for physical and emotional contact which is gradually leading her back towards her own forgotten humanity.

Once again it is the imagery of hands that functions as an index of her developing attitude. When she has been with Daniel, Rennie has yearned for "the touch of the hand that could transform you, change everything, magic." Passionately dedicated to helping other people, Daniel is virtually identified with the hands that Rennie comes to realize she herself has lost: "all she could imagine were his hands . . . his soul was in his hands." The morning after her arrival on St. Antoine Rennie wonders whether she, like other cancer victims, will resort to faith healing, "the laying on of hands by those who say they can see vibrations flowing out of their fingers in the form of a holy red light." Shortly afterwards she finds herself being pursued by a deaf and dumb man, whose inexplicable attentions strike her as being "too much like the kind of bad dream she wishes she could stop having." It is only when Paul explains that the man simply wants to shake hands with her in the conviction that the gesture will bring her good luck that Rennie realizes that "he's only been trying to give her something." Some time later Rennie witnesses an old woman on Ste. Agathe applying her healing powers to a tourist, and she too "wants to know what it feels like, she wants to put herself into the care of those magic hands." Immediately afterwards she quite literally puts herself into Paul's hands—he "reaches down for her. She takes hold of his hands; she doesn't know where they're going"—and after she and Paul have become lovers, finds her hands being taken by a group of native girls.

It is Paul who serves as the agency whereby Rennie is at last restored to her own body. At first she is afraid that the scar left by her operation will repel him as it has Jake, but

these fears are dispelled when she perceives his actual reaction, and understands that "he's seen people a lot deader
than her." The lovemaking scene that follows implicates
Rennie's final coming to terms not only with her physical
self, but also with the certain consciousness of her own inevitable decline and death:

> He reaches out his hands and Rennie can't re-
> member ever having been touched before. No-
> body lives forever, who said you could? This
> much will have to do, this much is enough. She's
> open now, she's been opened, she's being drawn
> back down, she enters her body again and there's
> a moment of pain, incarnation, this may be only
> the body's desperation, a flareup, a last clutch at
> the world before the long slide into final illness
> and death; but meanwhile she's solid after all,
> she's still here on the earth, she's grateful, he's
> touching her, she can still be touched.

This quasi-mystical moment of "incarnation" represents
the bridging of the gap between mind and body that Rennie has recognized in the dream in which she perceives her
own body "under glass." Having discovered that contact
with the world is still possible, that she can after all be
touched, Rennie herself is enabled in her turn to "lay on
hands." She begins with Paul himself: "She owes him
something: he was the one who gave her back her body;
wasn't he? . . . Rennie puts her hands on him. It can be,
after all, a sort of comfort. A kindness."

But the process of enlightenment in which she is engaged
does not reach its termination even here. Rennie may have
become reconciled to the perpetual threat of physical malignancy within herself, but she has yet to confront a still
more terrifying form of malignancy in the world about
her, a spiritual cancer menacing her very conception of
what it is to be human in the first place. This is the capacity for cruelty which she briefly glimpsed in Toronto, while
researching her article on pornography, and which so profoundly disturbed her on that occasion that she refused to
pursue her investigations any further. Once again the process of discovery expresses itself symbolically as a journey
of descent, assuming the form this time of Rennie's physical incarceration in a subterranean cell on the Kafkaesque
charge of "suspicion." When she first visits Fort Industry
in the company of Dr. Minnow, the underground corridor
he shows her is "too much like a cellar for Rennie." It recalls the cellar to which she was confined by her grandmother for real or imagined misdemeanours, a punishment which as we have seen is both psychologically and
symbolically linked with her preference for surfaces over
depths. "When I was shut in the cellar I always sat on the
top stair," Rennie recalls in connection with the ordeals
to which she was subjected as a child. Here she is afforded
no such option.

Rennie shares her cell with Lora, a woman she regards as
different from herself in every respect. Lora is deeply immersed in the life of the island, not excluding its criminal
aspects, and displays nothing of Rennie's own fastidious
detachment; when the old native healer on Ste. Agathe is
wounded, for instance, it is Lora who washes the blood
from her face, whereas Rennie herself feels squeamish at
the sight of blood and wants only to be let "off the hook."

Thrust into each other's company, the two women pass
the time by recounting their personal experiences; much
of the novel, indeed, as the reader only now learns, has in
fact consisted in these narrations. Listening to her companion, Rennie is chagrined to discover that "Lora has
better stories" than herself, that she has undergone experiences whose lurid authenticity contrasts vividly with the
pseudo-existence that Rennie has been living. Lora, it
turns out, has actually been raised in cellars of one kind
and another, and she is therefore conversant with the
depths that Rennie has always shunned. She has picked
up certain tricks for survival in the course of her adventures, and Rennie is disgusted to learn that she is prostitut-
ing herself in order to secure minor concessions from the
prison guards. Although she realizes quickly enough that
she is hardly in a position to pass judgement on Lora, she
is still unable to overcome her repugnance. "She looks
down at her hands, which ought to contain comfort. Compassion. She ought to go over to Lora and put her arms
around her and pat her on the back, but she can't."

Rennie's attitude begins to undergo a transformation once
she understands where the rope that has been left in her
apartment in Toronto in fact leads. The rope has been
rather smugly exhibited to her by two police officers, ostensibly the personifications of civilized order, who while
waiting for her return have ensconced themselves in her
kitchen like the faceless stranger himself. One of these
men asks questions concerning Rennie's personal life and
habits that are not altogether innocent of malice, and may
indeed betray a supressed voyeuristic streak. Rennie encounters subsequent pairs of policemen, none of whom inspire much confidence, at the air terminal on St. Antoine,
at a bar, in the street outside her hotel, and in her own
hotel room when she is arrested on the charge of "suspicion." After the uprising on Ste. Agathe has been quelled,
the local police have rounded up the insurgents and "tied
the men up with ropes." Some time later a number of these
prisoners are tortured by their police guards in a courtyard dominated by a scaffold, a structure which, dating
back to the British occupation of the island, recalls the use
civilization makes of ropes as instruments of social regimentation. One prisoner, who turns out to be the deaf and
dumb man met earlier, is treated with particular ferocity:
"The man falls forward, he's kept from hitting the pavement by the ropes that link him to the other men." As she
witnesses this orgy of gratuitous cruelty Rennie is overwhelmed by a dark revelation of universal complicity in
evil:

> She's seen the man with the rope, now she knows
> what he looks like. She has been turned inside
> out, there's no longer a *here* and a *there*. Rennie
> understands for the first time that this is not nec-
> essarily a place she will get out of, ever. She is
> not exempt. Nobody is exempt from anything.

After this climactic vision, which subverts the categories
of inside and outside, of here and there, by which she has
hitherto sought to confer moral immunity on herself, Rennie can no longer deny her own involvement in anything.
Depths have become surfaces. The diagrammatic simplicity of the victor/victim dichotomy is undermined by the
consciousness that the roles can be reversed without in the

least affecting the essential structure of relationships. As Paul, in some ways Rennie's mentor in her journey towards enlightenment, has earlier remarked, "there's only people with power and people without power. Sometimes they change places, that's all."

But although this obliteration of the tidy distinctions upon which her existence has been founded leaves Rennie feeling fatally implicated in everything she sees, it also has its positive aspect. When, shortly after the torture episode, Lora too is savagely beaten by the prison guards, Rennie finally finds it within herself to acknowledge her essential kinship with her companion and embody that recognition in a concrete act. At first Lora's mangled face seems to be "the face of a stranger"—the mask of the "faceless stranger" that Rennie has been fleeing from throughout the novel—but then she realizes that "it's the face of Lora after all, there's no such thing as a faceless stranger, every face is someone's, it has a name." She uses her own saliva to wash the blood off Lora's face, as Lora herself has earlier washed the blood from the face of the old healer. After this,

> She's holding Lora's left hand, between both of her own, perfectly still, nothing is moving, and yet she knows she is pulling on the hand, as hard as she can, there's an invisible hole in the air. Lora is on the other side of it and she has to pull her through, she's gritting her teeth with the effort . . . this is a gift, this is the hardest thing she's ever done.

> She holds the hand, perfectly still, with all her strength. Surely, if she can only try hard enough, something will move and live again, something will get born.

Rennie is thus duplicating in her own way the act that Daniel performed for her sake some time before, laying on hands in order to bring another human being back to life. By so doing she rediscovers the hands she forfeited in her youth, "feel[ing] the shape of a hand in hers . . . there but not there. . . . It will always be there now." The consequence of this crucial act of midwifery would seem to be that "something" is indeed "born," if not Lora herself then the new "subversive" reporter Rennie, who is capable for the first time in her life of seeing things not as society pretends they are but as they are in reality. "What she sees has not altered; only the way she sees it. It's all exactly the same. Nothing is the same." What remains uncertain is whether this "rebirth" is a purely private, existential event only, or one that might bring some benefit to the rest of mankind.

A number of critics have debated the question of whether Rennie is actually released from prison or not, as well as that of whether Lora is literally restored to life through Rennie's ministrations. Atwood's convoluted narrative design seems expressly calculated to generate doubts as to the "reality" of the final episodes, and as Carrington points out the "paradoxical statements" with which the novel concludes "suggest that these scenes of rescue and return represent only a fantasy ascent from the dark underground of the dungeon." Without wishing to go too deeply into this question, I would suggest that Atwood,

in shifting to the future tense to describe Rennie's release, intends to introduce an element of formal ambiguity which is essential to her meaning. For the clear implication of the work is that Rennie, whether she is physically liberated from the prison or not, can never escape the knowledge of human evil which that prison has come to symbolize. At the same time the recognition of human kinship which finds positive expression in Rennie's effort to revive Lora is one whose redemptive value is entirely independent of its practical consequences. In a certain sense, then, it is irrelevant whether Rennie is liberated or not, or whether Lora is resuscitated or not. Rennie remains imprisoned within the malignant cell even if she is free, and is freed by the capacity to lay on hands even if she remains in prison. It is this paradox that explains the apparently contradictory statements with which the novel concludes: "She will never be rescued. She has already been rescued. She is not exempt. Instead she is lucky."

Bodily Harm is, as Atwood herself once described it, an "anti-thriller," and frustrates the reader's conditioned expectation that suspense will be resolved in the customary manner. This refusal to play the game would seem to be part and parcel of Atwood's didactic point, for the conventions of the thriller (or of any other popular genre) might also be seen as culturally transmitted moulds through which raw experience is crystallized, neutralized and packaged for general consumption. Writing about life as if it were susceptible to thriller treatment is not much different from treating life as if it were simply a potential photograph or film or series of "lifestyles" articles. It is another way of not seeing, of confining one's experience to a fraudulent surface, a way which is parodied by Rennie's own abbreviated technique for reading mystery stories. But murder is real, as is human evil in all its manifestations, and an unmediated encounter with the crude actuality of bodily harm entails the shattering of the conventionalized modes of perceiving the world that genres of this kind exemplify. Looked at from a certain point of view, then, *Bodily Harm* is a self-deconstructing novel, to use an unwieldy but perhaps useful term. When Atwood says that her book takes the components of the thriller genre "and then pulls them inside out, as you would a glove," it is clear that the process she is describing mirrors that through which her protagonist is "turned inside out" during her climactic moment of vision in the prison. In overturning the very convention it implicitly invokes, denying its own generic postulates, the book enacts on a formal level the more general process of subverting those illusory categories that distance the perceiver from the world and from herself: the distinctions between aggressors and victims, depths and surfaces, here and there, mind and body, "I" and "thou." The structural ambiguity of the novel thus serves to reinforce a moral message which is very far from ambiguous, that only through a process of radical subversion is it possible to confront the malignant cell that lurks both within and outside the self, and to recognize in it the stranger's face which is our own.

Earl G. Ingersoll   (essay date October 1991)

SOURCE: "Margaret Atwood's *Cat's Eye*: Re-Viewing

Women in a Postmodern World," in *Ariel: A Review of International English Literature,* Vol. 22, No. 4, October, 1991, pp. 17-27.

[In the following essay, Ingersoll analyzes what he perceives as the autobiographical elements in Cat's Eye.]

Although one finds evidence of postmodernism in the manipulation of popular forms such as the Gothic in *Lady Oracle* and science fiction in *The Handmaid's Tale, Cat's Eye* is Margaret Atwood's first full-fledged "postmodern" work. Always the wily evader of critics' pigeonholes, Atwood, in a recent interview, has denied the classification of her work as "postmodern." She expresses her own amused disdain towards the critical-academic world for its attraction to "isms" in the discourse of *Cat's Eye* when Elaine Risley visits the gallery where her retrospective show is to be mounted. Risley dismisses the paintings still on display: "I don't give a glance to what's still on the walls, I hate those neo-expressionist dirty greens and putrid oranges, post this, post that. Everything is post these days, as if we're just a footnote to something earlier that was real enough to have a name of its own." At the same time, this novel is clearly Atwood's most postmodern in its play with form—the fictional autobiography—and in its continual self-referentiality as a text.

At the centre of this postmodern text is Atwood's complex use of her own past. Few writers have spoken out so vehemently against readings of their work as autobiography. As her interviews indicate, she is very aware that her audience is bent upon biographical readings of her fiction. With obvious amusement she tells how in question-and-answer sessions following her public readings she has often just finished disclaiming autobiographical roots for her characters when someone in her audience asks if she was overweight as a child like Joan in *Lady Oracle* or anorexic as a young woman like the unnamed narrator of *The Edible Woman.* For Atwood, there are clearly gender implications here since, as she has argued, women have traditionally been thought so imaginatively impoverished that all they could write about was themselves.

At the same time, although there is no Atwood biography—and she would be one of the last writers to authorize one—she is among the most interviewed contemporary writers. Thus, as she herself must know, serious readers of her work are familiar enough with the outlines of her family and her early life to be enticed into seeing the painter Elaine Risley—that stereotyped persona of modernist fiction—as at least partly her own reflection. Obviously she is not; and yet she *is,* despite the curious warning on the copyright page which reads in part as follows:

> This is a work of fiction. Although its form is that of an autobiography, it is not one. . . . with the exception of public figures, any resemblance to persons living or dead is purely coincidental. The opinions expressed are those of the characters and should not be confused with the author's.

It is easy enough to see that Atwood is attempting to protect herself from potential legal action generated by former friends or associates who might choose to see themselves as models for the less appealing characters in *Cat's Eye.* However, the attempt to deny *any* connection with Elaine Risley must encourage the reader to suspect that the lady doth protest too much. In this way, part of the enjoyment of this text involves a shifting back and forth between invention and the facts of the inventor's past.

Atwood has provided her audience with so many of those facts of her early life that it is next to impossible for the informed reader to dismiss as coincidental the roots of Elaine's childhood in Atwood's. She has told her interviewers, for example, about the summers she spent as a child living in tents and motels while the family accompanied her father, an entomologist, doing research in the Canadian north. On more than one occasion she has described to her interviewers how she and her brother would help their father collect insects he shook from trees. In this context, given the writer's having gone on record as frustrated with her audience's misguided autobiographical readings of her earlier work, it is difficult not to conclude that *Cat's Eye* is, among many things, a highly sophisticated expression of play with her audience's expectations. Atwood may plead ignorance of contemporary critical theory, but she is undercutting the conventional notion that autobiography privileges an autobiographical fiction as more truthful than other forms of fiction. She shows us in Elaine Risley, a painter/writer who may seem in a conventional sense to be exploring the truth of her past but who in a truer sense is creating, or writing, a past as she chooses now to see it, rather than as it might have once existed.

The novel begins with a definition of time, justified perhaps by Risley's having returned to Toronto, her home, for a retrospective exhibition of her art. She dismisses linear time in favor of "time as having a shape . . . , like a series of liquid transparencies . . . You don't look back along time but down through it, like water. Sometimes this comes to the surface, sometimes that, sometimes nothing. Nothing goes away." In the story she tells of her youth, Elaine offers a retrospective of the woman she has been and the women who have been important to her as she now sees herself and them. That past is very much seen through the cat's eye marble into which Elaine looked at eight and saw her future as an artist. The image of the cat's eye is central, since it represents a world into which she has been allowed access; at the same time, it is a world of inevitably distorted vision. Thus, the truth is not an entity to which we struggle to gain access so much as a way of looking and, in the process, creating the text of that truth.

Elaine Risley's retrospective allows her to re-view the people and relationships that have been important to the first fifty years of her life. In reconstructing her past—or the critical years from age eight to young womanhood—Elaine Risley is in large part deconstructing that past. The consequences of that deconstruction—what turns out to be the novel itself—is a complicated series of transformations through which the persona discovers that the past is only what we continue to reconstruct for the purposes of the present. And perhaps beyond that, Elaine Risley discovers that of all her relationships—with the opposite sex and with her own—the most important may have been the strange friendship with her tormentor/double Cordelia. By the end of the narrative, the persona will have finally exorcised the spirit of an alter ego who was perhaps primarily *that,* another self whom she no longer needs to fear, hate, or even love.

The focus of the early chapters is the very young Elaine Risley's struggle to find models in the two women who are crucial to her formative years. She begins her retrospective with her eighth birthday, a not surprising age for the onset of consciousness. For Risley, like Atwood, this was the time of her move to Toronto, and for Risley at least the end of happiness. Through the move to Toronto, a backwater of civilization in the 1940s, but still civilization, Elaine as a child is suddenly forced to confront "femininity." Having lived in tents and motels, she and her mother must don the costumes and the roles appropriate to their gender and put away their unfeminine clothes and ungendered roles until the warm weather when they return to the North. Overnight Elaine feels like an alien from another planet. The future of painful socialization is represented by the doorway in her new school marked "GIRLS," the doorway which makes her wonder what the other one marked "BOYS" has behind it from which she has been shut out.

We might expect Elaine to cherish the memory of a paradise lost of relatively ungendered life as a child in nature. Instead, she feels guilty for being unprepared to operate in a world of mothers who are housekeepers preoccupied with clothes and labour-saving devices. Although the mature Elaine mutes the resentment, the child Elaine suspects that her mother has failed her as the role model needed to help her find her way in a world of "twin sets" and wearing hats to church. The young Elaine's inability to fault the mother she loves forces her to internalize as guilt her sense of inadequacy. If she is suffering the pain of being out of place, it must be something that is wrong with *her;* certainly it cannot be anything wrong with the definition of womanhood embodied in the mothers of her friends, Cordelia, Carol, but especially Grace Smeath.

Clearly Mrs. Smeath is the Bad Mother that Elaine suspects her own mother of being for not having prepared her for socialization. In the Smeath household, Elaine and her friends are involved in that socialization; they study to be future housewives by cutting out pictures of "frying pans and washing machines" to paste into scrapbooks for their "ladies." A more important aspect of that socialization is represented by regular attendance at church. When the Smeaths invite Elaine to join them for the first of what eventually seems an endless series of Sundays, Atwood describes the interior of the church through the eyes of the young Elaine who might as well be a creature from Mars. One feature that becomes crucially important to Elaine are the inscriptions under the stained-glass pictures of Jesus—"SUFFER • THE • LITTLE • CHILDREN"— and of Mary—"THE • GREATEST • OF • THESE • IS • CHARITY."

Because she feels radically incapable of fitting into the world outside her home, Elaine becomes the victim of Cordelia's sadistic punishments for her incompetence as a student of womanhood. These punishments, which range from reprimands and shunnings to being buried alive, culminate in the scene of Elaine's almost freezing to death in a nearby ravine where Cordelia has thrown her hat. This is a ravine where *"men"* lurk to molest careless little girls. It is Elaine's victimization at the hands of other little girls, not those mysteriously dangerous men, which leads her to the nervous reaction of peeling the skin off her feet and hands, almost as though she is studying to become a child martyr by flaying herself alive. She is saved, she convinces herself, not so much by her own mother as by the apparition of the ultimate Good Mother, the Virgin Mary.

Mrs. Risley and Mrs. Smeath function then as variants of the Good Mother and the Bad Mother. Elaine's mother suspects that Cordelia and the other girls are tormenting her daughter, but she assumes that Elaine can tell her the truth and she never notices the marks of Elaine's flaying herself. Mrs. Smeath, on the other hand, *knows* that Elaine is being tormented but does nothing. In fact, Mrs. Smeath even *knows* that Elaine has overheard her saying that Elaine *deserves* to be punished for being at heart a graceless heathen. It is not until Elaine almost dies that Mrs. Risley acts. Somewhere down in the pool of the past lurks the monster of resentment against this Good Mother who should have known and acted sooner. Mrs. Risley becomes the representation, like her husband, of the well-intentioned, virtuous, but not terribly effective liberal humanists who *sense* that evil exists but refuse to acknowledge it, since a knowledge of evil would force them to find a place for it in their world.

Mrs. Smeath, on the other hand, is much easier for Elaine to deal with. Even as a child, Elaine can clearly see Mrs. Smeath's evil in the transparent world of that cat's eye which will be the emblem of her insight as an artist. She comes to see the crucial difference *within* Mrs. Smeath as a woman who professes to being a Christian—"SUFFER • THE • LITTLE • CHILDREN" and "THE • GREATEST • OF • THESE • IS • CHARITY"—yet believes that the greatest charity to little children who happen to be "heathens" is to make them indeed suffer. And, it is very much to the point that the individual who functions as Elaine's Muse is Mrs. Smeath, *not* Mrs. Risley. This variety of the Bad Mother, more in line with Freud's reality principle, generates a whole series of paintings through which Elaine vents her anger, hatred, and malice. Mrs. Smeath as the bad mother may very well represent much of what she finds most despicable in the conventional notion of Woman. At the same time, it is an evil which generates art and it is that art which liberates her from a self enslaved in anger towards and hatred of that image of "Woman."

That same indeterminacy is evident in Elaine's bizarre relationship with Cordelia. When she declares her independence, following Cordelia's move to another school, Elaine becomes powerful, assertive, verbally aggressive, and Cordelia fades into powerlessness, into the kind of silence which was Elaine's position early on in this power struggle veiled as a friendship. Elaine's enjoyment of a new facility with words, as though her tongue has been empowered by her earlier victimization, makes it clear how important the element of the retrospective is in this text. Told in a traditionally chronological fashion, Elaine's empowerment through language would have led the reader to anticipate that she would become a writer, rather than a painter.

In this symbiotic relationship, Elaine's friend/persecutor is given the name Cordelia. Most readers sense the irony in Atwood's borrowing the name of one of Shakespeare's innocent tragic heroines, but there are also implications of a transfer being transacted here. In the years following the Second World War, *King Lear* became one of our most attractive cultural myths in part because Cordelia reminds us how the innocent are swept up in the destruction of war and civil disorder and perhaps also that the innocent embody the redemptive power of love. At the same time, it is the refusal of Lear's single faithful daughter to speak, just as much as her sisters' hypocritical flattery, which sets in motion the machinery of conflict and destruction by which she and her family are overwhelmed. In this sense, Elaine, perhaps following her mother's example, is somewhat like Cordelia, choosing silence and martyrdom rather than risk the anxiety and guilt of self-assertion. Eventually, anger and resentment find their sublimated or socialized modes of expression, first in her verbal assaults on the imperfections of others and finally in her art, so often a visualization of her anguish at the hands of her tormentors.

More than anyone else, Cordelia is the one from whom she must free herself by acknowledging not only difference but kinship. Cordelia *is* a "secret sharer." Like her readers, Elaine keeps expecting her former tormentor to show up at the gallery, the most appropriate ghost to appear in this retrospective. Cordelia, however, does not need to appear: Elaine has already exorcized much of the guilt, hatred, and anger generated in her relationships with Mrs. Smeath and Cordelia through her art, conveniently brought together so that the artist, like her audience, can read this retrospective as a testimony to the transformative power of art. When Elaine returns to the bridge, the power of her creative consciousness calls up an apparition of Cordelia from the deeps of that pool of time with which we began. She tells us:

> I know she's looking at me, the lopsided mouth smiling a little, the face closed and defiant. There is the same shame, the sick feeling in my body, the same knowledge of my own wrongness, awkwardness, weakness; the same wish to be loved; the same loneliness; the same fear. But these are not my own emotions any more. They are Cordelia's; as they always were.
>
> I am the older now, I'm the stronger. If she stays here any longer she will freeze to death; she will be left behind, in the wrong time. It's almost too late.
>
> I reach out my arms to her, bend down, hands open to show I have no weapon. *It's all right,* I say to her. *You can go home now.*

In a strange and unexpected sense, Cordelia has become her name. Just as Elaine earlier was rescued from physical death in the icy stream below this bridge, this time she ac-

knowledges another variety of rescue. She confirms what this retrospective has been moving toward all along—the recognition that her art has rescued her from the spiritual death of a lifetime wasted in anger and resentment. Having recognized the power of Cordelia within herself, Elaine can at last release the Cordelia she has made to appear in the final hours before she prepares to leave home again. Perhaps she recognizes also that she and Cordelia had identities less distinct from each other than it seemed in childhood, that each had been fashioning the other in the image of a self she could not otherwise confront. Now Elaine herself can be a variety of the "Good Mother" and simply send Cordelia home before she freezes to death in "the wrong time."

In the end, *Cat's Eye* is postmodern in several interrelated ways. Atwood offers the informed reader the lure of a few well-known features of her own childhood and then proceeds to invent an autobiography which is the experience of Elaine Risley, a character who may bear only the most superficial similarities. Autobiography, even when intended, is obviously enough only another form of fiction. By offering us, in the words of the novel's preliminary note, a work of fiction whose form is that of an autobiography, she gives us a text which confirms that truth by showing how Elaine Risley has invented herself, constructed an autobiography, through her art. Elaine is even allowed to be amused by her critics' (mis)readings of her painting, one of whom writes of Risley's "disconcerting deconstruction of perceived gender and its relationship to perceived power, especially in respect to numinous imagery."

In addition, this text raises questions about the representation of women, about writing as a woman, about autobiography, and about mothers and daughters. As Barbara Johnson has argued, autobiography and its reflection in autobiographical fiction are a supplanting of the mother, a kind of giving birth to oneself through the creation of the text. Using the classic text of Mary Shelley's *Frankenstein,* Johnson argues that what a woman writer (the very term "woman writer" has traditionally been conceived of as a "freak of nature") creates has conventionally seemed a "monster." Johnson asks: "Is autobiography somehow always in the process of symbolically killing the mother off by telling her the lie that we have given birth to ourselves?" In telling us the story of her life, Elaine Risley foregrounds Cordelia as a monster only to show how she freed herself from Cordelia to become as a young woman monstrous in her own way, and appropriately, through *language,* with her "mean mouth." She offers us in Mrs. Smeath, the Bad Mother, whom she subsumes psychologically in her art, a kind of monstrosity which exorcizes the monstrous complicity of Mrs. Smeath in her persecution by Cordelia and the other girls. And she offers us in Mrs. Risley, the Good Mother, a failed guide to the intricacies of femininity in the outside world and, therefore, a mother who must be killed off before Elaine can achieve selfhood at fifty.

Why, we might ask, has it taken Elaine so long to give birth to herself, the sort of act managed by the Paul Morels and the Stephen Dedaluses of modernist fiction by their twenty-fifth birthdays? Part of the answer is obvious in the question. Elaine Risley is a female rather than a male character. In this context, a good analogue is Virginia Woolf who was well aware that she could not begin work on *To the Lighthouse,* dealing in part with the loss of her mother, until she was in her forties. As we have learned from sociologists like Nancy Chodorow, women must struggle to achieve a sense of self separate from others, in part because they are "mothered" or nurtured primarily by women. In this vein, Chodorow argues, mothers see themselves as continuous with their daughters:

> Because they are the same gender as their daughters and have been girls, mothers of daughters tend not to experience these infant daughters as separate from them in the same way as mothers of infant sons. In both cases, a mother is likely to experience a sense of oneness and continuity with her infant. However, this sense is stronger, and lasts longer, vis-à-vis daughters.

In these ways, the retrospective of her art is partly an invention to allow Elaine to achieve a sense of self, distinct from both Mrs. Risley and Mrs. Smeath. It is also a belated recognition of her mothering herself as the child and the young woman Elaine as well as her mothering of Cordelia whom she now can release from her hatred and her love. Having completed this retrospective of her life and given birth to herself, Elaine can acknowledge the separateness of her "daughters"—both the girl she was and Cordelia as her "other." At the risk of increasing Atwood's anxiety with yet another autobiographical reading of her fiction, it might be recalled that *Cat's Eye* is the revision and completion of a manuscript she began in her mid-twenties and finished as she approached her fiftieth birthday. Despite Margaret Atwood's disclaimer that the novel is not autobiographical, it is a text performing itself as a text, a text of the author's own struggle to achieve selfhood as a woman and as an artist.

Marilyn Patton   (essay date October 1991)

SOURCE: " 'Lady Oracle': The Politics of the Body," in *Ariel: A Review of International English Literature,* Vol. 22, No. 4, October, 1991, pp. 29-48.

[*In the following essay, Patton analyzes Atwood's use of goddess mythology in* Lady Oracle.]

> I search instead for the others
> the ones left over,
> the ones who have escaped from these
> mythologies with barely their lives

Margaret Atwood wrote these words as if they were spoken by the Circe persona in the "Circe/Mud Poems" section of her book of poetry called *You Are Happy.* Atwood's career as poet, storyteller, and critic has been a coming to terms with "these mythologies," a general term for myths about women and myths about gender relations which have been inscribed in our literature. Her career has been also a search for an escape from "these mythologies." Although numerous critics have analyzed Atwood's work with myths about women, their readings have been limited to primarily psychological interpretations. For the many

women who have escaped "with barely their lives," however, cultural myths about women are very much a form of "power politics." To do justice to Atwood's work, we must look beyond psychology to the politics of her work with—and against—myth.

By far the most potent myth in Atwood's imagination has been the White Goddess, a multi-faceted myth which reflects socially constructed images of women's roles. Ever since Atwood's first reading of Robert Graves's book, *The White Goddess,* when she was of college age, this Goddess has shadowed her thinking. One could easily argue that even her most recent novel, *Cat's Eye* (1988), is a reworking of goddess images. In fact, while she was working on *Cat's Eye* which is a novel of retrospectives, Atwood wrote a retrospective on her own career for *Ms.* magazine's fifteenth-anniversary issue. She described the influence of the Goddess:

> I read Robert Graves' *The White Goddess* which . . . terrified me. Graves . . . placed women right at the center of his poetic theory, but they were to be inspirations rather than creators . . . . They were to be incarnations of the White Goddess herself, alternatively loving and destructive. . . . A woman just might— might, mind you—have a chance of becoming a decent poet, but only if she took on the attributes of the White Goddess and spent her time seducing men and then doing them in. . . . White Goddess did not have time for children, being too taken up with cannibalistic sex.

The depth of Atwood's early obsession with this Goddess can be assessed by noting that her unpublished doctoral dissertation, "Nature and Power in the English Metaphysical Romance of the Nineteenth and Twentieth Centuries" (Atwood Papers), revolves around the idea of supernatural women and goddesses as manifestations of ideas about nature. Remnants of this thesis are visible in published materials such as **"Superwoman Drawn and Quartered: The Early Forms of *She"*** and **"The Curse of Eve,"** as well as the chapter on fictional women in *Survival,* her survey of Canadian literature. *Double Persephone,* Atwood's first collection of poetry, reflects the Demeter/Persephone myth, while other poetry, especially the "Circe/Mud Poems," utilizes the Goddess figure.

Robert Graves's version of the Goddess is a figure descended from earth mothers and grain goddesses from the matriarchal past, yet she often eats children, even her own. As Artemis or Diana, one of her major "incarnations," she is associated with the moon, and therefore is seen in three phases: virginity, fecundity, and hag. The Goddess is ambivalent, "both lovely and cruel, ugly and kind." Most important for Graves, she is *the* Muse, worshipped by all great poets. "Woman," writes Graves, "is not a poet: she is either a silent muse or she is nothing." The domestic is the enemy of the poetic for Graves; the worst thing that could happen to a poet would be that some "domestic Woman" would turn him into a "domesticated man." "The White Goddess is anti-domestic," he writes; "she is the perpetual 'other woman.' "

The myth of the White Goddess condenses, as myths do, many of the deepest, often unarticulated fears of women and men. Atwood's project is in part to articulate, to give form to, those fears—through reworking images of the Goddess. In her own versions of the Goddess, Atwood condenses fears of being large and fat, fears of being powerful, fears of devouring or overpowering lovers and children, and the fear of being a writer. Finally, because she is the Triple Goddess, of multiple identities, she represents the difficulty of coming to a sense of one "true" single identity, the Self, a goal which Western culture has invoked as the great desideratum.

Evidence in the Atwood collection of manuscript drafts and files of research materials (in the Thomas Fisher Rare Book Library) indicates that Atwood's novels are written both in terms of and also "against" the Goddess. I read Atwood's work as an attempt to come to grips with the hidden agendas of patriarchy, with socially constructed myths about women. Thinking back to Barthes's definitions of myths in *Mythologies,* that myth is "depoliticized speech" which "has the task of giving an historical intention a natural justification, and making contingency appear eternal," then the myth of the White Goddess represents exactly the sort of "depoliticized speech" which has historically been used to define, limit, and disempower women. She is one major instance of the myths, legends, and texts which have been used as tools in women's subordination. Atwood has begun to deconstruct, historicize, and reappropriate the myth of the Goddess; she has begun, in short, to politicize it.

While in her first novel, *The Edible Woman* (1969), Margaret Atwood transformed Robert Graves's fearsome "White Goddess" into a "delicious" cake, *Lady Oracle* (1976) represents a second major attempt to deal with the Goddess, who is in this text more powerful than ever before. Atwood comes to terms with the most terrifying aspect of the Goddess in the Graves text, the devouring, powerful cannibalistic Venus who mates with men and eats them. She is the power of nature made visible, and the poet's necessary muse.

Lady Oracle is a representation of the narrator's attempt to act out the role of the Goddess. By having her narrator become the Goddess, Margaret Atwood takes on the issue of cultural control of women (and women's bodies) as represented in literature and in prescribed images or roles for women; she does combat with Graves in particular and patriarchy in general. Atwood's reading of Graves emphasizes two aspects: the cannibalistic nature of the Goddess and her role as silent Muse. The poetic vocation is thus a key to *Lady Oracle,* and a continuation of the discussion about the relationship between the artist and her world raised in *Surfacing,* Atwood's second novel. How can a woman inhabit the space of literature without being overwhelmed by the ideological preconceptions of that literature? How can a modern woman live without becoming a victim of the ideological constructs of the Western world?

Lady Oracle, Atwood's third novel, is about the eating woman. The heroine, Joan Delacourt Foster, is an avid consumer who literalizes the "oral" in "oracle." As a noticeably overweight child, she imagines her mother's image of her, which "must have been a one-hole object,

like an inner tube, that took things in at one end but didn't let them out at the other." As she grew older, her mother "was tired of having a teen-aged daughter who looked like a beluga whale and never opened her mouth except to put something in it." Although Joan diets away her one hundred pounds of excess weight, she is occasionally haunted by nightmares of her fat childhood body and by meeting people who might remember her "Before" self. She earns her living writing "Costume Gothics," formulaic romance novels; sections of her latest book, *Stalked By Love,* are interpolated into *Lady Oracle.*

Joan's husband, a serious academic and political radical, does not even know about her Gothic romances; he also does not know that she is having an affair with "The Royal Porcupine," an avant-garde artist. He does know that she is becoming famous for a book published under her married name, a volume of automatic-writing poetry called *Lady Oracle.* Then a blackmailer threatens to reveal Joan's multiple identities. In an effort to disentangle herself from her complicated life, she enacts an imitation drowning death, flies to Italy, and buries her wet "drowning" costume, planning to begin a new life as easily as she usually begins writing a new book.

The Goddess is such a significant image to *Lady Oracle* that Atwood's research materials for the novel consist primarily of photocopied articles and references to the Goddess and to the Sibyl (another form of the Goddess). Basing my analysis upon the materials in these files, I argue against purely psychological explanations of Atwood's *use* of the mythological material, the route chosen by critics such as Barbara Godard, Roberta Sciff-Zamaro, and Sherrill Grace. Rather, the Goddess has both political and aesthetic dimensions for Atwood—she represents women's fears, but she also represents cultural constructions of women's roles. As Susan J. Rosowski notes, "In *Lady Oracle,* Atwood turns this tradition back upon itself, confronting the Gothic dimensions that exist within our social mythology" because "[o]nce established, fictional constructs become impervious to human reality."

Perhaps the most striking item in Atwood's research materials for *Lady Oracle* is the photocopy of a photo of a statue of the Goddess, labelled "Mother Nature," but generally known as the Artemis of Ephesus. This statue is, serendipitously, located within the enormous maze of the Villa d'Este, which she calls in her screenplay version of *Lady Oracle,* "the Tivoli Gardens, built by a Renaissance Cardinal for his dirty-weekend-palace. The Gardens are filled with statues that squirt water from various orifices of their bodies, run by hydraulic pressure." Atwood uses this figure in the published novel as part of the scenery. On a vacation in Italy, Arthur and Joan are wandering in the Villa D'Este when they suddenly come upon the Goddess:

> She had a serene face, perched on top of a body shaped like a mound of grapes. She was draped in breasts from neck to ankle, as though afflicted with a case of yaws: little breasts at the top and bottom, big ones around the middle. The nipples were equipped with spouts, but several of the breasts were out of order.

This is a significantly more provocative image of the White Goddess than that in the Graves text; Graves stresses the role of the Goddess as a beautiful muse and as a destroyer of men and children, but ignores her "nature goddess" shape. If we think critically about this passage, what stands out is the difference between the "serene" head and the incredibly grotesque body. Unlike the other statues in the Gardens, with normal human bodies attached to normal human heads, this monstrosity encapsulates the complete lack of fit between mind and body. The contrast emphasizes "Mother Nature's" (and woman's) alienation from her own body, as if the female function of the body (childbearing and breast-feeding) had gone completely out of control, usurping every other function. To have breasts, to be female, is compared by Atwood to a disease, yaws. And the unreliability of the female body is emphasized by the note that "several of the breasts were out of order." This cultural limitation of the female body is part of what troubles Joan Foster.

Chapter 25 of the published version of **Lady Oracle** concludes with the passage quoted above followed by a short paragraph in which the narrator says that she

> stood licking my ice-cream cone, watching the goddess coldly. Once I would have seen her as an image of myself, but not any more. My ability to give was limited, I was not inexhaustible. I was not serene, not really. I wanted things, for myself.

The complacent and distant attitude of the narrator in this published version is a reworking of a page of loose typescript in the files for **Lady Oracle** which gives a much more troubled version of this scene. It is apparent in the published version that Atwood has chosen to define the narrator as a person whose personal boundaries and self-definition are clear. In quite an opposite way the *unpublished* material emphasizes the conflicts, fears, and desires of Joan Delacourt Foster.

> If two breasts are a virtue in woman, why not three, why not a hundred? We stood hand in hand, licking up the last of our vanilla ice cream, regarding the goddess, who did not regard us. Her head rose from its nest of breasts like the head of a beautiful leper. What prayers could be addressed to such a deity? Something easy for the breasts to understand for the head was merely human, the body divine, its deformity made this obvious. Something repetitive and monosyllabic. Give. Give.

The interesting complexity in this section is that the point of view is not strictly limited. There is a dangerous sympathy with the Goddess, a connection that is too close. The narrator seems to be in part imagining herself as the Goddess, constantly asked to "Give. Give."

The emotional entanglement is signalled by the complex, contradictory language, the oxymoronic phrases: "a beautiful leper," the "body divine [because of] its deformity." The conflicting, intertwined emotions, the fear that one *is* the Goddess, the longing *for* the Goddess, the desire to escape *from* the Goddess, are all captured here. The very complexity of point of view, the multiple, mutually antag-

onistic desires suggest that the character of Joan Delacourt Foster which finally emerges in the published novel is in some sense a distillation of even wilder and less controlled versions.

The unpublished quotation continues in an even more vivid imaginative sequence:

> An image of inexhaustibility, and you looked at her with a certain longing, or so I imagined. Yet several of the breasts were not working, and the rest merely dribbled; think about that, the next time you treat a woman as the incarnation of the dream of largesse, and that goes for both of you. I know that I was two things for you, what you saw and what you would rather have seen; but how can I complain? We are never adequate to the dreams of others and these dreams infest our lives, like termites, like bloodworms. Any of these dreams come true would be a monster. Who carved this goddess? I can imagine her coming to life, reeling topheavily down the street, every breast wobbling, sprinkling lawns and flower borders as she passes, like a new portable irrigation system, her nurturing face twisted into a different expression, rage, the desire for revenge, seeking her creator. Women scream, men laugh in [page ends]

Leaving aside the issue of the addressee, the emotional weight of this passage in the final lines is terror, "women scream," a cry that may or may not have been displaced from the narrator onto other women. The terror is both personal and generic, both generalized fear of the Goddess as a "type," and also the particular fear of the narrator. The Goddess resembles not just a mythological figure, but also Joan's own former self, "reeling topheavily down the street." The Goddess is a terrible vision because of her "rage," "the desire for revenge." She is monstrous and linked to monsters—yet as a mythological archetype she is supposed to be *the* female, that which is part of, or a possibility in, every woman. Paradoxically, the narrator's fear is mixed with, as she says, "a certain longing," associated with the fact that she is "licking up the last of [her] ice cream," and worrying that the breasts are not inexhaustible. But these desires are repressed. The longing for breast milk, while licking on the breast-shaped and disappearing ice-cream cone, is transformed in the published version into an association with cold rather than nourishment, as the narrator watches "the goddess coldly."

We can see the degree to which the Goddess figure becomes a generalized "sign" of myths about women by connecting this unpublished material to Joan's attempt to bury her clothes, her former identity. The heroine has dug a hole under her rented "villa" in Italy in order to bury the wet clothes that were evidence of her faked death. Then she begins to imagine that the clothes are a buried body and that she is a murderer: "The clothes were my own, I hadn't done anything wrong, but I still felt as though I was getting rid of a body, the corpse of someone I'd killed." In fact, three hundred pages later, the clothes do return to haunt her. Her landlord's father digs them up and returns them, revealing the fact that he and the townspeople had been aware of her "buried" identity all along. But just before Mr. Vitroni returns the clothes, Joan has a revealing nightmare which ties together the buried clothes, her imaginary buried "body," and her vision of herself as fat.

> Below me, in the foundations of the house, I could hear the clothes I'd buried there growing themselves a body. It was almost completed; it was digging itself out, like a huge blind mole, slowly and painfully shambling up the hill to the balcony . . . a creature composed of all the flesh that used to be mine and which must have gone somewhere. It would have no features, it would be smooth as a potato, pale as starch, it would look like a big thigh, it would have a face like a breast minus the nipple. (ellipses in original)

The text has conflated the buried or murdered "body" with Joan's dieted-off fat. But there is also a striking similarity between "the creature composed of all the flesh that used to be mine" and the Goddess partially suppressed earlier, who came "reeling topheavily down the street," making every woman scream. The multiple breasts have been turned into a "face like a breast minus the nipple." She is enormously fat, featureless, wandering blindly "like a huge mole" as if she were magnetically attracted to Joan, as if she *were* Joan.

These passages constitute a climax to Atwood's ongoing obsession with the function of the Goddess as a "sign" of "woman" and of female possibility. They signify the terror of women, their fear that their own female bodies will overpower their minds, will search them out and destroy their lives—or that their bodies will become alienated from their heads, that their bodies will be "composed of flesh" which will "have no features." What is common to all of these terrifying images is the exaggerated size, the inhuman disproportion of the breast-covered Goddess, as if the fact of having a female body overpowered any other personal characteristics. As Atwood noted so clearly in her 1987 retrospective, **"Great Unexpectations,"** the images of what a woman could be scared her "to death." If women actually incarnated the characteristics attributed to them in myths such as the White Goddess, then one would not want to be female.

What is perhaps most significant, then, in the Artemis of Ephesus statue and in Atwood's writing about that statue is what we might call its "essentialism," that it *reduces* "Nature" to "Woman" (and "Woman" to "Nature"), that it defines both "Woman" and "Nature" by one characteristic (nourishment), and that the result is completely grotesque. It is as if Atwood took the most ludicrous examples of women embodying nature in the nineteenth-century romances she had studied in her doctoral dissertation, and then pushed those even further towards the grotesque. In a similar fashion, the philosophical import of Joan's childhood and adolescent obesity (and of her adult obsession with that discarded "Fat Lady") is that it is a sign, a grotesque reduction, of an individual to one single characteristic which erases all other meanings. This essentialism is perfectly incarnated in Joan's nightmare of the "body" which the clothes have grown, which has "no features," is "smooth as a potato," with "a face like a breast minus the nipple." As Molly Hite remarks, "this is a book in which fat is a feminist issue, and in which excess of body becomes symbolic of female resistance to a society that wishes to constrict women to dimensions it deems appropriate."

I have argued that Atwood sees amazing power in the White Goddess, but that in *Lady Oracle* she manages to take control over the goddess by rendering her powerless, even ridiculous. The "Fat Lady" in the pink skating costume, the sequence in which Felicia turns fat, the comic incident with the arrow in Joan's rear end, even—perhaps especially—the scene in which Joan and Arthur lick ice cream cones in front of the Goddess; these all appropriate and domesticate the Goddess. The powerless Goddess is even found inside of Joan's Costume Gothic, *Stalked by Love,* disguised as one of four women who sits in the maze; she is the one who is "enormously fat." The novel both constructs the Goddess and trivializes her, takes power over her, uses her. She may be a sign, but she is also just a sign.

Earlier I defined the myth of the White Goddess, using Barthes's terminology, as "depoliticized speech" which "has the task of giving an historical intention a natural justification, and making contingency appear eternal." Atwood's approach to mythologizing and essentializing of "woman" is to appropriate, deconstruct and domesticate that myth. Using Susan McKinstry's observation that Joan "is, precisely, a character" who has turned herself into fiction, we can see this manoeuvre as *political,* as turning the powerful Goddess into a figure one can control, manipulate, and parody. When Judith McCombs writes of *Lady Oracle* that "this is myth and genre upside-down, reflexive, parodied," one can think about those moves (parody, turning a genre upside-down) as acts of appropriation of cultural myths about women. If we look at the context in which Atwood wrote the novel, it is clear that the story may be interpreted as political, as taking seriously the social construction of "woman," especially the goddess figure, and rendering that construction powerless.

Thus far, I have noted the stimulating effect which the figure of the Goddess has on Atwood's imagination and have pointed towards evidence that this figure represents a kind of uncontrolled power which the text both uses and attempts to contain. The problem with the Goddess figure, as represented up until now, is her silence. Each image of the Goddess is speechless, inarticulate. She may have an expressive face, but she never shouts, curses, or yells, much less writes. She is, in short, Graves's perfect White Goddess, completely the Muse, never the inspired, never the poet.

Atwood solves the problem of the silenced Goddess by giving her a voice—by turning her into Joan Foster, author. We readers hear the Goddess speak through Joan. She tells us, at least, her side(s) of the story. Atwood's act of giving voice to the Goddess, her destruction of the myth of the silent Goddess, is enabled to some extent by additional material about the Goddess provided by her researcher. While one aspect of "woman" is epitomized by the silent statue, reduced to the single function of nurturing, other attributes are possible. The research file contains numerous entries from encyclopedias, dictionaries, and classical works which emphasize the role of the Goddess as "Sibyl," her position as "oracle." It includes excerpts from Virgil's *Aeneid* and Ovid's *Metamorphoses* (Book XIV), both of which concern the incident in which Aeneas consults the Sibyl in order to discover how to find his dead father's shade; the Sibyl gives information and prophesies at length. Some of the references discuss Diana or Artemis; others mention the Delphic oracle, naming Daphnis and Pythia; Ovid and Virgil simply call her "Sibyl."

Other names for the Goddess were Proserprine and Hecate, and the research even includes sketches of two statues of this triple Goddess. One entry notes that the "most famous of her temples was that of Ephesus. . . . She was there represented with a great number of breasts, and other symbols which signified the earth, or Cybele." The entry concludes with remarks that allude to a certain bloodthirstiness on the part of the Goddess, that some worshippers "cruelly offered on her altar all the strangers that were shipwrecked on their coasts" and that she "had some oracles."

Another entry from the *Classical Dictionary,* on "Pythia," describes in detail how "Pythia, the priestess of Apollo at Delphi" would deliver her oracle:

> . . . she was supposed to be suddenly inspired by the sulphureous vapours which issued from the hole of a subterranean cavity within the temple, over which she sat bare on a three-legged stool, called a tripod. In this stool was a small aperture, through which the vapour was inhaled by the priestess, at the divine inspiration, her eye suddenly sparkled, her hair stood on end, and a shivering ran over all her body. In this convulsive state she spoke the oracles of the god, often with loud howlings and cries, and her articulations were taken down by the priest, and set in order.

The similarity between Pythia's inspiration and Joan's "automatic writing" of "Lady Oracle" is quite striking; it is clear that Joan is acting as a sort of oracle. Her three-sided mirror substitutes for the tripod, the candle for the vapour, and her automatic writing takes the place of the priest.

But Joan is also partly modelled upon the Cumean Sibyl, an oracle of Apollo who spoke to Aeneas. Atwood used this excerpt from the C. Day Lewis translation of the *Aeneid,* with the Sibyl speaking from a cave:

> The Sibyl cried, "for lo! the god is with me. And speaking /
> There by the threshold, her features, her colours were all at once /
> Different, her hair flew wildly about; her breast was heaving, /
> Her fey heart swelled in ecstasy; larger than life she seemed, /
> More than mortal her utterance:

The significance of this Sibyl is that she is able to lead Aeneas into the underworld; her power opens up the "maze" of Hades, just as Joan's experiments with her candle and triple mirror conjure up a goddess/guide: "she lived under the earth somewhere, or inside something, a cave or a huge building; sometimes she was on a boat."

The intriguing connection between the marked excerpt from the *Aeneid* and Joan's Costume Gothic romances is almost parodic, since the romances make a formulaic routine of the heaving breast and flying hair. Yet the Cumean Sibyl does retain the power of prophecy and speech. She is woman unsilenced; in another passage from Atwood's excerpts from the *Aeneid,* "her voice came booming out of the cavern, / Wrapping truth in enigma; she was possessed."

The most significant materials of all are the xeroxed references (both from Robert Graves's *The Greek Myths*) to the silencing of the oracles which had belonged to women—in other words, to women's loss of the power of the word. In Graves's section on "Oracles," for example, he notes that "The Delphic Oracle first belonged to Mother Earth, who appointed Daphnis as her prophetess; and Daphnis, seated on a tripod, drank in the fumes of prophecy, as the Pythian priestess still does." Graves then suggests alternative explanations of why Mother Earth no longer controls the oracle, and the final explanation, that the priests of "Apollo robbed the oracle" seems definitive. This conclusion is substantiated by a note on the following pages that all "oracles were originally delivered by the Earth-goddess, whose authority was so great that patriarchal invaders made a practice of seizing her shrines and either appointing priests or retaining the priestess in their own service."

Margaret Atwood seems to be attempting to recover the Oracular or the Sibyllic role of the Goddess, to undo the overthrow of the "woman" (not lady) oracle by the priests of Apollo, and to reinstate the Goddess who is a poet. Paradoxically, she is empowered by the writings of Robert Graves, who most forcefully presented Atwood with her problem in her early years. By looking back to the legends of the original transition from matriarchy to patriarchy, Atwood is placing the almost trivial, definitely comic, story of Joan Delacourt Foster within the much more cosmic frame of the gendered arrangements of contemporary culture, which even today keep women as merely the priestesses and the Muses of patriarchal writing. These research materials, in other words, remind us that Atwood's primary obsession, as she framed it in *Ms.* magazine, is with the representation of the Goddess as the muse of the male poet, with Graves's contention that a woman could not be a poet. But what even Graves's own notes on "Oracles" hypothesize, and what the *Aeneid* demonstrates, is the power of a woman's voice, of the woman oracle, when she is allowed to speak.

I believe that if we think of the novel ***Lady Oracle*** as having sprung, in some sense, from musings upon the mythology of Artemis/Diana, Hecate/Mother Nature as represented in these excerpts and illustrations, then it becomes even more clear that one of the aims of the text is to reimagine the Delphic oracle again under the control of women. This is a figurative way of saying that the novel is attempting to imagine a way in which women can take back their rightful place as poets and writers. We can think of the various modes of writing in ***Lady Oracle*** as musings upon the place of gender in the politics of literary production, or even as musings upon the place of literary production in the realm of sexual politics. If we return to the published novel, we can see evidence that Atwood is, indeed, articulating the difficulties for women writers in assuming an equal place in the marketplace of literary production.

In *Lady Oracle,* the domination of publishing by editors who are primarily interested not in quality of writing but in sales, not in feminism but in money, is represented by John Morton, Doug Sturgess, and Colin Harper, the men who decide to publish Joan's poem. Sturgess's reduction of Joan Foster to a seductive object to decorate the bookjacket is typical: "Don't you worry your pretty head about good. We'll worry about good, that's our business, right?" Not only do men control women writers, but in addition, the modes of writing and creative expression practiced by men are presented as inherently repulsive: Fraser Buchanan's blackmail letters and avant-garde poetry of rejection slips, and the Royal Porcupine's "poetry" of frozen dead animals. This "art" is a burlesque, as McCombs says, [in *Women's Studies,* Vol. 12, 1986] of *"Survival's* colonial mentality, victims, dead animal and frozen Nature stories," but it is nevertheless unappealing to a woman writer. If we take these examples as representative, the role of men in the politics of literary production is to exploit women and animals.

Can women writers then enter into political writing? Atwood discusses this possibility through her description of *Resurgence,* the "small Canadian-nationalist left-wing magazine" which Arthur, Sam, and Don write. This journal provides an alternative form of literary production, and the fact that Marlene is the managing editor emphasizes the point that women can enter this sort of literary marketplace. Within the context of the novel, however, *Resurgence* becomes a joke because of the maelstrom created by the sexual politics of its staff, the merry-go-round of beds. Further, as Joan points out "Nobody . . . read *Resurgence* except the editors, some university professors, and all the rival radical groups who edited magazines of their own and spent a third of each issue attacking each other." Thus, as of 1976, Atwood did not see political writing as an attractive field for writing women.

Rejecting avant-garde art and political commentary, one discovers that the formulaic romance is possibly the most appealing field for women writers, so available to women that Paul has to disguise himself as Mavis Quilp in order to have his novels accepted. Further, as McCombs reminds us, the genre is definitely "natural" to Canada, since Harlequins are "Canada's most viable literary art, and a major publishing export." With female authors, female protagonists, and an enormous female audience, the market is ready for use.

At one point, Joan even considers the possibility of recuperating the Costume Gothic for political purposes. She knows that these formulaic stories (as compared to *Resurgence*) actually appeal to the masses which the left-wing radicals believe they want to reach: *"Terror at Casa Loma,* I'll call it, I would get in the evils of the Family compact, the martyrdom of Louis Riel, the horror of colonialism,

both English and American, the struggle of the workers, the Winnipeg General Strike."

The idea of the power of the cheap romance remains as one of the pleasures of reading *Lady Oracle.* The interpolated scenes from Joan's novel in progress are vividly written and enticing enough to engender desire for a satisfactory resolution of the plot, so that even the sophisticated reader feels the attraction of the genre. Her allusions to *fotoromanzi,* Italian love stories written almost like comic strips with voice balloons, but photograph pictures, point to a similar genre. In Margaret Atwood's letter to "Donya" requesting research materials for *Lady Oracle* she specifically requested a copy of a *"photoromanza"*: "In case you don't know what these are, they are cheesy magazines, sort of like True Romances except that the story is told in still black & white photos, with captions & cartoon balloons. The cheesier the better, and if you find several equally cheesy ones, buy all of them." No actual *fotoromanzi* have been preserved in the files but these "cheesy" romances, mentioned several times in *Lady Oracle,* have characteristics which clearly appeal to Joan: "The stories were all of torrid passion, but the women and men never had their mouths open . . . Italy was more like Canada than it seemed at first. All the screaming with your mouth closed."

Yet it is the popular appeal and the ephemeral nature of the *fotoromanzi* which distinguish them from high culture. With *Lady Oracle* and Joan's poem of the same name, Atwood begins her search for a mode of artistic expression which is anti-élitist in that it is deliberately designed for wide appeal, open to women authors and women characters, and which can also be opened up for larger purposes than escape.

Finally, Joan Foster's creation of her Gothic romances and her oracle poem is a story, like that of Atwood's strategies for appropriating to herself the potent image of the Goddess, in which the artist takes to herself the power of the Sibyl. Although the critic Frank Davey argues [in *Margaret Atwood: A Feminist Poetics*] that, as a narrator, Joan is "drowning in language," we could also say that she is letting loose the power of language.

The power of the Sibyl, however, is an ambiguous power. It is like the power of the mother, the power of creation. Yet on the other hand, it is also a giving away of one's self. Out of Joan's subconscious comes *Lady Oracle,* and after Joan's supposed suicide has been publicized in the media, the poem is turned into an item for popular consumption: "Sales of *Lady Oracle* were booming, every necrophiliac in the country was rushing to buy a copy."

The similarity between the many-breasted Goddess and the woman writer is apparent in this quoted sentence. Like the Goddess who offers her breasts, her substance, for public consumption, the poet offers herself, her ideas, her selves, and her fears for public consumption. Her novels or poems will be "condensed," "digested" by reviewers, "consumed" by the public, "devoured" by fans, "regurgitated" in literature classes—she will be metaphorically cannibalized.

Atwood is acutely aware of these possibilities. Her attention to the *fotoromanzi* suggests that she is meditating upon the role of the writer as producer of ephemera, thinking about the offering of a woman writer's created identities (of her "selves") for digestion by the public. The covers of Atwood's novels make the books resemble supermarket literature, which one might pick up along with the bread, milk, and fruit. A recent series simply has Margaret Atwood's face on every cover, as if the author were the product to be sold. The French language version of *Lady Oracle* has the real Margaret Atwood's face in a circular frame next to a parody of Margaret Atwood's face, with red hair and red eyebrows, in a rectangular frame.

Ultimately, I suggest, the writer is in the position of the narrator of the ice-cream-eating sequence, longing for the milk of an inexhaustible muse, Goddess and Mother, yet also in the position of the Goddess herself, constantly required to "Give. Give" of her self, to offer her heart to the public. An unpublished poem, entitled "Oracle Poem Three," poignantly raises this issue:

> What would you like today
> you who sit in rows
> and are bored
> and are hungry?
>
> Shall I describe a flower for you?
> Shall I describe a cripple?
> Would that make you feel better?
> I can do either.
>
> Or maybe you would like to kill me,
> that would be fun,
> that would be participation.
>
> Then you could divide me
> into segments, relics:
> that's what you do with saints,
> it makes them last longer.
>
> A finger
> to take home and place under your pillow
> and pray every night:
> perhaps it will cure you—
>
> But the heart, the golden heart,
> that's the element
> you will squabble over:
> wars have been fought for it.
>
> You think it will be secret,
> you think it will be magic,
> with the valuable heart
> you can do anything you want.
>
> But when you dig it out
> you are disappointed:
> it's scarcely larger than a chicken liver,
> it's pale, it's normal,
>
> and when you've swallowed it
> diamonds don't drop from your lips,
> you can't hear the trees talking.
>
> Is it because you have no faith?

The Delphic oracle is again under the control of a woman, a sibyl. She speaks. She may be devoured, she may devour, but at least she speaks.

In Lady Oracle, Atwood both destroys the Goddess (par-

odies her, makes her trivial) and celebrates her oracular powers, the force of her language. The triumph of *Lady Oracle* is that finally, after years of obsession with the Goddess, Atwood confronts her in her most horrifying aspect and, in Barthes's terminology, "vanquishes [the] myth from the inside."

James Wilcox   (review date 24 November 1991)

SOURCE: "The Hairball on the Mantlepiece," in *The New York Times Book Review,* November 24, 1991, p. 7.

[*Wilcox is an American-born short story writer and novelist whose works include* Modern Baptists *(1983),* North Gladiola *(1985), and* Miss Undine's Living Room *(1987). In the following review, Wilcox generally praises Atwood's* Wilderness Tips, *but finds some of the prose awkward and over-mannered.*]

In **"Hack Wednesday,"** one of the most engaging stories in Margaret Atwood's third volume of short fiction, *Wilderness Tips,* a middle-aged newspaper columnist sizes up men in an unusual way: "She can just look at a face and see in past the surface, to that other—child's—face which is still there. She has seen Eric [her husband] in this way, stocky and freckled and defiant, outraged by schoolyard lapses from honor." This uncanny ability applies just as well to Margaret Atwood herself. Almost every one of the 10 stories in this collection superimposes the past upon the present in an unsettling, often startling manner, which conjures up a sense of the mysterious in even the most banal relationships.

The first story, **"True Trash,"** a deceptively easygoing coming-of-age tale, accustoms us to the author's bold leaps in time. Set mainly in a summer camp on an island in Ontario's Georgian Bay, **"True Trash"** gives us a leisurely account of teen-age waitresses' fitful interaction with the "small fry" and counselors at Camp Adanaqui.

But it is only in a flash-forward of 11 years, when the former schoolboy camper Donny has dropped the last syllable from his name and grown a beard, that the story begins to take shape. During a chance encounter with him in Toronto, Joanne, a former waitress at the camp, begins to put together the missing pieces in a real-life *True Romance* story—or rather, as one of the waitresses called this type of magazine, *True Trash.* "The melodrama tempts [Joanne], the idea of a revelation, a sensation, a neat ending." But she is too sophisticated now for such a pat, "outmoded" story, and withholds from Don a revelation that would make him seem a *True Trash* character.

Information withheld gives a contemporary twist to another basically old-fashioned tale. In **"Death by Landscape,"** also set in a Canadian summer camp—Manitou is for girls, though—the mysterious disappearance of Lucy, one of the campers, during a canoe trip brings the disparate elements of the story into sharp focus. Cappie, the owner and director of Camp Manitou, cannot live with the unknowable. As Lois, Lucy's best friend, realizes later when she is a grown woman, Cappie had a desperate "need for a story, a real story with a reason in it; anything but the senseless vacancy Lucy had left for her to deal

Cover for Atwood's award-winning 1986 novel, The Handmaid's Tale.

with." Cappie's story is pure fiction, though, with no basis in fact. Lois's attempt to fill the "senseless vacancy" with some meaning leads beyond any literal rendering to a mythical landscape of her own disturbed mind.

This yearning for meaning in a post-modern world is further explored in **"The Age of Lead,"** Here the past that confronts Jane, a financial consultant in her 40's, is not just her youth. While watching a television program on the exhumation of a member of the Franklin expedition that was lost in the Arctic 150 years ago, Jane recalls her touching friendship with Vincent, a designer she had known since high school. Whereas it is eventually learned why John Torrington, the 20-year-old petty officer on the expedition, died, 43-year-old Vincent's recent death from "a mutated virus" cannot be explained by modern science. As Jane muses upon the two deaths, the more personal theme emerging from her school days with Vincent is united with the story's larger concern with indeterminacy: "She felt desolate. . . . Their mothers had finally caught up to them and been proven right. There were consequences after all; but they were the consequences to things you didn't even know you'd done."

If the frozen corpse of the petty officer seems "like a were-wolf meditating," so too does the 2,000-year-old man discovered by a peat digger in **"The Bog Man"** appear "to be meditating." Here again the past confronts the present in what at first seems a merely sensational, irrelevant way. Julie, a naïve Canadian student in love with her married archeology professor, goes to Scotland, where she endures boredom, "congealed oatmeal" and "rock-hard lamb chops" in order to be with her lover on a field trip. Trying to escape the boredom, Julie ventures out to the bog, where she is upset by the sight of the well-preserved corpse. This unearthing of the past seems to her "a desecration. Surely there should be boundaries set upon the wish to know, on knowledge merely for its own sake." Not surprisingly, she follows her instinct of leaving the past— or rather, the inconvenient parts of the past—buried when she later, as a mature, twice-married woman, tells the story of her affair to her women friends. "She leaves out entirely any damage she may have caused to Connor. . . . It does not really fit into the story."

Other characters in *Wilderness Tips* are more honest as they "sift through the rubble, groping for the shape of the past." In **"Isis in Darkness,"** a professor tries to revive the magic power that words held in his youth by writing about a brilliant woman poet who once had him under her spell. **"Uncles"** introduces us to Susanna, who ascends with the speed and ease of a romance-novel heroine from lowly newspaper obit writer to celebrated radio and television interviewer. Though she has considered herself a well-loved, deserving woman, the publication of a former colleague's memoir causes Susanna to wonder if she has "remembered my whole life wrong."

Kat, like Susanna, enjoys a slick rise to the top, though hers, in **"Hairball,"** is more easily explained. "When knives were slated for backs, she'd always done the stabbing." What would otherwise be an all-too-familiar tale of comeuppance in the dreary world of fashion magazines is given an uncanny aura by the presence of a benign tumor, dubbed Hairball, which Kat has preserved from an operation and given a place of honor on her mantelpiece. "The hair in it was red—long strands of it wound round and round inside."

Like the red-haired bog man and the frozen corpse haunting **"The Age of Lead,"** the pickled tumor opens up another dimension, revising the story of Kat's life in a way over which she, for once, has no control: "Hairball speaks to her, without words. . . . What it tells her is everything she's never wanted to hear about herself. This is new knowledge, dark and precious and necessary. It cuts."

Well constructed as these stories are, some may seem to belabor their themes with built-in explanations. At times, we're told what to make of the inexplicable, and such wonderful anomalies as the bog man or the frozen petty officer may wind up as too-convenient symbols. Now and then, the language itself can be troubling. In Ms. Atwood's previous collections, *Dancing Girls* and *Bluebeard's Egg,* the prose was supple, finely tuned with a variety of inflections. But in *Wilderness Tips* the stylized repetition of words and phrases ("Jane doesn't watch very much television. She used to watch it more. She used to watch comedy series") can seem mannered. And for a writer so abundantly talented, there are patches of curiously flat, unimaginative narrative, where we might encounter someone going "cold with dread" or bad luck gathering around a summer camp "like a fog."

These reservations, however, do not apply to such complex, beguiling stories as **"Wilderness Tips"** and **"Hack Wednesday."** In **"Wilderness Tips,"** the same themes are in evidence, but handled more deftly, with a buoyant irony that can keep even so ponderous an image as a sinking passenger liner afloat. Instead of a bog man or a dead English sailor, Ms. Atwood here serves up a roguish Hungarian émigré with the Anglicized name of George. The first time he visited Wacousta Lodge, the rustic lakefront house belonging to Prue's staid family, "he was led in chains, trailed in Prue's wake, like a barbarian in a Roman triumph. . . . He was supposed to alarm Prue's family." Nevertheless, Wacousta Lodge is conquered by the "barbarian" when George marries Prue's more docile sister Portia.

Browsing one day through the lodge's bookshelves, George comes across a book, published in 1905, called *Wilderness Tips.* "The book itself told how to do useful things, like snaring small animals and eating them—something George himself had done, though not in forests." This casual aside, suggesting so much about George's savage past, sets up a useful counterpoise to his wife's New World innocence. Portia "wishes she could go back a few decades, grow up again. The first time, she missed something . . . some vital information other people seemed to have." Here again is the familiar theme of life stories seeming incomplete because of missing information. But it is in many ways a willful ignorance that Portia lives with, refusing to explore the barbarian's own wilderness with any of the tips so conveniently at hand.

The barbarian hovering on the periphery of **"Hack Wednesday"** is perhaps the most disconcerting alien in this collection. It is Manuel Noriega himself, "his round face pocked and bleak as an asteroid." How Ms. Atwood works him so naturally into her tale of a middle-aged newspaper columnist at odds with her editor is storytelling at its best. Here a vision of the past helps bring about a sense of forgiveness, riot in any facile way, but with a tough-minded good humor that makes Marcia the columnist, one of Ms. Atwood's most appealing characters.

Merle Rubin   (review date 27 December 1991)

SOURCE: "Time Telescoping Tales," in *The Christian Science Monitor,* December 27, 1991, p. 14.

[*In the following review of* Wilderness Tips, *Rubin praises Atwood's ability to function as a "barometer" of the social climate of present and past decades in her writing, but faults her work for "a lack of energy and élan."*]

I find it hard to dislike Margaret Atwood's fiction, or even to offer serious criticism of it. Thoughtfully feminist, ecologically sensitive, a clear-eyed observer of social trends from urban alienation to rural isolation, Atwood is one of those writers who seem to function as barometers of their times.

One seldom feels one has wasted one's time in reading her. Often, one comes away from her work with a memorable insight or two. But I cannot say that I approach a new Margaret Atwood novel or story collection with a keen sense of anticipatory pleasure or excitement. Something about her gray, flat style communicates a damp, cold feeling of weariness, which is not simply the effect of her commitment to exposing the sometimes-depressing truth about living on an exploited, violence-prone planet, but also a lack of energy and élan in the way she does what she does.

Born in Ottawa in 1939, Atwood published her first book of poems in 1961, and now has about a dozen volumes of poetry to her credit. But it was the appearance of her novels throughout the 1970s and 1980s that gained her a wider audience. In poetry and prose alike, she has tackled a variety of modes, from the social realism of *Life Before Man* and *Bodily Harm* to the historical re-creation of her poetic sequence about a pioneer woman, *The Journals of Susanna Moodie,* and her dystopic futurist fantasy, *The Handmaid's Tale,* which was made into a film.

Wilderness Tips is Atwood's third collection of short stories. Many of these 10 neatly constructed, present-tense narratives unfold backward or forward over several decades. The characters define themselves—or fail to define themselves—in terms of the way they and the world have changed over the years.

The opening story, **"True Trash."** is set at a summer camp in the late 1950s, where a group of girls who have summer jobs as waitresses amuse themselves by reading and laughing at the stories in *True Romance* magazines. But life turns out to be more like fiction—even bad fiction—than they suspected. The innocent and not-so-innocent pleasures of summer flirtation and the scandal of a teenage pregnancy seem to lose their meaning over the years, however, as the story concludes: "You can do anything now and it won't cause a shock. Just a shrug. . . . A line has been drawn and on the other side of it is the past, both darker and more brightly intense than the present."

The hard-driving heroine of **"Hairball"** also changes with—or even slightly ahead of—the times. She begins as a "romanticized Katherine," dressed by her mother in frilly dresses, then sheds the frills in high school to emerge as a "bouncy, round-faced Kathy . . . eager to please and no more interesting than a health food ad." At university, she becomes "Kath" in her "Take-Back the-Night" jeans. By the time she runs off to England and lands a job with an avant-garde magazine, she's "sliced herself down to Kat . . . economical, street-feline, and pointed as a nail." Kat's toughness is shown to be a valuable asset, but in the hard-nosed world she's helped to create, even someone like herself can be tossed on the trash heap.

Richard of **"Isis in Darkness"** meets Selena in Toronto in 1960. Like other young people who hang out at the coffee-house there, Selena styles herself a poet. The difference is, her talent is real. Richard recognizes her quality and falls in love with her. It's not that he wants to marry her, or even that he feels the usual kind of desire for her. What he feels is a mysterious wish "to be transformed by her, into someone he was not." Richard marries a librarian and settles down to become an academic. But every 10 years, Selena turns up in his life, first as a living reminder of an existence dedicated to poetry, later as a walking emblem of discouragement and despair. Schematic as it is, this story achieves a measure of poignancy lacking in some of the other pieces.

The title story, about three sisters and the vaguely disreputable charmer who romanced the middle one but married the youngest, has a gloomy ending that left me as cold as its bloodless, stiffly drawn characters. Similarly, the childhood tragedy in **"Death by Landscape"** is such a literary cliché that any reader following the meanderings of this predictable story line would be more shocked if the troubled teenager had *not* met with misfortune on the camp canoe trip.

In **"Bog Man,"** a student's risqué affair with her archaeology professor in the early 1960s is a story that keeps changing as years go by. At first, it's a tale she tells only in confidence and only to other women: a story about the mysterious ways of men. Later, she tells the story more freely, emphasizing its comical elements, no longer idealizing the professor and feeling now a touch of sympathy for his hapless wife. The more time goes by, the more comical and cynical the story becomes and the less remains of her original emotions. "Connor [the professor] . . . loses in substance every time she forms him in words. He becomes flatter . . . more life goes out of him. . . . By this time he is almost an anecdote, and Julie [the former student] is almost old."

A similar process of disillusion is described in **"The Age of Lead."** As teenagers, Jane and Vincent mocked their mothers' joyless warnings about the dire consequences of deviation from the work ethic. But after the excitement of the 1960s and the expansion of opportunities for women in the 1970s, the 1980s fall like a ton of bricks: acid rain, urban decline, pollution, poverty, AIDS, and early death for many of Jane's contemporaries. "Their mothers had finally caught up to them and been proven right. There were consequences after all; but they were the consequences to things you didn't even know you'd done."

The bleakness of Atwood's outlook is underscored by the chilly third-person narration she favors: detached, slightly wry, often a little monotonous, but sometimes tightening to a dour sort of elegance. One can hardly fault Atwood for her pessimism or her resolutely pared-down style. But the vision offered here is a limited one: like a black-and-white television continuously tuned to nightly bad news.

What must be commended, however, is Atwood's ability to evoke the passing of entire decades—to convey how it feels to live at a given time and how it feels to view it in retrospect—all within the brief compass of a short story.

Jill LeBihan (essay date 1991)

SOURCE: *"The Handmaid's Tale, Cat's Eye* and *Interlunar:* Margaret Atwood's Feminist (?) Futures (?)," in *Nar-rative Strategies in Canadian Literature: Feminism and Postcolonialism,* edited by Coral Ann Howells and Lynette Hunter, Open University Press, 1991, pp. 93-107.

[*In the following essay, LeBihan analyzes the narrative technique and major themes in* The Handmaid's Tale, Cat's Eye *and some of the poems in* Interlunar.]

Margaret Atwood is nothing if not formidable in her utilization of different forms in her writing. Her two latest novels are strikingly different from one another in terms of the formal traditions within which they might be placed. *Cat's Eye* is a woman painter's cynical retrospective principally on her relationships with other women and feminism. *The Handmaid's Tale* is most often labelled 'feminist dystopian'. I intend to call into question the use of this title here, for the way in which it has been employed to place Atwood's novel against the mainstream of fiction, conveniently reading the location and label as marginalizing. Marginalization then becomes construed as having the function of undermining the subversive effects of the text. In what follows, I will suggest some alternative readings of location, which offer the possibility of serious challenges to mainstream thought from places other than from the conventional centres of power.

Her latest collection of new poetry, *Interlunar,* contains poems whose narrators speak from locations which find echoes in the setting of *The Handmaid's Tale.* They are voices that have been given to them, voices which aim to discover precisely where they have been put, voices which protest against the order which has this locational power over them. The voices in the poetry are nearly all weakened however, by disease, death, despair. *The Handmaid's Tale* is offered as a prediction of the future only if its warnings against oppressive central powers to mute protest are ignored. The world of Gilead is not quite an inevitable destiny. This kind of hope is not offered by the poetry of *Interlunar.* 'Letter From The House Of Questions' is not like the tale which has fortunately survived as proof that in some small, though ambiguous way, a protest has been registered. Instead it begins with a sense of its own inevitable annihilation:

> Everything about me is broken.
> Even my fingers, forming
> these words in the dust
> a bootprint will wipe out by morning,
> even these words.

Atwood has used a different writing genre or generic style for three of her most recent publications, then: poetry, 'feminist dystopian' novel and almost realist novel (since the bizarre or fantastic is never entirely missing from Atwood's work). I want to explore in this paper some of the connections between texts using different kinds of genre, of which Atwood makes use in her later writing: the speculative fiction and autobiographical confession of *The Handmaid's Tale,* the retrospective first person speaker of *Cat's Eye* and the less assertive narrational voices in the poetry of *Interlunar.* This study is an attempt to discover whether Atwood's work offers hope for feminist fiction in the future, whether it can challenge the position offered to it by the literary mainstream or whether its words in the dust will be obliterated by a savage bootprint.

Putting Margaret Atwood's name on a feminist agenda immediately causes problems. In refusing to overtly align herself with the women's movement, Atwood has been seen as a reactionary artist, separating her art from her politics and undermining feminist solidarity. This latter perceived fracturing of sisterhood has been welcomed by masculist critics, who see any kind of criticism and internal political division into factions as destructive wrangling or bitching. Pro-feminist critics have also begun to reject Atwood's work as a result of her apparent distance, despite the fact that her textual concerns are very relevant to many issues discussed as 'feminist', irrespective of her personal declarations of non-alignment to specific feminist groups.

The agenda of 'feminist (?) futures (?)', the reason for all the question marks relating to Atwood's work, converges for me at a much debated current critical problem. The questions meet at a spot marked by a 'post'. Does Atwood's writing exemplify postfeminism, postmodernism or postmodernist feminism? In what ways are these critical, political and chronological categories useful in reading her later fiction and in what ways does her writing help us better articulate these positions?

The post stands at a crossroads, as a sign pointing the (literary and critical) directions. The post marks one spot, its own stable site where it is embedded in concrete, but being a directional indicator, it is clearly attempting to order and to ease the transit of others, who look to it to learn where they are, where they have been and where they are going. Perhaps one of the biggest questions relating to the post is the one of who erects such a solid, stable, privileged signifier. For He who attaches the sign (and I use He advisedly) is the style merchant of today, the director of what is central and therefore of what is marginal. The presence of the post is a sign of the cultural times (just like fashion designer labels, it is a marker of who is in and who is out). The post is tagged to descriptions to indicate the contemporaneity of the signified. Postmodernism, Postfeminism and the like are titles which tell us the time.

But the chronological issue of the post is a vexing one, for it is a prefix which in addition to marking what is in vogue, what is current and up to date, is an attachment which also indicates time passing, and politics progressing beyond their starting points. As I read it, then, the post may seem static and upright, but in fact it is a moment of utter uncertainty. It relates at once to several planes of history, offering both a relevant connection with the movement from which it has evolved but also a distinction from those origins. The post is also generally an attachment which appears to offer some kind of engagement with current critical theory, a warning triangle—'Caution. Theory Ahead!'—or the post can even turn out to be a sign which points to reader in a misleading direction.

Elaine Risley, the narrator of *Cat's Eye*, comments upon the post problem with some bitterness. After procrastinating as far as possible, she finally enters the feminist art gallery where her retrospective collection is to be shown. She comments with irritation:

> I don't give a glance to what's still on the walls.
> I hate those neo-expressionist dirty greens and

putrid oranges, post this, post that. Everything is post these days, as if we're all just a footnote to something earlier that was real enough to have a name of its own.

Elaine Risley firmly rejects any attempt to make her a member of a post movement because she equates the post with the past. Elaine Risley distinguishes between the past, as something which is dated and irrecoverably lost, and history, which is a subjective reconstruction influenced by elements of that past, but which is by no means the same thing. But for her the post marks not a position in an historical continuum but rather a radical break in genre, style and politics. According to the formulation of Elaine Risley here, the post becomes a sign that the past is no longer a relevant or fashionable referent. Elaine Risley wants her paintings to be current, which is why she has such ambivalent feelings about the retrospective exhibition ('first the retrospective, then the morgue' she comments). But she wants to be current on her own terms, not in post terms. 'Language is leaving me behind', she says, which is precisely what she believes the action of the post prefix to be. To have her work termed postfeminist appears to Elaine Risley to specifically date her feminism, and thereby make it outdated. This post categorization process appears to make her feminism 'past it' when she still sees it as necessary and relevant. As Margaret Atwood herself says in an introduction to *The Edible Woman:*

> The goals of the feminist movement have not been achieved and those who claim we're living in a post-feminist era are either sadly mistaken or tired of thinking about the whole subject.

The Handmaid's Tale confronts the issue of postfeminism in a different way from *Cat's Eye,* by having the narrator speak from a time when postfeminism is no longer meaningful because the feminist precedent has all but been eradicated in a way that Elaine Risley fears might happen as a result of it being posted. References to preceding political, historical and artistic movements are still meaningful in all these discourses in Elaine Risley's era despite her fears that dating processes are used to relegate the past rather than make reference to it. The catalogue for her exhibition, for example, describes one of the paintings as:

> A jeu d'esprit . . . which takes on the Group of Seven and reconstructs their vision of landscape in the light of contemporary experiment and post-modern pastiche.

The post prefix can no longer be attached to politics, art or history in *The Handmaid's Tale* in the way it is used in *Cat's Eye* because there is no official recognition of any preceding movements. There has been an attempt to erase awareness of a multiple and subjective past through the institution of a single, approved version of history. Gilead orthodoxy replaces various perspectives on the past which are accessible only through different histories by equating its one history with the past; this history is appointed to give access to what it propagates as the only true past which, this orthodoxy says, is to be disowned because of its corruption and dissolution. The only acceptable reality in Gilead is the present. Fantasy and memory (the personal, subjective stories confessed by the narrator) do not conform to this orthodoxy—they challenge the single historical canon which purports to tell the past as it really was. Fantasy and memory are consequently the very strategies which the narrator uses as part of her resistance of contemporaneity, erupting through the Gilead period in the regular 'Night' episodes that haunt the novel with the narrator's consciously reconstructed, or her unconscious/dream worked personal history.

Like Elaine Risley's rejection of the post label, like the unconventional narrator of the tale, the Handmaid herself, who keeps at least one of her identities secret, *The Handmaid's Tale* similarly resists labels that position it within a particular generic stream. The maintenance of a covert or multiple identity is shown in the novel to be part of a policy of subversion of the dominant, as I shall discuss later. The projection of the novel into the 22nd century, then, the intervals of fantasy and nightmare, the shifts in temporal position, the narratorial insistence that the text is just one version of a story that can be told in different ways by other people, the multiple examples of women's communities with their different (and sometimes oppositional) political struggles, the perspective given by the final chapter that what we grasp as a single text is in fact a reassembled transcription from a surviving jumble of cassette recordings: through all these strategies the novel constantly reiterates its uncertain, problematic relationship with the concept of a single reality, one identity, a truthful history as propagated by both the political orthodoxy of Gilead and by much of literary criticism today.

There are four levels of narrative time in *The Handmaid's Tale:*

> 1) The pre-Revolution past, characterized by the narrator's memories of her childhood with her mother, her student days with Moira, her memories of her daughter and her relationship with Luke.
>
> 2) The period of the Revolution itself, and the time immediately subsequent to that, including the time spent training at the Red Centre.
>
> 3) The main narrative time, Gileadean time. It is this narratorial period that is interrupted by the dream sequences. The Gileadean present is what the narrator is telling her tale about, although the events of this present are still retold as past occurrences, narrated retrospectively on to cassette tape, a fact of which we are informed at the final textual time level.
>
> 4) The time of the 'present' (our future?), the period of the Symposium of Gileadean Studies—25 June 2195.

Apart from these textual times there is the question of the reader's own temporal context for the novel, her own recognition of events in the text and the placement of them within her own time scheme. For instance, some of the pre-Revolution period accounts of the novel deal with the narrator's mother's involvement in the women's movement of the late 1960s and the narrator's somewhat reactionary response to her mother's militancy. The narrator recalls witnessing the ritualistic burning of pornographic

publications, for example, and she remembers the return of angry and injured women from abortion demonstrations. This is an inclusion of what can be seen as 'real history' or rather, what is sometimes called 'faction': a fictionalization or generalized account of real occurrences. This is what Linda Hutcheon calls historiographic metafiction. The problem which I think this novel addresses is whether historical accounts can ever be more than 'faction'. The novel suggests that the privileging of history, notably in the form of 'authentic' first person narrative accounts of the past, as something more truthful and accurate than faction, is fallacious. The narrator insists that the tale she is telling is a 'reconstruction' which is always going to be at some level inaccurate, partial, incomplete, because it is retrospective and told by only one voice. But she suggests that this 'factitious' status, neither wholly fact nor complete fiction, is something that her story has in common with other historiographic metanarratives.

The novel operates on friction between narrative and theory, and between fiction and history. The story being told is one which comes from the personal experience of the narrating subject, although she does make use of stories told to her by others from their own lives. This first person confessional I rubs uneasily against the perspective provided by the viewing eyes of the academics which only cross the reader's field of vision at the conclusion of the novel. These organizing theoretical and editorial intrusions establish the text and 'establishmentarize' it. They drag the underground into the open, making public the story the Handmaid wanted to tell but they also attempt to uncover her secrets, trying to signpost her identity, giving her tale a stable location and thereby diffuse any resistance it might otherwise provide against the single authoritative, authentic history.

The preserved tapes on which *The Handmaid's Tale* is supposedly recorded can be viewed as vital records of the past, primary sources, a woman's voice speaking from a time when she should have been silent. The narration, because of its historical context, has become (like the scrabble game she plays) an act of subversion and rebellion. There is a level at which certain groups positioned within the women's studies category believe in these kind of recovered sources as challenges to a mainstream, canonical and patriarchal version of the past. But the narrative also consumes the past as it represents it, rewriting history by itself as its own fictional narrative, not The One Truth, but story, as the narrator insists.

The narrator's story is, on one level, a subversive act, because of the time in which she lived. She lives in a dystopian time when there is a patriarchal state domination of information. To withhold information, or to spread unauthorized material, is an act of treason for which the punishments are brutal and public. The narrator keeps a secret of her own name apart from the patronymic 'Of/fred'. Keeping this private knowledge forges a link with the past, but it is also an act of defiance, as the narrator is proving, at least to herself, that secrets can still be kept.

The private name has the same defiant linguistic pleasure for the narrator as her discovery of another piece of women's history. The carved incantation found in the bottom of her wardrobe, the pig latin joke 'Nolite te bastardes carborundorum' (don't let the bastards grind you down) is an example of women's history, literally staying in the closet. Women's history is as illicit in Gilead as homosexuality now, made subject to acts of suppression, under a similarly fearful state. The carving is a sign of the power of the secret in a time of oppression for the narrator, but the non-classically educated narrator has to ask the Commander for a translation of the coded message left by the previous Handmaid as a legacy to her follower.

The past is being reproduced at one level as a subversive act, but it is not a reproduction that is free of the determining factors of the prevailing ideology. Pig latin is a boy's school joke at the expense of classical teaching methods, but is a joke made from within the boys' school and interpretable only by the same classical scholars. Similarly, the recovery of the Handmaid's narrative by an academic institution in the 22nd century, the placing of the narrative in a literary continuum with Chaucer and all that that implies about a static canon, means that an act of feminist subversion has become part of the establishment. Elaine Risley is able to be self-conscious about this recuperation of her work since it happens in her own lifetime, and her comments are not without ambivalence:

> My career is why I'm here, on this futon, under this duvet. I'm having a retrospective, my first. The name of the gallery is Sub-Versions, one of those puns that used to delight me before they became so fashionable. I ought to be pleased by this retrospective, but my feelings are mixed; I don't like admitting I'm old enough and established enough to have such a thing, even at an alternative gallery run by a bunch of women. I find it improbable, and ominous: first the retrospective, then the morgue. But also I'm cheesed off because the Art Gallery of Ontario wouldn't do it. Their bias is toward dead foreign men.

Elaine Risley recognizes that she has become part of the feminist establishment, but she is still not taken seriously by the national art scene; that scene is still, as Atwood eloquently puts it, occupied by 'dead foreign men'.

Successful resistance for Elaine Risley depends upon standards of success set by her own culture and for Risley this means widespread, establishment recognition of her art. Risley's rebellion is public resistance to trends set both by the establishment and the 'alternatives' including mainstream feminism. For the narrator of **The Handmaid's Tale** resistance, if it is to be survived, has to remain underground. In the narrator's past, lack of public resistance was in part a result of her apathy. She writes:

> Is that how we lived then? But we lived as usual. Everyone does, most of the time. Whatever is going on is as usual. Even this is as usual, now.

> We lived, as usual, by ignoring. Ignoring isn't the same as ignorance, you have to work at it . . . The newspaper stories were like dreams to us, bad dreams dreamt by others. How awful, we would say, and they were, but they were awful without being believable. They were too melodramatic, they had a dimension that was not the dimension of our lives.

> We were the people who were not in the papers. We lived in the blank white spaces at the edges of the print. It gave us more freedom.

> We lived in the gaps between the stories.

The gaps between the stories told in black print can, despite their apparent blankness be read in a number of ways. They are not necessarily invisible to the reading eye (nor to the disciplinary one). The gaps are for the narrator in her earlier, pre-Revolution life, acquiescences to 'the usual', representing ways of surviving in an oppressive patriarchal state, where it is easier to keep a low profile than to draw attention to the way in which 'the usual' is formed according to gender.

Another way of reading the white spaces is to view them as being essential to the black print, a contrast which the human eye requires before it can recognize shapes and signs to read. Christopher Dewdney explains this lucidly in his *Immaculate Perception* in a section called 'Edge Features', and he also goes some way to showing here how the post can be used to illuminate and refer to the past, rather than just annihilating it:

> Our vision relies on discontinuity and change. It seems the majority of neural processing in the striate cortex consists of an analysis of edge-features. An object is perceived by its edges, the relationship of discontinuous lines. All written languages are the abstraction and distillation of only the essential edge-features necessary to perceive the form on which meaning is concomitant.

The black print never acknowledges its dependence on the white spaces with which it is discontinuous and thereby made perceptible. The consciousness has not been taught to focus on the white page against which the black letters are defined, and it is the print which is given the privileged attention as the unusual, the significant, not 'the usual' background.

The Handmaid is obliged to occupy the white space, and to live as usual. She can make this 'as usual' more than superficial by acquiescing completely, as Janine appears to do, at least initially, transforming herself into a semi-transparent blur (like 'raw egg-white',), to which no one pays attention. The narrator can, alternatively maintain only the superficial whiteness and have her own black spaces, her positive side. These do not challenge the orthodox centre page print; there is no question of their publication at that time. For the narrator in Gilead, the significances consist in the blackness of the 'Night' sequences which are as contrasts to the present white spaces in which she is supposed to invisibly subsist. By giving prominence to recollection of the subjective experience of the past, particularly as a private, illicit act, the narrator has found a way of providing Gilead with edge features.

The fantasy dream and memory of the 'Night' and the illicit relationship with Nick are the Handmaid's version of black print which has to remain invisible, whitewashed, at least while she is in Gilead. Finally, she goes the closest she can to taking over the black print and turning it to her own uses, by narrating her story in a form which clearly is intended to preserve it for others, although which others can never be known. But, of course, in this novel which is ever aware of determining power systems and the impossibility of escape from them, the controllers of the black print eventually take centre page. The mainstream academicians are the ones who transcribe, who organize, edit and publish the Handmaid's tale, and therefore relocate it firmly within the black print, once again neglecting the white ground.

I will reintroduce the post at this point. Up to now, the post has been discussed both as a signifier of chronological location—the prefix that indicates temporal movement away from origins—and it has also been discussed as the sign of the contemporary. The post has been seen, and feared (by Elaine Risley) as a marker of discontinuity and change, making the break with the past into a sign of fashion: the post as the designer label. In *The Handmaid's Tale* the character of Aunt Lydia is said to have a fondness for the either/or; that is, she cannot see the black print and the white spaces at the same time. In tune with Gilead orthodoxy, she would see the presence of the past as a threat to current stability, except that her either/or mentality enables her to deny that any vestige or reconstruction of a past remains. For Aunt Lydia there is only now.

The either/or viewpoint can be shown to be a fallacious one. The fusion of meanings into the word 'faction' shows that simple either/or divisions fail to operate at any linguistic or political level. *The Handmaid's Tale* itself proves the existence of a blend of what is considered historical fact and what is thought to be science fiction. The division of kinds of feminists into different political groups in the novel offers the possibility of feminist political, as well as literary, factions which are neither destructive bitchy squabbles nor pluralist utopias. I want to suggest that Dewdney's term 'edge-feature' is appropriate to the post because it functions as a marker of discontinuity and change, but one which illuminates the interdependence of the either/or, rather than insisting on the mutual exclusion of one term by the other.

A poem from *Interlunar* which recalls the quality of horror in some of the sequences from *The Handmaid's Tale* is **'No Name',** and it comments upon a moment of stasis between dream and reality, between life and death, a transition point where there is no firm post to cling to. The scene described in the poem is in a nightmare setting, a moment where the relationship and power between the man and the narrator, against whose door he is bleeding, is not established and is entirely uncertain:

> He is a man in the act of vanishing
> one way or another.
> He wants you to let him in.
> He is like the soul of a dead
> lover, come back to the surface of the earth
> because he did not have enough of it and is still
>   hungry
> but he is far from dead. Though the hair
> lifts on your arms and cold
> air flows over your threshold
> from him, you have never
> seen anyone so alive.

This man corpse returns with a powerful grip on the narrator, with his 'Please / In any language'. The haunting of the narrator in the poem is like those moments of the narrator's past that re-occur in *The Handmaid's Tale.* They have a narrative power over her, stories which demand to be told. She prefaces certain sections of the tale with the reluctant 'I don't want to be telling this', but somehow the narrator appreciates the necessity for her history to be recorded. **'No Name'** ends with the same suspended moment with which it begins, a poem of non-progression:

> Your door is either half open
> or half closed.
> It stays that way and you cannot wake.

In the poem a third position of stasis results from failing to occupy either one position, that offered by the fully open door, or another, that provided by the fully closed door. The narrator is locked into her dreamlike state apparently because she has refused the either/or. The half-open/half-closed state becomes just a third fixed term. But there is a fourth, more mutable condition where all the positions are potentially ones that can be taken, or even all occupied at once. In the poem the narrator is locked into a dream, in the novel she is locked into a nightmarish dystopic world from which dreams are sometimes an escape, sometimes a torture. In both novel and the poem there is a tangential location which is implicit, an alternative to the fixed either/or choices, but both texts arrive finally at the rigid third term. The choice ultimately appears to be between the white space, the black print, or the stasis of indecision. The option of recognition of the fourth 'edge-feature' does not appear as a possibility.

The Handmaids themselves are supposed to have, like the poem, 'no name', no stability. This is to make them interchangeable and replaceable. The stable, pre-Revolution name to which Offred attaches herself secretively is the name that the 22nd century academic researchers really require in their belief that it will give them not just another history but a fully open door to a single, retrievable past. Their attempts to discover the narrator's secret go precisely against the attempts of the Handmaid herself to preserve this one aspect of her private body and her private past in the face of the violations of freedom being perpetrated in the state of Gilead. The state of Gilead has removed the mythical private family unit and this is nowhere more obvious than in the figure of the Handmaid herself, announcing her function in her red robes. The sexual act is transformed from the containment of the nuclear family in the pre-Revolution, when two metaphorically fused to form one, into a multiple fission of the familial unit, with the Handmaid standing for the wife, but precisely positioning herself in between the wife and the Commander as a rupture in the once traditional coupling. Unfortunately, the potential of this rupture of the private unit to deconstruct the power and hierarchy of the monogamous patriarchal family is not realized. Rather, the intervening Handmaid simply reinforces the ties that bind the Commander and the wife. The Handmaid's role is subordinate to that of the privileged couple, and she is an item in the male-controlled chain of trade in women.

The biological division of power in *The Handmaid's Tale,* then, accordingly not only to gender but also fertility, is another symptom of what Aunt Lydia is fond of, the either/or. Gender ambiguity, bisexuality or plurality of sexuality are impossibilities in Gilead. The signposts are on the genitalia. The narrator is consistent in her attempt to undermine the division into the two gendered posts which keeps her attached to the powerless and subordinate half of the binary. One of the ways in which she does this is with the repeated motif: 'context is all'. The shock of the old, the specifically dated in the modern environment—for instance, the fashions in the *Vogue* magazine, the ridiculous garments retrieved for use in Jezebel's—prompts the very important recognition that versions of normality are not static. Elaine Risley, in a world whose versions of femininity are more contradictory and complex than those of Gilead, although by no means unrelated, of course, walks up to a drunk bag-lady on the street. The incident provides Elaine with a review of the language of gender and power:

> When I get up even, I see that this person is a woman. She's lying on her back, staring straight at me. 'Lady', she says. 'Lady, Lady.' That word has been through a lot. Noble lady, Dark Lady, she's a real lady, old-lady lace, Listen lady, Hey lady watch where you're going, Ladies room, run through with lipstick and replaced with women. But still the final word of appeal. If you want something very badly you do not say Woman, Woman, you say Lady, Lady.

The sign on the door of the toilet is run through with lipstick but the writing underneath can still be seen. The substitution of 'women' for 'ladies' as acceptable terminology does not mean that 'ladies' and all its baggage of meaning is eradicated, as the bag-lady is there to indicate with her plea. As Elaine Risley says at the beginning of the novel:

> Time is not a line but a dimension, like the dimensions of space . . . I began then to think of time as having a shape, something you could see, like a series of liquid transparencies, one laid on top of another. You don't look back along time but down through it, like water. Sometimes this comes to the surface, sometimes that, sometimes nothing. Nothing goes away.

The selective process of recovery of the past in *The Handmaid's Tale* is used as a characterization device for the narrator and it also becomes a damning indictment of the Gilead state organization. The commander is constructed as living in the past, with 'old-fashioned values', although in a less conscious way than the narrator, who actively reconstructs her past for herself as a political and personal survival tactic. The Commander takes Offred to a Disneyland version of a brothel, nicknamed Jezebel's by the women who work there. All the prostitutes have to wear sequinned, low-cut, frivolous attire that has been salvaged from the past: bunny-girl outfits, swimming costumes, frilly lingerie. The narrator recalls:

> 'It's like walking into the past,' says the Commander. His voice sounds pleased, delighted even. 'Don't you think?'
>
> I try to remember if the past was exactly like this. I'm not sure, now. I know it contained these

things, but somehow the mix is different. A movie about the past is not the same as the past.

Of all things the Gileadean statesmen could choose to replicate out of the past, these men choose prostitution. The sanctioned prostitution and surrogacy of the Handmaid system has its roots in the practices of many eras and cultures, but Jezebel's recreates a trade of sexual illegitimacy, a parody of sexual relations from the immediately pre-Revolution past. The narrator emphasizes the 'inauthenticity' of her mental reconstructions of the past in her stories. But the construction behind the Gilead system appears to believe in the annihilation of the Utopian 1960s permissiveness, and a replacement of the failed fabricated world from that era by a 'natural' system, the return to the 'usual' which means a system based on female subordination, with women as items in a complex scheme of ownership and reproduction.

The tale telling functions as a reassurance of the existence of the past, that things were different once. The need to juxtapose past and present is a desire for perspective, looking down through the waters of time rather than along the line as Elaine Risley sees it, reading the sign underneath the lipstick scoring. The Handmaid says:

> What I need is perspective. The illusion of depth, created by a frame, the arrangement of shapes on a flat surface . . . Otherwise, you live in the moment. Which is not where I want to be.

The perspective is provided by the white background to counteract the black print which fixes the subject in the moment. The subject needs to be able to see the frame, to be conscious that the arrangement of shapes on a flat surface is precisely that. Therefore there is an arranging subject in addition to an arranged one. The change of perspective is provided for the reader as much by the science fiction style of the novel and its future dystopian setting as by the narrator's recounting of her past. The shift in timescales in the novel is part of its emphasis on avoiding complacency, of avoiding the danger of accepting the present moment as usual when at another point in time its standards would have been rejected as appalling or horrific. The dystopian genre and temporal shifts are ways of drawing attention to the frame, the arrangers, and the white space and flat surfaces which make perception of the signs and shapes possible.

The Handmaid's Tale demonstrates the juxtaposition of past standards of normality with present 'usualness' and within this, the function of some kind of historical evidence to jog the memory into recognition of change. As the narrator reminds us: 'Nothing changes instantaneously: in a gradually heating bathtub you'd be boiled to death before you knew it'. In the 'Night' episodes of the novel, the narrator explains how she claims space for her thoughts, and more particularly for her past as a way of judging the temperature of the water. She recalls her mother urging her out of complacency, her mother's nagging insistence on the importance of the history of the women's movement, a selective version of the past:

> You young people don't appreciate things, she'd say. You don't know what we had to go through, just to get you where you are. Look at him, slic-

ing up the carrots. Don't you know how many women's bodies the tanks had to roll over just to get that far?

It is the 'Night' episodes of the novel, significantly, in which these stories from the past emerge. In the daylight, under the scrutiny of the Eyes, the narrator's recollection of the past puts her at risk. 'Night' becomes a definite, positive location from which to articulate resistance to the status quo, provided by the structural organization of the novel, interspersed as it is with these sequences which challenge the narrative of the present. Of course, Atwood does not allow this imposed structural division to go without examination. There is emphasis on the necessity of drawing attention to the frame throughout the novel and the final chapter, which claims to have organized the material in the tale, reincorporates into the academy what has up to this point been seen as a disruptive narrative strategy. But this demonstrates the impossibility of a clear division between the light and dark, the mainstream and the subversive, the inoperative 'either/or', something suggested also by the title poem from *Interlunar:*

> The lake, vast and dimensionless,
> doubles everything, the stars,
> the boulders, itself, even the darkness
> that you can walk so long in
> it becomes light.

The post as a chronological locator does not mean that its terms are divided off from the theories of literature that came before or that are to follow. The post does not give privilege to the prior theories either. Rather, it insists on recalling them and partially incorporating them within the present. The post does mark out the poles between which meanings shuffle, but the movement is not necessarily between only two signposts, and the movement can be back and forth: the post does not mark the entrance to a one-way street. 'The lake' is 'vast and dimensionless' as the poem says. The posts are used to mark out sections within it, making their own patterns and boundaries. Even this marking out of areas for concern does not prevent the darkness from turning into light, or the light from fading into dark. What this means for the future is uncertain, as the narrator of *The Handmaid's Tale* concludes:

> Whether this is my end or a new beginning I
> have no way of knowing: I have given myself
> over into the hands of strangers, because it can't
> be helped.
>
> And so I step up, into the darkness within; or
> else the light.

The compromise that 'can't be helped' is the relinquishing of privacy and the safe white spaces away from print, the giving of oneself into the hands of strangers through telling a story. The most recent of Elaine Risley's paintings in *Cat's Eye* is a similar recognition of the risks of constructing a central subject, a narratorial I (or 'an oversized cat's eye marble'). The adoption of another genre, another way of telling a story in Atwood's latest novel, that is the paintings put into words: these provide another perspective on the positioning of a public subject, a subject which is both an attempt to resist the mainstream but also requires recognition provided by convention in order to

achieve an effect. The frames can be stretched: Elaine Risley's latest painting, 'Unified Field Theory', is 'vertical oblong, larger than the other paintings'; *The Handmaid's Tale* is dystopian fiction, but also historiographic metafiction with a confessional journal-style first person narrator. The single identifiable generic frame is stretched to include as many different writing strategies as possible within its construction. But the story once in print or paint, as both novels' narrators accept, is not under the subject's control. Elaine Risley says, whilst looking around her exhibition:

> I walk the room, surrounded by the time I've made; which is not a place, which is only a blur, the moving edge we live in; which is fluid, which turns back on itself, like a wave. I may have thought I was preserving something from time, salvaging something; like all those painters, centuries ago, who thought they were bringing Heaven to earth, the revelation of God, the eternal stars, only to have their slabs of wood and plaster stolen, mislaid, burnt, hacked to pieces, destroyed by rot and mildew.
>
> A leaky ceiling, a match and some kerosine would finish all this off. Why does this thought present itself to me, not as a fear, but as a temptation?
>
> Because I can no longer control these paintings, or tell them what to mean. Whatever energy they have came out of me. I'm what's left over.

Elaine Risley lives to see how her work takes off without her, how it changes with each additional post attached to it, framing it, mildewing it. *The Handmaid's Tale* survives in a form as battered as those paintings of centuries ago. *Interlunar* is a reminder to pay attention to the lighting, to the way it colours and changes shapes, the way everything can be doubled in the reflection of that vast and dimensionless lake or else obscured and submerged without trace.

Peter Kemp   (review date 6 November 1992)

SOURCE: "The Atwood Variations," in *The Times Literary Supplement*, No. 4675, November 6, 1992, p. 20.

[*In the following review, Kemp praises* Good Bones *as a "sample-case of Atwood's sensuous and sardonic talents."*]

Pocket-sized and with sturdy covers, *Good Bones* looks a bit like a sketchbook in which an artist might jot caricatures, cartoons, preliminary studies, trial pieces and quick little exercises in catching the essence of a subject or delineating it from unusual angles. The miscellany with which Margaret Atwood fills its pages is, in fact, a writer's equivalent of this: a collection of lively verbal doodlings, smartly dashed off vignettes and images that are inventively enlarged, titled, turned upside down. Playing with the conventions of her narrative craft is a frequent pastime. Fiction's motives and motifs are outlined with witty flourish.

"Bad News", the opening piece, is a fantasia about the appeal of disaster tales. It's followed by a monologue in which The Little Red Hen, clucking with indignation, re-tells the story of her thrifty response to the grain of wheat as a cautionary tale of put-upon domesticity. Elsewhere, Gertrude gives her version of what happens in *Hamlet,* and an Ugly Sister and a Wicked Stepmother put in a good word for themselves. Political correctness is lampooned in **"There Was Once",** as the reciting of a standard fairy-tale gets subverted by progressive emendations and bowdlerizings. With sly funniness, a litany, **"Let Us Now Praise Stupid Women"**, lists everything fiction owes to unwise fe-males. As it catalogues the contributions to literature of "The Muse as Fluffball", aspects of genres like the fairy-story or the Gothic tale are captured in thumbnail sketch-es of impressionistic brio: "trapped inside the white pages, she can't hear us, and goes prancing and warbling and lol-loping innocently towards her doom . . . incest-minded stepfathers chase her through ruined cloisters, where she's been lured by ruses too transparent to fool a gerbil."

In other places, Atwood's pen prods verbal raw material around to see what it turns into in differing contexts. Three brief stories each incorporate, in the order they occur in the verse, the words of a stanza from John Mc-Crae's "In Flanders Fields the Poppies Blow". The title work, which ends the book, is a series of virtuoso varia-tions on the phrase, "good bones", using changing conno-tations—fine bone structure, hallowed relics, strong bones—to chronicle the phases of a life.

In its weird poeticizing of physiology, that piece is typical of many in the book (as well as some of the most haunting passages in Atwood's novels). Bodily life, male and fe-male, is inspected with jaunty acumen, and a cool eye is sent playing over its representations in fiction, sculpture and painting. These sections often call to mind that At-wood's father was an entomologist. Her stance in them sometimes jokily emulates scientific distance and dispas-sion, though her spoof zoologies of the human being and its gender habits soon mutate into sequences of gaudy, in-genious metaphor.

"No freak show can hold a candle to my father expound-ing Nature", Atwood wrote in an autobiographical essay in **Bluebeard's Egg.** In **Good Bones** to achieve and height-en a similar sense of the extraordinary, a vantage-point much favoured is that of the extra-terrestrial. **"Home-landing"** acquaints the inhabitants of another world with the behaviour-patterns peculiar to Earth's "prong people" and "cavern people". In **"Cold-Blooded"**, extra-planetary lepidoptera observe the activities of the "blood creatures" so surprisingly dominant on Earth, and note crude resem-blances to their own patterns of pupation and metamor-phosis: "At some indeterminate point in their life cycles, they cause themselves to be placed in artificial stone or wooden cocoons, or chrysalises. They have an idea that they will someday emerge from these in an altered state, which they symbolize with carvings of themselves with wings."

Death isn't the only phenomenon to receive this Martian treatment. One piece, **"Alien Territory"**, narrates the events of birth in terms of an adventure tale. Another turns the travelling of sperms towards an ovum into a sci-ence-fiction epic: "the mission becomes a race which only

one may win, as, ahead of them, vast and luminous, the longed-for, the loved planet swims into view. . . ."

Some of these flights of fantasy float away into buoyant humour. Gravity holds others closer to such global con-cerns as over-population, war and ecological catastrophe. As in Atwood's novels, the pervading style is fluently ac-complished, fluctuating between amusement and serious-ness, allowing mockery to meld affectingly into poetry: a meditation on bats moves with easy skill, for instance, from exuberant burlesque of the Dracula myth—"O flying leukaemia, in your cloak like a living umbrella"—to ten-der, exact evocation of the mammals "dank lazy half-sleep of daytime, with bodies rounded and soft as furred plums . . . the mothers licking the tiny amazed faces of the newborn". Mingling the incisive and the colourful, **Good Bones** makes a marvellous miniature sample-case of Atwood's sensuous and sardonic talents.

Nathalie Cooke   (essay date 1992)

SOURCE: "Reading Reflections: The Autobiographical Illusion in *Cat's Eye,"* in *Essays on Life Writing: From Genre to Critical Practice,* edited by Marlene Kadar, Uni-versity of Toronto Press, 1992, pp. 162-70.

[*In the following essay, Cooke explores Atwood's use of a fictional protagonist and an autobiographical form in* Cat's Eye.]

I have been told by friends, relatives, colleagues, and teachers—in fact, by everyone I know who has read it—that Margaret Atwood's *Cat's Eye* is 'more autobiograph-ical than her other books.' And, of course, they are right. It *is* more autobiographical—or, anyway, it is more obvi-ously about self-representation—than her other books. But it is autobiographical in the same way that **Lady Ora-cle** is gothic: it speaks to the form as much as it speaks from or within it.

The fascinating part about all this is that those experi-enced readers who would be embarrassed to classify **Lady Oracle** as just another costume gothic, or **Surfacing** as a simple unironic quest narrative, are the very same readers who seem to dismiss this novel by describing it as 'autobio-graphical.' They have been fooled by Atwood—yes—but also by the literary conventions she is exploring in this novel, those of autobiography itself. Most important, they have been fooled into looking at the autobiographical illu-sion that Atwood creates, and into overlooking the deft sleight of hand involved in its creation.

My argument is that autobiography is not so much a ge-neric category as it is a literary strategy. Atwood's readers must do more than classify **Cat's Eye** in terms of autobiog-raphy; they must focus their attention on the way autobi-ography is used in the novel. Accordingly, the emphasis of my discussion of the autobiographical elements in **Cat's Eye** lies more on Atwood's artistry than on the links be-tween Atwood's life and her art.

I am choosing my terms carefully because as critics have come to question their confidence in the 'referentiality of language' and the 'authenticity of the self' they have be-come increasingly uncomfortable about classifying autobiography at all, particularly about differentiating between autobiography, on the one hand, and fictional autobiography, on the other. After all, the project of categorizing various kinds of autobiographical writing places limits on a form that seeks to challenge limits—those between expression and experience, in particular. Northrop Frye, for example, traces autobiography back to 'a creative, and therefore fictional' impulse. And Paul Jay argues that 'the attempt to differentiate between autobiography and fictional autobiography is finally pointless. For if by "fictional" we mean "made up," "created," or "imagined"—something, that is, which is literary and not "real"—then we have merely defined the ontological status of any text, autobiographical or not.' However, by conflating forms of autobiography and fiction, Jay ignores the invitation that autobiographical fiction sends to its readers, to be read as *both* fiction and nonfiction—at the same time. Readers of autobiographical fiction, that is, are asked to read with a kind of double vision. I am by no means suggesting that such writing is any less fictional than fiction itself, just that we are invited to believe it might be. Herein, to my mind, lies all the difference.

What reason do we have to identify autobiographical elements as distinguised from fictional ones? I think we suspect that autobiography *reads* differently from fiction. Before we open the cover, for example, we find ourselves wanting to know whether a book is fiction or non-fiction. To be sure, when we say that a work is autobiographical we suggest that it has a claim to truth. This is why, as Alice Munro attests, those who classify a work as autobiographical go on to comment on its validity, and its author's 'good faith' or 'honesty.' In spite of ourselves, then, we readers check to see what shelf a book is on in the library; we read the dust jacket; we watch for markers within the text.

When we do these things with *Cat's Eye* we find quite a bit of evidence to suggest that it *is* autobiographical. Briefly, it is a first-person narratives about an artist who sanctions autobiographical readings of her own work. Then there is Margaret Atwood's dust-jacket biography that bears striking resemblances to the events of Elaine's narrative: the entomologist father, the brother, the summers in the countryside, the Toronto childhood, to name only a few things. Further, some of the episodes in Elaine's life cannot help but remind us of episodes in the lives of her fictional sisters. Take that Toronto ravine, for instance. It haunts Joan of *Lady Oracle* just as it haunts Elaine. And, by now, it has made a deep and lasting impression on all of Atwood's readers.

Ironically, too, Atwood's disclaimer only makes us focus our attention on the autobiographical elements within the novel. 'This is a work of fiction,' she tells us. 'Although its form is that of an autobiography, it is not one.' But we all know enough not to take Atwood's comments at face value, so we pursue the issue. In what way does *Cat's Eye* have the form of an autobiography? In what way is it fiction? Can we not assume that the incidents in *Cat's Eye,* as well as the first-person narrator, are grounded in Atwood's own life? I think we can; but how does that help us?

One answer is that *Cat's Eye* is both fiction *and* autobiography: a 'fictive autobiography,' to coin my own term, an autobiography composed by a fictional protagonist, which draws attention to its own problematical status as a fictive construct. As a result, we expect more from this book, and from Atwood herself: entertainment *and* honesty, craft *and* good faith. But that does not solve the problem. It is not enough for me to classify this *as* a fictive autobiography (as I have), as autobiography, as fiction, or, as Douglas Glover writes in his review (for *Books in Canada*), Atwood playing 'hide-and-seek at the place where autobiography and fiction meet, always ensuring there is a back door open for quick escapes.' More important than our trying to define *Cat's Eye* in relation to those two terms, fiction and autobiography, is our exploring the implications of Atwood's challenging us to try.

That is, Atwood is deliberately using the autobiographical form in her fiction. But why? I can think of at least three reasons for this: there are probably many more.

First, Atwood has always forced us to explore our assumptions as readers. When she writes, 'You fit into me / like a hook into an eye,' we are certain we understand the kind of relationship she is talking about: the solid, comfortable, close male-female kind. But then she makes us take another look. 'A fish hook,' she writes. 'An open eye' ('Epigraph,' *Power Politics*). What she is doing in *Cat's Eye* is an expanded version of this kind of pulling-the-rug-out-from-under-us. By now, in this post-Saussurean, post-post-modern literary era, we probably think that we can no longer be taken in by anything that has the ontological status of a literary text. However sophisticated we are as readers, though, we can all still be caught on the autobiographical hook. We think of ourselves as 'sophisticated readers,' after all, precisely because we enjoy reading; it satisfies an insatiable curiosity, a desire to solve questions, to find things out. And autobiographical fiction offers the lure of a particular individual's answers (in good faith) to the questions that concern him or her.

Further, when the writer is a woman, the temptation to ignore the distance between the text and the events represented in it seems to be even greater. Women have long been credited with the dubious honour of best being able to understand and communicate their emotions and personal experience. Mary Jacobus calls this the 'autobiographical "phallacy," '—with a "ph"—'whereby male critics hold that women's writing is somehow closer to experience than men's, that the female text *is* the author, or at any rate a dramatic extension of her unconsciousness.' But it is not only male critics who give credence to the 'autobiographical "phallacy" '; so too do feminists. Sylvia Plath proudly proclaims that women have long been associated with the 'blood-hot and personal.' And as Molly Hite quite rightly notes, 'many of the Anglo-American feminist critics who began with the intent of doing justice to women's fiction as a chronicle of female experience seem to have found themselves in the process purveying an exaggerated theory of mimesis in which authors are simply mirrored in their own texts.'

In fine, when we read *Cat's Eye* we are drawn by the prospect of the author within the text, of finding out about Atwood, or perhaps by having those stories we have heard about her confirmed, by her. It is not that this book is any less fictional than her others, but rather that the autobiographical elements in it suggest that it might be.

Atwood knows this. She has recognized that autobiographical fiction, by its very definition, forces its readers to do a kind of double-take—the same kind of double-take she has always demanded for her readers. At first glance, that is, generic classification seems to be a central issue. On closer inspection, however, it becomes apparent that this is no more than a red herring. When we read *Cat's Eye,* we are forced to redirect our attention from Atwood's presence or absence in this seemingly autobiographical text to ourselves and, in particular, to our assumptions about autobiographical fiction itself. This is indeed a book about self-reflection; and the reader's role is to reflect upon the various reflections of the self contained within it.

Another reason why Atwood uses the autobiographical in her fiction is that it provides one alternative to the narrative closure that seems to make her so uncomfortable. Cause of much critical anxiety, you will remember, was the absence of closure in Atwood's novel *Surfacing.* Hiding silently at the end of the novel, the still-unnamed protagonist is unable to move, let alone set about reintegrating herself into society. The conclusion of Atwood's next novel, *Lady Oracle,* is still more unstable. Not only do we find out that a stranger has probably recorded what we have so far taken to be Joan's first-hand account of her life, but we find that Joan is unable to impose closure on the book she herself is writing. If closure is anywhere to be found in this novel, it is in the opening lines, where Joan describes the death she has orchestrated for herself. As soon as we read further, though, we find that this ending, like all closure within the novel, has been exploded. Other endings are problematic as well: think of *The Handmaid's Tale* or *The Edible Woman.* Certainly, Atwood resists the two endings frequently reserved for a novel's heroine: marriage or death. This limited option, as Rachel Blau du Plessis has pointed out, is inadequate for any female writer. Instead, du Plessis argues, some women writers choose to 'write beyond' the traditional endings they inherit as a way of illustrating their problematic nature. And Atwood, in particular, has consistently shown her discomfort with narrative conventions by 'unwriting' the novelistic forms she takes up—the quest in *Surfacing,* the gothic in *Lady Oracle,* to name just two examples.

Of course, that *Cat's Eye* is a fictive autobiography would seem to eliminate the problem of closure: since the future is unclear to the autobiographer as well as to his or her audience, the ending of any autobiographical work is often ambiguous. And *Cat's Eye* is no exception in that the ending points to the limited nature of human perception:

> Now it's full night, clear, moonless and filled with stars, which are not eternal as was once thought, which are not where we think they are. If they were sounds, they would be echoes, of something that happened millions of years ago: a word made of numbers. Echoes of light, shining out of the midst of nothing.

> It's old light, and there's not much of it. But it's enough to see by.

But the autobiographical elements in *Cat's Eye* serve to challenge closure in a different way. As we recognize material from both *Surfacing* and *Lady Oracle,* we realize that Atwood draws upon and uses the autobiographical in these novels too. And surely, this is a way of forcing us to look beyond the text—to the unwritten world of Atwood's own experiences, perhaps, but certainly to other texts.

Finally, Atwood used the autobiographical as a tool in her ongoing challenge of classification, literary and otherwise. In her earlier novels, discomfort with rigid schemes of classification was voiced by the novel's heroines. Joan Foster, for instance, fights against the gothic as it begins to encroach upon her life and her art, seeing herself as a kind of 'escape artist.' Offred, too, attempts to escape from the prison-house that her society has created around biblical words and phrases. And even such an early protagonist as the Surfacer is uncomfortable with the restrictions society imposes upon women. To be sure, by alerting us to the fact that women in the Quebec countryside have no names, she emphasizes her—and yes, Atwood's—discomfort with naming. Neither the Surfacer nor the protagonist of *The Handmaid's Tale* have names (although Connie Rooke argues very convincingly that she has discovered Offred's 'real' name). Generally, though, Offred is called 'The Handmaid' by the academics of the text and within it who piece together her story. And, as they suggest, the name 'Offred' is itself only a 'patronymic, composed of the possessive preposition and the first name of the gentleman in question.'

For an Atwood heroine, though, Elaine Risley seems curiously resigned to the ways in which she and her art are classified. When Charna, one of the capital 'f' feminists in the book, describes *The Three Muses* as 'her disconcerting deconstruction of perceived gender and its relationship to perceived power, especially in respect to numinous imagery,' Risley agrees—up to a point. 'If I hold my breath and squint,' she says, 'I can see where she gets that.' As readers, though, we cannot help seeing that Charna's description of the painting is inadequate. It is not wrong, exactly; it is just limited. Because we see the paintings through Elaine's eyes, we are able to see more in them than feminist concerns.

What is happening, then, is that the heroine no longer has to battle against the hegemony of rigid classification precisely because the reader does it for her. Whereas, we readers are now very comfortable suggesting that the parodic elements in novels such as *Surfacing, Lady Oracle,* and *The Handmaid's Tale* are motivated by Atwood's 'feminist' concerns, we are suddenly uncomfortable with the term. Somehow that vexed tag 'feminist'—which means something different to Charna, Jody, Carolyn, Zillah, and Elaine, to name just a few examples—is more problematic than descriptive. And yet it is still necessary: for *Cat's Eye* is a book about the thoughts and images that make up Elaine's reflections—feminist, humanist, and personal.

To be sure, reviewers have already shown that they are uncomfortable putting any labels to *Cat's Eye.* Just as in the past they have been quick to categorize—and recategorize—Atwood's work, they are now hesitating. Even more surprising than this resistance to classification, however, are the grounds upon which that resistance is based: the sense that this is *more* than a feminist tract, *more* than a postmodern exploration of literary self-reflection, precisely, because it speaks from and about the autobiographical form.

In other words, Atwood is forcing us to rethink our position—again. Just as we had become comfortable with the idea that a biographical reading is a reductive one, Atwood shows us that it is quite the opposite. It is precisely the autobiographical aspect in and of *Cat's Eye* that makes us resist our temptation to master the text. We want to say that *Cat's Eye* is all of fiction and autobiography, feminist tract and personal meditation, contemporary metafiction and classical narrative precisely because it is *more* than these. But to say that would be to admit that Atwood has restored our faith in story and in the magic of literary illusion; and we are surely much too experienced as readers to say that.

Laura Shapiro (review date 8 November 1993)

SOURCE: "Mirror, Mirror, Who's the Evilest?" in *Newsweek*, Vol. CXXII, No. 19, November 8, 1993, p. 81.

[*In the following review, Shapiro praises Atwood's novel* The Robber Bride.]

Nobody maps female psychic territory the way Margaret Atwood does, sure-footed even in the wilds. Her latest novel, ***The Robber Bride*** takes its title from the Grimm fairy tale about the robber bridegroom who kidnaps maidens and carries them off to his house to be cut up and eaten. Here the malevolent suitor is a woman named Zenia, mysterious and alluring, who insinuates herself into other women's lives and carries off their husbands and boyfriends. If they're lucky, they escape.

At the center of the book are three women, longtime friends who became so after Zenia slashed and burned her way through each of their lives. Zenia herself lurks just out of sight until close to the end, when each of the women confronts her—and in her, their own worst demons. The three are classic Atwood creations, so vivid and idiosyncratic they could live next door, while perfectly evoking their time (now) and place (big Canadian city with a university). There's Tony, the maverick military historian enthralled by the human face of war, who lectures on such topics as fly-front fastenings and their effect on speed and efficiency in battle. There's Roz, the rich but desperately insecure business-woman. If only she were world-class at something, she frets—saintliness, or better yet, sin. "Mirror, mirror, on the wall, who is the evilest of us all?" she wonders. And it answers, "Take off a few pounds, cookie, and maybe I can do something for you." The third is Charis, born Karen, a name she left behind when she took up a life of herbal remedies, reading people's auras and oneness with nature. It's a measure of Atwood's great gifts that she can describe Karen's childhood experience of incest—a crime on the brink of becoming a literary cliché—so poignantly that it's freshly agonizing.

Moving amid these three women, touching up their portraits with one perfect detail after another, conjuring Zenia from their memories and fears, Atwood is in her glory. What a treasure she is, and what a fine new book she has written.

Margaret Atwood with Lauri Miller (interview date February-March 1994)

SOURCE: "On the Villainess," in *San Francisco Review of Books,* February-March, 1994, pp. 30-32, 34.

[*In the following excerpt, Atwood discusses her writing process and the role of the literary villainess in reference to her book* The Robber Bride.]

[*Miller*]: *In* **The Robber Bride,** *your character Zenia is cruel, cold-blooded and calculated, so able to manipulate the female protagonists in the book . . .*

[Atwood]: . . . And the male . . .

In a recent New York Times *article you said there has been a gap in the literary appearance of the villainess. Has this been particularly on the part of women writers, and have you met any resistance to Zenia from feminists?*

No. There is a whole list of manipulative characters, some of them written by women. We need go back no further than Edith Wharton. Have you read *The Custom of the Country?*

No, I haven't.

Well, you should. (She laughs.) It is about a manipulative, social climbing woman who steps on the bodies of all the men she climbs over. Also *The House of Mirth*, about an extremely evil women, the adulterer's wife, who essentially destroys the heroine of this book. So there are several such characters; when I was talking about it, it was that this character had disappeared in the fifties. I was at a feminist conference called 'Women Reviewing Women' in Wellesley; I was surrounded by feminists. They were buying this book like crazy. And I also get this a lot at readings, that it's so wonderful that women don't just have to be good and victims all the time because if you make women nice all the time that's the equivalent to making them powerless all the time. Of course, there have been many more villainesses created by men. And do you know why that is? Because there have been so many more characters created by men. And why was that? Because women really didn't start writing books until the late nineteenth century. Why was that? Because they couldn't write. If you want to see a villainess character, take a look at Toni Morrison's *Sula*.

So you don't feel there has been a recent gap in women writers depicting such evil in women?

There was a gap beginning in the fifties. The *femme fatale* disappeared for awhile, and I think the reason for that was that there was a big push to get women back into the home. And you can't set up housekeeping with the Marlene Dietrich of *The Blue Angel*. It's not going to work out. So women had to be made much more mommy-like, much more Doris Day-like or cute and pert and Debbie

Reynolds-like or sexual and stupid, like Marilyn Monroe and not a threat. But the threatening, smart, cunning, manipulative women, which Clare Boothe Luce's play *The Women* was all about—have you ever seen it?

No I haven't.

Well there's a movie version of it too. Take a look. All of the women in it are out scheming one another. There's never a man visible. It's very cleverly done. You see the women talking to them on the phone, but you never actually see a man in the whole movie. It's all women, and there are good ones and bad ones, and the plot finally turns when the good one decides to fight for the man that the bad one has stolen. And that was a forties movie, and I think it may have been a thirties play. This was a familiar character until the fifties, and then she disappeared. And then we got the sixties, and she wasn't around much then either because the sixties were the fifties until 1967, and then everybody was so focused on quote the sexual revolution that we weren't even thinking about that, and then came the women's movement with, "If you can't say anything nice about women, don't say anything at all." I think we're now through with all that, and we can put the full cast of characters back on the stage. Because to say that women can't be malicious and intentionally bad is to say that they're congenitally incapable of that, which is really very limiting.

For all her evil, it does seem that ultimately Zenia has a positive effect on the three female protagonists? Would you agree?

I like to leave judgments like that to the reader. Some people have said that; other people have said all kinds of other things that have nothing to do with that.

Well, their relationship to Zenia does seem to represent the fact that if one is not willing to look squarely at one's darker side, one is ultimately less able and less powerful.

Well, I would certainly take that point of view. I think you could say that. I don't know whether you're familiar with the opera *Tales of Hoffman*. There's a character in that who gets his shadow stolen from him, and in fact, to lose your shadow is to lose your soul. So insofar as Zenia is the shadow side of the characters, she is a necessary component. But you must realize that any character in a novel, if the novel is of any interest at all, has more than one dimension. Zenia is also a tricky con artist and a magician; by magician I mean the kind that says, "Look here," and while you're looking there, they're picking your pocket with the other hand. As an example, if I want to sell you the Golden Gate Bridge and you want to buy it, you give me the money. If it's a legitimate transaction, I give you the Bridge. If it's not a legitimate transaction, then you give me the money, and I skip town, and then you find out that I never had the Bridge in the first place. That's a con artist transaction, and that's what Zenia does. But notice that it is dependent on the desire of the person who gets conned. I can't sell you the Golden Gate Bridge unless you want to buy it. So Zenia has something to offer each of the characters that they want. And part of it is their notions of themselves as nice people, because in each case, she appeals to them for help, and because it is part of their image

of themselves and they help one another, they help her. And with one another, it's real help that they have to give, and it's needed, and all of those exchanges are legitimate exchanges. So it's not saying, "Don't be a nice person." I think it's saying, "Look in the bag or else you're going to get left holding the sack," or "A rattlesnake that doesn't bite teaches you nothing," or "Illusion is the first of all pleasures."

Would you say that you enjoy creating a certain amount of stir? In a past interview you said, "If you're not annoying someone, you're not really alive."

Well, I don't think it's cause and effect. In other words, I don't set out to annoy people. I set out to write books, and in all books there is conflict, in all books that hold your interest for more than ten pages. There is change, there is conflict, there are things that rub against one another, and that is just the nature of the novel. Wouldn't you say?

Yes I would.

Because if you have a book in which John and Mary get up in the morning and have a wonderful day, and they are very nice to each other, and their kids turn out well, and their dog is just terrific, and they have a great house, and they both have wonderful jobs, how much longer are you going to go on reading? Something has to happen. So it can be the invasion of monsters from outer space; it can be a flaw in their own characters or another character in the book, but something has to happen.

Politics and the relationship of the powerful to the powerless is a thread that runs throughout your work. You have commented in the past about how you don't like the distinction made between politics and art, as though one is sullied and the other is pure.

No, what I don't like is people thinking that they can't put politics into art because one is contaminated and the other pure, that art should only be about the psyche, that it should only be about the individual. Well, the novel has never only been about that because the novel shows people moving through time in society, and no matter what kind of novel it is, it always has that, and once you have society, you have power structure, and once you have power structure, you have politics. By that I don't mean that all novels should be about what goes on in Washington. That's not what I'm saying at all. What I am saying is that in the world that we observe, power is distributed unevenly . . . not a huge insight. (She laughs.)

Is the most interesting work for you personally that which is written by those who are disenfranchised in some way?

No, I don't make that kind of distinction. The most interesting work is that which is well done. In other words, you can't categorize things in that way in terms of subject matter or genre either. Some people think there is something called a legitimate novel and that there are other forms that aren't quite right, such as detective fiction or science fiction. I don't make those kinds of distinctions. If a book is well done and gripping, I don't care what kind of book it is, and I don't care what its arena is. It happens to be so that books in which a person is contending with forces may very well be about a person in a disadvantaged group contending with the forces of society. It may be about that or it could be about something quite different. You never know. But if we were to say these kinds of books are good because of their subject matter and these kinds of books are bad because of their subject matter, we would certainly generate a lot of mediocre literature about certain subject matter.

Who are some of the writers you presently feel a certain affinity with, whose books you most eagerly anticipate?

I just got hold of E. Annie Proulx, not because I have read any of her work but just because she sounds interesting and I will read her work. The lists get very long, and they also irritate those who happen to be left out. I hate giving off-the-cuff lists. I read so much, and there are so many books that have been memorable to me that in order to answer this question properly, I would probably have to sit down and write you a bibliography that would be at least ten pages. But let me mention a new writer that you probably haven't heard of—Barbara Gowdy.

What is the range of your reading?

Very broad. I read all kinds of books from all kinds of times from all kinds of countries and from all kinds of genres. And by all kinds of genders. In fact, I just checked out a book called *Lesbian Vampire Stories.* Now there's a category. And it's full of evil women, I have to tell you, and it's very much promoted as a feminist book. What do you make of that? (She laughs.) Literature is full of male anti-heroes; maybe Zenia is a female anti-hero. (Laughter.) Certainly my publicity person at Doubleday . . . she said, "Oh I love this book. You can use it as a sort of litmus test for your friends. You can say, this is a Zenia person; this is a Charis person; this is a Tony person; this is a Roz person." And I said, "And what about you?" She said, "Zenia." I said, "Oh, I'm shocked and horrified. Why do you think Zenia?" She said, "Because I am all of the others, and I want to be her." I said, "Why are you saying that?" She said, "Because she has power." And it's true; she has power, and power can be power to help, and it can be power to harm, but it also has to contain within itself a potential for harm, otherwise it's not power. I think that's one of the things women found out when they got some power, that once you have some power you're going to do some things that other people don't like.

What are the seeds for your novels and short stories?

I used to thrash around trying to think of answers for this, and another writer gave me the answer. When asked, "Where do you get your ideas?," she says, "I think them up." And that's what happens.

Do you work on your poetry, novels, and short stories at the same time, alternating between them?

When I'm working on a novel, I do almost nothing else; although with this one, I did a few pieces which are more or less unclassifiable: some are monologues, some are short prose pieces, one is a rewrite of "The Little Red Hen" story, and one is what Gertrude really said to Hamlet when he came into her dressing room and told her how to behave. And that you'll get next year. But apart from

that, when I'm writing a novel, I don't usually write poetry. And when I'm writing short stories, I seem to write nothing but short stories.

What is your next step in writing a novel? Once you have that seed of plot, do you concentrate then on developing characters?

Well, I don't even necessarily start with a seed of plot. I start with an image, a theme, a voice, a situation, a circumstance. I think writing a novel is a lot like making things out of mud, with the same amount of squashing it up and throwing it away and starting again all of those kinds of things. I don't think novels proceed from the top down. I don't think they start with abstract concepts and move down. Some have been created like that; certain kinds of experimental writing are like certain kinds of conceptual art in that people say, "Oh, I think it would be a good idea to dig a great big, circular hole in the ground and then line it with pink plastic." And in a way once you have that notion, it's almost secondary to create the object. But I feel that I build my novels up much more from the ground and from details than from saying, "Now I'm going to write a novel about this."

So in creating your characters you don't first start with a concept of what you would like them to embody?

I don't start with that thing that people always wish you to produce. They say, "What is the main idea of your novel?" They think that novels are how-to books or books of philosophy or that they are my-theory-of-life type books. If I wanted to write that kind of book, I would have written it. Novels are about people, people moving through time interacting with one another, and I don't think they can be reduced to "What is the theme in twenty words or less?" As one person said, "What would you like the reader to take away with her?" In other words, "What's the prize in the box of crackers? Why did I have to go through all this popcorn just to get this little plastic thing?" When I was in high school, we had to take a poem and then write a prose rendition of it. I think a lot of people still have this notion that a writer is an inarticulate person who can't get it out, that it takes them 500 pages to say, "War is hell" or whatever the message may be, and I don't think that fiction or poetry work like that. I think that what the book means is the experience that you bring to the book, and therefore it's going to have a somewhat different meaning to every single individual because everyone brings his or her totality to a book. I will see different things from the things that somebody else will see, just as I will see different things in a painting or different things in a film. "Mr. Shakespeare, tell us what is the reader to take with her from *Hamlet?* Never put off tomorrow what you can do today." And that's often what we're asked to do, summarize and condense and come out with this message.

Do you revise as you write or get it all down and then revise?

I write it through and then I revise it, often as much as six times. After you've done that and after you've gone through your editor, who is a very picky person, and then gone through the galleys and the page proofs, you've gone through it a lot of times. But to get into it, it means you have to, at least I do, write quite freely and that means I discard a lot and have a lot of crumpled pieces of paper.

Do you allow your editor to read your work while it's in progress?

Absolutely not.

Is there anyone you allow to read it?

No, I didn't go to creative writing school.

Are you surprised by the turns your characters take?

Well if I wasn't, I would get very bored.

Is that part of what fuels you to write?

Nobody knows what fuels him or her. It's an unknown mystery, and nobody knows in the writing department and nobody knows in the rest of life. That's another one of those crackerjack questions: "Where's the battery? Where's the little box with what makes you go in it?"

But is the surprise element one of the things you most enjoy about writing?

I certainly enjoy those when they occur. I don't know, I've been doing this since I was 16 years old. It's kind of useless by this time to ask me why I do it. And really why should anybody have to answer that question? I mean, why do you like running? Why do you like horseback riding? I like it. It's in my personality to like it.

Edna O'Brien has said that whether a novel is autobiographical or not does not matter, that what is important is the truth in it and the way that truth is expressed. Do you agree with that?

Yes, because in fact who knows? You will never know. I mean I could lie my head off and tell you that in fact I'm Charis or some other thing like that, and you would never know. We certainly don't know whether Shakespeare thought he was Richard III. We will never get to interview him. The author interview is a very recent phenomenon. Probably authors shouldn't be allowed to go out in public at all.

FURTHER READING

Criticism

Banerjee, Chinmoy. "Atwood's Time: Hiding Art in *Cat's Eye*." *Modern Fiction Studies* 36, No. 4 (Winter 1990): 513-22.
  Discusses the various narrative voices Atwood uses in *Cat's Eye.*

Bayley, John. "Dry Eyes." *London Review of Books* 13, No. 23 (5 December 1991): 20.
  Compares the stories in Atwood's *Wilderness Tips* favorably to the works of Nadine Gordimer and Elizabeth Bowen.

Beaver, Harold. Review of *Selected Poems II: Poems Selected and New, 1976-1986*, by Margaret Atwood. *The New York Times Book Review* (3 April 1988): 12.

Praises Atwood's insights into women's issues in *Selected Poems II.*

Berne, Suzanne. "Watch Your Back." *Belles Lettres* 7, No. 1 (Fall 1991): 43.
  Positive review of *Wilderness Tips* noting Atwood's "wry [and] disdainful" authorial voice.

Birch, Dinah. "Post Feminism." *The London Review of Books* II, No. 2 (19 January 1989): 3, 5.
  Explores Atwood's *Cat's Eye* and *Interlunar* as expressions of the author's "personal postfeminism" and praises Atwood's insights about the nature of suffering.

Givner, Jessie. "Mirror Images in Margaret Atwood's *Lady Oracle*." *Studies in Canadian Literature* 14, No. 1 (1989): 139-46.
  Analyzes Atwood's displacement of conventional literary imagery in *Lady Oracle.*

———. "Names, Faces, and Signatures in Margaret Atwood's *Cat's Eye* and *The Handmaid's Tale*." *Canadian Literature*, No. 133 (Summer 1992): 56-75.
  Discusses Atwood's use of autobiographical elements in the two novels.

Greene, Gayle. "Survival Strategies." *The Women's Review of Books* IX, No. 4 (January 1992): 6-7.
  Praises *Wilderness Tips* for combining "the power of [Atwood's] fiction with the complexity of her poetry."

Keefe, Joan Trodden. Review of *Selected Poems II: Poems Selected and New, 1976-1986*, by Margaret Atwood. *World Literature Today* 63, No. 1 (Winter 1989): 103-04.
  Praises *Selected Poems II* and calls attention to the literary significance of Atwood's career.

Makay, Shena. "The Painter's Revenges." *The Times Literary Supplement*, No. 4479 (3 February 1989): 113.
  Applauds Atwood's fidelity to childhood experience in *Cat's Eye* and calls the book "probably Atwood's finest novel to date."

Miner, Madonne. " 'Trust Me': Reading the Romance Plot in Margaret Atwood's *The Handmaid's Tale*." *Twentieth Century Literature* 37, No. 2 (Summer 1991): 148-68.
  Examines Atwood's treatment of heterosexual love in *The Handmaid's Tale.*

Norfolk, Lawrence W. "Do They Travel?" *The Times Literary Supplement*, No. 4507 (24 August 1989): 903.
  Praises *Interlunar* and analyzes Atwood's use of dark and light imagery.

St. Andrews, B. A. "Requiem for an Age." *Belles Lettres* 5, No. 3 (Spring 1990): 9.
  Calls Atwood "a master at distilling essences and delineating profiles of our age" and praises *Cat's Eye* as "a massive and moving novel."

Thurman, Judith. "Books: When You Wish Upon a Star." *The New Yorker* LXV, No. 15 (29 May 1989): 108-10.
  Finds Atwood's depiction of childhood in *Cat's Eye* to be truthful and compelling, but objects to the "bullying" tone of the book's prose.

Towers, Robert. "Mystery Women." *The New York Review of Books* XXXVI, No. 7 (27 April 1989): 50-2.
  Praises Atwood's attention to detail in *Cat's Eye.*

Additional coverage of Atwood's life and career is contained in the following sources published by Gale Research: *Bestsellers 1989,* No. 2; *Contemporary Authors,* Vols. 49-52; *Contemporary Authors New Revision Series,* Vols. 3, 24; *Contemporary Literary Criticism,* Vols. 2, 3, 4, 8, 13, 15, 25, 44; *Dictionary of Literary Biography,* Vol. 53; *DISCovering Authors; Major 20th-Century Writers; Poetry Criticism,* Vol. 8; *Short Story Criticism,* Vol. 2; *Something about the Author,* Vol. 50; and *World Literature Criticism.*

Hayden Carruth

1921-

American poet, critic, novelist, and editor.

The following entry provides criticism on Carruth's works from 1982 to 1994. For further information on his life and works, see *CLC*, Volumes 4, 7, 10, and 18.

INTRODUCTION

Carruth is a well-respected and prolific author, whose frequently autobiographical poetry encompasses a wide variety of emotions and forms and is noted for its unadorned, precise use of language. Often addressing such themes as the fragility of life, the fine line between sanity and madness, and the importance of social responsibility, Carruth has called his philosophy of poetry a "radical secular existentialism." Carruth's literary criticism, collected in such volumes as *Working Papers* (1982) and *Effluences from the Sacred Caves* (1983), is recognized for its directness and magnanimity, while *The Voice That Is Great Within Us* (1970), a poetry anthology edited by Carruth, is frequently used in university literature courses and is considered one of the best representations of contemporary American poetry.

Biographical Information

Carruth was born to Gorton Veeder Carruth, a newspaper editor, and Margery Barrow Carruth in Waterbury, Connecticut. He received a B.A. from the University of North Carolina at Chapel Hill in 1943 and earned an M.A. from the University of Chicago in 1947. During World War II, Carruth served for two years in the United States Army Air Corps, advancing ultimately to the rank of staff sergeant. Carruth worked as editor of *Poetry* magazine from 1949 to 1950, associate editor of the University of Chicago Press from 1950 to 1951, and project administrator for New York's Intercultural Publications from 1952 to 1953. In 1953 Carruth suffered an emotional breakdown and was admitted to Bloomingdale, the psychiatric branch of New York Hospital in White Plains, New York. Carruth kept journals and wrote poetry while hospitalized; these writings were encouraged by his doctors as a means of therapy until his condition worsened and he underwent electroconvulsive therapy. Carruth later acted as consulting editor of the *Hudson Review* and poetry editor of *Harper's*, and served on the faculties of the University of Vermont and Syracuse University. Carruth has won numerous literary awards, including the 1968 Morton Dauwen Zabel Prize, Guggenheim Foundation fellowships in 1965 and 1979, a senior fellowship from the National Endowment for the Arts in 1988, and the 1990 Ruth Lilly Poetry Prize.

Major Works

Carruth has published more than twenty-five volumes of poetry, some of which are single poems divided into sections. His long poem *The Bloomingdale Papers* (1975) was composed during his 1953 hospitalization and chronicles his experiences as a patient in a psychiatric ward. Carruth's poetic form, subject matter, and tone vary widely, even within a single collection, but he is almost entirely consistent in maintaining the importance of subject over poetic form. For example, in *The Bloomingdale Papers*, Carruth asserted: "I am a poet / whereby I mean no boast. / I want to / say simply, I am a poet, not a good one, / whereby neither do I mean any abasement. / Poetry is profuse and multinominal / the latency of action." In *For You* (1970) Carruth collects and revises five of his previously published long poems, the first of which, "The Asylum," treats the irony of the word "asylum" and is marked by stark, striking imagery and an apparent rejection of meaning. In "Journey to a Known Place" and "North Winter," the second and third poems in *For You*, Carruth forms a connection between the speaker and elements of the natural world, while in "Contra mortem" Carruth focuses upon a Vermont village and its inhabitants. In "My

Father's Face," the final poem in *For You*, Carruth departs from the contained, imagistic approach of the first four poems and gives voice to his distress over the loss of a parent. Considered by many critics to be one of Carruth's best poetry collections, *Brothers, I Loved You All* (1978) treats a variety of subjects and themes, including the madness inherent in society and the importance of the natural world in confirming thoughts and emotions. Carruth has commented: "By evolving into a state of self-consciousness, we have separated ourselves from the other animals and the plants and from the very earth itself, from the whole universe. So there's a kind of fear and terror involved in living close to nature. My poems, I think, exist in a state of tension between the love of natural beauty and the fear of natural meaninglessness or absurdity." *The Sleeping Beauty* (1982), another highly respected poetry collection, consists of 124 fifteen-line stanzas that address attitudes about women and love.

Critical Reception

Many critics have praised Carruth's honesty, integrity, and directness of approach in both his poetry and his literary criticism. He has been recognized for his ability to elicit intense emotional reaction in a variety of poetic forms and for the spare, tightly controlled language he uses to treat common subjects. Nevertheless, some critics have characterized Carruth's use of plain language as rigid and didactic, and they fault his poetry for lacking insight. Several commentators have noted that the quality of Carruth's verse tends to be uneven, but contend that Carruth captures basic human thoughts and emotions and expresses them in a sincere and unassuming manner. Alastair Reid has commented: "[Carruth's] poems have a sureness to them, a flair and variety. . . . His work teems with the struggle to live and to make sense, and his poems carve out a kind of grace for us." As a critic, Carruth has been praised for his extensive knowledge of literature, his open-mindedness, and his focus on social issues. As to the role of the literary critic, Carruth has stated: "Reviewers who use the space assigned them primarily for slopping out their own temperamentalities or for buttering up editors and readers by displaying their own cleverness at the expense of the authors whose works they are supposed to be considering, have no place—I emphasize, no place at all—in a responsible culture."

PRINCIPAL WORKS

The Crow and the Heart, 1946-1949   (poetry)   1959
Journey to a Known Place   (poem)   1961
The Norfolk Poems: 1 June to 1 September 1961   (poetry) 1962
Appendix A   (novel)   1963
After "The Stranger": Imaginary Dialogues with Camus (essays)   1964
North Winter   (poem)   1964
Nothing for Tigers: Poems, 1959-1964   (poetry)   1965
Contra mortem   (poem)   1967

The Clay Hill Anthology   (poetry)   1970
**For You*   (poetry)   1970
The Voice That Is Great Within Us: American Poetry of the Twentieth Century   [editor]   (poetry anthology) 1970
From Snow and Rock, from Chaos: Poems, 1965-1972 (poetry)   1973
Dark World   (poetry)   1974
The Bloomingdale Papers   (poetry)   1975
Loneliness: An Outburst of Hexasyllables   (poem)   1976
Brothers, I Loved You All: Poems, 1969-1977   (poetry) 1978
Almanach du printemps vivarois   (poetry)   1979
The Mythology of Darkness and Light   (poetry)   1982
The Sleeping Beauty   (poem)   1982
Working Papers: Selected Essays and Reviews   (criticism) 1982
Effluences from the Sacred Caves: More Selected Essays and Reviews   (criticism)   1983
If You Call This Cry a Song   (poetry)   1983
Asphalt Georgics   (poetry)   1985
Lighter than Air Craft   (poetry)   1985
The Oldest Killed Lake in North America   (poetry) 1985
Mother   (poem)   1986
The Selected Poetry of Hayden Carruth   (poetry)   1986
Sitting In: Selected Writings on Jazz, Blues, and Related Topics   (essays and poetry)   1986
Sonnets   (poetry)   1989
Tell Me Again How the White Heron Rises and Flies Across the Nacreous River at Twilight toward the Distant Islands   (poetry)   1989
Collected Shorter Poems, 1946-1991   (poetry)   1992
Suicides and Jazzers   (criticism)   1992
Collected Longer Poems   (poetry)   1993

---

*This volume contains revised versions of the previously published long poems "The Asylum" (which first appeared in *The Crow and the Heart*), "Journey to a Known Place," "North Winter," "Contra mortem," and "My Father's Face."

CRITICISM

Judith Weissman   (essay date 1982)

SOURCE: An introduction to *Working Papers: Selected Essays and Reviews* by Hayden Carruth, edited by Judith Weissman, The University of Georgia Press, 1982, pp. xv-xxiii.

[*In the following essay, Weissman surveys Carruth's critical works, concluding: "[Carruth's] progress has taken him continuously deeper into the knowledge of his own humanity, and of the humanity of literature."*]

It is difficult to write an introduction to the works of any living author, and it is particularly difficult to write about this selection of Hayden Carruth's essays and reviews. His work seems awesomely rich, full, complete—thirty years of essays that begin with Pound and end with numerous younger poets in mid-flight. But the appearance of completeness is illusory, for these essays are no more than a tenth of those Carruth has written. I am particularly sorry not to include a review of a group of critical books on Spenser and three notes on Pope, to whom Carruth brings the same sense of joyful discovery that he brings to poets whom he is actually reading for the first time. But some principles of selection were necessary, and one was that I would try to present, through these essays, a history of the last thirty years of literature. (Occasional departures from even this principle were made, as in the inclusion of the review of Casanova's memoirs. I included that review because it was thematically so well connected with others on love and aristocracy.) This selection concludes with a review that points toward the future, on what poets may do in the 1980s, because this volume should not appear to be nicely and neatly *finished*. Plenty of people are still writing, and Carruth is still reviewing them.

The title, **Working Papers,** modest as it is, was chosen by Carruth years ago, when he first planned to publish a collection of his essays. It is still appropriate now: it is modesty that characterizes these essays, and Carruth's poems, and Carruth himself. In addition, the subtle pun of the title, the several meanings of the phrase, are too important to abandon. It is true that this book is sketchy, a draft, in a way, of the polished book of literary criticism that Carruth might have written in another life. Most of these essays and reviews were written as real *work*—which, in our society, means labor performed in exchange for money. The reviews, particularly, were the work Carruth did instead of being part of a university—they got him out of school, like the working papers of sixteen-year-old boys in the 1930s.

In need of money, Carruth has taken review assignments as they came, on books which he did not choose. The few long, fully developed essays here—like those on Robert Lowell and on **"Poetry and Personality"**—make me wish that he had been able to write more of them, rather than being driven by necessity into doing so many brief reviews. But there is no reason to mourn over what he has done, or to treat this volume as one of promise rather than fulfillment, of frustration rather than realization. How many people in the privileged world of academia have written anything as good as this collection of reviews? Their genesis as work, as daily labor, has given them life. Carruth wrote them, not for the audience of scholarly journals, but often for newspapers or political magazines like *The Nation* or the *New Republic*. (Some, of course, were for more literary journals, though not academic ones, like *Poetry* and the *Hudson Review*.)

Some of the humanity of these essays and reviews also springs from Carruth's knowledge that he could help to determine the success of other people's books and affect how much money they made. The importance of reviewing, and of Carruth's reviewing in particular, became strikingly clear to me one evening when we attended a reading by a middle-aged poet who will never be rich or famous. He was amazed and delighted that Hayden Carruth had driven thirty miles to hear him, and after the reading, in private talk, recalled Carruth's review, many

years earlier, of one of his books. "My marriage was falling apart, I was cracking up. I had written what I knew was my best book, and no one would review it. Except you. You knew it was good. Man, you saved my life." The man was not joking.

A well-known reviewer has a lot of power. He can give outrageously high praise to his friends, who will then of course return the favor; he can put down rivals and newcomers who are potential rivals, and anyone who has dared to insult him; above all, he can advertise himself. Carruth never does any of this. The unspoken values of these essays and reviews—humility, modesty, generosity, self-effacement—are the most important values of all. Carruth occasionally acknowledges the flawed, human self which, like everyone else, he certainly has—as in the essay on Robert Lowell, when he says that he envies Lowell's wealth and privilege, and easy success and fame as a poet—but how miraculously free from the bitterness of self these essays and reviews are! How encouraging to the young, how respectful to the old and out of fashion, how sincerely interested in the work of other writers.

Everyone who has read Carruth's poems knows some of the troubles of his life and can figure out that he wrote these lucid and kind reviews under some of the most difficult of human circumstances. The tone and texture are so even, strong, almost imperturbable, that it is an effort to remember that Carruth's daily intercourse with the human world has been unusually painful and difficult, and that he lived most of the last twenty years in northern Vermont, an especially poor man in a place where nearly everyone was poor. These reviews do not have the feeling of loneliness, which always does harm, though it sometimes also does good. They are so friendly, social, communicative. They could not be more different from the cranky soliloquies that we might expect from someone who has lived Carruth's life.

That life is not entirely absent here, however. The changes in the essays reflect Carruth's own life as well as his participation in a general cultural life. Most important is a change in his language. At the beginning, he sounds like what he was, an ambitious young editor of a prestigious urban magazine, *Poetry*, located in a big city, Chicago. By the end, we can hear Vermont in his voice. He is looser, more colloquial, more concerned with everyday life, nature, agriculture. One sentence, from the last review, will be sufficient illustration: "Dullness sprang up in the fertile soil of American poetry during the seventies like colorless saprophytes in a damp pine forest." This is not the talk of a Vermont farmer. It is the talk of an extraordinarily intelligent and observant man who knows both the world of poetry and culture, and the plants of the Vermont woods, and understands both well enough to make use of one as an exceedingly precise metaphor for the other. A cultural tragedy is implied in this, a tragedy that informs Carruth's sense of the world. No one would bother to remark that Shakespeare or Milton or Wordsworth knew both culture and nature, but in our country the division has been growing deeper and deeper between the country and the city, agriculture and learning, the small community and the larger world. Carruth's life is extraordinary because he has known all of these possibilities so fully, and it has also been extraordinarily sad because he has known the pain of losing each of them.

Carruth never writes with the weary ease that often comes with self-confident skill and assured success. . . . Carruth has endured without settling into stoicism because he has refused to cease either suffering or hoping. His progress has taken him continuously deeper into the knowledge of his own humanity, and of the humanity of literature.

—Judith Weissman

Carruth's personal history is of less importance here than the other histories he writes about. The events of the world, as excluded from the New Criticism as the personalities of the poet and critic, are very much in evidence here. World War II, the Holocaust (before it became a fashionable topic), atomic weapons, racism in the United States (do other critics remember George Jackson?), and always, the suffering of the poor under the innumerable oppressions of government and bureaucracy. We hear occasionally about the problems of artists, too; but thank God we never hear that their sufferings are greater than those of the rest of the world. Justice and injustice, happiness and suffering, good and evil—yes, good and evil—and their consequences for the human race as a whole—those are always the final terms by which Carruth tests literature. These essays are not crudely utilitarian in any way; Carruth never says that some piece of writing is good simply because it contains some particular social idea or value. The utilitarianism (an unjustly disparaged philosophy in any case) is subtle and indirect. it lies in Carruth's refusal to let us forget that the ultimate context for art is the world—and that the world has been a very ugly place in the last thirty years. He has seen horror as clearly as anyone can, but has resisted the temptation to believe that an artist has the right to isolate and protect himself. He has held onto his vision of the sufferings of the world tenaciously, grimly, and above all, without cynicism.

The book, however, is primarily about neither Carruth nor the fall of the West. It is about literature and literary criticism. Carruth's interest in the literary criticism of the last thirty years has been more limited than his interest in poetry. He has not bothered with the bizarre explosion of academic criticism in the last few years, and we do not yet know what he has to say about the likes of Lacan and Derrida. Here he has written mainly about the New Criticism and some reactions to it, in his reviews of Karl Shapiro, Northrop Frye, Paul Elmer More, Joseph Frank, Martin Price, Eliseo Vivas, John Hall Wheelock, Edmund Wilson, George Steiner. Carruth shows the same respect and generosity toward other critics as he does to other poets; he admires intelligence, learning, scholarship, and love for

the tradition of literature, in others. He deplores readings that include no glance at the outside world or that rest on esthetic values alone.

Carruth's own criticism is always on the verge of becoming philosophy. And he writes comfortably, surely more comfortably than most poets would, about philosophical and historical prose. Camus, Sartre (on Genet), Genet, de Rougemont, Eliot, Eliot on Bradley, Casanova, Yevtushenko, Irving Singer, Gottfried Benn, Wyndham Lewis—a rather odd collection here, which, we must remember, Carruth did not choose. Such a disparate group does, oddly, belong together, for Carruth has unified them with two recurrent themes, the difficulties of human love, and the relation of art to the world. The European existentialists are among the heroes of this book, and surely its villains (I do not choose the word lightly) are Benn and Lewis. They are the primary examples of the evil to which men can come when they decide that they have the right to choose art over life. Carruth does not simply label them fascists and let them go, as a less conscientious critic might have done. He gives them the same intelligent care in reading that he gives to the others, and even praises them when they deserve praise. But he never allows their virtues—intelligence, skill, style—to obliterate his knowledge of the wickedness of what they believe. He cannot pardon them for writing well when what they say is evil.

Poetry is the subject of most of these essays, which constitute a perpetual reproach to the joylessness of academic criticism. There is joy in them. Read them—and remember what it was like to read for the first time Pound, Williams, Auden, Stevens, Muir, Ferlinghetti, Levertov, Aiken, Rukeyser, Duncan, Eliot, Perse, Lowell, Schwartz, Jarrell, Berryman, Zukofsky, Berry. Carruth is a graceful master of the myriad techniques of literary criticism, using them with ease to range widely, in lucid analysis of individual poems or poets, or the psychological development of a poet's work, or the poet's connection with a tradition which Carruth knows and reveres (a tradition which includes John Clare and William Barnes along with Shakespeare and Wordsworth). Though Carruth calls only a few human failings evil—cruelty, selfishness, fakery—he finds goodness in many places.

> *Paterson* . . . is a poem intense, complicated, and absorbing, one of the best examples of concision of poetry that I know.

> The love poems [of MacLeish], and there are many, written during every phase of the poet's career and under every aspect of feeling, are often splendid, composed with a restraint and exactness of language that is songlike, reproducing the sensuousness of ideas very evocatively, the basic eroticism of human thought.

> Opulence—it is the quality most of us would ascribe to the poetry of Wallace Stevens before all others; profusion, exotic luxuriance.

> This is hard substance, and the poems [of Muir] have about them, beyond their verbal utilitarianism, a kind of obduracy of spirit that we associate with the Scotch Presbyterian sensibility.

> Force, directness, affection for the separate word

and the various parts of speech (especially participles), knowledge of cadence and syntax, as components of meaning rather than vicissitudes of fabrication—there can be no doubt that Miss Rukeyser can write good poetry.

Perse writes a kind of pure poem of sensibility, an analytic of the heart, a conceptualizing poem. Without meter, without any rhythm except the self-sustaining verbal flow, his poetic principle, as one would expect in so abstract a composition, is pure grammar.

He has resolved to accept reality, all reality, and to take its fragments indiscriminately as they come, forging from them this indissoluble locus of metaphorical connections that is known as Robert Lowell.

In his war poems Randall Jarrell did rise, as if in spite of himself and at the command of a classical force outside himself, to his moment of tragic vision.

They all derive from his [Wendell Berry's] experience as a subsistence farmer, and they celebrate the earth and the strength a man gains from contact with soil, water, stone, and seed. Make no mistake, these are poems in praise of Aphrodite of the Hot Furrow, full of generative force, even though their manner is seldom rhapsodic.

What word can describe Carruth's way of reading? *Pleasure* and *joy* have become debased—perhaps the word I am searching for is *celebration*.

Finally, Carruth has written a few, late, precious essays on the general subject of poetry—**"The Writer's Situation," "Seriousness and the Inner Poem," "The Question of Poetic Form," "The Act of Love: Poetry and Personality"**—which I would not attempt to summarize. They are rich and graceful and lucid, and unashamedly intelligent. And so I return to Carruth's history—not, this time, the change from the city to the country or from privilege to chosen poverty—but the history of growth into simultaneous modesty and confidence, seriousness and humor, humanity and wisdom. Again, I look for a word: can *adult* or *mature* still mean anything good when they have come to mean "pornographic"? I cannot think of one word with which to express my recognition that all these qualities could not belong to a young man. The complementary qualities of these late essays are highlighted in two sentences in **"The Question of Poetic Form"**:

> Well, it seems to me that Plato made a very shrewd observation of human psychology when he conceived his ideals—if he was the one who actually conceived them (I am ignorant of pre-Socratic philosophy). . . .
>
> . . . I believe the closed pentameter couplet was natural to Pope, "organic," if you like, and if his poems are not as well unified *poetically* as any others of a similar kind and scope, if the best of them are not *poems* in exactly the same sense we mean today, then I don't know how to read poetry. (But I do.)

He feels free to offer an interpretation of Plato and also ad-

mits the limitations of his knowledge—an admission which itself establishes a breadth of knowledge which exceeds that of most current critics, who do not mention the fact that pre-Socratic philosophy exists. A younger and more anxious critic might have written a pompous little aside on where the interested reader might check up on pre-Socratic philosophy. Carruth can let it go. And he can also assert himself as a younger person could not, and say, in a biting parenthetical clause, that of course he knows how to read poetry. How good it is to read the work of someone whose knowledge and experience are so deep that he can make judgments without arrogance and without defensiveness.

But it would be wrong to make Carruth sound too much like the wise, good-hearted elder sage. There is always a more mysterious power in his writing, a power generated by the simultaneous existence of another pair of paradoxical qualities. I will use his own words, first on Lowell, second on Leroi Jones, to define those qualities: "this is tough, this is homely, this is American" and "our Shelley." Most of what I have praised in the essays belongs to the homely, American side of Carruth, to his affinity with Twain and Whitman, who never call people stupid or ugly, but only cruel or hypocritical or self-righteous, who value sanity and love, the natural world and the common man. Shelley is here too, in the combination of rage and spirituality, visions of horror and visions of ethereal beauty, and fury at the sight of wrong that can only be felt by someone who wants perfection. Parts of the first essay in the book, Carruth's defense of Pound, sound almost as if they were copied from Shelley's "Defense of Poetry."

> Poetry is the reason for all things humanly true and beautiful, and the product of them—wisdom, scholarship, love, teaching, celebration. Love of poetry is the habit and need of wise men wherever they are, and when for some reason of social or personal disadjustment they are deprived of it, they will be taxed in spirit and will do unaccountable things. Great men will turn instinctively to the poetic labor of their time, because it is the most honorable and useful, as it is the most difficult, human endeavor. Every spiritual faculty of man is a poetic one, and in poetry is that working of the spirit which engages man and his world in an intelligible existence. Only in poetry is man knowable to himself.

In the late essays the language is compressed, the tone, sober—but Shelley is still here, for example, in **"The Act of Love: Poetry and Personality"**:

> It follows that poetry is social, though not in any sense of the term used by sociologists. It follows that poetry is political, leaving the political scientists far behind. Maybe it even follows that if the substance of a poem, or part of it, is expressly though broadly social or political, this fact will reinforce the subjective communalism of the poet's intention in his transcendent act; but that is a question—the interrelationship of substance and the vision of form, or of moral and aesthetic feeling—to which twenty-five years of attention have given me no answer. Yet many, a great many, of our finest poems, especially as we read

backward toward the evolutionary roots of poetry, seem to suggest such a hypothesis, and in any event we know that political substance is not, and in itself cannot be, inimical to poetry. Finally it follows that the politics of the poet, in his spirituality, will be a politics of love. For me this means nonviolent anarchism, at least as a means; I know no end.

Carruth has none of the qualities that alienate some people from Shelley—frothy poetic excess, squeamish disdain for earthly life—but the two are alike in their deep, pessimistic, undying spirituality. Despite his personal suffering, Carruth's spirituality has endured, as Shelley's might not have. Carruth never writes with the weary ease that often comes with self-confident skill and assured success. The late essays are less joyful than the early ones but just as loving; they are less hopeful but more dogged in their vitality. Carruth has endured without settling into stoicism because he has refused to cease either suffering or hoping. His progress has taken him continuously deeper into the knowledge of his own humanity, and of the humanity of literature.

D. J. R. Bruckner (review date 23 May 1982)

SOURCE: A review of *Working Papers: Selected Essays and Reviews,* in *The New York Times Book Review,* May 23, 1982, p. 15.

[*Bruckner is an American journalist, editor, and critic. In the following review, he provides a positive assessment of* Working Papers.]

"Traditions come and go," Hayden Carruth wrote in 1973; ". . . they come and go in language. I am making a plea for courage among writers, and for a recognition that the means of poetry are what they are and what they have always been." But language is full of deceits; the temptation is to be dogmatic, "by insisting arbitrarily that part of the truth is the whole of the truth, and by pinning everything on an understanding of terms." Mr. Carruth, who is a poet, is undogmatic and often courageous. One could get the impression that he *will* find something to praise in any poet. But these reviews, [collected in ***Working Papers***], published over 30 years, remind us that his judgment is not soft and his ear does not err. He respects tradition and his readers.

"Respect" is the word. In 1958 he excoriated Lawrence Ferlinghetti's best poems ("easy stuff") and his claque ("an essentially frivolous audience"), while defending Gregory Corso as the best of the beatnik poets. He defined perfectly the purity of Denise Levertov's line in a review of her first book and 25 years later remains her best critic. In two 1960's essays, he made William Carlos Williams more accessible to the general public than any other critic had done, but he also noted Williams's faulty prosody, which most critics prefer to ignore. At the height of their reputations, he condemned Edmund Wilson for stooping to trivia and John Berryman for loading his poems up with his own vanity and self-indulgence. He has been a good guide, and candid about his own standards.

The morality of writers is a constant theme. "How shall our children live in a world from which first the spirit, then history, and finally nature have fled?" he asks. He is writing about poetry, mind you. In 1963 he counted all the poems appearing in *Poetry* magazine and expressed outrage that only three concerned nuclear annihilation. "Without morality, no myth; without experience, no convention," he wrote a few years later. And he defended his faith: "In great works of art we recognize a great and splendid light; perhaps not *in* the works but *behind* them, a luminosity beyond the realm of art. . . ." Writing about luminosity is a gutsy business nowadays.

Mr. Carruth acknowledges the relentless corruption of understanding by distraction, and he uses criticism to help readers become tough-minded, to give them a sense of dignity. "Love of poetry is the habit and need of wise men wherever they are," he writes, "and when for some reason of social or personal disadjustment they are deprived of it, they will be taxed in spirit and will do unaccountable things." He makes us love what he loves, with eyes wide open.

R. W. Flint (essay date Spring-Summer 1983)

SOURCE: "The Odyssey of Hayden Carruth," in *Parnassus: Poetry in Review,* Vol. 11, No. 1, Spring-Summer, 1983, pp. 17-32.

[*In the following essay, Flint surveys Carruth's body of work, paying particular attention to* The Sleeping Beauty *and* Working Papers.]

For at least two decades Hayden Carruth has been a poet of the first quality, no mythmaker or trend-setter in matters of style but a writer so well endowed with character, courage, stamina, honesty, and independence as to make whatever styles he has adopted or adapted peculiarly his own. He has also been a quirky anthologist (***The Voice That Is Great Within Us***), an occasional reviewer, and a writer of essays sometimes marked by a distinct evangelical fervor. Unlike one of his poetic stepfathers, Robert Frost, who spent his first eight years in California, he is a pure-bred Yankee, raised by an old-fashioned radical journalist in the town of Litchfield, Connecticut, that earlier gave us the Beecher family, a child of New England's own west coast as he moved northward and settled in Johnson, Vermont, a healthy distance from the centers of fashion. There he has supported himself by pen, part-time teaching, and a notably arduous brand of hardscrabble farming. Accident and fate, fortune and misfortune have kept alive in him a cast of mind that somehow joins the early nineteenth century of Shelley, Hazlitt, and Stendhal with the late twentieth. Like Shelley he has categorically exalted the profession of poet. Like Stendhal with little irony and less embarrassment he has taken love and music as his twin goads to action. Like all three he has been consistently, unblushingly political, albeit from the sidelines.

His new long poem, ***The Sleeping Beauty,*** in 124 intricately rhymed stanzas of fifteen lines each, his principal work of the last eight years, wonderfully assembles, unifies, and refines his leading themes. Its appearance is a signal event that throws a long backward light across his career and lifts to a high plane of accomplishment the work of a man whose single presence on the scene has sometimes seemed more latent than actual, whose fugitive publication by New Directions, Kayak, Tamarack, Sheep Meadow, and so on, has often obscured for lazy magazine readers his much greater skills as a poet than as a writer of prose. Not that the new sequence is line for line always better poetry than some splendid writing in its immediate predecessor, *Brothers, I Loved You All,* or in the better poems of *For You* and *From Snow and Rock, from Chaos;* only that just this vigorous new act of consolidation was necessary and, in hindsight, inevitable. He has always been expert in gentle reflective lyrics like minor Wallace Stevens, composed in a finely tempered mix of quantity and stress. But also like Stevens in major poems like "Esthétique du Mal" and "To An Old Philosopher In Rome," he has needed sturdier formal vessels to give range to his taste for abstraction. The deliberated fullness of his abstract vocabulary, most obtrusive in the essays but everywhere a strong native asset as it plays both for and against his keen sense of fact and relish for action, seems in retrospect to have made of *The Sleeping Beauty* one of the decade's essential poems.

During the sectarian late-late-modernist era just behind us, Carruth's oscillation among roles may have confused some readers—moralist, hedonist, exquisite epicure of country scenes, critic (a title he stoutly abjures, like Caesar pushing aside the crown of Rome), a raging enemy of illness, infirmity, lovelessness, industrial spoliation and mindless greed. No matter how "existential" his theory, no matter how closely he may have wanted to be in tune with poets like Ginsberg, Lowell, Levertov, Olson, or Creeley, who took the Pound/Williams route a long way back toward Whitman and Whitman's trust in self-creation through incremental autobiography, his actual practice, book by book, has passed freely between nominally hostile "camps." (The camps are chiefly chimeras of the camp followers.) Surely it has been a prime feature of the Romantic devolution in American poetry, this rotary, radar-like scanning of the possibilities, so much less dramatic than the knuckle-dusting warfare dreamed up by the press. We have witnessed a racking nostalgia for the lost coherences of the last four centuries, surprised and baffled at every turn by sudden subterranean eruptions.

How many habitual readers of his prose are aware that no less a connoisseur than James Wright is quoted on the back cover of *Brothers, I Loved You All* in praise of "the powerfully spare and precise lyricism of his songs; his almost spooky sensitivity to the voices of the people in his idyls; the larger music of his philosophical meditations; and everywhere, gathering all the other powers, the clear mind, Lucretian in its exact intelligence"? Wright puts the accent where it belongs. Like Wright in *Spoon River* and *Winesburg* country, Carruth settled in terrain that cried out for reconstitution in actual voices of its people or in the most scrupulous, clear-headed observation. Robert Frost could hardly be ignored in Vermont, but he could be sidestepped, amended, amplified. It may be that Carruth's early apprenticeship to Pound, in his opinion the century's supreme master of Style (upper case his), was the best protection he could think of against Frost and Whitman. He may also be right in supposing that a later

century will see Frost and Pound as close brothers just under the skin.

In the largest practical sense Carruth's eminent sanity has steadily dominated his great variability. We read him ecstatic, read him cynical, candid, temperate, fed up, whimsical, affectionate, and know him to be whole. Occasionally a trifle vain, a bit oblivious of the effect he may be having on urban skeptics, but master in his own house. He has made an absorbing story out of a fight against devastating odds, for which we are probably indebted to a companionable adhesiveness only slightly less intense than Dr. Williams'. For a man subject to severe depression he was lucky to have come of age at a moment when his country was not only successful in a general war against the devil but also vain in the consciousness of success. If historical phases in the arts seldom coincide—the United States, for instance, had a robust eighteenth-century classicism in architecture that still gives pleasure long after its counterpart in poetry has been mercifully forgotten—neither does the course of a single art ever seem quite in phase with public events. Confidence bred by victory in 1945 worked on poetry in mysterious ways indeed: gulfs deepened, rifts yawned, barrier reefs rose from hitherto calm lagoons. Henry Luce's American Century seemed to have no overt appeal whatever. Among poets the most aggressive were often the most sensible. It was raw ego and energy that made the difference, ego armed for battle, able to defy the mighty temptations to modesty preferred by the everlooming pre-war giants.

No one better expressed all this than Hayden Carruth, born in 1921. *The Bloomingdale Papers,* a brilliantly vivid verse diary of incarceration in a big private mental hospital during the winter of 1953-54, first published in 1975 after twenty forgotten years in the possession of a friend (the author suspects that repeated electroshock may have caused the amnesia) defines his chronic illness in the prevailing jargon as a deep anxiety psychosis leading to sudden paralyses and fits of the shakes. Not your usual literary melancholia but something Swiftian in effect. The same episode was later recast into the elegant, much more abstract *quinzains* of **"The Asylum"** in *For You,* and a decade after that the same intricately rhymed—ababaaccdedefef—fifteen-liners reappeared in the sequence **Contra Mortem.** Now, in **The Sleeping Beauty,** he has made the stanza, varied by prodigies of off-rhyming and eccentric paragraphing, into a medium as eloquently personal as Byron's *ottava rima.* But the plain-spoken, semi-journalistic **Bloomingdale Papers,** written in a cubbyhole during hours set aside for manual therapy, an officially sanctioned alternative to shuffle-board or basketweaving, has solid virtues not found again in his work until the memorable sequence **"Paragraphs"** in *Brothers* ("surely one of the few great poems written in English during recent years"—James Wright) and his portraits of upcountry cranks and crazies in the same book. But time flees and adequate short samples of this exuberant "realism" are unfeasible here. Instead let's have two sections of the beautifully sustained lyric cycle **"North Winter"** in *For You.*

45
In freshfallen snow

marks of pad and paw
and even partridge claw
go delicately and distinct
straight as a string of beads
but marks of a heeled boot
waver shuffle wamble
ruckle the snow define
a most unsteady line

then spell it out once

so

death knowledge being heady
it hath not the beasts' beauty
goeth tricksy and ploddy
and usually too damn wordy
but drunken or topsy-turvy
gladhanding tea'd or groovy
it arriveth
it arriveth
o you pretty lady.

50
When conditions of frost and
    moisture are just right
    the air is filled
with thousands and thousands
    of points of light
like the fireflies come back
only tinier and much more brilliant
    as if the fireflies
    had ghosts
to haunt a February night.

And in a graver mood, the entire poem **"The Loon on Forrester's Pond"** from *Brothers:*

Summer wilderness, a blue light
twinkling in trees and water, but even
wilderness is deprived now. "What's that?
What is that sound?" Then it came to me,
this insane song, wavering music
like the cry of the genie inside the lamp,
it came from inside the long wilderness
of my life, a loon's song, and there he was
swimming on the pond, guarding
his mate's nest by the shore,
diving and staying under
unbelievable minutes and coming up
where no one was looking. My friend
told how once in his boyhood
he had seen a loon swimming beneath his boat,
a shape dark and powerful
down in that silent world, and how
it had ejected a plume of white excrement
curving behind. "It was beautiful,"
he said.

The loon
broke the stillness over the water
again and again,
broke the wilderness
with his song, truly
a vestige, the laugh that transcends
first all mirth
and then all sorrow
and finally all knowledge, dying
into the gentlest quavering timeless
woe. It seemed
the real and only sanity to me.

The first of these lyrics is a young man's tribute to the elder Pound's kinetic fluency and delicacy in, say, *The Pisan Cantos;* "it hath not the beasts' beauty" makes the homage clear. The beauty of section 50 that follows can be better appreciated if one tries to think how, and by whom, it could be set to music. Each syllable does its work completely before yielding to the next. A quainter diction, say Shakespeare's "Come unto these yellow sands . . . ," easily welcomes the conventions of Elizabethan music which, in a manner of speaking, sober it up, pin it down. But nothing from Alban Berg to the most farfetched electronic shimmerings and twinklings could add anything to the shimmer of association just behind Carruth's utter straightforwardness in this lyric. It fully justifies Wright's adjective "Lucretian."

The gift of pregnant plainness is even happier in **"The Loon."** The whole poem might have collapsed into banality had he not had something intimate and interesting to say about loons, and had this something not shaped every cadence and line. One hears "sorrow" and "woe," "truly" and "me" quietly chiming in the background, like a well-prepared close in music. But a loon poem in the venerable Georgian style could never have resisted rhyming song with wrong, water with daughter, again with men, transcends with mends, mirth with dearth, until the bird was drowned by worse than pond water.

Long poems? Recent years have been kind to a number of poets whose appetite for them had so far been repressed. James Merrill's ouija board epic is one whose wildly eccentric philosophical framing sustained many appealing lyric and narrative progressions that would have been unthinkable without it. Last year Daniel Hoffman's *Brotherly Love* showed how the most sober, exact historical excavation can irradiate a set of digressions modest enough in themselves, can flood them with the light and warmth of a civilized intelligence. Adepts of north country poetry can hardly have missed the success of Carruth's friend David Budbill in *The Chain Saw Dance* and *From Down to the Village* in constructing out of many homely narratives, outwardly like the latest neo-realism in painting, a fascinatingly coherent musical whole.

The words "grace," "spirit," and "love" often appear as the guiding realities of *The Sleeping Beauty,* its subjective building blocks. Calling on his well-weathered proficiency in the writing of winterscapes (only Bly and Ammons are serious rivals in English), he concludes his first stanza:

> The flakes extremely fine
> And falling unseen, still make the bough
> Of the hemlock whiten. Here and now—
> Twig by twig, needle by needle—a plume
> Reached through the grayness,
> Intricate purity that somehow could assume
> Its own being in its own space,
> Out of nothing . . .
>   or out of a cold November
> Dawn that anyone could see, this grace
> That no one can ever quite remember.

The perfect beginning of a work that could hardly be more aware of its own fragility and arbitrariness, how it also reaches through the grayness and assumes "its own being in its own space, / out of nothing," or if not nothing then out of a Novemberish season in the history of the "spirit" it invokes.

The several incidental features *The Sleeping Beauty* has in common with Lowell's *History* and *For Lizzie and Harriet* and John Berryman's *Dream Songs* should delude nobody into assuming that Carruth has written another mildly surrealist daybook in verse. Many sections are indeed dream songs—but with a difference! Like Lowell he gives condensed, pared-down versions of the kinds of poems he is good at. Drama in late Lowell exists for the most part in the energy of separate phrases, lines, or metaphors in close vibration; in Carruth there is less local excitement but a much better plot. He is after a coherent dramatic lucidity of ideas. Whatever the justice of his picture of himself as an embattled commoner versus Lowell's "aristocratic" hauteur, as a lifelong radical anarchist versus the Bostonian's vaguely left-liberal moralism, the roads the two poets took on leaving the good town of *Paterson* veer in opposite directions.

About the poetry that followed *Life Studies,* in his essay **"A Meaning of Robert Lowell"** in ***Working Papers*** Carruth makes a point that touches the quick. Lowell, he says, increasingly succumbed to the vice of "extraneity" in an effort to appear objective, pushed the idolization of metaphor to preposterous lengths. Lacking an original, stringent, private vision of his age, he resorted to spectacular piecemeal effects, wonderful bits of worked-up observation that advance no inwardly plotted argument, that just lie there like so much curious sea-wrack. To illustrate this peculiarity, Carruth cites part of "The Scream" from *For The Union Dead:*

> One day she changed to purple,
> and left her mourning. At the fitting,
> the dressmaker crawled on the floor,
> eating pins, like Nebuchadnezzar
> on his knees eating grass.

About the fitness of this striking description of Lowell's mother's dressmaker in action, Carruth remarks: "Only when I stop to think do I realize that Nebuchadnezzar and what he stands for have only the remotest connection with this passage, and that the dressmaker is a figure of no importance in the poem. As an image, this is a brilliant extraneity: the defect at work." No doubt the poet was looking for an image of abjection commensurate with the social gulf between Lowells and dressmakers; the problem is that Nebuchadnezzar had gone mad but the dressmaker was in her right mind and quite oblivious of being or seeming demeaned by her action. She would have done no differently for her own mother.

Both men depend more than they might care to admit on the "existential" context of their earlier work, on the penetrating aura of gossip that clings to even the most fugitive poet of decent gifts and stamina. But whatever failings *The Sleeping Beauty* may have, Lowell's kind of scattershot brilliance is not among them. When the desired coherence fails to materialize, when Carruth seems to have less than he would like to add to received poetic wisdom about love, history, humanity, violence, pain, justice, and injustice, he falls back not on imagistic virtuosity, tortured syntax, or

labored free association but on the *sentiment* of coherence, much as Pound did, latent—or so he devoutly hopes—in his chosen general terms, which he then proceeds to draw together like strayed children as if propinquity would propagate a new higher synthesis.

One of the *The Sleeping Beauty*'s many merits is that it asks us to look back across the chasm that separates the applied incoherences we have either enjoyed or endured for the last quarter century to the straightforward Dante cult within which Pound and Eliot were nurtured, and behind that to Dante Rossetti's once popular translation of the *Vita Nuova,* to the prospective marriage of love and intellect, eros and mind, that captured the *fin de siècle* imagination and never ceased to shine behind even the wildest Swinburnian excesses. In considerable agony of spirit a thin, strong lifeline *can* be thrown back. Carruth's affinities often seem to be equally with those who have entertained the deepest despair of intellect, and with those who, no matter how painful their brush with chaos, cannot surrender their trust in the mysteriously integrating, self-rectifying natural qualities of language. In this he oddly most resembles not another poet, unless it be Pound, but Henri Beyle whose search for "happiness" through love, adventure, and philosophy, whose worship of the eternal feminine, whose science-bred secularity, taste for ecstasy and glory and contempt for war unless executed by genius for lofty ends, his lifelong hostility to his philistine father, his passionate love of music, are perhaps the most universally "American" phenomena in European literary history. Add Beyle's richly civilized *egotisme* and *espagnolisme* and you have a good prevision of the fix that men like Carruth find themselves in, bourgeois anti-bourgeois beyond evasion or masquerade whose fraternal good sense finally balks at institutional vengeance, who want the pleasures of revolution without the blood. Carruth's poem contains no "hell cantos" like Pound's, no gimmicks like Social Credit, no refined racism unless his fondness for certain black musicians is a benign form of it. A Jeffersonian pursuit of happiness seems finally to require a respect for the happiness of others. Wistfully repudiating Castro for his persecutions, embracing Hannibal (of all people) for his fabled magnanimity, Carruth's politics are strictly visionary.

The Sleeping Beauty is layered in tiers and swirls like a very good cake but with no frosting and no overabundance of sugar. Holding it together is a recurring meditation on the fixity and pervasiveness of beauty, mostly but not exclusively feminine. The princess is Rose Marie Dorn, his wife, who dreams up a storm, keeping alive the Old World *lacrimae rerum,* whose memories as an East German refugee steady herself and the poet/prince in their link with the past. In a conceit worthy of high German baroque she limits her dreaming to figures—poets, heroes, and horrors; Homer, Hesiod, Harlequin, Hermann, husband, holocaust, hydrogen bomb—whose names begin with the same letter as her husband's. This is certainly odd, but not crippling because it gives her a surprisingly long run. A scheme that includes Hannibal, Hegel, and Hitler is, to say the least, a challenge to ingenuity. The sleeper has her inanimate counterpart in a carved woman's face left in the bottom of a brook by a friendly sculptress; this coolest of beauty's effigies in turn joins wife and poem to Ophelia and thus to Hamlet, the poem's dominant enigma, unless beauty itself plays that role. True, in sections 107 and 123 beauty takes on, first, the terror of hermaphroditism, and then the Tieresian reconciliations of the androgynous:

> Androgyne! the forbidden
> Ancient of ancients granting that the poem glad-
> den
> In its free consciousness which burns
> With the whole selflessness of loving, its forms
> Risen profoundly from remembered voices, its
> tones
> Heard from the great silences,
> While the aurora ripples and flashes, while the
> snow
> Gleams with its own reflected innerness
> Of brilliance, brilliance, to the horizon, far
> Beyond the final extremities of distance
> In the beating universe,
> the poem alone and free . . .
> (from section 123)

But the healing, centering presence is still woman's:

> You lie in the center,
> The integration
> And the nowhereness of all things
> as seasons of being are separated
> by a winter/
> O northern princess,
> see these apparitions,
> How they gather in dreams, our history from the
> mist,
> The meaningless, mysterious images of your
> dreaming reason
> That you will know
> the instant you are really kissed.
> (from section 48)

As it rises from brookbed through the heroine's pregnant dreaming, the poem must negotiate two anchoring episodes of an entirely worldly, daylight nature. The first concerns the author's friendship with an ancient local "ugly," a farmer called Amos in honor of the fiercest of Old Testament prophets, a distillation in impeccable western Vermont dialect of the stalwart humor and character that just by surviving sufficiently reproach the new age of tourism and callously expensive retirement. What in other hands might have been the most awkward becomes instead one of the poem's most gratifying elements, thanks to Carruth's perfect ear and closeness to the subject. Amos has his own shy intimations of immortal beauty. And well understands the rascals among whom he is nevertheless quite happy to live. He is Marshall Washer of **Brothers** grown old and sibylline—a ghost, the ghost of the father that Hayden-Hamlet never quite had.

> Leaving? You don't want to see the end?
> *I seen it*
> *Already, and besides I ain't even*
> *Got enough Yankee meanness*
> *Left for talking about what's happened. And*
> *grieving—*
> *What's the use of it? I'll get off here. You needn't*
> *Stop. So long. I'll see you later.*

So long, Amos.

> Later?
> Stay here,
> Amos, for God's sake! DON'T GO NOW!
>
> Nowhere.
> And you, all of you,
> Are you gone? Where is the richness of the ma-
> nure
> That used to steam on the snow? Some chemical
> Rots the air. Are you gone? Is the land given
> To these mechanical monsters risen from hell?
> Look at them, the clones, smiling like Richard
> Nixon.
> (from section 118)

The other anchoring episode is the poet's extramarital adventures that make him, too, the remorseful rascal he needed to be in order to redeem the time with new love during the princess's dreaming, finally to bring on the torture of a last reconciliation:

> But still
> In his depression deepening toward paralysis,
> He has one more task.
> Driven in blindness, driven as the stars in their
> orbits,
> Knowing the outcome will be grotesque,
> A pain beyond bearing, and with nothing left to
> prove,
> He must go to the princess. With nothing left to
> ask,
> He must go,
> the prince who is human, driven, and filled
> with love.
> (from section 111)

Dreaming wife, lady of the brook, Amos *genius loci*, remorseful rapscallion prince, these are but preludes and interludes to the poem's weightiest concern, the seemingly disastrous effects of the code of Romance that in Carruth's view starts in southern Provence in *langue d'oc*. Resting his case on the troubadours' known heresies and their eclipse in the Albigensian Crusade, he freely exercises his poetic license in associating the Romantic spirit with most of the abuses that accompanied it from the twelfth century to the present. On this topic a reviewer is doomed to say either too little or too much. Carruth has by no means settled the matter to his own satisfaction. All is drama, suggestion, and surmise.

After the spouses' reconciliation and the dematerialization of Amos, the argument is simply dropped and the poem takes a last flight over the Canadian border into the absolute:

> In the flow of creation, short day and long night
> Mingling, past *la cité*, into the hills bright
> With the glorious instincts of the wolves,
> Dark with the forest's deepness, all selves
> Of history risen now in one true person, past
> The great white silent *lac*
> Where stars fade in the aurora, and at last
> Out onto the open north, ecstatic,
> Beyond earth and history, the nets of essence,
> Free, alone with every thing, the aurora flashing,
> Trumpets, the beat of the universe, immense,
> immense.
> (from section 122)

It *is,* without question or cavil, a romantic poem; it had to be before it could broach its mighty theme. It had itself to be a shining instance of what it pondered and deplored. If this seems an incongruous thought, in view of everything so far written about Carruth's hardheadedness, his ability to nail the action down to an entirely credible piece of real estate whose essence is often captured in a dramatic play of voices rather than in revery, then so be it. Nothing is less important than the label one affixes to a poem this various. Still, not only is the prince/princess fiction kept charmingly alive throughout, but the princess is never given the opportunity to blast the daylights out of her husband, never given a waking voice half as individual as Williams gave to his wife Flossie. A proper dramatic poem on the Williams order would surely have featured a tirade or two from the lips of the abused consort. One doesn't, finally, assume that Carruth is incapable of that much detachment, only that his meditation on the nature of Romance obliged him to reserve to himself as narrator just enough stumbling vanity and word-intoxication to allow the poem to illustrate its own thesis. This is a very subtle matter; no judgment of quality by category is intended, none at all.

One's final praise of the poem's incontestable beauties may be to remark for the last time on the sanity that disposes its parts with such laconic assurance, that sets one episode vibrating against another until all make a music like the great music of the blazing, jamming jazzmen and jazzwomen of better times.

Much of what might be said about **Working Papers,** a collection by Judith Weissman of about a tenth of Carruth's published reviews and essays, has been either said or implied already. His reluctance to be thought a critic is quite unjustified in detail—he is, in fact, one of the most fairminded, reliable journeyman critics still writing. Anyone would know what to expect by way of a welcome corrective kindness towards middle-range poets like Aiken, MacLeish, Edwin Muir, Robert Duncan, Denise Levertov, Muriel Rukeyser, Delmore Schwartz, whose reputations have often needed just the discriminating damage-control he brings to them. Most of his omnibus reviews of fledglings are models of their kind. And no poet-as-critic has tackled the big names with a more refreshing independence. No automatic reflexes here, no prudential trimming. The reader feels along his nerves the pain that certain polemical stands have cost him.

But on a wider scale he is right not to claim too much for his prose. Regarded as a critical history of the age's poetry, the book has a hollow center. No enemy of wit, he nevertheless (or his editor does) entirely ignores the contemporary line of wit—Tate, Wilbur, Nemerov, Simpson, Hecht, Merrill, Hollander, Ashbery, Koch, etc. Berryman appears only in the shambles of *Love and Fame.* Several poets like Roethke for whom he passingly expresses high admiration are not considered. And where is that heretical essay on Frost he once published in the *Hudson Review?* Does Ms. Weissman imagine he has spoken his last word on Frost in the semi-Frostian poem **"Vermont"** in **Brothers?** And those three published "notes" on Pope that Ms. Weissman mentions, was not one of them worthy of inclusion?

If this is indeed a mere tenth of his critical prose, obviously some principle of choice was operating. Judging by Ms. Weismann's reverent Introduction one suspects that it was largely moral, to make Carruth look abundantly positive in certain directions, silent in others. The book does amply demonstrate the "humility, modesty, generosity, self-effacement" that she thinks to have been "the unspoken values" of his prose. Unspoken may not be the best word; these qualities are rarely tacit, as for instance when he lights into Berryman's "boasting . . . cuteness . . . archness . . . arrogance . . . muleheadedness" in *Love and Fame.*

Most interesting is his defense of the "existential," subjectivist, holist, personalist line in modern thought. In a Yankee with natural ties to earlier Yankees like Paul Elmore More, this has its exotic aspect:

> If theism was anthropomorphic, if humanism was anthropocentric, then our era is anthropoeccentric; we exist on the edge of reality. There is no intellectualization, but a profound and popular ethologic retooling. The consequent shift of values is immense. Now we recognize that in meaninglessness we are our own sole value, and that art is our chief instrument in the imaginative creation of this value, the turning of human experience into human meaning, the making of selves.

That wraps it up very nicely. Written soon after the Lowell essay these remarks, slightly amplified elsewhere by the notion of "the autobiogenetic stance in art" (presumably his own), bring the potent philosophic *Drang* of the book to a climax. Virtually wrenched out of him in spite of his penchant for the "values of intelligence, decency, literacy, humaneness, civility, responsibility" of the English tradition that Auden represented for him (I counted eleven separate invocations of responsibility in the book), these ideas are not lightly taken up, nor lightly argued. This reviewer finds the cluster quoted above a lot more slippery and less persuasive today than it would have seemed only fifteen years ago when some kind of seismic shift did seem imminent. As a polemicist Carruth is gifted with a free-floating vehemence that, however many doubtful ukases it may generate, is somehow upward-looking, non-lethal, idealist in both the greater and lesser connotations of the word. The longer essays show a steady progress towards a largely rhetorical integration of the leading abstract talismanic terms that one finds more actively engaged in his verse. Prose philosophy for Carruth is largely assertion; for this reader it sometimes dangerously abuts on the exalted know-nothingism-amid-omniscience for which Hegel and his disciples have often been justly censured. Even in such seemingly innocent oppositions as subjective/objective the choice of either term as one's sole guiding star is likely to lead one astray. By "intellectualization" he clearly means the common assumptions about meaning and form that begot finished masterworks up to the end of the last century. But the notion that one can generate meaning and make up selves without resort to at least tacit abstract constructs of considerable width and depth is contradicted by his own practice in **The Sleeping Beauty.**

Is this not the dilemma of a would-be populist aesthetics,

or aesthetic populism, that it rarely considers its alternatives with unvarying seriousness? It waxes aesthetic when technical, professional issues seem paramount, populist when other sorts of issues impend. It lacks the will to treat the two impulses with simultaneous, undivided attention. Carruth's general essays, often persuasive in detail, usually evolve toward nodes of evangelical solemnity whose massed organ or trumpet tones are asked to do philosophy's more arduous tasks—moments not unlike similar oracles issued by Galway Kinnell, Robert Bly, Gary Snyder, Allen Ginsberg. Great names, every one; but the New Regionalism has begun to evince many properties of the old Victorianism.

At one point Carruth vigorously asserts that the only useful theory of poetry has been written by poets. Which is certainly true of men like Shelley or Coleridge who express genuine crises of thought and sensibility. But it may be fairly argued that the theories of autobiogenesis that seemed so provocative twenty or thirty years ago seem less so now, have begun to look like a convulsive attempt to recover the freshness and energy that marked the real revolution of nearly two hundred years ago.

Joe Ashby Porter   (review date Summer 1983)

SOURCE: A review of *Working Papers: Selected Essays and Reviews,* in *South Atlantic Quarterly,* Vol. 82, No. 2, Summer, 1983, pp. 330-31.

[*Porter is an American novelist, educator, and critic. In the following mixed review of* Working Papers, *he faults some of Carruth's essays as "glib and naive," but lauds the author's ability to write about poetry "with modesty, intelligence, and generosity."*]

Hayden Carruth's **Working Papers** provides a poet's-eye view of the literary and intellectual scene of the last thirty years, in his selected essays and reviews with an introduction by Judith Weissman. The forty-four works have been gathered from literary quarterlies such as *Hudson Review,* the monthly *Poetry* (which Carruth edited 1949-50), weeklies such as *Saturday Review* and *The Nation,* and from the *Chicago Daily News.* The reviews treat an assortment of philosophers, critics, and historians including Northrop Frye, Edmund Wilson, Eliseo Vivas, Eliot, Camus, and Sartre, and a larger group of poets including Pound (Carruth's hero), Williams, Auden, Stevens, Ferlinghetti, Levertov, Rukeyser, Eliot, Lowell, Jarrell, and Zukofsky. The essays address general questions of the relationships of poetry, love, and politics, and those of more narrowly focused subjects like **"Ezra Pound and the Great Style"** and **"A Meaning of Robert Lowell."**

Carruth, author of many books of poems since 1959, has also edited or co-edited three anthologies, including the important **The Voice That Is Great Within Us: American Poetry of the Twentieth Century** (1970). His considerable (and apparently wholly salutary) influence on poetry of the last three decades would alone justify this assemblage of some of his less readily accessible writing.

The book's weaknesses largely derive from its format. The collection does seem somewhat piecemeal and scattered.

Also, given some of the times and places of original publication, one is not surprised by occasional senses of the glib and naive. Carruth's 1963 characterization of Camus as "one of the great founders of the age" has a certain period breathlessness. Some of his judgments read a bit like dust jacket puffs. In one review we are told not only that Levertov's *The Poet in the World* "should be read by everyone who takes her poetry seriously" but also that it "should be read by every poet in the country—in the world!" "Every American who can read at all should read" a book by Wendell Berry.

Some of the book's strengths and virtues also derive from its genre. One that should go without saying, but doesn't always these days, is the freedom from jargon and obscurity. Another is the pleasure of watching a sensibility develop, a mind change through decades. After Carruth's 1969 passing assessment of George Steiner as "acute," one may begin his extended response in 1973 to Steiner with trepidation, only to find Carruth now recognizing muddle and confusion.

But the book's signal virtues seem specific to its author. The insider's and practitioner's viewpoint makes for marvellous flashes like "I am inclined . . . to say . . . that English poetry, meaning all poetry written in any kind of English, has been haunted for almost four hundred years by what Kit Marlowe . . . would have written if he had not been killed in a barroom fight at the age of twenty-nine." On poetry Carruth writes with intimacy and commitment, nowhere more notably than in the long 1967 essay occasioned by Lowell's *Near the Ocean.* After acknowledging his own envy of Lowell's advantages and acclaim, Carruth proceeds to work out what troubles him in Lowell, "the defect of pervasive extraneity" and "a faint odor of degenerate Freudian sentimentalism."

Carruth brings a commendable breadth of knowledge to bear on his tasks. He writes with modesty, intelligence, and generosity, and sees and states with a poet's own economy the distinctive excellences in very diverse kinds of poetry. These virtues often combine in **Working Papers** to give Carruth's prose something like what he attributes to Pound, a radiance.

Hayden Carruth   (essay date 1983)

SOURCE: An introduction to his *Effluences from the Sacred Caves: More Selected Essays and Reviews,* The University of Michigan Press, 1983, pp. 1-7.

[*In the following excerpt from his introduction to his* Effluences from the Sacred Caves, *Carruth reflects on philosophy and literature and discusses his approach to writing.*]

By heritage and inclination, I am not a Platonist. That is clear. I am forced to say it thus negatively, however, because I can define myself—to the extent possible at all—only *against* the Platonic and Romantic aspirations that still hold out to me a powerful, though I think false, allure.

I come from the western and northern hills of New England. Not the sunny arbors of Concord, the salons of Cambridge, nor even the dark, briny, death-haunted dockside of Ishmael's New Bedford; all unknown to me. My hills are sparse and rocky ground. John Dewey came from a town not far from mine in Vermont, and the James family, tough people in spite of their exoticism, from just over the border in Albany. I was raised a radical agnostic and relativist. Yet my father saw an angel in a tree and loved Blake beyond all other poets but Shakespeare. I myself have often heard angels, or at any rate soprano voices, singing in the treetops, and just as often have heard my name clearly and loudly called and have looked around, only to find no caller. And because the caller is not there, I have somewhat suspicioned the absence of the called.

Relativism was easy to abandon when I saw how it induces a hierarchical cast of mind, tending toward either intractable dualism or perturbing monism. I believe one's mind can go no farther than to acknowledge the equivalence of all things, including all values. For this reason I never had more than a working mechanic's interest in causality, and I loathed all concepts of determinism. I loathed the ego, that sick and changeable object created by refraction from the other objects of the determined world. My own was at best a collapsing kaleidoscopic image, at worst a cloud seen through a telescope. And so I caught the transcending fever, and I sought ways to rise above the objective ego and become a self in pure subjectivity, free and undetermined, an authentic existential independency. Yet at the same time my back-country hardheadedness made me vehemently disclaim any Transcendentalism in my transcension, and made me equally aware of the need for responsibility not only to the self but to others. I saw how in its moments of transcendent freedom the self is, in fact, a communion with the other, though how to define that other still escapes me. I think it may be the transcendent selves of all human imaginations not irreparably maimed by the life of machines in the objective world. I call it love.

At every step along the way I found how in books from the past my own thoughts, which had derived from the necessity of my own impairment, were written more clearly than I could write them. Camus, Kafka, Kant, Pope, Locke, Spenser, Dante, and many others. A writer whom I admire, Arthur Schopenhauer, wrote: "Genius, then, consists, according to our explanation, in the capacity for knowing, independently of the principle of sufficient reason, not individual things, which have their existence in their relations, but the ideas of such things, and of being oneself the correlative of the idea, and thus no longer an individual, but the pure subject of knowledge." How that struck me! Hadn't I known all along that what my Yankee forebears had called individualism was only the other side of corporatism, the two blind, sick egos of the objective world? Independence became in its true signification not the blustery, blowzy conceitedness of Ethan Allen but the sweetness of Piotr Kropotkin.

Another writer, the one whom maybe I admire most of all, Longinus, that hardheaded person from the classical world who still believed in sublimity and who had no historical identity (because no one has been able to discover who he—or she—was), this Longinus wrote: "Similarly from the great natures of the men of old there are borne in upon the souls of those who emulate them (as from sacred caves) what we may describe as effluences, so that

even those who seem little likely to be possessed are thereby inspired and succumb to the spell of the others' greatness." This is the inspiration that comes not as "originality," which in any case is a delusion, but as confirmation, the best and only reliable inspiration one may hope for.

When I was a young writer, just after World War II, I read and respected the works of the critics whose ideas were then still new: Pound and Eliot, of course, and Ransom, Tate, Winters, Burke, Warren, Richards, Blackmur, and others. Most of them were poets too, although of very differing accomplishments. I thought that since I was a poet, I would eventually also write full-scale essays and books in which I would develop a systematic view of art and experience. But then my life degenerated quickly into illness of the psychogenic kind, and I was forced to make my living at home as a hack reviewer and editor. At the time I resented this necessity very bitterly. But now, looking back, I wonder if I could have written such essays and books anyway. Hermann Hesse wrote that the born critic works "from grace, from innate acuity of mind and analytical powers of thought, from serious cultural responsibility." Far from grace, acuity, and power, my mind had not even enough ordinary assuredness to permit the act of sitting down to write an essay. Only "serious cultural responsibility" was left to me, left in bountiful measure by my Yankee ancestors, and I do not think it belongs to critics alone; it is as much the requisite quality of reviewers, not to mention everyone else. So for years I was a reviewer, working on assignment, and even the essays I wrote, all but two or three, came from the prompting of editors. Whatever ideas I had concerning art and experience were set down piecemeal, often in reviews of books I would not have chosen, myself, to read, much less to write about. In consequence this book of selected pieces [*Effluences From the Sacred Caves*] is miscellaneous and more repetitious than it should be, even though the things reprinted in it have been chosen quite rigorously from the total mess.

Well, I won't apologize for my life or work, because apologies are futile. [In a footnote, Carruth adds: "Nevertheless I do wish to apologize for, or at least explain, the omission of so many important poets from consideration in this book. It is precisely because my work has been done on assignment. Adrienne Rich is a good example. I have admired her work since the late 1950s, and have learned from it. I have reviewed many of her books. But the reviews have always been brief and most have been parts of larger reviews dealing with numbers of other poets. I tried to patch together some of these for this book, but the result was fragmentary, disconnected, and confused; it did justice neither to Rich nor to me. I have removed it. This means that a poet who is—I do not exaggerate—extremely important to me, far more important than many poets discussed here, has been left out, and that to this extent the book misrepresents what I really feel. I can say the same about several others: Jim Harrison, Tom McGrath, Hilda Morley, Robert Duncan, etc."] Moreover I did take my responsibility seriously. I was a reviewer, not a critic, but considered myself nevertheless a needed person in the confederation. I did my best, and I was honest.

I cannot recommend such a life as a good one for writers,

but since I cannot recommend any other life either, I'm not sure it matters. I worked. Don't think I didn't do everything, because I did: ghosting, rewriting, inventing blurbage, reading, proofing—once I typed manuscripts for a vanity publisher in New York for a dollar an hour. For a long time the number of books I put out that did not contain my name exceeded the number that did. Maybe this is still true, though I have lost count. It was hard. The pay was low. Many a month my family and I subsisted on a couple of checks from the *Nation* or the quarterlies. I wonder how we did it. As the inflation of the 1970s became acute, I found myself working long spates, twice around the clock often enough, especially when deadlines conflicted—and of course I never dared turn down an assignment. I remember many times when I walked from my writing-shack to put finished manuscripts in my mailbox at the hour when most of my neighbors, the farmers, were just getting up; the rosiness of summer dawn, the brilliant starry quiet of a winter morning with the temperature thirty below. Those were good moments, feeling alone in the world, tired but gratified. I miss them. Often I used to walk a half-mile up the road and back with my dog Locky, listening to the birds in their morning song or the trees creaking with frost.

I kept it up as long as I could. But I found myself working eighty or ninety hours a week and still not earning enough. When my illness abated sufficiently to permit it, I took a job as a professor in the city. It is very different, as thorough a change, almost, as I could imagine. Some aspects of my new life are welcome, but nothing replaces those peaceful early mornings.

A word is in order, I think, about the art of the reviewer. For if he or she is the humblest laborer in the vineyard, nevertheless the form in which the reviewer works is as exacting as those of the loftiest. Usually he is assigned a limit of length, often no more than five hundred or six hundred words, that makes the job fundamentally impossible to do. Many compromises are required. Even so, he must remember that he is first of all a journalist; he must report to his readers what kind of book, in substance as well as in structure, style, and mode, is under consideration. He must open with a "lead" that will hook the reader's attention. He must give some indication, though usually slight, of his own judgment of the book's success or failure, and he must do this not in terms of his own tastes but in terms of the author's intention. Finally he must hit upon some thematic figure or problem by means of which his review may acquire the same unity and integrity that any written work should posses. All this is not easy.

In fact, it is damned hard. It is too hard, and the rewards are never enough to recompense the labor; in this sense a review, though as demanding formally as a poem, is a useless effort. Moreover a good review happens, like good poems, only by luck; everything must come together in a fortuitous stroke of the imagination. One produces many failures, but unlike failed poems, which can be thrown away, failed reviews must be sent off in time to meet their deadlines, and usually they are published as they are, i.e., failures—except when officious undereditors pounce on them and make them even worse. Sometimes I have been

lucky. Sometimes I have put down on the page four hundred words so apt and lucid that they meet all the demands I have spoken of. It is like writing a good sonnet with that marvelous victory in the concluding couplet. But a good sonnet can keep me going for six months, while a good review gives no more than an instant's satisfaction.

That reviewing is truly an art may be negatively demonstrated not only in small literary magazines and local newspapers but equally in the flossiest quarterlies and the biggest mass-circulation weeklies. I see a hundred clumsy and obtuse attempts for every one that succeeds. Even the finest writers sometimes cannot turn out a readable, honest, useful, brief review. The best I know is Hesse's review of Sigmund Freud's *General Introduction to Psychoanalysis* in 1919, and it pleases me that Hesse for many years made his living, too, as a hack reviewer and editor, until finally his novels became popular enough to let him slack off. Another superb reviewer was Conrad Aiken. A third was Edmund Wilson, though only in his early work for such magazines as the *New Republic,* before the *New Yorker* spoiled him, and only when he was writing about fiction or literary theory, never about poetry. For reviews of poetry, read Louise Bogan.

And in spite of all I have said about its drawbacks, reviewing still can be a needed support for young writers and good training as well. If they wish to do it properly, I suggest they begin by acknowledging the review as a distinct literary genre, and then by reading and studying the reviews of the comparatively few great reviewers we have had since the introduction of the daily press. Remember, brevity is not merely a commercial, practical requirement, it is intrinsic to good reviewing, for a good short review is worth any number of prolix disquisitions. (Some of the worst reviews I have read are the pompous, long-winded self-indulgences published in the *New York Review of Books* and the *Times Literary Supplement,* or the even worse Macaulayesque maunderings in the "great" quarterlies of the nineteenth century.) Finally, never forget the reviewer's place, namely, the least. Author, publisher, editor, reader, all come first. Reviewers who use the space assigned them primarily for slopping out their own temperamentalities or for buttering up editors and readers by displaying their own cleverness at the expense of the authors whose works they are supposed to be considering, have no place—I emphasize, no place at all—in a responsible culture.

Thomas Swiss   (essay date Winter 1985)

SOURCE: " 'I Have Made This Song': Hayden Carruth's Poetry and Criticism," in *The Sewanee Review,* Vol. XCIII, No. 1, Winter, 1985, pp. 149-57.

[*In the following essay, Swiss surveys several of Carruth's collections of poetry and criticism and lauds the author for his technical skill and his earnest and straightforward approach in both genres.*]

Hayden Carruth is one of our most enduring writers; at sixty-three he continues to be prolific. Two collections of criticism, two full-length volumes of poetry, and a handsome small-press chapbook have all been published in the last two years. Even as I prepared to write about this recent work, a half-dozen new essays and poems appeared in the pages of some of our most respected magazines and literary journals.

In some quarters Carruth may be better known as a critic than as a poet. No doubt this situation is unavoidable in what remains—in Jarrell's phrase—an age of criticism. No matter. For Carruth writing and reviewing poetry are twin arts, activities he manages with equal intelligence and ease. In his poetry he writes with the practiced hand of a craftsman. In his criticism he explores the nuances and subtle processes in other writers' work as only a poet can do.

Carruth is one of our most useful critics. He comes to the work with an open mind, and he writes from the heart. In an age when many critics (those who are not writers) review within the closed circle of literary theory and jargon, and some critics (those who are writers) review mainly to defend their own work, Carruth's humane, careful, readable prose is particularly significant. You can, for instance, read an individual review or essay by Carruth without needing to know the *body* of his criticism. I'm not suggesting that Carruth in his criticism is simplistic or unmindful of theory. He is not. Carruth has merely chosen another path, a path ignored by some of the current crop of literary reviewers: he writes to explore earnestly the work itself.

Most of the material collected in **Working Papers** and **Effluences from the Sacred Caves** was written on assignment for a variety of magazines: *Saturday Review,* the *Nation,* the *New Republic,* and, of course, the literary quarterlies. Writing on assignment means writing to deadline: we can guess that most of these pieces were written quickly and with a particular audience in mind. The reviews tend to be brief; even the essays usually do not run longer than ten pages. At its worst, however, brevity can mean slightness, and one measure of Carruth's achievement is that no more than a small handful of his reviews lack significance.

Carruth's criticism, as collected in these volumes, falls into general categories: reviews of specific books of poetry; reviews of fiction as well as philosophical and historical prose; general essays on poetry and poetics; and personal essays that mainly entail his life as a writer and editor. Although Carruth has written engagingly about Camus, Casanova, Genet, Wyndham Lewis, and many others, I suspect most readers will be primarily interested in those pieces about poetry.

Working Papers was edited by Judith Weissman, who acknowledges the difficulty of editing and writing about the work of a living author but who then proceeds to gloss the collection in splendid fashion. Using figures supplied by Weissman, we see that these two collections represent no more than one-fifth of Carruth's criticism, a figure which attests to his productivity. **Effluences** contains an introduction by the author; a conversational self-reflective piece, it does not (as it should not) attempt to evaluate the work, but instead offers clues to the origins of the reviews and a description of his philosophical and literary interests.

Hayden Carruth is a generous critic, preferring to praise rather than condemn, to explain rather than debate. But Carruth takes a stand when he must; he does not defend or try to explain away bad philosophy, weak thinking, bad politics, or bad poetry. When he argues with, or objects to, something in a writer's work, he does so without being smug or condescending. He explains to the reader how the writer misfires in the work, but seldom presumes to tell the writer how he must change it.

Carruth is attracted to the work of the Black Mountain poets and some of those associated with the Beats— Creeley, Levertov, Ferlinghetti, Zukofsky, and others. I can't say he favors these "schools," for he seldom relies on name-tags or attempts to categorize writers. But Carruth admires writers influenced by Ezra Pound's theories of prosody.

The question of influence is notoriously slippery. Carruth himself takes up the topic many times in these pieces, especially in his writing on Pound (see **"On a Picture of Ezra Pound"** in *Effluences*), whom Carruth is fond of quoting. In the essay entitled **"Influences"** Carruth refreshingly describes "what is more important, yet at the same time more difficult to discuss . . . the influence on writing of the other arts; in my case, particularly the influence of jazz."

Carruth examines the work of Snodgrass, Ignatow, Ginsberg, Cummings, Hollander, Berryman, Lowell, Blackmur, Winters, Schwartz, Duncan, Aiken, Karl Shapiro, and others. He also presents appreciations of such writers as J. V. Cunningham, Archibald MacLeish, and James Laughlin.

Carruth has recently written more actively on poetry in general. Perhaps his new teaching position has freed him from the demands of assigned reviews, or perhaps only now does he feel confident enough to write closer to his own interests, to assert himself as only an experienced writer and critic can. At any rate he is now offering wide-ranging commentary, and these late essays are among the most interesting in the books.

I won't try to summarize many of the essays—a piece that begins with a discussion of metaphor might veer off to talk about the possibility of defining human nature before returning to its original topic. The essays that are particularly strong include **"How Not to Rate a Poet,"** in which Carruth explores the place of the "apprentice" and "journeyman" writer (his terms) in cultural history. A wonderful if cranky piece, it breaks new ground for our thinking about the relative importance of our writers.

"Here Today" is a cautionary essay in which Carruth argues that the "work of our good young poets . . . [is] being swept away by the mass of similar but inferior writing" because "the inferior writers have worked themselves into positions of power." This is a frightening if slightly overstated view that Carruth hints at in other essays. But even in an essay of such sweeping alarm Carruth returns finally to a less dramatic point—that many writers today have no sense of the poetic line. As he says elsewhere, "For me the line is the essential unit of verse, and I don't like to see it smudged." This recurring principle was inherited from his precursor Ezra Pound.

Other notable essays include **"The Act of Love: Poetry and Personality"** and **"Seriousness and the Inner Poem,"** in which he argues that it is the "quality of feeling" which is most important in a poem, not the seriousness of its topic. In all of the essays and reviews Carruth turns his subject over in his hands, commenting on this, touching that, feeling for rough spots and sometimes shaking it to see what falls loose, what remains in place. His is an inventive, appealing approach; these essays might serve as models for younger reviewers who would like to see a master at work.

Consider these two instances of self-criticism by Hayden Carruth: "I believe the best reader of my poetry will probably be a person who knows and loves jazz as I do," and "My best poems have all been written in states of transcendent concentration and with great speed." These comments point to characteristics in Carruth's *The Sleeping Beauty* and *If You Call This Cry a Song. The Sleeping Beauty,* written over a period of eight years, is Carruth's fifteenth volume of poetry, and it is a difficult book to describe.

The Sleeping Beauty is complexly and delicately organized: one long poem, it consists of one-hundred and twenty-four rhymed and off-rhymed lyrics in fifteen-line stanzas. This form Carruth had used in a poem appearing in his first book, *The Crow and the Heart* (1959). Commenting on that poem, **"The Asylum,"** in 1961, James Dickey called it "the finest sonnet sequence that I have read by a contemporary poet." *The Sleeping Beauty* is perhaps the long-awaited fulfillment of Dickey's conjecture that "Mr. Carruth might be one of the few modern poets capable of writing a good long poem."

Although no poem of merit can claim to need a prose gloss of the narrative appended to it as it travels into posterity or obscurity, I was grateful for the information on the dustjacket of the hardcover edition. The narrative behind Carruth's own is, of course, the Grimm brothers' fairy tale "The Briar Rose," and Carruth's poet-prince sets out on a journey to awaken the princess, Rose Marie Dorn, who is sleeping in a thorn hedge. Rose Marie Dorn in real life is Carruth's wife, and the prince is revealed to be Carruth himself in the last lyric (although we can guess earlier).

The poem ends with the poet addressing his wife, reconciling the mythical hallucinatory flights of the poem with their actual lives in the "authentic world":

> The sun
> Will rise on the snowy firs and set on the sleeping
> Lavender mountain as always, and no one
> Will possess or command or defile you where
>   you belong,
> Here in the authentic world.
>   The work is done.
> My name is Hayden and I have made this song.

Donald Hall has called *The Sleeping Beauty* "a life's knowledge set in order." It *is* that, even if the order is too personal at times, causing the poem to share some of the faults of obscurity contained in other recent book-length poems, including Robert Lowell's *History* and James Merrill's trilogy. As the poet-prince travels through Carruth's allegorical world, he moves inward: Carruth enters the sleeping beauty's dreams and fantasies. The figures in her dreams include, among others, social, business, and literary figures, poets and political leaders, all of whose names begin with the letter *H:* Homer, Hesiod, Hamlet, Heathcliff, Hitler, Hannibal, etc. The recurring initial, then, becomes a formal device for Carruth. If less restrictive than the recurring words in a sestina, the device serves a similar function: it is a "net" (to use Frost's familiar term), a way of ordering the poem through a finite set of possible alternatives.

Throughout the poem we hear "coincidental voices," all of them passing through the mind of the beauty, all of them invented (according to Carruth's notes), and all of them women. In some measure the poem explores our attitudes about women and, in a more general sense, about the idea of love. Another voice in the poem is that of Amos, a Vermont farmer who speaks in dialect. Amos represents sanity and wisdom, a wisdom that is being lost in our endless hurry to franchise, develop, and eventually ruin rural New England and other parts of the country.

The Sleeping Beauty would seem to fit into the genre M. L. Rosenthal calls "the modern poetic sequence," a lyric that can be judged only by the effect of the whole. *The Sleeping Beauty* resembles a piece of modern music— Carruth's beloved jazz in particular—improvisational (but not undisciplined), intimate, fragmented, and often self-analytical.

Although I'm tempted to describe many of the individual lyrics as "dreamsongs," Carruth's sequence shares little with John Berryman's work, work he criticizes as having "no real seriousness or creative force, but only a kind of edgy exhibitionism." The behavior of the sleeping beauty and her prince probably mirrors experiences in the poet's life, but Carruth warns us in endnotes that "nothing . . . in the poem needs to be construed as a personal reference." (Carruth's notes are sometimes a bit defensive, as if he were anticipating his critics.) Carruth's book is not an "autobiography in verse" (as Robert Lowell described his own later work), partly because *The Sleeping Beauty* opens out to a Poundian associativeness that enlarges the "I" and requires a complexity of points of view.

Hayden Carruth is among our most widely read poets, and his vocabulary is both large and sensitive. The first poem in *The Sleeping Beauty* (quoted here) and the next half-dozen establish an initial poetic pitch that (as Rosenthal says about poems in this genre) "creates its own dynamics, its object . . . neither to resolve a problem nor to conclude an action but to achieve the keenest, most open realization possible."

> Out of nothing.
>   This morning the world was gone;
> Only grayness outside, so dense, so close
> Against the window that it seemed no season,
> No place, and no thought almost,
> Except what preys at the edge of thought, un-
>   known;
> But it was snow. The flakes, extremely fine
> And falling unseen, still made the bough
> Of the hemlock whiten. Here and now—
> Twig by twig, needle by needle—a plume

Reached through the grayness,
Intricate purity that somehow could assume
Its own being in its own space,
Out of nothing . . .

If *The Sleeping Beauty* is Carruth at his inspired best, *If You Call This Cry a Song* represents the poet playing, most of the time, in a minor key. That's to be expected, I suppose, considering the nature of the book. The forty-five poems collected here were written over fifteen years (1964-79), and although most were published in magazines, Carruth did not collect them previously. *If You Call This Cry a Song* is the kind of book many prolific poets publish at least once in their careers; a miscellany published by a small press, the volume will interest mostly those readers already familiar with the poet's work.

As the title suggests, these poems embody many parallels between poetry and music. Of course all poetry must have an allegiance to music, but here the relationship is more self-conscious, resulting in poems which are often reflexive, calling attention to the very process of composing ("the dance of ink on paper"). Nearly a quarter of the poems use the word "song" or "singing"; others allude to specific musical genres or structures (including **"A Little Old Funky Homeric Blues for Herm," "Who Cares, Long as It's B-Flat,"** and **"The Cowshed Blues"**).

Like much of Carruth's work, the poems are personal, intimate, sincere. Many of the poems are dedicated to friends. The first poem is an invocation; others are addresses (**"The Winnower to the Winds," "Words to a Young Revolutionist"**). There are admonitions, meditations, adaptations, and several translations of poems by Gerard de Nerval, Alphonse de Lamartine, and Stéphane Mallarmé. Some have the same failings—they begin with promise, but lose energy and focus as they progress; finally the author must tack on an ending. Usually a question is tacked on, one that the poet might have worked harder to answer in the body of the poem.

Other poems get off on the wrong foot almost before they begin: Carruth falls into a style and diction that completely overwhelm, or in some cases clash with, the subject. The result inflates the mundane in the worst ways. In **"Picking Up the Beer Cans"** the subject and tone of the poem are colossally mismatched.

The poem begins:

> Twelve years   the obscene
> brown glint in the grass,
> the gleam of metal—I
> have hunted them.

And ends . . .

> In a few years my hunting
>   will be ended   and even
> now I cannot gather
>   the cans buried under leaves,
>   bottles broken by the snowplow.
>
> O my people . . .

Can this be the same poet who handled so gracefully the complex and delicate tonalities in *The Sleeping Beauty?* Some of these poems were collected, Carruth tells us, be-

cause they "have been important to other people." This gesture is hard to argue with, but other readers, coming fresh from the masterly *Sleeping Beauty,* will be disappointed. And yet isn't the unevenness of this collection practically a trademark of Carruth? Dickey observed that Carruth is a writer "with strange and terrifying shifts in quality." Beside the minor masterpieces in Carruth's first collection Dickey found "a great deal of ordinary, jargoning stuff which Mr. Carruth should have been ashamed to print in the same volume." One suspects that after twenty-five years of publishing the good with the bad, Carruth does so with a reason, however private it might be.

If You Call This Cry a Song includes a few jewels, such as **"Elaboration," "Our Northern Kind," "The Line,"** and my two favorites, **"My Meadow"** and **"Loneliness." "My Meadow,"** a poem of exquisite delicacy, is a meditation on one man's land that is soon twinned with a reflection on a life's discontent. The poem is quietly understated; the metaphors drawn from nature fall effortlessly into place; and the speaking voice—Carruth at his most relaxed, though one would never mistake the sprawling couplets with their beautiful rhymes and off-rhymes for prose—inspires the reader to trust the persona's commentary. Here are the first quarter and last quarter of the poem:

> Well, it's still the loveliest meadow in all Vermont.
> I believe that truly, yet for years have hardly
>
> seen it, I think, having lived too long with it—
> until I went to clean up the mess of firewood
>
> left by the rural electric co-op when they cut
> my clump of soft maples "threatening" their lines,
>
> this morning, the last day of September.
>
>   . . . . .
>
> I looked at my brook. It curled over my stones
> that looked back at me again with the pathos
>
> of their paleozoic eyes. I thought of my
> discontents. The brook, curled in its reflections
>
> of ferns and asters and bright leaves, was whispering
> something that made no sense. Then I closed my eyes
>
> and heard my brook inside my head. It told me—
> and I saw a distant inner light like the flash
>
> of a waterdrop on a turning leaf—it told me
> maybe I have lived too long with the world.

"Loneliness," subtitled "An Outburst in Hexasyllables," is a tour de force. Carruth describes the composition of the poem in an essay reprinted in *Effluences:* "For what it is worth, this is perfectly typical of the way I write: the first trance, then a second lesser one in which amplifications are made. Then after that only slight editorial changes, blue-penciling. I never disturb the structure of a poem once it is fixed, which usually occurs at the poem's inception, and I disturb the wording as little as possible."

"Loneliness" adumbrates remembered and projected experiences in the persona's life in Vermont. This sense of place informs the poem and manages to collect and illuminate the multitude of disparate images and actions of the poem. The formal structure of the poem—hexasyllables—seems just right, and this "outburst" is moving and memorable. "This poem arises directly from my experience that evening" Carruth tells us, and readers intuitively feel that presence in the poem. In an essay on Frost, Carruth argues for poems that spring from actual experience, not—as he calls them—"studio performances." It is because Carruth has always steered clear of studio performances in his criticism and his poetry that his work embodies the feeling of truth.

For readers not yet acquainted with Carruth's poetry I recommend his collection *Brothers I Loved You All* (1978). But *The Sleeping Beauty* may be his masterpiece. The entire body of Carruth's work is impressive: heartfelt, intelligent, vital. His goal, "to bring more people to poetry," he has pursued for a lifetime, and he has succeeded.

Hayden Carruth on "the natural world":

I have a close but at the same time uncomfortable relationship with the natural world. I've always been most at home in the country probably because I was raised in the country as a boy, and I know something about farming and woodcutting and all the other things that country people know about. That kind of work has been important to me in my personal life and in my writing too. I believe in the values of manual labor and labor that is connected with the earth in some way. But I'm not simply a nature poet. In fact, I consider myself and I consider the whole human race fundamentally alien. By evolving into a state of self-consciousness, we have separated ourselves from the other animals and the plants and from the very earth itself, from the whole universe. So there's a kind of fear and terror involved in living close to nature. My poems, I think, exist in a state of tension between the love of natural beauty and the fear of natural meaninglessness or absurdity.

Hayden Carruth, in an interview with Contemporary Authors New Revision Series, *Volume 4, Gale Research, 1981.*

Roger Mitchell **(review date November-December 1985)**

SOURCE: "Voice Is Everything," in *The American Book Review,* Vol. 8, No. 1, November-December, 1985, pp. 19-20.

[*Mitchell is an American poet, educator, and critic. In the following review, he applauds the skill with which Carruth employs a variety of voices and themes in* If You Call This Cry a Song.]

I would like to begin this review of Hayden Carruth's [*If You Call This Cry a Song*] by saying that voice is unim-

portant to poetry, but too many crimes are committed in such a remark, not the least of which is imprecision, since it isn't clear exactly what voice is. Whatever it is, though, a great deal is said about it, mostly in its defense. Those who use the word say, further, that true poets have their own—which is to say, a single—voice, and that the poet's worth can be measured precisely by this quality, possession of a unique and ubiquitous voice, like a brand label found in every shirt made by a given manufacturer. Departures from this voice are usually "regrettable," betraying either esthetic uncertainty or, worse, "insincerity" on the poet's part. To depart from one's voice is to depart from one's feeling and self and is thought therefore to be a sin against nature, a tampering with the givenness of life, an imposition of that hated, though human, quality—will—on a world of inviolable intuition and feeling. Thousands of poets are earnestly searching for *their* voices, and if I'm not mistaken, most are failing. The question is: Is this a real failure? Is voice, so conceived, an adequate measure of the value of poetry?

If my sense of voice is at all correct, it is chiefly a manifestation of the poet's originality. Voice is everything in speech or language that makes a poet that poet and no other. Like fingerprints, no two voices are supposed to be alike. Put this way, it seems that voice is really a property of the Romantic imagination, the underlying esthetic which values originality above nearly every other quality in the making of art. If this is so, and I believe it is, then voice is not an absolute requirement in the making of poetry but a negotiable one, a thing which some poets have and others do not. A. E. Housman, for instance, has voice, as has Hopkins, and a poem by Housman or Hopkins is instantly recognizable because of that voice. Robert Browning, on the other hand, has no voice, nothing in speech or language that would be unmistakably his. Poems of his are usually unmistakable, but it is not voice that makes them that way. That Housman had voice is vividly demonstrated when he argues against himself in "Terence, This Is Stupid Stuff " in a voice that is obviously not his own. But Housman had that other voice in him, strong and sure.

When the great reckoning is made a thousand years from now, Housman will be remembered, if at all, for the poem in which he let the other voice out, along with the one he cultivated as his own. I believe it is the natural state of the mind for it to be inhabited by voices, just as it is natural to feel many different things and to be puzzled and even divided by those feelings. Further, I believe it is a natural longing in us all to silence all but one of those voices, to be or to believe one thing, to not waver, to be sure. As readers, we like to hear what we've heard before in a poet. This, or something like it, accounts for two things in the poetry of Hayden Carruth: the diversity of modes and voices in his work and his anguish over that diversity. He says it plainly in **"Late Sonnet":**

> For that the sonnet no doubt was my own true
> singing and suchlike other song, for that
> I gave it up half-coldheartedly to set
> my lines in a fashion that proclaimed its virtue
> original in young arrogant artificers who
> had not my geniality nor voice, and yet

their fashionableness was persuasive to me,—
  what
shame and sorrow I pay!

On the other hand, we now have, in ***If You Call This Cry a Song,*** his wonderful variation on Frost's "Mending Wall," where the neighbor, Mr. Davis, "is entirely red pine, / / a stand of ranks / and files" while he [Carruth] is a "weedy / mixed-up clamor / / where all the voices / proclaim their own." Surely, among all its other possibilities, this is a defense of the natural multiplicity of voices in his work.

I am not one of those who believes (as I sometimes think Carruth himself believes) that he "found his voice" in ***Brothers, I Loved You All.*** The aging, embattled, Yankee dirt farmer of that book (as much fiction as fact, as far as I can tell) is simply one of the voices in his head, one he hears particularly well, but no more "real" or profound than the man who wished to make grand, Miltonic (or is it Homeric?) music in ***For You***:

    Colder than land is the random sea, shriveling
    Vein and sinew as the long tow took me, tum-
      bled me,
    Forward and down through the waves wheeling
      and plunging
    . . .

or the man who reinvented the romance and a language of the romance in ***The Sleeping Beauty:***

    And there in the sky is the known face half-
      hidden
    In rippling lights, askance, the eternal other
    Toward whom the poem yearns, maiden
    Of the water-lights, brother
    Of the snow-fields, Androgyne!

We have no reason to expect Carruth's newest book, ***If You Call This Cry a Song,*** to be the equal of the two previous books. ***Brothers*** and ***The Sleeping Beauty*** are, after all, two of this time's best. It is the nature of the new book, though it is not said, to be a gathering of what would not fit in the two earlier books. These poems span the years 1964 to 1979 and show us what sorts of things were passing through Carruth's mind as he wrote his way toward ***Brothers*** and ***The Sleeping Beauty.*** One or two seem rehearsals for the long neoromance. One or two are written in the Yankee voice of ***Brothers.*** **"Marvin McCabe,"** perhaps the best poem in the book, was probably written too late to be included in ***Brothers,*** where it would seem natural for it to be.

Aside from a few embarrassing attempts to write of or with the aid of jazz, ***If You Call This Cry a Song*** is a book of bright and near-bright moments, variations on what have come to be Carruth's necessary themes, spoken in his several voices. For instance, there are a number of poems that reach toward the "pure moment from an existence / in the other consciousness where time / is stilled." There are also the persistence yarns, **"Regarding Chainsaws"** and **"Marvin McCabe,"** celebrations of Yankee grit. There is Carruth's characteristic fascination with the inarticulate, the uneducated, the mentally deficient, animals, flowers, nature itself. Marvin McCabe wrecked his car after drinking too much. As a result, he can't speak. So,

Carruth gives him speech. "I have to rely on Hayden," he says,

    He's listened to me so much
    he knows not only what I'm saying but what
    I mean to say, you understand?—that thought
    in my head. He can write it out for me.

There are recurring bouts with loneliness and entropy— "work yet to be done— / / with a broken imagination." Little is right in Carruth's world. The retreat to the Vermont woods signifies that. Even there, though, "the vision of the void," existential loneliness, haunts him, just as the litter of beer cans outrages him, "the obscene / brown glint in the grass."

    I have been alone, always
    essentially alone,
    like the Indian now, and God,
    and everyone,

and one of the reasons for that has been the "rain of / metal and glass and plastic" that "falls to the earth undiminished." Finally, there is the antique lyric grace, the deliberate archaism, as in **"Bouquet in Dog Time"**:

    A bit of yarrow and then of rue,
    steeplebush and black-eyed susan,
    one fringed orchis, ragged and wry,
    some meadowsweet, the vetch that's blue,
    to make a comeliness for you.

Here, in faint outline, are the voice, the attitude, the awareness of language and people and nature which Carruth warns us we cannot do without, but which our whole way of life seems bent on eliminating.

This is a great deal from a book which is thought even by its maker to contain "former" favorites, "including a few I had in fact forgotten." A book and a career that demonstrates, as F. T. Prince has said, that "perhaps those poets who have most obviously become themselves in their art are those who have been made up of the most contradictory, wavering, clashing or simply alternating, selves."

Robert B. Shaw   (review date November 1986)

SOURCE: A review of *The Selected Poetry of Hayden Carruth,* in *Poetry,* Vol. CXLIX, No. 2, November, 1986, pp. 98-100.

[*In the following review of* The Selected Poetry of Hayden Carruth, *Shaw remarks: "Warts and all, this is a collection animated by a seriousness of purpose, a vocational commitment which few poets nowadays can match."*]

I wonder why Hayden Carruth has not made this selection of his poetry [in ***The Selected Poetry of Hayden Carruth***] himself. Galway Kinnell, who supplies an appreciative foreword, has done the job; it is unclear to what extent the author has been consulted. I can well imagine that someone who writes as copiously as Carruth might find the task of winnowing past work onerous. He is not only prolific but, as a stylist, extremely varied. In his readiness to experiment, to move on, he reminds one of the final lines of Frost's great poem, "The Wood-Pile":

I thought that only
Someone who lived in turning to fresh tasks
Could so forget his handiwork on which
He spent himself, the labor of his ax,
And leave it there far from a useful fireplace
To warm the frozen swamp as best it could
With the slow smokeless burning of decay.

Frost comes to mind for more than casual reasons. Many of Carruth's poems are set in Vermont, and we see in them the countryside Frost knew in his youth as it now is, nearly a century later. It is not a reassuring vision. The darker pieces depict a land from which the farms are disappearing, either bought up and gentrified or left to fester as rural slums. It is interesting (and melancholy) to compare the poems Carruth has written about work—elemental chores like cutting wood or baling hay—with those of Frost. For Frost such labor is the foundation of society—indeed, of human existence—and respect for it is assumed. Carruth, while he himself may share such a view, knows that lives spent in such labor are seen now by many as marginalized and quixotic. This consciousness, with the sorrow and anger it induces, gives his work a defiant, embattled air that is compelling. And when he can single out some aspect of the country or the life lived in it that has escaped ruin, he makes us feel the exhilaration of his small victory.

I like especially those poems of Carruth's which begin with rapt description and move, with delicate tact, into a more reflective mode. **"The Ravine"** starts out as brilliant inventory:

Stones, brown tufted grass, but no water,
it is dry to the bottom. A seedy eye
of orange hawkweed blinks in sunlight
stupidly, a mink bumbles away,
a ringnecked snake among stones lifts its head
like a spark, a dead young woodcock—
long dead, the mink will not touch it—
sprawls in the hatchment of its soft plumage
and clutches emptiness with drawn talons.

But by the end the poet is musing on his own painful gift for bringing together such noticings into a single composition: "These are my sorrow, / for unlike my bright admonitory friends / I see relationships, I do not see things." (To "see relationships": it is an unassuming but commanding summary of what the poet's work is all about.) Other fine poems of this kind include **"Once More," "The Cows at Night," "My Meadow,"** and **"The Loon on Forrester's Pond,"** with its wonderful capturing of "this insane song, wavering music / like the cry of the genie inside the lamp," which in the end, Carruth tells us, "seemed / the real and only sanity to me."

Sanity, and its fragility, are recurrent themes. Carruth's poems about mental derangement and time spent in an asylum are not his best, but they lend perspective to the rest of his work. We get the sense of one who can acknowledge vulnerabilities which once overwhelmed him, and can turn them to a creative purpose. I respect these poems; I do not like them. I feel a similar respect, and a similar lack of enthusiasm, for the pieces in which Carruth imitates Frost most closely, not merely in choice of landscape but in formal means. Such monologues and narratives in relaxed blank verse don't appear to know when to stop;

the pathos of the depleted lives they picture is exhausted long before they come to an end. I wish Carruth had imitated Frost's dramatic compression as well as his relaxed iambics. It should be said, though, that Carruth's unsuccessful poems have behind them more ambition than most poets' failures have. His lapses are courageous attempts gone wrong, and may often seem more worth reading than poems whose only distinction is that they have avoided obvious missteps. Warts and all, this is a collection animated by a seriousness of purpose, a vocational commitment which few poets nowadays can match.

Roderick Nordell (review date 19 March 1987)

SOURCE: "Words without Music about All That Jazz," in *The Christian Science Monitor,* March 19, 1987, p. 24.

[*Nordell is an American journalist, editor, and critic. In the following review, he determines that* Sitting In *provides "an uneven performance with a number of fine, thought-provoking moments."*]

It shouldn't be surprising that a poet here and there goes public with a fondness for jazz. Both poetry and jazz got rhythm, as the song says, and both have to make things new within established forms, whether the 14-line sonnet or the 12-bar blues.

Britain's late candidate for poet laureate Philip Larkin went so far as to write newspaper reviews of jazz, a collection of which was reissued not long ago. Recently a lesser-known American poet, Hayden Carruth, came out with [*Sitting In: Selected Writings on Jazz, Blues, and Related Topics*], in which he possibly goes further—saying that for him poetry has always been "second-best to jazz." Indeed, his criterion for almost anything is how close it comes to jazz.

Such daring judgment falls swingingly on the ear of a reader who tries, like Carruth, to play jazz with his betters on the bandstand from time to time—"sitting in," as the title of the book says. I feel as overromantic in the presence of thorough jazz artists as the poet in some of the verse that Carruth drops in among previously published prose pieces here. I appreciate his professorial wrestling (he teaches English at Syracuse University) with how to analyze a music that continues to tantalize intellectuals at home and abroad despite the folklore that you either understand jazz or you don't.

But some of his analyses seem subjective enough to be unconvincing. For example, "the blues" often has echoes of melancholy, as in "the blues ain't nothin' but a cold gray day," with certain flatted notes typically adding to the mood. But the genre includes too many romping, upbeat, even triumphant numbers to sustain Carruth's definition of the blues as "a sensual experience of seeking and failing, that is, of inadequacy."

The book's net effect is of an uneven performance with a number of fine, thought-provoking moments.

One important distinction Carruth offers is between the music called jazz and the culture of jazz, including its origins with black musicians, possible social meanings, and widespread influence. He notes that he first heard jazz as a child in a small farming community remote from the culture of jazz. He heard it as music, not cultural phenomenon. He must have been like those Europeans far from the US racial scene who heard the music and began to take it seriously before their American counterparts did.

Even if one disagrees with Carruth's verdict on the blues, it is interesting to see him reach it through scrutinizing the musical elements, apart from the lyrics. And you can see what he means when he says he has been given more aesthetic pleasure by poet William Butler Yeats and jazz clarinetist Charles Ellsworth Russell than by any other artists of this century. (Yes, he means Pee Wee Russell but avoids the nickname in a campaign against being condescending to jazz performers.)

Listen to Russell playing a "totally new and forever surprising counter-statement" to the melody on a recording of "Lulu's Back in Town." Carruth says this "is of the same genre as the 'Variations on a Theme by Haydn' of Brahms, and like that work is an assertion of creative independence made stronger, not weaker, by its relationship to the prior text."

And so another poet does his bit for what so many jazz musicians—and some of their classical counterparts—would like to see: a stage beyond categories where it's just all music, or maybe all jazz.

D. W. Faulkner   (review date Fall 1991)

SOURCE: "Homages to Life," in *The Sewanee Review,* Vol. XCIX, No. 4, Fall, 1991, pp. cii-civ.

[*The following excerpt is from Faulkner's laudatory review of* Tell Me Again How the White Heron Rises and Flies Across the Nacreous River at Twilight Toward the Distant Islands.]

For a good long while Hayden Carruth has been one of our best critics of contemporary American poetry. His reviews, whether appearing in literary quarterlies or major newspapers, have always borne a sense of kinship with his readers. He reads the way an attentive reader would want, with perspicacity and hindsight, as often offering the reader a close-but-no-cigar estimation of the work before him as he might the sense that he, as well as poetry, was seeing something welcome and new. Carruth can be tough, or laudatory, and often both, but he never praises mediocrity.

As a poet himself Carruth is much harder to pin down. His *Selected Poetry* (1985) is oddly uneven. Granted, it reflects more than thirty years of writing and ranges from his youthful salad days in the early sixties when he worked with James Laughlin and New Directions through and beyond his dark hours in the Bloomingdale psychiatric hospital in the seventies. At times in that collection he is dark and brooding, at others joyfully lyrical. A variety of writing forms seems to mirror his swings of mood: it is as though, like the great early modernist American painters, who moved from impressionism to fauvism to expressionism in the course of two decades, he was constantly shifting styles.

Carruth's new collection [*Tell Me Again How the White Heron Rises and Flies Across the Nacreous River at Twilight Toward the Distant Islands*], transcends the bumpy rhythm of his earlier work. In it he seems marvelously at home in the long breathy style that we have come to associate with Whitman's progeny. . . .

The book's title reflects its long-line form, which allows Carruth a majesty of perspective. He sets a tone by stating in self-reflection: "I became eventually, gradually, ashamed of my mind's incapacity, just I had once written / Poems to be read many times, but what was the use of that? Now I write poems to be read once and forgotten, / Or not to be read at all." The reader can only take this as a self-conscious demurrer from a writer who also says: "I believe there's a thing like over-tidiness, or call it / Over-cultivation, that's more the nub, old proven ways grown / Lopsidal and disproportionate, cultivation for no purpose / And too refined." What Carruth presents flies in the face of "the old ways," and yet it's symmetrical, full of proportion, and cultivated with the sharpest reason.

Although reflection on nature and experience dominates this fine collection, there are tips of the hat to Ovid, oriental poetry, and German philosophy, most particularly Schopenhauer, whom Carruth manages to incorporate into a reflection on everyday suburban life: "the Will of Schopenhauer's essay leaps out at me / in children-in-themselves, starker than stones or stars, / so that I cower; for the future is theirs, day by day / they remove it from the plastic wrap of not-being / and leave it on the death strewn lawns." These lines are typical of Carruth's ability to appropriate both his reflection on tradition and his awareness of the everyday and to blend them. The results are highly personal and refreshingly honest. Responding to an interlocutor who asks of the origin of dust, Carruth disarmingly reacts and demonstrates his newly won favor of the practical over the theoretical: " 'Generalized metaphysical fall-out,' I said. 'Dust to dust, etc.' / 'How do you know?' she said. / 'I don't,' I said. / 'Then kindly refrain from being so fucking authoritative,' she said."

The old rules of relying on tradition don't hold. The long-line style, possibly garnered from Galway Kinnell, is a shoehorn for Carruth here. With it he seems even more successful than Kinnell in that poet's recent efforts. There's also a poem in James Laughlin's "typewriter style" (**"When I Wrote a Little"**) that seems to confirm Carruth's developing sense that that freedom of form can support freedom of idea.

The backbone of this collection is a single poem originally published in [*The Sewanee Review*] that runs twenty pages and demonstrates every virtue of the long-line style that Carruth had laid out in the poems leading up to it. **"Mother"** is an elegy and a poetic investigation everywhere as powerful as Allen Ginsberg's "Kaddish"—and as eloquent as the best of Galway Kinnell's elegies in his *Book of Nightmares.* It is finely measured and profoundly moving. An homage to the life and death of the poet's mother, it includes, among its opening lines, "After the long years of my private wrecked language, when my mind shook in the tempests of fear, / After everything between us is done and never to be undone, so that no speech matters, / Nevertheless I must speak."

Carruth has spoken well in this collection. The reader, upon completing it, is left with a feeling that echoes its title, "Tell me again," we are tempted to respond.

Richard Tillinghast   (review date 27 December 1992)

SOURCE: "Chants and Chain Saws," in *The New York Times Book Review,* December 27, 1992, p. 2.

[*Tillinghast is an American poet, educator, and critic. In the following excerpt from a review of* Collected Shorter Poems, 1946-1991, *he asserts: "Something Hayden Carruth does as well as any living writer is to treat the reader as a friend, and to provide, through his poetry, hours of good company."*]

Hayden Carruth's *Collected Shorter Poems, 1946-1991* brings together in 417 pages what the author describes as "about two-thirds of my previously published shorter poems and perhaps one-fifth or less of all the poems I've written." Mr. Carruth is prolific. He revels in a capacity for writing in a wide range of styles and forms. Like other poets who came of age during the 50's, he started off imitating the formal style of the day, with its tendency toward a stiff, severe rhetoric:

> Stern and alone, I may endure.
> But memory though it slumber wakes,
> And deep in the mind its havoc makes.

As it did for others, the era of the 60's seems to have brought Mr. Carruth a sense of liberation. He experimented with free verse, and wrote in opposition to the war in Vietnam with a modesty not typical of the antiwar movement in poetry. In **"The Birds of Vietnam,"** first he speculates about the birds that might live there, then admits.

> but I have not seen you,
> I do not know your names,
> I do not know
> what I am talking about.

He writes about his periods of madness and his days spent in an institution, but this New England-born poet finds his sanity in rural Vermont. He communicates his love for the land and captures the essence of a landscape and weather that other observers would consider ugly:

> Rain
> soaks the fish-scale snow, the bloom
> of beer cans emerges beside the road.
> Another spring. You can think of nothing
> that is not rotten, see nothing
> not hideous.

Like Robert Frost, Mr. Carruth has attuned his ear to the ways and the talk of his neighbors in rural New England. In **"Regarding Chainsaws,"** a man named Stan has insisted on buying a chain saw of dubious utility from him—a chain saw that won't start. When the poet asks Stan how he is progressing with the saw,

> "Well," he says, "I token
> it down to scrap, and I buried it in three
> separate places yonder on the upper side

> of the potato piece. You can't be too careful,"
> he says, "when you're disposing of a hex."

Some of the talk Mr. Carruth records, particularly from *Asphalt Georgics,* can be less than intriguing. But part of his drift in these conversation poems, it seems to me, is that the New England farmers and town dwellers who are his neighbors are no longer—if in fact they ever were—the laconic rustics of Frost's pithy pentameters.

But Mr. Carruth is a poet of many moods. He writes about jazz with the affectionate familiarity of a long-time fan of the music. His pages abound with sensuous erotic poetry:

> You rose from our embrace and the small light
>   spread
> like an aureole around you. The long parabola
> of neck and shoulder, flank and thigh I saw
> permute itself through unfolding and unlimited
> minuteness in the movement of your tall tread,
> the spine-root swaying, the Picasso-like éclat
> of scissoring slender legs.

I'd trade a dozen asphalt georgics from this collection for one poem like the marvelous account of the author's attempt to make a pond on his property, **"Underground the Darkness Is the Light."** Mr. Carruth draws us into the narrative like a good storyteller whose strength is his companionable stance both toward his reader and toward the world of nature. As soon as he gets cranked up, with "When I first started out to make what later became known as Hayden's Runaway Pond," one sits back in expectation of a good yarn. And the poem does not disappoint. Something Hayden Carruth does as well as any living writer is to treat the reader as a friend, and to provide, through his poetry, hours of good company.

Allen Hoey   (review date Winter 1994)

SOURCE: A review of *Collected Shorter Poems, 1946-1991,* in *The Southern Humanities Review,* Vol. XXVIII, No. 1, Winter, 1994, pp. 101-05.

[*Hoey is a poet, educator, and critic who regularly writes the "Year in Poetry" essay for the* CLC Yearbook. *In the following review of* Collected Shorter Poems, 1946-1991, *he provides a positive assessment of the collection, commenting: "[T]his volume demonstrates what some readers have long known: Hayden Carruth possesses greater range of style, scope of subject, and diversity of formal skills than any other poet working in the United States today."*]

Since the publication of his first collection in 1959, Hayden Carruth has issued fifteen book-length volumes of poetry. Unfortunately, he has never had a consistent publisher (although New Directions has served him loyally, issuing three of the thirteen previously published volumes represented [in *Collected Shorter Poems, 1946-1991*], plus a collection of longer poems), and several of his books have been limited press runs with equally limited distribution. As a result, much of his best work has gone unnoticed or too little noticed; whatever level of benign neglect commercial publishers reserve for their poetry lists, at least they do provide a kind of high-profile promotion beyond the means of many of the independent presses which have kept Carruth in circulation. Readers familiar with one or two of Carruth's titles, or perhaps his commercially published *Selected Poems* of several years back, will be surprised to discover the fullness of his career.

Skimming the book, we notice his development from poems of the forties and fifties, which seem cut from the period fabric: compressed, metrically formal and usually rhymed, full of allusions to art, philosophy, and mythology. In the sixties, the forms begin to loosen, lines lengthening and shortening, some scattering across the page, as he creates a more personal style, public and professional in its rhetoric, written with careful attention to the oral aspect of language, though not necessarily, or even usually, seeming conversational. Carruth's voices range from backcountry Vermonters to Central New Yorkers, from backporch raconteur to elevated orator, yet his most successful poems employ rhetorical techniques of public presentation, while exploring the most private moments.

Most striking in this regard are monologues delivered by speakers clearly different from Carruth. Although the selection from his first volume, *The Crow and the Heart,* includes several poems spoken by historic or mythic personae, they seldom realize a complete character; most successful is **"The Fat Lady,"** a poem which, reminiscent of Frost, looks forward to the achievement of poems originally published in *Brothers, I Loved You All* (1978). Here, Carruth presents his Vermont neighbors either in monologues or in poems which quote or borrow locutions from the characters; as the speaker in **"John Dryden"** notes, "have you noticed / I can't talk about him without talking like him?" Like Frost, Carruth captures a sense of character and place while subtly presenting a complex set of meanings, discovering the kind of "natural symbol" ordinary people grapple with to understand their lives. Most haunting of these is **"Johnny Spain's White Heifer,"** in which the lost heifer comes to represent, through controlled digression, an ineffable lost purity. The opening lines introduce situation, locale, and character with elegant compression:

> The first time ever I saw Johnny Spain was
> the first time I came to this town. There
> he was, lantern jaw and broken nose, wall-eyed
>   and
> fractious, with a can of beer in one hand and a
> walkie-talkie in the other, out in front
> of the post office. And I heard someone saying,
> "Johnny, what in hell are you doing?" "I'm
>   looking,"
> he answered, in an executive tone, "for me god-
>   damn
> white heifer." "Run off did she?" "Yass,"
> he said. "Busted me south-side fence, the
>   bitch—
> if some thieving bastard didn't bust it for her."

Although Carruth loosens the pentameter more than Frost ever did, the sardonic humor and colloquial precision serve here as in the best of Frost to convey nuances of character—Johnny Spain's, the unnamed interlocutor's, and the narrator's. Other poems in this style include **"Lady," "Marshall Washer," "Regarding Chainsaws,"** and **"Marvin McCabe."**

Carruth's move to Syracuse, New York, in 1979 resulted in a shift of idiom and locale in *Asphalt Georgics* (1985),

a group of poems written in syllabic ballad stanzas employing frequently hyphenated enjambments. Set in Central New York, these poems lament the passing of the agrarian lifestyle that provided the basis for traditional georgics while celebrating the persistence of human life amid suburban sprawl that threatens that spirit. All lengthy, they build through strategies of apparent tangent and indirection, which does not allow easy excerpting; **"Names,"** the first poem of what might be read as a loose sequence, introduces the form and a sense of the intermingling of lives and histories as one speaker flows into another, the shift signalled by the changing names of what seems to be a single speaker over the poem's sixteen pages. The strict form allows Carruth considerable flexibility in presenting conversational speech. In **"Marge,"** for instance, a recovering alcoholic recounts the story of his divorce and business failure, his decline into alcoholism and recovery through the friendship of Marge, who took him in as a boarder and who has just died after a debilitating illness. Here are the opening stanzas:

> Look friend, you got troubles? Like it's
>   damn hard, figuring what
> it all means, right? Right. So let me
>   tell you. The Pizza Hut
>
> won't throw out a couple old guys
>   like us, it's a slow night,
> we had our supper, now we're just
>   gabbing, eh, with a mite
>
> more coffee if you can call this
>   coffee, and what would you
> give for a real old-time mug
>   right now instead of who
>
> knows what this cup is, pressed glue—why
>   hell, a lunger like me
> even could blow it out the door.

In these poems Carruth manages the peculiar mix of self-pity, understated humor, and blunt disclosure that characterizes strangers sharing intimacies because they have no one else to talk to.

Carruth's public rhetoric extends to the lyric, where his range of diction and vocabulary allows him to modulate easily from low to high style and to incorporate moments of humor in otherwise serious, even solemn poems without violating that tone. As in this passage from **"The Ravine,"** these lyrics most often grow out of careful observation of the natural world, not for the sake of seeing things but to consider "relationships of things":

> Stones, brown tufted grass, but no water,
> it is dry to the bottom. A seedy eye
> of orange hawkweed blinks in sunlight
> stupidly, a mink bumbles away,
> a ringneck snake among stones lifts its head
> like a spark, a dead young woodcock—
> long dead, the mink will not touch it—
> sprawls in the hatchment of its soft plumage
> and clutches emptiness with drawn talons.

As precise is this description from **"The Loon on Forrester's Pond"**:

> . . . this insane song, wavering music
> like the cry of the genie inside the lamp,
> it came from inside the long wilderness

of my life, a loon's song, and there he was
swimming on the pond, guarding
his mate's nest by the shore,
diving and staying under
unbelievable minutes and coming up
where no one was looking.

Typically, Carruth presents his observations through details objective enough to allow us to "see" the situation yet in language that renders the emotional construct of the subject, as the enjambment from the third to fourth line of this passage moves the action from outside to inside just long enough to suggest that we read the whole poem both internally and externally, then lets the focus shift back outward.

More recently, in poems gathered from his 1989 collection *Tell Me Again How the White Heron Rises and Flies Across the Nacreous River at Twilight Toward the Distant Islands,* Carruth's lines stretch across the page to Whitmanesque length in compositions that reflect the length in their looping discursiveness. Even more than in other poems, these structures accumulate, as does jazz, riffs and motifs that seem to diverge wildly from the "point" of the poem only to swoop around at the end to enlarge the idea of point. Many of these poems consider the poetic process from the vantage point of an aging poet who wonders what this life has meant, for himself as well as for aging or dead friends, James Wright, Raymond Carver, John Cheever, and Galway Kinnell among them. The close of **"A Post-Impressionist Susurration for the First of November, 1983"** gives some sense of the mode:

> . . . Because I could not name the colors I saw,
>   and I envied painters
> their knowledge of pigments,
> I studied the charts of colors and I looked up the
>   names—mallow,
> cerise—in the dictionary,
> I examined the meanings of *hue, shade, tone,
>   tint, density, saturation,
> brilliance,* and so on,
> But it did no good. The eye has knowledge the
>   mind cannot share,
> which is why painters
> So often are inarticulate. Is the eye ignorant, un-
>   educated? How absurd.
> That would be impossible.
> Hence I became eventually, gradually, un-
>   ashamed of my mind's incapacity,
> just as I had once written
> Poems to be read many times, but what was the
>   use of that? Now I write
> poems to be read once and forgotten,
> Or not to be read at all.

Also strong in this section are **"The Impossible Indispensibility of the Ars Poetica," "Ovid, Old Buddy, I Would Discourse with You a While," " 'Sure,' Said Benny Goodman,"** and **"Underground the Darkness Is the Light."**

These late masterpieces show a talent continuing to grow and mature well into Carruth's sixth decade. Unfortunately, this development is not consistent; both the selections from the late *Sonnets* and the section of new poems are less fully achieved. Although Carruth has proven himself an able sonneteer in other poems gathered here, and more

than capable of sustaining a sequence of sonnet-like poems (his masterful **"Paragraphs"** written in fifteen-line rhymed stanzas of his own devising), these sonnets swing, even in the same poem, from emotionality that too often smudges into sentimentality to excessive cerebration, ungrounded in the kind of specific detail or striking conceit at the heart of most powerful sonnets. The new poems suffer for being merely a collection of new poems in a volume otherwise characterized by intensive selection made from the vantage point of years if not decades from original composition. Slighter pieces and exercises that would go more easily unnoticed in a book are underscored in this context, especially when stronger poems, particularly from Carruth's most eviscerated collection, *The Oldest Killed Lake in North America,* have been excluded. The best of them, however, make a place for themselves, especially his moving poems about sexuality and aging. Particularly notable are **"Sonnet," "Essay on Death," "Sex," "Assignment," "August,"** and **"Block."**

Finally, a collected poems provides a perspective on a poet's career. And this volume demonstrates what some readers have long known: Hayden Carruth possesses greater range of style, scope of subject, and diversity of formal skills than any other poet working in the United States today. That is not to say that even in this rigorously assembled collection (a note informs us that this represents two thirds of his published shorter poems and one fifth of the poems he's written) Carruth's unevenness is not apparent; but even weaker poems evince qualities of mastery and fluency that make his strongest poems monuments to the human spirit.

This is the first of three projected volumes from Copper Canyon, to be followed by a collection of longer poems and one of essays. The second of these collections is especially essential, for any reader familiar with Carruth's work will regret in this *Collected Shorter Poems* only the sense of incompletion. So many of these poems, from the earliest volume through the poems of the late seventies and early eighties, point to Carruth's most ambitious undertaking, the neglected book-length poem *The Sleeping Beauty.* When completed, this project will preserve in compact from the accomplishment of one of our masters.

FURTHER READING

Criticism

Feder, Lillian. "Poetry from the Asylum: Hayden Carruth's *The Bloomingdale Papers.*" In *Literature in Medicine,* Volume 4, *Psychiatry and Literature* (1985): 112-27.
    Illustrates how Carruth's struggle for identity and selfhood while writing *The Bloomingdale Papers* contributed greatly to his growth as a poet.

Flint, R. W. Review of *Asphalt Georgics,* by Hayden Carruth. *The New York Times Book Review* (14 July 1985): 15.
    A laudatory appraisal of *Asphalt Georgics.*

Gardner, Geoffrey. "The Real and Only Sanity." *The American Poetry Review* 10, No. 1 (January-February 1981): 19-22.

Favorable review, in which Gardner surveys Carruth's earlier works and concludes that *Brothers, I Loved You All* is Carruth's most accomplished writing to date.

Howard, Ben. "New Englanders." *Poetry* CLVI, No. 6 (September 1990): 345-48.
    Extols Carruth's blending of disparate images and ideas in *Tell Me Again How the White Heron Rises and Flies Across the Nacreous River at Twilight toward the Distant Islands*.

McClatchy, J. D. "Labyrinth and Clue." *The Nation* 236, No. 5 (5 February 1983): 148-51.
    Brief positive assessment of *The Sleeping Beauty* in which McClatchy comments: "Carruth has fashioned a rich, complex poem on a human scale."

Oliver, Mary. "Gathering Light." *The Kenyon Review* VIII, No. 3 (Summer 1986): 129-35.
    Responds positively to *Asphalt Georgics*, asserting: "In a time when the poems of many poets are frighteningly similar in style, it is salutory and important to find work that strikes out in a different direction."

Weiss, David. "The Incorrigible Dirigible." *The Southern Review* 26, No. 2 (April 1990): 466-69.
    Characterizes the poems in *Tell Me Again How the White Heron Rises and Flies Across the Nacreous River at Twilight toward the Distant Islands* as "ungainly, temperamental, prosy, anecdotal, discursive, yet 'lighter than air,' " and asserts: "Only the helium of the poet's intelligence holds them impossibly up."

Additional coverage of Carruth's life and career is contained in the following sources published by Gale Research: *Contemporary Authors,* **Vols. 9-12 (rev. ed.);** *Contemporary Authors New Revision Series,* **Vols. 4, 38;** *Contemporary Literary Criticism,* **Vols. 4, 7, 10, 18;** *Dictionary of Literary Biography,* **Vol. 5;** *Major 20th-Century Writers; Poetry Criticism,* **Vol. 10; and** *Something About the Author,* **Vol. 47.**

Laurie Colwin

1944-1992

American short story writer, novelist, and essayist.

The following entry provides an overview of Colwin's career. For further discussion of her life and works, see *CLC*, Volumes 5, 13, and 23.

INTRODUCTION

Colwin is noted for her short stories and novels that portray the lives of attractive, well-educated, upper-class people. Although often faulted by critics for the limited range of her characters, themes, and settings, her fiction has been compared to that of Jane Austen for its concern with manners, privacy, and happiness in marital and familial relationships. As Robb Forman Drew asserts, Colwin "seems intent upon providing us with a witty, literate and intelligent entertainment, a commodity not so easily come by these days, and in that effort she has certainly succeeded."

Biographical Information

Colwin was born in New York City and grew up in Chicago and Philadelphia. She returned to New York City to attend the Columbia School of General Studies, and after graduation she worked on the editorial staff of several large publishing houses. Colwin published her first full-length work, *Passion and Affect*, in 1974. She died of a heart attack in 1992.

Major Works

Commentators generally agree that Colwin's novels and short stories are all similar in tone, setting, and theme. Amy Richlin has determined the defining traits of Colwin's fiction to be "good fortune for all characters, verging on magical realism; settings of equally unreal beauty, in terms of weather, domestic appointments, seasons; and a continuous metanarrative discussion of the problems of human happiness, change, time, nostalgia. These contents are packaged in a style of great rhetorical polish, intensely pleasurable to read." The plot of Colwin's *Family Happiness* (1982), for example, incorporates several of these elements; Polly, the protagonist of the story, is beautiful, happily married, and well-loved by family and friends, yet she enters into a love affair with an artist. Colwin explores Polly's inner conflict between familial obligations and the exhilaration of a new relationship, tracing her emotional development throughout the book. In Colwin's last novel, *A Big Storm Knocked It Over* (1993), a newly married woman, Jane, struggles with ambivalent feelings about her marriage, pregnancy, and the strong attraction she feels toward her boss. The narrative examines the relationship between Jane and her best friend as they both become new

mothers and as they attempt to define their roles in their respective marriages and professions.

Critical Reception

Several critics have derided Colwin for the limited scope of her fiction and have faulted her short stories and novels for their unsympathetic and self-involved characters. However, many commentators praise her works for their intelligent and humorous reflections on romance, family, friendship, and the effort to maintain privacy and self-awareness in the contemporary world. Regarding her predominantly domestic concerns, Willard Spiegelman contends: "Colwin has established herself as an anatomist of sanguinity in an age when unhappy families and desperate social lives have become the norm in fiction." Summarizing Colwin's contribution, Kate Lehrer asserts that she "gave us something of a cross between Noel Coward's drawing room and Jane Austen's domestic parlor, all wrapped in a most contemporary setting and sensibility."

PRINCIPAL WORKS

Passion and Affect (short stories) 1974
Shine On, Bright and Dangerous Object (novel) 1975
Happy All The Time (novel) 1978
The Lone Pilgrim (short stories) 1981
Family Happiness (novel) 1982
Another Marvelous Thing (short stories) 1986
Home Cooking: A Writer in the Kitchen (essays) 1988
Goodbye without Leaving (novel) 1990
A Big Storm Knocked It Over (novel) 1993

CRITICISM

Carolyn See (review date 19 September 1982)

SOURCE: A review of *Family Happiness*, in *The New York Times Book Review*, September 19, 1982, pp. 13, 42.

[*See is an American educator and novelist. In the following review, she faults the storyline of* Family Happiness *as weak and implausible.*]

Polly Solo-Miller Demarest is one of those heroines of American fiction who appear to have everything. She is married to a large, handsome, usually amiable husband, Henry; she has two sweet children, Pete and Dee-Dee; she lives in a Park Avenue apartment; she has graduated from a good school and holds down a high-level job, as Coordinator of Research in Reading Projects and Methods for the Board of Education ("This job combined some of the things Polly held most dear—service, children, and books").

What else does it take to make life perfect? The wonderful job only takes up three days of her week. Her husband makes more than enough money. Polly herself is beautiful, still young and powerfully cheerful. And she is a functioning part of a larger family that gathers together for big occasions and small—what a rarity!

The extended Solo-Miller family consists of her father, Henry Sr., who dwells in what Polly thinks of as "the realm of the higher mind"; that is, his mind is on his own concerns. Polly's older brother, Paul, is a priggish bachelor whose reputation for intelligence is so firmly entrenched that he no longer has to say anything bright. The younger brother, Henry Jr., has married the daughter of Czech refugees: "She and Henry, Jr., behaved more like brother and sister than like a married couple. They wore each other's clothes, did not plan to have children, played with their dog, and dedicated themselves to kite flying." The chatelaine of the extended court is the former Constanzia Hendricks, now called Wendy, a well-bred narcissist who has trained up her daughter, Polly, to be her perfect luncheon companion. Polly's place in the family is clear: "She had never given anyone the slightest pause. Her family doted on her, but no one felt it was necessary to pay much attention to someone as sturdy, upright, cheerful, and kind as she."

The situation, then, is perfection to start. Readers of Laurie Colwin will remember that her last novel, **Happy All the Time,** ended with just such a portion of domestic bliss: plenty of order, harmony, civility, good meals; plenty of champagne, good-looking young men and women in love and the implicit promise of a new generation. But . . . then what? Polly used to be in love with her husband, but Henry is a good provider, which means he spends a great deal of time at work and often is too tired to make love in the evenings or jokes in broad daylight. So Polly is in the position of a person who has bought a gorgeous car that doesn't run very well: It looks good (people express their envy to her constantly; they're convinced she's got life "aced"), but she knows that under the hood the motor's a lemon. The beautiful husband won't talk, the children are ephemeral, and the family that functions as a fortress for her is also, of course, a prison.

It will come as no surprise that Polly takes a lover. What else *can* she do? Not for her Peru, or the Peace Corps, or a Ph.D. It's a lover or nothing. Hers is out of a dream. He's well educated and from her class—a painter whose work and temperament dictate that he spend most of his waking life alone. His name is Lincoln Bennett, and he's madly in love with Polly. *Family Happiness* consists of the question, how happy can family happiness make you? Is it all right to want a little of your own happiness? Can a female human being expect to be seen as a human being instead of a family functionary—a robot who picks up the *baguettes* for a dinner party, who takes her husband's business suits to and from the cleaners, who can always be relied on "to provide something scrumptious for dessert"?

In many ways *Family Happiness* seems like a charming, ingratiating, beautifully written novel saved up from 50 years ago. Certainly the Solo-Miller family comes from predivorce days. Polly seems never to have heard of the feminist movement in any manifestation, and her moral scruples seem exaggerated for any decade of the 20th century. She is afraid to have Lincoln visit her at her apartment for even a "social" call, because she is afraid of what the doorman will say.

Polly and Lincoln's affair continues. Her family never notices because they never notice *her*. But her early euphoria turns to guilt, gloom, despair. She and Lincoln separate for a while, and Polly, driven by this series of devastating emotions, finds a girlfriend to confide in at her office, begins to talk to her husband again and—for the first time in her life—rather petulantly sasses her mother. After consolidating these gains, will Polly return to the straight and narrow, or will she keep her handsome, attentive lover?

This is "women's material" with a vengeance. But then what do most women have but marriage and children? How do they express freedom, despair, rebellion, mutiny, euphoria, abandon, except with a lover? It is certainly not Laurie Colwin's fault that these facts continue to pertain. It may be her fault, however, that the two men in Polly's life are cut from the purest cardboard. It never occurs to anyone, not Polly, not any of the in-laws, not even the author, that when Henry Demarest is on a business trip, he's on anything but a business trip. He's a large, boring, nice husband, period. And the "fact" that Lincoln Bennett, the other man, has to be alone—why does Polly believe it so implicitly? Why is the world famous painter so gaga about this sturdy, cheerful housewife that any other woman is out of the question for him? Because he must function here as part of a housewife's fantasy, that's why.

Something's wrong with the story of *Family Happiness.* Polly is so much a compendium of secondary virtues that she doesn't quite appear as a human being: "In the super-market, Polly harangued herself. People who shopped on Sunday were people who had let things get out of hand, who paid no attention to detail, who let themselves get lost. There were people who actually bought their *vegetables* at the supermarket." All this is very well in the way of scruples and refinement, but why won't Laurie Colwin let her Polly consider for a second what might happen to the rest of her life if indeed the doorman did let slip some-thing to her husband, or if, in some other way, the world discovered the cheerful housewife was having a serious af-fair?

People might get hurt, the situation might get out of hand. Such a new situation might approximate reality, but *Fami-ly Happiness* is safe in the realm of domestic fantasy; safe—safe as houses. Which is not to say that Laurie Colwin's next novel might not deal with just this problem.

Margaret O'Brien Steinfels   (review date 8 April 1983)

SOURCE: "Can We Stand Happiness?" in *Commonweal,* Vol. 110, No. 7, April 8, 1983, pp. 218-20.

[*In the following favorable review, Steinfels maintains that* Family Happiness *is "not great literature but an extremely satisfying read on a cold Saturday afternoon."*]

> "Happy families are all alike; every unhappy
> family is unhappy in its own way."

You have read that sentence before. The first clause holds your attention while you try to imagine the alikeness of happy families, but its plausibility soon fades. Is it their alikeness that is elusive or their happiness? The second clause is the stuff of great literature. *Anna Karenina* opens with that epigram, but so could the works of Dickens, George Eliot, Ibsen, O'Neill, etc. The diverse miseries of unhappy families grow in geometric proportion to the length of novel or play. Happy families whose good spirits we may enjoy at Christmas dinner, we will not endure for 750 pages. A novel about happy families, if it is not ironic, is necessarily brief.

Laurie Colwin's previous novel has the daft title, *Happy All the Time.* The hero, a foundation president, is led in the spirit of courtly love through an excruciatingly pro-tracted courtship while remaining ever hopeful, kind, and loyal. Happy all the time. I finished it smiling.

Family Happiness has some of its bedazzling qualities: not great literature but an extremely satisfying read on a cold Saturday afternoon. In fact, in the spirit of "domestic sen-suousness" that Colwin extols in her short story, **"The Lone Pilgrim,"** *Family Happiness* ought to be read while reclining with pillows on a plump old couch handed down from your maternal grandmother. You read, absorbed and

silent, wrapped in a nineteenth-century blue and white quilt stitched by a distant cousin on her marriage trip from Philadelphia to Boston in 1854. Colwin is big on families and family heirlooms. The domestic interiors of happy families are crowded with beloved objects. A sure sign of pathology in her fiction is a bare room.

The central proposition of *Family Happiness* is not that the Solo-Miller clan is similar to other happy families, but that the happy family ensemble has a life and rhythm of its own. Its happiness is not the mere sum of individual happinesses, nor is its vitality threatened by passing indi-vidual miseries. Polly Solo-Miller Demarest, daughter, wife, and mother, occupies the foreground. Her fall from grace and complacent happiness into bewildering unhap-piness and her ascent back to a guarded happiness consti-tute the plot. But her extended family is the background and anchor of the story.

There is one handsome, but distracted, husband; two dar-ling and wise children; a sometime neurasthenic mother; a crank of a father; two grown but pathetically immature brothers; their wives; and "branches in Boston, Philadel-phia, and New York, as well as London just like a banking house." Old, established, wealthy—financiers of the American revolution—the Solo-Millers enjoy nothing so much as their own company. The novel opens and closes with their ritual Sunday breakfast eaten at midday: for starters, "heavy white plates of smoked salmon, silver bas-kets of toast points, dishes of capers, lemon slices and scal-lions, and a cobalt-blue dish of niçoise olives." The sole difference between the novel's first breakfast and last is that Polly leaves the first early, ostensibly for a meeting, but actually for a brief tryst with her lover, Lincoln Ben-nett; in the last she does not leave. The story between is not filled with moral drama or passion but a subtle and fine moral suasion in which Polly refuses to find cause for her affair in the sometime neglect of her family. Lincoln Bennett, a recluse and a painter, is simply the first and dearest friend she has ever had. He lives beyond the fami-ly's reach.

The Solo-Millers are smug, or so Lincoln informs the un-critical Polly, and at moments are fairly wretched individ-uals. Still they are appealing; and it is easy to fall in love with the idea of the Solo-Millers. Their tribal life has not been touched by modernization except in small details; they own a Silex coffee pot, but cannot get it to work. Solo-Millers do not leave the family when they marry, their spouses join the family; nor do they divorce or approve of divorce. The apartments of the junior members are glow-ing satellites circling the parental hearth. They celebrate holidays and spend their vacations together. Their judg-ments are stern and their forbearance limited.

The matriarch Wendy, née Constanzia Hendricks, and the patriarch Henry Solo-Miller, Sr., preside at the Sunday breakfast as at a high liturgy. A concert or gallery opening is the occasion of a solemn procession and their single yearly attendance at synagogue on Yom Kippur "was with a sense of aristocracy. Anyone could be a Christian. Not anyone could be a Jew, and very few Jews were the sort of Jews the Demarests and the Solo-Millers were. It had been said of Grandfather Solo-Miller that he behaved as if he had chosen God, and not the other way around." Fealty, constancy, and excellence are the virtues of this clan. In addition, Polly is "sturdy, upright, cheerful, and kind." She is Polly the Good, accomplished and virtuous beyond appreciating. Naturally this condition poses the question that has worried all of us at some time or another, perhaps even Eve herself: is Paradise suffocating?

Polly's fall from grace is the occasion for her seeing, at last, the mixed blessing, but blessings nonetheless, of her tribe. "Family life is deflective: it gives everybody something to do. It absorbs sadness and sops up loneliness. It provides work, company, and entertainment. It makes tasks for idle hands and allows an anxious spirit to hide in its capacious bosom. With no one around her, Polly felt as if she had slipped out of earth orbit."

The possibility that the complacence of her family has pushed her into Lincoln's bed is tested and found wanting. To her plaintive, "I don't want to be the best anymore," her adoring husband, Henry, responds, "You can't help it, it is not something you do. It's something you are." The inevitability of Polly's virtue is like Iris Murdoch's "sovereignty of good"—"something of which saints speak and which any artist will readily understand. The idea of a patient, loving regard, directed upon a person, a thing, a situation, presents the will not as unimpeded movement but as something very much like 'obedience.'"

The ever-tasteful Sturm und Drang of the plot resolved—although her moral dilemma is not; Lincoln remains her lover—Polly sits at Sunday breakfast:

> This was her family, her tribe, her flesh. She felt not forced to love them, or condemned to be angry at them, but as if she were merely seeing them. Her place at this table was optional—she did not have to be there if she did not want to. But she did want to.

And later; "Her heart was full of love—for Henry, for Lincoln, for her brother and sister-in-law and parents and for her children." That is not a satisfactory ending, too much having-your-cake-and-eating-it-too. But it is very Solo-Miller. So the epigraph to *Family Happiness* must serve as its conclusion: "God setteth the solitary in families; He bringeth out those which are bound with chains; but the rebellious live in a dry land" (Psalm 68:6).

Robb Forman Drew (review date 13 April 1986)

SOURCE: A review of *Another Marvelous Thing*, in *The New York Times Book Review*, April 13, 1986, p. 14.

[*In the following mixed review, Drew discusses the characters and structure of the short story collection* Another Marvelous Thing.]

More often than not, in real life the love affairs of one's friends are heartbreaking to watch, no matter where one's sympathies or loyalties may lie. When couples begin resorting themselves into ill-considered combinations, it is quite painful to watch the flailing about of the children and spouses left in their wake. But Laurie Colwin's new book chronicles a charmingly romantic love affair in

> **Though *Family Happiness* gives a first impression of modesty and even sentimentality, the reader is best advised to beware: darker matters lurk beneath its glittering surface, and a wry appreciation of life's ambiguities that one does not expect to encounter in the pages of *Vogue*.**
>
> **—Jonathan Yardley, in his "Anna Karenina Comes to Manhattan," in** Book World—The Washington Post, *September 12, 1982.*

which there are no dire consequences whatsoever. There are really no consequences at all other than the creation of a sweetly isolated slice of memory to be shared only by the two people involved.

Another Marvelous Thing is a collection of eight stories that tells the tale from beginning to end of an affair between a determinedly tough-minded young woman, Josephine (Billy) Delielle, and an unabashedly sentimental older man, Francis Clemens, called Frank only by his sharp-tongued and irreverent mistress.

In the story **"Frank and Billy,"** Francis ruminates that

> Having a love affair . . . was not unlike being the co-governor of a tiny, private kingdom in some remote country with only two inhabitants—you and the other co-governor. This kingdom had flora and fauna, a national bird, language, reference, conceit, a national anthem . . . cheers, songs, and gestures. It also had national censorship—the taboo subjects are taboo. The idea that one of the co-governors has a life outside the kingdom always brings pain. For example, the afternoon Francis's eye fell on a thick air letter in an elderly hand. When pressed, Billy turned red and explained that for many years she had been having a correspondence with a retired schoolteacher in the town of Northleach whom she had met during one of her research periods in the Cotswolds. . . . This information left Francis speechless, like a blow to the stomach with a flat object. The moment he stepped out of her house her life without him began. Of course, the same could be said of him. What richness! what privacy! what sadness!

It's the sadness that we're not so sure about, although we're certainly willing to grant this couple their own pale and wistful melancholy, around which each of these stories is shaped. Their gentle mournfulness stems from the idea of the limits of their association, the irrefutable notion that each one has scant access to the other's life. But it is hard for the reader to grant them real sorrow; these two are the possessors of inordinately lucky lives, and they themselves have only the mildest and most ordinary of regrets. But I think Laurie Colwin knows exactly what she's about. After all, it is Francis, not necessarily the author, who infers sorrow from his condition, and she has effectively made him a rather touching character; he is a man who is nostalgic for his past before it is even concluded.

Throughout the book, and made clear in each story, is the understanding that Billy loves her husband, Grey, and that Francis is at least fond of his wife, Vera, although for all her virtues she seems curiously unappealing. In the first story in this collection, **"My Mistress,"** Francis sums Billy up.

> I know how she contrasts to my wife: my wife is affable, full of conversation, loves a dinner party, and is interested in clothes, food, home decor, and the issues of the day. She loves to entertain, is sought out in times of crisis by her numerous friends, and has a kind and original word for everyone. She is methodical, hardworking, and does not fall asleep in restaurants.

Billy, as it turns out, is none of these things and can claim not one of these attributes. What's more, she begrudges Francis every ounce of affection she feels for him. Only Laurie Colwin could make us like her, because Billy is smart and witty and *spunky* and it makes her feel a little bad to be in love with Francis and her husband at the same time. Billy's husband is a far more sympathetic character than Francis's wife, and so it is especially reassuring to the reader that Billy knows it will be difficult for her to carry on this affair without the possibility of a resolution. Francis, on the other hand, likes the romance so well that he is indifferent, if not opposed, to any final outcome. The tension between them provided by this difference of opinion is the line most clearly drawn through all these stories.

The stories in this slim volume are connected, and they often relay the same event from different perspectives, but each one is complete unto itself, and because of the frequent repetition of information, the book does not profit from being read straight through as if it were a novel. Besides, a great deal of the pleasure a reader derives from any of Laurie Colwin's work—novels such as **Happy All the Time** and story collections like **The Lone Pilgrim**—is a result of her fine craftsmanship, and it has always seemed to me that the short story is her strong suit. She understands its shape so well that she sees to it each one is a whole meal, not one course of a larger menu. These should be read one at a time, perhaps just before bed as a respite from an especially trying day.

A writer of Laurie Colwin's sensibility is surely familiar with both joy and tragedy of one kind or another, but **Another Marvelous Thing** does not attempt to investigate either one; these stories do not resonate with any strong emotion. The author seems intent upon providing us with a witty, literate and intelligent entertainment, a commodity not so easily come by these days, and in that effort she has certainly succeeded.

Martha Southgate   (review date 17 January 1989)

SOURCE: "Slim Pickings," in *The Village Voice,* Vol. XXXIII, No. 3, January 17, 1989, p. 58.

[*In the following review, Southgate offers a negative appraisal of* Home Cooking.]

Reading too much Laurie Colwin is sometimes like watching too many episodes of *thirtysomething:* The attractive and amusing surface starts to seem self-centered and narrow-minded. Even in her best work, like the novel **Happy All the Time** or the story collection **The Lone Pilgrim,** this is sometimes a problem, though those books are redeemed by a delightful sense of humor, fully drawn characters, and an often cutting emotional accuracy. Colwin has been compared to Jane Austen and the comparison, though overstated, is not entirely wrong. Her talent is the main reason that her latest, **Home Cooking,** a collection of essays about food, is so puzzling and disappointing.

Colwin clearly loves to cook and she communicates that enthusiasm even to this hardened kitchen avoider. The recipes sound delicious, but Colwin seems to have become a happy prisoner of her upper-middle-class milieu, rarely looking beyond the abundance that surrounds her or even examining it critically. Here's a sample, from **"How to Fry Chicken"**: "The lady who taught my sister and me, a black woman who cooked for us in Philadelphia, was of course the apotheosis: no one will ever be fit to touch the top of her chicken fryer." Why the "of course"? Is there some reason that a black domestic should have the edge in chicken frying? Colwin's editor should have had a little talk with her about the indigestible assumptions in this homey collection. They remove the charm from funny descriptions such as this one: "I have had all kinds of nasty fried chicken served to me, usually with great flourish: crisp little baby shoes or hockey pucks turned out by electric frying machines with names such as Little Fry Guy."

Colwin also misses the larger reason that people write about food: to take a look at the culture that's eating and see what lessons can be learned from the way we eat. She ignores this mission at her peril—the only culture she ends up examining is the upper-middle-class dinner party. Writing about her own life and friends allows Colwin to let all her worst tendencies run rampant, and doesn't leave much room for her natural good humor or her talent for observing men and women. She's a writer who needs to look beyond herself to be at her most interesting. That doesn't happen in this lightweight blend of recipes and anecdotes. They're not enough to satisfy a reader hungry for some real food for thought.

Jeanne Schinto   (review date Spring 1990)

SOURCE: "The Art of Eating Words," in *The Yale Review,* Vol. 79, No. 3, Spring, 1990, pp. 488-500.

[*In the excerpt below, Schinto discusses the the symbolic role of food and cooking in* Home Cooking *and in Colwin's fiction.*]

Occasionally, a novelist turns from fiction to recipes. Laurie Colwin's **Home Cooking: A Writer in the Kitchen,** a collection of essays, is exactly the kind of cookbook that Rachel Samstat would write. It's chatty and anecdotal, though the recipes are integral rather than incidental to its design. This truly is a cookbook, and proudly so. Having published novels and short stories, Colwin seems content to write in the cookbook genre for the length of one volume at least, though she can't suppress her skill as a writer of imaginative prose while doing so. From her chapter on flank steak: "My introduction to flank steak was a dreary one. I was invited for supper by a colleague who told me she was no cook, but that flank steak, according to the recipe of her sainted grandmother, was her one dish. Because I like to hang around in the kitchens of others, I watched while my colleague took a flat, blade-shaped piece of meat which she then rolled up and tied, like an old carpet."

Nor does this writer's passion for food come to us out of the blue, as did James M. Cain's recipes and food writing, for which, according to his biographer Roy Hoopes, he was perpetually trying to get assignments. Colwin's cookbook isn't out of character, because, unlike Cain's fiction, her other books are often illuminating about the symbolic roles that food and cooking play in modern life, particularly in the lives of women.

In *Another Marvelous Thing,* Colwin's female protagonist, nicknamed Billy, who is having an affair with Francis, is "indifferent" to food. "She hates to cook and will never present [Francis] with an interesting post-coital snack." Instead, they smear peanut butter on stale water crackers: "They were both ravenous and almost anything would have done." At a dinner party Billy gave, "it was clear that cooking bothered her." Vera, Francis's wife, on the other hand, is "an ace cook" who has been trained at a cooking school in France. Even so, she and Francis have a house-keeper who is "a marvelous cook." Vera does it only for fun.

In *Family Happiness,* dining-table scenes form a continuous series of tableaux, because, unlike many other modern American families, the extended family portrayed here still eats together regularly—Sunday brunch, for example, is a long-standing tradition. Polly Solo-Miller Demarest, a lawyer's wife who is having an affair with a painter, is the book's main character; at her peak moment of emotional distress—unable to decide between husband or lover—she has an epiphany in a supermarket. She sees a couple of teenagers buying chocolate and bananas with which to make a pudding and "felt as if she had been pierced with knives, as if the boy and girl had been sent to rub her nose in the face of young married love, full of silliness and improvised meals."

Polly . . . does not make a habit of shopping in supermarkets. "There were people who actually bought their *vegetables* at the supermarket—Polly did not believe that anything in a supermarket could really be fresh. . . . Shopping in a supermarket was a sign of bad housekeeping. How could these people bring themselves to admit their flaws publicly?" Of course, Polly's whole life, up until that moment, has been a public performance.

Readers of *Home Cooking* know that Colwin, unlike Billy, loves food. Readers also know that Colwin loves words as much as food—even preferring the bread-baking lessons of Elizabeth David's *English Bread and Yeast Cookery* to those of a friend. Still, she doesn't want people to simply read her cookbook. Her ingredients and directions make it plain that her book is meant for real people who shop in supermarkets and—unlike angels, anorexics, or the dead—really do need to eat.

Michiko Kakutani   (review date 4 May 1990)

SOURCE: "An Awful Time Living a Perfect Life," in *The New York Times,* May 4, 1990, p. C36.

[*In the following unfavorable review, Kakutani analyzes the characterization of Colwin's protagonist in* Goodbye without Leaving.]

Geraldine Coleshares, the heroine of Laurie Colwin's [*Goodbye without Leaving*], is a wife, mother and former backup singer with a rhythm-and-blues band. She describes herself as "a person who craved the marginal," a "nothing," who's "alone in the middle of the universe," "the harbinger of new life," "the innocent American, making trouble right and left—a microcosm of imperialism."

"I want to know," she says, "how to be what I am."

Geraldine's husband is her "Boy Scout from Mars," her "weirdo from Normalsville," who knew how to maneuver in the world," "the golden mean," who "managed to do good and make money at the same time."

Her best friend, Mary, is her "moral beacon."

Her lover, Leo, is "a school" who would turn her "into Hannah Arendt," someone who is "more like a destination than a person."

When we first meet Geraldine, she has just traded in her identity as a graduate student in English at the University of Chicago to join Ruby Shakely and the Shakettes—a Tina Turner-like group that's touring small towns around the country. Geraldine spends a lot of time on the tour bus "blowing reefer and playing cards," while her friends from school pursue more conventional lives: "getting married, having babies, being promoted, becoming White House Fellows or junior partners in their law firms."

Actually, a similarly conventional life is in store for Geraldine. She meets a lawyer named Jonathan, quits the Shakettes, and after much agonizing is married and has a baby. Her family and Jonathan's family get along beautifully, no doubt because they share (like so many earlier Colwin characters) identical tastes and backgrounds. Geraldine's mother is a children's book illustrator and the head of a county art center; Jonathan's mother is on a local library committee and gives an annual cocktail party that "was as regular an event as the bake sale, the Memorial Day parade or the Volunteer Fire Department chicken fry."

In time, Geraldine takes a job as a researcher at the Race Music Foundation in Harlem—an obscure organization devoted to preserving the work of early black musicians. She and Jonathan move to a bigger apartment in some unidentified but gentrified neighborhood in Manhattan, and they go to dinner parties where Geraldine attacks the liberal hypocrisies of the other guests.

> They wore snappy clothes and owned small European cars. They worked hard and took inter-

esting vacations in wilderness areas. They were healthy and hale and red-cheeked and they had never spent a minute of their lives worried about the essentials. The essentials had all been taken care of. Instead they had worried about grades, getting into college, law school. They worried when their cars didn't work and when cholera broke out in the some part of the world they had an impulse to go touring in. Later they had children and worried about early childhood development, what schools to send their children to. When they got together they talked about cooking equipment, and skiing, and gossiped about mutual friends. I was a total misfit.

It doesn't take the reader long to discover that Geraldine isn't a misfit at all; she only thinks she is. Like the people she says she loathes, she leads a privileged existence in which the essentials are happily taken for granted. Her marriage is pleasant and fulfilling. Her child is healthy and bright. She and Jonathan have no economic worries, no worries about their families, their jobs or their futures. Even her love affair with Leo is completely painless, devoid of guilt, conflict or emotional trauma of any sort. While unsatisfactory dinner party conversations are enough to elicit a litany of complaints, Geraldine never seriously assesses her life or her values, never achieves anything even approaching self-knowledge.

Indeed, the reader quickly begins to suspect that Geraldine is one of those people who are constantly inventing things to worry about to pass the time. Although she has wanted to be a rock-and-roll singer all her life, she worries, once she's got a job as a Shakette, that it's not a proper lifetime occupation. Although she's madly in love with Jonathan, she worries that marriage is incompatible with her career. Although she says she loves being a mother, she worries that people will look down on her for not having a high-powered job. It never seems to occur to her that being a wife and mother doesn't preclude being a singer.

To make matters worse, Geraldine is constantly turning her identity crises into annoying little aphorisms: "To be effortlessly yourself is a blessing, an ambrosia. It is like a few tiny little puffs of opium, which lift you ever so slightly off the hard surface of the world." Or: "I mean, people who really do things have professions, and vocations. Maybe I'm one of those meandering types and being in the music business was a form of meandering."

When Ms. Colwin steps away from Geraldine and her complacent, yuppified world, she succeeds in putting her eye for sociological detail to better use. Ruby Shakeley and some of Geraldine's other music-business friends are delineated briskly with a couple of lines of description, a couple of phrases of telling dialogue; and the European émigrés she later meets in New York are also observantly defined. Unfortunately, these characters are no compensation, in the end, for Geraldine's self-absorption, her cute, self-conscious whining.

Lorraine E. McCormack   (review date Winter 1991)

SOURCE: "Be True to Your School," in *Belles Lettres: A Review of Books by Women,* Vol. 6, No. 2, Winter, 1991, p. 13.

[*Below, McCormack offers a positive assessment of* Goodbye without Leaving.]

Like a lot of us, Geraldine Coleshares is having a little trouble finding her place in the universe. As a failed graduate student, successful rock-and-roll back-up singer, reluctant wife, and enchanted mother, never has a person with so rich a mixture of life experiences been so despairing of its value. In *Goodbye Without Leaving,* novelist Laurie Colwin gives us a comic version of the quest for life's meaning in which her main character is a combination of Woody Allen with rhythm and Janis Joplin on Prozac.

Disgusted with her dissertation and in love with rhythm and blues, Geraldine leaves the University of Chicago to tour as a back-up singer to black rock star Ruby Shakely. Being a Shakette seems to Geraldine the most authentic thing she's ever done; criss-crossing the country in a marijuana-fogged tour bus, dressed in day-glow fringe, living her dream. "Yes, I was myself. I was not black, I was not from the South, I was not funky. . . . I was not a Ph.D. candidate and I didn't care. I was a Shakette, and I knew my time had come."

Geraldine loves her two years on the road, but the group's camaraderie points up her feelings of rootlessness:

> Ethnic identity was slightly vulgar in my mother's eyes, or, at best, a kind of colorful peasant tradition. My father's mother had been a Jew from an old family that had intermarried until there was nothing much of anything left except a tree at Christmas time . . . a Judaism so reformed that it was indistinguishable from, say, the Girl Scouts.

Colwin surrounds Geraldine with a cast of characters who challenge her definition of herself every day. To Geraldine's amazement, almost to her dismay, her husband accepts her exactly as she is, a middle-class matron on the outside and a beatnik iconoclast on the inside. It is Johnny who validates the success of her marginal life style: "You can go to a dinner party and not lose your essential self. You can be true to your school and still make normal conversation. You can act like a regular person and still boogie in your soul."

Even after her marriage, Geraldine's truest feeling of connection in life comes from her encyclopedic collection of 45 rpm vinyl pressings of early rock and rollers. Her method of confronting any particularly stressful life situation is to spend several days prone, humming along to the obscure flip sides of ancient chart busters. This is the perfect therapy for a self-described wandering Jew and former Shakette, and for a while it dispels her feeling of being ethnically orphaned.

Geraldine bemoans her shallow roots to friends whom she sees as having primal connections to life that she doesn't have: black musicians, contemplative Catholics, Holocaust survivors. Each of them tries to set her straight. Unconvinced by their protests and intrigued by their legacies, Geraldine becomes the caretaker of other people's histories. As a researcher for the Race Music Foundation, she catalogues female blues singers of the twenties and thirties. One day a sound engineer called The Bopper plays Geraldine a tape of her own voice, a solo from her Shakette days. She is struck by the clarity and control in her voice, for these are qualities that seem missing from the rest of her life. The feelings her song expresses are heartfelt, but she doesn't feel she owns the music:

> "Let's make a million dollars. Let's record you singing some of those groovy old blues songs you catalogued. It'll be our big break."

> "I'm not a blues singer," I said. "Going on tour was a kind of lucky fluke. I went for the music, not to have a career. I'm not a singer. . . . I'm very flattered, Bopper, really I am," I said. "I just can't do it. I love this music with all my heart but I don't honestly believe it's mine to sing."

When Colwin's style flourishes, her characters reveal themselves in dialogue that makes you laugh out loud. Their exchanges are fresh and colorful, with none of the formulaic, sound-bite patter that leaks out of TV onto the page these days. Often the characters who are most clearly drawn get the least physical description, like Geraldine's friend "The Smoking Poet." The technique is so effective in the first two-thirds of the book that we feel rather distracted by the excessive physical descriptions of the characters who appear in the offices of the Hansonia Society, where Geraldine works as a secretary. This group of music preservationists are immigrants from Eastern Europe, and for a while the story proceeds as though Geraldine has stepped into a casting call for *Grand Hotel*, with everyone trailing silk scarves and brushing cigarette ash from their furs.

It is in the ethnic enclave of the Hansonia Society that Geraldine's longings for connections are nurtured, and she begins to sense her place in the grand scheme of things. She still sings her baby to sleep with "I Sold My Heart to the Junkman," but she feels comfortable adding a German Jewish lullaby now and then.

I found it easy to relate to Geraldine's feelings about music she could love but not really own. The memory I have of my parents swaying and beaming to "Moonlight Serenade" by Benny Goodman is certainly more dignified than the image I have of me at their age creaking my rocker to "Beast of Burden" by the Rolling Stones, but there you are. Instinct and honor keep you true to your school, and it was instinct and honor that drove Geraldine out of the University of Chicago and into the college of rock-and-roll knowledge, where surely she rated a full professorship. Her expertise is fun for the reader at first, but it gets frustrating not knowing which of the musical allusions are for real and which are made up: Brenda and the Tabulations, sure, but Baby Jean and the Jerelles? Oh well, maybe they were before my time; now there's a comforting thought.

Amy Richlin (essay date Spring-Summer 1991)

SOURCE: "Guilty Pleasures: The Fiction of Laurie Colwin," in *New England Review and Bread Loaf Quar-*

terly, Vol. 13, Nos. 3-4, Spring-Summer, 1991, pp. 296-309.

[*In the following essay, Richlin provides an overview of Colwin's fiction.*]

> "As for the book, it's no good writing about the upper classes if you hope to be taken seriously. You must have noticed that by now? Station masters, my dear, station masters."

> "I know, I know. Of course, I have noticed. But you see my trouble is that I loathe station masters, like hell I do. . . ."

> —Nancy Mitford, Christmas Pudding

Laurie Colwin occupies an odd position among American fiction writers. Like Ellen Gilchrist, she takes as her subject romantic love; like Alice Adams, she keeps to upper-class people located in comfortable places. Her prose is both elegant and witty, and at first her work gives the appearance of light fiction, no more. Yet something more seems to be going on. A glance over past reviews of her work finds uneasiness among the critics; one remarked that the depiction of so much easy happiness left the reader feeling vaguely unhappy. Has this been intentional all along? In her latest novel, *Goodbye Without Leaving,* is Colwin finally tipping part of her hand?

Complex currents of guilt beset the critical reader's pleasure in Colwin's text. We expect serious fiction to be openly class-conscious; the socially conscientious reader, however bourgeois, is looking for stories that at least problematize the bourgeois experience, or, even better, locate themselves entirely outside it. And we have become accustomed, these days, to a minimalist style that eschews the figures of rhetoric, describing bleak scenes in bleak sentences. It is ironic that Colwin's protagonists—academics, artists, products of good schools—are also the kind of women who read her books; yet these women, reading Colwin, meet guilt on all sides, as if they were eating chocolate instead of sprouts. The style is delicious, the settings are pleasant, the people are totally recognizable. These are stories about people you know. And, for the heterosexual reader, the assessments of heterosexual romance are equally recognizable, formulations that can be taken home and used; these are stories about yourself. How can this be great art?

Recent work on the romance has broached the possibility that even the popular fiction of women may be worth taking seriously. The fact that an author's work is restricted in setting, that it is pleasurable to read, even that it is comic, need not banish it from the critic's consideration. Moreover, a set of interrelated problems in Colwin's work suggests to me that she is producing more than a sort of fiction version of *The Preppy Handbook* (another product of a nice Jewish girl among WASPs). In *Goodbye Without Leaving,* this set of problems is writ large. First, the heroine is an assimilated Jew struggling to find her cultural identity; previous Colwin heroines have been happy being assimilated. But, where Colwin now problematizes happiness and Jewishness, she has always problematized happiness before; romance for her is not easy, however beautiful it may be; and she has often mediated on the artificiality of beauty itself. Her work is full of the pleasure of the romance plot, but it is also posted with signs calling this pleasure into question.

I write this as Colwin's ideal reader: a nice assimilated Jewish girl with a nice academic job and a lot of nice friends who went to good schools, always in and out of love. I would like to believe that the pleasure I have in Colwin's texts tallies with some kind of artistic merit, and I'm betting on the connections I've sketched above. I'll try to convince you, and myself at the same time, for the truth is that the whole thing makes me feel guilty. But maybe that just jibes with the widespread critical uneasiness I noted above; *we* all know we're not supposed to be happy all the time. And maybe that's the point.

Colwin's writing has always been marked by a high degree of wish-fulfillment in the plot line, and *Goodbye Without Leaving* must be the most extreme example. The heroine, Geraldine Coleshares, from a cultured and assimilated Jewish family, starts out as a bored graduate student in English literature at the University of Chicago, whose true passion is for black rock and roll. She haunts the (mostly black) clubs of Chicago, and shortly finds herself as a backup singer and dancer for Vernon and Ruby Shakely— as "the white Shakette." Her mentor gets her her first job with the introduction, "Here's a boss white chick who knows all your routines and she can *move*." Talk about bald-faced fantasy!

The two years that Geraldine goes on to spend touring with Vernon and Ruby prove to be the high point of her life; everything that follows is anticlimactic. Subsequent events include her marriage to a nice young lawyer from an assimilated Jewish family (Southern), who also loves rock and roll; the birth of their son, Little Franklin; a job at the Race Music Foundation, where Geraldine does research on female blues singers; and a job at the Hansonia Society, where Geraldine does further research, this time on the musicological endeavors of two Austrian Jewish expatriates who collected black music in the American South in the 1930's. Here she has the occasion to meet many Holocaust survivors, with one of whom she has an affair. But the significant thing about this final part of the book is that she begins to recover her roots, signs up for Hebrew lessons, and conducts her first Seder. Her cultural rootlessness has been a theme throughout the book; both as an American among Europeans and as an assimilated Jew among Christians, she feels a deep lack.

The experienced Colwin reader instantly recognizes many of the features of this book: good fortune for all characters, verging on magical realism; settings of equally unreal beauty, in terms of weather, domestic appointments, seasons; and a continuous metanarrative discussion of the problems of human happiness, change, time, nostalgia. These contents are packaged in a style of great rhetorical polish, intensely pleasurable to read. It seems worth considering here how these elements are interrelated and how they are connected with the Jewish question.

An old boyfriend of mine, a Northfield Mt. Hermon graduate then rowing on the Yale crew, used to describe himself as a WASH—a White Anglo-Saxon Hebrew. This is the culture in which Laurie Colwin has always set her work, and *Goodbye Without Leaving* is no exception. What is exceptional here is that, for the first time, she has written about Jewish assimilation as a problem rather than as an enviable blessing.

Geraldine Coleshares takes her place among a whole parade of similar Colwin protagonists. First to appear is Amelia ("Misty") Berkowitz, in two stories in *Passion and Affect* that form the basis for the novel *Happy All The Time.* The difference in cultural background between Misty and her beau, Vincent Cardworthy, is not made much of in the stories, but it looms in the novel, and the terms of the problem are set already in the stories: not just the problem of being an assimilated Jew, but the problem of being an assimilated Jewish young woman who loves and/or marries an upper-class WASP young man. Misty has colleagues already in *Passion and Affect*: probably Mary Leibnitz, who, in "Animal Behavior," falls in love with Raiford Phelps, known as Roddy; probably Jane Catherine Jacoby, in "Imelda," who (more exotically) has a boyfriend named Tito Ricardo-Ruiz, "an upper-class Argentinian whose father was with the embassy."

A more extreme example is the heroine of *Shine On, Bright and Dangerous Object*—"the little Marcus girl, Elizabeth Olive, nicknamed Olly" (many Colwin characters have prep-style nicknames). Olly marries into a family of New England WASPs right out of John P. Marquand; she dispenses with this problem early in the story: "my mother wondered if the Baxes would mind having Jews in the family, but they didn't care one way or the other." Misty, Mary, Jane Catherine, and Olly are joined in *The Lone Pilgrim* by Jane Mayer ("The Boyish Lover"), Elizabeth Leopold ("An Old-Fashioned Story"), Georgia Levy ("Delia's Father"), Rachel Manheim ("The Smile Beneath the Smile"), and Polly Solo-Miller ("Family Happiness"), who is also the protagonist of the novel *Family Happiness.* Rachel has her heart broken by a wealthy mathematician named Andrew Dilks. The Manhattan schoolgirl Georgia Levy describes her culture: "We came from good Jewish and Episcopalian families, and we grew up all alike" (*The Lone Pilgrim*).

The pleasure-loving English professor Jane Mayer has *her* heart broken by a physics professor named Arthur Corthauld Spaacks, known as Cordy, who comes from a wealthy but frozen New England WASP family, and the problem the story raises is precisely that of the clash between their cultures:

> The Mayers were a family of watered-down German and Dutch Jews who had once had a lot of money. Now they had things. They had Persian rugs, English silver, Limoges plates, and Meissen soup tureens. It was from Cordy that Jane learned the lesson so valuable to the *haute bourgeoisie:* that some people have a good deal of money and almost nothing else.

The things that the Mayers have go along with an ability to take pleasure in life; Cordy takes pleasure in depriving himself of good things, both material and spiritual (i.e., love). It is strongly suggested here that such an attitude is culturally determined; Jane yearns for Cordy nonetheless.

The consummate description of a Colwin heroine's family is that of Polly Solo-Miller. Here they are in the story **"Family Happiness"**.

> They gathered . . . on New Year's Day, on Christmas Eve as well as Easter Sunday. They were an old, old Jewish family of the sort that is more identifiably old American than Jewish. They gathered at Passover but not at Chanukah, and they went to synagogue twice a year on the two High Holy days. On Yom Kippur they did not fast but had family lunch in the afternoon. [Oy.]

In the novel, this is modified startlingly:

> Both [Polly's parents] were of old, old Jewish families, the sort that are more identifiably old American than Jewish. Solo-Millers and Hendrickses had come from Holland via Spain before the American Revolution, which they had either taken part in or helped to raise money for. (*Family Happiness*)

Presumably Polly belongs to the D.A.R.

There is an insistence throughout on two things: first, the identity in class status between the Jewish women's families and the WASP families into which they travel. Why make the Solo-Millers Jewish at all? Maybe that's just who Colwin writes about, as Hemingway wrote about white boys from the Midwest. But there does seem to be a subliminal voice here, and what it seems to be saying is, "See? There are Jews who don't look like Jews at all." Second, and connected: the non-problematic nature of the alliances between Jews and WASPs. Anti-Semitism just does not exist in these stories; this is all the more ironic considering that Colwin has chosen to write about one culture for which the exclusion of Jews has often been self-defining.

It is not that Colwin never recognizes the problem; it lurks in the background of *Happy All the Time.* Misty fights off Vincent's declarations of love, suggesting he might be happier with "someone who knows her way around a sailboat."

> "And besides that, there's the Jewish question," said Misty. "Oh, that," said Vincent. "I don't notice either of us being religious. Besides, my Aunt Marcia is Jewish. She married Uncle Walter. She's everybody's favorite relative. What's the big deal?"

Vincent's turns out to be the correct reading of the situation; everything works out perfectly, and Aunt Marcia sends them a Haggadah as a wedding present. But throughout the book, Misty remains pessimistic:

> In the real world, Misty knew, people like Walter Cardworthy and Fritz Berkowitz waged social warfare. In the real world, when people like Misty and Vincent got married their parents were horrified and tried to stop the wedding. . . . Living with Vincent made Misty re-

alize that she had spent a good deal of her life ready to ward off some terrible low blow.

The worst the text presents her with is a woman who knows her way around a sailboat, who makes her jealous: "Misty wore on her face an expression that Vincent called 'the only Jew at the dinner table look.' "

Yet Misty is hardly a Chassid. Like the other Colwin heroines, she is a Jew who resembles a familiar WASP type, her ancestors having been homesteaders rather than colonial fund-raisers. Her great-grandfather emigrated from Russia and wound up with a dairy farm in Medicine Stone, Wisconsin, and "[her] father and her Uncle Bernie were grandsons of the pioneers." Misty's family leans left and her father is a labor lawyer, but he gets along fine with Vincent's father, of Petrie, Connecticut—i.e., the Berkowitzes are Jewish, but they fit in. It thus jars slightly when we read that "Uncle Bernie said that when he wrote his autobiography he would call it *Jew Boy of the Prairie*." Somehow, despite all the happy assimilation, Misty feels alone at the dinner table as Uncle Bernie was alone on the prairie. Both feelings are turned into jokes, but persist nonetheless.

It is in this context (extreme but faintly uneasy assimilation) that we arrive at *Goodbye Without Leaving* and read Geraldine's explanation of why hymn singing always makes her cry:

> My parents were relentlessly secular. They believed that to be American was quite enough. Ethnic identity was slightly vulgar in my mother's eyes, or, at best, a kind of colorful peasant tradition. I had no church to go to. My father's mother had been a Jew from an old family that had intermarried until there was nothing much of anything left except a tree at Christmas time. We had some aunts on my mother's side—this side was of a Judaism so reformed that it was indistinguishable from, say, the Girl Scouts—who held the traditional Passover meal, but no one in living memory celebrated anything silly like Hanukkah. On the High Holy Days my mother dragged my father off to the local reformed synagogue, where the rabbi had a phony English accent and repeatedly intoned in his sermons that Jews were really nothing more than good Americans.

The attitude of Geraldine's mother, and of the rabbi, seems not much different from that of Colwin's own narrative voice in her earlier work, and is at bottom internalized anti-Semitism—which Geraldine here rejects. Can she turn a reclamation of Judaism for herself into a positive version of her endless longing for a lost past? Can she use it to claim a place at the dinner table? Can she find true happiness?

The problem of happiness and change is a leitmotif in Colwin's work. It shows up even in her titles—*Family Happiness, Happy All the Time*; these, especially the second, have always given me pause for thought. *Is* it possible to be happy all the time? This isn't really such a dumb question; this is the story of Solon and Croesus as told by Croesus. Colwin's characters often in fact are not happy, but angst-ridden, and this is certainly true of Geraldine

-243-

as Easter Sunday. They were an old, ~~old~~ *old* Jewish family of
the sort that is more identifiably old American than
Jewish. They gathered at Passover but not at Chanuka
and they went to synagogue twice a year on the two high
holy days. On Yom Kippur they did not fast but had
family lunch in the afternoon.

They had their Thanksgiving turkey, Easter ham,
Christmas goose and Passover capon off English Victorian
plates. Their silver was old Danish. They liked great big
~~cut~~ crystal glasses and ~~cut~~ crystal wine glasses. Proper
wine glasses seemed precious and rather <u>arriviste</u> to them.

On an early spring day, Polly sat in ~~her father's~~ *a big leather chair*
her father's study.
~~study~~ in ~~a big leather chair~~. The Solo-Millers had a duplex
apartment the study of which was on the second floor.
Polly ~~would~~ *could* faintly hear the sound of her children Pete,
Six
~~nine~~, and Dee-Dee, ~~five~~, *four downstairs* ∧ annoying their father and grandfather. The Sunday paper was on Polly's lap. She had
skimmed its contents and was now staring out the window,
past the big china bowl of paperwhite narcissis that Wendy
had set on a table in the corner. She was finishing her
coffee and waiting until it was the right time to call
her best beloved. Polly was having an affair with a man
her own age, a painter by the name of Lincoln Bennett. She
dialed his number, let it ring once, hung up, and dialed
again. It was her signal. He picked up instantly.

Revised typescript page for Family Happiness.

Coleshares, whose two years of perfect happiness as a Sha-kette seem to have made it impossible for her ever to be truly happy again. The contrast between the external circumstances of Geraldine and the rest, and their internal misery, is striking. It is as if Colwin were running a controlled experiment: let all circumstances *except* X be perfect—then what happens?

Again, it is *Happy All the Time* that provides the most clues to what is going on, and strongly suggests a tie between the Jewish question and the problem of happiness:

> "Life is never smooth to the great-grand-daughter of tin peddlers who were kicked out of Russia," said Misty. "It's no accident that all my family is in one embattled profession or another. We're just waiting for the Cossacks to come back. When the Cossacks come to Connecticut, you'll understand."

Suddenly we are on familiar ground—Woody Allen territory. Maybe the issue is not (just) whether *anyone* can be happy, but whether a *Jew* can be happy, and where. The horrible WASP family dinner in *Annie Hall* rises before our eyes.

Colwin's characters stage an endless debate on the question of whether happiness is possible, for whom, for how long. Pairs of characters square off; *Happy All the Time* in fact concerns two pairs, Misty (pessimist) vs. Vincent (optimist), plus Guido, Vincent's cousin (pessimist) vs. his wife Holly (a kind of Zen optimist). The book ends with this well-balanced quadrille toasting "a truly wonderful life"; but it is hard for the reader not to remember Misty's conviction that a blow may fall. In **"A Mythological Subject,"** in *The Lone Pilgrim,* the narrator (a pragmatic optimist) observes her puritanical cousin, the ironically-named Nellie Felix. Some characters need no interlocutor: Roddy Phelps in **"Animal Behavior"** breaks Mary Leibnitz' heart just because it's time for him to do it; Max Waltzer, in the Cheeveresque **"The Water Rats"** (*Passion and Affect*) sinks into madness as he broods over the perfection of his family life, and begins to lose it by holding it too tightly.

One of the main things that blocks Geraldine's happiness is a kind of nostalgia; for other Colwin characters, it works both over time and over the space between people, as with lovers who begrudge their beloveds the separation of sleep and dreams. Billy in **"Sentimental Memory"** (*The Lone Pilgrim*) says to the narrator: "I hate it that we live from one minute to the next. I want to keep everything. I don't want the minutes to fly away. I want to keep every second intact in my mind." The two schoolgirls in **"Imelda"** muse over the fact that their present will one day be their past; Jane Catherine differentiates herself from her boyfriend on this issue:

> ". . . He doesn't have any sentimental memory. When I think that a day is over and will never repeat, I get all ropy inside, but Tito thinks that life is a string that pulls you along." (*Passion and Affect*)

These themes figure prominently in *Goodbye Without Leaving,* the title of which encapsulates them. Geraldine is caught up in a literal *nostalgia*—a longing for return home; but it is compounded by her feeling that she has no home. She feels out of place in graduate school; while on tour as the white Shakette, she develops a crush on one of the black musicians, Doo-Wah Banks, who kindly turns her down; she rejects her parents; she fights off her marriage, drags her heels over having a wedding, moving to a grown-up apartment, having a baby. She feels most out of place at the dinners of her husband's law-firm friends—now not the only Jew but the only bopper at the dinner table. She cannot think of a career for herself (although, a true Colwin heroine, she lucks into two perfect jobs with a total of three contacts), and refuses all encouragement to return to singing, for which she is assured on all sides she has great talent. One reason that she gives is that she agrees with her boss at the Race Music Foundation that black music should not be co-opted by white singers: "I love this music with all my heart but I don't honestly believe it's mine to sing." She finds her first happiness after leaving the tour with her job there in Harlem, where she is both doing something she loves and also marginal; marginality seems to be her true metier.

This shows up most painfully in her longing for her own past, both personal and cultural. When she first meets Johnny, she says she will always be a Shakette. "Even when you're fifty?" he asks her. "I don't like to think about the future," she replies. (She here echoes an earlier Colwin heroine, Ann Speizer in **"The Achieve of, the Mastery of the Thing,"** who has a grim vision of herself as a fifty-year-old pothead.) Married to Johnny and musing over the old days, she reflects that the days of the girl groups are over: "Like an exile, I knew that I could never return to the home of my childhood." She explains to Johnny that the loss of her old self is just like the loss she feels in watching their baby turn into a little boy. But it also resembles her sense of lost culture: "I'm nothing," she says to Doo-Wah, "I'm a lapsed Jew from an assimilated family. I don't belong anywhere." As she begins her quest to practice as a Jew, she feels "spiritual longings as well as some desire for a historical context." At the Hansonia Society, she likens her new co-workers to the blacks at the Race Music Foundation: "They were all from a world I had never known and to which I had only the most minimal access." And when she finally finds her niche at the Hansonia Society, she measures her own sense of exile against the experience of real refugees; she calls her lover Leo Rhinehart "the man from Western Civ."—"He would kiss me and I would turn into Hannah Arendt."

This longing for what you cannot have lies at the center of everything for Colwin: romantic love, of which adultery is thus the epitome; life, which moves us inexorably away from the golden present. In *Happy All the Time,* Guido loves Holly and constantly cannot have her; her periodic retreats are only a physical expression of the true relationship between them. Two of the men in *The Lone Pilgrim*—Cordy Spaacks of **"The Boyish Lover"** and Andrew Dilks of **"The Smile Beneath the Smile"**—take pleasure in depriving themselves of what they love, while their hedonistic beloveds suffer. Rachel recites "They flee from me, that sometime did me seek" to Andrew. This poignantly beautiful mechanics seems, in Colwin, also to underlie *difference* itself: man vs. woman, and (implicitly) Jew vs. WASP, black vs. white.

The fact that *romantic* love is Colwin's subject is almost too obvious to mention, and yet the structure of romantic love—yearning, almost incapable of satisfaction—is a perfect example of Colwin's mechanics. Polly Rice, in **"The Lone Pilgrim,"** draws her illustrations for a deluxe edition of *The Art of Courtly Love* while longing for a lost lover who is far away in Greenland. An astronomer, he has a galaxy named after him, and she periodically looks up at the stars to try to spot it (she cannot). She works to the accompaniment of the Everly Brothers singing "Sleepless Nights," and a record of country hymns that includes one called "The Lone Pilgrim," in which a dead man sends a message to his loved ones. This overdetermined heap of separations is typical of Colwin's stories; when Geraldine in *Goodbye Without Leaving* longs for her own youth, the glory days of rock and roll, the babyhood of her little boy, a black man, a European culture she has never known, a sense of purpose in life, and religious faith, her yearning is the helpless longing familiar from Colwin's earlier work.

It is in this context that we can locate Colwin's obsession with adultery. Joyce Carol Oates, in a review of *The Lone Pilgrim,* singled out as odd what must be one of Colwin's most striking formulations of her creed: "falling in love outside of marriage is the ultimate and every other gesture is its shadow" (from **"A Mythological Subject"**). Adulterous love recurs throughout Colwin's work: it is the main subject of *Family Happiness* (which we thus see to be ironically named) and of *Another Marvelous Thing,* while in *Shine On* Olly first has an affair with her deceased husband's brother and then cheats on him with a married cellist. Adultery crops up in **"The Elite Viewer"** and in **"Children, Dogs, and Desperate Men"** (*Passion and Affect*), and in **"Sentimental Memory," "Intimacy," "Delia's Father," "A Mythological Subject,"** and **"Family Happiness"** (*The Lone Pilgrim*). In most of these cases, the extramarital passion acts to confirm the strength of the couple's marriage, provides a deeper love unavailable within the marriage without threatening the marriage or degrading it, and/or simply offers another pleasure in life's buffet. Geraldine's perfunctory affair with Leo in *Goodbye Without Leaving* is Colwin's nod to a habit she seems to be leaving behind—obligatory adultery.

But why does she call love outside marriage "the ultimate"? Colwin has a penchant for presenting her characters with significantly-titled books; we recall that Polly Rice, of the title story in *The Lone Pilgrim,* was illustrating *The Art of Courtly Love* (a "deluxe edition," mind you). And adultery is the *sine qua non* of courtly love—a love also set among lords and ladies, people with fancy manners. So Colwin is tapping into a traditional connection between class, behavior, and emotion. It suits her own themes, though; love without marriage provides the best example of love with separation. Even when the love is consummated, honorable lovers cannot be truly happy.

The anguish of such a lover is the theme of **"A Mythological Subject,"** which ends with the narrator watching her troubled cousin sleep:

> What a pleasant circumstance to sit in a warm, comfortable room on an icy winter's day and contemplate someone you love whose life has always been of the greatest interest to you. Procris in the painting [of Procris slain by Cephalus] is half naked, but Nellie looked just as vulnerable. It would be exceedingly interesting to see what happened to her, but then she had always been a pleasure to watch. (*The Lone Pilgrim*)

This passage combines Colwin's most important themes. The opening words, "What a pleasant circumstance," surely call into question the meaning of "pleasant." The narrator is Nellie's friend, yet she watches her with an almost cruel detachment. The distance between the two of them is like the distance between the warm room and the ice outside. The narrator (as now and again happens in Colwin) is consciously enjoying turning a lover into a work of art, in this case a dead woman in a painting. It seems to me to be at least possible that the dislocation of the assimilated Jew is the founding paradigm for the painful distance between the unnamed narrator and Nellie Felix.

One thing that makes Colwin's texts interesting is the sort of self-consciousness manifested by the passage just quoted. Her texts are *about* the intersection of pleasure with romance, and comment as they go on the aesthetic satisfaction of romantic pain—the beauty of longing. *The Lone Pilgrim* contains three brilliant stories on this theme: **"A Girl Skating,"** a meditation on the male gaze from the point of view of its object; **"A Mythological Subject";** and **"The Smile Beneath the Smile,"** in which female bystanders admire the visual effect of a couple tormented by romantic longing. The metanarrative in **"The Smile Beneath the Smile"** comments:

> It is no accident that love finds expression in poetry. Love has nothing to do with personality. It has to do with form. Translate this into emotional terms . . . and you find that romantic love has nothing to do with content . . . It only has to do with love.

This, I think, does a good deal to explain the highly marked aesthetic effect of a Colwin story. Her texts insist on beauty in surroundings, both in domestic interiors and in weather. The effect, on me at least, is a powerful nostalgia mixed with uneasiness. This is the same glossy, armored beauty David Lynch achieved in *Blue Velvet.* It looks normal, *perfectly* so; yet its inhabitants are often filled with pain and longing. It seems to me that Colwin is intentionally setting up an environment for her characters in a painterly way, and that the effect has something to do with effects like that created by the title of *Happy All the Time.* Colwin has a little joke with the reader when she picks a title for the dissertation of Harry Markham (who, in **"The Big Plum,"** sits and gazes longingly at a checkout girl in his supermarket); his dissertation is called *Vermeer and the Art of the Impossible* (*Passion and Affect*).

Certainly there is a good deal of the glossy impossible in *Goodbye Without Leaving.* Colwin diverts her energy from the usual weather effects and pretty interiors to pull off two tours de force of beautification: of the experience of American blacks and of the Holocaust.

The black experience in *Goodbye Without Leaving* is a far cry from Toni Morrison, or even Andrea Lee. Race prejudice is as removed from Colwin's world as anti-Semitism; drugs in the music business are turned into a running joke. Vernon and Ruby Shakely make a tame version of Ike and Tina Turner, with only vague hints that Vernon is not a nice fellow. All of Geraldine's former colleagues on the tour prosper; she runs into her fellow Shakette Grace at a fancy dinner party which Grace is catering. Doo-Wah Banks is putting his children through college when last seen. Most striking is Geraldine's first view of the Race Music Foundation: "housed in an old brownstone on one of Harlem's nicer streets." In a whole novel set in Manhattan, Geraldine hardly sees an unpleasant sight; she is once "almost mugged" near her old apartment, but she is rescued by her kindly Ukrainian neighbors. On her return to the Race Music Foundation after a three-year hiatus she does notice that the subway station exit looks worse, but the Foundation "looked positively rich." And Geraldine's first view of the neighborhood to which she is to move with Johnny, and which represents to her an uncomfortable degree of bourgeois solidity, includes the following vignette: "a handsome black woman took a wooden basket of apples out of the back of her station wagon"; now the blacks look like WASPs. It is almost incredible that this book is contemporary with Spike Lee's *Do the Right Thing* and Tom Wolfe's *Bonfire of the Vanities;* this is not New York as we know it. It's quite a trick to plunk your nice Jewish assimilated heroine down in Harlem as a switch on the Merion Cricket Club and have everything come out about the same.

The Holocaust survivors who populate the Hansonia Society also thrive. Colwin lavishes attention on their elegant clothing and food, both of which are frequent topics of discussion at the office. Geraldine has a chat with Hannah Hausknecht, the accountant, who tells about shopping at Saks and seeing there her best friend's aunt, who she had not known was still alive. As they talk Geraldine suddenly notices the tattooed number on Hannah's arm, and Hannah explains that she was in Auschwitz:

> "I will tell you something. I only remember the good times. I was in the children's section and it was near the end of the war. We made up songs about cakes. . . . But look!" she said. "I have grown up so plump and happy."

Later Geraldine makes another friend, Mrs. Hornung, who gets Geraldine into her special private swim club, where other refugees cheerily meet to swim and gossip:

> They had had everything taken away from them: their language, their landscape, their sense of stability, and here they were, greeting each other happily . . . , complaining about their hairdressers or dentists or stockbrokers, comparing the prices of shoes at Saks Fifth Avenue. . . .

During Geraldine's whole time at the Hansonia Society, delving into records of research in the rural South during the 1930's, the narrative never so much as mentions the Depression.

Considering that some have wondered whether there can be art after Auschwitz, it is a bit breathtaking to have this drawing-room comedy. Yet it seems to me that Colwin is not falsifying human experience. Frivolous, cheerful people went into Auschwitz, and some of them came out. That there should be a continuity of cakes and ale is a sort of miracle, and a joyous one. Toward the end of the novel, and her final decision that perhaps she will sing again, Geraldine swims laps and remembers herself singing her first solo as a Shakette: "I thought of Hannah Hausknecht, who had described sitting on the steps of the children's barracks at Auschwitz singing: *Was müssen das für Bäume sein / Wo die grossen Elephanten spatzieren gehen / Ohne anzustossen.*" The image of the little girl, who would someday turn into the lady in the Saks Fifth Avenue suit, sitting on the steps at Auschwitz singing a children's nonsense song, makes a serious statement about the place of silly cheerfulness in the face of the worst evil.

Music holds a special place in the hearts of those who grew up in the sixties. Rock and roll, as Bob Seger sings, never forgets. Geraldine Coleshares is not the first Colwin heroine to be haunted by tunes; Patricia Burr in **"A Road in Indiana"** (*Passion and Affect*) leaves her husband, prompted by a country and western album called *Closing Doors.* Jane Catherine Jacoby, in **"Imelda,"** who has a yen for Latin music along with her Argentinian boyfriend, is moved to tears by the music of Graucho Pacheco's Latin Band at the Bronx Music Palace. Polly Rice, in **"The Lone Pilgrim,"** sees music as a Proustian key to each person's private past: "It makes your past come back to you, and if you must pinpoint a moment in your life you can say, 'That was when "He's a Rebel," by the Crystals, was a hit.' " The kind of feeling for rock and roll that Geraldine has is immediately recognizable to a reader who lived through that time, and the feeling of outright, ecstatic joy produced by bopping always strikes me as one of the few metaphysical experiences available to ordinary people.

So it makes sense that, for Geraldine, the only pure experience is what she feels as a backup singer. For a person without a deeply felt religion, what could be more celebratory? Geraldine's best friend, Mary Abbott, a devout Catholic, several times compares her to a pilgrim, and says that being a Shakette (a female Shaker?) was not unlike being a nun—a form of pure being. Mary Abbott (appropriately named) knows this, because in the course of the novel she actually becomes a nun, in a Benedictine order; this caps a recurring appearance in Colwin's work of the *Rule of St. Benedict* (Holly reads it in *Happy All the Time,* as does the narrator of **"St. Anthony of the Desert"** [*The Lone Pilgrim*]). Geraldine knows this, too; she describes her feelings as Ruby sings her bravura number, "Jump for Joy": "The kind of ecstasy people find in religion, I found in being a Shakette. It was not an out-of-body experience, it was an *in*-body experience" (*Goodbye Without Leaving*).

In fact, in this book, rock and roll is what really comes off well as a religious experience. The scene that sticks in my mind takes place when Geraldine has gone to one of her loved haunts, an out-of-print record store near the Race Music Foundation, run by a zombie-like white rock aficionado named Fred Wood. She asks him for a record, which he produces and puts on the turntable:

> Bob and Earl were of the gospel-inspired school of rock and roll. As the first notes rolled over us, we froze. . . . The opening had heavy gospel riffs on piano and shadow guitar. I felt my hair stand on end. When it was over, a tear slid down Fred Wood's cheek. He took the record off the turntable with great tenderness and slipped it into its little paper jacket.
>
> "It's really beautiful," I said.
>
> "Oh, yes," said Fred Wood. He removed the dead cigarette from the corner of his mouth. He gave me the record in a used bag. "It is awesome."

What makes these white people freeze and cry? What does "beautiful" mean here? It helps to see it glossed by "awesome" rather than "pleasant." The song—"gospel-inspired"—is about love that you feel "Deep Down Inside." Though Colwin never uses the term "soul music" in *Goodbye Without Leaving,* maybe that is what Geraldine is looking for. In this book, almost everyone yearns: whites for blacks, Europeans for Americans, Americans for Europeans, humans for God, men for women, women for men and children. Music and all beauty are simply the expression of that yearning.

I have been a reader of Colwin's for a long time, and have often asked myself why I take her so seriously when her writing is, on the face of it, so unserious. Perhaps her concern has been, all along, with immanence and the problems it poses. Most people seek beauty, admit it as a positive good; and, in love, we seek the beautiful we bring into being in another by our very gaze. Colwin superimposes her hyper-real world of the Vermeer interior onto the ashcan reality more customarily seen in art today, and I think that by so doing she provides a meditation on the nature of art and love.

Or maybe I just take her seriously because I recognize my own experience on her pages. When Catherine Morland, in *Northanger Abbey,* says she finds history dull because you never see a woman, page after page, this is part Austen's vindication of the novel form—her own form. As a classicist, I deal with a tradition from which almost every woman's voice has been expunged. It is enlightening to read Ovid's *Ars Amatoria,* but how nice it would be to have more of Sulpicia's poems to go along with it. In two thousand years, I hope that, if John Cheever is still around, Laurie Colwin is there, too.

But it is thought-provoking that the elision of the unpleasant in Colwin's work stands in this same honorable tradition in English literature; another little joke of hers in the title of Geraldine's projected dissertation, *Jane Austen and the War of the Sexes* (*Goodbye Without Leaving*). Colwin's world is also the drawing-room world of English domestic comedy. In the epigraph to this essay, one of Nancy Mitford's characters, the upper-class ex-prostitute Amabelle Fortescue, tells the young writer Paul Fotheringay (a thinly disguised Evelyn Waugh) that to be taken seriously would entail a departure from the upper classes.

> Colwin superimposes her hyper-real world of the Vermeer interior onto the ashcan reality more customarily seen in art today, and I think that by doing so she provides a meditation on the nature of art and love.
>
> —Amy Richlin

Like the frustrated hero of *Vile Bodies,* Mitford's young hero has written a novel; his, meant as a tragedy, has been widely received as a comedy, much to his chagrin. Amabelle's comment applies not only to Paul's novel but, of course, to Mitford's. This sheltered world within the comfortable house has been marked for women writers and readers, and somehow at the same time lost its claim to be saying anything worth reading outside that world.

The elision of the unpleasant is not a denial of its existence; au contraire. Holly in *Happy All the Time* devotes her whole life to being a "domestic sensualist," a phrase that recurs in Colwin's work; toward the end of the novel, the skeptical Misty Berkowitz reaches an appreciative understanding of Holly's mission: "Even Holly worked: she worked to make life sweet. . . . she fought to keep the ugly, chaotic world at bay and to keep a sweet, pretty corner to live in." Like Holly, or like Stella Gibbons's Flora Poste, Colwin engineers a world in which the forces of disorder are kept at bay and the writer (or lover, or domestic artist) is free to see what is then possible. (The elegance of Colwin's style, and the pleasure it provides to the reader, are of a piece with her manipulation of her subject matter.) The omission of class issues, while it may prevent Colwin's novels from being universes, allows a sharp focus on moral and personal issues. It also suggests that aesthetics and class-consciousness cannot easily coexist. But the self-consciousness of Colwin's manipulations keeps the reader from lapsing into a comfortable compliance with the text's omissions, and both suggests and calls into question the effort that it takes to keep "chaos" at bay.

How wide her audience could be is another question. It is worth pondering that Colwin herself comes from a background marginal to the one she most often describes; she went to Cheltenham High School, a public school in an ordinary suburb of Philadelphia, and her high school yearbook picture shows her in black turtleneck, well on her way to Bard. To a nice assimilated Jewish girl from the suburbs, the world of Polly Solo-Miller is hyperbole: the carrying of a tendency to its extreme.

In *Goodbye Without Leaving,* Colwin does begin a consideration of race, class, and religion (however unsuccessful). Throughout the novel, it is Geraldine's rejection of the moral compromise she sees in the real world that makes her path so difficult. She loves Johnny because he loves rock and roll, and she is impressed with his ability to come to terms with the world of grownups, but all the same she fears he has sold out; she distrusts him when he tells her, "You can act like a regular person and still boogie in your soul." She despises the liberal politics of his law-firm friends, and invents a game called "Who Likes Negroes Most?" And she is even conscious that her own experience of being a Shakette is a luxury; to the others, it was a way out of the projects, as Grace reminds her when they meet again. In the face of her family's bourgeois values, Geraldine continues to pursue only what feels "fine, fine, super-fine" to her: rock and roll, the history of the blues, mother-hood (which she eventually embraces wholeheartedly). She sees the project of the Race Music Foundation, to pre-serve black music for black people, as right and noble. But the problem of relations between Jews and blacks never appears here—a thunderous omission.

Likewise, Colwin finesses the core problem with assimila-tion: not the denial of Judaism, but the denial of Jewish-ness. The Jews at the Hansonia Society are Western, not Eastern European; no one wears a *yarmulke.* They are Polly Solo-Miller with Auschwitz tattoos, and it is clear that the kind of internalized anti-Semitism that reflects hook-nosed caricatures still operates in Colwin's text. The old Colwin rises from the page when Geraldine finally takes courage to visit the "Neighborhood Synagogue" (not, you notice, Temple Beth Sholom), and remarks, "It was a square building that looked something like a Quaker meetinghouse." Now even the shul doesn't look like a shul. She takes her Seder seriously, but her husband and son hardly do. If she has a shot at finding Judaism, she gets nowhere near her Jewishness, which doesn't arise—except implicitly, in the continuing lostness of this main charac-ter. The failure here is like the failure to deal with black realities and Jewish/black realities; it may be an inevitable result of Colwin's aesthetic practice, but it shows where the weakness of that aesthetic practice lies.

Overall, the book is more successful in finally naming the problem and locating it in a nostalgic rock & roller than in resolving it, and is most successful in its evocation of the joy of rock in memory. But, uneasy and fascinated as ever, I for one will continue reading and re-reading Col-win; as she says of Nellie Felix, it will be interesting to see what happens to her, because she has always been a plea-sure to watch.

Pearl K. Bell   (review date Winter 1994)

SOURCE: A review of *A Big Storm Knocked It Over,* in *Partisan Review,* Vol. LXI, No. 1, 1994, pp. 93-95.

[*In the following excerpt, Bell furnishes a laudatory review of Colwin's last novel.*]

[Laurie Colwin's *A Big Storm Knocked It Over*] is a trea-sure beyond counting, the last of a series of novels in which she explored the domestic territory that was so dis-tinctly and memorably her own as a writer. The public world outside the boundaries of her private fiefdom is scarcely mentioned in her work: no politics, no social problems, no global turmoil. What fascinated Colwin was the agony and wonder of family life, the way clannish obli-gations shape an individual's pursuit of happiness, and bear down on the pain and pleasure of love. Few novelists these days pay much attention to happiness: it seems a bland idea (except for those who find it); it smacks of senti-

mentality; it blunts the sharp edge of irony; it's hard to de-fine and harder still to dramatize. (As Clifford Odets once in all seriousness remarked, "Happiness is no laughing matter.") But Laurie Colwin is neither embarrassed nor intimidated by the possibilities of this eminently desirable but elusive state of being.

In *Happy All the Time* (1978), *Family Happiness* (1982), and *Another Marvelous Thing* (1989), Colwin focused her wit and clear-eyed intelligence on men and women, on the whole likeable and decent, who ought to be perfectly con-tent with their lot but feel that something is missing. Yet they can't quite figure out what it is, or why they are rest-less and edgy. Most of them are well-educated, well-off New Yorkers, with good jobs and comfortable homes, without anything more distressing in their lives, it would seem, than an exasperating mother. Yet they tumble guilt-ily into adulterous love affairs without for a moment want-ing to break up their more or less contented marriages. As Jane Louise, the heroine of *A Big Storm,* ruminates: "A husband was someone you could hide behind. You could cover your head with a marriage. . . . You could stamp out unnecessary or wayward emotions. You could dispel untoward thoughts. You could pretend that all of your life was all of a piece and it was wonderful, wonderful, won-derful . . . ." (Note the word *pretend.*)

Colwin can be incisively ironic—and very funny—about oppressive parents, pretentious poseurs, and the philan-dering snakes that crawl into the most orderly gardens, and she harbors no illusions about the price most people may eventually have to pay for their willful self-deceptions. But neither her irony nor her comic sense is tainted with acid. What she captures with finely nuanced precision and generosity of spirit is the way perfectly sensi-ble human beings, seemingly without any cause for anxi-ety, become fretful about the direction their lives have taken, and berate themselves for their fretting. In Colwin's hands none of this ever smacks of self-pity or self-indulgence.

In her scrutiny of the domestic scene, she is particularly astute about the meaning of marriage and its awesome dis-turbances. As *A Big Storm* opens, Jane Louise, a success-ful book-designer in her late thirties, has just been married ("In sickness and in health, and in confusion"), and she can't stop gnawing at an invisible hangnail:

> Had she changed? Was there now some new creature named Jane Louise Parker who was older, wiser, more grown-up? Did married peo-ple look and smell different? . . . What an odd thing it was to have a husband. This person who was almost like a household object—a pillow or a lamp—who transformed you from a single en-tity into a unit, whose breathing at night was as reassuring as a clock, to whom you could, of an evening, pay almost no attention at all, and who in one minute, with one look, could turn into what a husband actually was: a sexual being.

Jane Louise's plaintive agitation about the metamor-phoses of marriage stems from her own and her husband's childhood traumas, which make her apprehensive about the giant step she has just taken. Neither of them has entirely recovered from the long-ago rancor of their parents' divorces and remarriages, and when they plan to have a baby, she is tormented by the thought that two "unprepared humans," of unhappy background, "were supposed to create some unswerving, stable, and dependable structure. How were they supposed to do that?"

A resourceful woman, this uneasy wife and reluctant mother climbs out of such sloughs of despond through heart-to-hearts with Edie, her dearest friend since college. The blessings of friendship—its compensations for the failures of family, its reassuring mortar of acceptance in a heartless world—play a vital role in Colwin's work. Like happiness, friendship is a fragile gift of life that few novelists bother to write about these days. When the two women give birth only weeks apart, Jane Louise, world-class worrier, asks Edie, "Do you suppose [the babies] will someday not be able to stand us?" Edie has the perfect answer: "Oh, doubtless. But they'll have each other."

The big storm of the title is a real tornado, but it is also Colwin's metaphor for the disruptive, unsettling changes enacted by marriage and parenthood. After the storm, the story ends in graceful tranquility on a country hilltop, as the two couples and their sleeping babies wait for the Fourth of July fireworks to begin—"that unexpected, magnificent, beautiful release, like the unexpected joy that swept you away, like life itself." We tremble, knowing what followed.

Soon after she wrote those closing words of her last novel, Laurie Colwin died of a heart attack. She was forty-eight years old. The loss is incalculable.

FURTHER READING

Criticism

Davenport, Gary. "The Two Worlds of Contemporary American Fiction." *Sewanee Review* 92, No. 1 (January 1984): 128-36.

> Contends that "except for occasional and slight traces of glibness *Family Happiness* bears witness to Laurie Colwin's continuing development as one of our most consistently intelligent and engaging novelists."

Duguid, Lindsay. "A Civilized Affair." *Times Literary Supplement*, No. 4377 (27 February 1987): 206.

> Mixed review of *Another Marvelous Thing*.

Eder, Richard. "First the Rhythm, Then the Blues." *Los Angeles Times Book Review* (6 May 1990): 3, 18.

> Summarizes the plot of *Goodbye without Leaving*.

Olshan, Joseph. "I Was a White Shakette." *New York Times Book Review* (13 May 1990): 12.

> Praises the style of *Goodbye without Leaving*, asserting that Colwin "is able to lend a comic voice to some rumbling social issues that would probably drown out a more conventional writer."

Thorne, John. "A Friend Indeed." *Book World—The Washington Post* 50, No. 50 (11 December 1988): 10.

> Positive assessment of *Home Cooking*.

Yardley, Jonathan. "Anna Karenina Comes to Manhattan." *Book World—The Washington Post* 12, No. 37 (12 September 1982): 3, 8.

> Laudatory review of *Family Happiness*.

Additional coverage of Colwin's life and career is contained in the following sources published by Gale Research: *Contemporary Authors,* **Vols. 89-92, 139 (obituary);** *Contemporary Authors New Revision Series,* **Vol. 20;** *Contemporary Literary Criticism,* **Vols. 5, 13, 23;** *Dictionary of Literary Biography Yearbook, 1980;* **and** *Major 20th-Century Writers.*

Léon-Gontran Damas

1912-1978

French Guianese poet, nonfiction writer, essayist, editor, and short story writer.

The following entry provides an overview of Damas's career.

INTRODUCTION

Best known for his poetry—particularly the collection *Pigments* (1937)—Damas was a co-founder of Negritude, a literary and philosophical movement begun in Paris during the early 1930s, which attacked European colonialism and racism and affirmed African traditions and Black identity. Damas's poetry features rhythms drawn from blues music, jazz, and the African drumbeat, and often addresses themes of alienation, loss, and racial persecution. In summarizing Damas's career, O. R. Dathorne stated that Damas "was a poet who fiercely believed in a cause, but he did not allow that cause to blunt his vision. . . . His poetry stresses not the collision of worlds but the manner in which humanity can triumph and overcome man-made obstacles."

Biographical Information

Damas was born in Cayenne, French Guiana, a French territory in South America. Raised in a middle-class, mulatto family, he was pressured by parents and teachers throughout his youth to accept French culture and customs. His antipathy toward assimilation emerged later as a major theme in his poetry, particularly *Black-Label* (1956). He attended elementary and secondary schools in Cayenne and in Fort-de-France, Martinique, before traveling to Paris in the early 1930s. There, he attended the Université de Paris, studying literature, oriental languages, history, law, economics, and ethnology. While in Paris, he associated himself with the Surrealist movement, publishing poems as early as 1934 in such prestigious French literary journals as *Esprit;* he also met Aimé Césaire and Léopold Sédar Senghor, with whom he founded Negritude and the short-lived journal *L'étudiant noir.* Damas published his first book, *Pigments,* in 1937. His second book, *Retour de Guyane* (1938), a nonfiction critique of French colonialism, developed out of an ethnographic study Damas conducted in 1934 on the Bush Negroes of French Guiana. After World War II, during which he was active in the French Resistance, Damas continued his research into African culture in the Caribbean and South America. From 1948 to 1951, Damas represented French Guiana in the French National Assembly, and beginning in 1966, he served as a representative for the *Société Africaine de Culture* in the United Nations Educational, Scientific, and Cultural Organization (UNESCO). He also taught modern and African literature at Federal City College and Howard University, both in

Washington, D.C. At the time of his death in 1978, he was a Distinguished Professor of African Literature at Howard University.

Major Works

The chief concerns of Damas's poetry are racism, the problems of self-identity caused by the French colonial policy of assimilation, and the weaknesses of Western culture and society. Narrated in the first person by a character who assumes the role of a victim, the poems in *Pigments* constitute Damas's most vehement and direct treatment of his major themes. In such poems as "Ils sont venus ce soir" ("They Came That Night"), with its image of slave traders interrupting an African dance, Damas constructs a dichotomy between blacks and whites, maintaining that blacks are an exploited people and that whites are the exploiters who wish to rob blacks of their African identity. "Solde" ("Sell Out") addresses the discomfort and alienation Damas feels as a member of Western society, while "Hoquet" ("Hiccups") laments his bourgeois upbringing and "Réalité" ("Reality") expresses his shame for feeling culturally white. In "S.O.S." he suggests that the relationship between colonized blacks and colonizing whites is similar to that between the Jews and Nazis during the years surrounding World War II. In other poems Damas attacks Western religion as hypocritical and ridicules the double standard of French society, arguing that even though a black may act white, he is always considered a second-class citizen. In "Contre notre amour qui ne voulait rien d'autre," for instance, he comments on the use of Noah's curse of Ham in the Old Testament as a justification for the subjugation of blacks. *Black-Label,* Damas's only book-length poem, documents the musings and reminiscences of an exiled black during an evening spent drinking Black-Label. Concerned with self-contempt and "negro lackeyism," the poem addresses what J. M. Ita calls "the crippling effects of being brought up to despise what one is, and cannot help but be." Damas's love poems, collected in *Graffiti* (1952) and *Névralgies* (1966), focus on loss and lack of fulfillment. His book-length prose works include *Retour de Guyane* and *Veillées noires* (1943), a collection of folktales that combine elements from African, Amerindian, and European storytelling traditions. These tales treat such themes as the ability of the powerless to survive and the injustice of social orders based on race.

Critical Reception

Critics generally concur that *Pigments* is Damas's most enduring and engaging work; none of his subsequent writings, they argue, equal its intensity and urgency. Most commentators tend to focus on the stylistics of Damas's poetry, particularly his use of humor, musical rhythms, repetition, and unorthodox typography. Poems such as "Bientôt," for example, are wholly structured on a repetitive form which invokes a sense of circularity, completeness, and musical rhythm. Such techniques sometimes give his poetry the appearance of extreme simplicity, which, many critics argue, demonstrates Damas's skill in manipulating language to achieve complex effects. Regarding the humor in his verse, commentators note Damas's reversal of stereotypes and frequent use of puns. The title of "Nuit blanche" ("Sleepless Night"), for instance, is an untranslatable pun for "sleepless night" and "night spent with whites." Critics disagree, however, about the ultimate significance of Damas's poetry. While some contend that Damas is simply a poet of Negritude, others claim that his poetry transcends its immediate context and that his love poems in particular are racially anonymous.

PRINCIPAL WORKS

*Pigments (poetry) 1937
Retour de Guyane (nonfiction) 1938
†Veillées noires (short stories) 1943
Poètes d'expression française: 1900-1945 [editor] (poetry) 1947
Poèmes nègres sur des airs africains [African Songs of Love, War, Grief and Abuse] (poetry) 1948
Graffiti (poetry) 1952
Black-Label (poetry) 1956

Névralgies (poetry) 1966
Nouvelle somme de poésie du monde noir [editor] (poetry) 1966
Hommage à Jean Price-Mars [editor] (nonfiction) 1969
Pigments, Névralgies (poetry) 1972

*A revised edition of this work was published in 1962.

†An enlarged version of this volume was published in 1972.

CRITICISM

Merle Hodge (essay date 1967)

SOURCE: "Beyond Négritude: The Love Poems," *Critical Perspectives on Léon-Gontran Damas,* edited by Keith Q. Warner, Three Continents Press, 1988, pp. 119-45.

[*Hodge is a Trinidadian educator, novelist, and critic. The following excerpt was drawn from her unpublished thesis, "The Writings of Léon Damas and Their Connection with the Négritude Movement in Literature," completed in 1967 at the University of London. Below, she examines the themes and tone of Damas's poetry, focusing on his work in* Graffiti, Black-Label, *and* Névralgies, *and remarks on the similarities between Damas and the French poet Jacques Prévert.*]

[*Graffiti*] at first disconcerts because it is all but racially anonymous—the burning preoccupations of *Pigments* are totally absent. A few years later in *Black-Label,* which had been in preparation all the while, the theme of race returns, but much of the work is strongly personal. His latest work, *Névralgies,* is also composed of personal poetry.

If we take the works *Pigments, Black-Label* and *Névralgies* (which incorporates *Graffiti*) as a trilogy, the three works show the poet progressively recoiling into himself. Although the poems of *Pigments* are intensely 'first hand' and are therefore poetry rather than standard-bearing, yet the angry *'moi'* of these poems is often meant as a collective voice, a cry from the poet assuming the fate of his whole race. A few of the poems of *Pigments* which are outside the field of race are hermetic poems. Some of the personal poetry of *Black-Label* is also quite private. A large proportion of *Névralgies,* which is entirely personal, remains in a tantalizing half-light.

The progression towards completely personal poetry reminds one of Sartre's prediction that the racial revolt and self-assertiveness of the Negritude movement would be but a necessary stage in the development of modern literature in the French ex-colonies. Damas, having vented his racial rage and asserted his identity (the latter being as much for his own benefit as in a gesture of revolt), moves towards poetry which has a wider human reference for delving deeper into the experience and feelings of one man. So that paradoxically his poetry opens out by becoming more egocentric. In *Pigments* he is vehemently black, proclaiming with all his might his racial identification and solidarity; in **Black-Label,** considerably mellowed, he takes up his narrower identity of a West Indian. In his love-poetry he is first and foremost a man.

The note of personal affliction which in **Pigments** remains a part of his racial awareness merges in his later works with a more general sadness and disillusionment with life. . . .

His love-poetry reveals a cause of his unhappiness. Damas is a poet of loss, deprivation, unfulfilment. His lament for his lost self, the loss of his 'black dolls', gives way to a lament on the loss of love. The happier aspects of love are totally absent from his love-poetry. It is almost in its entirety on the death or the absence of love. A poem in **Graffiti** is perhaps meant to explain the title of the volume, and might be the title-poem for all of Damas' love-poetry:

> Tandis qu'il agonise
> sans peur
> sans prêtre
> plus blanc que drap
> plus essoufflé qu'un train qui entre en gare
> d'un fabuleux parcours
> l'amour râle un poème
> comme d'autres
> confient un dernier acte
>
> Et
> d'eux-mêmes
> les vers
> s'inscrivent
> au fronton du mausolée marmoréen
> debout à l'image agrandi
> de ce qui fut
> au rythme d'une nuit
> afro-cubaine
>
> (On its very death-bed
> without fear
> without priest
> whiter than a sheet
> more breathless than a train coming in
> from a fabulous run
> love rattles a poem
> as others
> commit a final act
>
> And
> of themselves
> the lines
> are inscribed
> on the fronton of the marmoreal mausoleum
> erect in the enlarged image
> of that which was
> to the rhythm of
> an Afro-Cuban night)

The incident of the 'Afro-Cuban night' is presumably what is described in the beautiful third section of **Black-Label.** In the refrain repeated twice in this passage, an ominous note is sounded:

> IL A ETE PENDU CE MATIN
> A L'AUBE UN NEGRE COUPABLE
> D'AVOIR VOULU FRANCHIR
> LA LIGNE
>
> (HANGED THIS MORNING
> AT DAWN WAS A NEGRO

GUILTY OF WANTING TO
CROSS THE LINE)

In fact, the theme of the sexual taboo between the races does not loom very large in Damas' love-poetry. . . .

In **Pigments** there is a handful of poems in [a] . . . tender strain, revealing a side of his nature perhaps more fundamental than the intransigent anger which characterizes the book as a whole. . . .

This streak of tenderness comes into its own in Damas' love-poetry, where the grim combatant gives way to the quite gentle and sensitive man. Harshness, violent flashing anger subside into quiet sadness. In **Pigments** the effect of these few poems is heightened by the surrounding ones— they are pools of shade in a merciless light. And in the same way one perhaps appreciates Damas' love-poetry all the more when it is seen against his militant poetry. Against the fierce defiance of some of the poems of **Pigments,** a poem such as this has an even greater appeal—it is as though, divested of his armour and of his thunderbolts, he were left naked and vulnerable:

> Désir d'enfant malade
> d'avoir été
> trop tôt sevré du lait pur
> de la seule vraie tendresse
> j'aurais donné
> une pleine vie d'homme
> pour te sentir
> te sentir près
> près de moi
> de moi
> seul . . .
>
> (Longing of a sick child
> for having been
> too soon weaned from the pure milk
> of the only true tenderness
> I would have given
> a whole life-time
> to feel you
> feel you near
> near to me
> to me
> alone.)

But the spirit of the combatant never leaves him to fall, like the 'bâton qui soutient les vieux corps' (stick that holds up old bodies). Damas' poetry drifts into a claustrophobic nightmare of loneliness, regret, insomnia— 'névralgies', yet a certain stoicism remains to bolster up the tone. Never does he slip into self-pity. Much of the beauty of these poems lies in their restraint, the wistfulness born of resignation in sadness. Over-sentimentality finds no place in even the most melancholy of poems. It is outraged stoicism which accounts for the irritation of poems such as this:

> Je ne sais rien en vérité
> rien de plus triste
> de plus odieux
> de plus affreux
> de plus lugubre au monde
> que d'entendre l'amour
> à longueur de journée
> se répétant à messe basse . . .

(I know of nothing in truth
nothing more dreary
more hateful
more hideous
more lugubrious in the world
than to hear love
the live long day
repeating itself
in low mass . . .)

But in this poem and many others in the same strain Damas' irritation could well be directed at himself. His stoicism is by no means facile. It is achieved at the cost of constant effort and sometimes even betrays a hint of bravado. But his poems would be less moving if they betrayed a superman riding above his griefs, and in that case they would probably never have been written—many of these poems *are* his effort at rallying:

Il n'est pas de midi qui tienne
et parce qu'il n'a plus vingt ans
mon coeur
ni la dent dure
de petite vieille
pas de midi qui tienne
je l'ouvrirai
pas de midi qui tienne
je l'ouvrirai
pas de midi qui tienne
j'ouvrirai
pas de midi qui tienne
j'ouvrirai la fenêtre
pas de midi qui tienne
j'ouvrirai la fenêtre au printemps
pas de midi qui tienne
j'ouvrirai la fenêtre au printemps que je veux ét-
    ernel
pas de midi qui tienne

(Noon can never keep
and because it's no longer twenty
my heart
nor sharp-toothed
like a little granny

noon can never keep
I will open it
noon can never keep
I will open it
noon can never keep
I will open
noon can never keep
I will open the window
noon can never keep
I will open the window to the spring
noon can never keep
I will open the window to the spring that I want
    eternal
noon can never keep)

There are other poems [like **'Il n'est pas de midi qui tienne'** (quoted above)] where 'midday' and 'midnight' represent an elusive, precariously beautiful fulfilment. It is an image which often strikes his imagination, the noon of his childhood when the sun would hover for a moment at the highest point in the sky and all but abolish shadow. . . .

It is only in a handful of poems . . . that Damas approaches anything in the nature of overt moralizing. What emerges by way of a philosophy is a kind of protective near-pessimism which, far from leading to despair, favours acceptance and recovery. He debunks love as inherently precarious, and ends the book *Névralgies* on a note of resignation:

Citez-m'en
citez-m'en un
citez-m'en un
un seul de rêve
qui soit allé
qui soit allé
jusqu'au bout du sien propre

(Tell me then
tell me then of one
tell me then of one
one single dream
that went
that went
right to the end of its very own)

But the tendency in Damas' love-poetry is not towards generalizing. His poems are wrung out of a very particular experience, and if the woman addressed is not presented in very great physical detail, largely effaced into an absent 'ELLE' often thus written in capitals, she is not idealized into an abstraction of Woman. Some of the poems are made up of details and allusions which shut us out, but for the most part the fact that the *décor* of a poem is a very specific one makes for a quality of familiarity and intimacy whose appeal is quite the opposite of that of the more abstract forms of love-poetry, where a couple are sublimated into Eternal Man and Eternal Woman floating free of particularities. This poetry has its own attraction, lifting us out of the circumstantial into the vaguer realms of the Ideal (occasionally leaving us mere wondering spectators, staring up at figures who, in the process of sublimation, have become lamentably disembodied).

There is on the other hand love-poetry in which we are permitted to eavesdrop on the relationship of two individuals who are decidedly corporeal, firmly grounded in time and space and in the details of their experience, but who in their very particularity share in the nature of Eternal Man and Woman. Because they are palpably alive with their own particular life, they are part of the stuff out of which Eternal Man and Woman are fashioned. Damas applies no capital letters to his experience and delivers no homilies on Love. His poems remain intimate and untheatrical, never inflated by rhetoric or by conscious generality. In one or two cases he may be said to have fallen into the opposite sin, of insignificance, where he fails to call forth a response because the poem remains tied down by the smallness of its details. But usually the effect is the exact opposite. The reader may participate because the details are on such a scale as to fall within the scope of his own possible experience—they are recognizable. And so Damas' love-poetry assumes wider dimensions by proceeding from the un-pretentious small end of the telescope. He captures transitoriness—a mood, a reflection, a touch of frivolity—so intimate and so familiar that his poems of themselves rise out of the personal and private into the human:

Je te vois

je te sens
je te veux en tailleur gris
et non plus marron comme tes yeux qui semblai-
    ent
parfois invoquer dieu
parfois le diable
jusqu'à ce qu'ils eussent enfin
soumis les miens que tu m'auras souvent dit
toi qui incarnes le diable en diable
être à la fois et ceux de dieu
et ceux du diable.

(I see you
I feel you
I want you in tailored grey
and why the devil my god in tailored grey
and no longer brown like your eyes that seemed
sometimes to be invoking god
sometimes the devil
until at last
they had subjected mine that you so often said
you who incarnate the devil's own person
were all at once god's
and the devil's)

The sad smile in this poem is characteristic of much of his love-poetry. Throughout his personal poetry, joyless as the tale might be, his sense of humour does not desert him, and this is another factor contributing to keeping his poetry from being submerged in wearying complaint, in the same way that humour in *Pigments* makes bitterness palatable by tempering it into superb irony. There are still flashes of this familiar irony, but Damas' humour in his later personal poetry is, in general, not of the cutting type. It is considerably softened, subdued—it is a wry shrug rather than a whiplash. But in *Pigments,* from the detachment of irony he yet plunges into the occasional fit of rage. *Névralgies,* on the other hand, is the work of a collected man—it is on the whole consistent in its restraint, and the more bitter poems are among those reproduced from the earlier *Graffiti.* The overall impression of his personal poetry and of *Névralgies* in particular is a wry, dogged buoyancy:

Pas d'ombres
surtout chinoises
j'entends
j'entends rester seul et
maître
de la rade
seul maître du navire en rade
qui tangue et tangue et tangue
qui danse et danse et danse au lazaret de mon
    coeur en quarantaine . . .

(No shadows
above all shadow-theatre
I mean
I mean to stay alone and
master
of the ship's course
sole master of the laid-up ship
that bounces bounces bounces
that dances dances dances in the lazaret of my
    heart in quarantine . . .)

Not only does Damas withdraw into the isolation of self-reliance, but as we have noted, his tendency towards her-

metic poetry grows. Damas is a believer in metempsychosis. . . . The theme of metempsychosis would seem to shed light on a number of his decidedly esoteric poems, although it does not by any means provide crystal clarity. On the contrary, Damas maintains an intriguing half-light of equivocality over many of these poems, like the 'clair obscur' (dim brightness) which he evokes in one poem ['**Parce que la Comédie**'], a light reminiscent of that grey glare which is the setting of dreams—as in this poem for example:

Tant de vies
Tant de vies en une seule
gachées
Tant d'assiettes
tant d'assiettes
échouées
sous l'évier du drame
que l'homme fut seul à porter
à l'origine de toutes choses
dans le faux jour
dans le faux jour de la dernière invite.

(So many lives
so many lives in one
squandered

So many plates
so many plates
shattered
under the sink of the story
that the man carried all alone
at the very beginning of all things
in the false light
in the false light of the last round)

There are other similar allusions to a point lost in the mists of time, or simply a previous age—'la nuit des temps perdus proches' (the night of the lost ages nigh); 'de temps immémoriaux' (from time immemorial); 'à l'âge amérindien du monde' (in the Amerindian age of the world); 'une vie antérieure' (a former life). Reference to a 'dream recreated' might be interpreted in the context of metempsychosis or might be taken as allusions to what seems to be an actual dream which he relates in a passage of *Black-Label* and certain details of which recall ['**Captation**' in] *Pigments.* There is only one overt mention of reincarnation—this poem is addressed to his twin-sister who died in babyhood:

Qui pourrait dire
si ce n'est mort-né
l'autre moi-même

Qui pourrait dire
qu'en ce jour anniversaire
j'eusse à célébrer l'absence
de toi mon double

Qui pourrait dire
si ce n'est toi
autre moi-même
réincarné mon double
mort-né . . .

(Who could say
if not my still-born
other self

Who could say

that on this anniversary day
I would have your absence to celebrate
my double

Who could say
if not you
my other self
reincarnated my double
still-born . . .)

There are other poems where the idea is expressed of a mystical correspondence between himself and a woman. This is the suggestion throughout the passage from the third section of **Black-Label**. . . .

The theme of metempsychosis, or the repeated reincarnation of a soul until it has completed its term of transmigration, can be placed in the context of a theme which pervades all of Damas' poetry, that of fulfilment, or, more often than not, unfulfilment. His poems are full of metaphors and images of desire, of satisfaction out of reach—'Accoudés au désir de la veille insatisfait' (Brooding on yesterday's unfulfilled wanting—*Pigments*); there is the refrain of the section in **Black-Label** where he recalls the longing of his constricted childhood: 'Désirs comprimés' (Hankerings repressed); in **Névralgies** the theme of unfulfilment returns to dominate the book—the first poem is entitled **'Pour que tout soit en tout'** ('That all be in all'), and the last poem declares this fulfilment to be unattainable (the poem **'Citez-m'en'**), while the whole book abounds in images such as 'carrefour' (crossroads), 'midi' (midday), 'minuit' (midnight), 'mangue mûre' (ripe mango), 'fruit mûr' (ripe fruit) and other images of crisis of ripeness, of eating and drinking, hunger and thirst—'marron qui mange à sa faim' (marroon eating his fill), and there is also the longing for an end, an overdue climax or completion: 'le plaisir d'en finir avec un dilemme' (the satisfaction of having done with a dilemma), 'l'autobus pressé d'en finir au passage' (the bus in a hurry to have done with the trip), and in more than one poem the termination or fulfilment he longs for is no less than death: 'la mort dont je rêve' (the death I dream of).

But this his private mysticism, the belief in metempsychosis, does make him amenable to the mysteries of religion. The Church which in **Pigments** receives only the merest of amused sarcasm—in a poem about his upbringing—is suddenly the object of intermittent attacks in **Graffiti** and thereafter. The attention which the Church receives in his more personal works is perhaps not to be explained in the light of his bourgeois upbringing alone. Some poems suggest that he had had a more recent contact with the Church to which he was now reacting:

> Il me souvient encore
> de l'année foutue
> où j'eusse
> pu
> tout aussi bien sucer
> et le pouce
> et l'index
> du sorcier en soutane
> au lieu de l'avaler l'hostie
> ma foi mon dieu
> mains jointes

> (I still recall
> the rotten year
> when I
> could
> just as well suck
> both the thumb
> and the forefinger
> of the cassocked sorcerer
> instead of swallowing it the host
> oh faith my god
> hands joined)

He reduces the Church to a set of lugubrious and hypocritical forms and prohibitions, and in contrast to its 'Dieu unique et triple, implacable comme un grand prêtre due Temple de Jérusalem, et imbécilement bon comme un vieux sacristain de "La Croix" ' (God who is single and triple, implacable as a High Priest of the Temple of Jerusalem, and as imbecilically good-natured as an old sexton of "The Cross"), [**Retour de Guyane**], invokes some animistic god of his ancestors, whom his ancestors worshipped with joy and self-abandon. . . .

[Damas rejects] the god of Christianity as being part and parcel of Western civilization in its loss of contact with the life of the earth, its loss of humanity. His most frequent attack on the Church is the charge of hypocrisy, the accusation that worship has become largely formulae and regulation behaviour lacking in sincerity and meaningfulness. The third stanza here is obviously inspired by Etienne Léro's words in *Légitime Défense*:

> Langston Hughes et Claude McKay, les deux poètes révolutionnaires, nous ont apporté, marinés dans l'alcool rouge, l'amour africain de la vie, la joie africaine de l'amour, le rêve africain de la mort.

> (Langston Hughes and Claude McKay, the two revolutionary poets, have brought us, soaked in red alcohol, the African love of life, the African joy of love, the African dream of death.)

Damas evokes 'African' worship as being more vital and sincere than the ossified religion of Western civilization. One however hesitates to attribute to him a 'personal religion' on the strength of passages such as this. His allegiance to this god of his, one suspects, is a purely intellectual identification by reaction to Christianity, rather than a declaration of faith. . . .

Damas' deliberately coarse irreverence is only one characteristic which recalls the work of Jacques Prévert. In a mock prayer [from **Black-Label**], for instance, he enquires after the state of God's hearing, and offers a possible cause of His deafness, which seems to be his own very original and blasphemous interpretation of one of the 'Madonna and Child' poses:

> . . . SEIGNEUR
> à moins de les avoir bien sales
> pour n'avoir plus à vos côtes Marie-l'Unique
> à la fois Vierge et Mère
> qui avait l'oeil à votre oreille
> comme au jour le jour veille
> l'homme à la ruche . . .

> (LORD

unless they've got really dirty
for no longer having at your side Mary-the-
   Unbeatable
all at once Virgin and Mother
who kept an eye on your ear
like the day-to-day watch
of the bee-keeper . . .)

The book **Black-Label** is introduced as the work of 'un Prévert africain' (an African Prévert). Damas does not acknowledge Prévert as a master—he considers that he has been influenced, among modern French poets, above all by Desnos. Damas has known Prévert, and shows an unmistakeable enthusiasm for his work, where he discovers a kindred spirit; he was acquainted with Prévert's poems, published in reviews, sometimes in reviews with which Damas was associated, before Prévert collected them into *Paroles,* his first book of poetry, in 1945. Damas' first book of poetry had however already been published, nine years before, so that the question of influence can certainly be overdone, and the affinities to be established in the work of the two poets are perhaps for the most part to be traced to a confluence of aims and attitudes.

In the work of both men one finds the same impudence, the same sense of humour delighting in underlining accepted incongruities, the same rebelliousness and resentment of authority and restraint. As Prévert speaks contemptuously of 'le bon Dieu des flics' (the Heavenly Father of cops) so the uniformed defender of the established order [the police officer] figures more than once in Damas' work as the object of irritation or aversion. . . .

Prévert's attacks on the tedium and repression of school find an echo in Damas' evocations of his own school life, with lessons (in his case even more dry and devoid of relevance from the child's point of view) contrary to his inclination. Like Prévert's school children, the boy Damas longed for freedom from the prison of the classroom and its unpalatable fare. . . .

. . . CHARLEMAGNE en pied pendu a l'un
   des quatre murs
de la classe un Enfer . . .

                                    [*Black-Label*]

(CHARLEMAGNE in full-length hanging on
   one of the four walls
of the class; a Hell)

. . . tes nuits qu'agitaient
des leçons anonnées en dodine. . . .

                                    [*Black-Label*]

(your nights tossed about
with lessons mumbled in a trance)

Damas by reaction to his upbringing shares Prévert's anti-bourgeois attitude, his aversion for 'le Beau Monde'. The members of the social class in which Damas grew up did not differ substantially from the bourgeois caricatures which abound in Prévert's work. One particularly delightful passage in **Black-Label** on Damas' childhood recalls a poem of Prévert's ['Le beau langage', in *La Pluie et le beau temps,* 1955] in which a misdemeanour on the part of a child scandalizes the propriety of its elders and produces painful results:

. . . Les cris de joie feinte
   d'autres diraient de rage
   que tu poussais à perdre haleine
   à la toute dernière fessée recue pour t'être
   sous le regard acerbe de ta mère offusquée
   et à la gêne polie de tous
   farfouillé le nez
   d'un doigt preste et chanceux
   au goûter de Madame-La-Directrice-de-
      l'Ecole-des-Filles

(The cries of feigned joy
   others might call it rage
   that you kept up fit to make you breathless
   at the very last spanking you got because
   before the reproving eyes of your scandalized
      mother
   and to the polite embarrassment of all
   you rummaged in your nose
   with a nimble daring finger
   at the tea-party of Missus-Headmistress-of-the-
      Girls'-School)

Prévert's sympathy for the poor is matched by Damas' preoccupation in his writings with the poverty of his people. And in a passage [from **Black-Label**] where Damas evokes the peasant misery of the French Caribbean, he almost certainly has in mind a section of Prévert's 'Dîner de têtes'. . . .

One critic sums up Damas' work as 'resounding racism ending in an emotional cul-de-sac' [W. Feuser, 'Négritude—The Third Phase', *The New African* (April 1966)]. Despite this resounding inaccuracy, Damas' inspiration is at no point bounded by race, and far less by racism. His purely racial writing is as necessary and as justifiable as the whole Negritude movement, but his work follows a pattern which is the best direction that Negritude, in literary terms, could take. There is a limited number of successful works that can be written around the affirmation that one is black. Damas continues to engage himself actively in the cultural rehabilitation which has been an important aim of the Negritude movement, after his political involvement, which was another corollary of Negritude. His poetry does not end at the defense and exaltation of

---

Ellen Conroy Kennedy on *Pigments:*

[Though in his introduction to the 1937 edition Robert Desnos characterized] *Pigments* as Damas' "song of friendship . . . to his white brothers," this is true only by the most generous extrapolation. Why sweeten the pill? The short poems of *Pigments* are a bitter testimony, variations on themes of *pain.* They do reveal compassion for fellow-sufferers other than the Black man (the Jews under Hitler, for example). But nowhere in these pages does this reader find, nor does she ask for, "a song of friendship." If anger, tenacity and a certain despair are the impact of this first book of poems, this first major work of the Negritude group, they are valid, sufficient and important in and by themselves.

Ellen Conroy Kennedy, in Black World, *January 1972.*

his 'Negritude'. It is his common humanity above all which is revealed in his love-poetry, and it is a strange racism which moves a man to declare to one of the race which is the object of his racism:

> . . . nous ne sommes
> qu'une même somme
> qu'un seul et même sang . . .
>
> (We are but
> one same sum
> one same and single blood . . .)

J. M. Ita   (essay date 1970)

SOURCE: "On *Black Label*," in *Critical Perspectives on Léon-Gontran Damas,* edited by Keith Q. Warner, Three Continents Press, 1988, pp. 111-14.

[*Ita is a Nigerian educator and critic. In the following essay, which was originally published in the journal* African Arts/Arts d'Afrique *in 1970, he remarks on the themes of* Black-Label *and asserts that the poem has been largely misunderstood in the English-speaking world.*]

Black Label has, in the English-speaking world, the reputation of being a crude glorification of blackness, and a rather unintelligent example of black racialism. This undeservedly bad reputation is based on the fact, that of the whole poem sequence, the only part generally known to the English-speaking public are the following lines:

> The White will never be negro
> for beauty is negro
> and negro is wisdom
> for endurance is negro
> and negro is courage
> for patience is negro
> and negro is irony
> for charm is negro
> and negro is magic
> for love is negro
> and negro is loose walking
> for the dance is negro
> and negro is rhythm
> for laughter is negro
> for joy is negro
> for peace is negro
> for life is negro

These lines are, in fact, quoted by Mr. Gerald Moore in his introduction to *Seven African Writers,* where he prefaces them with the words: "The chief danger carried by Negritude is that of degenerating into a racialism as intolerant and arrogant as any other. At its fiercest, it can lead to the writing of defiant, if invigorating, nonsense like this: 'The White will never be negro . . .' "

By isolating Damas' lines, Mr. Moore has endowed them with a crudity which is not theirs when read in context. The lines are not, of course, intended to be an entirely self-contained poem, but constitute part of a sequence, representing the musings, reminiscences and vituperations of a negro in exile during a night spent drinking Black Label. This exile had begun, not in Paris, but in the colonies with the birth of a child deprived a maternal love, "that no maternal bosom will ever fail to nurse for lack of tenderness."

[In a footnote, the critic states that the phrase "that no maternal bosom will ever fail to nurse" is "a mistranslation. It should read 'which no maternal breast will ever nourish.' "] It was a child whose pram a stiffly uniformed nurse pushed endlessly from avenue to boulevard, and from park to square—a child perpetually drilled in the false gentility of a colonial bourgeoisie, in the hushed conversational tones and the fingers crooked over the teacup:

> At tea, the two pointed fingers
>   stabbing, pointing
> Exactly at the bourgeois sense of
>   conventions.

It is the *Negro-ness* of the child which nurse and parents, teachers and clergy all try to eradicate. Thus, the child's experiences force upon it (and temporarily upon the reader) an identification of negro-ness with all that is natural and spontaneous in its nature.

The lines "The White will never be negro . . ." are, in part, a summing up of identifications forced upon, and beaten into, the poet by his childhood experience. But the lines do not occur in the immediate context of the poet's convention-ridden childhood; they are a tirade provoked by the memory of fashionable Parisians in a metropolitan jazz dive aping what they suppose to be the natural spontaneity of the African.

> DO YOU REMEMBER
> The CUBAN CABIN
> The liveried page with the red parasol
> the stairs which gave sheer on to the giddying
>   darkness
> and threw you straight into the fevered rhythm
> the harshness of the blues
> the stomp . . .

Their immediate context is:

> The White at the Negro's school
> at the same time
> well behaved
> docile
> submissive and a mimic
> The White will never be negro . . .

The lines

> and negro is loose walking
> for the dance is negro
> and negro is rhythm

probably refer not so much to "loose walking" in general, but to an actual attempt of Parisians (seen or remembered by the poet) to imitate negro dance movements. For the Parisians search for the spontaneity of "Africa" through jazz and blues—that is to say, through the music and dance forms of the already exiled negro world. There is a fairly obvious irony in the situation: while the "fashionable" coloured colonial bourgeoisie cripple themselves in an attempt to adopt the norms of the white metropolis, the metropolis is struggling to imitate "African" spontaneity. But what the poet sees here is not merely *another* form of falsity and artificiality, but artificiality intensified to the highest degree; for surely no artificiality can be more artificial, and more of a mockery of all authenticity, than that which apes spontaneity. Besides this, the decision of Parisians to patronise Africa is doubly insulting. First, Paris has stunted and thwarted the development of the negro poet. Now its interests in "Africa" seem like an attempt to take over such crumbs of personality and vitality as had been left to him. The lines "The White will never be negro . . ." represent the forceful, if one likes, crude, outburst of the poet faced with phony Parisian Afrophilia.

There is a sharp contrast between the style of his passage, which is, superficially at least, straight forward and almost pompous in tone, and Damas' usual poetic style which is highly elliptical and shot through with *double entendre*. The passage in the framework of a more mannered sequence constitutes not only a denunciation, but a jeer at the folly of artificiality aping spontaneity.

Within the framework of **Black Label** genuineness and spontaneous life have become identified with the negro (that is, with the pre-exile negro) and artificiality with the white. But the poem cycle as a whole is not concerned with stating baldly the merits of the blacks and the demerits of the whites, or at least, not in the crude way which critics like Mr. Moore might be prone to suppose. It is little concerned with the whites. It is concerned with negro lackeyism, and the crippling effects of being brought up to despise what one is, and cannot help but be. Far from being crude, **Black Label** is a work of considerable complexity. Sprung from the negro experience, it burns that experience into its readers; but its treatment of negro self-contempt is relevant to all self-contempt, just as its treatment of the speciousness of the patrons of the Cabane Cubaine is relevant to all speciousness. It is a poem sequence whose complexity and scope entitle it to more serious and more sustained critical attention than it has so far received.

Léon-Gontran Damas with Keith Warner   (interview date July 1972)

SOURCE: An interview in *Critical Perspectives on Léon-Gontran Damas,* edited by Keith Q. Warner, Three Continents Press, 1988, pp. 23-8.

[*Warner is a Trinidadian educator and critic. In the following interview, which was conducted in July 1972 and originally published in the journal* Manna *in 1973, Damas remarks on his career and the Négritude movement.*]

[*Warner*]: *Do you think that when you started writing you did so mainly out of the urge to be productive from a literary point of view, or rather out of the urge to convey a particular message? If message there was, did you think that poetry was the vehicle to convey it?*

[Damas]: There was definitely a message. A cultural one first of all, and a political one. We cannot separate culture from politics. Nobody can do that. All the revolutions on the world succeed chiefly by the message of the poets.

You say by the message of the poets . . .

Poets and writers.

It is noticeable that most of the early négritude writing was by poets.

Yes, and thanks to négritude you had the end of French colonialism and the independence of Africa—thanks to négritude and to people who were not African, that's Césaire and myself.

I have found that in most of the talk of négritude, mention is made of the big three: Senghor, Césaire, and Damas, but I think you rank about the least known. Does this arouse any sort of feeling in you? How do you react to this?

There is no particular feeling. In Vermont at the Conference on Black Francophone Literature, they asked me, "Who is the father of négritude?" I said, "I'm fed up of all that. I don't understand why négritude needs so many fathers." Anyway I recalled an African proverb. I said that in Africa we don't know our fathers, we know our mothers. Now, the man who coined the word "Négritude" was Aimé Césaire, and Senghor has been obliged to admit this. But, for many reasons, Senghor is first now, the father of négritude. In Vermont they asked me who I was among the three. I said, "Perhaps I'm the Holy Spirit." But I can't be bothered by the attitude of some critics towards me. Why? Because I have the conviction that my work constitutes an important message, and **Pigments** has been not only the first book of its generation, **Pigments** has been the manifesto of the négritude movement.

More so than Césaire's Cahier d'un retour au pays natal?

Well, all the poets who came after **Pigments** were obliged to use material from the poems that *comprise* it. All the themes of **Pigments,** all the ideas in it have been taken, and from that period till now I see nothing new.

In other words you were way ahead of your time.

Yes. And at any rate, **Pigments** has been and still is a very big movement. I'm waiting for the new poets, the new writers and I'm waiting for what they can bring us that is new.

Can you point to a specific example of how **Pigments** *has become a movement?*

From **Pigments** you have a new movement in the United States—Soul Poetry. I'm not afraid to say that in my poetry you find rhythm. My poems can be danced. They can be sung. And what are they doing now? They sing poetry, soul music, soul literature, even soul food. At any rate you have a new generation in the states. I talk about the States because there are millions of black people living here.

I wonder though, whether bringing song and dance back into poetry, the new generation as you call them is not just going back to poetry in its true form. I am reminded of Paul Valéry calling a volume of poems Charmes, *using the word in its etymological sense, that is songs or poems from the Latin "carmen". Anyway, since you started to talk about American blacks, let me ask another question along that line. Do you see some more connections between your works and those of American blacks?*

Négritude has been the French expression of the New Negro movement and soul poetry is now the American expression of the négritude movement.

Now, the big three négritude poets all went into politics at

I think my best book is *Black-Label*. *Pigments* was a manifesto of the négritude movement, but the plain explanation of *Pigments* can be found in *Black-Label* and in *Retour de Guyane*.

— *Léon-Gontran Damas*

---

a particular time. Two are still there, while you have quit the political scene. What is the reason for this? Did you become disenchanted with politics or are you waiting for le coup final?

First of all we belong to different countries. I'm not an islander. I'm a man of the forest. I'm from a continent. We don't belong to the same social background. I'm from French Guyana and the problems there are not the same as the problems in Martinique or Guadeloupe or even Africa. Similarly, the problems of Africa are not the problems of the French West Indies. You see, I'm a man like my land—they accept me or reject me. And I accept or reject. I never vary in my position.

Is this why since **Pigments** *you have not published anything quite as forceful? Have you said it all in* **Pigments**?

No, I think my best book is ***Black-Label***. ***Pigments*** was a manifesto of the movement, but the plain explanation of ***Pigments*** can be found in ***Black-Label*** and in ***Retour de Guyane***.

Do you find that critics have misjudged what you were trying to say?

All the critics of négritude know nothing of the work of Senghor, nothing of the entire work of Césaire, nothing of my entire work. They just talk about négritude and about our works from pieces they read in anthologies. For example, they talk mainly about *Cahier d'un retour au pays natal*, ignoring *Corps Perdu, Ferrements, Cadastre, Discours sur le colonialisme,* etc. Now thanks to Senghor, Césaire and myself, we stayed the way we were in the beginning and all our books, after the first, were explanations of the first. And that's why, for many reasons, for political ones especially, Senghor has a big market now, Césaire is well known in Europe and elsewhere. As for myself, I'm as well known as Césaire and Senghor because we are the big three of négritude. They can't talk about Césaire and Senghor, and I'm fed up about that, without talking about Damas. At any rate, Senghor always pays us tribute, Césaire too, I suppose.

Speaking of Césaire, what can somebody like him do as a writer in a small country since he is fighting a world problem? Writing books cannot really help the situation in Martinique.

But Césaire's books are not read in Martinique.

Do you think they should be read in Martinique?

They refused.

Who refused?

His own people. First of all, the people who should read Césaire are illiterate, and that's why Césaire is obliged now to talk in créole. There is a cultural movement now, that's in créole. All the speeches are done in créole in Guadeloupe and Martinique. I don't know for French Guyana.

Do you see this as evidence of the fact that authors are finally realizing that they were above the level of the people? Are the writers finally coming down to the people?

No, that's another problem. It's the problem of education which obliged the people to read French authors, not native ones, and there is another problem—these people are not published in Martinique or Guadeloupe, they are published in France. Also the best readers of Césaire and myself are white French people.

As writers were you aware of this, that you were publishing for whites mainly?

You see, it's not the same situation as in the United States. You do not have as many readers in Martinique, Guadeloupe and French Guyana. You do not have a public, a mass of readers. You just have an elite, and you have people who can buy some of the books, and these books are very expensive.

What I want to find out is whether in writing for a white audience you did not subconsciously change what you were saying, whereas if you were writing for a black audience it would be quite different.

No, there was no conscious change.

Where do you find your readers?

You have some people who read Césaire and myself in French Guyana and in Martinique, but I suppose we are read by West Indians who live abroad in France or elsewhere but not in Martinique. And we shall be read now because in France at the Sorbonne they will organize a course on Négritude from next year. Perhaps the programme will be obliged to include the works of Césaire and other African writers. But in Martinique they are afraid to be confused with Africans. They criticize those writers for being too African.

The African writers?

No. They criticize Césaire and myself for our Africanness, our race consciousness because they tell you they are not Africans. They are créoles, they are French before being black, they are Martiniquans, they are Guadeloupeans, with nothing to do with Africa. And they say that if Césaire writes so many things about Africa, it's because he wants one day to be president of Martinique. Anyway, I suppose he's fed up with politics now and with the attitude of his brothers and sisters of Martinique.

And what about you? How do you stand in relation to the struggle?

I have to fight and will continue to fight. I help and continue to help. But I never published what I have to publish and what I shall publish now.

Is this more literary material? More essays?

More essays and poems. I now have to write the true history of the négritude movement. All those people who published, and chiefly Lilyan Kesteloot, recognise that they've been helped to publish what they did.

When you say that you are ready to tell the truth about the movement, it sounds as if we've been told a lot of lies. Is this so?

Yes. So many people have published books, theses and articles without knowing anything. They try to oppose me to Senghor and Césaire, but I can tell you that this will never happen. I know Senghor and Césaire. I know their foibles, their faults and they know my qualities and defects. But, as we began together, we have to stay together. They know that the historian of the movement will be Damas.

They know this?

Yes, and they are waiting.

I was about to ask whether we could expect the same type of revelation from Senghor and Césaire as well.

No. I suppose that they continue to work by themselves, but without doing what I am doing now—researching and studying our attitude, our way of life, but in a specific way. We can't talk of négritude if we don't take care of our psychological and sociological problems, our anthropological problem, our geographical problem.

Speaking of our geographical problem, what role does the West Indian play as a West Indian as opposed to as a black man?

He has to put out front chiefly West Indian problems, not African ones or problems of the négritude movement.

In other words we get back to the whole question of commitment.

Yes. The West Indian has to create something new based on the West Indian background. This he can do thanks to the race consciousness the awareness he received from us. We did not succeed on the political scene with the West Indian federation, but in the cultural field you will see many West Indians creating a new writing, and from this perhaps Africa will take something, the same way Africa received something from the French West Indies by way of the négritude movement.

Are you implying that Africa has more to learn from the West Indies than vice versa?

But even Senghor recognises that he discovered his Africanness through the West Indian Césaire and through me! He is not afraid to tell the truth.

Don't you think that the West Indian's race consciousness stems from the fact that he had undergone what the African had not, namely being taken away from his country?

Our experience has indeed been very great and the contribution of the West Indian to the liberation of the minds of black people has been very important.

Do you have a final word for your readers?

All I can ask is for people not to be in a hurry to see my publications.

Your works are there waiting to be published?

Yes, and there are many publishers waiting for my works. They don't understand why I'm not more published. But I don't publish merely to see my name on a book. I publish when I feel the need to say something.

Is this what motivated you in former publications?

I'm convinced that I contributed something by my studies in the literary field, in the political field. I'm not bothered about not being Député for French Guyana. There is plenty of time for that. That was a profession for others, not for me. It was just an occupation for me. I'm a writer, and when I decide, a teacher, like I am now.

So your message is now expounded in the classroom?

Teaching in the States is one way for me to help—to help today as I helped yesterday, and as I'm ready to help tomorrow.

Keith Q. Warner   (essay date 1973)

SOURCE: "New Perspective on Léon-Gontran Damas," in *Critical Perspectives on Léon-Gontran Damas,* edited by Keith Q. Warner, Three Continents Press, 1988, pp. 87-98.

[*In the following essay, which was originally published in the journal* Black Images *in 1973, Warner examines Damas's poetic techniques, particularly the poet's use of repetition, humor, and musical rhythm.*]

It is perhaps unfortunate that the name of Léon Damas is so often linked with those of Aimé Césaire and Léopold Senghor. The result is nearly always to the disadvantage of the French Guyanese poet, whose output is, to be candid, not as voluminous as that of the other two illustrious Negritude poets. The tendency seems to have been to study the various aspects of Césaire and Senghor while restricting analysis of Damas' works to his poems of protest in **Pigments.** This is not to imply that **Pigments** does not warrant analysis because of its great political and cultural impact, but those who examine Damas' poems solely for the Negritude manifesto they contain cut themselves off from some very refreshing aspects of the poems. Damas the fighter, the hater, the protester is well-documented, as are the reasons for the poet's wanting to fight, hate and protest. However, what about Damas the juggler of language, the subtle humorist, the singer of the blues, even the poet of love? It is thus interesting to examine these aspects of Damas along with the techniques and devices he used to achieve his aims.

In the years after the Second World War, and particularly in the theater in France, it became popular to show how writers were actually playing with the very language they were using. In this way, these authors showed how artificial language had become and also how modern man had ceased to fully appreciate the true impact of his language. Admittedly, the dramatists' use of language did vary from the poets', since, for the most part, their aim was not the same. The dramatists had other avenues open to them within the play, whereas the poets had to use the one poetic form, with only slight variations and innovations, whose very existence is its language. In the light of this, Damas must be credited with having had the foresight to re-direct our attention to the impact of language well-handled and to the vast potential of the "word". When of Damas, Senghor said that his poetry was unsophisticated, direct and brutal, it was a recognition of the fact that there was indeed power and vitality behind the apparently simple, everyday style of the poems.

In an interview that he accorded the present author in June 1972, Damas admitted that when he started writing poetry, it was out of a sense of commitment. The aspiring poet had a cultural and political message to convey, for, as he says, one cannot separate politics from culture. Thus, it is with justice that his admirers and critics have quoted passages like:

> Moi
> je leur dis merde
> et d'autres choses encore
>
> Me
> I say to them shit
> and other things as well

or:

> Alors
> je vous mettrai les pieds dans le plat
> ou bien tout simplement
> la main au collet
> de tout ce qui m'emmerde en gros caractères
> colonisation
> civilisation
> assimilation
> et la suite
>
> Then
> I'll stick my foot in it
> or quite simply
> grab by the throat
> everything that shits me up in capital letters
> colonisation
> civilisation
> assimilation
> and the rest

in support of their claim that Damas was full of fire and hatred in his dealings with white Europe, which had forced him to feel utterly ridiculous

> dans leurs souliers
> dans leur smoking
> dans leur plastron
> dans leur faux-col
> dans leur monocle
> dans leur melon
>
> in their shoes
> in their dinner jacket
> in their shirt-front
> in their collar
> in their monocle
> in their bowler hat

while having his hands horribly red with the blood of their "ci-vi-li-sa-tion". Those who have ever seen Damas read

his poems are immediately struck by the permanent smile on his face as he reads. There is certainly no visible venom, no loud denunciations, no table-banging or chest-pounding, only a slight frown and a mischievous smile. This outward appearance of the poet may indeed be misleading, and may not in fact truly represent what the young colonial felt at the time he was writing. It does, however, cause one to see in these poems another facet to which only sparse attention has been paid hitherto in the enthusiastic response to the written venom. One realizes how much the poet is playing with the language he is using.

Unlike the poetry of Senghor, with its long, flowing verset, full of images and explanations, Damas' poetry is almost abrupt, with frequent repetition, very short lines and numerous typographical variations. Damas' use of repetition goes beyond the normal desire for insistance or effect. He uses it as a potent linguistic weapon, elevating it to the level of a musical art form. The repetitions are of several types—of one word, of several words, of types of adverbs, adjectives, of whole stanzas, of nearly everything that catches the fancy of the poet at the moment of writing. Here, for example, is one of the simpler instances of repetition:

> Mes amis j'ai valsé
> valsé toute mon enfance
> vagabondant sur
> quelque Danube bleu
> Danube blanc
> Danube rouge
> Danube vert
> Danube rose
> Danube blanc
> rouge
> vert
> rose
> au choix
>
> Mes amis j'ai valsé
> valsé
> follement valsé
>
> My friends I have waltzed
> waltzed throughout my childhood
> wandering along
> some blue Danube
> white Danube
> red Danube
> green Danube
> pink Danube
> white Danube
> red
> green
> pink
> as you wish
> My friends I have waltzed
> waltzed
> madly waltzed

Apart from what one could term the normal repetitive process, there seems to be a sort of charm exerted by the words on the poet, so that he continues to explore every possibility open to him while he is using them. He seems, too, to enjoy the elements of surprise that he is introducing, in this case with respect to the Danube, as we can see from his re-introduction of the adjectives used to describe the river and his invitation to his readers to take their pick "au choix". We find this process of re-introduction of elements already used in another poem, **"Bientôt"**:

> Bientôt
> je n'aurai pas que dansé
> bientôt
> je n'aurai pas que chanté
> bientôt
> je n'aurai pas que frotté
> bientôt
> je n'aurais pas que trempé
> bientôt
> je n'aurai pas que dansé
> chanté
> frotté
> trempé
> frotté
> chanté
> dansé
>   Bientôt

> Soon
> I'll not only have danced
> soon
> I'll not only have sung
> soon
> I'll not only have rubbed
> soon
> I'll not only have soaked
> soon
> I'll not only have danced
> sung
> rubbed
> soaked
> rubbed
> sung
> danced
>   Soon

As can be seen, the entire poem is built on the repetitive form, which in turn gives it its circular movement, hence a feeling of completeness. For all this, the poem is extremely simple in form and once more manifests Damas' ability to juggle with the language he is using.

Repetition of key words and phrases sometimes leads to a dizzying complexity of terms which just fall short of being tongue-twisters. How else can one describe the beginning of **"Ils ont"**?

> Ils ont si bien su faire
> si bien su faire les choses
> les choses
> qu'un jour nous avons tout
> nous avons tout foutu de nous-mêmes
> tout foutu de nous-mêmes en l'air

> They did so well
> did their thing so well
> their thing that one day we completely
> we completely destroyed what we had
> just blew our thing sky high

It would be in fact difficult to read such lines very quickly and the slower reading that is forced upon us actually makes us aware of how much the poet succeeded in manipulating his language in order to achieve particular ef-

fects. It is obvious that when a poet begins eleven consecutive lines of verse with the same noun, as Damas does in the poem from the *Névralgies* collection, **"Sang satisfait du sens ancien du dit"**, he is doing so for more than a casual attempt at directing our attention to that particular word—"sang" in this instance. The poet seems to be prey to a quasi-obsession with extracting the fullest potential from the words on the page. This desire to extract to the fullest all that words are capable of at times leads Damas to the creation of unusual lines of verse, such as these from **"Pour toi et moi"**:

> Dos à dos je ne
> Dos à dos tu ne
> Dos à dos je ne sais
> Dos à dos tu ne sais
> je ne
> tu ne
> nous
> nous ne savons l'un autre
> plus rien de l'un
> plus rien de l'autre

> Back to back I do not
> back to back you do not
> back to back I do not know
> back to back you do not know
> I do not
> you do not
> we
> we know not you and I
> anything further about the one
> anything further about the other

In this case, one finds Damas using lines like "je ne" and "tu ne" which are definitely unusual and contrary to the expectations of popular usage in French.

An extension of the technique of repetition is the lengthy listings that the poet uses, especially when he is showing the faults of the oppressors or the attributes of his black brothers. In *Black Label*, Damas combines the two processes to come up with:

> car la beauté est nègre
> est nègre la sagesse
> car l'endurance est nègre
> est nègre le courage
> car la patience est nègre
> est nègre l'ironie
> car le charme est nègre
> est nègre la magie
> car l'amour est nègre
> est nègre le déhanchement
> car la danse est nègre
> est nègre le rhythme
> car l'art est nègre
> est nègre le mouvement
> car le rire est nègre
> car la joie est nègre
> car la paix est nègre
> car la vie est nègre

> for beauty is black
> and wisdom black
> for endurance is black
> and courage black
> for patience is black
> and irony black

for charm is black
and magic black
for charm is black
and hip swinging black
for dance is black
and rhythm black
for art is black
and movement black
for laughter is black
for joy is black
for peace is black
for life is black

There is a force in such listings that takes the ordinary statement and weaves it into poetic beauty. The same effect is noticeable in his poem **"Limbé"**, appropriately **"Blues"**, where Damas lists all that "they" have stolen from him, some twenty different things, each in its own line just the one noun: customs / days / song / rhythm / effort, etc. It is in poems such as these that one can readily perceive the difference between Damas and, say, someone like Césaire, or even Senghor. Whereas the uninitiated may often find it difficult wading through the wealth of complex images in Césaire and in Senghor, Damas does not waste words, that is assuming that one does not qualify deliberate repetition as waste. The poet goes directly to the point, driving home his "message" with a minimum of fuss.

If we have dealt at such length with Damas' use of repetition in the language of his poems, it is mainly because this process far surpasses the rest throughout Damas' poetry. But, as can be easily seen, there are in fact others—alliteration and pun among them. These all combine to produce a strain of humor which at times surprises the reader unfamiliar with Damas' techniques. One cannot escape the impression that in many of the poems, beneath all the suffering and pain, there still remains a sly dig at the enemy through more than a hint of a smile. This would indeed explain the surprising twist to so many of the poems. This is not to say that Damas takes his problems lightly, but he allows himself a degree of humor that the white enemy could not possibly attain or understand. In this he closely parallels the humor of early American blacks who for many years were forced, in the terms of Langston Hughes, a great personal friend of Damas, to laugh in order to keep from crying. His is therefore a personal humor and one that fellow blacks can understand and share. The colonizer, for example, would see nothing humorous in the last line of the following:

Terrain privé
Domaine reservé
Defense d'entrer
Ni chiens ni nègre sur le gazon

Private grounds
Guarded estate
No entry
No dogs or niggers on the grass

One has to be a part of the whole experience to fully appreciate how one could indeed view such (the lines actually represent warning signs) as something else beside insulting and tragic.

Perhaps the finest example of Damas' humor occurs in the poem **"Hoquet"** (**"Hiccups"**) which the poet says is his favorite. Here, all the techniques already mentioned blend to produce a neat indictment of the artificial upbringing that the Damas family strived for. There is repetition of the refrain "Désastre / parlez-moi du désastre / parlez-m'en" (Disaster / talk about disaster / tell me about it), a refrain in which the poet definitely has his tongue in his cheek as he breaks off from describing his mother's hypocritical admonitions. Damas resorts to some novel type lines as he pictures the mother extremely put out at the fact that her son should want to channel her precious music lessons into learning the banjo and guitar instead of the violin:

Ma mère voulant d'un fils très do
très ré
très mi
très fa
très sol
très la
très si
très do
re-mi-fa
sol-la-si
do
do

Il m'est revenu que vous n'étiez encore pas
à votre leçon de vi-o-lon
vous dites un banjo
comment dites-vous
un banjo
vous dites bien
un banjo
Non monsieur
vous saurez qu'on ne souffre chez nous
ni ban
ni jo
ni gui
ni tare
les *mulâtres* ne font pas ça
laissez donc ça aux *nègres*

My mother wanting a son very do
very re
very mi
very fa
very so
very la
very ti
very do
re-mi-fa
so-la-ti
do

I understand that once again
you missed your vi-o-lin lesson
a banjo
you said
a banjo
what did you say
a banjo
No sir
you must know that we do not allow in this
    house
neither ban
nor jo
nor gui
nor tar

mulattos don't do that
leave that for *black people*

This is Damas at his very best, using all that was dear to him as he moved along to the climax of the distinction between mulattos and blacks.

Naturally, it would be false to give the impression that Damas sees himself as a humorist. The main claim here has been that the poet's humor is an integral part of the whole make-up of the poems, especially those in **Pigments.** Even in those poems in which Damas is being admittedly hard on those who were responsible for his condition and that of his fellow blacks, the poet often slips in a line or two showing that he is still able to smile under the suffering. The poem **"S.O.S."** clearly demonstrates how Damas achieves this combination of pathos and humor simply by inserting the unexpected into his stanza:

A ce moment-là seul
comprendrez-vous donc tous
quand leur viendra l'idée
bientôt cette idée leur viendra
de vouloir vous en bouffer du nègre
à la manière d'Hitler
bouffant du juif
sept jours fascistes
sur
Sept

Then only then
will you all understand
when they get the idea
soon they'll be getting the idea
to want to stuff themselves with niggers
just like Hitler
stuffing himself with Jews
seven fascist days
out of
seven

It is not too difficult to imagine the poet silently smiling to himself as he wrote about this bizarre idea of "their" wanting to "bouffer du nègre" or, as he wrote later on in the same poem, to "couper leur sexe aux nègres pour en faire des bougies pour leurs églises" (to cut off black men's genitals to make candles for their churches). There are many other instances similar to this one, though they may not always be readily perceived unless the reader is willing to take a fresh look at Damas' poems.

Another aspect of the poems that could well be re-examined is that of their music. It has often been pointed out that Damas' poetry is full of rhythm and that it evokes the world of jazz. One could add that many of the poems are reminiscent of the blues songs of the American blacks, as they do have many of the elements common to the blues—the nostalgic first person recollection of things past, suffering, problems with the loved one, the constant yearning for better things to come. Just as the blues singer finds some solace in singing about his plight, so too does Damas lighten his internal burdens by writing about them in words that have only to be set to music. One has only to go back to the discussion of the poet's constant use of repetition to realize that some of these have an air of a lament about them, as if the poet were slowly singing to the strumming of a guitar or to the beat of a drum. The poem

"Bientôt", already quoted, would be a good example of this, as is the poem **"Limbé"** (**"Blues"**), with its repetitive insistence "Rendez-les moi mes poupées noires" ("Give me back my black dolls"). There are poems in which the sound of the words have a definite melodious air:

Nuits sans nom
nuits sans lune

. . . . .

sans nom
sans lune
sans lune
sans nom
nuits sans lune
sans nom sans nom

Nights with no name
nights with no moon
no name
no moon
no moon
no name
nights with no moon
no name no name

It is apparent that Damas is here exploiting the musical aspect of the French to the fullest. Fortunately, on this occasion the English version does manage to re-capture some of the same musicality. Whether Damas would have been as musical had he been writing in another language is not really important. The fact remains that he had to use the only language he knew, and this he did with dexterity, exploring the full potential of a language that lends itself to musical interpretation.

Nowhere does Damas indicate, like Senghor, whether he meant his poems to be accompanied by particular instruments. There is, however, frequent mention in the poems of a variety of dances and musical instruments: bolero, swing, tango, banjo, guitar, trumpet and, of course, the tom-tom, whose rhythm and beat are captured typographically in the poem **"Ils sont venus ce soir"**:

Ils sont venus ce soir où le
tam
   tam
  roulait de
    rythme
     en
       rythme

They came that evening when the
tom
  tom
  rolled from
    rhythm
     to
      rhythm

This typographical variation, already popular among the French Surrealist poets, was another device that Damas exploited whenever he felt it could be of help to him, as in the case in the poem cited where it helps turn the spoken word into song. Therefore, when Damas said, in the interview already mentioned, "my poems can be danced, they can be sung," it was no idle boast made from a lack of modesty. The poet must have known how he had constructed his poetry to be able to make such a statement.

There remains one final aspect of Damas' poetry that is hardly mentioned in most analyses—namely his variations on the theme of love, contained mainly in his collection *Névralgies.* Damas' poems of love show no trace of the poet's race, unlike those of Senghor which nearly always extol the virtues of the black woman. If, however, there is no trace of racial hatred or racial love, there is, nonetheless, the same technique that we have seen throughout the now typical Damas poem. This he uses to portray the universal lover in all his moods, happy when the loved one is near, sad when she is absent, jealous when he thinks that she is with someone else. The following lines may surprise those who have always thought of Damas as a poet of hate, those who have not looked beyond the Négritude manifesto of some of his poems, but should be easily recognizable as being from the type of lines that Damas would produce, with their repetition, juggling with words, typographical variations and their musicality:

> Quoique tu fasses
> ou que tu sois
> quoique tu veuilles
> et surtout
> quoique l'on dise
> quoique l'on fasse
> quoique l'on veuille
> et dise
> et fasse
> et veuille
> tu seras *ma chose*

> Whatever you do
> wherever you are
> whatever you wish
> and above all
> whatever they say
> whatever they do
> whatever they wish
> and say
> and do
> and wish
> you'll be *my thing*

Damas' poetry, therefore, should not be seen merely as an incitement to black consciousness, though this remains a very important part of it. If one were to return for a while to the old argument over the separation of form and function, one would find that, in Damas' poems, the function is effective mainly because of the form; there can be no separation of the one from the other. As such, it is doing the poet a disservice to continue to look exclusively at what he achieved without also examining the way in which he set out to achieve it.

E. A. Hurley   (essay date 1974)

SOURCE: *"Pigments—A Dialogue with Self,"* in *Critical Perspectives on Léon-Gontran Damas,* edited by Keith Q. Warner, Three Continents Press, 1988, pp. 99-110.

[Hurley is a Barbadian educator and critic. In the following essay, which was originally published in the journal Black Images *in 1974, he interprets* Pigments *as an internal dialogue.]*

It is understandable that it has been the practice to identi-

fy Léon Damas, the author of *Pigments,* as one of the leaders, along with Césaire and Senghor, of the Négritude movement. It is beyond question that the orientation of his first collection of poetry, published in 1937, around the themes of color and race, assimilation and colonization, as well as his expressed support of the ideals of Négritude lend weight to such a claim. It is true, too, that, like Césaire and Senghor, he demonstrated that his commitment to the principle of black liberation was not restricted to mere writing, however effective and important this may be, by engaging actively in politics in French Guyana. However, it would not be unfair to say of him that he lacks the poetic vision of Césaire and the cultural self-confidence of Senghor, or that, in the political sphere, he lacks the charismatic appeal of both of his colleagues. The simple fact is that he is not, either in politics or in literature, a leader.

As the present study will demonstrate, even though *Pigments* may be regarded as the first political statement in poetry by a French Caribbean writer, basically Damas is not speaking here on behalf of or to the particular racial group with which he identifies; he is really speaking for and to himself. *Pigments,* in fact, emerges as essentially a personal, if not private statement, which involves a conversation that the poet holds with himself. In order to understand this more clearly, we need to consider the components of the personality and sensibility of Damas which lead him to produce such poetry; we need to see Damas as an extremely sensitive individual, whose attitude to himself and to life in general was complicated by certain experiential factors: for example, his sickliness as a child, the assimilated bourgeois environment in which he was brought up, his experience of racial prejudice and ridicule in Paris, as well as, of course, his association with Césaire, Senghor and other black students in the metropolis. This list of factors, though obviously not comprehensive, is sufficient to suggest that racial consciousness should not be the sole or even major framework within which the poetry of Damas should be approached. His early physical fragility and his evident general psychological insecurity, strongly suggest repression and introversion as well as the constantly suppressed desire to react violently, and certainly predispose him to oversensitive responses to the stimuli provided by social contacts. This internal tension with which he has to cope can be observed throughout *Pigments* and in fact acts as the motive force behind his poetry. Whatever balance Damas is able to maintain depends on his self-control, on his exploitation of poetry itself as a kind of safety-valve, as is illustrated by his use of understatement and ellipsis, and ironic self-directed humor. It would therefore be a mistake to regard *Pigments* simply as committed "black" literature, created directly and deliberately out of the author's sense of responsibility towards his people. It would be fairer to Damas to consider it as a means of maintaining equilibrium, and as a dialogue between the poet and his inner self.

Pigments demonstrated Damas' concern over the two major problems which he is trying to resolve: on the one hand, the problem of defining his identity; on the other, that of examining the choices of response to his situation that are open to him. In other words, it is as if he continually asks himself both "who am I?" and "what am I to do?" Because there is no simple or straightforward answer to either question he is forced to enter into a kind of poetic dialogue with himself in order to clarify the issues involved.

It would be a mistake to regard *Pigments* simply as committed "black" literature, created directly and deliberately out of the author's sense of responsibility towards his people. It would be fairer to Damas to consider it as a means of maintaining equilibrium, and as a dialogue between the poet and his inner self.

—E. A. Hurley

As far as the first question is concerned, Damas' approach is to consider himself in relation to others, to base his identity on the recognition of a difference that exists between himself and a "they" that he not only does not have to qualify but also about whom he is rarely explicit. His answer to this question, therefore, is obviously "I am not 'they'". This accounts for the frequency with which this "moi"/"ils" ("I"/"they") distinction occurs throughout ***Pigments.*** In the first poem of the collection, **"Ils sont venus ce soir,"** the undefined "they" exist only in opposition to an "I" whose African identity is not stated, but merely suggested by the dedication of the poem to Senghor, by the reference to tom-toms, as well as by the implied historical fact of slavery:

> Ils sont venus ce soir où le
> tam
>   tam
>   roulait de
>   rythme
>   en
>   rythme
>   la frénésie
> des yeux
>
>   . . . . .
>
> DEPUIS
> combien de MOI MOI MOI
> sont morts

> They came that night when the
>   tom
>   rolled out from
>   rhythm
>   to
>   rhythm
>   the frenzy
> of eyes
>
>   . . . . .
>
> SINCE THEN
> how many I I I
> have died

In this case the "they", which he is not, are evidently the original European exploiters of the African continent. He makes the same distinction, between himself as African and exploited and Europeans as exploiters, in **"Limbé,"** as he expresses strong nostalgic longing for his "black dolls", the equally vague "they" being presented as thieves and robbers: "A l'oeil de ma méfiance ouvert trop tard / Ils ont cambriolé l'espace que était mien" (Before the eyes of my mistrust open too late / they have looted the space that was mine). The inner dialogue, therefore, enables him to define himself not only as being different from these "others" but also as having been exploited by them. As he pursues the conversation, he establishes a clear line of continuity between the original exploiters and contemporary "theys" (obviously white Europeans) who seek to rob him of a meaningful identity:

> Se peut-il donc qu'ils osent
> me traiter de blanchi
> alors que tout en moi
> aspire à n'être que nègre
> autant que mon Afrique
> qu'ils on cambriolée
>   **("Blanchi")**

> Is it then possible that they dare
> treat me as near-white
> when everything in me
> aspires to be only black
> as black as my Africa
> that they have looted

To the factor of the exploited/exploiter distinction is added that of a color, i.e. black/white, distinction and implicitly also an Africa/Europe distinction. This means that he further defines himself as African and as black. So far the conversational line is dependent mainly on Damas' historical perspective. What is of pre-eminent importance to him, however, is his relation to the world in which he is living. He has, therefore, to direct the topic to a discussion of his present situation, which is characterized for him by a feeling of acute discomfort, arising out of the fact of his assimilation into a society that he regards as alien, as his continued use of the "I/they" distinction illustrates:

> J'ai l'impression d'être ridicule
> dans leurs souliers
> dans leur smoking
> dans leur plastron
> dans leur faux-col
> dans leur monocle
> dans leur melon
>   **("Solde")**

> I feel ridiculous
> in their shoes
> in their dinner-jacket
> in their shirt-front
> in their collar
> in their monocle
> in their bowler-hat

Within the same contemporary context, the essentially existential discomfort he experiences within the alien society (which we know to be European, although he has not defined it expressly as such) is paralleled by a similar discomfort in the sphere of European political and racial chauvinism, as he realizes and implies that the relationship between colonized blacks and white colonizers (presumably French) is no different from that between Jews and Nazis:

A ce moment-là seul
comprendrez-vous donc tous
quand leur viendra l'idée
bientôt cette idée leur viendra
de vouloir vous en bouffer du nègre
à la manière d'Hitler
bouffant du juif
sept jours fascistes
sur
sept
                    ("S.O.S.")

Then and only then
will you all understand
when it occurs to them
and it will soon occur to them
to want to stuff themselves with niggers
just like Hitler
stuffing himself with jews
seven fascist days
out of
seven

He makes the further point to himself, therefore, that there exists a direct connection between the original enslavement and exploitation of his black African ancestors and the more recent colonization and assimilation and potential extermination of blacks like himself. As he attempts to clarify the issues involved, to establish a separate identity, he suggests another difference between the self he wants to isolate and preserve and a civilization which he can reject as having been and as still being degenerate and decaying:

et mon rêve qui se nourrit du bruit de leur
dé-
    gé-
        né-
            rescence
est plus fort que leurs gourdins d'immondices
                    ("Shine")

and my dreams that feed on the noise of their
de-
    gen-
        er-
            ation
is stronger than their cudgels of filth

This first part of the dialogue, in which he attempts to resolve the problem of his identity, is the only one which results in a definite conclusion; he is completely sure that he (exploited, black and African) is not "they" (exploiters, whites and Europeans); this is the only fact of the reality of his existence about which he has no doubt. As we shall see shortly, the other possible answers he suggests to the question "whom am I?" reveal a profound uncertainty, in the sense that in each case he seems to qualify whatever response he gives by saying to himself "yes, but I don't want to be". Every other aspect of his identity is affected by environmental factors which he has to concede grudgingly but which he should like to reject as alien. The poem **"Hoquet",** for example, admirably illustrates his unwillingness to accept the fact that he is as well the product of an early bourgeois upbringing which he despises and regards as one of the great tragedies of his life:

Et j'ai beau avaler sept gorgées d'eau
trois à quatre fois par vingt-quatre heures
me revient mon enfance
dans un hoquet secouant
mon instinct
tel le flic le voyou
Désastre
parlez-moi du désastre
parlez-m'en

And in vain I swallow seven mouthfuls of water
three or four times in every twenty-four hours
my childhood returns to me
in a hiccup shaking
my instinct
like a cop shaking a hooligan

Disaster
tell me about disaster
tell me about it

He realizes his impotence to escape the "disaster" of his early life, he is, as he is forced to admit, inevitably and involuntarily (as the "hiccup" image indicates) what particularly his assimilated, class-conscious mother made him. Similarly, despite his claims of being different from the "they" we discussed above, he has to face the bitter truth that he is assimilated into "their" civilization. What goes through his mind is that whilst he is not basically like "them", he has nevertheless become like "them", even though he does not want to be:

J'ai l'impression d'être ridicule
parmi eux complice
parmi eux souteneur
parmi eux égorgeur
les mains effroyablement rouges
du sang de leur ci-vi-li-sa-tion
                    ("Solde")

I feel ridiculous
an accomplice among them
a pimp among them
a murderer among them
my hands horribly red
with the blood of their
civ-il-i-za-tion

The discomfort which he experiences helps him to understand more clearly his own complicity. He has the courage, however, to face up to this aspect of his identity, which is brought out mainly through the honesty and lucidity with which the inner dialogue is conducted. Ironically, both his discomfort and his awareness of complicity help him to realize that he is, additionally, an exile in the alien environment of Paris; it is precisely because he has no desire to be that he conjures up visions of his own black women:

Rendez-les moi mes poupées noires
qu'elles dissipent
l'image des catin blêmes
marchands d'amour qui s'en vont viennent
sur le boulevard de mon ennui
                    ("Limbé")

Give them back to me my black dolls
to erase
the image of the pale sluts
dealers in love who walk up and down
on the boulevard of my boredom

The fact is that Damas' integrity and frankness with himself continually reveal to him and to us aspects of his identity which, literally, he can hardly stomach. It is for this reason that there are several references in *Pigments* to his experiencing sensations of nausea. [In a footnote, Hurley states that this is particularly evident in the poems **"Obsession"**, **"Il est des nuits"**, and **"Rappel"**.] This is related, too, to the fact that one of the most pervasive emotions felt by Damas when he looks clear-sightedly at himself is a feeling of shame, which finds its most direct expression in **"Réalité"**:

De n'avoir jusqu'ici rien fait
détruit
bâti
osé
à la maniére
du Juif
du Jaune
pour l'évasion organisée en masse
de l'infériorité

C'est en vain que je cherche
le creux d'une épaule
où cacher mon visage
ma honte
de
  la
    Ré
     a
      li
       té

Having so far done nothing
destroyed nothing
built nothing
dared nothing
like Jews
and the Yellow races
for the organized mass escape
from inferiority

In vain I seek
the hollow of a shoulder
to hide my face
my shame
of
Re
  a
   li
    ty

Evidently, in talking to himself, Damas is struck forcefully by the tragic futility of his existence. His analysis of his identity in *Pigments* may be regarded as both the result and the expression not only of a deep-rooted feeling of impotence, as far as revolutionary action is concerned, but also of, as he admits, an inability finally to move outside himself, to be anything but egocentric—a basic personality trait which he would like to reject:

Trêve un instant
d'une vie de bon enfant

et de désirs
et de besoins
et d'égoismes
particuliers

          ("Trêve")

Enough for a while
of a good boy life
and of private
desires
needs
and selfishness

This indicates clearly Damas' recognition of the essentially personal motives that lie at the root of most of his actions. The identity about which he is most concerned is not that of the mass of exploited black people but simply his own.

Having closely examined himself in an attempt to define who and what he is, Damas still has to explore the choices of action and reaction that are available to him. The second part of the dialogue, therefore, centers around discussion of the question which he poses to himself: "what am I to do?" Note that, as I am suggesting, *Pigments* is fundamentally a dialogue, so that whatever responses Damas makes are not intended to be stimuli to action that may be taken either by Damas himself or by others but simply as possibilities which he considers but which may finally be rejected. What emerges clearly from his examination of the question of his identity is his acute dissatisfaction with his condition as an exploited black man vis-à-vis European whites. It is to be expected, therefore, that he should want to change such a condition, even to react, and violently, against the unacceptable and unbearable situation in which he finds himself. There is, undoubtedly, running through *Pigments,* a strong suggestion of almost uncontrollable hatred and violent emotion. It is significant, however, in support of the contention that *Pigments* is really a dialogue, rather than an incitement to revolutionary action to be taken by blacks or even the expression of a commitment to the ideal of black liberation, that only once in the entire collection of poems, in **"Si Souvent"**, does Damas suggest directly the necessity for violent revolt as a solution to his present problems:

Et rien
rien ne saurait autant calmer ma haine
qu'une belle mare
de sang
faite
de ces coutelas tranchants
qui mettent à nu
les mornes à rhum

And nothing
nothing could still my hatred
as much as a fine pool
of blood
made
by those sharp cutlasses
which lay bare
the hills of rum

Even here, it must be noted, Damas' concern is purely personal; he is interested in the therapeutic value which violence, significantly performed by somebody else, may hold for him. In other poems, although Damas considers violent action, it is not regarded as a viable possibility in the present, but, as the tense he favors in this context indicates, as a possibility that belongs to the future:

> mais quelle bonne dynamite
> fera sauter la nuit
> les monuments comme champignons
> qui poussent aussi
> chez moi
>
>   **("Sur une carte postale")**
>
> But what good dynamite
> will blow up at night
> the monuments like mushrooms
> that grow too
> in my country

There are two points of interest here: firstly, the future tense and, secondly, the interrogative form used by Damas. They indicate not only that violence is not proposed as the form of action that he himself is prepared to undertake at the present time, but also simply that the whole idea is an almost random thought that crosses his mind in the course of his self-interrogation: Damas has not reached and will not reach the point of direct violent action; he is, and remains throughout *Pigments,* at the stage of reflection, of communing with himself. He suggests, nevertheless, that his own revolt is inevitable, but typically and significantly relegates this possibility to the future:

> Pour sûr j'en aurai
> marre
> sans même attendre
> qu'elles prennent
> les choses
> l'allure
> d'un camembert bien fait
> Alors
> je vous mettrai les pieds dans le plat
> ou bien tout simplement
> la main au collet
> de tout ce qui m'emmerde en gros caractères
> colonisation
> civilisation
> assimilation
> et la suite
>
> Sure enough I'll get
> fed up
> and not even wait
> for things
> to reach
> the state
> of a ripe camembert
> Then
> I'll put my foot in it
> or else simply
> my hand around the neck
> of everything that shits me up in capital letters
> colonization
> civilization
> assimilation
> and all the rest.

Once again, what stands out strongly is Damas' inner exasperation; the violence is all in his language and in his mind. Sometimes, characteristically, the frustration that seeks an outlet in violence is not even translated directly

into the language, but is only suggested, taking the comparatively mild form of an implicit, unspecific threat: "Bientôt / je n'aurai pas que dansé / bientôt" (Soon / I'll not only have danced / soon) (**"Bientôt"**). At other times, when the internal dialogue is centered on the notion of changing his situation as an alienated individual, revolt and violence are veiled to the point where they become little more than a vague hope, a possibility which, on the surface, appears to be the product of his optimism, but which deep down is merely the transposition of his despair for the present:

> Il ne faudrait pourtant pas grand'chose
> pourtant pas grand'chose
> grand'chose
> pour qu'en un jour enfin tout aille
> tout aille
> aille
> dans le sens de notre race à nous
>
>   **("Ils ont")**
>
> And yet it wouldn't take much
> yet not much
> much
> for one day finally everything to go
> everything to go
> to go
> in the direction of our own race

He is painfully aware of the hopelessness of the situation in which he finds himself and equally aware of his own selfishness and egocentricity (cf. **"Trêve"** quoted above), which prevent him both from moving outside himself and from taking effective retaliatory action. The doubts he has of himself inhibit him further, but he cannot repress the obsessive thought that he has to escape from this unbearable situation:

> nuits sans nom
> nuits sans lune
> où j'aurais voulu
> pouvoir ne plus douter
> tant m'obsède d'écoeurement
> un besoin d'évasion
>
>   **("Il est des nuits")**
>
> Nights with no name
> nights with no moon
> when I would have liked
> to be able to doubt no more
> so disgustingly obsessed am I
> by a need to escape

It seems as if Damas, in this dialogue with himself, reaches the conclusion that there is nothing to be done, since in the present all action is either futile or impossible. He is left, therefore, simply either expressing the anguish that results from this realization or shaking in impotent rage:

> Blanchi
> Abominable injure
> quand mon Afrique
> qu'ils ont cambriolée
> voudra la paix la paix rien que
> la paix
> Blanchi
> Ma haine grossit en marge
> de leur scélératesse

Near-white
Abominable insult
that they will pay me for very dearly
when my Africa
that they have looted
wants peace nothing but
peace
Near-white
My hatred grows along
with their villainy

It is clear that Damas' violent hatred, his feelings of frustration and impotence need to find some outlet. It is because of this that humor operates in *Pigments* as a kind of safety-valve. Damas' use of humor in language has already been commented on [by Keith Warner in "New Perspective on Léon-Gontran Damas", *Black Images* (1973)], but it can be argued additionally that what is important to an understanding of his intentions in this collection is not simply, although this is true, that Damas likes playing with words or that he laughs so as not to cry, but that, within the context of the dialogue which he has with himself, self-directed, ironic laughter is one of the logical responses to the question "what am I to do?" He cannot revolt, he cannot escape, he cannot move outside himself, he cannot even do nothing, he can only suffer, though not in silence, and laugh bitterly at himself. It is for this reason that he concludes the poem **"Pour sûr"**, quoted above, with anti-climactic self-derision: "En attandant / vous m'entendrez souvent / claquer la porte" (Meanwhile / you'll hear me often / slamming the door), since he fully realizes his impotence to do more than act symbolically.

It is important to note that the problems of identity and action are not resolved by Damas in *Pigments,* as they are by Césaire in his *Return to my native land.* Damas reaches only two definite conclusions in this collection: firstly that he is an exploited black man of African heritage and not a European, and secondly that something ought to be done about the unacceptable conditions of his existence which he shares with others like himself. Important as these conclusions doubtlessly are, they cannot however be regarded as firm statements of Damas' commitment to the ideal of black liberation which is one of the primary concerns of Négritude. The poems of *Pigments* are in their essence the product of an inner dialogue conducted between Damas the pseudo-European and Damas the newly-conscious black man, who in fact finds it necessary to hold this dialogue in order to be able to cope with the almost unbearable tensions that threaten to tear him apart. While it is true that he articulated in poetry, before either Césaire or Senghor, the feelings of the Négritude group, it is equally true that his sensitivity, affected by his unfortunate experiences as a student in Paris, played a larger part than for either of the others in determining his attachment to the ideals of Négritude. It is evident that his poetic vision is directed inwards rather than outwards. *Pigments* is the concrete expression of emotions that have been internalized; in this collection commitment is subordinated to emotionalism; the poems represent Damas' use of language as a personal means of escape and as a safety-valve rather than reflect his concern with awakening consciousness-in others. He is concerned less with laying the foundation for the liberation of oppressed black peoples than in achieving and maintaining a personal, inner harmony.

Damas's technique, whether his goal is direct social utterance or, . . . disinterested poetic utterance, or is a combination of the two, is best described as a jazz technique—endless theme and variation, incremental repetition, improvization, and a kind of verbal counterpoint that adds up to a most impressive expression of a trapped man's *négritude*.

—*C. E. Nelson, in a review of* Pigments, *in* Books Abroad, *Autumn 1963.*

Bridget Jones   (essay date 1975)

SOURCE: "Léon Damas," in *A Celebration of Black and African Writing,* edited by Bruce King and Kolawole Ogungbesan, Ahmadu Bello University Press, 1975, pp. 60-73.

[*Jones is an English-born Jamaican educator and critic. In the following essay, she provides an overview of Damas's career and works.*]

Léon Damas has received less attention than Senghor and Césaire. Out of a less abundant literary output, a few protest poems from *Pigments* (1937) are too often all that he is known by. Since his brief parliamentary career which ended in 1951, he has avoided the controversies of active politics and remained an exile whose main commitment is to the cause of international black consciousness. However, the complex personality of Damas cannot be reduced to the simplified image of Négritude's poet of hate, and there is much to celebrate both in his writing and in a teaching and publishing career devoted to promoting the liberation of black poets from the constraints of 'segregation, a slavishly imitative culture, colonization, spiritual assimilation' [introduction to *Nouvelle somme de poésie du monde noir*].

Born in Cayenne, French Guyana, in 1912, he shared philosophy classes with Aimé Césaire at the Lycée Schoelcher in Martinique, and moved on to Paris to study law in accordance with the ambitions of his middle-class family. He concentrates in his fragile person a racial sample of the Caribbean: there was Negro and Amerindian blood on his mother's side, and his father was a mulatto of partly European origin. He has expressed very forcibly his pain at being moulded into an *assimilé* by his upbringing as a child; the constant pressure from home and school to speak, behave and if possible think like a white Frenchman. Once a student he rebelled and affirmed himself a 'poète nègre', trying also by contacts and studies in ethnology to develop understanding of the African within him. It is later in life that he writes more calmly of the three rivers that run in his veins and stands 'upright in the triple pride of my mixed blood' [*Névralgies*], though never embracing Senghor's comfortable gospel of cultural synthesis.

Damas's first group of writings—the poems of *Pigments,* the French Guyanese folklore retold under the title *Veillées noires* (1935-43), and the report on his *Retour de Guyane* (1938)—combine to chart the same passionate self-discovery and rediscovery of the native land that we find in Césaire's *Cahier d'un retour au pays natal.* However, even a brief comparison highlights some of Damas's specific quality. He burst into print more quickly and fiercely; the poems 'Solde' and 'La complainte du nègre' for example, appeared in *Esprit* in 1934. Putting great emphasis on communicating his message, Damas prefers to use lucidly sarcastic prose to expose the failures of French colonialism and the assimilation policy. His deceptively naïve animal tales present a local folk culture in which African values triumphantly survive. The directness of his poetry is far closer in spirit and technique to an oral tradition than Césaire's subtle and erudite codes. His is an analytical intelligence gifted with a wickedly destructive wit, but unsuited to the sustained effort of will and imagination demanded by an epic poem. His work betrays the more radical self-doubt of the privileged colonial of mixed racial background and that indelible *rancune* he sees as specific to French Guyana.

Among a number of other factors, two influences seem especially strong in shaping Damas's attitudes and techniques. Firstly, he figures as the main heir to the spirit of *Légitime Défense,* an ephemeral little magazine produced in the margins of Surrealism in 1932 by Etienne Léro and other Martiniquan students. Their manner follows the Surrealist fashion for uninhibited abuse of the older generation, but their comments on the cultural situation are solidly founded on a Marxist analysis of their society. The pallidly imitative literature of the assimilated bourgeoisie is seen as a symptom of alienation. The Creole-speaking masses have no real access to education, and authentic local culture cannot flourish in a divided and exploited colonial society. René Ménil in particular uses the Surrealist conception of poetry for a very lucid critique of the 'écrivain antillais'. Damas responded deeply to these fighting words, re-using a number of the images and even syntactical tricks. However, he was not prepared to follow Léro and company in composing poetic exercises in the style of Breton or Dali.

A second major influence was Negro America. *Légitime Défense* had cited admiringly Afro-American poets, and included a key discussion from *Banjo.* As the researches of Michel Fabre have corroborated, Damas extended his knowledge of the New Negro movement through the *Revue du Monde Noir* (1929-32) and took advantage of personal contacts. With astute literary judgment he looked to Langston Hughes (later a personal friend) for a renewal based on the popular negro modes: blues, spirituals and the wealth of ballad and work songs. In McKay's novels he could find a heightened folk speech which caught something of the triumph of jazz rhythms in a sad white world. Hughes belonged to a loose fraternity of left-wing poets, Roumain, Guillén etc., often compulsive travellers, who were developing a new simplified rhetoric of black awareness, sharing key images and emotive proper names across language barriers. Damas responded to this outlook, adopting something of the footloose lifestyle of Hughes and McKay as well as the poetic conventions. The Afro-American writers and musicians also served him as a valuable argument against assimilation.

The themes of *Pigments* have become so much part of the Négritude heritage that most of them are now taken for granted and more interest attaches to Damas's poetic technique. It is a deliberately organized and militant collection, 'the manifesto of the negritude movement' as he called it in a 1972 interview [with Keith Warner that was published in *Manna* (1973)]. It begins where the old order of African life was shattered by the arrival of the oppressor: 'Ils sont venus . . .' and ends on a call to armed revolt. The theme of the black man's stolen African homeland is there: 'mon Afrique qu'ils ont cambriolée' ('Blanchi'), a secure ancestral community mapped out by the enumeration in 'Limbé' and still precariously surviving in the 'ancestrale foi conique' ('Shine') which shapes his hut roof in the New World. We notice how Damas dramatizes the traumatic experience directly, speaking in the first person role of the victim and inciting the audience to identify with him against THEM. The image of Africa remains tenuous enough to mark very clearly his distance from it, but since the oppressors are rarely specified Damas can canalize very powerfully a collective anguish of persecution by the white man.

This 'tribal' voice draws with more detail and immediacy on the experience of plantation slavery in the New World. The 'cargaisons fétides' of the Middle Passage, the whip and the red-hot iron, the hounds tracking the runaway, these memories seem to well up compulsively as the movement of a poem generates emotional intensity. Damas is particularly concerned with the persistence of psychic shock, the morbidly reduced vitality of a race whose blood has drained away to fertilize the cane-crop. The sluggish impotence of the present, hinted at in many *spleen* poems, is explicitly ascribed to the brutality and tortures of the slave master in 'La complainte du nègre'. 'En file indienne' comments obsessively on the strange resignation of the peasant women bearing burdens. In 'Rappel' Damas features ironically 'the good nigger (who) stretches out ten or fifteen hours in the sugar factory on his hard bed' and he returns to this theme more extensively in the first movement of *Black-Label.* It is the docility of his compatriots 'Morts pour la France' or the 'indéfectible attachment' of the Tirailleurs Sénégalais which provoke the infuriated call to arms in the last two *Pigments,* but he would not react with such violence if he did not recognize this same debilitated inertia within himself (cf. 'Réalité'). When he does envisage revolt it is in dreams of cathartic violence, like the image of the cane-cutter's cutlass raised in bloody revenge ('Si souvent', developed also in *Black-Label*).

Damas identifies the slave with the slavish cult of French culture. Most of his best poems evoke his own divided self, lifting the mask of exquisite Parisian manners to reveal the rebellious urges of natural Caribbean man underneath, or to expose the 'credibility gap' in French civilization itself. For *Pigments* has the self-awareness of Damas in France, giving voice to the loneliness and alienation of the colonial betrayed by the hollow *théories* on which he had been nurtured. It is this 'wind' no doubt which comes hiccuping up in **'Hoquet'**, just as he spits back **'Blanchi'**, or suffers 'l'indigestion / de tout morceau d'histoire de France'. He has been drilled to speak only 'le français de France'. His education has been French, including the favourite preposterous example of reciting 'mes ancêtres les Gaulois' (**'Nuit blanche'**). The poet ridicules the white behavioural model by using the trivial niceties of table manners or the high civility of taking tea in a Parisian salon, though he cunningly confuses distinctions of body language which relate to class as well as race. The image of European culture is similarly satirical: the Viennese waltz, a piano tinkling out 'un clair de lune à soupirs / tout format'.

Christianity is also placed among the irrelevant manifestations of the colonizer's culture. Several poems which begin with deceptive flippancy grow harsher in tone, as in **'Solde'** which culminates in a hysterical feeling of complicity in a vicious and bloodthirsty 'ci-vi-li-sa-tion'. Though he has been compelled to assimilate French culture, the eyes of the Frenchman will brand him irretrievably as other, as *nègre* (cf. **'Un clochard m'a demandé dix sous'**). He feels it his duty to warn of the link between mild racist mockery and violent persecution. His waltz conjures up as partners 'tonton Gobineau' and 'cousin Hitler', while **'S.O.S.'** warns of the fascist threat in terms designed to shock high-minded Francophiles.

The shared language and culture make more bitter the exclusion. Damas in blues mood paints sound pictures of night and darkness using physical malaise, especially cold, to convey inner solitude (see the rueful **'Pareille à la légende'** or sobbing melodies of **'Il est des nuits'**). His body remembers the warm *mornes,* his spirit is numbed by the chill *boulevards.*

One final theme has a specially close link with the Harlem-based protests against the artificial role that the white public imposes on the black artist: the musician, boxer, etc. allowed to perform but not develop independence. The image of the muted trumpet expresses this stifling in a minor key, but Damas also protests forcibly in **'Trêve'** and threatens in **'Bientôt'** some stronger action. Apart from a few earlier poems, *Pigments* has great internal coherence, allowing Damas to charge an individual pronoun or Creole term with the accumulated emotion of a whole racial experience.

Damas's poetic technique can be most positively assessed in terms of his own remarks on African poetry with its essentially sung nature and use of everyday language:

> (The African) does not compose for scholars. He composes so that the people can listen to him. This explains the jests, the puns, the word-play, the simplicity of expression.

> It is poetry where rhyme and syllable counts have no necessary role to play. Poetry which relies wholly on cadence and melody. On repetition which creates the rhythm. On effects of antithesis and parallelism in the ideas and images.

[Introductory note to ***Poèmes nègres sur des airs africains***]

Thus, unlike the more scholarly poets, Damas chose a medium to fit his message of solidarity with the black community. **'Et caetera'** was chanted in Baoulé as a call to rebellion in 1939, and there is an immediate audience response to Damas even across a degree of language unfamiliarity. Coming from a speech community where standard French was the language of the colonizers, and associated with formal and official situations, Damas is exceptionally sensitive to the choice of register. His slangy conversational idiom is a *prise de position* similar to the choice of Creole by contemporary Caribbean poets, but has the notable advantage of international currency. Damas was able to draw also on the poetic experiments with metropolitan spoken French being undertaken by Prévert, Queneau and others. In all his writing that 'décalage léger et constant' which Sartre mentions in *Orphée noir* is perceptible in the juggling with a range of spoken and written styles.

Most of what can be said about the techniques of *Pigments* holds good for all of Damas's poetry. Apart from *Black Label,* he works exclusively with the short or medium-length poem, at its best often a succint dramatic monologue or expression of mood. He has the two indispensable virtues which allow protest poetry to endure: a sense of humour and knowing when to stop.

His best poems are very skilfully constructed with a musical sense of the balance of pace and tone. Characteristically they have a forceful opening and end on a calculated dramatic shock (**'S.O.S.'**, **'Hoquet'**) or occasional diminuendo (**'Pour sûr'**, **'Position'**). His use of repetition, one of the structural features which govern folk literature, is very marked and would repay precise linguistic description. Typical protest poems are organised on an anaphora 'Trêve de. . . .' 'Passe pour. . . .' or a repeated plain assertion of the central idea:

> J'ai l'impression d'être ridicule
> Rendez-les moi mes poupées noires
> Ma mère voulant d'un fils. . . .

followed by a set of variations or paradigmatic substitutions which are often in a subordinate relation. **'Solde'**, despite its air of a folk-song stringing together improvised items by call and response (shoes on toes to bowler hat on top), shows a careful blend of easily understood phrases with more complex puns and metaphors (verses 2-3, 5-6), while developing the series: 'dans leurs (twice) / de leurs / parmi eux' essential to the meaning and rhythm (the pronoun allowing greater vocal emphasis than the possessive adjective). Repetition and refrains in a live speech event invite audience participation and are less quickly monotonous where the voice can add new units of meaning by ironical pauses, a higher pitch, etc. and vary pace and volume. The lulling repetition of past participles in **'Et caetera'** prepares the dramatic surprise of the bold expletive. The three printed versions of **'Un clochard m'a demandé dix sous'** offer a useful illustration of Damas at work: after the 1934 version he found 'hardes' to echo the stressed vowel of the key word 'clochard', then for the definitive version added three further emphatic 'Moi aussi' as well as a repetition to point the change in intonation contour from beggarly whine 'les yeux / le ventre / creux' to indignant revival of black pride. Many revisions also show increasing use of the rest for prosodic effects (typographical spacing and lines broken into shorter units), and heightened dramatization, especially of the climax to a poem; a last *noires* on **'Limbé'**, for example. Everything points to a poet progressively more conscious of constructing patterns for the spoken voice.

When using rhythm, password of the New Negro art, Damas delights in extravagant effects, preferring two feet for the 'poème à danser' to the twelve of the Alexandrine, as he jokes in ***Black-Label.*** In defiant poems his repetitions often suggest a strong 'drum-beat' by the use of duple time with frequent syncopation. An apparently slight piece like **'Bientôt'** (revised version) shows very dexterous stresses and patterning of oral [ɔ] [o] and nasal vowels with rapid consonants to give the key word onomatopoeic force as an urgent warning drum. The suspended high note of the unfinished sentence, and even the hint of the Creole: '(mó) pa ké dãsé', reinforce the message. ***Pigments*** suggested to Senghor 'un rythme de tam-tam instinctivement retrouvé' [1937 lecture collected in *Négritude et Humanisme,* 1964] and this point could well be explored systematically in terms of the persistence of African speech rhythms in Creolized French and the analysis of Damas readings by modern experimental phonetics.

Cover for the 1937 Paris edition of Pigments.

Though he writes in a relaxed standard French, Damas often seems as close to Creole as to Mallarmé when he uses the concision of a predicate without copula or allows the voice to punctuate the ambiguities of his syntax. Details like the high frequency of *foutre,* play on an opposition between *moi* (Creole *mó*) and *ils ont* (malicious echo of Creole *zòt?*), with the carefully selected lexical allusions, give Damas the flavour of a local entertainer, even though the firm simplicity of construction allows a wide appeal. Damas's masterpiece **'Hoquet'** has attracted many commentaries, but a less remarked feature is the scope it offers for an ironical play on Creole interferences in the mother's speech: the nasal vowels of *pain,* and [dž] of *banjo,* an expressive high note on the typical African reduplication of *français français,* etc.

Humour in Damas is an art of self-defence. He has the satirical imagination to reverse the stereotypes, and cast Hitler as cannibal, the European as trophy-hunting barbarian, the Christian God as an unfortunate who missed out on polygamy, and in **'Et caetera'** turn round the European's nightmare image of the Tirailleur raping white women to send him to attack colonialism in Senegal itself. In ***Pigments*** whimsical fancies often turn out to be serious weapons, like the Blue Danube motif in **'Nuit blanche'.** Disintegrating clichés and idioms, playing with satisfying sound patterns, and with a neat taste in puns, Damas seldom relaxes into verbosity, as if the underlying tension of his whole approach to things French kept his wit taut and short-winded.

Damas as poet dramatizing archetypal roles (the bogey man of **'Bouclez-la'** or the stern mother of **'Hoquet'**) and calling on so many of the techniques by which the storyteller holds his audience: jokes, sung interludes, rhythms and repetitions, prepares us for the *conteur* of ***Veillées noires.*** Even if folklore did not figure extensively in his own Cayenne childhood, Damas was doubtless keen to rediscover the oral sources which Dr. Price-Mars prized as the authentic voice of the Caribbean masses, and to add his own contribution to making known African survivals in the New World. These are enriched in the Guyanas by the presence of the reconstituted tribal groups of early escaped slaves ('Bush Negroes'). Damas is still promising to publish an enlarged collection of Afro-Amerindian tales, *La Moisson des Trois Domaines.*

The bulk of the material retold in ***Veillées noires*** demonstrates the resilience of African folk-tales in their New World setting. We find the range of animal characters, irrepressible Rabbit, Deer and Monkey, fierce but stupid Tiger, gossiping Bird and devious Turtle, common to so many areas of the black diaspora. (Anansi the spider-man was apparently reserved for a later collection.) They often express the art of survival of the powerless, in trickery, flattery and a hard-won humorous wisdom. The plots too are familiar, blending with African story or creation myth, elements of European devil tale, or Amerindian legend. They mirror the cultural diversity of a plural society, but one which has coexisted for centuries in the same natural habitat. Damas builds up a portrait of the local life-style with its particular ways of cooking, fishing, cultivating, practising magic. This is a land of rivers (Turtle and Alligator figure more frequently than in the Islands), where the deep forest, the *Yan-Man,* is a constant point of reference. This rural milieu has changed little since M. de Préfontaine wrote his manual for settlers in 1763.

Thus Damas offers a critique of assimilation policies simply by showing the richness of the native local culture they threaten. He is also more specific. A few stories deal explicitly with an unjust social order based on race: **'Aux premiers âges',** the old story of the magic fountain combining with a bitter parable of the talents in **'Les trois frères'.** More often a sharp aside brings a story into focus: the wicked mother offers her prettiest daughter to a Devil who apart from a slight limp might be any plantation owner (**'Grain de sel').** Such indications are sufficient to allow a second level of interpretation of all the stories satirizing the abuse of power. When Damas shows Little Pig learning class consciousness in the farmyard, or Monkey dressing up to pass for man, the parallels with **Pigments** are inescapable and direct us to decode in racial terms.

Naturally the extensive use of Creole songs and *dolos* (proverbs), stock jokes and riddles, underlines Damas's intention. Often the central figure of the tale is a musician, gifted like Ravet-Guitar with a subversive power to awaken the African vitality of the people in defiance of the landowner or ruler. The narrative incorporates these elements, usually without strain (though **'Echec et mât'** almost gets out of hand). Damas relishes playing off the Creole elements and apparently naïve content against a literary level of formal French, gracefully archaic in flavour (e.g. 'Papa Mouton eut le vin fort gai', etc.). The result is a seductive little book, with all the wit of the best of **Pigments** at the service of a more richly human and *guyanais* version of the same project.

The third pre-war volume, **Retour de Guyane,** originated in a 1934 ethnographic mission to study the Bush Negroes which exploded with passionate indignation into a full-scale critique of French policy and mismanagement. Damas fills in the background by a brief history of exploration and settlement, then looks at the contemporary situation. The long history of failed projects, the 'gangrene' of the penal settlements, so much potential frustrated by obtuse direct rule from Paris and corrupt or lazy officials, such factors have created a specific local mentality despite the internal divisions of race and class. This book is essential reading both for Damas's own commitment to his homeland, and for a partisan view of French colonialism from a writer unusually well-placed to evaluate assimilation. Most often he allows a damning series of facts to speak for themselves, but we recognize his flair for the telling detail: 'un vrai budget colonial' which spends 7,000 Fr. on a uniform for the governor's chauffeur and 4,000 Fr. on the Public Library, or so much convict labour expended on road-building, to achieve communication with the interior by the dug-out canoes of the Boni tribesmen. Damas disentangles the various issues involved in assimilation: political status as a French department (in fact achieved in 1946), social equality with white Frenchmen (a mirage), cultural uniformity (neither desirable nor possible). With a firm 'no' he concludes that the colonial is and can be an equal but remains *other.* He rejects a change

in political status as no more of a cure for the ills of French Guyana than suppressing the *bagne,* indeed such measures might serve to distract from vitally-needed economic development. An expert in the weight of words, he distrusts all the grandiose rhetoric, and warns against exchanging one set of labels for another on an equally empty package, or, to use his own image, 'pinning this *légion d'honneur* on a naked and starving breast'. Not surprisingly this book made Damas very unpopular both in official quarters and among some of his compatriots, though time has alas justified too many of his lucid commentaries on French policy in the Caribbean. The factual approach and well-argued position of **Retour de Guyane** is a valuable companion to the emotional rejection expressed in **Pigments,** and usefully relates the folklore of **Veillées noires** to the territory as a whole.

In the stimulating atmosphere of the pre-war black community Damas felt the pressure to contribute his message. Nothing he has published since shows quite the same urgent power. Indeed from 1947 on, a variety of enticing titles have been announced but not actually reached publication. Immediately after the war he worked on the first of the anthologies which collected the work of **Poètes d'expression française** not to the greater glory of French civilization but to promote awareness of a shared colonial experience. Damas makes his position clear by featuring Léro in his preface and work by the militant younger generation, Georges Desportes, Lucien Attuly, Guy Tirolien, etc. together with his own *compagnons de route,* Césaire and Senghor. However in compiling a manual on historical lines, 1900-1945, he also included too much mediocre and imitative versifying, and the resultant volume has been inevitably overshadowed by Senghor's excellent *Anthologie de la nouvelle poésie nègre et malgache,* published the following year.

During this, the heroic period of *Présence Africaine,* Damas expressed solidarity by a little collection of African songs [**Poèmes nègres sur des airs africains**] adapted from originals in indigenous languages. Though the themes are often close to his own songs of love, war or abuse, the tone is more confidently prosaic. Several tiny love-poems (**'Idylle', 'Sérénade', 'Prière'**) charmingly suggest an underlying order of stable human relations. Poems like the satirical **'Cocu et content', 'Parti-pris'** or **'La Maîtresse Servante'** illuminate the links between Damas's own poetic technique and folk-song originals with their well-defined social functions. However, the collection does not altogether avoid the quaintly stilted air of translation. In 1952 appeared Damas's own first collection of love-poems [**Graffiti**]. These nine lyrics modulating the pangs of 'mon coeur malade' with often a hinted context of exile or hostility, reappear in slightly revised form in **Névralgies.**

However, 1948-51 saw Damas engaged in the purposeful parallel activity of representing French Guyana, now an overseas Department, in the Chambre des Députés. His record is a workmanlike though not outstanding one of sensible proposals to develop the territory: tax relief, agricultural credit, electoral and judicial reforms, setting up of various bodies to promote forestry, agriculture and an 'Institut Français d'Amérique tropicale'. Damas took an active part in attacking the delay in extending French Social Security benefits to the D. O. M., and finally displayed his intransigence over the official enquiry into the troubles in the Ivory Coast. He held to his views and did not seek re-election. Although brief, this career offsets the picture of Damas as hysterical racist composing 'hate-filled diatribes' (Coulthard). For a period at least he made an attempt to work the system, and cooperate both with the socialist group in parliament and other bodies concerned with French Guyana. The poetic image is of the victim of persecution and censorship, having the courage to say *merde* instead of keeping meekly silent. The full picture is more complex and shows unexpected patience with the compromises of concerted action and the prose of officialdom.

Since the immediate post-war phase Damas has worked towards the cultural liberation of the black man in a more international sphere. He has written tributes to Dr. Price-Mars and René Maran for *Présence Africaine,* and edited a second anthology, ***La nouvelle somme de poésie du monde noir,*** which charts the enormous vitality of the poetic resurgence and also the expansion of Damas's own horizons. Though based now in the United States at Howard University, he has been a regular participant in cultural missions and congresses round the globe, looking back in addresses and especially public readings on the Négritude experience.

Damas's poetry since ***Pigments*** lacks that initial verve, though offering much to reward the reader or listener. Extracts from ***Black-Label*** appeared in the 1947-48 anthologies, and this sustained poem in four movements elaborates without significantly advancing Damas's long debate with himself and the world. It has a confessional quality, as if under the influence of alcohol the exiled poet yields up 'le film du rêve recréé', a long fluid series of flashbacks into his past. The first section develops from tears of exile by the waters of the Seine, to a long apostrophizing of all those who challenge him, men of the Caribbean who betray their own dignity, men of Africa who betrayed their brothers, then blames with humorous blasphemy the Christian God and bitterly reiterates his stance *against* all the forces of repression. The second canto concentrates more on the sentimental memories of the lonely heart: a pastoral vision symbolizing the distant Caribbean, a fiasco with the blonde Ketty, voices calling long distance. The round of partners quickens into the consoling rhythms of the Cabane Cubaine, the blues singer, and then the Afro-Brazilian beat triumphantly bombards Paris with the black man's revenge. Damas next develops one encounter into a sustained conversation, a *dédoublement* which allows him to give another self-addressed account of his childhood, the experience of **'Hoquet'** amplified and set in the real and ideal landscape of home. He ends in his favourite role as rebel, shouting 'Down with school' on behalf of all the underdogs and outcasts. In Section IV he pulls together many strands of experience to link his own poetic method to the *kamougué* folk-dance, trace his gift of language to the figure of Tétèche (the old woman storyteller presiding over ***Veillées noires***) and invoke the heritage of the Maskililis, the little men, free spirits of the woods, Amerindian or African. He takes care to dispel the Chris-

tian overtones of this *testament;* to the last he defies the system, glass in hand.

The form of ***Black-Label*** is hauntingly obsessive, patterns sustained beyond the point of saturation, refrains used to structure an elusive flux of mental experience. Critics point to the essentially musical nature of the construction. The notorious war-chant 'Jamais le Blanc ne sera nègre' achieves a very exciting beat by its double accent on the Creole syllable *nèg,* and the ambiguity of *est/et* finds a triumphant climax in the absolute statements of the last four lines. The context shows Damas ruefully conscious that this explosion of black power and joy is sited in a tiny Parisian dance floor. However, without the support of a musical accompaniment this poem flags. The absorption with his childhood and with protest for its own sake needs a less self-indulgent expression at this stage in the poet's career, though this is Damas's own favourite work.

Some of the love poems in ***Névralgies,*** like ***Black-Label,*** set a personal relationship into the tormented context of black-white relations. The title itself implies a bashful confession of weakness nagging at the soul. Memorable lyrics here are often the brief fixing of a mood, for example **'Par la fenêtre ouverte à demi'** with its unerring tense shift as the initial charm and consecrated attitudes of poet to the world and his muse give way to an avid urgency; **'Sur le sein'** playing ironically on the poet 'in whiteface', uses the metre to give a woeful emphasis to 'flasque' and 'blême'. Among longer pieces, **'Toute à ce besoin d'évasion'** constructs a lively pattern to ease the heartache: the woman totally absorbed in her holiday sunbathing, the poet just a key dangling in an empty pigeonhole. The verbal shrug of the final couplet is a typical play on an idiomatic nuance. Other pieces show in a more relaxed form the poet's sheer delight in language, whether punning on the European and Caribbean meaning of *marron,* composing nonsense proverbs and magic pass-words in the Surrealist manner (**'Nul ne se rappelle avoir vu'**), or building a collage on the sound waves (**'Et maintenant'**). Though a few poems stress race consciousness for lament or satire, overall this collection deals more playfully with the intimate sense of loss and lack of fulfilment. The urgent passion of ***Pigments*** is not there to direct the games.

The verdict of the general public is thus right in giving a special place to ***Pigments,*** even if it is unrepresentative of Damas's range of interests and abilities. His original contribution to Négritude may not be extensive in terms of ideas, but his temperament and Guyanese background add a valuable and distinctive note. Above all he is an authentic artist with words, in that heightened popular vein of other *poètes-gueux* from Villon to Verlaine, like them gifted with a poetic ear of rare subtlety and a sure sense of form. We value his sense of humour, his wit and satire, his astringent refusal to be mystified. He transmits the pain and passion of blackness simply and clearly enough to reach his chosen people, and the audience for his work continues to grow.

O. R. Dathorne on the differences between Aimé Césaire and Damas:

The past in Césaire's poetry is one long, grim night and when he refers to the glory of Africa, he does so almost with the modesty of the stranger. Damas, on the other hand, recognizes a past within the disturbed environment, for he feels that the efforts of misdirected currents of history were responsible for his dilemma. With anguish therefore he exclaims in "Limbed" that he wishes to be given back the black dolls so that he could play games that would restore his world of instinct. . . .

Damas's anger is quieter, more reflective than Césaire's; he can look back on the centuries and forgive. Another interesting point of comparison between Damas and Césaire is that although they share in common the same subject matter, there is a different expression of tone. Whereas Damas laments in "Reality" that he is almost a negative person because he has accomplished nothing, Césaire ironically celebrates those who do not invent anything. In Damas's poetry little attempt is made to vaunt racial superiority by stating negative virtues. When he does attempt this kind of writing, he does not succeed.

O. R. Dathorne, in his The Black Mind, *University of Minnesota Press, 1974.*

Daniel L. Racine   (essay date 1982)

SOURCE: "The Aesthetics of Léon-Gontran Damas," in *Présence Africaine,* Nos. 121 and 122, 1982, pp. 154-65.

[*Racine is a Guadeloupean-born educator and critic. In the essay below, he discusses the style of Damas's poetry.*]

What is meant by the "aesthetics of Léon-Gontran Damas" is, as one may guess, his art as a writer. This art is discernible in both his prose and his verse. Within the limits of this presentation, it is not possible to describe the talent of the brilliant essayist of *Retour de Guyane,* **"Misère Noire"** [*Esprit* (June 1, 1939)] or **"89 et nous les Noirs"** [*Europe* (May-August 1939)] nor to demonstrate the art of the griot-like story-teller of *Veillées Noires.* I shall focus my remarks on the verse of the poet whose touch can be perceived anyhow in most of his prose works.

It is not difficult for a discriminating reader of Damas's poetry to detect some of his literary devices and techniques. But this can best be done in the light of what I would identify as Damas's manifesto of African poetry and which can actually be proved to be his own poetics. In his introduction to a small volume of verse entitled *Poèmes Nègres sur des airs africains* (later translated as *African Songs of Love, War, Grief and Abuse*), Damas had this to say about African poetry:

> Traduits du *rongué,* du *fanti,* du *bassouto,* du *toucouleur* ou encore du *bambara,* les quelques textes que nous donnerons aujourd'hui, auront l'avantage de révéler les aspects multiples de la poésie nègre d'expression et d'inspiration. Poésie

dont la caractéristique essentielle réside dans le fait qu'improvisée, elle n'est jamais déclamée ni dite, mais *chantée.*

> Toute circonstance de la vie, tout événement qui excite l'attention du public est l'occasion d'un poème qui jamais ne différera du langage familier. C'est que l'Africain, qui est né poète et a vite fait d'improviser un chant, ne compose pas pour des savants. Il compose pour être écouté du peuple. Ce qui explique les moqueries, les calembours, les jeux de mots, la simplicité dans l'expression.

> Poésie où la rime et le nombre de syllabes n'ont forcément aucun rôle à jouer. Poésie qui attend tout de la cadence et de la mélodie. Tout de la répétition qui engendre des idées et des images.

> Poésie faite de subtilité, de délicatesse et de nuances, notait Gide dans son inoubliable *Voyage au Congo.*

One may summarize the chief articles of this profession of faith as follows:

> a) Africain poetry is improvised and must be sung rather than recited;

> b) the language of this poetry, which expresses everyday life, is colloquial; African poets do not improvise for scholars but for people; hence the use of mockeries, puns, plays upon words and simplicity in expression;

> c) African poetry does not count on rhyme and meter but, rather, on tempo, melody and repetition that engender rhythm;

> d) finally, antitheses and parallelisms of ideas are important parts of this poetry.

These features constitute for Damas the aesthetic cannons of black poetry and confer on it "subtlety", "delicacy" and "nuances". They are well illustrated in his own works.

In reviewing *African Songs* [in *Black Orpheus* (1962)], Professor Dathorne notes that "these poems were not translated from any African language into French by Damas, but are obviously inspired by African verse". If so, Damas's art had reached a point where it could be assimilated with its actual source of inspiration. Even if this were not so, Damas still proved to be an excellent interpreter since the adaptations given us do not sound like narrow translations. In fact, he had shown his talent as a translator on several occasions. *Veillées Noires* is a volume of collected Guyanese folk-stories remarkably translated from Creole into French. Professor Cook, reviewing *Névralgies* [in *African Forum* (Spring 1967)], observes:

> For several years, Damas has been translating Langston Hughes's poetry; this reviewer has seen some of these translations in manuscript, and they are magnificent. This is not surprising not only because of Damas's talent, but also because they are kindred spirits.

A sample of these translations can be found in *Retour de Guyane* (1938) where Damas quotes and translates with savour "I'm Makin' A Road", a poem improvised by L.

Hughes as a typical African piece. If Damas was first inspired by Hughes and other poets of the Harlem Renaissance, it was because, in their exile, they had been able to preserve traditional African poetry. By presenting himself as the translator of African songs rather than as a creator, he became the intermediary between oral and written cultures.

Of Damas's own creations, it is commonplace to say they follow African patterns. So much so, that some poems of *Pigments* were translated into Baoulé (an Ivory Coast language) and chanted by Africans as songs of revolt. This wonderful reward crowned his success in achieving in his own poetry the qualities and techniques he had long admired in the folk-poetry of Africa. There has been unanimous agreement among literary critics that, of all the poems born from the "Négritude" movement, Damas's are the most musical. Senghor refers to Damas's use of rhythm as "magic which, in the song-poems (. . .) as in the Blues, restores to words their life and strength".

In an interview given to Keith Warner in 1973, Damas declared about his work: "I am not afraid to say that in my poetry you find rhythm. My poems can be danced. They can be sung". The interviewer was so convinced that, in an article entitled "Léon Damas and the Calypso" [in *CLA Journal* (March 1976)], he was to observe that

> Léon Damas, although he used other techniques from the French literary tradition, used elements in his poetry which could fit very neatly into the realm of the calypso, just as he used elements from jazz idiom.

The opening poem of *Pigments* ["Ils sont venus ce soir"] describes rhythmically how the slave-traders intruded into the middle of a dance which they had interrupted to capture their prey:

> Ils sont venus ce soir où le
>
> tam
>   tam
>   roulait de
>   rythme
>   en
>   rythme   la frénésie
>
> des yeux
> la frénésie des mains
>
> la frénésie
> des pieds de statues
>
> DEPUIS
>
> combien de MOI MOI MOI
> sont morts
> depuis qu'ils sont venus ce soir où le
> tam
>   tam
>   roulait de
>   rythme
>   en
>   rythme   la frénésie

> des yeux
> la frénésie
> des mains
> la frénésie
> des pieds de statues

There is a dichotomy in this poem whose rhythm is suddenly broken in the middle with the word "DEPUIS", capitalized on purpose to stress repetitive disjunction and to force the mind to focus on a question that might be repeated indefinitely.

One of Damas's most lyrical poems closes with a lament on "le rythme, la cadence, la mesure" born in Africa. Their loss was among the privations wrought by the slave-trade.

Many of his poems have a drum-beat rhythm. This is the case, for instance, in the poem, **"Bientôt"**, where one imagines a duet of drums—the refrain "Bientôt" taken up by an ominous deep-voiced drum and the other lines in higher-pitched, staccato notes:

> Bientôt
> je n'aurai pas que dansé
> bientôt
> je n'aurai pas que chanté
> bientôt
> je n'aurai pas que frotté
> bientôt
> je n'aurai pas que trempé
> bientôt
> je n'aurai pas que dansé
> chanté
> frotté
> trempé
> frotté
> chanté
> dansé
>   Bientôt

While this poem ends abruptly with a defiant slap of the drum, the one entitled **"Limbé"** (**"Love sickness"**) gradually fades out in the end:

> Rendez-les-moi mes poupées noires
> mes poupées noires
> poupées noires
> noires
> noires

The diminishing sounds reflect nostalgia for a past which has slipped away irretrievably. Nonetheless, through rhythm, Damas attempted to link past and present, Africa and Guinea, in a rite of passionate union with the Motherland as illustrated in *Black Label*:

> POEME
> poème à danser que chantent
> Ceux dont je suis qui entendent être
> non pas les mots
> mais qui entendent
> être avec eux

au gré du rythme des heures claires
où dégainé le tambour-Ka
où débandé le tambour-Ka
enjambé le tambour-Ka
entouré le tambour-Ka
raisonné le tambour-Ka
cajolé le tambour-Ka
réchauffé le tambour-Ka
résonné le tambour-Ka
enivré le tambour-Ka
éreinté le tambour-Ka
essoufflé le tambour-Ka

It is easy to realize that a more direct, native rhythm, replaces an artificially elaborated meter. Damas did away with the restricting poetic conventions, with Alexandrine and Parnassian alike. His poetry relinquished metrical concerns and demands corporal, physical participation. Damas contended that he was happy with two feet and did not need the twelve of the Alexandrine:

DIEU SOIT LOUÉ
Il me suffit
d'avoir deux pieds.

J'en aurais beaucoup
beaucoup trop de douze
douze pieds comptés pesés
scandés d'un doigt
toujours le même
tout prêt à tout
bon à couper

This "pedestrian poetry" is clearly a reaction against learned stylization and literariness. Senghor has pointed out that "Damas's poetry is essentially unsophisticated". The latter's main concern seemed to be rhythm which he generated through many devices such as repetitions or parallelisms. For example, he would repeat the ending of each line at the beginning of the text:

Ils ont si bien su faire
si bien faire les choses
les choses
qu'un jour nous avons tout
nous avons tout foutu de nous-mêmes
tout foutu de nous-mêmes en l'air

or at the beginning of a line:

Moi aussi un beau jour j'ai sorti
mes hardes
de clochard

Moi aussi avec des yeux qui tendent
la main
j'ai soutenu la putain de misère (. . .)

Moi aussi (. . .)

or a list of single lines, often with parallel rhythms, which begin with the same words, to achieve cumulative effect:

. . . . . . la ligne
qui mène encore
aux Isles de l'Aventure
aux Isles à la Dérive
aux Isles de la Flibuste
aux Isles de la Boucane
aux Isles de la Tortue
aux Isles à Nègreries

aux Isles à sucreries
aux Isles de la mort-vive (. . .)

Another device used by Damas to emphasize rhythm is typography. Lines, and sometimes words, are cut and displayed on the page in a cascading way to suggest semiotically the rhythmic effect the poet wishes to create as we have seen above in the opening poem of *Pigments.*

Words can also be juxtaposed paradigmatically, sometimes in an apparent nonsensical fashion, just for the sake of their sounds. They may be adjectives, like:

roses effeuillées.
roses parfumées,
roses d'encens,
miraculées
Matriculées

They may be verbs:

Ceux qui se lèvent tôt
Pour que se lèvent tard
et se gavent
se dandinent
se pomadent
se désodorisent
se parfument
se lotionnent
se maquillent
se gargarisent
se jalousent
se débinent
s'enrichissent
d'autres (. . .)

In both examples, the paradigmatic arrangement creates a derogatory effect.

Damas took pleasure in juggling with words for their sound combinations. This is why his poems are often rich in alliterations. Consider, as a typical example, the reverberative echo in a line like "Le néant de mes nuits au néon à naître" or the search for sarcastic effect in "les deux doigts à thé pointus pointés et pointants".

Damas proved his mastery of the French language which he deliberately demystified by imposing upon words his own fanciful arrangements and meaning. This results most of the time in semantic shifts, amusing incongruities, grammatical deconstructions, syntactic disorders. He had a special gift for spoonerisms (the famous French "contrepetries") consisting of a transposition of unusual initial sounds of two or more words that generally creates a comic effect, as in the example "les bouches à mouches bées" instead of the expected "les mouches à bouches bées".

He tried all possible (even impossible) structures such as:

Le jeu coulant du noeud
le noeud coulant du jeu
le jeu du noeud coulant (. . .)

By nature a practical joker, Damas excelled in puns created by phonetic distortions or ambiguous associations of words. Such is the case of the poem **"Nuit blanche"**, untranslatable because one cannot find an expression meaning both a "sleepless night" and a "night spent among white people". The same difficulty occurs with the phrase "bon à rien" used in the same poem, and which can be "good for nothing" or "good Aryan". In both cases, the reader assumes the responsibility of transforming one interpretation into another.

This device may have been inspired by Claude McKay's *Banjo* but, here, the transformation is demanded by the writer. In a similar fashion, one of his characters transforms "United States" into "United Snakes".

Puns constitute one of the main elements of the humorous quality of this poetry which also consists of ellipses, allusions and unexpected associations. This aspect, which has been emphasized by many critics as one of the main characteristics of black poets in general and of Damas in particular, need not be insisted upon again here.

Finally, in his Introduction to **African Songs,** Damas referred to "simplicity of expression". He is quite at home with this principle. His poetry uses plain speech, colloquial words, those of everyday conversation, which gives the impression that the poet is actually talking directly to us without academic concern. Many poems can be read like sentences improvised on the spur of the moment, as for example:

> Pourquoi
> Grands dieux
> Pourquoi, pourquoi
> faut-il que tout chante
> fût-ce
> l'amour
> à tout jamais soudain
> d'une pureté d'albâtre

If anything, the extreme simplicity which characterizes this poetry bears testimony to its authenticity and its pressing sincerity. What can be simpler and more sincere than this love poem?

> Quand bien même
> Je t'aimerais mal
> en est-ce bien sûr
> au point d'en avoir mal
> pour sûr
> tu sais que je t'aime
> c'est sûr
> au point d'en avoir mal
> en est-ce bien sûr
> toi qui m'aimes
> toi qui m'aimes mal
> c'est sûr

What a difference indeed with the elaborate, sophisticated, learned and sometimes hermetic poetry of his peers in Negritude—Césaire and Senghor. The latter humbly admitted the superiority of Damas as a black poet when he publicly declared in an American television interview in 1966:

> To a certain extent, Damas is the most Negro among us all. In fact, I studied the rhythm of his verse; it is exactly negro rhythm and it resembles that of Langston Hughes.

Césaire has expressed the same view on many occasions.

The question has been asked why Damas, for more authenticity, did not use his native Creole (which is a mixture of French and African) to write his poetry. He answered this question several times in interviews and writings. His argument was the following:

> We do not deny our native language while continuing to write in French, but our truth must be reflected in the European language that we had learn and whose radiance is larger and may help to serve a better knowledge of man.

He also explained that

> Africans and West Indians have different languages complicated by countless dialects and a lack of a stable written literature. Thus, French like English for some and Portuguese or Spanish for others, offered itself as an excellent means for Negro expression. Like English, Portuguese and Spanish, French made it possible for all Negroes to communicate with some words and identifiable symbols.

Nevertheless, Damas was very often tempted to use Creole and one can find several passages where his native language will appear in his poetry even if he had to translate it into French such as in the following example:

> PIÈ PIÈ PIÈ
> PRIÉ Bondjé
> mon fi
> prié Bondjé
> Angou ka bouyi
> Angou ka bouyi
>
> Pierre Pierre
> Prie Dieu
> mon fiston
> prie Dieu
> mon fiston
> pour que soit fin prêt le maïs en crème
> à être savouré

He contended that Creole offers more rhythmic patterns, more affectivity and retains the linguistic memory of life on another continent at another time.

Damas is also said to have used surrealism as a means of access to identity. Because of his many connections with surrealist poets, one cannot deny some influences of this movement on his poetry, including a subrational layer of consciousness, dreams, fancies, snatches of incoherence and incongruous or gratuitous images. One may say, however, that Surrealism itself remains heavily endebted to Negro Art. What attracted Damas to this movement was precisely the possibility of aesthetic exchange between Blacks and Whites.

As a poet of Negritude, Damas made it a point to find out and express the essence of African aesthetics. He seems to have discovered an important part of it through African songs in different languages which he could learn, translate, interpret and assimilate to a point of identifying his own poetic expression with them. It was after their spontaneity in improvisation, their simplicity, their jocularity and their rhythmical patterns built up on repetitive segments that he created his song-like verse. By so doing he reached a coveted platform where his poetics became part and parcel of African aesthetics.

Thomas H. Brown　(essay date 1992)

SOURCE: "Filling in Reader Gaps in Poems by Léon-Gontran Damas," in *French Literature Series,* Vol. XIX, 1992, pp. 47-56.

[*In the essay below, Brown analyzes two of Damas's poems: "Ils sont venus ce soir" and "Contre notre amour qui ne voulait rien d'autre."*]

Black francophone writer, Léon-Gontran Damas, portrays in his poetry the sad results of black/white confrontations in his native French Guiana. Leaving spaces for reflection, gaps to be filled by a creative reader, Damas has developed an art of nonspecificity, a writing technique rich and provocative in powers of suggestion. Although Sartre identifies the intended reader of black francophone poetry as a black reader, this body of literature, including Damas' poems, has universal implications and is open to careful and imaginative scrutiny of readers everywhere.

It is certain that, if I was very much influenced by Mallarmé, I was even more so by Baudelaire (especially by his translations of Edgar Poe).

—Léon-Gontran Damas, in an interview in Jeune Afrique, 16 March 1971.

In his poem, **"Ils sont venus ce soir"** [from *Pigments, Névralgies*], Damas evokes the tragic, lamentable moment in time when outsiders came and disrupted forever the serenity of his life:

　"Ils sont venus ce soir"
　　Pour Léopold-Sédar Senghor

Ils sont venus ce soir où le
tam
　　tam
　　　　roulait de
　　　　　　　rythme
　　　　　　　　　en
　　　　　　　　　　rythme　　la frénésie

des yeux
la frénésie des mains
la frénésie
des pieds de statues

DEPUIS

combien de MOI MOI MOI
sont morts
depuis qu'ils sont venus ce soir où le
tam
　　tam
　　　　roulait de
　　　　　　　rythme
　　　　　　　　　en
　　　　　　　　　　rythme　　la frénésie

des yeux
la frénésie
des mains
la frénésie
des pieds de statues

What is stated in the poem? Only that "they" came one night when a tam-tam's beat produced the frenzy of eyes, hands, and feet, and that since this moment, much that is in the poet is dead. Who came? What did they do? What is dead in the poet? Why? The text does not say. It only suggests. It is up to the reader to discover these and other meanings.

Damas does not identify "ils" in the first line of the poem. Awareness of Damas' role in defining the concept of *négritude* provides a clue and helps the reader discover that "they" as unwanted outsiders represent the white race, the oppressors of blacks. With simplicity and brevity, Damas depicts a scene with double meaning. The arrival of strangers interrupts a festive moment, a joyous and ecstatic village dance, the symbol of the value and beauty of black African culture. When "they" come, the dance of joy is transformed into a *danse macabre*. The frenzy of eyes, hands, and feet now becomes a reflection of fear, of amazement, of pain, of death. Dancing feet are now "pieds de statues" (repeated twice), feet no longer capable of moving, glued, nailed down, suddenly transfixed, inert, lifeless. Damas could have given clues in his poem in order to represent a precise experience in place and in time. He does not do it. Too much precision would have diminished and stunted the meaning and impact of his poem. The nonspecificity of the poet serves a larger design, expanding the portrayal of the coming of whites among blacks. With unnamed perpetrators and unidentified act, the poem finally encompasses all the suffering and degradation of Damas and his people under French rule in his native French Guiana, plus any humiliation, any injustice, any scandalous, outrageous racial attitude or crime in any place, at any time brought against the black race by whites.

The very form of the poem, shown on the page in short, choppy fragments, toppling over each other to the ground, suggests a race brought low, separated from others and itself. Isolation and alienation are the inevitable results of the whites' coming. The words on the page illustrate the fracturing, the splitting. Tam-tam, a metaphor for black ancestral values, is cut in half. Eyes separated from hands and hands pulled away from feet show the extent to which the self has lost touch with itself. This body, broken, isolated, separated, disjointed, mutilated, represents the entire black race and demonstrates the enormity of Damas' tragic metaphor.

The words "DEPUIS" and "MOI MOI MOI" appear in capital letters, the only ones in the poem with such distinction intended to highlight their importance. "DEPUIS" stands in the middle of the poem so that in time and space it marks a joyous "before" and a wretched "after," a "before" of elation and fulfillment, symbolized by the dance before the coming of the outsiders, an "after" of sadness, lamentation, alienation, the dance turned to horror when "they" came. "DEPUIS" in this poem is a point of demarcation, a rupture in time and place, a sign in capital letters at midpoint, a meridian of time, the supreme moment at white heat which altered irrevocably and forever the destiny of the race. "MOI" in capital letters and repeated three times demonstrates the extent to which the poet is affected personally by the situation he is describing. He seems to be dying perpetually. "MOI" in a trilogy may also suggest the notion of trinity, a trinity of union, a complete black soul in harmony with itself, split, torn asunder by the advent of whites among blacks. "MOI" occurs in a question. How many "MOI," how many selves in the poet, how many precious parts of existence and being are dead since "DEPUIS," the most critical, the most crucial of all moments? The three "MOI" in capital letters stress the extent and repetition of hurt and injury. Damas asks the question, preferring it to a statement, because the issue, like a question, is open-ended. Damas is clearly searching. He cannot fathom the vastness of his loss. Can any black, man or woman, cut off, severed from past, culture, family, and self, measure the part of self which is dead and lost forever?

In **"Contre notre amour qui ne voulait rien d'autre"** [from **Pigments, Névralgies**], Damas contrasts the black wish for a free and peaceful life with white interdictions against these aspirations. A reference to Old Testament Patriarchs forces the reader to fill in a huge reader space in the poem, a gap which spans centuries and raises tragic and far-reaching implications for the entire black race:

"Contre notre amour qui ne voulait rien d'autre"

Contre notre amour qui ne voulait rien d'autre
que d'être beau comme un croissant de lune au
    beau mitan du Ciel à minuit
et pur comme le premier ris du nouveau-né
et vrai comme le verbe être
et fort comme la Mort d'où nous vient toute vie

Contre notre amour
qui rêvait de vivre à l'air libre
qui rêvait de vivre sa vie
de vivre une vie
qui ne fut
ni
honteuse
ni lépreuse
ni truquée
ni tronquée
ni traquée
ils ont invoqué NOE
et NOE en appela à SEM
et SEM en appela à JAPHET
et JAPHET s'en remit à NOE
et NOE en appela à MATHUSALEM
alors MATHUSALEM ressortit de l'arsenal
tous les oripeaux
tous les tabous
tous les interdits en fanal rouge

Attention
Ici Danger
Déviation
Chasse gardée
Terrain privé
Domaine réservé
Défense d'entrer
Ni chiens ni nègre sur le gazon

"Contre," the very first word of the title and the poem, establishes a tension, the opposition of "them and us." "Notre amour," which is black love, marks a sharp line of demarcation with third person plural "ils," unwanted outsiders who represent whites in general and the French in Guiana in particular, who have power, money, and privileges as ruling class.

Black hope is personified love with simple, reasonable desires; it wants to be, to be in the same sense that Erich Fromm describes being in preference to having or owning. A series of similes represents black love wanting to be "beau comme un croissant de lune au beau mitan du ciel à minuit (this love has intimate, tender contact with nature) / et pur comme le premier ris du nouveau-né (it recognizes the beauty and value of life) / et vrai comme le verbe être (it focuses on being, not possessing) / et fort comme la Mort d'où nous vient toute vie" (it finds strength and regeneration in death). Consistent with the cycle of birth, being, and death, black love moves in cadence with the archetypal rhythm of the seasons with death the necessary precursor of rebirth. Black love dreams, and the dream is to live in free air, to live its own life, an existence with its own uniqueness and at the same time in tender and natural harmony with the ebb and flow of all life forms. The grating repetitions of the consonant sounds in *truquée, tronquée, traquée* stand in contrast to the gentle, serene portrayal of black love and emphasize the harshness of whites' treatment of blacks.

Staunch, stern forces are marshalled against black wishes and dreams. "Ils," cold, methodical, impersonal "they," always as perpetrators, invoke a power higher than their own to secure divine sanction for white domination and cursing of blacks. "They" call on Biblical Patriarchs (Noah, Shem, Japheth, and Methuselah) and establish a collaboration with them. This is a long-standing alliance, and the scriptural authority of the Old Testament figures gives weight to their position and renders their strictures all the more imposing. The Patriarchs' names, the only words in the poem in capital letters, emphasize the far-reaching importance of their interdictions. Nevertheless, there is a hesitancy, a reluctance on their part to take responsibility for what they are doing. Noah refers to Shem, who calls on Japheth, who, coming full circle, turns the issue back to Noah. Finally, Noah, still unwilling to take a stand, defers to Methuselah, the oldest, the most venerable of all the Patriarchs. Methuselah does not hesitate. He acts. He "ressortit de l'arsenal / tous les oripeaux / tous les tabous / tous les interdits en fanal rouge." The "re-" in the verb, "ressortit," shows clearly that Methuselah's action is a recurring outrage. The word "arsenal" implies a full range of weapons, puts Methuselah's machinations in a war context, and demonstrates the might of the oppressors. The term, "oripeaux," has many meanings. They are copper blades (weapons) which at a distance look like gold. They are also old, tawdry clothes, rags, fabric, or embroidery with fake silver or gold. "Oripeaux" are thus symbols of things which try to be beautiful or authentic, but which are not. They represent the unfounded, false nature of Methuselah's declarations. The taboos and prohibitions, displayed in glaring red lights, take on an eerie, repressive, threatening presence. "Tous," used with "oripeaux," "tabous," and "interdits" indicates that the Patriarchs' repression is total.

White interdictions, listed in a series of street-sign messages (*"Attention / Ici danger / Déviation / Chasse gardée / Terrain priveé / Domaine réservé / Défense d'entrer / Ni chiens ni nègre sur le gazon"*) end the poem and at the same time bring closure to native hopes. The last sign, the most shameful of all, sums up the flagrant nature of the disgrace of white repression of blacks. These are French signs and French rules; blacks had no part in their formulation. They are not agreed upon; they are imposed. All together they represent every stricture, every regulation, every procedure, and pressure of a dominant class intent on keeping its favored status.

It is significant that Damas mentions only two of Noah's sons, Shem and Japheth, and omits the third, Ham. Traditionally, the world is shown divided among Noah's three sons: Shem received the Semitic nations, Japheth, the Indo-European lands, and Ham, Africa. In an ingenious and ironic reversal, Ham, traditionally portrayed as Noah's cursed son, does not participate in the nefarious activities of his brothers, his father, and Methuselah. Ham, the villain, is redeemed by his absence in the poem and finds himself aligned with the black race in Africa against all the other nations of the world assigned to Shem and Japheth.

How is it that Ham became Noah's cursed son, and what did this curse consist of ? The tradition starts in the Bible. The Old Testament account of Noah and his sons describes two events. In the first (Genesis VI-VIII), Noah is the hero of the flood story, the great Patriarch chosen by God to perpetuate the human race after its extinction. Noah's sons are married at this time, enter the ark with Noah, and are saved. After the flood, God blesses Noah, Shem, Ham, and Japheth to "be fruitful and multiply and replenish the earth" (Genesis IX, I).

The second narrative (Genesis IX, 18-27), which seems to be unaware of the flood story, deals with Noah's shameless drunkenness and Ham's apparent irreverent behavior toward his father. Ham sees his father's drunken state and nakedness and describes the experience to his brothers. Shem and Japheth show deference to their father's precarious predicament by approaching him backwards with averted eyes in order to cover his nakedness. Aware of Ham's unworthy conduct toward him, Noah curses Ham through Ham's son, Canaan. "And he (Noah) said, Cursed be Canaan, a servant of servants shall he be to his brethren. And he said, Blessed be the Lord God of Shem; and Canaan shall be his servant. God shall enlarge Japheth, and he shall dwell in the tents of Shem; and Canaan shall be his servant."

The traditional identification of Ham with Africa led to the notion that Noah's curse on Ham and his descendants was the mark of a black skin. But the geographical allocation to Ham stands on shaky ground. In Genesis X, XI, Ham's sons, Cush, Mizraim, Phut, and Canaan are also listed as lands belonging to Ham, and accordingly, Ham has four branches: Cush corresponds to Ethiopia, Mizraim to Egypt, Phut to Libya, and the fourth branch is Ca-

naan. Eventually, as we noted, Ham is identified with all the south lands known to the Israelites. A discrepancy arises because of Canaan's location outside of Africa. Moreover, at the time of the stories about Noah in the Bible, Ethiopia was not Negroid; Egypt and Libya were not either and are not to this day. A part of Palestine, Canaan lay between the Jordan River and the Dead Sea on the east and the Mediterranean Sea on the west. Canaan, which was mostly Semitic, not Negroid, was eventually conquered and assimilated by Israel. It would seem that the curse of black skin on Canaan (the Biblical personage) sufficed to categorize Canaan (the land) as black, too. Eventually, since it was impossible to regard Canaan a representative land of Africa, Egypt took its place. Ham in this interpretation, becomes equivalent to Egypt, and thus, Egypt is referred to as the home of Ham in Psalms 78:51, 105:23, 27, and 106:22.

Jewish legends, beginning in the second century A.D., provide more information on Ham's curse. They assert that Canaan received it instead of Ham because God's blessing on Ham placed him beyond Noah's curse. The stories about Canaan, as with Ham, stress his perverse nature. Canaan's last will and testament to his children encouraged them to love one another, love robbery, love lewdness, hate their masters, and never speak the truth.

There are other attempts to explain Ham's curse. The Talmudists represent Ham, the dog, and the raven, as the only ones in the ark who had sexual intercourse with their partners, while all the other humans and animals abstained. It is for this immoral conduct that Ham is cursed to be black.

Another reason for Ham's curse derives from his behavior during Noah's drunkenness. The Bible states simply (Genesis IX, 20) that "Noah began to be an husbandman, and he planted a vineyard." The legends amplify this account, indicating that Satan became a collaborator with Noah in the work of cultivating the vine and making wine. The story of Noah's drunkenness is also expanded in the legends, so that Ham witnesses his father in the act of sexual intercourse. Ham mocks his father before his brothers and adds to his irreverence with a greater outrage. He attempts to mutilate Noah to prevent his father's procreation. When Noah awoke from his wine, he cursed Canaan:

> Therefore he put the curse upon the last-born son of the son that had prevented him from begetting a younger son than the three he had. The descendants of Ham through Canaan therefore, have red eyes, because Ham looked upon the nakedness of his father; they have misshapen lips, because Ham spoke with his lips to his brothers about the unseemly condition of his father; they have twisted, curly hair, because Ham turned and twisted his head round to see the nakedness of his father, and they go about naked because Ham did not cover the nakedness of his father.

The belief in Ham as father of the Negro race became universal in early Christendom, and this tradition, passed on in church writings, stories, and folklore, persists to the present time. The Ham genealogy linking him and his descendants to the blacks of Africa exists in Muslim legends in which Noah damns Ham with a black skin, a concept which vindicated slavery of blacks by Muslims. The persistence of Noah's curse was particularly strong in the United States in the early nineteenth century where it served as justification for slavery, particularly in anti-abolitionist tracts and pamphlets. Several themes are repeated over and over in the pro-slavery literature: the natural and innate inferiority of blacks, their sexual depravity, states rights and constitutional sanction of slavery, and above all, scriptural justification for slavery because of Noah's curse on Canaan and its application to blacks.

In brief summary, the curse of Ham through Canaan starts with scanty information in the Bible. Jewish legends amplify and perpetuate the notion of a curse on the black race. The concept attains acceptance in Christianity and Islam and persists to out day in stories and folklore which have served as a basis for divine sanction of racism and subjection of blacks by whites. It is in this context that we must understand Damas' reference to the Biblical Patriarchs. The Methuselah, Noah, Shem, Japheth relationship, not a random listing by the poet, was the perfect metaphor to illustrate the everlasting, far-reaching influence and the overwhelming power of a white curse on the black race. Ham, the symbol of his race and the hero of the poem, is not even mentioned. This muted understatement by the poet intensifies and heightens the drama and impact of the poem. The reader has to discover Ham, conjure him up from a faraway past, imagine the unequal, ongoing, epic struggle between him and his children with an omnipotent white god and his prophets. It is the reader who must exorcise Ham of his curses, esteem his blackness, rehabilitate and ennoble him as the worthy father of the black race. In Damas' poems, less becomes more. Damas drives his message home simply and powerfully.

FURTHER READING

Criticism

Cook, Mercer. "The Poetry of Leon Damas." *African Forum* 2, No. 4 (Spring 1967): 129-32.

    Reviews *Névralgies,* noting its continuities with Damas's earlier works and its implicit treatment of race.

Kennedy, Ellen Conroy. "Léon Damas." In *The Negritude Poets: An Anthology of Translations from the French,* edited by Ellen Conroy Kennedy, pp. 39-61. New York: Thunder's Mouth Press, 1989.

    Presents a brief biographical and critical introduction to Damas along with fifteen poems from *Pigments.*

Kesteloot, Lilyan. "Léon Damas: *Pigments.*" In her *Black Writers in French: A Literary History of Negritude,* translated by Ellen Conroy Kennedy, pp. 123-58. Philadelphia: Temple University Press, 1974.

    Remarks on the style and themes of *Pigments.*

Racine, Daniel L. "Tribute to the Poet Léon Gontran Damas." *Research in African Literatures* 10, No. 1 (Spring 1979): 90-4.

    Comments on the distinctive traits of Damas's poetry.

Warner, Keith Q. "Léon Damas and the Calypso." *CLA Journal* XIX, No. 3 (March 1976): 374-81.

    Highlights elements in Damas's poetry that are similar to the calypso, a primarily oral genre of Trinidadian poetry.

————, ed. *Critical Perspectives on Léon-Gontran Damas.* Washington, D.C.: Three Continents Press, 1988, 178 p.

    Collects interviews and essays covering various aspects of Damas's career. The collection also contains a bibliography of works by and about Damas.

Additional coverage of Damas's life and career is contained in the following sources published by Gale Research: *Black Writers;* **and** *Contemporary Authors,* **Vols. 73-76 [obituary], and 125.**

John Grisham

1955(?)-

American novelist.

The following entry provides an overview of Grisham's career through 1994.

INTRODUCTION

An immensely popular author of "legal thrillers," Grisham is best known for his novel *The Firm* (1991), which centers around a recent Harvard Law School graduate who, after learning that his firm is heavily involved in organized crime, risks his life to help the FBI indict his associates and their Mob bosses. Although his novels are sometimes characterized as simplistic thrillers, lacking plausible plots and developed characters, Grisham is often praised for highly suspenseful, compelling narratives that display his extensive legal knowledge. Grisham has stated: "I write to grab readers. This isn't serious literature."

Biographical Information

Grisham was born in Arkansas, but during his childhood he and his family moved frequently so his father, an itinerant construction worker, could find employment. When Grisham was twelve, his family settled in Southaven, Mississippi. He earned a B.S. at Mississippi State University and went on to earn his law degree at the University of Mississippi. Shortly after graduating from law school, he and his wife, Renée, returned to Southaven where Grisham set up a small practice as a defense attorney. In the 1980s he was elected to the Mississippi House of Representatives, but he quit before finishing his second term, frustrated by his inability to enact changes in the state's education budget. Grisham left his law practice in 1990 in order to pursue a full-time writing career.

Major Works

Set in fictional Clanton, Mississippi, Grisham's first novel, *A Time to Kill* (1989), centers around the trial of a black Vietnam veteran who murders two white men after they brutally rape his ten-year-old daughter. The novel relates attorney Jake Brigance's defense of the grieving father before an all-white jury as well as the numerous attempts made on Brigance's life by the Ku Klux Klan. *The Firm, The Pelican Brief* (1992), and *The Client* (1993) all feature unsuspecting protagonists who are suddenly thrust into dangerous, life-threatening situations. In *The Firm* Mitchell McDeere struggles against Mob hitmen who work for his corrupt associates. While he desperately searches for evidence of their criminal activities, he is simultaneously trying to avoid being killed or framed. The action of *The Pelican Brief* begins with the murders of two United States Supreme Court justices. Darby Shaw, a law student at Tulane University, attempts to explain the motives behind

the two killings in a document that becomes known as "The Pelican Brief." When the criminals learn that Shaw has discovered the truth, they chase her across the eastern United States, making numerous attempts on her life. The hero of *The Client* is Mark Sway, an eleven-year-old who knows where a powerful Mob boss has hidden the body of a murdered United States senator. Mark hires defense attorney Reggie Love to assist him as he flees the law enforcement officials who want him to reveal his secret and the organized crime figures who want to silence him. Set in Mississippi, *The Chamber* (1994) concerns the defense of a Ku Klux Klan member in his late sixties. Convicted in his third trial of a 1967 fire-bombing of a Jewish civilrights lawyer's office, the man is sentenced to die in the gas chamber. In his appeal he is represented by his estranged grandson, who becomes obsessed with his grandfather's case.

Critical Reception

Upon its initial publication in 1989, *A Time to Kill* received very little critical attention, but the overwhelming success of *The Firm* sparked interest in Grisham's first novel, which was then praised by critics as forceful, dramatic, and thought-provoking. Commentators cited Grisham's legal expertise as well as his authentic portrayal of customs and values in the American South as some of the strengths of *A Time to Kill*. While *The Firm, The Pelican Brief,* and *The Client* have been faulted for implausible storylines, undeveloped characters, and simplistic, stilted dialogue, all three novels have been best-sellers, a phenomenon many critics attribute to Grisham's ability to captivate readers with his blend of intriguing legal predicaments, high tension, and unexpected plot twists. In a review of *The Client*, Christopher Lehmann-Haupt observed: "Mr. Grisham enraptures us with a story that has hardly any point. . . . What's most irritating is how deeply the plot hooks us." Some critics have argued that Grisham displays considerable talent as a writer, maintaining that his characterizations are accurate and well-developed and his dialogue arresting and realistic. Frank J. Prial, in a review of *The Pelican Brief*, asserted: "[Grisham] has an ear for dialogue and is a skillful craftsman. Like a composer, he brings all his themes together at the crucial moment for a gripping, and logical, finale." Like *A Time to Kill, The Chamber* has been praised for its compelling plot, use of complex legal details, and commentary on such controversial issues as racism and vigilantism.

PRINCIPAL WORKS

A Time to Kill   (novel)   1989
The Firm   (novel)   1991
The Pelican Brief   (novel)   1992
The Client   (novel)   1993
The Chamber   (novel)   1994

CRITICISM

David Keymer   (review date 15 June 1989)

SOURCE: A review of *A Time to Kill*, in *Library Journal*, Vol. 114, No. 11, June 15, 1989, p. 80.

[*The following is Keymer's positive review of* A Time to Kill.]

In this lively novel [*A Time to Kill*], Grisham explores the uneasy relationship of blacks and whites in the rural South. His treatment is balanced and humane, if not particularly profound, slighting neither blacks nor whites. Life becomes complicated in the backwoods town of Clanton, Mississippi, when a black worker is brought to trial for the murder of the two whites who raped and tortured his young daughter. Everyone gets involved, from Klan to NAACP. Grisham's pleasure in relating the byzantine complexities of Clanton politics is contagious, and he tells a good story. There are touches of humor in the dialogue; the characters are salty and down-to-earth. An enjoyable

book, which displays a respect for Mississippi ways and for the contrary people who live there.

West Coast Review of Books (review date February 1991)

SOURCE: A review of *The Firm*, in *West Coast Review of Books*, Vol. 16, No. 2, February, 1991, p. 17.

[*In the following review, the critic provides a laudatory assessment of* The Firm.]

How many different ways are there to use trite phrases like "gripping," "compelling," and all those other overused adjectives that fit this wonderful novel of suspense to a tee? Quite simply put, [*The Firm*] is one of the best thrillers to come along in a while and, to use a couple more cliches, it's a "real page-turner," a "roller-coaster ride" of adventure. I wince to say it, but "you won't be able to put it down." If this review is cliche-ridden, rest assured the novel is not.

Mitch McDeere, a recent graduate of Harvard Law School, is being recruited by several top firms. But none of the firms can compete with Bendini, Lambert & Locke, a Memphis-based firm that offers him a salary, a car and a lifestyle so incredible that Mitch jumps at the chance to work a 70-hour, six-day week in order to become a millionaire by age 40.

But all is not right at the firm which appears to be staffed by "Stepford Attorneys": No one ever leaves it, no one ever complains, and the longer the associates remain, the more they allow the firm to run their lives—even regarding such personal decisions as when to have children and where to live. Mitch is too busy to notice these irregularities until an FBI agent points out that there have been a number of "accidental" deaths in the firm, and he reveals the truth about it. Mitch must now choose whether to cooperate with the feds and lose everything he's worked for, or continue with a crooked firm, risking a prison sentence if the truth is exposed. Truly a man in the middle, he is forced to start running—from the firm, the FBI, and even from his own family.

The author is a criminal defense attorney by profession; but first and foremost, he is a wonderful storyteller. His characters are alive, and his plot unfolds with a chilling pace that does not let up for an instant.

There's no new way of expressing admiration for such a tight thriller without stooping to cliches. Just read it. It's damned good.

Bill Brashler   (review date 24 February 1991)

SOURCE: "Corporate Lawyers Who Lead Wild Lives," in *Chicago Tribune—Books*, February 24, 1991, p. 6.

[*Brashler is an American novelist, short story writer, biographer, and critic. In the following review, he praises Grisham's characterizations and literary strategy in* The Firm.]

Love a lawyer—no easy task in these litigious times—and you are usually enamored of a trial lawyer. At least in literature, where the zealous defender or prosecutor pursues the law in its purest form and shines on the page. Corporate and tax attorneys, those steel-lapeled "of counsels," usually languish in mahogany suites, out of metaphor's eye.

But that was before *L.A. Law* and other entertainments came along and somehow injected intrigue and spice into the lives of those on retainer. They do have blood as well as billable hours, as it turns out.

John Grisham's *The Firm* takes things a step further. It gives us Bendini, Lambert & Locke, a smug, rich Memphis, Tenn., tax firm so corrupt it makes the sleaziest ambulance chaser look honorable.

> What is impressive about the *The Firm's* narrative is Grisham's ability to show us the schemes of the bad guys along with those of the innocents. This is not a mystery, but a well-paced and, at times, harrowing thriller.
>
> —*Bill Brashler*

Bigwigs from BL&L appear on page one of this adept first novel as they try to recruit young Mitch McDeere, one of Harvard Law School's brightest. "It's an impressive firm, Mitch," says senior partner Oliver Lambert. "We're small and we take care of each other."

Do they ever. Their offer is $80,000 plus bonuses, a low-interest mortgage loan and a leased BMW. In return, McDeere simply has to work his tail off—70-hour weeks are expected—and toe the firm's line. By 45, he'll be a multi-millionaire.

Of course, all this is too good to be true. Then again, so is Mitch McDeere. Brilliant, tireless, witty and married to a looker, he also wows the firm's most insufferable partners and bills great heaps of hours.

Imagine McDeere's surprise when he is approached by an FBI agent who tells him that his new firm is rotten to its wingtips and that the recent vacation deaths of two partners were not accidental. The firm, McDeere later learns, is an active front for a Chicago—where else? —crime family.

Grisham is a criminal defense attorney in Mississippi—how does he know so much about the corporate law types?—and *The Firm* works on just about every level. Though it asks the reader to chew large chunks of disbelief in the name of collusion, conspiracy and ruthlessness, it makes up for that with savvy, crisp portraits of lawyers on the make. And McDeere is a likeable straight arrow who—even though he joined this crew in the first place—throws just enough back at his bosses to put us on his side.

What is impressive about the narrative is Grisham's ability to show us the schemes of the bad guys along with those of the innocents. This is not a mystery, but a well-paced and, at times, harrowing thriller. We are a small half-step ahead of McDeere and wife, but at the mercy of the villains and the train of events.

Grisham's villains shine, mainly because he has given them dimension and intelligence. The FBI's hat is not totally white; and even McDeere has his own agenda when things get tight.

There are glitches, however. We are to believe that the firm's lethal agents see and hear McDeere wherever he goes, yet he somehow conveniently manages to meet secretly with his few confederates and plan his survival. There is also a delicious diet of coincidence that books like this depend on.

But none of the nits, and the absence of even a grain or two of humor, keeps *The Firm* from reading like a whirlwind. Grisham knows his lawyers and hands them their just desserts. And how often does that happen?

Peter S. Prescott   (review date 25 February 1991)

SOURCE: "Murky Maneuvers in a Lethal Law Firm," in *Newsweek*, Vol. CXVII, No. 8, February 25, 1991, p. 63.

[*Prescott is an American editor, nonfiction writer, and critic. In the following review of* The Firm, *he lauds Grisham's ability to write a compelling, though frequently improbable, plot.*]

What Robin Cook did for hospitals, John Grisham does for a law firm in his highly entertaining thriller, *The Firm.* What evil lurks within the file drawers of Bendini, Lambert & Locke, a private tax outfit in Memphis? You'd think a bright fellow like Mitchell McDeere, third in his Harvard Law class, might be suspicious when the partners offer him $80,000 to start, plus bonuses, a BMW, low mortgage, two country clubs and his school debts paid off. He'll work 100 hours a week at first, they tell him, but he'll be a partner and a millionaire in 10 years—and as for job security, nobody ever leaves the firm. No, but five associates have met odd deaths in the past 15 years. Mitch, numbed by greed—so much money in Memphis!—signs on.

No sooner is he in place than the FBI rousts him out. They tell Mitch the firm is owned by the Chicago mob, which uses it to set up dummy corporations on Grand Cayman that launder countless millions. They offer him a choice: cooperate with the FBI and risk being murdered by his new colleagues, or refuse—and be sent to prison when the FBI moves in.

Improbabilities abound, the characters are ciphers—and yet the story has significant strengths. It contains useful information on such matters as how to send the massed troops of justice in the wrong direction, and how to move dirty money among numbered accounts. It also offers an irresistible plot. A plot that seizes a reader on the opening page and propels him through 400 more is much rarer in commercial fiction than is generally supposed. Like all such stories, it works best in its first half, when we're wondering how Mitch will be tripped up. Toward the end, the story gets physical, which requires another narrative skill. Grisham excels here, too.

Charles Champlin   (review date 10 March 1991)

SOURCE: A review of *The Firm,* in *Los Angeles Times,* March 10, 1991, p. 7.

[*A former correspondent for both* Time *and* Life *magazines, Champlin is a well-known American journalist and critic. In the following review of* The Firm, *he asserts: "The character penetration is not deep, but the accelerating tempo of the paranoia-driven events is wonderful."*]

Consider the premise of *The Firm,* a second novel by John Grisham, who is a criminal defense attorney practicing in Mississippi and living near William Faulkner's home town of Oxford.

A brand-new Harvard Law graduate, who finished high in his class, owes $23,000 in school loans but has a choice of job offers, each more lucrative than the other. Wall Street beckons, but so does a small, obscure firm in Memphis that promises a fat salary, a BMW, a low-cost loan to buy a house and the prospect of retirement at 50 as a millionaire.

Irresistible, despite a curious aura of secrecy and enforced conformity about the place. Mitch McDeere takes the job and has hardly scrawled his first brief when an FBI agent (a college classmate) sidles up, warns him that the firm is bad news and urges McDeere to become an informant. By a set of coincidences, no one has quit the firm alive, although there are a few cheerful retirees. The last informants, McDeere finds, died in a mysterious boating accident.

The firm, McDeere also learns to his horror, was founded and is owned and run by a crime family out of Chicago, the more or less legitimate tax work a cover for a huge volume of money-laundering involving the company jet, which carries vast bundles of cash to cooperative banks in the Caribbean to await repatriation.

Our boy is caught in a tightening vice between the FBI, extorting him to play on threat of prison when (not if) the firm goes down, and his murderous and suspicious partners with a frightening, efficient security system Capone would have envied.

The character penetration is not deep, but the accelerating tempo of paranoia-driven events is wonderful: clandestine meetings, predawn prowlings, a dangerous imposture and a final cat-and-mouse pursuit through the South to a down-market stretch of Florida coast, leading to a fine ironic finish.

Pagan Kennedy   (review date July-August 1991)

SOURCE: A review of *The Firm,* in *VLS,* No. 97, July-August, 1991, p. 7.

[*In the following review of* The Firm, *Kennedy faults Grisham's excessive reliance on popular culture, his weak characterizations, and offensive stereotypes.*]

Sit back, relax, and pretend it's the 1980s. Of course, you're male and fresh out of Harvard Law, stunningly handsome, and married to a gal with great legs who dreams of "furniture, and wallpaper, and perhaps a pool before too long. And babies." So when a law firm in Memphis offers you—even before you've passed the bar—a BMW, a house, and 80 grand a year, you don't suspect a thing. Hey, it's an offer you can't refuse, right?

The Firm is a thriller in which author John Grisham concentrates less on his characters than on their conspicuous consumption—BMWs, silk ties, BMWs, solid-cherry desks and leather wing chairs, BMWs, restaurants in "chic [i.e., white] East Memphis," and condos under the tax-sheltering skies of the Cayman Islands. The book is your standard late '80s/early '90s Power Novel: Like *Bright Lights, Big City, Bonfire of the Vanities,* and *American Psycho,* it simultaneously worships and demonizes money. But while those books make some stab at serious themes (though *Psycho* just stabs for the hell of it), *The Firm* is free of the literary oat bran of social commentary; instead it serves up a delicious pâté of designer labels, schlocky suspense, and six-figure salaries.

Grisham particularly likes to linger over large sums of money: "The average for associates was one-seventy-five per hour. For partners, three hundred. Milligan got four hundred an hour from a couple of his clients, and Nathan Locke once got five hundred an hour for some tax work that involved swapping assets in several foreign countries. Five hundred bucks an hour!"

Typically, Grisham chooses the trendiest bad guys of the moment: the Mob. When our hero, Mitch McDeere, signs on with the high-paying firm, he unknowingly joins a front for a Mafia family. Though the thugs run a sophisticated money-laundering operation, it seems they could benefit from some laundering of the old-fashioned soap-and-water variety—or at least better taste in clothes. Grisham condemns his Mafia guys with all the cruelty of the *Glamour* Fashion Dos and Don'ts page: "His wrinkled shirt was mercifully unbuttoned at the collar, allowing his bulging neck to sag unrestricted. A thick polyester tie hung on the coatrack with a badly worn blazer."

It takes impeccably dressed Mitch, who we're told is a genius, several chapters to figure out the firm's nasty secret. The reader is way ahead of him. In fact, astute readers may realize the Mafia's involved before opening the book. The cover shows a little business-suited guy hanging from puppet strings as he tries to scrabble up a corporate-style marble wall—a not-so-subtle reference to the puppet-string logo of *The Godfather* movies.

Before long, Mitch learns that the house and the BMW have strings attached, too: They're bugged. But even unmonitored, Mitch and Abby are a Stepford couple:

> "What would you like to talk about?" she asked.
>
> "Getting pregnant."
>
> "I thought we were going to wait a few years."
>
> "We are. But I think we should practice diligently until then."

Pretty soon, thank God, there's no time for repartee. Mitch is approached by the FBI, which wants him to help nail his employers; meanwhile the Mob suspects something's up. Caught between two ruthless organizations, Mitch takes the '80s way out: He plots an escape, outwits both the Feds and the Mob, and winds up with millions.

The plot moves so quickly, like a fine-tuned BMW, you almost don't notice the bumps in the road, namely, the author's racism. I had steeled myself for babes in high heels, but not for shuffling waiters named Roosevelt or this scene, where Grisham gives his theory about why Kentucky Fried tastes so bad on the Cayman Islands: "Colonel Sanders had the damnedest time teaching the island girls, though black or close to it, how to fry chicken. It was foreign to them." Gee, I guess only Southern blacks have that chicken-frying gene.

But offensiveness aside, *The Firm* has all the makings of a good TV movie, though it lacks women wearing huge shoulder pads who slap one another and say, "You scheming bitch." Reading this book was much like living in the '80s—you're repulsed, mesmerized, and glad it's over.

Jeffrey Toobin   (review date 23 February 1992)

SOURCE: "Still More Lawyer-Bashing from Novelist John Grisham," in *Chicago Tribune—Books,* February 23, 1992, p. 4.

[*In the following review of* The Pelican Brief, *Toobin asserts that while Grisham's characters "lack humanity" and situations in the novel are implausible, his plots contain a "narrative drive that welcomes readers to suspend disbelief."*]

John Grisham has done it again—for better or worse. Grisham's 1991 legal thriller *The Firm* tells the story of a young attorney lured by a high salary to a mysterious Memphis law firm where the new associates have a habit of dropping dead. After learning the dark secrets behind the firm's success, the hero worries less about blowing the whistle on his employers than about stealing their money. *The Firm* rang true with a public willing to believe everything awful about lawyers and took up seemingly permanent residence on the best-seller lists.

Grisham now seeks a bigger stage for his cynicism, turning his attention from a single corrupted-by-the-mob law firm to the White House and Supreme Court. *The Pelican Brief* begins late on an October night in the mid-1990s, when Justice Abe Rosenberg, the Supreme Court's 91-year-old liberal firebrand, is murdered in his home in Washington. Hours later, Justice Glenn Jensen, a dimwitted conservative, is garrotted in a gay porno theater. Whodunit?

Actually, that's not much of a mystery. The investigators—and the readers—learn quickly that a slinky terrorist-for-hire pocketed a few million bucks for the hits. The real question is who paid for it and why.

The surviving justices, as well as the FBI, begin scouring the Supreme Court's docket for litigants with large grievances, but Darby Shaw, a second-year law student at Tulane who is also "beautiful and brilliant," writes up a novel hypothesis in a paper she calls the "Pelican Brief." When Shaw's law professor-boyfriend passes the brief to a friend at the FBI, the professor is promptly blown to smithereens by a bomb clearly meant for Shaw.

As the brief circulates in Washington, everyone who sees it finds a reason to cover it up—particularly a top White House aide so evil that he makes H. R. Haldeman look like Beaver Cleaver. Everyone, it appears, is out to get Shaw. She sighs to a friend, "What would you do if you knew you were supposed to be dead, and the people trying to kill you had assassinated two Supreme Court justices, and knocked off a simple law professor, and they have billions of dollars which they obviously don't mind using to kill with?"

What Darby does is change her hair color and sip fancy coffee at a variety of picturesque New Orleans locales—something that makes sense only if you view this novel as a screenplay-in-waiting.

Indeed, the whole of *The Pelican Brief* is about as believable as an episode of "Mr. Ed." The White House aide warns a colleague about repeating the errors of Watergate, yet he installs a taping system in the Oval office—with the '90s touch of video as well as audio. The FBI and CIA obstruct justice as casually as they order office supplies. And so on.

Yet the new novel shares with *The Firm* a narrative drive that welcomes readers to suspend disbelief. Grisham knows how to drop hints and red herrings with the best of them, and he writes good dialogue. Grisham does cheat a little when he lets virtually every character in the novel know what's in the darned brief before he finally clues in his readers, near the end of the book. Still, he does keep some suspense rolling along and delivers a punchy, if not exactly surprising, conclusion.

What is most troubling about *The Pelican Brief*—and *The Firm,* too—is the universal loathsomeness of the characters. Grisham's law is, the more powerful the figure, the more sinister. Readers who believe that mad billionaires control armies of private assassins and that presidents view murder as a tool to improve their polling numbers will find a kindred spirit in Grisham.

That simplistic approach underlies the contrast between Grisham and his predecessor in legal-literary superstardom, Scott Turow. Think of Raymond Horgan, the once idealistic district attorney in Turow's *Presumed Innocent,* who in the midst of a tough political campaign betrays his former protege, murder suspect Rusty Sabich.

Horgan is troubled, flawed, real. Turow, recognizes that lawyers don't lack altruism; rather, like everyone else, they just suppress it a lot of the time. Grisham's characters don't just lack altruism, they lack humanity.

And, in *The Pelican Brief* they engage in a conspiracy so vast, so secret, so complex, so malevolent that. . . . Oliver Stone, call your agent.

Frank J. Prial   (review date 15 March 1992)

SOURCE: "Too Liberal to Live," in *The New York Times Book Review,* March 15, 1992, p. 9.

[*In the following review of* The Pelican Brief, *Prial declares: "Mr. Grisham has written a genuine page-turner. He has an ear for dialogue and is a skillful craftsman."*]

John Grisham hates lawyers. Really hates them. His impressive 1991 best seller, **The Firm,** exposed an imaginary Memphis law firm owned by Chicago Mafiosi. His new thriller, **The Pelican Brief,** takes aim at powerful Washington lawyers who front for a homicidal oil billionaire.

In **The Firm** the slimy lawyers were the story; this time around, they are usually just offstage. In the end, though, when the good guys win, the dotty oil man, with his prehensile Howard Hughes toenails, skips to Egypt or some place like that. Mr. Grisham couldn't care less about him. It's the evil corporate lawyers he's after and, since it's his book, he gets them.

Rapacious lawyers cannot, alone, a thriller make—at least not for a reviewer who has spent a substantial part of his life covering them in courtrooms. They are too commonplace. No, you have to have a rattling good story, too, and that Mr. Grisham provides.

> Grisham has an ear for dialogue and is a skillful craftsman. Like a composer, he brings all his themes together at the crucial moment for a gripping, and logical, finale.
>
> —*Frank J. Prial*

Two liberal Supreme Court justices have been assassinated. No one can come up with a motive. Darby Shaw, a young law student at Tulane University in New Orleans, has a theory: someone coming before the Court might want to give the conservative President an opportunity to replace the two liberals. Checking appeals pending in the Federal courts, she finds what she is looking for and produces a four-page memorandum. This is the pelican brief.

The investigation quickly involves the F.B.I., the C.I.A. and the White House, where the dull-witted President is, in fact, happy with his unexpected Supreme Court nominations. "I want young conservative white men opposed to abortion, pornography, queers, gun control, racial quotas," he says. "I want judges who hate dope and criminals and are enthusiastic about the death penalty. Understand?"

Soon people who have seen the brief, or even know about it, start to die. It's Darby the killers want, but the first to go is her law school professor and lover, blown up in his Porsche by a bomb intended for her. Darby hops around the country, changing airplanes, clothes and hair colors

and ducking into phone booths to give instructions to a Washington *Post* reporter who is trying to break the story.

There are improbabilities—like the elderly White House janitor who feeds state secrets (good ones) to a reporter, and Darby's pluck, which never flags. But this is an adventure story, isn't it?

The chase is fast-paced but not as fast as in **The Firm.** There Mr. Grisham dealt with two old-fashioned American preoccupations, paranoia and greed. This time around, he also tackles the court, the Government, the ecology and the newspaper business—among other things.

Just when the chase gets hot, we cut to the Oval Office, where the empty-headed Chief Executive is sinking putts on the carpet and being manipulated by his evil chief of staff, Fletcher Coal. Or to a lawyer's office or a hotel room or F.B.I. headquarters, where count on it, people are sitting around and talking, and—maddeningly—the action drags.

O.K., there are lapses. Even so, Mr. Grisham has written a genuine page-turner. He has an ear for dialogue and is a skillful craftsman. Like a composer, he brings all his themes together at the crucial moment for a gripping, and logical, finale.

John Grisham probably has a long and successful writing career ahead—if he doesn't get preachy. It could be a problem; he's a lawyer, too. And you know how they do go on.

Aric Press   (review date 16 March 1992)

SOURCE: "A Breach of Contract," in *Newsweek,* Vol. CXIX, No. 11, March 16, 1992, p. 72.

[*In the following review of* The Pelican Brief, *Press faults Grisham for failing to explain key occurrences within the plot.*]

Thriller writers make a deal with their readers. In return for a willing suspension of disbelief, the author sets off on a merry, roller-coaster plot, dropping hints, feinting at shadows, setting off surprises, all with the promise of a reasonable explanation at the end. In his last book, **The Firm,** John Grisham upheld his end of the bargain, with a hugely successful tale of a young lawyer from Harvard who makes the mistake of joining a Memphis law firm secretly controlled by the Mafia. Comes now Grisham's new book, **The Pelican Brief,** another of the catch-me-if-you-can genre. This time, it's a brilliant and attractive female law student who's staying one step ahead of the FBI, the CIA and a politically well-connected tycoon who has his own stable of killers. (And there are some fiendish lawyers to hiss at, too!) Grisham keeps the pages turning but, in the end, badly breaches the thrillermeister-reader contract.

After a shadowy killer assassinates two Supreme Court justices, the nation is stumped for suspects and motive. Working in the nether reaches of the Tulane law library— far from the lecherous glances of male law students or the boozy reach of her law-professor lover—Darby Shaw solves the crime. She explains her theory in a memo that becomes known as the pelican brief; the title refers to the endangered species at the heart of the lawsuit that sets off the killings. She thinks it's all pretty farfetched (she's right, of course) but her mentor passes it on to high-placed friends in Washington and the next thing the reader hears is bombs going off and body parts crashing to the pavement.

The setup is swell, and the chase is daring, but there's no brain food here. Why would anyone, even the richest scoundrel in Louisiana, want to kill two justices of the Supreme Court four years before his case might, *might,* be heard? Why, indeed, when one is 91 and barely alive, and the other is described as erratic at best? Grisham doesn't tell except to lay the idea off on some legal wizard who doesn't shed a clue either. Who leaked Darby's brief to the bad guys? Nobody knows and nobody much cares including the FBI director, even though the tip led to the death of the FBI's counsel. What's in the brief? Hard to say, since we never get to read the whole thing. The one chapter seemingly devoted to it is nifty but it doesn't match the early descriptions. And, by the way, how did Darby crack the case? As she says when she emerges from the law library, she didn't. All she had was a surmise, suggesting perhaps that where legal research fears to tread, legal fiction rushes in. Caveat emptor.

Karen Stabiner   (review date 5 April 1992)

SOURCE: A review of *The Pelican Brief,* in *Los Angeles Times Book Review,* April 5, 1992, p. 6.

[*In the following review of* The Pelican Brief, *Stabiner notes: "What makes this Hollywood fodder is Grisham's ability to mix and match the elements of commercial fiction. The symbiosis is almost irresistible."*]

Some books are born to movie deals, others have movie deals thrust upon them. [*The Pelican Brief*] bears the box-office chromosome. Grisham has fashioned a sexy (if oddly sexless) thriller about a gorgeous young law student who stumbles upon the identity of the man who hired an assassin to snuff out two Supreme Court justices. The ancient liberal justice Rosenberg and his conservative, closeted gay associate seem to have nothing in common, save that each man meets a gruesome death on the same evening. But dogged bibliophile Darby Shaw finds a connection that has eluded all of Washington—in part because she has a great mind, in part because the golf-playing President of the United States has good reason not to want anyone to solve the crime. What makes this Hollywood fodder is Grisham's ability to mix and match the elements of commercial fiction. The symbiosis is almost irresistible. Tom Clancy can write about political espionage, but Grisham does it with a woman-in-distress overlay. And what a woman. Darby Shaw is every boy's dream—red-haired and -toed, thanks to a lover with a pedicure fetish, tall (most of it great legs) and, in a nod to the demands of post-feminist America, brilliant, but still accessible. Even the predictable dips in the pace (How long is it going to take for the guys who can save her to figure this one out?) are fun.

James Colbert   (review date 28 February 1993)

SOURCE: "Grisham's Latest: Passing Judgment on *The Client*," in *Chicago Tribune—Books,* February 28, 1993, p. 7.

[*In the following review, Colbert provides a negative assessment of* The Client, *characterizing Grisham's works as "bland and inoffensive, . . . the literary equivalent of pureed potatoes or Muzak."*]

On a literary level, there is little to recommend John Grisham's new novel, **The Client.** The characters are wooden, and the plot is contrived. The pace is plodding and because the book never gathers any momentum, it seems painfully overlong.

It hardly seems worth the bother to read such a book—much less review it—but as the jacket of **The Client** proudly states, Grisham has written "three consecutive number-one bestsellers"—**A Time To Kill, The Firm** and **The Pelican Brief**—and "has become one of the most popular authors of our time." And that claim can be substantiated by a trip to any chain bookstore, where John Grisham posters and displays and whole racks of his books abound. That being the case, one has to wonder why such undistinguished work enjoys such popular success.

In **The Client** a black Lincoln appears in the woods where 11-year-old Mark Sway and his younger brother are playing. The driver has come to the woods to kill himself, but before he does, for reasons that are hard to fathom, he tells young Mark that he is a lawyer, that his client, Barry "The Blade" Muldanno, has killed a U.S. senator, and that The Blade has put the senator's body in concrete under his, the lawyer's, garage. This knowledge transferred, Mark escapes and the lawyer kills himself—which makes Mark the witness needed by Roy Foltrigg, the ambitious U.S. attorney who is prosecuting The Blade for the senator's murder.

Foltrigg "was the prosecutor, the people's lawyer, the government fighting crime and corruption. He was right, justice was on his side, and he had to be ready to attack evil at any moment. . . . He had pushed hard for a speedy trial, because he was right, and he would get a conviction. The United States of America would win!"

Well, maybe, maybe not. The outcome depends on whether Foltrigg can get Mark to divulge where The Blade hid the senator's body—a task made considerably more difficult when the boy hires a lawyer who is willing, for one dollar, to devote her entire practice to him.

And so it goes. Mark is threatened by the bad guys. His family's trailer home is burned. Held in detention, he may, after all, have to tell what he knows. But perhaps Mark can extricate himself. All he has to do is convince his lawyer to help him with his escape, scare off three Mafia legbreakers, back down the bungling FBI and work a deal to go into the Witness Protection Program.

If all that sounds a touch improbable, even for a precocious 11 year old, it is. So the question remains, how does such a book appeal to millions of fans, as Grisham's previous novels have done and as this one seems likely to do.

Well, in our consumer-oriented society, as any advertising person will tell you, there are certain items—including quite a few books and movies—that sell not because they are distinguished in any way but because they are bland and inoffensive, in this case, the literary equivalent of pureed potatoes or Muzak. And what John Grisham has attained is the perfect pitch of Muzak.

That is not to denigrate Grisham's achievement, for a product such as his can be created only if one has a certain marketing acumen. But if it is sad that such flawless lack of distinction achieves such success, one still wonders whether that occurs because the consumer has an innate taste for blandness or because the market is so good at selling particular pieces of it.

Lawrence J. Goodrich   (review date 5 March 1993)

SOURCE: "Topical Legal Thriller Spins an Intriguing but Improbable Tale," in *The Christian Science Monitor,* March 5, 1993, p. 10.

[*In the following review of* The Client, *Goodrich praises Grisham's treatment of the juvenile justice system and compelling plot, commenting: "If you can suspend disbelief long enough to accept an 11-year-old leading the adult world around by the nose for 422 pages, the rewards in* The Client *are worth it."*]

John Grisham is on a roll: He's had three No. 1 bestsellers in the two years since *The Firm* was published. His latest legal thriller, *The Client,* contains all the ingredients of a fourth consecutive winner.

The plot revolves around an unlikely hero: Mark Sway, an 11-year-old Memphis, Tenn., boy who, with his younger brother, witnesses the suicide of New Orleans lawyer Jerome Clifford. Mark and his brother are living with their young mother in a trailer park after her divorce from a husband who abused them all. This and the social frictions at school between the trailer-park kids and those from "better" homes are supposed to have made Mark "street wise" and mature beyond his years.

When Mark tries to intervene to keep Clifford from killing himself, he is captured by the suicidal lawyer, who decides they'll go together. In the process, he lets Mark in on a big secret: He is a lawyer for Mafioso Barry Muldanno, the murderer of a United States senator from Louisiana. Clifford tells Mark the FBI hasn't been able to locate the body, which Muldanno, in an unguarded moment, has let slip is currently located under the lawyer's garage floor.

Mark escapes from Clifford just before the suicide, which leaves him the only person beside Muldanno who knows the secret that can sew up the case. Soon the Memphis authorities, the US attorney in New Orleans, and the mob figure out that Mark probably knows something. The authorities want him to tell what he knows, but Mark has seen too many crime movies, and he's convinced that he's dead if he does.

With his brother lying in the hospital with traumatic stress syndrome from witnessing the suicide, and his mother spending every minute at the bedside, Mark decides he

needs a lawyer. Fortunately for him, he stumbles on Reggie Love, a self-made woman with a sad past who just happens to specialize in child-abuse and neglect cases. Together she and Mark modestly set out to outwit the system, the cops, and the mob.

The problem with this kind of thriller is the frequent implausibility of the plot. But if you can accept the premise of *The Client,* especially Mark's reasons for refusing to talk and a lawyer who takes him seriously, you're in for a great read.

The novel throws a spotlight on the treatment of juveniles by a system that, in trying to assist them often does more harm than good. The characters live in a messy world featuring the usual mobsters with no respect for life; sleazy prosecutors and hangers-on who see their jobs as mere stepping-stones to higher office; jurisdictional spats between federal and state authorities; and a veteran police reporter whose articles endanger Mark and land the reporter in jail for contempt of court.

But even if the good guys aren't always all that good, most of them are trying to do the right thing. This is not a novel of hopelessness: While there are ambiguities in the ending, there are many small acts of goodness along the way. A hero who emerges in the latter part of the book is Harry Roosevelt, a black juvenile-court judge who could have gone on to a more lofty position but declined to, and who really does try to find a solution that will place Mark and his family in the least danger.

If you can suspend disbelief long enough to accept an 11-year-old leading the adult world around by the nose for 422 pages, the rewards in *The Client* are worth it. Take it along with you to the beach this summer.

Christopher Lehmann-Haupt   (review date 5 March 1993)

SOURCE: "How Do You Fight the Mob? Get a Lawyer," *The New York Times,* March 5, 1993, p. C29.

[*Lehmann-Haupt is a prominent American critic. In the following review, he faults Grisham for frustrating readers with likeable characters and an undeveloped, implausible, but gripping plot, advising the reader to "settle into* The Client *for the captivating read it promises. Just don't look for any surprises. What you expect is more than what you get."*]

The opening of John Grisham's latest legal thriller, *The Client,* is irresistible. Eleven-year-old Mark Sway is leading his 8-year-old brother, Ricky, into the woods near their trailer-park home in Memphis, Tenn., to give him his first cigarette. While the boys are lighting up behind some bushes, a long, black, shiny Lincoln comes rolling up a dirt road close by and pulls to a stop. A chubby man in a black suit climbs out, removes a water hose from the trunk, attaches one end to the exhaust pipe, slides the other end through the partly open left rear window, climbs back into the car and starts the engine.

Little Ricky wants to run home, but Mark, being older and more streetwise, knows what he must do. He crawls to the rear of the car, removes the hose from the exhaust and sneaks back to the bushes. After a few minutes, the man climbs out again, weeping and mumbling and holding a bottle of whisky, reattaches the hose and climbs back into the car. Ricky begins to cry and to plead with his brother to take him home, but Mark pulls the hose loose again. This bizarre ritual continues until the man catches Mark and drags him into the car to die beside him.

Inside, the man threatens Mark with a gun and drunkenly explains why he's committing suicide. He's a lawyer who does work for the mob, and one of his clients, Barry (the Blade) Muldanno, has murdered a United States Senator. Nobody can find the body to use as evidence, but the suicidal lawyer has just learned that Barry hid it under the floor of the lawyer's garage. Besides Barry the Blade, he's the only one who knows, so his life is worthless.

While the lawyer is telling Mark all this and getting steadily drunker, Ricky removes the hose. Mark then escapes from the car and hides in the bushes again. The lawyer climbs out of the car once more, sees the detached hose and shoots himself in the head. The boys run home. Ricky goes into traumatic shock and has to be hospitalized. Both the police and Barry the Blade begin to suspect what the lawyer told Mark just before he died. They begin to press the boy to tell.

But what is most astonishing about this opening, which takes all of 20 pages, is how little Mr. Grisham does with it in the next 400 pages. *The Client* brings new force to the word anticlimax. It is as if at the outset the narrator had announced that he was about to conduct us on a journey across a desert with a cactus and a rock in it to a mountain range beyond, and that several surprises were in store. The surprises turn out to be that the cactus is a cactus, the rock is a rock and the mountain range is a mountain range. Once again, as he did in *The Firm,* Mr. Grisham enraptures us with a story that has hardly any point.

What's most irritating is how deeply the plot hooks us. Mark Sway is "a tough little kid, raised on the streets and wise beyond his years," as another character gratuitously informs us. Instead of letting himself be pushed around, Mark goes out and hires himself a lawyer, a woman who calls herself Reggie Love, and he tells her what he's feeling:

> "I'm really sick of this. Just sick of it. All my buddies are in school today, having a good time, being normal, fighting with girls during recess, playing jokes on the teachers, you know, the usual stuff. And look at me. Running around town with my lawyer, reading about my adventures in the newspapers, looking at my face on the front page, hiding from reporters, dodging killers with switch-blades. It's like something out of a movie. A bad movie. I'm just sick of it. I don't know if I can take anymore. It's just too much."

Reggie Love is feisty too, a former battered wife who has rebuilt her life and now looks out for abused children. In the novel's only engaging scenes, she outsmarts the various prosecutors and F.B.I. men who want her client to cease obstructing justice.

But instead of developing his plot, Mr. Grisham simply strangles it, gesturing hysterically all the while at the cactus and the rock as if somebody were hiding behind them. The reader keeps wondering why clever little Mark doesn't send some sort of message to Barry the Blade:

> "I'm not telling where the corpse is, but if anything happens to me or my family, a dozen lawyers around the country will reveal the contents of a dozen safety-deposit boxes I've told them to open in the event of my demise."

This would be as plausible as what actually happens in the story.

A third of the way into the plot, Mark recalls how he once attacked his father for abusing his mother. "When he came back to the trailer, the door was of course open, and I was waiting. I had pulled a kitchen chair beside the door, and I damned near took his head off with the baseball bat. A perfect shot to his nose. I was crying and scared to death, but I'll always remember the sound of the bat crunching his face."

You think this brutal recounting has to be a setup for some climactic scene to come. But guess again! It's just one in a whole arsenal of Chekhovian pistols on the mantelpiece that never do get fired.

So settle into *The Client* for the captivating read it promises. Just don't look for any surprises. What you expect is more than what you get.

Tom Nolan   (review date 12 March 1993)

SOURCE: "The Grisham Formula Revisited," in *The Wall Street Journal,* March 12, 1993, p. A6.

[*In the following review, Nolan finds the plot of* The Client *implausible and the characters unappealing.*]

John Grisham established a formula for generating suspense in his first runaway bestseller, *The Firm*: An innocent citizen is caught between the opposing and uncompromising forces of organized crime and federal law enforcement. The protagonist defies both camps to fashion a unique way out of the dilemma.

Mr. Grisham hews to the formula in his new novel, *The Client.* Here the innocent confronted with unappealing options is Mark Sway, an 11-year-old Memphis boy, who is present when mob lawyer Jerome Clifford commits suicide.

Clifford's hottest client, a New Orleans hood known as Barry "The Blade" Muldanno, has been indicted for the murder of a senator, although the apparent victim's body has not yet been found. Clifford knows the location of the corpse and reveals that information to young Sway before killing himself. Local and federal law enforcement officials want Sway to tell what he knows, but the mobster's minions warn him not to.

Afraid to talk lest he jeopardize the lives of his family and himself, Sway all on his own gets himself an attorney, retaining for the sum of $1 the services of 52-year-old Reggie

Love, a shrewd and capable advocate specializing in protecting children's rights.

Love has her hands full looking out for this urchin. Among those arrayed against Sway are a sanctimonious, publicity-hungry U.S. attorney and a gaggle of determined FBI agents. The tough fourth-year lawyer soon has them all tied in knots, though, including the FBI—"the Fibbies," as the gangsters call them, or "those clowns," in the words of Mark Sway.

A great deal of disbelief must be suspended in order for this plot to unfold. Does it make any sort of sense for the mobsters to "warn" this boy to keep quiet? Wouldn't they prefer to eliminate the potential witness outright? Too much heat would be generated were they to commit such an outrageous crime, one hood says. More heat than for the murder of a senator?

And how does keeping silent protect Sway at all? Surely telling what he knows is Sway's only way to safety. Why would the bad guys come after him once the secret was out? And if the villainous Muldanno can elude FBI surveillance in order to hire people to harass and threaten the child-witness and his lawyer, couldn't he just as easily persuade some cronies to move the corpse he's so worried will be found?

Eventually Muldanno does just that, but only in order to set up a contrived slam-dunk sequence in which Sway and Love outwit a bunch even clumsier than The Gang That Couldn't Shoot Straight.

Just as aggravating as these implausibilities is the personality of the book's "hero," a tot who is alternately smug, patronizing and whiny—probably the most obnoxious child in American fiction since the little terror in O. Henry's "The Ransom of Red Chief." By midpoint of *The Client,* this reader found himself rooting for "those clowns."

Tom Mathews   (essay date 15 March 1993)

SOURCE: "Book 'Em," in *Newsweek,* Vol. CXXI, No. 11, March 15, 1993, pp. 79-81.

[*In the following excerpt from an essay that includes commentary by Grisham, Mathews surveys Grisham's career through* The Client *and discusses critical response to the author's works.*]

Grisham is a straight arrow making his way along a very crooked path—a world of sleazy lawyers, fathead politicians and hot-dog G-men where something always stinks just below the surface of wealth and respectability. Grisham's law is as simple as Aesop and as old as Scheherazade: bore 'em and you die. In *The Client* his hero is Mark Sway, an 11-year-old who tries to stop a suicide only to learn a mob secret that could cost him his life. To save himself from the bad guys—and the good guys—Sway pays $1, all he has, to hire Reggie Love, 52, a street lawyer with a divorcée's past and a grandmother's soul. Dodging Mafia hoods, crazy neighbors and the police, vowing to join a health club and get in better shape if she ever gets

out alive, Reggie wonders whether she is "too old for this nonsense. The things lawyers do."

It was those things that drove Grisham right into fiction. "I'm pretty cynical about the legal profession," he says. "Thrilled to be out of it." *A Time to Kill,* his first and best novel, is also his most autobiographical. In Jake Brigance, you find the distillation of Grisham's own experience as a small-town ham-and-egger around the De Soto County courthouse. Before an all-white jury, Brigance defends a black Viet vet who took an M-16 and blew away two crackers who raped his 10-year-old daughter. Grisham took three years to write it, getting up at 5 a.m. and scribbling in a Sparco notebook, the kind court reporters use. "My motives were pure when I wrote *A Time to Kill,*" he says. "It's better because you can almost smell the biscuits and the eggs and the grits and hear the chatter in the Coffee Shop; the people are better, the setting is better; you can feel the sweat sticking to their shirts in the July heat around the courthouse."

But the book didn't sell, so Grisham wrote his second novel, *The Firm,* as "a naked stab at commercial fiction." He tells the story of Mitchell Y. McDeere, Harvard Law, seduced by an $80,000 starting salary and a black BMW into joining a top-drawer law firm that turns out to be a money laundry for the mob. Into this tale Grisham poured his own contempt for corporate lawyers in $1,200 suits who pay for their $245 Cole Haan loafers and solid-cherry desks by billing $300 an hour for 30-hour days. He wrote *The Pelican Brief,* partly to convince [his wife,] Renée, his most important critic, that he could invent a strong woman. When the world's deadliest terrorist bumps off two Supreme Court justices, it is left to Darby Shaw, a Tulane law student, to figure out a plot the FBI can't—and the White House won't—unravel. It's the quintessential Grisham formula: "You take some horrible, mean, vicious, nasty conspiracy over here," he says. "You put a very sympathetic hero or heroine in the middle of it, you reach a point where their lives are at stake—and you get them out of it."

Not exactly *Crime and Punishment?* Grisham pleads nolo contendere. He puts on no literary airs. And yet . . . something seems to be eating him. . . .

"These legal thrillers are driving me nuts," he says, a confession that should give his publishers heartburn. And Oxford bookseller Richard Howorth, whose grandfather once gave Faulkner a D in English, warns literary sourpusses not to do the same with Grisham. "Anyone who dismisses Grisham as 'commercial'," he says, "is making a big mistake.". . .

For a writer committed to thrills, Grisham practices only safe sex in his prose. "I cannot write about sex," he confesses. At one meeting with his editor in New York, the subject came up, and Renée said, "Johnny can't write about sex. He knows very little about it." Stifling a guffaw, David Gernert, his editor, said, "Don't even try."

So readers love his books, but are they art?

"Oh, there are a few literary snots in town who take shots at me," Grisham says mildly. Vernon Chadwick, professor of English at Ole Miss, argues that the market people in Hollywood and New York have seized on Grisham to water down American culture with the Southern-novel lite. But it isn't that easy. "Marketing can do many things, but it can't just *buy* a mass readership," says Gary Fisketjon, an editor at Knopf. "Readers detect crassness, the wrong touch." Like trout scrutinizing a badly tied fly, they may rise, but they won't take the offering.

Given the abundance of ego and the shortage of cash among so many "real" writers, the astonishing thing is how many around Oxford, where literary matters count, are willing to speak up in Grisham's defense. "I suppose I would have been more sullen if a bad book were taken as serious literary work," says Barry Hannah, whose own *Bats Out of Hell,* just out from Houghton Mifflin, is superb. "I liked the way John cleared the air." Donna Tartt, the author of *The Secret History,* who comes from nearby Grenada, observes that Dr. Johnson believed anyone who wrote for any reason but to make money was mad.

Let's not duck the literary issue: artists do something Grisham doesn't. The artist clearly enlightens where the commercial writer entertains. Consider the case of Larry Brown, another Oxford novelist, who tried to go commercial only to wind up an artist in spite of himself. Brown was a captain in the fire department. He once hoped to make a little money moonlighting in literature. Over eight years, he wrote five novels—the first, he says, was about "sex-starved women and man-eating bears in Yellowstone," an idea that should have turned the trick, but didn't. He also wrote 100 short stories, only to throw them all out before publishing *Facing the Music,* the collection that established him as one of the South's authentic new voices. In the best writing, Brown discovered, character counts more than plot. That may not have helped his bank account much; but he doesn't hold it against Grisham. "Everybody's glad for what happened to John," he says. "He paid his dues. He works harder than I do."

An astute justification of Grisham comes from Sydney Pollack, who directed the movie of *The Firm.* "This is a very suspicious, cynical decade," says Pollack. "All bureaucratic authorities are suspect. Part of the reason the book is so successful is you have an Everyman taken advantage of by the authorities and by the experts who are supposed to defend you against the authorities. And he beats them both." [In February 1993] Grisham told a chamber of commerce group that *A Time to Kill* was his best novel and that he had been going downhill ever since. "Was this wise?" wondered Hannah, for whom Grisham had inscribed a book: "To one of my heroes." The truth is that in the cluttered office Grisham calls "mission control," the only room on his spread that he won't let Renée redecorate, the place where he pins the deadline on the wall once a year, shooing out his son, Ty, 9, and his daughter, Shea, 7, for the duration, Grisham is restless.

Someone once asked him to explain the significance of the fact that where Faulkner, a complicater, invented Yoknapatawpha, Grisham, a simplifier, dreamed up Ford County in *A Time to Kill.* ("Give me a break," he replied.) Once upon a time, his plan was to alternate one Ford County novel with every thriller. His Ford County ideas brought

hems and haws from his agent and editor. The result was a three-book contract with Doubleday that holds him to legal thrillers. Now, he says, "what I'd really like to do is just go back to Ford County and never leave."

Of course, you can't go home again and bat out a Ford County novel in six months (*The Pelican Brief* took 100 days, *The Client* six months, and both show some damage). But Grisham says he's now so rich he could write a book every five years or maybe every 10 years. He doesn't intend to get into the ring with Count Tolstoy, as Hemingway would put it, or Faulkner. His idea is just to take more time, and in the tradition of Larry Brown, pay more attention to character. Whatever the case, he has what it takes to make the change. A while ago Bill Ballard sat in his law office near The Bookworm in Hernando, writing a review of *The Client* for the local library. Grisham, he wrote, now enjoys what Mark Twain called "the calm confidence of a Christian holding four aces." And it's never been a good idea to bet against him.

Ruth Coughlin   (review date 25 May 1994)

SOURCE: A review of *The Chamber,* in *The Detroit News,* May 25, 1994, p. 3D.

[*Coughlin is an American critic, who has served as a book editor and columnist for* The Detroit News. *In the following review, she declares* The Chamber *one of Grisham's best works to date, citing the novel's suspenseful plot and intriguing legal details as its strengths.*]

Since the publication of *The Firm* in 1991, you may have noticed that many critics think it's great sport to take potshots at the astonishingly successful John Grisham. Looks to me like the prevailing sentiment is that making fun of him is, as the kids say, the cool thing to do.

You know: He's unspeakably rich and famous. You can't be in an airport anywhere without seeing at least five people reading any one of his four books—*A Time to Kill, The Firm, The Pelican Brief, The Client.* In bookstores all over America, it appears as though the John Grisham displays occupy half the floor and shelf space. And it's somewhat obvious to me that when some of his harshest critics also turn out to be writers themselves, it comes across as though maybe they're suffering from that dreaded, green-eyed monster disease also known as jealousy. Not a pretty sight.

So, for the record, let's make a stab at being fair. *The Firm:* Terrific. *The Pelican Brief:* Much less terrific. *The Client:* Godawful. (Sorry, John, I've not yet read your very first novel, *A Time to Kill,* although people say I should, and no doubt I will).

Grisham No. 5, simply put, is one of his best.

On the other hand, whether I say it's swell or not makes no difference whatsoever. It probably doesn't matter one whit, either, if I tell you about the plot or why I think *The Chamber* is one of Grisham's best—because the lawyer from Mississippi has reached such a phenomenal level of success, he could fill up a book's pages with absolute drivel and still it would sell a zillion copies.

I am, however, supposed to be a book critic, so let us proceed.

Sam Cayhall is a murderer, racist, anti-Semite, terrorist and Klansman. In 1967 he was accused of bombing the law offices of Jewish civil rights leader Marvin Kramer. Kramer's 5-year-old twin sons were killed, and later Kramer committed suicide. Cayhall's first trial ended in a hung jury; so did his second trial, six months later, and he walked away from both a free man.

A dozen years pass, and an ambitious district attorney reopens the case, nailing Cayhall, as he should be nailed. He's sent to the Mississippi State Penitentiary at Parchman, where he will sit on Death Row for nearly 10 years. At 70, he's the oldest prisoner waiting to be led to the gas chamber and killed like an animal.

There's always a white knight, isn't there? Here, Grisham's savior is Adam Hall, 26, a young lawyer working for a huge firm in Chicago. He has been obsessed with the Cayhall case, and for good reason: Sam Cayhall is his grandfather, the father of Hall's own father, a tormented man named Eddie who ended up killing himself, the shame of his father's crimes overwhelming him.

Turns out the Cayhall lineage included generations of Kluckers. Turns out it's an evil, destructive family; that even though Sam Cayhall was just a gofer in the 1967 bombings, he partook in lynchings and once killed a black man who worked for him, a crime that went unpunished. Small wonder that Eddie Cayhall changed this illustrious group of rednecks' name to Hall.

When Adam Hall confronts the grandfather he's never met, he finds out that the execution is scheduled to take place in a month.

The race begins. And make no mistake: Grisham turns his plot into a heart-stopping, down-to-the-wire race, with the clock furiously ticking and the emotional terrain between grandfather and grandson moving like a seesaw.

In addition to suspense, he provides his readers an enormous amount of chilling and often gruesome information about what it's like to be on Death Row. And about how the complicated, last-ditch efforts a lawyer becomes involved in can be mind-numbing.

There's no love story and no sex in *The Chamber*—all to the good, since the romances in Grisham's previous novels have always seemed perfunctory to me.

Instead, there's just a good, old-fashioned, rip-snorting yarn, which is certainly all to the good, because it's what John Grisham does best.

John Mortimer   (review date 12 June 1994)

SOURCE: "The Devil's Advocate," in *The Sunday Times,* London, June 12, 1994, p. 1.

[*Mortimer is a noted English playwright, novelist, scriptwriter, lawyer, and critic. In the following review, he commends Grisham's storytelling ability and attention to detail in* The Chamber.]

All over the world, and particularly in America, lawyers are giving up trying to woo juries and are concentrating their powers of persuasion on the bestseller lists and film rights. Turning author has numerous advantages for the courtroom advocate; nobody will land on death row, or even in prison, if you fail. There's no need to put on a suit, leave home, crawl to your senior partner or be polite to judges. If you succeed, you may become rich beyond the dreams of even the most successful criminal defender.

Furthermore, you have, at your fingertips, material which most novelists would give their word processors to possess. No need to research a story of sex and skulduggery in the steamy world of international bridge; no reason to trawl back through your past life for a tale of suburban adultery; you can be spared the pain of writing, in coruscating prose, a study of family rivalry in 16th-century Portugal. Even the most inexperienced and moderately successful trial lawyer will have seen human beings at crises of their lives, taken part in dramas of action and suspense and heard the astonishing confessions of murderers, con men, petty thieves and swindling tycoons. Small wonder that authors such as Scott Turow start well favoured in the bestselling handicap.

John Grisham, from Arkansas, who left his law firm and no doubt lives in considerable comfort with his family in Oxford, Mississippi, has certainly won the big-money stakes. Thirty million copies of his books are now in print in the English language and Hollywood has paid an "industry record" for his latest offering, *The Chamber.* Such facts would lead you to suspect that it couldn't be much good and I embarked on it with low expectations.

For the first dozen pages they were fulfilled. We have come to expect much of some mystery writers; they are often the best performers on the page we have around. Raymond Chandler wrote brilliant prose and Dashiell Hammett managed the sickening inevitability of classical drama. Now Ruth Rendell shows an unparalleled understanding of human evil, and P D James gives her characters hearts and souls. None of these talents is perceptible at the start of Grisham's novel. Reading it is like hearing a young and pedestrian barrister opening a case to a bored jury on a dull day in court. You have little idea of what the characters look like or how they feel. There is no sense of place, no wryly accurate Chandleresque descriptions, none of the shivers down the spine which Rendell produces so expertly. The jury might consider falling asleep or covertly filling in the crossword puzzle, but then they begin to listen and the colourless account of the facts suddenly grabs their attention.

After 50 pages I could hardly wait to turn the rest over; because what Grisham can do, and this accounts for the 30m books in print (many of them may even have been sold), is to tell us a story. And a story, despite the opinions of many highly respected authors to the contrary, is what readers have paid to read. Recently, a writer I know who does, in fact, tell stories said that writers today can't be expected to "do" plots. Plots, it seems, went out with gaslamps and stone hot-water bottles. Mystery writers know quite well that this is not true, and that is why there are

30m copies of Grisham's books stacked up around the world.

His story is certainly compelling. A dreadful old Ku Klux Klansman, convicted, after two juries disagreed, of blowing up the office of a radical Jewish lawyer who defended blacks, and of killing his children, is on death row. He has run through nine years of the painfully complex and slow American appeals procedure. He has 16 days to go before entering the gas chamber. His grandson, a young liberal lawyer from a big Chicago firm, takes on the case. His aim is to find out the truth about his spiteful and racist grandfather and discover why his own father committed suicide. Like all good plots, from *Hamlet* downwards, it is exceedingly simple. Will he kill the king? Will they gas grandpa? Grisham may do without poetry, wit and style, and offer only the simplest characterisation. The young liberal lawyer may be colourless and the spooky old prisoner one-dimensional; but there is no doubt that this ex-lawyer knows how to tell a story.

It is more effective because the horrors of the death penalty are never overstated. All the lawyers hate it. The prison governor loathes it. The warders treat it with a rough and not unsympathetic humour. The only enthusiast is a sadistic deputy governor who is eagerly looking forward to his first execution. Those in favour of the death penalty are politicians with no experience of prisons or prisoners. Its ritual infliction, intolerably delayed by the American legal system, spreads corruption among all who have to take part in it.

In *The Chamber,* the conditions on death row (or, as it is euphemistically called, the maximum security unit) are relatively humane and the prison is in farming country. As in all such fiction, reality is sought by piling up minute, accurate detail; and the small facts, the hours of exercise, the dimensions of the cells, the prison menus (pretty good) and the strange, small kindnesses shown to the condemned man, are strangely fascinating. It's a piece of work that the authors on this year's Booker shortlist might examine in search of readability. The other 29,999,994 buyers will read this book just to find out how it ends.

FURTHER READING

Biography

Hubbard, Kim, and Hutchings, David. "Tales Out of Court." *People Weekly* 37, No. 10 (16 March 1992): 43-4.
> Traces Grisham's life and career, providing commentary by Grisham on his novels.

Criticism

French, Edward. Review of *The Client,* by John Grisham. *Books Magazine* 7, No. 3 (May-June 1993): 21-2.
> Positive review of *The Client.* French comments: "Another fascinating story from John Grisham, who scores a bull's-eye with every book."

Goodman, Walter. "Getting to Know Grandpa under Penalty of Death." *The New York Times* (29 July 1994): B10.
> Offers a mixed assessment of *The Chamber.*

Petersen, Clarence. Review of *A Time to Kill,* by John Grisham. *Chicago Tribune—Books* (8 September 1991): 10.
> Favorable assessment of *A Time to Kill,* which, Petersen asserts, "invites comparison to [Harper Lee's] *To Kill a Mockingbird* in its authenticity of setting and characterization."

Skow, John. "Legal Eagle." *Time* 139, No. 10 (9 March 1992): 70.
> Review of *The Pelican Brief.* Skow writes that the plot of *The Pelican Brief* is a near duplicate of that of *The Firm.*

———. "A Time to Kill?" *Time* 143, No. 25 (20 June 1994): 67.
> Praises Grisham's focus on capital punishment in *The Chamber* and discusses the book's relationship to Grisham's other works.

Stabiner, Karen. Review of *The Client,* by John Grisham. *The Los Angeles Times Book Review* (4 April 1993): 6.
> Faults Grisham for an undeveloped plot in *The Client.*

John Joseph Mathews

1894-1979

American novelist, biographer, historian, and autobiographer.

The following provides an overview of Mathews's career.

INTRODUCTION

Best known for the novel *Sundown* (1934), Mathews is highly regarded for his sensitive depictions of Native Americans who feel alienated from both their tribal heritage and American society. He is additionally remembered for his nonfiction works, in which he documented Osage history and culture, the settlement of Oklahoma by whites, and the impact this had on the region's Native Americans.

Biographical Information

Mathews was born in Pawhuska, Oklahoma, into an upper-class family. While only one-eighth Osage, Mathews had strong ties to the Osage nation: his great-grandfather, William Shirley Williams, was a missionary and "mountain man" fur trader who translated the Bible into the Osage language, and Mathews's family lived on an Indian reservation where his father managed the local bank and ran a trading post. In 1914 Mathews entered the University of Oklahoma, majoring in geology. His studies were interrupted by World War I; initially enlisting in the United States Cavalry, he served as a pilot in the Signal Corps. After spending part of the war in France, Mathews resumed his studies in the United States and graduated from the University of Oklahoma in 1920. He then attended Oxford University, earning a degree in natural science, and the University of Geneva, where he obtained a certificate in international relations. While in Geneva, Mathews did freelance work for the *Philadelphia Ledger,* frequently providing his editors with stories about the newly formed League of Nations. After extensive travel through Europe and Africa, Mathews returned to Oklahoma, where he began his career as a writer. In the years of his absence, Osage life had changed drastically—many members of the tribe had become "oil rich" and there was a much larger white population in Osage County—and Mathews felt compelled to preserve his people's history and beliefs. In addition to his literary efforts to document tribal culture, Mathews was elected to the Osage Tribal Council in 1934. An active spokesperson, he frequently represented the tribe in Washington, D.C., and helped the Osage attain rights to natural gas and oil deposits found on their lands. A United States representative to the 1940 Indians of the Americas Conference in Mexico, Mathews was also instrumental in establishing the Osage Museum in Pawhuska. He died in 1979.

Major Works

Incorporating events from Mathews's life, *Sundown* is set in the early part of the twentieth century and centers around Challenge Windzer, an Osage of mixed descent. Due to his education at the state university, his father's political activism, and the growing white population, Chal becomes increasingly familiar with the ways of white America and embarrassed by his tribe's customs. After his father's death and a brief stint as a pilot during World War I, the protagonist finds himself alone and alienated from both Osage and white society. Like *Sundown,* Mathews's nonfiction works focus on his heritage and the history of his people and home state. *Wah'kon-tah* (1932), in part the biography of Laban J. Miles, Indian agent to the Osage nation, focuses on the tribe's interaction with the United States federal government when the Oklahoma territories were being settled. History is also central to *Life and Death of an Oilman* (1951), the biography of the first governor of Oklahoma, and to the lengthy *Osages* (1961), which provides an overview of Osage traditions and beliefs as well as noteworthy events in the tribe's past. Relating Mathews's experiences in the Blackjack Hills of Oklahoma, *Talking to the Moon* (1945) likewise emphasizes

Osage culture, delineating Mathews's attempts to commune with the natural world and achieve greater spiritual harmony.

Critical Reception

Mathews's literary stature rests largely on *Sundown*, and scholars frequently credit him as being one of the first Native Americans to write fiction about Amerindians. Critics praise *Sundown* for its realism and argue that Mathews's objective treatment of the mixed-blood has universal relevance. His nonfiction works, while respected as evocative sociological and anthropological tracts about the Osage, have also been praised for their inherent literary qualities. *Talking to the Moon,* for example, has been favorably compared to Henry David Thoreau's *Walden* (1854) and John Muir's *My First Summer in the Sierra* (1911).

PRINCIPAL WORKS

Wah'kon-tah: The Osage and the White Man's Road (nonfiction) 1932
Sundown (novel) 1934
Talking to the Moon (autobiography) 1945
Life and Death of an Oilman: The Career of E. W. Marland (biography) 1951
The Osages: Children of the Middle Waters (history) 1961

CRITICISM

Kenneth C. Kaufman   (review date 8 November 1934)

SOURCE: "The Indian's Burden," in *The Christian Science Monitor,* November 8, 1934, p. 18.

[*In the review below, Kaufman provides a highly favorable assessment of* Sundown.]

No figure in the American scene is more inherently tragic than that of the young Indian who realizes fully the loss of his fathers' material and spiritual heritage, but who is unable to adjust himself to white civilization. Such a one is Chal Windzer [of *Sundown*], son of a mixed blood Osage father and of a full blood Osage mother, born about the turn of the century, when the Osages, Chal's father among them, were eagerly looking forward to the exploitation of their reservation in northern Oklahoma. He is molded by his heroic, tender, loyal mother and the old warriors into a typical little Indian boy.

But civilization comes to the Osage; first the cattle men, then the oil boom, with its attending demoralization. And his father's influence is at work. Chal wants to be a white man, but he does not know how. At his state university he is welcomed by the glad handers because of his handsome physique and his wealth; he feels the insincerity, the

emptiness back of much college life, but he has no refuge from it except lonely walks on the prairie.

The outbreak of the war is a relief. He understands the function of war; his people were warriors. Flying appeals to him; many Osages are named "Eagle." What he does not understand is the pettiness of discipline, the fuss and the fuming, the blatant sophistication which passes for progressiveness. He meets many types of American men and women; and he appraises them without malice, but unsparingly. Yet he realizes that the day of the old Indian life is over. Sometimes he even laughs at the old ways. In the end he goes back to the reservation, to the desolation of stagnation, to the artificial stimulus of drinking.

Mr. Mathews writes with complete objectivity; he is a superb realist. Not until near the close of the book does the reader realize that it is a merciless and inescapable indictment of our civilization, which has destroyed 'something sublime and beautiful, not only without providing a substitute for it, but without even knowing that it existed. Yet there is no pleading; even in his decay young Chal keeps something of that Indian mysticism which gives him a feeling of oneness with his environment.

Mr. Mathews is part Osage; one of his ancestors, Hard Robe, led General Custer's scouts at the Battle of Washita, and another was "Old Bill" Williams, mountain man and *compadre* of Kit Carson. He is not only an Indian, but a cultured white man, a graduate of Oxford. He has gone deeper into Indian consciousness and set down his findings more tellingly than any other writer of fiction known to me. Moreover, he is an artist with words.

Oliver La Farge   (review date 24 November 1934)

SOURCE: "The Realistic Story of an Indian Youth," in *The Saturday Review of Literature,* Vol. XI, No. 19, November 24, 1934, p. 309.

[*An American novelist, editor, nonfiction writer, autobiographer, and author of children's books, La Farge won the 1929 Pulitzer Prize for fiction for his novel* Laughing Boy. *Also the winner of the 1931 O. Henry Memorial Prize, La Farge has frequently written about Native Americans and has served as president of the National Association on Indian Affairs and the Association on American Indian Affairs. In the review of* Sundown *below, he praises Mathews's realistic and sensitive portrayal of Native Americans.*]

Mr. Mathews, himself part Osage and reared on the Osage Reservation, gave good evidence in **Wah 'Kon-Tah** that he could do that rare thing, write about Indians from the inside, and furthermore could make an interesting book of it with real literary value. One waited to see how he would follow up his first successful venture. In the present book [*Sundown*] he has taken up about where the other left off, a novel of the young Indian with some white blood, fundamentally Osage, bewildered by false values and caught in the devastating flood of gold which swept that mighty nation into the gutter.

But this is no mere historical study in novel form, nor just a literate protest against the foul conquest of a primitive civilization by an advanced barbarism; it is a full, rounded novel in its own right, reflective, at moments beautiful, at moments a little sloppy, carrying the reader with steady interest along its hero's story. In fact, I may do an injustice to *Sundown* by beginning with a statement of Indian themes and problems. The first consideration is that here is a well-written, well-planned, sensitive study of a young man. As such it stands on its own feet. Secondly, the young man is an Osage with one eighth of white blood (as near as I can calculate it) and too much white background for his own good, yet not enough to be useful to him—in this, typical of many. Such a novel, concerned with such a man, must then of necessity be also an unusual study of Indians in contact with whites. Since the writer is skilful, observant, and knows his material well, it is also an excellent literary document on Oklahoma, something to be taken, and enjoyed, as a little salt on Miss Ferber's too gorgeous *Cimarron.*

In a few spots, Mr. Mathews's grammar goes to pieces in a manner which suggests that the trouble may be bad proof-reading. He makes a good deal of the break-up of the Reservation and mentions various differences of opinion concerning allotment and oil leases, without giving the reader much, if any idea of what these signify, nor of what effects they produce. To one unfamiliar with the Osage's story, this should be extra confusing. I have some acquaintance with it in an academic way and found that part of the book somewhat so. One feels also, that the case has been possibly overstated when not a single attractive, or even reasonably decent, white American crosses the pages of the book.

Regardless of these faults, it is a relief to read a "sectional" novel of full realism, depicting oil towns, reservations, the state University, training camps, and so much else with remorseless conviction while giving one no sense of mere dirt-piling or of that fear of beauty which frustrates so many so-called realistic writers.

Most Americans do not realize in what a large part of this country Indians and whites are intermingled, nor have they any idea of the amazing, often grotesque effects of this contact on daily life, on politics, on morals and thought in every form. When thinking of Indians at all, we tend to visualize the old-time, independent hostiles, or the relatively remote and untouched tribes of the Southwest in whose stories, even today, but a few white men would appear. Mr. Mathews has turned to those others whose lives are twined in with cities and whole states, and in so doing has tapped for the first time a rich vein in the resources of our literature.

The New York Times Book Review **(review date 25 November 1934)**

SOURCE: "An Educated Indian," in *The New York Times Book Review,* November 25, 1934, pp. 19-20.

[*In the following, the critic offers a mixed review of* Sundown.]

The god of the great Osages was still dominant over the wild prairie and the Blackjack Hills when Chal Windzer was born. His Indian father, out of a vague and rather pointless ecstasy which assailed him on the night of his son's birth, had called him Challenge, saying: "He shall be a challenge to the disinheritors of his people." Though what it was the boy was to challenge, John Windzer never knew and his son never succeeded in finding out.

Sundown presents a very moving picture of the first years of Chal's life, his response to the legends of his race, his education as a day student at the reservation school, and his hero worship of his politically minded father. By the time Chal had grown to adolescence and had begun to face the problem of his future, there was plenty of money at his disposal. There were rich deposits of oil on the Osage land and the Indians, in spite of the best efforts of their white "guardians," had managed to get hold of some of the profits.

So Chal went to the State university, and because he was rather handsome and a good football player and reputed to be wealthy, he was immediately accepted into the collegiate social life. His adjustment to it, however, was a difficult one. He was intensely self-conscious, he couldn't master the small talk of his fraternity brothers and he was profoundly puzzled by their opinions and attitudes—their desire for good marks in classes, their nagging and furtive interest in the simple facts of love and mating. Believing the civilization of the white man to be superior, he grew ashamed of his Indian friends at college—constantly afraid, for some reason or other, that they would behave like Indians. For his part, he devoted himself to becoming as much as possible like his white companions.

Naturally active and intelligent, yet with no aim in life beyond the simple and momentary indulgences of drinking and love-making, Chal found a temporary respite in the outbreak of the war. He was sure of one thing—that he wanted to fly. He left college abruptly to join the aviation corps and remained in the service after the war, although by that time most of the zest and novelty had gone out of flying. At the death of his father he resigned and came home to the village where he had been born—now a garish and prosperous boom town.

In Kihekah there was no work for him to do and enough money so that he didn't need to look for any. Playing about with a group of young loafers, drinking and dancing all night, and tearing over the roads in his big car, Chal found himself unable to put a name to his spiritual discontent. He only knew that he came home as infrequently as possible and that he had grown to hate his mother. His sudden understanding that his own inertness, his own lack of purpose, is at the bottom of his mother's contempt for him, moves him to a satisfying boast: "I'm goin' to Harvard law school and take law—I'm gonna be a great orator."

Whether or not Chal has found himself this time, the reader—taking leave of him as he sits asleep in his chair—does not know. In view of his previous resolves, the enthusiasm with which he begins by regarding them and the fashion in which that enthusiasm later deserts him, the implication is that he has not. *Sundown* is a convincing study of a young Indian's attempt to adjust himself to a fundamentally alien civilization.

In spite of the fact that Mr. Mathews—who is the author of *Wah 'Kon-Tah* and himself part Osage—writes very ably, the book has a decidedly inarticulate quality, as if the problem he is trying to state had been only half comprehended and is hence not susceptible of clear statement. Perhaps this very quality, which mars the book as a novel, makes it an even more effective social study.

Mathews on *Wah'Kon-Tah*:

I wrote [*Wak'Kon-tah*] just as a woodthrush would sing. He's not conscious of how he sings; he just sings because he feels it. Sometimes I think of that first book and all the rest of them, I think of a violinist who has to express himself and he does it. He doesn't think of anything else or anybody else. I didn't have any idea that anybody would read it. I had no image in my mind of anybody or any group who might be interested in it. I just wrote it because I had to write it—suddenly. Having lived more or less a whimsical life from boyhood, this was my whim of the moment. If I hadn't finished it when I did, I might have gone deer hunting and forgotten about it.

John Joseph Mathews, in an interview with Guy Logsdon, in Nimrod, *1972.*

J. Frank Dobie (review date 21 October 1951)

SOURCE: "Black Gold and Roses," in *The New York Times Book Review,* October 21, 1951, pp. 3, 42.

[*Dobie was an American educator, critic, and editor who frequently wrote about Southwestern history and folklore. In the review below, he favorably assesses* Life and Death of an Oilman.]

Of all the filibusters, developers, demagogues (for no statesman of high rank can be named) cowmen, oilmen and other lusty figures who have played their parts on the vast earthen stage of the Southwest during the last hundred and fifty years, hardly half a dozen have received treatment in biographies that can be called mature. *Life and Death of an Oilman* is one of the scant half dozen. It is mature both in style and wisdom, in perspective, compass and interpretative power.

The oilman was E. W. Marland (1874-1941). As an "independent operator," which means that he was in constant combative contradistinction to the Standard companies, he represented perhaps the most vivid class of men who have made economic history in America during the present century. He wildcatted first in the Alleghenies under the Rockefeller shadow, rose to power exploiting virgin oil fields in Oklahoma, extended his operations to Texas, Colorado, California, Mexico and elsewhere, and then through the House of Morgan of New York saw the Marland Oil Company with all its ramifications become a mere feeder to Standard and himself cast out, to take impotent refuge in politics.

He never saw himself clearly, however. A partisan biographer might well have used him to indict Standard Oil. John Joseph Mathews, partisan only to truth and art, sees the cause of Marland's failure as lying within himself and in the ending of the "Age of Freedom" rather than in his stars or the ruthlessness of powerful competitors.

> He failed because of his vanity and a humanitarianism based upon the false premise that pleasure for others is an attainable goal. . . . He was the equal of any of the big boys (as he called them) in energy, in dreaming. in cleverness, and in acquisitive capacity, but his ruthlessness was vitiated by the fact that he had been born a gentleman. His father, moreover, had stimulated in him a feeling for the underprivileged, by any measure a weakness in those who create for themselves a single standard of money. He lacked the primitiveness of the others. Throughout his life he was too much burdened with artificiality. And if a single inclination could be said to have motivated him, it was hedonism.

He loved the clank-CLUNK of the well-drilling machine and the smell of crude oil was perfume in his nostrils, but he was a patrician. His mansion in Ponca City, which started out to be Pueblo-Spanish in style, had the repose of an English manor house. He planted miles of roses to lap it in soft Lydian airs. The hospital he built for the town had "the atmosphere of an eternal siesta." He gave stock to his lieutenants as prodigally as the miners of Nevada gave "feet" to Mark Twain.

He built houses for laborers who helped him get rich and made shares of company stock available to them on easy terms. He admitted the unwashed to his gardens and swimming pools, but for his sensitivities there were always too many of the common people in the same place at the same time. He advised associated to adorn their homes with oil paintings and Persian rugs. He was patron to Jo Davidson, the sculptor. He loved England and preferred dealing with the gentlemen governing the Hudson's Bay Company to the roughneck entrepreneurs of his own territory. Yet he was an intense patriot.

As Governor of Oklahoma—the final act in the drama of his life—he followed the humanitarianism of Roosevelt's New Deal and proposed many reforms, including separation of state schools from politics, but he had no patience for details and could not stomach officeseekers. The one thing he gave Oklahoma that will probably keep his name green is Bryant Baker's statue of the Pioneer Woman.

"It was the literary value of the man that struck one," Mathews says. The essentials of an oilman's financial and technical career are contained in this biography, but revelation of his character is what makes [*Life and Death of an Oilman*] compelling—gaudy achievement out of a complexity of desires, tastes, gestures, contradictions, energy, lightning perception, and then dénouement.

In three preceding books John Joseph Mathews has interpreted the land of the Southwest with a sensitiveness and understanding equaled only by Mary Austin. The peaks of his present drama of character rise out of that land as integrated background. Through the powers of thought, imagination and craftsmanship—powers always overlapping each other—he has fully realized the "literary value" of his subject.

John C. Ewers   (review date 24 September 1961)

SOURCE: "Tribal Tribute," in *The New York Times Book Review,* September 24, 1961, p. 24.

[*An American anthropologist, ethnologist, and prolific writer, Ewers is a specialist of Native American culture. In the following review, he praises the literary qualities of* The Osages.]

Oxford-educated John Joseph Mathews, great-grandson of an Osage woman and a missionary who translated the Bible into the Osage language, has written a sympathetic history of his great-grandmother's tribe [in *The Osages: Children of the Middle Waters*]. Likening his task to the reconstruction of a dinosaur from many scattered fragments, he has fitted together ingeniously the Indians' oral traditions and the writings of explorers, traders, travelers, missionaries, government officials and ethnologists, making allowances for white men's fragmentary knowledge, and the prejudices and special pleadings which impeded their understanding of Osage life and values.

Historians will question the author's heavy reliance upon tongue-to-ear Indian traditions to explain events that occurred centuries ago. Anthropologists will question his contention that Osage social and political organization and Osage religion, rich in natural symbolism and overburdened with ceremonial ritual, were entirely of their own making, uninfluenced by borrowings from other and closely related Siouan tribes. However, there can be no question of the literary merit of this sensitive account of an important Midwestern tribe.

The proud, warlike Osages were the dominant power in the lower Missouri Valley at the dawn of history in that region (1673). Yet these tall giants of men humbled themselves before their creator Wah'Kon-Tah by calling themselves The Little Ones. Theirs was a country teeming with game of both plains and woodland species, for which they thanked their creator and which they regarded as brothers.

For 140 years the Osages were involved in the conflicts among the French, Spanish and English for control of the interior parts of North America. They overcame their initial dislike for the body odors of heavily clad, hairy French traders who came among them, and whom they dubbed Hairy Eyebrows. They supplied Pawnee slaves as well as furs to the French. At the same time they prevented their French allies from carrying guns to their Indian enemies north and west of their villages on the Osage River. Spanish horses and French guns modified their culture, but the Osages clung tenaciously to their fine country and to their traditional religion.

Rivalry for their lucrative trade produced the first split in the ranks of the Osages when the Chouteaus (a family of fur-traders) persuaded about half the tribe to move south to the Arkansas in 1802. Pressures from Cherokee Indians resettled west of the Mississippi as well as from white settlers disturbed them after the United States acquired Louisiana. Resenting the killing of their game even more than the loss of their land, the Osages fought back.

Between the years 1808 and 1870 Federal commissioners, exploiting the vanity and ambitions of Osage chiefs, and professing to protect them from their Indian and white enemies, negotiated a series of treaties in which they gradually ceded all of their lands in Missouri and Kansas. They finally settled on land purchased from the Cherokees in northeastern Oklahoma.

After the buffalo disappeared, the Osages suffered from hunger on their new reservation, which was poorly suited to the growth of crops. Yet the present century witnessed both economic and spiritual revival among them. Oil and gas royalties brought undreamed-of wealth to these Indians who had stubbornly refused to relinquish the mineral rights to their reservation. By 1925 the Osage Nation had become the wealthiest nation in the world in terms of average individual income. Meanwhile conservative fullbloods found in the Peyote Cult an acceptable faith which combined traditional Indian religious values with some of the symbols of Christianity.

The predominant theme of [*The Osages*] is a spiritual one—the Osage Indians' struggle to achieve and to preserve a meaningful and satisfying system of beliefs and values, in the face of numerous strong and conflicting pressures. The author has dramatically and quite successfully portrayed this struggle from the Osage point of view.

Garrick Bailey on *The Osages*:

[*The Osages*] covers a wide range of topics: mythology, history, and culture. These diverse topics are integrated around a central theme, the relationship of the Osage to an ever changing world. What Mathews attempts to demonstrate is how the Osage viewed themselves in relationship to God, nature, and other men. He makes no attempt at being neutral with regard to the Osage and their relationship to other societies, particularly White society. To have done so would have defeated the primary purpose of the book. This is an Osage history, written from an Osage point of view, with events interpreted from an Osage cultural perspective. Because of this factor some people have said that *The Osages* is not a history, but rather a saga. In defense of Mathews and his approach to Osage history I am reminded of that oft-quoted dictum, "History is only mythology taken seriously, while mythology is merely some one else's history." Regardless of whether *The Osages* is a history, a saga, or a myth, it is one of the greatest examples of Native American literature and scholarship.

Garrick Bailey, in his "John Joseph Mathews: Osage, 1894-" in American Indian Intellectuals: 1976 Proceedings of The American Ethnological Society, *edited by Margot Liberty, West Publishing Co., 1978.*

Charles R. Larson (essay date 1978)

SOURCE: "Assimilation: Estrangement from the Land," in his *American Indian Fiction,* University of New Mexico Press, 1978, pp. 34-65.

[*Larson is an American critic, essayist, novelist, and editor. In the excerpt below, he discusses the themes of estrangement and assimilation in* Sundown.]

In the last chapter of John J. Mathews' *Wah'Kon-Tah* (a nonfiction account of life on the Osage Reservation during the tenure of its first federal agent, Major Laban J. Miles), there is a description of an Indian youth who returns from the white world affected by liquor, hot music, and fast cars. He is especially contemptuous of his parents:

> The young man looked with pity upon his parents. He thought of how old-fashioned they were: his father still wearing his buckskin leggings and his beaverskin bandeau, his pale blue silk shirt and his blanket; his mother in her shirt, moccasins and shrouding. They were certainly behind the time, all right. No matter how swell he dressed he was always embarrassed thinking of his parents sitting out at the ranch. They couldn't even speak English. He wished he didn't have to speak Osage with them—it sure made him feel funny when they talked together in public at the Agency.

The youth wears expensive tailored clothes, is indifferent to tribal customs and beliefs, and has become a kind of cultural half-caste, no longer seeing much value in his Indian origins, while aping the worst of the white man's object-oriented world.

Wah'Kon-Tah was published in 1932—two years before Mathews's only novel, *Sundown.* The unnamed Indian youth is easily identified as the precursor of Chal (Challenge) Windzer, the novel's main character. *Sundown* is the story of a mixed-blood Indian, from the night of his birth until his mid-thirties, during the Great Depression. It is the first novel by a Native American to follow a character's life from birth to maturity, to give us his story in retrospect with all of its failures and disappointments. Somewhat akin in structure to the traditional *Bildungsroman,* the novel is also the story of the corrupting natures of money and the white man's educational system.

There is not much of a story to *Sundown;* plot has, in fact, given way to character development. In the early chapters we see Chal's confusing feelings about his parents. His mixed-blood father considers himself one of the progressives, working to advance the Indian's standard of living by supporting allotment and the oil development of the Osage Reservation. Initially, he believes that the government in Washington can do no harm, yet by contrast, Chal's full-blood mother distrusts the government and most of the white man's ways on principle. As a child, Chal attends reservation schools and later goes to the state university, though he does not complete his degree because World War I breaks out and he enlists in the air force. The war ends, however, before he is mobilized, and shortly thereafter he returns to the reservation, where he becomes a kind of drifter with nothing to do. (There are a number of parallels here with Mathews's own life. Like Chal Windzer, Mathews also attended the University of Oklahoma, and he joined the air force during World War I.)

Chal's education, Mathews would have us believe, is the primary force that has cut him off from his tribal roots. This is true at every stage of his formal education—from primary school to the university, and even to flight school. Chal's earliest memories of the reservation school are, in fact, of its sinister-looking buildings. Even before he was old enough to attend the school, he had seen Indian boys in the schoolyard; "he had a feeling that they were like animals in a cage, and certainly there seemed to be much sadness in their faces." He thinks of the door of the school "as a mouth into which they [the students] were going; a big, black mouth, bigger and darker than a wildcat's." Mathews's picture of Chal's white teachers is hardly more flattering. One teacher, named Miss Hover, has come to the school because "she fell under the romantic spell of Fenimore Cooper." When her Indian students do not live up to Cooper's image, she quickly adopts a patronizing attitude toward them.

The reader begins to understand that it is education which is slowly severing Chal's ties to his cultural past. While in high school, on the days he has no classes, he is drawn to the country, where he feels a number of strong, almost uncontrollable forces pulling at him. "One day he stripped off his clothes and danced in a storm and sang a war song." On another occasion, "he took some paints and painted his face. . . ." These mysterious sensations come to him only when he is alone on the prairie, yet they continue during his years as a student at the university and later when he attends the air force flight school. Periodically, he has an uncontrollable urge to be alone in the country, where he can be close to the land. As his education occupies more of his time, however, he begins to feel guilty about these sensations, afraid that he is "reverting" to a kind of uncivilized past that typifies his people as a whole. These yearnings, he feels, must be controlled:

> Sometimes as he walked, the urge to pull off his clothes and trot came to him; the desire to play the role of coyote, but he dismissed such desires now with shame, and when they were most disturbing he would murmur aloud to drown the unconventional thought, and he would dismiss the thoughts of his first months at the University in the same manner. He was more civilized now and more knowing, and he was ashamed of his recent past.

By denying his basic affinity with the earth, Chal's education—like Chief Pokagon's in *Queen of the Woods*—cuts him off from the rich heritage of his people. Even worse, the white man's schooling makes him reject his Indian identity: "He didn't want to call attention to the fact that most of his blood was of an uncivilized race like the Osages. He believed that they didn't have any backbone, and he certainly wanted to make something out of himself." In his confusion, he becomes embarrassed that people identify him as an Indian, and he often feels uncomfortable because of the activities of other Indians around him. At the university, when two of his Indian classmates decide to drop out of school, he realizes that he is actually relieved to see them depart—for "fear that they would do something wrong." In time, he feels guilty about his appearance:

> He had often wished that he weren't so bronze. It set him off from other people, and he felt that he was queer anyway, without calling attention to the fact. It was embarrassing to attract attention, and when people looked at him he became shy. He thought he still might have black eyes and straight black hair that shone like patent leather when he put grease on it, if his face were only white.

At the height of his confusion, he mutters to himself, " 'I wish I didn't have a drop of God damn' Indian blood in my veins.' "

Eventually, Chal completely rejects his Indianness. The incident takes place at the air force school, when a white woman, with whom he will shortly have an affair, asks him " 'Are you Spanish or something?' " Chal replies, " 'Yes, Spanish.' " The narrator comments, "He should like to have indicated that he had a title, as well, but he thought he had better not." Mathews's picture of Chal Windzer is not so different from those of a number of characters in Afro-American novels who are light enough to "pass" as Caucasian. Like them, Chal renounces his racial origins, sides with the white world, and in the process alienates himself from both groups. He becomes a man with no identity at all, a cultural half-caste.

Chal's problems are in no way alleviated when he returns home after the war. His father has committed suicide, after realizing that by siding with the government he acted against his people; allotment and oil development have brought total disruption of traditional life to the Osage Reservation. Ignoring the example of his father's belated insight, Chal continues to be embarrassed by his mother's Indian ways (her manner of dress, the house she continues to live in in spite of the money she receives from the tribal government from its sale of oil). Even at his father's funeral, Chal "had been embarrassed during the ceremony . . . because some of the older Osages had come to the grave, and turning their eyes to the sky, had chanted the song of death." Chal was, in fact, moved by their act, "but there were so many new white people in town now, that he thought they shouldn't have gone through the primitive ritual after the Christian burial." Almost all of his activities are designed so he will not offend the whites around him, yet he has no clear idea what these people are like or what they expect of him.

If education has been the greatest factor in his estrangement from his people, it is money which adds to his total debilitation. From his father's estate Chal inherits $25,000—money that came from tribal sales of oil. There is, in fact, so much money that Chal does not have to do anything to earn a livelihood, yet the money keeps coming in. Mathews uses the black oil derricks as a ubiquitous symbol of the general disruption of traditional life; there is always another one looming on the horizon, no matter in which direction one looks. In one particularly moving incident, lightning strikes a derrick and sets it on fire. One of the Osage elders states that the " 'lightning struck that

---

Sundown **is the first novel by a Native American to follow a character's life from birth to maturity, to give us his story in retrospect with all of its failures and disappointments. Somewhat akin in structure to the traditional** *Bildungsroman,* **the novel is also the story of the corrupting natures of money and the white man's educational system.**

—*Charles R. Larson*

---

gas well 'cause the Great Spirit don't want the white people to come here any more.' " The earth has been polluted by the white man's rape of the land, and now this greed has spread to the Indians.

Chal's biggest problem is that he does not know "what to do with himself." In the last few chapters of the novel he drifts along, spending his time and money on fast cars, easy women, and binges with liquor that last a week or two at a time. He drives his automobile as fast as it will go; he moves from one woman to the next, finding little satisfaction in either of these diversions. Mathews implies that either liquor—his "senses were dulled . . . he was not acutely aware of anything"—or an automobile accident will finally destroy him.

Abruptly before the end of the novel, Chal makes one final attempt to reclaim his life. With an old friend named Sun-on-His-Wings, he goes to the sweathouse to purify his body. For his friend, this is the purification rite that precedes a service of the Peyote Church, but since Chal is not a member, he cannot attend the meeting. In the sweat lodge, one of the tribal elders named Watching Eagle speaks about the havoc that has been brought to the tribe.

> Long time ago there was one road and People could follow that road. They said, "There is only one road. We can see this road. There are no other roads." Now it seems that road is gone, and white man has brought many roads. But that road is still there. That road is still there, but there are many other roads too. There is white man's road, and there is road which comes off from forks. The bad road which no white man follows—the road which many of the People follow, thinking it is the white man's road. People who follow this road say they are as the white man, but this is not white man's road. People who follow this road say that road of Indian is bad now. But they are not Indians any more, these People who follow that road.

The effect on Chal is electrifying: "he was happy and contented, sitting there." He feels free, as if he is flying.

Yet the change is quickly reversed and, ironically, the sweat lodge ritual does not become preparation for spiritual renewal or a return to cultural roots—nothing akin to what Joseph Epes Brown has described as the function of this ritual [in his 1964 *The Spiritual Legacy of the American Indian*]:

> the "Sweat Lodge" . . . rites are carried out in preparation for all the other major rites, and actually are participated in prior to any important undertaking. They are rites of renewal, or spiritual rebirth, in which all of the four elements—earth, air, fire, and water—each contribute to the physical and psychical purification of man.

For Chal Windzer, the sweathouse cleansing becomes an ironic preparation for his final bodily humiliation. He returns to his bottle, drinking by himself in the countryside. When he is in a state of total inebriation, the old atavistic yearnings return to him; he begins to dance and sing, to feel that he is an Indian again. His body, however, has been destroyed by liquor, and shortly he falls over in a convulsion of great pain. The contrast that Mathews makes here with Chal's earlier yearnings is an important one: Chal has reached the stage where he only feels these forces pulling at him when he is drunk. Earlier, when he was still an adolescent, it was nature alone that created these sensations—not the artificial stimulus of liquor.

The ending of **Sundown** resolves nothing. Chal and his mother are sitting together, having a kind of nonverbal conversation. She breaks the silence and tells him, " 'Many white men are flying across the sea now.' " It is her attempt to rekindle his interest in flying, to get him interested in anything, yet Chal resents her remarks. " 'Ah . . . there isn't anything to flyin',' " he replies, then adds, " 'I'm goin' to Harvard law school, and take law—I'm gonna be a great orator.' " Though his statement silences her, she knows as well as Chal does that he has never thought about law school before, that he has no intention of becoming a lawyer. As the novel ends, she sits watching him ("She saw a little boy in breech clout and moccasins . . .") as he falls asleep. For all his indecisiveness, Chal might just as well be a little boy again.

Chal Windzer is a weak character, a questionable hero. He drifts along through life with little purpose or direction, never acting decisively but permitting himself, rather, to be acted upon. He attends the university because some of his high school friends are planning to; he joins the air force at the suggestion of one of his professors; he repeatedly says he is going to start working, but he never does. By the end of the story, he is utterly passive, plagued by guilt because of his feelings about his racial identity. Though he bears a certain affinity to a number of characters in subsequent novels by Native Americans, he is more directionless than they are. He has tried to assimilate into the white man's world, yet he has failed. By the end of **Sundown,** Chal Windzer has become a man without a culture, reduced to a life of frustration and existential loneliness.

Sundown is the most accomplished of the novels written by Native Americans exploring the assimilationist theme, the most significant early account of the clash of cultures, in large part because Mathews has moved beyond the element of plot (so important to Pokagon and Oskison) into the realm of character development. The reader comes away from the novel knowing quite clearly that Mathews never approves of Chal Windzer's attempts to become part of the white man's world, a stance that distinguishes the author from his predecessors. Unlike [John M.] Oskison's three novels, Mathews's work is almost totally concerned with Native American characters, with the problem of the obliteration of "Indianness" because of the white man's confusing world. Whereas Pokagon uses a proselytizing tone in *Queen of the Woods,* Mathews has chosen to tell his story for the most part without didactic commentary. The result may not always be totally successful; the pace of the narrative at times is slowed down by overwriting and the symbolism is somewhat inconsistent. Nevertheless, John J. Mathews has written a novel which still tells us something vitally important about the Native American and the problems of his identity more than forty years after it was written.

Martha Royce Blaine   (review date November 1979)

SOURCE: A review of *Talking to the Moon,* in *American Indian Quarterly,* Vol. 5, No. 4, November, 1979, pp. 362-64.

[*In the following, Blaine praises Mathews's treatment of nature in* Talking to the Moon.]

John Joseph Mathews is best known for his two works, **The Osages, Children of the Middle Waters** and **Wah' Kon Tah, The Osage and the White Man's Road. Talking to the Moon,** a lesser known work, was first printed in 1945 and recently reprinted. Mathews, a quarter-blood Osage, participated in the two cultures of his heritage. Born in 1894 at Pawhuska on the Osage reservation in Indian territory, he was reared there and observed both the traditional Osage ways as well as the effects of the ongoing and steady erosion by the white man's way superimposed upon them.

After spending years away from his native lands, as a student at Oxford in England, a pilot in World War I, and a writer, he returned in 1932 to his ranch to stay. As he says in the Foreword, "I have come to the blackjacks to live, as one who climbs out of the roaring stream of civilization onto an island, to rest and to watch."

To do this he built a small sandstone house in the blackjack oaks on his land away from man-created activity. Here he lived for ten years. Like others who have had the good fortune and a sense of appreciation of Nature's harmony, he was sensitive to each nuance of its constant and consistent laws of survival and change.

Elizabeth Mathews, his widow, who wrote the present edition's Foreword, states this book was his *Walden,* and it is, for the most part, a *Walden* of the forest and plains of the Middle West written with the added dimension of the Indian perception of the forces of the universe.

The book is organized in seasonal sections with chapters named after the Osage months or moons of the year, such as 'Just-Doing-that Moon,' 'Planting Moon,' 'Buffalo-Pawing the Earth Moon,' and 'Light-of-Day Returns Moon.' In this book the author does several things. He describes with great poetic beauty the great seasonal changes of this latitude in northern Oklahoma and the minutiae that comprise the total kaleidoscope of each season: trees, insects, mammals, weather—all beautiful—pass before our eyes and we feel the place and feel at home there, a part of Nature to which we belong. Such a sentence as "I stand in the silence with emotion that hurts and cannot be relieved by expression, either by word symbols or by physical action" illustrates Mathews' reaction to his environment.

Mathews was not a total recluse. Anthropologists and other professional friends from far and wide, neighbors, including cowhands, woodchoppers and Indian become known in part. We hear them talk, we see glimpses of their characters; we recognize in them that which we have seen in our friends and acquaintances through Mathews' perceptive descriptions. And those who know the Indian of that time will recognize them in the vignettes the author sketched of his Osage contemporaries. (Mathews was on the Osage Tribal Council and spent time in Washington doing tribal business in this period).

Hunting was more than a satisfying physical activity in which he participated. Frequent episodes are described in Oklahoma as well as in New Mexico and other places. Much joy came to him in both the hunt and the observation as a nonparticipant of the total action of animal, man and in some cases, the hounds that sounded through the woods and over the Osage hills. The clever coyote, who 'talks to the moon' is a central figure in this book, a survivor in Nature, as man himself will eventually have to learn to be, Mathews infers.

One begins to know the man. You see him running down the hill with his setters from his front door on a crisp autumn morning just for the pure joy of it. Then you see him riding in a round-up, then talking to the Old Men at Osage ceremonies, or you hear him thinking and comparing Nature's activities and wherein man *should* try to fit, but most often doesn't. The end of his retreat came as World War II developed. He gives serious attention to this and the role of nations one to another and men one to another. He discusses the proper relationships of all as he brings forth the ideas that have come to him in the backwaters of civilization.

One may or may not agree with his philosophical musings and conclusions, but as he said, "I didn't presume that I would come out of the blackjacks with the banner of truth flying, [but that] . . . I might find some connections between man's artificial ornamentation and the useless ornamentations among the creatures in my little corner of the earth. . . ."

The coyote's 'talking to the moon' is an example of ornamental expressions. They are those manifestations that are not vital to survival but are evidence of something beyond this in Nature's scheme. In man they are expressed in such behaviour as art and poetry. Mathews says much of value in this small book. [*Talking to The Moon*] is a treat and a retreat for the soul and poet in all of us.

Carol Hunter   (essay date Fall-Winter 1982)

SOURCE: "The Protagonist as a Mixed-Blood in John Jo-

seph Mathews' Novel: *Sundown,*" in *American Indian Quarterly,* Vol. 6, Nos. 3&4, Fall-Winter, 1982, pp. 319-37.

[*In the essay below, Hunter discusses Mathews's treatment of the theme of the "assimilated or mixed-blood Indian as an alienated character" in* Sundown.]

John Joseph Mathews' novel, **Sundown,** recreates as its setting Osage history from the period prior to the allotment of Osage Indian land in 1906 through the oil boom of the 1920s. It also traces the search for cultural identity of Challenge Windzer, a young mixed-blood from a wealthy Osage family. **Sundown,** initially published in 1934, is one of the earliest novels by an Indian author to present the theme of the assimilated or mixed-blood Indian as an alienated character.

Generally, Southwest regional and social novels of the 1930s focus on the unfortunate trials of white or immigrant Americans confronting a harsh environment. For example, more in common with the regional context of **Sundown** is Edna Ferber's *Cimarron* (1930), which attempts to recreate from a pioneer's perspective the early development of Oklahoma, including the oil boom of Osage County. Ferber concentrates primarily on the personal victory of a pioneer woman who survives the state's earliest development to become its first woman in congress. Similar to most American writers of this time, Ferber's Indian characters are stereotypes portrayed as part of the background of an untamed frontier setting.

During this same period, American Indian writers seldom identified with their tribal background. For instance, Lynn Riggs, who wrote *Green Grow the Lilacs,* was not identified as Cherokee. Around 1900, Simon Pokagon's *Queen of the Woods,* Charles Eastman's *From the Deep Woods to Civilization,* and Hum-ishu-ma's *Cogewea,* declared the advantages of an education in the white culture but, with the exception of D'arcy McNickle's *The Surrounded* (1936), none of these writers focused on the American Indian as being alienated in American society. Thirty years after Indian Territory had become the state of Oklahoma, however, Mathews came forth as the first American writer to present a novel which thematically portrays an American Indian—a mixed-blood—as a victim of a bi-culture identity.

Mathews was born November 16, 1894, on the Osage reservation near the Indian agency at Pawhuska, Indian Territory (Oklahoma). His great-grandmother was a full blood Osage Indian who married William Shirley Williams, a famous frontiersman known in western literature as "Old Bill Williams." Mathews' early childhood was spent in Osage County, the Osage reservation, observing events referred to in *Sundown;* moreover, his own youth parallels many of the experiences of the protagonist, Challenge Windzer. Like the protagonist, Mathews attended the University of Oklahoma, majoring in geology and later leaving school to serve as a pilot in the Army Air Corps. Unlike the protagonist, however, Mathews returned to the university, earned his degree, and later attended Oxford, studying related sciences. After several years abroad, he returned to Osage County in 1932, the same year in which his *Wah'Kon-Tah* was published which won the Book-of-the-Month award. *Wah'Kon-Tah* is a historical biography based on the career of Laban Miles, who was government agent to the Osage tribe after their removal from Kansas to the reservation in Northeastern Oklahoma. Later, Mathews wrote *Life and Death of an Oilman: The Career of E.W. Marland* (1951), the biography of Earnest Marland—a wealthy, flamboyant oil man who became Oklahoma's governor in 1936. *The Osage: Children of the Middle Waters* (1961) was Mathews' final publication—a voluminous epic on Osage history and culture from the prehistorical period to the period after the oil boom in 1930 in Osage County. Mathews' other work, *Talking to the Moon* (1942), is a biography written in a *Walden* context which tells about his experiences with nature while living in a one-room house he built in the isolated blackjack oaks of Osage County.

Sundown has, as its setting, the historical period at approximately where *Wah'Kon-Tah* concludes, and its historical and political background is concerned with the Osage allotment act. During this same period in Oklahoma's history, the Dawes Allotment Act of 1883 gave citizenship to Indians in Indian Territory in exchange for surplus land. Although tribal regulations varied, the procedure was to enroll adult members of the tribe so that each received approximately 160 acres for homesteading, dissolving reservations and opening surplused lands to white settlers. However, the Osage tribe had paid the Cherokee Nation for land in Indian Territory and resisted the Dawes Commission under those terms. No surplus lands were therefore available to white settlers; instead, the land was divided equally among the 2,229 Osages.

In the initial chapters of *Sundown,* the history of the Osage Allotment Act and the earliest economic development in Osage County after Oklahoma's statehood are recreated through the role of Chal's father, John Windzer, a mixed-blood. During the late 1800s, political unrest in Osage County history, as in the novel, over allotment had divided the tribe into two political parties: the "Progressives"—mixed-bloods who promoted personal ownership of land—and the "Non-Progressives"—full-bloods who were trying to maintain communal ownership of the reservation. John Windzer is characterized in *Sundown* as the prototype of the "Progressive" mixed-blood factor, those descendants of marriages between French trappers and Osage women during a much earlier period in Osage history. Rather than French background in the novel, however, John was English, the grandson of Sir John Windzer, an artist who married into the Osage tribe when the Osage lived near the Missouri River. Nevertheless, as the novel also suggests, these Osage mixed-bloods were the first among the tribe to adopt non-Indian customs, to learn the English language, and to accept the white culture's education. In the novel, as Mathews portrays the consequences, the mixed-bloods rejected the Osage tribe's older customs for what they believed was a more progressive and modern lifestyle and regarded the full-bloods as uncivilized or "backward."

In contrast to the full-bloods (who lived in villages), in *Sundown,* the mixed-bloods (who lived in homesteads scattered throughout the territory) gathered daily in town—usually in front of the trader's store—to gossip over the latest development in tribal politics: "From the earliest days of the Agency, they had sat in front of the trader's store during the summer, hunted during the Autumn and sat around the big-bellied stoves and spat into the sawdust during the winter." John Windzer was no exception; "each day he rode his pony one block to the trading post where he met the other mixed-bloods to talk about the allotment and Frazer oil lease."

> He had become a member of the Osage council and was proud to be one of the Progressives, who were mostly mixed-bloods with a few weak-spined and easily led full-bloods . . . They employed all the tricks of their white brothers to get what they wanted and had fought hard and long for allotment of the reservation, until with the influence of the ubiquitous whites waiting on the borders, they got the consent of the council for allotment. In reality the allotment was forced upon the tribe. John and the other councilmen took pride in their progressive principles and were pleased when government officials patted them on the back and approved of their work.

John Windzer was actually closer to full-blood than white ancestry, yet he preferred to identify as white. John was not so ambitious as he was a vulnerable and naive romantic, educated in the high ideals of Romantic and Victorian writers. His favorite verse was Lord Byron's "Childe Harold"; he also admired William Jennings Bryan's patriotic speeches. John was a dreamer who envied the articulation of the orator, Running Horse—a member of the Osage Council who vehemently opposed allotment. When John went with the Council to Washington to discuss the reservation oil lease and allotment, Running Horse effectively bruised the vanity of the Secretary of Interior in a brazen speech by calling him a "Judas" and a betrayer of Osage's trust. Consequently, the Osage Council was dismissed by the Department of Interior.

Humiliated and disillusioned, John could not believe that the government could be influenced by oil men competing for Osage oil leases as the Frazer oil lease expired. Ironically, after allotment, John was murdered by a car thief who killed him for his new automobile—the ultimate symbol of progress on the Indian reservation.

Challenge's full blood mother symbolized the older traditional Osage order. Perhaps also to symbolize the passivity of the Osage woman's role during this period, Mrs. Windzer remained unnamed throughout the entire novel. She proved, however, to be a stronger and more stable character than either John or Chal, even though she was tacit and submissive in her role as John's wife. For example, although she had a hired girl, she polished John's new boots each evening. Mrs. Windzer respected John's political role, but she was unimpressed by wealth and indifferent to the projected "reforms" which he so readily advocated and, as Mathews states, Mrs. Windzer did not see "the importance of all this business" in Washington. John was her "handsome lord," and she did not want him to be unhappy. When John wrote home that he could not believe that the government was dishonest, Mrs. Windzer decided she would not tell John the truth about the "white men up there in Washington." She knew that he was naive like "a little boy," who trusted everybody; furthermore, "he always believed in the guv'mint." But from Mrs. Windzer's perspective, "the white men talked from the end of their tongues and not from their hearts."

Mrs. Windzer views her son more in terms of his place in Osage society than does her husband. Because Chal was born under the signs of the Older clan system, his character would be influenced by the moon, wolf, and coyote—the symbols of the warrior. She recalled the howling of the wolf on the night Chal was born:

> She knew that she had heard him; the lone wolf that had howled from Cedarvale Hill. Even above the distant yapping of the coyote she had heard him. And at that moment she had given her son secretly to the wolf; the wolf had wanted him and she had given her son.

In common with most of the full-bloods, Chal's mother was suspicious of the white people on the reservation; she did not trust the government officials and was reluctant that Chal be sent to the Agency school. John felt formal education was a step toward equality with the whites, so Mrs. Windzer submitted to John's decision, although she planned for Chal to practice Osage customs:

> Some day she would put paint on his face and arrange his clothes and set the feather in his scalplock as they should be set; she would put the symbol of her family on him, and comb his hair as he looked at himself in the mirror.

When Chal reached the appropriate age, she and John would also pick his wife from one of the other villages, but until she could "find a good woman," she would dress and decorate her son for the Osage ceremonies.

In the Osage tradition, Chal would have been given an Osage name at birth identifying him with his father's clan for, until a child is given a name, he is not a person. John Windzer's rejection of Osage tradition weakened Chal's claim to Osage identity and, as a mixed-blood, Chal was neither a viable part of Osage culture nor of white society. Not only did his father emphasize the white ancestry in the Windzer family, but more importantly to Chal's perception, John Windzer promoted acculturation and its logical extensive assimilation.

These two diverse perspectives, personified through the roles of Chal's father and mother, were also the views the boy confronted in his environment before white encroachment and certainly after the territory was open to white settlers. Osage and white cultures created two realities for Chal so that his Indian values eventually conflicted with the values of the white civilization. Consequently, he became psychologically crippled, emotionally stunted and incapable of expressing his own character which resulted in alienation from his own self-worth and identity.

Chal's formative and impressionistic years occurred while the reservation was still restricted to Osage people. He came into contact with few whites, except for the traders, the government employees at the Osage agency, and the few poor white female servants and male farmhands who were given government permits to work for Osage families. The Osage reservation was in essence pastoral. Unfenced, this vast, hilly blue-stem prairie was open range for cattle and horses; Kansas ranchers merely branded their cattle for identification at roundup time. T. M. Finney, a well-known Grayhorse trader, describes the reservation in his historical memoirs [*Pioneer Days with the Osage West of 96'* (1925)]:

> . . . wild game and fowl of unlimited numbers were abundant as were deer, wild turkey, geese, ducks, prairie chickens, quail, snipe, plover, and wild pigeons. While the streams were well stocked with game fish. The otter, beaver, raccoon, opossum, coyote, and timber wolf were trapped and hunted for their pelts.

The novel portrays that Chal was unhindered by concepts of time and duty, that he spent most of the time riding on the "somniferous" prairies with Indian companions, Running Elk and Sun-on-his-Wings. Usually, he daydreamed or played make-believe roles, "whether in the form of man or animal." Mostly, Chal took the role of the coyote hiding in the tall blue-stem grass while he watched the antics of the prairie chicken; other times he pretended to be the wolf "who talked to the moon." Except for the red-tail hawk which circled tirelessly above, the novel implies that Challenge felt equal to all the prairie creatures. That Chal felt comfortable in the natural environment is indicated clearly by his casual reaction toward a tornado which hit Kihekah—he simply secured himself against the cyclonic winds in the manner of the full-bloods by holding on to a bush until the cyclone moved on. He also played alone at night on the prairie:

> Sometimes he would not get home until after dark, walking or riding over the prairie and into the belt of blackjack where the density of the darkness, or half-darkness of the twilight always produced other stimuli.

Chal's affinity with nature is interrupted, however, when he entered school. His impressions of the school were that "they were like animals in a cage"; the entrance to the school was a "dark door . . . a big, black mouth, bigger and darker than a wildcat's."

During Chal's adolescence, the reservation was incorporated as Osage County, the largest in the newly-formed state of Oklahoma; the railroads were completed and, as the derricks increased, so followed the white population. Mathews states that, except for the trader's and the miller's boys, Chal usually associated with Indian boys. In comparison to the taciturn nature of the Indian boys, Chal thought the new white boys in town chattered like "blackbirds"; furthermore, he thought the people moving into Kihekah strange but fascinating:

> He had always heard that the ordinary white people who came into the reservation, the white people not concerned with the Agency, were inferior. But if they were inferior as everyone said they were, why were they so sure of themselves, and why did they always get what they wanted?

With the increase in white population, the full-bloods were seen less frequently in town. By the time Chal was in high school, he associated mostly with whites, whom he imitated: "He simply copied the other boys because he thought it was the thing to do . . ."; but Chal's Indian friends, even though they, like Chal, were football stars, remained aloof: "After classes they would untie their ponies and trot off toward their villages." That Chal was beginning to reject his Osage heritage was indicated by his attitude toward Sun-on-his-Wings and Running Elk. He thought they were "out of step"; that they had "no get up" and that their attitudes "made him tired." They ignored the "civilized" school parties, yet "they danced at the Roundhouse in the village every June and September", and Chal felt "vicarious shame for them."

Sun-on-his-Wings and Running Elk are the "Non-Progressives," or the traditionalists, who resented the intrusion of the white man. In the annals of Osage County, the earliest settlers were essentially poor Irish, English, and Dutch, mostly protestant, often of the fundamentalist persuasion, who projected much of the ethos of the Victorian period. The Indian boys understandably would not compromise their Indian character in exchange for the affected manners of the whites, especially those of the younger generation at social functions.

Even though Chal believes he enjoyed the "Progressive" activities, the novel reveals that, in time, he perceived that the urban pressures began to have an effect. The noisy activities of the town—the hammering, sawing, and the noise from the oil drills—created in Chal a craving for the natural environmental "like one craves salt or sugar," with frequent periods of despondency. He notices that the wild life around Kihekah no longer existed. It had been several years since he had seen any wild turkeys along Bird Creek, and he had almost forgotten what the howl of the wolf was like. On occasion, however, Chal would hear the Osage drums and singers in the middle of a night when they mourned the death of a tribesman.

To escape from his moods and the "monotony of the fresh-painted environment of the new high school," Chal camped weekends on the prairie; yet he never told anyone, because "he felt ashamed." From Challenge's perspective, people did not go riding out on the prairie alone unless they were cowboys riding fence. Under the influence of the natural stimuli, however, Chal resumed his normal behavior of talking to the animals and personifying the hills and

---

> Thirty years after Indian Territory had become the state of Oklahoma, Mathews came forth as the first American writer to present a novel which thematically portrays an American Indian—a mixed-blood—as a victim of a bi-culture identity.
>
> —*Carol Hunter*

---

trees. Instinctively aroused by the moon one evening, Chal felt a profound urge to express himself:

> There was the moon, large and white, hanging in a gleaming sycamore. The coyotes stopped as suddenly as they had begun. A great unhappiness filled him, and for the briefest moment he envied the coyotes but he didn't know why. For some time he looked at the moon, and the more he looked, the more intense became the emotion that seemed to be trying to strangle him. He arose from his blanket and stood naked there in the light, then spread his arms toward the moon. He tried to think of all the beautiful words he had ever heard, both in Osage and English, and as he remembered them he spoke them aloud to the moon . . . He tried to dance but the hill was rock, then he chanted; chanted an Osage song, but the feeling that he was being overpowered caused him to stop.

Mathews suggests that Chal's reaction was a natural response to the beauty that his ancient ancestors respected and worshipped as a reflection of their maker. In contrast to his religious experience, however, Chal rejected this deeper facet of his character. Frustrated by his emotional response, ironically, he cursed: "Gawdam it."

The psychological conflict between Chal's internal and external reality emerged more pronouncedly in his teens, especially during his freshman year at the university. Because Chal and his Indian friends were highschool football stars, they were encouraged by their Kihekah white friends and the fraternities to enroll at the university. Soon after arrival, however, Chal was left to his own initiative because Sun-on-his-Wings and Running Elk departed after sensing the insincerity of the fraternity brothers "who talked with their teeth" rather than "from their hearts." The Indian boys' cultural background was so alien to university attitudes that, rather than attempt to cope or pretend, they packed and returned to the reservation.

Although Chal remained at the university, he soon believed that he was a "misfit." The fraternity's artificial social demands were demeaning to his self-concept; consequently, he became inhibited because of his inability to imitate the other young men. He felt "dejected" because he could not understand their emphasis on grades, nor their allusions to women. Chal eventually came to the conclusion that the attitudes and philosophies at the university were "just a projection of the strange attitudes of the white people who had come into the Osage to live." Yet inwardly, Chal felt ashamed of his shy behavior. To escape the mounting frustration, he sought the solitude of the nearby country where a river ran near the campus and, in this natural setting, he returned to his habit of daydreaming. On one occasion, he was suddenly astounded to discover that, as he trotted along the river, he had unconsciously been playing the coyote role and felt "humiliated" that he had reverted to his childhood game. "I guess I'm crazy all right," was his response.

Later the same day, while Chal observed the animal behavior and admired the scenery, he commenced to sing his favorite song, "Pawnee Crying On Hill"—the song which told the incident of his ancestor's killing a Pawnee brave. Chal's happy mood changed that evening back on campus, however; he became despondent again in retrospect of the day's experiences:

> He was disappointed with himself and felt distinctly that he was out of step, and he believed that on this particular night he knew the truth about himself: that he was hopeless.

When summer arrived, the effects of the past year were projected in Chal's attitude toward his father and mother. He no longer perceived his father as "a hero" and he detested his mother's broken English. The only person with whom Chal developed a rapport was Professor Granville, a geologist. The following school year, Granville, learning of Chal's interest in flying, recommended him for the Army Air Corps.

For Chal, the Air Corps represented self-respect and identity. The previous summer at Kihekah, he had objectively observed the Indians, the mixed-bloods and full-bloods, as though not aligned with either:

> Chal thought the little town was very dull and backward after the university . . . He was the only person not doing something, except the mixed-bloods and the full-bloods, but he believed that there wasn't much interest in them—he certainly didn't want to be like them.

Chal is three generations removed from his white ancestry yet, in his distorted perception, he placed himself outside Indian society. In the Air Corps, he felt less conspicuous because he blended in with the other men in uniform. Away from the suppression of Kihekah's provincial society and the university milieu, he developed more self-confidence; in retrospect, "he felt contempt for the people of the university, and certainly for the people of Kihekah." The social activities at the Air base "under the guise of patriotism," and the military uniform gave Chal a "polished veneer." He also discovered that his bronze skin was attractive to women.

In the Air Corps, Chal's day-dreaming diminished as his self-esteem rose with the new, meaningful role. He was an officer of his post, and flying satisfied his adventurous nature, but Chal's Osage background had not provided him with the discipline to master the rigors of routine. In the social context, the Osage customs of rearing children in which the parents enjoy yielding to children's demands and whims did not help in the development of self-

discipline. Thus, in the novel after the war ended, Chal became bored with army routine and, after his father was killed, he resigned his commission.

That Chal is spiritually and emotionally estranged from his Osage culture is apparent from the feelings he expressed at his father's funeral. He was "embarrassed" when his older relatives sang the Osage mourning chant at the gravesite. ". . . There were so many new white people in town now that he thought they shouldn't have gone through the primitive ritual after the Christian burial." Chal's spiritual sterility inevitably left him more vulnerable to the false values of materialism and consequently, as his character weakened, he became more passive and easily influenced.

Chal returned to Kihekah around 1920, which was the beginning of the oil boom in Osage county. Although John Windzer's estates had left him wealthy, Chal felt that mere opulence was no "honor" because almost everyone was rich. Mathews states that "the poorest newcomer of a year or two ago now drove about in his own car." Many people "rendered services" and "were guardians" for one, or more, restricted Indians. "Yet there were no refineries, no factories, nothing made and nothing produced by the citizens of the little town among the blackjacks."

Since Mathews is essentially focusing on Chal's character development, the allusions to the local crime, violence and corruption are subtle, yet the social environment is directly related to Chal's misdirection. During the decade, the news of Indian wealth invited infamous characters from the back alleys of civilization; Mathews alludes to this decadence through the events of John Windzer's and Running Elk's murders. Mrs. Windzer also revealed to Chal that the "guardians" appointed by the Osage Indian Agency were unscrupulously taking financial advantage of their wards.

Initially when Chal returned to Kihekah, he was impressed by the esteem shown toward the affluent businessmen, doctors and lawyers. Their success motivated him to seek an occupation:

> He wished he had something to do—some business, but there wasn't anything for him to do. He couldn't get a job. No one would give a job to an Indian. Certainly he wouldn't have any chance to run for a county office, 'cause the voters always said an Indian had too much money and he could get more respect if he had a job or was in some business for himself . . . There seemed to be another dignity somewhere that would be hurt if he worked . . . He guessed he must have two dignities, one tellin' him to do something, and one tellin' him not to do something.

To ward off boredom, Chal "cruised" main street, symbolically circling in his "new red roadster" from one end of the street to the other. Eventually, he took trips to Colorado to play golf and, finally, he and the other young Osages frequented the saloons in the oil town "under the impression that they were sophisticated people from Kihekah and were slumming." Inevitably, Chal's drinking became habitual. In contrast to his father who left the "rock and rye" on the kitchen table, Chal hid his liquor not in the pretended fear of the prohibition law, but rather so that his mother would not suspect how much he was drinking. On one occasion after attending a tribal ceremony with a young Osage woman and her white friend, Chal got intoxicated and became nostalgic about his Osage heritage. He decided to visit Sun-on-his-Wings. When he arrived at his friend's village, the Indian men were preparing to enter the "peyote Sweatlodge" and Sun-on-his-Wings invited Chal to join them.

In the lodge, Chal had two warnings which, had he been less insensitive, could have saved him from his own self-destruction. For one, he learned about the Big Hill murders; for another, while under the sedative influence of the peyote ceremony, he had a dream. During the initial part of the ceremony, Running Elk's father, White Deer, told the priest (the Roadman) that he knew who had murdered his son and Big Hill relatives and wanted revenge. The Roadman warned White Deer to forget his revenge and maintain his Indian values.

Chal was as impervious to the Big Hill experience, interpreted by the wisdom of the Roadman, as he was incapable of understanding the intrinsic meaning of his dream. After Chal drank the emetic tea, he and Sun-on-his-Wings left the lodge briefly to empty their stomachs (in this manner, along with the Sweatlodge, Chal purged his body of evil). After they returned to the ceremonial lodge, Chal's mood changed, "he was fascinated and calmed . . . his thoughts were light . . . like sycamore leaves dripping to the surface of calm water." Mesmerized, Chal began to dream. He imagined that he was on a twisted trail "like a lost rope" in which he was running with his arms extended wide . . . "suddenly he was flying." The air currents lifted him to "dizzy heights," but when he tried to come down, he would suddenly plunge "like a plummet" and thought that he would be crushed on the hills below. Spreading his arms wide, Chal tried to save himself and, once again, the air currents carried him upward. Flying higher and higher, Chal feared that he would never come down again.

Obviously, Chal's dream is an extension of his Air Force experience in which his career in the service had given him identity, self-respect and purpose. In contrast to his previous self-fulfillment, his present passive existence was leading him toward self-destruction.

After the Sweatlodge experience, there are indications that Chal might be regenerated. However, two days later after he saw the confident attitudes of the "serious businessmen" and compared them with the image of the "mystical Indians," he decided he was being too sentimental about the Osage past. Consequently, he joined Marie and her friends on another drinking spree in which the climax of the young Osages' decadence is depicted in the party scene. After a night of "tinny juke box music" at one of the oil towns, where they witnessed a cowboy brawling over "a transparent girlfriend," Chal awakened the next morning in a stupor at one of the Indian ranch homes. On the pretense of fishing, he walked down to a creek where his spiritual emptiness is personified by Mathews who described the water as "lifeless" and Chal, himself, as indif-

ferent to the water creatures and the natural scene which once had symbolized his Indian character. Finally, after more drinking and being deviously pursued by a white girl, Chal left the party in disgust only to purchase more corn liquor from an impecunious farmer trying to survive economic depression and crop failure. While drinking, Chal drove at a high speed to an isolated pasture where, in contrast to the past, he was now an intruder and a nuisance as indicated by the coyote "yapping" his complaint and a blue jay which seemed to be "screaming murder." Chal attempted to sing and dance an Osage song while a curious domesticated steer stared at him. In his drunkenness, however, he fell on the running board of his automobile:

> He was in pain and he danced for some sort of climax; that sense of completeness that consummates the creative urge; an orgasm of the spirit. The dance became wilder and suddenly, in his despair, he broke the rhythm of his singing and yelled, but still the emotion was choked in his body. He wanted to challenge something; to strut before an enemy. He wanted by some action or some expression, to express the whole meaning of life; to declare to the silent world about him that he was a glorious male; to express to the silent forms of the blackbirds that he was a brother to the wind, the lightning, and the forces that came out of the earth. He fell . . . Then he mumbled to himself the freighters' old phrase of impotence. "Goddamit," he said feebly.

While the novel began with the image of the sun—the Osage symbol of life—Mathews concludes by reflecting on Chal's inertness which compares starkly with his natural surroundings and the animals that continued to actively function around him. In the final chapter of *Sundown*, Chal returned home after having been intoxicated for two weeks with a bank robber at an isolated shack, unable to remember much of what he had done. Weary and confused, he sat down in the yard under a shade tree. In contrast to the years in which nature provided "stimuli" to Chal's imagination, his character now reveals how unaware and insensitive he had become to his surroundings. As he sat in the shade of the oak tree, "he was lazily indifferent to everything he watched while a sparrow approached a robin's nest and took one of the nestlings, carried it to the end of the branch and dropped it. Chal heard it spatter as it hit the earth."

The young robin symbolized not only Chal and his companions, of course, but a generation of young Indian men and women who were also lifted from the security of their Indian communities to be assimilated into white civilization. Government interventions took children from their homes and carried them to BIA schools where their traditional languages, values, and customs would be obliterated and replaced by Western European mores.

The pressure on Chal to assimilate or "imitate" frontier white society had its effect. In the final episode when Chal's mother casually alluded to his flying career, Chal feebly and ineffectually defended himself, saying that flying no longer interested him; instead, he had decided to go to Harvard and become a great lawyer and orator. Chal, whose character reflects the real experiences of some Osage men and women of past and present, thought that money could buy status. True to his father's character and to other young Osages of this period, Chal was proud and arrogant; he wanted to be equal to the best class in white society. But Chal was a failure. The protagonist in *Sundown* failed to meet the challenge of taking the best values of two worlds—Indian and white—and to adjust these values into a viable lifestyle. In the final images, the reader finds Chal sitting asleep in the shade of the "old postoak." The shadows of the morning gradually recede as the sun reaches midday. While Chal slept, nature in the image of the grasshopper and robin, continued to function all around his slumped figure.

Chal, like many of his contemporaries, lacked a sense of interior identity which forced him to rely on models. He perceived in his community two alternatives to emulate: the solid "practical" businessmen who projected what he viewed as "civilization," or the other Osages whom he viewed as "mystical, foolish, sentimentalist and uncivilized."

This study of *Sundown* reveals that the younger Osage generation in the early part of the century was burdened with guilt complexes that had been generated by the system, the missionary or government education, and the values of the frontier fundamentalist society in which one's worthiness was qualified according to wealth—a society which stressed that one "should" work to become a productive citizen of serious and disciplined character. Chal's generation did not have the cultural, puritanical foundation which emphasized sacrifice, work and reward, although they were taught in the white schools to abandon the Osage traditional ideologies in exchange for values stressing individual materialism. On the one hand, Chal's character clearly reflects that he had partially assimilated due to his internal conflict over having no occupation. On the other hand, he perceived clearly that in order to gain respect in the white community, he must work; however, Osage identity was not dependent upon occupation.

Individual Osage identity during the early part of the century was associated with the tribe's social system and its relationship to the natural environment. The essence of the Osage's purpose was experiencing shared communal activities which did not focus on any one individual. The Osage spent time feasting and visiting; for, as Indian agent Isaac Gibson recorded in 1900, the Osage "love to sing, to dance, to rest . . . They are aristocrats and like all wealthy people they don't care for manual labor." The protagonist in *Sundown* is a victim of an attempt to assimilate a people forced into a non-Indian world view which was the antithesis of the values of the white civilization. Chal could find no purpose in the new value structure erected by the white man.

The meaning of *Sundown* is apparent in Challenge Windzer's failure. His struggle for purpose represents the young Osage Indians who were caught in a complex socioeconomic environment during Osage County's early development. Throughout the novel, the author's caustic tone and bitter criticism toward the white value structure,

studied in conjunction with the protagonist's failure to find meaning in his life, demonstrates, in essence, that Mathews viewed Challenge's generation as tragic victims of abrupt assimilation.

Reginald and Gladys Laubin (review date August 1983)

SOURCE: A review of *Talking to the Moon,* in *Western American Literature,* Vol. XVIII, No. 2, August, 1983, pp. 179-80.

[*American critics, Reginald and Gladys Laubin have produced numerous films and works on Native American art and culture. In the following, they offer a positive assessment of* Talking to the Moon.]

[John Joseph Mathew's *Talking to the Moon*] is a timely book, beautifully written, and one that can be enjoyed just for its flow of beautiful English. It reminds one of the writings of Thoreau with its down-to-earth philosophy, keen and intimate observation of nature. But it is also full of native American comparisons, cowboy reflections and humor, and personal experiences.

To top all this, it was written by a native American, an Osage Indian. With all the interest that has developed in recent years in Indian authors and Indian literature it is strange that the name of John Joseph Mathews has seldom, if ever, appeared on the list of popular favorites. And yet here was an outstanding native American, who lived fully in two worlds. He went far in the white man's world—a Rhodes Scholar, a pilot in World War I, a rancher, and a noted writer on subjects other than Indian. But he was thoroughly acquainted with the lore of his own people, served on their tribal council, and brings forth little-known historical details of their existence. He knew the old people and was respected by them, often being called upon to represent them and to defend them before Congress.

Some of the experiences he records show deep insight into the ancient culture and an understanding of the problems of acculturation. There are of course differences in the attitudes of members of White and Indian cultures; these are described with high humor, but deep understanding, without prejudice or bitterness over the conflict.

The title, *Talking to the Moon,* is carried throughout the book with the chapters being named for the Osage moons or months. Although the Osage are a Siouan people their names for the moons, because of differences in geography and climate, are quite different from those of other Siouan tribes, but the author's use of these Osage terms is part of the fascination of the book and nicely ties in his account with the various characteristics of the seasons he is describing. His details of weather, storm, wind, temperature, rain, hail, sleet, snow, to say nothing of prairie fires and tornadoes, add greatly to his narrative and help a stranger to become acquainted with and to appreciate his beloved Oklahoma blackjacks.

Mathews' stories of many varieties of wild life prove him to have been a thorough student of nature. The many birds that lived in his "retreat" are most entertaining, and he even takes us to a prairie chicken dance. Some of his favorite local dwellers were mallard ducks. He said, " . . . nothing enjoys life more than a mallard. . . . It is a shame he can't sing." Although he was forced to consider the coyote his enemy, he admired him and played fair with him. He loved to hunt but regarded his hunting as part of the balance of nature for which he was striving, and always considered true sportsmanship ahead of taking game.

Philosophizing, he wrote, "The laws of the earth survival are laid down, and man is not far enough away from the earth to supersede them with those of his own creation; he can only go back to the earth to ascertain where he has diverged from the natural processes."

We knew Mr. Mathews personally. We were fortunate in meeting him and his wife several years ago in Oklahoma. So we naturally have a particular interest in this book, but had we never known him we would still find his writing delightful and his stories not only entertaining but valuable. He certainly was more interested in the "balance of nature" than were most people of his day and his comments and stories can help others who have a present-day interest in achieving similar goals. Mathews' own charming little sketches illustrate his text and we are happy to have had the opportunity to read this new edition of *Talking to the Moon.*

A. LaVonne Brown Ruoff   (essay date 1992)

SOURCE: "John Joseph Mathews's *Talking to the Moon:* Literary and Osage Contexts," in *Multicultural Autobiography: American Lives,* edited by James Robert Payne, The University of Tennessee Press, Knoxville, 1992, pp. 1-31.

[*An American educator and critic who specializes in Native American studies, Ruoff is the author of* American Indian Literatures: An Introduction, Bibliographic Review, and Selected Bibliography *(1990). In the following excerpt, she offers a stylistic and thematic analysis of* Talking to the Moon, *examining its relationship to other Native American autobiographies, its focus on Osage culture, and its similarities to Henry David Thoreau's* Walden *(1854) and John Muir's* My First Summer in the Sierra *(1911).*]

American scholars have increasingly emphasized the importance of American autobiographies to the study of American culture. In "Autobiography and the Making of America," Robert F. Sayre attributes this to American autobiographers having "generally connected their own lives to the national life or to national ideas" [*Autobiography: Essays Theoretical and Critical,* edited by James Olney, 1980]. Like their white and African-American counterparts, Native Americans have emphasized the connection between their lives and the larger community. Although their life histories emphasize the interrelationship between the individual and the tribe more than that with the United States as a nation, they also stress the impact of Indian-white relations on Indian life. Recognizing that life histories constitute one of the major genres of American-Indian literatures, scholars such as H. David Brumble III, Arnold Krupat, Gretchen Bataille, Kathleen Mullen Sands,

Lynne O'Brien, and Ruoff have increasingly turned their attention to the study of life histories and autobiographies. Because American-Indian written autobiographies reflect not only the personal and tribal history of the author but trends in popular literature and in Indian-white relations, they form a rich resource. This essay will focus on John Joseph Mathews's *Talking to the Moon* (1945), a highly sophisticated literary autobiography, and will discuss its place in the history of American-Indian autobiography. It will also examine the extent to which the form and content of Mathews's *Talking to the Moon* were influenced by Henry David Thoreau's *Walden* (1854) and John Muir's *My First Summer in the Sierra* (1911) as well as by Osage traditions and history.

Full-length confessions or autobiographies in the Western European literary mode are not part of American-Indian oral literary tradition. However, Brumble indicates in *American Indian Autobiography* that Native-American preliterate autobiographical narratives include a variety of forms designed to convey specific information or achieve a particular purpose. Among these are coup tales, which describe feats of bravery; tales of warfare and hunting; self examinations, which might consist of confessions required for participation in rituals or accounts of misfortunes and illnesses; self-vindications; educational narratives; and tales of acquisition of powers. Even today some Indians may decline to write or narrate full-length autobiographies because their tribes consider it inappropriate for individuals to speak about themselves in an extended fashion until after they have achieved a status acknowledged by the tribe.

American-Indian life histories and autobiographies often blend a mixture of tribal myth, ethnohistory, and personal experience. This mixed form was congenial to Indian narrators and authors accustomed to viewing their lives within the history of their family, clan, band, or tribe. In her introduction to *Life Lived like a Story,* Julie Cruikshank provides a contemporary example of this perspective. To her questions about secular events, three Athabaskan/Tlingit women responded by telling traditional stories because "these narratives were important to record *as part of*" their life stories. Their accounts included not only the personal reminiscences we associate with autobiography but also detailed narratives elaborating mythological themes, genealogies and lists of personal and place names that had both metaphoric and mnemonic value. She notes that these women talked about their lives using an oral tradition grounded in local idiom and a mutually shared body of knowledge.

In the early nineteenth century, publication of full-length American-Indian life histories was stimulated by the popularity of captivity and slave narratives. In the East and Midwest, it also resulted from renewed interest in "the noble savages," who no longer threatened whites because the Indians had been pacified or, under the provisions of the 1830 Indian Removal Bill, forcibly relocated to Indian Territory, now Oklahoma, and other areas west of the Mississippi. As Indians were removed, whites increasingly wanted to read about the vanished "noble savages" or about assimilated Indian converts to Christianity. Published in response to this interest, nineteenth-century American-Indian autobiographies became forceful weapons in Native Americans' never-ending battles against white injustice.

In 1833, the narrated American-Indian autobiography, a major literary form in the late-nineteenth and twentieth centuries, was introduced with the publication of *The Life of Ma-ka-tai-me-she-kia-kiak or Black Hawk*. Narrated by Black Hawk (Sauk) to translator Antoine Le Claire and revised for publication by John B. Patterson, this popular book went through five editions by 1847. The earliest published full-life autobiographies written by American Indians were *A Son of the Forest* (1829) by William Apes (Pequot, b. 1798) and *The Life, History and Travels of Kah-ge-ga-gah-bowh* (1847) by George Copway (Ojibwa, 1818-69). Like the slave narrators, Apes and Copway consciously modeled their autobiographies on the spiritual confessions and missionary reminiscences popular with white readers. The spiritual confessions linked Indian autobiographers to Protestant literary traditions and identified these authors as civilized Christians whose experiences were as legitimate subjects of written analysis as the experiences of other Christians. Apes, Copway, and later American-Indian autobiographers, like the slave narrators, used personal and family experiences to illustrate the suffering their people endured at the hands of white Christians.

Because he was apprenticed to whites after age four and was not raised in a traditional Indian culture, Apes, unlike later autobiographers, does not include a tribal ethnohistory in *A Son of the Forest*. This book is primarily devoted to Apes's spiritual journey toward salvation and to strong statements about white injustice to Indians. More representative of the evolving form of American-Indian written autobiographies than Apes's self-published *A Son of the Forest* was Copway's *The Life, History and Travels of Kah-ge-ga-gah-bowh* (1847). This popular autobiography went through six editions in one year. Although Copway used the structure of the spiritual confession and missionary reminiscence, he blended these with Ojibwa myth, ethnohistory, and personal experience. Copway also introduced descriptions of childhood experiences and portraits of family life designed to counteract the stereotype of Indians as "red devils" intent on killing as many innocent whites as possible.

From the early nineteenth century through the 1960s, more American-Indian life histories or autobiographies were published than any other genre of Native-American literature. However, subsequent Indian autobiographers abandoned the religious narrative as a model and in its place used versions of the blend of mythology, ethnohistory, and personal experience that Copway initiated. Instead of personal religious experience, Indian autobiographers emphasized tribal culture and history and Indian-white relations. *Life among the Piutes* (1883) by Sarah Winnemucca (Paiute, ca. 1844-91), exemplifies this shift in perspective. During most of the nineteenth century, Winnemucca was the only Indian woman writer of personal and tribal history. Her *Life among the Piutes* is particularly interesting for her characterization of her childhood terror of whites, her discussion of the status of women in Paiute society, and her descriptions of her role as a liaison between Indians and whites.

To the descriptions of tribal ethnohistory and growing up within a tribal culture included in earlier Indian autobiographies, later writers added accounts of Indian children's adjustment to white-run schools. *The Middle Five* (1900) by Francis La Flesche (Omaha, 1857-1932) exemplifies this trend. The most influential and widely read Indian autobiographer in the early twentieth century was Charles Eastman (Sioux, 1858-1939), who wrote two autobiographies. *Indian Boyhood* (1902), written for his children, describes his life as a traditional Sioux boy from infancy to age fifteen. *From the Deep Woods to Civilization* (1916) is a progress autobiography that traces Eastman's struggles to succeed, from his first days in a white school to becoming a medical doctor and an internationally known spokesperson on Indian issues. It also reflects his growing sense of Indian-ness and disillusionment with white society.

Mathews's *Talking to the Moon* differs from most earlier Indian autobiographies because it is a spiritual autobiography of a specific period in the author's life rather than a life history of growing up Indian or of adjustment to contact with non-Indians and their institutions. Unlike Copway and later Indian autobiographers, Mathews did not grow up within a tribal culture. Consequently, *Talking to the Moon* is not an exploration of Mathews's ethnicity but rather a chronicle of his attempts to find himself at a crucial time in his life through rediscovering the land, animals, and people of his native Oklahoma. In the course of this rediscovery, Mathews pays tribute to the Osage, whose traditional life had undergone tremendous change. One-eighth Osage by blood, Mathews spent his youth and much of his adult life after 1932 living among and working with them. Most of his books were devoted to describing their lives, heritage, and history.

While *Talking to the Moon* does contain the blend of myth, history, and personal experience that characterizes American-Indian autobiographies, it is modeled not on these books but rather on the works of Thoreau and John Muir. Mrs. Elizabeth Mathews makes this clear in her foreword to the 1981 reprint of her husband's book: "this is John Joseph Mathews's *Walden*. It is a book that a Thoreau or a Muir might write, but it is a *Walden* of the plains and prairies, of the 1930s and 1940s, by a Native American." By incorporating many elements of the form and content of Thoreau's *Walden* and Muir's *My First Summer in the Sierra*, Mathews deliberately places *Talking to the Moon* within a received literary tradition, which he adapts to incorporate aspects of Oklahoma and Osage culture and history. The result is the most sophisticated and polished autobiography by an Indian author to be published up to 1945. . . .

The period of his life covered by *Talking to the Moon* begins after the publication of *Wah'Kon-Tah*. Undoubtedly, Mathews's interest in what motivates humankind, his need to understand our relationship to nature, and his desire to observe nature closely led him to choose Thoreau's and Muir's works as his literary models. Like these authors, he withdrew from cities to overcome the separation he felt between himself and nature. For Mathews, this process involved restoring his relationship to his Oklahoma homeland and with the animals and humans, such as the Osage, cowboys, and ranchers, who inhabited it. Twenty-eight-year-old Thoreau settled near Walden Pond in 1845 and remained for two years. Thirty-eight-year-old Mathews settled and remained ten years in the "blackjacks" near Pawhuska, a region named for the tough oaks that covered the sandstone region. Clearly Mathews identified with Thoreau's statement of why he settled near Walden Pond: "I went to the woods because I wished to live deliberately, to front only the essential facts of life, and see if I could not learn what it had to teach, and not, when I came to die, discover that I had not lived." The influence of Thoreau's *Walden* is clearly reflected in Mathews's statement that he returned to the blackjack region in order to become part of the balance:

> . . . to learn something of the moods of the little corner of the earth which had given me being; to learn something of the biological progression and mysterious urge which had inspired it, until the biological changes within myself had dimmed the romance of it. I had kept my body fit and ready, but my perceptive powers had been dulled by the artificialities and crowding and elbowing of men of Europe and America, my ears attuned to the clanging steel and strident sounds of civilization, and the range of my sight stopped by tall buildings and walls, by neat gardens and geometrical fields; and I had begun to worship these things and the men who brought them into being—impersonalized groups of magicians who never appeared to my consciousness as frail, uninspiring individuals.

Mathews had long realized that the wonders of civilization, as well as "war and unnatural crowding of men, slavery, group fanaticism, and social abnormalities, were inspired by the biological urge manifesting itself in progression, as were the dreams of the few who created beauty, comfort, and tragedy." He emphasized that he did not return to the blackjacks because of political convictions but rather to devote a few years to pleasant and undisturbed living. There Mathews felt he might come to understand the relationship between humankind's primal and creative urges: "I realized that man's artistic creations and his dreams, often resulting in beauty, as well as his fumbling toward God, must be primal, possibly the results of the biological urge which inspires the wood thrush to sing and the coyote to talk to the moon." Unlike Thoreau and Muir, Mathews settled in a place where as a child he had felt a oneness with the ridges and prairies. The influence of Thoreau's *Walden* and Muir's *My First Summer in the Sierra* is reflected as well in the organization and content of ***Talking to the Moon.*** Mathews follows Thoreau's example by organizing his autobiography by seasons, which allows both authors to describe not only their observations of nature but their personal growth in terms of natural cycles. The focus of Muir's book is on the description of the changes in nature during a single summer and of his maturation during that period. Mathews follows Muir's example in using a month-by-month structure, which he bases on the Osage months of the year.

Mathews also includes topics similar to those treated by Thoreau and Muir. All three authors share a strong sense of place, revealed in Thoreau's loving descriptions of the area around Walden Pond, Muir's ecstatic world landscapes of the majestic Sierra Nevada, and Mathews's poetic descriptions of the ridges and prairies in eastern Oklahoma. Both Thoreau and Mathews chronicle the changes these places undergo through the seasons and years, emphasizing that these areas transcend and reflect time while Muir recounts in diary form his daily observations of his summer in the Sierra.

Thoreau examines the Walden Pond area and the soil of his beanfield to trace their history; Muir speculates about the origin of the boulders in the high mountains during the glacial period. Similarly, Mathews analyzes with the eye of the scientist and verbal landscape artist the limestone ridges and his post oak to learn the history of the rain, drought, and fire they endured over the passage of time. For Mathews, the ridges and the blackjacks link primordial nature with contemporary life. At the beginning of his book, Mathews focuses his description of the ridges on the blackjack oaks, whose dead limbs slant downward, "hard and tough as steel lances," protecting them from harm. In earlier days, buffalo rubbed against the trees to scratch their itching hides; now cows hide in their groves to deliver calves. Mathews's description of the blackjacks parallels Muir's numerous tributes to the fir, juniper, and pine trees of the Sierra.

Mathews's careful descriptions of animals, birds, and insects also reflect the influence of Thoreau and Muir. Thoreau's observations on his brute neighbors include his famous description of the mock heroic battle of the red and black ants. In attempting to come close to nature, Thoreau became an amateur scientist, observing under a microscope the movement of ants on a piece of wood, while Muir risked his life to observe a bear up close. Mathews is as curious about the creatures of nature as his predecessors were. Some of his experiments reveal a scientific detachment, as he himself seems to acknowledge. One is his futile attempt to tame a coyote whelp, which spent her days looking out of the pen with her yellow-green eyes filled with "hatred and courage." Mathews coldly comments that "She taught me nothing except the fact that even at her age her mother was still interested in her and made valiant attempts to save her. She also confirmed my experiences that coyotes suffer and die in silence and thus do not endanger the other members of the band by calling for help." Another example is his setting a chicken loose out on the prairie near a coyote den to determine the mother's reaction. Although the mother coyote clearly sees the chicken, she pretends the fowl is not there. The coyote both fascinated and frustrated Mathews, whose attempts to outthink it usually ended in failure. Like the Osage, Mathews regarded the coyote as "a symbol of cupidity and double-dealing." For Mathews these episodes exemplify the eternal battle between the intellect of humankind and the instinct of the animal as humans vainly and destructively attempt to control nature and all its creatures. Mathews is more conscious than Thoreau and Muir that his own efforts to control nature disturb the balance.

During his first year in the blackjacks, Mathews lived as part of this balance and was proud of his harmony with the life around him. However, under the influence of the Planting Moon (April), he broke the truce: "After bringing pheasants, guineas, and chickens to the ridge, I had to fight for the survival of my charges against my predacious neighbors, which was probably a more natural state and in the end more satisfying than the 'friends and neighbor' idea." The presence of his charges whetted the predators' desires and sharpened their cunning. He and the predators were caught in a struggle, pitting their wits against one another. Mathews wonders whether his position was unnatural since he did not live off the land; thus, he was then not part of the economic struggle of the ridge which results in the balance. Mathews vividly depicts this battle with predators in the chapter entitled "Little-Flower-Killer Moon" (May), in which he tells how he emptied the cylinder of his revolver into a skunk that slaughtered many of his chickens "from sheer lust." Mathews emphasizes that the skunk behaved abnormally, killing for enjoyment rather than survival and leaving behind his headless victims. Nevertheless, Mathews confesses that, when he held the muzzle of his gun to the skunk's head and emptied the cylinder, he gloried "in the nauseating musk odor that hung on the heavy air of night, transforming its glory with the sharp explosions that broke the silence of the ridge into a symbol of the mighty power of Homo sapiens when aroused and announcing his entrance into the struggle." For Mathews, the episode reveals the desire for revenge that lurks just beneath humankind's civilized veneer. He also acknowledges that this tragedy resulted from his bringing the chickens to his land, an act that interfered with the balance.

Like Thoreau and Muir, Mathews emphasizes sensory experience in nature, particularly hearing and sight. Just as Thoreau devotes a whole chapter of *Walden* to "Sounds" and gives detailed descriptions of animal sounds in "Winter Animals," and as Muir catalogs the animal and human sounds of the Sierra sheep camp, so Mathews includes descriptions of sounds: the April sounds of bird songs filled with "injured innocence and pessimism" and of long cattle trains that "come screaming into the little loading pens and stand panting from their exertion as the cattle bawl and the boys shout as they unload them." Mathews follows the examples of Thoreau and Muir in his emphasis on sight as well. Thoreau, in his chapter on "The Ponds" in *Walden* vividly describes the colors of shore and water while Muir, in *My First Summer in the Sierra,* paints verbal landscapes of the magnificent grandeur of this mountain range. Although Mathews includes far less geographic and landscape description than Thoreau and Muir, he includes some lovely descriptive passages in his chapter "Little-Flower-Killer Moon" of the thousands of little flowers that die away in May and of the flowering weeds that replace them, reinforcing the theme of the fragility of life in the cycles of nature elaborated in that chapter. Equally beautiful are the pictures of the prairies awash in the old-gold color of sunflowers, butterflies, and goldfinches that Mathews creates in the chapter called "Yellow-Flower Moon" (August). However, in both of these chapters Mathews uses these descriptions as introductions

to his observations on insects, birds, animals, and men, which are the focus of his interest.

Another parallel to Thoreau and Muir is Mathews's description of his living accommodations. For Mathews, as for Thoreau, his cabin and cultivated land represent personal space between the town and the wild. Whereas Thoreau recounts his labors in planting his garden and tilling his beanfield, Mathews describes his in planting kafir, a grain sorghum, for the prairie chickens and trees and shrubbery for his yard. Thoreau plants to eat while Mathews plants to encourage the presence of fowls and to shade himself from the parching Oklahoma sun and winds. Just as Thoreau pauses in tilling his beanfield to observe the hawks flying above him, Mathews pauses in his planting to observe the mockingbirds' return, the prairie chickens' dances, and the cocks' fights. Unlike Thoreau, Mathews does not use the description of building his cabin as a jumping-off point for discussing the history of man's attitude toward shelter. Instead, he uses it to introduce the human inhabitants of the ridges and prairies—Virgil, the most efficient hand on the ranch and Mathews's house builder, and other ranch hands who question why Mathews builds on a high ridge far from arable land and why he plans to live alone. Their attitudes set Mathews's own in relief.

There are parallels as well in the three authors' treatment of such subjects as solitude, neighbors, and visitors. For example, all three enjoy occasional visits with friends. Thoreau keeps three chairs for company; Mathews keeps a bountiful supply of food for his city guests. Mathews's descriptions of his pleasures in cooking echo those of Thoreau and Muir on bread making. The three authors also create memorable portraits of their visitors and neighbors. However, Muir and Mathews do not denigrate their neighbors or companions as does Thoreau in his description of the hapless Irish bogsman, John Field, whom he calls "honest, hardworking, but shiftless." Muir has little in common with his campmates, who are oblivious to the beauties of nature. He refers to Delaney as Don Quixote, because his sharp profile resembles that of the Spanish knight, and to Billy, the tobacco-chewing shepherd and camp butcher, as Sancho Panza. However, Muir is sympathetic to the hard life that Billy led.

Mathews creates several vivid portraits of locals. Especially memorable is that of Les Claypool, a former cowboy whose face was "like weathered granite"; "his steel-gray eyes and his silence, as he looked at his great gold watch with the hunting case," caused Mathews to feel like a guilty schoolboy when he was late for a meeting. Claypool staunchly clung to the past and resisted change. Thirty-eight years after he quit working on cattle drives and after he became a car owner, Claypool still kept his horse saddled, ready for emergencies.

Talking to the Moon shows the influence of Thoreau's *Walden* in its purpose, general structure, and content, and of Muir's *My First Summer in the Sierra* in its detailed, scientific descriptions of nature and sympathetic portraits of local characters. While it is clear that Mathews wished to write *Talking to the Moon* within the tradition of the pastoral, spiritual autobiography popularized by Thoreau and Muir, it is equally clear that he wishes to distinguish his work from theirs by adding an emphasis on Indian history and culture largely absent from their books. The difference in the focus of the autobiographies is evident in the authors' choice of titles. Whereas Thoreau and Muir select titles that refer to the places where they renewed themselves in nature, Mathews chooses one that alludes to the Osage's interrelationship with their natural gods. In *Walden,* Thoreau makes only a few fleeting references to the Indians near Concord, their simple shelters, and the ancient civilization that inhabited the soil Thoreau tills in his beanfield. Although Muir includes more descriptions of Indians he encounters in the Sierra, he is equally detached from them as people. This is especially clear in his comments about the Indian member of his sheep camp. Describing how the men chatted during breakfast, Muir remarks that the "Indian kept in the background, saying never a word, as if he belonged to another species." Unlike Billy, the shepherd, the "Indian" is neither given a name nor described in a character sketch. Later in *My First Summer in the Sierra,* Muir expands his reaction to Indian silence in the description of another Indian who arrived unobserved, "as motionless and weather-stained as an old tree-stump that had stood there for centuries. All Indians seem to have learned this wonderful way of walking unseen,—making themselves invisible like certain spiders I have been observing here." Muir also mentions the Digger Indians who inhabit the area and gives a short biography of Old Tenaya, the Yosemite chief and namesake of the basin.

By stressing the Indian heritage of the blackjack region, Mathews makes *Talking to the Moon* an account of the changes in the Osage culture that had survived for centuries as part of the balance of the blackjacks and prairie as well as an account of the changes in nature and himself. Mathews's sensitivity to the Osage is evident in his decision to pay tribute to his tribal ancestry not by exploring his own ethnicity as a mixed-blood but rather by focusing on the tribe's myths, history, customs, and elders. In fact, he does not mention his own Osage heritage, although his wife does in her foreword to the 1981 edition. As Terry P. Wilson points out in "The Osage Oxonian" [*Chronicles of Oklahoma* 59, No. 3 (Fall 1981)], Mathews was well aware of the antagonism of a faction of Osage full-bloods toward mixed-bloods. The full-bloods had not forgotten the fraud perpetuated in 1906, when many whites had their names included on the Osage rolls in order to get allotments of Osage land. Mathews realized that, although his own identity as an Osage was not tainted in this way, he was always "suspect in the minds of some." According to Wilson, the author's "elections to the tribal council said less about his identification as an Indian in the eyes of the Osages and more about their respect for his education, familiarity with the complexities of white society, and devotion to the tribe's interests." Wilson correctly concludes that this "reluctant dependence on Mathews and other mixed-bloods is typical of the ambivalence in most tribes and many Indian organizations."

Undoubtedly, Mathews realized that exploring his own ethnicity in this autobiography would have resulted in severe criticism from the Osages and would have undercut his efforts on their behalf. Instead, he chose to focus on recording what he learned from the Osages and on creating memorable portraits of tribal members. Mathews was all too aware that, since the beginning of the reservation period in 1878, the Osages had endured traumatic changes in their culture. In 1907, Oklahoma became a state and the Osage Nation reservation became Osage County. Unlike other Indian tribes in Oklahoma, the Osage had retained the mineral rights to their lands after allotment. The discovery of oil on Osage lands in 1897 led to boom times in the 1920s that threatened to extinguish traditional Osage culture and values. Oil companies, entrepreneurs, and scalawags poured into Osage County to take advantage of the Osages' oil and their new-found wealth. During what Mathews calls in *The Osages* the "Great Frenzy," some Osages spent their money freely. Other Osages were defrauded or murdered for their lands and oil money. Still others succumbed to alcoholism. By 1932, when Mathews settled in his cabin in the blackjacks, the boom of the 1920s was over. As Mathews notes in *The Osages,* the oil royalties peaked in 1925 at $13,000 per capita but slipped in 1932 to $712.

The traditional Osage were, in Mathews's view, the human inhabitants of the blackjack region most in tune with the land. The key to this oneness with nature was their religion:

> He [the traditional Osage man] built up in his imagination the Great Mysteries and he walked, fought, hunted and mated with the approval of them. When the Force urged him to expression, he turned his eyes to Grandfather the Sun; the colors he saw under his closed eyelids, he put into beadwork, quillwork, and painting, as inspirations from one of the greatest manifestations of the Great Mysteries, the sun, Father of Father Fire, impregnator of Mother Earth.

The Osage tribe symbolized the universe, and the Osages divided themselves and their universe into two parts: man and animal, spiritual and material, sky (Chesho; Sky People; Peace Division) and earth (Hunkah; Earth People; War Division). The Osage conceived of the moon as a woman because she periodically appeared twelve times a year; because of the moon's power over the earth; and because when she dominated the ridges, there was no disturbance by the male element: "Grandfather the Sun has gone to rest and even Father the fire is dim in her presence, as though out of a traditional understanding and deference, like a great warrior in camp where woman is supreme." As a good woman should, she leaves at dawn, taking her children, the stars, so as not to disturb Grandfather the Sun when he takes over the male world of daytime. Mathews incorporates the Osage concept of the moon as a woman into many chapters of *Talking to the Moon.* The opening passage of the chapter called "Single Moon by Himself" (January) illustrates how Mathews uses Osage concepts of the Moon Woman to set the mood: "The Moon Woman floats by herself now. There are no babies or fruits or flowers, say the Osage, and the Moon Woman is lonesome. She is not so gay and temperamental but dull and moody. Snow may stay on the ground for a long time, and there will be no sun, and the days as much alike, cold and gloomy. The moon is sometimes called Frost-on-Inside-of-Lodge Moon and long ago was known as the Hunger Moon."

For Mathews, traditional Osage life achieved a balance in nature which the white man never gained and which the Osage themselves lost when they were forced to abandon the old, free life and substitute the peyote cult or Christianity for the gods of their ancestors. Mathews describes the balance the Osage achieved in the chapter on the Planting Moon (April), the time for female ceremonies of planting and growth. Using Osage-style English, Mathews retells old Ee-Nah-Apee's story about Osage planting customs, which exemplify the tribe's belief in balance:

> Purty soon womens go to them little—hills, I guess, and they make hole with that pole on south side of that there hill. They used to say Grandfather sure would see them holes in them hills on south side, that-a-way. We put corn in them hills, in them little holes; and when we have all of 'em with corn in it, we put our feets on it. We stand on them little hills and make drum against the earth with the poles and sing purty song.

The women stamp the hills with the left foot for Chesho and the right for Hunkah. That the Osage have moved from these customs into the world of the white man is demonstrated by Ee-Nah-Apee laughing when she told the story, as "though she were embarrassed by recalling such primitive things that the tribe was now attempting to put away forever." The Osage recognized that the nature of the world and humankind included both of these polarities, which must be kept in balance. They also recognized that at various times one would dominate the other. Certainly this division of the Osage into Chesho (associated with peace and thought or imagination) and Hunkah (associated with war and physical action) influences Mathews's attitudes toward his own state of mind, which moves between these polarities. When the author first moved to the blackjacks, he exulted in the physical: "I wanted to express my harmony with the natural flow of life on my bit of earth through physical action." The planting song of the Osages runs through his head, stimulating him to the physical action of planting trees and shrubs. Another example of action during a Hunkah state of mind is his narrative, in the chapter called "Deer Breeding Moon" (October), of joining in a hunt to track down a bear which had killed some of a neighbor's sheep: "Bear hunting, with its frenzied action and the deep voices of the bloodhounds echoing from the savage walls of the mountain canyons, awakens every nerve to incautious action." He notes that, ten years later, his desire for action had been tempered. In the chapter "Single Moon by Himself" (January), Mathews describes his thoughts as "Chesho, as they should be, and there are no longer Hunkah thoughts of youth and action, when Single Moon by Himself comes to the blackjacks, and I am inside the dark little sandstone house by the fire."

Among the several Osage myths that Mathews blends into *Talking to the Moon* is that of the spider, the Osage symbol that Mathews uses on the spines of the books he has authored. Mathews indicates that the spider was formerly a clan symbol but is now used by a woman's secret society. According to the story, members of a clan could not make up their minds about which animal to choose as a symbol suitable to great warriors. During their search, they rejected many animals until one of their leaders walked into a spiderweb. The spider persuaded them to accept it as their symbol: "I am a little black thing; I have not the strength, the courage, the beauty of those you talk about, but remember this: wherever I go I build my house, and where I build my house all things come to it." Mathews also comments on the Osage use of the coyote in their stories that "depend on dignity made ridiculous as a basis for humor." The coyote also appears as a warning for children that they should never think of themselves as being shrewder than others, since "one may be outwitted through one's own vanity." For the Osage, the coyote was an indicator of something astir on the prairie, either enemy, friend, or quarry. They mimicked his yelping to deceive enemies: "He was an important person in the scheme of things, but he hadn't the proper virtues for symbolism."

> **Mathews's interest in what motivates humankind, his need to understand our relationship to nature, and his desire to observe nature closely led him to choose Henry David Thoreau's and John Muir's works as his literary models for *Talking to the Moon*.**
>
> **—A. LaVonne Brown Ruoff**

Mathews's most extended treatment of Osage history and culture is contained in the chapter "Buffalo-Pawing-Earth Moon" (June), focusing on the month when the Ee-lon-shescha, male ceremonial dances, are held at the villages of the three active branches of the original five physical divisions of the Osage. He vividly evokes the color and customs of these dances, describing the different costumes and steps used by dancers from various clans, the honoring songs, giveaways, and the storytelling. Mathews's activities and observations during the ceremonies reveal his relationship to the tribe. While he does not participate in the ceremonies, he observes proper etiquette by giving money to the drum keeper to help support the ceremonies and then joins the old men, who evidently welcome him: "Here I pick up many stories of the jealousy between the Peyote factions, and laugh with them over the stories of dignified men being humiliated. I like the sound of their voices and the graceful movements of their hands as they talk, in this setting of colorful activity." To illustrate Osage storytelling, Mathews recreates a scene in which an elder describes, in Osage dialect and within the hearing of the subject's grandson, how an arrogant Osage male was humiliated in the midst of his bragging. While the proud Osage was in the middle of a speech designed to impress some Sioux visitors, a louse crawled up his eagle feather headdress: "At the same time he finish his talkin' that feather make bow, ain't it? That little eagle feather make bow with louse ridin' on it—sure was funny." The story exemplifies Indians' use of humorous stories to enforce approved behavior.

Mathews confesses that he has never grown tired of watching the dancers, whom he has watched since he was a small boy—"a time when they wore nothing except breechcloths, moccasins, silver arm bands, and scalplocks and carried hand mirrors and war axes." Then the dancers were tall and lean. But now, despite the fat bellies and flabby arms and gorgeous costumes, "the dance is grave and the figures graceful, and in its dignity and fervency the dance is still a prayer" to Wah'Kon-Tah of the old religion, "not withstanding the symbols of peyote with which they adorn themselves." He comments that the June dances, which originally had ritual but at the time he describes had only social significance, and the gossip at the dances about conflict between peyote factions reinforce his sense of the drama in the world represented by the relentless movement of Christianity: "I feel the earth's drama all about me, but the conflict between Christianity and the old religion of the Osages forces itself upon my attention . . . ." Mathews feels extremely fortunate to witness the last struggle of a native religion and believes that his daily life in the blackjacks was as influenced by this as by any other struggle for survival: "The passing of a concept of God seems to be almost as poignant as the passing of a species."

Mathews illustrates this passing of the old religion, along with his own determination to preserve its artifacts, by recreating a scene between himself and the second son of Spotted Horse. The young man brings his father's message that, although it is all right to have a sacred medicine bundle in the Osage museum that Mathews is to establish, he should not open it: "He says you alltime ask too many questions about them bundles, he says. You oughtn't do that; it's bad. He says you' sure die if you fool with them things. Osage have put them bad things away, he says."

The confusion into which Christianity and industrialization have thrown the Osage is only part of that tribe's tragedy. Although old men lamented the destruction of the social structure, they lamented even more the consequent end of the tribe as a unit and the loss of their individual immortality. Their consciousness points out to them "the end of their race, the end of their god, the complete assimilation of their children, and the end of their immortality. It is the sheet-water of oblivion that washes their moccasin prints from the ridges and agitates their last thoughts."

Because the old Osage chief, Eagle-That-Gets-What-He-Wants, feared that tribal traditions would disappear from memory, unremembered by young Osage eager to adopt white ways, he arranged for his wife to interpret his accounts of Osage oral traditions, which Mathews wrote down. The chief's story about Tze Topah, his uncle and the chief of the Little Osages, illustrates how the Osage used oral tradition to keep their history and culture alive in the memories of their people. When old Tze Topah realized he would die soon, he spent many hours telling people what he knew and did when young. Unable to tell his sto-

ries to a band out hunting, Tze Topah dressed in his war finery and rode through the band's camp, singing so that all people would stop their work to hear his song and so that they would know him and remember him as long as they had tongues to talk and their children ears to hear.

For Mathews, the peyotism of the Native American Church represents a blend of Osage religion and Christianity. Many of the Osage elders felt that the religion of their god, Wah'Kon-Tah, was not strong enough to stand up against Christianity and therefore should be put aside. Mathews emphasizes that the Osage "adopted the Man on the Cross because they understand him. He is both Chesho and Hunkah. His footprints are on the peyote altars, and they are deep like the footprints of one who has jumped." Mathews enlivens his discussion of Osage culture with a series of verbal portraits of Osage elders. Many of these are contained in the chapter "Yellow-Flower Moon" (August), in which he describes how he helped an artist commissioned to paint the pictures of the old men for the Osage Museum. The proud Osage elder, Claremore, insists on posing for days in full regalia despite the withering July heat. The teasing Abbott, a member of the Osage tribal council, comments that the portrait of Claremore looks like a "white man that lost his money. Maybe someday when I look at it, I shoot myself." When Abbott poses for his own portrait, Mathews brings the desired twinkle to the council member's eye by recalling the story of how Abbott, who was always in debt, told a butterfly that landed on his shoulder, " 'Pay you next week.' " The incident also illustrates Mathews's rapport with the Osage elders. Other examples of Indian humor are provided by Nonceh Tonkah, the only elder to wear a scalplock. The old man instructs his daughter in Osage to tell the artist to bring his daughter to Nonceh Tonkah in exchange for his posing. The elder also asked the artist if he wants Nonceh Tonkah's head when he dies. His patronizing daughter refuses to translate these unseemly remarks. Mathews creates another memorable portrait in his characterization of Louie, a Cherokee who talks to owls, explaining that he does not have to hide from the owls because " 'them owls don't care 'bout nothin' when they do this here big talkin'.' " Louie hoots at the owls in a coaxing, seductive tone which they answer in kind. For Mathews, Louie embodies the unity between the Indian and nature.

Like Thoreau and Muir, Mathews sees himself as a mediator between man and nature. However, whereas Thoreau eschews identification with the purely natural man represented by Indians and non-Indian woodcutters, and Muir feels a bond with his shepherd but not with the Sierra Indians, Mathews praises both Indians and other men of nature for achieving a natural balance through instinct that he can achieve only through intellect. Each of the three writers attempts to achieve a balance between the polarities of the intellectual or imaginative and the physical or instinctual. Thoreau's concept of nature and of the balance between the polarities is rooted in the Romantic attitudes toward nature expressed by writers like Goethe and Wordsworth. As James MacIntosh points out [in *Thoreau as Romantic Naturalist: His Shifting Stance Toward Nature,* 1974], Thoreau shares with these writers a "powerful wish to love nature and even to merge with it, with a consciousness, sometimes explicit, sometimes concealed, of separation." MacIntosh notes that Thoreau shares the Romantics' secret fear of the destructiveness of nature—the natural cycle of growth, decay, death, and rebirth—and that he is wary both of the existence of nature within himself and of his realization that nature can sometimes exist as power or chaos rather than as life or growth. For Goethe, Wordsworth, and Thoreau, repeated experience is a "necessary way to enlightenment and truth." They are attracted by the "world of generation that brings pleasure and peace to the men of restless mind because it is both ordered and alive."

Muir shares with the Romantics an ability to express ecstasy in the presence of the natural sublime. Like Thoreau, he was influenced by both Wordsworth and Emerson. Harold P. Simonson suggests in "The Tempered Romanticism of John Muir" [*Western American Literature* 13, No. 3 (1978)] that the author tried in his work to reconcile the conflicting ideas that pertained, on the one hand, "to nature that conforms to the mind's eye and projects the drama of one's developing self; and, on the other hand, to nature as divine emanation, as revelation, as topological figure presupposing a distinctly separate and sovereign God." Simonson comments that Muir attempted to verify nature's higher laws, as did Thoreau, and found his epiphany in nature. Although Muir has less fear of the destructiveness of nature than Thoreau, he is nevertheless aware of its darker side. Simonson concludes that, despite Muir's affirmations about the flow and unity of nature's laws, Muir retained a dualized Christian cosmology, in which the soul is a divine spark known in a rapt state of wildness, and body was the bondage of society and morality, symbolized by life in the lowlands.

Mathews's sense of balance is rooted not only in the literary traditions represented by Thoreau and Muir but in the oral traditions of the Osage. Like Thoreau and Muir, he too deals with issues of duality—between the primal and the ornamental (a term he takes from Thoreau) or intellectually creative. Strongly influencing his thought, however, are the Osage principles of Chesho (sky, passivity, peace) and Hunkah (earth, action, war), which one must learn to balance. However, Mathews seems far less fearful of the dark side of nature than do Thoreau and Muir. In the chapter "The Single Moon By Himself" (January), Mathews comments on the constant battle to keep the balance:

> The peace of my ridge is not a peace but a series of range-line skirmishes and constant struggle for survival. The balance is kept by bluff and a respect for that power which backs it up, and it utilizes and protects an area large enough and fruitful enough to sustain that power. The laws of the earth for survival are laid down, and man is not far enough away from the earth to supersede them with those of his own creation; he can only go back to the earth to ascertain where he has diverged from the natural processes.

Thoreau and Muir lament that America destroys its soul and the land in its quest for material and industrial wealth. While recognizing these dangers, Mathews is also deeply concerned about the possible extinction both of Osage cul-

ture as a result of white pressure and of the free world as a result of World War II. Writing in 1942, when the survival of freedom in the United States and Europe was very much in doubt, Mathews concludes that the human race cannot have lasting peace, even though organized warfare seems to be human-created and therefore may be human-controlled: "Forced peace, which is the only kind of peace man can conceive of now in his present stage of development, cannot last any longer than the powers that impose it."

All three authors want to merge with and yet remain separate from nature. The differences between the philosophical positions of Thoreau and Mathews are exemplified in their attitudes toward hunting. In the chapter on "Higher Laws" in *Walden,* Thoreau stresses that hunting and fishing are usually a young man's introduction to nature. If he has the seeds of a better life in him, a man "distinguishes his proper objects, as a poet or naturalist it may be, and leaves the gun and fishpole behind" as did Thoreau himself. Meat eating, Thoreau feels, is a throwback to savage cannibalism—a reminder of a primitiveness that man must overcome. Muir treats the subject indirectly, through his description of the hunting techniques of David Brown, a gold miner and renowned bear hunter. Mathews, on the other hand, regards hunting as a form of ornamental play, a reminder of man's struggle for survival. The instinct to hunt remains strong in Mathews despite his progression to a sense of community with humanity and its renewal in nature. In the chapter "Deer-Breeding Moon" (October), Mathews describes the revitalizing power of a bear hunt:

> Somewhere ahead of that excited chorusing was a great black beast whose ancestors far back in time once hunted man, and man has a racial memory of having been the delicate, thin-skinned hunted instead of the hunter, which adds zest to bear hunting; the racial memory of the scratching and sniffing at his cave barrier is still deep in man's soul.

Thoreau, Muir, and Mathews use the cycles of nature as a framework for describing their own cycles of maturation and renewal, recalled for the benefit of the reader. All three authors emphasize, as did Wordsworth before them, that humanity must progress from physical to spiritual perceptions of nature but that close observation of the physical is a necessary stage to reaching the spiritual. Early in *Talking to the Moon,* Mathews stresses that, although humankind has the same natural urges as other species, he goes farther by acknowledging the progression of life through his dream of God. Mathews's attempts to protect his fowls from predators made him part of the life struggle and of the balance of the ridge: "Thus, I achieved a greater harmony with my environment and found that there is no place for dreams in natural progression, and it seems to me that I realized for the first time that with responsibility come enemies."

As the time and the seasons come and go, Mathews, like the other inhabitants of the ridges and prairies, is changed. Although he no longer wants to battle the natural elements, he becomes restless because just living and filling up his days are not enough: "First, I had to have responsibility and disturb the balance of the blackjacks: then, after a few years, I extended my activities beyond the ridges." Unlike Thoreau, he did not move away from his retreat, but instead he entered the world of social service by becoming a member of the Osage tribal business committee and a member of the Oklahoma Board of Education.

In explaining why he left Walden Pond, Thoreau says that "perhaps it seemed to me that I had several more lives to live, and could not spare any more time for that one. It is remarkable how easily and insensibly we fall into a particular route and make a beaten track for ourselves." Urging his readers to be a "Columbus to whole new continents and worlds within you," Thoreau wants them to open new channels, "not of trade, but of thought." Thoreau yearns for truth rather than for love, money, or fame. For Muir, the exploration of the Sierra Nevada is the first excursion into a sublime land, which ends only because the coming fall and winter necessitate his bringing the sheep back down from the mountains, not because he was psychologically ready to leave unspoiled nature. He remained in the Sierra for ten years.

Like Thoreau, Mathews matures sufficiently to end his isolation. He had begun to reenter the world of social re-

---

Terry P. Wilson on labeling Mathews an assimilationist:

Beyond the obvious parallels with his own life experience, Mathews wrote very accurately and compassionately about the Osages and their reservation. Critic Charles Larson mars an otherwise perceptive analysis of *Sundown* by classifying Mathews with two earlier Indian authors as an "assimilationist." The trouble is with the terminology. Certainly the novel's major theme centers on the problem of assimilation and the unresolved ending leaves the reader with the impression that an Indian heritage mixed with the white man's education most likely leads to an insoluble identity crisis. However, as Larson himself notes, Mathews's later life was a refutation of that hopeless helplessness syndrome portrayed in his novel. Mathews continued to write with the benefit of his formal education while engaging in tribal affairs and living an outdoors life closer to nature than did most twentieth century men, Indian or white. Doubtlessly, Larson was unaware of the political and emotional connotation of *assimilationist* in the national Indian community. The term is used to identify, and almost always to derogate, an individual who espouses and/or typifies the acculturationist thrust among Native Americans. Having this appellation applied to one's self would be abhorrent to virtually any Indian, regardless of its veracity, and it definitely does not apply to Mathews whose celebration of traditional Osage values in the face of intrusions from an Anglo-American "progressive" society expresses a decidedly anti-assimilationist philosophy.

Terry P. Wilson, in "Osage Oxonian: The Heritage of John Joseph Mathews," in Chronicles of Oklahoma, *Fall, 1981.*

---

sponsibility by becoming a member of the Osage tribal council and running, unsuccessfully, for the school board. His decision to conclude his retreat is dramatized in his vain attempt to enlist in active service during World War II, described in the last chapter, "The Light-of-the-Day-Returns or Coyote-Breeding Moon" (February). Turned down, Mathews was forced to recognize that he had indeed moved from the active Hunkah world to the inactive Chesho world. His "Chesho thoughts have the same roots as his Hunkah thoughts and the same roots as the Hunkah actions in all species, even though inspired by the Force as an urge to immortality." Not satisfied to feel and enjoy the flood of emotion that living inspires and expresses in action, he now wants to express the subtleties of world symbols.

In his conclusion, Mathews seems to take up the challenge offered by Thoreau to seek out new worlds of thought, which he will express in words, so that people will not only know that a great ego passed that way but that Mathews "heard the wood thrush at twilight—the voice disembodied in the dripping woods—that I have heard the coyote talk to the moon and watched the geese against a cold autumn sunset." By writing **Talking to the Moon,** Mathews recaptures the experience of renewal in nature earlier described by Thoreau in *Walden* and Muir in *My First Summer in the Sierra.* He also immortalizes in poetic prose the traditions of his beloved Osage, who achieved a harmony with nature that the three authors sought and that humankind must seek if we are to survive.

Louis Owens   (essay date 1992)

SOURCE: "Maps of the Mind: John Joseph Mathews and D'Arcy McNickle," in his *Other Destinies: Understanding the American Indian Novel,* University of Oklahoma Press, 1992, pp. 49-89.

[*Owens is an American educator, critic, and novelist of Choctaw and Cherokee descent. In the following excerpt, he provides an overview of* Sundown, *concluding that the novel "depicts starkly the consequences of oil and acculturation for the Osage while simultaneously refusing to accept the familiar pattern of simple doom for the Indian."*]

With the publication of **Sundown** in 1934, the mixedblood Osage writer John Joseph Mathews introduced the modern American Indian novel, laying out a pattern for novels by Indian writers that would be confirmed two years later when D'Arcy McNickle published *The Surrounded* (1936) and again and again during succeeding decades. Like *The Surrounded,* **Sundown** is the story of a mixedblood living both in and out of his tribal culture, and it is a nearly fatalistic tale that at a superficial glance seems to mesh neatly with the popular naturalism of the twenties and thirties. While Hemingway had chosen to emphasize at least an earthly continuum in his title for *The Sun Also Rises,* another novel of deracination and despair, at first glance Mathews would seem to focus starkly upon the other end of daylight, showing us the tragic results of the oil boom in Osage County—what had until only recently been the Osage Reservation.

Mathews himself served as an unlikely model for his protagonist, Challenge Windzer. Like Chal, Mathews was born on the Osage Agency of mixedblood parents, and like Chal, the author studied at the University of Oklahoma and went on to become a pilot during World War I. Like Chal, Mathews came of age amidst the oil boom that brought wealth and disaster to many Osage people, but unlike his character, Mathews graduated from the University of Oklahoma, served in France during the war, and later received degrees from both Oxford and the University of Geneva. Mathews, described by his publisher, Savoie Lottinville, as possessing "many of the qualities of the English gentleman blended with those of the gentleman Osage," may be in fact the most acculturated of all Indian novelists. After completing his degree in international relations at Geneva, where the League of Nations was in session, he toured France by motor bike and bummed around Europe. It was while on a big-game hunting trip in North Africa that, after encountering a wild group of Arab horsemen, he decided to return to his home and learn about his Osage relations.

With impressive tenacity and foresight, the Osage opposed the Dawes Severalty Act of 1887 (the General Allotment Act), which had such disastrous consequences for other tribes. According to Terry Wilson, "By steadfastly resisting a hasty application of the Dawes Act to its reservation, the tribe was able to protect the valuable mineral resources beneath the surface from individualization and to avert the loss of any of its territory through the expropriation of 'surplus' land by white settlers as had happened to Oklahoma tribes whose land was allotted earlier" so that when the Osage at last submitted to pressures for allotment in 1906 the tribe was able to keep its reservation holdings intact. Eventually, Osage County in Oklahoma retained the outline of the Osage Reservation boundaries. As an allotted member of the tribe, Mathews received 560 acres and a headright, and he came to take a deep interest in his heritage, writing about his people in *Wah'Kon-Tah: The Osage and the White Man's Road* (1932), in his autobiographical *Talking to the Moon* (1945), a kind of Osage *Walden,* and in *The Osages: Children of the Middle Waters* (1961). From 1934 through 1942 Mathews also served on the Osage Tribal Council.

Sundown seems to offer a quintessential postcolonial scenario, as described by [Bill Ashcroft, Gareth Griffiths, and Helen Tiffin], the authors of *The Empire Writes Back:* "A valid and active sense of self may have been eroded by *dislocation,* resulting from migration, the experience of enslavement. . . . Or it may have been destroyed by *cultural denigration,* the conscious and unconscious oppression of the indigenous personality and culture by a supposedly superior racial or cultural model." Like others in such a postcolonial drama, including nearly all Native Americans, Mathews's characters are beset by "a pervasive concern with . . . identity and authenticity." Prior to the opening of *Sundown,* the Osage, like Ridge's Cherokees and many other tribes, had been forcibly relocated by the federal government. Their culture had been exposed to the denigrating pressures of missionaries, including schools, and disruptive Euramerican values. And with the discovery of rich oil fields on tribal lands, this process had been accelerated enormously. The Osage in Mathews's novel

are finally overwhelmed by outsiders who (with their extreme sense of racial and cultural superiority) consciously and unconsciously destroy traditional values and attempt to displace the Indians yet further—through miscegenation, marriage, and simple murder in order to gain control of headrights and, thus, oil money.

Sundown begins with Chal Windzer's birth at a critical point of transition for the Osage Nation between old and new worlds. "The god of the great Osages was still dominant over the wild prairie and the blackjack hills when Challenge was born," writes Mathews in the novel's opening line. "He showed his anger in fantastic play of lightning and thunder that crashed and rolled among the hills; in the wind that came from the great tumbling clouds which appeared in the northwest and brought twilight and ominous milkwarm silence." The ecosystemic world of the Osage is intact in this scene and can be comprehended mythically. From these first sentences to the final lines of the novel, associations with the natural world—the sacred geography of the Osage people—will serve as an index to Chal Windzer's character and well-being. During those moments when, for a brief time, he is immersed in nature, he will feel nearly whole and close to something instinctual and sustaining; when he is removed from intimate contact with the natural world, he will become ever more displaced and confused.

"On this birthnight," Mathews continues as the novel begins, "the red, dim light which shone from the narrow window of the room where his mother labored, seemed faint and half-hearted in the moonlight; faint as though it were a symbol of the new order, yet diffident in the vivid, full-blooded paganism of the old; afraid, yet steady and persistent, and the only light in the Agency on this tranquil, silver night of silence." Associated with the sun, for the Osage the most powerful manifestation of the creator, the color red figures as a crucial link to the traditional Osage world in which the sun was honored in virtually every aspect of life. In this birth scene, the color seems to emanate from Chal's fullblood mother—the "only light in the Agency"—whose Indianness remains steadfast throughout the novel as a touchstone to unchanging and essential values. However, in its half-heartedness in conjunction with the sacred moonlight—also symbolic of the older, immutable Indian world—the red light underscores the tenuousness of even the mother's hold on traditional identity. Cast into this uncertain light at birth, Chal Windzer is born into the easily recognizable postcolonial and modernist position of deracination, alienation, and confusion.

Mathews's opening scene introduces the dialectic that will inform the novel's plot: the struggle between old and new—Indian and Euramerican—"orders." In keeping with this dialectic, the color red becomes sacred to Chal almost from birth, when he reaches out for the red dress of the Euramerican "har'd" girl. Red, Chal learns later, is the color of the Sun "who was Grandfather, and of Fire, who was Father, and of the Dawn, sacred to Wah'Kon-Tah."

John Windzer, Chal's father, declares at his son's birth, "He shall be a challenge to the disinheritors of his people.

We'll call him Challenge." Ironically, however, Chal never overtly challenges the new order, attempting instead to mold himself according to the new, non-Indian values, which he accepts but never comprehends. This attitude he inherits from his mixedblood father, who sits at home reading "Childe Harold"—a canonized artifact of the privileged culture and a romantic narrative that reinforces the Euramerican's "epic" and thus entropic view of the vanishing, historic past. This *"triste tropiques"* myth of cultural ruin and decay dovetails neatly, and ironically, with the Euramericans' desire to brush the Osage aside while appropriating Osage oil and land. Chal's father, one of the rapidly growing population of politically influential mixedbloods amongst the Osage, is proud to be a descendant of British nobility in the form of Sir John Windzer, an artist who lived among the Osage, and he boasts that "if it hadn't been for the progressives on the council, they never would have been any allotment, if it was left up to the fullblood party." With this declaration, Mathews is illuminating the bitter division between fullbloods and mixedbloods within the tribe, with the former generally struggling to retain traditional ways of life while the latter pushed increasingly for adoption of "civilized" values.

Serving as a pawn in the whites' maneuvers to control and rob the Osages, John Windzer facilitates the disfranchisement of the son he named Challenge. In the end, it is Mathews's depiction of Chal Windzer's descent toward ruin which challenges "the disinheritors of his people," a descent culminating when Chal swears to himself, "I wish I didn't have a drop of God damn' Indian blood in my veins."

In a recurring pattern throughout the novel, Chal identifies with animals and the natural world. As a child he imagines himself consistently as animal: "a panther lying lazily in his den" or "a redtail hawk circling high in the blue of the sky" or "an indefinite animal in a snug den" or a coyote stalking the prairie. On an almost unconscious level, he remains aware of the older Indian world outside of his parents' comfortable house and the increasingly civilized town:

> And then sometimes, when he waked early in the morning, he could hear some mourner on the hill which bordered the creek, chanting the song of death, and always some inscrutable sorrow welled and flooded him; something that was not understandable and was mysterious, and seemed especially fitting for the dense dark hours just before dawn; the hours most fitted for that questing, that feeble attempt to understand.

Chal's own unstated quest in this passage is for the impossible: an understanding of a world that has been made remote from him at birth. The song of death and the "inscrutable sorrow" are for the Osage world disappearing at astonishing speed in the course of Chal's life as oil money pours into what had been the reservation. This is the romantic posture toward American Indian existence adopted and celebrated by the non-Indian world. Writers from Freneau and Cooper to Faulkner and LaFarge would stop here, with a crocodile tear for the dying noble savage. Writing from within the supposedly "dying" culture rather than from the outside, however, Mathews goes beyond

such a stock response, making of Chal's story a more complex narrative of cultural survival. The "dark hours just before dawn" are Mathews's subject; a "feeble questioning" of the dilemmas of Indian existence and identity in the twentieth century is his method; and an awakening to a renewed sense of self—authenticity—for Native Americans would appear to be his goal.

Central to Chal's childhood is the nearby creek, where he swims and about which his life seems to revolve. And it is the creek which serves as an index to how far the destruction has progressed in the name of progress. Even as the oil boom is just beginning, Chal notices a change: "It had been several years since he had heard the wild turkeys flying up to roost along the creek, and he could scarcely remember what the howl of the wolf was like." As the "civilized" values of the town grow too intense for Chal, he invariably returns to the creek, still searching for that "something that was not understandable and was mysterious." One night he rolls up in his blankets to sleep beside the creek only to be awakened by the abrupt howling of coyotes: "There was the moon, large and white, hanging in a gleaming sycamore. The coyotes stopped as suddenly as they had begun. A great unhappiness filled him, and for the briefest moment he envied the coyotes, but he didn't know why." He rises and studies the moon and then

> he crossed the creek and climbed a little hill in the full flood of the ghostly light. He stood there, then spread his arms toward the moon. He tried to think of all the beautiful words he had ever heard, both in Osage and English, and as he remembered them he spoke them aloud to the moon, but they would not suffice it seemed; they were not sufficient to relieve that choking feeling.

Chal envies the coyotes because they know, instinctively, how to celebrate the sacral significance of the moon—nature—something he cannot do. In his desire to utter a polyphony of "beautiful words," Chal is attempting to create a prayer that would comprehend the potentially rich heteroglossia of his world, to fuse the "internally persuasive" language of his Osage heritage with the "authoritative" discourse of English in a syncretic utterance, and by speaking this hybridized utterance to the sacred Osage moon, to put the parts of himself together in an identity that can comprehend both worlds. Could Chal conflate the "beautiful" in both discourses, he might solve the painful dilemma of his inauthenticity and achieve a "temporal unification of the past and future with the present" that leads to a coherent sense of self. He is, with his desire to "think of all the beautiful words he had ever heard" and to speak them, attempting to emulate the coyotes. But Chal's dissociated sensibility cannot speak in one voice; he is choked into silence by his inability to articulate—to put the pieces of the self together into a coherent utterance. "But this mysterious unhappiness came to him only at times," Mathews writes, "and never except when he was alone on the prairie." At other times, Chal achieves a kind of transcendent awareness of his place in the natural order of the traditional, sacred Osage world:

> The sun was setting and the west looked like leaping flames that had been suddenly solidi-

fied. . . . Then, very suddenly, that mysterious feeling came over him. A mild fire seemed to be coursing through his veins and he felt that he wanted to sing and dance; sing and dance with deep reverence. He felt that some kind of glory had descended upon him, accompanied by a sort of sweetness and a thrilling appreciation of himself.

As the oil boom draws more of the "civilized" world to the Osage country, Chal grows more distant from the natural world. When he leaves for the state university with his friends, Sun-on-His-Wings and Running Elk, his disinheritance from his Osage identity becomes almost complete. From the beginning, he is annoyed with his childhood friends "for acting like Indians." When he flees the university to walk along the river, he daydreams about his future: "He couldn't dream fast enough to visualize all the honors that came to him. He even visualized a great feast and dance held in his honor by the Osages when he arrived back home for Christmas. They had made a song and invented a dance especially for him, and they gave him a name, but he couldn't decide what the name should be." In Indian cultures a name is earned—as Chal's father has told him earlier in the novel—and most crucially a name comes from the community to both confer an identity and confirm one's place within that community. Indian identity is communal, and Chal has lost his place within his Osage community; thus he cannot conceive of an Osage name. At this point the daydream evaporates, and in place of a rich heteroglossia Chal is left with only the authoritative discourse represented by the American dream of being "self-made": "As pleasant as the dream was, he decided to leave the Osage part of it out. He didn't want to call attention to the fact that most of his blood was of an uncivilized race like the Osages. He believed that they didn't have any backbone, and he certainly wanted to make something of himself." Chal's reflection mimics the observation of one J. E. Jenkins, an inspector for the Indian Office, who reported approvingly in 1906 that the Osage mixedbloods—who by the turn of the century outnumbered fullbloods—"act like white people, well educated and intelligent." A year earlier, however, Frank Frantz, the Osage agent from 1904 to 1905, had reported that if the fullbloods were an improvident lot, the mixedbloods was "a worse proposition" and did not "deserve any efforts in his behalf."

As Chal prepares to go to a college dance, he remembers his reflection: "At the last impression of his face in the mirror that evening, he had seen a bronze face in the black-and-white; the white making the bronze stand out, and he had wondered if he wasn't too dark." By the (white) values of the privileged culture, Chal finds himself unacceptable. However, Mathews does not allow Chal to completely repress his Osage way of viewing the world. As Chal dances with Blo, his beautiful (white) date, Mathews writes: "But this was a new experience, merging with someone in such fervency; someone like the Moon Woman, who, like many things beautiful, lived briefly. Like the Moon Woman of his childhood who reigned over the forgetfulness of the night; over the tranquil world of dreams; the world of Wah'Kon." Mathews adds later: "He wondered why he had a feeling that was something like a religious emotion when he thought of Blo. Of course it never occurred to him that it might be the tribal heritage of religion associated with beauty and dreams." For a moment, Chal's Osage self has achieved the upper hand in this political struggle, reversing the pattern that denigrates an Indian world-view, removing his date from the referential context that had made him feel "too dark" and displacing her into an Indian system of reference. She is made beautiful and given significance within the mythic paradigms of his tribal heritage.

Chal leaves the university to enlist in the Army Air Corps, and upon graduation from ground school, "he thought of himself as being separated by a great abyss from Sun-on-His-Wings and Running Elk, and from the villages and the people moving among the lodges." So separated is he that he tells a female admirer that he's Spanish rather than have her guess his real identity. Nonetheless, Chal is still profoundly Indian, and his ambivalence is underscored when he looks down from his airplane: "He had a feeling of superiority, and he kept thinking of the millions of people below him as white men." In the air, radically displaced, alone and controlling the most sophisticated example of American machinery, Chal fuses his resentment of the white man with a sense of having beaten the whites at their own game of individualism and machinery. Still, when he begins to gain self-assurance brought on by the admiration of women, "he felt that he had begun to be gilded by that desirable thing which he called civilization. He was becoming a man among civilized men."

When his father is murdered, Chal returns home and becomes another of the directionless Osages drinking and driving fast cars. In this aspect of Chal's malaise, Mathews reflects an accurate picture of the cultural disintigration besetting the Osage. In fact, while the bootleg liquor Chal drinks was a major problem among the Osage as among other portions of the American population, even drugs had become a scourge of the newly wealthy Indians, with morphine, cocaine and marijuana provided by an influx of "pushers." A seizure of fifty thousand dollars' worth of drugs in a single cache in Osage County in 1929 was reportedly the largest single drug seizure in Oklahoma prior to World War II. On a drinking spree, Chal goes in search of the old special place by the creek only to find that "several black wells stood about on the prairie above the trees and from each a path of sterile brown earth led down to the creek, where oil and salt water had killed every blade of grass and exposed the glaring limestone. Some of the elms had been cut down, and the surface of the water had an iridescent scum on it." Again, nature mirrors the condition of the Osage. Later, after an all-night drunk, Chal returns to the creek to try fishing, but "the water was lifeless."

While Chal was away, his friend Running Elk has also been murdered by whites trying to gain control of allotments. Before his murder, however, while drying out in a detoxification ward, Running Elk provides a vivid nightmare image of what has befallen his people. When Chal visits him, Running Elk describes a terrifying dream in which a "fat white man, completely naked and glistening, would stand at the door of his room with a spear in his hand." This nightmare vision illuminates the displacement of the Indian by the avaricious (fat) white man who has, as the spear and blocked doorway suggest, both looted Indian culture and trapped the Indian. The particularly deadly displacement of Indian males—which will be a concern of the next generation of Native American novelists—is suggested in the sexually aggressive posture of the naked white man with the phallic, appropriated spear. There would appear to be no place left for the Indian male except escape through alcohol and unconsciousness.

As foils for Chal, Running Elk and Sun-on-His-Wings stand at opposite ends of the spectrum of possibilities for the Osage. While Running Elk has sought oblivion through alcohol, Sun-on-His-Wings has turned toward Osage tradition and the new peyote church. Visiting his childhood friend, Chal takes part in a Sweat Lodge ceremony and is moved by the experience. After the ceremony, "they went back into the lodge, picked up their blankets, and dispersed. Chal drew his blanket closely around him." To Chal, as for others, the blanket has always been a sign of traditional, "primitive" Indians, and as such something to be scorned. Here, following the sweat and the prayers of the ceremony, Chal becomes, briefly, one of those scorned "blanket Indians." With this brief touch, Mathews hints at a potential return to traditional, immutable values through the new, syncretic peyote ceremonies.

The promise seems short-lived, however. During the Sweat Lodge ceremony, Watching Eagle, the Road Man, has told a man named White Deer: "Your son and those People who have been killed by these white men, followed that road which they thought was white man's road. Your son married white woman. You have children of your son, but they are not your children. They can never have a name among their people. They have no people." On a literal level, Watching Eagle is referring to the fact that according to tribal laws the offspring of Osage men and white women could not receive allotments or headrights, though children of Osage women married to white men could. Even though his mother is Osage, Chal, too, has no name among his people. As a mixedblood, he seems, in fact, to very nearly have no people. When he takes a group of drunken whites to see an Osage dance, Chal feels a strong urge "to go down on the floor and dance." He does not dance, however, because as Mathews writes, "he had never danced with his people." Chal's alienation is further emphasized when shortly after the Sweat Lodge ceremony he thinks that "he wanted to be identified with that vague something which everybody else seemed to have, and which he believed to be civilization."

Near the end of the novel, after drinking all night, Chal dances alone as he had in childhood:

> He stopped the car suddenly and climbed out and started talking to himself; talking nonsense. He kept repeating to himself, "Extravaganza," without reason, as the word was not associated with his frothy thoughts. . . . He arose with difficulty, with an intense urge for action. Suddenly he began to dance. He bent low over the grass and danced, and as he danced he sang, and as he sang one of the tribal songs of his people,

he was fascinated by his own voice, which seemed clear and sonorous on the still air. He danced wildly and his blood became hotter, and yet that terrific emotion which was dammed up in his body would not come out; that emotion which was dammed up and could not be exposed. As he danced he wondered why that emotion which had begun to choke him did not come out through his throat. He was an Indian now and he believed that the exit of all spirit and emotion was the throat, just as the soul came out through the throat after death.

Chal's solitary dance is an extravaganza, a frenzied celebration of nothingness rather than a ceremonial act expressive of one's place within the tribal community and natural world. In its frenzy, his dance contradicts the traditional poise and dignity of Osage dances, which never embraced the wilder "fancy dancing" of Plains tribes. Mathews's irony is heavy when he writes, "He was an Indian now," for in his extravagance (that is, *extra,* "outside," and *vagant, vagari,* "to wander about") Chal is far from his Osage people. He still cannot fathom that mystery he sensed as a child: "He wanted by some action or some expression, to express the whole meaning of life; to declare to the silent world about him that he was a glorious male; to express to the silent forms of the blackjacks that he was a brother to the wind, the lightning and the forces that came out of the earth." Drunk and without the teachings of his people, Chal has no language for such expression. He is inarticulate. His performance is, from the white perspective he has learned to value, simply another "extravaganza."

Sundown does not end on a fatalistic note. In the final scene, Chal boasts foolishly to his mother (while correctly associating linguistic facility with political power), "I'm goin' to Harvard law school, and take law—I'm gonna be a great orator." He then falls asleep with his head on his arms. Around him, in the novel's final lines, nature comes alive: "The nestlings in the nest above settled down to digest their food. A flamewinged grasshopper rose in front of Chal's still form, and suspended there, made cracking sounds like electric sparks, then dropped to the grass and became silent. The flapping and splashing of the mother robin, as she bathed in the pan under the hydrant, was the only sound of activity." The natural imagery of this conclusion, enveloping the sleeping Chal, strikes a positive note. Thus far, Chal has failed as a challenge to the disinheritors of his people. He has been disenfranchised culturally and is adrift in a wasted land. However, the novel, within which natural imagery has served consistently as an index to whatever is positive in Chal's world, ends with the purifying image of the bathing robin. A few lines earlier, a sparrow has pushed from the nest and killed one of the robin's young, but the mother goes on; she has other young and proceeds to cleanse herself. It is a small story of loss followed by renewal and hope. The flamewinged grasshopper sounds a more portentous note, rising like a warning before the sleeping Chal. In the grasshopper may also be seen a sign of hope, however, for in this image Mathews merges the natural world of the Osage—the sacred red, or flame color—and the "civilized" world of electricity. As the novel ends, unlike Running Elk, Chal is alive and sleeping peacefully near his mother in whom Osage values still live. The natural world, represented by bird and insect, remains intact.

Sundown ends on a somewhat ambivalent note, leaving the future of its mixedblood protagonist and of the Osage people unresolved. Just as the strong identity and self-assurance of the more traditional Sun-on-His-Wings balances the despair of Running Elk's disintegration and death, the novel depicts starkly the consequences of oil and acculturation for the Osage while simultaneously refusing to accept the familiar pattern of simple doom for the Indian, the "vanishing American" pattern so familiar to American literature and thought. In *Sundown,* Mathews leaves open the possibility of "another destiny, another plot" for the American Indian, refusing any romantic closure that would deny the immense difficulties confronting the displaced Native American, but simultaneously rejecting the cliché of the Vanishing American as epic, tragic hero. In this repudiation of the simple, entropic plot assigned to the American Indian by Euramerican myth-making, Mathews anticipates the major direction of Indian fiction into the 1990s. Perhaps the author saw other possibilities for Chal in the model that he, John Joseph Mathews, had to offer as a sophisticated, worldly, educated mixedblood and member of the Tribal Council. Perhaps Mathews is anticipating the possibility articulated by a member of a succeeding generation of Osages, Kenneth Jump, who wrote in 1979: "Could it be that Indian blood mixing with other bloods will create a new type of Indian? If this be true then the Osages will not be engulfed by present society but a new type of Osage Indian will emerge from this propagation." Chal may indeed represent the "new type of Indian" who figures so prominently in contemporary American Indian fiction.

FURTHER READING

Biography

Bailey, Garrick. "John Joseph Mathews: Osage, 1894-." In *American Indian Intellectuals: 1976 Proceedings of The American Ethnological Society*, edited by Margot Liberty, pp. 205-14. St. Paul: West Publishing Co., 1978.

> In-depth account of Mathews's ancestry, life, and writings.

Wilson, Terry P. "Osage Oxonian: The Heritage of John Joseph Mathews." *Chronicles of Oklahoma* LIX, No. 3 (Fall 1981): 264-93.

> Comprehensive overview of Mathews's life and career.

Criticism

Hunter, Carol. "The Historical Context in John Joseph Mathews' *Sundown*." *MELUS* 9, No. 1 (Spring 1982): 61-72.

> Discusses social and political aspects of *Sundown,* particularly Mathews's treatment of Osage history of the late 1800s and first part of the twentieth century.

———. Review of *Talking to the Moon,* by John Joseph Mathews. *World Literature Today* 57, No. 1 (Winter 1983): 152-53.

> Positive assessment of Mathews's autobiography. Hunter observes: "[There] is a spiritual essence conveyed through Mathews's acute and sensitive awareness of the esthetic but delicate balance so easily destroyed by man through greed and war. Nature lovers and environmentalists will appreciate Mathews, but *Talking to the Moon* is also an enriching experience for any reader."

Young, Mary E. Review of *The Osages: Children of the Middle Waters,* by John Joseph Mathews. *The American Historical Review* LXVII, No. 4 (July 1962): 1122-23.

> Mixed review of *The Osages,* in which the critic faults the volume's lack of documentation.

Tropic of Cancer

Henry Miller

American novelist, critic, short story writer, editor, and nonfiction writer.

The following entry presents criticism on Miller's novel *Tropic of Cancer* (1934). For further information on Miller's life and works, see *CLC*, Volumes 1, 2, 4, 9, 14, and 43.

INTRODUCTION

Tropic of Cancer (1934), Miller's most famous and acclaimed work, is a lyrical, profane, and surreal portrait of the author's experiences in the bohemian underworld of 1930s Paris. The novel was a personal and artistic breakthrough for Miller, who was an obscure and impoverished writer when it was first published. The theme of sexual and artistic liberation, which pervades *Tropic of Cancer*, manifests itself in its Whitmanesque poetic embrace of sexuality, its open disdain for the constraints of bourgeois society, and its declarations of antagonism toward the conventions of the modern novel. At one point Miller writes: "This is not a book . . . this is a prolonged insult, a gob of spit in the face of Art. . . ." While some critics have dismissed *Tropic of Cancer* as a merely autobiographical rant which is reckless and nihilistic in its abandonment of literary conventions, others have recognized Miller's notoriously liberal use of profanity and sexual description as an attempt to broaden the expressive means of the novel. The unusually polemical and partisan tenor of much early criticism on Miller's novel should be considered against the background of its publication history. Before Grove Press won its censorship struggle in the early 1960s, *Tropic of Cancer* was ruled obscene and its sale was banned in the United States and England.

Plot and Major Characters

Tropic of Cancer begins with the narrator describing his companions, whom he depicts as bohemian aesthetes living in varying degrees of squalor. He disdains Moldorf as a "word-drunk" poetaster and dismisses Van Norden and Sylvester as failed writers, reserving his praise for Boris and Carl, who are "mad and tone deaf . . . sufferers." The protagonist also sings paeans to the sex organs of Tania and Llona, describes his love of prostitutes, Parisian vistas, and food, and relates his methods for cadging meals from his wealthier friends. Interspersed among these thoughts are statements that reject the conventional standards of literature and art for the spontaneous stream of consciousness which eludes artistic representation. In a conversation with Van Norden, and in watching him make love to an impoverished prostitute, the narrator realizes that his companion's understanding of sex and women is adolescent, reductive, and mechanical. On visiting an art gallery to view the paintings of Henri Matisse,

the narrator expresses admiration for the vivacity and transformative power of the artist's work and recognizes a dramatic contrast between Matisse's vision and the lifeless materialism of Van Norden and Carl. After failing to seduce Tania, the narrator tries to alleviate his depression through drinking and brawling. He meets Fillmore, another neurotic American expatriate, whose attitude toward women is as degenerate as Van Norden's. Towards the end of the novel, the narrator travels to Dijon where he makes a cursory attempt at teaching a course in English. Upon his return, he accompanies a despondent and spiteful Fillmore to the train station before the latter departs for America. Pathetic in the naivete of his deflated idealism, Fillmore's whiny tirade against France allows the narrator to comprehend his own resilience in the "cancerous" environment of Paris.

Major Themes

A central theme of *Tropic of Cancer*, as suggested by its title, is the pervasive sickness and squalor of modern society and the resulting degeneracy of its literature. In reacting against conventional art and morality, Miller's protagonist adopts a Whitmanesque attitude of unblinking acceptance and affirmation and announces his intention of "recording . . . all that which is omitted in books." The novel's descriptions, animated by a celebratory, ribald tone, frequently linger on the deviant and sordid elements of Parisian life, particularly its prostitutes and vagabonds, and dramatize the protagonist's freedom from the lifestyles and conventions of mainstream society. This theme of personal emancipation accounts for the audacious liberties Miller takes with *Tropic of Cancer*'s style, a pastiche of poetic exultation, bland pornography, and the banalities of a personal diary. On occasion, Miller explicitly rails against conventional artists and denounces their adherence to established artistic norms as a lack of passion and verve. Erica Jong has suggested that this theme has strong autobiographical undertones since Miller's first attempts at fiction were derivative and unsuccessful, and *Tropic of Cancer* was written while he was "finding himself" as an artist.

Critical Reception

While *Tropic of Cancer*'s setting and some of its themes evoke comparisons with the works of other expatriate American writers living in Paris in the 1920s and '30s, Miller's experiments with form in this work signal a uniquely radical departure from the conventions of the modern novel, and its extremities of expression and style have elicited sharply divergent critical opinions. For some, Miller's blatant disregard for a coherent and linear plot and his exclusive adherence to autobiography are symptomatic of his failure as a novelist. A similarly dismissive and disdainful view is taken by critics who view Miller's liberal use of profanity as little more than impish prurience. At the opposite extreme, such professional associates and friends as Lawrence Durrell and Anaïs Nin circumvent aesthetic and formal objections to *Tropic of Cancer* by praising it as a "vitalizing" or "nourishing" antidote to the arid intellectualism and effete sentimentality of the modern novel. Because *Tropic of Cancer*'s legal troubles quickly made it a cause célèbre, early reviews of the novel tend to be compromised by an eagerness to either validate or indict Miller for his use of profanity and sexual candor. In the wake of other highly publicized victories over censorship, notably, Allen Ginsberg's *Howl* (1956) and William Burroughs's *Naked Lunch* (1959), numerous studies have appeared which focus more objectively on the literary merits of *Tropic of Cancer*. While some feminist critics attack Miller for what they view as his blatant sexism, others contend that *Tropic of Cancer* embraces an emancipatory conception of women, insofar as its celebration of sexual freedom flouts the social constraints of marriage and bourgeois morality. Other commentators have suggested that Miller's imagery and visionary rhetoric are more articulate and complex than would be suggested by the author's chaotic style of writing. Although there is little overall consensus on *Tropic of Cancer*'s literary value, novelist Norman Mailer argues that it is "one of the ten or twenty great novels of our century."

PRINCIPAL WORKS

Tropic of Cancer (novel) 1934
Black Spring (novel) 1936
Max and the White Phagocytes (essays and stories) 1938
The Cosmological Eye (essays) 1939
Tropic of Capricorn (novel) 1939
The World of Sex (essay) 1940
The Colossus of Maroussi (travelogue) 1941
Sunday after the War (memoir) 1944
The Air-Conditioned Nightmare (essays) 1945
*Sexus (novel) 1949
*Plexus (novel) 1953
Quiet Days in Clichy (essay) 1956
The Time of the Assassins: A Study of Rimbaud (criticism) 1956
Big Sur and the Oranges of Hieronymus Bosch (essays) 1957
*Nexus (novel) 1960
The World of Lawrence: A Passionate Appreciation (criticism) 1980
Crazy Cock (novel) 1992

*These works were published in one volume as *The Rosy Crucifixion* in 1965.

CRITICISM

Anaïs Nin (essay date 1934)

SOURCE: A preface to *Tropic of Cancer*, by Henry Miller, Grove Weidenfeld, 1961, pp. xxxi-xxxiii.

[*A French-born American autobiographer, novelist, short story writer, and educator, Nin established her early artistic reputation through experimental novels exploring the feminine psyche and through her association with Miller, whom she met in Paris in 1932 when he was writing the early drafts of* Tropic of Cancer. *In the following essay, which was originally published in 1934 as a preface to the first edition of* Tropic of Cancer, *she praises Miller for addressing the visceral roots of human experience.*]

Here is a book which, if such a thing were possible, might restore our appetite for the fundamental realities. The predominant note will seem one of bitterness, and bitterness there is, to the full. But there is also a wild extravagance, a mad gaiety, a verve, a gusto, at times almost a delirium. A continual oscillation between extremes, with bare stretches that taste like brass and leave the full flavor of emptiness. It is beyond optimism or pessimism. The author has given us the last *frisson*. Pain has no more secret recesses.

In a world grown paralyzed with introspection and constipated by delicate mental meals this brutal exposure of the substantial body comes as a vitalizing current of blood. The violence and obscenity are left unadulterated, as manifestation of the mystery and pain which ever accompanies the act of creation.

The restorative value of experience, prime source of wisdom and creation, is reasserted. There remain waste areas of unfinished thought and action, a bundle of shreds and fibers with which the overcritical may strangle themselves. Referring to his *Wilhelm Meister* Goethe once said: "People seek a central point: that is hard, and not even right. I should think a rich, manifold life, brought close to our eyes, would be enough without any express tendency; which, after all, is only for the intellect."

The book is sustained on its own axis by the pure flux and rotation of events. Just as there is no central point, so also there is no question of heroism or of struggle since there is no question of will, but only an obedience to flow.

The gross caricatures are perhaps more vital, "more true to life," than the full portraits of the conventional novel for the reason that the individual today has no centrality and produces not the slightest illusion of wholeness. The characters are integrated to the false, cultural void in which we are drowning; thus is produced the illusion of chaos, to face which requires the ultimate courage.

The humiliations and defeats, given with a primitive honesty, end not in frustration, despair, or futility, but in hunger, an ecstatic, devouring hunger—*for more life*. The poetic is discovered by stripping away the vestiture of art; by descending to what might be styled "a preartistic level," the durable skeleton of form which is hidden in the phenomena of disintegration reappears to be transfigured again in the ever-changing flesh of emotion. The scars are burned away—the scars left by the obstetricians of culture. Here is an artist who re-establishes the potency of illusion by gaping at the open wounds, by courting the stern, psychological reality which man seeks to avoid through recourse to the oblique symbolism of art. Here the symbols are laid bare, presented almost as naively and unblushingly by this overcivilized individual as by the well-rooted savage.

It is no false primitivism which gives rise to this savage lyricism. It is not a retrogressive tendency, but a swing forward into unbeaten areas. To regard a naked book such as this with the same critical eye that is turned upon even such diverse types as Lawrence, Breton, Joyce and Céline is a mistake. Rather let us try to look at it with the eyes of a Patagonian for whom all that is sacred and taboo in our world is meaningless. For the adventure which has brought the author to the spiritual ends of the earth is the history of every artist who, in order to express himself, must traverse the intangible gridirons of his imaginary world. The air pockets, the alkali wastes, the crumbling monuments, the putrescent cadavers, the crazy jig and maggot dance, all this forms a grand fresco of our epoch, done with shattering phrases and loud, strident, hammer strokes.

If there is here revealed a capacity to shock, to startle the lifeless ones from their profound slumber, let us congratulate ourselves; for the tragedy of our world is precisely that nothing any longer is capable of rousing it from its lethargy. No more violent dreams, no refreshment, no awaken-

ing. In the anaesthesia produced by self-knowledge, life is passing, art is passing, slipping from us: we are drifting with time and our fight is with shadows. We need a blood transfusion.

And it is blood and flesh which are here given us. Drink, food, laughter, desire, passion, curiosity, the simple realities which nourish the roots of our highest and vaguest creations. The superstructure is lopped away. This book brings with it a wind that blows down the dead and hollow trees whose roots are withered and lost in the barren soil of our times. This book goes to the roots and digs under, digs for subterranean springs.

George Orwell　(essay date 1940)

SOURCE: "Inside the Whale," in his *The Collected Essays, Journalism and Letters of George Orwell: An Age Like This, 1920-1940, Vol. 1,* Harcourt Brace Jovanovich, 1968, pp. 493-502.

[*An English novelist and essayist, Orwell is the author of such well-known works as* Animal Farm *(1945) and* 1984 *(1949) as well as the autobiographical narrative* Down and Out in Paris and London *(1933). His essays evince a profoundly moral concern for the victims of economic, political, and social exploitation. In the following excerpt from an essay that was originally published in* New Directions in Prose and Poetry *in 1940, he applauds Miller's use of vernacular and poetic language in* Tropic of Cancer *to vividly portray the lives of impoverished American expatriates in 1930s Paris.*]

When Henry Miller's novel, *Tropic of Cancer,* appeared in 1935, it was greeted with rather cautious praise, obviously conditioned in some cases by a fear of seeming to enjoy pornography. Among the people who praised it were T. S. Eliot, Herbert Read, Aldous Huxley, John dos Passos, Ezra Pound—on the whole, not the writers who are in fashion at this moment. And in fact the subject-matter of the book, and to a certain extent its mental atmosphere, belong to the 'twenties rather than to the 'thirties.

Tropic of Cancer is a novel in the first person, or autobiography in the form of a novel, whichever way you like to look at it. Miller himself insists that it is straight autobiography, but the tempo and method of telling the story are those of a novel. It is a story of the American Paris, but not along quite the usual lines, because the Americans who figure in it happen to be people without money. During the boom years, when dollars were plentiful and the exchange-value of the franc was low, Paris was invaded by such a swarm of artists, writers, students, dilettanti, sightseers, debauchees and plain idlers as the world has probably never seen. In some quarters of the town the so-called artists must actually have outnumbered the working population—indeed, it has been reckoned that in the late 'twenties there were as many as 30,000 painters in Paris, most of them impostors. The populace had grown so hardened to artists that gruff-voiced lesbians in corduroy breeches and young men in Grecian or medieval costume could walk the streets without attracting a glance, and along the Seine banks by Notre Dame it was almost impossible to pick one's way between the sketching-stools. It was the age of dark horses and neglected genii; the phrase on everybody's lips was "Quand je serai lancé". As it turned out, nobody was "lancé", the slump descended like another Ice Age, the cosmopolitan mob of artists vanished, and the huge Montparnasse cafés which only ten years ago were filled till the small hours by hordes of shrieking poseurs have turned into darkened tombs in which there are not even any ghosts. It is this world—described in, among other novels, Wyndham Lewis's *Tarr*—that Miller is writing about, but he is dealing only with the under side of it, the lumpenproletarian fringe which has been able to survive the slump because it is composed partly of genuine artists and partly of genuine scoundrels. The neglected genii, the paranoiacs who are always "going to" write the novel that will knock Proust into a cocked hat, are there, but they are only genii in the rather rare moments when they are not scouting about for the next meal. For the most part it is a story of bug-ridden rooms in working-men's hotels, of fights, drinking bouts, cheap brothels, Russian refugees, cadging, swindling and temporary jobs. And the whole atmosphere of the poor quarters of Paris as a foreigner sees them—the cobbled alleys, the sour reek of refuse, the bistros with their greasy zinc counters and worn brick floors, the green waters of the Seine, the blue cloaks of the Republican Guard, the crumbling iron urinals, the peculiar sweetish smell of the Métro stations, the cigarettes that come to pieces, the pigeons in the Luxembourg Gardens—it is all there, or at any rate the feeling of it is there.

On the face of it no material could be less promising. When *Tropic of Cancer* was published the Italians were marching into Abyssinia and Hitler's concentration camps were already bulging. The intellectual foci of the world were Rome, Moscow and Berlin. It did not seem to be a moment at which a novel of outstanding value was likely to be written about American dead-beats cadging drinks in the Latin Quarter. Of course a novelist is not obliged to write directly about contemporary history, but a novelist who simply disregards the major public events of the moment is generally either a footler or a plain idiot. From a mere account of the subject-matter of *Tropic of Cancer* most people would probably assume it to be no more than a bit of naughty-naughty left over from the 'twenties. Actually, nearly everyone who read it saw at once that it was nothing of the kind, but a very remarkable book. How or why remarkable? That question is never easy to answer. It is better to begin by describing the impression that *Tropic of Cancer* has left on my own mind.

When I first opened *Tropic of Cancer* and saw that it was full of unprintable words, my immediate reaction was a refusal to be impressed. Most people's would be the same, I believe. Nevertheless, after a lapse of time the atmosphere of the book, besides innumerable details, seemed to linger in my memory in a peculiar way. A year later Miller's second book, *Black Spring*, was published. By this time *Tropic of Cancer* was much more vividly present in my mind than it had been when I first read it. My first feeling about *Black Spring* was that it showed a falling-off, and it is a fact that it has not the same unity as the other book. Yet after another year there were many passages in *Black Spring* that had also rooted themselves in my memory. Evidently these books are of the sort to leave a flavour behind them—books that "create a world of their own", as the saying goes. The books that do this are not necessarily good books, they may be good bad books like *Raffles* or the *Sherlock Holmes* stories, or perverse and morbid books like *Wuthering Heights* or *The House with the Green Shutters*. But now and again there appears a novel which opens up a new world not by revealing what is strange, but by revealing what is familiar. The truly remarkable thing about *Ulysses,* for instance, is the commonplaceness of its material. Of course there is much more in *Ulysses* than this, because Joyce is a kind of poet and also an elephantine pedant, but his real achievement has been to get the familiar on to paper. He dared—for it is a matter of *daring* just as much as of technique—to expose the imbecilities of the inner mind, and in doing so he discovered an America which was under everybody's nose. Here is a whole world of stuff which you have lived with since childhood, stuff which you supposed to be of its nature incommunicable, and somebody has managed to communicate it. The effect is to break down, at any rate momentarily, the solitude in which the human being lives. When you read certain passages in *Ulysses* you feel that Joyce's mind and your mind are one, that he knows all about you though he has never heard your name, that there exists some world outside time and space in which you and he are together. And though he does not resemble Joyce in other ways, there is a touch of this quality in Henry Miller. Not everywhere, because his work is very uneven, and sometimes, especially in *Black Spring*, tends to slide away into mere verbiage or into the squashy universe of the Surrealists. But read him for five pages, ten pages, and you feel the peculiar relief that comes not so much from understanding as from *being understood*. "He knows all about me," you feel; "he wrote this specially for me." It is as though you could hear a voice speaking to you, a friendly American voice, with no humbug in it, no moral purpose, merely an implicit assumption that we are all alike. For the moment you have got away from the lies and simplifications, the stylised, marionette-like quality of ordinary fiction, even quite good fiction, and are dealing with the recognisable experiences of human beings.

But what kind of experience? What kind of human beings? Miller is writing about the man in the street, and it is incidentally rather a pity that it should be a street full of brothels. That is the penalty of leaving your native land. It means transferring your roots into shallower soil. Exile is probably more damaging to a novelist than to a painter or even a poet, because its effect is to take him out of contact with working life and narrow down his range to the street, the café, the church, the brothel and the studio. On the whole, in Miller's books you are reading about people living the expatriate life, people drinking, talking, meditating and fornicating, not about people working, marrying and bringing up children; a pity, because he would have described the one set of activities as well as the other. In *Black Spring* there is a wonderful flashback of New York, the swarming Irish-infested New York of the O. Henry period, but the Paris scenes are the best, and, granted their utter worthlessness as social types, the drunks and dead-beats of the cafés are handled with a feeling for character and a mastery of technique that are unapproached in any at all recent novel. All of them are not only credible but completely familiar; you have the feeling that all their adventures have happened to yourself. Not that they are anything very startling in the way of adventures. Henry gets a job with a melancholy Indian student, gets another job at a dreadful French school during a cold snap when the lavatories are frozen solid, goes on drinking bouts in Le Havre with his friend Collins, the sea captain, goes to brothels where there are wonderful negresses, talks with his friend Van Norden, the novelist, who has got the great novel of the world in his head but can never bring himself to begin writing it. His friend Karl, on the verge of starvation, is picked up by a wealthy widow who wishes to marry him. There are interminable, Hamlet-like conversations in which Karl tries to decide which is worse, being hungry or sleeping with an old woman. In great detail he describes his visits to the widow, how he went to the hotel dressed in his best, how before going in he neglected to urinate, so that the whole evening was one long crescendo of torment, etc etc. And after all, none of it is true, the widow doesn't even exist—Karl has simply invented her in order to make himself seem important. The whole book is in this vein, more or less. Why is it that these monstrous trivialities are so engrossing? Simply because the whole atmosphere is deeply familiar, because you have all the while the feeling that these things are happening to *you*. And you have this feeling because somebody has chosen to drop the Geneva language of the ordinary novel and drag the *real-politik* of the inner mind into the open. In Miller's case it is not so much a question of exploring the mechanisms of the mind as of owning up to everyday facts and everyday emotions. For the truth is that many ordinary people, perhaps an actual majority, do speak and behave in just the way that is recorded here. The callous coarseness with which the characters in *Tropic of Cancer* talk is very rare in fiction, but it is extremely common in real life; again and again I have heard just such conversations from people who were not even aware that they were talking coarsely. It is worth noticing that *Tropic of Cancer* is not a young man's book. Miller was in his forties when it was published, and though since then he has produced three or four others, it is obvious that this first book had been lived with for years. It is one of those books that are slowly matured in poverty and obscurity, by people who know what they have got to do and therefore are able to wait. The prose is astonishing, and in parts of *Black Spring* it is even better. Unfortunately I cannot quote; unprintable words occur almost everywhere. But get hold of *Tropic of Cancer*, get hold of *Black Spring* and read especially the first hundred pages. They give you an idea of what can still be done, even at this late date, with English prose. In them, English is treated as a spoken language, but spoken *without fear*, i.e. without fear of rhetoric or of the unusual or poetical word. The adjective has come back, after its ten years' exile. It is a flowing, swelling prose, a prose with rhythms in it, something quite different from the flat, cautious statements and snack-bar dialects that are now in fashion.

When a book like *Tropic of Cancer* appears, it is only natural that the first thing people notice should be its obscenity. Given our current notions of literary decency, it is not at all easy to approach an unprintable book with detachment. Either one is shocked and disgusted, or one is morbidly thrilled, or one is determined above all else not to be impressed. The last is probably the commonest reaction, with the result that unprintable books often get less attention than they deserve. It is rather the fashion to say that nothing is easier than to write an obscene book, that people only do it in order to get themselves talked about and make money, etc etc. What makes it obvious that this is *not* the case is that books which are obscene in the police-court sense are distinctly uncommon. If there were easy money to be made out of dirty words, a lot more people would be making it. But, because "obscene" books do not appear very frequently, there is a tendency to lump them together, as a rule quite unjustifiably. *Tropic of Cancer* has been vaguely associated with two other books, *Ulysses* and *Voyage au Bout de la Nuit,* but in neither case is there much resemblance. What Miller has in common with Joyce is a willingness to mention the inane squalid facts of everyday life. Putting aside differences of technique, the funeral scene in *Ulysses,* for instance, would fit into *Tropic of Cancer;* the whole chapter is a sort of confession, an *exposé* of the frightful inner callousness of the human being. But there the resemblance ends. As a novel, *Tropic of Cancer* is far inferior to *Ulysses*. Joyce is an artist, in a sense in which Miller is not and probably would not wish to be, and in any case he is attempting much more. He is exploring different states of consciousness, dream, reverie (the "bronze-by-gold" chapter), drunkenness, etc, and dovetailing them all into a huge complex pattern, almost like a Victorian "plot". Miller is simply a hardboiled person talking about life, an ordinary American businessman with intellectual courage and a gift for words. It is perhaps significant that he *looks* exactly like everyone's idea of an American businessman. As for the comparison with *Voyage au Bout de la Nuit*, it is even further from the point. Both books use unprintable words, both are in some sense autobiographical, but that is all. *Voyage au Bout de la Nuit* is a book-with-a-purpose, and its purpose is to protest against the horror and meaninglessness of modern life— actually, indeed, of *life*. It is a cry of unbearable disgust, a voice from the cesspool. *Tropic of Cancer* is almost exactly the opposite. The thing has become so unusual as to seem almost anomalous, but it is the book of a man who is happy. So is *Black Spring*, though slightly less so, because tinged in places with nostalgia. With years of lumpenproletarian life behind him, hunger, vagabondage, dirt, failure, nights in the open, battles with immigration officers, endless struggles for a bit of cash, Miller finds that he is enjoying himself. Exactly the aspects of life that fill Céline with horror are the ones that appeal to him. So far from protesting, he is *accepting*. And the very word "acceptance" calls up his real affinity, another American, Walt Whitman.

But there is something rather curious in being Whitman in the nineteen-thirties. It is not certain that if Whitman himself were alive at this moment he would write anything in the least degree resembling *Leaves of Grass*. For what he is saying, after all, is "I accept", and there is a radical difference between acceptance now and acceptance then. Whitman was writing in a time of unexampled prosperity, but more than that, he was writing in a country where freedom was something more than a word. The democracy, equality and comradeship that he is always talking about are not remote ideals, but something that existed in front of his eyes. In mid-nineteenth-century America men felt themselves free and equal, *were* free and equal, so far as that is possible outside a society of pure Communism. There was poverty and there were even class-distinctions, but except for the Negroes there was no permanently submerged class. Everyone had inside him, like a kind of core, the knowledge that he could earn a decent living, and earn it without boot-licking. When you read about Mark Twain's Mississippi raftsmen and pilots, or Bret Harte's Western gold miners, they seem more remote than the cannibals of the Stone Age. The reason is simply that they are free human beings. But it is the same even with the peaceful domesticated America of the Eastern states, the America of *Little Women, Helen's Babies* and "Riding Down from Bangor". Life has a buoyant, carefree quality that you can feel as you read, like a physical sensation in your belly. It is this that Whitman is celebrating, though actually he does it very badly, because he is one of those writers who tell you what you ought to feel instead of making you feel it. Luckily for his beliefs, perhaps, he died too early to see the deterioration in American life that came with the rise of large-scale industry and the exploiting of cheap immigrant labour.

Miller's outlook is deeply akin to that of Whitman, and nearly everyone who has read him has remarked on this. *Tropic of Cancer* ends with an especially Whitmanesque passage, in which, after the lecheries, the swindles, the fights, the drinking bouts and the imbecilities, he simply sits down and watches the Seine flowing past, in a sort of mystical acceptance of the thing-as-it-is. Only, what is he accepting? In the first place, not America, but the ancient bone-heap of Europe, where every grain of soil has passed through innumerable human bodies. Secondly, not an epoch of expansion and liberty, but an epoch of fear, tyranny and regimentation. To say "I accept" in an age like our own is to say that you accept concentration camps, rubber truncheons, Hitler, Stalin, bombs, aeroplanes, tinned food, machine-guns, putsches, purges, slogans, Bedaux belts, gas-masks, submarines, spies, *provocateurs,* press censorship, secret prisons, aspirins, Hollywood films and political murders. Not only those things, of course, but those things among others. And on the whole this is Henry Miller's attitude. Not quite always, because at moments he shows signs of a fairly ordinary kind of literary nostalgia. There is a long passage in the earlier part of *Black Spring,* in praise of the Middle Ages, which as prose must be one of the most remarkable pieces of writing in recent years, but which displays an attitude not very different from that of Chesterton. In *Max and the White Phagocytes* there is an attack on modern American civilisation (breakfast cereals, cellophane, etc) from the usual angle of the literary man who hates industrialism. But in general the attitude is "Let's swallow it whole". And hence the seeming preoccupation with indecency and with the dirty-handkerchief side of life. It is only seeming, for the truth is that life, ordinary everyday life, consists far more largely of horrors than writers of fiction usually care to admit. Whitman himself "accepted" a great deal that his contemporaries found unmentionable. For he is not

only writing of the prairie, he also wanders through the city and notes the shattered skull of the suicide, the "grey sick faces of onanists", etc etc. But unquestionably our own age, at any rate in western Europe, is less healthy and less hopeful than the age in which Whitman was writing. Unlike Whitman, we live in a *shrinking* world. The "democratic vistas" have ended in barbed wire. There is less feeling of creation and growth, less and less emphasis on the cradle, endlessly rocking, more and more emphasis on the teapot, endlessly stewing. To accept civilisation *as it is* practically means accepting decay. It has ceased to be a strenuous attitude and become a passive attitude—even "decadent", if that word means anything.

But precisely because, in one sense, he is passive to experience, Miller is able to get nearer to the ordinary man than is possible to more purposive writers. For the ordinary man is also passive. Within a narrow circle (home life, and perhaps the trade union or local politics) he feels himself master of his fate, but against major events he is as helpless as against the elements. So far from endeavouring to influence the future, he simply lies down and lets things happen to him. During the past ten years literature has involved itself more and more deeply in politics, with the result that there is now less room in it for the ordinary man than at any time during the past two centuries. One can see the change in the prevailing literary attitude by comparing the books written about the Spanish civil war with those written about the war of 1914-18. The immediately striking thing about the Spanish war books, at any rate those written in English, is their shocking dullness and badness. But what is more significant is that almost all of them, right-wing or left-wing, are written from a political angle, by cocksure partisans telling you what to think, whereas the books about the Great War were written by common soldiers or junior officers who did not even pretend to understand what the whole thing was about. Books like *All Quiet on the Western Front, Le Feu, A Farewell to Arms, Death of a Hero, Good-Bye to All That, Memoirs of an Infantry Officer* and *A Subaltern on the Somme* were written not by propagandists but by *victims.* They are saying in effect, "What the hell is all this about? God knows. All we can do is to endure." And though he is not writing about war, nor, on the whole, about unhappiness, this is nearer to Miller's attitude than the omniscience which is now fashionable. The *Booster,* a short-lived periodical of which he was part-editor, used to describe itself in its advertisements as "non-political, non-educational, non-progressive, non-cooperative, non-ethical, non-literary, non-consistent, non-contemporary", and Miller's own work could be described in nearly the same terms. It is a voice from the crowd, from the underling, from the third-class carriage, from the ordinary, non-political, non-moral, passive man.

I have been using the phrase "ordinary man" rather loosely, and I have taken it for granted that the "ordinary man" exists, a thing now denied by some people. I do not mean that the people Miller is writing about constitute a majority, still less that he is writing about proletarians. No English or American novelist has as yet seriously attempted that. And again, the people in *Tropic of Cancer* fall short of being ordinary to the extent that they are idle, disreputable and more or less "artistic". As I have said already, this is a pity, but it is the necessary result of expatriation. Miller's "ordinary man" is neither the manual worker nor the suburban householder, but the derelict, the *déclassé,* the adventurer, the American intellectual without roots and without money. Still, the experiences even of this type overlap fairly widely with those of more normal people. Miller has been able to get the most out of his rather limited material because he has had the courage to identify with it. The ordinary man, the "average sensual man", has been given the power of speech, like Balaam's ass.

It will be seen that this is something out of date, or at any rate out of fashion. The average sensual man is out of fashion. The passive, non-political attitude is out of fashion. Preoccupation with sex and truthfulness about the inner life are out of fashion. American Paris is out of fashion. A book like *Tropic of Cancer,* published at such a time, must be either a tedious preciosity or something unusual, and I think a majority of the people who have read it would agree that it is not the first. It is worth trying to discover just what this escape from the current literary fashion means. But to do that one has got to see it against its background—that is, against the general development of English literature in the twenty years since the Great War.

Henry Miller foresaw our world of restricted opportunity and widespread mediocrity and railed against it before it arrived. He understood that we would rather relegate sex to a commodity— alternately condemned and slavered over—than try to understand its deep and pervasive power in our lives.

—*Erica Jong, in her* The Devil at Large: Erica Jong on Henry Miller, *1993.*

Stanley Kauffmann   (essay date 1961)

SOURCE: *"Tropic of Cancer,"* in *The Critic as Artist: Essays on Books, 1920-1970,* edited by Gilbert A. Harrison, Liveright, 1972, pp. 211-16.

[*Kauffmann is an American dramatist, critic, and educator. In the following essay, which was written shortly after the first legal publication of* Tropic of Cancer *in the United States, he assesses Miller as a minor figure in American literature—a bawdy and funny provocateur, but one whose incessant use of scatological language and amateur philosophy reveals an immature and unsophisticated cast of mind.*]

Henry Miller's *Tropic of Cancer* is now published in this country in an unlavish edition of 318 pages set in big type at the price of $7.50—and this in spite of a large first printing. The interest of the price is that here it relates to the content of the book—not, as is usual, to its length or format. The publisher knows that the public knows the book's reputation and is willing to pay much more than

is currently charged for books of similar production cost. This gives, from the start, a different atmosphere to its publication. Rather than call it cashing in on prurience, let us say that the publisher is asking the purchaser to make a contribution to a defense fund in case of legal prosecution, although no provision is made for refunding, say, three dollars per copy if the publisher is unmolested.

The book itself, first issued in 1934 in Paris (in English) is an autobiographical first novel recounting the experiences, sensations, thoughts of Miller, a penniless American in the Paris of the early thirties. It is not so much a novel as an intense journal, written daily about what was happening to him daily, full of emotion recollected in proximity, as he scrounged for food, devoured books, conversed volubly, and flung himself into numerous beds. It is formless, in the sense that it could have continued indefinitely, but then Miller is an enemy of form. He writes of a Ravel composition:

> Suddenly it all dies down. It was as if [Ravel] remembered, in the midst of his antics, that he had on a cutaway suit. He arrested himself. A great mistake, in my humble opinion. Art consists in going the full length. If you start with the drums you have to end with the dynamite, or TNT. Ravel sacrificed something for form, for a vegetable that people must digest before going to bed.

The "full length" is Miller's ideal. Frankness of fact and devotion to truth are not always concurrent, but Miller has, within his powers, both of these. He says on an early page: "There is only one thing which interests me vitally now, and that is the recording of all that which is omitted in books."

He had been a husband and a hireling in various jobs in New York and elsewhere, always a hungry reader with literary ambitions, when at thirty-nine he broke loose and, without money, went alone to Paris to write. He swore he would never take a job again. In fact he takes two in this book—as a proofreader on the Paris *Tribune* and as an English teacher in Dijon. But the point was made—he had broken away.

Essentially that is what the book is: a mirror-image of the testimony which is given at revival meetings. There you can hear about men who got right with God; this man got right with art and sex and the use of his brain and time. Like all converts, he is on fire. Like all converts, he simply will not leave your lapels alone. Thus he is a bit tedious. Because he came fairly late in life to a personally valid ethic, he cannot believe that anyone he talks to has ever done it before him.

The book is a fierce celebration of his enlightened freedom, which is to say his acceptance of real responsibilities instead of merely respectable ones. But in the course of this paean he exhorts us mercilessly with such discoveries as: sex can be fun; America is commercialized and doomed; civilization must refurbish its values or perish. (Edmund Wilson has called the book "an epitaph for the whole generation that migrated to Europe after the war.") All this now suffers, of course, from the passage of time. These burning messages have been the commonplaces of novelists, most of them inferior to Miller, for at least a couple of decades. But could these views have been startling even in 1934? This was eight years after the publication of a much more widely read novel of Americans in Paris, *The Sun Also Rises.* Hemingway is as unlike Miller as is imaginable in temperament, but surely the new liberty and the dark apocalypse are in his book.

How Miller rages at us. And what is his chief complaint? That we are not like him, living like him, desiring and perceiving like him. A prime function of art is criticism, and if the artist in question has merit, he certainly is a superior person and modest coughs are out of order. But the smuggest bourgeois has no smugness like that of the self-consciously liberated bohemian. It tainted Gauguin and D. H. Lawrence; it infects Miller.

He is often compared to Whitman, which must please him because he thinks Whitman "that one lone figure which America has produced in the course of her brief life" (despite the fact that he began by worshipping Dreiser). There is considerable basis for the comparison, especially in attitude. Miller sees no democratic vistas and certainly does *not* hear America singing, but he, too, is a buddy of the universe and privy to its secrets, calling on the rest of us to be as open-shirted and breeze-breasting as himself. Also there is in Miller, although on a much lower level than in Whitman, a feeling of settled iconoclasm, of artistic revolt made stock-in-trade. There are attempts at bardic sweep, some of them successful, and there is Whitmanesque rejoicing in the smack of wine and flesh.

Sometimes Miller uses language stupidly (he calls Paris "more eternal" than Rome). Sometimes, as in the rhapsody on Matisse, he writes a symbolist poem with a heat that carries us across its weaker passages. Or he can transmute sensation into images that propagate like guppies. For example, one day, broke and hungry, he finds a concert-ticket and uses it.

> My mind is curiously alert; it's as though my skull had a thousand mirrors inside it. My nerves are taut, vibrant! the notes are like glass balls dancing on a million jets of water. I've never been to a concert before on such an empty belly. Nothing escapes me, not even the tiniest pin falling. It's as though I had no clothes on and every pore of my body was a window and all the windows open and the light flooding my gizzards. I can feel the light curving under the vault of my ribs and my ribs hang there over a hollow nave trembling with reverberations. How long this lasts I have no idea; I have lost all sense of time and place. After what seems like an eternity there follows an interval of semiconsciousness balanced by such a calm that I feel a great lake inside me, a lake of iridescent sheen, cool as jelly; and over this lake, rising in great swooping spirals, there emerge flocks of birds of passage with long slim legs and brilliant plumage. Flock after flock surge up from the cool, still surface of the lake and, passing under my clavicles, lose themselves in the white sea of space. And then slowly, very slowly, as if an old woman in a white cap were going the rounds of my body, slowly the windows are closed and my organs drop back into place.

I have quoted this at length because it is a good cross-section of his style. "The tiniest pin" and "after what seems an eternity" are careless spewing; but the "old woman in a white cap" is orphic.

The only person who could use four-letter words completely naturally would be a mental defective unaware of taboos. The foulest-mouthed longshoremen knows that he is using naughty words and is wallowing in them. Miller uses them in an exultation very much like that of a college boy away from home for the first time.

—*Stanley Kauffmann*

This is Miller. Narrative is not his forte; his characterizations are sketchy; his philosophy is jejune. It is in pressing his whole existence against the warm wax of his prose and leaving there its complete imprint that he is at his best—in following every quiver of sentience to its source or destination with phrases that sometimes add up to a gorgeous fabric. Karl Shapiro, in an introductory essay streaked with gibberish, says that "everything [Miller] has written is a poem in the best as well as in the broadest sense of the word." This is a sentimental and foolishly inclusive judgment, but it points in the right direction.

Shapiro says that Miller writes with "complete ease and naturalness" about sex, as Lawrence and Joyce did not. To me, there is (speaking only of this book) much less sex than bravado. As far as specific language is concerned, Lawrence thought there was something thaumaturgic in four-letter words and had Mellors speak them therapeutically. Joyce wrote down the words that his miraculous surgery of the psyche revealed. Miller employs them—mostly *outside* of dialogue—to demonstrate somewhat ostentatious emancipation and contempt for slaves of convention.

Anyway, to talk about complete naturalness in the use of those words by a member of our society is arrant nonsense. The only person who could use them completely naturally would be a mental defective unaware of taboos. The foulest-mouthed longshoremen knows that he is using naughty words and is wallowing in them. Miller uses them in an exultation very much like that of a college boy away from home for the first time.

Proof of his lack of naturalness about it lies in his avoidance of earthy language when he talks about his great love, Mona. Virtually every other girl in the book, well or lightly regarded, is referred to at some time or other as a c—t. Making Mona an exception seems to show not only some residual puritanism but exhibitionism in the other cases. In fact, before one is far along in the book, the plentiful four-letter words become either irritating or tiresome. I thought of Robert Graves' remark that in the British army the adjective "f—ing" has come to mean only a signal that a noun is approaching.

Lawrence Durrell, no more reluctant than numerous other foreigners to tell Americans what their best works are, says that "American literature today begins and ends with the meaning of what [Miller] has done." Further: "To read *Tropic of Cancer* is to understand how shockingly romantic all European writing after Rousseau has become." (Durrell, of all artists, must know that "romantic" is a qualitative not a pejorative term.) These statements are typical of the—to me—inflated praise that this book has evoked. I hazard a couple of guesses at extrinsic reasons for this. First, when a gifted man writes a prosecutable book, it is often over-lauded as a tactical move by those interested in the freedom of letters—especially those who hold that sex is Beautiful, not sexy. Second, possibly these statements are, as much as anything else, a tribute to Miller's purity of commitment, to his abhorrence of the pietisms of Literature and the proprieties of the Literary Life, to his willingness—if not downright eagerness—to suffer for the right to live and write as he chooses. His is no small spirit, it is just not as large as some have told us.

Here, then is his first novel, available (*pro tem,* at least) in his own country twenty-seven years after its publication abroad. Durrell believes that its place is next to *Moby Dick,* which seems to me a hurtful thing to say about a frisky minnow of a book that ought not to be compared with leviathans. Far from being "the jewel and nonpareil" of American literature (Durrell again), Miller cannot be put near such twentieth-century novelists as Dreiser, Fitzgerald, early Dos Passos, early Hemingway—let alone Faulkner—without unfair diminution.

This book belongs, modestly but securely, in the American tradition of profundity-through-deliberate-simplicities that has its intellectual roots in Thoreau and continues through such men as Whitman and Sherwood Anderson until, in a changed time, it thinks it needs to go abroad to breathe. Miller stands under his Paris street-lamp, defiantly but genially drunk, trolling his catch mixed of beauty and banality and recurrent bawdry—a little pathetic because he thinks he is a discoverer and doesn't realize that he is only a tourist on a well-marked tour. We see him at last as an appealingly zestful, voracious, talented hick.

Alan Friedman (essay date 1966)

SOURCE: "The Pitching of Love's Mansion in the *Tropics* of Henry Miller," in *Seven Contemporary Authors,* edited by Thomas B. Whitbread, University of Texas Press, 1966, pp. 129-53.

[*Friedman is an American critic and educator. In the following essay, he remarks on past critical opinion and legal actions concerning* Tropic of Cancer, *examines contradictions in some of the book's central themes, and concludes that* Tropic of Cancer *is ultimately a work of negation rather than affirmation.*]

More than any other year, 1926 climaxed the era of the so-called "Lost Generation" of American expatriate writers, although by then almost all their important docu-

ments, from Sherwood Anderson's *Winesburg Ohio* in 1919 to F. Scott Fitzgerald's *The Great Gatsby* in 1925, had already been written, published, and received. The year 1926 was climactic, however, since that year was Hemingway's—it was the year of *The Sun Also Rises* and it was the last of the *Moveable Feast* years—and Hemingway, despite his subsequent repudiation of Gertrude Stein's "dirty, easy labels," has come to epitomize the writers of his era, the writers we still glibly label "the Lost Generation."

Henry Miller, in 1926, was still in America, though he was "of" America far less than any of his self-exiled compatriots; for with the exception of the very early years, when he was growing up in Brooklyn, and the late years, when he was settled in his Big Sur Paradise, Miller has been consistently vehement in his opposition to everything he sees America symbolizing. "I can think of no street in America," he writes in *Tropic of Capricorn,*

> or of people inhabiting such a street, capable of leading one on toward the discovery of the self. I have walked the streets in many countries of the world but nowhere have I felt so degraded and humiliated as in America. I think of all the streets in America combined as forming a huge cesspool, a cesspool of the spirit in which everything is sucked down and drained away. . . . Over this cesspool the spirit of work weaves a magic wand, palaces and factories spring up side by side, and munition plants and chemical works and steel mills and sanatoriums and prisons and insane asylums. The whole continent is a nightmare producing the greatest misery of the greatest number. I was one, a single entity in the midst of the greatest jamboree of wealth and happiness (statistical wealth, statistical happiness) but I never met a man who was truly wealthy or truly happy.

And elsewhere he expresses his fears of America's influence on the entire world: "I see America spreading disaster," he writes [in *Black Spring*], "I see America as a black curse upon the world. I see a long night settling in and that mushroom which has poisoned the world withering at the roots."

But by 1926 Miller had yet to discover Paris, the Paris where, as he puts it, he was to be "born and reborn over and over. Born while walking the streets, born while sitting in a cafe, born while lying over a whore. Born and reborn again and again" (*Black Spring*). In 1926 Miller was not only still in America, still unknown and still spiritually isolated, but he was already thirty-five—nearly a decade older than Hemingway—and he was just beginning to write full time. Up to this point he had written, in addition to a series of prose-poems he attempted to sell from door to door, a single still-unpublished novel, and he was to produce two more before his fourth, *Tropic of Cancer,* was finally published, in Paris, in 1934.

Thus, although for the next quarter of a century he remained a kind of writer non grata in England and America, Miller the artist and Miller the cause had been simultaneously born, and born, it should be noted, to the sound of trumpets and a hallelujah chorus. Here, for instance, is

Lawrence Durrell, one of the many early hymnists, hailing *Tropic of Cancer* [in *A Private Correspondence,* 1963]:

> It strikes me as being the only really man-size piece of work which the century can really boast of. It's a howling triumph from the word go; and not only is it a literary and artistic smack on the bell for everyone, but it really gets down on paper the blood and bowels of our time. I have never read anything like it. I did not imagine anything like it could be written; and yet, curiously, reading it I seemed to recognize it as something which I knew we were all ready for. The space was all cleared for it. *Tropic* turns the corner into a new life which has regained its bowels. In the face of it eulogy becomes platitude. . . . I love its guts. I love to see the canons of oblique and pretty emotion mopped up; to see every whim-wham and bagatelle of your contemporaries from Eliot to Joyce dunged under. God give us young men the guts to plant the daisies on top and finish the job.

Granted, Durrell was only twenty-two at the time, and might not be expected to know any better, but, with almost undeviating consistency, such self-indulgent hyperbole has characterized his view of Miller ever since—and it has become an increasingly typical attitude as more and more voices have blended in an uncritical hailing of Miller's supreme significance.

But if Miller enthusiasts have tended to view him as a cause, as a banner around which they could rally in eager defiance of all the authoritarian taboos they glibly associate with Anglo-Saxon society, at least they have not gone the way of his equally vehement detractors who completely ignored the artist for the cause. For instance, according to Elmer Gertz [in "Henry Miller and the Law," in *Henry Miller and the Critics,* 1963], the trial lawyer who successfully defended *Tropic of Cancer* in Chicago, the self-righteous California judges who had earlier ruled Miller's two *Tropic* books obscene, "presumed to pass upon the character, or the morals, of Miller, the unorthodox ideas that outraged them, his sexual explicitness, and the use of four-letter words of Anglo-Saxon origin, and they gave little credence to the literary experts who held the *Tropic* books in high esteem." In writing of the landmark Chicago trial of *Cancer,* Hoke Norris has noted that time and again either hearsay or a quick glance at a page or two of the book was enough for the self-appointed guardians of community morality. "This sort of instantaneous literary and judicial judgment," he writes [in " 'Cancer' in Chicago," *Evergreen Review,* No. 25], "is to be found throughout the case, not only among police officials but also among some newspaper columnists, clergyman, and the writers of wrathful letters."

Norris goes on to cite various police actions against the book, as well as statements by the police chiefs involved; the following case is typical. One captain, the acting chief of a Chicago suburb, was asked if he believed he was enforcing the state obscenity law when, without a warrant and on his own initiative, he pressured local booksellers into removing *Tropic of Cancer* from their shelves. " 'No, I wouldn't say the state law,' replied Captain Morris. 'We were just enforcing a moral law which I believe has a place in a town such as ours where we have good, religious people and many churches.' " The full implications of such a statement are truly frightening to contemplate.

For many of us in the English-speaking world, then, the name Henry Miller conjures up thoughts of a more or less noble crusade against proper Bostonians and their ilk throughout the land; for, despite the hopes of Miller and his many fervent supporters, he has gained a reputation in his native country based not primarily on widespread recognition of his uncommon genius, but rather on his ability to rouse the shocked sensibilities of some and the civil libertarianism of others. The censorship war, of course, has been going on at least since the time of Plato, who feared the influence of the poets on his young Guardians, and it seems likely to continue a good while longer. In 1933, in response to Judge Woolsey's now historic decision on Joyce's *Ulysses,* Morris Ernst wrote that

> the *Ulysses* case marks a turning point. It is a body blow for the censors. The necessity of hypocrisy and circumlocution in literature has been eliminated. Writers need no longer seek refuge in euphemisms. They may describe basic human functions without fear of the law. . . . Under the *Ulysses* case it should henceforth be impossible for the censors legally to sustain an attack against any book of artistic integrity, no matter how frank and forthright it may be. We have travelled a long way from the days of Bowdler and Mrs. Grundy and Comstock. We may well rejoice over the result.

Unfortunately, in the afterglow of victory, Ernst mistook a single battle for the entire war—a war in which we have since witnessed the battles of *Lady Chatterley's Lover,* of *Fanny Hill,* of *Tropic of Cancer,* a war, in fact, which is far from ended. The Marquis de Sade, to mention only the most obvious, still looms in the future, as does perhaps a third of Miller's published writings.

One must assume, especially considering the many remarkable opinions written by various courts in the last few years, that the war is being won—and it need detain us no further. Still, it does warrant our consideration since Miller the cause—a Miller obviously noble, obviously on the side of the angels—tends to become inextricable from Miller the artist, a figure of still questionable stature. Stanley Kauffmann, in one of the most balanced reviews of *Cancer,* focuses on just this problem in considering the inflated praise the book has evoked. "I hazard a couple of guesses at extrinsic reasons for this," he writes.

> First, when a gifted man writes a prosecutable book, it is often over-lauded as a tactical move by those interested in the freedom of letters—especially those who hold that sex is Beautiful, not sexy. Second, possibly these statements are, as much as anything else, a tribute to Miller's purity of commitment, to his abhorrence of the pietisms of Literature and the proprieties of the Literary Life, to his willingness—if not downright eagerness—to suffer for the right to live and write as he chooses.

"His is no small spirit," Kauffmann concludes, "it is just not as large as some have told us."

Let us, then, examine that spirit Miller offers us in his early fiction, *Tropic of Cancer, Black Spring*, and *Tropic of Capricorn*, focusing primarily on *Cancer*, the first, most important, and best of this loosely connected trilogy. Two prefatory points should be made before continuing, however. First, it should be noted that Miller is extremely difficult to quote in brief, for what most characterizes his writing—and represents both the best and the worst thing about it—is his interminable jamming together of formless, exuberant imagery. Miller, in fact, writes like a Spasmodic poet, seemingly afraid that words are going out of style and, unless he employs them all immediately, they will be lost to us forever.

Second is the question of whether these books are novels at all. Miller insists they are not, even to the point where he writes an outraged response [a letter in *The New Republic* (18 May 1938)] to a highly favorable article by Edmund Wilson simply because the latter had assumed that *Cancer* is a work of fiction. [As Wayne Booth explains in *The Rhetoric of Fiction*:]

> Wilson praised Miller for his skilful ironic portrait of a particular kind of "vaporing" poseur, for making his hero really live, "and not merely in his vaporings or his poses. He gives us the genuine American bum come to lead the beautiful life in Paris; and he lays him away forever in his dope of Pernod and dreams." To all of this praise for irony, Miller replied:

> The theme of the book, moreover, is not at all what Mr. Wilson describes: the theme is myself, and the narrator, or the hero, as (Wilson) puts it, is also myself . . . the narrator . . . is me, because I have painstakingly indicated throughout the book that the hero is myself. I don't use "heroes," incidentally, nor do I write novels. I am the hero, and the book is myself.

Wayne Booth, in his brilliant study of the novel, cites this exchange between Wilson and Miller as exemplifying the contemporary critic's dilemma when considering the crucial question of distance between author and character, and he sympathizes with Wilson for making a very natural error. But there is overwhelming evidence that, despite Miller's protestations to the contrary, Wilson is basically right and Booth wrong. In *Cancer*, for instance, the protagonist writes that "I have made a silent compact with myself not to change a line of what I write. I am not interested in perfecting my thoughts, nor my actions." And yet the first draft manuscript of *Cancer* was three times the length of the published version, and three times Miller rewrote the book. [In a footnote, Friedman suggests that the reader see "the 'Chronology,' by Miller, for the year 1934, printed in *The Best of Henry Miller*, ed. Lawrence Durrell" and notes that in "the same book, Miller writes that *Cancer* 'was written several times and in many places—in Paris.' Durrell tells us that *Cancer* 'was distilled out of a colossal MS which I was lucky enough to read, and which could not have been less than fifteen hundred pages long. It seemed to me that there was enough material to make three or four *Tropic of Cancers* from it' ('Studies in Genius: Henry Miller,' in *Henry Miller and the Critics*, 1963)."] With regard to his Chronology, a supposedly fac-

tual account of his life, Miller has said: "Here and there I'm deliberately putting down a lie—just to throw the bastards off the track" [*Art and Outrage: A Correspondence about Henry Miller*, 1959].

The same, of course, goes for his "autobiographical romances," as he calls them—only more so. For instance, after vividly detailing an extensive series of sexual conquests, the protagonist of *Capricorn* says: "It was going on this way all the time even though every word I say is a lie." Samuel Beckett, in a perhaps apocryphal story, was asked if the title character of *Waiting for Godot* was meant to be God. "Of course not," he supposedly answered, "if I had meant God I would have said God; I meant Godot." Whether the incident actually occurred is beside the point; its moral remains loud, clear, and relevant: be wary when an artist speaks of what he intended by his work. Perhaps it would be best if, as E. M. Forster suggested, we read all literature as though it were written in a single room, simultaneously and in effect, anonymously. In practice, however, we need to strive for a satisfactory mean between the two extremes, especially when, as in Miller's case, author and protagonist have identical names and largely coextensive lives. As Kingsley Widmer, in [his *Henry Miller*, 1963,] the best book to date on Miller, had noted, "it is unavoidable in discussing Miller's work to call the central figure Henry Miller, as does Henry Miller, though this is not a claim that the experiences are literal fact . . . in all probability Miller's writings about Miller are not true, in several senses."

These early books, then, with their loosely connected, anecdotal narrative, deal primarily with an alienated aging American writer who divides his thoughts and energies between the intoxicating life of Paris and the frenzied life of New York, and who discovers that the world is essentially an uncongenial place for such sensitive, personable individuals as himself. *Cancer*'s similarities with *The Sun Also Rises* have been noted many times, as for instance in this comment by Samuel Putnam, a cohort of Miller's in the early Paris days and also a minor character in *Cancer*: ". . . whatever may be said of Miller, he has summed up for us as no one else has the expatriates' Paris of the second phase: and I think it may be said that the *Tropic of Cancer* is to that phase what *The Sun Also Rises* is to the preceding one" ["Henry Miller in Montparnasse," in *Henry Miller and the Critics*, 1963]. In addition, *Cancer* has affinities with *A Moveable Feast*, for both truly describe, to use Hemingway's words, "how Paris was in the early days when we were very poor and very happy." For even though hungry, Hemingway tells us, the young, eager, in love, expatriate writer of the 1920's found Paris "a moveable feast." But by the time of *Cancer* the hopeful twenties have given way to the forlorn thirties, and the prototype of the hungry writer has become a middle-aged lecher making nihilistic gestures at all the old romantic shibboleths. And thus the causes of Miller's happiness are more complex and more obscure than Hemingway's, for the latter is young and the work is going well and he is generally satisfied with the world he inhabits. If in *his* early writings, Miller ultimately achieves an affirmation of sorts, it is an affirmation predicated upon despair, for one by one he has rejected all the traditional values, all the consolations conceived by other men and other artists. The very point of *Cancer,* in fact, as Mark Schorer has put it [in his testimony in the case of "Commonwealth of Massachusetts vs. *Tropic of Cancer,*" printed in *Henry Miller and the Critics,* 1963], "is that he has divested himself of every connection and responsibility in order to be free to do nothing but live with no money, no obligations, no residence, nothing except himself for life, and at that point he says, 'I am the happiest man in the world'."

This world, Miller insists, is a cancerous zone, a hospital full of the dying and the deadly: "People are like lice," he says—"they get under your skin and bury themselves there. You scratch and scratch until the blood comes, but you can't get permanently deloused. Everywhere I go people are making a mess of their lives. Everyone has his private tragedy. It's in the blood now—misfortune, ennui, grief, suicide. The atmosphere is saturated with disaster, frustration, futility." And out of this misery his imagination thus imposes upon others, emerges a perverse kind of drunken glee, for "the effect upon me," he claims, "is exhilarating. Instead of being discouraged, or depressed, I enjoy it. I am crying for more and more disasters, for bigger calamities, for grander failures. I want the whole world to be out of whack, I want everyone to scratch himself to death." What Miller means, apparently, is that his spiritual malaise finds solace, even delight, in an external despair at least as negative as the one within.

In addition, *Tropic of Cancer* reads as a kind of scatological *Down and Out in Paris and London,* for like the Orwell book, it concerns the quest for food and shelter (among other things) during the days and nights of the Parisian Depression—only Orwell seeks even the most menial and degrading work in order to survive at any cost; Miller, on the other hand, becomes a parasite in order both to survive on his own terms (that is, without working) and, despite his protestations to the contrary, in order to make literature of the experience. At the beginning of *Cancer,* Miller offers us a miniature portrait of the artist and his art.

> It is now the fall of my second year in Paris. I was sent here for a reason I have not yet been able to fathom. I have no money, no resources, no hopes. I am the happiest man alive. A year ago, six months ago, I thought that I was an artist. I no longer think about it, I *am.* Everything that was literature has fallen from me. There are no more books to be written, thank God. This then? This is not a book. This is libel, slander, defamation of character. This is not a book in the ordinary sense of the word. No, this is a prolonged insult, a gob of spit in the face of Art, a kick in the pants to God, Man, Destiny, Time, Love, Beauty . . . what you will. I am going to sing for you, a little off key perhaps, but I will sing.

Art, then, becomes non-art, for it is not only formless and eclectic, negative and destructive, but it serves for the artist not as an end in itself but as a means to life. Elsewhere Miller writes that "art is only a stepping-stone to reality. It is the vestibule in which we undergo the rites of initiation. Man's task is to make of himself a work of art. The creations which man makes manifest have no validity in

themselves; they serve to awaken." Consequently, he concludes, the artist must cease "immolating himself in his work," must cease creating out of a martyrdom "of sweat and agony. . . . We do not think of sweat and tears in connection with the universe; we think of joy and light, and above all of play" [**"Of Art and the Future,"** in *Sunday After the War,* 1944]. And this is the kind of naysaying which, since it is ultimately affirmative, we can readily accept—for even if art is not simply a spontaneously formed outpouring, even if art is not simply unrecollected and untranquilized emotion, it is pretty to talk as if it were.

Of Miller's semiautobiographical fiction, there are, to date, a total of nine excessively large volumes. They are unified primarily by similarities of mood and atmosphere, and only secondarily by subject matter, by, for instance, the dual theme of loss of innocence and initiation into manhood—an initiation which Miller's picaro has undergone enough times to become a fraternity unto himself. From time to time he renders this theme explicit, as when he discusses the effect upon himself of Henri Bergson's book, *Creative Evolution:* "When I think of the book now, and the way I approached it, I think of a man going through the rites of initiation. The disorientation and reorientation which comes with the initiation into any mystery is the most wonderful experience which it is possible to have" (*Capricorn*). Nonetheless, and despite the rather earthy form such initiation usually takes in these writings, Miller's central concern in them "was not with sex . . . but with the problem of self-liberation" [*The World of Sex,* 1940]. Richard Ellmann, in testimony given during the Chicago trial of *Cancer,* expressed essentially the same view of that book when he said that "there is nothing which is attractive about sexuality as represented in it." Very much unlike, for example, *Fanny Hill,* a book which exalts sex, joyfully delighting in it and the life devoted to it, *Cancer* is rather "a criticism of life in Paris at that time and, by extension, a criticism of life throughout the world at that time."

Miller's focal theme, and he expounds it at lengths sometimes painfully graphic, sometimes enormously funny, is disgust and revulsion at the stupidity and ugliness he sees all about him—and because his disgust and revulsion are both profoundly felt and often ineffectually transmuted into art, and because disease must, after all, be represented by disease, Miller rages on like a tidal wave of sewerage:

> If there were a man who dared to say all that he thought of this world, there would not be left him a square foot of ground to stand on. When a man appears the world bears down on him and breaks his back. There are always too many rotten pillars left standing, too much festering humanity for man to bloom. The superstructure is a lie and the foundation is a huge quaking fear. If at intervals of centuries there does appear a man with a desperate hungry look in his eye, a man who would turn the world upside down in order to create a new race, the love that he brings to the world is turned to bile and he becomes a scourge. . . . If any man ever dared to translate all that is in his heart, to put down what is really his experience, what is truly his

truth, I think then the world would go to smash, that it would be blown to smithereens and no god, no accident, no will could ever again assemble the pieces.

And because Miller would be this man and because he is a frustrated romantic whose vision of reality bears virtually no resemblance to the stagnant world he sees about him, his naïveté and his disillusionment give way, at times, to strident nihilism and profound despair. "I can't get it out of my mind," he says in *Cancer*, "what a discrepancy there is between ideas and living." Nonetheless, the romanticism, the wide-eyed wonder of youthful innocence, not only clings but at times breaks forth into lyric passages of perhaps surprising beauty, as in the following passage from *Big Sur*, a much later book by a much mellower Miller:

> There were always birds: the pirates and scavengers of the blue as well as the migratory variety. (At intervals the condor passed, huge as an ocean liner.) Gay in plumage, their beaks were hard and cruel. They strung out across the horizon like arrows tied to an invisible string. In close they seemed content to dart, dip, swoop, careen. Some followed the cliffs and breakers, others sought the canyons, the gold-crested hills, the marble-topped peaks. . . . From the ocean depths there issued strange formations, contours unique and seductive. As if the Titans of the deep had labored for aeons to shape and mold the earth. Even millennia ago the great land birds were startled by the abrupt aspect of these risen shapes.

Even as early as *Cancer*, however, the lyrical Miller is not only present, but present when we might expect him. Perhaps despite himself, his bubbling enthusiasm for life, for all of life, is self-infectious, and he continually breaks out in a hives-like joyfulness. Having written, "we're all dead, or dying, or about to die," he almost immediately refers to himself as "incurably optimistic! Still have one foot in the 19th century. I'm a bit retarded, like most Americans. . . . The mere thought of a meal—*another* meal—rejuvenates me. A meal! That means something to go on—a few solid hours of work, an erection possibly. I don't deny it. I have health, good, solid, animal health. The only thing that stands between me and a future is a meal, *another* meal."

Food, in fact becomes *Cancer*'s one transcending standard of value. Art may be an intrusion, love a diseased prostitution, and the world a rotting corpse, but food, that divine inspiration, is God's glory on earth. "Food," Miller writes with gusto, "is one of the things I enjoy tremendously." And perhaps it is the only thing he enjoys tremendously always, for Miller, who often seems obsessed with the fact that he is not Jewish, adopts the traditionally Jewish belief in the therapeutic powers of food, in food as a nostrum for all the ills of life. Upon his long-delayed return to his parents' home in Brooklyn, a guilt-ridden Miller writes elsewhere, he feels a sudden compassion for the lower-middle-class sterility of their lives. But then, after the tears of this necessarily temporary reunion have been shed, the family turns, as usual, to the inevitable next meal. "The table was set; we were to eat in a few moments. It seemed natural

that it should be thus, though I hadn't the slightest desire to eat. In the past the great emotional scenes which I had witnessed in the bosom of the family were nearly always associated with the table. We pass easily from sorrow to gluttony" ["**Reunion in Brooklyn**," in *Sunday After the War*, 1944].

The problem in *Cancer*, however, is far less likely to be that of gluttony than that of hunger. At one point, Miller's hunger becomes so acute that, despite his essentially passive, nonassertive nature, he feels constrained to initiate corrective action. Realizing "that no one would refuse a man a meal if only he had the courage to demand it," he writes to a dozen or so acquaintances, asking each the day of the week it would be convenient to have him come to dinner. Not only do none refuse him, but even those who can't stand him wine and dine him royally. "They were all obviously relieved," he writes, "when they realized that they would see me only once a week. And they were still more relieved when I said—it won't be necessary any more.' They never asked why. They congratulated me, and that was all. Often the reason was I had found a better host; I could afford to scratch off the ones who were a pain in the ass." Miller, for his part, never thinks to ask why his hosts do give him up so readily, but it is apparent that his feelings for them were mutual. Miller, however, continues blithely on. "'Life,' he quotes Emerson as having said, 'consists in what a man is thinking all day.' If that be so," he adds, "then my life is nothing but a big intestine. I not only think about food all day, but I dream about it at night."

But Miller's dreams and fantasies are as much sexual as they are gastronomical, and Paris serves equally well as caterer and procurer. "I have never seen a place like Paris," Miller comments, "for varieties of sexual provender." And for the picaro of *Cancer*, life in Paris becomes, as much as anything else, an attempt to sample as much as possible of this so generously provided provender. The whorey hordes, like marching Chinamen four abreast, parade incessantly down the streets of Miller's cities—streets he associates, both literally and figuratively, with life in the raw and, therefore, with life unclothed in the devitalizing dehumanizing raiments worn by everyone who is not of the streets. As Miller puts it in *Black Spring*: "What is not in the open street is false, derived, that is to say, *literature*." And he adds, "I was born in the street and raised in the street. . . . To be born in the street means to wander all your life, to be free."

And thus Miller seeks out his whores, creatures of the street par excellence, and romanticizes them as fellow free spirits: Tania, with her "fat, heavy garters," her "soft, bulging thighs," "a Tania like a big seed, who scatters pollen everywhere," a Tania who is the loveliest Jew of them all, and for whose sake, Miller exclaims, "I too would become a Jew" (*Cancer*); Germaine, who bore all the obvious signs of her way of life (the boozy breath, the cheap jewelry, the rundown heels, the pasty rouge accentuating what it was meant to conceal), and yet like Molly Bloom exhibits in bed such an earthly joyousness—a joyousness clinically or cynically called nymphomania—that Miller quite naturally finds her delightful; and Claude, who, unlike Germaine, was not really cut out for this line of work, who was, at bottom, "just a good French girl of average breed and intelligence whom life had tricked somehow," and who "had a soul and a conscience . . . (and) refinement, too, which is bad—in a whore," and whom for a while Miller thought he loved.

There are, of course, innumerable others—enough in *Cancer* and *Capricorn* to people a street of brothels—and with a comic detachment, a saving irony of vision which is one of the outstanding features of Miller's writing, he records them all—the fat whores and the lean whores, the immoral and the amoral, the predatory, buzzardlike whores who are fundamentally man-haters and the merely hungry ones who, with both belly and bed warm and full, care nothing at all for a man's money. And because, like Yeats's ultrarational Crazy Jane, Miller can never forget that love has pitched its mansion in the place of excrement, his amatory encounters read like a series of experimental investigations into the accuracy of her assertion. Necessarily, Miller emphasizes those human organs, traditionally unmentionable and even at times unthinkable, which serve dual functions for Crazy Jane—and for everyone else. The duality is central when Carl, for whom Miller has been ghost-writing love letters for six months, at last goes to meet his rich, widowed correspondent. Although the lady is not only willing but downright eager, the luckless Carl spends the entire evening unable to find a delicate way of telling her that his bladder is full to bursting.

Later on in *Cancer,* when Miller gives us a description of Carl's room, he notes that "in the *bidet* were orange peels and the remnants of a ham sandwich." The convenient and, in France, omnipresent *bidet* is, of course, the perfect symbol of the dual functioning of the sex organ, and Miller makes good use of it as when he rails at Claude's offensive delicacy. "Who wants a *delicate* whore!" he demands. "Claude would even ask you to turn your face away when she squatted over the *bidet!* All wrong! A man, when he's burning up with passion, wants to see things; he wants to see *everything,* even how they make water."

The *bidet* also plays a key role subsequently when in a typical surrealistic flight of fancy, Miller imaginatively abstracts from his picaresque narrative and arrives at an existential epiphany in which, suddenly "inspired by the absolute hopelessness of everything," he envisages a new world where he can burrow fully and freely into life. As usual, he writes of the experience in terms of a symbolism both powerful and stridently abstruse:

> I made up my mind that I would hold on to nothing, that I would expect nothing, that henceforth I would live as an animal, a beast of prey, a rover, a plunderer. . . . At this very moment, in the quiet dawn of a new day was not the earth giddy with crime and distress? Had one single element of man's nature been altered, vitally, fundamentally altered, by the incessant march of history? . . . I have reached the limits of endurance. . . . The world which I have departed is a menagerie. The dawn is breaking on a new world, a jungle world in which the lean spirits roam with sharp claws. If I am a hyena I am a lean and hungry one: I go forth to fatten myself.

All this quasi-mystical self-aggrandizing is as much pompous posturing for an effect as it is a serious attempt to find proper expression for an ever-recurring sense of hopelessness. But then, considering Miller's point of departure, what else could we expect? The scene Miller had been describing occurs, not surprisingly, in a brothel where, perhaps despite his better judgment, he had conducted a rather dandified and panting disciple of Gandhi's. The young Hindu, despite his eagerness, is obviously out of his depth. Turning his head away and blushing violently, he asks Miller to do the choosing from among the "bevy of naked women" surrounding them. Then, in an awkward violation of decorum, he has Miller switch girls with him. Finally, he commits the ultimate *"faux pas"* in confusing the functions of the *bidet* and the toilet—and it is the resultant unflushable mess which actuates Miller's readily stimulated imagination, for he freely associates it not merely with his erstwhile companion, but with all disciples of any faith, and hence with all man's hopes for a better life either in this world or in the next. Miller believes not only that things are rotten, but that they are bound to get a good deal worse. And thus his incessant wallowing in filth and degradation, the so-called seamier aspects of life, as a kind of objective correlative for his despair.

One of the would-be burners of *Cancer* has said that it is "like a slut walking down a neighborhood street, half undressed and spewing filth to those near her," and that it "deals heavily with carnal experiences, with perversion, with human filth and excrement" [Jack Mabley, quoted in " 'Cancer' in Chicago," *Evergreen Review,* No. 25]. Deal with these things it does, of course, yet such a statement is misleading. For one thing, sexual perversion occurs rarely in Miller's fiction (unlike, for instance, Lawrence Durrell in his never-banned *Alexandria Quartet,* Miller is not fascinated by incest and homosexuality). At one point in *Cancer* he even expresses revulsion at a friend's espousal of masturbation, and in *Capricorn,* describing a boyhood attack on a sissy of a choirboy, he says, "it was a disgraceful performance, but it made us feel good. Nobody knew yet what a fairy was, but whatever it was we were against it."

The Miller of the *Tropics* is a man who has trained himself to care for no one— and rather than run the risks of emotional involvement attendant upon normal intercourse, he reduces all such contact to the simply sexual.

—*Alan Friedman*

Even his seemingly endless pursuit of females—or, more precisely, of the sex organs of prostitutes—must be examined in context; for, although obviously obsessed with the "idea" of sex, Miller, especially in *Cancer,* is largely indifferent to it in reality. Despite his concern with his physical needs, he almost never goes out of his way to satisfy them. Taking a woman to bed—although he does so at every opportunity—seems always to be someone else's idea: the various women who accost him in the streets or the cafes, the blushing Hindu afraid to go upstairs alone, the friend who offers him the loan of his own latest bed-mate. Miller's reaction to the latter is typical: "I didn't know whether I wanted to or not," he says, but of course he does. It is free, it is convenient, and besides it saves him the cost of a night's lodging.

Miller's essential passivity regarding sex receives full treatment much earlier in *Cancer*. He is with Van Norden, an agreeably unsavory character who functions as a kind of alter ego, and who, in contrast with Miller, literally does think and talk of nothing but sex. Bessie, the only woman he cannot take to bed, correctly characterizes him as "just a worn-out satyr" who does not "know the meaning of passion." With Miller in tow, he engages for both of them the invariable nameless and hungry prostitute. The three of them, all equally passionless, retire to Van Norden's room, where Miller's passivity casts him into the role of *voyeur*. "As I watch Van Norden tackle her," he writes,

> it seems to me that I am looking at a machine whose cogs have slipped. . . . I am sitting on a chair behind him, watching their movements with a cool, scientific detachment. . . . It's like watching one of those crazy machines which throw the newspaper out. . . . The machine seems more sensible, crazy as it is, and more fascinating to watch, than the human beings and the events which produced it. My interest in Van Norden and the girl is nil. . . . As long as that spark of passion is missing there is no human significance in the performance. The machine is better to watch.

Here, undoubtedly, is the crux of Miller's problem, for his sexual passivity and general malaise result from that absent spark of passion. In general, as we have seen, he attempts to make the sterility of the world about him into the villain of the piece—even to the point of faulting Paris, the one place where life has been possible for him. At times, however, Miller will attempt a more specific self-analysis, a more intimate delving after the roots of the cancerous growths within him. Of a much earlier period he writes: "things were wrong usually only when one cared too much. That impressed itself on me very early in life. . . . This caring too much—I remember that it only developed with me about the time I first fell in love. And even then I didn't care enough. If I had really cared I wouldn't be here now writing about it. . . . It was a bad experience because it taught me how to live a lie" (*Capricorn*).

The Miller of the *Tropics*, then, is a man who has trained himself to care for no one—and rather than run the risks of emotional involvement attendant upon normal intercourse, he reduces all such contact to the simply sexual. Concomitantly, when every woman becomes a whore and every whore a single anatomical feature, the process, as Miller has suggested, is a lie, or rather, the poetic technique of synecdoche. Like food, then, the simple animalistic response to sexual stimulus serves as a safe standard, for it actually involves only a minute fraction of the real personality buried beneath the brutish exterior.

But the buffoon-lecher mask slips occasionally, revealing a Miller who cares very much indeed. For throughout the autobiographical fiction, as Kingsley Widmer has indicated, there runs the pivotal theme of

> the misery and inspiration connected with the Dark Lady of passion. She is partly the "femme fatale" of the romantic, and inverted traditional muse of the artist, the Eve-Lilith of primordial knowledge, a witch-goddess of sexuality and power, and, according to Miller's insistence, his second wife. Under the names of Mona and Mara, she haunts most of Miller's work; and she appears, at least briefly, in almost every book he has written.

Certainly her appearances are brief and intermittent, for her story is as fragmented as everything else in Miller's discontinuous narrative. Nonetheless, Miller's treatment of her constantly emphasizes her emotional centrality to his life and to his work. For one thing, the Mona/Mara passages are remarkably free of both censorable language and excremental references. Descriptions of Mona and of scenes with her, unlike those of other women in the *Tropics*, never become flights of nihilistic, semiabstract imagery indulged in for their own sake. Of the significance of Mona, the "Her" to whom *Capricorn* is dedicated, Miller writes: "Everything I endured was in the nature of a preparation for that moment when, putting on my hat one evening, I walked out of the office, out of my hitherto private life, and sought the woman who was to liberate me from a living death."

In *Cancer* she appears initially as a figure of almost virginal purity, a kind of antiwhore who embodies love rather than sex. Miller has been eagerly awaiting her return to Paris when "suddenly," he writes,

> I see a pale heavy face with burning eyes—and the little velvet suit that I always adored because under the soft velvet there were always her warm breasts, the marble legs, cool, firm, muscular. She rises up out of a sea of faces and embraces me passionately. . . . I sit down beside her and she talks—a flood of talk. . . . I hear not a word because she is beautiful and I love her and now I am happy and willing to die.

Then in bed their intense passion finds expression, as do Miller's tenderness and love—and a new emotion, fear.

> She lies down on the bed with her clothes on. Once, twice, three times, four times . . . I'm afraid she'll go mad . . . in bed, under the blankets, how good to feel her body again! But for how long? Will it last this time? Already I have a presentiment that it won't. . . . Finally she drops off and I pull my arm from under her. My eyes close. Her body is there beside me . . . it will be there till morning surely. . . . My eyes are closed. We breathe warmly into each other's mouth. Close together, America three thousand

miles away. I never want to see it again. To have her here in bed with me, breathing on me, her hair in my mouth—I count that something of a miracle. Nothing can happen now till morning.

But in the morning everything happens. They wake to find each other crawling with bedbugs; Mona, needing a bath, food, and adequate clothing, loses her temper at Miller's having forgotten to provide for money; and, although Miller does not detail the rest of the sequence of events, by the next page Mona disappears from the narrative—not to be even mentioned again for some 120 pages. Again he longs for her, wondering how different life might be with "a young, restless creature by (his) side"; but his image of her has altered drastically and, bitterly, he sees her as alien to his European world. If she ever should return, he wryly speculates,

> she'll probably tell me right away that it's unsanitary. That's the first thing that strikes an American woman about Europe—that it's unsanitary. Impossible for them to conceive of a Paradise without modern plumbing. . . . She'll say I've become a degenerate. I know her line from beginning to end. She'll want to look for a studio with a garden attached—and a bath-tub to be sure. She wants to be poor in a romantic way. I know her. But I'm prepared for her this time.

Exactly what is good about being poor in an unromantic way Miller never explains, but certainly he is correct about being prepared for her—for he manages, at least for the moment, to blot from his mind everything that belongs to the past, especially those few years when they were together and life was, if not edenic, at least vital and intense. Now when he thinks of her—and he is not able to keep himself from doing so entirely—it is "not as of a person in a definite aura of time and space, but separate, detached, as though she had blown up into a great cloud-like form that blotted out the past." Regardless, he adds,

> I couldn't allow myself to think about her very long; if I had I would have jumped off the bridge. It's strange. I had become so reconciled to this life without her; and yet if I thought about her only for a minute it was enough to pierce the bone and marrow of my contentment and shove me back again into the agonizing gutter of my wretched past.

And yet, no matter what the reason, a man who wilfully destroys his past, as Miller begins to realize, commits spiritual suicide: "It seems as if my own proper existence had come to an end somewhere, just where exactly I can't make out. I'm not an American any more, nor a New Yorker, and even less a European, or a Parisian. I haven't any allegiance, any responsibilities, any hatreds, any worries, any prejudices, any passion. I'm neither for nor against. I'm a neutral" (*Cancer*). But this statement serves first as manifesto and only subsequently as actual fact, for after the climactic moment when he recognizes the irrevocable loss of Mona, he gives way to a despairing loneliness so profound and so terrible that all else seems irrelevant. Yet in his hopelessness he comes full cycle, rediscovering his affinity with all the sordid and cancerous aspects of Paris, a city that "attracts the tortured, the hallucinated,

the great maniacs of love," a Paris that "is like a whore. From a distance she seems ravishing, you can't wait until you have her in your arms. And five minutes later you feel empty, disgusted with yourself. You feel tricked." Ultimately, there are only the streets for refuge, for the streets take every man's torments, every man's raging despair that is so precious because it confirms his significance as an individual capable of suffering, and the streets make something of it neither for nor against, but simply neutral. Miller, as we see him last, is a vastly diminished figure wondering "in a vague way what had ever happened to (his) wife." "A vague way"—the phrase is significant—for it suggests, and this is borne out in the later writings, that the failure of the relationship may well have resulted from Miller's intrinsic inadequacies. As Widmer has put it: "While his version of the Dark Lady myth aims to show Miller as the victim of love, he really presents himself as the victim of his own lovelessness."

Thus Miller's passionless passivity, his apathetic indifference to the things that most of us value in life. He begins his *Tropics* triad as a rebel without a cause—as "a James Dean character, a Hemingway of undisciplined creative yearnings"—and even though he is often ludicrous and ineffectual we are sympathetic, for he is saying things that need to be said; we have heard them before, but they bear the repeating. For, as Miller puts it in *Capricorn*, "even if everything I say is wrong, is prejudiced, spiteful, malevolent, even if I am a liar and a poisoner, it is nonetheless the truth and it will have to be swallowed."

Before very long, however, he is worn out and used up, a causeless nonconformist maintaining the old postures merely because they have become habitual. By the end of *Cancer*, Miller has even run out of defiant gestures. He is sitting in a cafe, idly watching the Seine; his pockets bulging with money—the filthy stuff he has always claimed to despise—money, moreover, he has stolen from a friend. And, perhaps strangest and unkindest cut of all, he speaks the tired conservatism of the *nouveau riche*: ". . . you can't create a revolution," he writes. "You can't wash all the dirt out of your belly" (*Cancer*). Thus in *Capricorn* Miller has nowhere to go. "To want to change the condition of affairs," he writes at the beginning of that book, "seemed futile to me; nothing would be altered, I was convinced, except by a change of heart, and who could change the hearts of men?" Miller had thought that he could, but he was wrong. "For a man of my temperament," he adds later in the same book, "the world being what it is, there is absolutely no hope, no solution."

Miller claims that the *Tropics* are about regeneration— "the Dionysian theme which . . . must be the theme for the writers to come—the only theme permissible, or possible." Miller does occasionally employ redemptive imagery—for example, the quietly flowing Seine at the end of *Cancer*—but he seems ultimately incapable of rising from negation to affirmation, incapable of transcending his long dark night of the soul (the very word "soul", in fact, he finds ludicrous). In *Capricorn* he writes that "whoever, through too great love, which is monstrous after all, dies of his misery, is born again to know neither love nor hate, but to enjoy. And this joy of living, because it is unnaturally acquired, is a poison which eventually vitiates the whole world." The *Tropics*, then, is not about redemption at all, but only about the death of love—and the irrevocable finality and waste of one man's spiritual suicide.

Certainly only the naive would attempt to deny that love has indeed pitched its mansion in the place of excrement, but only those uncompromisingly bitter and self-defeating—and Miller is both in these books—attempt to exalt an excremental or merely animalistic standard over that of love. Miller, it seems, would have the cancerous growths of his *Tropics* block out the light entering love's mansion, just as his own memory conveniently blotted out more and more of his painful past. But fortunately, and perhaps despite his intentions, Miller demonstrates that such a perverse disordering is invariably doomed to failure—and this demonstration may well be the one permanent edifice in the jungles of Henry Miller's *Tropics*.

George Orwell on Miller's attitude toward politics:

I first met [Henry] Miller at the end of 1936, when I was passing through Paris on my way to Spain. What most intrigued me about him was to find that he felt no interest in the Spanish war whatever. He merely told me in forcible terms that to go to Spain at that moment was the act of an idiot. He could understand anyone going there from purely selfish motives, out of curiosity, for instance, but to mix oneself up in such things *from a sense of obligation* was sheer stupidity. In any case my ideas about combating Fascism, defending democracy, etc etc were all boloney. Our civilisation was destined to be swept away and replaced by something so different that we should scarcely regard it as human—a prospect that did not bother him, he said. And some such outlook is implicit throughout his work. Everywhere there is the sense of the approaching cataclysm, and almost everywhere the implied belief that it doesn't matter. The only political declaration which, so far as I know, he has ever made in print is a purely negative one. A year or so ago an American magazine, the *Marxist Quarterly,* sent out a questionnaire to various American writers asking them to define their attitude on the subject of war. Miller replied in terms of extreme pacifism, but a merely personal pacifism, an individual refusal to fight, with no apparent wish to convert others to the same opinion—practically, in fact, a declaration of irresponsibility.

George Orwell, in his An Age Like This, *Harcourt Brace Jovanovich, 1968.*

Ihab Hassan (essay date 1967)

SOURCE: "The Life in Fiction," in his *The Literature of Silence: Henry Miller and Samuel Beckett,* Knopf, 1967, pp. 59-67.

[*Hassan is an Egyptian-born American critic and educator who has written numerous books on modernist and postmodernist literature, including* Radical Innocence: The Contemporary American Novel *(1961) and* The Dismem-

berment of Orpheus: Toward a Postmodern Literature *(1971). In the following excerpt, he analyzes the themes and technique of* Tropic of Cancer, *characterizing the novel as a profane yet lyrical paean to the chaos of raw experience.*]

The trilogy that begins with *Tropic of Cancer* (1934) is still Miller's most compelling work. *Cancer* itself is primarily an act of obedience to flow; it shows neither recognition on the part of its hero nor conversion in his outlook. There is no "hero" and no central "point," and there is no form but the shape of disintegration, the rhythm of humility and rage endured by human flesh. If the book makes a plea, it is the eternal plea of the self: more life! We need to look at the book, as Anaïs Nin put it, "with the eyes of a Patagonian for whom all that is sacred and taboo in our world is meaningless."

It is the second year in Paris for the narrator; he has no money, no illusions. In the Villa Borghese, where he lives, everyone is alone and everyone is dead. This is the beginning. But how can there be a beginning when Time is not the hero, as Miller insists, only Timelessness? The narrator pretends that he has sloughed off the dross of the world; he has found himself. The discovery, however, must be put in writing though it claims the spontaneity of a curse or song:

> This is not a book. This is libel, slander, defamation of character. This is not a book, in the ordinary sense of the word. No, this is a prolonged insult, a gob of spit in the face of Art, a kick in the pants to God, Man, Destiny, Time, Love, Beauty . . . what you will. I am going to sing for you, a little off key perhaps, but I will sing. I will sing while you croak, I will dance over your dirty corpse. . . .

The song is dedicated to Tania, "my chaos," who appears but briefly in the book, and it progresses while the world, like a cancer, is eating itself out. The progress of the book, then, is the movement of a personal song that grows from day to day with increments of action and recollection, moving toward no end. The book and the life pretend to be acts of discovery; celebration and expectation have become one.

We are introduced early to a gallery of grotesque or desperate figures—Tania, her husband Sylvester, Moldorf, Lucille, Borowski, Mona, Cronstadt, Elsa, Boris, Marlowe, Carl, Paula, Van Norden, etc.—who move on the edges of the city, jostle in its streets and disappear in its catacombs. They all seem like end-of-the-world figures, shadowy caricatures erupting suddenly into humor and life. Most of them are Jewish or half-Jewish. This is significant, Miller insists, because for the Jew, as for the narrator himself, the world is a cage filled with wild beasts. Paris is sperm and vomit; across the ocean, America is a foetus smoking a cigar. Meanwhile, the narrator feels "The Last Book" growing in him, 'the book that must include everything left out in other books. The whores come and go obscenely while the narrator fumbles for some key to the mystery and violence of creation. The tattered souls he meets in the depths glow with a secret, indestructible light. You can't put a fence around a human being, Miller believes, recognizing in his fellow men—though he may spit at their feet—the freedom of his own spirit. The spectacle of decadence and despair in Baudelaire's "fourmillante cité" is constantly relieved by sudden accesses of laughter and health. "Walking along the Champs-Elysées I keep thinking of my really superb health. When I say 'health' I mean optimism, to be truthful. Incurably optimistic! Still have one foot in the nineteenth century. I'm a bit retarded, like most Americans," the narrator confesses. Even in the heart of darkness, which is the modern city, the American can still retain his radical innocence.

The narrator does more than retain his innocence; he experiences epiphanies, usually in dives and whore-houses. A hilarious series of episodes presents him wandering through the underworld of Paris, in the company of Hindu disciple of Gandhi, and culminates in a vision. It is a vision of the justification of all things, roses and dung heaps; the sheer hopelessness of existence becomes for him proof of its many miracles. "For the fraction of a second perhaps I experienced that utter clarity which the epileptic, it is said, is given to know. In that moment I lost completely the illusion of time and space. . . . On the meridian of time there is no injustice: there is only the poetry of motion creating the illusion of truth and drama." Released from hope, from the vanity of human wishes, the narrator is also released from affliction. But his anger and his rejection of the social lie persist:

> I made up my mind that I would hold on to nothing, that I would expect nothing, that henceforth I would live as an animal, a beast of prey, a rover, a plunderer. . . . I have found God but he is insufficient. I am only spiritually dead. Physically I am alive. Morally I am free. The world I have departed is a menagerie. The dawn is breaking on a new world, a jungle world in which the lean spirits roam with sharp claws. If I am a hyena I am a lean and hungry one: I go forth to fatten myself. . . .

Freedom, not spiritual rebirth, is what our hero finds; in his jungle world of violence and deceit a black apocalypse gathers slowly.

Yet the cunning narrator is not quite as spiritually dead as he claims. The intensity of his anger, the vitality of his written testament, are proof to the contrary. The proof is also in the contrast between him and the desperadoes, Van Norden or Fillmore, who seek his company. They, too, have laid their illusions bare and picked their souls clean; they, too, seek pleasure for pleasure's sake. But their anguish remains undiminished and their joys arid. They cannot love; nor can they disport themselves with the casual animal grace of the French toughs they meet. Unlike Miller himself, they are all undisturbed by the visions that haunt him: the earth moving out of its orbit, the deltas and river beds drying, the snow blowing in huge drifts. "A new day is dawning, a metallurgical day, when the earth shall clink with showers of bright yellow ore . . . at the periphery the light waves bend and the sun bleeds like a broken rectum." Visions come and go; the oscillations from one mood to another are endless. At night, the narrator works at his grubby job as proofreader for an American paper, and facts oppress his spirit. But when he hits the morning air, his imagination runs wild, releasing itself in extravagant poetry and echolalia. Soon again, memories come crowding in, and the image of Mona, the wife he has left behind in America, shuts out the light. The narrator is back in "the agonizing gutter of my wretched past"; like an abyss, lost love beckons him to the bottom. Then the fierce image of some artist, Strindberg, say, emerges from the depths:

> And, as I ruminated, it began to grow clear to me, the mystery of his pilgrimage, the flight which the poet makes over the face of the earth and then, as if he had been ordained to re-enact a lost drama, the heroic descent to the very bowels of the earth, the dark and fearsome sojourn in the belly of the whale, the bloody struggle to liberate himself, to emerge clean of the past, a bright, gory sun god cast up on an alien shore.

If the narrator is reborn, we do not see it. Rebirth implies the experience of a unique moment of crisis. There is no such crisis in *Cancer*. There is only the experience of flow. Pain and ecstasy follow one another as surely as night follows day. We see the antics of the hero, sick and dying, in Kruger's studio; we see next his antics in bawdy houses or barroom brawls, Joy and tenderness erupt in the most unlikely places; so does misery. The vision, on the profane level of the action, remains crudely comic. When the narrator cheats a "midwife" of her fees or Fillmore entertains his Russian "princess," we follow each incident with riotous disbelief, as if the whole world had suddenly gone mad and we had been gleefully released. Anarchy prevails in its most clownish forms; the "genito-urinary friendships" of Paris mix ugliness with raucous laughter and incessant surprise. Sordid, depleted, absurd, the cankered world of Miller still swarms with the wonder of profane being.

There is also, on another level of action and vision, a sacred sense of being. To paint pre-Socratic man, a creature part goat, part Titan—this is the aim of Miller. On this level, the obscene contains the mystery of creation itself. Contemplating the door of creation, fissure and womb, Miller invokes archetypal images, which come, pell-mell, like a burst of surrealistic poetry:

> Out of that dark, unstitched wound, that sink of abominations, that cradle of black-thronged cities where the music of ideas is drowned in cold fat, out of strangled Utopias is born a clown, a being divided between beauty and ugliness, between light and chaos, a clown who when he looks down and sidelong is Satan himself and when he looks upwards sees a buttered angel, a snail with wings. . . . If anyone knew what it meant to read the riddle of that thing which today is called a "crack" or a "hole," if anyone had the least feeling of mystery about the phenomena which are labeled "obscene," this world would crack asunder.

The rhapsody of creation and destruction, dedicated now to the Female Principle and now to the lost image of Mona, is sustained for page after indiscriminate page with shattering effect. Standing in the midst of reeking humanity, Miller suddenly steps aside and apart, knowing that true artists and visionaries alike are condemned by their race. He belongs not to men but to the earth. He belongs with the monsters of creation. Whining, childish at times, cowardly and self-indulgent, the narrator snaps out of his sweaty condition to say: "Side by side with the human race there runs another race of beings, the inhuman ones, the race of artists who, goaded by unknown impulses, take the lifeless mass of humanity and by the fever and ferment with which they imbue it turn this soggy dough into bread and the bread into wine and the wine into song." Men of this race stand with their feet in a pool of blood and tears, their hands empty, clutching always for the god out of reach; and they stand on high places, with gibberish in their mouths, ripping out their entrails. How else is humanity to be redeemed?

What finally distinguishes Miller is a peculiarly American attitude, generous, violent, prodigal toward both art and life. In his radical innocence, he sees as much truth in harlot or wife, stray object or charged symbol, seeing that everything points to, and beyond, itself to the ground of being.

—*Ihab Hassan*

Once again, agony is followed by peace. The apocalyptic seer screams doom with defiance in his scream: "It may be that we are doomed, that there is no hope for us, *any of us,* but if that is so then let us set up a last agonizing, bloodcurdling howl, a screech of defiance, a war-whoop! Away with lamentation! Away with elegies and dirges!" This is the song of *Cancer* on the upper registers. On another register, the song comes to us less as a howl than a purr.

This latter note is struck toward the inconclusive ending of the book. After a funny and horrible experience as a lycée teacher in Dijon, which is rendered even more vividly in [*Henry Miller: Letters to Anaïs Nin*], the narrator flees back to Paris. There he sets about helping Fillmore to escape from the clutches of his wild and greedy mistress, Ginette. After pocketing the huge sum that Fillmore leaves with him to give to Ginette, the narrator wanders happily on the banks of the Seine. He is in a state of euphoria for which there is no dramatic or objective correlative—except the stolen money. "Inside me things were running smoother than any Rolls Royce ever ran. It was just like velvet inside. Velvet cortex and velvet vertebrae. And velvet axle grease, what!" He is not thinking about Mona now, and even his bitterness toward America vanishes. There is space around him, and peace within. The Seine flows by him quietly, peacefully, like a great artery through the human body.

One is forcefully struck by the passive quality of the book, its refusal to control experience or evaluate it, the silence beneath bitterness and beatitude. "I love everything that flows," Miller quotes, and flow seems all he can love. Where can such a love lead us? To a new sense of the wholeness or even holiness of all experience? Again and again, the discrepancy between triviality of event and loftiness of reflection jars our expectations. Is this but another subterfuge to erase distinctions and level life? Then again, one wonders about the narrator himself. Is he left with a fuller knowledge of his situation? What, precisely, motivates his bursts of rage or reconciliation? And does anything really *happen* to him?

A partial answer to these questions may be discovered in the anti-form of *Cancer*. On the plane of actual experience, no "question" is really valid; things are what they are, events simply happen. But knowledge is another matter; it requires that experience be given form and value. This is the pride of the mind, seeking always some grip on the slippery stuff of life. Now *Cancer* is not raw experience; it is rather a *song* of experience. As such, it implies a kind of form. Its form, nevertheless, is almost preartistic. It rejects the ideas of purpose and control; it denies the conventions of comedy and tragedy; and it defies the abstract patterns of quest, conversion, or reversal long honored in Western literature. The anti-form of *Cancer* amounts simply to this: a complex gesture of the imagination that renders in language the unity of mind and nature, knowledge and experience, artist and man.

The gesture in Miller's work can be analyzed into its component elements. Considered closely, these elements do not always appear to us original. Miller's use of time is an example:

> In reading my books, which are purely autobiographical, one should bear in mind that I write with one foot in the past. In telling the story of my life, I have discarded the chronological sequence in favor of the circular or spiral form of progression. The time sequence which relates one event to another in linear fashion strikes me as falsely imitative of the true rhythm of life. [*The World of Sex*]

Time moves obedient to the rhythm of the emotions, not the logic of history, Miller claims. But after the examples of Proust, Joyce, and Mann, this hardly seems a shattering insight. Likewise, Miller's literary point of view owes something to the romantic egoism of Walt Whitman and Thomas Wolfe in America even more than to the romantic pessimism of Céline. Furthermore, his abrupt shifts of tone find a precedent in the Symbolist and Surrealist poets before him. In Miller's work, we have seen, nausea yields to ecstasy, comic incident to solemn vision. A simple description of a scene or an action suddenly blends into surreal poetry, images crackling and twisting, words rushing and piling, language itself exploding in outrageous mockery. At times, the whole lexicon is let loose on us, marshaled by howling neologisms. Yet this technique, striking as it may seem, climaxes a literary tradition that extends from Rimbaud and Laforgue to Apollinaire and Cendrars. Miller brings that tradition to a close less by revolution than by sheer indiscriminacy.

For what finally distinguishes Miller is a peculiarly American attitude, generous, violent, prodigal toward both art and life. In his radical innocence, he sees as much truth in harlot or wife, stray object or charged symbol, seeing that everything points to, and beyond, itself to the ground of being. *Cancer*, which begins as a dirge to Western civilization, ends therefore as a hymn to natural man. The life of the book is in its savage texture, the pulsing surface of a rowdy and occasionally nasty egoism. For the egoism is undoubtedly there, marring the sacramental view. Presumably, the egoism is that of the narrator who relates himself haphazardly to everyone, seldom to anyone. This is his existential flaw. The limitation—or should one say uniqueness?—of the book is that it has no perspective on itself: its author, Henry Miller, has no more wisdom or art than the flawed narrator of *Cancer* possesses.

William A. Gordon   (essay date 1967)

SOURCE: "The Volcano's Eruption," in his *The Mind and Art of Henry Miller,* Louisiana State University Press, 1967, pp. 85-109.

[*In the following excerpt, Gordon discusses the imagery, style, and themes of* Tropic of Cancer, *arguing that the novel is a documentation of Miller's struggle for self-liberation.*]

Tropic of Cancer, which came out in 1934, was Miller's first published full length work. He had written several "novels" before this, but those who have read them, including Miller, agree that they lack his essential quality, that they are derived and imitative. Although *Tropic of Cancer* is not part of the central work which Miller had planned in 1927, it is a kind of spontaneous bursting forth of feeling which had been bottled up for years. It is significant for several reasons, not the least being that it is still one of his most readable books. In *Cancer* Miller found and developed the role of hero-narrator which he has maintained throughout his writing career. This narrator, even when he is describing his own personal experiences and feelings, remains detached and relatively free of his environment. He is what Miller has always said of himself even as a child, at once a part of and totally independent of the life around him. He is gregarious and totally alone. He is Dostoievski's "underground man" who is filled with violence, but he lacks the self-doubts and tortured inner struggle that mark Dostoievski's heroes. He is presented to us as a man who has finally, once and for all, burst out of the confines of his culture, who has himself become the arbiter of values, who is the herald of a new world to come after this present world shall finally have been destroyed. *Tropic of Cancer* accepts that destruction and celebrates the affirmation of individual life. Its various sections explore the undiscovered life which belongs to the self but has been covered over in the effort to come to terms with a corrupt civilization.

He is the Nietzschean man who wakes one day to exclaim rapturously with Rabelais, "Fay ce que vouldras!" Having discarded the values which he inherited from his culture, hero Miller faces life in Paris in an effort to establish new values. In the process he regresses to almost infantile levels of demand. He is consumed with the desire for food. Everything in life that he wants becomes the object not of

will or desire, but of voracious appetite. The first rule of life is survival, and he takes all the means he can find to this end. He sets up a list of friends who will share the responsibility for feeding him, and he calls once a week at the house of each, until he outstays his welcome. He begs and scrounges and yet all the while seems to enjoy life to the full. Everyone worries; he is serene.

Besides developing the character of the hero, *Tropic of Cancer* establishes the style which will be characteristic of Miller from then on. There are generally three elements which he combines in different proportions. The first element is the life of the hero-narrator in the present, which includes his sense of body and mind, the continual rendering of the feeling of living here and now. Secondly there are the anecdotal elements which make Miller's novels one of the great collecting places of strange and unusual characters. Sometimes these anecdotes seem to be told for their own sakes, like the story of Max, the destitute refugee. But usually they function as a foil for the narrator to show his own view of life or to compare the developing values of the hero with the obsessive concerns of the unredeemed. In *Cancer* this role is reserved mainly for Van Norden, who occupies one long chapter besides lengthy passages later in the book.

On the third level and woven into the other material are the free-flowing fantasy-like associations by which the hero-narrator interprets the world in which he lives. These passages are not as fully developed as in later works, but they are still a significant part. They generally arise either out of the narrator's present experience of felt life or out of his anecdotes about others. The fantasy of Miller's shorter works like **"Into the Night Life"** is pure surrealism, but fantasy as a technique in the major novels is highly integrative. Symbols enable the narrator to reach beyond the present moment to the past and future, and beyond the present limited geographical location to the universe. The fantasy passages allow the narrator to integrate his own past life and the episodes and characters of the present with his major themes—the birth of independence, the discovery of the lines of the body. *Tropic of Cancer* seems to be a less-unified book than *Tropic of Capricorn* because the fantasy passages do not unite and integrate the material into themes as completely as they do in *Capricorn*. Despite this fault, however, *Cancer* has an excitement about it of something new; it is crude but fresh.

Miller tells us something of his own view of *Tropic of Cancer* in *The World of Sex:* "The *Tropic of Cancer* is a sort of human document, written in blood, recording the struggle in the womb of death. The strong sexual odor is, if anything, the aroma of birth, disagreeable, repulsive even, when disassociated from its significance." Miller calls *Tropic of Cancer* a work of the moment, "the volcano's eruption" [*Art and Outrage*, 1959]. Yet it is important because it emphasizes more than other works one aspect of Miller's development, that is, the purposeful treatment of what is ugly, repulsive, and distasteful in life. Miller's struggle in the womb of death is well worth recording, but easily misunderstood. His attitude in *Tropic of Cancer* is not peaceful acceptance as it will become later. It is rather the first assertion of the self against all that seeks to enslave that self, against disgust for the forms that life may take, against conventional easy adjustments to reality, against sentimentalism, self-deception, and obsessions of every sort. It proposes to face frankly the biological facts of existence and especially to treat these facts in the most immediate concrete terms available. It is against art, as Miller saw it practiced in his own day, because it refuses to gloss over anything; it is against all sentimental conceptions of God or religion, against all conventional notions of man, destiny, time, or eternity. It is *for* very little except the complete honesty and integrity of the individual.

As Miller has emphasized in his study of D. H. Lawrence, the refusal to face animal life leads to that idealization which is yet another form of death, because it denies the fundamental nature of man and cuts him off from his source of vital energy. The law of life is growth, and for man that means freeing himself from the womb, achieving independence. Life is a process in which man is constantly being born. The refusal to be born is the acceptance of death.

In the light of what we have already seen of Miller's early life the rebellious sexuality of *Tropic of Cancer* is something of a paradox. We can easily imagine a highly repressed individual breaking loose as Miller does in this book, but there is no evidence that Miller had ever been particularly repressed. Passages in other books about his early life show a freedom of approach to sexual experience and an ability to tolerate sexual images which would seem to indicate an almost total lack of repression. Yet we must assume on the basis of the imagery of *Tropic of Cancer* that a great release of instinctual energy is taking place, and that enabled Miller to move on to another level of experience.

We can better understand the nature of Miller's rebellion if we examine his situation at the time of writing *Tropic of Cancer*. Early in *Tropic of Capricorn*, that is while the narrator was working at Western Union, we find a discussion of the bottled up rebellion directed against all the forces of society which hero Miller felt was keeping him from achieving his full potentiality as an individual. There was at this time a tremendous upsurge of aggression which as yet had not been channeled in any constructive direction. A second great emotional upheaval takes place in *Sexus* when he breaks loose from the depressing relationship with his first wife to enter a new kind of relation with Mona. The relationship with Mona, however, does not free Miller; it enslaves him. He finds himself with time to write, but he is dependent upon a woman who so dominates his life that he is unable to use the time constructively. The "Land of Fuck" Interlude of *Tropic of Capricorn* shows us a descent to the level of instinct, but does not show us the emergence from that state. At the end of *Nexus*, just before Miller left for Paris, his aggressive feelings are still largely unchanneled and violent, and his sexual energies are tied up in a frustrating relationship which has progressively deteriorated. It is clear that Miller has not yet arrived at a state of free and spontaneous awareness of life which can operate effectively in achieving his full potentiality as a person.

As the great explosion in which both sexual and aggressive energy are released into the work of art, *Tropic of Cancer* is a disturbing book. Its violence has become heavily charged with sexual feeling, and for this reason it is a cathartic of the most violent kind. It has been attacked fanatically and defended in the same way. It is only right that it should be. A rebellion of the nature of Miller's does not usually evoke a lukewarm reaction. Some readers, caught up in Miller's mood to the extent that they feel the same release, love the book; others, disturbed by the raw state of its emotion, dislike it intensely. Such in fact, has been the history of critical reactions to *Tropic of Cancer*.

The hero-narrator of *Tropic of Cancer* is in many ways the Nietzschean hero par excellence, but his rebellion has other elements which we have touched upon. In a symbolic sense the rebellion of the hero is an effort to escape from the womb of the mother. There are many sources, as we have seen, for Miller's womb imagery; but his attitude in *Cancer* seems closest to that which he expressed much later in *The Time of the Assassins,* his study of Rimbaud, and in his comments on James Joyce. In the Rimbaud study Miller draws a character sketch of the man who is striving to break free of the mother, and he associates that effort with violence.

Failure of the individual to free himself from the mother, Miller says, means that the dark side of his nature had not been faced early in life. He explains how man rejects the dark side of life out of fear that he will lose his individuality, unique identity, and freedom. Man thus becomes a rebel striving for the "freedom to assert his ego unrestrained." The search for freedom then takes the form of a rebellion against life itself, which conceals the bondage to the mother:

> All this has one meaning for me—that one is still bound to the mother. All one's rebellion was but dust in the eye, the frantic attempt to conceal this bondage. Men of this stamp are always against their native land—impossible to be otherwise. Enslavement is the great bugaboo, whether it be to country, church or society. Their lives are spent in breaking fetters, but the secret bondage gnaws at their vitals and gives them no rest. They must come to terms with the mother before they can rid themselves of the obsession of fetters. "Outside! Forever outside! Sitting on the doorstep of the mother's womb." . . . No wonder one is alienated from the mother. One does not notice her, except as an obstacle. One wants the comfort and security of the womb, that darkness and ease which for the unborn is the equivalent of illumination and acceptance for the truly born. [*The Time of the Assassins*]

Fulfillment of man's destiny, that is, the achievement of man's potentialities for freedom, means that one must leave the security of the mother's womb and accept the world as the true matrix of his development. The world then becomes a womb and man repeats in a different way the process of growth from conception to birth. Miller points out the dangers of remaining linked to the mother in his discussion of James Joyce. Of man's two choices, to accept the world as womb and be born again, or return to the womb of the mother and lose the world forever, Miller has elected the first and recorded his struggle to be born. Joyce, Miller claims [in **"The Universe of Death,"** in his *The Cosmological Eye,* 1939], has elected the second; he has returned to the womb of the mother, symbolized in the person of Molly Bloom. His fight is with the mother, symbolized for him in family, country, and church. In his revolt he rejects the world once and for all and returns to this mother, who has become for him "the veridic whore of creation." In the person of Molly Bloom the mother becomes "the quintessence of the great whore which is woman of Babylon, the vessel of abominations. Floating, unresisting, eternal, all-contained, she is like the sea itself. Like the sea she is receptive, fecund, voracious, insatiable. She begets and she destroys; she nourishes and she devastates. With Molly Bloom, *con anonyme,* woman is restored to prime significance—as womb and matrix of life." Joyce's hero is unable to free himself from this woman-matrix. The hero returns to the womb at last:

> And so, with final, triumphant vengeance, with suicidal glee, all the threads which were dropped throughout the book are recapitulated; the pale, diminutive hero, reduced to an intestinal worm and carried like a tickling phallus in the great body of the female, returns to the womb of nature, shorn of everything but the last symbol. In the long retrospective arc which is drawn we have the whole trajectory of man's flight from unknown to unknown, the rainbow of history fades out. The great dissolution is accomplished. After that closing picture of Molly Bloom a-dreaming on her dirty bed we can say, as in Revelation—And there shall be no more curse! Henceforth no sin, no quiet, no fear, no repression, no longing, no pain of separation. The end is accomplished—man returns to the womb.

What Miller was trying to avoid at the time he arrived in Paris was the fate which he has assigned to James Joyce, the return to the womb, the flight from life to security. Growth, he was beginning to discover, must be to greater differentiation, to freedom, to independence, and it is precisely that image of woman which he attacks in the person of Molly Bloom that he is attacking in *Tropic of Cancer.* His violence and his sexualizing of experience are a part of his attempt to control his own destiny, which also accounts for his prevailing womb imagery and for his attacks on sexual obsession of all kinds.

Miller's first task in *Tropic of Cancer* is to establish a sense of the self and a sense of the world. He must cling resolutely to the sense of self, a self which is free and independent of external events as the source of his well-being and happiness. The world is a chaos, but the self lives:

> It is now the fall of my second year in Paris. I was sent here for a reason I have not yet been able to fathom.
>
> I have no money, no resources, no hopes. I am the happiest man alive. A year ago, six months ago, I thought I was an artist. I no longer think about it. I *am.* Everything that was literature has fallen from me. There are no more books to be written, thank God.

Miller is here in Paris, abandoned by Mona to find himself as best he can. The first year in Paris was a year of suffering; now comes the violent birth. "I had two beginnings really, one here in America, which was abortive, and the other in Europe. How was I able to begin again, one may well ask? I should answer truthfully—by dying. In that first year or so in Paris I literally died, was literally annihilated—and resurrected as a new man" [*The World of Sex,* 1940].

It would be premature at this point to go much further into the implicit significance of Miller's rebirth in *Tropic of Cancer.* He has said himself that he was not aware of the significance of these events at the time. In fact development in reflective power and insight provides the principal thematic unity in Miller's work. The very imperfection of his knowledge and his growth to greater awareness creates the essential autobiographical form.

To understand Miller's situation in *Tropic of Cancer* we need not go outside of the book itself. Miller has been in Paris for a year, and he has been estranged from Mona during most of that time, though she has not been absent continuously. During that year, we presume, Miller was still very much attached to her and felt her absence very keenly.

> For seven years I went about, day and night, with only one thing on my mind—her. Were there a Christian so faithful to his God as I was to her we would all be Jesus Christs today. Day and night I thought of her even when I was deceiving her. And now sometimes, in the very midst of things, sometimes when I feel that I am absolutely free of it all, suddenly, in rounding a corner perhaps, there will bob up a little square, a few trees and a bench, a deserted spot where we stood and had it out, where we drove each other crazy with bitter, jealous scenes. . . . When I realize that she is gone, perhaps gone forever, a great void opens up and I feel that I am falling, falling into deep black space. And this is worse than tears, deeper than regret or pain or sorrow; it is the abyss into which Satan was plunged.

But reflection upon Mona, though it leads to misery, brings about a salutary awareness, and the conversion of life into art. Life with Mona had been a descent into hell, the hell depicted by Strindberg, "in that wild carnival of maggots he reveled in, in that eternal duel of the sexes, that spiderish ferocity which endeared him to the sodden oafs of the northland. . . ." It was that duel between the sexes which brought them together. "We came together in a dance of death and so quickly was I sucked down into the vortex that when I came to the surface again I could not recognize the world. When I found myself loose the carnival was over and I had been picked clean. . . ." Now it is time to convert life into art, and even this brief recollection of Mona leads to a reflection on art:

> . . . I began to reflect on the meaning of that inferno which Strindberg had so mercilessly depicted. And, as I ruminated, it began to grow clear to me, the mystery of his pilgrimage, the flight which the poet makes over the face of the earth and then, as if he had been ordained to reenact a lost drama, the heroic descent to the very

bowels of the earth, the dark and fearsome sojourn in the belly of the whale, the bloody struggle to liberate himself, to emerge clean of the past, a bright, fiery sun god cast up on an alien shore.

The drama of rebirth, re-enacted over and over in world history, must continue to be enacted in every man's life, and this is the stuff out of which poetry is made. Miller, we assume, has already sojourned in "the belly of the whale"; now the experience must be converted into art. His first book begins with the explosion, the emerging being, ravenously hungry. His first thoughts are aggressive, hostile, primitive, sexual. He dedicates the book to Tania:

> It is to you Tania that I am singing. I wish that I could sing better, more melodiously, but then perhaps you would never have consented to listen to me. You have heard the others sing and they have left you cold. . . . The world around me is dissolving, leaving here and there spots of time. The world is a cancer eating itself away. . . . I am thinking that when the great silence descends upon all and everywhere music will at last triumph. When into the womb of time everything is again withdrawn chaos will be restored and chaos is the score upon which reality is written. You Tania are my chaos. It is why I sing. It is not even I. It is the world dying, shedding the skin of time. I am still alive, kicking in your womb, a reality to write upon.

Hunger dominates the mood of *Tropic of Cancer,* hunger for life, for food, for sex. And all of Miller's hunger has sexual overtones. He associates with Tania his desire for food, and his preoccupation is transformed into sexual imagery which itself is expressed in images of eating:

> At night when I look at Boris' goatee lying on the pillow I get hysterical. Oh Tania, where now is that warm cunt of yours, those fat, heavy garters, those soft, bulging thighs. There is a bone in my prick six inches long. I will ream out every wrinkle in your cunt, Tania, big with seed. I will send you home to your Sylvester with an ache in your belly and your womb turned inside out. . . . I am fucking you, Tania, so that you'll stay fucked. And if you are afraid of being fucked publicly I will fuck you privately. I will tear off a few hairs from your cunt and paste them on Boris' chin. I will bite into your clitoris and spit out two franc pieces.

From Tania and sex his voracious appetite moves to hunger for food, and never a meal, "Coffee without milk or sugar. Bread without butter. Meat without gravy, or no meat at all. Without this and without that!" In one of the most sensual passages in any of Miller's writing, the opening of a wine bottle becomes the equivalent of a sexual experience: "Boris is rubbing his hands again. Mr. Wren is still stuttering and spluttering. I have a bottle between my legs and I'm shoving the corkscrew in. Mrs. Wren has her mouth parted expectantly. The wine is splashing between my legs, the sun is splashing through the bay window, and inside my veins there is a bubble and splash of a thousand crazy things that commence to gush out of me now pell mell. I'm telling them everything that comes to mind, everything that was bottled up inside me and which Mrs. Wren's loose laugh has somehow released."

The sequence of imagery is easily converted into sexual symbolism, the bottle between the legs, shoving the corkscrew, the liquid feeling of the splashing wine, the liquid feeling of Mrs. Wren's laugh, her parted mouth. Food, wine, sex, Europe, the sun splashing are all the subject of voracious appetite and convertible, one into the other.

The association between birth and hunger, sex and appetite, is natural. In the world of dreams and fantasy they are easily enough converted into each other. Miller has recognized this and dealt with it specifically in **"Uterine Hunger."** The world, he says, has seemed as if it were "An artificial womb, a prison, it seems as though everybody and everything were conspiring to pull me back into the womb from which I broke loose too soon."

> And always I am hungry, voraciously hungry. I am insatiable. It is a hunger on all fronts: alimentary, sexual, spiritual. I don't eat—I attach myself, like the amoeba, to whatever morsel of food presents itself. Once I have ingested it I split—double, triple, multiple selves floating off in search of fresh morsels of food. It goes on like that *ad nauseam.* Women—they too seem morsels of food. After I attach myself to them I devour them. I fuck my way through body, brain and soul, and then I split up again.

With hunger, with this voracious appetite for experience, Miller associates passion. What is missing in the world is passion; there is nothing but ideas, and ideas are bloodless; they do not support life:

> Nobody as far as I can see is making use of those elements on the air which give direction and motivation to our lives. Only the killers seem to be extracting from life some satisfactory measure of what they are putting into it. The age demands violence, but we are getting only abortive explosions. Revolutions are nipped in the bud, or else succeed too quickly. Passion is quickly exhausted. Men fall back on ideas *comme d'habitude.* Nothing is proposed that can last more than twenty-four hours. We are living a million lives in the space of a generation. [*Tropic of Cancer*]

Miller's later work will become more transcendental, in the manner of Whitman. In *Tropic of Cancer* he is principally concerned with restoring the acceptance of bodily function to the realm of human experience. Man must restore the unity of experience; love and excrement must be felt on the same plane of existence, equally acceptable. *Tropic of Cancer,* however, has little to say about love, though it has a great deal to say about excrement and the failure of life. Aside from Miller's own reflections on life, the principal subject matter of the book concerns the failure of others to live fully and freely, that is, with the failure in passion. The characters in *Tropic of Cancer* indulge freely in sexual experience, but that experience does not flow freely from a unified life; therefore it is obsessive. The most obsessed of all the characters is Van Norden. We are given a succinct summary of his character early in the book: "I like Van Norden but I do not share his opinion of himself. I do not agree, for instance, that he is a philosopher, or a thinker. He is cunt-struck, that's all."

At first glance it might appear that there is little difference between Miller and Van Norden. They are both irresponsible, both in search of a good time. Miller is as avid for a woman as Van Norden, as eager for an orgy. But Miller takes it as it comes. He has a great sex drive, but he is not obsessed. His sexual drives can be mobilized in an instant, even his passion, his desire for love. But when he is not actively engaged sexually, he is free to do other things, to eat, to walk, to work. Van Norden is never free. Sex haunts him like another self. Yet fundamentally he is passionless. There are two major episodes which show Van Norden's deficiencies. The first is when he is trying to have intercourse with a woman and is unable, evidently, to penetrate. Miller says:

> "for God's sake Joe, give it up! You'll kill the poor girl." "Leave me alone," he grunts. "I almost got it in that time." The posture and the determined way in which he blurts this out suddenly brings to my mind, for the second time the remembrance of my dream. . . . He's like a hero come back from the war, a poor maimed bastard living out the reality of his dreams. Wherever he sits himself the chair collapses; whatever door he enters the room is empty; whatever he puts into his mouth leaves a bad taste. Everything is just the same as it was before; the elements are unchanged, the dream is no different than the reality. Only between the time he went to sleep and the time he woke up, his body was stolen. He's like a machine throwing out newspapers . . . the front page is loaded with catastrophes . . . but he doesn't feel anything. If somebody doesn't turn the switch off he'll never know what it means to die. You can't die if your own proper body has been stolen. You can get over a cunt and work away like a billy goat until eternity; you can go to the trenches and be blown to bits; nothing will create that spark of passion if there isn't the intervention of a human hand.

What is wrong with Van Norden's performance is that passion is missing, and therefore it is meaningless and, more than that, it is uninteresting:

> My interest in Van Norden and the girl is nil; if I could sit like this and watch every performance going on at this minute all over the world my interest would be even less than nil. I wouldn't be able to differentiate between this phenomenon and the rain falling or a volcano erupting. As long as that spark of passion is missing there is no human significance in the performance. The machine is better to watch. And these two are like a machine which has slipped its cogs. It needs a touch of a human hand to set it right. It needs a mechanic.

Van Norden's disintegration is completed in the last episode, which might be called the descent into meaninglessness. Like most of Miller's handling of the tragic, there is a spirit of clowning which makes the episode farcical. He has just met Van Norden again after several month's absence from Paris:

Van Norden still bellyaching about his cunts and about washing the dirt out of his belly. Only now he's found a new diversion. He's found that it's less annoying to masturbate. I was amazed when he broke the news to me. I didn't think it possible for a guy like that to find any pleasure in jerking himself off. I was still more amazed when he explained to me how he goes about it. He had "invented" a new stunt, so he put it. "You take an apple," he says, "and you bore out the core. Then you rub some cold cream on the inside so it doesn't melt too fast. Try it some time! It'll drive you crazy at first. Anyway, it's cheap and you don't have to waste much time."

This is life viewed in the crazy mirror of an amusement park. The meaning is that there is no meaning in a world inhabited by such as Van Norden because they are not rooted in reality.

Miller's own feelings about life jar sharply with those of his friends. For him the chaos of modern life is no less, but he has a source of inner strength. In a sense Miller has been brought to the absolute bottom of life at this point, but still finds he can live and be happy. The secret of life is that it must be lived on all levels, not excluding the physical. It is the wedding of ideas to action: "Still I can't get it out of my mind what a discrepancy there is between ideas and living. A permanent dislocation, though we try to cover the two with a bright awning. And it won't go. Ideas have to be wedded to action; if there is no sex, no vitality in them, there is no action. Ideas cannot exist alone in the vacuum of the mind. Ideas are related to living: liver ideas, kidney ideas, interstitial ideas, etc."

This wedding of thought and action is the basis not only of Miller's subject matter, but of his technique. In *Tropic of Cancer* he first explores the technique which he will perfect in later books. In general Miller's approach to the union of thought and action is to juxtapose concrete experience and fantasy life.

There are three levels of awareness which are interwoven in Miller's works: present actual experiences, present fantasy, and past experience, both fantasy and actual. Shifts in time are far more rare in *Tropic of Cancer* than in later works, and for this reason the work has a cruder structure than, say, *Tropic of Capricorn*. In *Cancer* the shift is from external to internal, in which the external taken up into fantasy acquires some universal quality. What makes Miller different is principally the kind of material he chooses to universalize. Emerson, no doubt, would have had misgivings about Miller's material, but the choice is not unlike what he advocated: "The meaner the type by which a law is expressed, the more pungent it is, and the more lasting in the memories of men."

This conversion of the base into the universal is exemplified in Miller's episode with a Hindu, a friend of the Hindu with whom he was leading his usual submarginal existence. The Hindu wishes Miller to accompany him to a house of prostitution, and Miller does. While there the Hindu expresses the need for a toilet. Miller tells him that it is usual to use the bidet for such purposes, assuming the Hindu wished to urinate. Miller next hears a tremendous racket coming from the Hindu's room. Everybody in the house is jabbering away in French, obviously outraged. Miller hurries into the Hindu's room. There in the bidet are "two enormous turds floating in the water." This is a clear violation even of whorehouse etiquette. The episode is converted into a dream sequence a few pages later, a fantasy about the illusion of absolute truth and justice.

> And so I think what a miracle it would be if this miracle which man attends eternally should turn out to be nothing more than these two enormous turds which the faithful disciple dropped in the *bidet.* What if at the last moment, when the banquet table is set and the cymbals clash, there should appear suddenly, and wholly without warning, a silver platter on which even the blind could see that there is nothing more and nothing less than two enormous lumps of shit.

It might well be objected that Miller could find other, more acceptable terms in which to express his disillusionment, but that would be to mistake the point and the style. The fact is that the crude and realistic terms which Miller uses, the material out of which he creates his fantasies, are the terms in which fantasy life often works. This is not the social level upon which Miller is communicating, but the most private level of the most private thoughts of all men, the level on which the obscene and the sacred meet. These crude Anglo-Saxon terms are precise because they are the most concrete words in the language, and fantasy is always concrete.

A similar aspect of Miller's writing which has been widely attacked is his bald and often elaborate discussions of sexual organs. *Cancer* has few descriptions of actual sexual activity, what might be called detailed accounts of sexual play. But he does use explicit descriptions in other ways and they are worth a comment. Since Miller's general object is to record those aspects of experience which have been left out of books, then the fascination and significance of the organs of sex are bound to be a part of his material. Our culture lives mainly by denial, and descriptions or pictures of sexual organs usually arouse the righteous to full-scale attack. Children, however, are endlessly fascinated by their own and others' bodies, and it is doubtful that adults have lost much of this fundamental voyeurism. Miller's descriptions are of both the female and male genitalia throughout his work, but in *Cancer* it is mainly the female who comes under consideration.

It is a well-known psychological fact that the female genitals have a significance for the male far beyond their simple biological function. They are of course stimulating to the man's sexual desires, but they can be on occasion the object of fear or of obsessive curiosity. They harbor mysteries which the man seeks to solve but to which he can never find the answer, or they may symbolize fecundity in a very primitive way. Miller shows us in *Cancer* two different attitudes to sexual organs, one self-defeating, the other supposedly successful.

Van Norden represents the inadequate development. For him a woman does not exist as a person, simply as a set of genitals, his "Georgia cunt" or his "Danish cunt." For Van Norden the genitals are "the empty crack of the prematurely disillusioned man." For Miller the female geni-

tals are the occasion for one of the longest fantasy passages in *Tropic of Cancer,* one in which he explores all of the fecundating energy of the cosmos.

The scene occurs when Miller and Fillmore are entertaining two whores, who are acrobats. Miller finds himself suddenly with two legs around his neck and gazing into "a dark hairy crack . . . set in a bright, polished billiard ball." The sight suddenly opens up a corresponding fissure in his brain out of which pours an elaborate flood of images. The mother becomes the great whore of creation, the obscene horror. Sex and obscenity and the destruction of the world become intermingled. It is the underlying reality that he discovers in these moments of revery; once again the sacred and the obscene are united, reconciling the most basic contradiction of our culture. Thus Miller has always insisted that he is for obscenity and against pornography. The obscene we ignore at our peril, the pornographic he seems to feel is worse than useless.

When obscenity has been used in modern literature, it has usually been in a Manichean revulsion from sexuality, as in Baldwin's *Another Country.* Miller tries something which seems to me different; he attempts to make the obscene a part of life, accepted, but without losing any of the raw shock of the primitive origins. It is the same with sex and love. We read a great deal nowadays about the need for preserving love and tenderness in sexuality, and of the many disastrous ways in which they may become separated. Miller, like Rank, points out the dangers inherent in identifying love and sexuality. For Miller sexuality must first exist fully for itself before it can take part in a love relationship. Tying sexual activity exclusively to a love relationship seems to bring the danger of diminished potency. In fact the internal split in modern man which creates the problem of psychic impotence appears, from Miller's point of view, to come more from an overemphasis on love virtue, the sacredness of marriage and the purity of mothers and sisters, than from the full appreciation of sexuality for its own sake. For him, the modern world is dried up like the whore, but the reawakening must be sexual. The writer puts "the live wire of sex right between the legs. . . . if there is nothing but a gaping wound left then it must gush forth though it produce nothing but toads and bats and homunculi."

Tropic of Cancer, like *Quiet Days in Clichy*, is concerned with Miller's present activities at the time of writing. The point of view is that of the man in the street, the man to whom these things are happening. Virtually nothing of the past appears in either book. Similarly there is little exploration of the creative process as such. The creative process is associated in Miller's mind with gestation, birth, fertilization, in general the whole sexual process and its overflow into all the areas of life. For the most part in *Tropic of Cancer* the emphasis is on Miller's immediate relationship with people. The urge to write, when it does appear, is an alienating rather than a unifying element. "Tania is in a hostile mood—I can feel it. She resents me being filled with anything but herself. She knows by the very caliber of my excitement that her value is reduced to zero. She knows that I did not come this evening to fertilize her. She knows there is something germinating inside me which will destroy her." The work to be created remains a minor theme in *Tropic of Cancer*. Miller has not settled yet on the major theme of his later work, the birth of the artist.

On two other occasions Miller touches on this creation theme. The first is in the form of a revery, confronting the works of Henri Matisse. Matisse becomes a symbol of life created in color and light, a change from "the habitual gray of the world." Miller has the impression of being immersed in the very "plexus of life." It is Matisse, "if any man today possesses the gift, who knows when to dissolve the human figure, who has the courage to sacrifice an harmonious line in order to detect the rhythm and murmur of blood. . . . Behind the minutiae, the chaos, the mockery of life, he detects the invisible pattern. . . . No searching for formulation, no crucifixion of ideas, no compulsion other than to create." For Miller creation is inevitably associated with biological processes: "Even as the world falls apart the Paris that belongs to Matisse shudders with bright, gasping orgasms, the air itself is steady with a stagnant sperm, the trees tangled like hair."

With the desire for creation comes the fear of being born. As life is taken up into art, so art is being converted into life. And the birth through creation is analogous to the birth of the self. To create is to become whole and separate, independent, but this independence is also our chief fear.

> Going back in a flash over the women I've know. It's like a chain which I've forged out of my own misery. Each one bound to the other. A fear of living separate, of staying born. The door of the womb always on the latch. Dread and longing. Deep in the blood the pull of paradise. The beyond. Always the beyond. It must have all started with the navel. They cut the umbilical cord, give you a slap on the ass, and presto! you're out in the world, adrift, a ship without a rudder. You look at the stars and then you look at your navel. . . . What is distant becomes near, what is near becomes distant. Inner-outer, a constant flux, a shedding of skins, a turning inside out. You drift around like that for years and years, until you find yourself in the dead center, and there you slowly rot, slowly crumble to pieces, get dispersed again. Only your name remains.

The struggle, the misery, is still there. Mona is absent, but he is not yet self-sufficient. His awareness has increased; he can deal with a self—a real not a false self.

> For a fraction of a second, perhaps, I experienced that utter clarity which the epileptic, it is said, is given to know. In that moment I lost completely the illusion of time and space; the world unfurled its drama simultaneously along a meridian which had no axis. In this sort of hair-trigger eternity I felt that everything was justified, supremely justified; I felt the wars inside me that had left behind this pulp and wrack; I felt the crimes that were seething here to emerge tomorrow in blatant screamers; I felt the misery that was grinding itself out with pestle and mortar, the long dull misery that dribbles away in dirty handkerchiefs.

This is the self which senses on the deepest level that it is capable of love, of crime, of any monstrosity, of unlimited generosity, in short the true self. Man begins to live when he ceases to depend upon external events for his happiness, secure in the knowledge and awareness of the self.

> Somehow the realization that nothing was to be hoped for had a salutary effect upon me. For weeks and months, for years, in fact, all my life I had been looking forward to something happening, some extrinsic event that would alter my life, and now suddenly, inspired by the absolute hopelessness of everything, I felt relieved, felt as though a great burden had been lifted from my shoulders.

> . . . Walking toward Montparnasse I decided to let myself drift with the tide, to make not the least resistance to fate, no matter in what from it presented itself. Nothing that had happened to me thus far had been sufficient to destroy me; nothing had been destroyed except my illusions. I myself was intact. The world was intact . . . . Had one single element of man's nature been altered, vitally, fundamentally altered, by the incessant march of history? By what he calls the better part of his nature, man has been betrayed, that is all. At the extreme limits of his spiritual being man finds himself again naked as a savage. When he finds God, as it were, he has been picked clean; he is a skeleton. One must burrow into life again in order to put on flesh. The word must become flesh; the soul thirsts. On whatever crumb my eye fastens, I will pounce and devour. If to live is the paramount thing, then I will live, even if I must become a cannibal.

Miller has returned from the complexity of the life presented to him by his environment, particularly of his early life, to the simple natural fact. At this point he says, "I have found God, but he is insufficient. I am only spiritually dead. Physically I am alive. Morally I am free."

To be secure in that inner happiness we must first be convinced that there is nothing to be hoped for from the world; it has nothing to offer but misery and pain. To accept the world as chaos is to stand on the threshold of total acceptance, of deliverance from the womb. Miller's reasoning in this argument is not hard to follow. Dependence on the mother, that is, refusal to leave the womb, is characterized by a desire to be taken care of, to be fed, to be nursed, to receive good things. As long as one looks to the world to provide those things which are in essence infantile, there is no deliverance. Deliverance comes when we look at the world for what it is and see that it gives nothing; it destroys. If we can face this fact and still be happy, then we seek nothing; we are secure in ourselves; we become fathers, capable of fathering ideas, or children, of accepting responsibility. In *Tropic of Cancer* Miller looks hard at the world and sees nothing but chaos. At the end, as he sits by the banks of the Seine and feels the flow of history, a serene mood of peace comes over him. He accepts life.

> After everything had quietly sifted through my head a great peace came over me. Here, where the river gently winds through the girdle of hills, lies a soil so saturated with the past that however

far back the mind roams one can never detach it from its human background. Christ, before my eyes there shimmered such a golden peace that only a neurotic could dream of turning his head away. So quietly flows the Seine that one hardly notices its presence. It is always there, quiet and unobtrusive, like a great artery running through the human body. In the wonderful peace that fell over me it seemed as if I had climbed to the top of a high mountain; for a little while I would be able to look around me, to take in the meaning of the landscape.

An excerpt from *Tropic of Cancer:*

I have made a silent compact with myself not to change a line of what I write. I am not interested in perfecting my thoughts, nor my actions. Beside the perfection of Turgenev I put the perfection of Dostoevski. (Is there anything more perfect than *The Eternal Husband?*) Here, then, in one and the same medium, we have two kinds of perfection. But in Van Gogh's letters there is a perfection beyond either of these. It is the triumph of the individual over art.

There is only one thing which interests me vitally now, and that is the recording of all that which is omitted in books. Nobody, so far as I can see, is making use of those elements in the air which give direction and motivation to our lives. Only the killers seem to be extracting from life some satisfactory measure of what they are putting into it. The age demands violence, but we are getting only abortive explosions. Revolutions are nipped in the bud, or else succeed too quickly. Passion is quickly exhausted. Men fall back on ideas, *comme d'habitude.* Nothing is proposed that can last more than twenty-four hours. We are living a million lives in the space of a generation. In the study of entomology, or of deep sea life, or cellular activity, we derive more . . .

The telephone interrupts this thought which I should never have been able to complete. Someone is coming to rent the apartment . . . .

It looks as though it were finished, my life at the Villa Borghese. Well, I'll take up these pages and move on. Things will happen elsewhere. Things are always happening. It seems wherever I go there is drama. People are like lice—they get under your skin and bury themselves there. You scratch and scratch until the blood comes, but you can't get permanently deloused. Everywhere I go people are making a mess of their lives. Everyone has his private tragedy. It's in the blood now—misfortune, ennui, grief, suicide. The atmosphere is saturated with disaster, frustration, futility. Scratch and scratch—until there's no skin left. However, the effect upon me is exhilarating. Instead of being discouraged, or depressed, I enjoy it. I am crying for more and more disasters, for bigger calamities, for grander failures. I want the whole world to be out of whack, I want everyone to scratch himself to death.

Henry Miller, in his Tropic of Cancer, *Grove Weidenfeld, 1961.*

George Wickes   (essay date 1969)

SOURCE: "Cancer and Delirium," in his *Americans in Paris,* Doubleday, 1969, pp. 239-61.

[*Wickes is a Belgian-born American critic and educator. In the following excerpt from his study of American expatriate writers of the 1920s and 30s, he discusses the crucial influence that the avant-garde, bohemian atmosphere of Paris had on Miller's artistic growth, and the personal tribulations and friendships which contributed to the genesis of* Tropic of Cancer.]

On March 4, 1930, a slight, bald, middle-aged American arrived in Paris. Mild-mannered and bespectacled, he had the air of a college professor. Café waiters often took him for a German or a Scandinavian. "I lack that carefree, audacious air of the average American," he wrote in a letter at the time. "Even the Americans ignore me. They talk English at my elbow with that freedom which one employs only when he is certain his neighbor does not understand." Like so many Americans during the previous decade he had come to write, but his circumstances were altogether different. They came mostly from families which could afford to support their idleness. They usually sowed a very small crop of unpublishable literary oats and indulged in mild libertinage with their own kind along the Boulevard Montparnasse: got drunk in the American cafés for a season or two, mastered a few dozen French clichés, read a little, wrote a little, then went home to bourgeois respectability. They were the university wits of their day, following the pleasant fashion of their class, but their creative impulses were largely wishful and soon dissipated.

Henry Miller came from another world. An outcast from the lower middle class, a dropout after two months of college twenty years before, an outsider in his native land, he had worked at a succession of odd jobs and seen more of life than most men. He had no desire to associate with his compatriots in Montparnasse when he first arrived, referring to them scornfully as "the insufferable idiots at the Dôme and the Coupole." And this was more than the usual reflex of the American abroad, to whom all other Americans were a source of embarrassment. Miller had a deep-seated hatred of all things American. For him the United States represented "the air-conditioned nightmare" of technology without a soul. He had come to Europe to get away from America and to find a way of life that would answer to his psychic needs. Like most Montparnasse Americans he was a sentimental expatriate. Unlike them he found what he wanted and succeeded as a writer.

Miller had been to London and was on his way to Madrid, according to his later accounts, when he ran out of money. But the letters he wrote at the time reveal no intention to travel any farther. On his first Sunday in Paris he wondered, "Will I ever get to really understand the true spirit of this people?"—not a question asked by the casual transient. A few weeks later he wrote, "I love it here, I want to stay forever." Paris was the destination toward which he had been moving for years, ever since his friend Emil Schnellock had described it to him. Schnellock, whom Miller had known as a schoolboy, had lived abroad and become a painter. To Miller it was incredible that his friend, "just a Brooklyn boy" like himself, should have been magically transformed into an artist and cosmopolite. No doubt his example more than anything else affected Miller's decision to become a writer at all costs. Years later in *Tropic of Capricorn* Miller was to write:

> Even now, years and years since, even now, when I know Paris like a book, his picture of Paris is still before my eyes, still vivid, still real. Sometimes, after a rain, riding swiftly through the city in a taxi, I catch fleeting glimpses of this Paris he described; just momentary snatches, as in passing the Tuileries, perhaps, or a glimpse of Montmartre, of the Sacré Coeur, through the Rue Laffitte, in the last flush of twilight. . . . Those nights in Prospect Park with my old friend Ulric are responsible, more than anything else, for my being here today.

Miller's wife June also played a crucial role. As Mona or Mara she appears in *Tropic of Capricorn* and other autobiographical romances, an enigmatic figure who entered his life in the early twenties, a Broadway taxi dancer with literary aspirations. Their love was often tempestuous, but through it all she was determined that he would become a writer. She persuaded him to quit his job at Western Union, she worked so that he could write, she found patrons for his work among her admirers by passing herself off as the author. Thus she raised money for a trip to Europe, convinced that he would be able to write there. They went together in 1928, but only on a tour. In 1930 she found the money to send him alone, intending to join him when she had more. As she knew better than Miller, he had reached a dead end in New York.

In one of his first letters from Paris in 1930 he voiced his deep sense of frustration: "I can't understand my failure. . . . Why does nobody want what I write? Jesus, when I think of being 38, and poor, and unknown, I get furious." By the time he landed in Paris he had been writing for eight years. He had completed four books and countless stories and articles. Only three articles had ever been published. Discouraged by poverty, debts, and the fact that his wife had to work so that he could lead "the true life of the artist," he still yearned for the comforts of bourgeois life. These contradictory feelings of guilt and self-pity, the compulsion to succeed and the interpretation of success as money, were all neuroses of Protestant America, with its gospel of work and wealth. In Paris Miller was never troubled by such worries. Though he lived more parasitically and marginally than ever, he was psychologically liberated as he had never been in New York. Hence the euphoric mood that marks all his writing during the decade he spent in Paris. There at last he was able to write, on the first page of *Tropic of Cancer:* "I have no money, no resources, no hopes. I am the happiest man alive. A year ago, six months ago, I thought that I was an artist. I no longer think about it, I *am.*"

Miller's first impressions of Paris—and the most reliable account of his first eighteen months there—are to be found in the letters he wrote to Emil Schnellock at the time. His first letter, written three days after his arrival, announces: "I will write here. I will live quietly and quite alone. And each day I will see a little more of Paris, study it, learn it as I would a book. It is worth the effort. To know Paris is to know a great deal. How vastly different from New York! What eloquent surprises at every turn of the street. To get lost here is the adventure extraordinary. The streets sing, the stones talk. The houses drip history, glory, romance." From the start he liked everything about the city, its cosmopolitan atmosphere, the variety of people, their nonconformity. "Here is the greatest congregation of bizarre types. People do dress as they please, wear beards if they like, and shave if they choose. You don't feel that lifeless pressure of dull regimentation as in N. Y. and London."

The letters written within a month of his arrival are full of wonder and delight. Everything is new and charming, the language, the way of counting, the procedure in the restaurants, the tipping. The police are allowed to smoke on duty. Gourmet meals are cheap. The writing in the newspapers and magazines is intelligent and sophisticated. Miller was prepared to see good in everything, from the fifty thousand artists of Paris selling their work to an appreciative public to the custodian in the underground toilet writing a love letter, happy with her lot, unlike the silly stenographer in a New York skyscraper. As on his previous visit he was overcome by the setting, particularly at night. "I am on the verge of tears. The beauty of it all is suffocating me. . . . I am fairly intoxicated with the glamour of the city." His second letter, sixteen pages long, describes that emotion peculiar to the place, *la nostalgie de Paris,* nostalgia that can be experienced at the moment itself.

At the same time Paris gave him an inexhaustible supply of material and the urge to write. Within three weeks of his arrival he reported, "I have added a hundred pages to my book and done excellent revision work also. No water colors. I am overwhelmed yet by the multifarious, quotidien, anonymous, communal, etc. etc. *life!*" The program announced in his first letter of exploring the city and writing about it was carried out in a number of long letters written during his first two months or so. Actually these were not letters at all, but feature articles for circulation to magazine editors and for eventual use in a book on Paris Miller planned to write. Bearing such titles as "Spring on the Trottoirs" and "With the Wine Merchants," they usually described itineraries in quest of local color.

Paris was always a great city for walkers, and Miller was one of its most tireless pedestrians, covering enormous distances in his search for the picturesque. The paintings he had seen colored his vision so that wherever he went he found scenes from Monet, Pissarro, Seurat. In painting even more than literature Paris has always drawn its lovers back toward the past. Miller was particularly susceptible to this nostalgia for a city he had never known, regretting that he had been born too late. Many years later, in *Big Sur and the Oranges of Hieronymus Bosch,* he was still wishing he had been there as a young man:

> What would I not give to have been the comrade

or bosom friend of such figures as Apollinaire, Douanier Rousseau, George Moore, Max Jacob, Vlaminck, Utrillo, Derain, Cendrars, Gauguin, Modigliani, Cingria, Picabia, Maurice Magre, Léon Daudet, and such like. How much greater would have been the thrill to cycle along the Seine, cross and recross her bridges, race through towns like Bougival, Châtou, Argenteuil, Marly-le-roi, Puteaux, Rambouillet, Issyles-Moulineaux and similar environs circa 1910 rather than the year 1932 or 1933!

Actually the world he yearned for was older than 1910; it was the impressionists' Arcadia painted in that string of sparkling villages along the Seine before they were industrialized into grimy suburbs.

Although somewhat self-conscious as literary compositions, the Paris letters marked an important stage in Miller's writing. They were good exercises, and they provided him with plenty of material that he was soon to use in his own way. Miller thought he was writing a book on Paris to match Paul Morand's slick guided tour of New York, which he had been reading with considerable envy at its success. He hoped his impressions might amount to "something popular, saleable, palatable." Unwittingly he was already at work on *Tropic of Cancer*. The letters contain the earliest writing that was to go into that book. One of them in particular, entitled "Bistre and Pigeon Dung," contains several passages that Miller saved and later wove into the fabric of his book. Here is one that reappears on one of the opening pages of *Tropic of Cancer*, only slightly revised:

> Twilight hour, Indian blue, water of glass, trees glistening and liquescent. Juares station itself gives me a kick. The rails fall away into the canal, the long caterpillar with sides lacquered in Chinese red dips like a roller-coaster. It is not Paris, it is not Coney Island—it is crepuscular melange of all the cities of Europe and Central America. Railroad yards spread out below me, the tracks looking black, webby, not ordered by engineers but cataclysmic in design, like those gaunt fissures in the Polar ice which the camera registers in degrees of black.

Another passage in the same letter describes a nude by Dufresne with "all the secondary characteristics and a few of the primary," likening it to a thirteenth-century *déjeuner intime,* a vibrant still life, the table so heavy with food that it is sliding out of its frame—exactly as it appears at the beginning of the second chapter of *Tropic of Cancer*. Still another passage describes the animated street market in the rue de Buci on a Sunday morning, then moves on to the quiet Square de Furstenberg nearby, providing a page at the beginning of the third chapter of the book. Here is Miller's original description of the Square de Furstenberg, a spot that particularly appealed to him:

> A deserted spot, bleak, spectral at night, containing in the center four black trees which have not yet begun to blossom. These four bare trees have the poetry of T. S. Eliot. They are intellectual trees, nourished by the stones, swaying with a rhythm cerebral, the lines punctuated by dots and dashes, by asterisks and exclamation points.

Here, if Marie Laurencin ever brought her Lesbians out into the open, would be the place for them to commune. It is very, very Lesbienne here, very sterile, hybrid, full of forbidden longings.

When he incorporated this passage into *Tropic of Cancer,* Miller revised for economy and sharpness of outline, but kept the imagery unchanged. The original, written in April 1930, shows his particular vision of the city; he had yet to discover how to use it.

"Bistre and Pigeon Dung" was probably rattled off in one day, like other fifteen- or twenty-page letters. Under the stimulation of Paris Miller was indefatigable: "I feel that I could turn out a book a month here. If I could get a stenographer to go to bed with me I could carry on twenty-four hours a day." Walking in the city was a creative act in itself. He was forever composing in his head as he walked, the writing as vivid to him as if he had put it down on paper. Sometimes he could not remember what he had actually written and had to ask Schnellock. His books of the thirties were all to be written in this state of exaltation, as he walked around Paris in the present tense.

Other letters anticipate *Tropic of Cancer* even more in spirit. Miller lost no time in getting acquainted with the most squalid sights. He had always been attracted to the ghetto and the slums; now he often painted the ugliest street scenes.

> I looked around and there stood a brazen wench, leaning against her door like a lazy slut, cigarette between her lips, sadly rouged and frizzled, old, seamed, scarred, cracked, evil greedy eyes. She jerked her head a few times inviting me to come back and inspect her place, but my eyes were set on a strange figure tugging away at some bales. An old man with enormous goitres completely circling his neck, standing out below the hairline like huge polyps, from under his chin hanging loosely, joggling, purplish, veined, like gourds of wine—transparent gourds. Here the breed is degenerate and diseased. Old women with white hair, mangy, red lips, demented, prowl about in carpet slippers, their clothes in tatters, soiled with garbage and filth of the gutters.

This was Quasimodo's Paris, he pointed out, visible from the towers of Notre Dame, the inhabitants no different from those in the Middle Ages. But there was nothing romantic about the way he saw them. "They have bed-bugs, cockroaches and fleas running all over them, they are syphilitic, cancerous, dropsical, they are halt and blind, paralyzed, and their brains are soft."

Picturesque and sordid, this is Miller's Paris. Here even more than in the passages he actually used can *Tropic of Cancer* be anticipated. Again and again he dwelt with relish on the cancerous street scenes he found in the old quarters. He also explored the uglier regions of the modern industrial city, walking through endless dead stretches of suburb, bleak neighborhoods like those of his native Yorkville or Brooklyn. Paris provided local color of the particular kind that appealed to his imagination. Some six or seven weeks after his arrival he listed the topics he wanted to write about, including in addition to such standard items as the flea market, the six-day bicycle races, and the Grand Guignol, some that appealed to his rather special tastes: the slaughterhouses, the mummies at the Trocadéro, the Moslem cemetery, sexual perversions, the pissoirs, a comparative study of toilets on the Left Bank and toilets on the Right Bank. As this list suggests, Miller took particular delight in all that was unappetizing and macabre.

Miller's accounts of his first two months in Paris are full of enthusiasm. His feelings never changed, but the idyll soon ended. The troubles recorded in *Tropic of Cancer* were just beginning: the long walks to American Express for the check that never arrived, the constant change of address, the search for cheap hotels, soon followed by homelessness and hunger. He had arrived with enough money to last him till the middle of April and with expectations that his wife would send more. By the latter part of April his money had run out, and he had to go without food for five days. Then he received a small amount, not enough to last long, for in early May he was penniless again and desperate enough to think of looking for a job. A week later he was solvent again, quoting prices and urging Schnellock to come to Paris where he would show him how to live on less than twenty-five dollars a week. Miller's standards were still fairly grand.

As his circumstances grew progressively worse, his notions of poverty became more realistic. In August he was living with Monsieur Nanavati, the Hindu he calls Mr. Nonentity in *Tropic of Cancer,* and complaining of his lot as a servant: "Life is very hard for me—very. I live with bed-bugs and cockroaches. I sweep the dirty carpets, wash the dishes, eat stale bread without butter. Terrible life. Honest!" After that his friend Alfred Perlès took care of Miller off and on, sneaking him past his concierge and hiding him in his hotel room; Perlès worked at night, so Miller could sleep in his bed then.

He became well acquainted with hunger and vagrancy and discovered that the climate was miserable most of the year. October was rainy and cold. June came for a visit, but she brought no money and stayed only three weeks under wretched circumstances. Miller began to realize that he could not live on hopes indefinitely and resigned himself to leaving before long. Several letters mentioned plans to return to New York. But he managed to hang on till December, when he found a friend who took him in for the winter. Then his constant obsession was food: "What we artists need is food—and lots more of it. No art without food." Phagomania, his chronic complaint, is as prominent as lust in *Tropic of Cancer.*

He spent the winter months in a studio with a view of the Eiffel Tower. Ten years later he dedicated *The Wisdom of the Heart* to the man who took him in, Richard Galen Osborn, "who rescued me from starvation in Paris and set my feet in the right direction." Osborn was a Connecticut Yankee who worked in a bank by day and indulged his fondness for French culture in all its forms by night. He liked to talk with Miller about modern French writers, he liked to drink Anjou, and he had a weakness for the ladies. One day he added a third member to the household, the Russian princess who appears in *Tropic of Cancer* as

Masha. The book presents a fairly faithful portrait of their absurd *ménage à trois* based on a letter Miller wrote to Schnellock at the time: "Irene has the clap, Osborn has bronchitis, and I have the piles." The letter records Irene's dialogue for four pages, later reproduced almost verbatim when the episode was expanded into half a chapter. Osborn wrote his own story about their life together, "No. 2 Rue Auguste Bartholdi," presenting the same basic circumstances from another point of view and rather unexpectedly portraying Miller as a man who worked all the time.

In the same letter Miller described the full beard he grew that winter, a shaggy, dark red beard that would soon make him look like Dostoevsky. According to *Tropic of Cancer,* he grew the beard at the request of a painter, who then did his portrait with his typewriter in the foreground and the Eiffel Tower in the background. The painter was John Nichols, a great talker who regaled Miller with anecdotes about the artists he knew and who accompanied him to that favorite resort of painters, the Cirque Médrano, where they had "a fine Seurat night." Miller, who always sought the company of painters, acquired many artist friends in Paris. When Osborn had to give up the studio, Miller went off to stay with a sculptor, Fred Kann, who lived near the Montparnasse cemetery.

Nichols' portrait has vanished along with the beard, but a verbal portrait survives from about the same period in an article that appeared in the Paris edition of the *Chicago Tribune* with a caricature of Miller by the Hungarian artist Brassaï. The writer was an American newspaperman with the unlikely name of Wambly Bald who wrote a weekly column called *"La Vie de Bohème."* What he had to say was not particularly memorable, except as evidence that Miller was already a notorious character who in his daily life enacted the role he was about to turn into literature. The role came to him naturally; he was simply acting himself as a *clochard,* a Paris bum. He was of course fully aware of the impression he created and capable of exploiting it. He could even have ghost-written the article himself, for he often wrote Bald's weekly column; and certainly the man who wrote *Tropic of Cancer* was not above self-portraiture. Miller returned the compliment by depicting Bald—probably without the least malice—as his most scabrous character.

After a year in Paris Miller calculated that he could live on six dollars a week, if only he had it, but actually he was living on nothing at all. How he managed is explained by Alfred Perlès in *My Friend Henry Miller:* "Henry was always to be seen at one or the other of the terraces, the Dôme or the Coupole, surrounded by people he had just met or was just meeting. Impossible to say how he picked them up and where and why." After his first few months in Paris Miller had overcome his prejudices against the Montparnasse cafés, finding them good places to cadge food and drink. He had a great talent for making friends, and as he explains in *Tropic of Cancer,* "It's not hard to make friends when you squat on a *terrasse* twelve hours a day. You get to know every sot in Montparnasse. They cling to you like lice, even if you have nothing to offer them but your ears." Eventually he worked out a rotating dinner schedule with his friends, dining with a different friend every evening of the week. Sometimes he performed small services in exchange, giving English lessons or walking a child in the Luxembourg Gardens. But usually his friends were only too willing to feed him for the pleasure of his company. He was a most ingratiating person, a spellbinding talker, and a man of completely unaffected charm. Perlès observed that people loved to watch him eat and drink.

Miller did not begin writing *Tropic of Cancer* until the end of August 1931, but everything he experienced during that first year and a half in Paris went into the book as substance or style, the world's rottenness or his crazy hallucinated vision of it, that particular combination of "cancer and delirium" which gives the book its own very special atmosphere. By the time he began writing the book he had thoroughly explored the lower depths. What he had seen and heard would have depressed any other man beyond words; Miller was fully alive to it but buoyed up by his sense of humor, and because he had gone to rock bottom himself, elated that he had survived, more alive than ever. Then at last he succeeded in writing what had been bottled up inside him for so many years.

Toward the end of his first year in Paris he took stock of himself and his writing. To Schnellock he reported the opinions of friends who urged him to stay on: "I'm supposed to be a guy with promise. Besides that, I'm supposed to be a *romantic*. People wonder and shake their heads. How is it that things happen to that guy the way they do? Always in the midst of exciting things, adventures, confessions, etc. But the question in my mind is: what am I doing for literature?" He was still trying to finish the manuscript he had brought with him from New York, probably the novel called "Crazy Cock," [published as *Crazy Cock*, 1991] but was disgusted with it, unable to express his true feelings, boxed in by too much careful plotting and form. When he finished he wanted to burst through all such barriers. "I will explode in the Paris book. The hell with form, style, expression and all those pseudo-paramount things which beguile the critics. I want to get myself across this time—and direct as a knife thrust." In another letter written about the same time he gloried in the life he was leading: "Great days—full of missing meals—but rich in paint, verbiage and local scenery. Getting into such a bummy condition that people everywhere nudge one another and point me out." Despite hunger and hardship he felt he had lived more richly during one year in Paris than in all the rest of his life. Here is the protagonist of *Tropic of Cancer:* "I feel now exactly as all the great vagabond artists must have felt—absolutely reckless, childish, irresponsible, unscrupulous, and overflowing with carnal vitality, vigor, ginger, etc. Always on the border of insanity, due to worry, hunger, etc. But shoving along, day after day." Finally on August 24, 1931, having finished his novel at last, he announced that he was ready to go to work on the book he had been wanting to write: "I start tomorrow on the Paris book: first person, uncensored, formless—fuck everything!"

At the end of his second summer in Paris, Miller worked for a time as a proofreader for the Paris edition of the *Chi-* *cago Tribune*. His friend Perlès, who earned his small income as a proofreader, got him the job. Miller disapproved of jobs on principle but liked this one. He enjoyed the atmosphere of the newspaper office, the noise of the machinery, and the company of his fellow workers, especially the typesetters who were all like characters out of a French novel. Working at night had a charm all its own. Every evening he, Perlès, and Wambly Bald would make their long walk across Paris to the newspaper office. After work they would eat in a nearby bistro, the favorite haunt of pimps, whores, newspapermen, and others who worked by night. Then in the early morning hours, when all Paris was deserted, they would walk home again. Though Miller worked only a short time for the newspaper, the impressions of that time remained among the most vivid of his Paris years. Of the many writers and would-be writers who worked on the *Tribune* or the Paris edition of the *New York Herald,* only Miller and Bravig Imbs have given any sense of the atmosphere. Most of the journalists' accounts are full of sophomoric clichés.

Although Miller preferred the subterranean drudgery of proofreading to the more exalted editorial work upstairs, he was only too willing to be published in a newspaper, even anonymously or pseudonymously. Long before he was employed by the *Tribune* he wrote feature articles for that paper's Sunday edition. Only employees were supposed to contribute such articles, so Perlès submitted them as his own. In his biography Perlès reprints one of these articles, "Rue Lourmel in Fog," which is very much like the impressionistic compositions Miller had sent to Schnellock when he first arrived in Paris. Other articles appeared in the *Tribune* or in the *Herald* during his first year in Paris: "The Cirque Médrano," "The Six-Day Bike Race," "Paris in *Ut Mineur.*" The usual rate was fifty francs, and once Miller received three hundred and fifty francs, but the important thing was that he was getting his work published readily for the first time in his life. He had tried to write for newspapers and popular magazines in the past, but with no success.

During his second year in Paris Miller's work also appeared in a literary magazine for the first time, Samuel Putnam's recently founded *New Review*. Putnam was a scholarly newspaper correspondent who had come to Paris in 1926 to translate Rabelais. Besides the standard modern translation of that difficult author, he produced translations of contemporary authors ranging from François Mauriac to Kiki. For all his mastery of the written language, Putnam spoke French with such an abominable accent as to be almost unintelligible. He was a steady customer of the Montparnasse bars, where Miller probably met him about the time he quit as associate editor of *This Quarter* and decided to found his own quarterly. Miller appeared twice in the *New Review* and edited one issue with Perlès. Putnam made the mistake of asking them to see the magazine through the press when he had to go to America for a visit. They promptly threw out some of the contents they found boring, including a long article by Putnam, and put in material they thought livelier, including a story by Miller. They also decided to add a supplement, a bawdy, vituperative, nonsensical parody of all manifestoes called "The New Instinctivism," denouncing everything: "A proclamation of rebellion against the puerilities of art and literature, a manifesto of disgust, a gob of spit in the cuspidor of post-war conceits, a healthy crap in the cradle of still-born deities." When the printers sent proofs to Putnam, he quashed the supplement, but the review appeared with the contents Miller and Perlès had chosen.

Miller first appeared in the *New Review* as a film critic. The second number, which came out in the summer of 1931, included his review entitled **"Buñuel or Thus Cometh to an End Everywhere the Golden Age."** Miller, who had been a cineast since childhood, was delighted to be in Paris where he could see avant-garde films that were never shown in New York. On the first Sunday after his arrival he had made a pilgrimage to Studio 28 in Montmartre to see one of the great surrealist films, *Un Chien Andalou,* made by Buñuel in collaboration with Dali the previous year. A week or so later he went to a ciné club meeting and was impressed by the brilliant discussion. By October 1930 he had made friends with the film maker Germaine Dulac, who promised June an important role in a talkie that was to be made in two or three months; nothing ever came of this proposal, and Madame Dulac, whom Miller described as "one of the celebrated Lesbiennes of Paris and all Europe," may have had only a passing interest in June. Toward the end of October he saw the new Buñuel-Dali film, *L'Age d'Or,* and in December he sent Schnellock a draft of his article for the *New Review*. His admiration for Buñuel never diminished. In the mid-thirties he paid tribute to him again in a long article on the cinematic art entitled **"The Golden Age."** Less explicit but even more pervasive is the influence of Buñuel's films on certain surrealist sequences in Miller's writing, particularly "Into the Night Life" in *Black Spring*.

Miller's first published story, **"Mademoiselle Claude,"** appeared in the third number of the *New Review* in the fall of 1931. That story marks the actual beginning of his literary career, announcing all the characteristics of the *Tropics*—the first person monologue, the progressive narrative moving into the present tense, with events happening and time passing as the story unfurls. Here too are the tropical moral values—the generous whore who is almost an angel, the narrator-*maquereau* who wants to be a saint. He finds her customers to keep her from being sad, and they end up going to the clinic together every day, more in love than ever. Even the imagery is here: "Paris looks to me like a big, ugly chancre. The streets are gangrened. Everybody has it—if it isn't clap it's syphilis. All Europe is diseased, and it's France who's made it diseased."

The style anticipates *Tropic of Cancer* with its flowing rhythms:

> The idea, though, of waking up in the morning, the sun streaming in the windows and a good, faithful whore beside you who loves you, who loves the guts out of you, the birds singing and the table all spread, and while she's washing up and combing her hair, all the men she's been with and now you, just you, and barges going by, masts and hulls, the whole damned current of life flowing through you, through her, through all the guys before you and maybe after, the

> flowers and the birds and the sun streaming in and the fragrance of it choking you, annihilating you. O Christ! Give me a whore always, all the time!

Miller liked that long sentence well enough to quote part of it in *Tropic of Cancer.*

Miller was fascinated by the Paris whores. On his first Sunday in Paris he had noted with surprise: "Montmartre is simply lousy with whores. Little bars, hardly bigger than a coffin, are jammed with them." The imagery is typical, if not the reaction. "Wow! they make you shiver those dolled-up spectres. They sit in the cafés and beckon to you from the window, or bunk smack up against you on the street, and invite you to come along." By May he had found his first girl friend, a whore named Germaine. In December he wrote, "And who is Mlle. Claude? Ah, the prettiest, juiciest, cleverest little cocotte in Montparnasse. Osborn and I share her once in a while. Such taste, such discretion, such politesse." He found her intelligent, well-read, animated, and refined. He recommended her to Schnellock, who could address her in care of the Coupole. Though the letter ends half-humorously, sounding like an advertisement, Claude is described in similar terms in *Tropic of Cancer,* but compared unfavorably with that ordinary hustler Germaine, who according to the book, served as the real model for the story. "She was a whore all the way through," Miller concludes, "and that was her virtue!"

By the time **"Mademoiselle Claude"** appeared in print Miller had started writing *Tropic of Cancer*. He had already met most of the characters and had most of the experiences that went into the narrative. But there is more to that book than mere storytelling; *Tropic of Cancer* dramatizes a particular outlook, a satiric blend of humor and iconoclasm, a fiercely critical view of the world. In the fall of 1931 Miller was being exposed to some of the ideas that gave the book its philosophical bias. He then lived for a time with Michael Fraenkel, a prophet of doom whose theories appear in the first two chapters and elsewhere. On the opening page Miller summarizes Fraenkel's death philosophy, complete with Fraenkel's favorite weather metaphor.

> Boris has just given me a summary of his views. He is a weather prophet. The weather will continue bad, he says. There will be more calamities, more death, more despair. Not the slightest indication of a change anywhere. The cancer of time is eating us away. Our heroes have killed themselves, or are killing themselves. The hero, then, is not Time, but Timelessness. We must get in step, a lock step, toward the prison of death. There is no escape. The weather will not change.

There is usually a note of ridicule in Miller's treatment of Fraenkel's ideas, but he also admits that Fraenkel is one of the two writers he respects, the other being Perlès. The reason he takes them seriously is that, unlike other writers he knows, these two have fervor. "They are possessed. They glow inwardly with a white flame. They are mad and tone deaf. They are sufferers."

Fraenkel was a small intense man with a goatee who bore

a marked resemblance to Trotsky. Born in Russia and brought to the United States as a boy, he became the greatest book salesman in America and saved enough money to retire at the age of thirty in 1926. He had always wanted to write, and Paris seemed the best place for a writer to go. His writing was the product of a philosophical mind obsessed with one subject, the spiritual death of modern man as symbolized by the millions of deaths of the Great War. His friend Walter Lowenfels plays upon the central paradox of Fraenkel's life in an unpublished biographical sketch, "The Life of Fraenkel's Death," pointing out that Fraenkel earned his living in America so that he could retire in Europe to write about death.

Lowenfels himself followed a similar pattern. He too had been in business in America, the family butter business which he later treated as something of a joke, contrasting butter with poetry, and which he quit at the age of twenty-nine, having decided to go to Europe to write. His ideas were akin to Fraenkel's, though not nearly so extreme. At the time they became friends he had just finished an elegy on Apollinaire. Under the influence of Fraenkel he then took death as his central theme and wrote a sequence of elegies called *Some Deaths,* lamenting the suicides of poets such as Hart Crane and Harry Crosby, René Crevel and Jacques Rigaut. Fraenkel and Lowenfels also formed what they called an anonymous school, writing books together anonymously in the spirit of French writers and painters before them. In *Tropic of Cancer* Miller jokes about an anonymous collaboration proposed by Fraenkel, to be called "The Last Book," and some years later Miller and Fraenkel actually did collaborate on a book, the *Hamlet* correspondence, which was published by Fraenkel's Carrefour Press.

Miller became acquainted with Fraenkel about the time he started writing *Tropic of Cancer.* Lowenfels and Fraenkel had already been in league for two years or more. Now the three of them formed what Lowenfels calls "the avant-garde of death." Neither he nor Miller took Fraenkel's monomania altogether seriously. "Henry and I really joked about Fraenkel's death business—turning it into something else, something we could use in our business, which was, say what you like, writing." Fraenkel was useful to Miller in more immediate ways, for he owned an apartment building at 18 Villa Seurat and was better off than Miller's other friends. A number of people have claimed an influence on Miller when he was still unknown, but their most important contribution at this time was keeping him alive. This was Lowenfels' motive in bringing Miller and Fraenkel together, this and Fraenkel's need for an intelligent audience, which was as great as Miller's need for bed and board.

The Miller-Fraenkel relationship was a strange and amusing one, founded on phagomania and the death obsession and kept alive by talk. Both men were prodigious talkers. Miller remembers that Fraenkel used to drop in at breakfast time, stay through lunch, through dinner, and far into the evening, talking, talking all the time, leaving Miller exhausted. Fraenkel in turn was overwhelmed by Miller's talk. "It was extraordinary, amazing, incredible. A compulsion mechanism, a kind of sickness, if you like, something pathological." But he also adds, "It was talk of the highest order I ever heard." Though by nature stingy and indifferent to food, Fraenkel would occasionally buy Miller a meal just to be able to keep talking. In *Tropic of Cancer* Miller complains that there is not a scrap of food in the house. He also registers a feeling of impermanence, fearing his chair will be pulled out from under him as he types. Fraenkel, ever the businessman, rented out apartments and soon evicted Miller by renting the room he occupied. Miller liked the Villa Seurat and returned there to live three years later; meanwhile his discussions with Fraenkel continued and turned into correspondence when Fraenkel traveled about the world.

Years later, in an article entitled "The Genesis of the *Tropic of Cancer,*" Fraenkel reminisced about the beginning of their acquaintance: "And then one day Walter told me about a strange man he had run across in Montparnasse, a fellow called Miller. He was described as one of tremendous vitality, zest, enthusiasm, an amazing talker, without visible means of support, a kind of derelict, but gay and happy withal, alive. 'Not alive exactly,' he said, 'but certainly not dead. Alive in a kind of confused, old-fashioned way. An interesting chap. Why not drop him a line, a *pneu?* He is down and out and maybe he can do some typing for you.' And then with a twinkle in his eye: 'Take him on. Just your meat.' Did he perhaps see a possible disciple in him?" According to Fraenkel there were no preliminaries between them, no reservations; they immediately talked to each other like old friends. Fraenkel gave Miller his book *Werther's Younger Brother,* a self-portrait ending in suicide. Miller responded with a long enthusiastic fan letter which Fraenkel quotes: "You say things that no one in America is saying—that I would dearly love to say myself." Miller, who had been told that Fraenkel's book was pessimistic and confused, "found everything touched with a wild beauty, and if there were disorder, then it was, as Bergson said, an order of disorder which is another order."

Though Fraenkel claims too much credit for his influence on *Tropic of Cancer,* he gives the best explanation on record of Miller's state of mind at the time. And though he was only the latest in a series of friends to advise Miller to write spontaneously, his insight may have been the clearest. Certainly his advice was most timely. Beneath Miller's restless confusion Fraenkel detected a determination to be himself. Miller had come to Paris to make a new start but had not yet found himself. When Fraenkel read Miller's novel in manuscript, "Crazy Cock," he immediately saw that Miller was trying to write for the publishers, not for himself.

> By this time I knew the sort of person he was, impulsive, erratic, anarchic, a mass of contradictory moods, ideas, feelings, and I told him to sit down before the machine and white paper and write anything and everything that came to his mind, as it came, red-hot, and to hell with the editors and the public. Write as you talk, I told him. Write as you live. Write as you feel and think. Just sit down before the machine and let go—tell everything you are going through now; you've got all the material you want right in this,

in what you are thinking and feeling and going
through *now.*

As they talked endlessly of death, Miller found the theme
that could integrate his creative impulses and give him the
direction he lacked. His obscenity, his violence, his inner
chaos, and love of corruption are all expressions of "The
Death Theme." So Fraenkel thought at any rate, though
at times his disciples may have had their little joke at his
expense. Lowenfels wonders whether the Fraenkel they
remember is not a creature of their imagination. He feels
that Fraenkel did not come through very well in his own
writing. A greater thinker than writer, he left more of himself in the writings of others, in Miller's early work and
Lowenfels' poems written between 1929 and 1934. Lowenfels also remarks that Fraenkel was at his best when writing under the stimulus of Miller. No doubt they inspired
each other, but long before he met Fraenkel, Miller was
steeped in the thinking of Oswald Spengler, whose apocalyptic view he had taken as his own. Miller had in fact re-
read the first volume of *The Decline of the West* since coming to Paris and in doing so had concluded that Spengler
was the greatest of contemporary writers, greater than
Joyce, Mann, or even Proust. "There is great music, great
literature, great ideas." Surely his thinking in *Tropic of
Cancer* was fired by Spengler, though Fraenkel undoubtedly fanned the flames.

The book that most immediately anticipated *Tropic of
Cancer* was Louis-Ferdinand Céline's first novel, *Voyage
au Bout de la Nuit.* Not only the Spenglerian sense of
doom is there, but the very idiom and tone, the picaresque
narrative and the gallows humor that Miller adopted. Céline's *Voyage* is another episodic autobiographical novel
that dwells on all that is vicious, treacherous, sadistic, obscene, diseased, and repulsive in human nature. The central character is an underdog adventurer who lives by luck
and by his wits. Céline's favorite setting is the ugly, working-class Paris where he was born and where he practiced
medicine, though he also traveled about the world like
Candide, finding inhumanity wherever he went. His experience eventually drove him to bitter misanthropy, but his
first book achieved a balance between laughter and pessimism that is much the same as Miller's comic treatment
of inherently tragic matter. After reading *Voyage au Bout
de la Nuit* it is easier to understand *Tropic of Cancer,* for
Céline's war experience exposes the "civilization" that
both writers attacked. Céline lost his innocence in the
Great War, suffered shell shock, was cured of his illusions,
learned to distrust all ideals and to place the law of self-
preservation above all others. Miller, despite his imagery
of trench warfare and poison gas, had no direct experience
to compare with Céline's, yet he had gone through the
same process of disenchantment, emerging with even
fewer scruples. He too had become a militant anarchist,
declaring war on society.

Despite the many striking parallels between the two
books, Céline and Miller produced their works quite independently. Miller had finished the first draft of *Tropic of
Cancer* before the publication of *Voyage au Bout de la
Nuit* in November 1932. He read the book soon after it appeared and was overwhelmed, although he found it difficult reading and had to spend a week isolated in a hotel

room with a dictionary to decipher its colloquial French.
During the next two years he was to revise his own book
three times before it appeared in print, so conceivably Céline could have influenced the rewriting. But the letters to
Schnellock reveal that Miller had found his style and subject matter before he had ever heard of Céline. It was simply another case of two writers responding to their time
and place with the same perceptions.

Like Céline's novel, *Tropic of Cancer* is autobiographical,
but it is not to be taken as documentary. Although Miller
protests that he is writing the plain unvarnished truth, this
gambit is one of the oldest in fiction. He is closer to fact
than most novelists, but his method is theirs, his powerful
imagination producing a metamorphosis as it colors and
heightens the original circumstances. Miller has confessed
that he has difficulty remembering what he imagined and
what actually happened.

Tropic of Cancer gives a more or less fictionalized account, then, of the adventures of a character named Henry
Miller who explored the lower depths in Paris during the
depression. The book is a jumble of sensations, reflections,
conversations, encounters, and hallucinations, all filtered
through the consciousness of its narrator in the first person, present tense. The chaos is deliberate, for Miller
wanted to put down impressions and thoughts as they occurred to him, to depict a man "in the grip of delirium."
He also wanted "to get off the gold standard of literature,"
to write without revising, and to record "all that which is
omitted in books."

Tropic of Cancer is sometimes compared to *The Sun Also
Rises,* not for the similarities but for the differences between them. The comparison is absurd yet apt, for it
shows how much the world had changed between the mid-
twenties and the early thirties. Henry Miller's adventures
in Paris present a burlesque of the expatriate romance. Instead of a potentially tragic hero, the protagonist is a
clown whose escapades mock all sense of human dignity.
Instead of investing his characters with a glamour that ex-
cuses their faults, Miller caricatures his friends, bringing
out all that is grotesque, ludicrous, or contemptible in
their private lives. He also sees his surroundings in a jaun-
diced light and thereby makes more meaningful use of his
Paris scenery. For Hemingway Montparnasse provided an
appropriate backdrop, a likely setting for the lost generation, but his characters stayed on the surface and could
just as well have dissipated elsewhere. Miller penetrated
far deeper into Paris than any other American writer and
projected a vision of the city that was altogether different.
He succeeded only as Céline had done in making its ugliness symbolic of private and universal anguish, a sordid
modern-day inferno, a labyrinth of cancer and despair.

Jane A. Nelson   (essay date 1970)

SOURCE: "Fragmentation and Confession in *Tropic of
Cancer,*" in her *Form and Image in the Fiction of Henry
Miller,* Wayne State University Press, 1970, pp. 19-49.

[*Nelson is an American critic and educator. In the following excerpt, she analyzes the structure of* Tropic of Cancer
using Jungian theories of unconscious, primitive archetypes

> [What Miller articulated] was the disgust, the contempt, the hostility, the violence, and the sense of filth with which our culture, or more specifically, its masculine sensibility, surrounds sexuality. And women too; for somehow it is women upon whom this onerous burden of sexuality falls.
>
> —*Kate Millett, in her* Sexual Politics, *1969.*

and Erich Neumann's writings on ancient myths about the "primordial Great Mother."]

The demonic, obsessive quality of the erotic experience in Henry Miller's fiction has been sufficiently recognized, as have the Medusa characteristics of his women. This recognition, however, has not led his critics to examine the formal functions these darker aspects of the erotic have in his work. Kingsley Widmer in his remarks on Miller's obsession with the Dark Lady even asserts the contrary, arguing [in his *Henry Miller,* 1963] that this important theme does not provide a significant measure of concentration in individual works. Instead, in a chapter devoted to an analysis of **Tropic of Cancer,** he finds the disorder of Miller's world the only important ordering principle:

> If the discrete fragments, as in the first two chapters of **Tropic of Cancer,** seem beyond order, then the very disorder, by imitative form, gives the quality of his "anecdotal life."

Probably the term *fragmentation* best describes what happens in these first two chapters of **Cancer,** but not in the sense Widmer intends when he charges that this and the following sections have no formal unity. The moments sharply and brutally created by the imagery are not as entirely discrete as Widmer finds them. Many of them are part of a constellation of images revealing the outlines of a single archetypal image. The presentation of these images may be described as an attempt to dramatize the hero's confrontation with the archetypal and primordial figures of the Terrible Mother, the negative aspect of the Great Mother archetype described by Jung and others from their studies of myth, literature, religion, and clinical phenomena. Erich Neumann's account of the psychological process of fragmentation [in *The Origins and History of Consciousness,* 1954] suggests the parallel literary process in **Tropic of Cancer** through which this archetypal figure begins to emerge:

> The power of the primordial Great Mother archetype rests on the original state where everything is intermingled and undifferentiated, not to be grasped because ever in flux. Only later do images emerge from this basal unity, forming a group of related archetypes and symbols revolving about this indescribable center. The wealth of images, qualities, and symbols is essentially a product of the fragmentation effected by a con-

sciousness which perceives, discriminates, divides, and registers from a distance. *Determinatio est negatio.* The multiplicity of images corresponds to a multiplicity of possible attitudes and possible reactions of consciousness, contrasted with the original total-reaction that seizes upon primitive man.

> The overpowering dynamism of the archetype is now held in check: it no longer releases paroxysms of dread, madness, ecstasy, delirium, and death. The unbearable white radiance of primordial light is broken up by the prism of consciousness into a multicolored rainbow of images and symbols. Thus from the image of the Great Mother the Good Mother is split off, recognized by consciousness, and established in the conscious world as a value. The other part, the Terrible Mother, is in our culture repressed and largely excluded from the conscious world.

The archetype appears in groups of symbols, some human, some not:

> Delayed reaction and de-emotionalization run parallel to this splitting of the archetype into groups of symbols. The ego ceases to be overwhelmed as consciousness becomes more capable of assimilating and understanding the individual symbols. The world grows clearer, orientation is more possible, and consciousness is enlarged. An anonymous and amorphous primal deity is inconceivably frightful; it is stupendous and unapproachable, incomprehensible and impossible to manipulate. The ego experiences its formlessness as something inhuman and hostile, if indeed it ever tackles the impossible task of experiencing it. So we often find an inhuman god at the beginning in the form of a beast, or some horrid anomaly and monster of miscegenation. These hideous creatures are expressions of the ego's inability to experience the featurelessness of the primal deity. The more anthropomorphic the world of gods becomes, the closer it is to the ego and the more it loses its overwhelming character. The Olympian gods are far more human and familiar than the primeval goddess of chaos.

I am making extensive use of this convenient correlation between mythology and psychology for two reasons. First, Neumann's explanation of the fragmentation of the archetype describes one significant and controlling aspect of form in Henry Miller's **Tropic of Cancer:** the movement from a vaguely defined and surrealistically expressed representation of the Terrible Mother to a more sharply focused but stylized description of human figures who represent the archetype and establish the patterns by which the *I* can become aware of its relationships to these chthonic forces. Second, Neumann's description of the process by which the contents of the psyche are made available to consciousness defines and reveals precisely the nature of *confession* and *anatomy* as Miller employs these forms.

Many readers of Miller's fiction have understood that they were reading an account of the author's life, close to actual in some instances. His intimate disclosures of sexual activity are still dear to the cultist who wishes to attack American puritanism. But it is necessary to take seriously his comments on *Tropic of Cancer* in *The World of Sex:* "Liberally larded with the sexual as was that work, the concern of its author was not with sex, nor with religion, but with the problem of self-liberation." To define the nature of this self-liberation is more difficult than seems immediately apparent.

The question of Miller's form, moreover, becomes important if one recognizes in his work an unmasking of the contents of the unconscious. Simon O. Lesser suggests [in *Fiction and the Unconscious,* 1957] that Miller fails as a writer because he fails to "disguise and control" his revelations. His fictional unconscious brings us too close to the real:

> In its zeal to do justice to our repressed tendencies fiction is in constant danger of overstating the case for them. Particularly if it does this too directly, with a minimum of disguise and control—we think at once of such a writer as Henry Miller—it is likely to arouse aversion rather than pleasure. But it is not always easy to say whether a work of fiction or a reader is responsible for a failure of this sort. A work which in the perspective of time may seem well balanced may cause us to recoil because it insists on telling us more of the truth, above all more of the truth about ourselves, than we are prepared to accept.

The control and disguise exercised by form will not be recognized in Miller if one approaches his fiction expecting the conventions of novel and romance. Even George Orwell, whose essay on Miller ["Inside the Whale"] remains one of the best, insists that the tempo and narrative method of *Cancer* are those of the novel. He does recognize that *Cancer* is fiction, however, not autobiography.

Kingsley Widmer castigates Miller for failing as a novelist, objecting to the weakness of Miller's narrative patterns and to his lack of narrative coherence. He finds the surrealistic episodes simply escapes from reality lacking relevance in structures of individual works. He objects to characterization which does not provide sufficient "past, future, and depth" for the characters. Nor can he accept Miller's own shady moral character.

For several reasons, such a response to Miller must miss or distort whatever formal elements might be available to analysis. Widmer, for example, overlooks the significance of the seasons in *Cancer,* the descent into winter and the return to spring, which serve to organize the work more than may be immediately apparent. One cannot insist on a past or a future for his characters, moreover, because many are deliberate abstractions identified by stylized analyses of their weaknesses. Others are images of archetypes. His surrealistic episodes are not an escape from the reality of a dirty Paris and the everyday monotony of Bohemian existence (a reality which is not external at all—Paris, for example, has only symbolic existence), but a movement into an inner reality in which certain images bring us close to the archetypes Jung described. Here the fragmentation described by Neumann is especially operative.

In neither *confession* nor *anatomy,* as Northrop Frye has pointed out [in *The Anatomy of Criticism,* 1957], is narrative pattern the important means of organization; hence, to insist on sustained narrative in Miller is irrelevant. In *confession,* the coherence of the author's character and attitudes and his integration of the significant events in his life provide the fictional pattern. In *anatomy,* moreover, people are not people, but representatives of mental attitudes. To insist on realistic characterization in such a form is also irrelevant. In neither form is the actual structure of society a concern, as it is for the novelist. Much more remains to be said on all these points in connection with *Cancer.* But at the beginning it is necessary to consider formal devices not usually identified with the analysis of the novel. Fragmentation is such a device.

The fragmentation of the Archetypal Feminine permits Miller to present or bring into "consciousness" the chthonic forces of the unconscious which are, according to Jung, symbolized by the feminine. Miller's *I* must come to terms with these forces before it can be liberated or integrated. In fact, it is by means of this fragmentation that the events in the "author's" life are integrated and the requirements of the confession form are met. The literary presence of the Great Mother figure is manifested not only in human forms, but in almost all congeries of images in *Cancer,* including the inorganic and animal. These elemental symbols of the Archetypal Feminine are more important in *Tropic of Cancer* than in *Capricorn,* in which a later stage in the process of the integration of the *I* is dramatized.

The central symbol of the Archetypal Feminine in *Cancer* is not a human figure but Paris itself. Miller's world is a city world. But his harlot-thronged streets and filthy alleys do not provide the reader with a tourist's guide to a Paris nether world. In passage after passage the symbolic significance of the city emerges with such insistence that a real Paris never appears. This characteristic led one of Miller's critics [Homer K. Nicholson, Jr.] to complain [in his Ph.D. dissertation "O Altitudo: A comparison of the writings of Walt Whitman, D. H. Lawrence, and Henry Miller," 1957] that Miller is incapable of developing a sense of place:

> So extreme is this defect that it is often difficult to remember which of the *Tropics* deals with Paris, and which one with New York. When Miller describes a scene, he injects so many of his personal intellectual responses that the scene scarcely exists as a visual entity any longer.

Frank Kermode, who recognized that Miller's Paris is pointedly symbolic, saw the city [in *Puzzles and Epiphanies,* 1962] as representative of twentieth-century American and European civilization, especially (and oddly) the "puritan cultures" of the North. However, his subsequent insight—the basic situation is that of the artist in a slum civilization—is too narrowly sociological. Interpretations which see Miller's nightmare city-world as symbolic of the diseased cultures of an unfortunate century do not explain why his descriptions of this city-world reproduce it almost exclusively in images and symbols that are traditional representations of the Archetypal Feminine.

Womb, cave, underworld, city, house, abyss, sea, and fountain are elemental symbols of the Archetypal Feminine. As a maternal symbol, the city is the harborer of her inhabitants But the faithful city can also become a harlot, the diseased organism that Miller describes:

> The city sprouts out like a huge organism diseased in every part, the beautiful thoroughfares only a little less repulsive because they have been drained of their pus.

Miller's Paris is also a womb, the belly of the whale into which the artist must descend before he can be reborn or transformed:

> After leaving the Pension Orfila that afternoon I went to the library and there, after bathing in the Ganges and pondering over the signs of the zodiac, I began to reflect on the meaning of that inferno which Strindberg had so mercilessly depicted. And, as I ruminated, it began to grow clear to me, the mystery of his pilgrimage, the flight which the poet makes over the face of the earth, and then, as if he had been ordained to re-enact a lost drama, the heroic descent to the very bowels of the earth, the dark and fearsome sojourn in the belly of the whale, the bloody struggle to liberate himself, to emerge clean of the past, a bright, gory sun god cast up on an alien shore. It was no mystery to me any longer why he and others (Dante, Rabelais, Van Gogh, etc., etc.) had made their pilgrimage to Paris. I understood then why it is that Paris attracts the tortured, the hallucinated, the great maniacs of love.

The journey into the belly of the whale is fraught with danger, for the female figure is terrible as the representative of death for the individual. For Jung the belly of the whale is the land of the dead where the monster Mother figure must be conquered before transformation or rebirth can occur.

> The Feminine is the belly-vessel as woman and also as earth. She is the vessel of doom, guiding the nocturnal course of the stars through the underworld; she is the belly of the "whale-dragon," which, as in the story of Jonah, swallows the sun hero every night in the west; she is "the destroyer at eventide."
>
> The Great Mother as Terrible Goddess of the earth and of death is herself the earth, in which things rot. The Earth Goddess is "the devourer of the dead bodies of mankind" and the "mistress and lady of the tomb." Like Gaea, the Greek Earth Mother, she is mistress of the vessel and at the same time the great underworld vessel itself, into which the dead souls enter, and out of which they fly up again. [Erich Neumann, *The Great Mother,* 1963]

Such is the significance of the remainder of the passage in *Cancer* in which Miller compares his sojourn in Paris to the journey into the belly of the whale:

> One walks the streets knowing that he is mad, possessed, because it is only too obvious that these cold, indifferent faces are the visages of one's keepers. Here all boundaries fade away and the world reveals itself for the mad slaughterhouse that it is. The treadmill stretches away to infinitude, the hatches are closed down tight, logic runs rampant, with bloody cleaver flashing. The air is chill and stagnant, the language apocalyptic. Not an exit sign anywhere; no issue save death. A blind alley at the end of which is a scaffold.
>
> An eternal city, Paris! More eternal than Rome, more splendorous than Nineveh. The very navel of the world to which, like a blind and faltering idiot, one crawls back on hands and knees. And like a cork that has drifted finally to the dead center of the ocean, one floats here in the scum and wrack of the seas, listless, hopeless, headless even of a passing Columbus. The cradles of civilization are the putrid sinks of the world, the charnel house to which the stinking wombs confide their bloody packages of flesh and bone.

The first descriptions of the city to appear in *Cancer* are found in section one, in what may fairly be called intense, separate, and distinct moments.

But there is a substratum to be explored in these first two disorderly sections of *Cancer*. We are moving in a twilight world of semi-consciousness, and symbolic relationships among the numerous images can be mapped.

In the first two descriptions of Paris, for example, the traditional symbols of the Archetypal Feminine appear and hence the forces of the unconscious which the Feminine represents. In the first of these passages the city is realized as a watery, darkening world in which spider web and serpent figures are dimly suggested:

> Twilight hour. Indian blue, water of glass, trees glistening and liquescent. The rails fall away into the canal at Jaurès. The long caterpillar with lacquered sides dips like a roller coaster. It is not Paris. It is not Coney Island. It is a crepuscular melange of all the cities of Europe and Central America. The railroad yards below me, the tracks black, webby, not ordered by the engineer but cataclysmic in design, like those gaunt fissures in the polar ice which the camera registers in degrees of black.

The theriomorphic emblem of the spider appears throughout *Cancer* associated with the female figure: ". . . I could no more think of loving Germaine that I could think of loving a spider; and if I *was* faithful, it was not to Germaine but to that bushy thing she carried between her legs." Elsewhere Miller describes "the great sprawling mothers of Picasso, their breasts covered with spiders, their legend hidden deep in the labyrinth." Erich Neumann discusses the symbolism of spider and web in connection with the witch characteristics of the negative Mother: "Net and noose, spider, and the octopus with its ensnaring arms are here the appropriate symbols." He points out that these images appear in situations in which an individual is struggling to free himself from the Great Mother. Jung, commenting on the significance of this symbol, fixed its meaning for the passage we have been examining: "The center of the unconscious process is . . . often pictured as a spider in its web, especially when the conscious attitude is still dominated by fear of unconscious processes" [*The Collected Works,* Vol. XII: *Psychology and Alchemy,* 1953]. An example of this symbolism in Jung's text is similar to the formation of the symbol in Miller's passage; a section from the frontispiece of a collection of Brahminic sayings is reproduced, showing a web encircled by the uroboros, the figure of the snake biting its tail. The parallel is not as important here as the observation that serpent, water, and spider—traditional symbols of the Archetypal Feminine—are the symbols chosen for the first impression of Paris and are symbols which appear again and again in connection with the city. Whenever the movement in *Cancer* is toward a "surreal" description of events or psychic states, these symbols and other equally important ones emerge. And they are related to the movement toward the frozen, motionless world of ice developed at great length in the episode when Miller visits Dijon, the penultimate episode of the book.

In the second passage describing Paris in the first section of *Cancer* equally significant images appear:

> Indigo sky swept clear of fleecy clouds, gaunt trees infinitely extended, their black boughs gesticulating like a sleepwalker. Somber, spectral trees, their trunks pale as cigar ash . . . For the moment I can think of nothing—except that I am a sentient being stabbed by the miracle of these waters that reflect a forgotten world. All along the banks [of the Seine] the trees lean heavily over the tarnished mirror; when the wind rises and fills them with a rustling murmur they will shed a few tears and shiver as the water swirls by. I am suffocated by it. No one to whom I can communicate even a fraction of my feelings. . . .

The mixed figures of speech destroy any illusion of an actual scene, and it is only in context that the river described can be identified as the Seine. The scene is experienced entirely in terms of the observer's reactions to images of sky, water, trees, and wind. These images produce a sense of isolation and of suffocation. The *I* is aware of feelings which cannot be communicated. But the symbols have important traditional values which are unmistakably involved here. [In *The Collected Works,* Vol. IX, Part I: *The Archetypes and the Collective Unconscious,* 1959] Jung has identified water as "the commonest symbol of the unconscious. The lake in the valley is the unconscious, which lies, as it were, underneath consciousness, so that is often referred to as the 'subconscious'. . . ." Water is also one of the most persistent archetypal symbols of the maternal and the feminine. The Archetypal Feminine is identified by Jung with the positive forces of the unconscious: "The water that the mother, the unconscious, pours into the basin belonging to the anima is an excellent symbol for the living power of the psyche." But the unconscious is also the terrifying and destructive Terrible Mother.

In the passage in which Miller walks along the Seine, he is walking along a dreadful river—a tarnished mirror, lined by somber and spectral trees, trees that shiver in the wind that rises and fills them. Jung has described the archetypal pattern of such experience as the apprehension of the autonomous nature of the spirit rushing over dark waters. The mirror at the bottom of the water is the unconscious into which consciousness must look. Jung comments on the need for this experience in the symbolically impoverished twentieth century:

> Whoever has elected for the state of spiritual poverty, the true heritage of Protestantism carried to its logical conclusion, goes the way of the soul that leads to the water. This water is no figure of speech, but a living symbol of the dark psyche.

The appropriateness of these comments for Miller's quest, although their language is perhaps too religious or vaguely "mystical" for literary analysis, is confirmed by the overwhelming repetition of such experience in *Cancer*.

The city scenes of *Cancer* represent only one group of symbols which make the figure of the archetypal Terrible Mother available to the consciousness of the *I*. The process of fragmentation also produces monstrous female figures which combine animal and human features or coalesce with the streets and buildings of the city itself. The symbolic role of the city as representative of the Archetypal Feminine is verified in these figures, for the identification of the two permits them to coalesce, the parts of the female revealing the feminine significance of the city. Such almost human figures belong to the grotesque iconography of Miller's world, and in their archetypal dimension are interchangeable with images of the city scene:

> Tania is a fever, too—*les voies urinaires,* Café de la Liberté, Place des Vosges, bright neckties on the Boulevard Montparnasse, dark bathrooms, Porto Sec, Abdullah cigarettes, the adagio sonata *Pathétique,* aural amplificators, anecdotal seances, burnt sienna breasts, heavy garters, what time is it, golden pheasants stuffed with chestnuts, taffeta fingers, vaporish twilights turning to ilex, acromegaly, cancer and delirium, warm veils, poker chips, carpets of blood and soft thighs.

The destruction of spatial barriers between entities is even more apparent in the description of Llona:

> She had a German mouth, French ears, Russian ass. Cunt international. When the flag waved it was red all the way back to the throat. You entered on the Boulevard Jules-Ferry and came out at the Porte de la Villette. You dropped your sweetbreads into the tumbrils—red tumbrils with two wheels, naturally. At the confluence of the Ourcq and Marne, where the water sluices through the dikes and lies like glass under the bridges. Llona is lying there now and the canal is full of glass and splinters; the mimosas weep, and there is a wet, foggy fart on the windowpanes.

Several of these visually fragmented female figures appear in the twilight consciousness of section one in *Tropic of Cancer*. By different names—Tania, Irène, Llona—they are manifestations of a devouring, castrating, chthonic Aphrodite, fascinating and deadly aspects of the Terrible Feminine. But their effect on the *I* can be positive: Tania is equated with chaos, which is destructive but also the source of the writer's inspiration. Her "Jewishness" makes her both fascinating and hateful. Irène is another deadly figure: "The trouble with Irène is that she has a valise in-

stead of a cunt. She wants fat letters to shove in her valise." The letters here are creative efforts, productions, aspects of the individual which are devoured. Of Llona:

> Men went inside her and curled up. . . . She
> would cut off your prick and keep it inside her
> forever, if you gave her permission. . . . her
> tongue was full of lice and tomorrows. Poor
> Carol, he could only curl up inside her and die.
> She drew a breath and he fell out—like a dead
> clam.

The roles of these figures as wives and mistresses in the
Bohemian fringe world Miller appears to inhabit are inci-
dental to their function as symbols of the unconscious.
They share this function with the city.

Like the whores and hags which throng the streets of Miller's Paris, these women are stylized by terms which insist
on outlining their sexual functions. Scientific or discreet
references to human anatomy could scarcely serve as effectively to underline the sexual characteristics of the
human figure. Such stylization emphasizes their symbolic
possibilities as efficiently for the contemporary reader as
did the crude reproductions of the female exposing herself
carved on the doorways of Irish churches or the ritual exhibitionism of an Etruscan goddess for those in other ages.
The terms used are not those of the medical textbook,
which would suggest a dead world of clinical abstractions.
On the contrary, in certain circumstances they are quite
ordinary and would pass unnoticed. Only in a literary context from which they are ordinarily excluded can they
serve to effect the kind of stylization needed to render the
significance of these half-realized figures. For the figures
themselves are taboo.

The Gorgonesque quality of the chthonic feminine is
clearly recognized in the figure of Mona, a character of
even greater significance in *Tropic of Capricorn.* She never
becomes a realistically developed character, for it is the
outline of her symbolic role that is important. In her manifestation in *Cancer,* she belongs to the same configuration
of images as the other female figures and the city. Like
Aphrodite, she rises

> . . . out of a sea of faces and embraces me, em-
> braces me passionately—a thousand eyes, fin-
> gers, legs, bottles, windows, purses, saucers all
> glaring at us and we in each other's arms obliv-
> ious. I sit down beside her and she talks—a flood
> of talk. Wild consumptive notes of hysteria, per-
> version, leprosy. I hear not a word because she
> is beautiful and I love her and now I am happy
> and willing to die.

The "sea" from which she rises is itself created from a
number of non-human symbols of the Feminine. In a later
passage her Gorgonesque nature is revealed:

> I wake from a deep slumber to look at her. A
> pale light is trickling in. I look at her beautiful
> wild hair. I feel something crawling down my
> neck. I look at her again, closely. Her hair is
> alive. I pull back the sheet—more of them. They
> are swarming over the pillow.

The figure of the Gorgon is one of the most familiar representations of the Terrible Mother in ancient mythology,
and the symbolism of this figure is intimately related to the
significance of the other symbols I have pointed out:

> Among the symbols of the devouring chasm we
> must count the womb in its frightening aspect,
> the numinous heads of the Gorgon and the Me-
> dusa, the woman with beard and phallus, and
> the male-eating spider. The open womb is the
> devouring symbol of the uroboric mother, espe-
> cially when connected with phallic symbols. The
> gnashing mouth of the Medusa with its boar's
> tusks betrays these features most plainly, while
> the protruding tongue is obviously connected
> with the phallus. The snapping—i.e., castrat-
> ing—womb appears as the jaws of hell, and the
> serpents writhing round the Medusa's head are
> not personalistic—pubic hairs—but aggressive
> phallic elements characterizing the fearful as-
> pect of the uroboric womb. The spider can be
> classified among this group of symbols, not only
> because it devours the male after coitus, but be-
> cause it symbolizes the female in general, who
> spreads nets for the unwary male. [Erich Neu-
> mann, *The Origins and History of Consciousness*]

The crawling vermin in Mona's hair, the serpents and spiders, the lice and bedbugs of the "filthy" scenes of *Tropic
of Cancer* represent only a few of the important theriomorphic images in the book, but images peculiarly appropriate to the demonic world of the Terrible Feminine. [In
The Grotesque in Art and Literature, 1963] Wolfgang
Kayser has noted their appearance as one of the distinguishing motifs of grotesque literature:

> Certain animals are especially suitable to the
> grotesque—snakes, owls, toads, spiders—the
> nocturnal and creeping animals which inhabit
> realms apart from and inaccessible to man. Part-
> ly for the same reason (to which their uncertain
> origin is added) the same observation applies to
> vermin.

The appropriateness of the images is clear if we remember
Kayser's final definition of the grotesque as "an attempt
to invoke and subdue the demonic aspects of the world."
It is the power and scenery of this world that Miller's fragmentation is attempting to describe in *Tropic of Cancer.*
The demonic underworld is inescapable. It is another
"fragment" in which the Archetypal Feminine, the persistent symbol of the unconscious and its dangerous but fecund character, appears.

Often the filthy world in which these vermin thrive erupts,
like the autonomous and powerful unconscious, into the
world of cleanliness and order, as in the opening section
of *Cancer:*

> I am living at the Villa Borghese. There is not
> a crumb of dirt anywhere, nor a chair misplaced.
> We are all alone here and we are dead.

> Last night Boris discovered that he was lousy.
> I had to shave his armpits and even then the
> itching did not stop. How can one get lousy in
> a beautiful place like this? But no matter. We
> might never have known each other so intimate-
> ly, Boris and I, had it not been for the lice.

The filthy world is necessary to the "sterile world," for

without it, fertility, creation, and life are impossible. At the end of the first section, Mona and Miller leave the "filthy" Paris hotel for the Hôtel des Etats-Unis: "No more bedbugs now. The rainy season has commenced. The sheets are immaculate." But encounters with the demonic world are dangerous and unpleasant. Just before an important scene in which the hero confronts the surrealistically developed figure of the Terrible Feminine, the filthy world is described in terms which register his fear and aversion:

> When I sit down to eat I always sit near the window. I am afraid to sit on the other side of the table—it is too close to the bed and the bed is crawling. I can see bloodstains on the gray sheets as I look that way, but I try not to look that way. I look out on the courtyard where they are rinsing the slop pails.

The crawling vermin belong to the archetype of the Terrible Mother, clearly apparent in the serpentine hair of the Gorgonesque Mona.

Much of the animal imagery also belongs to the primordial world of the Great Mother archetype and thronging animal images in *Tropic of Cancer* are one of the means by which Miller dramatizes twilight states of consciousness. Even the theriomorphic significance in the title of the book is appropriate to its thematic concerns. Cancer, the crab, is first of all a feminine sign in the zodiac. It is the sign in which the sun begins to retreat and the days grow shorter, a cold sign. Jung speaks of its significance in astrology as "feminine and watery." Cancer is also the house of the moon, Luna, believed to secrete the dew or sap of life, and when all the planets are in Cancer, the end of the world by water will occur.

Not all of the animal images in *Tropic of Cancer* delineate or belong to the archetypes of the Great Mother or the Terrible Mother, however. The animal figures or images can also be the symbolic carriers of the archetype of the self, Jung's "supraordinate personality" which includes the unconscious as well as the "ego":

> Because of its unconscious component the self is so far removed from the conscious mind that it can only be *partially expressed by human figures;* the other part of it has to be expressed by *objective, abstract symbols.* The human figures are father and son, mother and daughter, king and queen, god and goddess. Theriomorphic symbols are the dragon, snake, elephant, lion, bear, and other powerful animals, or again the spider, crab, butterfly, beetle, worm, etc. Plant symbols are generally flowers (lotus and rose). These lead on to geometrical figures like the circle, the sphere, the square, the quaternity, the clock, the firmament, and so on. The indefinite extent of the unconscious component makes a comprehensive description of the human personality impossible. Accordingly, the unconscious supplements the picture with living figures ranging from the animal to the divine, as the two extremes outside man, and rounds out the animal extreme, through the addition of vegetable and inorganic abstractions, into a microcosm. These addenda have a high frequency in anthropomorphic divinities, where they appear as "attributes."

However, among those which appear in section one of *Cancer*—and the list is long—many symbolize or "decorate" the world of the Archetypal Feminine. In the following passage, for example, the lion is emblematic of the forces which destroy the figure of the over-intellectualized Jew who refuses to recognize their reality:

> There are people who cannot resist the desire to get into a cage with wild beasts and be mangled. They go in even without revolver or whip. . . . [The Jew's] courage is so great that he does not even smell the dung in the corner. The spectators applaud but he does not hear. The drama, he thinks, is going on inside the cage. The cage, he thinks, is the world. Standing there alone and helpless, the door locked, he finds that the lions do not understand his language. Not one lion has ever heard of Spinoza. Spinoza? Why they can't even get their teeth into him. "Give us meat!" they roar, while he stands there petrified, his ideas frozen, his *Weltanschauung* a trapeze out of reach. A single blow of the lion's paw and his cosmogony is smashed.

As a primordial image of powerful forces—forces which oppose the independence of consciousness—the lion is a primitive symbol frequently associated with the figure of the Great Mother, often in her terrible aspect as goddess of night, evil, and death. To single out one image for comment, however, only draws attention to the entire complex of animal images in Miller's prose and their significance for the process of fragmentation in Miller's development of the confession.

The male figures of *Tropic of Cancer* are the subject of later discussion except that I wish to point out here that their significance in *Cancer* is not in their social roles of Jewish intellectual or Bohemian playboy but in their relationship to the chthonic feminine. Castration, dismemberment, and mutilation are the motifs which define this relationship in the descriptions of Paris and the accounts of various male "characters." The narrator draws attention to *A Man Cut in Slices,* the title of a book placed in a Paris shop window. In a dream he sees Van Norden, one of the important male figures, "about to walk away when suddenly he notices that his penis is lying on the sidewalk. It is about the size of a sawed-off broom-stick." Paris streets "remind one of nothing less than a big chancrous cock laid open longitudinally."

It is the relationship with a smothering, castrating, dismembering aspect of the Terrible Feminine that is important in Miller's description of Moldorf, who appears briefly in sections one and two. The archetypal nature of this relationship is underlined by the characteristics of Moldorf: Moldorf, Miller writes, is God. He is a dwarf: "Moldorf, multiform and unerring, goes through his roles—clown, juggler, contortionist, priest, lecher, mountebank." His fate is to be symbolically dismembered in a fantasy scene in section two which ends when his wife Fanny consumes him: "There is something inside her, tickling, and tickling." The entire scene, the figure of the dwarf himself, produces a curious melange of images and events that appear to justify one critic's characterization of Miller's fiction as an "overflowing surrealist cocktail" [Isaac Rosenfeld, "Henry Miller," in *An Age of Enormity,* 1962].

But reduced to its elements, the archetypal pattern emerges. The devouring destructive Feminine is represented in Moldorf's life by a domestic and conventional wife. But she shares with her whorish sisters in *Cancer* a destructive role described in almost the same terms as the others I have mentioned. Moldorf's "fate," his dwarf's stature, his designation as "God"—even perhaps Miller's choice of the sacred dung-beetle image to describe him (the Egyptian scarab was the emblem of the sun as the God who begets himself)—suggest an archetypal pattern familiar in the mythology of the Great Mother. Moldorf is the companion God of the Great Mother:

> The young men whom the Mother selects for her lovers may impregnate her, they may even be fertility gods, but the fact remains that they are only phallic consorts of the Great Mother, drones serving the queen bee, who are killed off as soon as they have performed their duty of fecundation.

> For this reason these youthful companion gods always appear in the form of dwarfs. The pygmies who were worshiped in Cyprus, Egypt, and Phoenicia—all territories of the Great Mother—display their phallic character just like the Dioscuri, the Cabiri, and the Dactyls, including even the figure of Harpocrates. [Neumann, *The Origins of Consciousness*]

The young God-dwarf was killed or castrated as soon as he performed his function of fecundating the Great Mother:

> Death and dismemberment or castration are the fate of the phallus-bearing, youthful god. Both are clearly visible in myth and ritual, and both are associated with bloody orgies in the cult of the Great Mother.

Moldorf's experience is similar to Van Norden's:

> "I tell you, when she climbs over me I can hardly get my arms around it. It blots out the whole world. She makes me feel like a little bug crawling inside her." [*Tropic of Cancer*]

Moldorf is the traditional homunculus, belonging, as does the satyr Van Norden, to the figure of the Terrible Mother and representing one of the "human" figures in terms of which the power of the Terrible Goddess is demonstrated.

I have been speaking somewhat indiscriminately of the Great Mother and the Terrible Mother archetypes as representation of the Archetypal Feminine. Although they are related, these figures should be separated insofar as their "literary presence" is important for an analysis of the fragmentation of archetypes in *Tropic of Cancer*. For the Jungian psychoanalyst, the archetype *an sich* cannot be visually represented, and I am describing only the "perceptible, actualized representation or 'archetypal image." The attempts to make the archetype perceptible to consciousness through a variety of images is called *fragmentation,* a term I have borrowed to describe the proliferation of

Front wrapper for the first edition of Tropic of Cancer, *designed by Maurice Girodias.*

"archetypal" images in Miller. The form of his fiction should not be considered a transcription of a psychic process, or a "case history," however. Such exclusive focus and concentration on certain experiences which could be called "archetypal" would seem unlikely to occur in a case history.

Yet such focus and "unity" are familiar formal characteristics of works of literature. If at the end of this study the reader is convinced that the images and experiences analyzed can be described acceptably in Jungian terms, then he may also be willing to see in the total form of Miller's work a unified allegorical structure. Miller's technical problem was one of making archetypal processes and experiences plausible to his audience. This he accomplishes in part by creating the illusion of a twentieth-century city world in which his isolated protagonist wanders on an endless "quest." The nature of this city world, however, is clearly archetypal, rendered in images which reveal the character of the Archetypal Feminine, the most inclusive term of those I have used. In *Tropic of Cancer* these images are traditionally those which have symbolized the archetype in myth, dreams, literature, and art. They appear in several strata.

The least ordered of these projections produces the archetype in elemental terms:

The world around me is dissolving, leaving here and there spots of time. The world is a cancer eating itself away. . . . I am thinking that when the great silence descends upon all and everywhere music will at last triumph. When into the womb of time everything is again withdrawn chaos will be restored and chaos is the score upon which reality is written. You, Tania, are my chaos. It is why I sing. It is not even I, it is the world dying, shedding the skin of time. I am still alive, kicking in your womb, a reality to write upon.

The symbolism of this passage is that of the Great Round, the womb of chaos; even the figure of the circular snake that bites its own tail is suggested in the cancer eating itself away and the world that sheds its skin of time. Spatial entities do not exist in the "womb of time." This chaos is fertile for the self, "the score upon which reality is written."

This symbolism develops into the differentiated symbolism of the Archetypal Feminine, which has both negative and positive significance: tomb and womb, underworld and cave; symbols of containing and protection such as shield, veil, bowl, grail, earth, and water. When human forms, however monstrous, begin to emerge in the symbolic representations of the Feminine, the Terrible Mother appears in the Gorgons and other destructive goddess figures; the Good Mother appears in quite different projections. All of these projections are manifestations of aspects of the transpersonal unconscious, especially the negative forces of the unconscious, which are seen as feminine antagonists to the efforts of consciousness to free itself. Moreover, these figures are alternately frightening and fascinating. From the unconscious, with its intermingling of positive and negative forces, must flow not only what is evil, but what is vital. The integration of the individual, the transformation of the artist "in the belly of the whale," the confrontation of the deadly aspects of the Feminine and the escape from them—these are the patterns into which the images of Miller's confession are arranged.

The *I* cannot escape confrontations with the deadly aspects of the Archetypal Feminine. In *Cancer,* the androgynous, Gorgonesque figure at the center of Paris, who first appears in Miller's description of the Lesbian Madame Delorme, reappears in a later surrealist episode unmistakably parallel to the first. In his encounter with Madame Delorme, he must penetrate deep into a palace in the city:

> How I ever got to Madame Delorme's I can't imagine any more. But I got there, got inside somehow, past the butler, past the maid with her little white apron, got right inside the palace with my corduroy trousers and my hunting jacket—and not a button on my fly. Even now I can taste again the golden ambiance of that room where Madame Delorme sat upon a throne in her mannish rig, the goldfish in the bowls, the maps of the ancient world, the beautifully bound books; I can feel again her heavy hand resting upon my shoulder, frightening me a little with her heavy Lesbian air.

All the symbolic possibilities of this scene are realized in the later episode:

> Standing in the courtyard with a glass eye; only half the world is intelligible. The stones are wet and mossy and in the crevices are black toads. A big door bars the entrance to the cellar; the steps are slippery and soiled with bat dung. The door bulges and sags, the hinges are falling off, but there is an enameled sign on it, in perfect condition, which says: "Be sure to close the door." Why close the door? I can't make it out. I look again at the sign but it is removed; in its place there is a pane of colored glass. I take out my artificial eye, spit on it and polish it with my handkerchief. A woman is sitting on a dais above an immense carved desk; she has a snake around her neck. The entire room is lined with books and strange fish swimming in colored globes; there are maps and charts on the wall, maps of Paris before the plague, maps of the antique world, of Knossus and Carthage, of Carthage before and after the salting. In the corner of the room I see an iron bedstead and on it a corpse is lying; the woman gets up wearily, removes the corpse from the bed and absentmindedly throws it out the window. She returns to the huge carven desk, takes a goldfish from the bowl and swallows it. Slowly the room begins to revolve and one by one the continents slide into the sea; only the woman is left, but her body is a mass of geography.

Miller's familiarity with the experiments of surrealism may have influenced his choice of images here, but the relationship with the earlier scene would argue against considering it an irrelevant literary exercise. The symbols clearly outline the archetype of the Terrible Feminine:

> The terrible aspect of the Feminine always includes the uroboric snake woman, the woman with the phallus, the unity of child bearing and begetting, of life and death. The Gorgon is endowed with every male attribute: the snake, the tooth, the boar's tusks, the out-thrust tongue, and sometimes even with a beard.
>
> In Greece the Gorgon as Artemis-Hecate is also the mistress of the night road, of fate, and of the world of the dead. As Enodia she is the guardian of crossroads and gates, and as Hecate she is the snake-entwined moon goddess of ghosts and the dead. . . .
>
> . . . As Good Mother, she is mistress of the East Gate, the gate of birth; as Terrible Mother, she is mistress of the West Gate, the gate of death, the engulfing entrance to the underworld. Gate, door, gully, ravine, abyss are the symbols of the feminine earth-womb; they are the numinous places that mark the road into the mythical darkness of the underworld. [Neumann, *The Great Mother*]

This is the enthroned, androgynous, frightening figure that Miller descends to meet symbolically in the cellar of a Paris courtyard. A mistress of the dead, deep in cave or palace, behind doors, a figure that can coalesce with continents that slide into the sea (itself one of the most persistent symbols of the Feminine)—here in many of its manifestations is the archetypal figure of the Terrible Feminine. The motif of swallowing underscores the deadliness of this figure for the *I* is symbolized by the fish in its womb-like vessel. Another ancient symbol of the self, the eye, appears in this passage. In the "courtyard," however, the eye is inadequate—a glass eye that sees only half the world.

Miller's ubiquitous mistress of the dead, her body a mass of geography, is a figure of fantasy; her symbolic trappings belong to the surreal world. But in the passages immediately preceding the cellar scene, the androgynous figure is suggested by the "character" Olga, apparently a part of the "real" world, the filthy Paris which both attracts and repels the *I*, filled as it is with the odors of rancid butter and halitosis, crawling with vermin and misshapen human figures. It is a Paris in which Miller sees Notre Dame rising like a tomb from the water.

The figure of Olga is unmistakably marked by masculine characteristics and even plays a masculine role in the filthy world, although the maternal, providing role of the Archetypal Feminine figure—its positive aspect—is more apparent than the destructive:

> It was just a few days ago that Olga got out of the hospital where she had her tubes burned out and lost a little excess weight. However she doesn't look as if she had gone through much suffering. She weighs almost as much as a camel-backed locomotive; she drips with perspiration, has halitosis, and still wears her Circassian wig that looks like excelsior. She has two big warts on her chin from which there sprouts a clump of little hairs; she is growing a mustache.

> The day after Olga was released from the hospital she commenced making shoes again. At six in the morning she is at her bench; she knocks out two pairs of shoes a day. . . . If Olga doesn't work there is no food.

The "Madame Delorme" fantasy scene is an inner experience of the Archetypal Feminine. The external world in *Cancer* reveals a less direct (because it is projected on the outside world) but nevertheless similar relationship between the *I* and aspects of the Archetypal Feminine outlined in this analysis. The movement between this inner and outer world is part of the action of the book.

Appropriately, at the center of Paris the *I* finds an androgynous symbol of the elemental Feminine. In *Cancer*, moreover, elemental symbols dominate. In the later *Capricorn*, Mona/Mara appears in almost human form and dominates the symbolic structure. New York (the negative Feminine) is not quite as important in *Capricorn* as Paris is in *Cancer*. And the difference should be noted, for Paris, although deadly and destructive, is also a city of creation and birth. The negative and positive aspects of the Feminine lie side by side.

Although the confrontation of the negative can occur in Paris itself, Paris is contrasted with an entirely negative city in *Cancer:* Dijon. Winter is the season in which the hero of *Cancer* leaves Paris for Dijon, where he has secured a position as teacher of English. The stay in Dijon is a "descent into Hell," into a winter land where he confronts most directly the images which haunt the book. Only by such a descent and confrontation, however, can the *I* be truly integrated. Isolation drives him far into himself, where he must meet the implications of the archetypal experience:

> Who am I? What am I doing here? I fall between the cold walls of human malevolence, a white figure fluttering, sinking down through the cold lake, a mountain of skulls above me. I settle down to the cold latitudes, the chalk steps washed with indigo. The earth in its dark corridors knows my step, feels a foot abroad, a wing stirring, a gasp and a shudder. I hear the learning chaffed and chuzzled, the figures mounting upward, bat slime dripping aloft and clanging with pasteboard golden wings; I hear the trains collide, the chains rattle, the locomotive chugging, snorting, sniffing, steaming and pissing. All things come to me through the clear fog with the odor of repetition, with yellow hangovers and Gadzooks and whettikins. In the dead center, far below Dijon, far below the hyperborean regions, stands God Ajax, his shoulders strapped to the mill wheel, the olives crunching, the green marsh water alive with croaking frogs.

Miller finds himself in the dark corridors of the earth. The archetypal labyrinth is suggested by these dark corridors, and by the corridors through which the *I* must grope every night, seeking his room in darkness. Its image belongs to the Archetypal Feminine:

> The labyrinthine way is always the first part of the night sea voyage, the descent of the male following the sun into the devouring underworld, into the deathly womb of the Terrible Mother. This labyrinthine way, which leads to the center of danger, where at the midnight hour, in the land of the dead, in the middle of the night sea voyage, the decision falls, occurs in the judgment of the dead in Egypt, in the mysteries both classical and primitive, and in the corresponding processes of psychic development in modern man. Because of its dangerous character, the labyrinth is also frequently symbolized by a net, its center as a spider.

> In the rites of Malekula, the monster Le-hev-hev, as negative power of the Feminine, is also associated with the spider; with the man-devouring "mythical ogress," "the crab woman" with two immense claws; with the underworld animal, the rat; and with a giant bivalve that when opened resembles the female genital organ, and in shutting endangers man and beast. [Neumann, *The Great Mother*]

We are often in a similar world in *Cancer*. In descriptions of Paris, for example, the web of the spider appears in scenes where it is not deliberately emphasized:

> The railroad yards below me, the tracks black, webby, not ordered by the engineer but cataclysmic in design, like those gaunt fissures in the polar ice which the camera registers in degrees of black.

In the Dijon episode, Ajax labors at the negative wheel of life, for the mill and loom are symbols of fate and death; this symbol has appeared before in *Cancer* when it is clearly at the center of the land of the dead:

In the middle of the street is a wheel and in the hub of the wheel a gallows is fixed. People already dead are trying frantically to mount the gallows, but the wheel is turning too fast. . . .

In Dijon Miller comes to a sterile dead world that is figuratively his "voyage to the land of the dead," the winter world into which he must descend before he can obtain the equilibrium he reaches in the last section of the book. Here he recognizes that he has to live "separate," not separate from others, but separate from the psychic pull of the unconscious, the symbol of which is the Archetypal Feminine:

Going back in a flash over the women I've known. It's like a chain which I've forged out of my own misery. Each one bound to the other. A fear of living separate, of staying born. The door of the womb always on the latch. Dread and longing. Deep in the blood the pull of paradise. The beyond. Always the beyond. It must have all started with the navel. They cut the umbilical cord, give you a slap on the ass, and presto! you're out in the world, adrift, a ship without a rudder. You look at the stars and then you look at your navel. You grow eyes everywhere—in the armpits, between the lips, in the roots of your hair, on the soles of your feet. What is distant becomes near, what is near becomes distant. Inner-outer, a constant flux, a shedding of skins, a turning inside out. You drift around like that for years and years, until you find yourself in the dead center, and there you slowly rot, slowly crumble to pieces, get dispersed again. Only your name remains.

The eyes that he grows everywhere are symbols of the self, the inner self, the Purusha, "thousand-eyed," the Rudra with eyes on all sides, symbols of consciousness and of the creative powers of the soul, hence separate from the Great Mother, which in her devouring, paradisaical aspect is deadly, and destroys the individual. The *I* finds himself in the dead-center of winter Dijon, the land of the dead. In this penultimate section of *Cancer* he has reached the bottom. With spring he returns to Paris, and finally (after an episode in which he encourages and assists his young friend to escape from a predatory French girl) he reaches the equilibrium of the final section of the confession:

After everything had quietly sifted through my head a great peace came over me. Here, where the river gently winds through the girdle of hills, lies a soil so saturated with the past that however far back the mind roams one can never detach it from its human background. . . . So quietly flows the Seine that one hardly notices its presence. It is always there, quiet and unobtrusive, like a great artery running through the human body. In the wonderful peace that fell over me it seemed as if I had climbed to the top of a high mountain; for a little while I would be able to look around me, to take in the meaning of the landscape.

Human beings make a strange fauna and flora. From a distance they appear negligible; close up they are apt to appear ugly and malicious. More

than anything they need to be surrounded with sufficient space—space even more than time.

The sun is setting. I feel this river flowing through me—its past, its ancient soil, the changing climate. The hills gently girdle it about: its course is fixed.

Its course is fixed to the sea. One has only a brief time on the mountain. The river here seen is positive, fecundating, flowing, connecting the individual with the past, especially the human past. But the *I* has achieved a certain independence and equilibrium in this last scene in *Cancer:* a considerable transformation has occurred. The flowing of the river through his body suggests that the creative power of the unconscious is now available to him, whereas in Dijon all was frozen and dead.

The flowing imagery of *Cancer,* one of the most important of the non-human forms into which the Archetypal Feminine is fragmented, is complex and polysemous. These images belong to the water symbolism associated with the Great Mother. They are among the most primordial representations of her essential nature, and reflect the ambivalent response of man to the forms and powers of his unconscious. As "water" she is the source of life and—in dissolution—transformation and death.

Neumann has summarized the forms taken by this figure in ancient mythology and religion:

The Great Goddess is the flowing unity of subterranean and celestial primordial water, the sea of heaven on which sail the barks of the gods of light, the circular life-generating ocean above and below the earth. To her belong all waters, streams, fountains, ponds, and springs, as well as the rain. She is the ocean of life with its life—and death—bringing seasons, and life is her child, a fish eternally swimming inside her, like the stars in the celestial ocean of the Mexican Mayauel and like men in the fishpool of Mother Church—a late manifestation of the same archetype.

Such images of the Great Mother may be fearful and repellent at times, dangerous to the individual consciousness. Yet they are incestuously attractive in the promise of a womb-like release from the shocks sustained by consciousness.

The images of flowing have been noticed by most readers of *Cancer,* as have the womb symbols. But for the most part, Kingsley Widmer's comment on the meaning of these symbols is typical. They have been considered emblems of the flux of the events in life, an interpretation which can explain the river imagery but which seems inadequate if one considers the traditional meanings associated with fountain, urine, sweat, menstrual blood—in fact all flowing, fluid substances in Miller. Widmer's reading, moreover, does not explain the ambivalence of the *I* toward this imagery, and the different relationships the *I* establishes with it. His comments [in *Henry Miller*] on the relationship between the central imagery of flowing and the events of *Cancer* illustrate my point:

Miller seems defeated by the sordidness of the place [Dijon], the futility of teaching, the loneliness of the displaced bohemian among the pedants, and even by a childish fear of the dark and the foreign. His exuberance falters; he recognizes "a fear of living separate, of staying born." Though the message throughout **Cancer** turns on the acceptance, even embracement, of the flowing chaos of life, here the "constant flux" brings the shipwrecked sailor of the American voyage to "dead center, and there you slowly rot." Unable to accept the flux in its ordinary round of misery or to continue shouting King of the Hill from the top of the quite unmiraculous pile of everyday excrement, Miller abruptly flees Dijon and goes back to Paris where he can play the artist as burlesque and apocalyptic confidence man. The meaningless world can best be accepted in romantic and rebellious terms, as an artistic-religious vision, and not as the ordinary substance of life. Perhaps partly in spite of himself, Miller makes a striking confession in this episode which just precedes the final chapter of the book and which helps explain his culminating refusal to return to ordinary American life: the excremental absurdity of life demands that one have a rebellious role as the outsider abroad.

If one considers the archetypal significance of Miller's images, he reaches quite different conclusions.

These conclusions affect the reader's recognition of Miller's form. The essential formal element of *confession,* according to Northrop Frye, is that the author's "mind" be integrated on subjects that are introverted but intellectualized in content. Hence the passages in which the "inner" meaning of the Dijon episode is examined by Miller and the relationship of the self to the images in which the archetype appears are central. Just before the Christmas holidays (again, it is in the winter of the year that the "hero" leaves for Dijon) Miller had visualized in brutal sexual imagery the obscenity of contemporary experience—paralysis, inertia, and the attempt to make the earth into an "arid plateau of health and comfort." These are obscenities because they indicate that the source (the crater—the familiar womb symbol, feminine symbol of the unconscious) is dry:

> The dry, fucked-out crater is obscene. More obscene than anything is inertia. More blasphemous than the bloodiest oath is paralysis. If there is only a gaping wound left then it must gush forth though it produce nothing but toads and bats and homunculi.

(Toads, bats, and homunculi are the familiars of the grotesque world, for the unconscious must have negative as well as positive aspects.) Even if the dark forces produce only the demonic, at least we are in touch with the sources of "reality." It is not the impermanence of life, filled with horror and hell as well as heaven, that dismays the hero, but the denial of its source and the loss of its vitality.

The *I* must free for himself the "flow" of the unconscious, by challenging its threat to overwhelm consciousness (the desire to return to the womb) and by confronting its negative as well as its positive character:

> "I love everything that flows," said the great blind Milton of our times. I was thinking of him

this morning when I awoke with a great bloody shout of joy: I was thinking of his rivers and trees and all that world of night which he is exploring. Yes, I said to myself, I too love everything that flows: rivers, sewers, lava, semen, blood, bile, words, sentences. I love the amniotic fluid when it spills out of the bag. I love the kidney with its painful gallstones, its gravel and what-not; I love the urine that pours out scalding and the clap that runs endlessly; I love the words of hysterics and the sentences that flow on like dysentery and mirror all the sick images of the soul; I love the great rivers like the Amazon and the Orinoco, where crazy men like Moravagine float on through dream and legend in an open boat and drown in the blind mouths of the river. I love everything that flows, even the menstrual flow that carries away the seed unfecund. I love scripts that flow, be they hieratic, esoteric, perverse, polymorph, or unilateral. I love everything that flows, everything that has time in it and becoming, *that brings us back to the beginning where there is never end:* the violence of the prophets, the obscenity that is ecstasy, the wisdom of the fanatic, the priest with his rubber litany, the foul words of the whore, the spittle that floats away in the gutter, the milk of the breast . . . *all that is fluid, melting, dissolute and dissolvent,* all the pus and dirt that in flowing is purified, that loses its sense of origin, *that makes the great circuit toward death and dissolution. The great incestuous wish is to flow on, one with time, to merge the great image of the beyond with the here and now. A fatuous, suicidal wish that is constipated by words and paralyzed by thought.*

All symbols of creative power in this passage acknowledge the fecundity of the "crater," the womb, the great Feminine Archetype of the unconscious. But the lines in italics point out the danger facing the self: the powerful, incestuous wish. The "acceptance" without differentiation of this flow and flux leads to "death," and the wish for such dissolution is primordial. Here is a clear statement of the intellectual recognition of the nature of the fecund depths of the individual, and of the necessity of avoiding the "fatuous, suicidal wish." The relationship described is elemental (certainly all the images in the passages support such an interpretation) and dangerous: the incest described suggests the uroboric incest outlined in Neumann's analysis of the elemental representations of the Great Mother archetype, along with the problem of "transformation" on the elementary level which faces the development of the individual consciousness.

> The life feeling of every ego consciousness that feels small in relation to the powers is dominated by the preponderance of the Great Round that encompasses all change. This archetype may be experienced outwardly as world or nature or inwardly as fate and the unconscious. In this phase the elementary feminine character, which still contains the transformative character within it, is "worldly"; natural existence with all its regular changes is subservient to it. The central symbol of this constellation is the unity of life amid the change of seasons and the concurrent transformation of living things. . . . the death character of the material-maternal is an expression

of this archetypal domination of nature and the unconscious over life, and likewise over the undeveloped childlike, or youthfully helpless, ego consciousness. In this phase the Archetypal Feminine not only bears and directs life as a whole, and the ego in particular, but also takes everything that is born of it back into its womb of origination and death. [Neumann, *The Great Mother*]

When the narrator speaks of the incestuous wish to dissolve in the flow, he is not advocating a simple acceptance of the flow of life; he is speaking of what has been described as *uroboric incest*:

> Uroboric incest is a form of entry into the mother, of union with her, and it stands in sharp contrast to other and later forms of incest. In uroboric incest, the emphasis upon pleasure and love is in no sense active, it is more a desire to be dissolved and absorbed; passively one lets oneself be taken, sinks into the pleroma, melts away away in the ocean of pleasure—a *Liebestod*. [*The Origins of Consciousness*]

Neumann is not speaking of the personal mother:

> This incest reflects the activity of the maternal uroboros, of the Great Mother archetype, mother of life and death, whose figure is transpersonal and not reducible to the personal mother. [*The Origins of Consciousness*]

Miller's desire to escape the Mother, a theme which pervades his fiction, is a desire to escape the dissolution of the self that surrender to the unconscious would demand.

The relationship with the "flow" that the *I* must establish if it is to become independent and escape the frozen wastes of the "dead center" requires an assertion of independence and at the same time a winning of creative energy from the unconscious. Equilibrium, or integration of the *I*, establishes just such a relationships, although it is only temporary. No real end to the glittering and deadly power of the unconscious exists, nor would such an end be desirable.

Only by experiencing the archetype through the images into which it is fragmented and arriving at conscious or intellectual recognition of "divisions" of the Archetypal Feminine is the *I* "born." And this integration and intellectualization provides the integrated pattern which identifies the confession form.

Leon Lewis   (essay date 1986)

SOURCE: "*Tropic of Cancer:* The Journal of a 'Year' in the Surreal City," in his *Henry Miller: The Major Writings*, Schocken Books, 1986, pp. 75-103.

[In the following excerpt, Lewis provides an overview of the major themes of Tropic of Cancer.*]*

Henry Miller's first book, *Tropic of Cancer*, remains startling and unique. The radiant spirit and exuberant anger which Miller projected from the opening sentences of *Cancer* are as alive now as the day when they were released. Twenty-five years after its first publication in the United States, and half a century after Miller began his final revi-

sions on the manuscript, *Cancer* is one of the best exemplars of Pound's definition of literature: News that stays news. Many writers have taken advantage of Miller's victories in the war against censorship and suppression, but Miller does not look like a pioneer who is interesting only as a precursor.

In an age when nothing is "outrageous" any more, Miller still has the power to *out* rage almost anyone writing today. As Mailer notes, "a revolution in style and consciousness" was taking place in *Cancer*, and like any real revolution, it has not been entirely absorbed. *Tropic of Cancer* is still threatening and elusive, perhaps more so than works by Miller's famous contemporaries. Miller, in *Cancer*, is still at least a little dangerous, still strangely exciting, still curiously liberating.

The mock invocation with which Miller opens *Cancer* seems dreadfully timely in the mid-1980s amidst economic uncertainty, international tension, political incompetence and social disintegration—is it the 1930s come back to haunt us in a terrible new form? Instead of cringing in fear, Miller, his own "rebellion" giving him the will to declare himself, snarls: "This then? This is not a book. This is libel, slander, defamation of character. This is not a book, in the ordinary sense of the word. No, this is a prolonged insult, a gob of spit in the face of Art, a kick in the pants to God, Man, Destiny, Time, Love, Beauty . . . what you will." This, indeed, is a declaration of human necessity, a prophetic demand that man must resist all the so-called "solutions"—the neat, packaged answers of the advertising world, the offers of all the salesmen and spokesmen who represent official versions of religion, politics, business and culture. It is an attack on what purports to be scientific rationality (educational *science*, managerial *science*, and so forth) and it leads to a countercommitment to mystery and ecstasy, anticipating and inspiring the social delirium of the 1960s. It is also, in somewhat less obvious terms, an exhortation to preserve the principle of free inquiry and to reject the security of any totalitarian system. Because Miller hardly provides a conventional argument in analytic steps, this is generally overlooked, but what Miller has done is less familiar and more effective. *Cancer* is not a tract but a demonstration, an exhibition of psychic survival.

When he crossed the Atlantic, Miller must have entertained some picture of Paris as an international refuge for the eager artist, but instead of finding a community of kindred spirits, Miller found a city crawling with the detritus of America's spiritual decay. The fabled City of Light was there too, but it took him quite a bit longer to find it. As the book opens, the artist/hero who is Miller's narrator and protagonist has given up the idea of living in any sort of conventional manner and has become a kind of Dostoevskian underground man. We see him first in *Cancer* prowling through the bottom strata of a civilization in decomposition, recording disasters to which he remains immune. His rage cuts through the lachrymose posturing of his fellow expatriates like a sword, while his dream/vision is drawn around him like a shield. His isolation is his protection, but it has its costs. He has no real friends (how different from the corporeal Henry Miller!), just acquaintances he spends time with, gets drunk with, gets laid with and so on, and his relationship with women is ghastly. But *Tropic of Cancer* is not a cosmos—it is a picture of a time and a place from the perspective of a person who is so delighted to feel and show his strength that everything else is secondary. The book is a product of careful calculation, and some sacrifices have been made. Because Miller knew that *Cancer* was just the beginning, a part of a larger story, he made his artist/hero, as Nin pointed out, mostly sex and stomach, although there is plenty of heart too, if one looks closely. And of course, the book is relentless in its refusal to put a good face on anything.

It is this tone of absolute candor that originally upset so many people. To a world that had shut its ears to all accounts of sexual adventure in fear that it might be reminded of its own inclinations, Miller gleefully raised his voice to sing, just as Allen Ginsberg, to a world deteriorated somewhat further, felt compelled to *Howl.* "I am going to sing for you," Miller boasts, "a little off key perhaps, but I will sing. . . . To sing you must first open your mouth. You must have a pair of lungs, and a little knowledge of music. It is not necessary to have an accordion, or a guitar. The essential thing is to *want* to sing. This then is a song. I am singing." But this is not a "Song of Himself," that will come later, in the *Rosy Crucifixion.* Here, Miller's most active and intense personal reactions are primarily contemplative or fantastic since he is basically an observer. His reverie about Tania, his muse of "chaos," is typical: "I will ream out every wrinkle in your cunt, Tania, big with seed. I will send you home to your Sylvester with an ache in your belly and your womb turned inside out. Your Sylvester! Yes, he knows how to build a fire, but I know how to inflame a cunt. . . . I will tear off a few hairs from your cunt and paste them on Boris' chin. I will bite into your clitoris and spit out two franc pieces." Although there is a sense of the immediate about these promises (or threats), Miller's artist/hero is contemplating what he *will* do (or what he has done), not what he is doing. The "song" that runs through the book is a song of the world, and the most erotic verses involve the damaged men and women who live in that world, desperate and weakened creatures who resort to sexual frenzy to reclaim the life they are losing. Passages like the address to Tania are crude and vicious, but they are designed to establish Miller's fierce, defiant stance toward the culture that has been responsible for this human erosion. Unlike Tania, Boris, Sylvester and the others, Miller is not a citizen of this world, although he moves easily there and knows it well. He is more like an explorer, and the bitter humor with which he describes it is a reflection of his disengagement:

> Llona—a wild ass snuffing pleasure out of the wind. On every high hill she played the harlot— and sometimes in telephone booths and toilets. She bought a bed for King Carol and a shaving mug with his initials on it. She lay in Tottenham Court Road with her dress pulled up and fingered herself. She used candles, Roman candles, and door knobs. Not a prick in the land big enough for her . . . *not one.* Men went inside her and curled up. She wanted extension pricks, self-exploding rockets, hot boiling oil made of wax and creosote. She would cut off your prick and

> keep it inside her forever, if you gave her permission. One cunt out of a million, Llona! A laboratory cunt and no litmus paper that could take her color. She was a liar too, this Llona. She never bought a bed for King Carol. She crowned him with a whiskey bottle and her tongue was full of lice and tomorrows. Poor Carol, he could only curl up inside her and die. She drew a breath and he fell out—like a dead clam.

This is a hard passage to read without experiencing a feeling of uncertainty. Is this the only way Miller's artist/hero sees women? Is it true, as Kate Millett claims [in *Sexual Politics,* 1970], that Miller "is a compendium of sexual neuroses, and his value lies not in freeing us from such afflictions, but in having had the honesty to express and dramatize them." I believe that Millett's comments might be most appropriately applied to a discussion of the books in the triad, "The Formation . . . ," because the distance between author and "character" is considerably narrowed there. In *Cancer,* as I hope will become more apparent, both the *men* and the *women* Miller spends time with are treated with similar harshness. The contempt, disgust and fear which Miller exhibits in the passage on Llona is matched by equally contemptuous descriptions of men throughout *Cancer.* The element of fear is another matter, and it lends credence to Millett's claims. I will refer to this aspect of Miller's attitude while examining the triad, but it should be mentioned here that because of Miller's determination to maintain the tone of great confidence in his "I" narrator, some very significant facets of his life are purposefully excluded.

The point of the passage about Llona and King Carol is that the social landscape is very bleak. The women seem to have magic powers locked in their bodies but the men lack the proper keys. The myth of the fertile, life-giving earth/mother female figure has been distorted so that woman is now an insatiable, self-absorbed, castrating whore. The myth of the male as a noble warrior and a pillar of dignity, integrity, justice and reasoned discourse has been distorted so that man is now a frightened, ego-inflated phallus without feeling or wisdom. The film of *Cancer* by Joseph Strick had Rip Torn play Miller's artist/hero as this kind of man—all cock and no heart. But Miller's "I" narrator is not like these men. He can step out of the cancerous domain at any time. Between the passages on Tania and Llona, the artist/hero, sounding like Joyce Cary's Gulley Jimson, sees another "world" altogether:

> Indigo sky swept clear of fleecy clouds, gaunt trees infinitely extended, their black boughs gesticulating like a sleepwalker. Somber, spectral trees, their trunks pale as cigar ash. A silence supreme and altogether European. Shutters drawn, shops barred. A red glow here and there to mark a tryst. Brusque the façades, almost forbidding; immaculate except for the splotches of shadow cast by the trees. Passing the Orangerie I am reminded of another Paris, the Paris of Maugham, of Gauguin, Paris of George Moore. I think of that terrible Spaniard who was then starling the world with his acrobatic leaps from style to style. I think of Spengler and of his terrible pronunciamentos, and I wonder if style, style

in the grand manner, is done for. I say that my mind is occupied with these thoughts, but it is not true; it is only later, after I have crossed the Seine, after I have put behind me the carnival of lights, that I allow my mind to play with these ideas. For the moment I can think of nothing—except that I am a sentient being stabbed by the miracle of these waters that reflect a forgotten world. All along the banks the trees lean heavily over the tarnished mirror; when the wind rises and fills them with a rustling murmur they will shed a few tears and shiver as the water swirls by. I am suffocated by it. No one to whom I can communicate even a fraction of my feelings.

This is the *Paris* of Henry Miller—a timeless realm of wonder which the artist/hero can share with no one else, except perhaps the eternal company of artists with whom Miller wishes to establish kinship. This Paris is like the prelapsarian America of his imagination, but it is something more at the same time, a place which he can actually observe and enjoy. There is a certain sadness about this Paris too, because he cannot enjoy it with his "friends" ("No one to whom I can communicate. . . ."), but that makes it a kind of sanctuary for him, a refuge from the rot. He is sustained in his pleasure and wonder at this world by his confidence that one day he will be able to join the land of light to the rest of his existence, but in *Cancer*, the two worlds stand apart. And for the moment, that is sufficient, especially since he is comfortable in both of them. With his identity as the man with the most extreme passion staked out and secure, the artist/hero walks through both worlds, one dying and the other "busy being born" (in Bob Dylan's words), his outlook in very sharp contrast to all the inhabitants of the dying land:

> Walking along the Champs-Elysées, I keep thinking of my really superb health. When I say "health" I mean optimism, to be truthful. Incurably optimistic! Still have one foot in the nineteenth century. I'm a bit retarded, like most Americans. Carl finds it disgusting, this optimism. "I have only to talk of a meal," he says, "and you're radiant!" It's a fact. The mere though of a meal—*another* meal—rejuvenates me. A meal! That means something to go on—a few solid hours of work, an erection possibly. I don't deny it. I have health, good solid, animal health.

Although Miller means "meal" literally, since he often didn't know until it appeared where the next one was coming from, his appetite is clearly for experience itself, and his optimism is based on his belief that any experience will be nourishing for the artist/hero. While *Cancer* describes a world that is perishing, Miller sees beyond it to a time when art ("a few solid hours of work") will give man his soul, and love (unavailable here, only an "erection" is a possibility now) will give him his heart. In order to survive until that time comes, in fact to work to make it happen, the artist/hero needs the strength to live through the cancerous time of his life, and as Martin points out [in *Always Merry and Bright: The Life of Henry Miller—An Unauthorized Biography,* 1978], "at the end of the book the man who can write the book is born." In other words, *Cancer* is a record of Miller's resistance to the squalor which he could easily have slipped into. He is susceptible to the various disorders that have infected the people of *Cancer*—has, as a matter of fact, been infected himself throughout most of the previous decade—and he needs all of his devices (scorn, casual cruelty, the withdrawal of sympathy) to remain relatively healthy ("good solid, animal health"). His relationships with both men and women should be seen in this light. Without this "health" as a base, Miller could never get out of the Villa Borghese, where, as he says on the first page, "We are all alone here and we are dead."

Cancer is divided into fifteen "sections" but they are not *chapters,* just as *Cancer* is definitely not a *novel.* Rahv speaks of the "dissolution of genre" in Miller, but he is not particularly specific about what this amounts to. *Cancer* is really a mutant of sorts, a journal that resembles a diary, a packet of sketches, a rough collection of essays, an assemblage of anecdotes—"what you will," as Miller says. The narrative consciousness of the artist/hero gives it some continuity, but it does not have any real character development, a chronological linear progression, a plot one could outline, or any dramatic denouements or even a "conclusion" that ties things up. The word *novel* confuses the issue and tends to induce expectations that are not satisfied, as Miller may have sensed when he disagreed strongly with Edmund Wilson's review of *Cancer.* I think the word *journal* is most useful, and it might be helpful to call *Cancer* a journal of the surreal city, with its implications of a kind of newspaper that has many departments or features reflecting different concerns and modes of activity, especially if one also recognizes a parallel with the so-called "new journalism" of the 1970s. This journal, however, is not a "daily" in any sense, or regular in its record. The span of time which is covered is very elastic, and the edges are purposely hazy, as are the various divisions. It opens during the "fall of my second year in Paris," which we discover is 1929, and seems to end in the spring of 1931, but those "years" might be months, or decades. The entire concept of a calendar is burlesqued as Miller starts sections by saying, out of nowhere and with no further point, "Easter came in like a frozen hare"; or "I think it was the Fourth of July"; or "It was close to dawn on Christmas Day." One of the points behind this technique is that the artist/hero has very little to do with the demarcations of a conventional society. There are other rhythms in his life, and they gradually become apparent.

Within each of the fifteen sections, four motifs are repeated with varying emphasis. They are:

> 1. Rage at "a world crumbling and polished like a leper's skull," expressed sometimes as loathing, sometimes as hilarity.
>
> 2. Male bonding, including passages of men together eating, drinking, debating, scheming, fighting and fornicating.
>
> 3. Lust, primarily from the point of view of the conventional male narrative consciousness, with women as its object, but also as its inspiration.
>
> 4. Quasi-philosophical excursions about art, nature, religion and cosmology, including some fairly powerful lyric "poetry."

These four motifs occur to some extent in each section, and are like four threads interwoven in complementary fashion throughout the book. Whichever one is used to begin the section, the fourth motif is employed in its conclusion in nine of the last ten sections. A systematic analysis of the entire book following this pattern would be possible, but it would become dreary after awhile, just a recitation of the already understood. A brief outline of the fifteen sections, followed by a closer examination of four representative ones, will suffice. The separate sections of *Cancer* are organized in the following manner [the page references are from the 1961 Grove Press edition]:

> I (1-19): The scene, mood and style of the book are set. Tania, Llona ("a wild ass snuffing pleasure out of the wind"), Carl and Boris, writers like Miller ("They are possessed. They glow inwardly with a white flame. They are mad and tone deaf. They are sufferers"), and Moldorf ("Thyroid eyes. Michelin lips. Voice like pea soup") are introduced. Mona's departure for America is recalled as a cutting of ties, the removal of connections to previous concerns.
>
> II (20-33): Domestic chat; cultural baggage recorded in homes of people where artist/hero cadges meals, a bed, social contact. Attack on America as cause of rot everywhere.
>
> III (34-43): Germaine, the whore the artist/hero finds most compatible.
>
> IV (44-48): Carl and Marlowe, neurasthenic expatriate Americans defeated by life in Paris; Marlowe returning to America directly, Carl looking for a pension or similar sinecure ("I hate Paris! . . . All these stupid people playing cards all day . . . look at them!").
>
> V (49-62): More domestic conversation; the artist/hero finds various households stifling, his distaste for acquaintances is growing, his sense of himself as an artist is clarified ("The artist, I call myself. So be it.").
>
> VI (63-71): He is grateful for help offered by a fellow he meets, but is obliged to reject the companionship of this boring if well- meaning person whose mattress for the artist/hero is "a morgue for lice." Attends a concert, reflects on aesthetic experience of music, its hold on the audience, and what the audience might do if the artist (Ravel) did not hold back at some point.
>
> VII (72-90): A somewhat sympathetic but also destructively comic account of young Hindu man visiting brothel with Miller as guide; parody of Dante, parody of any religious commitment, debunking of blind faith, spiritualism as a solution to the mess and filth of world.
>
> VIII (91-150): Fabulous description of Van Norden, the anti-Colossus of *Cancer*, a polar-opposite of the Hindu of the previous chapter; the nonspiritual man as mechanical monster and something of a psychic double for Miller's worst impulses.
>
> IX (151-167): Tentative effort at liaison with Tania—no real relationship develops; he recalls

> life with Mona through prism of selective nostalgia, and recognizes an irrevocable commitment to the present in Paris and suffers momentary depression.
>
> X (168-188): He attempts to overcome depression with booze, brawls, broads in company of men—much brutality.
>
> XI (188-197): No satisfaction with whore who offers interesting persona when dullness beneath mask becomes apparent. Tends to equate unsatisfactory woman with city of Paris, dwelling on disappointment. Fails, momentarily, to see how one's outlook colors incidents and locations.
>
> XII (199-215): The artist/hero is living with Fillmore, another desperate expatriate. Fillmore's crudity and ugliness point toward dead end inherent in the artist/hero's worst behavior with women.
>
> XIII (216-233): Grand apostrophe to art and life: A reemergence from chaos, the lowest point of *Cancer* now firmly in permanent past.
>
> XIV (234-259): Visit to Dijon as commitment to art, work, the possibility of viable community. Dijon episode mostly unsuccessful, but effort is worthwhile in itself.
>
> XV (260-287): Fillmore's pathetic return to America. A man who has been crushed, returning in ruin. Artist/hero helps him on his way, recognizes his own survival, emerges from "year" in world of cancer stronger and fitter.

The four sections I will examine more carefully each concentrate on one of the four motifs I have described, although the others are still present as a kind of muted background. Section III deals primarily with lust, VIII with the male impulse at its worse, XIII is Miller's most serious attempt at a prolonged metaphysical discourse and XIV is concerned with the social order Miller despises.

Kate Millett calls Germaine "the archetypal French prostitute of American tourism," and quotes eight passages out of context in which woman is assigned to a "mindless material capacity." Although I would suggest that the artist/hero and the corporeal Henry Miller are not quite equal entities here, and that all of *Cancer* presents people living under circumstances of considerable nastiness which Miller describes to illustrate things as they ought *not* to be, Millett makes a pretty convincing case that Germaine is treated, like so many other women in Miller's work, with "anxiety and contempt." And yet, there is Norman Mailer arguing [in *Genius and Lust: A Journey through the Major Writings of Henry Miller*, 1976] that *lust* "takes over the instinct to create life and converts it to a force," and that Miller "captured something in the sexuality of men as it had never been seen before, precisely that it was man's sense of awe before woman, his dread of her position one step closer to eternity (for in that step were her powers) which made men detest women, revile them, humiliate them, defecate symbolically upon them, do everything to reduce them so that one might dare to enter them and take pleasure of them." Although Mailer wrote his essay on lust almost as a direct response to Millett's attack on his thinking in *Sexual Politics,* the two are not listening to or talking to each other at all. Mailer's conclusion is that passages like those that Millett condemns are "screams [of] his barbaric yawp of utter adoration for the power and the glory and the grandeur of the female in the universe." When they are read separately, *both* arguments seem convincing. But "utter adoration" is surely nothing like "anxiety and contempt." A close look at the section in *Cancer* where Germaine appears is in order.

The section begins with the artist/hero pretending not to be hungry so as to avoid disturbing the Cronstadts (actually the family of Walter Lowenfels) who are sitting down at a special meal just as he arrives. He mockingly calls himself *"delicat"* in his pretense, but adds poignantly, "On the way out I cast a lingering glance at the bones lying on the baby's plate—there was still meat on them." As he walks down the Rue de Buci, he notices "The bars wide open and the curbs lined with bicycles. All the meat and vegetable markets are in full swing." The streets are seething with life, "a fresh hive of activity. Long queues of people with vegetables under their arms, turning in here and there with crisp, sparkling appetites." Amidst the people rushing to satisfy their appetites, the artist/hero is both delighted by the motion and color and troubled by his own persistent hunger. The dual nature of his reaction is caught by his comparison of the Square de Furstenberg as he sees it now "at high noon" and as he saw it, "the other night when I passed by . . . deserted, bleak, spectral." He compares the trees at night to T. S. Eliot's poetry, calling them "intellectual," trees with their roots in stone, bare branches not yet in bloom. Images of aridity are overcoming the artist/hero's delight in the sensuality of the world.

As the day continues and the artist/hero wanders on through the streets, "guts rattling," it begins to rain and the light and joy of the city are replaced by images of confusion and disease. In a bookstore window, he sees the title, *A Man Cut in Slices* and recognizes its applicability to his life since he is often so completely occupied with the tasks of finding food, lodging, good company that he cannot see any larger picture of things. The title suggests food again, but the food seems to be spoiling now, less enticing since he can't get it anyhow. The street begins to look like a wax reproduction of organs "eaten away by syphilis," suggesting the reversal in *Hamlet* where the prince describes Polonius at supper, but where he is "food" for maggots.

The "beautiful day" has turned 180 degrees, and the artist/hero pauses "a few minutes to drink in the full squalor of the scene." Food has become repulsive as he describes "a clump of decrepit buildings which have so rotted away that they have collapsed on one another and formed a sort of intestinal embrace. The ground is uneven, the flagging slippery with slime. A sort of human dump heap which has been filled with cinders and dry garbage. . . . There is the shrill squawk of children with pale faces and bony limbs, rickety little urchins marked with the forceps. A fetid odor seeps from the walls. . . ." The images here are of rot, starvation, indigestion and waste. But it is not just the visible world that has been spoiled. The artist/hero

turns away from the Place du Combat, and his mind "reverts to a book I was reading the other day." The book describes a town in a shambles, "corpses, mangled by butchers and stripped by plunderers, lay thick in the streets; wolves sneaked from the suburbs to eat them." The town is Paris during the days of "Charles the Silly," and the artist/hero mentions that he has "thought long and ruefully over the sad fate of Charles the Silly. A half-wit, who prowled about the halls of his Hôtel St. Paul, garbed in the filthiest rags, eaten away by ulcers and vermin, gnawing a bone, when they flung him one." A debased monarch, without proper food, eaten away by his own hunger, reminding the artist/hero of *his* need for nourishment. And then, in a typical application of associative logic, the artist/hero mentions the main "diversion" of Charles the Silly, "card games with his 'low-born companion' Odette de Champdivers."

Here, then, is a picture of a man in an ugly world who is a little desperate and very hungry. "It was a Sunday afternoon, much like this, when I first met Germaine," he recalls. Miller has spent several pages showing how one of the most basic of the natural appetites has been perverted. It would be nice to be able to choose one's food, not to have to scramble for it and accept what you can get. It would also be nice to be able to develop a relationship with a woman under ideal conditions, but in the world of *Cancer,* both the men and women Miller knows are operating under less than ideal conditions. Maybe it is arrogant to condemn the behavior of these people from the comfort of an academic cloister. In a landscape where one is either starving or being "eaten," there are different orders of primacy. And even in this setting, Germaine stands out among her "colleagues."

The artist/hero remembers that he was walking on the Rue du Pasteur-Wagner, on the corner "of the Rue Amelot which hides behind the boulevard like a slumbering lizard," when he sees, continuing the image of eating; "a cluster of vultures who croaked and flapped their dirty wings, who reached out with sharp talons and plucked you into a doorway. Jolly, rapacious devils who didn't even give you time to button your pants when it was over." "Germaine was different," he says, although, "There was nothing to tell me so from her appearance." What distinguishes her is the fact that amidst a clearly commercial transaction ("It was not difficult to come to terms"), she notices and responds to those things which make a person distinct as an individual, "she liked the knickerbockers I was wearing. *Très chic!* she thought." Just the sort of statement to make a person feel a bit special, although that could be construed as part of her "job." However, when Germaine presents herself to the artist/hero, he describes her pride in herself as an aspect of a kind of dignity that cannot be demolished by the rude manners of others. "There was something about her eloquence at that moment and the way she thrust that rose-bush under my nose which remains unforgettable." Germaine's pride in her sexuality is very sad in that she has nothing else that the world values, but her courage is impressive. And whether it is lust alone, or something more, the artist/hero says, "That Sunday afternoon, with its poisonous breath of spring in the air, everything clicked again." The starving man has found food. After their assignation, the artist/hero is ready to look on her with his cold, discerning eye again, but in spite of his defensive stance, some humane instinct has been ignited in both of them:

> As we stepped out of the hotel I looked her over again in the harsh light of day and I saw clearly what a whore she was—the gold teeth, the geranium in her hat, the run-down heels, etc., etc. Even the fact that she wormed a dinner out of me and cigarettes and taxi hadn't the least disturbing effect upon me. I encouraged it, in fact. I liked her so well that after dinner we went back to the hotel and took another shot at it. "For love," this time.

The artist/hero is not prepared for much more than a satisfying of appetites, but he is forced to admit that he liked Germaine's sexuality and that he liked *her* too. "I liked them separately and I liked them together," he says. When she discovers the artist/hero's "true circumstances," she offers him food and a kind of friendship, and it is at this stage of the narrative that Kate Millett begins to quote Miller's final estimation of Germaine. I would suggest an alternative interpretation. The words which describe Germaine as "a whore from the cradle," and refer to "her whore's heart which is not really a good heart but a lazy one." are an indictment of the artist/hero at this point in the narrative. He has been rendered unfit to judge the nuances of a person's motivation because of his own reduced vision. All he can admire in Germaine are those things which he values in himself—guts, fire, stamina, courage and cunning. That she may have more to offer, a complex, caring, sharing side; possibly a reflective, even philosophic inclination, distresses the artist/hero because he has become accustomed to regarding sex as he regards food—the answer to a physical urge to be satiated however possible. In comparing Germaine to Claude, another prostitute, the artist/hero mentions to Germaine's "credit" that "she was ignorant and lusty, she put her heart and soul into her work. She was a whore all the way through—and that was her virtue." Claude troubles the artist/hero because she "had a soul and a conscience; she had refinement, too, which is bad—in a whore. Claude always imparted a feeling of sadness; she left the impression, unwittingly, of course, that you were just one more added to the stream which fate had ordained to destroy her." Without any explanatory message, Miller has made it pretty clear that the artist/hero, at this early point in the narrative, has shut down a vital part of his sensory apparatus because he is not capable of dealing with a woman beyond certain prescribed, formulaic rituals of passion-plus-commerce. Millett claims that this is Miller "giving voice to certain sentiments which masculine culture had long experienced but always rather carefully suppressed." I would disagree to some extent, and suggest that within the context of the entire section, Miller is not just "giving voice" to these sentiments, but criticizing them by showing the narrowness and fear of the person who is delivering them. The dismissal of Germaine's qualities as a person at the end of the section are not the words of a person we can trust on this subject, but of someone who has been temporarily warped by the accumulated pressures of living "down and out" in an urban wasteland.

Miller's attitude toward this kind of man becomes more clear in the section (VIII) that presents the bizarre Van Norden, a character with many discomforting similarities to the artist/hero at his worst. The long section is one of the most vivid in *Cancer*. What kind of a country, what kind of a civilization could produce such a monster, it almost demands to know? Van Norden is not a murderer in the conventional sense, but he is a killer of the soul, and his homicidal tendencies extend to everyone he meets, including himself. The fact that he goes unpunished, that he is not even discouraged in any way, is a clear indication that something is drastically wrong. This man is, in Millett's words, the one who "yearns to effect a complete depersonalization of woman into cunt," and the one who turns sex into "a game-fantasy of power untroubled by the reality of persons or the complexity of dealing with fellow human beings." The opening paragraphs of the section introduce him and also establish at the outset a separation between him and the narrator:

> At one-thirty I called on Van Norden, as per agreement. He had warned me that if he didn't answer it would mean that he was sleeping with someone, probably his Georgia cunt.

> Anyway, there he was, tucked away comfortably, but with an air of weariness as usual. He wakes up cursing himself, or cursing his job, or cursing life. He wakes up utterly bored and discomfited, chagrined to think that he did not die overnight.

The artist/hero often gets angry or discouraged, but he invariably wakes up in high spirits and stays that way until worn down by some problem. He never curses "life."

The first few pages of the section are taken up entirely by a rambling monologue in which Van Norden makes his attitude toward women all too clear. These pages are a masterful example of gruesome comedy, and the comedy is at Van Norden's expense. His pathetic self-centeredness and his simplistic reduction of everything make him a parody of a man. Miller does not have to comment at all as Van Norden is condemned in his own words:

> "My teeth are all rotten," he says, gargling his throat. "It's the fucking bread they give you to eat here." He opens his mouth wide and pulls his lower lip down. "See that? Pulled out six teeth yesterday. Soon I'll have to get another plate. That's what you get working for a living. When I was on the bum I had all my teeth, my eyes were bright and clear. Look at me now! It's a wonder I can make a cunt any more. Jesus, what I'd like is to find some rich cunt. . . ."

Vain, stupid, consumed by self-pity—and in Paris, he doesn't like the bread! And lacking in both ideals and faith: " 'The married ones! Christ, if you saw all the married cunts I bring up here you'd never have any more illusions. They're worse than the virgins, the married ones. They don't wait for you to start things—they fish it out for you themselves. And then they talk about love afterwards. It's disgusting. I tell you, I'm actually beginning to hate cunt!' " In their basic outlook, Van Norden and the artist/hero are at polar opposites, and even though they share each other's company and go whoring together, this should be apparent immediately. If the tone of Van Norden's whining doesn't get the point across, then his incredible statement, "Would you believe it, I've never been to the Louvre—nor the Comédie-Française. Is it worth going to those joints?", must separate him from Miller whose reactions to the work of painters approaches reverence.

Miller listens to Van Norden rather noncommittally, but when Van Norden starts to invite him to various social engagements, the artist/hero begins to demur ("I can't tomorrow, Joe. I promised to help Carl out . . ."), and when Van Norden proposes they "share" a mother and daughter, his reluctance is apparent ("Listen, Joe, you'd better find somebody else . . ."). At this point, Van Norden becomes almost desperate, practically pleading with the artist/hero for companionship: " 'What do you do with yourself all day? Don't you get bored? What do you do for a lay? Listen . . . come here! Don't run away yet . . . I'm lonely. Do you know something—if this keeps up another year I'll go nuts. I've got to get out of this fucking country. There's nothing for me here. I know it's lousy now, in America, but just the same. . . .' " Van Norden's monologue concludes, and during the next few pages, the same theme is played again with minor variations as Carl tells the artist/hero about his visit to a woman named Irene whom he has been courting by letter for months. Miller mentions at one point that as Carl headed for Irene's apartment, "he threw me a last despairing glance, one of those mute appeals which a dog makes when you put a noose around its neck. Going through the revolving door I thought of Van Norden. . . ." Carl's hesitancy and confusion as he relates the details of their meeting become steadily more preposterous and then gradually pitiful:

> "And that's not all. I promised her a letter in the meantime. How am I going to write her a letter now? I haven't anything to say. . . . Shit! If only she were ten years younger. Do you think I should go with her . . . to Borneo or wherever it is she wants to take me? What would I do with a rich cunt like that on my hands? I don't know how to shoot. I am afraid of guns and all that sort of thing. Besides, she'll be wanting me to fuck her night and day . . . nothing but hunting and fucking all the time . . . I can't do it!"

Both Carl and Van Norden are cases of arrested development, adolescents who need constant reassurance because they have so little sense of who they are. Miller is wryly sympathetic, almost like an older brother ("Maybe it won't be so bad as you think. She'll buy you ties and all sorts of things. . . ."), but Carl is a defeated man, and his last words have the stuff of horror about them: " 'That's it—that's the best solution for a writer. What does a guy want with his arms and legs? He doesn't need arms and legs to write with. He needs security . . . peace . . . protection. . . . All I'd want is a good wheelchair and three meals a day. Then I'd give them something to read, those pricks.' " Obviously, Miller himself does not believe "that's the best solution for a writer." And similarly, he does not share Van Norden's view of women, even if there is some overlapping. The first fifteen pages of this section show plainly that Miller does not endorse Van Norden's

rampant sexism or Carl's pitiable retreat from life. On the other hand, he does not quite condemn them either. His attitude is somewhat ambiguous because he has experienced several crises himself that have brought him, momentarily, rather close to their psychic states. What interests Miller is the way they behave, and the world which must be partially to blame for this kind of behavior.

As I have noted previously, Miller is an observer in this book. Following Carl's account of his night with Irene, Van Norden tells Miller the whole story again, repeating the details that Carl told him. The next few pages are as imaginatively pornographic as anything Miller has written, and they present an interesting double perspective because Carl is inclined to put a romantic gloss on things while Van Norden has a fixation for specific anatomic detail. Neither man can see the woman herself: In Carl's case she is lost in fantasy, while in Van Norden's she is never more than a collection of erotic accessories. Although Miller does not attempt to psychoanalyze Van Norden, there is one very revealing moment when Van Norden, in a moment of "overwhelming futility," confesses, "I want to be able to surrender myself to a woman. . . . I want her to take me out of myself. But to do that, she's got to be better than I am; she's got to have a mind, not just a cunt. She's got to make me believe that I need her, that I can't live without her." Of course, such a woman will never exist for Van Norden. He does not know how to share any part of himself with anybody, much less "surrender," and he has such an inflated sense of his own "qualities" and such a superficially critical view of all women that he would never admit one is "better" than he is. Miller does not tell us any of these things, but Van Norden's words make it all apparent. (In this section, the artist/hero hardly ever ventures an opinion on anything and rarely explains character except to say why Van Norden cannot write at all.) By the time Van Norden expounds upon the limitations of all women, it is obvious he is not speaking either for the narrator of *Cancer* or for its author, as Millett claims. His "philosophy" is presented as the false gospel of a failure:

> The thing is this—they all look alike. When you look at them with their clothes on you imagine all sorts of things; you give them an individuality like, which they haven't got, of course. . . . Listen, do you know what I did afterwards? I gave her a quick lay and then I turned my back on her. Yeah, I picked up a book and I read. You can get something out of a book, even a bad book . . . but a cunt, it's just sheer loss of time. . . .

What follows this bit of wisdom is one of the most harrowing scenes in modern literature, an emblem of an age much like Chaplin's berserk assembly line in *Modern Times*. Van Norden has persuaded Miller that they should pick up a whore, and the artist/hero, once again the observer, watches "with a cool, scientific detachment":

> As I watch Van Norden tackle her, it seems to me that I'm looking at a machine whose cogs have slipped. Left to themselves, they could go on this way forever, grinding and slipping, without ever anything happening. Until a hand shuts

the motor off. The sight of them coupled like a pair of goats without the least spark of passion, grinding and grinding away for no reason except the fifteen francs, washes away every bit of feeling I have except the inhuman one of satisfying my curiosity. The girl is lying on the edge of the bed and Van Norden is bent over her like a satyr with his two feet solidly planted on the floor. I am sitting on a chair behind him, watching their movements with a cool, scientific detachment; it doesn't matter to me if it should last forever. It's like watching one of those crazy machines which throw newspaper out, millions and billions and trillions of them with their meaningless headlines. . . . As long as that spark of passion is missing there is no human significance in the performance. The machine is better to watch. And these two are like a machine which has slipped its cogs. It needs the touch of a human hand to set it right. It needs a mechanic.

For Miller, the "mechanic" is the artist, the person who can see the infinite variety of the cosmos, the endless intricacy of the human heart and mind—what a piece of work is man. After several more pages commenting on the great richness of Paris and his almost relentless desire to see, to know, to contemplate (à la Whitman), Miller concludes the section by showing just how far from Van Norden he is. If the world of *Cancer* is to be "drawn back again to the proper precincts of the human world," then it is artists like Matisse (and Miller himself) who will be instrumental in the process. Miller describes the effect of Matisse's work on his own sensibility (an effect that Van Norden and the other damaged figures in *Cancer* could not feel) in terms of light versus darkness, one of the most prevalent patterns of his writing. The light is a symbol of creative energy, and when it is present, the full range of imaginative possibility of the human mind is brought into play so that everything is seen as marvelous and fascinating. For Matisse, the world could never be boring.

The artist/hero enters the art gallery on the Rue de Sèze as if he were entering a genuinely new world. He has come from what he calls "the world of men and women whose last drop of juice has been squeezed out by the machine—the martyrs of modern progress." The transition from the cancerous world of Van Norden, Carl and the others to "a world so natural, so complete, that I am lost"—the world of Matisse's paintings—is literally staggering: "On the threshold of that big hall whose walls are now ablaze, I pause a moment to recover from the shock which one experiences when the habitual gray of the world is rent asunder and the color of life splashes forth in song and poem." Miller attempts to find verbal equivalents for Matisse's images, knowing that there is no real substitute for seeing the paintings, but trying to capture the spirit behind their creation in his writing. It is the attempt that is most significant, because by his own efforts here he is displaying the active response and total involvement that an artist hopes for but rarely receives from his "public." In doing this, Miller is trying to show that, like Matisse, he can also see a world alive with color and light; and he is also trying to indicate that his own real audience is composed of people who share his knowledge of and appreciation for what Matisse has accomplished. All of these ideas are a part of

his strategy to separate himself momentarily from his existence amongst the damaged people he lives with in *Cancer,* the people to whom he can't "communicate even a fraction of" his feeling.

For several paragraphs, Miller engages in what might be called an appreciative participation in Matisse's art: "Vividly now I recall how the glint and sparkle of light caroming from the massive chandeliers splintered and ran blood, flecking the tips of the waves that beat monotonously on the dull gold outside the windows. On the beach, masts and chimneys interlaced, and like a fuliginous shadow the figure of Albertine gliding through the surf, fusing into the mysterious quick and prism of a protoplasmic realm, uniting her shadow to the dream and harbinger of death." Beneath or beyond the paintings themselves, Miller sees the figure of Matisse, an emblem for the artist as one who is "capable of transforming the negative reality of life into the substantial and significant outlines of art." "He stands at the helm peering with steady blue eyes into the portfolio

Henry Miller's list of streets and places in Paris.

of time. Into what distant corners has he not thrown his long, slanting gaze? . . . He is a bright sage, a dancing seer who, with a sweep of the brush, removes the ugly scaffold to which the body of man is chained by the incontrovertible facts of life." The section concludes with several images of women in Matisse's work, women who are seen with an awe and wonder diametrically opposite from Van Norden's view. It is true that Miller is not writing with sympathy and understanding of one particular woman, but his evocation of Matisse is a part of a vision that is as exalting as Van Norden's is degrading. For the artist/hero, women are never interchangeable, they do not "all look alike":

> But in Matisse, in the exploration of his brush, there is the trembling glitter of a world which demands only the presence of the female to crystallize the most fugitive aspirations. . . . I stumble upon the phantom odalisques of Matisse fastened to the trees, their tangled manes drenched with sap. . . . Even as the world falls apart the Paris that belongs to Matisse shudders with bright, gasping orgasms, the air itself is steady with a stagnant sperm, the trees tangled like hair. . . .

What is missing from *Cancer* until the Dijon section, the next to last one, is even the most tentative suggestion that the artist/hero can operate anywhere between the tremendous extremes of the hell of "the incontrovertible facts of life" and the heaven of "the significant outlines of art." This may be seen as a weakness, but *Cancer* has been conceived of as a book of absolutes, and its lack of a subtle investigation of human relationships in the middle ground is a part of its character and design. I will reserve comment on Miller's failure to deal with these matters effectively until I examine those books of the triad, "The Formation . . ." in which they become the central subject. What is important here is to continue to investigate Miller's vision of the world of art as an antidote, or a redemptive force, to be employed against the nightmare of a machinelike people locked into a sterile land. The paean to Matisse is like many of the concluding passages to the separate sections of *Cancer,* a rhapsodic celebration of not only the life-giving powers of art, but also of what Charles Feidelson has called the "symbol-making intelligence" of the human consciousness. It is the ability to see with wonder the endless phenomena of the universe and the desire to try to find language to convey this feeling of "wonder" that marks Miller's sensibility here. It is his relish for naming things and for placing them in bizarre juxtapositions which create new and unusual harmonies that keeps Miller's artist/hero inviolate in the worst sectors of *Cancer*'s awful blight.

It is in his passages of "impure poetry" that Miller comes closest to actually offering a "philosophy" of existence, and because his writing is much closer to the form of poetry than traditional philosophic discourse, to consider it in terms of philosophic strictures can only lead to misunderstanding and even condemnation. These passages are not logical arguments but attempts to create a mood in which some idea might be seen, or felt or understood. They work, if at all, by the strength and originality of their imagery,

by the establishment of a certain ethos through the use of rhythm and structure and by their ability to generate a kindred emotion in the reader. They are, obviously, dependent on the willing participation of a reader with similar sympathies, and as such, their appeal is much more to the mystical than the rational. In other words, they have the very personal, singular and difficult to defend attributes of much contemporary poetry. The section (XIII) which precedes the Dijon trip offers some of this "poetry" at its best and worst.

Miller opens the "poem" with a statement of the conditions that led to its genesis:

> And now it is three o'clock in the morning and we have a couple of trollops here who are doing somersaults on the bare floor. Fillmore is walking around naked with a goblet in his hand, and that paunch of his is drumtight, hard as a fistula. All the Pernod and champagne and cognac and Anjou which he guzzled from three in the afternoon on, is gurgling in his trap like a sewer. The girls are putting their ears to his belly as if it were a music box. Open his mouth with a buttonhook and drop a slug in the slot. When the sewer gurgles I hear the bats flying out of the belfry and the dream slides into artifice.

The time, the place, the company, the activity, all these are inducements to shut down the mind and turn up the skin/senses; but not for Miller. The artist/hero is seemingly inspired to mental intensity by just those things which encourage sensual abandon for most people, which is a partial explanation of his "philosophy"—a kind of emotional *reasoning* that parallels a heightened sensory indulgence; a progression by instinct and a building of the argument by repetition of related images in increasing intensity.

The subject of this "poem" is woman, and how she contains the mystery of life. Millett uses it to suggest that Miller is reducing women to sexual apparatus, Mailer to prove that Miller is a genius. I would suggest that it is an extraordinary series of images, a catalog of passionate responses like the lists of Rabelais, and in terms of "meaning," a tribute to a sort of Lawrentian life force and a prayer of appreciation for Blake's God of Energy as Eternal Delight. My temptation is to quote ten full pages of it, but instead, here are some selections of what I feel are the most effective "stanzas" with a few comments.

First, blending art, literature, archetype and inspired nonsense, Miller indicates his awe at woman as the living incarnation of some universal power:

> I see again the great sprawling mothers of Picasso, their breasts covered with spiders, their legend hidden deep in the labyrinth. And Molly Bloom lying on a dirty mattress for eternity. On the toilet door red chalk cocks and the madonna uttering the diapason of woe. I hear a wild, hysterical laugh, a room full of lockjaw, and the body that was black glows like phosphorus. Wild, wild, utterly uncontrollable laughter, and that crack laughing at me too, laughing through the mossy whiskers, a laugh that creases the bright, polished surface of the billiard ball.

Great whore and mother of man with gin in her veins. Mother of all harlots, spider rolling us in your logarithmic grave, insatiable one, fiend whose laughter rives me!

Then, like chaos swirling into shape, Miller narrows the focus and makes one mode, the mathematical, the controlling vessel in which to concentrate the rampage:

When I look down into that crack I see an equation sign, the world at balance, a world reduced to zero and no trace of remainder. Not the zero on which Van Norden turned his flashlight, not the empty crack of the prematurely disillusioned man, but an Arabian zero rather, the sign from which spring endless mathematical worlds, the fulcrum which balances the stars and the light dreams and the machines lighter than air and the lightweight limbs and the explosives that produced them.

One wishes that Miller had followed Pound on the principle of *condensare,* because the "poem" is surrounded by sentences of murky theorizing and awkward expostulation. At times, it lapses back into mere argument, and these tend to destroy the mood because, as Mailer pointed out, "his polemical essays read like sludge." But then the poem picks up again, extravagantly extending the image of woman still further:

The earth is not an arid plateau of health and comfort, but a great sprawling female with velvet torso that swells and heaves with ocean billows; she squirms beneath the diadem of sweat and anguish. Naked and sexed she rolls among the clouds in the violet light of the stars. All of her, from her generous breasts to her gleaming thighs, blazes with furious ardor. She moves amongst the seasons and the years with a grand whoopla that seizes the torso with paroxysmal fury, that shakes the cobwebs out of the sky; she subsides on her pivotal orbits with volcanic tremors.

This is a classic apostrophe to great Venus, the goddess of love, and it is very specifically from a male point of view. Perhaps Miller realized that it was a bit superficial, because the next "stanza" describes woman in her sorrow:

And then her sorrow widened, like the bow of a dreadnought and the weight of her sinking flooded my ears. Slime wash and sapphires slipping, sluicing through the gay neurons, and the spectrum spliced and the gunwales dipping. Soft as lion-pad I heard the gun carriages turn, saw them vomit and drool: the firmament sagged and all the stars turned black. Black ocean bleeding and the brooding stars breeding chunks of fresh-swollen flesh while overhead the birds wheeled and out of the hallucinated sky fell the balance with mortar and pestle and the bandaged eyes of justice.

Miller might have actually set this as a poem if he hadn't been bound by the typological barriers of typeset prose. Consider this arrangement:

And then her sorrow widened
like the bow of a dreadnought
and the weight of her sinking

flooded my ears

Slime wash and sapphires slipping
sluicing through the gay neurons
the spectrum spliced and the gunwales dipping

Soft as lion-pad
I heard the gun carriages turn
saw them vomit and drool:

the firmament sagged [and]
all the stars turned black
black ocean bleeding
and the brooding stars breeding
chunks of fresh-swollen flesh

Overhead the birds wheeled [and]
out of the hallucinated sky fell the
balance with mortar and pestle [and] the
bandaged eyes of justice

A few "ands" have been removed, but essentially, this is the "stanza" that Miller wrote. It reminds me of Hart Crane, particularly *The Bridge,* which was composed about the same time as **Tropic of Cancer.**

From page 228 through the middle of page 231, the "poem" hovers on a back burner while Miller delivers some more "argument," but then it concludes with some of his best and most powerful writing. Here, he is no longer talking about woman, but about an aspect of women's nature, and about its significance in the world for both men and women. The mood is regenerated by a rhapsody on rivers as the symbolic carriers of life—indeed, the water of life:

I want a world of men and women, of trees that do not talk (because there is too much talk in the world as it is!) of rivers that carry you to places, not rivers that are legends, but rivers that put you in touch with men and women, with architecture, religion, plants, animals—rivers that have boats on them and in which men drown, drown not in myth and legend and books and dust of the past, but in time and space and history. I want rivers that make oceans such as Shakespeare and Dante, rivers which do not dry up in the void of the past.

Then, Miller shifts from the specific, *water,* to one of its basic properties. Beginning with a generous nod to Joyce (an invocation to the muse?), Miller sings in his most powerful voice of a world at once awful and wondrous; a world in which the artist/hero can thrive and his art can prosper:

"I love everything that flows," said the great blind Milton of our times. I was thinking of him this morning when I awoke with a great bloody shout of joy: I was thinking of his rivers and trees and all that world of night which he is exploring. Yes, I said to myself, I too love everything that flows: rivers, sewers, lava, semen, blood, bile, words, sentences. I love the amniotic fluid when it spills out of the bag. I love the kidney with its painful gallstones, its gravel and what-not; I love the urine that pours out scalding and the clap that runs endlessly; I love the words of hysterics and the sentences that flow on like dysentery and mirror all the sick images of the soul. . . . I love everything that flows, everything that has time in it and becoming, that brings us back to the beginning where there is never end: the violence of the prophets, the obscenity that is ecstasy, the wisdom of the fanatic, the priest with his rubber litany, the foul words of the whore, the spittle that floats away in the gutter, the milk of the breast and the bitter honey that pours from the womb, all that is fluid, melting, dissolute and dissolvent, all the pus and dirt that in flowing is purified, that loses its sense of origin, that makes the great circuit toward death and dissolution.

As Mailer says, "No, there is nothing like Henry Miller when he gets rolling."

Cancer concludes with two sections, one almost an interlude and the other as close to a summary of his faith as Miller gets. The interlude (IXV) involves the artist/hero taking a job at a lycée where he is supposed to teach French schoolboys the English language. The section is something of a practical demonstration of how one can actually work toward the realization of a community that has its roots in the life-flow Miller loves. It is set in Dijon, significantly outside Paris, and Miller uses the school as a model for the world he has just left. The dull, oafish, small-minded professors stand for the mind-numbing establishment wisdom which has led to a cultural catastrophe. The boys are still young enough to be saved, and Miller is a guide to and exemplar of an alternative life vision. He attempts to wake the boys up, to make them aware of the world and of themselves. "Here I was," he says, "the emissary of a corpse who, after he had plundered right and left, after he had caused untold suffering and misery, dreamed of universal peace":

> What did they expect me to talk about, I wonder? About *Leaves of Grass,* about the tariff walls, about the Declaration of Independence, about the latest gang war? What? Just what, I'd like to know. Well, I'll tell you—I never mentioned these things. I started right off the bat with a lesson in the physiology of love. How the elephants make love—that was it! It caught like wildfire. After the first day there were no more empty benches. After that first lesson in English they were standing at the door waiting for me. We got along swell together. They asked all sorts of questions, as though they had never learned a damned thing. I let them fire away. I taught them to ask still more ticklish questions. *Ask anything!*—that was my motto. I'm here as a plenipotentiary from the realm of free spirits. I'm here to create a fever and a ferment.

Miller doesn't really save the boys, possibly because he is too busy trying to save himself. Since Dijon offers him no excitement, he must flee back to Paris to stay alive, but he has made his mark and other forays will follow.

On the last pages of *Cancer,* the artist/hero seems to step permanently away from the dying people and the doomed culture of the surreal city and into a landscape of gentle hills rising serenely above a great river. First, Miller helps poor Fillmore onto a boat headed back to England and then America. Fillmore has succumbed and is returning to his home a beaten man. In contrast, Miller has sur-

vived, and thus can feel at home anywhere. Although he feels sorry for Fillmore, he can't help noticing that his own strength has been proven in a dangerous combat zone that has produced many casualties. After the dark, depressing winter world in Dijon, "Paris had never looked so good to me," he says. With money meant for Fillmore's pregnant mistress divided in two shares so that he might have a reward for his good offices, the artist/hero calls for a cab and magnanimously tells the driver to go "anywhere. . . . Go through the Bois, go all around it—and take your time, I'm in no hurry." The cab cruises around Paris for awhile, and Miller eventually directs it toward the Seine. As he looks at the great river, he experiences a sense of peace that is unlike anything he had known anywhere in *Cancer.* For the first time, he has actually succeeded in transcending the terrors of the immediate present and is able to turn off the tremendous flow of energy that has been driving him. And in doing this, with his defensive network not acting as an impedance, the artist/hero is able to merge for a moment with a much greater energy flow—the river of light from the natural world. The moment may not last, but it augurs well for the future:

> Christ, before my eyes there shimmered such a golden peace that only a neurotic could dream of turning his head away. So quietly flows the Seine that one hardly notices its presence. It is always there, quiet and unobtrusive, like a great artery running through the human body. In the wonderful peace that fell over me it seemed as if I had climbed to the top of a high mountain; for a little while I would be able to look around me, to take in the meaning of the landscape.

Linda R. Williams (essay date 1991)

SOURCE: "Critical Warfare and Henry Miller's *Tropic of Cancer,*" in *Feminist Criticism: Theory and Practice,* edited by Susan Sellers, Harvester Wheatsheaf, 1991, pp. 23-43.

[*Williams is an English educator and critic. In the following excerpt, she criticizes Kate Millett's influential attack on Henry Miller's misogyny as theoretically naive and ineffectual. Williams proposes a feminist reading which takes account of the sexual ambivalence implied by Miller's masochism and suggests that Miller embraced a desire for self-annihilation.*]

Tropic of Cancer is Henry Miller's polemic of antihumanism. It is an attempt to write 'The last book', an affirmation of extremity in the forms of transgression, disease and violence. For the Miller of *Tropic of Cancer* life is war, with Paris as its theatre. Men and women fight each other on the sexual battlefield of its pages, with a violence which makes the impossibility of impartial reading explicit: if we read the book at all, it is hard not to take sides. Want, sexual warfare, and a lack of sentiment about humanity interconnect in the cravings of the selves which populate *Tropic of Cancer,* and Miller's exploration of the savage and exploitative battles or contracts between men and women has made him an obvious target for feminists. The novel's grim opening movement—'toward the prison of death. There is no escape'—is a kind of perverse come-on to those of us who would not be deemed faint-hearted readers. Thus Miller begins his attempt to show a world revealing itself 'for the mad slaughterhouse that it is', in which desire becomes ultimately the desire for annihilation, a nirvana in which the hero screams exultantly ' "*I am inhuman!*" ' It is a book which wants to be literally 'beastly', setting itself an extreme aesthetic agenda which aims to violate the coherence and the ethical priorities of the conscious self. Miller's universe is apocalyptic: 'The age demands violence', and sex prowls on the volcano's edge.

Much of the novel's reputation for offensiveness can be put down to the moral perspectives of the left and right at the time of its first attempted publication (its actual American publication was delayed until 1961); the judgments against sexual explicitness and language would not be so clearly made now, and *Cancer* retains little of the power to shock it held for the Judge who tried it for obscenity at a failed attempted publication in 1951: 'If this be importable literature, then the dignity of the human person and the stability of the family unit, which are the cornerstones of our systems of society, are lost to us' [Louis Goodman, 'District Judge of the US, Louis Goodman on the "Tropics," ' in *Henry Miller Between Heaven and Hell,* 1961]. To be deemed dangerous is, however, exactly the critical response Miller sought; in *Tropic of Capricorn* he wrote 'I look at people murderously', and his novels invite readers to look back with critical knives at the ready. In the first section of this essay I hope to show that Miller defines the terrain of sexual warfare on his own terms, terms which are not fully challenged by early feminist critique in its hostile engagements with him, before suggesting how other readings might combat this problem. Miller delights in outrage, but outrageousness is ever more difficult. Perhaps the only reader who would now not disappoint him in this is the feminist critic.

Feminist outrage at Henry Miller has characteristically engaged with him according to that familiar dialectic of shocking fiction countered by shocked critical response. This is not difficult. *Tropic of Cancer* tries very hard to be nasty, embracing in its frenzy of violation an ambitious range of objects. Miller promises us a novel which is 'a prolonged insult, a gob of spit in the face of Art, a kick in the pants to God, Man, Destiny, Time, Love, Beauty . . . what you will'. However, this anti-metaphysic is not pointed enough for Miller, and he proceeds to mark out more specifically the recipient of the text's outpourings, an implied reader who will submit to a readerly 'libel, slander and defamation of character' in receipt of the text. The ideal forms insulted above soon become pin-pointed as a 'you': 'I will sing while you croak, I will dance over your dirty corpse.' Who, then, is this 'you' which the novel invokes in order to trample on? Who is created as listener only to become a corpse?

> It is to you, Tania, that I am singing.

The 'you' that croaks and is buried, and the 'you' that listens, is of course a woman. But she is woman as reader, as muse and inspiration, as Miller's necessary victim and—as a key inhabitant of the 'mad slaughterhouse'—the mediator of his desired annihilation. Through a death-ly sexual communion which uses Tania, Miller touches 'his own' non-existence. She is the 'dirty corpse' but also the Tania who does not die, who returns and recurs as an obscure object of desire throughout the novel, one of the vilified recipients of Miller's heinous aphorisms. For whilst this Tania is the object of one of Miller's most notorious streams of violent intentions (' "I will send you home to your Sylvester with an ache in your belly and your womb turned inside out. . . . I shoot hot bolts into you. . . . I will bite into your clitoris and spit out two franc pieces" '), she is also something quite other. The tension between the violent 'intentions' of the 'I' which rants so purposefully here, and his desire for a Tania who offers him a 'chaotic' self-subversion, is a key area which I will explore. ' "You, Tania, are my chaos" ', Miller writes, in tandem with the key statement,

> Chaos is the score upon which reality is written.

How, then, can feminist criticism respond to such an impossible network of identifications?

The link between sexuality and death in Miller connects explicitly with Freud's theory of the death drive. Miller admits in *The World of Sex* that he cannot write about one without calling upon the other:

> Sex and death: I notice how frequently I couple them. . . . For the poet, the final ecstasy does not lead into the daylight of God, but into the nocturnal darkness of passion. Sometimes life itself takes over, writes its own poem of ecstasy, signed 'Death'.

Whilst the Romantic force of this eulogy to the erotics of annihilation is characteristic of Miller, the coupling of Eros and Thanatos is not of course unique. Miller's lack of originality is of little interest to me, however; what is more important is the way in which sexual violence, aggression and submission come together in his corpus, and the implications of this for feminism. My concern here is to show how that plexus in *Tropic of Cancer* can unlock and illustrate questions which still nag feminist criticism and theory; indeed, the poetics of sexuality and violence which Miller struggles to activate impinges on territory occupied not only by feminism, but also by psychoanalysis and military science. Miller offers a key articulation of the kind of desire made explicit in Freud's last topography, in which the sexual model of libido is subordinated to that of the death drive. What happens when feminism, late Freud and strategic theory come together in relation to Miller's *Tropic of Cancer* is the subject of this essay.

· · · · ·

> Men and women come together like broods of vultures over a stinking carcass, to mate and fly apart again. . . . A huge intestinal apparatus with a nose for dead meat. *Forward!* Forward without pity, without compassion, without love, without forgiveness. Ask no quarter and give none! More battleships, more poison gas, more high explosives! More gonococci! More streptococci! More bombing machines!

Henry Miller writes his way into the front line of the sex war, declaring that peace is only possible on the other side of conflict. If *Tropic of Cancer* as a whole is the war in which Miller tries 'fighting with ink' (to borrow his phrase about D. H. Lawrence), its sexual passages are the individual battles or bouts. As I will explore when I look at the disruptions in Miller's language, this inky battle is not fought to enshrine a sexist self in writing, but to fend off the 'self', ostensibly made coherent by grand narratives. Miller—for the hero of *Tropic of Cancer* is called 'Henry Miller'—goes to Paris like a war correspondent going straight to the front line; but he is not an innocent reporter. Paris invades him and makes him participate, intoxicating like a poison or addiction; he is a delirious but willing victim infiltrated by 'her' contagion or drug. Some of Miller's most passionate writing is reserved for Paris, which he is both inside of and, in reading her, 'other than'; she is a city which 'attracts the tortured, the hallucinated, the great maniacs of love'. But the city's importance lies in its openness to the conflicts which obsess Miller—it is his vision of a city which says Yes to everything, and as such it is both dubiously feminised and acts as an externalisation of the affirmative Freudian unconscious. At another point Paris is the maternal incubator of reality: 'Paris is the cradle of artificial births'. The whole novel is then enacted within the body of a voracious woman, for 'Paris is like a whore': 'From a distance she seems ravishing, you can't wait until you have her in your arms. And five minutes later you feel empty, disgusted with yourself. You feel tricked.'

This five-minute fuck is elsewhere in the novel likened to an exhausted military operation:

> It's like a state of war: the moment the condition is precipitated nobody thinks about anything but peace, about getting it over with. And yet nobody has the courage to lay down his arms, to say, 'I'm fed up with it. . . . I'm through.'

Sex between a prostitute and her client is like taking up arms, when both agree on a price and begin to fulfil the contract from positions of enmity. It is important to recognise the complex way in which *Cancer*'s metaphorics of warfare work; the opposition is not simply that of hatred between men and women, who hardly engage on an emotional level but instead lock themselves into a pattern of opposition already historically marked out for them. In *Cancer* prostitutes are mercenaries, paid to 'fight', so that sex-as-contract is simultaneously sex-as-battle, and winning is getting one's money's worth or getting the contract fulfilled. The individual encounter between whore and customer thus becomes a microcosm of wider human relations for Miller; the whore's space, the woman herself, is the city scaled down and intensified. Miller is keen to emphasise that this particular state of war is not passionate or *personally* aggressive; both opponents are forced to engage not because of individual desire or human feeling but because of their conflicting roles. Whore and client are the foot soldiers of the sex war, whose own egoistic priorities are irrelevant. Whilst it is often said that Miller's women do not have their own identities and are seldom even named (' "Imagine that! Asking me if I loved her. I didn't even know her name. I never know their names" '), in Miller's world personal characteristics are ruthlessly subjected, either to the ecstatic experience of loss which I will explore later (' "Sometimes I get so lost in my reveries that I can't remember the name of the cunt or where I picked her up" '), or to the roles which history has ascribed men and women and which render them simply active servants of the war (in this sense Miller's men can be equally nameless, like ' "that cute little prick who drives me bats about his rich cunt" ').

In the whore's world the exchange of money becomes 'the primal cause of things' which opens hostilities, and thus three forms of exchange, of sex and bodies, of money, and of violence, are conflated: ' "She's got her mind set on the fifteen francs and if I don't want to fight about it she's going to make me fight." ' The sexual contract between prostitute and client signifies a declaration and acceptance of war, which silences any pacific voice of reason. They are locked in a tunnel-vision of the inevitability of conflict:

> rather than listen to one's own voice, rather than walk out on the primal cause, one surrenders to the situation, one goes on butchering and butchering and the more cowardly one feels the more heroically does he behave, until a day when the bottom drops out and suddenly all the guns are silenced and the stretcher-bearers pick up the maimed and bleeding heroes and pin medals on their chest.

Whilst Miller's mind might be 'on the peace treaty all the time', he must nevertheless proceed in the knowledge that the armistice can only come when the battle is over.

Simply because of the explicitness with which Miller shows the violence of sex and gender relations in their unfeeling extremity, *Tropic of Cancer* is an important novel for feminist criticism. What happens between the whore and her customer makes Miller's attitude to war more explicit than his attitude to sex, even if it does both at the same time. Her bed is the theatre of war, and a space within which the public/private division explicitly breaks down; it is a microcosm of Paris as 'an artificial stage, a revolving stage that permits the spectator to glimpse all phases of the conflict'. Making love with a whore can be synonymous with waging war in a frenzy of territorialism against those who have come before. The man who fucks her 'fights like a thousand devils . . . to wipe out that regiment that has marched between her legs'. It is 'a fight in the dark, a fight single-handed against the army that rushed the gates, the army that walked over her, trampled her, that left her with such a devouring hunger that not even a Rudolph Valentino could appease.' Here again there is no question of love; it is an impersonal engagement which subordinates sexuality to the death drive, and Miller never even bothers to tell us who won. She is trampled but she also devours. And just as individual personality is immaterial to the conflict, there is never any question that 'pure' sexual desire—Freudian Eros, or libido in the form of a life instinct—has led to this.

In order to explore more fully this loveless engagement, I want to look at the way in which Miller's sexual writing can be seen as a literary encounter with the death drive. The callous tone of *Cancer* comes from its blithe disregard for the humanism of self-respect; bodily drives and the active role one fulfils, neither of which one necessarily

> **Feminist outrage at Henry Miller has characteristically engaged with him according to that familiar dialectic of shocking fiction countered by shocked critical response. This is not difficult. *Tropic of Cancer* tries very hard to be nasty, embracing in its frenzy of violation an ambitious range of objects.**
>
> **—Linda R. Williams**

chooses, are more important and determining. In his sado-masochistic world personal bodies are political in the sense that they are cannon-fodder in a conflict which they do not control and which subordinates personal identity to the exigencies of sexual warfare. What is important for a feminist reading of Miller is not, however, the position he occupies in relation to this struggle, but rather his obsession with it in the first place. A feminist understanding of the 'origins' of this war require, for me, a detour via Freud's late analysis of 'devouring hunger'. If there is any 'truth' in Miller's representation, it emerges from the way he brings together his disturbing vision of desire with a strong image of the exploitative manner in which men and women relate to each other. This is a representation which requires an equally complex feminist response—one which can incorporate not only the wealth of feminist work on the social and historical bases of hostile gender relations but which also makes use of the more controversial aspects of psychoanalytic theory. Encountering a disturbing vision of desire like Miller's, which embraces sadism, masochism and the desire to 'let go' of the self, requires a theory which disturbs any notion that libido is a healthy, humanistic life-instinct.

Miller articulates sexuality through the metaphorics of warfare because it allows him to bring together the violent and violating forms of sexual desire which are given a particular power within the historical framework which enlists men and women against each other. Existent conventional patterns of gender enmity are energised by and enter into a grim alliance with sado-masochistic violation. The materially fixed gender relations upon which Miller's sexual warfare is mapped is combined with a celebration of desire which violates or disregards the self, painfully and sadistically or, as I shall explore, ecstatically. These apparently *separate* forms of desire—first, to enter erotically into a painful scenario, and second, a desire which seeks nirvana as the 'zero-point' of self—are what Freud attempted to explain together, as two forms of the same drive, in the theory of the death drive, developed in his work during the First World War, introduced most fully in *Beyond the Pleasure Principle* (1920), and then maintained as the basic structure of his theory of the instincts. What we have seen so far on Miller's battlefield is the first kind of desire—the sado-masochistic desire for pain, restraint or simply the battle for domination; what I shall explore next is the second kind of desire—the desire to

abolish subjective unities and to enter the blissful extinction evoked by the nirvana principle. The death drive becomes the exemplary instinct for Freud; desire is the desire for non-self, a state of equilibrium, or, more radically, the desire to take the self back to its 'original' inorganic state of zero tension. Only this ultimate trajectory could explain to Freud the sexual expressions of sadism and masochism, as elaborate or warped forms of the desire to return. Despite its obvious importance in the analysis of the sexual power-relations with which feminism is concerned, the death drive has proved to be one of Freud's most controversial theories and has been largely ignored by feminists interested in psychoanalysis, except by those explicitly concerned with the taboo areas of feminine masochism and dangerous pleasures.

Bringing historical constructions and the form of desire explained by the death drive together in this way needs to be worked through more fully. Whilst feminism has used psychoanalysis productively, and has showed the political gaps at certain moments in the history of psychoanalysis, the discussion which occurs in later Freud of sadism, masochism and the transgression of egoistic boundaries has not been extensively linked to the needs of feminism. *Tropic of Cancer* requires this link to be made. Whilst any discussion of the violence of heterosexual sex is interesting to feminism, what is at stake in the literalisation of the sex war in *Tropic of Cancer* is more disturbing and less clear than has been acknowledged. Miller is exploring an at times confused conflation of the history of gender conflict and a form of desire closer to the death drive than to straightforwardly sexual models of libido.

Miller is clear, then, that sex is war when men and women come together—the fact that the woman is being paid only clarifies what exists for him implicitly in all cross-gender encounters. When Freud explores the warfare of sexuality, however, he does so via a series of discussions of sadism and masochism, forms of erotic violation which Miller enthusiastically indulges. Nevertheless it is not only, or even primarily, Miller's women who want to be violated. For instance Mona (the long-time love of several Miller novels) recognises that Miller's masochism matches her understanding of Strindberg's, who she reads voraciously, delighting in an image of *masculine* desire which meets her sadism:

> I can see her looking up from her book after reading a *delicious* passage, and, with tears of laughter in her eyes, saying to me: 'You're just as mad as he was . . . you *want* to be punished!' What a delight that must be to the sadist when she discovers her own proper masochist! When she bites herself, as it were, to test the sharpness of her teeth. In those days, when I first knew her, she was saturated with Strindberg. That wild carnival of maggots which he revelled in, that eternal duel of the sexes, that spiderish ferocity which had endeared him to the sodden oafs of the northland, it was that which had brought us together.

The obvious point to be made about this is that it reverses the sado-masochistic model so familiar to our culture; it is more often Miller's men 'who cannot resist the desire to get into a cage with wild beasts and be mangled'. Here it is Mona, like the original Wanda in Sacher-Masoch's *Venus in Furs,* who finds in Miller her masochist; she is the sadistic lover and reader. At another point in *Cancer* Miller's (male) friend Van Norden talks about sex in this curiously masochistic way:

> 'I get so goddamned mad at myself that I could kill myself . . . and in a way, that's what I do every time I have an orgasm. For one second like I obliterate myself. There's not even one me then . . . there's nothing . . . not even the cunt. It's like receiving communion.'

> 'But what is it you want of a woman, then?' I demand.

> ' . . . I want to be able to surrender myself to a woman,' he blurts out. 'I want her to take me out of myself. But to do that, she's got to be better than I am. . . .

This takes up the idea of orgasm as a 'little death' but twists it in the service of an expression of masculine masochism, a male character's manifest desire to submit to an experience of absence, at the same time as his submission to a woman. Thus the point when Van Norden says in the middle of this discussion, ' "There's something perverse about women . . . they're all masochists at heart" ', has to be read as a moment of audacious self-irony. What is surely more important for feminism here is the way Miller finds himself—perhaps despite himself—asking his own version of Freud's famous question, which becomes 'What does the *man* want?' This is not at all obvious; the composite image of masculine desire formed across the whole of *Tropic of Cancer* is bizarrely diverse. Miller is exploring forms of masculine sexuality which incorporate the ostensibly feminine desire for submission, as well as a variety of experiences of self-loss towards which masochism can form a pathway.

This exploration is important for feminism because as a representation or fantasy of masculine sexuality it challenges what Jessica Benjamin [in *The Bonds of Love: Psychoanalysis, Feminism, and the Problem of Domination,* 1990] calls the 'major tendency in feminism [to construct] the problem of domination as a drama of female vulnerability victimized by male aggression'. It is a 'tendency' in readings of misogynous literature which is exemplified by Kate Millett.

. . . . .

Miller's talent for irritating everyone does not fail him in his encounter with Kate Millett. She takes the bait and fights back venomously in her highly combative reading of Miller in *Sexual Politics,* which exemplifies an early moment of feminist criticism. Millett's work on Miller became a model for feminist readings of violently sexual 'masculine' writing. She fights back, but she fights on Miller's terms, and all too often reads like a repetition of Miller; her extensive quotes and enraged comments would hardly be destructive of a writer already so keen to offend. In Millett one senses that Miller found his perfect reader, one who offers back revitalised images of 'gender relations according to Miller' which have been freshly charged with

the energy of feminism. Miller may have met his match, but the battle continued to rage on the terms he set up.

A more effective feminist strategy, for me, would be one which either rewrites the rules of 'conventional' hostile encounter—the strike and counter-strike which occurs in the open from clearly opposite sides—or a kind of critical guerrilla operation which uses the 'arms' of the text against it to show how the text capitulates and contradicts itself. The latter strategy is perhaps most appropriate to a text like *Cancer* which offers such a contradictory range of masculine images. Whilst these responses may seem bizarrely violent ways to read books, violence is already present in Miller's writing, and in a whole history of feminist critical responses to the literature of misogyny. Reading Miller is often a painful experience, and if we read through the lens of identification with a character of the female sex, we are put in the position of the nameless 'cunts' and whores Millett defends, when defence is unnecessary: Miller's women can surely look after themselves. What, then, would an effective strategy of engagement be? Miller revels in the voracious desire both to consume and to be violated which is taken to extremes in his representations of masculine and feminine sexuality. Crucial questions of identity are raised when the masculine 'I' of *Tropic of Cancer* repeatedly calls for his own sexually engineered non-existence. But what for Miller is a positive 'impersonality' for Kate Millett is a necessarily negative dehumanisation: 'The perfect Miller "fuck" is a biological event between organs, its hallmark—its utter impersonality.' Any desire to explore psychic and sexual splitting is in Millett's language 'a pathological fear of having to deal with another, and complete human personality.' Her priorities are integrative and holistic, prescribing the humanisation of erotica against Miller's 'cheap dream of endlessly fucking impersonal matter . . . a childish fantasy of power untroubled by the reality of persons or the complexity of dealing with fellow human beings'.

Thus the grotesqueness of Miller for some women readers, taken at face value, easily provokes engaged repulsion—Millett's combative response—if not a bizarre masochistic identification, which casts the text in the role of sadist who inflicts a painful experience on the reader. Miller's obsession with warfare, conflict and disease imagery (the enemy within) on a metaphoric and a narrative level, provokes Millett to set up his corpus as an enemy. But Miller fights dirty, inconsistently and apparently unsystematically, so that ascribing a motive or model to his attack is difficult. Disturbed by one who characterises himself as a murderous and 'roving cultural desperado' ('Blow it to hell! Kill, kill, kill! . . .' he writes in *Capricorn*), Millett is poked into indignant defensiveness.

What happens when someone marks out another as their enemy? Despite the pleas of some pacific women, feminism has had to affirm the act of taking sides and recognising the need for strategies. Kate Millett is right to deploy a criticism of conflict with reference to Miller, both because this is what Miller invites and because we often use a military lexicon when we discuss criticism (strategies, defences, engagements, etc.). But what is at stake in the notion of a feminist critical *strategy?* Feminism engages with the sex war on the page in its critical writing and in the academy, and it does so through deploying the language and tools of a number of military strategies. At its strongest, feminist literary criticism is not applied feminist theory, which would approach texts through a pre-ordained perspective, practising secondarily what it theorises first. If we are to take terms like 'critical strategy' at all seriously, it is necessary to make critical militarism explicit. Both the practice of playing on the contradictions of a political force until it capitulates, and the practice of meeting the opposing force straight on in conventional terms, armed with a coherent strategy, are military operations. Attacking the text head-on with a critical strategy developed prior to a knowledge of that text produces responses which perhaps inadequately meet the 'enemy' threat since they lack a tactical understanding of its form. This conventional attack/defence approach is much less appropriate to reading than are the operations of guerrilla or 'people's war'. Military theorist Carl von Clausewitz, writing in his seminal 1832 text *On War,* characterises a 'people's army' as a diffuse, subversive and non-totalising force which overturns the balance of power not by 'cracking the nut' but, having ascertained the nature of the terrain of encounter and the form which the enemy force takes, by deploying a strategy based on the strength of dispersal, unpredictability and difference, not like a conventional 'platoon of soldiers . . . [who] cling together like a herd of cattle and generally follow their noses'. The flexibility of this approach is important, and it requires a knowledge of the other which is like reading, but reading as reconnaissance. Constructing one's enemy at his strongest point requires the space to imagine, listen to, and 'know' him, and precludes the existence of combative theories constructed prior to the event—theory is engendered in practice. Projecting thought beyond the enemy lines is a powerful exercise in reading. The success of a guerrilla war is described by Clausewitz in these terms: 'The flames will spread like a brush fire, until they reach the area on which the enemy is based, threatening his lines of communication and his very existence.'

If one has already set up a text as a threatening or aggressive force, this would surely be the desired result—a reading which sets the text on fire, and allows that fire to destroy the text as culturally important if it is not strong enough to survive the attack. At its most dextrous, feminist criticism listens to the other voices of writing, finding sources of power—points at which literature becomes something other than it seems—as well as showing how texts position themselves politically. Feminist criticism deals most effectively with violently misogynous writing when it opens up paradoxes where the text promises certainty, when it shows inconsistencies beneath a ruthless logic, and finds fault-lines in monoliths. There is something far more satisfying in showing how a piece of sexist writing trips over its own doubts and, in its ideological capacity, self-destructs, than in meeting that writing head-on with a pre-formed theory, often deploying the opponent's rules of engagement, and battling it out at the risk of losing. A more subversive strategy acts 'Like smouldering embers, it consumes the basic foundations of the enemy forces . . . a general conflagration closes in on the enemy'. A feminist reading of Miller is, then, more complex and more successful if it kindles the doubts already inherent in *Cancer*—a novel so obsessed with disease as an internal other, the cancer of its title—causing the text to burn itself out or capitulate to the gnawing enemy within.

. . . . .

When a feminist reads a writer like Henry Miller she engages in a kind of critical warfare. Oppositional feminism like Millett's holds Miller up as the exemplary fiction of misogyny, a fit enemy for feminist critique to pit itself against. Miller is 'offensive' to some feminists because he is seen to go on the offensive against women in his writing: he offers an example of Klaus Theweleit's dictum in *Male Fantasies*: 'the erotic woman is the terrain of warfare.' However, we need to distinguish between what happens when women such as Millett find Miller 'offensive', and the moral castigation of Miller's obscenity which underpinned the debate about whether he should be published, in order to avoid once more evoking that uneasy and paradoxical alliance of feminism and the Right which has occurred in recent debates on pornography. This is a question which has been opened up particularly strongly since the early 1980s, and two critical anthologies, the Barnard collection *Pleasure and Danger* and Snitow, Stansell and Thompson's *Desire: The Politics of Sexuality* contain especially important feminist work carried out recently on the question of dangerous pleasures, showing Millett's early position clearly in relief. The difference between Millett on Miller and, say, Alice Echols or Muriel Dimen on more recent anti-porn feminist positions represents a crucial historical move. Echols discusses feminism's emphasis on forms of 'politically-correct sex' which would prohibit not only pornography but sexual fantasy *per se*. Dimen succinctly writes: 'When the radical becomes correct, it becomes conservative', although whether this makes Miller's rampant incorrectness radical is another question.

The cultural feminisms Echols discusses would consign Miller to the censor's bonfire not only for his violence but also for his exploration of psychological aberration, and for his insistence on the politically difficult notion that sexual desire and conscious intent do not always work together: the danger of desire is that what I want is not necessarily good for me, and I might want it more if it isn't. The alternative propounded not only by Millett but more recently by writers such as Susan Griffin, Andrea Dworkin and Adrienne Rich is an idealised notion of 'loving and being loved by women in mutuality and integrity', a 'love' which is consciously ordained, simultaneously enforcing psychic coherence and prohibiting fantasy: ' "Integrity", their answer to patriarchy's dangerous dualism, entails the transformation of all aspects of our lives into one seamless, unambiguous reflection of our politics. Such a view assumes that we can and should be held accountable for our desires.' Echols's question, 'How has it come to pass that some lesbians are in the forefront of a movement which has resurrected terms like "sexual deviance" and "perversion" . . . ?' opens up an incisive discussion of the alliance between forms of lesbian cultural feminism and the New Right. But in pin-pointing the polemic against porn as also a fear of fantasy, she moves the debate one stage on: 'in advocating sexual repression as a solution to violence against women, cultural feminisms resort to mobilizing women around their fears rather than their visions.' Jessica Benjamin in her excellent volume *The Bonds of Love,* which uses late Freud in its analysis of sadism and masochism, puts it in this way: 'a theory or a politics that cannot cope with contradiction, that denies the irrational, that tries to sanitize the erotic, fantastic components of human life cannot visualise an authentic end to domination but only vacate the field.'

Benjamin's whole book is written with a Hegelian vision of 'an authentic end to domination' as its goal, taken through a thorough analysis of contradiction. Any approach to Miller which cannot cope with his insistence on irrational sex and dehumanised bodies, or which would sanitise his erotics, as conventional Miller criticism has done, into a transcendence of bodies and disease in a wholesome and integrative experience of self-liberation, is obviously a non-starter. However there is no straightforward reason why what Gore Vidal [in 'Women's liberation meets Miller-Mailer-Manson man', in *Collected Essays 1952-1972,* 1972] calls 'Miller's hydraulic approach to sex and his dogged use of four-letter words' should a priori be offensive to feminists. The problem is rather what misogynous machinery runs on Miller's hydraulic power. For Millett this is clear; her Miller is a 'brutalised adolescent' whose 'formula is rather simple': 'you meet her, cheat her into letting you have "a piece of ass", and then take off. Miller's hunt is a primitive find, fuck, and forget.' Miller is indeed a gift to Millett, since his insistence on sex as an inhuman and dissolute experience, and on women as cunts, acts as a perfect foil for Millett's plea for wholesome sexual relations, for women's right to integrated subjectivity. She eloquently develops her position as the negative of Miller's and D. H. Lawrence's misogynies:

> Lawrence had turned back the feminist claims to human recognition and a fuller social participation by distorting them into a vegetative passivity calling itself fulfilment. His success prepared the way for Miller's escalation to open contempt. Lawrence had still to deal with persons; Miller already feels free to speak of objects. Miller simply converts woman to 'cunt'—thing, commodity, matter.

Henry Miller was notoriously sexist, and thus if one is interested only in producing a chamber of sexist horrors he is a soft if eager target. When Millett identifies Miller as enemy she unwittingly allows him to choose the weapons. Taking on his lexicon of warfare she fights his game rather than her own. But it is one thing for feminism to engage with misogyny on *its* terms, and quite another when feminism appropriates those terms as armaments—fighting *with* its terms. When Millett identifies with Miller's representations of femininity she prosecutes him for winning a sex war for which he has written the strategic rules of engagement. For Millett Miller is something of a case history: an example to diagnose, the articulation of the offensive position: 'Miller does have something highly important to tell us; his virulent sexism is beyond question an honest contribution to social and psychological understanding which we can hardly afford to ignore'. This is the nearest Millett gets to defeating Miller, using his corpus in service of the project of *Sexual Politics.* But this is also the point at which she ceases to read him; not only is the essay about to end, but here he becomes important only as a piece of pathological evidence. This leaves feminist criticism in a position of impasse which is hard to break. Once the terrain of engagement has been set up as either attack or defence, Millett's defensiveness means that in the end she ceases to read.

[In *Self and Form in Modern Narrative,* 1989] Vincent Pecora offers a clarification of critique which is less defensive than Millet's and thus offers a powerful purchase on the text: 'The objective of critique is then to read a specific narrative . . . as if it were *the* narrative a contradictory social order told to itself to make sense of its own inconsistencies.' I have said that the key 'experience' for Miller is the desire to escape into a nirvana space of inhumanity; he paradoxically *wants* his 'lines of communication' to be consumed and inflamed. But not, presumably, by feminist flames: the means of destruction has to be of his own choosing. My task is then to read Miller's desire for annihilation, which I shall now look at briefly, as a theory of his self-inconsistency, first as a possibility of anti-humanist and perhaps 'feminine' disruption, and secondly as possibly a means of closet-reintegration—the absurdity of a masculinity beyond death.

. . . . .

> The man watching the clock was shackled and gagged; inside him were a thousand different beings tugging for release. . . . My only recourse—I no longer had a choice—was to lose my identity. In other words, flee from myself. [*The World of Sex*]

Millett has identified Miller's writing as murderous but its misogyny is not on any obvious level taken to the point of death—the male 'I' fucks an awful lot of women, but they are not fucked to death. On the other hand Miller's 'own' desire for annihilation, or the erasure of personal identity, is a form of ecstatic self-violation which Millett ignores. Whilst sex and violence might be inextricable, death in Miller is more likely to be an exultant male suicide than murder; 'vast relief' comes with violence to the self not to woman as other. What obsesses Miller is what has been characterised as a feminine state of openness, and an inability to identify with any conventional image of humanity. His 'I' wants to be *not* an 'I', in a novel which is about want.

What I am interested in is how Miller desires to lose in the sex war he fights. His desire becomes, despite itself, not the desire for victory over the enemy, but the desire for an experience of emptiness, the annihilation of restrictive economies, and an affirmation of a position which, according to the rules he is working with, is uncannily feminine; he is blamed for stripping women of their identities, but then reclaims this loss as his own in a struggle to lose himself. His concern is to plunge into a state of radical self-loss, an experience of 'letting go' which at one point he calls the Absolute. His openness to suffering is a craving for orgasmic negation, the emptiness of the 'spent', suffering as literally 'allowing'—being open to anything. The novel is written on the knife-edge of loss; on one side Miller wanders the streets in 'the splendour of those miserable days . . . a bewildered, poverty-stricken individual who haunted the streets like a ghost at a banquet', whilst on the other this loss turns inside out into an ecstatic experience of egolessness which comes close to the writing of *jouissance*. By risking feeling loss painfully, he gains access to its freedom and weightlessness, unencumbered by the spirit of gravity.

Millett discusses Miller's euphemistic use of 'spending', but prefers to concentrate on its contractual aspect rather than the fact that it affirms a state in which he is in possession of nothing, reaching out to a point as near as possible to his own non-existence. Miller has nothing, and nothing to lose: 'I am the one who was lost in the crowd.' This is indeed part of a longer project, picked up again in his essay **'My life as an echo'**: 'My ideal is to become thoroughly anonymous—a Mr What's-his-name . . . I am at my best when nobody knows me, nobody recognises me.' 'I' is, of course, still present here, paradoxically calling for its own extinction; it is a paradox incorporated into his statement 'I am inhuman', where the 'I' militates against its proclaimed inhumanity. Miller is primarily exploring desire as that which *wants nothing,* which is directed toward radical self-destruction. Nothing, therefore, is quite tangibly attractive: 'No appointments, no invitations for dinner, no program, no dough. The golden period, when I had not a single friend.' Austere as this may sound, this is no stoical sensual deprivation but Miller's road of excess, driving him towards his culminative affirmation of dehumanised sex.

In his famous essay **'The Brooklyn Bridge'** Miller shows the characteristic mechanism of transgression which inverts an opposition—here emptiness and possession, or loss and gain—in an attempt to fracture that whole economy, gouging a gap into which he can jump, a point at which he is neither lost nor found: 'in the city I am aware of . . . the labyrinth. To be lost in a strange city is the greatest joy I know; to become oriented is to lose everything.' By throwing away one's egoistic compass one can find one's way to a labyrinth of 'joy' inaccessible to the psychically 'oriented'. The moment one *recognises*— boundaries, pathways, identities and landmarks—one 'loses everything'. At this point, Miller wants not to map out enemy territory so as to wage war more effectively, but to jump into its strangeness—'the city is crime personified, insanity personified'—so that sides are forgotten. The experience of poverty in a strange city is valuable in the way that it estranges self from self, and facilitates desire as loss of self:

> It was only in moments of extreme anguish that I took to the bridge, when, as we say, it seemed that all was lost. Time and again all was lost, irrevocably so. The bridge was the harpy of death, the strange winged creature without an eye which held me suspended between two shores.

Suspended between two shores, he is unfixed and positioned over a flow rather than stasis—as he tells us in his eulogy to movement in *Cancer,* 'I love everything that flows.' But this is a *repeated* experience of all being lost,

one which recurrently fulfils his anonymous ideal. Death never comes to the textual Miller as an absolute end; rather it is an interruption of identity which manages to return. This uncanny 'Time and again' sensation is what gives the self its discontinuity, and it is what gives *Cancer* its formal fragmentation. Here is perhaps another example of a male writer producing *écriture féminine,* for *Cancer,* like its central 'I', is discontinuous; it slips into repeated narrative deaths so that its identity as a 'whole' novel is problematic. It jumps across time with no warning, allowing half-notions to spread like a disease, expanding into streams of elements (Miller's famous raving lists). At the risk of turning Miller into a postmodernist, his surreal collage of disparate sexual landscapes can be understood as being engendered by an 'esthetic of interruption which structures contemporary consciousness' in the terms used by Sylvere Lotringer in *Pure War:*

> it's the death of intimacy. All the reflection of these last years on an exploded, 'schizophrenic' model of subjectivity corresponds to the great esthetic of the collage. The ego is not continuous, it's made up of a series of little deaths and partial identities which don't come back together, or which only manage to come back together by paying the price of anxiety and repression.

Tropic of Cancer is a montage of bodies and cheap hotel rooms, of formal disruptions and narrative gaps partly created by Miller's aphoristic style (Lotringer again: 'It's . . . by interruptions that writing is worked on. . . . aphorisms . . . are interruptions of thought.') Formal disunity emphasises the 'I' as a possible source of coherence, but it is here that Miller would defy our need for an old-fashioned great narrative most, when the 'I' itself insists on slipping away, apparently at will. But then 'he' comes back, denying even the certainty of absolute disappearance.

Clearly, then, this 'blissful' experience is an important moment for Miller, but that does not make it in itself important for feminism. And what has become of his gendered vision? One simple answer is that the interruption of identity which Miller slips into in this reverie is, negatively speaking, a self-violation—a turn-about in the fortunes of war, when the 'I' transgresses the terms of gendered combat and turns upon himself—and, positively, a 'feminine' gap, both of which render a monolithic feminist critique problematic. Miller is one site upon which we can question the priorities of feminism when confronting what at first seems to be a straightforwardly misogynous text.

In his notes on D. H. Lawrence, written in his Paris Notebooks at the same time as he was writing *Tropic of Cancer,* Miller conflates his 'aesthetics of death' with sexual warfare:

> [With t]he great sexual interpretation of all things . . . comes the silent admission. . . . that death can not be averted. It can only be glorified. It gets *aestheticized.* And men forget too, that in this final period which Lawrence represents *woman must fight man* desperately.

For Miller the desperate fight comes at the same moment as the aestheticisation of death; political conflict is part of the historical 'final period'—as the moment of *Cancer*'s writing is apocalyptically identified—which is more important for Miller because it is also the moment at which loss or ecstasy is given an artistic rather than a religious or ethical importance. This is the key to what the 'I' says he is doing in writing 'The last book': the prioritisation of an ostensibly unlimited artistic self-overcoming over political battles: the 'complete release' which Clausewitz calls 'Going to extremes', and which can only come when the limits of political expediency are abandoned. This is what Virilio [in *Pure War*] terms 'an infernal tendency'

> heading toward an extreme where no one will control anything. There, Clausewitz says something fundamental: 'Politics prevents complete release.' It's because war is political that there is not complete release. If war weren't political, this release would reach total destruction.

In attempting to abandon the political limits of social morality and, apparently, the imperatives of the reality principle, Miller-as-'writing machine' desires this extreme point of release.

What is at stake in the loss or interruption Miller defies is not simply subjective sensation, or the radical lack of it. This final moment of annihilation takes Miller to the space of writing, and at this point the moral response of certain feminisms comes into its most direct confrontation with Miller's aesthetic, for when he becomes 'a writing machine' he casts off everything except irresponsibility. 'The last book' is the death of him: 'I have simplified everything. . . . I am throwing away all my sous. What need have I for money? I am a writing machine. The last screw has been added. The thing flows. Between me and the machine there is no estrangement. I am the machine. Once the machine is turned on it is inhuman; the body it uses dies as a human being, the book it produces is written 'anonymously', and Tania, who has humanly invested in him, is destroyed too: 'She knows there is something germinating inside me which will destroy her.' So when *Tropic of Cancer* plays out its conflict between artistic production and personal ethics, it sets up an extreme agenda which separates inhuman artists from ethical humans:

> Side by side with the human race there runs another race of beings, the inhuman ones, the race of artists who, goaded by unknown impulses . . . turn . . . everything upside down, their feet always moving in blood and tears, their hands always empty, always clutching and grasping for the beyond, for the god out of reach: slaying everything within reach in order to quiet the monster that gnaws at their vitals.

The morality of personal relations which so concerns Millett is subordinated to the needs and desires of the writing machine. This is clearly a problem for a feminist criticism which in its political readings has been most concerned with ethical fair play. *Tropic of Cancer* is important to this discussion not because it actually is 'The last book', but because it keeps returning to the question of the amoral psychic and sexual conditions which would engender such a book. When feminism subordinates writing to morality the call for politically correct sex becomes a call for politically correct art. This is not a priority I am happy to echo.

At the end of a long and violent meditation on a girl's 'dark, unstitched wound' Miller has a vision of 'The story of art whose roots lie in massacre'. It is this image which *Cancer* celebrates. Whilst many feminisms have confronted and analysed massacre, the writing which violence produces cannot be understood through a blindly ethical perspective. To borrow again from Lotringer, *Tropic of Cancer* is a text written in 'the discourse of war': 'It's a whole politics of writing. It's not an organised discourse of war, even less a discourse *on* war, it's a discourse at war. Writing in a state of emergency.'

FURTHER READING

Bibliography

Moore, Thomas H., ed. *Bibliography of Henry Miller*. Minneapolis, Minn.: Henry Miller Literary Society, 1961, 33 p.
    Comprehensive primary and select secondary bibliography, with sections listing doctoral dissertations on Miller's works, recordings by Miller, and the locations of early first editions of his works.

Shifreen, Lawrence J. *Henry Miller: A Bibliography of Secondary Sources*. Metuchen, N.J.: Scarecrow Press, 1979, 477 p.
    Extensive secondary bibliography.

Biography

Brown, J. D. *Henry Miller*. New York: Ungar Publishing Co., 1986, 147 p.
    Critical biography which includes three chapters on Miller's formative years in Paris when he wrote *Tropic of Cancer*.

Dearborn, Mary V. *The Happiest Man Alive: A Biography of Henry Miller*. New York: Simon & Schuster, 1991, 368 p.
    Contains several chapters focusing on Miller's life in Paris and his experience in writing *Tropic of Cancer*.

Ferguson, Robert. "1933-34: *Tropic of Cancer* and 'a Half-dozen Terrifying Words.' " In his *Henry Miller: A Life*, pp. 208-234. London: Hutchinson, 1991.
    Offers a detailed account of Miller's life during the composition of *Tropic of Cancer*.

Martin, Jay. *Always Bright and Merry: The Life of Henry Miller*. Santa Barbara, Calif.: Capra Press, 1978, 560 p.
    An unauthorized biography that questions Miller's claim that such books as *Tropic of Cancer* are strictly autobiographical.

Tytell, John. "Henry and June and Anaïs." In his *Passionate Lives: D. H. Lawrence, F. Scott Fitzgerald, Henry Miller, Dylan Thomas, Sylvia Plath—In Love*, pp. 143-197. New York: Birch Lane Press, 1991.
    Views Miller and his lovers as "Dionysian" romantics whose bohemian lifestyles inspired the orgiastic, visionary rhetoric of *Tropic of Cancer* and his other works.

Criticism

Dick, Kenneth C. *Henry Miller: Colossus of One*. The Netherlands: Alberts-Sittard, 1967, 218 p.

Praises Miller's artistic achievements, particularly *Tropic of Cancer*, and offers a portrait of his relationships with Anaïs Nin and June Miller.

Gottesman, Ronald, ed. *Critical Essays on Henry Miller.* New York: G. K. Hall, 1992, 411 p.

Comprehensive critical anthology which includes essays on the genesis of *Tropic of Cancer*, the sexual dimensions of Miller's novel, and its relation to "Orphic" or visionary poetry.

Hutchison, E. R. *"Tropic of Cancer" on Trial: A Case History of Censorship.* New York: Grove Press, 1968, 300 p.

Offers a detailed account of the legal struggles in the early 1960s between Grove Press and the numerous censors who sought to ban *Tropic of Cancer* on grounds of obscenity.

Jackson, Paul R. "Caterwauling and Harmony: Music in *Tropic of Cancer*." *Critique: Studies in Modern Fiction* XX, No. 3 (1979): 40-50.

Discusses the metaphorical significance of musical references in *Tropic of Cancer*, asserting that Miller's howling, cacophonous lyricism forms a thematic counterpoint to the insipid popular and classical music which symbolize the effete, decadent sensibility of European culture.

Jong, Erica. "Crazy Cock in the Land of Fuck." In her *The Devil at Large: Erica Jong on Henry Miller*, pp. 81-118. New York: Random House, 1993.

Extensive analysis and appreciation of *Tropic of Cancer*.

Millett, Kate. "Henry Miller." In her *Sexual Politics*, pp. 294-313. New York: Doubleday & Co., Inc., 1970.

Influential feminist analysis and attack on *Tropic of Cancer* which delineates the nature and extent of Miller's misogyny. See the excerpt reprinted in *CLC-43*.

Wickes, George, ed. *Henry Miller and the Critics.* Carbondale, Ill.: Southern Illinois University Press, 1963, 194 p.

Anthology of Miller criticism which includes such critics as Lawrence Durrell, Kenneth Rexroth, Harry Levin, and Kingsley Widmer. The book is divided into three periods covering Miller's life in Paris and America, and the publication history and reception of *Tropic of Cancer* in America.

Widmer, Kingsley. "The Apocalyptic Comedian." In his *Henry Miller*, pp. 17-40. New York: Twayne, 1963.

Critical analysis of *Tropic of Cancer* which views Miller as a comic nihilist whose rebellion against convention represents a critique and reversal of traditional values.

Woolf, Michael. "Beyond Ideology: Kate Millett and the Case for Henry Miller." In *Perspectives on Pornography: Sexuality in Film and Literature*, edited by Gary Day and Clive Bloom, pp. 113-128. London: MacMillan Press, 1988.

Argues that Kate Millett's feminist opposition to Miller in her *Sexual Politics* is contradicted by her embrace of sexual liberation in her novel *Flying*, which shares with *Tropic of Cancer* an understanding of sex as a means of escape from ideological and social constraints.

Additional coverage of Miller's life and career is contained in the following sources published by Gale Research: *Concise Dictionary of American Literary Biography 1929-1941; Contemporary Authors*, Vols. 9-12, rev. ed., 97-100; *Contemporary Authors New Revision Series*, Vol. 33; *Contemporary Literary Criticism*, Vols. 1, 2, 4, 9, 14, 43; *Dictionary of Literary Biography*, Vols. 4, 9; *Dictionary of Literary Biography Yearbook 1980; DISCovering Authors; Major 20th-Century Writers*; and *World Literature Criticism*.

Christopher Okigbo

1932-1967

(Full name Christopher Ifenayichukwu Okigbo) Nigerian poet.

The following entry provides an overview of Okigbo's career. For further information on his life and works, see *CLC,* Volume 25.

INTRODUCTION

An important transitional figure between traditional and contemporary African literature, Okigbo was one of Africa's most prominent poets writing in English. Chinua Achebe stated: "While other poets wrote good poems, Okigbo conjured up for us an amazing, haunting poetic firmament of a wild and violent beauty." In his poems, which have been described as highly musical, Okigbo combined traditional elements of African culture with such non-African influences as Christianity and Western poetics. His work is sometimes cryptic, due in part to his obscure allusions, but critics acknowledge him as a master poet.

Biographical Information

Born in Ojoto, Nigeria, Okigbo graduated from the University of Ibadan and worked as a teacher and librarian before beginning a literary career. Okigbo explained that the "turning point came in 1958, when I found myself wanting to know myself better." For Okigbo, poetry would always remain a highly personal endeavor. Thus, his interest in social and political change in Nigeria, which is an integral part of many of his works, derived from his belief that it is impossible for the artist to examine his or her own identity in isolation. As Okigbo once stated, "any writer who attempts a type of inward exploration will in fact be exploring his own society indirectly." His concern for social justice was perhaps best expressed in his commitment to the Biafran secession. In July 1967, at the outbreak of the Nigerian Civil War, he enlisted in the Biafran Army. He was killed in action in August 1967.

Major Works

During his lifetime Okigbo published only two collections of poetry: *Heavensgate* (1962) and *Limits* (1962). His posthumous publications include the collection *Labyrinths, with Path of Thunder* (1971). Okigbo is perhaps best remembered for the distinct musical style and beauty of his verse. Paul Theroux advised readers to *listen* to Okigbo's poetry in order to appreciate it fully, asserting that "looking is confusion: what we see in the poem may be an impenetrable mystery, and there are words and phrases in Okigbo's poetry that are nearly impossible to figure out. Listening is simpler and more rewarding; there is music in [his] poetry." Okigbo's practice of infusing poetry with rhythm and song has been imitated by subsequent African writers. Sunday O. Anozie observed: "Nothing can be more tragic to the world of African poetry in English than the death of Christopher Okigbo, especially at a time when he was beginning to show maturity and coherence in his vision of art, life and society, and greater sophistication in poetic form and phraseology. Nevertheless his output, so rich and severe within so short a life, is sure to place him among the best and the greatest of our time."

Lee Hunt

Critical Reception

Because Okigbo used myth, ritual, and dense symbolism, critics were initially divided in their reactions to his work. Some argued that Okigbo's poems evoke humanity's quest for divinity; others viewed them as an attack on Christianity; and a few regarded them as testimonies of Okigbo's social and political views, especially those poems concerning the cultural and religious alienation of Nigeria during the colonial period. Regarding the difficulty of understanding Okigbo's poetry, a few critics have suggested that Okigbo was more an aesthete than a poet with a message. Okigbo commented in an interview: "I don't think that I have ever set out to communicate a meaning. It is enough that I try to communicate experience which I consider significant."

PRINCIPAL WORKS

Heavensgate (poetry) 1962
*Limits (poetry) 1962; published in the periodical *Transition*
†*Poems: Four Canzones* (poetry) 1968; published in the periodical *Black Orpheus*
Labyrinths, with Path of Thunder (poetry) 1971
Collected Poems (poetry) 1986

*This work was published as a volume in 1964.

†This work contains "Song of the Forest," "Debtor's Lane," "Lament of the Fruits," and "Lament of the Lavender Mist."

CRITICISM

Christopher Okigbo with Marjory Whitelaw (interview date March 1965)

SOURCE: An interview in *The Journal of Commonwealth Literature*, Vol. 9, July, 1970, pp. 28-37.

[*In the following excerpted interview, which originally took place in March, 1965, Okigbo discusses such topics as négritude, religion, African culture, and his own poetry.*]

[*Whitelaw*]: *Christopher, do you think of yourself as an African poet?*

[Okigbo]: I think I am just a poet. A poet writes poetry and once the work is published it becomes public property. It's left to whoever reads it to decide whether it's African poetry or English. There isn't any such thing as a poet trying to express African-ness. Such a thing doesn't exist. A poet expresses himself.

What about poets who express négritude?

Yes, but that is different because it is a particular type of poetry. It is platform poetry. It is platform writing. It is just like being invited to deliver a lecture on a particular subject. But it is valid as poetry when it is good, because we do in fact have this sort of thing in our own poetry in the oral tradition. The poetry of praise, for instance. Platform poetry. You go to a king's palace to praise him, and you build up images in praise of him. That sort of poetry is valid provided it is good.

In other forms of poetry . . . the most regular form that is written by young African poets, writing in the English language, is in fact written to express, to bring out a sense of an inner disturbance. We are trying to cast about for words; whether the words are in Ibo or English or in French is in fact immaterial . . . We are looking for words to give verbal concreteness, to give verbal life to auditory and visual images . . . I think this is a separate form of poetry from platform poetry. It just happens that one form is written more here, among English-speaking poets, and one more among French. But the two forms are valid, and I don't quarrel with négritude. . . .

You say you go back to village festivals—I know you write a great deal about these.

Yes, I do. And I do not feel that in fact as a Christian I have ever been uprooted from my own village gods. We have a goddess and a god in our family, our ancestral gods. And although I do not worship these actively, in the sense of offering them periodic sacrifices, I still feel that they are the people protecting me.

But the way in which I think Christianity can be reconciled with this aspect of paganism is that I believe in fact all these gods are the same as the Christian God—that they are different aspects of the same power, the same force.

What shape do these gods take in your family?

Well, we have a carved idol representing a man, and another carved idol representing a woman, and the man we call Ikenga, and the woman we call Udo. And the man is the father of the entire family, for several generations back; the woman is the mother of the whole family, several generations back. And in a large extended family we have just these two gods, Ikenga and Udo.

We offer sacrifices to them periodically. I am here at Ibadan; I don't live at home at Ojoto. So my parents or my uncles will offer sacrifices to them periodically. And the women of the family will from time to time scrub the walls of the shrine where these gods are housed, with fresh mud (the walls of the shrine would be of a mud mixture, a very satisfactory and inexpensive building substance), and the men of the family will repair the thatched roof to prevent it leaking. And once in a while they offer a white hen, or eggs laid by white hens, or kola nuts, or pods of alligator pepper. And I feel, you know, that we still belong to these things. We cannot get away from them.

This is purely a family shrine, is it?

This is a family shrine. We have the ones worshipped by the whole town. The whole town, for example, worships the python and the tortoise. The python, I imagine, represents the male deity, and the tortoise represents the female deity. And the whole town worships these two idols, and they (the creatures) are sacred to the whole town. I mean they are sacred to their particular shrines, and we cannot kill them. If in fact you find a python that is dead, you give it a ceremonial burial. Oh, yes. This still happens, even now. And Christianity cannot wipe this out.

What does the python symbolize, then?

The python represents the penis. And the tortoise represents the clitoris. One for the male organ and the other for the female.

Do you also go to the Christian church?

I haven't gone to church for a long time.

Neither have I. This is a rather theoretical question . . . But you think of yourself as a sort of nominal Christian, do you?

I think that over the years I have tried to evolve my own personal religion. The way that I worship my gods is in fact through poetry. And I think that each poem I write is a ceremony of innocence, if you like. The creative process is a process of cleansing. And since I began actively to write poetry, I have never gone to church. So I don't think it would be right for me to say I am a Christian or I am a pagan. I think my own religion combines elements from both. . . .

Do you think that for a lot of Africans today it is difficult to be African?

I don't see why it should be difficult. I don't think there is any culture in the world that doesn't have borrowed elements. There is this multivalence in all cultures. Africa happens to be a new society, new in the sense that people are just beginning to know about Africa. So this multivalence is emphasized. It is just like holding something under a microscope—it becomes enlarged. Africa is now under the world's microscope; everybody sees Africa, and nobody bothers to look at any other place.

I think most Europeans have the idea that if any writer should be 'committed' (to use this literary cliché) it should be the African writers. I mean committed to writing about social change, about discovery of identity—that is, he should not be working in isolation, in an ivory tower; he should not have removed himself from the preoccupations of the people of his own time.

Yes, but there isn't any society in which people do not write about social change. Social change is not only taking place in Africa; it's taking place everywhere in the world.

Yes, but in North America particularly there are writers who feel that the writer has a duty to discover himself rather than to discover the world. Thirty years ago writers like Thomas Wolfe were writing about the great panorama of American life, but today they seem, many of them, to be isolated from their contemporaries, to be concerned with self-exploration. They feel no responsibility whatever to their own society. Now the point I want to make is that we in the West might suppose that (because Africa is under such violent pressures of change) it would be difficult for African writers to evade this responsibility.

Yes, but I don't think that this sense of responsibility is fulfilled only by writing directly about the change in society, about social change. I believe that any writer who attempts a type of inward exploration will in fact be exploring his own society indirectly. Because the writer isn't *living* in isolation. He is interacting with different groups of people at different times. And any inward exploration involves the interaction of the subject with other people, and I believe that a writer who sets out to discover himself, by so doing will also discover his society.

I don't think that I like writing that is 'committed'. I think it is very cheap. I think it is the easy way of doing it. Much more difficult than that, of course, is inward exploration.

I hope that ultimately people will start doing that sort of thing in Africa. They haven't started doing it yet.

What would you say, then, is the function of the writer in Africa?

Oh, the writer in Africa doesn't have any function. That is, personally I can only say what I conceive as my own function. I have no function as a writer; I think I merely express myself, and the public can use these things for anything they like. I mean . . . you read a poem to a child; a child may weep. You may read the same poem to other people, and they may burst out into laughter. I don't in fact think that it is necessary for the writer to assume a particular function as The Messiah or anything like that . . . Well, as an individual he could assume this sort of role, but I don't think that the fact that he's a writer should entitle him to assume a particular role as an educator. If he wants to educate people he should write text books. If he wants to preach a gospel he should write religious tracts. If he wants to propound a certain ideology he should write political tracts. . . .

Who reads your poems?

I don't know. But I've read my poems to different groups of people. I went to Kano once (in the Northern Region [of Nigeria]) and I was invited to give a talk at a school, to the whole school. And because I had not prepared a talk, I read one or two poems, and the children burst into tears. I felt that . . . at least they had had experience of the agony I had gone through . . . You know the process of writing the particular poems I read to them had been agonizing. And I thought that they had had a share of the agony of composition. I don't know who reads my poems and I don't think I care. I think that once I've written a poem I've given it a life of its own and the poem should go to anyone it likes. Anybody who is prepared to open his door to it.

The poem should go to anybody it likes . . . ?

Well, anybody who is willing to let it in. After all, if you go to somebody's house and knock on the door he may open the door or he may not; he may open the door and say, 'Good afternoon; I am sorry, I'm resting, I'm busy.' Well, I mean the poem should just be treated as a person having its own life, a life of its own. This is the way in which I think of my work.

I think that when a word is committed to print it develops legs, wings even, and goes anywhere it wants to go. It is the same as a talking drum. You may want to speak to someone in a different village; when you play the drum and give him the message, he is not the only one who is listening to it. Anybody who is awake at the time listens to it. And those who wish to take the message will take it. I think the poem has this sort of existence, quite apart from the author.

How old were you when you wrote your first poem?

My first published poem . . . Well, my first poem, I believe I was about fourteen. But I haven't preserved it. When I was at school, I contributed poems to our school magazine, but I believe most people did that. We were just learning to speak English at the time. But my first published poem was written when I was twenty-five. My first published poem—it was very short. It is in a back number of *Black Orpheus*.

Was there a stage in your life when you decided that you definitely wished to be a poet?

There wasn't a stage when I decided that I definitely wished to be a poet; there was a stage when I found that I couldn't be anything else. And I think that the turning point came in December 1958, when I knew that I couldn't be anything else than a poet. It's just like somebody who receives a call in the middle of the night to religious service, in order to go and become a priest of a particular cult, and I didn't have any choice in the matter. I just had to obey.

From where did the call come?

(*Laughing*) I don't know. I wish I knew. I wish I knew. I can't say whether the call came from evil spirits or good spirits. But I know that the turning point came in 1958, when I found myself wanting to know myself better, and I had to turn around and look at myself from inside.

And when you say 'self', does this mean not only self but also the ancestors, the background?

(*Emphatically*) No. I mean myself, just myself, not the background . . . But you know that everything has added up to building up the self. So when I talk of the self, I mean my various selves, because the self itself is made up of various elements which do not always combine happily. And when I talk of looking inward to myself, I mean turning inward to examine myselves. This of course takes account of ancestors . . . Because I do not exist apart from my ancestors.

In fact I am generally believed, at home, to be a reincarnation of my maternal grandfather, my mother's father . . . although I don't know if this is true, because I didn't meet him in this world. But I know that people return to the world after they are dead, in different forms.

But when I talk of myself, I mean the whole—everything that has gone to make me what I am, and different from somebody else. And this takes account of the ancestry. One cannot escape from that fact. And I don't think this is an entirely African idea.

No, no. I am much involved with my own ancestors.

It is unimportant that I don't go to the family shrine to sacrifice the fruits of the soil. My creative activity is in fact one way of performing those functions in a different manner. Every time I write a poem, I am in fact offering a sacrifice. My *Heavensgate* is in fact a huge sacrifice.

As I said, I am believed to be a reincarnation of my maternal grandfather, who used to be the priest of the shrine called Ajani, where Idoto, the river goddess, is worshipped. This goddess is the earth mother, and also the mother of the whole family. My grandfather was the priest of this shrine, and when I was born I was believed to be his reincarnation, that is, I should carry on his duties. And although someone else had to perform his functions, this

other person was only, as it were, a regent. And in 1958, when I started taking poetry very seriously, it was as though I had felt a sudden call to begin performing my full functions as the priest of Idoto. That is how it happened.

The opening passage of *Heavensgate,* my first volume of poems published in 1963, is as follows:

> Before you, mother Idoto,
> naked I stand,
> before your watery presence,
> a prodigal,
>
> leaning on an oilbean,
> lost in your legend . . .
>
> Under your power wait I
> on barefoot,
> watchman for the watchword
> at heavensgate;
>
> out of the depths my cry
> give ear and hearken.

And there is another part of *Heavensgate.* This is entitled **'Lustra',** in other words, the rites I perform periodically. And I wrote this when I moved from one house to another. This was the first one I wrote in the new place. And I had to start once more, performing these functions. I will read a part of it and then explain it so that you will understand my own idea of the creative process. There wasn't any question of my taking a decision, you see. It is that I found myself some time ago ready to assume the full responsibilities of a religious priest—a religious priest in the very serious sense of the word:

> So would I to the hills again
> so would I
> to where springs the fountain
> there to draw from
>
> and to hilltop clamber
> body and soul
> whitewashed in the moondew
> there to see from
>
> So would I from my eye the mist
> so would I
> through moonmist to hilltop
> there for the cleansing
>
> Here is a new-laid egg
> here a white hen at midterm . . .

(*Here Christopher stopped reading and began once more to talk.*) And the new-laid egg of course is the poem. And the white hen at midterm is the poem . . . And this poem in fact appears in the middle of *Heavensgate.* A white hen at midterm—I mean midterm in the sense of this poem being written in the middle of a longer work. (*Long pause.*)

I take my work seriously because it is the only reason I am alive. I believe that . . . I believe that writing poetry is a necessary part of my being alive, which is why I've written nothing else. I hardly write prose. I've not written a novel. I've not written a play. Because I think that somehow the medium itself is sufficiently elastic to say what I want to say, I haven't felt the need to look for some other medium.

Paul Theroux   (essay date 1965)

SOURCE: "Christopher Okigbo," in *Transition,* Vol. 5, No. 22, 1965, pp. 18-20.

[*Theroux is an expatriate American novelist, critic, and travel writer who has extensive knowledge of Africa and has set several of his works in Kenya and Malawi. In the following essay, he analyzes the theme of movement in Okigbo's poetry.*]

Ordeal. Ending on the edge of new agonies. Beginning again. And the poet wrapped only in nakedness goes on, deliberately, mostly conscious because he is half-carried by the nightmare winds, half-carries himself with his own home-made, wild, tangled-wood tales.

'Logistics,' says Okigbo in the **'Initiation'** section of *Heavensgate,* 'which is what poetry is.' The art of movement, says the dictionary. And here is the key—Okigbo's art is in moving, movement, being moved, a lived-through victimisation full of symbol and logic and accident and the poet's own plots. It is pure motion because he does not presume and force himself over the ordeal, but suffers it and summons at the end all his energy to resume and carry us all on to continuous illuminations all along the way to death.

At the beginning Okigbo finds himself before the 'watery presence' of *Idoto.* He is naked, a supplicant, offering himself as a sacrifice to his own poetic impulse; he is prepared to suffer creation.

And again, in **'Passage,'** there are the classical 'Dark waters of the beginning,' 'Rays . . . foreshadow the fire that is dreamed of,' and

> On far side a rainbow
> arched like boa bent to kill
> foreshadows the rain that is dreamed of.

The rainbow, the Covenant, is seen as a snake, capable of both leading and devouring the poet. The symbol that will lead the poet is seen as the embodiment of good and evil. The dual vision of Okigbo's occurs all through his journey; the saint would see only the rainbow, the profligate would see the snake—but the visionary Okigbo sees both.

O. R. Dathorne wrote in *Black Orpheus* 15, 'Christopher Okigbo's poetry is all one poem; it is the evolution of a personal religion.' Dathorne goes on to say that Okigbo's poems are narrating the 'progress towards *nirvana'.* But, although Okigbo speaks of being cleansed and desires the 'cancelling out', it seems he is acting on a larger desire to work himself through the ordeal of accepted religiosity and mythology to a new way of seeing rather than to evolve 'a personal religion'. It is not so much evolution of a religion as the *sublimation* of religion in himself that he seems to seek. Surely he begins with all the religious trappings, but the objective is to be released from them, and this can only be had by a complete acceptance and understanding of them. The very fact that Okigbo is always left on the edge seems to indicate that he will never finish 'the eight-fold path' toward true *nirvana.* At the beginning of **'Distances'** (*Transition* 16) he says:

> I was the sole witness to my homecoming.

Yet, many lines later, the last line of the poem is

> I am the sole witness to my homecoming.

This seems proof that there is more than one home and that the poet is doomed always to be the only witness to his arrival at a temporary state of perception. There are different layers of perception, but they must be continually obscured or the poet will be paralysed with all the new rituals of his 'religion'. Once found, the perception must be abandoned.

Okigbo has to conspire with God to reach a state of perception, but always it is the act of writing that serves to release him:

> Stretch, stretch O antennae
> to clutch at this hour
> fulfilling each moment in a
> broken monody.

At the beginning of **'Newcomer'** he has begun to assume a new identity:

> Mask over my face—
> my own mask
> not ancestral—

He has thrown off the curses and blessings of the ancestral identities and says simply, 'Time for worship' several times in this first section of **'Newcomer'**. The most meaningful and direct lines in the book come next:

> O ANNA of the panel oblongs
> protect me
> from them f—n angels
> protect me
> my sandhouse and bones.

Those 'f—n angels' that have become love-locked in a death-grip with so many believers *must* leave him alone. The strength of the above lines comes from his confident examination of his powers as a seer in the previous section, **'Lustra.'** His spirit is 'in ascent' and with confidence he muses:

> I have visited
> on palm beam imprinted
> my pentagon—
> I have visited, the prodigal . . .

Throughout the poem he views himself as a prodigal, yet he returns again and again to confirm this in order to release himself in the confirmation. His visitations meditated upon in **'Lustra'** give him the strength to cry out in **'Newcomer.'** The voice in **'Newcomer'** comes from a newly realised identity.

He has not become a 'newcomer' without sacrifice. He has been, as Dathorne says, crucified (**'Initiation i'**—the repeat of the crucifixion image, the impossibility of forgetting 'the scar of the crucifix') after becoming 'newly naked', and finally he ends the **'Initiation'** section with the explicit:

> And he said to the ram:
> disarm.
> And I said:
> except by rooting,
> who could pluck yam tubers

from their base?

Dathorne calls the reply 'the pain of self-knowledge'. It is the knowledge of lust's presence spoken in reply to a severe command. The ram can only become innocent, lamb-like, by disarming; the disarming of the ram means the removal of his horns—the poet's reply shows us that he understands, for in both the command and the reply there are different castration images. The destructive and distracting sexual appurtenances must be removed. The poet replies in parable: he can only rid himself of 'yam tubers' by 'rooting', dig in order to pluck, immerse himself deeply in his own glands. This process of disarming would not be acceptable to the adherents of conventional religion who are supposed to pluck out the eye if it offends. The poet in **'Initiation'** will pluck by digging, which implies a concentration on the damnable fixtures (Augustine stares at the sour flesh of a fat whore and achieves sainthood in the rejection of it). Okigbo is guilty of all the things he is *capable of doing*. A blind man can hardly be praised because he is not a peeping-Tom.

The next section is a **'Bridge'** in the metaphorical-religious sense and also in the jazz meaning of the term—some music between the main choruses in the piece. And then

> in the teeth of the chill Maymore
> comes the newcomer.

Most of the symbols Okigbo has established in **Heavensgate** are repeated in the first section of **'Siren Limits'** (the first 'part' of **Limits**). He is at the edge, 'talkative'

> like weaverbird
> Summoned at offside of
> dream remembered
> Between sleep and waking

And:

> Queen of the damp half-light,
> I have had my cleansing,
> Emigrant with air-borne nose,
> The he-goat-on-heat.

The ordeal has ended at 'offside of / dream remembered' yet he is sure of only his nose being 'air-borne'. His feet are planted on earth as he is aimed at a vague idea of perception. Certainly the cleansing is real (the best poems in **Heavensgate** come after the disconnected images of the vision fragments; he assumes the new strength immediately after purification), but the 'he-goat-on-heat' is the ram disarming himself in his own way (the ram trying to wrench his horns free in his moment of heat, oestrous). And he goes on 'feeling for audience'—both the audience of listeners that will not be present at his homecoming, and the 'audience' with the force that drives him on, up into his head.

With the new cleansing comes new agony. The poet does not let us forget:

> *& the mortar is not yet dry*
> Then we must sing
> Tongue-tied without name or audience,
> Making harmony among the branches.
> And this is the crisis point,
> The twilight moment between

sleep and waking;
And the voice that is reborn transpires
Not thro the pores in the flesh
but the souls back-bone.

The agony is again partially resolved, in the old way with a new consequence: the traditional groves of **Heavensgate** bathed with the hard light that he has realised in his passage. No one will watch, he must accept the anonymity of the artist and the visionary. Okigbo demands humility of himself, and so, soon after the 'crisis point', he calls for us to 'Hurry on down—'.

In the last section of **'Siren Limits'** we glimpse how incomplete the cleansing has been

> AN IMAGE insists
> from the flag pole of the heart
> The image distracts
> with the cruelty of the rose . . .

Desire has led him back through the 'soul's backbone'. Sexual baggage, the pole, the rose insist on the memory of 'my lioness' (the same image as in **'Watermaid ii'** of **Heavensgate:** 'Bright / with the armpit-dazzle of a lioness, / she answers'):

> Distances of your
> armpit-fragrance
> Turn chloroform,
> enough for my patience—
> When you have finished,
> and done up my stitches
> Wake me near the altar,
> *& this poem will be finished.*

In these eight lines Okigbo plunges backward into **Heavensgate** (the lioness) and forward into **'Distances'** where the last four lines are used as an epigraph. The lioness, the whole sexual operation haunts the sensually anaesthetised poet. In realising that it is an image that has insisted and in giving way to this insistence he is again granted the perception. This perception turns into disappointment because no one is capable of sharing it. In the **'Fragments of the Deluge'**

> HE STOOD in the midst of them all
> and appeared in true form,
> He found them drunken, he found none
> thirsty among them.

And later,

> They cast him in a mould of iron,
> And asked him to do a rock-drill:
> Man out of innocence—
> He drilled with dumb bells about him.

The 'Man out of innocence' drills through experience. 'Dumb bells' can be interpreted as the set of weights that strong men lift to show they are strong; or as 'dumb bells'—morons (American slang); or as instruments capable of producing sound, now silent. In the context it is actually *all three!*

In section VII of **'Fragments'** he has reached the high point of the poem; the rest, as he says in **Heavensgate,** is 'anagnorisis'. In this section comes the deification,

> which is not the point;

> And who says it matters
> which way the kite flows,
> Provided movement is around
> the burning market,
> The centre—

The wisdom that he has practised throughout the poem comes upon him in a phrase, consciously; the logistics of staying near the flame no matter what the mask. This is more than an approach to sexual action—it is commitment to it. So we are not surprised to find in the vision of IX ('Then the beasts broke . . .') the careful preparation and final orgasmic violence ending in division and death. Neither does the final ambiguity of the return of the 'Sunbird', mixed with the image of 'Guernica', startle. He has entered 'the burning market' as he predicted. After it, a quiet moment:

> The Sunbird sings again
> From the LIMITS of the dream,
> The Sunbird sings again
> Where the caress does not reach

Quiet, though mixed with unspoken torment, for it is this 'caress' of the Sunbird (no longer the Lioness that he can devour) which he cannot manage that will release him from the *Limits* and press him into the **'Distances'** where

> At this chaste instant
> of delineated anguish,
> the same voice, importunate,
> aglow with the goddess
>
> . . . . .
>
> strips the dream naked,
> bares the entrails;

The Sunbird still out of reach agonises him. And the litany:

> I have fed out of the drum
> I have out drunk of the cymbal
> I have entered your bridal
> chamber; and lo,
> I am the sole witness to my homecoming.

The repeated pattern all through **'Silences,'** *Heavensgate,* *Limits* and **'Distances'** has shown the concern for movement *through* and not necessarily a movement *to.* The fat state of perceptivity has been gotten, he is 'symbiotic with non-being' (Dathorne) but it is a 'chaste instant', impermanent, and it is this short-lived purity that delivers him again into the pain of the 'homecoming', and that will continue to deliver him into pain.

It is impossible to do justice to Okigbo's erudition in such a short space. His sources can be found in Ibo mythology, the Bible, Allen Ginsberg's *Howl,* Pound's *Cantos* and in his own impeccable craft coupled with a soaring imagination. Okigbo, poet, prophet, prodigal; the consistency of his vision throughout his work.

He passes 'from flesh into phantom', from holy groves to the hospital bed. This is *nirvana*? No. It is a hell of revelation in which the reader sees Okigbo become a disembodied existential eyeball scorching itself on the ordeal. He cannot be picked up at random and thumbed through; we have to follow his progress from pain to perception and back to pain. Okigbo can be considered from the point of view of all theologies, mythologies—each yields an interpretation. But better we too suffer the ordeal, ending on the edge of new agonies.

Beginning again.

> after we had formed
> then only the forms were formed
> and all the forms were formed
> after our forming . . .

John Povey   (essay date December 1967)

SOURCE: "Epitaph to Christopher Okigbo," in *Africa Today,* Vol. 14, No. 6, December, 1967, pp. 22-3.

[*Povey is an English educator, critic, and the editor of* African Arts. *In the following excerpt, he surveys Okigbo's works, highlighting the poet's lyricism and praising his wide emotional range and subject matter.*]

Okigbo was a far-ranging writer, eclectic, with a poetic strength which moulded the apparently piecemeal sources of his inspiration into a personal and sensitive vision. He is acknowledged as an intellectual poet, making the fullest statement through rigidly cerebral images that recall inevitably that old imagist master, Ezra Pound. Yet this assertion may exaggerate Okigbo's difficulty and make us underrate the tenderness that flecks his work and that directness of vision which takes beauty as its aim. There is an immediate loveliness in the half jocular spring image of:

> when the draper of May
> has sold out fine green
> garments; and the hillsides
> have made up their faces. . . .

The following lines, though both verbally and intellectually compressed, have that same directness of the emotively visual:

> now breaks
> salt-white surf on the stones and me,
> and lobsters and shells in
> iodine smell—
> maid of the salt-emptiness.
> sophisticreamy, native . . .

The most famous image in all Okigbo's poetry evokes Africa's tense glaring beauty:

> Bright
> with the armpit-dazzle of a lioness,
> she answers,
> wearing the light about her;
> and the waves escort her,
> my lioness,
> crowned with moonlight.
> So brief her presence—
> match-flare in wind's breath—
> so brief with mirrors around me.

But one can almost imagine that Okigbo cautiously suspects such lushness. He uses it consciously, even while he recognizes that it directs his poetry into forms that may be self defeating. In the following lines one recognizes how carefully selected are the critical verbs:

An image insists
from the flag pole of the heart,
The image distracts
with the cruelty of the rose . . .

Okigbo seeks a more precise evocation than the sensual one, though one wonders whether the repetition of his definition of poetry exposes a partial doubt about an interpretation that would deny so much of his work.

And I said:
The prophet only,
the poet.
And he said:
Logistics.
Which is what poetry is.
Which is what poetry is.

Okigbo's created style must encompass his dual experience. Although the division in the heart of the African has become the worst kind of sloppy cliche, it has the validity that rests at the center of any truism. Okigbo stands between those two cultures of which he is inevitably and brilliantly the dual heir. He is an African educated within the European tradition, for better or for worse, and the double channels of historical theology press into all his work. He can begin **Heavensgate** with an impassioned celebration of the tribal figure Idoto:

Before you, mother Idoto,
naked I stand,
before your watery presence,
a prodigal
leaning on an oilbean;
lost in your legend. . . .

But before the brief poem concludes, there is the anguished Christian cry, "out of the depths . . ." Okigbo can begin a poem with "Lacrimae Christi" and go on to the "Messiah will come again, / Lumen mundi . . ." but the last verse of this lyric takes one into that African dimension of:

Fingers of penitence
bring
to a palm grove
vegetable offering . . .

And he contemplates himself with that ultimate self-awareness, recognizing that if, as for all social men, there must be, "Mask over my face," it will not be the traditional one. It will be, "my own mask / not ancestral—"

It is this new poetic self behind its own "persona" which brings together a duality of belief and a multiplicity of style that must speak of the nature of modern Nigeria. It succeeds with a prescience so exact that it must be an accident of revelation rather than the foreknowledge of event. In describing the eternal disaster he appears to describe his experience during the last few weeks.

And they took the hot spoils off the battle,
And they shared the hot spoils among them:
Estates among them;
And they were chosen
mongrel breeds,
With slogan in hand, of
won divination . . .
And you talk of the people

And there is none thirst among them.

The last published lines in Okigbo's book raise a noun that was once the ultimate evocation in Europe, "Guernica." It became, in the thirties, a symbol of the senseless cruelty of man—and during a civil war. The young people today, hardened to mass slaughter, must smile to imagine our concern with such relatively minimal damage from the sky; such small bombs. But that symbol stays though the dimensions of destruction expand; the protests of other poets thirty years ago, remain just as valid as ever. That is why the word Guernica is so evocative still in the lines of this young African poet, a baby during the Spanish war. His nation has been able to learn from history only by the painful penalty of reliving history's suffering.

The Sunbird sings again
From the LIMITS of the dream,
The Sunbird sings again
Where the caress does not reach,
of Guernica,
On whose canvas of blood,
The newsprint-slits of his tongue
cling to glue . . .
and the cancelling out is complete.

"The cancelling out is complete." So must it remain with Okigbo.

Yet although he personally died fighting for a savage partitioning of his country, his spirit ranged more widely than the tribe into a totality of brotherhood. Perhaps the urge for brotherhood in such shattering civil strife seems almost madness. If so Okigbo beautifully accepts that madness for it joins him to his neighbor in a tender unity that moves above politics. In a poem for Peter Thomas the last lines are infinitely gentle, yet no less strong:

I am mad with the same madness as the
moon and my neighbour,
I am kindled from the moon and the
hearth of my neighbour.

Such lines take on a different dimension of hope in these dark days but that must be for others, not Okigbo in this absurd and tragic death.

When you have finished,
and done up my stitches,
Wake me near the altar,
and this poem will be finished.

But Christopher Okigbo will never wake and all his poems are finished.

In a context far removed from war but now so desperately relevant he once wrote:

Thundering drums and cannons
in palm grove:
the spirit is in ascent.

This statement becomes both the opening and concluding stanza of a brief lyric, so significant does the poet find its emphasis. We wish that we could share the optimism as we hear those cannons that tear Nigeria. It asserts the poet's capacity to range above the narrowness of day-to-day events. Later there must be an ascent of spirit that will reaffirm its continuance amongst the horrors of a civil war.

That spirit, alas, will not be that of Christopher Okigbo but it will declare the same idealistic priorities for all men.

Okigbo on *Heavensgate* and *Limits*:

My *Heavensgate* was influenced by the Impressionist composers. It is curious how this happens, but this is the truth or part of it. I wrote several parts of *Heavensgate* under the spell of Debussy, Caesar Frank and Ravel. My *Limits* was influenced by everything and everybody. But this is not surprising, because the *Limits* were the limits of a dream. It is surprising how many lines of the *Limits* I am not sure are mine and yet do not know whose lines they were originally. But does it matter?

Christopher Okigbo, in Transition, *July 30-August 29, 1962.*

Wilfred Cartey (essay date 1969)

SOURCE: "Belief and Man's Faith," in his *Whispers from a Continent: The Literature of Contemporary Black Africa,* 1969. Reprint by Heinemann Educational Books Ltd., 1971, pp. 315-84.

[*Cartey was a West Indian critic and educator. In the following excerpt, he examines Christian imagery in Okigbo's poems.*]

The reality of Christopher Okigbo's *Heavensgate* is not within the realm of nature, but moves through and modifies many Christian ordinances, soaring into the realm of belief and of spirit. The prodigal poet stands a naked supplicant, seeking to elucidate the mystery of the genesis, of his initiation, of his purification. Time is not only a linear chronological progression from innocence to spiritual awareness, but also a structurally lyrical moment in which the poem arcs from the dark waters of the beginning across the waters of noon to the fountain of lustration, to its final descent as the moon goes under the sea, bringing the song's ending. Yet, before the end, the eyes of the prodigal open:

> Eyes open on the sea,
> eyes open, of the prodigal;
> upward to heaven shoot
> where stars will fall from.

His spirit is in the ascent and with the returning cycle of nature's rebirth, a newcomer is born:

> In the chill breath
> of the day's waking
>
> comes the newcomer
>
> when the draper of May
> has sold out fine green
> garments, and the hillsides
> have made up their faces

The invocation at the beginning of *Heavensgate* immediately introduces the linear imagery on which the poem is based, the finely etched spatial indications introducing less clearly defined metaphysical concepts:

> Before you, mother Idoto,
> naked I stand,
> before your watery presence.
> a prodigal,
>
> leaning on an oilbean;
> lost in your legend . . .
>
> Under your power wait I on barefoot.
> Watchman for the watchword at
> HEAVENSGATE;
>
> out of the depths my cry
> give ear and hearken.

From the beginning, innocence is confounded by the divergent promises of the elements, fire and water:

> Dark waters . . . foreshadow the fire that is
>   dreamed of.
> . . . a rainbow . . . foreshadows the rain that is
>   dreamed of.

The image of innocence is mirrored in the picture of "the young bird at the passage." The image is carried forward and is now presented on two levels—the bird has learned the power of flight and the boys the joys of innocence:

> And when we were great boys . . .
> we sang words after the bird—
>
> And we would respond,
> great boys of child—innocence

Soon the song of the bird, which stood indecisively at the passage, moves under a lamp, becomes a stale song:

> still sings the sunbird
> under the lamp,
> stale song the dumb bell
> loud to me.

Within "the hot garden where all roads meet," the song becomes a canticle of pipe organ music, introducing a festival of mourning. Forgiveness to the newly naked at Pentecost does not lead to resurrection but merely opens to a "vision of the hot bath of heaven / Among reedy spaces."

In the second section, initiation is the crisscrossing of lines in the synthesis of religion and belief. The initiation ritual reaffirms innocence through the purity of line:

> Scar of the crucifix
> over the breast
> by red blade inflicted
>
>   . . . . .
>
> witnesseth
> mystery which I initiate
> received newly naked
> upon water of the genesis
>
>   . . . . .
>
> Elemental, united in vision
> of present and future,
> the pure line, whose innocence
> denies inhibitions.

Intuition and sensation blend and save man from the un-natural, from sham. Through his initiation moral man is led to free living, away from sophistry, and saved from "the errors of the rendering" that distorted logic or religion produce.

In **"Bridge"** all movement is momentarily suspended as the poet, treading water at noontide, waits in listening anticipation:

> I am standing above you and tide
> above the noontide,
> Listening to the laughter of waters
> that do not know why:
> Listening to innocence . . .
> I am standing above the noontide
> with my head above it

In **"Watermaid"** the waiting soon is replaced by an effervescent, momentary encounter with a presence. Images of containment, of vertical movement, the play of reflected light and shadow splice together the poet's swiftly fleeting, but experientially necessary, sensations:

> and the waves escort her,
> my lioness,
> crowned with moonlight.
>
> So brief her presence—
> match-flare in wind's breath—
> so brief with mirrors around me.

Yet after this brief encounter, the poet is once more left alone, aspiring to fulfill his monody:

> The stars have departed,
> and I—where am I?
>
> Stretch, stretch, O antennae,
> to clutch at this hour,
>
> fulfilling each moment in a
> broken monody.

Lustration now takes place, and the poet accepts the ritual of a newly laid egg performed with "thundering drums and cannons in palm grove," and the spirit is in the ascent to the hills, "to where springs the fountain," and "body and soul white-washed in the moondew" clamber to the hilltop. The newcomer arrives, even though in the chill May morning the welcome is synthetic. Yet the fledgling that had stood at the passage on one leg, now a heron, attempts a perilous flight toward the infinite:

> in flight into the infinite—
> a blinded heron
> thrown against the infinite—
> where solitude
> weaves her interminable mystery

Man's journey is at an end; his spirit freed, he goes searching for essences.

D. S. Izevbaye   (essay date 1973)

SOURCE: "Okigbo's Portrait of the Artist as a Sunbird: A Reading of *Heavensgate* (1962)," in *African Literature Today*, No. 6, 1973, pp. 1-14.

[*In the excerpt below, Izevbaye delineates the interplay of sources Okigbo employs in* Heavensgate *and* Limits.]

The year 1971 saw the publication by Heinemann Educational Books of *Labyrinths with Path of Thunder,* a collection which is in one respect the final edition of Okigbo's work although, because of the omission of the Canzones and at least two of the later poems, its finality consists not in completeness but in saving editors of Okigbo's poems the trouble of having to decide what the poet actually wrote or intended to write. An additional value of this collection is the poet's introductory interpretation or, as interpretations are never known to be final, a description of the design of the poems which should become the basis of future interpretations. By thus providing the reader with an outline map of *Labyrinths,* Okigbo has cleared some of the paths to his poetic experience and has probably helped to arrest the growing tendency to regard the experience as something that is not available to the reader. This view of the poems as an impenetrable territory has been encouraged by reports of Okigbo's early view of poetry as a type of cult from which the uninitiated is excluded and by the cautious critical explications—often necessarily cautious, admittedly—in which the critic and the reader are unmasked as intruders. This impression of a closed world has been a potential inhibition to response, and the poet has thrown down this psychological barrier by offering the elucidations in *Labyrinths.*

The poetry remains a genuinely difficult one by itself, of course. To be able to find their way through the labyrinths of allusions to personal myths and forgotten cultures many readers will have to rely on the thread of meaning provided in the introduction and the notes. However, this change in respect of the poet's attitude to the reader reflects the difference between *Labyrinths* and the discrete earlier versions of Okigbo's poetry. In the earlier versions the uninitiated reader is understandably excluded from the poetic experience because the poet is himself still being initiated. *Labyrinths* follows the path of exploration or inquiry leading to discovery or revelation. With the poet's discovery of the true pattern of his initiation the reader can now be taken through the different stage until he too is finally admitted into the sanctuary. Each of the earlier sequences is incomplete by itself because it is only an investigation of the poet's partial glimpse of an experience, and only the complete group of sequences can provide a reliable blueprint from which a reader might reconstruct the poetic experience. The earlier poems are not then the true gateways; or if they are gateways they often lead to blind alleys, though they are useful as reflections of the poet's own wanderings and losses of direction before the surer path of his pilgrimage is revealed in the continuity of *Labyrinths.*

The revisions which result in *Labyrinths* are, like most revisions, necessary for a clearer and more accurate statement of the poet's experience. Nevertheless the earlier poems are of value because they tell a fairly accurate story of the process of composition. An interpretation of the revisions shows that in addition to the need for an efficient performance the final version required the tailoring of the old poems in order to fit the new need. One of the most important changes in *Labyrinths* is the cutting out of 'Transition' from *Heavensgate.* Without necessarily committing oneself to a fallacy by describing as the poet's intention what is really an effect of the final revision, one may justify the excision of 'Transition' by arguing that its triumphant tone is not quite consistent with the humble and exploratory spirit of *Heavensgate,* and that this tone is contradicted, in 'Siren Limits', by the poet's use of the image of the shrub or the low growth which confesses a striving towards maturity rather than claim a full maturing of poetic powers. However if there is something inconsistent about the claims of 'Transition' in the light of the actual performance of *Heavensgate* this section of the poem is itself less out of place in the original sequence than it would have been in *Labyrinths* within which the *Heavensgate* sequence itself is mainly an introduction or a prelude. In other words it was necessary to eliminate an end which has turned out to be a true end no longer.

If the 1962 version of the sequence would not fit into *Labyrinths* without modification it nevertheless has its own completeness, and the different sections have their justification for being in the poem, although the question that has most frequently been raised is that of the relevance of the parts. The organic unity of Okigbo's poems should seem a fairly commonplace idea by now, since it was emphasized in the earliest as well as in the most recent comments on the poetry—in Anozie's review [*Ibadan,* March, 1963] as well as in Okigbo's introduction. But although this underlying principle of composition has long been recognized it has not always been accepted as generally applicable to all the poems. For example, 'Newcomer', the fifth movement of *Heavensgate,* is sometimes seen as separate from the rest of the poem because its sections were originally composed as separate poems and at different times [O. R. Dathorne, *Journal of Commonwealth Literature,* July, 1968].

The ground for such a doubt is of course Okigbo's method of composition which creates the impression that each poem is an assemblage that may be dismantled and reassigned to the various sources, like Tutuola's Complete Gentleman. For example, it seems as if some of the units in an Okigbo sequence can comfortably be moved to other positions especially when, because of the omission of existing parts or the addition of others, a new relationship is created between the parts which makes it necessary to reexamine the meaning conveyed. Such a reassignment is evident in both *Modern Poetry from Africa* (1963) and *Labyrinths* where 'Bridge' is moved from its place in the middle of *Heavensgate* to the end in order to link the sequence with *Limits.* A discussion of Okigbo's poems therefore should assume the reader's acceptance of the essential looseness of structure arising from this method of composition. In this respect the sequences have a kinship with primitive epics because the poems appear to be a series of predetermined *forms* which attract independent poetic compositions to themselves. An important factor in the composition of extended traditional poems, especially primitive epics, is the fact that poems originally created as separate compositions cease to be considered independent units after they have been organized into larger units. The process of composition appears to be the adoption of

a conventional, but fairly loose, structure within which individual experiences may establish a logical relationship with one another. The most favoured structures are usually those connected with social institutions or with religious or ritual performance. The relevance of this to a discussion of *Heavensgate* is obvious. The poem deals with the personal experiences of the hero. Its theme is the growth of a poet's mind. To the extent that the poem has a biographical—or autobiographical—structure, each of its movements represents the moments of crisis in the hero's life. So it is possible to regard any equivalent structure—like the basic stages of a man's life, Childhood, Adolescence, and Maturity—as the scaffolding around which the poem is constructed. The period of composition notwithstanding, poems about various experiences fit into the various stages whether as crises, or as the cause or the resolution of crises. The act of creation may thus be seen to consist mainly in a structural arrangement which makes each unit of the poem subordinate to, and a functional part of, the overall organization.

This emphasis of organization also makes it necessary to adopt a more flexible view of originality with regard to the problem of the literary influences or borrowings in the poems. For the purpose of this essay it is useful to make a distinction between literary echoes and literary borrowings. Literary echoes are resonances of an original, and to get a full experience of the poem the reader requires some knowledge of the original. And although such a poem might have an independent existence, like *The Waste Land,* the poems which it echoes are often part of the aesthetic experience of the poem, since the echoes are adaptations of an accepted context the knowledge of which, while not being essential, is invariably enriching.

In literary borrowing, on the other hand, knowledge of the original context contributes little or nothing to the experience of the new poem. It might in fact be a hindrance to proper critical response. The borrowed phrase or sentence is often used with little regard for its source, as in some of Okigbo's poems where not much is gained from a knowledge of the original poem. For usually Okigbo's interest in his borrowings seems limited to the beauty and the utility of the phrase itself, and the 'meaning' or 'experience' of the poem is often controlled by its immediate context. This is mostly true even when, as in the title *Heavensgate,* the borrowed word affects the reader's response in the right direction before the context has had a chance to do its work. The discussion which follows is based on the text of 1962. . . .

The title *Heavensgate* appears to be a word abstracted from a context, and the context that readily suggests itself is Shakespeare's twenty-ninth sonnet where the bard is lifted from a mood of depression to sing 'hymns at heaven's gate' by the thought of love. There is the same movement from despair to elation in the two poems. In both cases the central symbol is a singing bird. Even the image of the importunate outcast at the ears of deaf heaven in the sonnet seems reflected in the prodigal's apparent return to a starting point after an abortive attempt at entry. But it is not essential to see the title as a literary echo in order to notice that the sunbird is the central image of the poem, or that the whole poem is conceived as a musical form in which much value is attached to the interplay of sounds.

The conception of the poem as musical form is apparent in the opening invocation which is used as a prelude to introduce the main motif of the piece. This function is more apparent in the anthology by Moore and Beier where the adopted title 'Overture' provides an apt musical analogy by emphasizing the introductory function of the invocation as well as describing the relationship between the suppliant and the goddess. Since the first movement, **'Passage'**, deals with the period of passage from boyhood to manhood, the prelude is appropriately a physical dramatization of an attempted entry into a spiritual or aesthetic state. The central movements of the poem are concerned with such attempts in the present time. The events of the present are explained in the past, which is the period dealt with by the first two movements, **'Passage'** and **'Initiation'**. **'Transition'**, which is the coda to the whole sequence, anticipates the hero's passage into a future state, a state which is never really achieved in Okigbo's poetry except in **'Distances.'** Although **'Transition'** foretells a state which **'Distances'** enacts, the vision which it presents—the uninhibited release of unlimited song—is not achieved in the poem itself, as is made clear in the structure of *Heavensgate.* In fact the effective mood of Okigbo's first two sequences is not fulfilment but anticipation. So that even by the end of **'Siren Limits'** the resolution of the crisis is deferred to future time:

> When you have finished
> & done up my stitches,
> Wake me near the altar,
> & this poem will be finished . . .

'Passage' as a whole deals with the hero's early childhood responses to experience. But although there is an attempt, in **'Passage (ii)'**, to recapture childhood experience by reproducing sounds mimicked by the boys, both **'Passage'** and **'Initiation'** deal with experience in retrospect. Although 'the young bird at the passage' is the observer of the spectacle in **'Passage (i)'** (probably the onset of a thunderstorm), it is the mind of the mature artist which now interprets this scenery as a reproduction of the creation scene, and takes us back to that period 'when we were great boys' and 'sang words after the birds'.

This second section is central to the first two movements of the poem because of the way it uses the symbols of bird and light establishes their significance for the rest of the poem. After the associations built up by this section, light and bird would together herald the lyric impulse in both *Heavensgate* and *Limits.*

Meanwhile **'Passage (iii)'** picks up the image of the bird with which the preceding section closes, and with it defines and enlarges the theme of creation with which the first section opens. It does this by presenting the two major forms which the boy's introduction into the act of creation has taken. These are represented as at play at the blacksmiths' forge, and at work with the teacher at school. Since these introductions to experience take the form of response, there is possibly a third situation in which it oc-

curs—that of worship in church. But this is not introduced until later.

The emphasis on response as the main factor in the boy's formative period shows that in **'Passage (ii)'** the boys are passing through a period of pupilage. Those gifts which are to survive into their adult life are already in evidence here—the fascination which song holds for them is evident in their imitation of bird sounds—'kratosbiate'. There is also the identification of these sounds with other fascinating sounds the children are made to imitate at school, as in their dutiful response to the sing-song recitation of their teacher, *'Etru bo pi a lo a she . . .'* The metonymy, 'white buck and helmet', shows the teacher himself as seen through childhood eyes. As if to show that both experiences are really part of the same experience in spite of their separate locations at school and at play, the flames of the forge become metaphor for the shaping influence of school where boys are pulled through innocence, and the smith's workshop becomes a new setting for learning. The boys show a preference for the latter setting, since the symbols of school influence are consigned to the flames. That is why 'burn' is possibly ambiguous in the following extract:

> And we would respond,
> great boys of child-innocence,
> and in the flames burn
> white buck and helmet
> that had pulled us through innocence. . . .

The lines would normally be read to mean, 'we would burn white buck and helmet in the flames'; but it could also imply, 'we would burn [be shaped] in the flames'.

If religion does not feature as an important influence in those two sections it sounds the dominant note in the rest of **'Passage'** and **'Initiation',** and helps to define the unpleasant experiences which force the prodigal to accept the necessity for homecoming. In **'Passage (ii)'** the real centre of the Christian procession is the overwhelming bewilderment which the poet feels on arriving at a crossroads or a turning point in his development. This mood is achieved through an emphasis on the solemnity and on the mourning colour which marks the procession and which identifies the poet's mood with the traditional feeling of loss and alienation associated with mournings. The fragments of melody, the appeal to a personal saint, 'Anna of the panel oblongs', and the refuge in the cornfields among the wild music of the winds complete the mourner's feeling of a broken emotional anchor. Thus begins the prodigal's progress from separation through bewilderment and alienation which are the preludes to his renunciation of the Christian religion.

'Passage (iii)' outlines the hero's initial objections to Christianity; its foreign origin is emphasized in the drama of the seven-league boots striding over distant seas and deserts; its oppressiveness is implied in the designation of Leidan as 'archtyrant of the holy sea' (an obvious pun); and the aversion which he feels for Christian ritual and its reward is present in the report on the fate of people like Paul, who, after conversion, become subjected to the:

> smell of rank olive oil
> on foreheads,

vision of the hot bath of heaven
among reedy spaces.

Having had a foretaste of various forms of experience in
'Passage' (play, education, religion), the poet recalls, in
'Initiation', his formal introduction into the adult world
of religion, poetry, and sex. His introduction to the first
takes the form of a ritual initiation, but his introduction
to the other two areas of experience occurs as a form of
discovery. As might have been anticipated in the previous
section, the prodigal's first significant experience of religion takes the form of a painful initiation which he sees
rather resentfully as a branding that has the claims of a
legal agreement:

> Scar of the crucifix
> over the breast
> by red blade inflicted
> by red-hot blade on right breast
> witnesseth

The pain itself is not the cause but the consequence of his
resentment. The cause stems from his conception that ideally, the initiated should be

> Elemental, united in vision
> of present and future,
> the pure line, whose innocence
> denies inhibitions.

Instead of this promised transformation the initiated ones
turn out to be worthless or corrupt adherents whom the
poet has arranged in categories which include lifeless morons, fanatics, and self-seekers. This perversion of good intentions is imputed to cultural differences. Maybe that is
why the hero seeks refuge in the memory of a childhood
experience in the third section.

The second and central theme of the poem is presented in
'Initiation (iii)' and **'Initiation (iv)'. 'Initiation (iii)'** returns us the poet's childhood. The theme is music making,
with Jadum the minstrel singing cautionary songs from
the fairyland of youth till late into the night. The opening
lines are a suggestion that Jadum got his name from the
sound of his music, 'JAM JAM DUM DUM'. The emphasis is not so much on his madness as on the music he
makes. The power of his minstrelsy over the childish listener is the theme of the section. And yet the fact of his
madness is important too, for the identification of poetry
with madness is also the theme of **'Newcomer (ii)'** where
the hero is 'mad with the same madness as the / moon and
my neighbour'.

'Initiation (iv)' focuses attention directly on the art of poetry by formulating a poetic. The formulation takes the
form of a dialogue with 'Upandru'. The first item defines
Okigbo's technique, his delight in mystifying the reader
with recondite references. Obscurity is a technique for hiding the poet's thoughts: 'Screen your bedchamber
thoughts / with sunglasses'. The second item, the view
that only poets may penetrate beyond this mask, might explain why, as was once reported, Okigbo claimed, 'I don't
read my poetry to non-poets':

> who could jump your eye
> your mind-window?

And I said:
The prophet only,
The poet.

The bedchamber is introduced in the fifth section where
the poet screens his thoughts with a riddle. In this introduction of the third theme, the sexual, the poet rejects the
Christian call of **'Initiation (i)'** for a 'life without sin'. In
his conviction that freedom from lust can come only
through indulgence the prodigal has found a philosophy
to live by. By this rejection of an alien religion and the
adoption of poetry and of a personal code of existence, the
prodigal-poet considers his initiation into a new personal
world complete, and feels ready for union with Watermaid. **'Bridge'** represents this stage of the anticipation of
her influence.

The desired union with Watermaid is however not consummated in the third movement. There is a stage missing
in the ritual of the prodigal's return, and that is, an identification of the source to which he is returning, and a performance of the requirements for readmission. **'Initiation'**
has turned out a misleading experience. What he describes
in the first section is merely an abortive initiation; and although he achieves something in the first two sections by
completing the renunciation of his prostituted allegiance,
he does not go further than an examination and a discovery of his own purposes in the last two sections. In fact no
adequate preparation for the meeting with Watermaid has
taken place. That is why, as the poet discovers, **'Bridge'**
has been a premature stage in his homecoming. So although the goddess responds to the prodigal's cry, the revelation is too evanescent to be of permanent value to the
poet who now watches the loss of the harvest:

> So brief her presence—
> match-flare in wind's breath—
> so brief with mirrors around me.
>
> Downward . . .
> the waves distil her:
> gold crop
> sinking ungathered.

The lament in **'Watermaid (iii)'** involves not merely alienation but also a loss of the expected harvest. In **'Watermaid (iv)',** for example the departure of the stars is used
not only as a backdrop to the isolation of the poet, it is also
a reference to **'Watermaid (i)'** in which poetic blessing is
expected when the eyes of the prodigal 'upward to heaven
shoot / where stars will fall from'. That is why the prodigal-poet strives to recapture the fleeting strains of poetic
inspiration in a passage that anticipates the second movement of **Limits:**

> Stretch, stretch, O antennae,
> to clutch at this hour,
>
> fulfilling each moment in a
> broken monody.

The reason for the failure to achieve full union with
Watermaid has been revealed earlier where the suppliant
hid the secret in beach sand. The goddess has discovered
that the candidate for initiation is ritually unclean and
therefore unfit for her presence. All he has done is to go
through an adapted form of Christian confession without

using a priest—an unsuitable ritual, for Watermaid is unambiguously presented as 'native'—in a renunciation of the Christian experience. That is why, in spite of being from the sea, she is 'Watermaid of the salt emptiness'. Salt water has become distasteful because of its supposed association with the baptismal rites of primitive Christianity:

> so comes John the Baptist
> with bowl of salt water

Since Watermaid is not a Christian goddess we may assume that she belongs mainly to a non-Christian, even pre-Christian, religion or community.

It follows, then, that the particular defilement we are concerned with is non-Christian and even non-ethical, and that the state of impurity should not be linked with the prodigal's rejection of Christian insistence on continence in the **'Initiation'** movement. In fact the recurrence of the he-goat-on-heat motif in *Limits* reinforces this view that the uncleanliness which drove Watermaid away from contact with pollution, and makes the **'Lustra'** movement of *Heavensgate* necessary, is a ceremonial rather than an ethical or moral purification. Ritual offering is necessary only because the poet-hero has been a prodigal and is therefore technically a stranger requiring ritual cleansing before being readmitted into communion with his goddess.

It is this purification feast that is variously celebrated in the three parts of **'Lustra'**: first the traditionally prescribed objects of purification in the first part; then the spirit's hopeful ascent towards acceptance to an accompaniment of ceremonial drums and cannons in the second part; finally, the vegetable and chalk that are offered in the third part as an act of penitence to complete the requirement partially fulfilled by the performance in the earlier sections. Although the offerings are all traditional ones, they possess the attributes of moistness and whiteness which have been associated with the goddess. Also like the goddess, the attitude is 'native'. It will be noticed that in the line, 'whitewashed in the moondew', a common Christian moral attitude has been purged from the word, 'whitewash', which is now reinvested with a non-Western, traditional ritual meaning. We may assume that his renunciation is final at this stage.

In the third section the poet adopts the underlying faith of the religion from which he is a refugee; the rejection of the source of the faith is explicit in the attitude of 'After the argument in heaven'. The doctrine has relevance for the prodigal because it provides reassurance in the analogy drawn with the Christian belief in the Second Coming—the reappearance of his Watermaid, after the fulfilment of the lustral requirements.

It is this expected second coming of Watermaid which makes the fifth movement, **'Newcomer'**, a necessary conclusion for *Heavensgate.* Having lost his first opportunity to achieve communion with Mother Idoto, it is only in 'Newcomer' that the poet gets another opportunity to hold himself open to poetic inspiration from his native muse, after his blunder in the **'Watermaid'** movement. Although 'Newcomer' suffers from repetition in the context of the poem since the first two sections take the reader over some old ground, on the whole it moves us a step further towards the close of the hero's development. For example, in the opening lines the peals of the angelus recall the prodigal's state of exile, and the involuntary sign of the cross which accompanies these bells becomes transformed into a gesture of defiance against the usual response. It also serves him as a protective mask to insulate his new individuality from being swamped by communal values:

> Mask over my face—
> my own mask
> not ancestral—

Thus, the internalized allegiance which makes it irresistible for the Christian to respond spontaneously at the sight or sound of Christian symbols is tested against the hero's new-found identity. The appeal to the personal 'Saint', Anna, for succour is a desperate step which he takes because he is threatened by the danger of succumbing to the Christian call to worship.

'Newcomer (ii)', by no means the happiest section, repeats the theme of identity just presented in the first section. It is dedicated to a kindred spirit. Both 'spirits' are isolated from the generality of men by their madness—for what is madness but a deviation from commonly-accepted norms of behaviour. It is this common 'insanity' of creative spirits which unites the hero and Peter Thomas with Jadum, the mad minstrel of **'Initiation (iii)'.**

The final section of **'Newcomer'** is also a dedicatory piece: 'For Georgette', written as a kind of nativity poem. Although, like the section dedicated to Peter Thomas, this piece was originally occasional, it finds a logical context in *Heavensgate.* Its burden is the final arrival of the much-longed-for inspiration which gave the whole of the *Heavensgate* sequence its exploratory structure and the strongly expectant tone first dictated by the 'Watchman for the watchword' in the overture. But this section is not a description of the composition of *Heavensgate,* as Anozie pointed out in the review. It only heralds the arrival of poetic inspiration, for *Heavensgate* is an account of its own uncompleted quest only, and the reader is left at that point of elated expectancy just as inspiration descends—a point just one stage ahead of **'Watermaid (i)',** and one behind **'Watermaid (ii)'.** A suitable setting to have the muse delivered has been created in 'May', 'green', and 'garden'. The 'synthetic welcome' suits the experimentation with words and form which gets the poet ready to welcome inspiration when it arrives.

We are now ready for the actual manifestation of the poetic impulse. The blinded heron of **'Transition'** proclaims the birth of song, and anticipates the fulfilment of the goal towards which *Heavensgate* has been developing. The poem closes by the use of images with which the poet initially dramatized the problems of creation. The heron is of course the 'sunbird' of **'Passage'** now developed into a mature bird, and it is to become the talkative weaver-bird of **'Siren Limits'**. We are also to meet him in **'Fragments out of the Deluge'** as the martyred songster who arose, like the phoenix from its ashes, to hymn new songs of its own immortality.

The song of *Heavensgate* ends as darkness descends over the setting, a contrast with the sunrise scene of the opening movement. This is achieved by a tempering of the dominant colours of the poem—transparency replaces the brilliant white of **'Watermaid'**, and soft leaf green replaces the bright, violent colours of the creation scene—i.e. the red, violet and orange of **'Passage (i)'**. Natural phenomena, too, undergo this change: the moon goes under the sea—and it will be remembered that in **'Newcomer (ii)'** the moon is the source of madness and inspiration, and that the sea is the home of Watermaid, goddess of inspiration. When the song is over, the inspirer goes home to rest, leaving the poet spent but sane; leaving only the shade to cloud the play of colour and sound.

And we have to wait until **Limits** when the poet is seized in a new poetic frenzy, his tongue having been liberated after appropriate purification.

Chinua Achebe on Okigbo's poetic gift:

Okigbo is such a bewitching poet, able to cast such a powerful spell that, whatever he cares to say or sing, we stand breathless at the sheer beauty and grace of his sound and imagery. Yet there is that undeniable fire in his last poems which was something new. It was as though the goddess he sought in his poetic journey through so many alien landscapes, and ultimately found at home, had given him this new thunder. Unfortunately, when he was killed in 1967 he left us only that little, tantalizing hint of the new self he had found. But perhaps he will be reincarnated in other poets and sing for us again like his sunbird whose imperishable song survived the ravages of the eagles.

Chinua Achebe, in his Morning Yet on Creation Day: Essays, *Anchor Press/Doubleday, 1975.*

Donatus I. Nwoga   (essay date Spring 1975)

SOURCE: "Plagiarism and Authentic Creativity in West Africa," in *Research in African Literatures,* Vol. 6, No. 1, Spring, 1975, pp. 32-9.

[A Nigerian educator and critic, Nwoga edited and compiled Critical Perspectives on Christopher Okigbo *(1984). In the following excerpt, he addresses the issue of plagiarism in Okigbo's poetry, comparing Okigbo's works with those of other poets.]*

Perhaps I should start in the matter of "plagiarism" with our authentic poet, Christopher Okigbo. Sunday Anozie, in his book, *Christopher Okigbo: Creative Rhetoric,* writing of Okigbo's earliest poems, the **"Four Canzones,"** talks of the four-movement division in each of the Canzones, which continues in the 4th Canzone, "each movement introducing a new variation upon the central theme, and all rounding off in that last ritual exorcism inspired by Miguel Hernandez," the Spanish author of "El amor ascendia entre nosotros . . ." "Inspired," writes Anozie, but look at the similarities:

Okigbo

"Lament of the Lavender Mist"

The moon has ascended between us—
Between two pines
That bow to each other;
Love with the moon has ascended,
Has fed on our solitary stem;
And we are now shadows
That cling to each other
But kiss the air only.

Hernandez

"El amor ascendia entre nosotros"

Love ascended between us like the moon between two palms that have never embraced
Love passed like a moon between us and ate our solitary bodies
And we are two ghosts who seek one another
And meet afar off.

Anozie comments later, in summary, of these early poems:

Okigbo's poetic language at the same period is both unoriginal and diffident, vacillating between different, often conflicting traditions, and adapting whichever poetic forms and diction may have appealed to his curious and impressionable mind. It is evidence of Okigbo's genius and labour that he practically overcame in his later poetry most of these difficulties and succeeded in creating a poetic technique and an idiom purely his own.

Yet, Okigbo's last set of poems ends with:

Okigbo

An old star departs, leaves us here on the shore
Gazing heavenward for a new star approaching;
The new star appears, foreshadows its going
Before a going and coming that goes on forever

Alberto Quintero Alvarez

What departs leaves on the shore
Gazing seawards at the star foreseen;
What arrives announces its farewell
Before a coming-and-going that goes on for ever.

Various sections of Okigbo's poetry are traced by Anozie to various authors and poets. Here is one that he did not trace. The two later versions of **"Lament of the Drums"** (*Black Orpheus* and **Labyrinths**) start with invocations. The **Labyrinths** version starts:

LION-HEARTED cedar forest, gonads for our thunder,
Even if you are very far away, we invoke you:

Give us our hollow heads of long-drums . . .

Antelopes for the cedar forest, swifter messengers

Than flash-of-beacon-flame, we invoke you:

Hide us; deliver us from our nakedness . . .

Many-fingered canebrake, exile for our laughter,

Even if you are very far away, we invoke you:

Come; limber our raw hides of antelopes . . .

This is clearly an adaptation of the drum invocations of the Ashanti drummers recorded in 1926 by Rattray:

> Kon, kon, kon, kon,
> Kun, kun, kun, Kun,
> Spirit of Funtumia Akore,
> Spirit of Cedar tree Akore,
> Of Cedar tree, Kodia,
> Of Kodia, the Cedar tree;
> The divine Drummer announces that,
> Had he gone else where
> He now has made himself to arise . . .
> We are addressing you,
> And you will understand;
> We are addressing you
> And you will understand.

Much of the material of this stanza is repeated in following stanzas in which the Earth, the Elephant which supplies the hides for the drums, the fibre with which the hides are tied to the drums, the pegs that tense the fibres, and the kokokyinaka bird, the totem of drummers, are invoked. These drum incantations are the first things played in the morning before the formal drumming of the Drum-History of Mampon. Kwabena Nketia gives the title of this drum piece as "The Awakening" and gives another version of the invocation of the elephant.

Obviously the forms of words differ greatly, and Okigbo makes explicit request for the functioning of the various invoked elements which the original drum piece takes for granted, and it is antelopes, not elephants, that Okigbo asks for hides. But there can be no doubt that he was inspired by the traditional "The Awakening," followed its pattern starting from the invocation of the cedar tree, and abbreviated some of its ideas.

Now, I doubt very much that Dr. Anozie, if he had known this, would have desisted from his comment which gives stylistic and thematic validity to the introduction of this invocation into the poem. What he does say is:

> that the new versions of Movement I of **"Lament of the Drums"** should start in each case with an invocation and a prayer is a clear sign of greater visionary consistency and an improvement upon the original version. For example, by invoking their own proper elements . . . and also by drawing attention to their own traditional roles of communications . . . the Drums assert themselves as the principal actors in the present drama.

It would appear that Sunday Anozie was not disturbed by the sources of Okigbo's material, only that the material should stylistically and thematically conform with the total poem in which it appears.

Another source of borrowing in Okigbo from traditional literature is represented by his poem for Yeats. *The Centenary Essays for W. B. Yeats,* edited by D. E. S. Maxwell and S. B. Bushrui and published in Ibadan in 1965, contains his **"Lament of the Masks: For W. B. Yeats: 1865-1939."** This is a long poem in four sections. From Section II one begins to hear echos. The lines:

> How many beacon flames
> Can ever challenge the sun? . . .
> Ten thousand rivers
> Can never challenge the sea.

echo Ewe religious poems that I have seen but I cannot immediately recall their place of publication. However, the parallel to the Yoruba *Oriki* of the King of Ikerre is quite close:

> Two hundred needles do not make a hoe
> Two hundred stars do not make a moon

The next lines:

> Thunder above the earth,
> Sacrifice too huge for the vulture

take the second line from the Yoruba *Oriki* to Shango, which, in Ulli Beier's translation starts

> Huge sacrifice,
> too heavy for the vulture
> it trembles under your weight

In Section III, the following lines form the second stanza:

> They put you into the eaves thatch
> You split the thatch
> They poured you into an iron mould
> You burst the mould.

These remind one of a section of the Yoruba *Oriki* to Eshu, again translated by Ulli Beier:

> Eshu slept in the house—
> But the house was too small for him.
> Eshu slept in the verandah—
> but the verandah was too small for him.

It is worth noting here that the Yoruba poem continues

> Eshu slept in the net—
> at last he could stretch himself.

which introduces an element of paradox, consistent with the trickster nature of Eshu, but which Okigbo did not need and therefore did not use.

A definite "plagiarism" in this section is that from the Yoruba salutation poem to the Timi of Ede. The third stanza reads:

> For like the dog's mouth you were never at rest,
> Who, fighting a battle in front,
> Mapped out, with dust-of-combat ahead of you,
> The next battle-field at the rear—
> That generations unborn
> Might never taste the steel—.

Christopher Okigbo was the Cambridge University Press representative in Nigeria and was living in Ibadan in 1965. Ulli Beier's *African Poetry,* published in 1966 by Cambridge University Press, must have passed through his hands. Ulli Beier's translation of the *Oriki* of the Timi of Ede, published in this collection, contains the following lines:

> Fighting a battle in front
> You mark out the next battle-field behind.
> My Lord, please give the world some rest.

Okigbo took the two lines and left the third, and concluded his stanza with words very reminiscent of J. P. Clark's line in "The Imprisonment of Obatala."

> And generations unborn spared the wrong.

Incidentally, I did a study in another context which showed that quite a few of the images and lines in Okigbo's **"Fragments from the Deluge"** were derived from and paraphrased and reworked from J. P. Clark's little-known long poem "Ivbie" in his collection *Poems,* which was published by Mbari in Ibadan in 1962.

It is an interesting scholarly exercise tracing these borrowings and parallels. But I have yet to see any critic who is so bothered with them that he casts doubt on the creativity of Okigbo and his "authentic Africanness."

Robert J. Stanton (essay date Winter 1976)

SOURCE: "Poet as Martyr: West Africa's Christopher Okigbo, and His *Labyrinths: With Path of Thunder,*" in *Studies in Black Literature,* Vol. 7, No. 1, Winter, 1976, pp. 10-14.

[*In the following excerpt, Stanton describes how events in Okigbo's life seem to have informed his poetry and influenced his poetic style.*]

Okigbo claims the following:

> I don't think that I have ever set out to communicate a meaning. It is enough that I try to communicate experience which I consider significant. [*African Writers Talking,* 1972]

This rejection of giving "meaning" to his poetry denies us the use of logical analysis to interpret his work. He is known to be influenced by the French Symbolists, especially by Mallarme who also wrote poetry without regard to logical meaning. Symbolic poetry is a poetry which strives to create a mood. Such poetry is a presentation of a particular state of mind.

Another possible influence upon the direction of Okigbo's work is the work of abstract artists. This was first pointed out by Ali A. Mazrui. Abstract art had reached its height during the time within which Okigbo wrote poetry. Abstract art also is not meant to be "meaningful." It appeals to the emotions and deep inner experiences of mankind. If an abstract painting is "seen" correctly it will evoke an emotional reaction which is triggered by an authentic "experience" of the painting. Okigbo once read his poetry to school children who cried in agony upon hearing it. He believed that this reaction is a correct response to his poetry.

In December, 1958 he learned that he could not be anything other than a poet, . . . "when I found myself wanting to know myself better, and I had to turn around and look at myself from inside." Chinua Achebe points out that this statement must be taken lightly, since, for example, Okigbo eventually became active as an army officer. But, then again, he may have become an army officer when he could no longer exist as a poet. (This point will be supported when we come to look at his **"Elegy for Alto."**)

He saw himself having many selves within, including the whole of the society of which he is a part:

> I believe that any writer who attempts a type of inward exploration will in fact be exploring his own society indirectly . . . I believe that a writer who sets out to discover himself, by so doing will also discover his society.

He states that his writing of inward exploration is more difficult than "committed" African writing as expressed in the "negritude" writers for example. He did not see any African writer, other than himself, doing any sort of inward exploration, but he hoped for its beginning in others.

Okigbo's Introduction to his [*Labyrinths, With Path of Thunder*] takes on many of the concerns that we see in the poetry of T. S. Eliot. In both poets there is a reaching out towards spiritual fulfillment. Both poets must find this fulfillment by rising above the wasteland that surrounds their respective places in history. Both poets attempt to purify themselves before and during their respective quests which takes them through the rot of modern culture. Both poets reach stages wherein movement ceases to be. (In Okigbo's work this occurs in the **"Silences"** sequence.) Eliot, in "Ash Wednesday," learns that purification and the will to gain salvation are still not enough to gain such. He learns that he must wait in silence in a world between worlds, a twilight world, a rose garden, the place of solitude wherein he prays for salvation to a woman wearing white light. He awaits the Divine Word which will allow him to enter the spiritual heaven of god. He awaits total destruction of Self. Yet he cannot enter because he cannot rid himself of the memories of sensuous distractions.

Okigbo, on the other hand, makes it. In the final poem of **"Distances"** he tells us this in highly sensuous metaphors:

> . . . and in the orangery of immense corridors,
> I wash my feet in your pure head, O maid
>
> . . . I have entered your bridal chamber; and lo,
>
> I am the sole witness to my homecoming.

He is the sole witness to his homecoming because the attempt towards salvation is strictly a matter between the candidate and his god. One finds one's own way to salvation.

In **"The Passage,"** the first poem of *Labyrinths,* we see the candidate at the gate of his goddess. He has wasted his time in the world (therefore he is a prodigal) but he claims that he has achieved a state of humiliation ("Under your power wait I"). He has stripped himself of past illusions ("Before you, mother Idoto, / naked I stand"). He awaits the word to enter ("watchman for the watchword at Heavensgate"). He is barefoot before the goddess because he considers himself pure, humble, and yet vulnerable before her.

The second poem **"Dark waters of the beginning"** elaborates upon the first. The candidate tells us what it is like at the gate. Dark waters exist because the state of salvation is not known. Weak light from the sun attempts to pierce the gloom of darkness. This weak struggling light is a foreshadowing of "the fire that is dreamed of." The light is a promise of great warmth. There is a rainbow present also. The rainbow "foreshadows the rain that is dreamed of."

The promise of fire and water is the sign of future fulfillment. The word "orangery" comes up again. In the last poem of the Labyrinths series we saw that it is "in the orangery" wherein the candidate has finally reached salvation. Here, in this second poem, we see that he, a "wagtail," has been invited to the "orangery" inspired by his state of solitude which is the necessary condition of all poetic creation. He is called forth to be a poet of mourning. He is to tell the complicated "tangled-wood-tale." In this position he will undergo a metamorphosis. He will lose his "wagtail" identity for that of a sunbird.

Beginning with the third poem in **Heavensgate,** the last of **"The Passage"** poems, Okigbo begins to turn back to the past in an attempt to show what he has experienced before reaching his present position before the Heavensgate. The word "crossroads" plays an important part in this poem. The candidate is himself at a crossroads. There is the choice between Christianity or the choice of a more natural religion:

> . . . in cornfields
> among the windplayers,
> listening to the wind leaning over
> its loveliest fragment.

Should he go to the new religion which has already attracted a "festivity in black"? Should he take up the gospel, "the light years held in leather"? This is not answered in the poem. Both choices contain "lovely fragments." Okigbo states that he does not consider himself either a Christian or a pagan, but rather that he holds to a personal religion which "combines elements from both." We note here the polar opposites which attract Okigbo. He is humble before his goddess, yet maintains a self-confidence which allows him to cry out to her to "give ear and hearken." He may be common (thus he calls himself a wagtail), but nevertheless he is urged forth towards a special destiny, i.e., to become a prophetic sunbird. He describes a "festivity in black" (a funeral ceremony?) meeting "behind the bell tower" (in a churchyard?) in "the hot garden" (a cemetery?) "where all roads meet" (at death?). Here he includes himself among others who listen attentively to the music of a church organ. Does he consider Christianity to be rooted in death, and motivated by it too? But next to these "Christian" images he places himself in cornfields wherein he listens to the natural music of a wind moving through cornfields. From Christianity, then, Okigbo may have satisfied his unconscious will to die; from paganism, he may have satisfied his unconscious will to live.

"Initiations," the next poem in the sequence, gives us an answer to his early religious dilemma. He has made the choice to join the Christians. He has been baptized "upon waters of genesis" by a shallow sort of person named Kepkanly who left him with the "scar of the crucifix / over the breast." Looking back in retrospect he sees faults in those "committed" to Christianity. We are given four angles in the practices of Christianity. These are difficult to determine because the syntax is ambiguous. Before we come to the first angle, however, we have the "pure line" which appears to be nothing more nor less than a straight line "whose innocence / denies inhibitions." At the first

angle "man loses man, loses vision." Does this imply that Christianity is too heaven-oriented? Does Okigbo warn us here that our "angle" should not move in a direction away from the presence of our fellow men? The second angle, a consequence of the first, is "life without sin, without life." The literal meaning of this is that a sinless "life" is death. If this second angle is accepted and taken up then a third angle is reached which also leads to a death (an intellectual one here, in contrast to the spiritual death of a life without sin) because our hypothetical Christian finds himself "avoiding decisions" once sin is totally rejected from his life. Okigbo is surely having fun here, drawing out the logical consequences of a life dedicated to orthodox Christian morality. A fourth angle results from the duty and obligation of "loyal" Christians. This angle produces morons, fanatics, priests, popes, organizing secretaries, party managers, brothers, deacons, liberal politicians, "selfish selfseekers," and finally the followers of these Christian leaders. The Christian leaders who do things in the name of Christ "are good / doing nothing at all." Achebe points out that Okigbo is using geometry to show the different degrees of rigidity in Christian practice. The square shape produces the greatest rigidity; the straight line "denies inhibitions."

The final two poems of **"Initiations"** present pagan aspects of his initiation which are used to balance off the Christian initiation. But both poems end by stating: "And there are here / the errors of the rendering . . ." Jadum from Rockland, the speaker in the first of these poems, is "A half-demented village minstrel." His identification with Rockland is a reminder of the mad Carl Solomon in Ginsberg's *Howl.* The second of these poems consists of a repartee between the candidate and a village explainer. The entire poem seems to closely imitate the stylistic design of Gregory Corso's dialogue poetry. The gist of these two poems may be that the advice of authorities, which is given in a mad world, cannot help but be in error and appear mad itself.

"Watermaid" is next. The poem expresses the poet's desire for purgation. The poet-protagonist stands before a goddess "Bright / with the armpit dazzle of a lioness." She is a water goddess as is Idoto, the goddess at Heavensgate. Perhaps they are the same? She appears to him only momentarily. He wishes to express his "secrets" to her. But she will not accept him with "mirrors around me." He is rejected, it seems, for his lack of maturity. He is too self-centered. The mirrors around him reflect only himself.

"Lustra" is a successful attempt at cleansing. He climbs to a hilltop to offer sacrifice to the gods. The act of giving frees him from himself and makes purgation possible. Okigbo tells us that the "new laid egg" and the "white hen" are both the poem itself. "My **Heavensgate** is in fact a huge sacrifice" [*Journal of Commonwealth Literature,* No. 9, 1970]. The offer of his poetry is his way of fulfilling his role as the priest of Idoto. This cleansing in **"Lustra"** brings some new satisfaction to the candidate as indicated by the refrain "the spirit is in ascent." It is reiterated here that in this poem the candidate first finds that sacrifice is the necessary act for purgation which is in turn necessary for salvation. It is understandable, then, that the candidate will offer up his life as the greatest of sacrifices. Indeed, he "dies" at the end of *Labyrinths* (in the **"Distances"** sequence) in order to be reborn as the poet of his people. He celebrates this in **"Elegy for Slit-drum,"** a late poem in *Path of Thunder:*

> the mythmaker accompanies us (*the Egret had
>   come and gone*)
> Okigbo accompanies us the oracle enkindles us
> the Hornbill is there again (*the Hornbill has had
>   a bath*)
> Okigbo accompanies us the rattles enlighten
>   us—

But when his warnings to his people fail to fully move them towards necessary action against their exploiters the poet then moves towards the destruction of his poetic self (this he does in the last poem of *Path of Thunder*). Okigbo may have been motivated, in turn, to sacrifice his own life (and therefore placed himself in the front line of battle) when he discovered within himself that he had somehow failed in his public role as poet of his people.

"Newcomer" recalls another Christian initiation. He has been an exile from the church. And he still cannot give himself fully over to it. He asks his mother Anna to protect him "from them fucking angels." His exiled state is emphasized in his identification with Moses waking "behind the bulrushes." "The cock's third siren" suggests the eventual betrayal of Christ. Nevertheless, a newcomer comes to birth "in the chill breath of the day's waking." The last section of **"Newcomer"** finds him in a high spiritual state "above the noontide" wherein time itself seems to have been transcended: "Under my feet float the waters / Tide blows them under . . ."

> Okigbo . . . chooses to no longer be
> "just" a poet. A careful reading of
> ["Elegy for Alto"] will show that Okigbo
> has totally abandoned his early subtle
> poetic style. The poem is almost one long
> howl of agony written in obvious
> condemnation of the exploiters. But it is
> now rhetoric rather than poetry.
>
> —*Robert J. Stanton*

The **"Siren Limits"** sequence (i.e., *Limits* I-IV) deals with the rise of the candidate from wagtail to sunbird identity. But the new sunbird poet finds himself still too weak to deal with the problems of his culture.

In *Limits* I the poet reaffirms the cleansing process he has recently passed through: "Queen of the damp half light, / I have had my cleansing. . ." He makes a sacrifice of "the he-goat-on-heat." He also hangs up his egg-shells as a sacrifice. Throughout the poem the tone is one of confidence.

In *Limits* II the candidate describes his difference from

other men. He has greater need of "roots" and "sap," for his goal is to gain full sunlight, the source of life and knowledge. He becomes the sunbird in this poem made up entirely of metaphors. His "selves" unite into one soul and the voice of this soul is prophetic.

In *Limits* III the young sunbird poet looks out onto chaos and negligence: "Banks of reed. / Mountains of broken bottles." The refrain *"and the mortar is not yet dry . . ."* suggests that the poet is not yet strong enough to deal with this situation. Quietly, like Adam and Eve's departure from Eden, the poet (selves-soul-voice) becomes an exile: "So we must go, eve-mist on shoulders." The "brand burning out at hand-end" suggests a state of spiritual impotency. In such a condition the poet sings "tongue-tied. / Without name or audience." The voice attempts to be reborn in an intense dream which is dissipated into "Hurry on down" unfulfilling situations. At the end of these dissipations the refrain is repeated twice consecutively, and we are told that the dream has been "like a shadow, / Not leaving a mark." The poetic process has been attempted but is yet too weak to be effective in a prophetic capacity.

In *Limits* IV we see the poet confronted by the image of a goddess. Her image is first suggested as one of great beauty which "distracts / With the cruelty of the rose." But this image is replaced by its polar opposite, a terrifying "sea-weed / Face, blinded like strong-room." He asks to be wounded by this last image. He may be in need of full knowledge of the goddess which, like himself, has more than one self. The image of the goddess grants him the ability to create energy for his upcoming quest which he sees will bring harm to himself. The last two lines— "Wake me near the altar, / and this poem will be finished . . ."—suggest that the fulfillment of the poetic achievement involves an unconscious active pursuit of the truth. Only in truth is he worthy to ask for salvation from Idoto.

The **"Fragments out of the Deluge"** sequence (i.e., *Limits* V-XII) deals with an almost total destruction of the poet's culture.

In *Limits* V-VII the poet speaks of a death and the failure of rebirth. He identifies with Christ who is denied and betrayed by followers who lack a thirst for the "seed [the Divine Word?] wrapped in wonders [prophesy?]" *Limits* VI presents us with this denial of Christ; *Limits* VII presents us with the rebirth of Christ among the spiritually decadent: "And to the cross in the void came pilgrims; / Came, floating with burnt-out tapers." The pilgrims are without thirst, i.e., without inspiration. They perform a ritual without true mourning.

In *Limits* VIII the poet as sunbird speaks prophesy to his people just as Christ spoke to his people. The "fleet of eagles" are the planes of the colonial imperialists. They will come to the sacred place "over the oilbean shadows" and enslave the people with their ideology "under curse of their breath." The colonialists will come in planes and bring fear to the native people:

> The eagles ride low,
> Resplendent . . . resplendent;

And small birds sing in shadows.
Wobbling under their bones . . .

Limits IX is another poem of prophesy. "A blind dog howls at his godmother." But the innocent (represented by Eunice singing in the passageway) are not disturbed. The poet-prophet is not heard: "Give him no chair, they say."

In *Limits* X destruction comes upon the fearful, innocent people. The colonialists kill the sunbird, and the twin-gods of the forest, the tortoise and the python. Okigbo states: "The whole town . . . worships the python [the male penis] and the tortoise [the female clitoris] . . . They . . . are sacred to the whole town . . . we cannot kill them . . . And Christianity cannot wipe this out." The colonialists are described in their sweeping acts of destruction. They destroy tree totems and the gods of the underworld. After this destruction they occupy the land and exploit the wealth they find at the houses of the gods. The prophesy is fulfilled.

In *Limits* XI we find the gods without voice, and the people unable to mourn them.

In *Limits* XII we see the sunbird in the act of being reborn. He sings from the soul "where the [physical] caress does not reach." The destruction, then, has not been complete. However, the sunbird has lost its power to speak clearly: "The slits of his tongue / cling to glue . . ." The sunbird is like Eliot's Philomel, changed into a nightingale which can only sing Jug Jug to dirty ears. Direct reference is made to Picasso's *Guernica* which we all know is a powerful painting which depicts the agony of war.

The **"Lament of the Silent Sisters"** sequence is given to us in highly ambiguous terms which are sung by a Crier and a Chorus. The songs lament the destruction. Music more than image is important in this sequence. It is the expression of a deep sadness in the mind.

In **"Silent Sisters I"** the crier and chorus search for a way to say "NO [to death?] in thunder."

In **"Silent Sisters II"** there is a lament for the destruction caused by war, and there is a search for a rebirth from it.

"Silent Sisters III" describes the chorus in an act of silent agony lifting up such to the night heavens. The crier calls this "our swan song," i.e., a song of death.

In **"Silent Sisters IV"** beliefs of possible hope (e.g., "I see many colours in the salt teeth of foam"; "The rainbow they say is full of harmonies") appear in six lines. But ten other lines express fear of loss (e.g., "Wild winds cry out against us"; "The salt water gathers them inward"; "Will the water gather us in her sibylline chamber?"), making fear stronger than hope in this struggle of polar opposites.

In **"Silent Sisters V"** the chorus and crier see that their music contains visions of both good and evil. Hawthorne's influence comes into sight here just as it did in the opening poem of this sequence when it was asked how to say NO in thunder (Melville states that Hawthorne is able to do so). They accept Hawthorne's view of the world. They recognize that one must equally accept both the good and evil

in this world if there is ever to be inner growth. Accepting this, there is a growth of silent songs of light:

One dips one's tongue in the ocean;
Camps with the choir of inconstant
Dolphins, by shallow sand banks
Sprinkled with memories;
Extends one's branches of coral,
The branches extends in the senses'
Silence; this silence distils
in yellow melodies.

So, we see that the sunbird has been made dumb, silent like the mourning sisters. Through the visual and auditory senses a rebirth may come about. The spirit, but not the voice is alive. The music exists without words.

The **"Lament of the Drums"** sequence describes the waste-land which confronts the poet and his people. Drums are used here because they approximate the human voice. But neither they nor the human voice of the poet is yet able to speak effectively of the agony in the soul of the people. Later, however, in *Path of Thunder,* Okigbo will speak directly to his people, and his voice will be so clear that he shall be faced with immediate danger:

If I don't learn to shut my mouth I'll soon go to
hell,
I, Okigbo, town-crier, together with my iron
bell.

"Drums I" is the invocation of the people to the forest and to the antelopes within it to produce drums which will be used to speak for them in their agony.

"Drums II" shows the drums coming alive, "but how shall we go? / The robbers will strip us of our tendons!" There is no hope for rebirth in "a Babylonian capture" which is forced upon them in the name of Christ: "the martyrdom / Blended into that chaliced vintage."

"Drums III" tells of the attempt of Palinurus to keep the soul alive by song in a time of destruction and profanation. It is an invocation by him who has overcome despair, who now receives "tears of grace, not of sorrow." The voice of the drums, however, is like a "stifled sneeze." Since no voice is able to be generated a call goes out for laughter so that at least the shame of the vulnerable, silent people might be covered in disguise.

"Drums IV" and **"Drums V"** clearly show that the drums cannot speak. They are, we are told, exiled, disjointed, raped, bleeding, and empty. Their voice is null, cacophonous, and void. The spirit of the Great River (the people's source of life) still begs for a voice, but the fear of the colonialist powers (described as 'pot-bellied' despoilers) denies such a voice, and denies the spiritual rebirth of a people as a consequence.

In the **"Distances"** sequences the poet arrives at his salvation.

In **"Distances I"** he enters "the white chamber" of death, going "from flesh into phantom on the horizontal stone [his bier]."

In **"Distances II"** he describes his own physical death and describes the place of Death wherein we see Her (i.e.,

Death) quietly watching ("in a cloud of incense, / paring her fingernails . . .") the riotous confusion of Her victims. When She moves "She bathed her knees in the blood of attendants; / her smock in entrails of ministrants . . ."

"Distances III," "Distances IV," and **"Distances V"** describe the candidate's journey to hell (in III), at the gate of hell (in IV; recall that he is at the gate of heaven in the very beginning of *Labyrinths,* so we understand that he is now at its polar opposite), and his existence in hell (in V). There is absolutely no logical sense in these three poems. The lines rightly give us the impression of madness and chaos. The form of these three "hell" poems reflects a sort of endless anarchy. There is no real beginning to any of them, nor does there exist a true ending. There is no period punctuation to be found within these poems until we get to a false one near the very end of **"Distances V."** Nothing is ever developed to or from any one point. **"Distances III"** consists of phrases connected together mainly by prepositions; **"Distances IV"** depends on conjunctions and prepositions to lead us "to the catatonic ping-pong" (another Ginsberg allusion) wherever that may be; **"Distances V,"** the poem which is meant to give us an experience of hell itself, is a poem which destroys all possibility of comprehension in each and every one of its twenty-one lines. Here is its first "stanza":

> Sweat over hoof in ascending gestures—
> each step is the step of the mule in the abyss—
> the archway the oval the panel oblong
> to that sanctuary at the earth's molten bowel
> for the music woven into the funerary rose
> the water in the tunnel its effervescent laughter
> the open laughter of the grape or vine
> the question in the inkwell the answer on the
>   monocle
> the unanswerable question in the tabernacle's si-
>   lence—

In **"Distances VI,"** the last poem in *Labyrinths,* the poet arrives "home" to his solitary salvation as a poet. He has discovered the voice necessary for the rebirth of his people who stand on an "anti-hill." He has made an inner exploration of his and therefore his society's own living hell, and in this journey he has found the living words (to be spoken in *Path of Thunder*) of an "incarnate voice."

Labyrinths, then, is concerned with the development of a national poet's VOICE. Okigbo is telling us how he has gone through various stages of his inner growth which is formed by a series of deaths and rebirths. The language he is using is one that tells of an inner landscape which is why his poetry may seem difficult to read at first. He seems to also make use of cubism in that he is showing us his inner selves (e.g., as sunbird, crier and chorus, drums) from different perspectives at different points in his development. Only by reading *Labyrinths* at least twice does the full instantaneous perspective become comprehensible. Eventually, each poem unites in our mind with all the other poems in *Labyrinths* to form a total picture of Okigbo's "incarnate" voice which is so because he has united all polar opposites in his sacrifice to and for his people.

In **"Thunder Can Break,"** the first poem in *Path of Thunder,* a celebration of victory occurs. The war with the colo-

nialists has resulted in a victory for and in a unification of the people of Nigeria:

> Fanfare of drums, wooden bells; iron chapter;
> And our dividing airs are gathered home.

But the poem concludes with a warning from the poet to himself that he must keep himself "down to earth," must keep from over-celebrating the victory lest he lose his prophetic vision:

> Thunder can break—Earth bind me fast—
> Obduracy, the disease of elephants.

"Elegy of the Wind" is written in the same poetic style that we find in the early *Labyrinths* poems. This poem celebrates the "incarnate" voice of prophecy and the acts of purification which give birth to it.

"Come Thunder" is a warning to the people of Nigeria that danger to their freedom exists, even as they celebrate their freedom from colonial rule:

> And the secret thing in its heaving
> Threatens with iron mask
> The last lighted torch of the century . . .

"Hurrah for Thunder" speaks out, in metaphorical terms, against the pettiness and political shallowness of Nigeria's leaders who apparently are exploiting their political positions to gain personal wealth.

"Elegy for Slit-drum" shows the people in their preparation for civil war.

"Elegy for Alto," the final poem in *Path of Thunder,* ends in a tone of despair:

> The glimpse of a dream lies smouldering in a
>   cave,
> together with the mortally wounded birds.
> Earth, unbind me; let me be the prodigal; let this
>   be
> the ram's ultimate prayer to the tether . . .
>
> An old star, departs, leaves us here on the shore
> Gazing heavenward for a new star approaching;
> The new star appears, foreshadows its going
> Before a going and coming that goes on
>   forever . . .

The poet has suffered through the destruction of his peoples' land and culture and has lost the incarnate voice. He has a vision of cyclical movement which will destroy all evil, but will destroy all good as well. The only thing we may be sure of, he seems to say, is the continual struggle between opposing forces. This is why the poet asks for a release from the pain of living ("Earth unbind me") and from all hope for salvation: "let me be the prodigal." These two requests are in direct contradiction to his earlier requests when his spirit was in the ascent. His present place in time is controlled by "robbers" and politicians who are on the warpath to destroy in their selfish desires to dominate all others. Okigbo therefore chooses to no longer be "just" a poet. A careful reading of this last poem will show that Okigbo has totally abandoned his early subtle poetic style. The poem is almost one long howl of agony written in obvious condemnation of the exploiters. But it is now rhetoric rather than poetry.

Obi Maduakor (essay date 1979-1980)

SOURCE: "The Poet and His Inner World: Subjective Experience in the Poetry of Christopher Okigbo and Wole Soyinka," in *UFAHAMU,* Vol. 9, No. 3, 1979-80, pp. 23-41.

[*In the following excerpt, Maduakor examines the retrospective quality of Okigbo's poetry and comments on its significance in relation to modern African poetry.*]

In an interview with Marjory Whitelaw published in 1965, the Nigerian poet Christopher Okigbo made a distinction between what he called "platform poetry," and the lyric mode he referred to as the poetry of "inward exploration." Platform poetry, he felt, is declamatory and rhetorical; but it deserves, nevertheless, the labour of the poets who write it. Still, it is a less difficult kind of poetry to write than the poetry of inward exploration:

> Much more difficult . . . of course is inward exploration. I hope that ultimately people will start doing that sort of thing in Africa. They haven't started doing it yet. [*Journal of Commonwealth Literature,* July, 1970]

Okigbo believed, on the other hand, that his poetic career began with a poetry that is inwardly oriented. As he says, "the turning point came in 1958, when I found myself wanting to know myself better, and I had to turn around and look at myself from inside." Without doubt, Okigbo has the question of his own identity as an African poet in mind in this declaration; but the confession has a relevance that is applicable too to his inner world. In his first published work *Heavensgate* (1962), the assertion of his own identity is very much in evidence. But in such pieces as **"Siren Limits"** and **"Distances"** the poet journeyed inwards.

The self that Okigbo wished to explore is susceptible to forces that fragment:

> When I talk of the self, I mean my various selves, because the self itself is made up of various elements which do not always combine happily. And when I talk of looking inward to myself, I mean turning inward to examine myselves.

The tragic tone of this passage may account for the mood of despair that pervades much of Okigbo's poetry. The various elements of which the self is made up do not always combine "happily." There is here an echo of the Yeatsian theory of the divided self, and the consequent search for unity of being.

The conflict within is for Yeats the human inheritance of the Fall. He refers to it in the poem "Vacillation" as "those antinomies / Of day and night." Okigbo seems to subscribe to this opinion when he says that the poetry of inward exploration is written "to bring out a sense of inner disturbance." Such a poetry explores the poet's inner world, which is a world of conflict and tension. Thus, Okigbo can talk of the "self that suffers, that experiences." The suffering self is, in his case, the creative self; and its agony is of a dimension that amounts almost to a physical dissolution of the self. Equilibrium may be regained only when the poet is exorcised of the demon that lacerates his inner being.

The creative artist's constant warfare with the demon within may explain Okigbo's admiration for legendary heroes, such as Aeneas and Gilgamesh. Okigbo admires their heroic exploits but he is even more fascinated by their courage to dare the abyss within. That confrontation with the dark forces of the self is mythologized in the motif of descent into the underworld of death. Witness Maud Bodkin in *Archetypal Patterns in Poetry:*

> Before any great task that begins a new life and calls upon untried resources of character, the need seems to arise for some introversion of the mind upon itself and upon its past—a plunging into the depths, to gain knowledge and power over self and destiny. It is, I think, of such an introversion that the underworld journey of Aeneas is symbolic.

The literary counterpart of the epic heroes is Orpheus. Okigbo mentions him twice in the Introduction to *Labyrinths.* The poet-protagonist in the volume is an Orphic figure, a personage with "a load of destiny on his head," and one who "is about to begin a (creative) journey." In his study, *Descent and Return,* the German critic, Walter Strauss, sees Orpheus as the traditional image of the agony of poetry. That agony is linked up with Orpheus's descent into the underworld of death. The descent is for Strauss a metaphor for the creative artist's journey into the world of his own interior:

> Orpheus is not only poetry; he has become, in modern times, the agony of poetry. . . . He is the figure, the myth, entrusted with the burden of poetry and myth. His metamorphosis is the change in poetic climate itself, placed against an ever-darkening sky in which poetry recedes more and more toward secret and unexplored spaces, spaces that are obscure and must be illuminated by constellations of the mind ever threatened by disaster and extinction.

In the companion poems, **"Siren Limits"** and **"Distances,"** Okigbo descends into the spaces of the mind in the effort to reconcile the discordant elements of the self. The inner disturbance that plagues the poet originates from a sense of his own creative sterility. Okigbo believes that the creative thoroughfare can be opened to the questing poet only when he has annihilated his being. The annihilation is a prelude to rebirth. Therein lies the paradox of what he calls the "live-die proposition":

> **"Limits"** and **"Distances"** are man's outer and inner world projected—the phenomenal and the imaginative, not in terms of their separateness but of their relationship—an attempt to reconcile the universal opposites of life and death in a live-die proposition: one is the other and either is both.

Okigbo's statement here has far-reaching implications. Opposites, he implies, are mutually interdependent: the inner world is related to the outer; life recalls death. The reconciliation of these opposites is the synthesis from which the cycle begins again. Thus, although **"Siren Lim-**

its" and **"Distances"** explore Okigbo's inner world, the surfacing from the depths of the poet's own interior brings him into contact with the world of physical reality. The surfacing may take the form of an awakening from dream, or it may imply that consciousness has been regained, and that the poet is once more in contact with the material world. In the case of Okigbo, to whom physical dissolution is a metaphor for the struggles of the creative mind, the awakening or the return from the journey into the interior signals the end of creative agony. Borrowing a phrase from Joyce, Okigbo calls this condition "a state of aesthetic grace":

> The self that suffers, that experiences, ultimately finds fulfilment in a form of psychic union with the supreme spirit (muse) that is both destructive and creative. The process is one of sensual anaesthesia, of total liberation from all physical and emotional tension, the end result, a state of aesthetic grace.

Dream and trance prepare the way for Okigbo's entry into the inner landscape of creative tension. Yeats refers to this landscape as the imagination's dim Kingdom, and he holds that all visionaries have entered into it in a state of trance [*Essays and Introductions,* 1969]. In Okigbo's **"Siren Limits I,"** the poet-protagonist is "Summoned at offside of / dream remembered." The subsequent stanzas insist on the importance of dream-condition as a necessary prelude for the poet's exploration of his inner world:

> Between sleep and waking
> I hang up my egg-shells
> To you of palm grove.

The Nigerian critic, Donatus Nwoga, has noted that the function of **"Siren Limits I"** is "prefatory." It creates, in his own words, "a pervading atmosphere of time and setting, describing a state of half-dream, half-reality" [*Journal of Commonwealth Literature,* No. 7, June 1972]. The atmosphere evoked in the verse in question is predominantly oneiric. The "you" of the last line is the personage addressed later in the poem as "Queen of the damp half-light" [*Labyrinths*]. She is the poet's muse, or Mother Idoto. In the Introduction to *Labyrinths* Okigbo associates her with Robert Graves's "White Goddess."

The image of "half-light" locates the poet further in the twilight zone between night and day, and between dream and reality. To enter into this zone of experience, the poet must be "disembodied," that is, go out of the body. The elimination of the body is what Okigbo talks of as hanging up "my egg-shells." One will recall that Okigbo said in the Introduction to *Labyrinths* that his protagonist would become "disembodied" in his pursuit of the white elephant.

In Okigbo's **"Siren Limits,"** the exploration of the landscape of the poet's inner world begins in section II:

> Into the soul
> The selves extended their branches,
> Into the moments of each living hour
> Feeling for audience
>
> Straining thin among the echoes.
>
>   [*Labyrinths*]

Poetry such as this, wrote [Wole] Soyinka in an indirect homage to Okigbo, is the work of a poet who can confront the "world beneath the matter, the realities of the mystic kingdom in which other black writers are wont to explore lineaments of body or soul" [*African Forum,* No. 1, Spring, 1966]. Other critics have associated this stanza with Okigbo's need for a literary audience at one time in his career. This view is not being contested. But important too is the fact that Okigbo must have been convinced that the kind of work which would rank him among the great authors of the past (those referred to as "poplars" in a preceding stanza) must be of a quality that is born out of the anguish of the soul. For, did not Yeats say that "all the great poems of the world have their foundations fixed in agony" [*Uncollected Prose by W. B. Yeats,* Vol. 1, 1970]. In the first stanza of **"Siren Limits II,"** Okigbo is "a shrub among the poplars." In order to attain to light (to grow to the size and stature of the "poplars") his plant-roots must seek the "sap" of life from the soil of his own soul:

> FOR HE WAS a shrub among the poplars,
> Needing more roots
> More sap to grow to sunlight
> Thirsting for sunlight,
>
> A low growth among the forest.
>
>   [*Labyrinths*]

The line "Thirsting for sunlight" in the above quote, and "Straining thin among the echoes" in the previous, are metaphorical expressions of the agony of composition. Caught up in a similar creative throes in *Heavensgate,* Okigbo lamented "Stretch, stretch, O antennae." In **"Siren Limits I,"** the agony of the dance is no longer stated but dramatized. The self descends into the soul's abyss in order to fulfill "each moment in a / broken monody." "Straining," "thirsting," and "stretching" are metaphors for the artist's battle with himself. Okigbo wrote in the Introduction to *Labyrinths* that such battles can be as fierce as the "swell of the silent sea, the great heaving dream at its highest, the thunder of splitting pods." The high moments of this interior battle he calls the "crisis point" in **"Siren Limits III":**

> And this is the crisis point,
> The twilight moment between sleep and waking.

The ordeal has its own reward; for the dissolution of the self is a prelude to rebirth:

> And voice that is reborn transpires,
> Not thro' pores in the flesh, but the soul's back-
>   bone.

"Transpire" may at first suggest evaporation. But Okigbo has in mind the gradual emergence of the reborn voice (the art-work itself) into light:

> And out of the solitude
> Voice and soul with selves unite
> Riding the echoes,
>
> Horsemen of the apocalypse;
>
> And crowned with one self
> The name displays its foliage
> Hanging low

A green cloud above the forest.

That inner turmoil out of which works of "changeless metal" are born (to quote Yeats once more) is suggested with images of combat in **"Limits IV."** A poetic image rooted like a flagpole in the poet's own heart clamours for articulation, but this privilege is denied the poet until he has done battle with the "supreme spirit that is both destructive and creative." That spirit is the muse to whose cruelty the poet surrenders himself willingly as a gesture of self-immolation:

> AN IMAGE insists
> From flag pole of the heart;
> Her image distracts
> With the cruelty of the rose . . .
>
> Oblong-headed lioness—
> No shield is proof against her—
> Wound me, O sea-weed
> Face, blinded like strong-room—

Creative effort is for Okigbo as difficult as the attempt to recapture the outlines of an important but elusive dream. As he puts it in the Introduction to *Labyrinths:*

> The present dream clamoured to be born a cadenced cry: silence to appease the fever of flight beyond the iron gate.

In the first stanza of the passage from **"Siren Limits IV,"** the poet's clamouring voice is muffled by the indifference of the midwife muse who is unwilling to assist the pregnant poet at the moment of labour. The images that suggest the struggles of the creative mind in stanza two include "shield," "wound," and "lioness." Since the battle is not a physical one (the poet is still in a state of trance) the scene is as internalized as the soil of the heart on which the poetic flagpole is rooted. The interior struggle here is the counterpart of the descent movement in **"Limits II."** Here, however, the trance is prolonged. There is no surfacing as yet from the deep. The poet is still exiled to the limits of his interior world. "The LIMITS," Okigbo wrote elsewhere, "were the limits of a dream" [*Transition,* No. 5, 1962]. Thus both the poet himself and the reader await his final resurrection. **"Siren Limits"** comes to a close on this note of waiting:

> When you have finished
> & done up my stitches
> Wake me near the altar,
> & this poem will be finished . . .

The transitional links between **"Siren Limits"** and **"Distances"** are provided by Okigbo both in his Introduction to *Labyrinths* and in the main body of **"Siren Limits"** itself. In the Introduction he writes:

> **"Distances"** is . . . a poem of homecoming, but of homecoming in its spiritual and psychic aspects. The quest broken off after **"Siren Limits"** is resumed, this time in the unconscious.

The poetic quest is broken off at the point when Okigbo says at the end of **"Siren Limits":**

> When you have finished
> & done up my stitches,
> Wake me near the altar,

& this poem will be finished . . .

The elliptical periods at the end of the last line suggest that the quest has been suspended.

Okigbo says that the quest in **"Distances"** has taken place in the unconscious, by which he means the world of the interior. I have argued on the evidence of the poem itself and on the evidence of Okigbo's testimony elsewhere that the experience related in **"Siren Limits"** took place also in a world of the interior. On the question of connection between the two poems, there is this significant passage from **"Siren Limits":**

> Distances of her armpit-fragrance
> Turn chloroform enough for my patience—

These lines occur in one of the closing stanzas of **"Siren Limits."** From the first word of the above verse, Okigbo borrowed the title of the poem **"Distances"** which is the culmination of the experience begun in **"Siren Limits."** The word "Distances" has a connotation that is related to "Limits." Both suggest that which is distant and far away. In both poems the poet is spiritually away, lodged in imagination's dim kingdom. The dream motif is what Okigbo calls the "spiritual and psychic aspect" of his quest.

That the transition achieved earlier in **"Siren Limits"** from life to death, from the physical world to the spiritual, and from the external landscape to the interior, is still in force in **"Distances"** is indicated by the strategic statement in the first line of the poem that "flesh" has been transformed into "phantom":

> FROM FLESH into phantom on the horizontal
> stone
> I was the sole witness to my homecoming . . .

The second line strikes the note of homecoming, of the poet's arrival at the palace of his muse. The first line is only a brief suggestion of the trials that must accompany that final moment of spiritual illumination. Still, the motif of departure is central in **"Distances"** in its overall effect:

> For in the inflorescence of the white chamber,
> a voice from very far away, chanted, and the
> chamber descanted the birthday of earth,
> paddled me home through some dark labyrinth,
> from laughter to the dream.

"Laughter" is for Okigbo a feature of the waking life, while "dream" is associated with the unconscious. Okigbo's muse, whether she is "lioness" or "Idoto," seems to have been abstracted into the single image of "white goddess" by the evocation in the above stanza of the image of "white chamber." Okigbo betrays this tendency when he says that

> several presences haunt the complex of rooms and ante-rooms, of halls and corridors that lead to the palace of the White Goddess, and in which a country visitor might easily lose his way.

The "country visitor" is the questing poet; and the "rooms and ante-rooms" stand for what Yeats called the "still cave of poetry." They are the "dark / labyrinth" through which the poet is to be paddled home to the celestial palace of the muses. This palace is a place of joy and of song. Its chambers are lighted, and they resound with the song of life: "the birthday of earth." Ironically, however, the poet can reach it only after he has passed through the gates of hell symbolised by the image of "anti-hill" (abyss):

> Miner into my solitude,
> incarnate voice of the dream,
> you will go,
> with me as your acolyte,
> again into the anti-hill . . .

In the companion poems, "Siren Limits" and "Distances," Okigbo descends into the spaces of the mind in the effort to reconcile the discordant elements of the self. Okigbo believes that the creative thoroughfare can be opened to the questing poet only when he has annihilated his being. The annihilation is a prelude to rebirth.

—Obi Maduakor

Okigbo will descend a second time into the underworld of his being for such is the penalty that awaits the creative endeavour of every subjective artist. **"Distances II"** is therefore pervaded by images of death and of self dissolution. Okigbo speaks in this section of his "anguish," his "solitude," and of his "scattered / cry". Death, who had ambushed both the questing poet and his fellow pilgrims at the beginning of this section, has, by the end of it, literally torn them to pieces:

> At her feet rolled their heads like cut fruits;
> about her fell
> their severed members, numerous as locusts.
> Like split wood left to dry, the dismembered
> joints of the ministrants piled high.
>
> She bathed her knees in the blood of attendants
> her smock in entrails of ministrants . . .

The image of "crucifix" in Sections III and IV reemphasizes the ordeal of the suffering poet. In his quest for poetic secrets, the poet must journey through what is called in **"Distances IV"** the "hollow centre" of awareness. The creative secret itself Okigbo couched in a language that is both magical and esoteric: "the catatonic pingpong / of the evanescent halo . . ." Engulfed within the "intangible void" of the self, the poet pictures himself in **"Distances V"** as a mule trying to ascend the edges of an abyss:

> SWEAT OVER hoof in ascending gestures—
> each step is the step of the mule in the abyss—

Poetry, which is the objective of his quest, is invested with multiple attributes. It is the "music woven into the funerary role," the "water in the tunnel," the "open laughter of the grape or vine," the "question in the inkwell." The poet, we are told is heading

to that sanctuary at the earth's molten bowel
for the music woven into the funerary rose
the water in the tunnel its effervescent laughter
the open laughter of the grape or vine
the question in the inkwell the answer on the
    monocle
the unanswerable question in the tabernacle's silence—

The "sanctuary at the earth's molten bowel" becomes a "cavern" in **"Distances VI,"** to which the poet is summoned by his muse:

> Come into my cavern.
> Shake the mildew from your hair;
> Let your ear listen:
> My mouth calls from a cavern . . .

The summoning implies that the poet who has been hovering on the twilight zone between sleeping and waking is to regain full consciousness. His awakening from dream, an awakening the reader may have awaited from the end of **"Siren Limits,"** is accompanied with a rhythmic intensity appropriate for a moment of an illuminating creative epiphany. In the second half of **"Distances VI"** the awakened poet is "darkening homeward" from dream into consciousness, from hell into outer space, from the interior landscape into the external, with the energy of a startled wolf:

> And at this castle instance of delineated anguish,
> the same voice, importunate, aglow with the
>   goddess—
> unquenchable, yellow, darkening homeward
> like a cry of wolf above crumbling houses—
> strips the dream naked,
> bares the entrails.

Having been so uproariously aroused, that is, fully inspired, the poet-lover can boast of gaining entry into the muse's bridal chamber:

> I have fed out of the drum
> I have drunk out of the cymbal
> I have entered your bridal
> chamber; and lo,
> I am the sole witness to my homecoming.

D. S. Izevbaye (essay date Spring 1982)

SOURCE: "Death and the Artist: An Appreciation of Okigbo's Poetry," in *Research in African Literatures,* Vol. 13, No. 1, Spring, 1982, pp. 44-52.

[*In the essay below, Izevbaye examines the ways in which the theme of death influences the form of Okigbo's poetry.*]

The attempt to understand death and the need to master its sorrow have given birth to various African forms of artistic expression, whether these occur as "the ambivalence, often found in funeral songs, [which] helps to adjust the shock and grief which death brings to the living" [Gerald Moore, *Africa,* Vol. 38, 1968], or as a representation of the language of the dead in the speech of *mmonwu,* the masquerade. Such a representation is logical in the context of Uche Okeke's view [*Tales of the Land of Death,* 1971] that the basis for the representational art of the mask makers may be found in the Igbo world view that the land of the dead corresponds in pattern to the land of the living, having "its own kind of activities and things similar to these that exist in the land of the living." Furthermore, the dead could not possibly have gone into oblivion, and their land is the eventual home for the living.

The two kinds of response to death—the probing of its nature and the attempt to master the grief of death—influence the imagery and the form of Okigbo's poetry. The subject of death produces two basic forms in his poetry: the lament for the dead, and the poem that has its setting in the land of the dead.

Generally, in literature, the lament can take the form of a dirge, a form that concentrates on the lot of the dead person, or an elegy, with its concern for the effect on the living of the loss of the deceased. The concern for the dead is less important in Okigbo's poetry than the attention paid to the living, as in his **"Lament of the Silent Sisters,"** a poem about social reform and individual responsibility. The closest that we get to the dirge-like concern for the dead is in Canto III of **"Lament of the Drums,"** his most formal poem. Even **"Elegy for Slit-drum"** and **"Elegy for Alto,"** the two poems that he composed in May 1966 soon after the killings, are more about the politics of the living than the fate of the dead. Although the tone is that of the dirge, the theme of death alternates with reference to the political background of the theme. In **"Elegy for Slit-drum"** he writes,

> The elephant has fallen
> the mortars have won the day
> the elephant has fallen
> does he deserve his fate
> the elephant has fallen
> can we remember the date—
>
> Jungle tanks blast Britain's last stand—

The social and political background remains constant in Okigbo's laments, although the earlier, revised poems do not contain the kind of topicality we find in the last line of the above quotation. Still, the social concern remains in the **"Silences"** group of laments, especially in lines like "how does one say NO in thunder?" and "Her pot-bellied watchers / Despoil her. . . ." So, although Okigbo's favorite form is the elegy or lament, poems in this genre are at once an expression of public grief and a criticism of society. The one exception is his poem on Yeats, **"Lament of the Masks,"** which is not a true lament but an *oriki* or praise poem, being a less mournful poem than **"Silences."** **"Lament of the Masks,"** is really a panegyric because it contains only two short references to death in Canto III ("For we had almost forgotten / Your praise-names—", and "[You] will remain a mountain / Even in your sleep. . . .").

Although **"Lament of the Masks"** is less social and more personal in its tributes than **"Silences,"** it is less despairing because it draws consolation for the living from the idea of the poet's literary legacy. This idea is conveyed in the allusion to an African folktale about how Dog brought fire to man as protection from the harmattan. In the context of the panegyric this allusion implies that the legacy of po-

etic technique left by Yeats for the generation of poets coming after him has made their work easier for them. The dead poet is thus given the status of Prometheus among poets.

The second kind of response to death, the attempt to probe and understand its nature, produces the other kind of poetic form we find in Okigbo's work: the personal pilgrimage to the land of death. We find this form in the ***Heavensgate***—"Siren Limits"—"Distances" group. These poems differ from the Laments in two respects. First, they are not about the bitter effect of death on the living, but about the useful experience of death. Consequently, not only are they not about grief, they are about "divine rejoicing" at the hero's homecoming. Their tone is one of exultation; the tone of **"Distances"** is even ecstatic and celebrative, in contrast to the mood of despair and world-weariness of **"Silences."**

Ecstacy at finding oneself in the realm of death is not unusual in the literature of Africa. By chanting the theme, "may death be familiar to your spirits," Samba Diallo, the hero of Cheikh Hamidou Kane's *Ambiguous Adventure,* seeks to mark out an area of central concern for Africans influenced by the materialism of the West. In traditional Igbo literature, the heroic stature of man is ultimately measured by his exploits in the land of the dead. Ojadili, like Uko, is the hero who "wrestled in the land of the dead [and] . . . beat the dead in their land." Okigbo makes such a venture into the underworld the basis for deifying his hero, and such journeys always have a fruitful conclusion in his poems:

> On an empty sarcophagus
> hewn out of alabaster,
> A branch of fennel on an
> empty sarcophagus. . . .

Like the Christian image of an empty tomb at Easter, the fennel on an empty sarcophagus is the hero's victory over death; and the alabaster material of the sarcophagus, like the horizontal stone that similarly opens **"Distances,"** is not treated as a barrier, but as a gateway through death to a new life. This suggests that death is being treated not as a termination but as a transition. The importance of death in Okigbo's poetry may be seen in the fact that even ***Heavensgate,*** a pastoral, was "conceived as an Easter sequence" according to Okigbo in his introduction, thus implying that life comes after death or that death comes before life. The heavensgate of the poem is the physical expression of the hero's passage from innocence to knowledge. ***Heavensgate*** is prevented from being completely idyllic by the presence of various symbolic suggestions of death on the path of the hero's progress, beginning with the wagtail-sunbird's retreat into mourning in an orangery, through the memorial silence for Kepkanly and "for him who was silenced," to the deathly image of man in the acknowledgement that man's body is merely "sandhouse and bones."

Thus, unlike the laments, poems about the hero's personal pilgrimage describe, by anticipation or by speculation, the experience and knowledge of death. **"Distances"** is the key poem on this theme, for it attempts to convey both a sensory experience of death and its imagined physical form.

"Distances" cannot be read at a purely literal level, as can *Heavensgate,* for example, because ordinary persons and events are continuously identified as the avatars of death throughout the poem. Okigbo tells us that this poem is based on his "experience of surgery under general anaesthesia," but the surgical atmosphere ("camphor iodine chloroform / ether") and the presence of the surgeon ("in smock of white cotton") are identified with the presence of death. The hero's loss of consciousness becomes both a figurative recreation of the original experience and a different imaginative experience. The section itself seems an ironical anticipation of the death of Okigbo himself:

> Death lay in ambush that evening in that island;
> voice lost its echo that evening in that island.
>
> And the eye lost its light,
> the light lost its shadow. . . .
>
> until my eyes lost their blood
> and the blood lost its odour.

The vision of the priestly figure of Death is reproduced in a clear and memorable portrait:

> and behind them all,
> in smock of white cotton,
> Death herself,
> the chief celebrant,
> in a cloud of incense,
> paring her fingernails. . . .
>
> At her feet rolled their heads like cut fruits;
> about her fell
> their severed members, numerous as locusts. . . .
> She bathed her knees in the blood of attendants;
> her smock in entrails of ministrants. . . .

This section of **"Distances"** uses death as a metaphor for the aesthetic cleansing or purification of the poet's language and emotion. If **"Siren Limits"** (which employs the same technique of superpositioning to effect the coexistence of the original experience and its value as a poetic image) contains some of the most effective writing among this group of poems, it is difficult to deny to **"Distances"** the power to reveal the meaning of Okigbo's spiritual pilgrimage.

It has been argued above that the main forms Okigbo's poetry takes—the elegy or lament and the pilgrimage-poem—have been influenced by two kinds of response to death, the expression of grief and the attempt to unriddle the character of death. Because the expression of these two responses occur in Okigbo as forms of public statements and private explorations, they may appear as two distinct aspects of his poetic development. It is necessary to show the continuity between the two by suggesting that Okigbo is like Okolo the wrestler:

> Eze the chief . . . ordered Okolo to go to a smithy who lived in the land of the dead and bring back the famous twin gongs. . . .
>
> [In the land of the dead] Okolo seized a pair of gongs and sneaked out of the spirit's house. . . .
>
> Okolo . . . reached the land of the living. He beat his shrill-sounding gong triumphantly. All

the villagers rushed out to welcome him and dance to the music from the gong.

If we use this folktale as a metaphorical interpretation of **"Distances"** in relation to *Path of Thunder* and Okigbo's influence on the work of the younger Igbo poets who have been writing since the beginning of the Civil War, the private poetic quest to death's realm can be seen as Okigbo's preparation for duty as town crier.

To restate part of this argument in more prosaic and factual terms, it can be seen that the poems about the hero's personal pilgrimage generally retain and make use of the original occasion for their composition, especially in the references to persons like Kepkanly, Haragin, and Upandru. The method is at its most effective in **"Siren Limits"** where the images operate simultaneously at different levels.

"Siren Limits" can be read, for example, at the literal or autobiographical, the psychological or emotional, and the imaginative or aesthetic, levels. The image of the "siren" recalls the original alarm bell of the ambulance conveying the poet to hospital, but the experience is also given a sexual meaning in the dream of the queen who bewitches the hero and thereby turns him into a "he-goat-on-heat." The merging of these two experiences in the idea of **"Siren Limits"**—i.e., the original experience of the poet on the ambulance stretcher with the allusion to Ulysses straining at the mast of his ship—produces a complex image that suggests the imaginative life at the frontier of fulfilment:

> When you have finished
> & done up my stitches,
> Wake me near the altar,
> & this poem will be finished. . . .

The link between the private quest and the public pronouncement now becomes clearer. What needs to be eradicated from the former kind of poem is the private element. Still using the image of Ulysses tied to the mast, Canto IV of **"Siren Limits"** begins with the theme of self-surrender, the painful and enforced giving up of self-esteem for the greater glory of the muse:

> An image insists
> From flag pole of the heart;
> Her image distracts
> With the cruelty of the rose. . . .

In the elegies, on the other hand, what Okigbo refines out of existence is the immediate occasion for the poem's composition, that is, those elements that would emphasize the topicality of the poems. The second part of *Limits,* **"Fragments out of the Deluge,"** is an exception in this regard, being an experimental attempt to fuse personal involvement with public issues. *Path of Thunder* is also an exception because, although it is unrevised, there is good reason to believe that the group is a new and more effective attempt than **"Fragments"** (which in fact anticipates *Path of Thunder*) to combine the private statement with the use of the poet-as-public-hero. The antithesis of the truly private poems are the sequences in **"Silences"** in which there are no explicit references to the immediate subjects of the two laments, Chief Obafemi Awolowo and Patrice E. Lumumba.

In other words, there have been two separate but related strands of development in Okigbo's poetry: the private, concerned with the perfection of his art, and the public, aimed at making pronouncements on the public issues of the day. **Path of Thunder** is an integration of both strands. The fact that the poet was killed before revising these last poems suggests that perhaps the problem was never quite solved for him. Not wanting to be like Usu the Bat who survived a war by being neither bird nor beast, Okigbo abandoned his poetic calling to answer the call to arms. There he tasted the forbidden food of the dead and that, ironically, yielded to him the true and final knowledge of Death herself.

The literary and critical reactions to Okigbo's death contain themes and motifs that we commonly find in many African folklore explanations of the origin of death. Two folktale motifs in particular recur in these reactions—those which Frazer once described as the Two Messengers and the Two Bundles [*The Worship of Nature*, 1926] to which one might add a third, that of the Forbidden Fruit and the Tree of Death.

The theme of the Wrong Message, that of death delivered to Man by the faster of two messengers, occurs in J. P. Clark's threnody, "Death of a Weaverbird" [*Casualties*, 1970], where, in a reference to the clear-voiced Weaverbird, Clark says that

> When plucked,
> In his throat was a note
> With a bullet for another.

In the motif of the two bundles, Man is offered two bundles and asked to choose one. Man chooses the bundle containing death and becomes mortal thereafter, unlike the serpent who can cast off his old skin and live eternally because he chose the right bundle. Certainly, the recurrent motif of death in Okigbo's poems sometimes makes one feel that like Samba Diallo, he is seeking to make death familiar to men's spirits by constantly singing about it. In *The Trial of Christopher Okigbo* Ali Mazrui raises the issue of the poet's responsibility to his art and presents the choice between art and social involvement in the riddle of the two bundles, like all questions about the rightness of a poet's choice of a warrior's role. Mazrui's presentation makes Okigbo's choice a questionable one, for which he sets up judges in After-Africa to try the poet. A different interpretation of the choice occurs in a poem by Obiora Udechukwu, one of the second generation of Nsukka poets who were still writing under the influence of Okigbo by the end of the civil war. Udechukwu addresses Okigbo in his "Lament of the Silenced Flute" as

> YOU.
> Who changed your lunar flute
> for a gun
> that future generations
> might not bite the sand.

A slightly more ironical verdict occurs in Soyinka's "For Christopher Okigbo" in which the choice that leads to martyrdom is justified—with some qualification in the tone—with emphasis on the poet's role as a torchbearer who has to tell his society plain truths as they are revealed to him.

Choosing to speak out plainly is itself enough of a hazard for the committed poet at certain periods in society's history. Okigbo saw the possibility of a purely literary alternative to social action in the obscure language of private poetry that he equated, in **"Lament of the Silent Sisters,"** with the making of musical patterns or the choice of silence. The penalty for eating off the tree of knowledge is the fall of man. This much is acknowledged in the closing couplet of **"Hurrah for Thunder"** that welcomed the army coup of January 1966:

> If I don't learn to shut my mouth I'll soon go to hell,
> I, Okigbo, town-crier, together with my iron bell.

Wole Ogundele   (essay date June 1983)

SOURCE: "From the Labyrinth to the Temple: The Structure of Okigbo's Religious Experience," in *Okike: An African Journal of New Writing*, No. 24, June, 1983, pp. 57-69.

[*In the following essay, Ogundele argues that Okigbo's religious views, as expressed in his works, were much broader and more autobiographical than critics have considered them to be.*]

The exact place and function of 'religion' in Christopher Okigbo's poetry has been until lately, generally misrepresented. The misrepresentation of course stemmed from what critics and some writers held, in the last two or so decades, to be one of the imperatives of the then nascent neo-African literature: cultural assertion. Even when the writers themselves, Okigbo inclusive, insisted to the contrary, their views were either derided, denounced with anger or pity, or simply judged to be of no account in the whole business of discovering relevances and functions.

This theoretical distortion led to two types of Okigbo criticism. First are those critics who represent Okigbo as rejecting one religion for another; second are those others who pitch meaning against imagery in the poems—most notable in this group are Ali A. Mazrui and the Chinweizu troika [in *Zuka*, September, 1967, and *Transition*, Vol. IX, 1975]. For the purpose of its arguments the first group chooses to define and understand 'religion' in a narrow sense, thereby inadvertently projecting Okigbo as a negritude poet. [R. N. Egudu, *African Literature Today*, Vol. 6, 1973] for instance sees evidence in the poems that Okigbo could not be accommodated in the Catholic faith and he therefore went back to revive the indigenous one. He concludes his own defence of Okigbo's "defence" as follows:

> The 'good' for him is traditional African culture with its own religion, and the native African talent in him which has enabled him to revive and preserve that culture irrespective of the efforts of the foreign agencies to suppress it.

This is far from being true of either the mind or art of Okigbo the poet. Worse still, the impression created of the poetry by this kind of interpretation is that the poet had settled his religious conflicts prior to the poetic experience—that in fact the poetry is only an account of the conflict, in which traditional religion triumphed. This may be biographically true, but the poetry presents it otherwise. The conflict and aesthetic sensibilities are presented, rather, as two kinds of consciousness, indistinguishable from one another, and forming an indissoluble compound. Secondly, Egudu's interpretation contains the implicit view that the experience of one religion is fundamentally different from, even hostile to, that of another. But such hostilities between the foreign and the traditional gods were, needless to recall, created by missionary zealotry; the deities themselves were not averse to assimilation or shared accommodation, and mutual strengthening.

Okigbo right from the start intuitively perceived this, seeing that the corrupting element in the foreign religion was its earthly agents and the elaborately irrelevant impediments they had set up, and not in the spiritual experience itself: the ecclesiastical intermediaries block that creative encounter between man and god, thereby preventing the experience of divine presence that is at the core of the truly spiritual conversion.

Thus the poet-protagonist acquired protestant inclinations which he carries back with him to the traditional rites and belief. The poetry, right from **"Four Canzones"** up to **"Distances,"** is shot through with intellectual, emotional, and spiritual ambivalencies, therefore: denial of Christianity even while assimilated by, and assimilating, it; acceptance of indigenous religion as desirable, but in a form modified to suit personal purposes. Okigbo's poetry is therefore a long exploration and casting off of these inimical contrarieties, and a search for personal belief. It demonstrates in the process that all religions, indigenous or foreign, collective or personal, have a common structure of experience; that religious experience can be identical with aesthetic experience; and too that the language of religion can also be the language of poetry.

It is of course true that Okigbo's poetry is the poetry of quest for the vanishing African traditions and forgotten gods; it is also true that the poems record the wanderings of the exile amidst alien idols and his return to roots; but no less true is it that this poetry is essentially an autobiographical excursion into a past that acquires significance only because personal, and into a present that is not totally communal. It is also important to remember that both in fact exist more in the psyche of the poet than in reality—that is, the past has been poetically recreated through individual memory. The quest itself is a lonely one undertaken, not on behalf of the community but of the self—and into his own soul.

Thus, the quest plot, the autobiographical design, and the allegorical trope of the prodigal son, all combine to make Okigbo's poetry a poetry of personal responsibility and salvation, the concomitants of which are self-revelation and personal search for transcendent absolutes. This claim may appear rather large, especially in view of the slimness of his output; it should however be remembered that the vast and rapid cultural changes brought about by colonialism did create a metaphysical vacuum in the African's

universe. Okigbo in his poetry embarks on a quest for salvation through a personal encounter with a chosen deity and in the process fills his own little space in the vacuum. But he attains salvation not outside but within the historical realities produced by subjugation and colonialism, and by a demonstrated autonomy of an intensely conscious and creative mind which synthesizes traditional with Christian modes of apprehending the metaphysical as well as ontological dimensions of reality.

Okigbo's mode of resolving and transcending his dilemmas—and of apprehending higher realities—is the ritual mode, a mode that fuses the religious with the aesthetic. Annemarie Heywood has recently tackled Okigbo's poetry as ritual in an illuminating and instructive essay, "The Ritual and the Plot: the Critic and Okigbo's *Labyrinths*" [*Research in African Literatures,* Spring, 1978]. Characteristics of this *"poetry as ritual"* (her emphasis) are: the non-communicative and non-expressive function of language that is yet concrete but not natural; and the manipulation of words for their sensuous impact rather than logical meaning. This mode calls for simultaneous use of verbal and nonverbal forms of self-expression such that the resulting performance is a "medium of revelation and ritual." The whole poem is, in other words, one long ritual performance or extended dramatic symbol, enclosing smaller symbols.

On meaning, Heywood's observations are also noteworthy: the plot enacted by Okigbo's ritual experience is that of "the heroic monomyth," with definite universal patterns. This plot, she goes on, accords with the immemorial historical purpose of rituals and ritual poetry: "a means of participating in the sacred and attaining the divine." Thus Okigbo, through deliberate manipulations of symbols, magic, and ritual gestures, re-establishes the primordial kinship between man and god; through a re-enactment of the sacred drama of pain and suffering, he metamorphoses into the latter.

Furthermore, the ritual nature and form of the poetic experience helps the protagonist achieve several aesthetic ends. In the first movement of **"The Passage,"** the prodigal is in the sacred grove, weak, naked, and leaning on an oilbean for support, and waiting. In these positions and gestures are expressed the attitudes of humility, absolute contriteness on the one hand, and expectancy on the other. Also aroused are the contradictory emotions of regret and despair, and hope. All these are yet canalised in a particular direction:

> Under your power wait I
> on barefoot,
> watchman for the watchwood
> at *Heavensgate;*
> out of the depths my cry:
> give ear and hearken . . .

Thus even at this moment of total passivity and surrender, an activity more intense and of a superior kind is going on: physical and emotional contraction facilitates the expansion and availability of being to the other world. One must bear in mind that this section deals as much with childhood awakening of aesthetic sensibilities as with the early awareness of "hidden possibilities and potentialities" [B.

Gunn, *Journal of Religion,* July, 1970], behind common reality.

But as made clear in **"Initiations,"** this incipient disposition was diverted and stultified, hence the long and tortuous journey he undertakes is not just for the recovery of this pre-recognition, but also for the realisation, in adult life, of such possibilities. Therefore, even though the poetry is ritual, it is not ritual performed along established, orthodox lines to link yet again man with god; its plot and structure are those of a man in search of an altogether new deity whose presence he alone has felt in ways no inherited metaphors can exactly capture. It is unique also in the sense that Okigbo the sensualist refused to give way to the redeemed prodigal who has renounced the world (**"Four Canzones"**) but instead, deftly performs the synthetic operation of making the deity sensual—

> Shadow of rain over sunbeaten beach,
> shadow of rain over man with woman.

with he himself an incontinent god—

> And he said to the ram: Disarm.
> And I said:
> Except by rooting,
> who could pluck yam tubers from their base?

The ritual structure explores these uniquely contradictory desires while its holistic plot dramatizes the pursuit of the deity.

"Religion," maintains John E. Smith, "wherever we find it, manifests a threefold structure that can be set forth in generic terms" [*Religious Studies,* October, 1965]. The three elements of the structure are: the Ideal, the Need, and "the saving power"—the Deliverer. To summarise very briefly, the *Ideal* is the absolute and goal of life against which actual life is measured. Through the resulting *"contrast-effect,"* personal limitations are realised and possibilities of fulfilment known. Its nature provides guiding principles for realisation of fulfilment while participation in it is the ultimate, teleological end hoped for. It is possible to know its nature because it makes itself manifest in phenomena which it at the same time transcends. The *Need* starts from awareness that both present life as it exists, and the self living it, are flawed. The flaw is first sensed as a void, the urge to fill it leads to recognition of its nature as a gulf separating the self from the Ideal. Once recognized for what it is, this obstacle must then be encountered and overcome. This is the office of the *Deliverer* who, in helping to overcome the Need, "establishes the Ideal on the far side . . . of distorted existence." The nature and functions of the Deliverer are of course determined by the nature of the Ideal that needs to be established, and in turn by the nature of the obstacle that stands in the way. Where the self can on its own overcome that obstacle, he is his own Deliverer.

Applying this structure to Okigbo's religious experience as embodied in his poetry up to and including **"Distances,"** several interesting discoveries are made. First, the deity Mother Idoto, though cultural, is not so traditional after all. Second, Okigbo's religious experience is in character closely bound up with contemporary Africa's experience: it is both ontological and temporal. It cannot

therefore be a return to atavism—the logical implication of the arguments about the poet's defence of and return to traditional religion. In short, Okigbo's "religious poetry" contains the truth about contemporary African experience because, to quote Smith again, "it acknowledges the reality of time and relates the progress of human life to the cosmic process of redemption." Third, Okigbo is his own Deliverer whose ultimate self-discovery is metamorphosis into god, as is underlined by his use of the Egyptian belief about the Pharaohs, the Gilgamesh-Enkidu myth (*Limits* V), and Calvary.

To start with the Ideal. Her identity is very clear: Mother Idoto, the stream deity of Okigbo's village community. But in the poems she is a veritably complex deity with many facets and aspects. She is muse and embodiment of poetic sensibilities and illuminations. Since the poet-protagonist's quest is for the psychic, creative self sundered and lost in early life, she also stands for the lost self and the unity to be effected. Since this unity can only come through a return to cultural roots, she is the "cultural mother"—the source and origin of creative intuition. Furthermore, she is the sole reminder of that Elysian past when harmony between man, nature, and god obtained:

> etru bo pi alo asshe e anando we quandem . . .

> And when we were great boys
> hiding at the smithies
> we sang words after the bird—

> Kratosbiate . . .

Her nature too is sufficiently delineated:

> BRIGHT
> with the armpit-dazzle of a lioness,
> she answers,

> wearing white light about her;

> and the waves escort her,
> my lioness

In spite of this fierce moral purity, she is a woman sexually desired

> Her image distracts
> With the cruelty of the rose . . .

> Distances of her armpit-fragrance
> Turn Chloroform enough for my patience—

ardently pursued and eventually possessed:

> I have entered your bridal
> chamber; and lo,

> I am the sole witness to my homecoming.

Sexual penetration, which consummates the hunt, brings the quest to an end. In symbolic terms, this sacred sexual union between man and deity does not only signify interpenetration of the two realms for this poet-prophet, it also means ascent into the divine plane and assumption of divinity. Sensual yet puritanically pure, Mother Idoto stands for the abundant life of the senses which, cultivated, is an avenue to perception of ontological realities, and for the continual self-sacrifice of the poet to his vocation in order to attain immortality through the poem. Thus she embodies the total meaning of the poet-pilgrim's religious and aesthetic search, plus the goal and ultimate purpose of his life.

From the above then, the watermaid is a new deity evolved as a result of a combination of several spiritual and creative needs. In all such exigencies, the need to draw sustenance from cultural roots and thereby re-establish continuity, is a constant. This goddess has been created anew and invested with tremendous powers, much like the Umuaro communities got together and created Ulu at a time of acute stress. Hence, some of the items of worship are traditional:

> Mask over my face—
>
> My own mask, not ancestral—I sign:
> remembrance of calvary,
> and age of innocence, . . .

But the form is not and accordingly, the Need is also different for the quester. *Limits,* **"Silences"** and **"Distances"**, are the poems which reveal the nature of the Need through history. Their contents need not delay us here, but their religious and aesthetic modalities must be dwelt upon. The three groups of poems project "man's outer and inner worlds" which, to Okigbo, are equivalents of the phenomenal and the imaginative. In other words, reality is not restricted to mere sense-data experience but, symbolist that he is, Okigbo feels it as 'presences'. Thus the three sequences present instances of a religio-aesthetic view of the universe. The factual journey from Nsukka to Yola becomes a mythic quest "of several centuries." Real characters and places are also mythicised and invested with dark, mysterious powers. In **"Siren Limits (III)"** it is the Cable Point at Asaba while in **"Fragments out of the Deluge (VII)"** it is Flannagan and the nuns who drowned in 1875:

> And to the cross in the void came pilgrims;
> came, floating with burn-out tapers;
>
> Past the village orchard where
> Flannagan
> Preached the Pope's message,
> To where drowning nuns suspired
> Asking the key-word from stone;

About the cable trope, Anozie has commented that the "Rockpoint of cable" image "may serve as a good illustration of the quasi- religious fascination which physical presences near the sea had for Okigbo" [*Christopher Okigbo,* 1972]. While still retaining its sense-data thingness, the point shows itself as a mysterious presence and landmark in the quester's psycho-spiritual journey: its super-natural quality is enhanced by the purely symbolic (non-material) level on which the journey has up to that point proceeded, by the hauntingly repetitive hypnotic phrase "Hurry on down." Similarly, through the poeticization of a historical character Okigbo exhibits an aesthetic that responds to the general and the metaphysical essence that exists behind the particular. The source of the drowning nuns image is a religious one. Hopkins has already mythicized the actual event and seen it as a manifestation of God's mysterious ways. His aesthetic experience is of course totally spiritual, and as the poem expands, his increasingly

ecstatic response to nature produces an intuitive awareness of Divine power and mystery. In working transitive events into the structure of myth, Okigbo like Hopkins, sees beyond the temporality of things into their permanence. Okigbo's aesthetic experiencing of things therefore combines with his symbolistic creed of seeing reality as a revelation of "supernal presence" to produce a poetic belief in the essence of things. **"Lament of the Drums"** especially testifies to this conviction that ontological reality is of supreme importance. His disclaimer on the drums is therefore within the logic of his overall aesthetic. The drums and the sisters have become independent realities. It is their essence as spirits of the ancestors that is invoked:

> Lion-hearted cedar forests, gonads for our thunder,
>
> Antelopes for our cedar forest, swifter messengers
> Than flash-of-beacon-flame, we invoke you:
>
> Many-fingered canebrake, exile for our laughter

Particularly apposite is the gonad image—an organ producing other substances. This is further underlined in sequel II where the messenger drums declare themselves

> Liquid messengers of blood,
> Like urgent telegrams,

Okigbo's ritualization of factual events and their integration into a mythical epic (*The Aeneid*) which stresses the spiritual over the material, shows the paramountcy of ontological reality in his poetic.

What all these point to is that Okigbo's ritual mode is not just a technique for writing poetry; rather is it a mode of perceiving and apprehending reality such that all are categorized and given *meaning*. Two categories emerge: experiences of the Ideal and those of the present, flawed world; or those of the sacred and those of the profane. These two worlds are, in the poems, distinct but not mutually exclusive—experiences of the secular world constitute the obstacles the poet-pilgrim must encounter in his ascent to the sacred peak. Both types of experience are integrated in ritual action, which progresses through the labyrinth into the temple. The two symbols and their variants respectively express the two categories of experience and they are worth considering at some length.

The symbols and their archetypes circumvent the entire quest, which begins in a shrine (a grove of trees) with the acolyte in a rite-of-passage act of homage. This grove, with its totemic symbols, is a microcosm of the unpolluted African past, culture and Religion and the world. Within it all actions and items are symbolic: the contrite posture of the priest in **"Passage (i);"** his return to the hill-top in **"Lustra"** (i) and (iii) with offerings:

> Fingers of penitence bring
> to a palm grove
> vegetable offering with five
> fingers of chalk.

His priestly ministrations create an air of expectation. Thus the ceremonial hero in **"Passage (i)"** is not just leaning and awaiting the divine word; he actually expects the goddess. The expectation also takes a teleological form:

> Dark waters of the beginning
>
> Rays, violet and short
> piercing the gloom,
> foreshadow the fire that is dreamed of.

In this holy space all items and actions are symbolic of the primordial beginning. Time is isolated and holy, acquiring the dimension of stillness. Because of this multi-dimensional holiness, it is to the temple that the hero always runs:

> So would I to the hills again
>
> there for the cleansing

and is actually purified:

> Thundering drums and cannons
> in palm grove:
> the spirit is in ascent.

As an isolated, holy place, it emphasizes spatial and temporal limit, edge and closure, in *Limits* (XII)—the limit beyond which profanity cannot go, a place of order at the edge of chaos, and the home of the Sunbird. It is also the spatial equivalent of the spiritual solitude and dream state that is the womb of creativity and prophetic power, as already made clear in **"Initiations (iv)"** through Upandru's advice. In **"Distances"** the temple symbol takes the architectural form of a maze-like chamber whose sanctuary is at the nave of the chapel. Here it is home, emphasized again and again:

> I was the sole witness to my homecoming . . .

As home then, the temple becomes the pilgrim's resting place, centre of the world and of the self. It is here that the psychic self takes over to effect the spiritual rebirth much sought after:—the resurrection that is prelude to apotheosis:

> Miner into my solitude
> incarnatae voice of the dream,
> you will go,
> with me as your chief acolyte
> again into the anti-hill . . .

The climactic union with the watermaid also makes the temple symbolic of desire gratified.

Starting at the shrine, the quest ends in another holy place—the bridal chamber. Between these two terminal poles is the labyrinth, a continuum and a state of becoming. **"Passage"** represents several episodes of wandering. The first of which is the innocent wanderings of the "great boys" in their rural setting—**"Initiations (ii)."** While this one may be right but pathless, the others are both an error and in lost directions. In (iii) it is "Silent faces at crossroads" and in (iv) it is in wasted landscape. The initiatory experiences are dramatized as circular wanderings in a poetic landscape, or labyrinth; they also present their own images of wandering: Jadum the mad minstrel advises against wandering "in speargrass / after the lights." In *Limits* and **"Distances"** the labyrinth symbol rises to new levels. *Limits* is both a temporal and a spatial journey the

fruitlessness of which is emphasized by its labyrinthine nature. It is a journey between two temples—between the edges of sleep, or two sacred spots. The wanderings here thus become, for the protagonist, a state of continual growth or becoming:

> For he was a shrub among the poplars
>
> A low growth among the forest

The interaction of the temple and the labyrinth symbols enables Okigbo the conscious artist to use his own personal quest as pivot around which motifs from different myths revolve. The labyrinth symbol for instance allows the quester to re-experience the colonial invasion by representing it as an intrusion of the profane world of commerce and lust into the Sunbird's hallowed precincts of essences. The disaster is seen apocalyptically—the gods are dead and abandoned, not in the shrine but behind it—and penetration of the temple by the profane world of labyrinths marks the end of a cosmic order. Hence "the cancelling out is complete"; but the Sunbird resurrects in a new form.

Also at work in **"Lament of the Drums,"** this same symbol allows the poet to mythicize political happenings of the day. It also facilitates integration of public, external events into the motifs of quest for personal fulfilment. The analogy between Aeneas' pelagic wanderings and the tragic fate of Palinurus his helmsman, with Nigeria's own political journey and the misfortunes of one of her helmsmen becomes a metaphor of public lament for unreached destinations and the consequences thereof.

These twin symbols of temples and labyrinths emphasize Okigbo's conception of time. His poetic attitude, says Anozie, "moves spiritually round a belief in the restoration of a peaceful social and moral order, a new epoch; sometimes it affirms a disintegration of all existing social and moral codes in favour of a new and more sublime creative reality." That is, between an apocalyptic vision and an eschatological one. The symbols express between them these visions of personal versus collective history and time. Through *Heavensgate* to **"Distances"** Okigbo sees history as a unity moving through not so different labyrinths toward one templar end. So it is that in Okigbo's poetry everything participates in the sacred.

By consistent and sustained employment of the ritual, the poet's ultimate purpose is of course abolition of the entire profane time, which purpose is in keeping with both the "heroic monomyth" theme of the poems, and the self-deification purpose of the quest. It is also consistent with the autobiographical design: memory used to discover the self, redeem time, and reintegrate both. Which is what the parable of the prodigal son is about.

Taking our cue from both John E. Smith and Annemarie Heywood, we have sought to demonstrate that poetic experience and religious experience are indeed consubstantial in Okigbo; that the poet in him perceives and feels reality (history and politics inclusive) religiously; that Okigbo does not push any particular creed, indigenous or foreign, but instead is creatively eclectic in his choice of means for responding to and framing the welter of historical and cultural realities within and without. It is also clear that the autobiographical design infuses the poems with a self-consciousness that makes Okigbo the inventor and artificer prevail over Okigbo the submissive worshipper—this revolutionary apperception quickly grows into a revelatory experience the consequence of which is the creation of a monoreligion with he himself as the object of worship.

Peter Thomas remembers Okigbo:

In private, the mask of mischief and bonhomie would sometimes be discarded—though seldom for very long—and I could see why it was that most of the poems made such profoundly sad, often nostalgic, music. For one thing there was his wife, bonded to a school in the North, up near Lake Chad. "Every time I meet her," he told me once, "I fall in love all over again." And I remember his radiant face and contagious joy when he announced the birth of his daughter. Then there was the matter of the professional work that kept him from his writing—and the worse matter of wanting to write but feeling unready or unable. That was what brought us together over the making of *Heavensgate;* perhaps it lay behind the inscription on the *Limits* MS; but talking with me or having me read to him would somehow set him to work again—or temporarily exorcise the paralysis that beset him.

Peter Thomas, "Ride Me Memories," in African Arts, *1968.*

James Wieland   (essay date Spring 1984)

SOURCE: "Beginning: Christopher Okigbo's 'Four Canzones,' " in *World Literature Written in English,* Vol. 23, No. 2, Spring, 1984, pp. 315-27.

[*In the following essay, Wieland examines Okigbo's early poetry, arguing that the "Four Canzones" contains the essential elements of all his works.*]

It is unfortunate that Christopher Okigbo's first serious poems, **"Four Canzones (1957-1961),"** have become separated from the rest of his poetry, for they are contiguous with it, providing a fine prelude to the more substantial poetry of *Labyrinths* and *Path of Thunder.* It is apprentice work but it is important, offering an introduction both to the metaphysics that underpins his work and to his thematic and formal preoccupations.

The brutal directness of the *Path of Thunder* poems—"Politicians are back in giant hidden steps of howitzers, of detonators"—appears a less radical departure from his main body of work when read in the context of a poem like **"Debtors' Lane":**

This is debtors' lane, this is
the new haven, where wrinkled faces
watch the wall clock strike each hour
in a dry cellar.

Similarly, the language, imagery, private symbolism and

structural organization of **"Lament of the Flutes"** and **"Lament of the Lavender Mist"** prepares the way for the mode of *Labyrinths.*

Tidewash . . . Memories
fold-over-fold free-furrow
mingling old tunes with new.
Tidewash . . . Ride me
memories, astride on firm
saddle, wreathed with white
lilies and roses of blood . . .

Sing to the rustic flute:
Sing a new note . . .
("Lament of the Flutes")

And the specific musical accompaniment recommended for several of the *Path of Thunder* poems—there a component in an increasing use of traditional form and a more publicly directed poetry—is a reintroduction of experiments with form first explored by Okigbo in the **"Canzones,"** where it is to be seen in the context of his attempts to forge a "new note" "to the rustic flute."

"Four Canzones" also raises the question of Okigbo's use of sources. Vergil and Eliot are put to work as models of kinds of poetry, adding tonal nuances to the work, and there is no attempt to hide the influence. We may think ahead to the second part of *Limits,* **"Fragments out of the Deluge,"** or note that an early version of **"Lament of the Silent Sisters"** was introduced by an epigraph from Mallarmé's *Herodiade,* but, of course, Okigbo's "borrowings" are comprehensive. Often the allusion or influence calls upon the reader to bring an experience of the other work to the poem being read. Resonances are established between works internal and external to the poem. One of the first of these borrowings concludes **"Lament of the Lavender Mist";** it is a close translation of Miguel Hernandez's "El amor ascendia entre nosostros . . ." but knowledge of the source gives little to the poem. Frequently, however, the echoes add to the ambience of the poem, forming an element in its complex psychic life—the allusion to Proust, for example, in **"Lament of the Lavender Mist"**—and neither the echoes nor the borrowings, if they deepen the mental event of the poem, can be said to inhibit the creativity behind the poem. Indeed, they add to the open-endedness, the centrifugal force of much of his poetry. Donatus Nwoga sums up the question, placing it firmly in an African tradition: "Originality, in African tradition, has not much to do with where the artist derived his material. The essence of originality is the use to which the artist puts his material, both borrowed and invented" [*Critical Perspectives on Nigerian Literature,* ed. Bernth Lindfors, 1976]. Hernandez's lovers "seek one another / And meet afar off "; Okigbo's "cling to each other / But kiss the air only": this is a crucial variation.

As this suggests, and implicit in the lines quoted above from **"Lament of the Flutes,"** integral to the poetry from the start are vital questions about the nature of poetry and the role of the poet in the dynamically changing Nigerian society of the late 1950s. Being both a poet and a member of the priest's family in Ojoto, Okigbo felt acutely the tensions underlying Nigerian society, and while at one level his protagonists' pilgrimage is to make sense of the changes he sees about him and to renew contract with his heritage, at another, it has many parallels with the psychology of the creative act: as the physical and psychic anguish serve as metaphors for creativity; as the questor moves from isolation or ignorance towards knowledge and reunion, towards continuity. By the end of the **"Canzones"** the exile has begun to apprehend the extent of his isolation from the source of his being and the poet has begun to find a language and a form that can accommodate his experience. Thus, **"Lament of the Lavender Mist"** signals the beginning of *Labyrinths,* not the completion of **"Four Canzones"**; becomes a point of departure, not a place of arrival as, implicit in the failure to realize the union—"we are now shadows / That cling to each other / But kiss the air only"—is the need to find a new attitude to Idoto. **"The Passage"** opens with the exile, now "a prodigal," humble and reverent:

> Under your power wait I
> on barefoot,
> Watchman for the watchword
> at *Heavensgate.*

Lying between the lines of the **"Canzones"** are accidents of personal and public history. The poems log various physical and psychological displacements—shifts from Lagos, to Fiditi, to Ojoto, to Nsukka and the emotional turmoil associated with these moves—and catch something of the tensions between rural and urban, traditional and westernized Nigeria in post-colonial African society. Such pressures impinge, of course, upon the whole spiritual and intellectual fabric of the people and they provide a substance for the poet-exile's equivocation and ambivalence. We sense also the obligations Okigbo may have felt to the various influences of his education. He never lost contact with his village of Ojoto, absorbing tribal chants, laments, songs and dances, but he attended English-medium schools, took an honours degree in classics at Ibadan and was widely read in Western literature. These are some of the dualities of his being and they resonate behind the tentative questions of **"Lament of the Flutes"**:

> Shall I answer their call
> creep on my underself
> out of my snug hole, out of my shell
> to the rocks and fringe for cleansing?
> Shall I offer to *Idoto*
> my sandhouse and bones,
> write no more on snow-patch?

Okigbo makes it clear that any attempt to renew contact with an elemental heritage is as much a journey into the present and the future as it is into the past. His rifling of traditional and arcane sources, so much a part of the texture of *Labyrinths,* begins in the **"Canzones"** and stems from his struggle to find a language for his poetry and symbols which may give an order to existence, or fictions which will suffice for the present. Implicit in a search for coherence is always the possibility that it is available and *Labyrinths,* after numerous false starts and blind alleys, moves towards the ecstatic resolution of **"Distances"**:

> I have fed out of the drum
> I have drunk out of the cymbal
>
> I have entered your bridal

chamber; and lo,

> I am the sole witness to my homecoming.

Path of Thunder, however, offers no comparable sense of synthesis. The final poem leaves "us"—poet and audience—responding to a universe in seemingly endless process:

> An old star departs, leaves us here on the shore
> Gazing heavenward for a new star approaching;
> The new star appears, foreshadows its going
> Before a going and coming that goes on forever.

This is a knowledge, and it embodies what Wole Soyinka calls "the reality of African metaphysical systems" which possess "a natural syncretism." He continues [in *Myth, Literature and the African World,* 1976]:

> Where . . . the mediation of ritual is required,
> it is performed as a human (communal) activity,
> not as a space-directed act of worship . . . And
> the literature that is based on this conception
> differs from others by betraying an exaltation of
> constantly revolving relationships between man
> and his environment above a rigid pattern of existence mandated by exteriorised deities.

Offering a similar report on metaphysical reality, Leopold Senghor says that "the African conceives the world, beyond the diversity of its forms, as a fundamentally mobile, yet unique, reality that seeks synthesis." While such a view of reality receives its most explicit articulation in Okigbo's last writing, it is implicit in the openness to change of the prodigal's inner world in *Labyrinths,* and it is influential in the design and matter of the **"Canzones,"** in their constant shifts of perspective and form and their openness to interdependent levels of life and literature.

In addition to a mode of knowing that accepts the "fundamentally mobile" nature of reality, there is a dynamism that seeks this synthesis of which both Senghor and Soyinka speak, that struggles to concentrate and to unify disparate forces into a comprehensive but accessible body of knowledge, keeping open the necessary channels between poet, audience and "traditional wisdom" [T. S. Eliot, *After Strange Gods,* 1934]. Okigbo does, however, recognize that these links are tenuous and, being acted upon by social, political and personal pressures, are in continual flux. For not only does he have access to a metaphysical system built on a notion of process, but also he lives in a society whose entire fabric has been subject to extreme pressures of change for at least two hundred years. His poetry, then, manifests no closed system. Words, images, metaphors, even traditional symbols carry multiple meanings as the poet seeks to capture the essence of his world and to make contact with an audience that is no longer homogeneous.

Almost from the outset, it seems, central to the order and coherence, to the continuity which Okigbo seeks in self and society, is an awareness of change. This awareness underwrites his treatment of Idoto, source and object of his protagonist's pilgrimage. In **"Watermaid"** she is "match-flare in wind's breath" and throughout *Labyrinths* she is characterized by her transience and numerous metamorphoses, but this elusive, transient quality is with her from her first appearance in **"Four Canzones"** where, even in her most substantial form, she is evoked as the "Lady of the lavender— / mist." Similarly, the relationship between the water spirit and the protagonist, who is also in continual process, is figured by its protean character. And while the repeated new beginnings at their deepest level reflect the struggle of the poet to find a suitable synthesis of social, historic and aesthetic imperatives, all the time working towards a reintegration into his traditional culture and seeking a poetic, they may be seen also as a part of a larger pattern of movement and change, central to which is the awareness that it is the journey, and not its completion, which provides access to knowledge.

In **"Watermaid,"** the poet-prodigal pleads that his poetry might

> Stretch, stretch . . .
> to clutch at this hour,
>
> fulfilling each moment in a
> broken monody.

But the monody begins in **"Four Canzones"** where the poems grow out of each other, answer or overturn each other, in an open-ended and continuing dialogue on the predicament of the exile.

The exile figure is launched in **"Song of the Forest,"** a poem which borrows situation, elements of structure and imagery from Vergil and is to be heard against the "warm meditative" music of the _ubo_. The _isolato_, who "must leave the borders of [his] / land, fruitful fields," is framed between lines celebrating the pastoral bliss of the one who stays behind:

> You loaf, child of the forest,
> beneath a village umbrella,
> plucking from tender string a
> song of the forest.

But while it uses one of the traditional tensions of the pastoral mode, the poem is about choices—the poet-exile "must leave," he will not stay behind to "loaf" in the forest—and it is about poetry. The "child of the forest" will "teach[-] the woods to sing a / song of the forest" but when the exile contemplates "the rustic flute" in **"Lament of the Flutes"** and hears again the lure of the pines and the creatures of the forest, he speaks of the need to "Sing a new note." The poem sets in motion equivocations which are to expand and resonate throughout the sequence and the canon.

Drawing on the second stanza of the first poem, **"Debtors' Lane"** offers an Eliot's-eye view of the city "away from home," but while the economic, social and industrial forces of an emerging urban society form a backdrop to these two poems, the focus remains firmly on human frailty. In apparent conformity with the pastoral, the hollow life-illusion of the city is condemned, but, by implication, the poem questions also the inactive and passionless introspection of the recluse who has found a "new haven" away from the "blasts" and "buffets / of a mad generation." The "new haven," however, is a "dry cellar" and its occupants languish, "watching the wall clock strike each hour."

The next poem, **"Lament of the Flutes,"** written after Okigbo's return to Ojoto, has at its centre the possibility

of an order in the universe. "Dawn" comes "gasping thro worn lungs," the day breathes, winds point directions and the "talkative pines" speak a language the _isolato_ understands. He is absorbed once more in the landscape, and yet he is far from "the child of the forest" of the first poem. There is about him something of that sense of destiny which Okigbo suggests is the characteristic of his persona in **_Labyrinths;_** he is

> a personage . . . much larger than Orpheus; one with a load of destiny on his head, rather like Gilgamesh, like Aeneas. Like the hero of Melville's _Moby Dick_, like the Fisher King of Eliot's _Waste Land;_ a personage for whom the progression . . . is like telling the beads of a rosary; except that the beads are neither stone nor agate but globules of anguish strung together on memory.

The poet-protagonist of **_Labyrinths_** and the "Okigbo" figure of the last poems is coming into focus: the poetry has begun to acquire a voice and a form.

Released from the myopia of youth and the exclusive idealism of **"Debtors' Lane,"** the exile wants his memories to guide him—"Ride me / memories"—and this leads neither to pastoral simplicities nor to the solution thrown up by the _ubi sunt_. The complex tensions felt by the poet-exile as he makes the ritual journey back into his social and cultural inheritance—it is much more than the progression into "nostalgia" which Anozie suggests—are manifested in the ambivalence he attributes to the water spirit: "What will the / Watermaid bring at sundown / a garland? A handfull of tears?" As the questions suggest, he is not yet able to surrender himself unconditionally to Idoto. When the exile re-emerges in the first movement of **_Heavensgate,_** now "a prodigal" and prepared for a ritual cleansing, there are no qualifying questions: "Before you, mother Idoto, / naked I stand."

Formally, the choices and contradictions explicit in the structure of the first two canzones become a part of the dramatic organization of **"Lament of the Flutes"** as the poem, in its diction and structure, embodies the notice of intention embedded in the chorus: "Sing to the rustic flute. / Sing a new note." There is now a sympathetic and instinctive, rather than a logical, wedding of image and symbol, and a poetic diction which begins to answer the call of two traditions. The search is not for an assimilation of traditions but for a language which retains the integrity of each while catching the experience that initiated the poem. The Englishness of "Maytime flowers" rests easily with the locally evocative "Watermaid . . . at sundown," and while the poem can be spoken of in terms of the structure of modern poetry, it is, as Anozie points out, "in the style of a _griot_ incantation" [_Christopher Okigbo_, 1972]. The form is apposite, since the _griot_—an interpreter of history—has the power to reach back to the source of being; thus we have the sense of a mind searching for meaning.

Just as the form of old Provence gives way to a lyric form as much in debt to the lyric conventions of modern poetry and traditional Igbo forms, the exclusive choices of the pastoral are found to be inappropriate to Okigbo's exile. His Eden is stained with blood: "Remembrance of things past" initiates nightmare recollections of "Eagles in space and earth and sky, / Shadows of sin in grove of orange," and "A song of Christmas" sets off "Echoes in the prison of the mind" (**"Lament of the Lavender Mist"**). The lines gain added resonance when read in the context of **"Fragments out of the Deluge,"** which details the theft and desecration of the outward symbols of the local religion by the colonial missionaries:

> Their talons they drew out of their scabbard,
> Upon the tree trunks, as if on fire-clay,
> Their beaks they sharpened;
> And spread like eagles their felt-wings,
> And descended upon the twin goods of Irkalla
>
> And the ornaments of him,
> And the beads about his tail;
> And the carapace of her,
> And her shell, they divided.

The language alludes to the imperial division of Africa but it is, perhaps, in a poem like **"Elegy for Alto,"** from the *Paths of Thunder* poems, that the threatening eagles are most clearly equated with imperialist force. (In the specific political context of the late poems, "the eagles" of British imperialism continued to influence the direction of Nigerian politics long after Independence was brought down.)

> And the horn may now paw the air howling
>   goodbye . . .
>
> For the Eagles are now in sight:
> Shadows in the horizon—
>
> The Robbers are here in black sudden steps of
>   showers, of
>   caterpillars—
>
> The Eagles have come again,
> The eagles rain down on us. . . .

As is the case with the eagles, other resonant images (rain, lighting, shadows, leaves, the moon, thunder) accumulate significance by repetition and variation until, in *Paths of Thunder,* they carry their own compelling force. Okigbo has made them his own: they never lose their natural significance but they acquire a powerful symbolic energy from their repeated use. In many instances, as I have suggested, the rich images and metaphors of *Labyrinths* and *Paths of Thunder* have their source in **"Four Canzones":** indeed that beginning helps to define them.

"Lament of the Lavender Mist" adds to the question posed in the previous poem: "What will the / Watermaid bring at sundown?" What is it to return to one's culture? When Idoto finally appears in this later poem—she is at first heard, she is a "voice / Returning from a dream," waking poet and audience into recollections of things past and present—her dual aspect is manifest. Anticipating her treatment in **"Watermaid,"** she is at once ominous—

> Lady of the lavender—
> mist, scattering
> Lightning shafts without rain,
> came forging
> Thunder with no smell of water

—and a figure of potential, of birth or rebirth:

> And she took me to the river
> Believing me a child—
> Spirit of the wind and the waves.

While on the one hand, the exile seems stunned—"Abyss of wonders"—on the other, he wishes, like Prometheus, to steal this portent of vision: "Take her to an island in the sun . . . Take her to a mountain waterfall." By part four of the poem the exile is "led" to "the water," with all its traditional and Christian symbolic significance, but the hoped-for genesis—"Echoes of the waters of the beginning"—founders:

> . . . the outstretched love
> Dried as it reached [him]—
> Shadows of the fire of the end.

In explicit contrast to the generative forces of wind and water, the poet-exile, a type of fisher king, is left on the waste land, "kissing the air only." We are forced to consider some deficiency in the exile. For, although the poem has at its centre a ritual union and draws on local and Christian religious metaphor, the union does not come to fruition. Too anxious to embrace his object and lacking in humility, he fails to make the necessary spiritual reparations to Idoto. When he next approaches her, his attitude is transformed: he is "lost in . . . legend" and under her spell (**"The Passage"**) as, through the immediacy of the scene and a complex of allusions, the timeless ritual of renunciation is evoked. The significance of the moment is conveyed through the conjunction of the ritual—the youth, naked, giving himself to his sacred stream in the presence of an oilbean totem—with the biblical echo of Daniel calling to his Lord: "out of the depths of my cry: / give ear and hearken."

As these lines suggest, the reunion with Idoto must come from within: this stage of the journey is to be played out in the poet's mind. But this speaks also of form, and the change has been signalled in the resilient, organic poetry of the last two canzones. It is here that we begin to see the centrality to Okigbo's work of metaphor—its fusing, transposing, synthesizing energy—as his poetic fictions call for an intuitive response. There is a developing tendency to use imagery in an interdependent way and what develops is a give and take, an emotional and psychic flux—a current—energizing the entire sequence (and later uniting the canon). As a consequence of this flow of associations the images do not remain in isolation, but are organized into metaphors drawing into their field disparate forms of experience which are still part of an enlarged reality.

"Four Canzones," then, gives early notice of the matter and manner of Okigbo's poetic fictions. In the process of moving from the simple pastoral variations of the first two poems to the private emotive contexts of the two laments, motifs, images, key words and ideas are repeated, experimented with and explored for underlying textures of meaning which establish a dialogue between poems, with other works that are drawn into the ambience of the sequence by allusion or echo, and between the poetry and neo-African affairs. So that while **"Debtors' Lane"** feeds off its affinities with "The Hollow Men" and its use of a pastoral mode, the musical accompaniment extends the poem's scope, as its social and didactic impetus is played out through the telegraphy of the drum and the declamation of the whistle. Similarly, **"Lament of the Flutes"** blends a *griot* incantation with modern lyric conventions to make a poetry which is unique and which forms the basis of *Labyrinths.*

Such explorations of traditional and contemporary Western form and traditional Nigerian form and presentation provide access to a mind struggling to find its way, and to a poetry seeking a form. At what may be termed the narrative level of these four poems, we follow a figure confronting his exile and resolving to find a way back to Idoto, while at the level of allusion and image and the underlying movement of a mind (that more subliminal level), there are early indications of the search for a synthesis which informs and is the goal of the later work.

Okigbo's poetic world corresponds to what Soyinka calls "the dark continuum of transition": it is no fixed world. From **"Song of the Forest"** his protagonist has been looking for symbols to live by, looking for perspectives that will make sense of his world and, inevitably, the gleanings he has—brief moments of psychic or physical arrival—become points of departure as one perception opens the way for others, in a process of continuing discovery "in each living hour." Hence, the beginning which forms the substance of **"The Passage,"** when placed in the context of the **"Canzones,"** is just one in a series of beginnings which begins with the departure of the exile figure in the **"Song of the Forest,"** is implicit in the statement of intention in the choric refrain of **"Lament of the Flutes,"** and which does not end: "The new star appears, foreshadows its going / Before a going and coming that goes on forever . . ." (**"Elegy for Alto"**).

> One dips one's tongue in the ocean;
> Camps with the choir of inconstant
> Dolphins, by shallow sand banks
> Sprinkled with memories;
> Extends one's branches of coral,
> The branches extend in the senses'
> Silence; this silence distills
> in yellow melodies.
>
> (**"Silences"**)

John Haynes (essay date Spring 1986)

SOURCE: "Okigbo's Technique in 'Distances I,' " in *Research in African Literatures,* Vol. 17, No. 1, Spring, 1986, pp. 73-84.

[*In the essay below, Haynes analyzes Okigbo's poem "Distances I," offering a line-by-line account of its meanings and techniques.*]

The following commentary deals with **"Distances I"** from the point of view of Christopher Okigbo's handling of reference, allusion, textual unity, and speech acts. But I begin with some preliminary remarks by way of justification, since Okigbo's work has been the subject of much polemic. He is said to be obscure, un-African, and elitist and to rely too heavily on an unassimilated modernism derived from the American poets, Ezra Pound and T. S. Eliot. The last charge, when directed at the earlier books of *Labyrinths,*

is well founded, but in the "middle" work which includes **"Distances,"** Okigbo transcends his earlier imitativeness and writes some of his best pieces. Unlike Goodwin (*Understanding African Poetry,* 1982), I find **"Distances"** successful. Also, it provides the philosophical center to Okigbo's quest. The other charges—obscurity, un-Africanness, elitism—seem to me to be somewhat confused in conception.

Okigbo's central philosophical idea deeply involves modernity and its mixture of clash and mesh with his traditions. Okigbo adopts a modernist technique as his way of articulating that radical undercutting of older foundations and certainties that even the fullest independence cannot reinstate. True, Okigbo derives his style from the West, but two points must be remembered about this: first, that the imagist method he uses came to the West itself largely from China and Japan; second, that modernist verse is not the monopoly of elitist and/or capitalist-oriented poets. The communists, Mayakovski, Macdiarmid, and Neruda—all employ modernist styles; and in the first phase of Bolshevik rule, modernist art and literature were equated in their radical disruptiveness and their subversion of received (bourgeois) canons as a further expression of the political revolution. It is with the rise of Joseph Stalin and the demise of the original conception of the Soviet that doctrines of writing which in effect went back to nineteenth-century realism became "official," and modernism was seen by Lukács as a symptom, not now of radical departure, but of bourgeois decadence.

Okigbo's obscurity is attacked now by African critics who count themselves of the left (not the only critics of his obscurity, of course) for the same reasons that Lukács attacked Joyce and Kafka or the surrealist poets of the 1920s. While this criticism has stimulated our interest in forging a radical populist poetry—with all the technical problems that brings—it would be a mistake to take such poetry as the only kind worth reading, especially for the radical. It may be argued that the "simple" neo-Soviet kind of poetry (sometimes simplistically aligned with traditional oral poetry in Africa) is, in fact, more conservative, ultimately, than modernism. The latter is subversive of received commonsense categories as encoded in habitual language usage. This common sense, after all is what our rulers have taught us. A really revolutionary poetry must help its audience to think and to perceive in new ways, not merely to invert or to reshuffle the old "certainties." This kind of poetry is necessarily philosophical and demanding, but not necessarily "elitist." Philosophizing is not intrinsically elitist: it is so only in certain societies where not working with the hands is overrewarded and overprivileging.

It is often said that Okigbo is "obscure" by critics who seldom look into what this obscurity might consist in. In fact, as I hope to show later in this account, obscurity certainly cannot be taken in an absolute way, as "in" the poems. Perhaps the more important aspect of Okigbo's difficulty is his use of the English language rather than Igbo. His own command of English can seldom be matched, especially in more recent times, by second-language speakers who not only do not acquire English until after their earliest intimate years, when rhythm and intonation loom so large, but also do not use English as a language of affect and intimacy. The present paper aims to interpret the complexity of **"Distances I"** by looking *into* the language which the art of poetry, "simple" or not, demands almost by definition, poetry being utterance that realizes the "grain of language" itself, and thus undercuts all other discourses.

Here is the poem itself:

1 FROM FLESH into phantom on the
  horizontal stone   (1)
2 was the sole witness of my homecoming . . .

3 Serene lights on the other balcony: (2)
4 redolent fountains bristling with signs—

5 But what does my divine rejoicing hold?(3)
6 A bowl of incense, a nest of fireflies? (4)

7 I was the sole witness to my
  homecoming . . .   (5)

8 For in the inflorescence of the white (6)
9 chamber, a voice, from very far away,
10 chanted, and the chamber descanted,
  the birthday of earth,
11 paddled me home through some dark
12 labyrinth, from laughter to the dream.
13 Miner into my solitude,   (7)
14 incarnate voice of the dream,
15 you will go,
16 with me as your chief acolyte,
17 again into the anti-hill . . .
18 I was the sole witness to my
  homecoming . . .   (8)

I begin with a discussion of the way in which Okigbo represents the situations of this poem. Although Okigbo frequently does not refer to an immediate physical situation, we know from his introduction to *Labyrinths* that the scene in **"Distances"** is an operating theater. The scene is represented by the poet from the viewpoint of himself as a patient on the "horizontal stone," or operating table, under anesthetic. At the same time, and in the same words, Okigbo also refers to an inner dreamscape experienced by the patient as he moves into unconsciousness. The skill Okigbo shows here is in the double reference to an outer physical world and an inner psychic one.

This is particularly clear at the beginning of the poem when the outer world is still near to consciousness. As the poet sinks from consciousness, the inner world too sinks deeper, becoming a traditional shrine and then, further into the psyche, a mythical landscape.

Let us first look at this double reference. It is realistically motivated, since it follows the course of actual anesthesia (a variation on the idea of the poet's vision as being a dream). The first two lines set the double scene clearly enough. "From flesh into phantom," from the bodily to the intangible and imagined, as if the body is dissolved and the utterer becomes a ghost. "Phantom" has connotations also, of course, of surgery—connotations of "phantom limbs." But in addition it suggests the world of spirits and death, which anyone undergoing surgery feels much closer to. In the same line Okigbo's metaphor of the "horizontal

stone" represents both the actual operating table and an altar, perhaps pyre. That it is an altar is encouraged by similar depictions in other parts of *Labyrinths.* For example, in **"Siren Limits IV"** which, in some ways, preludes **"Distances,"** Okigbo writes

> When you have finished
> & done up my stitches,
> Wake me near the altar,
> & this poem will be finished
>   (27)

And in the poem immediately following **"Distances I,"** we read

> And in the freezing tuberoses of the white
> chamber, eyes that had lost their animal
> colour, havoc of eyes of incandescent rays,
> pinned me, cold, to the marble stretcher
>   (54)

where the "white chamber" is the scene of the "marble," or stone, "stretcher."

This first line, then, makes simultaneous reference to a modern operation and to an "altar" in a traditional religious ceremony. In each situation the poet lies passively under the ritual attendance of figures in special clothing, with specialized skills. The "white chamber" is equally interpretable as a shrine or an operating theater.

However, these very similarities also highlight the contrast between modern scientific medicine and traditional worship. In his anesthetized fantasy the speaker moves back, or "down," to an earlier stage in his biography, to a prescientific and un-Western "homecoming," an inner journey back in cultural time and individual experience. It is solitary because the experience, encompassed in the dream, is inaccessible to anyone else. The wanness of Okigbo's refrain, "I am the sole witness to my homecoming," testifies to the fact that this homecoming in fantasy is by no means the same thing as an actual resumption of earlier norms or an earlier sense of cultural certainties. The refrain, too, comes from a voice which is not in the scenes "within" the poem. It is an artistically self-conscious comment on the experience of the poem as a whole, totalizing, and addressed to a reader.

The poem moves on to mention "serene lights on the other balcony." This also may have double reference, as the lights of the operating table, "serene" because seen with anesthetized vision; but also the illuminations in the religious scene, in the "white chamber" thought of as a shrine. "Signs" may also be religious, or scientific in the sense of screens, dials, charts, and so on. The "divine rejoicing" represents, together with the "laughter" of line 12, the effects of the gas and also a religious experience. "Incense" also suggests religious ritual but may also stand for the scent of the gas; the speaker inhales both. The "voice from very far away" is both priestly "chant" and "descant" and also the request and reply as the surgeon calls for this or that instrument whose name is repeated by the assistant who hands it to him, another ritual.

The operating theater and the shrine, in modern terms, contrast with one another, but not in a traditional context, where they are not distinguished. Both spiritual and physical, science and spell, aim at a more global healing than does the surgical. Okigbo's inner journey begins, naturalistically, in the modern medical world and moves toward what is both deeper and nearer to his youth. The return to the traditional shrine might seem to comprise the "homecoming," but such an interpretation is premature because the journey continues, deeper than the individual biography, psyche, culture, till it comes to a fundamental, mythical ambience, which may be related to Jung's "collective unconscious" in which certain mythical stereotypes, the "archetypes," express the deepest levels of the human mind, beyond any particular culture. For Jung, civilization depends on the individual's gaining this contact with archetypal images. In presenting this idea Okigbo is not, of course, necessarily committed either to an adherence to Jung's notions or to the idea that any actual man can really live outside, or beyond, a specific society. The poetic image represents an impossible archimedean point which may be imagined in order to throw actual lives and cultures into sharper perspective, thus to bring out their contingence.

The double reference remains more sporadically now, as Okigbo, for the mythical journey, relies on allusion. The double reference can still be felt in the "voice from very far away," but this "voice" now begins to carry us forward, allusively, into the mythical landscape—"paddled me home through some dark / Labyrinth"—on a journey by water. The allusion appears to be to the "Epic of Gilgamesh," which Okigbo suggests elsewhere by mention of the names of various gods and men in that myth. Here the connection is more tenuous, but a number of factors suggest it.

Gilgamesh himself makes a journey to the land of death, and it ends in failure, like Okigbo's "journey of several centuries from Nsukka to Yola in pursuit of what turned out to be an illusion" (*Labyrinths*), the illusion in Gilgamesh's case being the belief that a man may achieve immortality by dint of effort and determination. He too makes a journey over water in this quest and meets the figure of Utnapishtim, who is known as "The Faraway," a name echoed in the "voice from very far away" which guides Okigbo here, as Utnapishtim acts as Gilgamesh's guide. Furthermore, Utnapishtim tells Gilgamesh that the gods had decreed that he, Utnapishtim, should "live in the distance," again echoing Okigbo's poem, this time its title. Perhaps too, in the earlier part of the poem, the Gilgamesh motif is foreshadowed in the "horizontal stone," which we have seen as an operating table and an altar, but it is also similar to a sarcophagus, which is similarly associated with the journey into death in the ancient Egyptian cosmology. This sarcophagus is mentioned in **"Fragments out of the Deluge"** (*Labyrinths*), and the title suggests the Middle Eastern myth of the flood which occurs in a nonbiblical form in the Epic of Gilgamesh, Utnapishtim being the equivalent of Noah (Nuhu). Almost in the same breath, in **"Fragments out of the Deluge,"** Okigbo mentions Enkidu, the "wild man" who, he says, is the "companion and second self of Gilgamesh." This interpretation of Enkidu as Gilgamesh's alter ego is not to be found in the myth itself. It represents a modern psychoanalytical approach put forward by Jung in "Symbols of Transfor-

mation," where he refers to "the higher and lower man, ego-consciousness and shadow, Gilgamesh and Enkidu," and says of this myth, that it "could probably be paraphrased thus: just as man consists of a mortal and an immortal part, so the sun is a pair of brothers, one of whom is mortal, the other immortal." Gilgamesh, of course, is identified by Jung as a "sun hero."

Just as Okigbo as the poet-hero ("sunbird") enters the underground realm of the labyrinth after a sea journey and comes to the "anti-hill," so Gilgamesh makes a similar sea journey and comes to the mountain that leads to the underworld, symbolizing, for Jung, the unconscious. This mountain is called "Mashu," and Sandars notes, in his glossary, that it has twin peaks and is regarded as the place of the sun's return to the world in the dawn, and it was identified with the "Anti-Lebanon Mountains." "Anti-Lebanon" seems to be echoed in the otherwise very puzzling "anti-hill."

Perhaps I have said enough to establish a prima facie case for taking Okigbo's technique of allusion, whatever else it may suggest, to be related to the Gilgamesh epic. This, of course, widens the significance of the poet's individual journey and suggests an intercultural dimension to what began as a personal confrontation with the unconscious and a visit to the kingdom of death (Okigbo refers to the Sumerian goddess of the underworld, Irkalla [or Ereshkigal].) This is an image of a universal psychic depth and, in this sense, a kind of "home." It suggests what Okigbo calls a "nameless religion" (*Labyrinths*). There is, of course, every danger that what seems to be universal may turn out to be a Western imposition. But the process of the poem shows a progression from the concrete individual in the operating theater to the first culture, and beyond; so we see the archetypal end in terms of, and we reach it through, the particular *contingent* culture. And the whole mission is placed in the mind of a specific African.

Characteristic of Okigbo's technique is the use of grammatically disjointed sentences, a technique particularly associated with modernism, especially imagism.

Sentence 1, for example, trails away into dots and is not overtly connected to sentence 2, which is moodless (without subject or finite verb) and also breaks off, this time in a dash. Two questions follow, which are related by their parallelism, sentences 3 and 4. Sentence 3 seems to be connected to sentence 2 by the conjunction, "But." However, this is a slightly unusual type of "but," since it is brought to bear by fiat of the poet, rather than by the internal logic of the connection. The difference may be illustrated by

> (1) He put on his hat. But it didn't fit.
> (2) He put on his hat. But that was foolish.

(2) uses "But" to represent the speaker's judgment, while (1) marks the internal logic of the two sentences.

Sentence 5 breaks in on the second of these questions, sentence 4, and also ends in dots. Sentence 6 begins with a conjunctive "For," similarly motivated to the "But" in sentence 3 but more attenuated (A suggestion as to what is linked by "For" is made later).

The relation between sentences 7 and 6 is more straightforward than has been the case so far because they have the same topic, "voice" for which "miner" is a near synonym. But still there is no other connection besides this one through vocabulary. Then sentence 7 ends with more dots and is itself broken into by the refrain, sentence 6, closing the poem and ending in dots also.

Okigbo's sentences are thus consistently disjointed, except in the two cases where conjunctions occur between them. But these conjunctions are themselves somewhat untypically used, and the links they make are not immediately obvious. This disjunction, in fact, sends the reader the more intently back to the vocabulary, making him read it more imaginatively than he might otherwise, in order to find the dynamic "thread" of meaning. The reader begins to notice, for example, that "miner" in line 7 is semantically related to "labyrinths" (sentence 6), to "homecoming" (sentence 5), which also occurs in sentences 1 and 8. "Homecoming" is more remotely connected to "birthday" and more closely to "home" (sentence 6). "Voice" in sentence 7 harks back to sentence 6 which contains "laughter," "descanted," and "chanted," the last two of these being associated with religion and so with "acolyte" (sentence 6, or line 16), and with "incense" in sentence 4 and also to "voice" itself. In sentence 7, also, "dreams" recalls "dream" in sentence 6, "serene" in sentence 2, and "phantom" in sentence 1; and these are related contrastively to "incarnate" in sentence 6, line 14, and "flesh" in sentence 1.

It is on the basis of these lexical ties that we can construct the representational narrative, as this affects the relations between sentences. The sentences are linked, also, in a different way, which we can see if we consider the basis of a recital for the poem from the point of view of its potential intonation.

I shall not attempt an analysis of a performance of the poem, mainly because an intonational analysis would not reveal the meanings carried. And there is the complexity that a number of intonational interpretations are possible. Yet the essential dynamic of the poem, which will be realized in performance by one intonational pattern or another, can be traced by looking at the text as a succession of speech acts. Although the individual sentence is not necessarily a unit of intonation (and certainly is not in sentences 4 and 6), it can be taken as a speech act unit, at least at the primary degree of complexity, which reveals the main lines of the poem's interpersonal (or attitudinal) development, the succession of emotional attitudes and roles.

In the first sentence the poet speaks in the first-person role and adopts a totalizing perspective. The speech act may be described as "revelation" in which the poet addresses his audience or reader directly. This role differs from all the other roles in the poem, except, of course, where the refrain is repeated. It is as if the poet alternates between the roles of chorus and actor. The repetitions of the refrain change in significance as they accumulate. First, there is an annunciative force to it, then it becomes reassertive, and in the last line retrospective, the fact of repetition modulating the meaning each time.

Sentence 2, being moodless, has no explicit speech role,

since no "person," in the grammatical sense, is mentioned. Just this serves to express lack of person, lack of finiteness, a floating disorientation, mirroring the subjective experience of the speaker sinking into his dream. This disorientation is replaced, in the third and fourth sentences, by self-questioning, a self-doubt which perhaps is also doubt about the status of the self. Then in sentence 5 the refrain returns, reassertively. Sentence 6 follows this refrain with narrative explanation, this being the basis of the function of interpersonal "For" at the beginning of it. Then sentence 6 switches to the third person, with the poet now in the role of observer in relation to the "voice," the poet's "I," for the first time takes a subsidiary position, recurring in line 11 with "me" as one part of the main topic, which is the "voice." In sentence 7 the speech role changes yet again, the poet now adopting a second-person position and addressing the "voice" in an assertion of commitment to it. Leaving aside the comprehensive point that ultimately the whole poem is addressed to a reader, since it *is* a poem, we can still distinguish, within the poem's world, a difference between the poet as observer, hearer of the voice, and its more intimate relation to him in sentence 7. The difference is between an I/it relation and an I/you one. The tone of commitment contrasts too with the earlier disorientations and self-questionings. It matches the more detached definiteness of the refrain which ends the poem, sentence 8. The sequence of attitudinal meanings is summarized below.

SEN-TENCE	SPEECH ROLE	ATTITUDE
1	First person to reader	Prospective, annunciative revelation
2	No person or time (tense)	Disorientation
3-4	First person to self	Questioning self-doubt
5	First person to reader	Reassertive revelation
6	Third person to self and reader	Narrative explanation
7	Second person to voice	Commitment
8	First person to reader	Retrospective revelation

Clearly, once the poem has been understood at the lexical level, a recital which brings out these shifts in role and speech act can perform a unifying function similar to that often, but not here, performed also by nonlexical types of cohesion. The speech act unity of poems has been little studied as yet, possibly because critics tend to think in terms of the written page and possibly because those aspects of sound they do take into consideration, such as rhyme and "stress," are to be found at definite points in the text, while the rise and fall of intonational pitch contours is not; it is cumulative and overarches other more atomistic units of language. In this overarching lies its unifying function, a kind of unity which is more often associated with music, perhaps.

The techniques we have looked at are, of course, related to Okigbo's obscurity, but not necessarily so. It is quite possible to employ double reference and allusion without causing problems for readers. But such an achievement depends on the readers' having a common "community," both culturally and intellectually speaking, which the poet can rely on their drawing upon when he makes his oblique references and allusions. For the reader who happens to know about Okigbo's village and about the mythology he alludes to, his poems are, of course, not obscure. This is true, even though, in practice, there may be relatively few such readers. They may be dubbed "elitists," but looking at intellectual interests in this way, as I have already suggested, is to presuppose a necessary connection between thinking and privilege, since this obtains in particular societies.

I suggest, also, that many of the attacks on Okigbo's obscurity are motivated by a dislike of, and a lack of perception of the relevance of, his sources, of what I have oversimplified as his affinity for Jung's ideas. We need only look at a different kind of allusion such as the following from Idi Bukar's poem "Necessity."

> They forgot
> that truth's necessarily illegal
> that the torturer's breath falls upon it
> He tests it on the expensive dials of pain
> in memory of Lenin
> who had warned them
> him
> in 1903
> when there were still fourteen more years
> of that same uncertain and dangerous necessity
> still to survive

The allusions to Lenin's "What Is to Be Done?" will be plain to the Marxist reader. But—and this is perhaps the point—it will be seen as an educative and "relevant" allusion which the student who does not pick up can explore to extend his knowledge of the poem's community because the poem is, in part, a lesson, the poet a teacher, and learning about Lenin is valid in a way learning about Jung and Sumerian mythology is not. It seems to me, however, that what Okigbo says through his "depth" allusions *is*, in fact, valid for the African Left, but here is not the place to argue that case.

What I have tried to do here is, perhaps, merely to suggest that, even though our ideas are not quite the same as theirs, we can learn from our ancestors.

Romanus N. Egudu (essay date 1986)

SOURCE: "Christopher Okigbo and the Growth of Poetry," in *European-Language Writing in Sub-Saharan Africa, Vol. 2,* edited by Albert S. Gerard, Akademiai Kiado, 1986, pp. 750-54.

[*In the essay below, Egudu characterizes Okigbo as "the most significant poet" of his generation.*]

Christopher Okigbo is obviously the most significant poet of [1960s Nigeria] not only because of his national relevance but also because of his artistic excellence. He can rightly be described as the poet of Nigerian history, for there is a movement in his work which parallels that of the history of Nigeria from her contact with the white man to the early stages of the civil war, when Okigbo died. *Heavensgate* and *Limits* are a re-enactment of the cultural (especially religious) alienation which the country experi-

enced during the colonial era; **"Distances"** is a conclusion to *Heavensgate* and *Limits,* and a final reversion to indigenous traditional religion; **"Silences: Lament of the Silent Sisters"** and **"Lament of the Drums"** are a study in Nigeria's post-colonial politics with its confusion and lack of any sense of direction which led to the disillusionment of the masses; and **"Path of Thunder"** is an assessment of the *coup d'état* of January 1966 and a verdict that is also a prophecy of war.

If Okigbo's poetry is "one long elaborate poem" as one critic remarked, [O. R. Dathorne, *Journal of Commonwealth Literature,* No. 5, 1968], or if it has "organic relatedness" as another observed [S. O. Anozie, *Christopher Okigbo,* 1972], and as the poet himself stated the binding link must be sought in the story of the country from the colonial period to the beginning of the civil war rather than in any other source. In spite of Anozie's argument that what makes all of Okigbo's poems one long poem is verbal linkage, the fact remains that each sequence of poems except perhaps **"Four Canzones"** crystallizes around a chapter in Nigeria's historical experience. If Okigbo is the hero of most of his poems, he is so only in the sense that he carries the burden of his people's cultural and historical evolution. The sufferings of a nation can also be seen as those of any one man in the country.

Okigbo's poetry is therefore much less personal than many people think. The religious conflict which is dealt with extensively in *Heavensgate* and *Limits,* for example, is grounded in firm historical reality. In Chinua Achebe's *Arrow of God* which (like *Things Fall Apart*) deals with the same period of Nigerian history, we read as follows:

> Mr. Goodcountry told the converts of Umuaro about the early Christians of the Niger Delta who fought the bad customs of their people, destroyed shrines and killed the sacred iguana. He told them of Joshua Hart, his kinsman, who suffered martyrdom in Bonny.
>
> "If we are Christians, we must be ready to die for the faith", he said. "You must be ready to kill the python as the people of the rivers killed the iguana. . . . It is nothing but a snake, the snake that deceived our first mother, Eve. If you are afraid to kill it do not count yourself a Christian."

We may compare this passage with the following lines from *Limits,* which show a similar hostile attitude toward the animal totems that represent the gods of the indigenous religion:

> Their talons they drew out of their scabbard,
> Upon the tree trunks, as if on fire-clay,
> Their beaks they sharpened,
> And spread like eagles their felt-wings,
> And descended upon the twin gods of Irkalla
>
> And the ornaments of him,
> And the beads about his tail,
> And the carapace of her,
> And her shell, they divided.
>
> *Limits* (XI)

> AND THE gods lie in state

And the gods lie in state
Without the long-drum.

And the gods lie unsung,
Veiled only with mould,
Behind the shrinehouse.

Limits

The twin gods here are the same "twin gods of the forest" mentioned earlier in the poem Okigbo tells us in a footnote that they are "the tortoise and the python." Their religious significance as totems is similar to that of the sacred iguana and the royal python in *Arrow of God*.

Besides, in *Heavensgate* and *Limits,* Okigbo mentions two Christian historical characters by name: Leidan and Flannagan. The Rev. Fr. Leidan and the Rev. Fr. Flannagan were missionaries at Onitsha early in the 1940s. They thus took part in the suppression of indigenous religion. In *Heavensgate* (IV) Leidan is referred to as the "archtyrant of the holy sea," the phrase being a pun on "Holy See," and in *Limits* (VII) it is Flannagan who

> Preached the Pope's message,
> To where drowning nuns suspired,
> Asking the key-word from stone;
> and he said:
>
>> To sow the fireseed among grasses,
>> and lo, to keep it till it burns out . . .

It is significant that these examples of historical relevance and factual links are found in Okigbo's early poetry, for it is often with reference to his early work that critics have asserted that Okigbo was pursuing "art for its own sake" [*Christopher Okigbo,* 1972], or that "meaning" was not his concern [*Studies in Black Literature* 1, 1976]. Okigbo himself gave this impression that he did not care for meaning: "Personally I don't think that I have ever set out to communicate a meaning. It is enough that I try to communicate experience which I consider significant". In spite of this statement, however, there is meaning in his poetry—meaning that is historical, not just personal, though it is coloured by personal experience. Indeed even **"Four Canzones,"** Okigbo's earliest poem which has no overt historical links still has much social relevance. The first and third canzones compare and contrast the city and the village and find that the latter possesses all the blessings which the former lacks. The second canzone is a social comment, while the fourth deals with a private love experience. In this way **"Four Canzones"** constitutes a logical introduction to Okigbo's later poetry, giving an early hint of the three major areas of experience which were to be developed in his poetry: namely, cultural atavism (nostalgia), socio-political problems, and the nature of carnal love. Thus of all Nigerian poets, Okigbo can be said to be the most Nigerian from the point of view of not just nationality alone but, most importantly, of comprehensive national consciousness. Hence his central position in the growth of Nigerian poetry.

This consciousness is not limited to the content of Okigbo's poetry; it is also present in the form of his verse. More than any other Nigerian poet writing in English, Okigbo has explored and exploited the art of his indigenous (Igbo) traditional oral literature and the vernacular rhetoric of his people. The incantatory quality of his poems derives from the musical nature of Nigerian oral poetry, at times adopting its very form. Okigbo has also drawn some of his images from Nigerian folk tales and from the local environment. For example, the image of a bird standing "on one leg" in the second section of **"The Passage"** recalls the story of a fowl that went to a strange land and stood on one leg because it did not understand the customs of the people of that place. The experience re-enacted in the poem is that of solitude in spiritual (religious) exile, when, though the protagonist had been initiated into Christianity, he was ignorant of the customs of the new religion, and had therefore to stand apart, at a loss, like a bird on one leg. Examples of imagery based on the local environment are rife in Okigbo's poetry. Many of his poems are set against the background of shrines in groves which are customarily the scene of traditional religious worship and sacrifice. He can also fashion a specific image out of a particular feature of his rural surroundings: "Faces of black like long black columns of ants" [**"The Passage"**]. Furthermore, Okigbo enhances the form of some of his poems by working into them vernacular expressions which have been translated literally. In **"Lament of the Lavender Mist"** for example, he equates the lady of the poem with "Kernels of the waters of the sky"; this is a word-for-word translation of the Igbo term for hailstone, itself an object considered by the Igbo people to be a symbol of purity and delicate beauty. Also the expression "shadow of rain" in "Eyes watch the stones" is a direct translation of the Igbo term for the nimbus cloud which is the harbinger of rain.

By means of these and other artistic devices, Okigbo gave his poetry the imprint of Africanity, and subsequent poets nave seen this as a major factor in making Nigerian poetry truly Nigerian in spite of its being written in English.

Paul Theroux on the manner of Okigbo's death:

He was an unlikely solider, but so was Byron, so was Rupert Brooke, so were many of the classical poet-heroes that Okigbo idolised. People believed that the Biafran War should not have been fought. But what was Nigeria? It was a jumble of alienated regions. Okigbo would have jeered at the way the country's name had been coined in a despatch by a British woman journalist in 1897. But Biafra was Igboland: one language, one culture, one people. There was every reason for it to exist as a sovereign state. Okigbo did not care for politics, but he was greatly attached to the past and very certain of his identity. He was intelligent, open-minded, self-assured—the sort of person who is thrown into jail in Africa, or is speared to death or deported for being difficult. He was just the sort of person every country needs. Characteristically—in a war that few people here now remember—he died fighting for his village.

Paul Theroux, "A Free Spirit," in West Africa, *23 June 1986.*

Elaine Savory Fido (essay date 1986)

SOURCE: "Okigbo's *Labyrinths* and the Context of Igbo Attitudes to the Female Principle," in *Ngambika: Studies of Women in African Literature,* edited by Carole Boyce Davies & Anne Adams Graves, Africa World Press, Inc., 1986, pp. 223-39.

[In the following excerpt, Fido traces Okigbo's treatment of female characters in his poetry and links Okigbo's view of women to Igbo tradition and familial influences.]

Igbo culture is a complex entity, and the boundaries which define it are diffuse. Igbo people have intermarried with peoples along their borders, and the colonial intrusion and its aftermath has so changed things that it is hard even for scholars bent on determining essential facts to find them. The process of disentangling colonial influences and non-Igbo influences from the core of traditional Igbo culture is ongoing, but debates persist as to whether one element or another is old Igbo or is the product of a continually changing and adapting cultural ambience. To be sure, there are deep-seated blendings of the traditional and the modern and the Igbo have become known for their capacity to accept and absorb change. One major area of this debate concerns Igbo attitudes to women.

Christopher Okigbo was born at Ojoto, a town near Onitsha in which a local but powerful goddess, Idoto, had her shrine. Many of the riverine areas of Igboland and of Eastern Nigeria in general have goddess cults of various kinds, including the Mammy Water and the sea-goddess *Owu-Miri,* who is worshipped around Oguta and Egbema. This prevalence of female deities is in accordance with the theory that the Igbo traditional religion was based around the female principle, centrally around the Earth Goddess Ala, described by Michael Echeruo as the most likely deity to be called supreme god of the Igbos. This theory is not unchallenged since Chukwu, a male deity, is often described as having become more important than Ala. However, some theologians claim that this was only a response to Christian missionaries and Igbo Christian theologians need to find a supreme god amongst the Igbo pantheon (one is tempted to add a supreme *male* god). There is also a view that the Arochukwu people extended Chukwu's power in the service of their own aggressive expansionism. Other Igbo theologians argue that "the supremacy of Chukwu has never been challenged by any divinity in the Igbo religious pantheon." Whatever the precise history of Chukwu and Ala may be, the fact is that female deities figure largely in the culture and literature of the Igbo people, right up to this day and even in literature written by men in the English language.

Eastern Nigeria has produced a number of significant writers, including the most well-known of all African writers at this date, Chinua Achebe. It is notable that Igbo women as a group are the most numerous and productive of African women writers. Whilst it is difficult to say for certain what factors predispose Igbo culture to encourage the development of women as creative writers, it is clear that they exist, and it is also apparent that male Igbo writers are particularly concerned with the balance of male and female values in society and write about the results of inequities in male and female principles as being dangerous to social health. Igbo culture is favorable to the development of relative individualism, and the variations in dialects and customs between villages reinforce an impression of social flexibility, a factor which played a part in Igbo attitudes to established colonial rule and education. But beyond that circumstance which might give rise to female independence and development within cultural restraints, there are definite links made by Igbo people between strong women and specific social and cultural realities. For example, asking where the Igbo novelist Flora Nwapa was born, I was told that she comes from a place where the women are very strong (namely Oguta).

A few years after Okigbo was born, in 1932, a woman anthropologist published a study of Igbo women in which she detailed their close bonding with one another and their sense of independence and identity, as well as their closeness to the female Earth Goddess, acknowledged by their men [Sylvia Leith-Ross, *African Women,* 1939]. Her comment on Igbo male attitudes to women is important:

> One hears it said that the Igbo man 'does not respect women'. He does: he even respects her in a way so original and so modern that Europeans have only just begun to think of it.

Leith-Ross' study covered both rural and urban Igbo communities and included Port Harcourt, Onitsha and the intervening area. Her findings importantly point to what amounts to a women's sub-culture amongst the Igbo, with councils which almost amount, she suggests, to the power of secret societies, belief in the fecundity of women being linked to that of the yam deity, and a relation to the male world which was easy enough to permit men to say they would not mind being reincarnated as women, which could scarcely be the case in a really sexist society. Leith-Ross' position also supports the current arguments of the Bendel Igbo dramatist Zulu Sofola who argues that tradition benefitted women more than the modern postcolonial situation. Furthermore, the research of the Yoruba historian J. F. Ade Ajayi corroborates the idea that colonialism worsened the situation of the African woman. This is not surprising since the British colonialist period was marked in Britain itself by strong sexism.

There is some evidence that the traditional role of Igbo culture concerning gender might have been somewhat androgynous. Androgyny is defined in this sense as the capacity emotionally and intellectually to accept every human being as a mixture of male and female elements, with ideal human social relations permitting both sexes to utilize the 'other' in their nature freely and usefully. Certainly there is much psychological evidence that androgynous people are more mentally healthy than those who subject themselves to extremes of gender roles, and this may have an effect on creativity. Leith-Ross, at any rate, found that there was an androgynous flavour to Igbo culture: she describes "glimpses of some peculiar conception of sex or of a thread of bisexuality running through everything . . . or of a lack of differentiation between the sexes—or of an acceptance of the possibility of the transposition of sex." Chinua Achebe deals centrally with unbalanced maleness in *Things Fall Apart,* and Carole Boyce

Davies argues that he seems to be saying that survival involves man in unifying male and female qualities [unpublished]. In one interview, Achebe said: "There is always some kind of war between the sexes, you know, but in the traditional society it was good-humored." This focus on male-female relations as the underpinning of society seems to characterize both female and male writers from Eastern Nigeria, such as Flora Nwapa, Buchi Emecheta, Zulu Sofola, Christopher Okigbo, Cyprian Ekwensi and Onuora Nzekwu, who are Igbo and Elechi Amadi who is Ikwerre.

Yet for all the suggestions of possible advantages to women in traditional cultures, tradition was certainly not ideal, and modern influences such as British sexist colonialism further complicated gender relations. Some writers, like Amadi, have specifically written on women's issues, but only to reveal their own conflicts. Amadi's essay on the Nigerian civil war, *Sunset in Biafra* reveals his adherence to British-style army training, not surprising since he undertook that himself. But perhaps it partly explains why, when he talks of women, he sounds very much like a Western man:

> Because man recognises instinctively that feminine powers are overwhelming, he is reluctant to concede any further powers and privileges to woman . . . This is the feminine sexual power which men fear. The women who oppose the feminist movement are mostly those who recognise this power . . .

The same authoritarian, anti-emotional tradition which shapes soldiers in the Western style also makes men incapable of giving up their rigid surface controls to enjoy intimacies and equalities with women. Okigbo, whilst not a professional soldier, was killed in the Biafran war and his poetry clearly articulates the stress of determining identity amidst cultural crisis and gender crisis. In his work, fear of women can also be clearly perceived. Anxiety about the female principle is in fact a strong element in male Eastern Nigerian writers' work, whereas in writers such as Flora Nwapa, there is a profoundly different perception, an engagement with the reality of trying to be female and an individual in a society which constantly tries to mythologize about women to distance any danger they might pose. Nwapa's *Efuru* shows a woman trying to come to terms with loss of husband and child through her relation to a water-deity, a sort of divine role-model who helps her to decide that childlessness is not the end of the world. There is a great difference between using myth to make reality more workable and endurable and using myth to create fantasies which deny the reality. Much recent critical work by women has found the latter tendency strong in male creative literature, and of course the anger which women have begun to express can sometimes lead to intense hostility to men, itself a social divisive force. Buchi Emecheta's work, influenced as it is by her British experience, is characterised by a greater element of what one might call Western style feminism than is true of other African women writers in Nigeria. So it is possible to see that on both sides, male and female, there is a mixture of dissatisfaction with present male-female relations based on the central belief in Eastern Nigerian cultures that society is built on these relations and that something is presently wrong. A variety of solutions based not only on knowledge of tradition but also on colonial and post-colonial cultural influences from Britain have further polarized the sexes.

Okigbo's poetry ought to be seen in this context, for his presentation of his own spiritual odyssey is framed by the developing images of a female principle which shapes and informs the adult male psyche. *Labyrinths* is a spiritual journey to rebirth as an adult consciousness and a creative voice. The creative artist who made the poetry was himself a collection of contradictory elements: poet and man of action who was killed in war; mystic with ambitions to be a financier; proud Igbo and yet lover of European poetry; a man ambivalent about *négritude* but extremely attracted to symbolism and committed to the rehabilitation of his race and culture after colonialism; and Christian trained yet an adherent of older religions. The creative process made it possible for him to find coherence in himself, and his poetry shows the stages of integration of the disparate elements of his vision.

In his life, Okigbo had problems in his relations with women. He tried to save his marriage by making one last trip to visit his wife at Yola, a trip described in his preface to *Labyrinths* as being "in pursuit of what turned out to be an illusion". Yet women or the concept of the feminine in various forms shape the major images in his poetry. People who were close to Okigbo believe that the poems are all or almost all based on real relations with women. Yet the emotional tone of the poems is often agonized, as if when faced with the physical and emotional reality of sexual love Okigbo found great pain and self-doubt tormented him. Ideals and abstractions are, in that case, a good deal easier. Sunday Anozie has written that Okigbo adored his wife and daughter [*Christopher Okigbo,* 1972]. But that surely is too simple a statement. When the poetry is closely examined, there seems to be running through all of its emotional textures a tension between love and fear, desire to submit to intensities of emotional and physical love and desire to remain separate, adoration of the mother and terror of the sexual partner. Also evidenced is a need to restore the ancient mother-ruled images of traditional religious cults and so rid his culture of colonialism, countered by a need to be an adult male, independent of needs for softness and protection given by a woman. In many ways, Okigbo's twists and turns of desire are those characteristic of man in many if not all cultures, where mother-domination in early childhood creates a fear of woman's power and a desire to dominate women in order to be adult and a man. But there is a vital aspect of his agony which is particular to modern post-colonial African man, and indeed to Igbo man, with his history, it seems, of close and relatively balanced relations with the feminine. That is, while the feminine is closely intertwined with his idea of traditional religion, the male-dominated Christian ethos shaped his public idea of himself as a man in colonial and post-colonial society, and that is antithetical to Igbo tradition. In addition, British culture portrays the male poet as an effeminate man, someone less than fully developed as a masculine figure.

Okigbo's commitment to poetry coincided with his conviction that he was the reincarnation of his maternal grandfather, who was a priest of the goddess Idoto. Thus his ethnic and spiritual identity was bound up in his poetic development. His return to tradition was a return to the 'Mother' Idoto and a rejection of the male god of patriarchial Christianity. The very androgynous quality which often characterises highly developed creative writers is arguably the result of imaginative effort to transcend gender in order to create a full human canvas: Okigbo makes no attempt to depict real woman in his poetry, but instead deals with the mythic and symbolic qualities which she can hold for a male imagination. Yet his poet-protagonist's strivings for self-creation seem to point to a desire for androgyny, a sensuous and emotive union with the 'other'. Chukwuma Azuonye links Okigbo's woman symbols with Jungian psychology, but resists the idea that Okigbo expresses fear of the feminine. However, the masochistic quality noted in the poetry by Sunday Anozie derives its force from the painful dilemma of the sensitive man—whether to submit to sensuous experience and give up control of the woman or to risk the loss of self-possession which must come in surrender to sexual experience. The fear of woman which informs Okigbo's images of the Lioness is an ambivalent one, but nevertheless there is an anxiety within it that the man will be castrated by the act of surrender.

Let us examine the spiritual quest which shapes *Labyrinths.* Critics have discussed Okigbo's use of the Idoto cult and Christianity, and occasionally note has been made of Okigbo's references to ancient Middle Eastern cultures. But there is a major thread of meaning in the poems which relates to Okigbo's knowledge of ancient history and which ties Idoto to the cults of an ancient Egyptian goddess, Isis, who was in her various incarnations Isis, Ishtar, Inanna and finally, much reduced, the Virgin Mary, the most widespread deity in the ancient world. There are in fact three religions intertwined in the poetry: Idoto-worship and traditional Igbo worship of the feminine; Christianity and the worship of Isis-Ishtar.

The very title, *Labyrinths,* is best interpreted through the ancient Cretan culture which Okigbo himself refers to in his preface. The Cretan goddess is of course connected to the legends of the Labyrinth and Nor Hall has explained it well:

> A Minoan statue of the mother goddess from Crete embodies this message in archaic form . . . With a snake in one hand and a tool (her double-edged axe) in the other, the goddess connects the chthonian realm of matter (the Mother) and the upper world of the sky-god, who calculates, measures and perceives . . .

> The axe came to mean many things. It is called *labrys* and is related to *labyrinth,* the underground dwelling of the goddess. In order to pass through the labyrinth it was necessary to make a full 360-degree turn, to turn completely round on oneself to go out the way one came in. In the ancient world this action was meaningful on what we would call a psychological level, as evident in the conjecture that it was the crossing sweeper *Labys* who is credited with the maxim 'know thyself'.

Okigbo links the double-edged axe of Crete with the Aro culture of the Igbo people in his preface, thus connecting the ancient Middle East/North Africa together with his own ethnic traditions. The labyrinth is of course the ancient symbol of the womb, and there is a strong theme of rebirth and initiation in Okigbo's poem cycle. But that initiation takes place in the world of the Mother, opposed to which, in *Labyrinths,* is the measuring, geometric world of Kepkanly, the primary school teacher of the colonial Mission school. Earth and sky, the water goddess and the Christian sky god, are the poles of spiritual existence at the beginning of *Labyrinths.*

Okigbo's poems are obscure, symbolical, full of personal allusions and unexplained references to foreign poets and to political events or Igbo cultural traditions. Nothing is clearer than Okigbo's intention not to be fully understood, even to himself. There has been complaint about this. But perhaps it is best to accept that when a writer is deliberately obscure, out of competence rather than out of failure to be clear, there is good reason. Then, perhaps, the most appropriate way to approach Okigbo's work is as if he was writing the kind of mystical, gnomic verses which characterize ritualistic poetry in African cultures, e.g. in Ifa worship amongst the Yoruba. Okigbo's relation to spiritually tormented poets like T. S. Eliot (who also uses the symbol of a powerful and threatening woman associated with myth in his poetry) has long been recognized. If the complexity of spiritual truths felt and explored by a finely tuned intelligence is added to the complexity of Okigbo's socio-political and historical context, then it is not particularly surprising that his work is difficult.

The relation of the three religions in *Labyrinths* is difficult to disentangle for Okigbo's method of composition is associational and he does not provide explanatory links. But much of the imagery has several layers of meaning which connect religious traditions at a deep symbolic level. For example, the Igbo folktale which tells of a monkey dazzled by the armpit of a lioness until he destroys himself clearly accounts for the image of the 'armpit dazzle of the lioness' in *Labyrinths.* But it is also true that one of the titles of Isis, Queen of Heaven, was Lioness of the Sacred Assembly, and that Sakmet was the lioness-headed goddess of Ancient Egypt who was symbolic of war and pestilence and who annihilated her enemies. Similarly, eggs, which are important in the worship of Igbo water-goddess and which figure largely in the ritually important symbolisms of the poetry, were one of the important symbols of Isis. White light, which surrounds the Watermaid in *Labyrinths* is not only the dazzle of the Lioness, but the moonlight which has always been associated with female deities, including Isis and her various forms. Other clusters of images have this syncretic overtone, including those of water, the sea, corn and associated golden objects (the gold crop, ears of the secret, amber, golden eggs, yellow memories), Nature, snakes and birds. Most of these are strongly associated both with Igbo traditions and with Isis and goddess worship in the ancient world.

It is important to place these connections in the context of Igbo legends that the Igbo people came originally from Egypt. These legends, which are said to explain the celebrated terra-cotta skin of many Igbos as well as their relatively small land area and their migratory tendency to resettle and intermarry with other peoples, as well as their sense of being different from other peoples in Nigeria, might well have been the original impetus behind Okigbo's fascination with ancient history.

In *Labyrinths,* Okigbo interweaves Christianity complexly with Igbo traditions. In the opening cycle of poems, the protagonist submits to Idoto as a 'prodigal' with all the Biblical overtones of that term. He thus points to the conflict within him which is again expressed strongly when he begs his dead, saintly mother, Anna Okigbo, to protect him from "them fucking angels." Anna is a particularly important name itself to carry ambivalences if one remembers . . . that Anna was not only Okigbo's mother's actual name but a major part of Jung's 'anima' term. Yet again, Christianity significantly appears as the colonialist eagles who rape Igbo culture, bringing with them their God who silences the longdrums and causes the forest gods to be forgotten and their shrines abandoned. Yet their violence is in the service of a religion which teaches love (and we know from Achebe the impact of a new faith which could release some Igbos who felt themselves persecuted by Igbo religious principles). Similarly the old cults of Isis could involve the sacrifice of males. So men must have feared the power of women within that context. There is therefore a good deal of violence in *Labyrinths,* much of it linked to female cruelties to men via the dangerous experience of sexual attraction as well as to the Christianizing/colonising experience. Christianity first taught toleration and love, then suppressed women, of course, with increasing ferocity, waging a war on the remnants of pagan cults which often reflected the place of women in the ancient world and which seemed to give them greater power and freedom than Christianity was willing to permit. Instead of a sexually active ideal of women, Christianity created an ideal of virginity/chastity and motherhood and Okigbo's poetry communicates these images together with a great deal of ambivalence toward female beauty (linking it to power and cruelty to men). Sunday Anozie quotes a passage from Robert de Montesquieu which deals with the story of John the Baptist in a way very reminiscent of Okigbo's treatment of male fear of women:

> The secret is none other than that the mystery of her being is to be violated by John, who catches sight of her and pays for this single sacrifice with his life; for this free spirited virgin will only feel pure again, when she is holding the head of an executed man . . .

This passage seems to be to capture Okigbo's spirit of fear in the poems which relate to sexual woman. But, Christianity, after all, suppressed women so much so that such violence against men was virtually impossible to conceive of, and the sexual strictures against women subdued their sexual nature to the service of their god. Celibacy replaced sexuality as the spiritual centre of physical devotion to God.

The relation of sexuality to religion is crucially important in *Labyrinths.* The poet-protagonist develops from his rebirth as Idoto's returned son to a sexual awakening with the Watermaid and afterwards as agonised adult experience with the Lioness, which culminates in his 'homecoming' as the bridegroom of this powerful and destructive female presence, seen paring her fingernails amidst the carnage of dismembered limbs and blood. Even small details in the poetry bring the reader to link violence, sex and religion. In the poem to Awolowo **'Lament of the Drums',** the reference to Celaeno and her harpy crew, the image of the sea as raped and the waters as sultry all conjure up a disturbed female sexuality, which is either threatening or violated and thus hurt. The language of the poetry abounds with images of the fruitfulness of the goddess, of her connection with water, and with powerful and threatening nature, as in **'Distances III'** where she is associated with a molten centre of earth and her labyrinths are connected with violence. The androgynous forest gods are raped. There is a strong castration theme which runs through the poetry, and which links it with the old world of self-castration associated with the cult of Cymbele, a Greek version of Isis, and Attis, who was castrated and who gave rise to the custom of self-castration by priests of Cymbele.

The origins of this connection between sexuality, religion and violence was the necessary death and rebirth of vegetation along the Nile valley as the great river ebbed and flowed. The river was Isis, the vegetation Osiris, who died and was resurrected each year. The legend went that Osiris, Isis' brother-lover was torn to pieces and Isis put his body together again, but his penis was missing. She created him whole and blew life into him and he caused her to conceive her son, the god Horus. Afterwards, the goddess' husbands and lovers were always associated with death and rebirth. But the Babylonian goddess, Ishtar, had as her consort her son, Tammuz, whose death she did not cause but rather mourned. Okigbo includes in *Labyrinths* the lament of Ishtar for Tammuz, which was identified by Dan Izevbaye as a virtual translation of an ancient Sumerian song [*The Critical Evaluation of African Literature,* 1973]. In Biblical times, Hebrew women performed a ritual lament for Tammuz, showing how ancient traditions of goddess worship had permeated even their male-oriented religious culture. It is plain that historically, men gradually resisted the self-surrender and death-rebirth myths associated with the goddess' consort. The myth of Gilgamesh, often described as the first epic, tells how Gilgamesh refuses to become the goddess' lover, saying that Ishtar has hurt too many lovers before. He goes off to become the first patriarchal hero and Enkidu is sacrificed in his stead. Okigbo weaves mention of the Gilgamesh epic into **'Fragments out of the Deluge'.** Christianity was the triumph of male ascendency and also the triumph of a gentle, loving god-figure in Christ himself, yet of course it has been a bloody and oppressive religion to those ground down by colonialism and slavery and forced to accept the god of those who exploited them. Okigbo's sense of conflict in relation to his Mother Idoto and to the powerful goddess images is made very clear by his references to Christian violation of Igbo culture and even by references to the drowning nuns who represent womanhood totally submissive to a god who does not save them.

Fertility, associated of course with creativity and therefore with the poet, is associated with the female deity. In the lament for Tammuz, there is mention of special concern for the loss of various kinds of fruition: 'fields of crops', 'fields of men', children in reference to 'barren wedded ones' and 'perishing children'. The sinister 'potbellied watchers' who despoil 'her' in this poem suggest a male violation of the goddess' plenty. Here Okigbo's sympathy appears to be with a hurt maternal Nature, but he seems to have ambivalence towards the feminine in many other places. When the poet-protagonist finally achieves his 'birthday of earth', there is an overtone still of fear and adoration at the same time for the goddess who has been his inspiration and his mate. It is as if the poet risks his manhood and his existence to achieve his poetic vocation through union with the Lioness. In the sensuous passage of sexual encounter with the Watermaid, the poet is a submissive and loyal subject. Even the sea is 'spent', presumably from loving her. When he washes his feet in the 'maid's pure head' at the end of *Labyrinths,* he is afraid of her variegated teeth. These tensions are characteristic of the poetic journey of the protagonist, in which he becomes, for example, a skeletal oblong, (the oblong is associated with both his mother Anna through the church organ panels, and with the Lioness' head), a shape created by his attraction to the female deity he follows but reduced to a skeleton. For patriarchy depends on potency, on domination of women, in fact, and the poet stands between the matriarchal world of Idoto and the patriarchal colonial one of Christian education and culture: submission to woman risks potency, yet provides fusion with the Igbo traditions which the poet desires, and also promises a delicious and masochistic pleasure of domination by another and release from the responsibility of domination.

The geometric shapes which are a linked series of images in the poems are connected to notions of rigidity and excess, hypocrisy and exploitativeness found in both religious and secular leaders and men of responsibility. The cross itself functions as a complex symbol, and a huge fiery cross links itself with geometric shapes in the poet's mind as he dreams in **'Distances'** IV. Initiation ordeals, including the knife (circumcision and also the old Igbo ritual of cutting the face to prove endurance on the part of the initiate) are linked with the idea of Christian ritual. Kepkanly, who presides over the initiation of the young poet into the Catholic catechism, is the god of the schoolroom, but the world he promises is one where precise thinking and rigid attitudes (symbolised by various geometric shapes) seem to Okigbo to betray the mysteries of the spirit and put pragmatisms, and therefore moral corruptions, to the forefront. The fiery cross of **'Distances'** is reminiscent of the KKK, the racist American organization which more than any other has publicized the Christian involvement with prejudice and hatred, including killing innocent people because of their colour or ethnic identification. The young poet is scarred by Christianity in the way that the old Igbo ritual scarred its initiates to prove courage on their part. In **'Distances'** IV there is a surreal vision of geometric shapes in a cosmic setting, and in V Okigbo links the 'kiss' which is so much associated with Christ to the scar, and to two swords. As in the Isis myths and in Igbo religion, Christianity is a mixture of violence, sexuality and spiritual purity, a dangerous environment for the unwary.

The image of the Mother is crucial to the poems. Idoto is the deity who is symbolic mother to the young poet returning to his culture and to his spiritual base. But also Anna, the poet's earthly mother, whose funeral is the theme of the lovely poem "SILENT FACES at crossroads", in **"The Passage",** becomes associated by the shape of the oblong with the Lioness herself. **'Distances'** V brings together the idea of form as a cosmic and religious frame for the soul with the 'panel oblong', associated with the church organ and the coffin of Anna's burial and the Lioness' head, and the sanctuary at the centre of the earth where Mother Earth will receive her children, where water runs through tunnels (with the obvious suggestion of female sexual secretions), and this looks forward to **'Distances'** VI. There is a constant interweaving of symbols and thus the sexual overtones of the Lioness are interwoven with the maternal aspects of Idoto/Anna. It is interesting that Isis cults, too, had this dualism, where the female deity was both protective and nurturing and destructive and threatening to man. Similarly also Isis worship was finally destroyed (her temples sacked) and her identity subsumed into the Virgin Mary by Christianized Rome in much the same way as Idoto and the forest gods were destroyed by Christian British imperialism and its local Igbo adherents. In **'Fragments Out of the Deluge'** Okigbo makes reference to the Flood, which was associated with the goddess before it was Biblical (she is supposed to have sailed on the waters in a crescent moon boat and her symbols included the dove). Also in this poem, Okigbo mentions the Lioness and in a footnote explains that she had killed the hero's second self, which is a clear reference to the epic of Gilgamesh and a clear identification of the poet with Gilgamesh himself (the sacrificed Enkidu being the second self of Gilgamesh). So there is here a dualism within one poem which is repeated over and over again in *Labyrinths:* the female principle becomes the creative-protective-destructive cosmic centre of the universe.

Fear plays a major role in Okigbo's poetry, whether it is fear of the void or the abyss, fear of woman, fear of becoming or of dying. The fear is caused by the ambivalence which a person such as the poet-protagonist must feel, for his psyche is partly shaped by colonialism and Christianity which he regards as "fireseed", i.e. destructive to him. Of course his attitude to woman must be equally ambivalent, for she is essential to his being as well as on an ongoing threat to his potency and domination. The fear motivates the poetry in creative and constructive ways, for courage, whether creative or physical is not the absence of fear but the capacity to act despite it. *Labyrinths* was a brave thing to do, just as Okigbo's involvement with Biafra was direct and cost him his life. He was never a coward. In his last poems **"Path of Thunder",** he returns to the image of the ram tethered for sacrifice as presenting his own situation in the War, and in a moving and prophetic statement, indicates knowledge of likely death:

> O mother mother Earth, unbind me; let this be
> my last testament; let this be
> The ram's hidden wish to the sword the sword's
> secret player to the scabbard—

Once again, the Mother image becomes instrumental in presenting the realities of the poet's psychic condition: he is victim again, and in need of the protection of "Earth", of becoming once more the 'prodigal', and the hints of parallels with Christ's Passion which are prevalent in **Labyrinths** seem relevant again here. The poet is one of the "stars" which come and go, as poets, prophets and leaders come, do their work and die. Okigbo's presentation of the religious vocation of poet brings him to perceive suffering and even death as a necessary offering of experience which has to be made by those who seek greater understanding and knowledge, and who seek to serve their culture in times of stress. His ambivalence about Christianity does not prevent him from seeing the isolation, self-discipline and suffering of Christ himself as a model for the fate of the poet-prophet in other conditions and times. In the syncretic world of Okigbo's poetry, however, the Christ figure is close to the male sacrificial victims of the old goddess cults, where the death and resurrection of a chosen man meant renewal of crops and life for the community, a necessary triumph for the life principle in defiance of seasonal changes. The effect of the power of the goddess in **Labyrinths** on the poet is like the relation of Isis and Osiris, so that the submission to her cruelty, her deathly aspect and her power is like a voluntary self-sacrifice in the service of greater knowledge and poetic experience. The poet becomes, as it were, the earthly servant of both Idoto and the other female deities who inhabit the poetry, and in this way becomes a kind of Christ-victim figure, serving a lone apprenticeship in preparation for his own Calvary, and being ultimately sacrificed, not, as in **Labyrinths,** in a psychic and sexual sense subsumed into the goddess' power in order to rise again, but in the final sense of his mission being completed, his star leaving the heavens, as a casualty in war.

Okigbo was self-consciously a mystic, fully accepting of the romantic ideal of the poet as seer. His own comment on the composition of his work, although perhaps misleading given the erudite texture of borrowings from European and American poets which characterizes his earlier work, suggests a reconfirmation of the spiritual core of his poetry:

> . . . all I did was to create the drums and the message they deliver has nothing to do with me at all.

It remains true that his work is essentially religious and mystical, but it should be recognised that the centre of that mysticism is the poet's complex relation with a series of female deities and with his own maleness in that context.

FURTHER READING

Bibliography

Anafulu, Joseph C. "Christopher Okigbo, 1932-1967: A Bio-Bibliography." *Research in African Literatures* 9, No. 1 (Spring 1978): 65-78.

  Combines an extensive bibliography of Okigbo's work with a brief biography.

Biography

Lindfors, Bernth. "Okigbo as Jock." In *When the Drumbeat Changes,* edited by Carolyn A. Parker and Stephen H. Arnold, pp. 199-214. Washington, D.C.: African Literature Association and Three Continents Press, 1981.

  An account of Okigbo's school years which focuses on his athletic achievements.

Thomas, Peter. "Ride Me Memories: A Memorial Tribute to Christopher Okigbo (1932-1967)." *African Arts* 1, No. 4 (1968): 68-70.

  Thomas, a close friend of Okigbo, relates anecdotes characterizing the poet as a lively, generous man sometimes subject to the deep sadness he expressed in his poetry.

Criticism

Akporabaro, Fred. "Christopher Okigbo: Emotional Tension, Recurrent Motifs, and Architectonic Sense in *Labyrinths.*" *Nigeria Magazine* 53, No. 2 (April-June 1985): 6-13.

  Highly laudatory examination of the themes and techniques of Okigbo's poetry.

Anozie, Sunday O. "Christopher Okigbo: A Creative Itinerary, 1957-1961." *Présence Africaine,* No. 64 (1967): 158-66.

  Examines the rhetorical and thematic structure in Okigbo's *Poems: Four Canzones.*

———. *Christopher Okigbo: Creative Rhetoric.* Evans Brothers Limited, 1972, 203 p.

  Critical survey of Okigbo's work, including *Poems: Four Canzones,* by the founder of the Okigbo Friendship Society.

Cooke, Michael G. "Christopher Okigbo and Robert Hayden: From Mould to Stars." *World Literature Written in English* 30, No. 2 (Autumn 1990): 131-44.

  Traces "a particular affinity in imagery, outlook, and even experience" between poets Robert Hayden and Okigbo.

Dathorne, O. R. "African Literature IV: Ritual and Ceremony in Okigbo's Poetry." *Journal of Commonwealth Literature,* No. 5 (July 1968): 79-91.

  Describes *Heavensgate* as a work that "shows man in the process of striving towards a god."

———. "Okigbo Understood: A Study of Two Poems." *African Literature Today,* No. 1 (1968): 19-23.

  Briefly examines two untitled poems from different periods in Okigbo's career.

Egudu, Romanus. "Defense of Culture in the Poetry of Christopher Okigbo." *African Literature Today,* No. 6 (1968): 14-25.

  Explores the theme of "literary struggle" in Okigbo's poetry.

———. "Ezra Pound in African Poetry: Christopher Okigbo." *Comparative Literature Studies* VIII, No. 2 (June 1971): 143-54.

  Traces the influence of American poet Ezra Pound on Okigbo's poetry.

Jones, Le Roi. Review of *Heavensgate,* by Christopher Okigbo. *Poetry* 103, No. 6 (March 1964): 400.

  Brief, mixed review of Okigbo's first collection of poetry.

Knipp, Thomas R. "Poetry as Autobiography: Society and Self in Three Modern West African Poets." In *African Litera-

ture in Its Social and Political Dimensions, edited by Eileen Julien, Mildred Mortimer, and Curtis Schade, pp. 41-50. Washington, D.C.: Three Continents Press, 1984.

Argues that Okigbo's poetry reflects the values and common experiences of African culture, thereby making his poetry a type of autobiography.

Leslie, Omolara. "The Poetry of Christopher Okigbo: Its Evolution and Significance." *Studies in Black Literature* 4, No. 2 (Summer 1973): 1-8.

Traces Okigbo's poetic development within the social and political milieu of Nigeria around 1960.

Moore, Gerald. "Vision and Fulfillment." In his *The Chosen Tongue: English Writing in the Tropical World*, pp. 163-76. New York: Harper & Row, 1969.

Briefly places Okigbo in the tradition of modern African literature.

Ngaté, Jonathan. "Senghor and Okigbo: The Way Out of Exile." In *Explorations: Essays in Comparative Literature*, edited by Makota Ueda, pp. 253-77. New York: University Press of America, 1986.

Maintains that Okigbo's frequent use of the theme of "the prodigal son returning to the goddess-mother Idoto" symbolizes the poet's desire to identify himself with African traditions and society and to reject the Christian aspects of his education.

Nwoga, Donatus Ibe, ed. *Critical Perspectives on Christopher Okigbo.* Washington, D.C.: Three Continents Press, 1984, 367 p.

Collection of essays on Okigbo's life and works, including reprints of interviews with Okigbo and bibliographies of major secondary studies.

Okpaku, Joe Ohi. "The Writer in Politics—Christopher Okigbo, Wole Soyinka, and the Nigerian Crisis." *Journal of the New African Literature and the Arts* 4 (Fall 1967): 1-13.

Examines the role of the creative artist in African politics.

Theroux, Paul. "Christopher Okigbo." In *Introduction to Nigerian Literature*, edited by Bruce King, pp. 135-51. Reprint. Lagos, Nigeria: Africana Publishing Corporation, 1972.

Proposes two methods for studying Okigbo's poetry: "one is to look at his poems, the other is to listen to his music."

Arthur M. Schlesinger, Jr.

1917-

(Full name Arthur Meier Schlesinger, Jr.; born Arthur Bancroft Schlesinger) American historian, essayist, biographer, and memoirist.

The following entry provides an overview of Schlesinger's career through 1991.

INTRODUCTION

Schlesinger is a contemporary American historian known for his encyclopedic knowledge of history, his uniquely perceptive and often controversial analyses of events, and his engaging literary style. His ability to trace the social and cultural influences surrounding historical events has made his writings both compelling to the general public and well regarded among critics. Among his many honors, Schlesinger received the Pulitzer Prize for *The Age of Jackson* (1945) in 1946 and *A Thousand Days* (1965) in 1966.

Biographical Information

Born in Columbus, Ohio, in 1917, Schlesinger graduated summa cum laude from Harvard in 1938. After the publication of his critically acclaimed thesis, *Orestes A. Brownson* (1939), and *The Age of Jackson,* Schlesinger, then twenty-eight years old, joined his father as an associate professor in Harvard's history department. A liberal and a Democrat, Schlesinger served as a special assistant to Presidents John F. Kennedy and Lyndon B. Johnson. In 1966 Schlesinger returned to teaching and joined the staff of City University of New York. He has remained active in a variety of political and historical organizations, including the Robert F. Kennedy Memorial, the Society for Historians of American Foreign Relations, and the American Civil Liberties Union.

Major Works

The publication of *The Age of Jackson* in 1945 established Schlesinger as a new and authoritative voice in American history. He not only examined the many social trends that laid the foundation for the Jacksonian era, but also traced their influence on post-Jacksonian history. Schlesinger's advocacy of liberalism and American democratic views was voiced in *The Vital Center* (1949), a collection of essays arguing against communism and promoting American democratic principles. Following the assassination of President Kennedy, however, Schlesinger incited controversy with his intimate memoir of the workings of the Kennedy White House entitled *A Thousand Days*. With the escalation of the Vietnam War and the advent of Richard Nixon's presidency, Schlesinger wrote *The Bitter Heritage* (1967), a critical evaluation of America's Vietnam policy, and *The Imperial Presidency* (1973), which traced

the expansion of presidential power in the twentieth century. In the midst of the Reagan presidency, Schlesinger published *The Cycles of American History* (1986), a collection of essays exploring the cyclical rise and fall of liberal and conservative leadership in America as well as other issues. Schlesinger's recent *The Disuniting of America* (1991) criticizes the current emphasis on minority groups and multiculturalism, which he views as threats to the individual rights and liberties that are the basis of constitutional democracy in the United States.

Critical Reception

Most critics, like George Dangerfield and Richard Rovere, praise Schlesinger's literary style and his ability to condense and interpret widely disparate pieces of information in a meaningful, accessible way. Jeanne Kirkpatrick and other commentators, however, fault Schlesinger's liberal and political bias as obstacles to a balanced presentation of contemporary historical events. While his interests continue to be directed toward contemporary issues, critics nearly unanimously agree that Schlesinger remains tenaciously devoted to liberalism and to the guiding principles of America's constitutional democracy.

PRINCIPAL WORKS

Orestes A. Brownson: A Pilgrim's Progress (nonfiction) 1939

The Age of Jackson (nonfiction) 1945

The Vital Center: The Politics of Freedom (essays) 1949

The General and the President and the Future of American Foreign Policy [with Richard H. Rovere] (nonfiction) 1951

*The Crisis of the Old Order, 1919-1933 (nonfiction) 1957

*The Coming of the New Deal (nonfiction) 1959

Kennedy or Nixon: Does It Make Any Difference? (nonfiction) 1960

*The Politics of Upheaval (nonfiction) 1960

The Politics of Hope (essays) 1963

A Thousand Days: John F. Kennedy in the White House (memoirs) 1965

The Bitter Heritage: Vietnam and American Democracy, 1941-1966 (essays) 1967

The Crisis of Confidence: Ideas, Power, and Violence in America (essays) 1969

The Imperial Presidency (essays) 1973

Robert Kennedy and His Times (biography) 1978

The Cycles of American History (essays) 1986

The Disuniting of America: Reflections on a Multicultural Society (essays) 1991

**These works are collectively referred to as *The Age of Roosevelt*.

CRITICISM

Paul L. O'Connor (review date 17 June 1939)

SOURCE: "The Mystery of a Bronze Head," in *America*, Vol. LXI, No. 10, June 17, 1939, p. 237.

[*In the following review, O'Connor maintains that Schlesinger's* Orestes A. Brownson *is "the history of [America's] intellectual development, the biography of a mind in its lonely search for truth."*]

Two years ago a bronze head, knocked off a pedestal by a group of playful boys and found rolling down Riverside Drive, New York, started zealous reporters searching for someone who knew something about the name "Brownson" on the monument. Only after a hectic day of interviews and research—a sad commentary on American Catholic scholarship—was the search concluded with the knowledge that the original head belonged to Orestes A. Brownson, 1803-1876, philosopher, controversialist and convert to Catholicism. The bronze head brought Brownson back to public attention; Mr. Schlesinger's biography [***Orestes A. Brownson***] will keep him there.

For Brownson's career was as violent, as astonishing, as unpredictable to the people of his day as his rolling like-

ness to Riverside Drive residents. At an early age he renounced Presbyterianism for ordination as a Universalist minister. His unorthodox preaching and rebel theology jarred his congregation. Rejected, he fell into agnosticism, rose to announce himself an independent minister. He dabbled in politics, sifted and discarded Transcendentalism, edited controversial reviews, and attempted to reform Unitarianism. He shocked staid Boston with his avowed purpose of making religion an ally of the laboring classes and with his untiring quest for the Church of the Future, which his logical mind and passionate love of truth led him to find in the Church of the Past and the Church of the Present—the Catholic Church.

This book is not a biography of the man Brownson. It is rather the history of an intellectual development, the biography of a mind in its lonely search for truth. Practically devoid of comment, of easy humor, of charm, it is, as was Brownson himself, swift, eager and rugged. The author prefers to let Brownson speak from his own formal essays, but occasionally the reader catches a fleeting glimpse of the man behind the pen, enthusiastic, worshiping logic and honesty, irascible, puzzled, lonely. In the author's annotated exposition of Brownson's doctrinal viewpoint several minor faults occur. The development is sketchy, and usually only one side of Brownson's many controversies is given. Too much reverence is paid, unwittingly I think, to the epistemological system of Hegel and Marx. But the book not only fills a gap in the history of prominent American Catholics but will go a long way toward accomplishing what the mystery of the bronze head started, making Brownson a part of our national heritage.

Allan Nevins (review date 16 September 1945)

SOURCE: "At the Roots of Democracy," in *The New York Times Book Review*, September 16, 1945, pp. 1, 26.

[*In the following review, Nevins praises Schlesinger's* The Age of Jackson *for its broad scope, but criticizes it for being "excessively hostile" toward the Whig party.*]

When American democracy is most kinetic, when its transitions are most abrupt, and when its ideas take on their most revolutionary hue, then it is best worth studying. The so-called Jacksonian revolution has always made a deep appeal to the American imagination. The tremendous *bouleversement* which dislodged the old ruling class typified by John Quincy Adams and brought to power an untried aggressive set of leaders with a new backing, was mightily dramatic. Jackson's imperious personality was the most ruggedly picturesque that public life had yet known, and his election opened a series of political battles which shook the country. But the chief reason for our interest in the Jacksonian overturn lies deeper than these considerations. It lies in the fact that it brought up from the depths of American life a set of powerful new forces; it revitalized our politics by the impact of profound impulses from below.

Behind such political forces always lie ideas, and it is remarkable that the ideas of the Jacksonian revolution have waited until now for adequate analysis. Those of the Revolution and Constitution-making periods, for example, have long ago been sifted and examined. One reason for the delay is that the rough and tumble of Jacksonian days has tended to obscure the role of ideas. Another is that the energies behind the overturn came from a rough Western population and an inarticulate body of Eastern workingmen, both long supposed to be strong in emotions but weak in reasons.

In due time, however, the whole range of Jacksonian doctrine, and its relationship with antecedent Jeffersonian theories and subsequent Wilsonian and Rooseveltian thought, was certain to receive attention. A long list of recent writers—Parrington, Van Wyck Brooks, Abernethy, Curti, Gilbert H. Barnes, Carl Swisher, Turner, Charles Warren—have dealt with various facets of the thought of the time, and they have proved that it was much more important than old style historians supposed.

The old conventional explanation of Jackson's rise to power was simple. "A mob of malcontents," as John W. Burgess put it, got together, gave a strong pull, and brought the old order toppling in ruins. This mob represented a combination of South and West against the propertied, conservative East; but the group also held control of two Eastern States—New York, where the wily Van Buren had gained power, and Pennsylvania, where Jackson's martial feats had given him immense popularity.

The revolution, according to stock explanations, emphasized frontier "individualism" and Western "egalitarianism." In its inception it was purely political, a revolt against the old monopoly of office holding by the rich, the well-born, and the well-educated.

When the mob filled Washington in 1829 to roar applause of the old hero and romp through the White House, there was little indication that the change would sharply modify economic policies and social structures. The fact that it did, according to the old view, was largely an accident. It resulted from the personal conflicts, Jackson vs. Clay and Biddle, which precipitated the war against the Bank of the United States.

Mr. Schlesinger's service, performed not merely adequately but brilliantly [in his *The Age of Jackson*], is to reinterpret Jacksonian democracy in the light of an immense body of facts which had previously been ignored. Examining the politics of the era not in terms of "party battles" but of animating ideas, he makes the period far more richly instructive. The whole force of the Jacksonian movement takes a new orientation. Mr. Schlesinger argues that it stemmed more largely from the Eastern working man than the Western settler; that it was more intimately connected with the Industrial Revolution than with the transAppalachian frontier. Jackson, as he puts it, struck fire with the working classes because he seemed to them the embodiment of political democracy. There was plenty of radicalism in the West, but it was the spasmodic and opportunistic radicalism of an unstable society, where men might enjoy prosperity one year and wilt under hard times the next. The discontented Eastern workers, however, developed a stable and permanently fruitful body of radical doctrine.

The West, according to this interpretation, furnished the old hero, Jackson himself, a man of far broader vision, acuter judgment, and better education than the Whig historians had ever dreamed of. It furnished some subordinate leaders of importance: Thomas Hart Benton of Missouri, Polk of Tennessee, Robert Dale Owen of Indiana and Benjamin Tappan of Ohio. It and the South furnished the great initial agitation in a revolt against the "Tariff of Abominations," against monetary stringency, and against Eastern snobbery and privilege; but when the time came to transmute agitation into a reform program, asserts Mr. Schlesinger, Eastern leaders and ideas rose to control. It was in the East alone, among the embittered working men who, toiling for a few shillings a day, saw their union movement snuffed out by employers, courts and police while corporate wealth grew arrogant, that the spirit of revolt had perdurable power. The East "had the consistent and harsh experience which alone could serve as a crucible of radicalism."

As the Jacksonian program developed, Mr. Schlesinger admits, it actually tended to estrange the old hero's original supporters. Jackson's opposition to the use of Federal money for local improvements, written into his Maysville Road veto, displeased Michigan and Illinois, where Democrats no less than Whigs liked to spend national money on roads and canals. Jackson's ultimate financial policy was equally repugnant to the West, and was accepted there only because its real intent was well cloaked. The West wanted paper money, and plenty of it; as a debtor area it liked inflation. Jackson's advisers wanted hard money, and his "old bullion's" war on the bank culminated in deflationary measures. But the Eastern workers and shopkeepers, hating corporate monopoly, demanding the right to organize, and wishing the Government to vindicate its powers as against business and banking, were satisfied with the trend of the Jacksonian Administration. The new spirit, with its emphasis on the rights of the masses, and the practical reforms, with the crushing of the Bank and promotion of general incorporation laws, delighted the toiling millions. Such spokesmen as the fiery William Leggett and the class-conscious George H. Evans geared the Jacksonian movement to a new social conscience. And Jacksonianism in the East shot up as a vital force in politics, political theory and literature. Mr. Schlesinger's most interesting section treats the movement in relation to intellectual trends, religion, the law and letters. In polemics it produced a striking figure in William M. Gouge, Philadelphia editor and economist, who wrote the classic indictment of paper currency, formulated a set of hard-money theories, applied them to the new finance capitalism, and devised means to give them practical effect. In political theory the movement brought forth a galaxy of controversialists—Orestes Brownson, C. C. Cambreleng, Theodore Sedgwick Jr. and Thomas Brothers—who sharply revised the old Jeffersonian gospel. They wrote of the economic element in government where Jefferson had written of political equality; they dilated upon the worker's needs and the control of industrialism instead of the virtues of rural independence. In law, Roger Taney and David Dudley Field shook out the banner of reform and codification.

Most striking of all was the way in which the Jacksonian crusade, thus oriented toward the new economic problems, the town worker and a novel concept of governmental control, captured a broad segment of literature. It flowered out into new magazines, notably the *Democratic Review* and *Boston Quarterly*. It found a brave voice in Fenimore Cooper, hater of Whig editors and the commercial oligarchy, until he became worried lest the radicals go too far. It gave fire to the editorials of William Cullen Bryant and Walt Whitman, and sang in their verse.

Emerson refused to commit himself between Democracy and Whiggism, thinking the former had the best principles and the latter the best men; so did Thoreau. But Hawthorne had more nerve and decision. Most notable of all in some ways was the work of George Bancroft. Most critics have been content to quote J. Franklin Jameson's remark that Bancroft's *History* voted for Jackson and let it go at that, supposing that he offered some rhetorical generalities about democracy and the common man. But Bancroft, as Mr. Nye's recent life showed, and as Mr. Schlesinger points out, had a true philosophy, and several of his chapters embodied no little profundity of thought on modern democratic trends.

All in all, [*The Age of Jackson*] is a book which gives the Jacksonian movement new meaning. Treating it primarily as the outgrowth, not of frontier development but of new economic strains and torsions, and describing it as pivoted upon the relations between the state and the business corporation, it links the Jacksonian doctrine with ideas of our own day. Before Jackson's aides and successors could codify their philosophy of state interference with economic life in the interests of the common man, the slavery struggle supervened and national attention was riveted on the sectional clash.

But in due time the Wilsonian and Rooseveltian democracy, intent upon the general welfare, suspicious of corporate power, and hostile to Jefferson's doctrine of the weak state, revived the philosophy of Jacksonian radicals. That philosophy, Mr. Schlesinger believes, holds high promise for the future. It is not a philosophy of regimentation, but it holds that no one group or class shall dominate the Government in such a fashion as to sacrifice liberty to its own interests. It holds that there is a perpetual tension in society, a doubtful equilibrium which breeds problems that demand constant vigilance and effort.

Crisply written, full of pungent comment and quotation, and abounding in vivid thumbnail sketches of important figures, Mr. Schlesinger's book possesses unflagging interest. Parts of it will excite dissent. It perhaps overemphasizes the East as against the West; equal attention to Western utterances and opinions would furnish a different view. It is excessively hostile to Whig leaders and Whig ideas, the caustic treatment of Daniel Webster and Horace Greeley seeming especially unfair. It sometimes rides its thesis a bit too hard. But it is a remarkable piece of analytical history, full of vitality, rich in insights and new facts, and casting a broad shaft of illumination over one of the most interesting periods of our national life.

Sydney E. Ahlstrom   (review date Spring 1950)

SOURCE: "Mr. Schlesinger's *Vital Center*," in *Religion in Life*, Vol. XIX, No. 2, Spring, 1950, pp. 205-12.

[*In the review below, Ahlstrom contends that the liberal, democratic outlook defined in Schlesinger's* The Vital Center *is based on a relativistic ethic that denies the fundamental tenets of the democratic system it advocates.*]

One of the minor tragedies of the present time is that most descriptions of our crisis have become clichés. It was, therefore, very fortunate that Professor Arthur M. Schlesinger, Jr., should have written a terse volume on the "politics of freedom." *The Vital Center* is a statement of "mid-twentieth-century liberalism," an outlook that has been shaped by "the hope of the New Deal, the exposure of the Soviet Union, and by the deepening of our knowledge of man." More explicitly it is a study of the circumstances that now demand a center position between the business-oriented politics of Calvin Coolidge and the politics of the total planner. Of central importance for this program is Mr. Schlesinger's desire to maximize freedom within the limitations of the social needs of an industrial age and to improve the general welfare to the extent that freedom is not endangered. All of these considerations of public policy, however, he relates directly to the concept of Western man adrift in an "age of anxiety." Accordingly, the irrationality and depravity of man, which have been traditional justifications for authoritarianism, are here used to strengthen the case for democracy. It is also in this context of despair, impersonality, and conflict that he outlines the past attempts of the Right and the Left to cope with the problems which industrialism and urbanism have created.

Conservatives have failed, by his analysis, because they have too often heeded the counsels of the business mind and yielded to the acquisitive instincts of the "plutocracy." They have not displayed the concern for the public weal that has characterized leaders of the "aristocratic" tradition from Alexander Hamilton to Theodore Roosevelt. Moreover, following Joseph A. Schumpeter's thesis, he sees capitalism itself to be bringing about its own undoing. The failure of the Left, the nature of totalitarianism, and particularly the "case of Russia" are given more extended analysis. For these purposes Mr. Schlesinger abandons the traditional device of polarizing Right and Left on a linear scale, and uses instead the diagram of a full circle in terms of which divergences that begin as conservative versus liberal or radical versus reactionary finally meet, as Communist *and* Fascist, 180 degrees around from the "vital center" on a common ground of violence and terror. Mr. Schlesinger takes no chances that the absolute tragedy of totalitarianism will be underestimated, nor does he have any doubts about the impossibility of co-operating with Communists or fellow-traveling progressives whom he terms Doughfaces—"democratic men with totalitarian principles."

Affirming the value of freedom, welcoming the aid of conservatives more than doughfaces (because they value freedom more), and recognizing the well-nigh insuperable problems that confront sinful and erring man, the book is a summons to liberal action, not a blueprint for Utopia.

In foreign policy, Mr. Schlesinger asks for active support of the non-Communist Left wherever it is found and world-wide action in behalf of freedom. Domestically, he emphasizes the responsibilities of government for maintaining freedom, extending its social services, and restoring the sense of community. Although the details and institutional aspects of these proposals could hardly be charted in so brief a compass, the book is a comprehensive and compelling formulation for radical democratic men with libertarian principles.

. . . . .

This essay, however, is not concerned with the program of action which the book outlines, but rather with its theoretical and presuppositional structure. Although Mr. Schlesinger has stated in his Foreword that "novel or startling political doctrines" have not been set forth, he does present a very considerable theoretical foundation for his program. These aspects are especially important because the book has been very widely read and because it is a "report on the fundamental enterprise of re-examination and self-criticism" which virtually a whole generation of liberals has undergone in the last decade. It is, therefore, an important case study. Despite the wide acceptance of the outlook presented in this volume, it is my conviction that a long-term basis for hope has not been presented; and that the church must not only concern itself with this liberal analysis in general, but conduct the re-examination and reaffirmation of doctrine that will give substance and vitality to such a program and to our collective hopes.

The *Leitmotiv* of this book is moral crisis and the flight from freedom of modern man. Its basic demand is for recharging the moral resources of man. This is in itself a departure from the cant of most American liberalism, and appearing thus in what is *primarily* a discussion of public policy, it actually confers on the book a certain pioneering status. Nor has Mr. Schlesinger stopped with the mere announcement of a moral problem.

In diagnosing our ills, he has presented an interpretation of the human predicament which has in it much that is Pauline, although it has been phrased in the terminology of psycho-socio-economic theory. The message is an old one, a hard one, and a tough one. With a certain Calvinistic fervor it exposes the great liberal fallacy about the nature of man. Though often couched in terms of frustration, it says with the Apostle:

> Now then it is no more I that do it, but sin that dwelleth in me.
>
> For I know that in me (that is, in my flesh,) dwelleth no good thing: for its will is present with me; but how to perform that which is good I find not.
>
> For the good that I would I do not: but the evil which I would not, that I do. (Romans 7:17-19)

This approach constitutes a fundamental revision of the ideas of man's benign goodness and his inexorable progress to a kingdom of heaven on earth.

Again, in finding the basis for man's anxiety in the social complexities that leave man homeless and rootless, without sense of communion or brotherhood, Mr. Schlesinger suggests a New Testament theme. To be sure, there is no citation of Holy Writ and he is not trying to bolster dogmas relating to the Mystical Body of Christ; but as one reads in page after page of the lonely, torn, unintegrated mass-man that industrial society has created, one sees a new richness in the words of St. Paul:

> . . . . God hath tempered the body together, ... that there should be no schism in the body; but that the members should have the same care one for another. And whether one member suffer, all the members suffer with it; or one member be honoured, all the members rejoice with it. (I Cor. 12:24-26)

None of my remarks which follow could detract from the value of this insight.

As will soon be made clear, however, Mr. Schlesinger has not written a biblical interpretation of our predicament. Nor has he allowed the profoundest spirit of the Hellenic tradition to inform his basic conceptions. The resulting philosophical orientation, therefore, seems inadequate to the needs imposed by present-day pressures. It is entirely possible, nonetheless, that a few of the following criticisms would be unnecessary if Mr. Schlesinger had depended less on a psycho-sociological notational system, and if it had been possible for him to amplify some of the theoretical problems and to define more adequately certain concepts. With these reservations in mind, and from a point of view which is essentially evangelical, though eschewing the anticlassicism and antirationalism of much modern orthodox thought, a more detailed explication of what seem to be the shortcomings of Mr. Schlesinger's analysis can be considered.

The reader is not left long to doubt that the basis of the politics of freedom is essentially relativistic. Liberalism, we are told, must not be disdainful of the "pragmatic compromise"; there is the familiar insistence on the overarching importance of "results" as the final test of the validity of our ideas; and we are not spared the deprecation of logic common to emergent philosophies from Emerson to James. Mr. Schlesinger also commits himself to a social interpretation of history. "The state and the factory are inexorable"; James Madison's statement of the economic interpretation of history (before Marx was born) is applauded as "magistral"; and Joseph de Maistre and Edmund Burke are praised not so much for the articles of their faiths as for their insights into the function of social myths—Paretos before their time, as it were. We hear of the "manic-depressive cycle" of American business, the "capitalist death-wish," and the "compulsive mass escape from freedom [of industrial man] into the deep, womb-dark sea." We are bidden, finally, to have hope that "cultural pluralism" and "spontaneous group activity" will satisfy "those irrational sentiments once mobilized by religion" and, thus supplying "outlets for the variegated emotions of man, ... restore meaning to democratic life."

This is a capitulation to that very approach which Mr. Schlesinger criticized in such strong terms while reviewing a recent study of the psychology of the American soldier. The review filed a protest against the methods, language, and pretensions of the "Social Sciences." It may be suggested, however, that were his animadversions taken literally, a very considerable portion of this book would suffer the maledictions its author himself pronounced. One can readily agree with him about the importance of "American study of village sociology" in problems of world reconstruction; but in the present theoretical framework the democratic idea of freedom is seriously vitiated and individual dignity in either the classical or the Judeo-Christian sense tends to lose its meaning. These matters must, therefore, be considered briefly.

Although not as a direct result of this social interpretation of man, the ideal of freedom tends to become a muscular rather than a rational concept. Democracy in the Western tradition has always been linked inseparably with the idea of free man reasoning. The emphasis is now changed. Democracy becomes not a reasoning faith but "a fighting faith." We are given frequent citations to the effect that praiseworthy aristocrats have not failed to love the sword whereas plutocrats have preferred "tranquillity." Without questioning for one moment the need to defend our heritage, one can wonder how this view differs from the somewhat less than profound message of Carl Sandburg's recent novel (which, for that matter, reiterates much of Walt Whitman's demand for "a large and resolute breed of men"): have faith in continuity and struggle—so it has been and ever shall be. The problem of freedom, however, is related more directly to the idea of individual dignity; and here Mr. Schlesinger's social interpretation is revealed again. The "essential strength of democracy," he admits, lies in its "startling insight into the value of the individual"; but in the same paragraph he asserts that "individualism derives freely from the community," Freedom, too, it is said, "has acquired its dynamism from communion in action."

Yet there is another dimension in which **The Vital Center** must be evaluated, because it has been supplemented by the author's appreciation for the philosophical temper that can be traced from Pascal, Dostoievsky, and Kierkegaard to Sartre and Niebuhr. All of these men have made the predicament of the individual a crucial fact and each of them, judging by frequent citations and references, has informed Mr. Schlesinger's present conclusions. We must "strengthen the human will," he says, following Albert Camus. "The reform of institutions can never be a substitute for the reform of man." "The death pallor" will come over free society "unless it can recharge the deepest sources of its moral energy." This insight, however, is insufficient in itself. In fact, study of the combined effect of these views of freedom, the individual, and our ethical problem reveals the deepest tragedy of Mr. Schlesinger's analysis.

This tragedy lies in the fact that the value of his trenchant statement of our crisis is doubly canceled by the contradictions brought on by his sociologism. On the page after his affirmation of the anterior need for the "reform of man" he asserts that "the hope for free society lies. . . . in the kind of men *it creates.*" (Italics mine.) Furthermore, the goal is shifted: it is not moral man but "emotional and psychological stability" that is wanted. Man is *"instinctively*

anti-totalitarian." (Italics mine.) What he lacks is "profounder emotional resources" and effective group activity.

Now nobody would dismiss the anxiety and loneliness of modern, industrial man or deny that he would be happier if he were less lonely. He is often made happier even now by joining the Rotarians. He would be happier still if by some miracle the medieval village (or even the nineteenth-century American town!) could be made a much more significant factor in the total social pattern. To the extent that practical corrective measures are possible they should be undertaken. But these considerations are *in the strictest sense of the word peripheral.*

In the first place, this idealization of "rich emotional life," whether in context or out, seems deficient in explicitness, and insofar as it is a poetic summons to a stronger *Volksgeist* it is actually dangerous. But more important, it overlooks the central issue. Human dignity is our real concern and this rests on other things than the pragmatic value of an erect, intelligent animal. The insights of our "classical and religious past" must be consulted. Yet, except for occasional references, Mr. Schlesinger seems to place more confidence in social psychoanalysis. This resort is not entirely successful, for it is never made clear why the totalitarian methods of providing "emotional resources" are *categorically* wrong. Stalin has appealed to those "irrational sentiments once mobilized by religion," promising a way, a truth, and a life, complete with *parousia* and paradise. He has integrated his converts socially: cells, collective farms, and a nationalistic mission. There seems to be no shortage of "group activity." Nor is there a love of tranquillity! And the conclusion drawn is that ultimately this abolition of freedom is wrong only because it will not work. Due to the nature of Mr. Schlesinger's philosophy of the individual, the crucial weapon is lacking.

What *are* the "spontaneous sources of community," the "springs of social brotherhood" which we must tap again? If there is something in man which unfreedom thwarts even if it could remove his anxiety, we must define it. Moreover, a moral crisis is a demand for ethics—not just a choice between "conflict and stagnation." We must turn reason to the task of erecting a logical framework of principle. Neither man, the will of man, nor society is going to be made moral by minimizing the frustrations brought on by urbanism! This merely suggests a new optimistic fallacy. There is more than a simple faith in progress that needs to be revised. There will be no "rededication to concrete democratic ends," no "revival of the *élan* of democracy," no "resurgence of the democratic faith" until man, rational man, defines the ends of democracy in terms that do justice to his rationality and to his dignity. We must not think that illogical reasoning is going to "get results." Using every concept and technique that the sciences can give us, we must try to transcend ourselves and our culture in search of what Plato called the "outline of virtue." This means that we must direct our intellectual energies to defining what Mr. Schlesinger calls "the values which distinguish free society from totalitarianism." A check-list of political freedoms is insufficient. It is also essential that we do not blur our responsibilities by suggesting, as he does, that "the advocate of free society defines himself by telling what he is against." We cannot let it be said of us as Henry Adams said of another generation of liberals: they considered the intellectual difficulties in their path to be unessential because they were insuperable.

. . . . .

No one can deny Mr. Schlesinger's insistence that these are times requiring bravery. But one is reminded of Cicero's advice to his son: "It is impossible for the man to be brave who pronounces pain to be the greatest evil, or temperate who proposes pleasure as the highest good"[*Moral Duties of Mankind,* Book I]. We cannot scorn the rationalists or deprecate reason: there is too much glory in the "elevated and unsubdued mind." This liberating force of Hellenism the modern liberal needs in his search for principle and for his proper estimate of man.

Yet there is another response to the need for bravery, and the admonition of St. Paul imposes itself: "Wherefore take unto you the whole armor of God, that ye may be able to withstand in the evil day, and having done all, to stand." (Eph. 6:13.) It is true that Mr. Schlesinger, in his critique of Encyclopedist or Social Darwinist optimism, has sounded a Pauline note. But he has not emphasized the paradox of man's predicament and his anxiety *regardless* of social adjustment. Nevertheless his exposition points to the fact, and understanding the fact we can resort to the wisdom of our heritage.

An excerpt from *The Vital Center*

[World] government, in a sense, cannot emerge too soon; for the people of the world cannot long afford to expend their energies in squabbling with each other. The human race may shortly be confronted by an entirely new range of problems—problems of naked subsistence whose solution will require the combined efforts of all people if the race is to survive. We have raped the earth too long, and we are paying the price today in the decline of fertility. Industrial society has disturbed the balance of nature, and no one can estimate the consequences. "Mankind," writes William Vogt, "has backed itself into an ecological trap." Vogt, Fairfield Osborn, and Sir John Boyd Orr have described some of the dilemmas awaiting us as the world population presses hard upon our vanishing agricultural and mineral resources. The results of industrialization and introduction of public health standards in Asia, for example, may well be calamitous, unless they are accompanied by vigorous birth-control policies and by expanded programs of land care and conservation.

In the light of this epic struggle to restore man to his foundations in nature, the political conflicts which obsess us today seem puny and flickering. Unless we are soon able to make the world safe for democracy, we may commit ourselves too late to the great and final struggle to make the world safe for humanity.

Arthur M. Schlesinger, in his The Vital Center, originally published in 1949, reprinted in 1962 by The Riverside Press.

Jacques Maritain has written that "democracy needs. . . . evangelical ferment in order to be realized and in order to endure" [*Christianity and Democracy*]. This implies a faith in man—to use our best metaphor—as created in the image of God. It implies that sin involves more than Aristotle's Punch-and-Judy show between reason and the appetites. It implies that the dignity of man is, in the last analysis, a spiritual truth. "We are endowed by our Creator with certain inalienable rights." They are really rights: no man and no government can legitimately take them away. Democracy, as Bergson said, is evangelical. Without the inspiration of Christianity, it is just another formula—a reasonable formula, but ultimately caught in a paradox that only faith can resolve.

This, it seems to me, is the real sermon of our times, and modern political thought must be invested with its meaning. If the center holds, it will not be because men grounded their hopes in ephemeral psychic satisfactions, but because they searched for and found principle in the universe. If we fail—and we may fail—we must face the judgment of Hosea: "for the Lord hath a controversy with the inhabitants of the land, because there is no truth, nor mercy, nor knowledge of God in the land. . . . . Therefore shall the land mourn, and everyone that dwelleth therein shall languish." (Hosea 4:1-3.)

C. Vann Woodward   (review date 2 March 1957)

SOURCE: "*The Crisis of the Old Order,*" in *The Saturday Review,* New York, Vol. XL, No. 9, March 2, 1957, pp. 11-12.

[*Woodward is an American historian, editor, and professor emeritus who has written extensively on the American South. He is the author of several books on American history, including* The Strange Career of Jim Crow *(1955) and* The Burden of Southern History *(1960). His* Origins of the New South *(1951) won the Bancroft Prize for American History in 1952 and Mary Chestnut's* Civil War *(1981), which Woodward edited, was awarded a Pulitzer Prize in 1982. In the following review of Schlesinger's* The Crisis of the Old Order, *Woodward offers a favorable assessment of the book's treatment of fifty years of political and social trends that culminated in the 1933 election of Franklin Delano Roosevelt to the presidency of the United States.*]

"This is, I suppose, a bad time to be writing about Franklin Roosevelt," says Arthur M. Schlesinger, Jr., in an apologetic foreword to his *The Crisis of the Old Order.*

Nonsense! As a matter of fact the Harvard history department, of which Mr. Schlesinger is a member, has for several years devoted a large part of its man-hours to the production of books on FDR and the military and political aspects of his period. Such industry could only have been based on the theory that this is a most excellent time to be writing about Franklin Roosevelt.

Weighing advantages against disadvantages, and using the book under review as a test case, one can find much to justify the theory. The obvious disadvantage is, of course, want of perspective. The compensating advantage is the opportunity for the exploitation of living memory. Assuming all the considerable risks involved in the foreshortened perspective, and by no means avoiding all the pitfalls, Mr. Schlesinger has made brilliant use of the compensatory advantages. The result of his daring gamble is a permanent enrichment of our historical literature.

Actually, most of the present volume is not about Roosevelt at all, but about the early years of a rather specially defined "Age of Roosevelt"—which turns out to be even longer than the "age" it seemed to the Roosevelt-haters. According to the author it embraced "half a century of American life." In this long volume he only gets down to the first inauguration in 1933. He goes back to the Populists for a bow to the founding fathers, then in turn pays his respects to contributions by the muckrakers, reformers, and progressives at the start of the century, as well as the accomplishments of the Republican Roosevelt and of Woodrow Wilson. Only with the end of the First World War, however, does he dig in for more than an impressionistic survey, and only with the crash of 1929 does he become systematic and detailed.

The special quality that gives Mr. Schlesinger's history the fillip of an intellectual cocktail is his use of analogy, a rather sinful indulgence in the eyes of orthodox historians. It was his bold assertion of the freedom to analogize that distinguished his *Age of Jackson,* in which there was an implied analogy between the 1830s and the 1930s. His analogies are not obvious and explicit, but subtle and implicit. The present work on Roosevelt is not so heavily seasoned with analogy as was the earlier one on Jackson, but there is enough to lend it a distinctive flavor. When he writes about the disillusionment over a lost peace that followed the First World War, about the effect of war upon reformers and their ideals, about the spread of anti-intellectualism, the excesses of the Red scare and the witch hunters, and the alienation of the intellectuals, he does not need to spell out the implications for the analogous phenomena of a later postwar era. "The old Wilsonians watched the New Era in indignation and contempt," he observes. And the alert reader can see the lips of the old New Dealers curl with scorn over subsequent goings on.

Another special quality of this gifted historian is his talent for perceiving and capturing the interplay between ideas and action, between abstract theory and concrete event, between thought and politics. We are shown how the imagination of a generation was fired by idealism, then chilled by disillusionment, anesthetized by cynicism, and finally all but alienated from the native heritage of freedom and drawn toward an alien creed. The account of the defection of artists, writers, and intellectuals in the early Thirties is especially perceptive. Shrewd also is the author's identification of certain influences in this process, particularly that of Lincoln Steffens's *Autobiography,* John Chamberlain's *Farewell to Reform,* and John Strachey's *The Coming Struggle for Power.*

For a historian whose primary interest is analytical and interpretative, Mr. Schlesinger shows no little ingenuity in evoking the mood and drama of time and place. A period that ranges between such extremes of hope and despair, luxury and bankruptcy, optimism and pessimism as the period between 1919 and 1933 offers plenty of scope for

such ingenuity. The author is convincing in his portrayal of the gross complacency and Philistinism of the Harding and Coolidge era. But he is downright moving in his picture of the depths of depression: of Pennsylvania miners "freezing in rickety one-room houses, subsisting on wild weed-roots and dandelions, struggling for life in black and blasted valleys"; or of Kentuckians who "ate violet tops, wild onions, and the weeds which cows would eat (one wrote, 'as cows won't eat a poison weeds'), while wan children attended school without coats, shoes, or underclothes"; or of the thousands of "wild boys" who wandered the country. "I don't want to steal," a Pennsylvania man wrote Governor Pinchot, "but I won't let my wife and boy cry for something to eat. . . . How long is this going to keep up? I can't stand it any longer. . . . O, if God would only open a way."

The only questionable allocation of space in the book would seem to be the hundred pages devoted to a brief biography of Franklin Roosevelt down to 1933. This is skillfully enough done but interrupts the narrative unduly without contributing anything very new about the subject. A real contribution does appear, however, in a penetrating analysis of the FDR behind the public mask of grin and gusto and exuberant optimism. Even intimate friends rarely glimpsed the enigmatic and complex hidden man, an inscrutable combination of craftiness, hardness, and private sadness, "a man without illusions." A thesis is advanced about this man and his times. It is that the traditions of liberal reform were continuous from Populism to the New Deal, and that the antithetical elements of that tradition—agrarian and urban, Bryan and T.R., trust-busting and government regulation, New Freedom and New Nationalism—all found expression and apparent reconciliation in Franklin Roosevelt. It is too early to criticize the thesis, for it remains to be established in later volumes.

This is a long running start for a big jump: from 1933 to 1945. The publisher predicts it will be accomplished in three more volumes. It looks like more than that to me. At any rate, this book clearly launches one of the important historical enterprises of our time.

George Dangerfield   (review date 31 January 1959)

SOURCE: "The Promise of the Blue Eagle," in *The Nation,* New York, Vol. 188, No. 5, January 31, 1959, pp. 100-02.

[*Dangerfield is the author of the Pulitzer Prize-winning study* The Era of Good Feelings *(1953). In the following review, Dangerfield contends that the in-depth analysis of politics and economics in Schlesinger's* The Coming of the New Deal *is complemented by a "detailed exposition of theory and philosophy being put to work during a highly critical period" of the Roosevelt presidency.*]

The exhilarating arrival of the New Deal; its introduction to the public at large of so many able, energetic, controversial, eccentric and brilliant figures; its vitality; the dramatic, visible, audible gallantry of the President himself—all of these are here [in *The Coming of the New Deal*], as might be expected. Schlesinger's previous books assure the reader in advance that the personalities behind those names once so familiar—Roosevelt, Wallace, Ickes, Johnson, Tugwell, Hopkins, Richberg, Perkins, Morgenthau, Douglas and all—will be brilliantly presented. The author is a master of historical characterization, which is, to be sure, the easiest kind of writing if one has a flair for it; he is also good at narrative, at compressing dense and resisting material into a formal and intelligible sequence, and that is by no means so easy.

Readability is important, literary skill is valuable; but history has been known to get along without either. What matters, obviously and finally, is the author's interpretation of the New Deal as a transforming force. The present volume deals chiefly with the years 1933 and 1934, when the New Deal was in its first phase, still searching in all directions for possible solutions, not yet in open conflict with the Court. Here a reviewer is in some difficulty: this is a work in progress, and in his final evaluation the author may well modify his conclusions on any phase of the Age of Roosevelt in terms of its relation to the period as a whole. So far Schlesinger appears to take the conventional view that the New Deal at this stage should be judged as much by its promises as by its performances; and that the more questionable of its performances—the National Recovery Administration is the most obvious of them—are to be examined by the light of the promises contained in them. I see no reason to cavil at this view: to be conventional in these days sometimes requires a strong mind.

But what were the promises? Here one is obliged to do a little guessing. *The Coming of the New Deal* implies that the New Deal did not at any time hold out the promise of a radical reorganization. It might have done so. In all our history, no reforming party had hitherto come to power at a time of economic collapse. But the legislation exacted from an obedient Congress during the Hundred Days, though profuse and exciting, could all be traced back to precedents in American history. What was breathtaking was the speed and the scope of the performance. Three followed a long search for the restoration of Demand—of consumers' purchasing power—and this gave the opposition time to shake itself back into what might be called respectable shape.

Sackcloth is not a robe banking and business wear with pleasure, still less with distinction; and the season of repentance was brief. Once it was over, the old ritualistic cries, the mating calls of sterile ideas, were heard again: back to the gold standard—a balanced budget—economy in government—hands off business. It was not here, however, that the really dangerous criticism lay. The really dangerous criticism was directed toward the relief aspects of the emerging program. At its most strident, this criticism sounds absurd today; it did not sound absurd then: such is the abyss which the New Deal has dug between the present and the immediate past.

> When someone asked him about homeless boys riding the rails in search of employment, Henry Ford said equably, "Why, it's the best education in the world for those boys, that traveling around. They get more experience in a few months than they would in years at school." Even a liberal businessman like Robert E. Woods of Sears, Roebuck could identify relief as

the New Deal's "one serious mistake." "While it is probably true that we cannot allow everyone to starve (although I personally disagree with this philosophy of the city social worker)," Wood wrote, "we should tighten up relief all along the line. . . ."

The old equation between starvation and genius, or that infinite capacity for taking pains which was sometimes held to have something to do with genius, was handily transferred to the economic scene and easily related to national character. For the federal government to save people from starvation and intolerable anxiety was to destroy initiative, and so on and so forth. One need not trouble oneself with these primitive cries, uttered by comic millionaires who went to the Translux to hiss Roosevelt. Submarginal living might produce an Andrew Carnegie or a Jack Dempsey; the whole experience of America said that it had never, for example, produced a good farmer. What is significant is that this kind of thinking was not confined to primitive minds; men like Hopkins were troubled by it; the President was too. What is important is that these men never succumbed to their uneasiness.

Indeed, the later criticism that Roosevelt was an "enemy to his class" was only superficially (if savagely) concerned with banking reform or civilizing the Stock Exchange or soaking the rich: it was always directed toward the objectives for which the rich were being soaked. The rich, in any case, were not Roosevelt's class, though he had lived with them all his life and had little respect and certainly no veneration for them: he belonged to the Hudson River squirearchy. Far back in the past of this squirearchy there was a tradition of scientific farming and quasi-feudal landowning; so that Roosevelt's soil conservation program, in the history of which he was deeply read, did not spring only from the example of his cousin T. R.; it was quite in the tradition of the Hudson River squires. What was not in this tradition was his concern for the people who lived on the soil. And this concern, which proclaimed him a traitor to his class and which was odious to the rich who were not of his class, did not come so easily as regards the urban unemployed, whose lives could not be touched by the rehabilitation of TVA. It is of the first importance, in contemplating the changes which took place within the first New Deal, to consider that, in 1933 and 1934, it may have been difficult even for men of good will to rid themselves of the notion that there was something debilitation, something anti-historical (i.e., anti-American) about the welfare state.

Ultimately, when all the debates had taken place between men of conflicting philosophies inside and outside the Administration, it was the President who decided what should be the nature and speed of the New Deal. Schlesinger here takes the administrative view and, with all the limitations which such a view implies, it is the correct one: what greater, unadmitted and unrecognized pressures dictated the President's decisions we are unlikely ever to know. His direction of events is naturally best observed in the field of foreign relations, where Presidents traditionally have a free hand; and here the story of the London Economic Conference of 1933 is full of interest.

Schlesinger admits that Roosevelt's handling of this conference was "deplorable"; but, to simplify an argument which he refrains from making very complex, he sees the issues involved in these terms. On the one hand, there were the gold countries, intent upon stabilizing the exchanges and restoring the gold standard; on the other hand, there was Roosevelt's determination that nothing should hinder America's drive for recovery. At the same time the author says, rather casually, that Roosevelt did think about the possible synchronization of world spending, with a view to raising world prices. In this way, he could be said to have favored a policy of international cooperation: one could discover, lurking in the recesses of his being, a personage who resembled a Wilsonian internationalist.

The conference was, no doubt, doomed from the start: yet Roosevelt's wrecking of the conference, a deliberate act if ever there was one, does suggest that at this time he was an isolationist. The Johnson Act of 1934 almost, if not quite, hardens the suggestion into a certainty. Not that there was, at this period, anything incompatible between isolationism and old-fashioned progressivism. First things first as a national policy—at least until 1936 when Hitler re-occupied the Rhineland and Franco started his insurrection—had merit, considering what Schlesinger calls the "controlling realities," and chief among the controlling realities was America's desperate need for recovery. First things first was light years away from "America First." But Schlesinger's interpretation of Hull's tariff policies in terms of "the triumph of reciprocity" is not too persuasive. In short, it is difficult to see the New Deal in its heyday as anything but isolationist: part of the fascination of Roosevelt is his ability to change, even gradually, even if it took a war situation to change him and, incidentally, to rescue the New Deal.

A similar gradualism can be seen in Roosevelt's attitude toward NRA. Just as, at the beginning of the Hundred Days, he refrained from nationalizing the banking system, so on this larger industrial scene he persisted in the belief that recovery could be achieved through a partnership between business and government: the result was the big-business formula of scarcity and high prices. It took him some time to realize all this, and he might not have realized it as soon as he did if the Court had not ably assisted him by striking down NRA. In the same conspectus one may place his attitude toward organized labor. "He sympathized with organized labor more out of a reaction against employer primitivism than as necessarily a hopeful new development in itself. . . . Neither politically nor intellectually was the New Deal much interested in the labor movement during Roosevelt's first years." The elements necessary for a change of thinking were all there, and specifically in clause 7a of the National Industrial Recovery Act: they had not yet come together in the President's mind.

In the extraordinary ferment of the first Administration, and of Roosevelt's own mind, it is not surprising that so much that was cautious and conservative should have been found side by side with so much that was experimental, pragmatic and progressive. The promises of the first

New Deal, like the performances of the second, can be interpreted in terms of a conflict between reform and recovery. Roosevelt only hinted at really basic reforms of the capitalist state: he was interested in the practical means and the logical consequences of recovery. That is to say, he tried to impose upon the repellent features of the capitalist state, as he found them, the benign image of the welfare state. He did not succeed wholly; but to the extent that the image has become ineffaceable, he succeeded magnificently.

This conflict was partly responsible for the administrative confusion of the New Deal; and *The Coming of the New Deal* stresses, very rightly I think, the question of Roosevelt as an administrator. He could be called a very poor administrator or an artist in administration; poor because he was wasteful; an artist because he was flexible. He believed in bringing into his government men of all kinds of economic and political beliefs: in this sense his Administration was one prolonged debate; but the debate was so arranged that the best information was made available to him and the last word was left with him. He had himself no discernible philosophy; he knew how to put conflicting philosophies to work. In the extraordinary chaos of temporary agencies, which so often overlapped or even nullified one another, he maintained, somehow or other, some kind of positive direction. His way of pitting one man against another, of leaving everyone uncertain as to the security of his position in the government, of subjecting people to a sadistic teasing, kept his advisers on their toes; just as his warmth and his charm held them together.

It was a personal triumph, and the personality behind was complex and baffling. Schlesinger, going back to Archilochus' distinction between hedgehog and fox, says that Roosevelt was all fox. He was devious, evasive, at times untruthful. Not even his intimates could be sure that they knew anything about him; there was, at the heart of the labyrinth, a solitary reserve which could not be entered. Schlesinger believes, however, that "one cannot exhaust the Roosevelt mystery by saying that he was complicated . . . he was complicated everywhere except in his heart of hearts." In his heart of hearts lay a simple, a rather naive idealism.

It was certainly this which the public sensed, or that majority of the public which listened to him with pleasure and voted for him without pain. It was because of his idealism, not in spite of it, that Roosevelt was able to dramatize so successfully one great constitutional event—the transformation of the Presidency from an organ of government into an influence which should pervade every corner of the national life. If we had not experienced the immanence of a Roosevelt, we might not today feel so crippled by the remoteness of an Eisenhower.

History is, in one sense, a translation. It takes the complex of the past and carries it across—makes it understandable—to those who think and live in the complex of the present. Obviously, it is an incomplete translation at best. There is a good deal in the past that is too idiomatic for a successful rendering, and a good deal more that is simply irrecoverable. Nor can any single work give more than a fragment of what *is* recoverable. I don't see much virtue in criticizing a book for not being what its author never intended it to be. One could remark on the absence of any intellectual history in this work; but then that may come, and presumably will come, in a later volume. What is more serious is the relative poverty of its social history— we are left with a very indistinct idea of the condition of the people under the first New Deal. But that would require another kind of book. *The Coming of the New Deal* presents an administrative and political study: not a close analysis of economic theory and political philosophy, but a detailed exposition of theory and philosophy being put to work during a highly critical period. As such it is a powerful, a memorable, an important book.

An excerpt from *The Politics of Hope*

This point—the quality of life—suggests the great difference between the politics of the '60's and the politics of the '3o's. The New Deal arose in response to economic breakdown. It had to meet immediate problems of subsistence and survival. Its emphasis was essentially quantitative—an emphasis inevitable in an age of scarcity. But the '60's will confront an economy of abundance. There still are pools of poverty which have to be mopped up; but the central problem will be increasingly that of fighting for individual dignity, identity, and fulfillment in an affluent mass society. The issues of the new period will not be those involved with refueling the economic machine, putting floors under wages, and farm prices, establishing systems of social security. The new issues will be rather those of education, health, equal opportunity, community planning—the issues which make the difference between defeat and opportunity, between frustration and fulfillment, in the everyday lives of average persons. These issues will determine the quality of civilization to which our nation aspires in an age of ever-increasing wealth and leisure. A guiding aim, I believe, will be the insistence that every American boy and girl have access to the career proportionate to his or her talents and characters, regardless of birth, fortune, creed, or color.

Arthur M. Schlesinger, in his The Politics of Hope,
Houghton Mifflin Company, 1963.

Lewis A. Coser   (review date July 1963)

SOURCE: "New Frontiers," in *Commentary*, Vol. 36, No. 1, July, 1963, pp. 76-8.

[*In the review below, Coser argues that Schlesinger's* The Politics of Hope, "*attempts to define the lineaments of a new pragmatic liberalism,*" *but that Schlesinger's conclusions are often partisan and do not reflect the "critical and unattached" judgment characteristic of his earlier works.*]

This collection of essays [*The Politics of Hope*], written in the 1950's and early 1960's for a variety of magazines, reflects the amazing catholicity of Mr. Schlesinger's tastes and interests. His range is wide indeed. There are pieces here on the virtues of dissent (written in the age of Eisen-

hower) and pieces on the need for greatness and heroic leadership (written at the onset of the Kennedy age). Mr. Schlesinger has discussed the Oppenheimer case (in the *Atlantic*), Whittaker Chambers (in the *Saturday Review*), and in *Esquire* he raised the question, "What has unmanned the American man?" Other essays comment on the careers of Walter Lippmann and Reinhold Niebuhr, on the causes of the Civil War, and on numerous other subjects. This variety makes an assessment of the book difficult enough; the difficulty is compounded when one realizes how much Mr. Schlesinger's role on the intellectual scene has changed during the period covered. He used to be a critical and unattached intellectual. He is now attached—to the White House. Hence one must distinguish carefully between the old Schlesinger and the new, even though the book's organization, topical rather than chronological, plainly was not meant to invite such distinctions.

The earlier pieces, those written in the 1950's, continue in the vein of the author's *Vital Center.* They show a genuinely curious and troubled mind trying painfully to define a new liberal politics after the collapse of some of the traditional liberal certainties. Persuaded by Reinhold Niebuhr of the futility of utopian visions in an immoral society of sinful men, Mr. Schlesinger here attempts to define the lineaments of a new pragmatic liberalism in tune with realistic requirements and the conduct of practical affairs. Aware of the stubborn recalcitrance of political facts before the grand schemes of certain of the older liberal thinkers, Mr. Schlesinger counsels caution, a politics of responsibility, a plunge into the course of history rather than a desperate struggle against its current. If his translation of the somber pessimism of certain theological thinkers into the idiom of high-level political journalism often sounds rather shallow, this is perhaps not entirely Mr. Schlesinger's fault. He evidently does the best he can. And it remains that certain of these essays, those on Lippmann, De Voto, Niebuhr, and Chambers, for example, are perceptive, engaging, and sympathetic examinations of the life and thought of these men. In addition, certain of the polemical pieces of the 1950's—against the New Conservatives, against *Time*'s disparagement of intellectuals, against those "revisionist" historians who would persuade us that the Civil War could have been avoided had everybody but been a bit more reasonable—are fine examples of the polemicist's craft. But all these are products of a phase of his career which Mr. Schlesinger has now left behind. His newer pieces are no longer questioning and tentative; instead, they bristle with new-found muscular certainties.

The new style reveals the new man. Invigorated by the sweet taste of power, Mr. Schlesinger writes now with aplomb. His more recent essays abound in "forward motion," "revived national energies," "faith in leadership," and long strings of similar clichés. Take, for example, the essay on **"The New Mood in Politics,"** written in 1960. Here Mr. Schlesinger assures the reader that "From the vantage point of the 60's, the 50's . . . will seem simply a listless interlude, quickly forgotten, in which the American people collected itself for greater exertions and higher splendors in the future." Does this sound like political analysis or does it sound like campaign oratory? In fact, it *is* campaign oratory, indistinguishable from the highfalutin speeches of Mr. Schlesinger's master and hero—which, come to think of it, were at least partly written by the same author.

The old Schlesinger often probed deeply and was aware of the complicated ambiguities of political action. The new Schlesinger has wholly succumbed to self-congratulatory certainty. He can now write: "Our national leadership is young, vigorous, intelligent, civilized, and experimental. . . ." All this is a bit hard to take, coming as it does from the pen of a man whose official address is the White House. Were there no self-employed trumpeters available?

The new Schlesinger, perhaps because of what John Dewey called "an occupational psychosis," seems to have developed a trained incapacity to perceive the somber side of the American experience in the 1960's. His complacency is formidable. He can now write, for example: "There are still pools of poverty which have to be mopped up; but the central problem will be increasingly that of fighting for individual dignity, identity and fulfillment. . . ." Some pools these! A spate of recent books—see Dwight Macdonald's superb discussion of them in a recent issue of the *New Yorker*—have shown that at least one-fourth of the American population still lives in poverty. Reading Mr. Schlesinger's cultivated prattle about identity, fulfillment, and the like, one cannot help recalling Bertholt Brecht's *"Erst kommt das Fressen, dann kommt die Moral."* Brecht was often vulgar, but at least he was never smug.

If one is to believe Mr. Schlesinger, a truly remarkable transformation has occurred in American within a very short time span. In 1958 it was "a pompous society," the 50's were a "decade of inertia [when] we squandered, for example, a commanding weapons' lead until our own officials now frankly concede that by the early 60's the Soviet Union . . . will have a superiority in the thrust of its missiles and in the penetration of outer space." Things were falling apart, and the vital center did not hold. But enter the 60's and everything has changed: "We have awakened as from a trance; and we have awakened so quickly and so sharply that we can hardly remember what it was like when we slumbered." The old Schlesinger was much given to attacks against the alleged "deterministic" explanations of sociology and to the vindication of "human freedom"; but the new Schlesinger's belief in indeterminacy runs riot. Everyone has the right, I suppose, to invoke "heroic leadership" and to believe in the seminal and history-making actions of great men. But Mr. Schlesinger abuses the privilege. It is asking a bit much to have us believe that the mere advent of Mr. Schlesinger's employer on the scene has, as with one wave of a magic wand, changed the major characteristics of an era and of a society. This is no longer social analysis, even if it is dressed up in terms of an alleged law of historical alternation between Innovation and Conservatism "discovered" by Mr. Schlesinger's father a generation ago; it is just plain *chutzpah*. Are we really to believe that mass society with all its attendant signs and characteristics suddenly disappeared from America at the moment John F. Kennedy and Arthur Schlesinger, Jr. entered the White House? "Few," writes the author, "would

describe American society any longer in last decade's condescending vocabulary of conformism and homogenization." Is he kidding himself or is he trying to kid us?

Finally, I wish to comment on Mr. Schlesinger's leading essay which carries the pretentious title **"On Heroic Leadership and the Dilemma of Strong Men and Weak People."** This is an important essay, not because it says anything important, but because it seems to express the ideology which is now dominant among the President's intellectuals in Washington. Here Mr. Schlesinger calls for a reconstitution of democratic theory since "maintained in rigid purity, it has been an abundant source of trouble." The citizen in a democracy, he says, simply cannot play the role in which classical democratic theory has cast him. This has led to political estrangement and frustration. Hence, Mr. Schlesinger argues, we need to rely on heroic leadership, we need to divest ourselves of our instinctive distrust of such leadership if the democratic polity is not to flounder in a sea of mass emotions. This, I submit, is a detestable doctrine.

I share Mr. Schlesinger's view that the American political process has been characterized in recent years by a devolution of democracy, and that at least one of the major reactions to this has been an increase in political alienation. But Mr. Schlesinger's heroic leadership doctrine, far from decreasing this alienation, would make it a permanent condition. It would institutionalize reliance on the tutelary powers of a government headed by heroic leaders. We would then truly have reached the condition that de Tocqueville always feared would threaten democratic nations: "As each member of the community is individually isolated and extremely powerless, no one of the whole body can either defend himself or present a rallying point to others; nothing is strong in a democratic country except the state." In such a condition, de Tocqueville thought, "the people shake off their state of dependence just long enough to select their master, and then relapse into it again." According to Mr. Schlesinger, the crisis of democracy can be cured only by a strong injection of personalist appeals by a political hero. This is a pernicious remedy. What is needed is *more* participation in decision-making by the citizens, not less. If existing institutional restraints prevent such wider participation, they will have to be abolished. In the meantime, lunch-counter demonstrators and Freedom Riders, not Schlesinger's managerial demiurges, maintain one's faith in the possibilities of democracy. The future of democracy in America is tied to the chances of breaking up those illegitimate and irresponsible centers of power, both economic and political, which have grown up within the interstices of the democratic polity, and which effectively thwart the exercise of democratic decision-making, even as they strangle economic growth and equal access of the whole population to the good things of life. So far, one waits in vain for Mr. Schlesinger and his Washington co-thinkers to even mention, let alone deal with, this problem. Unless they do so soon, one will be forced to conclude that all this talk about heroic leadership is an ideological smokescreen behind which business can be conducted as usual.

All that I wanted to convey in this review has, in effect,

already been said, and in the book itself. It occurs in a passage from Walter Lippmann's *The Method of Freedom* which Schlesinger quotes in his essay on its author:

> It is only knowledge freely acquired that is disinterested. When, therefore, men whose profession is to teach and to investigate become the makers of policy, become members of an administration in power, become politicians and leaders of causes, they are committed. Nothing they say can be relied upon as disinterested. Nothing they teach can be trusted as scientific. It is impossible to mix the pursuit of knowledge and the exercise of political power and those who have tried it turn out to be very bad politicians or they cease to be scholars.

So be it.

James MacGregor Burns (review date 28 November 1965)

SOURCE: "JFK: A Memoir and More," in *The New York Times Book Review,* November 28, 1965, pp. 1, 84.

[*In the following review, Burns praises Schlesinger's* A Thousand Days *for its scholarship, its encyclopedic account of events, and "diamond-bright" portraits of White House and Congressional leaders. However, Burns contends that the broad scope of the book prevents any significant in-depth analysis of the Kennedy era.*]

More than any other people, perhaps, Americans like to leave issues to the "verdict of history." When some problem seems too opaque or some leader too inscrutable, we comfort ourselves with the thought that some day the historians will decide the merits of the case or take the final measure of the man. The trouble is that historians never come in with a final verdict; usually they are a hung jury. History is written by the survivors—but new generations bring new survivors.

The great historian combines the feel and immediacy of the participant with the distance and perspective of the critic who can put events in their broadest context, tap wide sources of data and judgment, and enjoy all the blessings of hindsight. He can accompany the main actors down the rutted, twisting road and feel—as well as record—the bumps and turns. But he can also step back, and, with his fellow historians as his jealous and watchful constituency, he can gain a perspective that sees a man and his era against the long prologue and epilogue of events.

Such a historian is rare. I doubt that Arthur Schlesinger Jr., with all his self-confidence, expected at the outset that he would write virtually a history of the Age of Kennedy. He describes his work [*A Thousand Days: John F. Kennedy in the White House*] as a "personal memoir by one who served in the White House during the Kennedy years," and one notes that he faithfully records his own background (O.S.S., Stevenson aide, etc.) and his own White House activities (mainly foreign relations) as well as his chief's. His work ends up, however, as a remarkable feat of scholarship and writing, set in the widest historical and

intellectual frame—and all the more astounding for having been written in something less than 18 months.

It is exciting in this book to see the historian take over, to see the mere chronicler of events, at first content to use his limited and staccato exposure to great events, give way to the scholar of contemporary America. Certainly Schlesinger's presence in the White House helped give him *Verstehen*—that quality of being able to feel one's way into complex situations and to know, if not how things were done, how they could not have been done.

Yet I think that Schlesinger's achievement is due less to his having been a member of the Kennedy White House than being a member of the Kennedy era. He shared with Kennedy, though from a different perspective, the worlds of Boston, Harvard, military power, state and national politics, convention rooms, Washington. Like Kennedy, he was born during World War I, came of age in the Great Depression, knew, admired and criticized the New Deal, rejected many of the old liberal stereotypes, suffered through the platitudes of the Eisenhower years and embraced the politics of modernity.

In this long volume Schlesinger has caught both the sweep and the ferment of the thousand days. He has chronicled Kennedy's long and skillful nomination campaign, the battle with Nixon, the feverish preparations for office, the scintillating inaugural days, and then the burdens of power—Latin America, Berlin, Southeast Asia, Africa, and always Moscow and Peking; and at home, economic recovery, the civil rights revolution, the fight with Big Steel, and all the rest. Nor does he ignore the disappointments—the burning humiliation after the Bay of Pigs, the frustrations on Capitol Hill, and the immovability—as Schlesinger sees it—of the bureaucracy in general and of the State Department very much in particular.

The chronicle is fresh, vivid and informative, but what the historian has done is to re-create the historical, political and personal context in which the events take place. He reaches back into the Truman and Eisenhower years to dissect the web of forces that variously empowered and constrained the Administration. He has a sure grasp of the party rivalries, factional quarrels, intellectual and policy differences and quirks of personality in which issues and policies were entangled.

His closeness to White House aides, bureaucrats, and Congressional politicians has not dulled the author's ability or willingness to portray them in diamond-bright vignettes. The result is a continuously fascinating but almost encyclopedic treatment not only of the big events and of the less crucial but still instructive topics like Laos, the Congo, the Skybolt missile mixup, Santo Domingo (Kennedy came close to occupying it), Goa, and even relations with South Africa.

Thus the United Nations:

> Not until I began making regular visits to that great glass tower glittering above the East River did I start to grasp the intensity of the UN life. It was a world of its own, separate, self-contained, and in chronic crisis, where a dozen unrelated emergencies might explode at once,

demanding immediate reactions across the government and decisions (or at least speeches) in New York. It had its own ethos, its own rules and its own language: delegates would argue interminably over whether to "note" or to "reaffirm" a past resolution, to "deplore" or "regret" or "condemn" a present action. . . . Stevenson, presiding over this hectic outpost in American diplomacy, had a far more arduous and exhausting job than most Washingtonians appreciated; and, because he had the grace of making everything look easy and the habit of disparaging his own success, people in Washington did not realize how superbly he was discharging an impossible assignment.

Nehru: By 1961

Nehru, alas, was no longer the man he had once been. It has all gone on too long, the fathership of his country, the rambling, paternal speeches to his flock, the tired aristocratic disdain in New Delhi, the Left Book Club platitudes when his face was turned to the world. His strength was failing, and he retained control more by momentum of the past than by mastery of the present.

The difficulty of opposing the Bay of Pigs:

The advocates of the adventure had a rhetorical advantage. They could strike virile poses and talk of tangible things—fire power, air strikes, landing craft and so on. To oppose the plan, one had to invoke intangibles—the moral position of the United States, the reputation of the President, the response of the United Nations, "world public opinion" and other such odious concepts.

Robert Kennedy:

When, to the general indignation of the bar and press, he was appointed Attorney General, he was widely regarded as a ruthless and power-hungry young man devoid of principle or scruple, indifferent to personal freedom or public right, who saw life in rigidly personal and moralistic terms. . . . And Bobby's public bearing— the ominous manner, the knock-the-chip-off-my-shoulder look, the stony blue eyes, clenched teeth, tart, monosyllabic tongue—did not especially dispel the picture of a rough young man suddenly given national authority. I do not know of any case in contemporary American politics where there has seemed to me a greater discrepancy between the myth and the man.

It is not accidental that these examples relate mainly to foreign affairs, for so does the book. Schlesinger, being "only irregularly involved" in domestic matters, felt that he had less to say about them. This conclusion stemmed from a mistaken premise, as I see it, that the author could describe best what he had most witnessed. Here again, Schlesinger the historian is not dependent on Schlesinger the White House aide.

He handles domestic policies and politics superbly when he finally comes to them, but the treatment is relatively too brief. Schlesinger makes perceptive judgments about Kennedy's relations with Congress, the radical right, various groups and personages of the left, the leadership of labor, the intellectuals—but there is simply not enough background and depth. Incredibly, this long book is not long enough. Or perhaps it should be in two or even three volumes to do justice to the Age of Kennedy.

What manner of man emerges from these pages? Clearly Kennedy was a hero to Schlesinger, as he was, evidently, to all his friends and aides (we have yet to hear from his valet). Like other biographers, Schlesinger was struck by Kennedy's detachment, coolness, restraint, self-control, distaste for emotional display. But these qualities, he feels, overlay deep feelings, involvement, commitment.

The President feared to make an unnecessary display of himself, to seem to be histrionic or corny. He saw no sense in knock-down and drag-out fights if he did not win them. "There is no sense," he said, "raising hell, and then not being successful. There is no sense in putting the office of the Presidency on the line on an issue, and then being defeated." He would rather compromise and win a bill than lose dramatically and win a heightened moral issue.

Kennedy regarded crowds as irrational, the author says. He did not want to play on a mob's emotions, as Franklin Roosevelt had done so brilliantly and demagogically in his Madison Square Garden speech at the climax of the election of 1936. He was fearful of the proposed march of civil rights forces on Capitol Hill (but pleased when the rally around the Lincoln Memorial turned out to be one of the most luminous moments in the nation's life). He violated his own restraint only once, in Berlin (*"Ich bin ein Berliner!"*) and was afterward worried about it. Why this fear of arousing mass feeling, of using popular emotion as a tool in politics?

The author finds a more basic reason for this quality than the usual explanations of rationalism or pragmatism. The "basic source may have been an acute and anguished sense of the fragility of the membranes of civilization, stretched so thin over a nation so disparate in its composition, so tense in its interior relationships, so cunningly enmeshed in underground fears and antagonisms, so entrapped by history in the ethos of violence." It was this kind of sensitivity that Kennedy brought to civil rights. His relation to this issue in the 1950's, the author suggests, was more a matter of intellectual and political commitment than of emotional identification.

By the 1960's American Negroes were in a state of semi-revolution. Kennedy used a wide array of executive powers, but he used them slowly and prudently, and he did not come to command the nation's mood and conscience, as Franklin Roosevelt had done in coping with protest born of depression. "A sweeping revolutionary force is pressed into a narrow tunnel," Martin Luther King complained. Only after the crises in Oxford and Jackson and countless other Southern towns did the President take his place in the Negro revolution.

Schlesinger feels that his timing was right—that the President could act only after the nation's attention was focused on civil rights. Some Negro leaders still believe that Kennedy should have moved earlier and more boldly— that the leader must set in advance the moral tone that will inform a people's perspective and in turn strengthen the President's hand.

History will continue to render "verdicts" on such questions, as we try to learn more about the interrelations of Presidential deeds, the people's moods and the political process. History will also bring new evaluations of Kennedy the man, as we hear more, for example, from the "Irish mafia" types who saw Kennedy's robust, earthy and less cerebral side. History will reassess both the Thousand Days and *The Thousand Days.* But I will offer one man's verdict now. This is Arthur Schlesinger's best book. A great President has found—perhaps he deliberately chose—a great historian.

John M. Blum (review date 4 December 1965)

SOURCE: "Schlesinger's Kennedy," in *The New Republic,* Vol. 153, No. 23, December 4, 1965, pp. 21-4.

[*In the following review, Blum argues that Schlesinger's* A Thousand Days *accurately depicts "the spirit and the style of the New Frontier, and its leader," and gives the reader a personal glimpse into the workings of the seat of government.*]

For Andrew Jackson, so we learned from Arthur Schlesinger, Jr., the sun broke through the clouds as he set out for his inauguration; for Franklin Roosevelt, the mist and wind under a sullen sky were witness to the nation's applause for buoyant call to action; for John F. Kennedy, Schlesinger tells us now, "it all began in the cold," as so soon thereafter it was all so tragically to end. In *A Thousand Days,* Schlesinger, as he did before for Jackson and for Roosevelt, brings his sure knowledge, his lucid prose, and his unmatched gift for understanding the endless adventure of governing men to the analysis of the Administration of a great President. The book, Schlesinger says at the outset, is "not a comprehensive history of the Kennedy Presidency. It is a personal memoir." But the intensity of the author's personal experience with Kennedy does not, in spite of the disclaimer, diminish the range, the quality, and the authority of the history recorded. Schlesinger's is the first account of the Kennedy years to catch and convey the spirit and the style of the New Frontier and its leader. It will be for many years the account against which all others must be measured, and on which all others will in some degree depend.

Kennedy, as Schlesinger portrays him, served both as the agent and the symbol for an indispensable reformation of public policies as those policies were made and applied and understood at home and abroad. "Let us," the President said of the Alliance for Progress, as by implication he often said of his own country, "let us once again transform the American continent into a vast crucible of revolutionary ideas and efforts—a tribute to the power of the creative energies of free men and women—an example to all the world that liberty and progress walk hand in hand." The Kennedy whom Schlesinger reveals believed in those possibilities and dedicated himself to their fulfillment. He did so even though his political perceptions told him how perilously slow the course of progress had to be, and—more important—even though his reading of histo-

ry and his consequent sense of irony reminded him always of the distance that lay between the noblest, most vigorous intentions and their invariably lesser products. That sense of irony contributed to Kennedy's humor, which he wryly turned against himself, without in the least reducing Kennedy's stamina, born partly of rare courage, partly of confidence, and essential to his imperturbability in crisis.

Irony has meaning only to man thinking, only to an intellectual, and Kennedy, as Schlesinger demonstrates, was the most incisive intellectual of the whole brilliant galaxy of men whom he summoned to his side. More than any one of them, he commanded the entire array of difficult subjects to which he adverted. Yet Kennedy, even in repose, exuded the poised grace of a man trained and resolved to act. His command of his mind—thorough in its instruction, jugular in its drive to the essence of a problem—whetted his impatience to be on with his tasks. The impulse to action, the swift concentration on the practicable, the mistrust of the rhetoric of idealism, the unhesitating recourse when circumstances so indicated to the power of the military or of the Irish Mafia—all these led some intellectuals, particularly those who did not know Kennedy or who disagreed with him, to misread his high purpose and to underrate his arresting capabilities, to disown their closest kin to hold the Presidency since the time of Thomas Jefferson. For his part, Kennedy was hurt and puzzled when intelligent but cloistered men in 1960 found him neither less nor more than Richard Nixon. As Schlesinger observes, two years later no one could properly any longer confuse the adversaries; Kennedy in office had proved his right to the margin of support the electorate ultimately awarded to his successor.

Schlesinger's vignettes serve the New Frontiersmen well, especially Averell Harriman whose wise and selfless engagement merited the unstinted admiration it receives. Some thirty years the senior of most of his colleagues, Harriman nonetheless shared their ebullient youth. Adlai Stevenson, as Schlesinger portrays him, was less at home in Kennedy's Washington, but the picture of Stevenson that emerges captures his spirit, even though Schlesinger ruefully admits the continual uneasiness of Stevenson's relationship with Kennedy. A lesser President might have failed to enlist Stevenson in the common cause which the older man had defined and clarified while the younger was preparing himself for the responsibilities of power. Those who, as Schlesinger describes them, perhaps best represented the essential qualities of Kennedy's use of power, his preferred processes of government, and his goals for the United States were the trenchant, systematic, indefatigable McNamara, and the tough, steady Attorney General—hungry to learn, more and more the most effective and reliable liberal in the Cabinet.

Others fare less well. Lyndon Johnson, for one, whose strength Schlesinger gladly recognizes, appears, as he was, at some remove from the center of affairs—restless, egocentric, but an impressively loyal soldier to an army he had only reluctantly joined. In Los Angeles in 1960, Schlesinger writes, after Kennedy had won the nomination, Johnson was "far from Isaiah," and for the heathen Schlesinger adds, in a footnote other historians will envy,

" 'come now, and let us reason together'. Isaiah 1:18. L.B.J. *passim.*" But Johnson is the object only of respectful fun, while Dean Rusk is the object of exasperated disappointment.

The American Establishment (the subject of a puckish footnote that pays special respect to Richard Rovere) has questioned Schlesinger's taste, even his patriotism, for reporting Kennedy's private statement that Rusk would be permitted to resign. In the full context of Schlesinger's book, that report is neither tasteless nor unpatriotic nor undeserved. Schlesinger devotes a major portion of his total narrative and analysis to examining the inertia of the State Department, the Joint Chiefs, and the CIA, and to explaining Kennedy's efforts to break through the depressing influences of those agencies. The crisis for the President arose with the Bay of Pigs, an episode that Schlesinger makes a kind of fulcrum for his own critique of government as Kennedy inherited it. The implications of the story Schlesinger tells are as disturbing now as they must have been to the President at the time. State, CIA, and the Joint Chiefs displayed an invincible inability to question the premises from which the original planning of the operation had proceeded. In a series of small decisions built upon those rigid premises, a series that became irreversible in its momentum (in precisely the manner discussed by D. Braybrooke and C. E. Lindblom in *A Strategy of Decision*), they led the new Administration to the calamity of the invasion. That affair, shattering the gay confidence of the spring of 1961, opened a long season of gloom that spread with the troubles in Berlin, Laos, and Africa. But the travesty of the Bay of Pigs had reminded Kennedy that specialists in intelligence and weaponry and protocol were attached to the particular interests they represented and, with singular exceptions, were incapable of comprehending or of representing the general interests of the Presidency or of the United States. Accordingly Kennedy turned increasingly to generalists in whom he had personal confidence, men charged with the dual duty of prodding the bureaucracies to perform at a high level of energy and imagination, and of transcending the advice of bureaucratic expertise. As the White House took over the strings of policy, Kennedy gained the initiative and scope necessary for his later achievements, especially for his superb resolution of the second Cuban crisis and for his delicate diplomacy for the test ban. But Rusk, apparently by his own choice, ordinarily stood apart from involvement in those and other major issues, and Rusk only hesitatingly, if at all, endeavored to purge his department of its sluggishness, parochialism and banality. Thus Kennedy's statement about Rusk's resignation, and thus Schlesinger's report.

After the Bay of Pigs, Kennedy's largest difficulties in foreign policy, as Schlesinger sees it, derived not from American weakness or fumbling but from the strength and will of adversaries or off-and-on friends, particularly the Soviet Union and France. The accounts of Kennedy's trials with Khrushchev and de Gaulle profit alike from Schlesinger's care with details and his prefatory excursions into the backgrounds of Russian and French policy. Here and elsewhere in the book—for example, in sections on Latin America, Africa, Italy and Great Britain—the author's grasp of the past enhances his rendering of the immediate. His candor, moreover, exposes certain failures of the Administration which he views more generously than will some of his readers—for one, the lapse in communication with and consideration for an ally that intensified British disappointment over the cancellation of Skybolt; for another, the preoccupations that kept Kennedy from reversing the flow of decisions about Vietnam, decisions that originated in large part with various New Frontiersmen. Though no apologist for Diem, Schlesinger suggests in the intractable case of Vietnam how crippling were the limits of Kennedy's available choices. In that and other cases, Schlesinger tends to applaud the practicable and meliorative, and tends to deplore the radical and millennial. Here he reflects the tough but creative mood of the New Frontier. Yet that mood leaves, perhaps, too little room, not for agreement with, but for sympathy for those theorists who help to preserve a millennial vision against which the impact of the practicable can be measured. And Schlesinger, without being necessarily wrong, is nevertheless harsh in his asides about H. Stuart Hughes and those of like mind.

Schlesinger's more gentle but still critical treatment of the radicals in the civil rights movement appreciates their success in advancing their cause. At the same time, the Kennedys and their associates lent considerable thrust to that accelerating movement, and the Attorney General, in Schlesinger's assessment, receives the credit that his detractors have refused to grant him. Still, some of Robert Kennedy's admirers, including Schlesinger, for their part have not discussed the significance of the New Frontier's judicial appointments with the skeptical detachment of Alexander Bickel in his *Politics and the Warren Court.* Overall, however, Schlesinger's approach to civil rights and other domestic issues is distinguished by its clarity and balance. Indeed his discussion of economic policy provides a model for any general exploration of technical questions. Most important, with marked restraint Schlesinger shows conclusively that Kennedy did get the country moving again. The accomplishments of Lyndon Johnson rose from the strong foundations Kennedy built, for Kennedy's celebrated style was no trick of public relations but the graceful expression of a powerful mind, a powerful person, and a powerful program, admirably timed.

"Is there some principle of nature," Richard Hofstadter asked in a question Schlesinger quotes, "which requires that we never know the quality of what we have had until it is gone?" Perhaps. Those close to Kennedy knew before that dreadful day in Dallas. Many others did not. It is the special triumph of Schlesinger's [*A Thousand Days*] that those who read it, now or years from now, will know the quality of Kennedy. They should then conclude, with Schlesinger, that above all Kennedy "gave the world for an imperishable moment the vision of a leader who greatly understood the terror and the hope, the diversity and the possibility, of life on this planet and who made people look beyond nation and race to the future of humanity." In a sense, then, it did not come to an end in the cold.

David Schoenbrun (review date 11 February 1967)

SOURCE: "Vietnam Legacy," in *The New Republic,* Vol. 156, No. 6, February 11, 1967, pp. 25-8.

[*In the following excerpt, Schoenbrun examines* The Bitter Heritage, *focusing on Schlesinger's controversial interpretation of the escalation of the Vietnam War.*]

The Bitter Heritage is a bitter-sweet essay that will please few but stir all who read it. Despite some serious flaws, it is by far the best short history and analysis of the war in Vietnam available in book form. It is not, strictly speaking, a book. It totals less than 40,000 words, most of them previously published in three magazine articles. One whole chapter, "On the inscrutability of history," first published in *Encounter,* is a long, brilliant discursion with minimal relevance to the subject. . . .

Its sweetness is found in its dedication and its last chapter. It is dedicated "for those fighting in Vietnam." (The hawks are by no means the only patriots, the only supporters of our soldiers.) And the last chapter, "Vietnam and American Democracy," is a moving, lucid appeal to reason and the best democratic traditions of responsible dissent, as well as a warning against a recrudescence of McCarthyism in the course of the increasingly bitter national divisions on the war.

The bitterness is there, too, if well concealed by the "cool" style of the sophisticated pamphleteer that Schlesinger has become. He uses his pen as a rapier, "that silent, white weapon of the gentleman," swiftly, skillfully and with deadly precision. The man he slashes most deftly is Secretary of State Dean Rusk but his principal victim is President Johnson.

Scholar-duelist Schlesinger does not confine his thrusts at Rusk to Vietnam. He goes far back into the records to make Rusk look foolish, such as this quote from May 18, 1951, when Rusk was an Assistant Secretary of State: "The Peiping regime may be a colonial Russian government—a Slavic Manchukuo on a larger scale. It is not the government of China. It does not pass the first test. It is not Chinese." In the light of the current Sino-Soviet split and China's competition with Russia for world communist leadership, Rusk's 1951 estimate is grotesque. Mr. Schlesinger might have strengthened his case, largely built on hindsight, by pointing out that the then Secretary of State, Dean Acheson, was already talking publicly about a Sino-Soviet rift, predicting the split that followed. Rusk was wrong by almost any standard, hindsight or foresight.

The most devastating use of quotations to cut a man to pieces is directed against President Johnson:

> Some others are eager to enlarge the conflict. They call upon us to supply American boys to do the job that Asian boys should do. They ask us to take reckless actions which might risk the lives of millions and engulf much of Asia. (August 12, 1964 election campaign speech)

> I have had advice to load our planes with bombs and to drop them on certain areas that I think would enlarge the war and result in committing a good many American boys to fighting a war

that I think ought to be fought by the boys of Asia to help protect their own land. And for that reason I haven't chosen to enlarge the war. (August 29, 1964)

> There are those who say you ought to go north and drop bombs, to try to wipe out the supply lines, and they think that would escalate the war. We don't want our American boys to do the fighting for Asian boys. We don't want to get involved in a nation with 700,000,000 people and get tied down in a land war in Asia. (September 25, 1964)

> We are not going north and we are not going south; we are going to continue to try to get them to save their own freedom with their own men, with our leadership and our officer direction, and such equipment as we can furnish them. (September 28, 1964)

> We are not going to send American boys nine to ten thousand miles from home to do what Asian boys ought to be doing for themselves. (October 21, 1964)

Perhaps the cruelest cut of all is Schlesinger's quoting Senator Johnson's criticism of President Eisenhower's brief attempt to obtain congressional approval to intervene to save the embattled French legions in Dien Bien Phu. The then Minority Leader charged that the United States "is in clear danger of being left naked and alone in a hostile world. . . . Our friends and allies are frightened and wondering, as we do, where we are headed." Mr. Schlesinger might, here again, have strengthened his case had he pursued his research more carefully in a longer study, for he overlooked the more telling fact that it was Minority Leader Johnson who led the opposition against the Eisenhower-Dulles intervention scheme by demanding prior consultation and consent of our allies, notably the British. Winston Churchill and Anthony Eden—no appeasers—were appalled by the proposal and turned it down flat. Eisenhower could not deliver to the Senate the guarantee Johnson had demanded and therefore had to abandon the idea.

Schlesinger's faults of omission become grave and injure his otherwise effective essay when he commits serious errors in a reference to the Geneva Conference of 1954: ". . . And negotiations in Geneva, in which the United States *declined to take part,* resulted in the de facto *partition of Vietnam at the 17 parallel*" (italics added).

The phrase "declined to take part" would leave the uninformed reader with the impression that the United States had no part in the Geneva Conference, was not even there. In fact the United States delegation, headed by General Bedell Smith, was not only there but participated in the Conference. Schlesinger is correct only in the very narrowest and most unimportant sense of the phrase "to take part"; the US was indeed not an *official* participant in the Conference. But General Smith did attend the meetings as an interested party and, at the concluding session, when the final agreement, now known as the "Geneva Accords," was read, he spoke on behalf of the United States and pledged that we would not take any actions against those accords if they were not forcibly violated by others.

This is a most important point, for it has been falsely argued that we were in no way committed by the Geneva Accords.

It is also regrettable that Schlesinger states there was a de facto partition of Vietnam. The Geneva Accords very precisely stated that there was to be only a "temporary, military demarcation line," for the purposes of regrouping hostile troops on either side, leading to a period of calm that would permit free elections and unification of the country. A *temporary demarcation* is legally and morally very different from a partition. It is true that the divisions of Berlin and Korea became partitions but there was not much doubt that this was the Soviet intention. Partition was not the intention of the Geneva conferees. Schlesinger should also have recalled the agreement on free elections. How can the public judge the validity of the Geneva Accords, so often referred to as a possible solution today, if its most basic clauses are not precisely stated?

Schlesinger is on much firmer ground when he attacks the Administration argument that we are legally committed, under SEATO, to defend South Vietnam. He cites the Dulles testimony at the original SEATO hearings in November '54: "If there is a revolutionary movement in Vietnam or Thailand, we would consult together . . . but we have no undertaking to put it down: all we have is an undertaking to consult." He also cites the transcript of August 1964, of the Senate Foreign Relations hearings, when Rusk testified: "We are not acting specifically under the SEATO Treaty." And Senator Morse's statement that Rusk had twice told the Committee, in Executive Session, "that we are not acting in Vietnam under SEATO."

Schlesinger succeeds in angering hawks and doves both in his argument about the validity of our involvement in Vietnam. First, he knocks down the SEATO commitment argument, stating that "No President of the US before President Johnson interpreted the SEATO Treaty as compelling American military intervention, and no other signatory so interprets the treaty today . . . [it] is an exercise in historical and legal distortion." Having shot down the hawks' favorite argument he then shoots at the doves by arguing that Eisenhower's offer of economic aid to Diem plus the special protocol of SEATO "did draw a line across Southeast Asia," and that, although this did not "in any legal way compel American military intervention," it did, "in a political way," involve the United States in holding that line. In other words, Schlesinger feels the intervention was not legal, it involved "no vital strategic interest," but it was drawn, "for better or for worse," and "we must deal with the situation that exists."

The best and most important chapters are II to VI, some fifty pages of tightly written, finely reasoned answers to the most fundamental questions that Americans are asking more and more insistently. These chapters are entitled: "What We Did There," "Where We Are Now," "The Price We Are Paying," "The Roots of Our Trouble," and "Is China the Enemy in Vietnam?" Briefly these are Schlesinger's answers:

What We Did There

Eisenhower on Dulles advice, offered South Vietnam's Premier Diem economic aid, on condition that he carry out political and economic reforms. He took the aid but not the advice. Kennedy then increased the number of our "advisors," less than 1,000 under Eisenhower, to 10,000 and gave them arms and authorized them to shoot back if fired at. Schlesinger, a devotee of Kennedy, puts the blame for the escalation on General Maxwell Taylor and Walt Rostow and absolves Kennedy. He is less considerate of Eisenhower and Johnson. He blames them, not their advisors.

Where We Are Now

Johnson took the final decisive plunge over the brink increasing Kennedy's 10,000 advisors by geometric proportions to 25,000, 75,000, 150,000, 400,000, now on the way to a half million. He carried the war from the ground to the air, from the South to the North, from purely conventional weapons to chemical weapons, napalm, fire bombs and defoliation bombs, practically everything short of A-weapons. We are, says Schlesinger, carrying out "the physical obliteration of the nation" in the course of protecting it. Schlesinger wonders "what other country, seeing the devastation we have wrought in Vietnam, will wish American protection?" Finally he wonders whether we are really fighting to save the Vietnamese, or "are we doing it for less exalted purposes of our own?"

The Price We Are Paying

At the time Schlesinger was writing, the war was costing a billion-and-a-half dollars a month. Since he closed his book it has shot up over two billion a month. "Everything is grinding to a stop" in domestic programs, Schlesinger asserts. He states that Johnson was on his way to "a place in history as a great President, for his vision of a Great Society; but the Great Society is now, except for token gestures, dead." We are estranged from our allies, divided among ourselves, putting great strains upon the loyalty of a wonderful new generation of American youth, risking a revival of McCarthyism, weakening our economy, infecting the body politic.

The Roots of Our Trouble

We have been imprisoned by "old illusions—the illusion of American omnipotence and the illusion of American omniscience." Johnson does not have the "knack for discrimination in his use of power." "His greatest weakness is his susceptibility to overkill." "The appearance of flim-flam showmanship and manipulation in Washington has created a crisis of credibility from which it may take the nation a long time to recover."

Is China the Enemy in Vietnam?

Schlesinger charges that, "hovering behind our policy is a larger idea," that this is a "fateful test of wills between China and the United States." The proof that the real enemy is China, advanced by "our leaders," is, in Schlesinger's view, "exceedingly sketchy and almost perfunctory." Most of the countries directly threatened by Chinese expansion—Russia, Japan and India—"apparently do not accept it" (the proof, that is). We have not understood that communism is not monolithic but polycentric, which is why we profess to see China as the real reason for revolution in Vietnam.

Schlesinger points up the absurdities of official analogies between Southeast Asia and aggressions in Manchuria by the Japanese or Czechoslovakia by Hitler. Vietnam will "not be solved by bad historical analogies," Schlesinger insists. He states that "the containment of China will be a major problem for the next generation," but wisely warns us against confusing "the prevention of Chinese aggression with the suppression of nationalist revolution."

Schlesinger's natural allies among those who oppose Administration policy in Vietnam will find excellent documentation and argument to serve their cause in the five chapters cited above. They will also respond warmly and gratefully to his closing chapter on American democracy and his plea to "preserve mutual trust among ourselves as Americans." It is these chapters that make one hope that this valuable, if uneven, essay will enjoy the widest possible circulation. It comes so close to being exactly the right book, at the right length, by the right man, whose byline commands national attention and respect, that it is altogether lamentable to find in the very heart of the essay— his proposals for a solution, "A Middle Course"—so many grounds for controversy not only with the hawks but with the doves. Perhaps Schlesinger is right to stop flying around and propose a middle ground on which to alight. But his middle ground proposals suffer from the weakness of most middle-of-the-road ideas: they please neither side. And he puts his proposals in such a manner as to provoke angry argument.

For example, Schlesinger, having disposed of the spurious legal argument that we are committed under SEATO, goes on to say that we have taken "moral obligations" to those South Vietnamese who, because of collaboration with us, would be imprisoned or suffer "death" if the Viet Cong should take over South Vietnam by force. Many Americans would not agree that the Administration has committed us all morally to its errors. Many remember that this same argument was long used by the French to justify their refusal to pull out of Algeria. But, were there mass arrests and killings when the French left Algeria? There were not. There is also another alternative which he does not even mention. Those who were most marked by collaboration with us can be offered asylum by us rather than our having to commit more men to fight and die because an error has been made.

There are many flaws of this kind in his reasoning, but the most glaring and controversial is Schlesinger's treatment of the question of our bombing North Vietnam. He impressively reviews all the arguments and demonstrates that the bombing is not only cruel, inhuman, destructive of those we are trying to protect, but that it is basically futile as a military means of winning the war or even bringing about a negotiation. Having proved that, does he therefore conclude that we should stop bombing? No, Schlesinger concludes: "Let us therefore taper off the bombing of the north as prudently as we can." Basically, Schlesinger proposes a general tapering-off: a reduction of bombing, a de-escalation which is, "of course, something a good deal less than withdrawal." He proposes recogni-

tion of the Viet Cong as a legitimate indigenous group entitled to share in an interim regime that would prepare for elections after a negotiated truce, but says that they must first lay down their arms and open their territories. He suggests generous amnesty provisions such as those "which worked so well in the Philippines"—where the communists were defeated. He approves the theories of Generals Ridgway and Gavin who argue that "it is possible to slow down a war without standing still." Finally, he suggests that we should accept a "neutralization under international guarantee," as our "long-run objective in Vietnam." Unfortunately this last proposal is glossed over in a very few words without any attempt to make a strong, thoughtful case for neutralization. That is the main trouble of this chapter's reprint of the *New York Times* article in which it was originally published. It is sometimes brilliantly but often too briefly argued. It goes too far to placate the hawks and not far enough to satisfy the doves.

Most of us, it seems to me from frequent traveling and lecturing across the nation, are confused, worried and frustrated by the war in Vietnam. The majority lies between the hawks and the doves. Whether this middle group will find a new place to stand in Schlesinger's middle ground is a question that can only be answered if and when millions of citizens read his book. One can always argue with and try to perfect an excellent presentation. Without one, nothing can be done. This is so very good a presentation that it is a pleasure to be able to argue with it, to hope for its great success and, eventually, a more thorough, bolder advance by Arthur Schlesinger, a man who has already served his country well and has made a valuable contribution to liberal democracy.

Richard H. Rovere   (review date 10 December 1973)

SOURCE: "Downward the Course of Empire," in *The New Yorker,* Vol. XLIX, No. 42, December 10, 1973, pp. 190, 193-94, 196.

[*Rovere collaborated with Schlesinger on* The General and the President and the Future of American Foreign Policy *(1951). In the following review, he examines Schlesinger's* The Imperial Presidency, *commending his thoroughness and commenting on his blatant democratic partisanship.*]

No other American institution has held as much fascination for either Americans or foreigners as the Presidency. In its Constitutional and separation-of-powers setting, it is an American invention. Though certain attributes of it have been put to use elsewhere, it is still uniquely American. Perhaps it has already seen its best days, but it has endured and worked well for by far the better part of two centuries. "Not many Presidents have been brilliant," Lord Bryce wrote in 1921. "Some have not risen to the full moral height of the position. But none has been base or unfaithful to his trust, and none has tarnished the honor of the nation." Warren G. Harding became President that year, and if the former British Ambassador had written a bit later he might have added a few words to this judgment. It is doubtful, though, whether the case of Harding would have led to any significant alteration of that judgment. What Bryce wrote a half century ago expressed the opinion of most students of the office until at least the late sixties. Far more than any other aspect of the American polity, the Presidency has been under constant scrutiny—hence Watergate—since the early days of the Republic, and it has been the subject of a truckload or two of books, nearly all of them admiring. Yet during the last years of Lyndon Johnson and the first five of Richard Nixon, things have changed greatly, and generalizations by the hundred have been undermined. In domestic affairs, Johnson rose in moral stature, but this was no compensation for the evil that he did in foreign affairs. Bryce's "base" may be rather too strong a word to characterize the motivations of these two men (though a good many Americans have used much stronger terms of condemnation), yet the honor of the nation has been tarnished—not for good and all, one may hope, but for the better part of a decade, and in particularly ugly ways.

After Harding died and Bryce wrote, the cult of the Presidency flourished again, despite pedestrian performances by Calvin Coolidge and Herbert Hoover, and no American celebrated the office more enthusiastically than the historian Arthur Schlesinger, Jr., who, when he was a very young man, wrote a laudatory account of the stewardship of Andrew Jackson. Then, some years later, he went on to produce three volumes of a still uncompleted work in praise of Franklin D. Roosevelt, and followed that with a lengthy account of the brief tenure of John F. Kennedy, in whose Administration he served. Though never a cultist in the true sense and almost always judicious as a chronicler, Schlesinger has probably had more to say than anyone else in praise of the Constitutional arrangements that provide, with a certain amount of elasticity, the powers of the Presidency; it is therefore most fitting that Richard Nixon's career in the White House and on beaches here and there should be examined by Schlesinger, and it is reassuring to find him several times conceding some of the errors of his own earlier generalizations. In his **The Imperial Presidency,** there are more mea culpas than are to be found in the works of many professional historians. This book, which, like several of its predecessors, is huge and compact, can serve as both a history of the Presidency—particularly the role it has played in wars and foreign policy—and an almost up-to-the-minute study of the present regime. When he gets to Nixon, however, the author spends nearly as much time on domestic as he does on foreign affairs.

Schlesinger is, as he always has been, at once partisan and judicious, and he gives one the feeling that his distaste for the character and methods of Nixon would be about the same even if they were ideological twins and co-chairmen of Americans for Democratic Action, though he is a good deal more generous and impersonal than most severe critics of Nixon. He concludes that "Nixon's Presidency was not an aberration but a culmination"—a judgment that, I expect, a good many readers will be unable to accept. The opinion, though, grows out of the stress Schlesinger places on foreign affairs. The word "imperial" in his title is basic to his view of what has happened over the years. Most of the conflicts between the Executive and the Legislative have in one way or another been related to the roles assigned each on war and foreign policy by the Constitu-

tion; it has been the tendency of Presidents almost from the start to place a broad construction on their powers of military command and diplomatic negotiation, while Congress has done the same thing with its control over expenditures and the Senate's powers of advice and, more notably, consent. In the early days these conflicts led to some heated disputes, but we were a distinctly minor power for a century, and such threats to our "security" as there were came mostly from powers that were even more minor or, if major, remote. Meanwhile, though, we were growing in strength, and just before the start of this century the word "imperial" became us. Wilson, the second Roosevelt, and those who followed after Roosevelt had troubles that involved at least some of the issues that have bedevilled Nixon. The language of the Constitution is on the whole admirable, but it is almost two centuries old, and in two centuries not only the country but the precise meaning of words has changed in many respects. For example, the Constitution accords the House the authority to "declare" war, but it is not altogether clear whether "declare" means to initiate war or to "declare," in the sense of "acknowledge," the existence of a state of hostilities. Over such matters there have been several polite tussles and some less than polite ones, but until lately, according to Schlesinger, they were, with the assistance of large-minded men from the third branch, the Judiciary, worked out in the spirit of an old-fashioned word that Schlesinger seems determined to restore to everyday usage—"comity." (I doubt whether any other book published in recent years has used the word as frequently as this one does. A somewhat coarser and more snobbish phrase, "gentlemen's agreement," is closer to today's fashion.) Schlesinger does the language as well as history a service by insisting on comity as the spirit that has so far kept the Constitution alive instead of becoming the series of mere "parchment barriers" that Madison feared it would become unless it embodied the spirit of the people and held their respect. And Schlesinger holds that many of Nixon's shortcomings are the result of his failure to understand the comity and civility that have been essential to making the system function satisfactorily. He not only lacked them himself but staffed almost the entire executive branch with men who were not necessarily less honest or competent than professional politicians but who had not come to understand that ignoring certain rules by which the game is played can make the separation of powers unworkable.

In an uncharacteristic mood of near-despair, Schlesinger, who would like very much to see Nixon out of office, examines the ways in which he could be forced or induced to clear out, and finds all of them lacking. He favors impeachment—the "genius" of which, he says, is to be found in the "fact that it could punish the man without punishing the office"—but he would rather not try it than try it and have it fail, and he is afraid that Nixon has so arranged things that he is sheltered from charges of deliberate complicity in any of the crimes of which the Administration and various of its members have been accused: either he has not been directly involved or, realizing the dangers of complicity, he has destroyed the evidence that would be needed for conviction. Moreover, regarding the Administration as a culmination rather than an aberration, Schlesinger thinks what should be sent to the cleaners is not merely one branch of our government but most of our public and private institutions, which have been for some time in a state of decline that made Nixon inevitable. It is an odd approach, and I, for one, cannot go along with it: Vietnam has been a demoralizing influence, and may in the end prove, particularly since it was so swiftly followed by Watergate, to have been thoroughly destructive. But Schlesinger, like his eminent father, is a cyclical theorist, and he notes that corruption on a grand scale has a way of turning up in our society every fifty years—1823, 1873, 1923, 1973. This seems at odds with his belief that Nixon is a kind of Spenglerian phenomenon, and he offers no evidence that the institutions he finds to be in advanced decay right now will have rejuvenated themselves sufficiently to be ready for another ride down the slippery slope in 2023. Moreover, he feels that Watergate—the investigation, not the developments under investigation—is the best thing that has happened in a long time, since it has alerted us to the wickedness all about us. (Applying his numerology, he writes, "Around the year 2023 the American people would be well advised to . . . start nailing down everything in sight.") But he fails to point out that the corruption of Watergate was on a scale never before known, and its chastening effect could be on a similar scale. At the moment, there seems to be an opportunity for death and an opportunity for revival.

The foregoing should not suggest that this is a book heavy with speculation and prophecy. What there is of that comes at the very end, and some, though not all, of it is in a spirit of playfulness. This is a work of substantial historical scholarship written with lucidity, charm, and wit.

Jeanne Kirkpatrick   (review date 6 April 1974)

SOURCE: "Politics by Other Means," in *Saturday Review/World*, Vol. 1, No. 15, April 6, 1974, pp. 25-7.

[*Kirkpatrick is a former professor of political science and American ambassador to the United Nations. In the following review of* The Imperial Presidency, *Kirkpatrick finds that Schlesinger's analysis of the expansion of the power of the president of the United States lacks balance and is clouded by his political loyalties.*]

We move quickly in America from political conflict to constitutional controversy. The authority and ambiguity of the Constitution encourage recourse to its provisions to strengthen an argument or to prove a point. Since no given division of powers can be proved to be exactly what the Founding Fathers had in mind, dissatisfaction with incumbents is readily translated into dissatisfaction with the balance of power among the branches of government. Not only does constitutional debate seem more serious, more elevated, than simple criticism of personalities, but also the constitutional argument can be made to reinforce the case against particular incumbents. Thus, in the Thirties liberals were not content to excoriate the conservative judges who found the New Deal unconstitutional; they also questioned whether the Constitution had *really* given the Supreme Court the power to review statutes passed by the representatives of the people, and they proposed reforms ranging from packing the court to outlawing judicial review. Three decades later it was conservatives, stimulated by the "permissive" decisions of the Warren court, who worried about the judicial usurpation of legislative power. We are witnessing today a comparable shift in attitudes toward the presidency. Liberals, who for decades were articulate champions of presidential power, have become increasingly sensitive to the dangers of concentrating power in the executive department, while conservatives, long jealous of executive encroachments on congressional power, have lately opposed bills that aim to limit presidential initiative in foreign affairs. The Nixon presidency has won more liberals to the cause of legislative supremacy than have all the constitutional arguments of the century.

Arthur Schlesinger, longtime friend and warm supporter of presidential power, understands this very well, but the knowledge does not inhibit him. In his new book, ***The Imperial Presidency,*** Schlesinger argues that presidential power has finally been so expanded and abused that it threatens the constitutional system. Richard Nixon, he asserts, ". . . not only had an urgent psychological need for exemption from the democratic process. He also boldly sensed a historical opportunity to transform the presidency—to consolidate within the White House all the powers, as against Congress, as against the electorate, as against the rest of the executive branch itself, that a generation of foreign and domestic turbulence had chaotically delivered to the presidency."

An excerpt from *The Imperial Presidency*

A constitutional Presidency, as the great Presidents had shown, could be a very strong Presidency indeed. But what kept a strong President constitutional, in addition to checks and balances incorporated within his own breast, was the vigilance of the nation. Neither impeachment nor repentance would make much difference if the people themselves had come to an unconscious acceptance of the imperial Presidency. The Constitution could not hold the nation to ideals it was determined to betray. The reinvigoration of the written checks in the American Constitution depended on the reinvigoration of the unwritten checks in American society. The great institutions—Congress, the courts, the executive establishment, the press, the universities, public opinion—had to reclaim their own dignity and meet their own responsibilities. As Madison said long ago, the country could not trust to "parchment barriers" to halt the encroaching spirit of power. In the end, the Constitution would live only if it embodied the spirit of the American people.

"There is no week nor day nor hour," wrote Walt Whitman, "when tyranny may not enter upon this country, if the people lose their supreme confidence in themselves,—and lose their roughness and spirit of defiance—Tyranny may always enter—there is no charm, no bar against it—the only bar against it is a large resolute breed of men."

Arthur M. Schlesinger, in his The Imperial Presidency, *Houghton Mifflin Company, 1973.*

Nixon, Schlesinger argues, not only expanded presidential power in the manner of many of his predecessors but also usurped power, violating the requirements for separation of powers, threatening to replace constitutional government with executive autocracy. To prove his case, he goes where everyone concerned with the proper distribution of power in American government must go—back to the Founding Fathers.

It is not hard to demonstrate that the farsighted, creative men who wrote the Constitution feared the concentration and abuse of political power and took pains to devise a political system which divided power vertically, between the states and national government, and horizontally, among the branches of the latter. Nor is it difficult to trace the expansion of presidential power through successive more or less real emergencies, more or less clear and present dangers. Edward S. Corwin's masterful work on the office and powers of the President (much cited by Schlesinger) broke this ground several decades ago. Schlesinger warns us in the foreword that much of his material is "a thrice-told tale" but feels that it provides the necessary context for the consideration of contemporary problems. Of course, Schlesinger does not merely recount constitutional history; he selects, interprets, and judges.

Bertrand Russell once noted that all the observation and experimentation of animal behavior had produced few surprises because "one may say broadly that all the animals that have been carefully observed have behaved so as to confirm the philosophy in which the observer believed before his observations began." So it is with Schlesinger's Presidents. Those whom we knew to be his heroes—especially Franklin Roosevelt and John F. Kennedy—fare very well in this new recapitulation of the development of the presidency. And vice versa. It is not entirely clear why this should be the case. Franklin Roosevelt was hardly a strict constructionist. Instead, he combined an expansive conception of presidential powers with a nearly total disdain for the Supreme Court and its constitutional requirements. The famous "destroyer deal," undertaken in May 1940 in disregard of an explicit congressional injunction against providing matériel to belligerents, may have been desirable and farsighted, but Corwin was probably right when he called it "an endorsement of unrestrained autocracy in the field of our foreign relations." (At least those new converts to strict construction, Senators Fulbright and Church, think so.) Schlesinger, who is especially concerned that Presidents should not have the power to involve the nation in war, justifies as legitimate uses of emergency powers the "destroyer deal" and a series of subsequent unilateral presidential initiatives that took the United States to the edge of war. He does not apply to Roosevelt's acts the tests by which he judges Truman, Lyndon Johnson, and Nixon guilty of the illegitimate use of emergency powers.

The judgment merits scrutiny. However monstrous, Hitler in early 1940 did not constitute a "sudden," "direct," or "immediate" threat to the United States. In issuing the "shoot on sight" orders to our convoys, Roosevelt did not act "in the case of a neighboring country or an imminent invasion of the United States." In early 1940 it was Britain

whose life was threatened, not the United States. The purpose of these remarks is not to suggest that Roosevelt was wrong, but to recall that in the year-and-a-half before Pearl Harbor, Roosevelt, claiming emergency powers in a situation in which the survival of the nation was not immediately threatened, repeatedly took actions that risked involving the nation in war and took them, moreover, without consulting or accurately informing a Congress which would certainly have disapproved. Schlesinger's willingness to accept Roosevelt's justification for these and later unilateral claims of presidential power illustrates the flexibility of his criteria.

Indeed Schlesinger applies not a double standard but a whole host of standards in approving and disapproving Presidents' behavior. Though very tough on other cold-war Presidents, he hardly glances at John F. Kennedy. The Bay of Pigs, a clear-cut case of unilateral presidential action that might have involved the nation in war, is brusquely dismissed with a reference to the prevailing atmosphere. That atmosphere, incidentally, had some curious characteristics. Almost no one seems to have been himself. Congress was "mesmerized" by the "supposed need for instant responses," and Congress and the executive alike accepted executive supremacy "as if under hypnosis." This hypnosis hypothesis contributes a fascinating new dimension to our understanding of how "the best and the brightest" made so many mistakes in those years. Otherwise, Schlesinger finds Kennedy's action in the Cuban missile crisis an example of the justified and successful use of emergency powers.

Kennedy is the only one of the post-World War II Presidents who on this reading is not found guilty of having arrogated new powers to the presidency. Even Eisenhower, when he finally got around to resisting Joe McCarthy's guerrilla war on the executive departments, made new claims—"the most absolute assertion of presidential right to withhold information from Congress ever uttered to that day in American history." Korea "beguiled" Truman into making, and Congress into accepting, "an unprecedented claim for inherent presidential power to go to war." Meanwhile the Taft-Coudert Amendment, which prohibited committing U.S. troops abroad "in advance of aggression solely by executive decision," was beaten back by such presidential liberals as Paul Douglas, J. W. Fulbright, Herbert Lehman, Wayne Morse.

Under Lyndon Johnson, violation and distortion of the Constitution proceeded apace. John Kennedy's dispatch of 16,000 American "advisers" to Vietnam "took place under familiar arrangements for military assistance based on congressional legislation and appropriation," and so created no problem even though a good many of these "advisers" found their way into combat. But "there were no serious precedents" for Johnson's decision to send 22,000 combat troops and to start bombing without a declaration of war by Congress. "There was of course the Tonkin Gulf resolution, rushed through Congress in August 1964 in a stampede of misinformation and misconception, if not of deliberate deception." But Johnson, Schlesinger confides, "did not believe for a moment that the resolution provided the legal basis for his action."

Schlesinger does not doubt that Johnson could have had a declaration of war for the asking, but he does not give him any credit for the desire to limit the conflict by not formally declaring war and "scaring the hell out of the people."

Bad as they were, Johnson's offenses pale beside those of his successor. For Schlesinger, Watergate is only the symptom of a much more serious constitutional crisis. Schlesinger's Nixon is a "genuine revolutionary" bent on transforming the American system of government by checks and balances into a plebiscitary presidentialist regime with himself cast as Louis Napoleon or Charles de Gaulle. Watergate symbolizes the revolutionary presidency, the theory of presidential power that places the President above the Constitution.

It is easy enough to demonstrate that Richard Nixon has attempted to arrogate new, objectionable, and probably unconstitutional powers to the presidency. But, in a context that stresses the progressive concentration of powers in the chief executive and the questionable actions of his predecessors, it is not easy to demonstrate that Nixon is a "revolutionary." There is also the problem of the relationship between the "imperial presidency," which the author tells us was "essentially a creation of foreign policy," and the "revolutionary presidency," which presumably is the creation of the present incumbent. Sometimes the terms are used as if synonymous. Perhaps the explanation is that Schlesinger's distress with the Nixon administration has led him to exaggerate when he calls Nixon a revolutionary. Perhaps he means to say that Nixon's new claims accelerated the trend to executive autocracy and that the cumulative impact on the system of concentrating so much power in the presidency has produced a constitutional crisis.

Certainly Schlesinger's distress is acute. He deplores Nixon's staff, his style, his policies. He reproaches Nixon for constitutional offenses: attempting to circumvent the will of Congress by impoundment, abusing executive privileges, continuing the war in Vietnam after the repeal of the Tonkin Gulf resolution, conducting an air war in Cambodia after the withdrawal of American troops. He holds him squarely responsible for the criminal offenses of his subordinates. He reproaches him for his solitary habits; for his immoderate concern with leaks; for his tendency to see enemies everywhere, to exaggerate dangers, to misuse "national security"; for his choice of a cabinet; for his expansion of the White House staff; and above all for his debasement of the White House ethos ("this was not the White House we had known"). Repeatedly Schlesinger raises the question, Has not the time come for impeachment? His answer: "Only condign punishment would restore popular faith in the presidency and deter future Presidents from illegal conduct." Laws limiting presidential authority will not solve the problem and might, furthermore, have the undesirable effect of limiting some future Roosevelt. Only impeachment, as object lesson as well as punishment, can make Watergate "the best thing to have happened to the presidency in a long time." That, plus the reinvigoration of Congress and the people, would ensure

us against the revolutionary presidency—provided that we also elect the right sort of man to the office.

Writing books (like making war) may be a continuation of politics by other means. This is a political book written to influence the way we feel and think about the current scene. It is as timely as the moment, and the passion of the author adds zest to his writing. But the fact that Arthur Schlesinger is one of the most prolific and honored historians of the period does not make this a scholarly work. Schlesinger is also a political man who has strong views and a personal stake in many of the events of our times.

His antipathy for Richard Nixon is of long standing and great intensity. It leads him to some omissions, some hyperbole, some purple prose, and some unfair argument. To describe the establishment of a volunteer army as though there had been no popular discontent with the draft, no clamor in Congress for its end, as though the whole policy derived from Nixon's desire to "solve the problem of the undependable army" and "liberate Presidents for a wider range of foreign adventure," is to engage in fantasy. So is the suggestion that price and wage controls were undertaken as a way to gain "even more power."

To imply that if it were functioning properly, the U.S. government would more nearly resemble the Fourth, rather than the Fifth, French Republic is quite simply incredible. To assert that the American middle class was unconcerned about the Indochina war "as long as the Americans killing and dying in Vietnam were sons of poor whites and poor blacks" is an unhistorical calumny (albeit a fashionable one). To argue that the Tonkin Gulf resolution did not constitute congressional authorization for the Vietnam war but that its repeal made the war less legal is far-fetched.

The list could easily be extended, but its only purpose is to illustrate what a knowledgeable reader will readily see for himself: that, in *The Imperial Presidency*, Arthur Schlesinger is writing as a partisan of a particular interpretation of recent times. Some Nixon haters will love this book, and supporters of the Nixon cause (if such remain) will scorn it. Persons seeking a balanced discussion of the presidency are advised to look elsewhere.

Garry Wills (review date 12 November 1978)

SOURCE: A review of *Robert Kennedy and His Times,* in *The New York Times Book Review,* November 12, 1978, pp. 7, 54, 56.

[*Wills is an American syndicated columnist and the author of books on such widely diverse subjects as Jack Ruby, race relations in America, and G. K. Chesterton. He is probably best known for his incisive political commentaries, especially those contained in his* Nixon Agonistes: The Crisis of a Self-Made Man *(1970) and* Confessions of a Conservative *(1979). A critic of both the American liberal and conservative establishments, Wills has been described by one critic as "an undogmatic conservative who is ready to let his experiences influence his conclusions" and who is "cheerfully resigned to being a singular conservative, a renegade in the eyes of others who crowd under that rubric." In the follow-*

ing review of Schlesinger's Robert Kennedy and His Times, *Wills praises Schlesinger's presentation of the complexities of Robert Kennedy's character and milieu.*]

[In **Robert Kennedy and His Times**] Arthur Schlesinger has a kind of proprietary right to this subject. He was the craftsman of the framework within which Kennedys have been most often studied—the claim that Kennedys mature late; but that the maturity, when it comes, is spectacular. That was the theme of the books appearing just after Robert Kennedy's death. Authors like Jack Newfield, David Halberstam, Jules Witcover, William vanden Heuvel and Milton Gwirtzman granted that there had been a "ruthless" edge on the younger Robert Kennedy, but they maintained that tragedy and experience had mellowed, had deepened him by the time tragedy claimed him. Unfortunately for that thesis, Mr. Kennedy's last political act was to launch the charge at Eugene McCarthy in their television debate before the California primary: "You say you are going to take ten thousand black people and move them into Orange County." The authors I mention muted this problem by neglecting to quote the sentence. Mr. Schlesinger, to his credit, not only quotes it but adds: "This sounded, and was, demagogic." One comes to respect Mr. Schlesinger's confidence that Robert Kennedy does not need special pleading. All Kennedy critics are quoted frequently and fairly. The challenging, somewhat prickly charm of Mr. Kennedy is by this means more forcibly conveyed than in more protective works.

The last part of Mr. Schlesinger's title, referring to "His Times," is as important as the treatment of Mr. Kennedy's own character. He takes this opportunity to rewrite, in large part, his version of the Kennedy Presidency in **A Thousand Days.** A great deal more is known than when he wrote his 1964 history of Camelot. Squalid characters from the C.I.A. and the under world now move among the knights and princesses. Names like Judith Exner and Sam Giancana must be included, and Mr. Schlesinger does not balk at his duty. The Church Committee's findings are drawn on, along with material released under the Freedom of Information Act.

The C.I.A. findings are important in a biography of Robert Kennedy, because Mr. Schlesinger recognizes that the Attorney General, after the Bay of Pigs, became the principal cheerleader for Operation Mongoose, the campaign of terror and sabotage directed at Castro. Mr. Kennedy's own notes of a White House meeting on Nov. 4, 1961, present his determination: "My idea is to stir things up on island with espionage, sabotage, general disorder, run & operated by Cubans themselves with every group but Batistaites & Communists. Do not know if we will be successful in overthrowing Castro but we have nothing to lose in my estimate."

Two months later, Mr. Kennedy met with the C.I.A. organizers of Mongoose and told them their work was "top priority," that "no time, money, effort—or manpower—be spared." Chemicals to incapacitate sugar workers were discussed, and the encouragement of "gangster elements" in Cuba. When an opportunity for reassessment arose, Mr. Kennedy wrote: "I am in favor of pushing ahead rather than taking any step back." Mr. Schlesinger concludes

that Mr. Kennedy wanted Mongoose to unleash "the terrors of the earth" on Cuba because "Castro was high on his list of emotions." Like others, Mr. Schlesinger can find no direct evidence that Mr. Kennedy knew of the assassination plots against Castro. But the C.I.A. was being urged to acts of secret war that involved killing; it probably felt authorized by what Mr. Schlesinger calls "a driven sense in the administration that someone ought to be doing something to make life difficult for Castro." "Mongoose was poorly conceived and wretchedly executed. It deserved greatly to fail. It was Robert Kennedy's most conspicuous folly."

The one place where Mr. Schlesinger seems to hedge a bit on the evidence is his treatment of the missile crisis. *A Thousand Days,* preceding Mr. Kennedy's own book on that crisis (*Thirteen Days*), could report Robert's private pledge to remove the Jupiter missiles from Turkey after a decent interval ("I mentioned four or five months"), so long as this was never presented as a quid pro quo. Mr. Schlesinger thinks this offer invalidates the argument (of I. F. Stone and others) that President Kennedy did not, as he claimed, "make every effort to find peace and every effort to give our adversary room to move." But the Russians knew as well as Americans that the Turkish missiles were obsolete (they had already been recalled, but the order had not gone into effect). The missiles' bargaining potential was only as a "quid pro quo" that would allow Russia to back off with better grace; their withdrawal sacrificed nothing, militarily, on our part. Robert Kennedy quotes his brother as saying, "I am not going to push the Russians an inch beyond what is necessary." But in risking nuclear war rather than admit the private deal he was making, John Kennedy pushed them hard indeed, and backed up that push with an arbitrary deadline of 48 hours. Mr. Schlesinger tried to defend the deadline as prompted by fear that nuclear warheads might be delivered to Cuba within that period. But it was not known for sure that they had not been delivered, or that 24 hours one way or the other made any difference.

Mr. Schlesinger's difficulties in this area are complicated by the fact that his own Watergate-era book, **The Imperial Presidency** denounces secret Presidential pledges as a device of executive diplomacy. To say that Mr. Kennedy *did* make a deal on the missiles (and so was being pacific), he has to admit what critics like Richard Nixon accused Mr. Kennedy of—some secret concession. The Kennedy Administration, when it denied that charge, was both usurping power and lying about it—the very thing Mr. Schlesinger's **Imperial Presidency** finds distasteful in the Nixon Administration. Mr. Schlesinger nods warily to "those who think that no President would ever make a secret commitment," slips into the supposition that "perhaps there may be a place for secret diplomacy," then sprints hopefully toward the conclusion that "the missile crisis was a triumph, perhaps the only triumph of flexible response." Mr. Gwirtzman and Mr. vanden Heuvel say that Robert Kennedy considered the missile crisis his finest hour, and Mr. Schlesinger makes it clear that Mr. Kennedy took a stand far more sensible than that of his own hero, Maxwell Taylor. But Mr. Kennedy joined others in "jumping on" Adlai Stevenson for proposing an open bargain of Turkish missiles for those on Cuba.

There is no denying that Robert Kennedy was fierce in his enmities—toward, Roy Cohn, Jimmy Hoffa, Lyndon Johnson, Eugene McCarthy; or that he personalized struggles, even at the highest policy level (as in turning the C.I.A. loose to get Castro.) He was also fierce in his loyalties, and paradoxically, fiercer in tenderness. Mr. Schlesinger quotes Shirley MacLaine on the way his "psychic violence" produced gentleness. Mr. Kennedy had the scrapper's instinct for underdogs, and a restless desire to know about the different forms of human suffering. All these aspects of the man are captured in this learned and thorough, balanced yet affectionate book. I don't know if Mr. Schlesinger is right about the gradual but inevitable improvement of Kennedys with age; but his own books about Kennedys keep getting better. The one on Edward, when he gets around to it, should be a gem.

Mr. Schlesinger is most admirable in his restraint when it comes to the "might-have-beens" of 1968. Others indulge the hope that Mr. Kennedy could have made sense of that year's chaos—won his party's nomination and the Presidency, ended the Vietnam war and brought us peace, with ourselves as well as other nations. I doubt all that, for reasons strengthened by a reading of Mr. Schlesinger. People do not want to remember how torn and angry the nation was; and Robert Kennedy polarized, at his best as well as his worst. The war was losing popularity in 1968, but the critics of the war were losing popularity more dramatically. Mr. Nixon and Mr. Wallace, between them, took a landslide number of votes.

Mr. Kennedy was not popular in the South because of his civil rights achievements as Attorney General. He would have been even less popular when he arrived there trailing his antiwar "kids." And no Kennedy would move in 1968 without Mayor Daley. Through all his in-again-out-again lunges and withdrawls of 1968, Mr. Kennedy thought constantly of Mr. Daley, consulted and cultivated him. How would he be able to keep Mr. Daley and keep his kids?

President Johnson's anger and will to sabotage would have been something on an entirely different scale with Mr. Kennedy than it was with Hubert Humphrey's late not-quite rebellion.

To say Mr. Kennedy could not have put the nation together again in 1968 is less an indictment of him than of the nation. Richard Nixon actually looked moderate between the kids of Mr. McCarthy and the anti-kids of George Wallace.

Mr. Schlesinger, an adviser during the time when Mr. Kennedy felt drawn both to run and to withdraw, reflects the dragon flying of his spirit as new depths paradoxically tossed him on the surface. The feckless gestures to Mr. McCarthy, the meetings where Edward Kennedy said "I don't know what we are meeting about," the insomniac pacing of Mr. Kennedy from those he wanted to urge him on and those he wanted to hold him back—all show that the man of narrower earlier focus was giving way to a free-dom that felt the chaos but made him helpless to handle it with Mr. Nixon's nasty efficiency.

Mr. Kennedy had become a person gulping at delayed knowledge with an almost haunted ferocity. Some of the signs looked like delayed adolescence—the Tennyson quotes, and sudden tears; the maudlin use of post-Camelotisms. "His favorite song—one heard it so often blaring from some unseen source in his New York apartment—was 'The Impossible Dream.' " This was the Kennedy who slandered Mr. McCarthy while he envied him, who wondered if there was not something to Adlai Stevenson after all. Death did not take away a successful candidate in 1968, but something more interesting.

An excerpt from *The Age of Jackson*

From the start of the century, first in banking and insurance, then in transportation, canals, bridges, turnpikes, then in manufacturing, the corporation was gradually becoming the dominant form of economic organization. The generation of Jackson was the first to face large-scale adjustment to this new economic mechanism. For owners and large investors, the adjustment presented no particular problem. But those on the outside had a feeling of deep misgiving which was less an economic or political than a moral protest: it was basically a sense of shock. . . .

For a people still yearning for an economy dominated by individual responsibility, still under the spell of the Jeffersonian dream, the corporation had one outstanding characteristic: its moral irresponsibility. "Corporations have neither bodies to be kicked, nor souls to be damned," went a favorite aphorism. Beyond good and evil, insensible to argument or appeal, they symbolized the mounting independence of the new economy from the restraints and scruples of personal life.

Arthur M. Schlesinger, in his The Age of Jackson, *Book Find Club, 1945.*

Carroll Engelhardt   (essay date Spring 1981)

SOURCE: "Man in the Middle: Arthur M. Schlesinger, Jr., and Postwar American Liberalism," in *South Atlantic Quarterly*, Vol. 80, No. 2, Spring, 1981, pp. 119-38.

[*In the following excerpt, Engelhardt examines Schlesinger's concept of liberalism as it is developed in many of his writings, contending that Schlesinger, by maintaining a centrist position, has tried to value "realism more than idealism." Yet, Engelhardt argues, "by stressing the role of pragmatic intellectuals, he has made a fetish of empiricism . . . and has identified too closely with the existing power structure."*]

During the 1950's many American intellectuals believed in the exhaustion of political ideology, the pluralist theory of politics, and the consensus interpretation of United States history. As a leading intellectual, Schlesinger not only shared these beliefs, he anticipated them with *The Age of Jackson* (1945) and *The Vital Center* (1949), two highly influential works that did much to shape the new liberalism. "Professor Schlesinger," Arthur Mann [in "The Progressive Tradition," *The Reconstruction of American History,* edited by John Higham, 1962] has said, "writes history as he votes and votes as he writes." Clearly there is a connection between Schlesinger's liberalism, his conception of the intellectual as political activist, and his historical scholarship. Just as he has sought to combine ideas and politics in his career as political commentator, so he has combined intellectual and political history in his studies of the Jackson, Roosevelt, and Kennedy administrations. Narrative history in the grand style, these works are also partisan in extolling the virtues of strong Democratic presidents who, aided by the reform ideas of leading intellectuals, carried on the liberal tradition in America. Schlesinger's choice of historical subjects is significant because it reveals his predilection for the charismatic leaders he sees as essential for achieving liberal reforms.

The foreword of *The Age of Jackson* established the book's contemporary relevance by suggesting that "the world crisis has given new urgency to the question of the 'meaning' of democracy," and by insisting that "the key to that meaning is . . . to be sought in the concrete record of what democracy has meant in the past." From his study of the concrete record Schlesinger concluded that the tradition of Jefferson and Jackson—and in fact the basic meaning of American liberalism—involved the movement on the part of other sections of society to restrain the power of the business community. He emphasized the role of eastern intellectuals and labor reformers in giving intellectual coherence to the demands of the common man for social change. Faced with the new problems of industrial development, the Jacksonians, a coalition of reformers and the disadvantaged groups of society, rejected the antistatism of Jeffersonian tradition and resorted to a strong president and government intervention to restore relative economic equality among the classes of the country. Thus the Jacksonians were pragmatic realists who recognized the basic issue of power: the need for a liberal government strong enough to resist the demands of the business community. In response to this realistic revision of liberalism some orthodox Jeffersonians were so committed to their agrarian, antistatist ideology that they abandoned the Jacksonian cause and condemned themselves to political irrelevance, a sin which pointed up the dangers of ideological commitment and which Schlesinger could not forgive in Jackson's time or his own.

For Schlesinger the historical lessons of Jacksonianism to contemporary liberals were clear. To preserve democracy and achieve social justice, liberals must be pragmatic, nonideological, and have a realistic view of human nature. Although supporting strong government to restrain business, they should be pluralists, committed to a multi-interest state, seeking to preserve as much variety within the state as is consistent with energetic action by government. The balance of government, business, and other interests can be achieved not by some rigid ideological system but only by "an earnest, toughminded, pragmatic attempt to wrestle with new problems as they come, without

being enslaved by a theory of the past, or a theory of the future." And finally, Schlesinger admonished liberals facing the problems of postwar America to remember that man is neither all brute nor all angel, and that there are no easy solutions to social problems.

Historical scholarship, represented by *The Age of Jackson,* marked Schlesinger's first step toward redefining American liberalism as the vital center. Two further steps in this process were his participation in the formation in 1947 of Americans for Democratic Action—the organizational expression of centrist liberalism—and the appearance in 1949 of *The Vital Center,* which provided the intellectual justification for a new liberalism appropriate to the realities of the postwar world. In Schlesinger's view, mid-twentieth-century liberalism required restatement because of three developments: first, the New Deal, which demonstrated the success of pragmatic reforms in making capitalism work; second, the exposure of the Soviet Union, which revealed the excesses of a messianic ideology that sacrificed individuals to its vision of a future utopia; and third, a deepening knowledge of man, which reflected Reinhold Niebuhr's emphasis on sinfulness as a basic quality of human nature. To preserve freedom amidst the terrors of technology that produced the alienation leading to totalitarianism, both the democratic Right and Left must overcome past failures. Because of their close identification with business, American conservatives had neglected their social responsibilities, while liberals' sentimental beliefs in beneficent human nature and automatic social progress had blinded them to the realities of power. Suggesting that a successful defense of the vital center required the cooperation of the democratic Right and Left, Schlesinger was sufficiently skeptical of the extreme right wing of the business community to insist upon a revived liberalism that would reject totalitarian solutions to the problems of industrial societies, reassert its faith in the integrity of the individual, and seek to protect both the liberty and security of individuals through the "mixed system" of the welfare state. Although the vital center must of necessity be both anti-Fascist and anti-Communist, in the book Schlesinger emphasized the latter because it seemed a greater contemporary danger.

In a chapter entitled "The Communist Challenge to America," Schlesinger analyzed the twofold menace: the external threat of Soviet power in the world and the internal threat of Communist subversion from within. Schlesinger attributed the start of the Cold War to Soviet aggression, which he saw rooted in traditional Russian expansionism made more ominous by a dynamic Communist ideology. It was more dangerous because "Communism can rally its fifth columns in any corner of the world where injustice and poverty give it a foothold." Moreover, "nothing less than the entire world can in the end satisfy totalitarian imperialism, for totalitarianism charges imperialism with the fear and frenzy of an ideological crusade. . . ." Given the inherent expansive logic of the Russian system, Schlesinger feared that "tomorrow Soviet power will surely spread everywhere that it meets no firm resistance."

The anxious tone of Schlesinger's rhetoric indicates the

temper of postwar liberalism. Obviously liberalism had to become increasingly toughminded to survive. To meet the external threat Schlesinger argued that Soviet expansion could best be checked by the realistic policy of containment (Truman Doctrine) and the idealistic policy of reconstruction (Marshall Plan and Point Four) in both Europe and Asia. It was necessary to build up Western military capabilities to deter the Russians from further aggression acts, but Schlesinger recommended stopping short of outright intimidation because that would only unite the Soviet people behind a totalitarian regime. Schlesinger shared George Kennan's hope that containment of Soviet expansion would eventually generate internal pressures forcing modification of their system. Further, by abandoning colonial imperialism, supporting nationalist movements, and furthering technological progress through programs like the Marshall Plan and Point Four, the West could provide an attractive alternative to communism in the Third World and frustrate its messianic hope for world-wide revolution.

Thus in his initial statement of liberal foreign policy objectives, Schlesinger was at one with the Realist school of American diplomacy in recognizing the necessity for use of power in foreign relations but restrained in his recommended uses for that power. Yet idealism was combined with realism; Schlesinger saw containment as more than a military policy and urged the creation of a non-Communist Left throughout the world to reform the social evils that give communism its toehold in society. The Left must be non-Communist because the Soviets aimed at subverting the independent Left in order to advance the interests of Soviet foreign policy and to destroy existing social systems. Therefore, liberals must exclude Communists from their organizations and regain their "radical nerve," which meant being as progressive, realistic, and toughminded as the Communists. To this end Schlesinger attacked and rejected the sentimentality of the "Doughface Progressives"—those Popular Front liberals who had supported Henry Wallace in 1948 and who were "fellow travelers" as a consequence. Because of their sentimental belief in progress and their unwarranted optimism about human nature, Schlesinger charged, the Progressives were "soft," "shallow," and "impotent." Because their philosophy did not have room "for the discipline of responsibility or for the danger of power," the Progressives could not be trusted to deal with the internal and external Soviet dangers.

When viewed together it is clear that *The Age of Jackson* and *The Vital Center* were both shaped by Schlesinger's revulsion at the ideological excesses of fascism and communism and that both assumed that democratic capitalism, when tempered by realistic reforms, provided an acceptable alternative to totalitarian systems. Both demonstrate Schlesinger's commitment to pluralism by suggesting that competition among several groups is essential for preserving freedom in a democratic-capitalist state. Finally, *The Age of Jackson* established a reputable political ancestry for the new liberalism articulated in *The Vital Center.* Thus the new liberalism was not so new; it had deep roots in the American past. Although Schlesinger is seemingly at odds with the consensus school because of his stress on conflict and discontinuity in United States history, these two books show that for him conflict takes place within carefully circumscribed limits and that his discussion of the vital center implies belief in a consensus of opinion on the value of freedom and the continuity of this widely shared commitment from the nation's founding.

Taken by itself *The Vital Center* indicates that anticommunism has been fundamental to Schlesinger's analysis of the postwar world and his reassessment of American liberalism. His anticommunism was frequently expressed in terms of a hostility to ideological thinking in general. The problem with ideology, according to him, is its rigid and dogmatic abstraction from the untidy reality of human experience. He insists that the most vital American social thought has been empirical and pragmatic and that American liberalism has functioned best when it has been open to a variety of ideas and has avoided hardening into an ideology. To provide a respectable philosophical pedigree for the new liberalism's hostility to ideology, Schlesinger appealed to the ideas of William James and Reinhold Niebuhr. Following James he insisted that liberals must be empirical and pragmatic because social reality is complex and constantly changing; empiricism and pragmatism are methods which keep liberals free from frozen ideological patterns of thought, enable them to test their ideas against experience, and allow them to keep abreast of the changing world. Schlesinger credited Niebuhr's combination of political pragmatism and Christian theology with reshaping postwar liberal thought and acknowledged his own intellectual debt to Niebuhrian assumptions about the mixed nature of man, the necessity of power and dangers of moral absolutes in politics, and the impossibility of achieving social utopia.

Given his hostility to ideology, it is ironic that Schlesinger's defense of centrist liberalism as a "fighting faith" constituted an ideology in Karl Mannheim's classic definition of the term [Karl Mannheim, *Ideology and Utopia*]. During the 1950's it came to represent the dominant outlook of most American intellectuals, and in their hands it became an interest-bound defense of existing United States society as an acceptable alternative to communism and fascism. Borrowing insights from neoorthodoxy, sharing anti-ideological, pluralist, and consensus beliefs, Schlesinger, among many American intellectuals, became a liberal with conservative assumptions: a pessimistic view of human nature, a fear of radicalism and mass democracy, a reliance on groups and their leaders that became a force for moderation and compromise, and a belief in slow, moderate change within the framework of a stable society.

Schlesinger's anticommunism, with its correlative rejection of ideology and blindness to his own ideological assumptions, has had several serious consequences for his liberalism. By rejecting ideology, Schlesinger not only excluded from consideration radical ideas he did not like, but he also neglected the utopian and idealistic elements of his own liberalism. His empiricism, pragmatism, and realism led him to identify closely with the existing structure of American society. Whether it is possible to achieve meaningful social change from a position of such close identification with society is questionable; it may be necessary to take a more critical stance and give more attention to the "ends" of reform than Schlesinger has done in his defense of centrist liberalism. Anticommunism also led Schlesinger and other liberals to emphasize the issues of foreign policy and loyalty at the expense of domestic reform. Since the United States stressed military containment and national security in the 1950's and neglected the progressive social change Schlesinger had so strongly advocated in *The Vital Center,* one must ask why his liberal objectives were not achieved? Were liberal intellectuals like Schlesinger in some way responsible for the conservative drift of American policies? For his part he has denied liberal responsibility and has blamed conservatives for these developments. Whether liberals must share responsibility for the excesses of military containment and national security, despite Schlesinger's denials, can be determined by the examination of Schlesinger's anticommunism and its impact on his thinking about foreign and domestic policy.

On the anti-Communist issue Schlesinger characteristically mediated between extremes: how does one eliminate Communists from positions of influence in the United States and yet preserve civil liberties? He wanted to avoid the witch-hunting tactics of right wingers Martin Dies and Joseph McCarthy on the one hand, while on the other he rejected the "sentimental" idea of "Doughface Progressives" that prosecution of Communists or fellow travelers in any circumstances is a violation of civil liberties. As an alternative to repression he maintained that reform was the best way to combat communism, which could be defeated in the long run "only by removing the internal sources of its appeal." In two magazine articles published in 1952, Schlesinger defended his reform position from right-wing attacks by arguing that New Dealers had been anti-Stalinist and that communism had failed in the 1930's because "the New Deal showed that reform and recovery were possible within the framework of free institutions."

Schlesinger also distinguished himself from the Right by his greater concern for procedural safeguards to protect the civil liberties of the accused. For example, he advocated following the doctrine of "clear and present danger," which suggests that freedom of speech can be curtailed in the interests of national security and yet limits any restrictions to genuine national emergencies. On these grounds Schlesinger thought Communists in strategic government positions—the State Department and National Security agencies—constituted a "clear and present danger" and could therefore be dismissed. This did not violate civil liberties, because the First Amendment did not give the Communist party the constitutional right to be a secret espionage network nor did American citizens have a constitutional right to work for government. Although Schlesinger supported government loyalty investigations, he did not want government loyalty programs to degenerate into purges of liberals and nonconformists. He did criticize Truman's Executive Order and the State Department for lack of procedural protection for the accused, and he did propose criteria he hoped would prevent witch-hunting and correct abuses in the Truman Loyalty Program.

In taking this stand Schlesinger did not consider the effectiveness of his proposed measures for protecting the constitutional liberties liberals traditionally have sought to preserve. He ignored the possibilities that greater procedural safeguards actually increase the potential damage to anyone adjudged disloyal by an administrative tribunal and that by focusing on Communists as a special case the clear-and-present-danger doctrine actually threatened the rights of free speech for everyone else. Schlesinger neglected to reflect on these issues because like right wing anti-Communists he believed communism to be a genuine internal threat to the security of the United States—a questionable assumption given the small size of the Communist party and the failure of the FBI and the Truman Loyalty Program to discover a Communist espionage network—and he was therefore willing to sacrifice traditional liberties in order to meet this perceived danger.

Schlesinger also applied the doctrine of clear and present danger to the issue of employing Communists as college teachers. In 1949 he criticized the University of Washington for dismissing three faculty members—two Communists and one fellow traveler—without recourse to the doctrine which placed their proceedings outside the American civil liberties tradition, transformed "those wretched nonentities into living evidences of the capitalist assault against freedom," and made them "far more powerful in martyrdom than they were in freedom." As Schlesinger's shrill language indicates, he had no sympathy for the "loathsome ideas" of "these wretched nonentities," but he insisted that tenured Communists could not be dismissed on grounds of beliefs alone short of clear and present danger. Free discussion in the market place of ideas was Schlesinger's final defense against Communist influence: "if democratic ideas are as good as we believe them to be, this is the testing which will prove it beyond all doubt" [**"Right to Loathsome Ideas,"** in *Saturday Review* (14 May 1949)]. But if the market place were really so effective in excluding "loathsome ideas," then why restrict the hiring of teachers at all? It seems that on this point Schlesinger significantly moderated his liberal principles, conceded some important ground to right-wingers, and contributed to the anti-Communist hysteria of the late 1940's and early 1950's.

Despite his agility Schlesinger's attempt to maintain a middle position has not satisfied everyone. Over the years radicals like Carey McWilliams, Christopher Lasch, and Ronald Radosh have argued that liberals like Schlesinger shared many common assumptions with right wing anti-Communists. There is some merit to the radical critique in that liberals did agree with conservatives that communism represented a serious internal danger and that the Truman Loyalty Program, the official listing of subversive organizations, and the prosecution of Communist party leaders were necessary to meet the threat, but radicals blur essential distinctions between the two species of anticommunism. Unlike the McCarthyites, Schlesinger did condemn hysterical forms of anticommunism, did criticize the poor procedures of the Truman program, did urge better procedural safeguards to protect innocent victims from witch-hunts, and did stress social reform as the best way to combat communism. One may question the effectiveness of these actions, but their existence does indicate that Schlesinger attempted to preserve some elements of his liberal heritage and does distinguish him from right-wing anti-Communists.

Schlesinger's anticommunism also had a significant impact on his thinking about foreign policy. His responses to the Korean and Vietnam crises reveal the problems of his attempt to maintain the vital center in foreign affairs. In reacting to the Korean War in 1950 Schlesinger revealed an important characteristic of postwar liberalism: its tendency to support limited objectives with unlimited rhetoric. What threatened United States national security in Korea, according to Schlesinger, in a book coauthored with fellow-liberal Richard Rovere [***The General and the President,*** 1951], "was not the possible conquest of South Korea but the possible conquest of millions of minds throughout the world." If the United States had not challenged North Korean aggression, "millions of people . . . would have found rich confirmation of their fear that Russian power was in fact invincible, that American big-talk was a shameless bluff, and that the UN was a snare and a delusion. . . ." Notwithstanding that containment had originally been developed to check Soviet expansion in Europe, Schlesinger and Rovere now argued that the policy required fighting a limited war in Korea to discourage Russia from expanding elsewhere, thus making manifest the globalism inherent in the Truman Doctrine. Although Schlesinger and Rovere assumed the existence of monolithic World Communism and their defense of the Korean war had global implications, they rejected the alternative of unilaterialism posed by General MacArthur because it involved an unlimited ideological crusade that would risk atomic war with the Soviet Union. Whereas MacArthur wanted "total victory" over communism in Korea, Schlesinger and Rovere supported Truman's more limited goal of negotiated settlement. While the conservative MacArthur and the liberal Schlesinger and Rovere shared common assumptions about the global nature of the Communist menace, their shared commitment to unilateral action was less apparent to the liberals. Misled by the terms "collective security" and "UN action," Schlesinger and Rovere ignored the fact that Truman's decision to intervene was made unilaterally without consulting the UN or the European allies of the United States.

As a good empiricist Schlesinger subsequently modified his stand somewhat in response to changing world realities. By 1960 he was writing about the varieties of communism but still insisted that the Soviet Union was a theological society characterized by commitment to a dogmatic ideology. Then the Vietnam crisis further contributed to the modification of his thinking at the same time it forced him to defend his earlier position.

As the Vietnam War escalated after 1965, the New Left and revisionist historians increased their criticism of both the war and Cold War liberalism, charging that Vietnam was the logical result of the excessive anticommunism and aggressive United States foreign policy of the postwar period. Schlesinger responded to these attacks by defending his anti-Communist stance of the 1940's and by denying a necessary connection between liberal anticommunism

and containment policy of that time and the Vietnam disaster. As he said in 1967, "I write as an unrepentant anti-Communist—unrepentant because there seems to me no other conceivable position for a liberal to take." He argued that official and intellectual reactions of the 1940's have legitimacy if one understands that communism at that time meant Stalinism, which was brutal, repressive, and in secure control of Communist parties throughout the world. Schlesinger cannot accept the revisionist argument "that Russia was moved only by a desire to protect its security and would have been satisfied by the control of Eastern Europe." Schlesinger still insists, as he did in 1949, that "postwar collaboration between Russia and America . . . [was] inherently impossible" because Communist ideology committed the Soviet Union to a steady expansion of its power and to a distrust of capitalist democracies like the United States. Although Schlesinger regrets that the United States eventually exhibited its own forms of excessive self-righteousness, he maintains that given the dynamic of a totalitarian ideology plus Stalin's paranoia, even "the most rational of American policies could hardly have averted the Cold War."

Vietnam posed special problems for Schlesinger because of his commitments to anticommunism, containment, and the foreign policy of the Kennedy administration. In late spring 1966, alarmed at the growing Americanization of the war, he switched to moderate opposition. One result of his decision was the publication in early 1967 of ***The Bitter Heritage,*** a book intended to stir public opinion against widening the conflict and for a negotiated settlement. Both the book and Schlesinger were destined to become quite influential in shaping the views of the intellectual community on Southeast Asia. From his study of the problem Schlesinger concluded that Vietnam represented the illegitimate extension of two legitimate assumptions of American foreign policy: that the United States has an obligation to maintain international collective security and to spread democracy throughout the world. This illegitimate extension dated from the 1950's when Secretary of State John Foster Dulles defined the issues of the Cold War in absolutist moral terms, pitting the virtuous Free World against an evil, monolithic communism bent on world revolution. Dulles' absolutist philosophy, a perfect example of ideological dogma, became institutionalized in the State Department, the Defense Department, and the CIA, all of which acquired a vested bureaucratic interest in resisting communism on a global scale. Consequently the doctrine of collective security was transformed. The United States, unilaterally, began to apply it in areas where major power involvement was slight, where no balance of power existed, and where there was internal revolt rather than external aggression. The culmination of this process, and the ultimate perversion of America's democratic mission, was Lyndon Johnson's attempt to apply the Great Society to Southeast Asia, which, Schlesinger maintains, was a fantastic overcommitment of American power. Implicit in Schlesinger's analysis is the notion that this overcommitment would not have occurred if John Kennedy had lived. Indeed, in his recent biography of Robert Kennedy, Schlesinger argues explicitly that John Kennedy had decided to withdraw American advisers by

1965 but that the mood of the country compelled him to defer action until after the 1964 election.

Schlesinger's Vietnam analysis rests on a distinction he articulated in 1967 between obsessive, conservative anticommunism and rational, liberal anticommunism "graduated in mode and substance according to the threat." With this overly neat distinction Schlesinger asserted rational anticommunism as a moral necessity for all liberals, absolved Kennedy liberals of liability for the war, and placed blame on conservatives. In other words, military containment and loyalty investigations were a rational response to the genuine threat of Stalinism in the 1940's, but conservative anti-Communists erred in applying military solutions to Vietnam. Unfortunately for Schlesinger his argument is shaky on at least two counts: first, the men who formulated Vietnam policy (Johnson, McNamara, Rusk, the Bundys, and the Rostows) were Kennedy advisers and liberals, not conservatives; second, they proceeded in what they considered to be a rational manner in steadily escalating the pressure on North Vietnam. The problem is that the difference between "obsessive" and "rational" anticommunism on foreign policy issues is not as great as Schlesinger would like to believe. Both groups started from the same assumption of monolithic World Communism as a moral evil to be resisted around the globe. It is true that liberals like Schlesinger and Kennedy were "Realists" who argued that the United States should pursue its national interests within the limits of its power and should avoid the extremes of capitulation to communism or the messianic moralism of right-wingers who advocated total victory. Yet it was difficult for liberals to maintain a middle position. Given their hostility to communism, their global assumptions, and the generalizing tendencies of their anti-Communist rhetoric, liberals were also susceptible to moral crusades, as Schlesinger's support for Korea and his initial support for Vietnam indicates. One might say that Schlesinger has introduced his own ideological abstractions in distinguishing between rational and obsessive anticommunism and thus is blind to the reality of liberal culpability for the Vietnam War.

Vietnam and its aftermath was a time of reassessment for Schlesinger, but his basic presuppositions changed very little as a result. Like that of most intellectuals who turned against President Johnson's policy, Schlesinger's opposition was based on pragmatic rather than moral grounds. One consequence of this pragmatic opposition, as Charles Kadushin has pointed out, "is that it allowed old Cold Warriors to have opposed the war in Southeast Asia . . . and yet continue to hold views of the world that are not appreciably different from those they held in 1960" [Charles Kadushin, *American Intellectual Elite,* 1924]. The major change in United States policy produced by the Vietnam experience, according to Schlesinger, was a retreat from the messianic globalism which had dominated United States diplomacy in the 1950's and 1960's. This change was dictated by a realistic recognition of the practical limits of United States power and by a realization that "in this new age of polycentrism the extension of Communism no longer means the automatic extension of Russian or Chinese power." Despite substituting polycentric for monolithic communism, Schlesinger's thinking

Caricature drawing of Arthur Schlesinger, by David Levine. Reprinted with permission from The New York Review of Books. *Copyright (c) 1986 Nyrev, Inc.*

about foreign affairs retained its global assumptions and its peculiar blend of idealism and realism. The United States must pay attention to the realities of national self-interest and power, it should continue to contain communism where its vital interests are threatened and where it has the power to do so successfully, and it ought to advance the moral goals of human freedom and welfare around the world. Faced with circumstances in the 1970's far different from those which confronted him in the 1940's, Schlesinger still urged liberals to seek a foreign policy based on "realistic idealism," a foreign policy immune from the excessive moralism of the Right and the New Left, one "which will at once protect the national interests of the United States and advance the welfare of a diverse and suffering humanity" [**"New Liberal Coalition,"** *Progressive* 31 (April 1967)].

Although the Communist challenge in the postwar period led liberals to be preoccupied with foreign affairs and to neglect domestic issues, Schlesinger did his best to keep the lamp of domestic reform burning bright as a necessary precondition to a successful foreign policy. He concluded *The Vital Center* with a chapter entitled "Freedom: A Fighting Faith," intended as a stirring call to action for liberals of his generation. Unfortunately for Schlesinger, liberals had to wander in the wilderness of the 1950's before beholding the promised land of the New Frontier. Facing the conservatism and complacency of the Eisenhower presidency, Schlesinger responded by working for presidential candidate Adlai Stevenson, by studying the "Age of Roosevelt," and by writing several essays in which he articulated new tasks for liberalism. He also derived solace from his father's cyclical theory of "the tides of national politics," in which periods of liberalism and conservatism alternated throughout American history. Liberals could thus take heart that their time would come again.

As with *The Age of Jackson,* Schlesinger's *The Age of Roosevelt* was intentionally relevant to contemporary politics. The first three volumes, published between 1957 and 1960, attempted to provide Schlesinger's beloved Democratic party with a reawakened interest in the New Deal tradition at the same time they implied some striking parallels between Republican conservatism in the 1920's and the inaction of the Eisenhower administration in the 1950's. Consistent with Schlesinger's views of what American liberalism required, he saw Franklin D. Roosevelt as a strong president and as a pragmatic realist, a man who avoided the ideological extremes of "either/or," who was open to the ideas of intellectuals, and who took an experimental approach to politics. When the national planning and structural reforms of the First New Deal did not end the depression and when the Supreme Court demonstrated its hostility to structural reform by striking down the first agricultural Adjustment Act and the National Recovery Administration, Roosevelt's pragmatic realism led him to adopt the Keynesian approach which became the Second New Deal. Thus the genius of Franklin D. Roosevelt is that he "always resisted ideological commitment," and the significance of the New Deal is that it combated the depression in a practical, experimental way without resorting to ideology.

Notwithstanding that it repeated several themes of *The Age of Jackson*—commitment to a strong president, emphasis on the role of intellectuals, preference for ideas over ideology, and stress on realistic pragmatism—*The Age of Roosevelt* revealed the increasingly moderate character of Schlesinger's liberalism and its growing accommodation to the existing system of corporate capitalism. The historical lesson of the New Deal for American liberals is that American society can be improved by moderate Keynesian reforms; the goals of the society need not be questioned nor the structure changed.

Schlesinger did not limit his political activities during the 1950's merely to writing the history of past liberal accomplishments, however. As part of the regular revision for liberalism to meet new social needs, required by his empirical and realistic premises, Schlesinger attempted to distinguish between "quantitative liberalism," which had so brilliantly met the economic needs of the 1930's, and "qualitative liberalism" now needed to fight for individual dignity, identity, and fulfillment by improving the quality of life in a mass society. Despite his attempt to distinguish between economic and cultural issues, "qualitative liberal-

ism" implied no repudiation of "quantitative liberalism," as is seen in Schlesinger's list of new issues for 1956: education, medical care, the well-being of the sick and aged, equal opportunity for minority groups, urban planning, slum clearance, better housing, bettering the mass media, and improvement of popular culture. Essentially this list represents the unfinished business of the New Deal wrapped in an attractive new slogan. Quite clearly these programs would require increased government spending to improve the quality of life for groups that lacked economic resources. Even though quantity and quality, economic and cultural, tended to blur, Schlesinger's phrases "new America," "quality of life," and "qualitative liberalism," growing out of his work with the Finletter group, were his particular contributions to Stevenson's 1956 campaign and helped prepare the way for the New Frontier and the Great Society of the 1960's. Schlesinger's call for renewed reform at home was tied closely to his concerns about foreign affairs: "a truly creative and progressive foreign policy can only come from a truly creative and progressive America—we can't further freedom, equality, and opportunity in the world unless we further it at home."

Undeterred by Stevenson's second defeat, Schlesinger carried his "qualitative liberalism" into the 1960 campaign. Attaching himself to John Kennedy as the strong leader to fulfill these expectations, he worked to convince dubious liberals of the validity of Kennedy's reform credentials by numerous speeches and by the publication of *Kennedy or Nixon: Does It Make Any Difference?* As was clear at the time, and became even more clear in retrospect with the publication in 1965 of the third installment of Schlesinger's historical treatment of liberalism—*A Thousand Days: John F. Kennedy in the White House*—Kennedy's presidency was the answer to Schlesinger's liberal hopes and indeed represented the high tide of "qualitative liberalism." The book made explicit the connection between Roosevelt and Kennedy. It praised the New Frontier for its toughmindedness and realistic use of power in the Laos negotiations, the Berlin Crisis, and the Cuban Missile Crisis; for breaking with the Republican's rigid ideological view of a polarized world (the free world vs. communism) and presenting the alternative pluralistic idea of a "world of diversity"; and for respecting intellectuals and the world of intellect. Schlesinger insisted that "both the New Frontier and the Great Society [which was the result of John Kennedy's initiatives] have done a good many things to improve the quality of American life—and of American lives."

Schlesinger's apologetics for John Kennedy vividly reveals his commitments to strong presidents and to pragmatic intellectuals as means of furthering liberal reform. Both commitments, however, raise serious questions. Schlesinger's historical analysis and political career suggest that American liberals have been unable to develop programs which attract sufficient popular support and therefore must rely on charismatic individuals—Jackson, Roosevelt, Kennedy—to achieve political change. This is a weak and dangerous position for two reasons: first, there is the authoritarian potential of a strong president—a danger Schlesinger belatedly recognized during the Johnson and

Nixon years; second, it leads to constant compromises of position because loyalty to a strong leader is so crucial. These weaknesses have attracted the attention of radical critics. Ronald Radosh, for example, recently attacked Schlesinger for his service to power in the Boy of Pigs invasion. Radosh charges that Schlesinger lied to newsmen in the interest of national security, helped President Kennedy fabricate a cover-up, and distorted the historical record by his less-than-truthful account in *A Thousand Days.* In reply Schlesinger simply states that he initially opposed the venture and that he did not resign because he trusted Kennedy, who would not have planned the Bay of Pigs invasion and who held out great promise for the future of the country. This debate illustrates what Schlesinger has called the irresolvable conflict between the two types of intellectuals, pragmatists and utopians, who represent the major social roles intellectuals have played throughout American history. Schlesinger, the pragmatic realist, risks the corruptions of power by trying to change society from within; Radosh, the utopian idealist, risks irrelevance by attempting to change society from without. Their mutual disdain is evident as are the weaknesses of their respective positions. On the one hand, the intellectual is condemned to impotence; on the other, infidelity.

Facing the unacceptable ideological alternatives of the New Left and the New Right, Schlesinger responded in 1968 by resurrecting the political strategy of the vital center in the form of "the New Politics" personified by a new charismatic liberal, Robert Kennedy. The New Politics bypassed the traditional political intermediaries—political bosses, trade unions, ethnic federations, and trade associations—and relied on mass involvement aided by the mass media. Schlesinger thought Kennedy promised "a basic reconstruction of American liberalism—a reconstruction that had he become President, might have marked as emphatic a stage in the evolution of American democracy as that wrought in other times by Andrew Jackson and Franklin Roosevelt." As the last liberal politician who could communicate with students, nonwhites, the middle class, and the white working class, Kennedy had the power to reconstruct the Roosevelt coalition. Moreover, Kennedy's commitment to a strong presidency was essential for securing racial and social justice.

Unfortunately Robert Kennedy's assassination left Schlesinger's great expectations unfulfilled. Complicating an already troubled political scene, the abuses of presidential power during the Vietnam War and Watergate forced Schlesinger to reconsider his position in *The Imperial Presidency.* Characteristically he sought a moderate solution between two extremes: "The American democracy must discover a middle ground between making the President a czar and making him a puppet. . . . We need a strong Presidency—but a strong Presidency within the Constitution." Schlesinger insisted that politics, not law, was the best means of control. He rejected institutional arrangements such as an executive-congressional commission to oversee foreign policy because he feared it might introduce dangerous rigidities into the American system. A first step toward restoring constitutional comity, he maintained, was impeachment. The Nixon White House must be held legally accountable for its illegal behavior in

Watergate or all hopes of constitutional limits would be lost. In addition, the American people should develop a less reverent, more skeptical attitude toward the office; skepticism leading to withdrawal of support by Congress, by the press, and by public opinion could effectively limit presidential power. Thus, despite the imperial presidency of Lyndon Johnson and the revolutionary presidency of Richard Nixon, Schlesinger still hoped to preserve a strong presidency under the Constitution. This is not surprising because, as we have seen such a president is essential for furthering Schlesinger's liberalism. Less apparent, perhaps, is the weakness of his proposed political restraints. Given his adulation of Jackson, Roosevelt, and the Kennedys, one wonders if Schlesinger would adopt a less reverent, more skeptical attitude toward the presidency if it were held by a liberal Democrat.

Much to Schlesinger's regret no great leader has appeared on the American political horizon since Robert Kennedy's death. Lamenting both candidates' lack of public vision in the 1976 election, Schlesinger reluctantly voted for Jimmy Carter, but he later had several occasions to criticize his lack of leadership: Carter was no innovator; he had no unifying vision and consequently no coherent policy. Worse yet, Carter appeared to be drifting into conservative Republicanism by advocating a balanced budget and free market solutions to the problems of energy and inflation. In opposition to Carter's policies Schlesinger, as he did in the 1950's, stressed the priority of qualitative liberalism, the necessity of affirmative government, and the need for a strong president to generate action. Reaffirming his belief in the cyclical pattern of American politics, Schlesinger maintains that the 1980's will witness a resurgence of liberalism to deal with the unresolved issues created by the conservative 1970's.

Schlesinger has pursued the political strategy of vital center and has remained a "man in the middle" throughout his career; characteristically he adopted middle-of-the-road positions between what he defined as unacceptable extremes. Liberal intellectuals like Schlesinger, moreover, have provided the rationale for the most important government policies since World War II. The global policy of containment which resulted in Vietnam, the strong presidency which culminated in Watergate, and the welfare state which yielded a cumbersome bureaucracy have all produced a storm of criticism in recent years. Yet Schlesinger has been reluctant to modify his political position; he denies that liberalism is in any way responsible for American disasters. Containment is a valid liberal policy to check communism, Vietnam a perversion of its principles; the strong presidency is necessary to advance reform and guide foreign policy, Watergate a misuse of power; the welfare state is essential to achieve social justice, bureaucracy a technical problem to be overcome. Through all the disturbing events of the postwar period, Schlesinger has been steadfast in his liberalism. He argues that his political pragmatism and Niebuhrian assumptions about human nature are validated empirically by the facts of history and are the only possible grounds on which to base a realistic politics. Stripped of unrealistic, utopian assumptions, Schlesinger's liberalism is a peculiar blend of realism and idealism: it is confident that society can be improved and freedom maintained by human effort, but like French existentialism it knows that the struggle will be unending and that the perfect society will never be achieved. These are the historical lessons Schlesinger has gleaned from his studies of the Jackson, Roosevelt, and Kennedy administrations. These are the liberal principles he believes can guide humankind toward a better future in an endlessly troubled world.

But one may ask whether the vital center is a relevant position for a person seeking social change in American society. In adopting centrist liberalism it would appear that Schlesinger has valued realism more than idealism. By avoiding ideology and by stressing the role of pragmatic intellectuals, he has made a fetish of empiricism, has blurred the distinction between *is* and *ought,* and has identified too closely with the existing power structure. This is a strange stance for a liberal to take; perhaps the fact that Schlesinger's brand of realistic liberalism dominated the postwar intellectual scene helps to account for the absence of serious social debate and the lack of meaningful social reform in America since 1945.

Arthur Schlesinger, Jr.   (essay date Spring 1981)

SOURCE: "A Reply," in *South Atlantic Quarterly,* Vol. 80, No. 2, Spring, 1981, pp. 139-42.

[*In the following essay, Schlesinger responds to Engelhardt's essay "Man in the Middle: Arthur M. Schlesinger, Jr., and Postwar American Liberalism" (see above), commenting that Engelhardt "is essentially fair-minded" but misinterprets Schlesinger's positions regarding ideology, the dangers of Communism in the United States, and the role of private property under social control.*]

It is a bit disconcerting for an historian to find himself the target of history. But, as we were long ago authoritatively informed, "All they that take the sword shall perish with the sword"; so I accept the occupational risk and thank the *South Atlantic Quarterly* for the opportunity, before the sword finally falls, to comment on the comment.

Let me say at once that I do not envy anyone the awful task of reading a forty-year flow of words, some historical in purpose, some biographical, some polemical. I think Mr. Engelhardt's piece is essentially fair-minded and often generous, though not always, in my view, quite accurate.

Early on, for example, he credits me with anticipating the alleged belief of the intellectuals of the 1950's "in the exhaustion of political ideology, the pluralistic theory of politics, and the consensus interpretation of United States history." I am unquestionably a pluralist in my view of politics, and of life as well. As William James said, temperaments determine philosophies; and, like James, I temperamentally abhor monisms. I agree with Isaiah Berlin in doubting "a final harmony in which all riddles are solved, all contradictions reconciled" and in seeing conflicts of value "as an intrinsic, irremovable element in human life."

But I must demur on the other two charges. My point has been not the exhaustion but, on the contrary, the *danger* of political ideology. Mr. Engelhardt goes on to suggest that I am a closet ideologue myself. Not by my definition

of ideology, a word I have always used to denote an all-encompassing, all-explanatory, monistic system; but Mr. Engelhardt evidently prefers to blur what I continue to regard as the useful distinction between a systematic and rigid body of dogma on the one hand and a cluster of general ideas and ideals on the other. Karl Mannheim had a bizarre definition of ideology—one that would, for example, exclude Marxism.

As for the consensus interpretation of American history, I am more commonly—and I am sure more correctly—regarded as the author of one of "probably the last. . . historical studies to be written squarely in the Progressive [i.e., anticonsensus] tradition" (Richard Hofstadter, *The Progressive Historians*). My historical as well as my political writings have always opposed the notion that the American past was devoid of conflict and that there was no substantial difference between, say, Jackson and Biddle or Roosevelt and Hoover.

Am I, as Mr. Engelhardt darkly suggests, "a liberal with conservative assumptions?" Only if one accepts the idea that liberalism requires faith in the perfectibility of man and society. If Mr. Engelhardt really believes that this is what modern liberalism is about, he misses the whole point. The postwar generation premised its liberalism on Reinhold Niebuhr's mighty dictum: "Man's capacity for justice makes democracy possible, but man's inclination to injustice makes democracy necessary." Even before I started reading Niebuhr, I regarded the recognition of human limitations as providing the firmest intellectual foundation for liberalism (see the last paragraph of **The Age of Jackson**).

Like many younger scholars, Mr. Engelhardt displays a mysterious queasiness when confronted by the phenomenon of anti-Stalinism. Why this should be, I do not know. Even post-Stalin Russia is nobody's prize, surely not Mr. Engelhardt's (though he does appear to criticize me for "still" insisting, as late as 1960, "that the Soviet Union was a theological society characterized by commitment to a dogmatic ideology," as if this were not an accurate description of the Soviet Union even in 1981); and Stalin's Russia was beyond all dispute a horror. Why does Mr. Engelhardt suppose a liberal could have been anything but anti-Stalinist?

He is quite wrong in writing that liberals like myself considered communism, apart from Soviet espionage, "a genuine internal threat to the security of the United States." As we used to put it at the time, communism was a danger *to* the United States, not a danger *in* the United States. Mr. Engelhardt, however, dismisses the distinction between rational and obsessive anticommunism and seems dubious about the feasibility of "a middle position" between sober defense of national interest on the one hand and messianic crusades on the other. What would his recommendation have been? To have renounced anti-Stalinism altogether?

On the whole, he does not deal with anti-Stalinism on its merits but rather rests his disapproval on alleged secondary effects: not only messianic crusades against communism at home and abroad; but emphasis on foreign policy at the expense of domestic reform; undue identification with the existing structure of American society; responsibility for the conservative drift of American policy.

In my own case, far from favoring foreign policy at the expense of domestic reform, I argued for domestic issues so insistently in the 1950's that Max Ascoli excommunicated me as an isolationist in the pages of his magazine *The Reporter*. As for the American social structure, I do indeed believe that a free society requires the diversification of ownership. In that sense, I suppose, I am a defender of the existing structure. Indeed, I would very much like to see someone explain sometime how the means of political opposition and of free expression can survive the abolition of private property.

Individual freedom surely requires two conditions: economic resources relatively safe from the state, and a system of justice relatively independent of the state. The nationalization of the means of production and distribution would, so far as I can see, destroy both these conditions. Nor do syndicalist fantasies of decentralization, workers' control, etc., seem to me to provide any realistic answer to the power drive of the modern communist state. In short, I see no way of protecting autonomous institutions if they have no property base from which to defend themselves against the state. So I conclude that the Bill of Rights requires the retention of private property and that the problem of politics is to place private property under social control. Does Mr. Engelhardt disagree with this line of thought? If so, he should stand forth and declare himself. If not, why is my position so reprehensible?

Within the framework of mixed ownership, I remain, as I have always been, an opponent of business domination and an advocate of affirmative government on behalf of the poor and powerless. "One must ask," Mr. Engelhardt writes, ". . . were liberal intellectuals like Schlesinger in some way responsible for the conservative drift of American policies?" My answer to this, only briefly noted by Mr. Engelhardt, is that liberalism and conservatism ebb and flow in American politics according to a discernible cyclical rhythm. As the reform activism of Theodore Roosevelt and Wilson wore out the American people after two decades and ushered in the do-nothing twenties, so the activism of Roosevelt and Truman was followed by the Eisenhower lull, and the activism of Kennedy and Johnson by the Nixon-Ford-Carter-Reagan stasis. (In this connection, I should note that I did *not* vote for Carter in 1976. I expected to vote for the Democratic candidate, as I had always done in the past, but, once in the booth, could not bring myself to pull the lever for a man so hostile to the Roosevelt-Truman-Kennedy tradition and consequently did not vote at all for president. In 1980 I voted for John Anderson.)

Little is more predictable than that seasons of action, passion, idealism, and reform should give way to seasons of apathy, hedonism, cynicism, and recuperation—and that these latter periods should continue until the national batteries are recharged and until the problems recently neglected demand a new burst of social innovation. It is this cyclical rhythm, not the sins of liberal intellectuals, that in my view accounts for conservative swings in American politics.

Mr. Engelhardt seems unhappy that the liberal periods should rely on strong leadership. I wish, by the way, that he and everybody else would stop using the word "charismatic." Max Weber, who invented the word, applied it to medicine men, warrior chieftains, and religious prophets, leaders ruling by magic, miracle, and revelation. The concept of charisma has nothing to do with leadership in a democracy, where, as Wilson said, "the dynamics of leadership lie in persuasion." Leadership has always seemed to me to have an indispensable role in the democratic process, both practically—in order to get things done—and morally—in order to affirm human freedom against the supposed inevitabilities of history. "The appearance of a great man," wrote Emerson, "draws a new circle outside of our largest orbit and surprises and commands us." Is this so terrible? Can Mr. Engelhardt really regard Washington, Jackson, and Lincoln, the Roosevelts and the Kennedys, as threats to American democracy?

Mr. Engelhardt's besetting problem is the Slippery Slope argument: don't do a good thing now lest it lead to someone else doing bad things later. So one must not contain the Soviet Union lest it result in Vietnam, nor favor a strong presidency lest it produce Watergate, nor support the welfare state lest it yield a bureaucracy. This is an argument for doing nothing at all. I don't suppose this is really where Engelhardt ends up. But he is singularly vague about his alternatives. Before rushing to judge others, historians surely have the obligation to consider what their own standards are and what choices they themselves would have made in the circumstances.

Alan Brinkley (review date 1 December 1986)

SOURCE: "Conflict and Consensus," in *The New Republic*, Vol. 195, No. 22, December 1, 1986, pp. 28-31.

[*In the following review, Brinkley asserts that the essays collected in Schlesinger's* The Cycles of American History *are eloquent reminders of the importance of history in forming an understanding of the present.*]

It is a tribute to Arthur M. Schlesinger Jr.'s immense talents and protean accomplishments that he seems to defy conventional classification. In the course of his 40-year career, he has been a political activist (one of the founders of Americans for Democratic Action), a public official (an assistant to President Kennedy), a campaign strategist (for Adlai Stevenson and the Kennedys), a memoirist, a political essayist, and even for a time a film critic. Above all, of course, he has been a historian—perhaps the best known and most widely read American historian of his generation. But even within the historical profession, the unusual range and variety of his work have made him difficult to categorize. His most familiar works are those examining American public life in the 20th century: his magisterial three-volume *The Age of Roosevelt* (a fourth volume is reportedly in progress), his celebrated studies of John and Robert Kennedy, his analysis of the modern presidency. Yet his first book was a highly regarded study of the 19th-century New England cleric and political activist Orestes Brownson. And probably his most influential work—a book that shaped scholarly discussion of an entire field for more than a generation—was *The Age of Jackson,* published in 1945 and recipient of the first of Schlesinger's two Pulitzer Prizes. (The second came 20 years later, for *A Thousand Days.*)

This new collection of essays [*The Cycles of American History*] reveals another area in which Schlesinger resists conventional categorization: his relationship to the dominant schools of interpretation within the historical profession. Politically, he is a well-known liberal, and his political convictions inform his scholarly work in countless ways. But liberalism takes many forms, and Schlesinger's does not fit neatly within any major scholarly camp. He has carved an interpretive niche for himself that is firmly his own.

In some respects, he is one of the last of the great "progressive" historians whose work dominated American scholarship during most of the period between World War I and World War II, and among whose most distinguished representatives was Arthur M. Schlesinger Sr. The progressives (whose ranks also included Charles A. Beard and Frederick Jackson Turner) saw American history as a vast battleground in which economic or regional rivalries created continual conflicts and in which democratic elements fought constantly against the forces of entrenched privilege. Although the progressives never embraced the economic determinism of later Marxist historians, they did place economic inequality (and the struggles it inspired) at the center of the American past.

Among scholars of the postwar generation, the younger Schlesinger's own generation, the most powerful force in American historiography was a reaction against this approach and the emergence of what came to be known as "consensus" history. Consensus scholars emphasized not conflict but (in Richard Hofstadter's words) "the common climate of American opinion," the shared belief among almost all Americans in "the rights of property, the philosophy of economic individualism, the value of competition . . . the economic virtues of capitalist culture." Conflicts there had been, to be sure, but they had rarely been fundamental conflicts. Americans were in basic agreement even when they thought they differed. Schlesinger never accepted, however, the approach that came to enchant so many of his contemporaries. He never believed that surface controversies are mere distractions from broader agreement. The battles that seemed important to their contemporaries, he has always argued, should seem equally important to historians. And in his most influential historical works—his study of Jacksonian politics, his history of the New Deal—he has emphasized not continuity and consensus, but the centrality of conflicts between democratic forces and special interests.

The importance of such struggles remains very much at the center of his thinking in this book, perhaps most notably in the title essay ["**The Cycles of American History**"]. The idea that American history moves in "cycles," that periods of social activism alternate with periods of retreat in a reasonably predictable pattern, is not a new one. Emerson referred to it obliquely in the 1840s; Henry Adams developed it explicitly in the 1890s; and Schlesinger's father made it central to his own work. Schlesinger himself

has insisted for many years on the importance of the cycle—"a continuing shift in national involvement, between public purpose and private interest"—as a key to historical explanation. The evidence, he claims, lies in the ebbs and flows of public life in the past, and particularly in the 20th century. The public activism of the early 20th century (the "progressive era") ultimately gave way to the conservatism of the 1920s, which gave way in turn to the renewal of energy of the New Deal. The postwar conservatism of the Eisenhower years succumbed in the early 1960s to the dynamism of the New Frontier and the Great Society, to be followed by another withdrawal into private interest in the 1970s and 1980s.

Troubling questions have always accompanied this theory. Schlesinger faces them squarely here. The cyclical pattern works reasonably well as a description of at least part of the American past. But can it serve, as its advocates like to claim, as a predictive device? Is the pattern simply coincidence (like the causally meaningless fact that presidents elected at 20-year intervals since 1840 have all, until now, died in office)? Or is there an internal dynamic, which makes the cycle self-generating? Schlesinger argues here that the cycle is, in fact, self-sustaining. "There is a cyclical pattern in organic nature," he notes, as well as "a cyclical basis in the very psychology of modernity." Most of all, however: "It is the generational experience that serves as the mainspring of the political cycle." Members of each generation shape their political assumptions in response to the public climate of their adolescence and early adulthood. When they come of age, usually some 20 years later, they attempt to give voice to assumptions shaped at an earlier time:

> Young men and women whose ideals were formed by TR and Wilson—Franklin and Eleanor Roosevelt, Harry Truman—produced the New and Fair Deals in their own maturity. The generation whose ideals were formed by FDR—John Kennedy and Lyndon Johnson—produced in their maturity the New Frontier and the Great Society. In the same way the age of Kennedy touched and inspired a new generation. That generation's time is yet to come.

Schlesinger has not answered, certainly, all the objections scholars have raised to the cycle as a basis of interpretation. He concedes, for example, that the generational view of the past must confront the fact that babies are born continuously, that "the division of people into generations seems arbitrary." His only answer is to say that most other social divisions—economic classes, for example—are to some degree arbitrary as well. The predictive possibilities of the cyclical argument would seem brighter, moreover, if there were more compelling evidence that the generation shaped by the "age of Kennedy" seemed about to produce a crusade for a restoration of public purpose. Still, he has in this essay provided a challenging basis—generally absent from earlier arguments for the "cycle"—for exploring the pattern not simply as a historical fact, but as a historical force.

Whatever the strengths or weaknesses of this argument, however, Schlesinger's commitment to it reveals an important facet of his own historical instincts: his emphasis on discontinuity as the central feature of the past. Not for him the consensus view of a history unbroken by fundamental conflict. The alternations in American public life between public purpose and private interest, he suggests, are not meaningless blips on the surface of broad continuities. They are the main event.

They are, moreover, to be welcomed. Some (although by no means all) consensus historians came to celebrate the absence of conflict, to welcome what they believed to be America's happy freedom from the class divisions and social turbulence that have beset other societies. But to Schlesinger (as to the progressive historians of the 1920s and 1930s), it is conflict that keeps the hope of progress and social justice alive. Indeed, he gives evidence throughout these essays of his preference for a sharply competitive, even turbulent politics over a consensual public life in which popular aspirations might not find adequate channels for expression. In his discussion of the American presidency, for example, he rejects proposals to insulate the president from the pressures of politics (through, for example, a single six-year term or a shift to a more purely parliamentary system). If anything, he argues, presidents should be *less* insulated from politics, more subject to the checks and balances of the electoral process and the separation of powers.

The most unusual essay in this book discusses the vice presidency, an office he proposes to abolish in favor of speedy "special elections" in the event of the death of a president. Again, the suggestion (implausible as it may be) is rooted in a belief that leadership must be subjected constantly to the healthy ferment of democracy. Perhaps that is why Schlesinger, although he has often been contemptuous of New Left historiography, is not as harshly critical of American radicals and not as aghast at their excesses during the 1960s as are many of his contemporaries. Wrongheaded as revolutionaries have been, he suggests, their agitation "exposes the hypocrisies of the standing order and sharpens objections to it." And the threat they pose "undermines the obstacles of imbecility and vested interest."

The belief in discontinuity is particularly clear in one of the book's best essays, **"Vicissitudes of Presidential Reputations,"** in which Schlesinger takes on a generation of revisionists. For nearly two decades now, historians have been restoring the reputation of Herbert Hoover, portraying him as an important progressive whose policy innovations in the 1920s and early 1930s laid much of the groundwork for the New Deal. The inauguration of Franklin Roosevelt, they imply, was not a major turning point in our political history but another step along a broad continuum. The Eisenhower presidency, revisionists similarly argue, was not simply a somnolent interregnum between periods of dynamic reform but a time of wise and prudent restraint and healthy progress.

Schlesinger has little patience with either argument. He concedes the revisionist point that Hoover was not in all respects a hardened reactionary and that Eisenhower was more than an amiable stumblebum. But in most essential respects, he clings tightly to his own longheld views. Those familiar with his earlier discussions of the Hoover administration (in *The Crisis of the Old Order*) and the Kennedy administration (*A Thousand Days*) will recognize that Schlesinger sees no reason to recant. The New Deal and the New Frontier were, he insists, both dramatic breaks with a stagnant conservatism—evidence again of the importance of the "cycle" and the centrality of discontinuity in American history; and evidence too of his own refusal to accept the consensus view of a relatively unbroken, unconflicted past.

It would be a mistake, however, to view Schlesinger as somehow set apart from the major intellectual currents of his generation. Although he has balked at some of the assumptions of postwar historiography, in other respects his ideas have not only matched but shaped those of his contemporaries. Nowhere is that clearer than in the debate over "ideology" that did so much to guide American intellectual life in the 1940s and 1950s. Postwar intellectuals, appalled by the horrors they had seen millenarian ideologies (fascism, Stalinism, and later Maoism) produce in other societies, came to see in the more ideologically neutral world of liberal democracy a healthy antidote to dangerous political fervor. Americans, they argued, are a pragmatic, not an ideological, people. And it has been their ability to resist the appeal of fervent crusades and "total solutions" that has allowed democracy to flourish and prosper. Schlesinger himself produced one of the most eloquent expressions of this idea in his 1949 book, *The Vital Center,* which challenged the popular assumption that the center was a barren place, incapable of generating any real commitment or political energy. On the contrary, he argued, the center was not only the best defense against the dangers of millenarian excess; it was itself a vital stance, which could rely on its commitment to personal freedom to inspire social progress and public purpose.

He continues to advance that argument today, as the eloquent concluding essay in this volume makes clear:

> The vast pervasive resistance of the psyche and of society leads some to forsake incremental change in favor of the millennial hope, "a new heaven and a new earth," the Kingdom of God or the kingdom of the proletariat. . . . Those who profess to execute the mandates of God or of History are menaces to humanity. . . . Reform avoids the arrogance of revolution. . . . The consent of the majority is essential if both the fabric of society and the freedom of the individual are to survive.

His commitment to that idea may help to explain some of his own most conspicuous political attachments. John Kennedy, for all the public passion he helped to produce, considered himself a cool pragmatist uninterested in the claims of ideology. Franklin Roosevelt, similarly, was openly and boastfully experimental, willing to tolerate any number of ideological currents but unwilling to commit himself irrevocably to any one of them.

Although certain themes are recurrent through much of [*The Cycles of American History*], it is a diverse collection, with no single concern. It begins with an evocative essay emphasizing the self-consciously experimental origins of American democracy and debunking the idea (now enshrined in presidential rhetoric) that the founders saw the republic they were creating as the expression of a God-given plan, a "divine consecration." It includes six important essays on facets of American foreign policy, which together sharply challenge the economic determinism of some New Left historians but which reject as well the missionary vision of the nation's international role so popular among conservatives and neoconservatives. It recapitulates many of the ideas Schlesinger developed in *The Imperial Presidency* about the nature (and abuses) of presidential power, and extends the examination to the post-Nixon era. It offers some of the author's own prescriptions for dealing with our present problems. (He favors, for example, a Felix Rohatyn-like industrial policy modeled vaguely on the New Deal's National Recovery Administration.) And it expresses repeatedly one of Schlesinger's most important convictions: a rejection of historical determinism—of the idea that innate social forces ensure that events will develop in a particular way—in favor of a belief in the importance of individuals and their capacity to alter the course of history.

Like most collections of previously published work, this one suffers occasionally from redundancy. And despite a substantial effort by the author to reshape old material in light of new scholarship and recent events, there is a dated quality to at least some of these essays. The book abounds with examples of characteristics that have often irritated Schlesinger's many critics within the historical profession: frequent invocations of personal friends (John and Robert Kennedy, Reinhold Niebuhr, Averell Harriman), easy shifts back and forth between scholarly detachment and partisanship, harsh dismissal and sometimes ungenerous characterizations of historians with whom he disagrees, abundant and at times perhaps excessive displays of erudition.

But this collection reveals as well why Schlesinger, despite the countless ways in which he has violated the conventions of his profession, remains one of its most important voices. It is not simply because he possesses a literary grace that few American scholars can match, and not simply because the range of his interests and knowledge far exceeds that of most historians in this age of narrow specialization. It is because he possesses a rare ability to make history seem important, because he is willing to argue that the search for an understanding of the past is not simply an aesthetic exercise but a path to the understanding of our own time. He is a reminder to professional historians of the possibilities of reaching beyond their own ranks to the larger world in which they live.

Kenneth S. Lynn   (review date March 1987)

SOURCE: "The Schlesinger Thesis," in *Commentary*, Vol. 83, No. 3, March, 1987, pp. 46-52.

[An American literary scholar whose works evidence his conservative principles, Lynn is the general editor of Houghton-Mifflin's "Riverside Literature" series and the author of numerous essays and books on American life and letters. In the following essay, Lynn censures Schlesinger for allowing his political loyalties to bias his historical accounts.]

Once upon a time, the books of the historian Arthur M. Schlesinger, Jr. were worth reading. In *The Vital Center* (1949), for instance, he spoke with a fog-cutting scorn of those "progressives" who still clung to the miasmic dreams of the 1930's and were still blind, in consequence, to Soviet imperialism and the malevolence of the American Communist party. The modern liberalism which he represented was much more tough-minded. Thanks to a "restoration of radical nerve," he explained, in words that revealed how much he owed to the wisdom of Reinhold Niebuhr, modern liberalism recognized the complexity of reality, the ineradicable sinfulness of human nature, the corruptive consequences of power, the narrow possibilities of all historical endeavor, the virtues of gradualism, and the horror inherent in every form of totalitarianism.

Today, having lost his nerve and so much else, Schlesinger speaks of the United States and the Soviet Union in the same breath as "international menaces," acting out fantasies of "innate superiority." In the American case, Schlesinger argues in his new book, *The Cycles of American History,* a messianic dream of America as the redeemer nation has flowed into the vacuum created in the national mind by the erosion of our sense of history and its attendant consciousness that all secular communities are finite and flawed. So far as interest and knowledge are concerned, we have become "an essentially historyless people," the author of *Cycles* complains. "Businessmen agree with the elder Henry Ford that history is bunk. The young no longer study history. Academics turn their back on history in the enthusiasm for the ahistorical behavioral 'sciences.' "

Precisely which contemporary businessmen the professor has in mind, he does not say—for the simple reason that he hasn't any; in characterizing their attitude by reference to a drearily familiar wisecrack tossed off by an automobile tycoon born in 1863, Schlesinger is not telling us something he has actually learned about executives in Lee Iacocca's Detroit and elsewhere; to the contrary, he is merely indulging an animus, on the flip side of which can be found, not incidentally, a striking tendency to worship men of inherited wealth, such as Averell Harriman, to whom *Cycles* is dedicated. " 'My father always told me that businessmen were sons-of-bitches,' " the author of *Cycles* remembers John F. Kennedy saying in 1962, at the time of the young President's wage-price battle with the steel companies, and the relish with which Schlesinger repeats that unlovely epithet testifies to his own belief in its applicability to the social class in question.

But what is even more revealing about Schlesinger than his willingness to rely on prejudice instead of evidence in his judgment of businessmen is his unwillingness to engage in self-criticism while lamenting the current state of affairs in academia. For although there is truth in his assertion that students nowadays have a diminished interest in history and that many scholars prefer to work in the behavioral sciences, he need not have turned to grandiosely vague allusions to a national "tradition" of "narcissistic withdrawal from history" in order to account for these developments. More modestly and more usefully, he might have begun by asking whether the faded appeal of history in our colleges and universities is not the result of intellectual disorder in the historical profession, and from there he might have proceeded to take a hard look at his own special field of 20th-century American political history, which has declined to the point where senior-faculty positions in the field have gone unfilled at Harvard, Johns Hopkins, and other institutions, for want of candidates who have proved themselves as scholars. How, and when, and why, did the discipline fall into such woeful difficulty? Conceivably, the author of *Cycles* could have filled at least a chapter with enlightening answers to these questions, except that doing so would have required him to rethink his most cherished assumptions about the American past.

The academicians who came to dominate 20th-century American political history in the decade and a half after World War II—Schlesinger at Harvard, Walter Johnson at the University of Chicago, Eric Goldman at Princeton, Frank Freidel at Stanford and Harvard, John Morton Blum at MIT and Yale, and William Leuchtenburg at Columbia may be taken as gifted representatives of the type—were men who had grown up during the New Deal and had been indelibly marked by their enthusiasm for it. Some of them, indeed, became personally involved in liberal politics. Walter Johnson played a role in persuading the Hamlet-like governor of Illinois to run for President, a feat which he later described in *How We Drafted Adlai Stevenson* (1955). Among Schlesinger's many *engagé* acts was his work as a speechwriter for Stevenson. Leuchtenburg held directorial posts both in New England and New York with the liberal pressure group, Americans for Democratic Action, and with New York's Liberal party as well. Goldman, in the fullness of time, would serve as a special consultant in Lyndon Johnson's White House.

Much more significant, though, is the fact that fond memories of FDR constricted the sense of history of this group of historians, whether they concentrated on the boom-and-bust years between the world wars, or on the era of Theodore Roosevelt and Woodrow Wilson, or attempted to cover the whole first half of the century. In the collective view of these chroniclers, the most exciting way to tell the story of 20th-century America was to orchestrate it around what they regarded as the intermittent triumph of presidentially-conducted crusades for reform, with true reform being equated in their minds with the unfolding agenda of liberal thought.

From Johnson's portrayal in charming detail of *William Allen White's America* (1947) to Leuchtenburg's clear and thoughtful survey, *Franklin D. Roosevelt and the New Deal* (1963), the group published a stream of books. Goldman's panoramic *Rendezvous With Destiny* appeared in 1952, along with the first of the three solidly documented biographical volumes on the early FDR that Freidel would produce in the 50's. During the close-out year—1954—of his associate editorship of eight volumes of Theodore Roosevelt's letters, Blum deftly distilled his encyclopedic knowledge of TR's Presidency into *The Republican Roosevelt.* In 1957, Schlesinger launched a projected multivolume study of the age of Franklin Roosevelt by

dramatically recounting *The Crisis of the Old Order: 1919-1933,* and he reached even higher levels of narrative tension in *The Coming of the New Deal* (1959) and *The Politics of Upheaval* (1960), the latter a recreation of the turbulence of 1935-36.

The blurb by Blum on the back of the dust jacket of *The Politics of Upheaval* represented the sort of encomium that Schlesinger's Rooseveltian labors had already accustomed him to, and that served to set his work somewhat apart from that of his confreres, even though their books, too, were extremely well received. "As he has before," glowed Blum,

> the author in this book commands the complexity, the contradictions, the vibrancy of the New Deal years. His astute judgments and his skillful organization clarify the meaning of those years for Americans then and now. His literary talents, unsurpassed among historians, recreate the richness and vitality of the period. He is the master of the vignette. Here are incisive portraits of Father Coughlin, Huey Long, Alf Landon, and the New Dealers, too. Here, above all, Franklin Roosevelt moves through history, now indecisive, now grandly constructive, always marvelously alive. This is an indispensable book for all Americans, not just for historians.

Yet for all the compliments that were lavished on their work, these liberal rhapsodists did not have much success with the best graduate students of the period. With only a scattering of exceptions, none of the young people with genuine historical interests was drawn more than briefly to their specialty, while the broad-gauged students who viewed political history as an aspect of social, economic, or intellectual history generally chose to write their dissertations in the latter disciplines under mentors who had their political allegiances, whatever they may have been, under firm control. Thus, the mediocritization of 20th-century American political history began thirty years ago with the failure of a group of specialists in the field to accumulate a critical mass of recruits who came up to their own level of analytical competence, flawed though it was. And the most likely reason for their pedagogical failure was the political bias that drastically narrowed their conceptions of what reform was and kept them from seeing that in modern America virtually every President has been a reformer. There was good theater, to be sure, in the group's vision of marvelously alive liberal leaders summoning the electorate to one rendezvous with destiny after another, but as a means of cutting into and understanding American history, it was an instrument of limited usefulness, and most of the intellectually sophisticated graduate students—that saving remnant—avoided having it thrust upon them.

The group's theoretical assumptions were buried in the stuff of their work and did not receive explicit statement as a creed—except by Schlesinger, whose favorite smear word, ironically, is dogma. Not only did he enunciate his black-and-white ideas, but he claimed that they applied to the whole sweep of American history. "Every great crisis thus far in American history," Schlesinger wrote in the closing pages of *The Age of Jackson* (1945), the book that brought him a permanent appointment at Harvard well before he was thirty,

> has produced a leader adequate to the occasion from the ranks of those who believe vigorously and seriously in liberty, democracy, and the common man. . . . In the past, when liberalism has resolved the crisis and restored tranquillity, conservatism has recovered power by the laws of political gravity; then it makes a new botch of things, and liberalism again must take over in the name of the nation. But the object of liberalism has never been to destroy capitalism, as conservatism invariably claims—only to keep the capitalists from destroying it.

Although the author of **Cycles** deplores those who conceive of America as a redeemer nation with a mission to save the world, he himself passionately believes that liberalism has been the historic redeemer of America.

Schlesinger acquired his Manichean model of the American past from his historian father, Arthur Meier Schlesinger. As early as 1924 (when his precocious son was a lad of seven), the elder Schlesinger set forth in a lecture his growing conviction that American history had always been bound, and would forever be, by an oscillation of political sentiment between periods of concern for the rights of the few and periods of concern for the wrongs of the many, between eras of quietude and rapid movement, between emphasis on the welfare of human beings and the welfare of property. In 1939, after six years of the New Deal (whose advent he was sure he had predicted), Harvard Professor Schlesinger was more confident than ever that his theory was right, at which point he elaborated it in an essay in the *Yale Review,* entitled "The Tides of National Politics." Ten years later, he updated the essay and collected it in *Paths to the Present.*

Beginning with the Stamp Act Congress of 1765, the elder Schlesinger found that American history had gone through eleven alternating periods of liberalism and conservatism lasting an average of 16.55 years. The latest period of liberalism had begun in 1931, when the Democrats took over the House of Representatives to the discomfiture of President Hoover, and terminated in 1947, the year in which a Republican-controlled Congress "proceeded to reorient the country in a conservative direction." (For some reason, the author of *Paths to the Present* did not regard Truman's upset victory over Dewey in 1948 as a new lease on life for liberalism. Could it be that *Paths to the Present* had gone to press before the election?) Major deviations in the time span had occurred only in two instances: the eight-year "liberal span" from 1861 to 1869, encompassing the Lincoln and Andrew Johnson administrations, and the ensuing "thirty-two-year reign of conservatism" ending with the assassination of William McKinley in 1901. The likelihood of further deviations was not great, in Schlesinger *père's* judgment: ". . . [W]e may expect the recession from liberalism which began in 1947 to last till 1962, with a possible margin of a year or two in one direction or the other." "The next conservative epoch," the Nostradamus of Harvard proclaimed, "will then be due around 1978."

What generates these mass drifts of sentiment? the elder Schlesinger asked himself. No observable correlation existed with the peaks and valleys of the business cycle, he was honest enough to observe; two bad depressions had occurred in the 1869-1901 period without cessation in the "groundswell of conservatism," while the New Deal had held sway in an interval of almost unrelieved bad times. Nor was there any correlation, he continued, with foreign wars, or with enlargements of the electorate, or with the physical growth of the country, or with improvements in transportation and communication. Finally, in his puzzlement, he fell back on mass psychology, a difficult subject to deal with in the best of circumstances and especially so for a historian known for his suspicion of Freud and other explorers of the invisible world of the psyche. The oscillations spring from "something basic in human nature," Professor Schlesinger vaguely ventured. "Apparently the electorate embarks upon conservative policies till it is disappointed or vexed or bored and then attaches itself to liberal policies till a like course is run."

But if human nature was the key to the shifts, why did the electorate get bored at a different rate of speed from the electorates in other democracies? And what did the terms used to describe the shifts mean anyhow? What did it mean to say that Lincoln's Presidency was liberal, when everything in his administration from the day it began was subordinate to the conservative cause of preserving the Union? What sense was there in characterizing the post-Civil War period as an "era of quietude," when even Professor Schlesinger had to admit (albeit in a vocabulary scarcely in touch with the well-nigh revolutionary industrial violence of the late 1870's) that "the years from 1869 to 1901 were constantly disrupted by the reform agitation of agrarian groups and labor elements?"

"The Tides of National Politics," in sum, was a murky piece of work which raised far more question about the dynamics of American politics than it answered. But perhaps the least well-thought-out aspect of the essay had to do with the explanation of why the author preferred the image of a spiral to that of a pendulum as a symbol of the oscillation process. The chief governmental gains of any liberal era, Professor Schlesinger pointed out with unalloyed satisfaction in his voice, generally remain on the statute books when the conservatives recover power, and are duly added to when the liberals come back into office, with the result that "liberalism grows constantly more liberal and, by the same token, conservatism grows constantly less conservative." Hence the aptness of the spiral image. But was there a point at which the spiraling expansion in the size of the federal government would fundamentally alter the nature of the government, so that no democratic leader would be able to make himself master of it? Alas, the question never came up in *Paths to the Present,* even though by 1949 a bureaucratic political order was clearly emerging in Washington, D.C., in fulfillment of James Burnham's somber prophecy eight years earlier that the United States was destined to endure a "managerial revolution."

In the course of his career, the elder Schlesinger had written some highly valuable books and articles, most of them dealing with social and economic issues and ranging impressively over two hundred years of American history. Thus there was ample reason for his son to be proud of him, even if he found "The Tides of National Politics" embarrassing. But in fact he did not find it so, for the degree of identification between father and son would seem to have been so intense as to preclude such a disagreement. At birth, the son had been named Arthur Bancroft Schlesinger, in honor of his mother, a collateral descendant of the historian George Bancroft, as well as of his father. But when he was eleven or twelve, dusty volumes of *Who's Who in America* reveal, it was decided—presumably with the concurrence of all concerned—that he would thenceforward be known as Arthur Meier Schlesinger, Jr. To this day he still signs himself Junior—and still thinks of himself as the "legatee," to use his own word, of the theory of American history propounded by his father.

Thus, in *The Age of Jackson,* the first and by far the best of his big books, the twenty-eight-year-old younger Schlesinger made a whole era come alive by dint of keen attention to ideas and a perspicacious evocation of a host of individuals of different political stripes—and yet was dead wrong in his central thesis. "Jacksonian democracy," he insisted, "was . . . a second American phase of that enduring struggle between the business community and the rest of society which is the guarantee of freedom in a liberal capitalist state." How could such an alert historian have been incapable of figuring out that the democratic surge of Jacksonism was intimately linked to the expansion of wide-open, laissez-faire capitalism and was not a phase in the restraint thereof? Part of the answer is that his devotion to Franklin Roosevelt led him to conceive of Jacksonian democracy as an earlier version of the New Deal. But the young authors false thesis mainly derived from an even more intense devotion. In the *Yale Review* version of "The Tides of National Politics," published six years before *The Age of Jackson,* the years 1829-1841 had been denominated as a period in which emphasis on the welfare of property had given way to an emphasis on human welfare, and for Arthur M. Schlesinger, Jr., that was that.

At times in his age-of-Roosevelt series Schlesinger again showed that he was capable of a bias-free perspicacity, as in his splendid sketch of Alf Landon. And although his basic judgments of leading New Dealers were all too often predictable, he sometimes dressed them out with fascinating qualifications, even in the case of Roosevelt, while his trackings of the permutations of New Deal policy were admirably careful and clear. As noted earlier, John Morton Blum in his blurb called the third volume of the series an indispensable book for all Americans; indispensable or not, *The Politics of Upheaval* surely kindled an eagerness in thousands of American readers for the volumes that would carry the story forward to Roosevelt's death in 1945 and possibly as far as the end of the Truman administration—for had not the time span of *The Age of Jackson* extended through Van Buren's Presidency and beyond?

The Politics of Upheaval, however, came out in the same year John F. Kennedy was elected President. Following that event, various liberal historians were quick to compare JFK to TR and FDR. Here once more was a leader in the heroic mold of other liberal Presidents of the century. For Schlesinger, though, the Kennedy victory had an even headier meaning. Schlesinger *père*'s historical timetable had called for a new liberal tide to come in in the early 1960's and here it was, more or less right on schedule. By the ineluctable laws of human nature that ruled American politics, a liberal hegemony of 16.55 years was clearly about to begin.

In the coruscating opening pages of *The Best and the Brightest* (1974), David Halberstam argues that the hubris of the New Frontiersmen was rooted in the good breeding and cerebral hotshotism to which his title refers. But certainly in Schlesinger's case, if not in others as well, lack of humility also derived from an intoxicating sense of moving to the beat of a powerful historical pulse. Reinhold Niebuhr, of course, had warned of the perennial tragedy of human history. Still and all, to a true believer in "Tides" the prospects for liberal governance looked extraordinarily bright, and never more so than on the gray, chilly afternoon of January 9, 1961, in Schlesinger's house on Irving Street in Cambridge, when the President-elect at last asked his host if he was ready to work at the White House. Schlesinger in *A Thousand Days: John F. Kennedy in the White House* (1965) remembers replying, "I am not sure what I would be doing as Special Assistant, but, if you think I can help, I would like to come." Neither in word nor in thought, evidently, did he register the slightest regret at having to put aside his age-of-Roosevelt series, in which he had barely reached the end of FDR's first term in office.

In the days following his acceptance of Kennedy's remarkably unspecific invitation, Schlesinger was reputed to have invested a fair amount of time trying to convince colleagues in the Harvard history department that active involvement in politics would deepen his understanding of the subject and make him a better historian. But if these reports were true, he was profoundly self-deceived. Far from becoming a better historian, he would never again, for the next twenty-six years, be able to think critically, and the field of 20th-century American political history would be further damaged as a result. The proposal that he join the New Frontier constituted a test of his will to stay the course as a historian—and he flunked it, even as the test posed by the Vietnam war would snap his vaunted "radical nerve" and cause him to quail before St. Augustine's certainty, as restated by Niebuhr, that "to the end of history, the peace of the world must be gained by strife."

Schlesinger's confession of confusion about his duties as Special Assistant was waved off by Kennedy. "Well, I am not sure what I will be doing as President either," he said, "but I am sure there will be enough at the White House to keep us both busy." A graceful joke surely, and Schlesinger retells it well. Nevertheless, his account of that gray afternoon on Irving Street reads strangely. For Kennedy to have been unclear in his mind about the role he expected Schlesinger to play in Washington would have been totally out of character for him, and Schlesinger could not have been so naive as not to realize that he was being tacitly asked to take copious notes on the Kennedy administration and eventually to write its history. In the 1980's Edmund Morris, literarily the most gifted of living biographers of American political leaders, would also be granted access to a sitting President so that he might portray him in print, but both sides would recognize the problem of protecting the biographer's intellectual independence; wherefore it was proposed and agreed that Morris would have regular contact with the Reagan White House, but would not be of it. That kind of ethical concern, however, had never been characteristic of Joseph P. Kennedy's way of doing business, and it did not affect his son's. The Kennedys coopted people, if necessary they bought them (to ghostwrite a book or whatever), and when the President-elect created a slot on his staff for the eager Schlesinger he thereby made him his creature—and his family's.

A Thousand Days—published a mere two years after Kennedy's death—runs to more than a thousand pages and is crammed with excerpts from documents, quotes of conversations, and intricately detailed recapitulations of events. As such, it is a valuable historical source. Unfortunately, the memoir also warrants comparison with Parson Weems's pamphlet biography of George Washington, the purpose of which, Weems explained to a publisher in 1800, was to bring out the President's "Great Virtues." Not from *A Thousand Days* can the reader learn about Kennedy's dalliances, during his assignment as a fledgling naval officer in 1941 and early 1942 to the Office of Naval Intelligence, with a married blonde of Danish birth who was suspected of being a German agent; or about his personal friendship with Senator Joe McCarthy; or about the rockiness of his marriage ("Like all marriages, this one may have had its early strains," says Schlesinger in dismissal of the subject); or even about the full extent of the disease he suffered from and the daily implantation of deoxycorticosterone acetate pellets in his thighs that it required before the arrival of cortisone in a form that could be taken orally.

Minimizing threats to Kennedy's luster and making pitiless cracks about his opponents, especially Nixon, became the unseemly devoirs of a once-honorable historian. But that was only the beginning of his degradation. As the assassination of the President proved to be but a prelude to his brother's, as situation-room confidence in counterinsurgency was eaten away by guilt about body counts, as the civil-rights movement led to black power, Keynesian full employment to runaway inflation, and the poverty program to social pathology, as the entire liberal dream took on the aspects of nightmare, Schlesinger surrendered to sheer fantasizing. The most egregious example was the 900 pages of treacle entitled *Robert Kennedy and His Times* (1978), which argued that in the role of tribune of the dispossessed young Kennedy came to haunt the American imagination and did so still, a decade after his death. Of how many imaginations besides those of Roosevelt Grier and Anthony Lewis could Schlesinger have been actually thinking?

With *The Cycles of American History,* the extent to which the historian has internalized his father's point of view becomes clearer than ever. In his central essay, **"The Cycles of American Politics,"** the author sets forth a new

version of what he refers to as "the Schlesinger formulation" of American politics. The emphasis now falls on 20th-century American history rather than the full run, and instead of being broken down into sixteen-year tides it is presented in three cycles, each of thirty years' duration. The first two cycles follow the same pattern: each began with two stirring decades (1901-20 and 1933-52) of "public action, passion, idealism, and reform," and were succeeded by one deplorable decade (the 1920's and the 1950's) of "materialism, hedonism, and the overriding quest for personal gratification." (Yes, that's right. Arthur M. Schlesinger, Jr. deplores personal gratification.) The third cycle, however, began with a foreshortened period of commitment to larger purposes, extending only from the advent of Kennedy to the early 1970's, after which the "compass needle . . . swung toward private interest and the fulfillment of self."

Beneath the streamlined chassis, the chrome fender guards, and the body stripes, **"The Cycles of American Politics"** is the same old Tin Lizzie in which the elder Schlesinger took American history for a ride. As before, a view of human nature that stops at the borders of the Republic is invoked as the force governing everything. "A nation's capacity for high-tension political commitment is limited. Nature insists on a respite. People can no longer gird themselves for heroic effort. They yearn to immerse themselves in the privacies of life." But thanks to the miracle of mass psychology, people eventually "grow bored with selfish motives and vistas, [they] weary of materialism as the ultimate goal. The vacation from public responsibility replenishes the national energies and recharges the national batteries. People . . . ask not what their country can do for them but what they can do for their country." Which is why Schlesinger can speak of the future with the same air of authority as his father. The national batteries will soon be recharged, he prophesies. "Shortly before or after the year 1990," Manichean America is going to get moving again.

But recent swings in American politics have been so erratic and so frequent as to make a mockery of the cycle concept. In a preemptive strike against this horrid idea, Schlesinger acknowledges the seeming anomaly that the Environmental Protection Act, the Occupational Safety and Health Act, and the Comprehensive Employment and Training Act became law on the dreadful Nixon's watch, and that Nixon even proposed a guaranteed minimum income in his Family Assistance Program, as well as indexing social-security benefits, imposing wage-and-price controls, and presiding over the fastest increase in social payments since the New Deal. Not to fret. Even though by the terms of the cycle theory an era of selfishness surely ought to have begun with Nixon's inauguration in 1969, the "liberal tide of the 60's [was] still running strong."

It may further seem anomalous, Schlesinger goes on to say, that a Democrat was elected President in 1976, smack in the middle of an otherwise Republican line-up. Not to fret. The four-year Carter Presidency did not represent an inexplicably brief recrudescence of the reign of the good guys, for Carter was "the most conservative Democratic President since Grover Cleveland." He was a throwback, this Georgian, and from "a longer perspective, the differences between Carter and Reagan will seem less consequential than the continuities." So much for the fact that, for all his skepticism about big-government solutions, Carter significantly extended liberalism's domestic agenda in a number of areas, such as education, energy, and urban development (the action-grant program), while in foreign policy it would be hard for anyone to deny that he was a liberal for almost three years, inasmuch as liberalism in this realm has been equated since Vietnam with the abnegation of national power. Moreover, the alleged throwback to Grover Cleveland was actually a portent of things to come, for the streaky combination of conservatism and liberalism for which Carter stood is evident nationwide in today's Democratic party, and may well provide oratorical themes for its presidential nominees in the era dead ahead that Nostradamus, Jr. likes to think will touch off a new cycle of his kind of politics.

"Power is poison," Henry Adams darkly remarks in *The Education of Henry Adams* (1918), but if those sobering words are quoted in the pages of *Cycles* it is only because the author wishes to quarrel with them. Which is ironic, because being close to the President of the United States in the early 1960's unquestionably poisoned the wells of Schlesinger's historical imagination. The stories of Blum, Freidel, and Leuchtenburg (and of the other members of their historical group) unfolded somewhat differently; nevertheless, a grim complementarity to the fate of Schlesinger obtained.

There may be other reasons—there almost surely are—why Blum's later career would be distinguished principally by his service on one of Harvard's governing boards rather than by scholarship; and why Freidel, after churning out three volumes on FDR, bing, bing, bing, in 1952, 1954, and 1956, should not have been able to come up with volume four, *Launching the New Deal,* until 1973 and has since fallen silent as Roosevelt's biographer; and why the intellectual promise of Leuchtenburg's *Franklin D. Roosevelt and the New Deal,* published in the final year of Camelot, remains unfulfilled. Yet at the same time that we must concede the likely presence in their lives of other coercive factors, it is difficult not to believe that as historians these three men—and many others like them in universities across the nation—were disabled by the political events of the 1960's and their reverberating sequels in the 1970's and 1980's. History, it would seem, betrayed a whole generation of specialists in 20th-century American political history because it smashed their working model of the American experience, as constructed by them out of the New Deal in their impressionable youth.

Although this generation is now passing from the academy, its successors for the most part remain wedded to the study of presidential elections as the only way to understand the political scene. There is, however, another way, as a good many political scientists, economists, and sociologists have discovered. While the electorate in the past forty years has switched allegiances time and again, the linear development of a leaderless, bureaucratic government has proceeded unbrokenly. In the middle and late 1940's, the consolidation of the administrative apparatus

of the New Deal, the emergence of a national-security establishment, and the recruitment into federal service of experts from the natural sciences and the social sciences had the effect of placing much of the government beyond the control of elected officials.

Schlesinger, in *Cycles,* creates the impression that because the liberal Presidents of the postwar period, Truman, Kennedy, and Johnson, kept their White House staffs small and served as their own chiefs of staff, they were very much in charge of things. The quantum leap in size of the White House staff took place under Nixon and was the product, Schlesinger avers, of his paranoiac insecurity as President. These vaporings merely illustrate the pathos of Schlesinger's intellectual situation, as does his anti-Nixon, anti-Vietnam war diatribe, *The Imperial Presidency* (1973). In fact, the only postwar President who has come even close to asserting presidential control over the executive bureaucracy was Eisenhower, and that was because he governed through a general-staff system with which he, as a long-time Army officer, was eminently familiar. And if the White House staff was enlarged during Nixon's Presidency, it was because he, too, sought to bring the bureaucracy to heel.

Today, an elaborate staff exists in the houses of Congress as well as in the White House, and the modus operandi for the staffs of the vast federal agencies is to lobby their counterparts on the Hill, rather than the Congressmen themselves. Meanwhile, "iron triangles" linking executive bureaus, congressional committees, and interest group clienteles protect their stakes in federal programs by frustrating the efforts of Presidents and their appointees to horn in on the policy-making action. Ramifying out beyond the Washington Beltway are the intermediary organizations—the consultants, the contractors, the city and state governments—through which the federal bureaucracy prefers to act so as to keep down its numerical strength (and thus silence protests about it), while at the same time expanding its political strength. And "issue networks," as the political scientist Hugh Heclo calls them, further politicize the nation at large by enabling such variegated people as the businessman with shady international contacts, the renowned economist sitting by the telephone in his book-lined study, and the citizens' group voicing its outrage at a planning-commission hearing to plug into the Washington power frame.

We like to think that when a new President comes into office he takes full command. Vertically and for brief periods, presidential authority has indeed been felt in the furthest reaches of the bureaucracy, most recently under the budget-cutting and deregulating Ronald Reagan. Horizontally and consistently, however, it has not.

In an age of bureaucracy, more historians ought to join the effort of their social-science colleagues to follow the connections between politics and administration. Many benefits might result from the rise of such a scholarship. It could serve to rejuvenate a badly ailing academic discipline. It might help to create a general appreciation of why so many of the episodes that have shaken the American Presidency in the past twenty-six years, from the decision to go forward with the Bay of Pigs invasion to the Watergate debacle to the Iranian arms scandal, have been bureaucratic dramas. On a considerably lower level of importance, it could also make even more apparent than is already the case that the prefabricated political responses of Arthur M. Schlesinger, Jr. have very little bearing on the world that lies around him.

C. Vann Woodward (review date 15-22 July 1991)

SOURCE: "Equal But Separate," in *The New Republic*, Vol. 205, Nos. 3-4, July 15-22, 1991, pp. 41-3.

[*In the following review of Schlesinger's* The Disuniting of America, *Woodward examines Schlesinger's view that the recent emphasis on ethnic and linguistic separatism will not exhaust the unifying ideal of the American republic.*]

The current upsurge of American minorities goes under several names, each designating a different aspect of the movement and varied attitudes toward it: ethnicity, diversity, pluralism, multiculturalism, Afrocentrism, anti-Westernism. All these aspects have found lodgement in the universities, where their most vocal spokesmen are often concentrated and where students provide their most volatile followers. It was natural, therefore, that the current debate and concern should have focused first on academic questions such as who shall be admitted, what they should be taught, and who should teach them. And it is well that this should be so, for higher education is most immediately affected, and the discussion of the effects must continue.

In his brief and brilliant book, Arthur Schlesinger Jr. is certainly not unaware of the academic aspects of the problem, and in fact he has a chapter titled "The Battle of the Schools." But Schlesinger is mainly concerned with larger and more lasting implications and their national consequences. The jacket of *The Disuniting of America* bears a subtitle, *Reflections on a Multicultural Society,* that is not carried on the title page but helps to indicate the nature of the book, while the main title suggests its graver and wider implications.

The outburst of minority assertiveness in the United States is taking place against a background of explosions of the sort within nation-states around the globe. Those abroad are often marked by old hatreds and deeply entrenched linguistic and religious differences; they take separatist forms, and use organized violence that threatens the existence of the nation in which they occur. On the larger scale one thinks of the Soviet Union and India, and with many variations the smaller examples include South Africa, Canada, Lebanon, Yugoslavia, Ethiopia, Sri Lanka, Burma, Indonesia, and even the most recent liberated generation of nation-states, such as Czechoslovakia. History in the *real* new world order is made not primarily by what nations do to each other, but by what is done to nations by divisive ethnic feuds within.

Against this background of current foreign divisiveness and (until lately) in sharp contrast to it, Schlesinger brings to bear a historical perspective on the American tradition. He begins aptly with the celebrated question posed in 1782 by J. Hector St. John de Crèvecoeur in his *Letters from an American Farmer.* "What then is the American, this new man?" And he follows with the familiar example cited by the Franco-American author, of one couple that in three generations united in marriage American citizens of eight different national origins. "From this promiscuous breed," continued Crèvecoeur, "that race now called Americans has arisen." He follows by coining in the same paragraph the melting-pot metaphor: "Here individuals of all nations are melted into a new race of men," a race that had turned its back on "ancient prejudices and manners." Crèvecoeur's *Letters* were translated into several languages and became a favorite text for prominent America-watchers of Europe in the next two centuries, including Alexis de Tocqueville in 1835, James Bryce in 1888, and Gunnar Myrdal in 1944. All of them marveled at a unique capacity of America, what Bryce called "the amazing solvent power which American institutions, habits, and ideas exercise upon newcomers of all races."

Americans themselves proclaimed assimilation to be an ideal of the national creed from the start. Washington welcomed "the oppressed and persecuted of all Nations and Religions" not as groups or ethnic enclaves, but as individuals who would be "assimilated to our customs, measures, and laws: in a word, soon become *one people.*" Wilson echoed him during World War I: "You cannot become thorough Americans if you think of yourself in groups. America does not consist of groups." What with more than 27 million immigrants pouring in between 1865 and 1917—more than the total population of the country in 1850—it is just as well for the national welfare that the tradition of assimilation generally continued to prevail. America seemed to have made diversity a source of unity.

It is true that the melting pot met with resistance from time to time. Assimilation was not automatic, and ethnic enclaves were formed in metropolitan quarters. Foreign languages and newspapers persisted, and so did a suspicion that the melting pot was a WASP device for imposing on newcomers from other nations the dominant Anglo-centric culture. And apart from European newcomers, certain oldcomers were held unassimilable from the start. Crèvecoeur answered his own question, "What then is the American, this new man?" in his very next sentence: "He is either an European, or the descendant of an European." That silently defined blacks out of an American identity. Later Tocqueville deplored the omission. The exclusion was supported by a consensus among whites for a long time to come, but for whites themselves—for newcomers as well as oldcomers—assimilation remained the goal. Even among the majority of blacks, down through Martin Luther King Jr., the fight was against segregation and separatism, and for desegregation and integration.

Then came the growing cult of ethnicity, the passion for "roots," for ancestral voices, for separate and inviolable group identities. As Schlesinger describes this shift from integration and assimilation to separatism:

> Instead of a transformative nation with an identity all its own, America increasingly sees itself as preservative of old identities. Instead of a nation composed of individuals making their own free choices, America increasingly sees itself as

composed of groups more or less indelible in their ethnic character. The national ideal had once been *e pluribus unum.* Are we now to belittle *unum* and glorify *pluribus?* Will the center hold? Or will the melting pot yield to the Tower of Babel?

Schlesinger readily admits that the republic, long dominated by white Anglo-Saxon males, owes overdue acknowledgement to the contributions of women, black Americans, Hispanics, Asians, and Indians, and that their demands have had some healthy consequences. What he fears is the "disuniting" effects of overdoing both demands and responses. In 1989, for example, the New York state commissioner of education appointed a Task Force on Minorities to report on a history curriculum for the public schools. With no historian among its seventeen members, and with ethnic representatives in charge, the task force denounced as "terribly damaging" to the psyche of ethnics a prevailing emphasis on Eurocentric tradition and Western culture and demanded a new curriculum containing four other cultures to teach "higher self-esteem" to their children. The report contains no reference to the ideas of individual freedom and political democracy to which most of the world now aspires. Such ideas, along with their unifying effect, are presumably too Western. Instead the report sanctions racial tension and deepens racial divisiveness.

While numerous groups have joined in to voice their own grievances and claim redress as victims, black Americans, the largest minority with the oldest and most tragic grievances, have been the most prominent. To them Schlesinger devotes most of his attention in this book. The self-appointed spokesmen whom he quotes are not presented as typical or representative, but as pacesetters and extremists. A black psychiatrist attributes white racial inferiority to a genetic inability to produce the skin pigments of melanin that account for black racial superiority. Another black psychologist contends that the black mind works in genetically distinctive ways. Some argue that biological and mental differences make blacks "process information differently" and prove the need for teaching in "black English." This explains black learning difficulties under the present system. The solution is to break with white, racist, Eurocentric culture and embrace "Afrocentricity." Leonard Jeffries of the City College of New York offers his people a choice between the cold, materialistic "ice people" who brought "domination, destruction, and death" to the world, and the warm, humanistic "sun people" and their intellectual and physical superiority.

The multiracial curriculum conceived by the New York task force has inspired similar efforts in many parts of the country. An educational psychologist, Asa G. Hilliard III of Georgia State University, who conceived the collection *African-American Baseline Essays,* contends that "Africa is the mother of Western civilization," that Egypt was a black African country and the source of the glory that was Greece and the grandeur that was Rome. Africans also discovered America and named the waters they crossed the Ethiopian Ocean, long before Columbus. Adopted first by the public school system of Portland, Oregon, Hilliard's ideas have inspired Afrocentric curriculums in Milwaukee, Indianapolis, Pittsburgh, Richmond, Atlanta, Philadelphia, Detroit, Baltimore, Washington, D.C., and other cities.

How fully and faithfully all these metropolitan school systems have followed the Portland example framed by Hilliard and his six collaborators I have no means of knowing. As published in a revised edition of 1990 by the Portland Public Schools, *African-American Baseline Essays* runs to a total of 486 pages. All parts follow the common thesis that Africa gave birth to Western civilization, and that it was the birthplace of architecture, mathematics, medicine, music, and philosophy—not to mention the arts and sciences in general, social studies and history included. The theory of origins relies heavily on identifying Egyptians through the millennia as black Africans, an identification that leading American Egyptologists consulted by Schlesinger firmly reject—as firmly as classical scholars reject the dependence of Greek civilization on Egypt.

American blacks are not the first racial group with wounded pride to seek comfort in myths of a glorious past. The Irish also claimed to have discovered America before the Vikings and Columbus. Perhaps it is because the wounds of black Americans are so much deeper than those of white minorities, or because contemporary Africa offers little but famine, civil wars, and police states, that they reach back so desperately to mythic antiquities for solace. Their purpose is therapeutic, to instill pride and self-esteem in black children. That is a misuse of education and an abuse of history, and it will not work. The trouble is not the teaching of Afro-American history or African history. "The issue is the teaching of *bad* history under whatever ethnic banner," as Schlesinger puts it, and goes on to observe: "Surely there is something a little sad about all this."

One of the sad things is a seemingly unconscious resort to a type of racism of which American blacks have themselves been the main victims: the theory that biology or race determines mentality, once a favorite apology for slavery. But even sadder is the crippling effect of the Afrocentric therapy on the children it is designed to help. In Schlesinger's words:

> The best way to keep a people down is to deny them the means of improvement and achievement and cut them off from the opportunities of national life. If some Kleagle of the Ku Klux Klan wanted to devise an educational curriculum for the specific purpose of handicapping and disabling black Americans, he would not likely come up with anything more diabolically effective than Afrocentrism.

The adoption of Afrocentric curricula for public schools from Portland to Baltimore illustrates the manipulability of white guilt and the danger of taking paths paved with good intentions.

Reflective black Americans must often find themselves embarrassed by the present rage for Africanization. They know that Americanization and rejection of Africa has long been the dominant message of black leaders from David Walker in 1829 to Martin Luther King, who declared unequivocally, "The Negro is American. We know nothing of Africa." W. E. B. DuBois noted a "fierce repugnance toward anything African" among his associates in the NAACP, who "felt themselves Americans, not Africans"—this before he moved to Africa himself in his last years. Among outstanding contemporary black scholars, John Hope Franklin draws a sharp distinction between propaganda "on the one hand and the highest standards of scholarship on the other," and Orlando Patterson scornfully denounces the "three Ps" approach to black history: princes, pyramids, and pageantry. At least one black journalist, William Raspberry of *The Washington Post,* begs his people "not to reach back for some culture we never knew but to lay full claim to the culture in which we exist."

Other minorities—brown, yellow, red, white—each with its own separatist slogans, myths, and programs of ethnicity, have joined in the common cult of victimization, inflammable sensitivity, alibi-seeking, and self-pity. Hispanic Americans, increasingly at odds with black Americans, reject "black English" but promote bilingualism, another source of fragmentation and ethnic separatism. Minorities do not congregate, they self-segregate. Sometimes they are assisted in this on university campuses by administrations that furnish separate dormitory, dining, study, and social facilities. Stanford boasts "ethnic theme houses." Where Chief Justice Earl Warren held in 1954 that segregation "generates a feeling of inferiority," ethnics now hold that integration generates such a feeling and segregation is the cure.

A more realistic view of ethnic separatism is that it fosters sensitivities, resentments, and suspicions, setting one group against another. With more reasons for suspicion against whites than others, blacks may have acquired the greatest susceptibility to paranoia. Alarming evidence of this is provided by a poll of New Yorkers in 1990 that showed that 60 percent of black respondents thought it "true or possibly true" that the government was making drugs available in black neighborhoods to harm black people, and 29 percent thought it true or possible that the AIDS virus was invented by racist conspirators to kill blacks.

The cult of ethnicity and its zealots have put at stake the American tradition of a shared commitment to common ideals and its reputation for assimilation, for making "a nation of nations." At stake as well are Washington's goal of "one people," Crèvecoeur's "new race," Tocqueville's "civic participation," Bryce's "amazing solvent," and Myrdal's "American Creed." With this attack comes a contemptuous assault on Western culture in general as a curse to mankind. It appears, as Schlesinger suggests, that "white guilt can be pushed too far."

For all that, Schlesinger believes that "the campaign against the idea of common ideals and a single society will fail," and that "the upsurge of ethnicity is a superficial enthusiasm stirred by romantic ideologues and unscrupulous hucksters whose claim to speak for their minorities is thoughtlessly accepted by the media." It is his "historian's guess" and his personal conviction "that the resources of the Creed have not been exhausted. American-

ization has not lost its charms." Whether his guess and conviction prove justified or not, we owe Arthur Schlesinger a great debt of gratitude for his reflections on the subject.

An excerpt from *The Disuniting of America*

The genius of America lies in its capacity to forge a single nation from peoples of remarkably diverse racial, religious, and ethnic origins. It has done so because democratic principles provide both the philosophical bond of union and practical experience in civic participation. The American Creed envisages a nation composed of individuals making their own choices and accountable to themselves, not a nation based on inviolable ethnic communities. The Constitution turns on individual rights, not on group rights. Law, in order to rectify past wrongs, has from time to time (and in my view often properly so) acknowledged the claims of groups; but this is the exception, not the rule. . . .

Within the overarching political commitment, people are free to live as they choose, ethnically and otherwise. Differences will remain; some are reinvented; some are used to drive us apart. But as we renew our allegiance to the unifying ideals, we provide the solvent that will prevent differences from escalating into antagonism and hatred.

Arthur M. Schlesinger, in his The Disuniting of America, *originally published in 1991, reprinted by W. W. Norton & Company in 1992.*

Heather MacDonald (review date June 1992)

SOURCE: "Toward Yugoslavia?" in *Commentary,* Vol. 93, No. 6, June, 1992, pp. 61-3.

[*In the following favorable review of Schlesinger's* The Disuniting of America, *MacDonald discusses Schlesinger's concern that multicultural emphasis in America is both separatist and segregationist in scope and intention.*]

Originally published by Whittle Direct Books and now re-issued with an expanded foreword, ***The Disuniting of America: Reflections on a Multicultural Society*** is an uncompromising look at the fraud of multiculturalism and Afrocentrism. Arthur M. Schlesinger, Jr.'s eminence as a historian—he currently holds the Albert Schweitzer chair in the humanities at the City University of New York—has not protected him, or his book, from the usual smears. Ishmael Reed, a novelist who teaches English at Berkeley, has denounced Schlesinger as a "follower of David Duke," and Henry Louis Gates, Jr., professor of English and Afro-American studies at Harvard, has caricatured Schlesinger's arguments as a "demand [for] cultural white-face."

While predictable, the hostile response to ***The Disuniting of America*** is nevertheless particularly discouraging, for it is difficult to imagine a book expressing greater compassion for the racial frustrations which Schlesinger sees as fueling Afrocentrism, or greater candor about the past injustices of American society and historiography. If such a book—as frank about America's failings as about those of multiculturalism—is dismissed as neo-Nazi propaganda, then good-faith discussion has been all but foreclosed.

Schlesinger's thesis is that the current cult of ethnicity imperils the very basis of the American experiment. Although multiculturalists may think they own the patent on "diversity," Schlesinger shows that diversity has been America's trademark since inception. Our unique admixture of peoples has prompted both native-born and foreign observers to ask: what can hold so variegated a nation together? From the 18th to the 20th century the answer has remained constant: the "American Creed." As Gunnar Myrdal wrote in 1944, Americans hold in common "the *most explicitly expressed* system of general ideals" of any country in the West: the ideals of equality and the inalienable rights to freedom, justice, and opportunity. It is adherence to those ideals, not one's race, original nationality, or ethnicity, that makes one an American.

Today, says Schlesinger, the American identity is in jeopardy as multiculturalism and Afrocentrism elevate racial and ethnic over national affiliation. At the end of this road, he warns, lie Yugoslavia and other contemporary battlegrounds of racial and ethnic separatism. While the analogy may seem a touch overwrought, there can be no question that multiculturalists are playing with weapons that can wreak havoc on our already inadequate schools, our social structure, and economy.

Separatist ideas of history are among those weapons. To be sure, today's multiculturalists and Afro-centrists are hardly the first to revise history. During previous waves of American ethnic consciousness, Schlesinger points out, underdog groups similarly fabricated their own "compensatory" versions of history—what the historian John V. Kelleher calls the "there's-always-an-Irishman-at-the-bottom-of-it-doing-the-real-work approach to American history." The crucial difference, however, is that those earlier movements never sought to impose their ethnocentric mythologies on the public-school curriculum.

By contrast, Afrocentrists, who place Africa at the source of the world's cultural and scientific achievements, view the teaching of history in the schools as a tool for group empowerment and for the advancement of group self-esteem. Such "therapeutic" uses of history undermine what Schlesinger sees as the true purpose of historical study: "the recognition of complexity and the search for knowledge." Moreover, as Diane Ravitch, now an Assistant Secretary of Education, has warned, "Once ethnic pride and self-esteem become the criterion for teaching history, certain things cannot be taught" in the schools. Proscribed subjects include (in Schlesinger's formulation) "the tyrannous authority [of African emperors], the ferocity of their wars, the tribal massacres, the squalid lot of the common people, . . . [and] the complicity with the Atlantic slave trade."

As for what *is* being taught, the twin pillars of Afrocentrism are the claims that the West stole its culture from Egypt, and that Egypt was black. Schlesinger debunks both these fallacies, and disproves as well the relationship between ethnocentric education and self-esteem or academic achievement. Self-esteem, he notes, originates not in racial pride but in personal achievement and family encouragement, while the presence or absence of ethnic role models in the curriculum has no known correlation with academic success.

The connection between Afrocentric education and American black identity is even more tenuous, Schlesinger boldly argues. Since the early 19th century, most black leaders have repudiated the notion that they are Africans first, Americans second. The current cult of "self-Africanization," among a people who no longer have an authentic relation to Africa, Schlesinger dismisses as "play-acting." Most damning of all, he concludes, Afrocentric pedagogy works against the very goals it claims to be pursuing, since nothing could be more cunningly designed to retard the social and economic progress of black children than the new form of segregation represented by black-only public schools, the deemphasis of logic in favor of emotive forms of expression, and the encouragement of "black" English.

In defense of their policies, multiculturalists routinely cite the sins of the European "canon" against which they are rebelling, an allegedly monolithic, exclusive, and intellectually repressive structure which, in the words of a leading Afrocentrist, is "killing [black] children, killing their minds." Western culture as a whole, they add, is the world's leading source of racism, imperialism, sexism, and all-around nastiness. Yet as Schlesinger points out, the Western canon—a fluid, immensely complex cultural inheritance that contains voices of rage and protest as well as voices of celebration and devotion—is precisely what has inspired the great black political theorists and philosophers, not to mention innumerable critics of the West both white and black.

What sets Europe apart from the rest of the world is not oppressiveness—its sins have been more than matched by Asia, the Middle East, and Africa—but rather the fact that Western oppression has "produced [its] own antidote":

> Whatever the particular crimes of Europe, that continent is also the source—the *unique* source—of those liberating ideas of individual liberty, political democracy, the rule of law, human rights, and cultural freedom that constitute our most precious legacy and to which most of the world today aspires. These are *European* ideas, not Asian, nor African, nor Middle Eastern ideas, except by adoption.

And though Schlesinger can be severe about the West's failure to live up to its ideals, including the treatment of blacks and other minorities, he is scathing on the relative merits of other cultures compared with ours:

> There is surely no reason for Western civilization to have guilt trips laid on it by champions of cultures based on despotism, superstition, tribalism, and fanaticism. In this regard the Af-

rocentrists are especially absurd. The West needs no lectures on the superior virtue of those "sun people" who sustained slavery until Western imperialism abolished it (and, it is reported, sustain it to this day in Mauritania and the Sudan), who still keep women in subjection and cut off their clitorises, who carry out racial persecutions not only against Indians and other Asians but against fellow Africans from the wrong tribes, who show themselves either incapable of operating a democracy or ideologically hostile to the democratic idea, and who in their tyrannies and massacre, their Idi Amins and Boukassas, have stamped with utmost brutality on human rights.

The eloquence and erudition of *The Disuniting of America* make its hostile reception all the more disturbing. Reading this book, one is torn between admiration for its arguments and the sad conviction that they are utterly futile. To warn against the dissolution of our common national ideals and our common culture holds little threat for people who claim, however speciously, that they never shared those ideals and were never part of that culture.

One of the most pernicious effects of multiculturalism has been to destroy the linguistic ground necessary to debate it. For such a debate would have to invoke terms like "we" and "commonality." Yet multiculturalists, aided by the sophisticated deconstructive efforts of literary theorists like Stanley Fish and Barbara Herrnstein Smith, reject any such appeal to an American "we" as an act of imperialist violence. The only language that remains is that of an increasingly narrow "us" versus an increasingly alien "them." This is the language of civil war.

FURTHER READING

Criticism

Brogan, D. W. "General Jackson: Rehabilitation." In his *American Themes*, pp. 219-26. New York: Harper & Brothers, n. d.
  Favorable assessment of Schlesinger's history of Andrew Jackson's presidency.

Brogan, Hugh. "The Uses of American History." In *Reviews in American History* 15, No. 4 (December 1987): 521-26.
  Review of *The Cycles of American History* in which Brogan praises Schlesinger's ability to present history with humor, balance, and clarity, and lauds his treatment of the themes of liberalism and presidential power.

Commager, Henry Steele. "Two Years That Shaped Our Lives." *The New York Times Book Review* (4 January 1959): 1, 16.
  Favorable review of Schlesinger's *The Coming of the New Deal*.

———. "Should Historians Write Contemporary History?" *Saturday Review* XLIX, No. 7 (12 February 1966): 18-20, 47.
  Questions the appropriateness and accuracy of Schlesinger's White House memoir, *A Thousand Days*.

Cowan, Paul. "RFK: The Official Version." *The Nation* (30 September 1978): 316-18, 320.
  Contends that Schlesinger's *Robert Kennedy and His Times* is filled with information, but fails to lend insight into Kennedy's significance in American history.

Cunliffe, Marcus. "Arthur M. Schlesinger, Jr." In *Pastmasters: Some Essays on American Historians*, edited by Marcus Cunliffe and Robin W. Winks, pp. 345-74. New York: Harper & Row, 1969.
  Examines Schlesinger's theme of liberalism from his early works to *The Crisis of Confidence*, contending that Schlesinger's liberal bias does not usurp the credibility of his presentation of history.

Fall, Bernard B. "The American Commitment in Vietnam." *Saturday Review* L, No. 5 (4 February 1967): 39-41.
  Review of Schlesinger's *The Bitter Heritage* praising his grasp of the complex history surrounding the Vietnam War.

Schneider, Robert W. "A Relative Certainty: A Modern Liberal's View of Man." *Journal of American Culture* 5, No. 4 (Winter 1982): 96-106.
  Examines Schlesinger's conception of liberalism.

Williams, William Appleman. "Schlesinger: Right Crisis—Wrong Order." *The Nation* 184, No. 12 (23 March 1957): 257-60.
  Contends that Schlesinger's *The Crisis of the Old Order* fails to take a position on Herbert Hoover's administration and unjustifiably blames the Depression on the economic collapse of the old order.

Interviews

Brandon, Henry. "On Writing History." In his *Conversations with Henry Brandon*, pp. 40-54. London: Andre Deutsch Ltd., 1966.
  Relates Schlesinger's views concerning his works and their place in modern historical scholarship.

Garraty, John A. "Political and Social Change: 1941-1968." In his *Interpreting American History: Conversations with Historians*, pp. 265-88. London: Macmillan, 1970.
  Interview in which Schlesinger discusses his theory of political cycles, the role of the intellectual in government, and the style and ability of the American presidents from Franklin Roosevelt to Richard Nixon.

Luis Valdez

1940-

(Born Luis Miguel Valdez) Chicano dramatist, scriptwriter, nonfiction writer, essayist, editor, and director.

The following entry provides an overview of Valdez's career through 1992.

INTRODUCTION

Considered the originator of modern Chicano theater, Valdez is best known as the founding director of El Teatro Campesino, a seminal, grassroots theater group initially formed to convince California migrant farmworkers of the value of unionization. Valdez, who writes some works in English and others in a blend of English and Spanish, is credited with having provided momentum to the Chicano theater movement through his highly vivid style and his ability to place the Chicano experience within a universal American framework.

Biographical Information

Born into a family of migrant farmworkers in Delano, California, Valdez began working in the fields at six years of age. Although his education was frequently interrupted by his family's constant travel, Valdez finished high school and subsequently attended San Jose State College. After graduating in 1964, Valdez joined the San Francisco Mime Troupe, from which he gained an appreciation of "agitprop" theater, which makes use of political agitation and propaganda to protest social injustice. Valdez returned to Delano in 1965 to assist César Chávez and the United Farmworkers Union in their efforts to unionize migrant workers. There Valdez organized the strikers into a performing group to dramatize the exploitation of farmworkers and to demonstrate the necessity of unionization for their financial survival. In 1967 Valdez and El Teatro Campesino began touring nationally, expanding their focus on the plight of migrant farmworkers to include the Chicanos' roots in Native American history, music, and myth. In the early 1970s Valdez's emphasis on mysticism and indigenous concerns eventually resulted in a split between El Teatro Campesino and the overall Chicano theater movement. Since the mid-1970s Valdez has become additionally involved in writing and directing for television and film productions.

Major Works

Valdez was credited early in his career with creating the *acto,* a short, often humorous dramatic sketch that employs the language of working-class Chicanos to present a lucid social or political message. Valdez's early *actos,* generally written or created with other members of El Teatro Campesino, often make use of humor and simple representational strategies, including signs imprinted with

characters' occupations that are hung around actors' necks or masks that actors exchange to reverse their traditional roles. Valdez's plays of the late 1960s and early 1970s, including *No saco nada de la escuela* (1969), *Vietnam campensino* (1970), and *Soldado razo* (1971), deal with such subjects as the American school system's tendency to force cultural assimilation on minorities and the over-representation of Chicanos in the Vietnam War. Traditional Native American and modern issues converge in *Dark Root of a Scream* (1971), in which the death of a Chicano soldier is treated as a sacrifice to the gods, paralleling Aztec culture and history. By the mid-1970s El Teatro Campesino had become more commercially oriented. In 1978 Valdez's drama *Zoot Suit* enjoyed a highly successful run in Los Angeles. Considered the first play to draw large Mexican-American audiences to a mainstream American theater production, the drama is metatheatrical and documentary in nature. In this work Valdez uses Latin-American music, sections of courtroom transcripts, and quotes from newspaper reports to examine the Sleepy Lagoon murder case, in which several young Chicanos in east Los Angeles were convicted of murder and sentenced to life imprisonment based on circumstantial evidence. In subsequent works, such as his play *I Don't Have to Show*

You No Stinking Badges (1986) and *La Bamba* (1987), a film concerning Chicano pop star Ritchie Valens, Valdez has continued to deconstruct negative stereotypes regarding Chicanos and Mexicans within a mainstream perspective that avoids exclusive minority concerns.

Critical Reception

Although sometimes faulted for his overly idealistic rendering of Native American culture, Valdez has been credited with providing the impetus that led to the genesis of the Chicano theater movement and with creating the now-accepted genre of Chicano theater, as based on the *acto.* A leader and innovator, Valdez is widely recognized as one of the few dramatists who have been able to change the way Chicanos are perceived by white America. As Gerald C. Lubenow has noted, Valdez "has succeeded by shaping the experience of Chicanos into drama that speaks to all Americans."

PRINCIPAL WORKS

The Shrunken Head of Pancho Villa (drama) 1963
Las dos caras del patroncito (drama) 1965
La quinta temporada (drama) 1966
Los vendidos (drama) 1967
La conquista de México (drama) 1968
I Am Joaquín (screenplay) 1969
The Militants (drama) 1969
No saco nada de la escuela (drama) 1969
Bernabé (drama) 1970
Huelguistas (drama) 1970
Vietnam campesino (drama) 1970
Dark Root of a Scream (drama) 1971
La gran carpa de la familia Rascuachi (drama) 1971
Soldado razo (drama) 1971
Aztlan: An Anthology of Mexican American Literature [editor, with Stan Steiner] (anthology) 1972
El fin del mundo (drama) 1972
Los vendidos (screenplay) 1972
Pensamiento serpentino: A Chicano Approach to the Theatre of Reality (poem) 1973
El baile de los gigantes (drama) 1974
El corrido [adaptor; from his drama *La gran carpa de la familia Rascuachi*] (television script) 1977
Zoot Suit (drama) 1978
Bandido (drama) 1981
Corridos (drama) 1982
Zoot Suit (screenplay) 1982
I Don't Have to Show You No Stinking Badges (drama) 1986
*La Bamba (screenplay) 1987
Corridos! Tales of Passion and Revolution (television script) 1987
Luis Valdez—Early Works: Actos, Bernabé, Pensamiento serpentino (essays and dramas) 1990
Los mineros (television script) 1991
Zoot Suit, and Other Plays (dramas) 1992

*Valdez also directed the film.

CRITICISM

John Harrop and Jorge Huerta (essay date March-May 1975)

SOURCE: "The Agitprop Pilgrimage of Luis Valdez and El Teatro Campesino," in *Theatre Quarterly,* Vol. V, No. 17, March-May, 1975, pp. 30-9.

[*An American professor and critic, Huerta has written many books on Chicano literature and drama in addition to serving variously as founder, director, and actor in many Chicano theater groups in California. In the following essay, he and Harrop provide an overview of Valdez's career with El Teatro Campesino, focusing in particular on his development as a playwright.*]

San Juan Bautista is a very ordinary, small town in central California. Its chief attraction to outsiders is the Catholic Mission—one of those churches the Spanish priests dotted along the coast of California in their eighteenth century odyssey, with cross and sword, to claim the heathen Indian for Christ. An odd place to find Peter Brook and his International Centre for Theatre Research—among the arid hills where, for the mere wages of survival, expatriate Mexicans now work the land that once belonged to their ancestors.

But here, for six weeks in the summer of 1973, Brook and his acolytes came to work with and to learn from one of the most remarkable theatre groups now working in the United States. For San Juan Bautista is the present home of Luis Valdez and his Teatro Campesino—farmworkers' theatre—which, since it was founded in late 1965 to protest against the economic and spiritual exploitation of the Chicanos, has managed to retain its popular integrity while achieving an artistic stature that has won it awards in the United States and appearances at international festivals in Europe.

Valdez, the founder and guiding spirit of El Teatro, is himself the son of a migrant farm worker, and spent his youth fruit picking around central California while gleaning sufficient education to gain entrance to the California State College. Here an earlier interest in theatre (stimulated by a kindergarten play in which masks and physical movements had compensated for the fact that Valdez couldn't speak English) manifested itself again, and he wrote and had produced two plays during his undergraduate years.

Uncertain what his future would be after graduation, Valdez happened upon a performance by the San Francisco Mime Troupe and, immediately taken by their physically direct and dynamic style, he moved to San Francisco and joined the company. Those were the heady days when the civil rights movement and the anti-war movement were gathering momentum, and street theatre such as performed by the Mime Troupe (and the Bread and Puppet Theatre in New York), was beginning to be seen as a natural tool of non-violent protest. Theatre was being 'brought back to the people' on portable stages set up in parks; with marching bands and puppet shows in the streets; and with a broad and bawdy physicality that went for the guts and the heart.

While Valdez was with the Mime Troupe, the atmosphere of protest in America reached the migrant Mexican farmworkers in central California: they went on strike against wages and conditions in the grape fields. These were Valdez' fellow Chicanos—indeed, part of his family was striking—and he came down from San Francisco to join with Cesar Chavez' United Farmworkers Union in a protest march in Delano, California.

As a result of that experience, Valdez conceived the idea of a theatre which would support and further politicize the Mexican farmworkers in their struggle. In November 1965, with the blessing of Chavez, he held a meeting at which he broached the idea of a theatre to the striking workers. The first response was uncertain—chiefly because none of the workers had ever been to a theatre—and Valdez realized that to interest the workers he had to relate directly to their own experiences. So he had some signs made—Esquirol (scab), Huelgista (striker), Patroncito (grower) and Contratista (contractor)—and hung these around the necks of some of the workers, telling them to enact the characteristics of their signs. The results far exceeded his expectations:

> The scab didn't want to at first, because it was a dirty word at that time, but he did so in good spirits. Then the two strikers started shouting at him, and everybody started cracking up. All of a sudden people started coming . . . they filled up the whole kitchen. We started changing signs around, and people started volunteering . . . imitating all kinds of things. We ran for two hours just doing that.

Thus was El Teatro Campesino born.

From this beginning Valdez gathered a small group to work with each other each evening after the day's picketing. This group evolved what they called 'actos'—short scenes dealing with some specific element of the strike. The actors started with a real life incident, character or idea, and improvised around this in commedia dell'arte fashion, using no scripts or scenery. For simplicity of communication and ease of identification they kept the original idea of wearing signs around their necks to indicate the characters or attitudes bring represented. Props or costumes were used only as a basic reinforcement of character or situation. Valdez was careful not to disguise the fact that the actors were themselves strikers engaged in the same cause as the people for whom they were performing. He was also concerned not to alienate his audience by requiring any political or theatrical sophistication: the actors always appealed directly and simply to the immediate experience of the striking farmworkers.

Typical of the early *actos* was *Three Grapes*. A green, a ripe, and a rotten grape come onto the stage and squat. Each wishes to be picked by a scab who has not joined the strike: but each time the scab attempts this he is driven away by a striker with a 'Huelga' (strike) sign. Finally all the grapes become rotten. The scab then realizes that the grower has lost his economic power and joins the strike. The simple lesson gets across: if a grower cannot harvest his crop he must concede to the strikers.

The *actos* always contained a great deal of physical business and broad humour. The farmworkers are a straightforward, simple, and ebullient people: they respond to largeness of style and comic situations. So Valdez used comedy for its direct appeal—and because, as he said, 'you can't do tragedy on the back of a truck.' The social points came across through the comic situations and the broad but recognizable reality created by the actors:

> When I speak about comic and dramatic images, I'm speaking about visions of reality. Our comic images represent the reality that he (the farmworker) sees. It's not a naturalistic representation: most of the time it's a symbolic, emblematic presentation of what the farmworker feels. But we can't be stuffy about it, so we use slapstick. Very often the slapstick is the image.

A particularly powerful example of what Valdez meant by 'emblematic presentation' occurs in another early *acto* called *The Fifth Season,* where Summer is represented by an actor wearing an old shirt covered in dollar bills. To the farmworker Summer is the time when the fruit on the trees turns to money. The orchards and vineyards are heavy with clusters of dollars, there for the picking. But the dream of paradise is never realized: nor could it be in the present relationship of the workers to the growers. So the workers laugh at the image of Summer not because it is funny in itself, but because they recognize the irony of the situation—that the joke is on themselves.

For several months after its establishment, El Teatro picketed during the day and worked on the *actos* during the evening, giving weekly performances for the strikers in Delano. Then, in April 1966, Valdez and his actors joined the great march of strikers from Delano to the state capital of Sacramento, performing nightly in all the small towns on the route. This experience both honed their technique and extended their repertoire. It also gained them a wider reputation, which led to their first commercial performance at the Committee Theatre in San Francisco, on 2 May 1966.

For the next year El Teatro lived in Delano, but toured Chicano population centres throughout California to raise support and funds for the continuing strike. The first national tour came in July and August 1967, when the company performed in union halls across the United States—and in the courtyard of the Senate building in Washington, at the Newport Jazz Festival, and at the Village Theatre in New York. [On July 24, 1967] the *Wall Street Journal* spoke of their 'provocative, lively, and entertaining theatre,' and *Newsweek* of their 'ardent and sometimes grim gaiety' [July 31, 1967]. The *Newsweek* critic went on to say:

> The young people of El Teatro are full of racial pride, social and political fervour, and . . . they know exactly what they mean. As in the old Everyman morality plays, each character has a clear identity, is caught in a sharply defined situ-

ation, and is presented with a clear choice of destinies.

All of the New York critics drew parallels between the impact of El Teatro Campesino and that of the Federal Theatre and Labour Union Theatre in the 1930s, when economic and social distress had turned theatre into a powerful political weapon.

The New York tour, for which the company received an Obie, established it nationally, and confirmed that this kind of theatre, though still based in and geared to the aims of the striking Chicano farmworkers, was capable of a dynamic relationship with a much broader spectrum of people. This faced Valdez with an important decision:

> The strike in Delano is a beautiful cause, but it won't leave you alone . . . it's more important to leave a rehearsal and go back to the picket line. So we found we had to back away from Delano to be a theatre. Do you serve the moment by being just kind of half-assed, getting together whenever there's a chance, or do you really hone your theatre down into an effective weapon?

So, in September 1967, Valdez moved the company away from Delano and its direct link with the Farmworkers' Union, and established El Centro Campesino Cultural in Del Rey, California.

The initial success of El Teatro had been based on a bitter truth: its work was rooted in the everyday facts of the farmworkers' lives. Now Valdez wished to keep this truth—the life blood of the worker—running through his theatre, but to reach out beyond the strike to deal with the life of the Chicano in more general terms of his human rights and self respect.

In coming to this expanded theatrical consciousness, Valdez was aware of several facts concerning the cultural identity of the Chicano. First the Spanish had come and deprived the Mexican Indians of their Mayan and Aztec ancestry—had colonized them, robbed them of their pride and wealth, and in return imposed upon them a Christianity which had taught them meekly to accept second-class citizenship in their own country. Later, the Spanish masters had been exchanged for American, and pressures to take on a set of Anglo values.

More than this, many Chicanos living in the USA are not immigrants, but living in a land which is ancestrally theirs, and while there is no separatist movement on the part of the Chicanos in these territories, there is a strong movement to resist anglicization and to retain ethnic traditions. It was to this understanding of the true Chicano cultural and spiritual identity that Luis Valdez turned in taking El Teatro to Del Rey and establishing a Chicano cultural centre, to explore the music and political history of the Chicanos as well as the drama. The new purpose was to embrace and revive the culture of their ancestors, and to create a pride in being a Chicano.

Valdez recognized that to deal with these broader and more abstract issues in his theatre would require a greater technical sophistication on the part of the actors, who would now have to deal with and communicate ideas which, while related to, were no longer a direct part of their immediate experience. He therefore instituted a training programme for the company, on similar lines to those which many 'new' theatre groups were undertaking in the later 'sixties.

There was a great deal of ensemble work—trust and sensitivity exercises—plus work upon physical movement and, above all, a sound technical base for the improvisational work which still formed the starting point of El Teatro's creative efforts. Of one of their exercises, Valdez wrote that it 'must clearly establish characters and their relation to each other. Such things as language, movement, and the strict adherence to the reality of inter-relationships are important. Disciplined clean characterizations are the objective.' Again, 'The emphasis is upon wit and quick thinking, as well as movement, characterization, and stage presence.'

Thus, while clarifying and disciplining the work of the company, Valdez was concerned to retain the great ebullience, energy, and fundamental truth of their work. While becoming conscious of the need for theatrical technique, El Teatro never lost the sense of being a people's theatre, performed by and for the Chicano people—aesthetics never got in the way of direct communication.

What Valdez achieved was a strengthening of impact due to the disciplined channelling of the energies of his troupe, and a cleaner and quicker way of making the point, due to the greater clarity of the stage action. The earlier reliance upon signs hung around actor's necks gave way to more use of masks and the actor's own physicality. The use of props was subtler, and there was a more sophisticated sense of theatrical rhythm and timing. But the vivid sense of humour, the broad physical style, the energy spilling from the stage to sweep up the audience, and, at root, the sharing of fundamental truths by actor and audience, continued to be the hallmark of El Teatro Campesino.

After the move to Del Rey and subsequently (in 1969) to Fresno in the central farmland of California, the broader consciousness and capacity of El Teatro became apparent in the *actos* of that period. The earlier pieces were clearly geared towards the strike. *Three Grapes* has already been described, and other *actos* of the first period were **Huelgistas** (**The Strikers**), **Las Dos Caras del Patroncito** (**The Two Faces of the Boss**), and *Papellecion* (*Playing Games*). These *actos* were all very short, and to the immediate point. *Papellecion,* for example, has a grape grower with a sign, 'Smiling Jack', who tells his picker how much he loves his Mexican workers. As he talks, the sign changes to 'Liar', 'Gringo', 'Jackass', and finally 'Huelga', as the worker comes to see through the platitudes of the boss.

The new work looked at the Chicano in a wider social perspective. ***No Saca Nada de la Escuela*** dealt with the problems of young Chicanos in American schools, where the language and cultural barriers have left them at the bottom of the class, and encouraged a poor self-image and delinquency. ***Los Vendidos*** (***The Sell-Outs***), which was given a national television presentation by NBC, dealt with problems of those Chicanos who had tried to reject their backgrounds and became anglicized, or at least to call themselves 'Mexican-Americans.'

The inequities in the draft system in the United States during the Vietnam War were also dealt with by El Teatro. The play in which this was done, **Soldado Razo (*The Chicano Solider*)**, was concerned with the death of a Chicano soldier in Vietnam. It treated the 'macho' syndrome and the other forces which conspired to send him there, the absurdity of one brown slave being sent thousands of miles to kill other brown victims, and the total ugliness of the Vietnam circumstance. This was perhaps the first complete example of the new consciousness underlying the work of Valdez and El Teatro. While still based in the truth and uniqueness of the Chicano situation, it proclaims its relationship with the larger anti-war movement in the United States, and its brotherhood with all colonized peoples.

Soldado Razo also illustrates the evolution of the company's work in production terms. The fundamental physical elements of the early *actos* are retained. There is no attempt to create an artificial physical environment. The stage is bare, with the exception of a simple curtain suspended from a pole upstage centre, and above the curtain is a huge sign—El Teatro Campesino de Aztlan. The emphasis is still upon actors, and actors who are people like their audiences. But the simple cardboard signs have now disappeared, to be replaced by fully fleshed-out characters created with broad and simple strokes.

A further element has also appeared. Symbolic figures, masked and costumed, create a universal environment within which particular characters work out their individual destinies. In **Soldado Razo,** Valdez employed Death as his narrator, a kindly-ironic skeleton in a monk's robe, whose mocking eye fell upon actors and audience alike.

A triple consciousness is now operating in El Teatro's work: a sense of a particular man in a local situation (the Chicano); a universal man in a world situation (the poor, or underprivileged, or oppressed), and those spiritual, cosmic, and mythological forces of man's primitive psyche which give him a common humanity. In a review of **Soldado Razo** [that appeared September 23, 1971], the drama critic of the *Los Angeles Times* wrote: 'Agitprop theatre? I guess so, if we need a definition, but equally close to *Everyman* and the great medieval chronicles. Something very complicated, and very simple, and very rare is going on. . . .'

On another occasion, the *Los Angeles Times* spoke of the work of El Teatro Campesino as being 'a stunning mixture of Brechtian presentation and Chicano folklore,' [July 5, 1971], and as Valdez has himself referred to El Teatro's style as 'somewhere between Brecht and Cantinflas,' a brief comparison with Brecht might provide insights into Valdez' own work. The most apparent relationship is in the similarity of the early *actos* to Brecht's *Lehrstucke*. Both are short pieces with a didactic purpose in which the actors *present* characters rather than assume them. Both are geared to completely simple presentation—for Brecht in the classroom, for Valdez on the back of a truck. Both are meant to politicize an audience and inspire them to action.

But here, perhaps, any close analogy ends, for whereas Brecht's impact was geared to the intellectual and rational, based upon the dialectic of Marxism from which he also derived the structure of his pieces, Valdez' appeal is much simpler and more visceral. He has said: 'For our political and personal salvation we don't have to scurry to Marxism or Socialism. We can go to our own roots.'

Certainly, Valdez wished to heighten his audience's understanding of experience, but it was an understanding to be gained with body and soul, rather than through an intellectual process. Nor was the structure of Valdez' *actos* based upon any intellectual conceit: it came wholly from the necessities of the circumstances in which the actors first worked. It had the basic appeal and technique of the earliest forms of popular theatre.

Valdez' simplicity was a response to fundamental human reactions and beliefs, while Brecht's was more calculated, disciplined, and cerebral. Brecht's choice of a parabolic form and destruction of theatrical illusion was self-conscious, whereas Valdez simply took what he found and gave it theatrical impact. Above all, Teatro Campesino eschewed the revolutionary humourlessness of Brecht's didactic pieces—it took its cause seriously, but never itself. Valdez remained close to Cantinflas while Brecht had ignored Hanswurst.

Both Brecht's *Lehrstücke* and Valdez' *actos* turned to historical circumstances, and to folklore or myth. But whereas with Brecht these were neither a part of his own sensibility nor that of the audience for which he was writing, Valdez had the advantage of finding his ideas within the spiritual ethos of the Chicano people. He could continue to make use of contemporary experience, but go beneath that to touch common beliefs and attitudes based in the experiences of a still-believed Christian religion, and a Spanish colonial culture. Beneath this again, Valdez believed he could make a direct appeal to the Mayan and Aztec culture which was the deepest part of the Chicano spiritual identity.

During the years from 1969 to 1971, while this broadening of El Teatro's purpose from the concentration upon Huelga to that of Raza (national identity) was taking place, and the company was moving to its present home in San Juan Bautista, it took part in the Seventh World Theatre Festival in Nancy, France, toured Mexico, and was constantly involved in tours on behalf of the farm-workers throughout the south-western United States.

In 1970 the company also made its first film, **I Am Joaquin,** based upon an epic poem by Corky Gonzales. The film won first prize at both the San Francisco and Monterey Festivals. But perhaps the most significant event in El Teatro's early history took place in May 1970, when it sponsored the first Chicano Theatre Festival in Fresno, California. Since 1968 small companies had sprung up in Chicano areas in the United States, emulating El Teatro Campesino in their attempt to politicize and raise a Chicano consciousness. Thirteen companies attended that first festival, which has been repeated in each subsequent year.

As a result of the success of these festivals, Luis Valdez has been instrumental in creating Tenaz (El Teatro Na cional de Aztlan), to establish communication between the companies, to provide a means for sharing material, and, above all, to hold workshops at which members of El Teatro Campesino could share their skills with the newer companies which, at first, were founded upon enthusiasm and commitment, but scant theatrical ability. There are now more than 75 companies across the United States, and the work they are doing, catalyzed and encouraged by El Teatro Campesino, is helping to create a Chicano consciousness, dignity, and sense of purpose.

While the Teatros spawned by El Teatro used the *acto* form originated by Valdez, he himself, after 1971, created what he called the *mito,* moving further in the direction of myth and symbolism, and relating to the great religious sense and spiritual intuition deep-seated within the Chicano self. Valdez became ever more convinced that the Chicano must grasp his indigenous heritage as the spiritual key to his existence and purpose in life.

The *mito* was a theatrical form with roots in the many-layered culture of the Chicano. It drew upon Aztec ritual, Mexican folklore, and Christian drama. The *auto sacramentale* structure was familiar to many Chicanos, and Valdez used elements of this in a conjunction with the basic folk-ballad form of the Chicano—the *Corrido,* 'handed down from generation to generation . . . a living part of the Chicano's cultural heritage. Love, hate, jealousy, courage, pride—all of the universal themes of man's existence on earth are expressed in these songs.'

El Teatro took some of these well known ballads and acted them out to the accompaniment of the guitar and singing, and then incorporated this into the *mito* structure. Thus the *mito* became the playing and singing of a narrative idea, which was illustrated by emblematic symbolism and ritual taken from the medieval religious drama, the whole being salted by the vigorous, earthy humour which had formed a dynamic element of the secular medieval theatre.

The *mito* was still geared to the making of direct points about the everyday experience of the Chicano, while this was now seen in the much wider perspective of a total Chicano sensibility. To educate the Chicano to a fuller understanding of himself, to ennoble him in his own eyes, this was the function of the *mito,* in which Valdez was using traditional religious forms to proselytize a contemporary religion—*La Raza.*

The levels of consciousness at work in the *mito* are well illustrated by the setting Valdez calls for in his play **The Dark Root of a Scream.** This play followed **Soldado Razo,** in which Valdez was moving towards his new form. The stage directions ask for:

> a collage of myth and reality. It forms, in fact, a pyramid with the most real artifacts of barrio life at the broad base and an abstract mythical-religious peak at the top. Above these scenes (of barrio reality) some images are made of iron and the hard steel of modern civilization—guns, knives, automobile parts; others reveal a less violent, more spiritual origin—molcajetes, rebozos, crucifixes, etc. Finally, the very top of the pyramid is dominated by ancient indio images:

conches, jade, the sunstone, feathered serpent heads.

The circumstances of this play are the wake for a dead Chicano soldier, killed in Vietnam, whose coffin is set at the top of the pyramid. The action concerns the response to the death of the solider, whose name is Quetzalcoatl Gonzales, from his family, three youths who were his friends, and the Catholic priest who has come to 'comfort' the family.

Moving in and out of the various levels of physical reality, the play touches upon the wasted lives of the youths, removed as they are from any sense of cultural identity; the passivity of the family who have settled for a colonized existence; and the stupidity and futility of the priest, whose fear of the Church leads him to reinforce the situation by explaining it as God's will. At the climax of the play a heartbeat is heard from the coffin and, when it is opened by the mother, feathers and Quetzalcoatl's heart are discovered. This final symbolism relates to the early Aztec sacrifices to the Sun God, when the heart was torn out of a living body, and to the significance of Quetzalcoatl as the redeemer of the Indian people—here still living, despite being killed by the colonizers.

In **The Dark Root of a Scream,** as in all his most recent plays, Valdez is attempting to reach the deepest levels of Chicano consciousness by his use of elements of Mayan and Aztec rituals, and their Christian equivalents. As was the case in all pagan societies, when the Indians of Mexico were converted to Christianity many of their rituals were simply overlaid with the new Christian sacraments. Thus, in the Mayan ritual of Quetzalcoatl, the God is sacrificed and rises again, so that the analogy with Christ can readily be made.

There is also a close analogy between the Virgin of Guadalupe and the Aztec's own earth mother Tonantzin. The first appearance of the Virgin, to Juan Diego in 1531, was on the very hill which was the traditional home of Tonantzin. El Teatro Campesino has treated this idea which closely binds the Christian Chicano to his pre-Columbian ancestors, and has adapted a play, **La Virgen del Tepeyac,** from an original manuscript of the appearance to Juan Diego, written in 1531.

The play opens with the *corrido* idea—a traditional song dealing with the adoration of Tonantzin, to which new lyrics have been written. This is followed by a dramatization of the arrival of Cortez, the destruction of the old religion, and the yoking of the Indians to Christianity. One of the climactic moments, and most powerful images of the play, is the appearance of the Virgin out of a symbolic womb made up of the slaughtered bodies of the Indians. Lofted high on a platform the Virgin speaks to Juan Diego and tells him that she has come to end the injustice.

El Teatro's play deals with the true economic nature of the Spanish conquest, under its cloak of religious conversion, and, more importantly, suggests that the Chicano can discover his true roots and spiritual identity through the symbol of the Virgin of Guadalupe-cum-Tonantzin. That same mother earth from which we must all derive our inner strength, a sense of unity and universal love.

Possibly the most complete example of the structure and impact that Valdez is now seeking is to be found in **La Carpa de los Rasquachis (*The Tent of the Underdogs*)**, of which Valdez has said, 'It's everything we have ever done, with this whole extra dimension, the spiritual.' The play begins almost casually, with the members of the company coming on stage, clowning, chatting up the audience and erecting their 'tent' backdrop—a curtain made up of potato sacks and torn burlap. This suggests a basic simplicity and poverty—but more than that for the tent recalls those used by shows which toured small Mexican towns in the 1930s. The tent is the home of the under-privileged Rasquachi family in the play, and also houses the whole cultural history of the Chicanos. Three separate but interrelated levels of reality are thus established.

The play proper begins with the narrative musical choruses, which tie all the scenes together. Then a religious procession makes a formal entrance. Christ, with a halter round his neck, is led by a black-masked figure, overpainted with a white skeleton, wearing the helmet of the sixteenth-century Spanish Conquistadores. Devil-masked executioners surround the Christ-figure, who is ritualistically crucified.

The awesome silence attending this action is broken by lively mariachi rhythms, and we are swept into the life of poor Jesus Rasquachi, a Chicano farm-worker who is lured across the border to the United States by hopes of economic advancement and the collusion of corrupt customs officials and labour agents. The play follows the fortunes of his family through the typical experience of such a worker. One son becomes a dope addict, another a pusher; a brother becomes a dupe for an Anglo political machine, and is killed for his pains. Finally, a worn-out shell, Rasquachi dies on the floor of the welfare office while being forced to make belittling statements about himself in order to get the state's pittance.

The play is performed in Spanglish by the company of twelve players, who change hats and props with skilled panache and act with great physical agility and comic flair. Nothing escapes El Teatro's eye as it exposes all that it believes to stand in the way of the full realization of Chicano individuality. It satirizes equally the puffed-up machismo of posturing revolutionary activists, and the corruption of the Catholic Church—here symbolized by a bishop with a dollar sign upon his mitre.

As in **The Dark Root of a Scream,** the essence of the play is an appeal for a return to a kind of atavistic spirituality. As a reviewer put it:

> El Teatro finally advocates a militant non-violence, a compassion which is not synonymous with compromise, and a religious innocence which is not naivety. Transcendence for the Chicano cannot be attained through Catholicism, but rather through a uniting of the White Christ with the Aztec God Quetzalcoatl.

A scene exemplifying this idea takes place at the end of the play, when Quetzalcoatl is reborn, magnificent in his Indian dress, transcending the tattered, materialism around him. In his absence, there has been no peace, no hope for the Chicano. He brings an end to universal discord with a simple philosophy: you are my other self, if I do harm to you, I do harm to myself. If I love and respect you, I love and respect myself. It is this philosophy that El Teatro is now attempting to live and to propagate.

Luis Valdez' move from active political involvement to a more personal and seemingly passive form of spiritual approach has brought criticism from some radical Chicano quarters. Valdez himself sees El Teatro's present orientation as a logical extension of its development from a theatre dealing with specific problems of the striking farmworkers, through the wider material problems of the Chicano minority to more fundamental human goals.

> Now our acts are the acts of human beings living and working on this earth. . . . We are still very much the political theatre, but our politics are the politics of the spirit—not of the flesh, but of the heart.

In this search for spiritual rebirth, Valdez is greatly influenced by the myth of Quetzalcoatl, who has appeared in all the recent plays. The God of positive force, Quetzalcoatl was defeated by the God of negative force, Tezcatipoca, more than a thousand years ago. The rebirth of Quetzalcoatl is due, according to the Mayan calendar, towards the end of this century, when the world will once again enter a period of peace and positive dynamic. Valdez believes the current task of El Teatro to be the bringing of people to a spiritual understanding which will prepare them for Quetzalcoatl's return.

This purpose informs the life-style and work of the company in its communal existence in San Juan Bautista. It still 'combats poverty and oppression in the heart of the richest agricultural valley in the world,' but now does this in the context of La Raza and a wider universal brotherhood. El Teatro's roots are more than ever in a Chicano reality, for the capacity for powerfully simple religious belief is as much a part of the Chicano's daily existence as the soil from which he draws his living. The same hands pray and pick grapes with equal honesty. It is to the full consciousness of this reality that El Teatro now appeals.

While discovering a soul, El Teatro Campesino has not lost its vulgar energy. While affirming man's sublimity, it still laughs at his human absurdity. The theatre remains as funky, beautiful, coarse, delicate, commonplace, and cosmic as La Raza itself. Words written by Luis Valdez in 1970 connect the past with the present, and to the future of El Teatro:

> Beyond the mass struggle of La Raza in the fields and barrios of America, there is an internal struggle in the very heart of our people. That struggle too calls for revolutionary change. Our belief in God, the Church, the social role of women—these must be subject to examination and redefining on some kind of public platform. And that again means teatro. Not simply a teatro composed of actos or agit-prop, but a teatro of ritual, of music, of beauty and spiritual sensitivity. A teatro of legends and myths. A teatro of religious strength. This type of theatre will require real dedication.

Such dedication to theatre, to his people, and to all humanity has always been the guiding spirit and sustaining force of Luis Valdez and El Teatro Campesino.

Valdez without question has been a major catalyst in the renaissance of Chicano art and poetry as well as self-pride within the youth sector of the Mexican American community in the United States.

—*Richard A. Garcia, in* A Decade of Hispanic Literature: An Anniversary Anthology, *1982.*

R. G. Davis and Betty Diamond (essay date January-March 1981)

SOURCE: *"Zoot Suit*: From the Barrio to Broadway," in *Ideologies and Literature,* Vol. 3, No. 15, January-March, 1981, pp. 124-33.

[*Davis is an American critic with a special interest in the theater. In the following essay, he and Diamond trace the evolution of* Zoot Suit *from its inception to Broadway and examine the reasons for its failure.*]

Zoot Suit, by Luis Valdez, was the first Chicano play on Broadway. Valdez chose as his subject an actual event—the Sleepy Lagoon Murder case. On August 2, 1942, José Díaz was found dead in a dirt road near Los Angeles. There were no witnesses and no murder weapon, but twenty-four Chicanos were indicated for the murder of this one boy. The Hearst papers played it up as a "Mexican crimewave," and in the trial the Chicanos involved were referred to as members of a "gang." The prosecution charged that one of the members of the gang, Henry Leyvas, was beaten by members of a rival gang at the reservoir nicknamed "Sleepy Lagoon," and that Leyvas and his gang returned armed and organized for the purpose of revenge on the rival gang. Admitted as evidence was this statement from a report written by Capt. E. Duran Ayers, Chief of Foreign Relations Bureau of the Los Angeles County Sheriff's Department:

> The biological basis is the main basis to work from. Although a wild cat and a domestic cat are of the same family, they have certain biological characteristics so different that while one may be domesticated, the other would have to be caged to be kept in captivity; and there is practically as much difference between the races of man as so aptly recognized by Rudyard Kipling when he said when writing of the Oriental, 'East is East and West is West and never the twain shall meet,' which gives us an insight into the present problem because the Indian, from Alaska to Patagonia, is evidently Oriental in background—at least he shows many of the Oriental characteristics, especially so in his utter disregard for the value of life.

Ayers traces the "utter disregard for the value of life" back to the Aztec sacrifices. Of the twenty-four Chicano boys indicted, seventeen were convicted. Three were found guilty of first degree murder; two of second degree. One, asleep in his car through the whole incident, was given five years to life. All were sent to San Quentin. Two boys who had enough money for their own lawyers demanded separate trials, and their cases were dismissed for insufficient evidence. On October 4, 1944, the District Court of Appeals, in a unanimous decision, reversed the conviction of all the defendants and the case was later dismissed due to lack of evidence.

Valdez' choice of subject was thus clearly a political one. *Zoot Suit,* a docu-drama with music, focuses on the trial of Henry Reyna—the fictionalized Henry Leyvas and leader of the pachuco gang—on Reyna's relationship to his family and friends, and on the relationship of the pachuco to the Mexican-American community. The play gets its name from the exaggerated clothing that was the badge of the pachuco—high-waisted, baggy, pegged pants; square-shouldered, oversized jacket; and long, dangling key chain.

Zoot Suit began as an experimental production of the Mark Taper Forum's "New Theatre for Now" series in April, 1978. The response to the original fourteen performances was electric enough to convince Gordon Davidson, the Forum's artistic director, to move it to the theatre's main space, rework it, and have it open the Forum's twelfth season.

In October, 1978, after a successful six-week run at the Forum, *Zoot Suit* moved to the 1200-seat Aquarius Theatre in downtown L.A. where it remained until [summer, 1980]. It brought in an average of $90-100,000 a week. While still playing in L.A., a modified version opened on Broadway at the Winter Garden on March 25, 1979, and closed April 29, after 17 performances, at an $800,000 loss.

It is possible the play failed on Broadway, as Valdez contends, because of racist reviewers. Even though plays can endure despite negative reviews, New York reviewers are extremely influential figures and they almost universally panned the play. Focusing on the issue of racism, however, diverts us from a far more significant issue: that *Zoot Suit,* as presented on Broadway, was in fact a bad play, politically and aesthetically.

In case anyone has any doubts about this being "Brechtian" theatre—and we mention this because the work of Valdez is constantly described as being "somewhere between Brecht and Cantinflas"—Valdez opens the play with the disclaimer, mouthed by El Pachuco, the interlocutor and Spirit of the pachuco, that the theatre by nature is a place of pretense, a place of fantasy. The docu-drama is thus undercut before the newspapers which form much of the set (symbolizing the complicity of the Hearst papers in the racist hysteria of the period) are brought on stage. And at the end of the play, Henry Reyna, released from jail, finds himself in a dilemma: shall he marry Alice Bloomfield, the Jewish Communist working for the Defense Committee which grew up around the Sleepy Lagoon case, or his faithful Chicana, Della Barrios? (With such a name, Henry's ultimate choice is predestined.) The false love story between Alice and Henry, a love which never happened in the real case, is so badly written that the progressive Alice—and in turn her politics—is laughed at.

In the thirteen years of his work with El Teatro Campesino, Valdez was conscious of his social role, and in *Zoot Suit,* many social and political issues are touched upon: the complicity of the Hearst press, the racism of the judicial and penal systems, the nature of Chicano family relationships. But rather than politicizing the events by deepening the analysis, Valdez adds musical dance numbers to keep the spirits up, leaves the barrio behind, sentimentalizes all relationships in order to make his "message" palatable and saleable, and invests his Pachuco with Indian and Existential consciousness.

It is the pachuco, the 1940's street youth, who is the central focus of the play. In addition to the pachucos who make up Henry's gang, there is the larger than life character—El Pachuco—who speaks directly to the audience, wittily introduces and interrupts the play, criticizes the action and acts as Henry Reyna's inner voice, El Pachuco is the mythic spirit of "pachuquismo." Valdez claims this existential rebellious youth is the predecessor of the Mexican-American consciousness of the early '70's Chicanismo. This mythic interpretation of the real-life pachuco is one of the central political problems of the play.

To understand where this interpretation of the pachuco comes from, it is helpful to look briefly at the history of El Teatro Campesino. When Valdez started El Teatro Campesino in 1965, he was responding to immediate material needs: the U.F.W. needed workers to leave the fields and Anglos to send money for support. So Valdez and his campesinos created "actos," agit-prop pieces to do just that. After two years, he and his teatro left Delano and the U.F.W. because he wanted to devote more time to teatro; because he wanted to deal with broader issues—Viet Nam, racism, imperialism, the situation of the urban Chicano; and because he wanted to do teatro only about Chicanos, a position clearly untenable in the multi-ethnic U.F.W., yet in keeping with the increasingly nationalist thrust of the chicano movement at that time. Accordingly, the earliest works of Campesino are peopled by campesinos, patrones, coyotes, and esquiroles, but it is not long before the figure of the pachuco appears.

At first a minor character whose "bilingualism" consists of the ability to say both "En la madre la placa" and "Fuck you," and whose money is made by "liberating" purses, the pachuco becomes, in the person of the "vato loco," the contemporary street dude, a rebel-hero who, allied with a Black Panther, "liberates" the college that has refused him admission.

Once separated from the U.F.W., Valdez' plays come more and more to treat the question of ethnic identity and national consciousness. Actos begin to be accompanied by "mitos," religious rituals and plays with metaphysical themes. The shift in theme is not as dramatic as it first appears, however, for even in his U.F.W. days Valdez spoke

of Chicano identity in terms which included Aztec Mayan and Christian religious thought, mysticism, and mythification.

Accordingly, the pachuco is, in one play, the character who is most sympathetic to the revolutionary cries of "Viva Villa" which emanate from a bodiless head with a Villa moustache and a voracious appetite for cockroaches; but in another, he appears as the unseen central character, Quetzalcoatl Gonzales, a cultural nationalist and community leader, whose name and activities suggest this vato is linked to the Aztec savior-god, Quetzalcoatl. The pachuco is rebel/hero/savior.

In 1974, by the way, because of such mitos, Valdez came under attack for "misleading the people" and ultimately left TENAZ, an association of Chicano theatres which he helped found, because he did not accept the increasing criticism of his essentially religious solutions to material problems.

It is in the 1976 touring version of *El Fin del Mundo* that the character of the vato, played, as in *Zoot Suit,* by Daniel Valdez, is given its closest examination. The story of Raymundo Mata, while a naturalistic story of union organizing in "Burlap, California," is also encased in an obvious symbolic framework. It is the story of the "end of the world" as we know it today, and of the literal "end"—the death—of Raymundo Mata, known in the barrio as "el Mundo." In the play, although Mundo is held up as a potential model, there is a serious study of the contradictions within him and of the complications of using such a figure as hero. Mundo, the local drug dealer, arrogant, rebellious in the face of authorities, violent, sexist, egocentric, is willing to do anything for money, even disrupt the U.F.W.'s organizing. Ultimately, he learns compassion, faith, and brotherhood, but at the very moment of his apotheosis, he is killed. It is clear that as a street dude, he is useless, even harmful, to his community. It is only after he has harnessed his rebelliousness that he becomes useful and admirable.

In *Zoot Suit,* however, the complexities are lost and the historical facts, distorted, in the service of mythification. El Pachuco is presented as a model, but just what does he model? In an interview with Valdez in New York City on December 30, 1978, R. G. Davis pointed out that El Pachuco is like Superfly, and that Superfly, the pimp hustler of Black exploitation films, is different from the working class Blacks moving up and buying a house in the white ghetto of Lorraine Hansberry's *Raisin in the Sun.* The regressing Superfly is a no-work character much like *Zoot Suit's* Pachuco. Neither one shows or demonstrated work; in fact, they secret their labor. How did they get their two hundred dollars for those threads? Such a model is not useful.

Furthermore, as Yvonne Yarbro-Bejarano and Tomás Ybarra-Frausto point out in an unpublished paper entitled "Un Análisis Crìtico de *Zoot Suit* de Luis Valdez," not all pachucos were "lumpen." Some worked and "eran como pachucos de fin de semana." Thus, they continue, Valdez' portrait of El Pachuco and the pachuco gang members furthers a simplistic stereotype. (Valdez must have been somewhat aware of this criticism because he tries to avert it by having Communist Alice comment to Henry: "You're an excellent mechanic. You fix all the guy's cars. Well, at least you're not one of the lumpen proletariat." Her analysis is, at best, weak.)

The pachuco is also presented as a defender of Chicano pride and culture, as a rebel. He is meant to be seen, as we are repeatedly told, as the "home front warrior." But to what end? The only value he articulates is that he "takes no shit from anyone." True, the pachuco possesses a rebelliousness, but it is totally without direction; it is a blind lashing out. Richard A. Garcìa, a Chicano historian at UC-Irvine, argues with Valdez' interpretation of the pachuco. In a *Los Angeles Times* article [published on August 27, 1978], he wrote that pachucos are regarded by some as:

> The first Mexican-Americans to have consciously celebrated their bicultural heritage. This view is dangerously romantic and historically false. Indeed, *pachucos*—far from being progressive—were among the most reactionary segments of the Mexican-American community. . . . The failure to distinguish clearly between criminal behavior and authentic political action underlies current attempts to turn *pachucos* into Chicano folk heroes.

Valdez' elevation of the pachuco to the status of social bandit is like Norman Mailer's encomium of subway graffiti as a grand existential assertion of "I am." There is much energy and much anger in such scrawling, but when the graffiti cover up the subway map, you get lost.

Valdez realizes that he has distorted the character of the pachuco. In the Davis interview, Valdez states that the pachuco is a creation of 1978, not of 1942; that he represents a consciousness that is present today. He also says that the pachuco does not represent an ultimate solution, but is only a phase, a symbol that change is possible, that Chicanos can do something with their lives. In *Zoot Suit,* however, the fact that the pachuco must be transformed before he can do something useful is undercut. One of the pachucos in San Quentin turns to the audience and declaims naively that he has come to a grand realization: when he gets out of jail, the thing he can do is become a union organizer (audience laughter)—or a professional baseball player (more audience laughter). The "message" is played for a laugh. Similarly, that the pachuco can become useful only when he changes and ceases to be a pachuco is contradicted by the insistence upon the mythic, i.e., static, nature of El Pachuco.

Valdez wants the figurative character and the documented imitation of Henry Reyna to carry all the weight of his own Chicanismo and Mayan Aztec mysticism. Henry is a tough blowhard, but loves his family. El Pachuco is a tough blowhard, but is beaten up by Marines and Sailors and ends up naked, except for a loincloth, on stage in a pool of light. The loincloth is supposed to represent, if you know Campesino's mitos, the Indian under the clothes of the city dude. The image is barely understood by those of us who know, giggled at by Chicanos in the Los Angeles audience, and viewed as melodramatic and confusing in

New York City. Thus the confused politics produces confused art.

The other political problems in the play are also inseparable from the aesthetic problems. When a cultural nationalist goes to Broadway to reach a "wider audience," his message, which previously gained much of its force precisely from its cultural specificity, must be diluted to be intelligible to those not a part of that culture. Valdez, in other words, had to professionalize the "rasquachiness" that gave the works of El Teatro Campesino their unique force and vigor.

According to Valdez, the major changes in *Zoot Suit* were made before the trip to Broadway, between the original version as played on the Taper's experimental stage, and the version as performed on the main stage of the Forum. It is at this juncture that the barrio disappeared from the set and the Las Vegas shiny dance floor stage emerged; the love story between Alice Bloomfield and Henry Reyna came to dominate the historical/political material; and the production staff, formerly members of Campesino, was changed. (Pat Birch of *Grease* fame, for example, became principal choreographer; Thomas A. Walsh, a set designer, replaced Bob Morales; and Abe Jacob, a sound designer, was added.)

But the play was a great success in L.A. even after the professionalization and homogenization began. There is another, very slippery, issue here. The success of *Zoot Suit* in L.A. was due, in part, to the California audience—Chicano and non-Chicano—which could read the geography and personal Chicano experiences into the play, however simple the characterizations, just as Campesino's original farmworker audience could read into the agit-prop "actos" in Delano.

In Valdez' earliest works, the people on stage and the people off-stage were the same. They came from the same place and their concerns were specifically those of the Huelga. Even when those concerns broadened, the effect of the actors and plays was great because the Chicano performers' persona gave an additional dimension to the plays. They were speaking the language of the audience, legitimizing its culture. So when someone on stage said "Chale, ese," the audience roared at hearing its private language in a public place; there was the laughter of recognition, of complicity.

Similarly, in Los Angeles, when El Pachuco came on stage and preened in his Zoot Suit, the largely Chicano audience went wild. In New York, however, there was an embarrassed silence, perhaps a chuckle or two. As Clive Barnes wrote, "Broadway is not the street where it lives." Though Barnes' comment may have been motivated by East Coast snobbery, it has a certain validity. Take away the Chicano audience and the Chicano actors, take away the Chicano locale, and all you have left is the play itself, a play which does not hold up to critical scrutiny.

Also, once on Broadway, the play had to be changed even further to reach not merely a wider "audience," but a wider "market." Culture, politics, become part of a product that must be packaged and sold. The Shubert Organization, owners of seventeen theatres on Broadway and the producers of *Zoot Suit,* was interested in developing the newly discovered Hispanic market, a market which Hollywood has also recently discovered (*Gang, Boulevard Nights, Up in Smoke.*)

The show had to be changed to fit both the white New York theatre scene, and to attract the Puerto Rican, Cuban, Dominican audience. Accordingly, it was cut and reshaped to fit what Valdez and Davidson would "work" in New York. But it is a tricky problem to reach a wider audience rather than cater to it, as one moves from local community to state and on to the national stage. "Once the Broadway machinery takes hold, other things happen," said Davidson.

The first problem was that of language. The *Wiz, Ain't Misbehavin', Eubie, Timbuctoo* are "Black" shows, but they are big musicals that attract both Blacks and whites to the theatre. But if a play is in Spanish, only the Spanish speaking will attend. Political problem: in the actos, one way in which the Good Guys were distinguished from the Bad Guys was their embrace of Chicano Spanish. We know "Miss JIM-enez" is a villain because she denies her culture and anglicizes the pronounciation of her name. However, the more *Zoot Suit* belonged to the Spanish speaking, the less it could be understood by the English speaking. And the more Chicano slang, the less it could be understood by Puerto Ricans, Cubans, and Dominicans. Thus to reach a wider audience market, the language had to change. One political point down. Spanish/slang out: sentimentalized English in.

A different set of problems resulted from the marketing scheme of placing *Zoot Suit* in the Winter Garden, a large theatre which demands musical extravaganza. The play was too small for the house. In addition, the 1943 Zoot Suit riots in which white sailors and marines attacked pachucos in L.A. seemed a bit distant in this docu-drama interrupted by dance and song. The historical importance of these events was buried by flashback and flashy gimmicry. (The "minority" play most recently at the Winter Garden was *Comin' Uptown,* an all Black musical version of *A Christmas Carol.* Its politics? Scrooge is a black tap dancing slum landlord.)

Finally, problems in the play also came from Valdez' politics of cultural nationalism. He did not want Anglos to walk out,—to get his "message" to them and to sell them tickets. However, because Valdez does still experience the world as divided between "us" and "them," his ability to understand those outside his culture is limited. We get recreations of others experiences, i.e., characters from bad movies. In *Zoot Suit,* we have the heroic white liberal lawyer whose startling message is that the system works, and the feisty Jewish Communist who of course falls in love with Henry, ever true to the cheap theatrics that two who are antagonists at the beginning of a show will become lovers by its end.

Also, Valdez' cultural nationalism relies heavily on the "spirituality" that is, in his view, the inheritance of the Chicanos from their Indian past. He believes in his "mission": *Zoot Suit,* he said to R. G. Davis when asked how the play was going in L.A. "is doing what it is supposed

to do, what it has to do." He has faith. He, by himself, would change Establishment theatre. Campesino would take over, though just how the takeover was to be accomplished and what would happen once it had, was vague, rather like the unfocused rebelliousness of the pachuco hero Henry Reyna. Valdez has faith, rather than a proposal. So too *Zoot Suit.*

It is not Valdez' success one criticizes, for who in the good world of the liberal left dare proclaim poverty is moral? But what *Zoot Suit* offers us is ultimately the pachuco. While the performance of Eddie Olmos on Broadway lent an alluring stature to El Pachuco, the real life pachuco was a kid, a clothes model, an image of political reaction and temporary identity rebelliousness. To select as truth only those elements one wishes to see as true, to ignore the historical reality of the central characters of a drama based on political fact, is to create a model of the Chicano as useless as the Frito Bandito.

Gerald C. Lubenow   (review date 4 May 1987)

SOURCE: "Putting the Border Onstage," in *Newsweek,* Vol. CIX, No. 18, May 4, 1987, p. 79.

[*In the following excerpt, Lubenow favorably appraises*

Poster for the Broadway revival of Zoot Suit.

Valdez's work as a playwright as well as his role as script-writer and director of the film La Bamba.]

When playwright Luis Valdez withdraws to rewrite a script, he envisions himself not as some great Spanish playwright, but like Moss Hart and George S. Kaufman in a stuffy room in New York City smoking cigars and eating Hershey bars. The only difference is that he loves cigars and hates chocolate. "I'm as American as the next guy," he says. "It's just a question of being perceived as such."

In the theater, where that very question can make or break you, Valdez has come triumphantly into his own. With a new immigration law creating millions of hyphenated Hispanic-Americans, he is a powerful interpreter of their search for identity in an Anglo culture. He has succeeded by shaping the experience of Chicanos into drama that speaks to all Americans. His latest work, *I Don't Have to Show You No Stinking Badges,* has been cheered in Los Angeles and San Diego. *Corridos,* a series of Mexican folk ballads that won critical acclaim on the stage, will air as a special on PBS this fall. *La Bamba,* a movie about '50s rock-and-roller Ritchie Valens that Valdez wrote and directed, is being talked about as one of this summer's hot movies.

Badges is as middle-American as Archie Bunker. Buddy Villa, the testy father in the play, even complains of Asians ruining the San Fernando Valley neighborhood where he and his wife have made a comfortable home as the "silent-bit king and queen of Hollywood." Their son drops out of Harvard Law School to find himself. Determined to become a movie star, he attacks his parents for playing anonymous stereotypical Chicano roles.

If *Badges* has ethnic origins, its dreams are mainstream. The play is as much a story of generational conflict as of assimilation. Jorge Huerta, an expert on Chicano theater, is struck by the distance between *Badges* and *The Shrunken Head of Pancho Villa,* an early Valdez work about Mexican parents trying to find themselves in America. "These people in *Badges* are middle class," says Huerta. "This is an American conflict. All Americans have gone through it." What Chicanos don't have to do, *Badges* says, is apologize for wanting to assimilate.

La Bamba is set in the '50s. Ritchie Valens is all-American, a poor boy who makes it on raw talent and honest ambition. A third-generation southern California kid who doesn't speak Spanish and has never seen Mexico, he becomes a star and records "La Bamba," the first song in Spanish to be a rock-and-roll hit. The film soars from its grainy documentary-style opening to the final crash everyone knows is coming. It has established Valdez, 46, as an accomplished filmmaker and prompted talk of other movie projects.

From the time Valdez first made it to Broadway with *Zoot Suit,* no one has done more to change how America perceives its Hispanic citizens. With *Corridos,* he brings to television the tradition of the Mexican-American folk ballad—densely textured weavings of story and song. "My work comes from the border," he says. "It is neither Mexican nor American. It's part of America, like Cajun music." With songs in Spanish and dialogue in English, *Corridos* features Linda Ronstadt, who is half Mexican. Smiles Valdez, who went over Ronstadt's songs with her word by word, "She sounds very authentic. You wouldn't know she doesn't speak Spanish."

Valdez's early plays mix Spanish and English. "I was on my way to being acculturated," he says of growing up in San Jose, Calif., in the '50s. "By the time I graduated from high school, my Spanish was in tatters. I got it back because I wanted it back." His ultimate concern, however, is not which language he uses, but what he has to say: "I'm writing in English now. It took me a long time to get to that. I needed a few Spanish words as an anchor." He switched when he found Chicano audiences, particularly the young, didn't want Spanish, didn't understand it. "My characters can speak English and be very Chicano at the same time," he says. His message is his medium: "I have something to give. I can unlock some things about the American landscape."

Valdez started as a migrant worker picking cotton and staging agitprop skits on the back of a flatbed to support Cesar Chavez's farm workers' union. His success and the direction of his recent work have caused some critics to accuse him of selling out. He admits to ambition. "There was a time when I spoke only to Chicanos. Now I want a national audience." But he also retains a firm grasp on his roots. During the filming of *La Bamba,* he was intrigued by the thought that he and Valens may have worked together in the orchards near San Jose. When the labor camp set was built, he took his parents on a tour. "It was so real," he says, "it was like stepping back into the past."

Anthony DeCurtis   (review date 16 August 1987)

SOURCE: "Flawed 'La Bamba'," in *Rolling Stone,* Issue 506, August 16, 1987, p. 13.

[*In the following film review of* La Bamba, *DeCurtis criticizes Valdez for artificially inflating the already powerful story of Valens's life.*]

A variety of problems plagues *La Bamba,* the new film about the life of Ritchie Valens, the Mexican American rocker who was killed at age seventeen in the 1959 plane crash that also took the lives of Buddy Holly and the Big Bopper. Casting in the major roles is the movie's most obvious problem. Newcomer Lou Diamond Phillips is likeable but far from riveting as Valens, while Danielle von Zerneck, who plays Valens's girlfriend and the inspiration for his hit "Donna," is almost laughably blank. In contrast, Rosana De Soto and Esai Morales, as Valens's mother and half brother, give performances that are operatic in their histrionic excess.

But the movie's most damning flaw is in its handling of Valens's death. *Sweet Dreams,* the 1985 movie about country singer Patsy Cline, who died in a plane crash at age thirty, worked because it made Cline's life seem so recognizably ordinary. When her plane slams into a mountain, it hits with all the pointless shock that violent, accidental death delivers in real life.

Writer and director Luis Valdez takes a much less effective tack in *La Bamba,* in which the circumstances surrounding Valens's death are laden with portentous clichés. The singer is haunted by prophetic dreams of plane crashes and reels off lines like "I'm gonna be a star, and stars don't fall from the sky, do they?"

The mystical inflation of Valens's story may be the result of the difficulties Valdez faced in dramatizing the life of someone who died as a teenager. But Valens's life hardly requires this degree of aesthetic shaping to have its impact. The child of an impoverished and broken family, Valens had already scored hits with "Donna," "La Bamba" and "Come On, Let's Go" at the time of his death and seemed poised for greater things. The loss of such a seminal figure should provide power and pathos enough for any film.

Luis Valdez with David Savran (interview date January 1988)

SOURCE: An interview in *American Theatre,* Vol. 4, No. 10, January, 1988, pp. 15-21, 56-7.

[*In the following interview, Valdez discusses his career as a playwright and the roles of politics and mysticism in his work.*]

One month into the 1965 Delano grape strike, which solidified the power of the United Farm Workers, 23-year-old Luis Valdez met with a group of union volunteers and devised a short comic skit to help persuade reluctant workers to join the strike. He hung signs reading *Huelgista* (striker) on two men and *Esquirol* (scab) on a third. The two *Huelgistas* started yelling at the *Esquirol* and the audience laughed. Thus began Valdez's career as founder and director of El Teatro Campesino—a career that in the more than two decades since has thrust him to the forefront of the complex and politically charged Hispanic search for identity in the Anglo culture of the United States.

Riding the wave of growing Hispanic numbers and influence, Valdez has come into his own in no less than three media: his latest play, the comedy *I Don't Have to Show You No Stinking Badges,* drew cheers in recent seasons at the Los Angeles Theater Center and San Diego Repertory Company; *Corridos,* a series of staged Mexican folk ballads, was videotaped and aired as a PBS-TV special in October; and *La Bamba,* a movie about '50s rock-and-roller Ritchie Valens that Valdez wrote and directed was released over the summer (in English and Spanish versions) to critical accolades and box-office success. "There was a time when I spoke only to Chicanos—now I want a national audience," Valdez admits. But the recent mainstreaming of his work has not obscured the continuity or clarity of Valdez's intention: to communicate the Chicano experience in all of its political, cultural and religious complexity.

That intention was shaped in El Teatro Campesino's early history and fired by its struggles. During the company's first years it was a union tool, performing in meeting halls, fields and strike camps. Drawing on *commedia dell' arte* and elements of Mexican folk culture, Valdez created

actos, short comic sketches designed to raise political awareness and inspire action. *Los Vendidos* (*The Sellouts,* 1967), for example, attacks the stereotyping of Chicanos and government-sanctioned tokenism. A Chicano secretary from Governor Reagan's office goes to Honest Sancho's Used Mexican Lot to buy "a Mexican type" for the front office. She examines several models—a farm worker, a young *pachuco* (a swaggering street kid), a *revolucionario* and finally a Mexican-American in a business suit who sings "God Bless America" and drinks dry martinis. As soon as she buys the last, he malfunctions and begins shouting "*Viva la huelga,*" while the others chase her away and divide the money.

At the same time that he was writing and performing agit-prop for the Farm Workers, Valdez turned to examine his pre-Columbian heritage, the sophisticated religion and culture of the ancient Mayans. The Teatro settled in two houses in San Juan Bautistas in 1971, where they farmed according to Mayan practices and Valdez developed the second of his dramatic forms, the *mito* (myth), which characteristically takes the form of a parable based on Indian ritual. For Valdez the *mito* is an attempt to integrate political activism and religious ritual—to tie "the cause of social justice" to "the cause of everything else in our universe." *Bernabe* (1970) is a parable about the prostitution of the land. It opposes the pure, mystical love for La Tierra (the Earth) by the mentally retarded *campesino* of the title against its simple possession by landowners and banks. At the play's end Bernabe is visited by La Luna (the Moon, dressed as a 1942 *pachuco*), La Tierra and El Sol (the Sun) in the guise of Tonatiuh, the Aztec sun god. In a final apotheosis, the "cosmic idiot" is made whole and united with La Tierra, at last revealed to be Coatlicue, the Aztec goddess of life, death and rebirth.

In the 1970s Valdez developed a third dramatic form, the *corrido* (ballad), which, like the *mito,* is intended to claim a cultural heritage rather than inspire political revolution. The *corrido* is Valdez's reinvention of the musical, based on Mexican-American folk ballads telling tales of love, death and heroism. *Zoot Suit* (1978) is perhaps his best known *corrido* and was the first Hispanic play to reach Broadway, after a long and successful run in Los Angeles. Mixing narrative, action, song and dance, it is the story of members of a zoot suit-clad pachuco gang of the '40s, their wrongful conviction for murder and the "Zoot Suit Riots" that followed.

I Don't Have to Show You No Stinking Badges takes on the political and existential implications of acting, both in theatre and society. It takes place in a television studio in which is set the suburban southern California home of Buddy and Connie Villa, two assimilated, middle-class Chicanos, "the silent bit king and queen of Hollywood." Their son, Sonny, who has just dropped out of Harvard Law School and has returned home with his Asian-American girlfriend, tries to find work in Hollywood, but despairs at having to become one of the many "actors faking our roles to fit into the great American success story." With Pirandellian sleight of hand, Valdez uses a director to interrupt the scene (which it turns out is an episode of a new sitcom, *Badges!*) in order to debate the social function of art. "This isn't reality," Sonny protests. But the director assures him, "Frankly, reality's a big boring pain in the ass. We're in the entertainment business. Laughs, Sonny, that's more important than reality."

Although closer to mainstream comedy than mystery play, Valdez's exploration of role-playing represents more a development of than a break with the technique of his early *mitos*. Both *Bernabe* and *Badges* eschew naturalism in favor of a more theatrically bold style, the earlier play drawing upon a naive former model and the later a sophisticated one. *Bernabe,* in keeping with the conventions of religious drama, opts for a simple, mystical ending, while *Badges* refuses the pat resolution of television sitcom by offering several alternative endings. Both examine the spiritual implications of material choices; both are celebratory despite their socially critical vision.

Deep connections are evident in Valdez's uniquely diverse collection of plays. As he shapes the experience of Chicanos into drama that speaks to all Americans, he is also examining the interrelationship between the political and the metaphysical, between historically determined oppressive structures and man's transhistorical desire for faith and freedom.

I spoke with Valdez in May 1987, in his El Teatro Campesino office in San Juan Bautista.

[*Savran*]: *How did you get interested in theatre?*

[Valdez]: There's a story that's almost apocryphal, I've repeated it so many times now. It's nevertheless true. I got hooked on the theatre when I was six. I was born into a family of migrant farm workers and shortly after World War II we were in a cotton camp in the San Joaquin valley. The season was over, it was starting to rain, but we were still there because my dad's little Ford pickup truck had broken down and was up on blocks and there was no way for us to get out. Life was pretty meager then and we survived by fishing in a river and sharing staples like beans, rice and flour. And the bus from the local school used to come in from a place called Stratford—irony of ironies, except it was on the San Joaquin River [laughs].

I took my lunch to school in a little brown paper bag— which was a valuable commodity because there were still paper shortages in 1946. One day as school let out and kids were rushing toward the bus, I found my bag missing and I went around in a panic looking for it. The teacher saw me and said, "Are you looking for your bag?" and I said, "Yes." She said, "Come, here," and she took me in the little back room and there, on a table, were some things laid out that completely changed my perception of the universe. She'd torn the bag up and placed it in water. I was horrified. But then she showed me the next bowl. It was a paste. She was making papier-mâché. A little farther down the line, she'd taken the paper and put in on a clay mold of a face of a monkey, and finally there was a finished product, unpainted but nevertheless definitely a monkey. And she said, "I'm making masks."

I was amazed, shocked in an exhilarating way, that she could do this with paper and paste. As it turned out, she was making masks for the school play. I didn't know what

a play was, but she explained and said, "We're having try-outs." I came back the next week all enthused and auditioned for a part and got a leading role as a monkey. The play was about Christmas in the jungle. I was measured for a costume that was better than the clothes I was wearing at the time, certainly more colorful. The next few weeks were some of the most exciting in my short life. After seeing the stage transformed into a jungle and after all the excitement of the preparations—I doubt that it was as elaborate as my mind remembers it now—my dad got the truck fixed and a week before the show was to go on, we moved away. So I never got to be in the Christmas play.

That left an unfillable gap, a vacuum that I've been pouring myself into for the last 41 years. From then on, it was just a question of evolution. Later I got into puppets. I was a ventriloquist, believe it or not. In 1956 when I was in high school, I became a regular on a local television program. I was still living in a *barrio* with my family, a place in San Jose called Sal Si Puedes—Get Out if You Can. It was one of those places with dirt streets and potholes, a terrible place. But I was on television, right? [laughs], and I wrote my own stuff and it established me in high school.

By the time I graduated, I had pretty well decided that writing was my consuming passion. Coming from my background, I didn't feel right about going to my parents and saying, "I want to be a playwright." So I started college majoring in math and physics. Then one day late in my freshman year I walked to the drama department and decided, "To hell with it, I'm going to go with this." I changed majors to English, with an emphasis on playwriting, and that's what I did for the rest of my college days.

In 1964 I wrote and directed my first full-length play, *The Shrunken Head of Pancho Villa.* People saw it and gave me a lot of encouragement. I joined the San Francisco Mime Troupe the following year, and then in '65 joined the Farm Workers Union and essentially started El Teatro Campesino. The evolution has been continuous since then, both of the company and of my styles of playwriting.

During that period, what was your most important theatre training—college, the Mime Troupe?

It's all important. It's a question of layering. I love to layer things, I think they achieve a certain richness—I'm speaking now about "the work." But life essentially evolves that way, too. Those years of studying theatre history were extremely important. I connected with a number of ancient playwrights in a very direct way. Plautus was a revelation, he spoke directly to me. I took four years of Latin so I was able to read him in Latin. There are clever turns of phrases that I grew to appreciate and, in my own way, was able almost to reproduce in Spanish. The central figure of the wily servant in classical Roman drama—Greek also— became a standard feature of my work with El Teatro Campesino. The striker was basically a wily servant. I'd also been exposed to *commedia dell' arte* through the Brighellas, Arlecchinos and Pantalones. I saw a direct link between these *commedia* types and the types I had to work with in order to put together a Farm Workers' theatre. I chose to do an outdoor, robust theatre of types. I figured it hit the reality.

My second phase was the raw, elemental education I got, performing under the most primitive conditions in the farm labor camps and on flatbed trucks. In doing so, I dealt with the basic elements of drama: structure, language, music, movement. The first education was literary, the second practical. We used to put on stuff every week, under all kinds of circumstances: outdoors, indoors, under the threat of violence.

There was a period during the grape strike in '67 when we had become an effective weapon within the Farm Workers and were considered enough of a threat that a rumor flashed across the strike camp that somebody was after me with a high-powered rifle. We went out to the labor camp anyway, but I was really sweating it. I don't think I've sweated any performance since then. It changed my perspective on what I was doing. Was this really worth it? Was it a life-and-death issue? Of course it was for me at the time, and still is. I learned that in a very direct and practical way. I was beaten and kicked and jailed, also in the '60s, essentially for doing theatre. I knew the kind of theatre we were doing was a political act, it was art and politics. At least I hope I wasn't being kicked for the art [laughs].

What other playwrights had a major impact on you in those days?

Brecht looms huge in my orientation. I discovered Brecht in college, from an intellectual perspective. That was really the only way—no one was *doing* Brecht back in 1961. When Esslin's book, *Brecht: The Man and His Work,* came out in 1960, I was working in the library, so I had first dibs on all the new books. Brecht to me had been only a name. But this book opened up Brecht and I started reading all his plays and his theories, which I subscribed to immediately. I continue to use his alienation effect to this day. I don't think audiences like it too much, but I like it because it seems to me an essential feature of the experience of theatre.

Theatre should reflect an audience back on itself: You should think as well as feel. Still, there's no underestimating the power of emotional impact—I understand better now how ideas are conveyed and exchanged on a beam of emotion. I think Brecht began to discover that in his later works and integrated it. I've integrated a lot of feeling into my works, but I still love ideas. I still love communicating a concept, an abstraction. That's the mathematician in me.

How has your way of writing changed over the years?

What has changed over the years is an approach and a technique. The first few years with the Teatro Campesino were largely improvisational. I wrote outlines. I sketched out a dramatic structure, sometimes on a single page, and used that as my guide to direct the actors. Later on, I began to write very simple scripts that were sometimes born out of improvisations. During the first 10 years, from '65 to '75, the collective process became more complicated and more sophisticated within the company—we were creating longer pieces, full-length pieces, but they'd take forever to complete using the collective process.

By 1975 I'd taken the collective process as far as I could. I enjoyed working with people. I didn't have to deal with the loneliness of writing. My problem was that I was so much part of the collective that I couldn't leave for even a month without the group having serious problems. By 1975 we were stable enough as a company for me to begin to take a month, two months, six months, eventually a year. I turned a corner and was ready to start writing plays again.

In 1975 I took a month off and wrote a play called *El Fin del Mundo* (*The End of the World*). We began to create it the year before and did it through 1980, a different version every year. The characters were people born of my experience, and they are still alive for me. Someday I'll finish all of that as a play or else it will be poured into a screenplay for a "major motion picture" [laughs]. Shortly after that, in 1977, I was invited by the Mark Taper Forum to write a play for their New Theatre for Now series. We agreed on the Zoot Suit Riots as a subject. *Zoot Suit* firmly reestablished my self-identity as a playwright. Essentially I've been writing nonstop since '75. That's not to say I didn't write anything between '65 and '75. *Soldado Razo,* which is probably my most performed play around the world, was written in 1970, as was *Bernabe. The Dark Root of a Scream* was written in 1967. These are all one-acts. But I used to work on them with a sense of longing, wanting more time to be able to sit down and write.

Now I'm firmly back in touch with myself as a playwright. When I begin, I allow myself at least a month of free association with notes. I can start anywhere. I can start with an abstract notion, a character . . . it's rarely dialogue or anything specific like that. More often than not, it's just an amorphous bunch of ideas, impressions and feelings. I allow myself to tumble in this ball of thoughts and impressions, knowing that I'm heading toward a play and that eventually I've got to begin dealing with character and then structure.

Because of the dearth of Hispanic playwrights—or even American playwrights, for that matter—I felt it necessary to explore the territory, to cover the range of theatre as widely as I could. Political theatre with the Farm Workers was sometimes minimal scale, a small group of workers gathered in some dusty little corner in a labor camp, and sometimes immense—huge crowds, 10,000, 15,000, with banners flying. But the political theatre extends beyond the farm worker into the whole Chicano experience. We've dealt with a lot of issues: racism, education, immigration—and that took us, again, through many circles.

We evolved three separate forms: the *acto* was the political act, the short form, 15 minutes; the *mito* was the mythic, religious play; and the *corrido* was the ballad. I just finished a full-length video program called *Corridos.* So the form has evolved into another medium. I do political plays, musicals, historical dramas, religious dramas. We still do our religious plays at the Mission here every year. They're nurturing, they feed the spirit. Peter Brook's response when he saw our Virgin play, years ago, was that it was like something out of the Middle Ages. It's religious for many of the people who come see it, not just entertainment. And of course we've gone on to do serious plays and comedies like *I Don't Have to Show You No Stinking Badges.*

It seems that a play like **Bernabe** *aligns the* mito *and the* acto, *the politics and the myth. It uses religious mysticism to point out the difference between simply owning the land and loving it. The political point is made by appeal to mystical process.*

The spiritual aspect of the political struggle has been part of the work from the beginning. Some of that is through Cesar Chavez, who is a spiritual-political leader. Some people—say, the political types—have had trouble dealing with the spiritual. They say, "It's distortion. Religion is the opium of the masses." But it seems to me that the spiritual is very much part of everyday life. There's no way to exclude it . . . we are spirit. We're a manifestation of something, of an energy.

The whole fusion between the spiritual and the material is for me the paradox of human existence. That's why I connected with Peter Brook when he was here in '73—his question was, "How do you make the invisible visible?" To me myth is not something that's fake or not real. On the contrary, it's so real that it's just below the surface—it's the supporting structure of our everyday reality. That makes me a lot more Jungian than Freudian. And it distinguishes me, I think, from a lot of other playwrights. A lot of modern playwrights go to psycho-analysis to work out their problems. I can't stop there, that's just the beginning for me. I've had to go to the root of my own existence in order to effect my own salvation, if you will. The search for meaning took me into religion and science, and into mythology.

I had to sound out these things in myself. Someone pointed out to me the evolution a couple of years ago. *The Shrunken Head of Pancho Villa* is theatre of the absurd. One of the characters, the oldest brother, is a disembodied head, huge, oversized. And he eats all of the food that the family can produce. So they stay poor. He has lice that turn out to be tiny little cockroaches that grow and cover the walls. He sings *La Cucaracha* but cannot talk. And he can't move. He's just kind of there. In a metaphorical sense, that was me back in the early '60s. That's the way I felt—that I had no legs, no arms. By 1970, when I got to **Bernabe,** I was the idiot, but I'd gotten in contact with the sun and the moon and earth. Fortunately, out of these grotesque self-portraits, my characters have attained a greater and greater degree of humanity.

I've always had difficulty with naturalism in the theatre. Consequently, a lot of people have looked at my work and said, "Maybe he just can't write naturalism. His is the theatre of types, of simplistic little stick figures." What I needed was a medium in which to be able to do that, so I came to film. *La Bamba* is naturalism, as well as of the spirit. There I wanted the dirt, so I got the dirt. I wanted intimate realistic scenes between two real people. I can write that stuff for the stage too, but it just doesn't interest

Valdez as the narrator for Corridos! Tales of Passion and Revolution, *which he also wrote and directed. The program was aired by the Corporation for Public Broadcasting in 1987.*

me. The stage for me—that box, that flat floor—holds other potentials; it's a means to explore other things.

As much a ritual space as anything else.

Most definitely. It seems to me that the essence of the human being is to act, to move through space in patterns that gives his life meaning. We adorn ourselves with symbolic objects that give that movement even more meaning. Then we come out with sounds. And then somewhere along the line we begin to call that reality—but it's a self-created reality. The whole of civilization is a dance. I think the theatre celebrates that.

So religion functions in your work as a connection with the past, with one's heritage and one's bond to all men.

Sounding out those elemental drums, going back into the basics. I was doing this as a Chicano but I was also doing it as someone who inhabits the 20th century. I think we need to reconnect. The word religion means "a tying back." The vacuum I thought I was born into turned out to be full of all kinds of mystery and power. The strange things that were going on in the *barrio*—the Mexican things, the ethnic things—seemed like superstition, but on another level there was a lot of psychic activity. There's a lot of psychic activity in Mexican culture that is actually political at times.

Zoot Suit is another extremely spiritual, political play. And it was never understood. People thought it was about juvenile delinquents and that I was putting the Pachuco on the stage just to be snide. But the young man, Henry Reyna, achieves his own liberation by coming into contact with this internal authority. The Pachuco is the Jungian self-image, the superego if you will, the power inside every individual that's greater than any human institution. The Pachuco says, "It'll take more than the U.S. Navy to beat me down," referring to the Navy and Marines stripping zoot suiters in the 1940s. "I don't give a fuck what you do to me, you can't take this from me. And I reassert myself, in this guise." The fact that critics couldn't accept that guise was too bad, but it doesn't change the nature of what the play's about. It deals with self-salvation. And you can follow the playwright through the story—I was also those two dudes. With *Zoot Suit* I was finally able to transcend social conditions, and the way I did it on stage was to give the Pachuco absolute power, as the master of ceremonies. He could snap his fingers and stop the action. It was a Brechtian device that allowed the plot to move forward, but psychically and symbolically, in the right way.

And Chicanos got off on it. That's why a half-million people came to see it in L.A. Because I had given a disenfranchised people their religion back. I dressed the Pachuco in the colors of Testatipoka, the Aztec god of education, the dean of the school of hard knocks. There's another god of culture, Quetzalcoatl, the feathered serpent, who's much kinder. He surfaces in *La Bamba* as the figure of Ritchie Valens. He's an artist and poet and is gentle and not at all fearful. When my audiences see *La Bamba,* they like that positive spirit. The Pachuco's a little harder to take.

But these are evolutions. I use the metaphor of the serpent crawling out of its skin. There's that symbolism in *La Bamba*—it's pre-Columbian, but it's also very accurate in terms of the way that I view my own life. I've crawled through many of my own dead skins.

Although **Badges** *and* **Bernabe** *are very different, in both of them the metaphysical is given a political dimension.*

I like to think there's a core that's constant. In one way, what I have to say is quite basic, quite human. In another way, it's specifically American, in a continental sense. I'm reaching back to pre-Columbian America and trying to share that. I feel and sense those rhythms within me. I'm not just a Mexican farm worker. I'm an American with roots in Mayan culture. I can resonate and unlock some of the mysteries of this land which reside in all of us. I've just been in the neighborhood a little bit longer.

What about the endings of your plays? **Zoot Suit***'s seems very Brechtian, a happy ending immediately called into question. Then you present three different possible futures for the characters. And* **Badges** *is similar. You present what could happen, depending on the choices the characters make.*

Multiple endings—multiple beginnings, too—have started to evolve in my work. I don't think there's any single end. I firmly believe that, we exist simultaneously on seven levels—you can call them *shakras* if you're so inclined, or you can call them something else. In the Mayan sculptures, there's a vision of the universe in those ancient head-dresses, in which you see the open mouths of birds with human heads coming through them, and then something else going in through the eyes and coming out again. That's a pulsating vision of the universe. It might have been born from the jungle but is, nevertheless, an accurate description of what is going on below the surface, at the nuclear level, in the way atomic particles are interacting. To me the universe is a huge, pulsating, enormously vital and *conscious* phenomenon. There is no end. There is no beginning. There's only an apparent end and an apparent beginning.

We had an ending and beginning to *La Bamba,* which I had scripted and seemed right on paper. But our first preview audiences rejected them. So eventually we snipped them. What we had was not exactly a Brechtian turn, but it was a stepping back and looking at the '50s from the perspective of the '80s. They wanted to stay in the '50s. I had been trying, on some level, to alleviate the pain of Ritchie Valens' death, but audiences told us, "Leave us with the pain." So that's where we left it.

Can you describe how you work as a director with your own material?

As a director I switch gears. Writing is a solitary process—you're in there with the words, and I love that. But I also love directing, getting out of myself and into other people. As a director—and this again comes from my experiences in the Farm Worker days—I have to know who I'm working with. And what they are like. If I have four actors, or a dozen actors, plus crew, my first job as a director is to get them to become one, to get them hot enough about doing the project so that there's a lot of enthusiasm.

More and more the first thing I want to establish in character development is movement. You can't have a feeling, an emotion, without motion. You can pick up a lot from the associative school, referring back to your own experiences, but I think it's also possible to get people to laugh and cry through what they do to their bodies.

Very often that's the difference between acting for film and acting for the stage. You can't get away with "acting" on film. You have to cut it so close to the bone, you have to *be,* to get down-and-dirty. It's "the Method," to be sure. So you have to make it small, intense and real. On the stage, because you have to project, things sometimes get out of whack. And you have to switch to a new mentality. This is where ritual comes in. Performance on the stage is much more like dance than anything else. Dance is real. You can't fake dance. But somehow a lot of people start acting as if they're "acting," and think they're doing it right. In fact, acting is something totally different: it's a *real* act. Which gets back to politics, in that our first theatrical acts were real political acts. That's why that dude was out there with a high-powered rifle—he wasn't seeing theatre, but a threatening political act.

Now it seems that the political dimension has become sublimated, less explicit. You're no longer writing agitprop.

There is a time and place for all forms. It's 20 years down the road. But the political impact is still there. The only difference is that I'm being asked to run for governor now, which I'm not interested in doing. My purpose is still to impact socially, culturally and politically. I'm reaffirming some things that are very important to all of us as Americans, those things that we all believe to be essential to our society. What I hope is changing is a perception about the country as a whole. And the continent as well.

I'm just trying to kick my two cents into the pot. I still want El Teatro Campesino to perform on Broadway, because I think that's a political act. El Teatro Campesino is in Hollywood, and I don't think we've compromised any social statements. We started out in '65 doing these *actos* within the context of the United Farm Workers. Twenty-two years later, my next movie may be about the grape strike. My Vietnam was at home. I refused to go to Vietnam, but I encountered all the violence I needed on the home front: People were killed by the Farm Workers' strike.

Some critics have accused you of selling out.

I used to joke, "It's impossible for us to sell out because nobody wants to buy us." That doesn't bother me in the least. There's too much to do, to be socially conscious about. In some ways, it's just people sounding me out. I don't mind people referring back to what I have been. We're all like mirrors to each other. People help to keep you on course. I've strayed very little from my pronounced intentions.

In '67 when we left United Farm Workers and started our own cultural center in Del Rey, we came out with a manifesto, essentially stating that we were trying to put the tools of the artist in the hands of the humblest, the working people. But not just 19th-century tools, not clay and straw or spit and masking tape or felt pens. We were talking about video, film, recording studios. Now we're beginning to work in the best facilities that the industry has to offer. What we do with them from here is something else.

Do you read the critics?

Sure. I love listening to the public. They're the audience, who am I to argue with them? They either got it or they didn't. The critics are part of the process. I do have some strong feelings about the nature of American criticism—I don't think that it's deeply rooted enough in a knowledge of theatre history. Very often newspapers just assign reporters, Joe Blow off the street. Perhaps it would be too much for the public to have somebody that's overly informed—is that possible?—about the theatre.

How do you see the American theatre today?

The overwhelming impression for me is that theatre's not nearly as interesting as it could be, that it's been stuck in its traces for many, many years. Broadway has not moved out of the '20s, from what I can see. It might be due to the fact that so many of the houses on Broadway are 19th-century playhouses. But much of the material that I see—

As Valdez shapes the experience of Chicanos into drama that speaks to all Americans, he is also examining the interrelationships between the political and metaphysical, between historically determined oppressive structures and man's transhistorical desire for faith and freedom.

—*David Savran*

and I don't see nearly enough—is too anemic for my tastes. I have trouble staying awake in the theatre, believe it or not. I can barely stay awake at my own plays.

I feel that the whole question of the human enterprise is up for grabs. I don't think this country has come to terms with its racial questions, obviously. And because of that, it has not really come to terms with the cultural question of what America is. There are two vast melting pots that must eventually come together. The Hispanic, after all, is really the product of a melting pot—there's no such thing as a Latin American race. The Hispanic melting pot melds all the races of the world, like the Anglo melting pot does; so one of these days, and probably in the United States, those two are going to be poured together—probably in a play, and it could be one of my own [laughs].

There's a connection with the Indian cultures that has to be established in American life. Before we can do that, however, we have to get beyond the national guilt over the genocide of the Indian. What's needed is expiation and forgiveness, and the only ones that are in a position to forgive are the Indian peoples. I'm a Yaqui Indian—Spanish blood, yes, but largely Yaqui. I'm in a position to be able to forgive white people. And why not? I think that's what we're here for, to forgive each other. Martin Luther King speaking in 1963 at the Lincoln Memorial was a beginning. It didn't reach nearly far enough. We're still wrestling with it. Deep fears, about miscegenation and the despoliation of the race, have to be dealt with. I'm here, through my work, to show that short, brown people are okay, you know what I mean? We've got ideas, too, and we've got a song and a dance or two. And we know something about the world that we can share. I'm here to show that to other brown people who don't think very much of themselves, and there are a lot of those.

I wish there were more plays that dealt with the reality of this country. The racial issue is always just swept aside. It deserves to be swept aside—once it's been dealt with. We cannot begin to approach a real solution to our social ills—a solution like integration, for instance, or assimilation—without dealing with all our underlying feelings about each other. I'm trying to deal with my past, not just with respect to Anglos, but to blacks and Asians. I draw on the symbolism of the four roads: the black road, the white road, the red road and the yellow road. They all meet in the navel of the universe, the place where the upper road leads into the underworld—read consciousness and subconsciousness. I think that where they come home is in America.

What are your plans for the future? And goals.

I'm into a very active phase right now, as writer and director, but with writing as the base. I have a number of very central stories I want to tell—on film, on television and on the stage. I want to be working in the three media, on simultaneous projects that feed each other. I like the separation between film, television and theatre. It makes each a lot clearer for me. In theatre, there are a number of ritualistic pieces I want to do that explore the movement of bodies in space and the relation between movement and language. That sphere I can explore on film, too, or television. What film gives me is movement around the actor—I can explore from any viewpoint, any distance. But theatre's the only medium that gives me the sheer beauty, power and presence of bodies. Ritual, literally.

I've got a piece that I've been working on for many, many years, called *The Earthquake Sun,* about our time. All I can tell you is that it will be on the road one of these days. I have another play called *The Mummified Fetus.* It takes off from a real incident that happened a couple years ago: an 85-year-old woman was discovered with a mummified fetus in her womb. I have a couple of plays that the world has not seen, that we've only done here with the company.

In television I have a number of projects. *Corridos* has begun to open up other possibilities. I talk about video as electronic theatre. I'm getting into the idea of doing theatre before cameras, but going for specifically theatrical moments as opposed to real cinematic moments. *Corridos* is an example of this.

I hope a more workable touring network will develop in this country. The links between East and West must be solidified. I think it's great for companies to tour. We're very excited about the possibility of our company plugging into the resources of the regional theatres, as we've done with *Badges* in San Diego and at the Los Angeles Theatre Center, even with the Burt Reynolds Playhouse in Jupiter, Fla. We hope to be able to go from regional theatre to regional theatre all the way across the country, including New York. In that way, we'll be able to reach a national audience.

I still want to experience the dust and sweat occasionally. I'm trying to leave time open for that. This month we're going to celebrate the 25th anniversary of the United Farm Workers, and we'll be back on a flatbed truck, doing some of the old *actos.* I don't want to lose any of our audience. I want worldwide audience. We had that—up until 1980 we were touring Europe and Latin America. We want to tour Asia with the Teatro Campesino. Essentially, I would like to see theatre develop the kind of mass audience—it's impossible of course—that the movies have. I wish we could generate that enthusiasm in young people and in audiences in general, get them out of their homes, away from their VCRs, to experience the theatre as the life-affirming, life-giving experience that it is.

Luis Valdez   (essay date 1990)

SOURCE: *Early Works: Actos, Bernabé and Pensamiento Serpentino,* Arte Publico Press, 1990, pp. 6-13.

[*In the following excerpt, Valdez defines "Chicano theatre" and discusses the significance of the* acto *in its development.*]

What is Chicano theatre? It is theatre as beautiful, rasquachi, human, cosmic, broad, deep, tragic, comic, as the life of La Raza itself. At its high point Chicano theatre is religion—the huelguistas de Delano praying at the shrine of the Virgen de Guadalupe, located in the rear of an old station wagon parked across the road from DiGiorgio's camp #4; at its low point, it is a cuento or a chiste told somewhere in the recesses of the barrio, puro pedo.

Chicano theatre, then, is first a reaffirmation of LIFE. That is what all theatre is supposed to be, of course; but the limp, superficial, gringo seco productions in the "professional" American theatre (and the college and university drama departments that serve it) are so antiseptic, they are antibiotic (anti-life). The characters and life situations emerging from our little teatros are too real, too full of sudor, sangre and body smells to be boxed in. Audience participation is no cute production trick with us; it is a pre-established, pre-assumed privilege. "¡Que le suenen la campanita!"

Defining Chicano theatre is a little like defining a Chicano car. We can start with a lowriders' cool Merc or a campesino's banged-up Chevi, and describe the various paint jobs, hub caps, dents, taped windows, Virgin on the dashboard, etc. that define the car as particularly Raza. Underneath all the trimmings, however, is an unmistakable product of Detroit, an extension of General Motors. Consider now a theatre that uses the basic form, the vehicle, created by Broadway or Hollywood: that is, the "realistic" play. Actually, this type of play was created in Europe, but where French, German, and Scandinavian playwrights went beyond realism and naturalism long ago, commercial gabacho theatre refuses to let go. It reflects a characteristic "American" hang-up on the material aspect of human existence. European theatre, by contrast, has been influenced since around 1900 by the unrealistic, formal rituals of Oriental theatre.

What does Oriental and European theatre have to do with teatro Chicano? Nothing, except that we are talking about a theatre that is particularly our own, not another imitation of the gabacho. If we consider our origins, say the theatre of the Mayans or the Aztecs, we are talking about something totally unlike the realistic play and more Chinese or Japanese in spirit. *Kabuki,* as a matter of fact, started long ago as something like our actos and evolved over two centuries into the highly exacting artform it is today; but it still contains pleberìas. It evolved from and still belongs to el pueblo japonés.

In Mexico, before the coming of the white man, the greatest examples of total theatre were, of course, the human sacrifices. *El Rabinal Achi,* one of the few surviving pieces of indigenous theatre, describes the sacrifice of a courageous guerrillero, who rather than dying passively on the block is granted the opportunity to fight until he is killed. It is a tragedy, naturally, but it is all the more transcendent because of the guerrillero's identification, through sacrifice, with God. The only "set" such a drama-ritual needed was a stone block; nature took care of the rest.

But since the Conquest, Mexico's theatre, like its society, has had to imitate Europe and, in recent times, the United States. In the same vein, Chicanos in Spanish classes are frequently involved in productions of plays by Lope de Vega, Calderón de la Barca, Tirso de Molina and other classic playwrights. Nothing is wrong with this, but it does obscure the indio fountains of Chicano culture. Is Chicano theatre, in turn, to be nothing but an imitation of gabacho playwrights, with barrio productions of racist works by Eugene O'Neil and Tennessee Williams? Will Broadway produce a Chicano version of *Hello, Dolly* now that it has produced a Black one?

The nature of Chicanismo calls for a revolutionary turn in the arts as well as in society. Chicano theatre must be revolutionary in technique as well as content. It must be popular, subject to no other critics except the pueblo itself; but it must also educate the pueblo toward an appreciation of *social change,* on and off the stage.

It is particularly important for teatro Chicano to draw a distinction between what is theatre and what is reality. A demonstration with a thousand Chicanos, all carrying flags and picket signs, shouting CHICANO POWER! is not the revolution. It is theatre about the revolution. The people must act in *reality,* not on stage (which could be anywhere, even a sidewalk) in order to achieve real change. The Raza gets excited, simón, but unless the demonstration evolves into a street battle (which has not yet happened but it is possible), it is basically a lot of emotion with very little political power, as Chicanos have discovered by demonstrating, picketing and shouting before school boards, police departments and stores to no avail.

Such guerrilla theatre passing as a demonstration has its uses, of course. It is agit-prop theatre, as white radicals used to call it in the '30's: agitation and propaganda. It helps to stimulate and sustain the mass strength of a crowd. Hitler was very effective with this kind of theatre, from the swastika to the Wagneresque stadium at Nuremburg. At the other end of the political spectrum, the Huelga march to Sacramento in 1966 was pure guerrilla theatre. The red and black thunderbird flags of the UFWOC (then NFWA) and the standard of the Virgen de Guadalupe challenged the bleak sterility of Highway 99. Its emotional impact was irrefutable. Its political power was somewhat less. Governor Brown was not at the state capitol, and only one grower, Schenley Industries, signed a contract. Later contracts have been won through a brilliant balance between highly publicized events, which gained public support (marches, César's fast, visits by Reuther, Robert and Ted Kennedy, etc.), and actual hardass, door to door, worker to worker organizing. Like Delano, other aspects of the Chicano movement must remember what is teatro and what is reality.

But beyond the mass struggle of La Raza in the fields and barrios of America, there is an internal struggle in the very

corazón of our people. That struggle, too, calls for revolutionary change. Our belief in God, the church, the social role of women, these must be subject to examination and redefinition on some kind of public forum. And that again means teatro. Not a teatro composed of actos or agit-pop, but a teatro of ritual, of music, of beauty and spiritual sensitivity. This type of theatre will require real dedication; it may, indeed, require a couple of generations of Chicanos devoted to the use of the theatre as an instrument in the evolution of our people.

The teatros in existence today reflect the most intimate understanding of everyday events in the barrios from which they have emerged. But if Aztlán is to become a reality, then we as Chicanos must not be reluctant to act nationally. To think in national terms: politically, economically and spiritually. We must destroy the deadly regionalism that keeps us apart. The concept of a national theatre for La Raza is intimately related to our evolving nationalism in Aztlán.

Consider a *Teatro Nacional de Aztlán* that performs with the same skill and prestige as the Ballet Folklórico de Méico (not for gabachos, however, but for the Raza). Such a teatro could carry the message of La Raza into Latin America, Europe, Japan, Africa—in short, all over the world. It would draw its strength from all the small teatros in the barrios, in terms of people and their plays, songs, designs; and it would give back funds, training and augmented strength of national unity. One season the teatro members would be on tour with the Teatro Nacional; the next season they would be back in the barrio sharing their skills and experience. It would accommodate about 150 altogether, with 20-25 in the National and the rest spread out in various parts of Aztlán, working with the Campesino, the Urbano, the Mestizo, the Piojo, etc.

Above all, the national organization of teatros Chicanos would be self-supporting and independent, meaning no government grants. The corazón de la Raza cannot be revolutionalized on a grant from Uncle Sam. Though many of the teatros, including El Campesino, have been born out of pre-established political groups, thus making them harbingers of that particular group's viewpoint, news and political prejudices, there is yet a need for independence for the following reasons: objectivity, artistic competence, survival. El Teatro Campesino was born in the huelga, but the very huelga would have killed it, if we had not moved sixty miles to the north of Delano. A struggle like the huelga needs every person it can get to serve its immediate goals in order to survive; the teatro, as well as the clinic, service center and newspaper, being less important at the moment of need than the survival of the union, were always losing people to the grape boycott. When it became clear to us that the UFWOC would succeed and continue to grow, we felt it was time for us to move and to begin speaking about things beyond the huelga: Vietnam, the barrio, racial discrimination, etc.

The teatros must never get away from La Raza. Without the palomilla sitting there, laughing, crying and sharing whatever is onstage, the teatros will dry up and die. If the raza will not come to the theatre, then the theatre must go to the raza.

This, in the long run, will determine the shape, style, content, spirit and form of el teatro Chicano. Pachucos, campesinos, low-riders, pintos, chavalonas, familias, cuñados, tíos, primos, Mexican-Americans, all the human essence of the barrio, is starting to appear in the mirror of our theatre. With them come the joys, sufferings, disappointments and aspirations of our gente. We challenge Chicanos to become involved in the art, the life style, the political and religious act of doing teatro.

· · · · ·

Nothing represents the work of El Teatro Campesino (and other teatros Chicanos) better than the acto. In a sense, the acto is Chicano theatre, though we are now moving into a new, more mystical dramatic form we have begun to call the mito. The two forms are, in fact, cuates that complement and balance each other as day goes into night, el sol la sombra, la vida la muerte, el pájaro la serpiente. Our rejection of white western European (gabacho) proscenium theatre makes the birth of new Chicano forms necessary, thus, los actos y los mitos; one through the eyes of man, the other through the eyes of God.

The actos were born quite matter of factly in Delano. Nacieron hambrientos de la realidad. Anything and everything that pertained to the daily life, la vida cotidiana, of the huelguistas became food for thought, material for actos. The reality of campesinos on strike had become dramatic, (and theatrical as reflected by newspapers, TV newscasts, films, etc.) and so the actos merely reflected the reality. Huelguistas portrayed huelguistas, drawing their improvised dialogue from real words they exchanged with the esquiroles (scabs) in the fields everyday.

> "Hermanos, compañeros, sálganse de esos files."
> "Tenemos comida y trabajo para ustedes afuera
>   de la huelga."
> "Esquirol, ten vergu enza."
> "Unidos venceremos."
> "¡Sal de ahi barrigón!"

The first huelguista to portray an esquirol in the teatro did it to settle a score with a particularly stubborn scab he had talked with in the fields that day. Satire became a weapon that was soon aimed at known and despised contractors, growers and mayor-domos. The effect of those early actos on the huelguistas de Delano packed into Filipino Hall was immediate, intense and cathartic. The actos rang true to the reality of the huelga.

Looking back at those early, crude, vital, beautiful, powerful actos of 1965, certain things have now become clear about the dramatic form we were just beginning to develop. There was, of course, no conscious deliberate plan to develop the acto as such. Even the name we gave our small presentations reflects the hard pressing expediency under which we worked from day to day. We could have called them "skits," but we lived and talked in San Joaquin Valley Spanish (with a strong Tejano influence), so we needed a name that made sense to the raza. Cuadros, pasquines, autos, entremeses all seemed too highly intellectualized. We began to call them actos for lack of a better word, lack of time and lack of interest in trying to sound like classical Spanish scholars. De todos modos éramos raza, quién se iba a fijar?

The acto, however, developed its own structure through five years of experimentation. It evolved into a short dramatic form now used primarily by los teatros de Aztlán, but utilized to some extent by other non-Chicano guerrilla theatre companies throughout the U.S., including the San Francisco Mime Troupe and the Bread and Puppet Theatre. (Considerable creative crossfeeding has occurred on other levels, I might add, between the Mime Troupe, the Bread and Puppet and the Campesino.) Each of these groups may have their own definition of the acto, but the following are some of the guidelines we have established for ourselves over the years:

> Actos: Inspire the audience to social action. Illuminate specific points about social problems. Satirize the opposition. Show or hint at a solution. Express what people are feeling.

So what's new, right? Plays have been doing that for thousands of years. True, except that the major emphasis in the acto is the social vision, as opposed to the individual artist or playwright's vision. Actos are not written; they are created collectively, through improvisation by a group. The reality reflected in an acto is thus a social reality, whether it pertains to campesinos or to batos locos, not psychologically deranged self-projections, but rather, group archetypes. Don Sotaco, Don Coyote, Johnny Pachuco, Juan Raza, Jorge el Chingón, la Chicana, are all group archetypes that have appeared in actos.

The usefulness of the acto extended well beyond the huelga into the Chicano movement, because Chicanos in general want to identify themselves as a group. The teatro archtypes symbolize the desire for unity and group identity through Chicano heroes and heroines. One character can thus represent the entire Raza, and the Chicano audience will gladly respond to his triumphs or defeats. What to a non-Chicano audience may seem like over simplification in an acto, is to the Chicano a true expression of his social state and therefore reality.

Jorge Huerta (essay date 1992)

SOURCE: An introduction, in *Zoot Suit and Other Plays* by Luis Valdez, Arte Publico Press, 1992, pp. 7-20.

[*In the following excerpt, Huerta traces Valdez's maturation as a playwright and director, and discusses the defining qualities of his work.*]

For some, Luis Valdez needs no introduction; for others, his name may only be associated with his more widely seen films and television programs. No other individual has made as important an impact on Chicano theater as Luis Valdez. He is widely recognized as the leading Chicano director and playwright who, as the founder of El Teatro Campesino (Farmworker's Theatre) in 1965, inspired a national movement of theater troupes dedicated to the exposure of socio-political problems within the Chicano communities of the United States. His output includes plays, poems, books, essays, films and videos, all of which deal with the Chicano and Mexican experience in the U.S.

[Before discussing *Zoot Suit, Bandido!,* and *I Don't Have to Show You No Stinking Badges!*], I would like to briefly trace the director/playwright's development, placing him and these plays in their historical context.

Luis Valdez was born to migrant farmworker parents in Delano, California, on June 26, 1940, the second in a family of ten children. Although his early schooling was constantly interrupted as his family followed the crops, he managed to do well in school. By the age of twelve, he had developed an interest in puppet shows, which he would stage for neighbors and friends. While still in high school he appeared regularly on a local television program, foreshadowing the work in film and video which would later give him his widest audience. After high school, Valdez entered San Jose State College where his interest in theater fully developed.

Valdez's first full-length play, **The Shrunken Head of Pancho Villa,** was produced by San Jose State College in 1964, setting the young artist's feet firmly in the theater. Following graduation in 1964, Valdez worked with the San Francisco Mime Troupe before founding El Teatro Campesino. Valdez became the Artistic Director as well as resident playwright for this raggle-taggle troupe of striking farmworkers, creating and performing brief comedia-like sketches called *"actos"* about the need for a farmworker's union. The *acto* became the signature style for the Teatro and Valdez, inspiring many other teatros to emulate this type of broad, farcical and presentational political theater based on improvisations of socio-political issues.

Within a matter of months El Teatro Campesino was performing away from the fields, educating the general public about the farmworker's struggle and earning revenue for the Union. By 1967 Valdez decided to leave the ranks of the union in order to focus on his theater rather than on the demands of a struggling labor organization. As a playwright, Valdez could now explore issues relevant to the Chicano beyond the fields; as a director, he could begin to develop a core of actors no longer committed to one cause and one style alone.

Although he and his troupe were working collectively from the beginning, the individual playwright in Valdez was anxious to emerge. Discussing the process of writing plays outside of the group, Valdez recalled: "I used to work on them with a sense of longing, wanting more time to be able to sit down and write." In 1967, the playwright did sit down and write, creating what he termed a *"mito,"* or myth, that condemned the Vietnam war, titled **Dark Root of a Scream.** This contemporary myth takes place during a wake for a Chicano who died in Vietnam, an ex-community leader who should have stayed home and fought the battle in the barrio. The dead soldier becomes symbolic of all Chicanos who fought in a war that the playwright himself objected to. "I refused to go to Vietnam," Valdez said twenty years later, "but I encountered all the violence I needed on the home front: people were killed by the farmworkers' strike."

In 1968 the Teatro was awarded an Obie, off-Broadway's highest honor, and the following year Valdez and his troupe gained international exposure at the *Theatre des Nations* at Nancy, France. In 1970 Valdez wrote his second *mito,* **Bernabé.** This one act play is the tale of a *loquito del pueblo* (village idiot), Bernabé, who is in love with La Tierra (The Earth) and wants to marry her. La Tierra is portrayed as a *soldadera,* one of the women who followed and supported the troops during the Mexican Revolution of 1910.

Bernabé is a wonderfully written play that brings together myth and history, contemporary figures and historical icons. The allegorical figure of La Luna, brother to La Tierra, is portrayed as a Zoot Suiter. This is Valdez's first theatrical exploration of this 1940's Chicano renegade, foreshadowing one of his most powerful characters, El Pachuco, in **Zoot Suit. Bernabé** tells its audience that Chicanos not only have a history of struggle but *are* that struggle. Bernabé "marries" La Tierra and becomes a whole person; he symbolically represents all men who love and respect the earth.

Also in 1970, even as Valdez, the playwright, was scripting his individual statement about the Chicano and his relationship to the earth, Valdez, the director, was guiding the collective creation of an *acto* dealing with the war in Vietnam: **Soldado Razo (Buck Private).** **Soldado Razo** carefully explored some of the reasons young Chicanos were willing to go fight in Vietnam. Reflecting the influences of Bertholt Brecht's theories, the playwright uses the allegorical figure of La Muerte (Death) as a constant presence narrating the action, continually reminding his audience that this is theater and that the soldier's death is inevitable.

Soldado Razo complemented and expanded the earlier *mito,* **Dark Root of a Scream,** looking at the same issue but from a different viewpoint and in a distinct style. In Valdez's words, the *acto* "is the Chicano through the eyes of man," whereas the *mito* "is the Chicano through the eyes of God," exploring the Chicanos' roots in Mayan philosophy, science, religion and art. While **Soldado Razo** methodically demonstrates the eventual death of its central figure, **Dark Root of a Scream** begins after a soldier's death, exploring the cause from a mythical distance.

In 1971 the troupe moved to its permanent home base in the rural village of San Juan Bautista, California, where the Teatro established itself as a resident company. During this period Valdez began to explore the idea of adapting the traditional Mexican *corridos,* or ballads, to the stage. A singer would sing the songs and the actors would act them out, adding dialogue from the corridos' texts. Sometimes the singer/narrator would verbalize the text while the actors mimed the physical actions indicated by the song. These simple movements were stylized, enhancing the musical rhythms and adding to the unique combination of elements. The *corrido* style was to appear again, altered to suit the needs of a broader theatrical piece, **La carpa de los Rasquachis** (**The Tent of the Underdogs**).

Developed over a period of years, **La carpa de los Rasquachis** stunned the audience at the Fourth Annual Chicano Theater Festival in San Jose, California in 1973. This production became the hallmark of the Teatro for several years, touring the United States and Europe many times to great critical acclaim. This piece is epic in scope, following a Cantinflas-like (read "Mexico's Charlie Chaplin") Mexican character from his crossing the border into the U.S. and the subsequent indignities to which he is exposed until his death.

La carpa de los Rasquachis brought together a Valdezian aesthetic that could be defined as raucous, lively street theater with deep socio-political and spiritual roots. The style combined elements of the *acto, mito* and *corrido* with an almost constant musical background as a handful of actors revealed the action in multiple roles with minimal costumes, props and set changes. This was the apogee of Valdez's "poor theater," purposely based on the early twentieth-century Mexican tent shows, otherwise known as "carpas."

In an effort to define his neo-Mayan philosophy, Valdez wrote a poem, *Pensamiento Serpentino,* in 1973. The poem describes a way of thinking that was determining the content of Valdez's evolving dramaturgy. The poem begins:

> *Teatro*
> *eres el mundo*
> *y las paredes de los*
> buildings *más grandes*
> *son* nothing but scenery.

Later in the poem Valdez describes and revives the Mayan philosophy of "In Lak Ech" which translates as *"Tú eres mi otro yo* / You are my other me." The phrase represents the following philosophy:

> Tú eres mi otro yo / You are my other me.
> Si te hago daño a ti / If I do harm to you,
> Me hago daño a mí mismo / I do harm to myself;
> Si te amo y respeto / If I love and respect you,
> Me amo y respeto yo / I love and respect myself.

In the opening lines Valdez describes Chicano theater as a reflection of the world; a universal statement about what it is to be a Chicano in the United States. Recognizing the many injustices the Chicano has suffered in this country, the poet nonetheless attempts to revive a non-violent response. Valdez creates a distinct vision of a "cosmic people" whose destiny is finally being realized as Chicanos who are capable of love rather than hate, action rather than words.

While *La carpa de los Rasquachis* continued to tour, Valdez made another crucial change in his development by writing *Zoot Suit* and co-producing it with the Center Theatre Group of Los Angeles. Once again at the vanguard, Valdez began the mainstreaming of Chicano theater, or, for some observers, "the infiltration of the regional theaters."

The director/playwright did not abandon El Teatro Campesino by getting involved with a major regional theater. The Teatro was still touring and *Zoot Suit* was co-produced by both theater organizations, thus including the Teatro in all negotiations and contracts. But this was a first step towards an individual identity that Valdez had previously rejected by working in a collective.

As advertised in the Los Angeles press, "On July 30, 1978, the Second Zoot Suit Riot begins," and it did. *Zoot Suit* played to sold-out houses for eleven months—breaking all previous records for Los Angeles theater. While the Los Angeles production continued to run, another production opened in New York on March 25, 1979, the first (and only) Chicano play to open on Broadway. Although audiences were enthusiastic, the New York critics were not, and the play was closed after a four-week run. Hurt, but undaunted, Valdez could have the satisfaction that the play continued to be the biggest hit ever in Los Angeles and a motion picture contract had been signed.

Zoot Suit marked an important turning point in Valdez's relationship with El Teatro Campesino as he began to write for actors outside the group. This experience introduced Valdez to the Hollywood Latino and non-Latino talent pool, suddenly bringing him into contact with a different breed of artist. With a large population of professionals at his disposal, Valdez's vision had to expand. No longer surrounded by sincere, but sometimes limited talent, Valdez could explore any avenue of theater he desired. The success of the Los Angeles run of *Zoot Suit* enabled our playwright/director to move more seriously into film making. Valdez adapted and directed *Zoot Suit* as a motion picture in 1981.

The collaboration with a non-Hispanic theater company and subsequent move into Hollywood film making was inevitable for Valdez; the natural course for a man determined to reach as many people as possible with his message and with his art. Theater was his life's work, it was in his blood, but so was the fascinating world of film and video.

With the financial success of *Zoot Suit,* Valdez purchased an old packing house in San Juan Bautista and had it converted into a theater for the company. This new playhouse and administrative complex was inaugurated in 1981 with a production of David Belasco's 1905 melodrama *Rose of the Rancho,* adapted by Valdez. This old fashioned melodrama was an ideal play for San Juan Bautista, because it was based on actual historical figures and events that had occurred in that town in the nineteenth century. Played as a revival of the melodrama genre, the play could be taken for face value, a tongue-in-cheek taste of history replete with stereotypes and misconceptions.

The experiment with *Rose of the Rancho* served as a kind of motivation for Valdez, inspiring him to write the second play in this collection, *Bandido!* which he then directed in 1982 in the Teatro's theater. This was Valdez's personal adaptation of the melodrama genre but with a distinctly Valdezian touch as we will see later.

Valdez wrote and directed *Corridos* for the 1983 season, producing this elaboration of the earlier exercises in San Francisco's Marine's Memorial Theater, a large house that was filled to capacity for six months. The San Francisco production garnered eleven awards from the Bay Area Theater Critics Circle before moving on to residencies in San Diego and Los Angeles.

All of his interaction in Hollywood and his own sense of history inspired Valdez to write the final play in this collection, *I Don't Have to Show You No Stinking Badges!*, first produced by El Teatro Campesino and the Los Angeles Theatre Center in 1986. This production represented the beginning of yet another phase for Valdez and his company. El Teatro Campesino was no longer a full-time core of artists, living and creating collectively under Valdez's direction. Instead, the company began to contract talent only for the rehearsal and performance period. El Teatro Campesino became a producing company with Valdez at the helm as Artistic Director and writer. After great success in Los Angeles, *Badges!* was co-produced with the San Diego Repertory Theater and the Burt Reynolds Dinner Theatre in Jupiter, Florida. While the Teatro continued to produce, Valdez began to focus his efforts more on writing and directing films.

Valdez directed *La Bamba,* the sleeper hit of the summer of 1987, finally opening up the doors that had been so difficult to penetrate for so many years. "When I drove up to the studio gate," Valdez related, following the success of his film, "the guard at the gate told me that the pastries were taken to a certain door. The only other Mexican he ever saw delivered the pastries." That same year our playwright adapted and directed the earlier *Corridos* into a PBS version titled *Corridos: Tales of Passion and Revolution,* starring Linda Rondstadt and featuring himself as narrator. This production won the Peabody Award, the Pulitzer Prize of broadcasting.

Following the success of *La Bamba* and *Corridos,* Valdez continued to work on other projects for television and film as he also took his position as the leading Chicano filmmaker in Hollywood. Ever the activist, Valdez helped form the Latino Writers Group, which he hoped would pressure the studios to produce films written by Latinos. "The embryo is the screenplay," he said. "The embryo, in fact, is what is written on the page. This is where you begin to tell the difference between a stereotype and reality."

In 1991, Valdez adapted and directed *La Pastorela,* or *Shepherd's Play* for a great performances segment on PBS. This television production is based on the traditional Christmas play, which El Teatro Campesino has produced in the mission at San Juan Bautista for many years. That same year, Valdez and his wife, Lupe, co-scripted a motion picture based on the life of Frida Kahlo, for production in 1992. Plans were also underway for a revival of *Bandido!* in San Juan Bautista during the 1992 season as well as a re-mounting of *Zoot Suit* for a national tour.

Valdez's impressive career can be separated into the following four periods: Phase One, the director/playwright of the original group of farmworkers; Phase Two, a Teatro Campesino independent of the Union; Phase Three, a professional Teatro and co-productions such as *Zoot Suit*; and the current, Fourth Phase, Luis Valdez, the filmmaker alongside El Teatro Campesino, professional productions across the country and community-professional productions at home.

Zoot Suit is the logical culmination of all that Valdez had written before, combining elements of the *acto, mito* and *corrido* in a spectacular documentary play with music.

> **Valdez taught us to laugh at ourselves as we worked to improve the conditions in our barrios and our nation. In particular, he urges us to embrace life with all of the vigor we can muster in the midst of seemingly insurmountable obstacles.**
>
> *—Jorge Huerta*

Unlike any of his previous plays or *actos,* however, *Zoot Suit* is based on historical fact, not a current crisis.

By illuminating an actual incident in the history of Chicano-Anglo relations in Los Angeles, *Zoot Suit* does not have the immediacy of an *acto* about today's headlines. The politically aware will know that the police brutality and injustices rendered in this play are still happening; others may lose the point. Most significantly, this play illuminates events that had a major impact on the Chicano community of Los Angeles during World War II, incidents that are carefully ignored by most high school history books.

Like the *acto, Zoot Suit* exposes social ills in a presentational style. It is a play that is closer to the docu-drama form, owing more to Brecht than to Odets as the action reveals the events surrounding the infamous Sleepy Lagoon Murder Trial of 1942. By employing a narrator, Valdez is discarding a totally representational style in favor of this more direct contact with his audience. El Pachuco's almost constant presence, underscoring Henry's inner thoughts and tribulations, skillfully captivates the audience and serves as a continual commentator on the action.

Just as La Muerte did in *Soldado Razo,* El Pachuco will stop the action entirely in order to make a point, telling Henry (and the audience) to listen again when the judge rules that the "zoot haircuts will be retained throughout the trial for purposes of identification . . ." It is a kind of "instant replay" that is only used once for maximum effect. Countering the figure of El Pachuco is the allegorical character of The Press which descends directly from the *acto* as well.

Like the *corrido,* there is a musical underscoring in *Zoot Suit,* placing the events in a historical context by employing the music of the period. El Pachuco sings some of the songs, as in a *corrido,* setting the mood through lyrics such as those that introduce the "Saturday Night Dance" in Act One, Scene Seven. While El Pachuco sings, the actors dance to the rhythms he creates, transforming from youthful fun to vengeful intensity gone wild by the end of the scene.

Some of the songs are original while others are traditional Latin or Anglo-American tunes, such as Glenn Miller's "In The Mood." Unlike the *corrido,* in which the music was played by live musicians, however, the music is pre-recorded. The choreography is also more like that of a musical comedy during the dance numbers, staged with historical authenticity to enhance the theatricality and further engage the audience.

Most importantly, this play places the Chicanos in a historical context that identifies them as "American," by showing that they, too, danced the swing as well as the mambo. Valdez is telling his audience that the Chicanos' taste for music can be as broad as anyone's. He is also revealing a cross-culturalism in the Chicanos' language, customs and myths. As Valdez so emphatically stated when this play first appeared, "this is an *American* play," attempting to dispel previous notions of separatism from the society at large. He is also reminding us that Americans populate The Americas, not just the U.S.

Valdez will not ignore his indigenous American ancestors, either, employing elements of the *mito* very subtly when the Pachuco is stripped of his zoot suit and remains covered only by an indigenous loincloth. This image suggests the sacrificial "god" of the Aztecs, stripped bare before his heart is offered to the cosmos. It is a stunning moment in the play, when the cocky Pachuco is reduced to bare nakedness in piercing contrast to his treasured "drapes." He may be naked, but he rises nobly in his bareness, dissolving into darkness. He will return, and he does.

The character of El Pachuco also represents the Aztec concept of the *"nahual,"* or other self as he comes to Henry's support during the solitary scene in prison. Henry is frightened, stripped emotionally bare in his cell and must rely on his imagination to recall the spirit of El Pachuco in order to survive. The strength he receives from his other self is determined by his ability to get in touch with his *nahual.*

The documentary form of the play is influenced by the Living Newspaper style, a documentary theater that exposed current events during the 1930's through dramatizations of those events. The use of newspapers for much of the set decoration, as well as the giant front page backdrop through which El Pachuco cuts his way at the top of the play is an effective metaphor for the all-pervading presence of the press. When Dolores Reyna hangs newspapers on the clothesline instead of actual laundry, the comment is complete.

Like most of Valdez's works, this play dramatizes a Chicano family in crisis. Henry Reyna is the central figure, but he is not alone. His *familia* is the link with the Chicano community in the audience, a continuing reminder that the Chicano *is* a community. Unlike the members of his family, however, Henry's alter-ego brings another dimension to this misunderstood figure. El Pachuco represents an inner attitude of defiance determining Henry's actions most of the time. El Pachuco is reminiscent at times of the Diablo and Diabla characters that permeated the *corridos,* motivating the characters' hapless choices as in Medieval morality plays.

El Pachuco's advice is not based on a moral choice, as in the *corridos,* but rather, on judgments of character. Mostly, El Pachuco represents the defiance against the system that identifies and determines the pachuco character. Sometimes, Henry does not take El Pachuco's advice,

choosing instead to do what he thinks is right. At times, Henry has no choice, whether he listens to his alter-ego or to another part of himself, he will still get beaten. Interestingly, El Pachuco is sometimes more politically astute than the defendants themselves, allowing Henry an awareness his fellows do not have. In other instances, such as when the boys debate whether to confide in George, the boys' instincts are better for the whole and Henry must ignore El Pachuco's advice.

Now available in video, the motion picture of *Zoot Suit* is a vivid record of elements of the original stage production, because it was filmed in the Aquarius Theatre in Hollywood where it had played. The motion picture recreates and reconstructs the play. At times we watch the action unfolding as if we, too, are one of the hundreds sitting in the audience, watching the play; then suddenly the characters are in a realistic setting, as in a sound stage and we are enveloped in social realism. Just as the Pachuco continually reminds the audience that "this is just a play" in the stage version, the film also prompts us to remember that this is a *demonstration of actual events,* urging us to think about it as we watch the action moving back and forth between realities. *Zoot Suit* is also a rewriting of history, as is the central issue of the next play, *Bandido!*

Bandido! is an exploration and expurgation of old clichés about the early California bandits. Valdez's intent is to alter history by demonstrating his version of the exploits of one Tiburcio Vásquez, the last man to be publicly hanged in California. The play is therefore didactic like an *acto* or a docu-drama but goes beyond those forms to become a "melodrama within a play." The playwright creates a construct in which audience sees Vásquez through different eyes. Vásquez is sympathetic when observed through the playwright's eyes and a stereotype when seen through history's distorted characterization.

The key to a successful production of *Bandido!* lies in an understanding of the satiric nature within the form of the play. Valdez's introductory notes state the challenge to director and actors most clearly: "The contrast of theatrical styles between the realism of the jail and the *trompe l'oeil* of the melodrama is purely intentional and part of the theme of the play . . . their combined reality must be a metaphor—and not a facile cliché—of the Old West." The actors must therefore represent real people in the jail scenes and stereotypes of those characters and others in the melodramatic scenes.

Valdez is no stranger to stereotypes, as is illustrated in one of the playwright's most enduring *actos, Los vendidos (The Sellouts),* which he first wrote in 1967. In this very funny and popular *acto,* the playwright turns stereotyping around, making the audience reassess their attitudes about various Chicano and Mexican "types." We laugh, but also understand that the characteristics exposed are a reflection of Anglo perceptions and, yes, even sometimes our own biases as Chicanos. In both *Los vendidos* and *Bandido!* the playwright is portraying these characters *with a clear understanding that they are stereotypes.*

The characterization of Tiburcio Vásquez will vary according to the point of view of who is re-creating him on stage. If he is perceived as "real" in the jail scenes and a stereotype in the melodrama, the audience will distinguish the playwright's bias. They might also understand that their own biases come from the Hollywood stereotype of a "bandido." The actor, too, must delight in demonstrating the exaggeration, commenting upon his character even as he explores the exaggerations. This is a Brechtian acting technique, asking the actor to have an opinion about his character's actions and choices. Within the construct of the melodrama within the play, this can be effectively displayed.

Valdez clearly thinks of Vásquez as a social bandit, a gentleman who never killed anyone but who was forced into a life of crime by the Anglo invaders of his homeland. The playwright's goal here is to make Tiburcio Vásquez more than a romantic figure cloaked in evil, to present us with a reason for his actions instead of only the results.

Valdez's first play, *The Shrunken Head of Pancho Villa,* featured a young Chicano social bandit named Joaquín, symbolic of that better known *"bandido,"* Joaquìn Murrieta. Labelled a pachuco by the police, Joaquìn steals from the rich to give to the poor. Neither Joaquìn nor Vásquez are clearly understood by the authorities, but they fascinate their communities. As Pico says to Vásquez in the second act: "You've given all of us Californios twenty years of secret vicarious revenge."

The Shrunken Head of Pancho Villa offers hope for the community through unified social action, although the fate of *Bandido!*'s central figure is predetermined by history. Valdez knows that nobody can change the inequities of the past, but offers the suggestion that the future can be altered for the better, if misrepresentations of the Chicano are altered.

It is not that Valdez is attempting to completely whitewash Vásquez, either. When the Impresario asks him, "Are you comic or tragic, a good man or a bad man?" Vásquez responds: "All of them." To which the playwright might respond: "Aren't we *all* comic and tragic, good and bad?" It is perhaps the degree of evil that fascinates our playwright here, that degree always determined by who is being asked. Thus, the opposing views of this comic, tragic, good and bad man.

Valdez's style here is reminiscent of Luigi Pirandello, the Italian playwright and novelist whose works often turn reality inside out, leaving the reader or observer to ponder the nature of reality. Again, the Impresario states the obvious when he tells Vásquez, "Reality and theater don't mix, sir," as we watch a play that is watching its own melodrama.

Above all, *Bandido!* is *theatrical,* offering the audience a delightful mixture of songs and dances that narrate the story as in the *corrido,* as well as characters that can be hissed or cheered as they would have been in the nineteenth century. Melodramas were extremely popular in Mexican theaters and *carpas* of the nineteenth and early twentieth centuries in this country, a fact that histories of U.S. theater neglect to report. In other words, the genre belongs to all of us.

What makes this play truly Valdezian, however, is the fact that it is not simply a play presenting us with villains and heroes in conflict. The conflict is the melodrama itself— the distortion the Impresario wants to present for profit. "The public will only buy tickets to savour the evil in your soul," he tells Vásquez, a truism that cannot be denied. It is more fun to watch the villain than the hero in an old fashioned melodrama. In Valdez's play, however, the villain is the Impresario, precursor to a legion of Hollywood producers. If history cannot be changed in either *Zoot Suit* or *Bandido!,* the next play looks to the future as the only hope.

The Valdezian questioning of reality reaches its pinnacle in *I Don't Have to Show You No Stinking Badges!* In this play the playwright presents us with a world that resembles a hall of mirrors, sometimes catching this picture, other times another view. One never knows for certain if what we are observing is real or an illusion. Instead of *Bandido!*'s "Melodrama within a play," we are now given a much more complex vision as Valdez explores the different levels of reality between the world of the stage and the realm of television. Like *Zoot Suit,* this play was written for a fully-equipped theater. Furthermore, it requires a realistic set, designed to look like a television studio setting, including video monitors hanging above the set to help the audience understand its transformation into a "live studio audience."

Badges! focuses on a middle-aged Chicano couple who have made their living as "King and Queen of the Hollywood Extras," playing non-speaking roles as maids, gardeners and the like. The couple have been very successful, having put their daughter through medical school and their son into Harvard. They have, in effect, accomplished the American Dream, with a suburban home complete with swimming pool, family room and microwave.

The major conflict arises when Sonny, alienated from the Ivy League reality, comes home from Harvard unexpectedly and announces that he has dropped-out. To make matters worse, he decides he will become a Hollywood actor. His parents, his girlfriend and the audience know his fate will be the same as his parents', playing "on the hyphen" in bit parts as thieves, drug addicts and rapists. Or will he? Like *Zoot Suit, I Don't Have to Show You No Stinking Badges!* does not give a distinct ending, but rather, leaves the solution up to the audience members to decide.

While *Zoot Suit* takes us from a presentational style to a representational style as a play, *Bandido!* explores both styles transferring from the "real" Tiburcio Vásquez to the melodramatic version: Vásquez through the eyes of Luis Valdez and Vásquez through the eyes of Hollywood and dime novels. *Badges!,* on the other hand, takes us on a much more involved journey, by remodeling the theater to look like an actual television studio with all of the paraphernalia of the medium. To add to the effect, when the action begins it begins as an actual taping in progress.

As soon as the action begins in *Badges!,* we begin to think of it as a play, performed in the style of a sit-com, not a taping, but rather, a *play,* until the final scene. This is when it becomes difficult to tell if what we are seeing is a part of Buddy and Consuelo's "sit-com," or if what we are witnessing is Sonny's "sit-com," or his "play," existing only in his mind.

Just as we saw Tiburcio Vásquez attempting to write the true version of his story, we now see Sonny Villa recreating his reality. "Is it real, or is it Memorex?" he asks, underscoring the premise of the play itself. Are we, the audience, a "live studio audience?" Are they really taping this? Did Sonny really rob a fast food restaurant? Questions mount as we watch Sonny's transformation, his angst or his drama.

What is real to Sonny is the fact that he must find himself within this society, the son of parents whose very existence has depended on portraying the marginalized "other." When Connie tells her son "I'd rather play a maid than *be* a maid," she makes a point but cannot escape the fact that maids are all she ever will play. Sonny knows that he, too, will not be given greater opportunities unless he writes and directs his own material, to his standards and not some Hollywood advertising agency's.

From melodrama-within-a-play to video-within-a-play, the playwright takes us on theatrical explorations that offer no easy solutions. The earliest *actos* offered clearly defined action: "Join the union," "Boycott grapes," etc. But what to do about distorted history or negative portrayals of Chicanos in the media? Can any of us, as Sonny Villa proposes to do, write and produce films and videos that cut through the biases of generations? Only a select few will ever have that opportunity and Luis Valdez is one of them.

Ultimately, these three plays present us with different aspects of the playwright himself. Valdez is the Pachuco of Broadway, the social bandit of the media and the brilliant student who will change the face of Hollywood portrayals of his people. He laughs at himself as much as at historians and Hollywood in these plays, exploding myths by creating others, transforming the way in which Chicanos and Chicanas view themselves within the context of this society. Each of these plays is finally about a search for identity through the playwright's quest for what is reality—past, present and future. "How can we know who we are," he continually asks, "if we do not know who we were?"

In the twenty-six years since he founded El Teatro Campesino, Luis Valdez has made an odyssey few theater artists in the United States can claim. This course could not have been predicted, yet the journey was inevitable. Yes, Valdez has gone from the fields of Delano to the migrant labor of a theater artist, to the even more complex world of Broadway and Hollywood. But he has never forgotten his roots, has never abandoned the beauty of his languages, both *Inglés* and Spanish.

Nor has he forgotten about his people's troubles and triumphs.

Valdez taught us to laugh at ourselves as we worked to improve the conditions in our barrios and in our nation. In particular, he urges us to embrace life with all of the vigor we can muster in the midst of seemingly insurmountable obstacles. May these plays inspire others to follow in his footsteps.

FURTHER READING

Criticism

Review of *Aztlan; An Anthology of Mexican American Literature,* edited by Luis Valdez and Stan Steiner. *Choice* 9 (January 1973): 1451.
    Maintains that although the collection "is informative, dignified, and energetic, it is overbalanced by nonliterary matter."

Corliss, Richard. "Rock Fable or Teen Ballad?" *Time* 130, No. 7 (17 August 1987): 62.
    Unfavorable review of *La Bamba.*

Garcia, Nasario. "Satire: Techniques and Devices in Luis Valdez's *Las dos caras del patroncito.*" *De colores Journal* 1, No. 4 (1974): 66-74.
    Explores how Valdez's early play *Las dos caras del patroncito* makes use of theatrical techniques and devices to satirize the relationship between farmworkers and their exploiters.

Garcia, Richard A. "Chicano Intellectual History: Myths and Realities." In *A Decade of Hispanic Literature: An Anniversary Anthology,* edited by Nicolás Kanellos, pp. 285-89. Houston: Revista Chicano-Riqueña, 1982.
    Refutes Valdez's contention that the pachucos were the prototype of Chicano consciousness, asserting that "pachucos were not the precursors of the Chicano movement and *Pachuquismo* was not the source of the Chicano intellectual thought."

Milleret, Margo. Review of *Luis Valdez—Early Works: Actos, Bernabé, Pensamiento Serpentino,* by Luis Valdez. *Theatre Journal* 43, Vol. 4 (December 1991): 546-47.
    Laudatory review.

Novick, Julius. Review of *Zoot Suit,* by Luis Valdez. *The Nation* 227, No. 3 (22 July 1978): 88, 90.
    Mixed review of the 1978 Los Angeles production of the drama.

Steiner, Stan. "The Cultural Schizophrenia of Luis Valdez." *Vogue* 153, No. 6 (15 March 1969): 112-13, 143-44.
    Overview of Valdez's life and career.

Tatum, Charles. Review of *Zoot Suit and Other Plays,* by Luis Valdez. *World Literature Today* 67, No. 2 (Spring 1993): 384.
    Praises the collection as "an essential acquisition for anybody interested in contemporary Chicano literature."

Additional coverage of Valdez's life and career is contained in the following sources published by Gale Research: *Contemporary Authors,* Vol. 101; *Contemporary Authors New Revision Series,* Vol. 32; *Dictionary of Literary Biography,* Vol. 122; *Hispanic Literature Criticism,* Vol. 2; and *Hispanic Writers.*

Banana Yoshimoto

1964-

(Pseudonym of Mahoko Yoshimoto) Japanese novelist, short story writer, and essayist.

The following entry provides criticism on Yoshimoto's works that have been translated into English as of 1994.

INTRODUCTION

Yoshimoto is best known to English-language readers for fiction that features young, offbeat Japanese characters and concerns such sensationalistic topics as incest, suicide, transsexuality, and mysticism. Despite earning a reputation for a hip sensibility, her works are pervaded by traditional themes of loss, love, friendship, and isolation.

Biographical Information

Born in 1964, Yoshimoto is the daughter of renowned philosopher and literary critic Ryumei Yoshimoto. A resident of Tokyo, she attended Nihon University and has won numerous literary prizes. In addition to her works of fiction, Yoshimoto has also published essay collections in her homeland.

Major Works

NP (1991; *NP*) and the novella and short story that comprise *Kitchin* (1988; *Kitchen*) focus on young Japanese women. In the novella *Kitchen* a young woman named Mikage moves in with her friend Yuichi and his transsexual father after her grandmother dies. Mikage, for whom kitchens, food, and cooking have cathartic properties, studies the culinary arts, eventually using them to help Yuichi cope with his father's unexpected death. In the short story "Moonlight Shadow" the protagonist's boyfriend dies in a car accident on a bridge. Obsessed with his death, she returns daily to the site until a mysterious woman conjures a vision of her lost lover. *NP* revolves around a woman, Kazami, who befriends a brother, sister, and step-sister whose father, a well-known author, mysteriously committed suicide after publishing a collection of short stories entitled *NP*. Employing a metafictional approach, Yoshimoto creates an intricate web of interpersonal relationships and coincidences as Kazami's life begins to parallel that of the author and several of his characters. The plot is further complicated by many twists, including affairs involving the step-sister and her half-brother, her father, and Kazami.

Critical Reception

Although Yoshimoto's fiction has been received enthusiastically in Japan, the response among English-speaking critics has been mixed. Detractors have found *Kitchen* little more than charming, arguing that the dialogue is unrevealing and the protagonists' introspective ruminations about life are insipid and sentimental. Several commentators, however, have expressed appreciation of Yoshimoto's youthful perspective on modern Japanese life, praising her focus on social fragmentation, her blending of Japanese and Western cultures, and her openness to eccentricity. Citing *Kitchen*'s use of fantasy, its lack of conventional parental figures, and its emphasis on androgyny and idealized love uncomplicated by sexual encounters, Deborah Garrison has observed: "Yoshimoto's attraction to weirdness and her unpretentious approach to it—she's not trying to be hip, just faithful to her sense of people as they are—are what might make Western readers want more of her." *NP* is generally regarded as less successful than *Kitchen*, with critics mentioning unsympathetic characters and unconvincing treatment of weighty issues as the novel's flaws. Donna Seaman, however, has observed that the events of *NP* "deepen our wonder at the dangers and idiosyncrasies of love."

PRINCIPAL WORKS

Kitchin [*Kitchen*] (novella and short story) 1988
Tugumi (novel) 1989
NP [*NP*] (novel) 1991

CRITICISM

Nick Hornby (review date 8 January 1993)

SOURCE: "Mystical Mundane," in *The Times Literary Supplement,* No. 4684, January 8, 1993, p. 18.

[*In the following excerpt, Hornby contends that Yoshimoto blends prosaic and extraordinary elements in* Kitchen, *yet the desired effect of this fusion is unapparent in translation.*]

Kitchen comes to us almost bent double with the weight of its success in its native country. Banana Yoshimoto's slim volume, which consists of the title novella and **"Moonlight Shadow,"** a matching short story, has sold "millions" of copies in Japan, and won two prestigious literary prizes. Works like this always appear strangely attractive in translation, promising as they do the contradictory virtues of accessibility and exoticism.

The book is certainly exotic. Indeed, anyone who has been deterred by the self-conscious eccentricity of some recent Japanese writing (particularly the work of Haruki Murakami) might find themselves dispirited by the novella's *dramatis personae* alone: one of the central characters, Yuichi, lives with a mother who was formerly his father.

Yoshimoto's writing is much more understated than this isolated example of narrative flamboyance suggests. Her stories possess a clarity and simplicity that can seem lightweight. The reliance on mood and a kind of ingenuous directness means that the author is perilously dependent on her translator. "The endless sea was shrouded in darkness. I could see the shadowy forms of gigantic, rugged crags against which the waves were crashing. While watching them I felt a strange, sweet sadness", we read at the climax of the title novella. By this stage in the story there is little else going on apart from the quality of the writing, and yet, with its safe, limited and predictable combinations of noun and adjective, this is irredeemably ordinary.

Both *Kitchen* and **"Moonlight Shadow",** each narrated by young women, are about loss. In the longer story, Mikage, the female narrator, moves into the house of Yuichi and his mother/father after the death of her grandmother; in the second, the girl has lost a boyfriend in a car crash, and is granted a vision of her beloved by a mysterious lady on a bridge. There are other thematic ties. The interest in transsexuality is given further expression in **"Moonlight Shadow"** (the dead boy's brother, who lost his girlfriend in the same accident, has taken to wearing her clothes around town); more importantly, both tales attempt to fuse the mystical and the mundane.

It is here, presumably, that Yoshimoto has scored in Japan. *Kitchen* (the title refers to Mikage's favourite room) attempts to locate a heartbroken, breathy longing where the rest of us find only a kettle and a dirty oven. In the final pages of the story—which for British readers may have unhappy echoes of the television advertisement for Milk Tray—Mikage makes a death-defying climb to bring her beloved Yuichi an unusually good deep-fried pork and rice dish.

One can imagine the langorous, puzzled sorrow that Yoshimoto intended to conjure up (**"Moonlight Shadow",** shorter and more intense than *Kitchen,* achieves genuine poignancy), but in the end, the translation only succeeds in summarizing, rather than capturing, a mood.

Scott Shibuya Brown (review date 10 January 1993)

SOURCE: "Adrift in the New Japan," in *Book World— The Washington Post,* January 10, 1993, p. 8.

[*A journalist, Brown was the 1990-91 recipient of the Gannett fellowship in Asian Studies. In the following review, he provides a thematic analysis of* Kitchen.]

In an interview, the architect Arata Isozaki once remarked that Tokyo's massive sprawl rendered the ideas of "center" and landmarks superfluous. One could easily set down in any of its several urban areas and not know (or care) that, in most major cities, geographical meaning was supposed to radiate from a singular locus. While initially discomfiting, for Isozaki, the effects of such decentralization are strangely appealing, when one gets used to them.

This psychological state of living without defining landmarks, of decentralization and dislocation, is also at the heart of *Kitchen,* [a novella and a short story] that represent the first English translation of Banana Yoshimoto, a young and extraordinarily popular chronicler of the 20-something crowd in Japan. Like the geography of Tokyo, Yoshimoto's characters exist at random, denied any possibility of order by the death of their loved ones. Alienated and withdrawn, they linger in the wake of these deaths, grappling with the transition from order into emotional chaos.

Kitchen, the better of the two [pieces], concerns a young cooking student, Mikage, who loses her grandmother, her only surviving relative. Taken in temporarily by a young mutual acquaintance, Yuichi Tanabe, and his transsexual mother, Eriko (who used to be Yuichi's father), Mikage slowly regains her sense of self by extracting pleasure from mundane things—sleeping on her hosts' enormous sofa, listening to their living noises, and simply finding peace, as she puts it, in the mother and son's "strange cheerfulness."

Most of all, what becomes her touchstone of healing is the Tanabes' well-maintained kitchen, where Mikage, in her endless preparation of food, steadily fills the vacuum in her existence. Although Yoshimoto's metaphorical equation of food with life is, on one hand, overbearingly apparent, she writes about the kitchen and cooking as if she were in love with food—that is, artlessly and with much

> Yoshimoto's characters exist at random, denied any possibility of order by the death of their loved ones. Alienated and withdrawn, they linger in the wake of these deaths, grappling with the transition from order into emotional chaos.
>
> —*Scott Shibuya Brown*

enthusiasm: "Every day I thrilled with pleasure at the challenges tomorrow would bring. Memorizing the recipe, I would make carrot cakes that included a bit of my soul. At the supermarket I would stare at a bright red tomato, loving it for dear life. Having known such joy, there was no going back."

There are, however, things that Yoshimoto does less well. The dialogue of her characters, while possibly distorted by the translation, is too often banal, hinting at nothing but the obvious, in the manner of bad television. Similarly, Yoshimoto's characterizations are frequently facile and not particularly telling, again calling to mind the pervasive influence of video culture (Yoshimoto herself belongs to the *shinjinrui* generation, those born in the 1960s under the twin auspices of a strong GNP and explosive technology). Her second [story], **"Moonlight Shadow,"** which also revolves around the death of loved ones, is especially dependent on cliches. In it, a young woman and a young man struggle to carry on after losing their lovers in a car crash; through an other-worldly intervention, they see the continuous path of life, which allows them to accept the nature of death.

Yet, there is also an engaging and deceptive lightness, even slightness, in **Kitchen** that surprises, given its rather grim subject matter. Indeed, what becomes clear midway through is that while **Kitchen** ostensibly is about loss, what the novellas truly represent is another turn on the classic Japanese theme of *mono no aware,* or evanescence: beauty as an ever-transitory, perpetually fading, bittersweet phenomenon (this connection with the classical, I suspect, has generated the book's overwhelming popularity in Japan—57 printings according to the jacket blurb). As a meditation on the transience of beauty and love, **Kitchen** is often melancholy and lovely, consistently striking a delicate balance in delineating the emotions that surround death without becoming emotional in turn.

In the end, that delicacy remains **Kitchen**'s most beguiling charm. Though its context is matter-of-fact modern and Western (as the buzz of technology hovering unobtrusively in the background reminds us), Yoshimoto in many ways has written a work shaped by the most traditional of aesthetics. Of course, it must be said as well that in the brief tradition of modern Japanese literature, which dates back 120 years, flux and the hardships of transition have been oft-celebrated themes. But so long as the Japanese concept of beauty is defined by ephemerality, the appeal of tradition is not likely to change—not for someone as currently popular as Banana Yoshimoto, nor for future Japanese authors willing to tackle the subject of love and loss.

Todd Grimson (review date 10 January 1993)

SOURCE: "The Catcher in the Rice," in *Los Angeles Times Book Review,* January 10, 1993, pp. 3, 7.

[*Grimson is an American novelist and short story writer. In the following review, he perceives a youthful, innocent quality and an emphasis on family life as both the strengths and weaknesses of* Kitchen.]

I had been really looking forward to reading Banana Yoshimoto. I've long been a fan of Japanese fiction, from the emotionally cryptic but cumulatively powerful work of Nobel Prize-winning Yasunari-Kawabata to the "most Western," sex-and-violence-obsessed Yukio Mishima, plus Tanizaki, Kobo Abe, Yoshiyuki—almost everything translated has been worth reading, with many surprises to be savored along the way.

Banana Yoshimoto has been mentioned along with Haruki Murakami (author of *Hard-Boiled Wonderland and the End of the World* and *A Wild Sheep Chase*) as part of a new generation of Japanese novelists, and Murakami is amazing, just what the art calls for, so I presumed **Kitchen,** Yoshimoto's first book to be translated would be, well—*important.*

Instead, **Kitchen** is light as an invisible pancake, charming and forgettable, showing every sign of having been written when the author was only 23. It starts out engagingly enough, the young female narrator telling of her love for kitchens: "White tile catching the light (ting! ting!)."

Our heroine, Mikage, has recently been orphaned; her grandmother has died; her parents passed on long ago. A boy she knows, Yuichi, asks her to come live with him and his mother, Eriko. Mikage cannot take her eyes off Yuichi; he seems to glow with white light.

When Eriko appears, she is so beautiful Mikage is stunned. As it turns out, Eriko is a transsexual: She is Yuichi's father, and changed sex many years ago when Yuichi's mother died. This circumstance is treated with no particular thought or examination; it just *is.*

Mikage moves in with them, sleeping on the huge couch. The kitchen passes inspection, and Mikage begins to cook in it the very next day. "That whole summer I went about it with a crazed enthusiasm: cooking, cooking, cooking. . . . And if something came out wrong I'd do it over till I got it right. Complicated omelettes, beautifully shaped vegetables cooked in broth, tempura—it took a fair amount of work to make these things."

Later on, rather abruptly, we are informed that Mikage has moved out and that Eriko has been dead for a month. Yuichi is in mourning; he and Mikage are both orphans now, yearning for each other chastely, dreaming at one point (amazing!) the same vaguely psychic dream.

The release of information to the reader seems unskilled, or immature, weak in narrative or plot. But that's helpful for establishing and holding the central mood of the *very* innocent yearning of the two orphans for each other; there's no story to get in the way.

It's entertaining when Yuichi's former girlfriend shows up at Mikage's work (she is suddenly revealed to have had a job for some time now, as an assistant to a famous cooking teacher), although Mikage rather too easily maintains the upper hand in the confrontation. "When I imagined the workings of her mind, the senseless anger that spurred her to come here," Mikage reflects, "I pitied her from the bottom of my heart."

Later on, separated from Yuichi, Mikage decides to surprise him with *katsudon* pork and rice. That is, she delivers some takeout as proof of her love. It's actually quite sweet.

The title novella is only 105 pages long, so another story is included, **"Moonlight Shadow,"** which shares similar themes with the first. "A lover should die after a long lifetime. I lost Hitoshi at the age of twenty, and I suffered from it so much that I felt as if my own life had stopped . . . I loved Hitoshi—I loved Hitoshi more than life itself."

OK, so we're young here. Really young. We're no Raymond Radiguet (whose *Count D'Orgel* is probably the best 20th-Century novel by anyone around the age of 21). There is really no point, either, in comparing Yoshimoto at this point in her development to Haruki Murakami.

The similarly young Japanese-American writer Cynthia Kadohata might be the best reference point. Both share a certain innocent likability in their writing—not to be underestimated or dismissed—along with a certain insipidity.

In Japan, the notion of being an orphan may have different, much more harrowing connotations than it has over here. Early on in **Kitchen,** Mikage says, "I was tied to no creature in the world, I could go anywhere, do anything. It was dizzying."

In American culture, such a situation, however sad, is often seen as liberating, giving one the opportunity to reinvent oneself, conquer the world. In Japan, the portrayal of Mikage's situation may have satisfied some deep, resonant idealized identification, even longing, in the book-buying public.

Family is everything. But family, whether in the form of relatives, employer or school, may not continue to be everything in the brave new future, and it is this possibility of breaking free, of individuality in the Western sense, that Mikage represents. And yet, Mikage does not choose this fate, she is innocent, and in fact, she spends much of her time bemoaning the loss of family connection. Consciously, at least, she believes she misses this comforting tie. She tells herself (and the reader) she does. The truth may be much more complex. She can have it both ways. And she thus serves as a bridge between reassuring order and frightening disorder (which is not without its allure). She is both as blameless and as innocently subversive as Holden Caulfield was over here in 1951 and has been ever since.

The phenomenal success of **Kitchen** in Japan (published there in 1987) is therefore easily understandable. If "Bananamania" is exportable to the United States, I think it will be largely on the basis of this marketable, pleasurable name, Banana Yoshimoto. It has the sound of fun.

An excerpt from *Kitchen*

"Hey, look! Isn't that a pretty moon?" Yuichi pointed to the winter moon with his chin.

"Oh, isn't it," I said sarcastically (his diversionary tactics were so obvious), but as I stepped into the building I turned to glance at it. It was almost full and shed an incredible brightness.

In the elevator on the way up, Yuichi said, "Of course there's a relationship."

"Between what?"

"Don't you think that seeing such a beautiful moon influences what one cooks? But not in the sense of 'moon-viewing *udon*,' for instance."

The elevator stopped with a little jerk. When he said that, my heart faltered for an instant. He spoke as if he knew my very soul. As we walked to the door, I asked, "In what sense then? In a more profound way?"

"Yes, yes. In a more human sense, you know?"

"I agree. That's absolutely true," I said without hesitation. If they asked a hundred people on a quiz show, a hundred voices would reverberate as one: "Yes! Yes! It's true!"

"You know that I think of you as an artist. For you cooking is an art. You really do love to work in the kitchen. Of course you do. Good thing, too."

Yuichi agreed with himself again and again, carrying on a one-man conversation. I said, smiling, "You're just like a child."

A moment before, my heart had seemed to stop. Now that feeling voiced itself in my mind: If Yuichi is with me, I need nothing else. It flashed for only an instant, but it left me extremely confused, dazzled as I was by the light given off by his eyes.

Banana Yoshimoto, in Kitchen, *translated by Megan Backus, Grove Press, 1993.*

Elizabeth Hanson   (review date 17 January 1993)

SOURCE: "Hold the Tofu," in *The New York Times Book Review,* January 17, 1993, p. 18.

[*In the review below, Hanson values* Kitchen *as a work about modern, young Japanese.*]

A Japanese maxim warns that "A gentleman does not go near a kitchen." Traditionally a cramped, dingy place—

even in an otherwise well-appointed home—the old-fashioned kitchen revealed the low status of the women who spent much of their time there. Yet today, though still small by American standards and still largely the domain of women, kitchens are the showcases of Japanese consumer affluence.

Banana Yoshimoto's first novel evokes this modern opulence even in its title, which uses the trendy English loanword *kitchin* rather than the Japanese term, *daidokoro.* Ms. Yoshimoto was all of 24 years old when *Kitchen* was published in Japan in 1988; with its kooky young woman protagonist, Mikage Sakurai, the novel—a best seller that is now in its 57th printing—clearly has spoken to the author's contemporaries.

"The place I like best in this world is the kitchen," Mikage announces in the very first line. "I love even incredibly dirty kitchens to distraction—vegetable droppings all over the floor, so dirty your slippers turn black on the bottom." Left alone in the world when her grandmother dies, Mikage finds that her saddest moods are dispelled by the chance to scrub a refrigerator or even glimpse a busy kitchen from the window of a bus. She is befriended by a young man, Yuichi Tanabe, and his glamorous transsexual "mother," Eriko, and in this household finds some peace—at least for a time.

"Moonlight Shadow," the less satisfying story that fills out this volume, tells of a mysterious stranger who leads the young woman narrator—her voice sounds exactly like that of Mikage Sakurai—to a reunion with her deceased boyfriend.

Unfortunately, the endearing characters and amusing scenes in Ms. Yoshimoto's work do not compensate for frequent bouts of sentimentality. The English text feels choppy—this may be due to the author's style rather than the translation—and the translator, Megan Backus, uses Americanisms that sometimes sound odd coming from the mouths of Japanese characters.

For English-language readers, the appeal of *Kitchen* lies in its portrayal of the lives of young Japanese. Here are characters who disdain traditional meals made of tofu and pickled vegetables and instead tuck into doughnuts, sandwiches from Kentucky Fried Chicken and pudding cups from the local mini-mart. Yuichi and Eriko offer Mikage a huge sofa to sleep on, not a futon, and gleefully fill their apartment with electronic gadgets. And Mikage herself typifies the confusion of young Japanese women, attracted as she is to kitchens and cooking as symbols of comfort and womanliness, yet trying to live independently.

Observing the women pupils at a cooking school, Mikage feels how different she is: "Those women lived their lives happily. They had been taught, probably by caring parents, not to exceed the boundaries of their happiness regardless of what they were doing. . . . What I mean by 'their happiness' is living a life untouched as much as possible by the knowledge that we are really, all of us, alone."

Deborah Garrison   (review date 25 January 1993)

SOURCE: "Day-O!" in *The New Yorker,* Vol. LXVIII, No. 49, January 25, 1993, pp. 109-10.

[*In the following review, Garrison perceives the novella* Kitchen *as a quirky and oddly upbeat examination of a young person's emotional trials.*]

Banana Yoshimoto's ***Kitchen*** is a tangy, imperfect little snack. The book, though it appears to be a short novel, is really a pair of stories—the first, called ***Kitchen,*** is just long enough, at a hundred and three pages, to be classed as a novella. A literary prize-winner and long-running best-seller in Japan a few years ago, it arrives here translated, somewhat doggedly, by Megan Backus and attended by a small but irresistible fanfare of cuteness. There's a photograph on the mint-and-dark-peach jacket of a bright-eyed Japanese girl in a white eyelet dress, her hair stylishly longer on one side than the other—someone it might be fun to know. She's not Banana, but the packaging doesn't entirely lie. The author was only twenty-four when ***Kitchen*** was first published, and reading it, along with its less ambitious companion, **"Moonlight Shadow,"** gives you the sense that you're meeting a real young woman, who is, among other things, cute. Both stories are told by a naïve, occasionally goofy first-person narrator, whose bursts of energetic resolve are as girlish as her cries of passionate despair.

What makes this girlishness palatable—what counterbalances it—is the author's preoccupation with grief. "When my grandmother died the other day, I was taken by surprise," Mikage, the twentyish heroine of ***Kitchen,*** explains at the start of her strange tale. "The fact that time continued to pass in the usual way in this apartment where I grew up, even though now I was here all alone, amazed me. It was total science fiction. The blackness of the cosmos." An only child whose parents died when she was little, Mikage was brought up by her grandmother. But her musings on her plight are mostly uplifting and practical in nature. She acknowledges, for example, the relief: "To live alone with an old person is terribly nerve-racking, and the healthier he or she is, the more one worries." She confesses the battier aspects of her search for comfort: "Steeped in a sadness so great I could barely cry . . . I pulled my futon into the deathly silent, gleaming kitchen"—and she sleeps there, curled like a forlorn family pet at the base of the refrigerator. "However!" she continues. "I couldn't exist like that. Reality is wonderful." She's the opposite of the depressive who masks pain under a noisy (and transparent) cheerfulness: she keeps telling you she's depressed, listless, and tearful, but she can't hide her essentially sunny nature.

Yoshimoto's writing isn't itself very complex; it skips lightly over the surface of even Mikage's darkest hours. But what she's trying to describe—happiness—*is* complex, and is much trickier to evoke convincingly than misery, maybe because the sources of true contentment are more obscure. Obviously, reality isn't as wonderful as Mikage claims: she is utterly without family, and she has to find a way to manage on her skimpy inheritance. But she is graced with the stubborn happiness of the survivor, which can crop up out of nowhere after a death in the family and thrive like a weed.

What also crops up out of nowhere for Mikage is an invitation to live, rent-free, at the Tanabe residence. Yuichi Tanabe, a reserved young man about Mikage's age, visits her after her grandmother's funeral and proposes that she come to live with him and his mother. (Yoshimoto's way of effecting this and all transitions is so matter-of-fact you can't decide whether it's charming or dopey. "*Dingdong.* Suddenly the doorbell rang," she writes.) Mikage's reaction to Yuichi's polite appearance on her threshold—"I couldn't take my eyes off him. I think I heard a spirit call my name"—is a bizarre blend of teeny-bopper and Zen: love at first sight, non-Western style. Mikage also takes an instant liking to Yuichi's stunningly pretty mother, who turns out, to the reader's baffled delight, to be a man. Yuichi delicately introduces the subject to Mikage with "Guess what else . . ." His mother was his father—before plastic surgery. This is a wonderful touch, not because it's played for laughs (it isn't) or because it's a big surprise (strangely, it's not that, either) but because it's a piece of superfluous inventiveness on the author's part; it lends everything around it an air of cheerful unreality that mirrors Mikage's state of mind.

> Yoshimoto's attraction to weirdness and her unpretentious approach to it—she's not trying to be hip, just faithful to her sense of people as they are—are what might make Western readers want more of her.
>
> —*Deborah Garrison*

Yoshimoto, for all her narrative exuberance, understands the one-step-forward, two-steps-back emotional indirectness of a young person in crisis. The death of Mikage's grandmother is only the prelude to the more shocking, untimely death of Yuichi's mother, and the news of it causes Mikage, who has since moved into her own place, to appreciate the powerful solace of her days at the Tanabes': of sleeping on their couch and hearing Yuichi's mom clatter in on her heels, humming a tune; of perfecting her cooking skills in their underutilized kitchen; of waking up in the middle of the night at the same time as Yuichi and comparing dreams with him. The reader learns of these moments only in retrospect because it is only in retrospect that Mikage comes into full possession of their significance. Most of *Kitchen* occurs not in real time but in mental hyperspace—the virtual rather than chronological aftermath in which events are digested and understanding is gained.

But the story finally seizes on a down-to-earth matter: whether Mikage and Yuichi, in their shared orphanhood, should become lovers or remain fast, sibling-like friends. Yoshimoto can't render it a very compelling question: the intimate rapport between Mikage and Yuichi simply fails to be as interesting as the lively, perfectly achieved completeness of Mikage taken by herself. Her outburst following a good long cry over her grandmother ("I implored the gods: Please, let me live"); her remark at the sight of clouds blowing around in a strong wind ("In this world there is no place for sadness")—these rarities will stay with the reader.

Mikage is, throughout, a little bit weird, and so are the other characters. Yoshimoto's attraction to weirdness and her unpretentious approach to it—she's not trying to be hip, just faithful to her sense of people as they are—are what might make Western readers want more of her. (Two novels and two collections of essays have come out in Japan since *Kitchen.*) And Banana Yoshimoto herself seems an odd one; it's hard to know what genus to put her in. She can't be called a Japanese counterpart of members of the American literary brat pack. She's not jaded enough—she's too adorably nerdy, and she's way too friendly. She's not a brat. In fact, she makes you wonder if bounce-and-shine is still a standard feature in the artistic youth of other nations; you just don't see too much of it around here. Yoshimoto even includes an afterword to the American edition of *Kitchen,* in which she expresses the hope that the book will be a balm to those who have known setbacks in their lives; there's a generous, therapeutic impulse somewhere inside this fiction writer. "Surely we will meet someday," she closes her message to the reader, "and until that day, I pray that you will live happily." Such graciousness feels weird, too—it's foreign, anyway. But why be wary of a kind wish?

Penelope Fitzgerald (review date 28 January 1993)

SOURCE: "Ninjo," in *London Review of Books,* Vol. 15, No. 2, January 28, 1993, p. 20.

[*An English novelist, biographer, and critic, Fitzgerald is the author of several novels, including* The Golden Child *(1977),* Offshore *(1979), and* Innocence *(1986). She is known for combining a humanistic approach and a compressed, witty narrative style in her fiction to reveal the strength and nobility of her characters as they cope with life in contemporary society. In the following review, she contends that the pieces included in* Kitchen *emphasize the theme of coping with loss.*]

Banana Yoshimoto contributes a respectful preface to her book [*Kitchen*], dedicating it to her publisher, and thanking the manager of the restaurant where she supported herself while she was writing it and the professors who voted her a prize—'it made me so very happy.' This dutifulness sounds traditional. Traditional, too, when you get to the novellas themselves, are the violent emotions restrained within cramped but manageable limits and the compelling need for analogy between the human predicament and the natural world. 'I understood it from the colour of the sky, the shape of the moon, the blackness of the night sky under which we passed.' 'The sky outside was a dull gray. Waves of clouds were being pushed around by the wind with amazing force. In this world there is no place for sadness.' 'The scratching of our pens mingled with the sound of raindrops beginning to fall in the transparent stillness of evening.'

But at the same time the two novellas in **Kitchen** are the work of an original, a truly determined individual. 'For a very long time,' Yoshimoto says, 'there was something I wanted to say in a novel, and I wanted, no matter what it took, to continue writing until I got the saying of it out of my system. This book is what resulted from that history of persistence.' When it first came out in Japan five years ago (the publishers tell us) the country was swept by Bananamania and **Kitchen** spent a year on the best-seller list. They also suggest that it recalls the early Marguerite Duras. This I don't quite see, although both writers are concerned with the formidable barriers of loneliness. Loneliness for Duras, however, is a personal disability which leaves her characters not communicating, but talking endlessly to themselves. For Yoshimoto, to feel lonely is to share the universal sense of mortality. 'Someday, without fail, everyone will disappear, scattered into the blackness of time,' she writes. 'The space that cannot be filled, no matter how cheerfully a child and an old person are living together—the deathly silence that panting in a corner of the room, pushes its way in like a shudder. I felt it very early, although no one told me about it.'

Mikage Sakurai, who tells her own story in **Kitchen,** is in fact left alone, when her grandmother dies, in their Tokyo apartment. She quits college to train as a catering instructress, and from this point of view can manage her life well enough, but feels she 'was tied by blood to no creature in this world'. Enter, with a ring on the doorbell, an unexpected saviour, Yuichi Tanabe, a college boy a year younger than herself. He works in the evenings at the shop where Mikage's grandmother had often bought flowers; he had adored the old lady, and now invites Mikage to come and live for as long as she wants to in his own home. The delicate relationship between the two, which never quite defines itself, is described, day by day, with a kind of touching persistence, as though the narrator's life depended on the reader understanding it exactly. Meanwhile the translation, with what accuracy I can't tell, alternates rather bewilderingly between the (more or less) contemporary and the magical. 'It sounds like I was possessed. His attitude was so totally "cool", though, I felt I could trust him. In the bleak gloom before my eyes (as it always is in cases of bewitchment), I saw a straight road leading from me to him. He seemed to glow with white light.'

Although she is anxious to govern her life by free will and choice, Mikage accepts his invitation almost without giving it thought. Yuichi, however, does not live alone, but with his mother, a dazzlingly beautiful woman, too strikingly dressed for any ordinary daytime job. She works, it turns out, in a nightclub, and, as Yuichi tells Mikage with barely concealed amusement, she is really his father. 'After my real mother died, Eriko quit her job, gathered me up, and asked herself: "What do I want to do now?" ' What 'she' decided was to 'become a woman'. With the help of a plastic surgeon she had 'everything done' with singular success, and with the money left over from the surgery she bought the nightclub. Here then is willpower in action. Eriko is presented as having true greatness, with

the physical attraction of greatness. Whatever Mikage feels, or doesn't feel, about Yuichi, she is certainly in love with Eriko. Both of them lie awake in anxiety until they hear the sound of humming and the click of high-heeled shoes as she comes back, sometimes drunk, in the small hours. But Eriko is murdered, stabbed by one of the club's unbalanced customers who fancied her as a woman. She manages, before she dies, to beat this man to death with the bar-bell. 'That makes us even.' Yuichi is proud that his mother (or father) died fighting. If the Tokyo police make any sort of enquiry, we don't hear about it. Violence, for this novelist, is not significant either socially or morally. Like everything else, it is a matter for the emotions. Both Yuichi and Mikage, left without their protector, experience a sickness to the depth of the soul, and the rest of their story is concerned with the ordeal of rehabilitation.

For Yoshimoto, to feel lonely is to share the universal sense of mortality.

—Penelope Fitzgerald

When Mikage first comes to live in the Tanabe household, she sleeps on an outsize sofa ('a dog too big to keep in Japan could stretch out across it sideways') next door to the kitchen. This kitchen is not the traditional 'Japanese room' of the apartment—that is kept for the TV. On the contrary, it has fluorescent lighting, a Silverstone frying pan and a German-made vegetable peeler, while in the fitted cupboards 'all kinds of plates silently awaited their turn'. To Mikage all kitchens are of importance. 'A kitchen,' she says, not at all ironically, 'represents some distant longing engraved on my soul.' She would like, when the time comes, to die in one, so that she could feel 'How good'. And from its opening paragraphs this novella proposes food and cooking as a metaphor for love. English readers got used to this device in Dickens—the supreme example is the fowl which Captain Cuttle cooks for Florence Dombey—but not to this strangely obsessive effect. Even in the depths of her grief for her grandmother's death (although she has the feeling that she isn't weeping for one sad thing, but rather for many), Mikage feels soothed by the sound of knives clattering and the voices of people at work the other side of a brightly-lit kitchen window. At the sight of it she implores the gods, after all, to let her live. During her stay at the Tanabes' she teaches herself to cook, driving herself to make her dishes resemble the illustrations in the book, or staring sometimes at a single red tomato, 'loving it for dear life'. When she is left living alone in the apartment with Yuichi, now an orphan like herself, they don't make love, they buy enormous quantities of food from the supermarket and eat for many hours. 'Deep-fried tofu, steamed greens, bean-thread with chicken (each of them with various sauces), chicken Kiev, sweet and sour pork, steamed Chinese dumplings . . .' Much of one's life history, Mikage reflects, is etched on the senses. A nightmare banquet

(Yuichi gets very drunk) cannot resolve the situation between them, but she has been right to recognise food's power. She is selected for her job as assistant to an august cookery instructress, in preference to the other candidates, for the singular reason that she lives on the edge, whereas the rest have been taught, 'probably by caring parents, not to exceed the boundaries of happiness'. When Yuichi goes missing and takes refuge in a country inn, Mikage climbs into his room by moonlight to bring him a pork-and-rice *katsudon* from the take-away. In this way, and in no other, she touches the springs of his grief. The *katsudon* is excellent, and 'the darkness no longer harbours death.'

"Moonlight Shadow" is the companion [story] to ***Kitchen.*** It is set in a provincial university town, so that instead of the skies of Tokyo you look for the soul's reflection at the river and its bridge and the rows of waterside houses 'which hung in a faint mist, as though submerged in an ocean of blue air'. The elements of ***Kitchen*** recur—the violent incident which is reported rather than seen directly, the very young protagonists whose emotional life is threatened almost before it has begun, the background of part-time jobs, college classes and tea-houses, the mysterious (and in this case magical) intervention of an odd woman. Hitoshi and Satsuki (still a schoolgirl) are student lovers. 'Children that we were, we hurt each other many times over,' but Yoshimoto effectively shows that for four years this could only be described as true love. They live on op-

posite sides of the river; the bridge is their meeting-place. Hitoshi has a younger brother, Hiiragi, who is regarded as eccentric. He, too, has a girlfriend, Yumiko. The four of them are often together. One night, when Hitoshi is giving Yumiko a lift home, both of them are killed in an accident on the bridge. As she does in ***Kitchen,*** Yoshimoto shows a brilliant, delicate discernment between the stages of the agonies of loss. These begin 'without a prospect in sight. Day after day went by, like losing one's mind bit by bit.' Satsuki feels that, at 20, she is undergoing one of the things it is 'better not to have to experience in a lifetime—abortion, prostitution, major illness'. (War is not mentioned. Yoshimoto was born in 1964.)

Satsuki's resource, rather than lying awake waiting for the sky to grow light, is an early-morning run. The Japanese national uniform is now a two-piece sweat suit, and she buys one, and a container for hot tea. Her run always takes her to the bridge, the fatal spot of the accident, but also, at the dawn hour, the most beautiful place in the city. Here, one morning out of so many which seem alike, she is 'spoken to' by a stranger asking to share her tea, a woman whose age can't be guessed, and who gives her name as Urara. Yoshimoto's technique in this story is less assured (though even more touching) than in ***Kitchen,*** and the reader sees through Urara as soon as her eyes are said to be 'knowing and serene'. She is the wise woman, necessary in many a fairy tale to assist chance or fate.

Since the 18-year-old Hiiragi has also lost his lover in the accident, Satsuki feels an affinity with him, and arranges to meet him in the coffee-shop of a department store. 'In he came, wearing a sailor-style girl's uniform, complete with middy blouse and skirt.' Hiiragi's sailor suit, like Eriko's cross-dressing, is unsettling, but the correct reaction is compassion. His classmates, it seems, are understanding, recognising that the suit belonged to his lost sweetheart. Both Satsuki and Hiiragi, then, are the victims of obsession, in need of deliverance from the dead who captivate them. Urara, waiting again by the bridge, tells Satsuki that, for an unexplained moment, the dimensions of time and space are going to shift: 'Got it?' To which Satsuki can only reply: 'Got it.' What she gets will be the spirit-seeing of the classic ghost story. It doesn't seem out of place. Throughout these two moving novellas Yoshimoto has concentrated less on crowded contemporary Japan than on *ninjo,* the impulses of the human heart.

Ian Buruma   (review date 12 August 1993)

"Weeping Tears of Nostalgia," in *The New York Review of Books,* Vol. XL, No. 14, August 12, 1993, pp. 29-30.

[*Buruma is a Dutch-born critic who has written several nonfiction works on Asian culture. In the following excerpt, he claims that* Kitchen *draws upon aspects of traditional Japanese literature and current popular tastes.*]

Japan can easily give the impression of a country of fag hags. Comic books for young girls feature beautiful youths falling in love with aristocratic men, or androgynous rock stars. Japanese girls like David Bowie at his most camp. The film of E. M. Forster's *Maurice* played to full houses, mostly of young girls. Luchino Visconti was a teen-age idol, as was his star, Helmut Berger. The most popular theater company for young girls is the all female Takarazuka, based in a dreamlike little spa near Osaka, with pink bridges and pink houses, and a large pink theater. One of the most popular Takarazuka roles—apart from Rhett Butler and Lieutenant Pinkerton—is that of a young woman at the court of Louis XVI, who grows up as a boy named Oscar. As a dashing military officer, Oscar falls in love with a Swedish aristocrat, who is already in love with Marie-Antoinette. But Oscar in turn is adored by her/his groom, who is unaware of his master's female identity. The play is entitled *Rose of Versailles.*

All this would be camp, if it were knowing. But it is not. Young Japanese girls appear to find the pink bridges, the gay romances, the rock stars in drag, the girls dressed as boys who fall in love with other boys, beautiful. *Akogare,* romantic longing, is the term they use for this dream world, far removed from the demands of reality. What would be the highest of camp in another context can become cute in Japan, redolent of childhood. It is rather like the chosen name of [Yoshimoto Banana]. Banana is the kind of sobriquet that would suit a Brazilian drag artist. But the publicity photograph of Yoshimoto Banana, hugging her little puppy dog, is cuteness personified. The fact that her father is the most famous philosopher of the 1960s new left gives her name an extra air of incongruousness, as though there were a young German novelist called Banana Habermas.

Yoshimoto Banana's extraordinary success—more than six million books were sold in two years, and she is still in her twenties—has made her so famous that the Japanese foreign ministry was handing out copies of her book to foreign visitors at the G-7 Summit in Tokyo. They may not realize what peculiar fantasies lurk behind Yoshimoto's cute exterior.

Yoshimoto Banana's stories are clearly related to the androgynous teen-age universe of Takarazuka and girls' comics. The characters in **Kitchen,** a book of two short stories, include a transsexual father and a boy who dresses up in his dead girlfriend's school uniform. Yet there is nothing overtly kinky about these transformations. In the first story, entitled **Kitchen,** a young girl called Mikage, who is left alone in the world after her grandmother dies, goes to live with Eriko, the transsexual, and his/her son, Yuichi. She more or less lives in their kitchen, cooking delicious food, trying to soothe her lonely heart. In a way, the kitchen is to Mikage what drag is to Eriko: a refuge from loneliness after the death of a loved one. Yuichi explains how his father became his mother:

> "After my real mother died, Eriko quit her job, gathered me up, and asked herself, 'What do I want to do now?' What she decided was, 'Become a woman.' She knew she'd never love anybody else. She says that before she became a woman she was very shy."

In the second story, entitled **"Moonlight Shadow,"** Hiiragi's taste for wearing his dead girlfriend's clothes is equally matter-of-fact. And it, too, is an escape from loneliness. His girlfriend, Yumiko, died in a car crash, together with his brother Hitoshi. Hitoshi's girlfriend is called Sat-

suki, and the story is told in her voice. She wants to know why Hiiragi insists on going around in Yumiko's school uniform:

> When I asked him if he wore it for sentimental reasons, he said that wasn't it. "Things are just things, they can't bring back the dead. It just makes me feel better."

What cooking is to Mikage, jogging is to Satsuki. As Satsuki says: "His sailor outfit—my jogging. They served exactly the same purpose. . . . Neither recourse was anything more than a way of trying to lend some life to a shriveled spirit. It was a way to divert our minds, to kill time."

The Italian scholar Giorgio Amitrano pointed out the connection with girls' comics in his introduction to the German edition of **Kitchen.** He wrote that Yoshimoto's stories, with their odd sexual disguises and morbid emotions, are not only like many Japanese girls' comics, but also owe much to horror movies and the impressionistic style of Kawabata Yasunari's novels. This is more weight than the book can possibly carry, but the point is well taken. For a fascination for horror and death is as much part of girls' comics as the cuteness and androgynous fantasies.

The tone of Yoshimoto's stories is strange, for it veers from childlike naiveté to flights of bizarre fancy, which is just like most Japanese comic books for teen-agers. Sometimes her prose is direct and simple, and sometimes it reads like a young girl's diary, filled with poetic sadness: "Suddenly, to see that the world was so large, the cosmos so black. The unbounded fascination of it, the unbounded loneliness . . ."

Children often dream of flying out the window of their

Lucy North on *Kitchen:*

Both stories [in *Kitchen*] are modern fairy tales, told in the sometimes cheerful, sometimes despairing voices of young girls who have suffered the loss of someone dear (a grandmother in the first; a boyfriend in the second), and who overcome that loss and face up to "carrying on." Underneath the stories' simplicity, it is possible to discern gentle explorations of gender. Both have as subsidiary figures a person who blurs gender boundaries; in *Kitchen* it is Eriko, a beautiful, nurturing, powerful mother who was once a man; in "Moonlight Shadow" it is a boy who wears his dead girlfriend's school uniform. This theme of androgyny is an important trace from young girls' comic books, which have some cultural if not literary significance in Japan, and some of whose writers are taken increasingly seriously by feminist critics. There are also important messages for life: how to deal with obsessions, how to nurture others and live for oneself at the same time, how to be generous, how to use one's talents, and how to be strong.

Lucy North, in her review of Kitchen, *in* Belles Lettres, *Spring 1993.*

bedrooms, following some fairy or another, to a never-never land without parents, to a new family of children and freaks. Yoshimoto's characters are a bit like the children in such tales—except that they are not children; they just dream like children. Instead of fathers and mothers, there are the surrogate fathers and brothers, dressed in women's clothes.

But neither of her stories celebrates or even suggests new sexual possibilities, as one might assume. Indeed, sex, like real parents and siblings, is absent. Yuichi never becomes Mikage's lover, and neither does Hiiragi in Satsuki's case. Not sex but death permeates both tales: the death of Eriko, stabbed by a mad suitor; the death of Mikage's grandmother; and the deaths of Satsuki's boyfriend and Hiiragi's girlfriend. Death, loss, the melancholy fleetingness of life, these are brooded over endlessly with the feverish sensibility of Victorian children's tales. This is where **Kitchen** is both contemporary and very traditional—hence, perhaps, the perceived shades of Kawabata, who, incidentally, wrote some of his stories for an audience of young girls. But it is a pop version of Kawabata, as though *The Izu Dancer,* or *Snow Country,* were written for the Takarazuka theater.

The two most common phrases in classical Japanese literature, as well as in modern pop songs and in Yoshimoto's book, are sadness (*kanashimi*), and nostalgia (*natsukashisa*). Translated into English, this can sound odd: "The sound of his voice made me want to weep with nostalgia." Or: "Somewhere deep in my heart I felt I had known her long ago, and the reunion made me feel so nostalgic I wanted to weep tears of joy." Weeping tears of nostalgia is not something one comes across often in Western literature. Not that the emotion doesn't exist, but it is not usually so histrionically expressed; or rather, what sounds histrionic in English is perfectly ordinary in Japanese. Perhaps nostalgic isn't even quite the right word for *natsukashii,* but I wouldn't know of a better one.

Nostalgia is closely linked to that other key element of Japanese aesthetics: *mono no aware,* the sadness of things, *lacrimae rerum.* Sadness about the transience of life, is, in Japanese art, a thing of beauty. Again, like nostalgia, it is not easy to translate. But you find instances of it all through Yoshimoto's book: "When I finished reading I carefully refolded the letter. The smell of Eriko's favorite perfume tugged at my heart. This, too, will disappear after the letter is opened a few more times, I thought. That was hardest of all."

Nostalgia is one reason why so much in Japanese art is about reliving the past, or fixing the flow of time, as in a haiku. The ghosts of the dead appear in Noh plays, rather as Christ did to his disciples after the crucifixion. Sometimes they return to torment or exact their revenge, and sometimes to liberate the living from being haunted by death. And sometimes just to say goodbye. In **"Moonlight Shadow,"** Satsuki sees her dead boyfriend for one last time, when he appears one night on a river bank: "My tears fell like rain; all I could do was stare at him. Hitoshi looked sadly back at me. I wished time could stop—but with the first rays of the rising sun everything slowly began to fade away."

The beautiful sadness of things is linked to the Japanese cult of purity, of uncorrupted youth, of the cherry blossom in full bloom. It is the fleetingness of the cherry blossom's life (about a week in Japan), and the speed at which decay and corruption spoil the pure beauty of a young boy or girl, that bring on the sense of exquisite sadness. Here is where classical Japanese aesthetics meets the world of Takarazuka, girls' comics, and Yoshimoto's stories. For in all these instances, there is a deep nostalgia for the purity of youth, before sex roles are clearly defined, before social hypocrisy corrupts, before the rot sets in. In Japanese fiction of the seventeenth and eighteenth century, homosexuality was often celebrated for this reason: boys' love was considered to be purer than the heterosexual kind; it was uncontaminated by the demands of reproduction and other family duties.

Since family duties are (or at any rate were) particularly onerous in Japan and the sexes so rigidly defined, it is no wonder that young girls so often long to stop time, and retreat into a fantasy world of purity, androgyny, and prepubescence. Yet, of course, women have written about sexual love. Lady Murasaki wrote about little else in her *Tale of Genji.* But even she, who still enjoyed a high status in the rarefied sphere of the Heian court, was filled with sadness: she pined, she longed, she was nostalgic. Since then the status of Japanese women steadily declined and women's stories, whether written by women or men, became sadder and sadder. Love so often ended in tragedy, because there was no room in Japanese society for love. Marriage had nothing to do with romantic love. And women who loved outside the home, in fiction and in fact, overstepped their social borders, and their passion had to end in death. Sex, in the fiction of the Edo period (1603-1867), was almost entirely confined to the licensed quarters. But only men wrote about this floating world of paid love. Ihara Saikaku's *The Life of an Amorous Woman* (1686) is one of the masterpieces of this genre. Women, being confined to the brothel or the home, hardly wrote anything at all. They were the sacrificial victims of love in the male imagination, and often in reality too.

Love, wrote Tanizaki Junichiro in 1932, was liberated for the Japanese by European literature. He meant that romantic love in modern Japan had become a serious subject, not an excuse for dramatic suicide. Before there was only sex, with prostitutes, actors, boys; now sexual love would strike a blow for individual freedom. Women writers took up this theme too. But it is interesting that one of the greatest literary masterpieces of the early modern period (and indeed of modern Japanese literature *tout court*) should still be so traditional, in content and in form. It is a novella, entitled *Growing Up,* written by Higuchi Ichiyo and published in 1895. It is the story of a young girl growing up in a licensed quarter of Tokyo. What makes her sexual awakening, her growing up, so sad is that we know how she will end up, in the brothel with her elder sister. Freedom, as this story shows, belongs to the child. The loss of innocence means bondage not freedom. To become a woman is to enter the prison that society has provided, in this case a whorehouse, but it could just as well have been the home.

Things have changed since 1896, to be sure. Japanese women have more freedom than ever before. One of the most remarkable statistics of modern Japan is that since a few years ago, more women than men initiated divorce proceedings. (In Higuchi Ichiyo's time, a woman did not even have the right to ask for a divorce.) And yet, as far as sexual love is concerned, things have not changed as much as it may seem. For the alternative to pure sex is still very often a sad nostalgia for lost innocence.

What has changed is that the description of sex, from a predatory point of view, is no longer a male preserve. A young woman writer called Yamada Emi made her reputation by writing novels about working as a dominatrix in an SM club, and her passion for black men. In *Bedtime Eyes,* she describes her lover, a black GI, as a sweating sex object. His character is as flat and featureless as the courtesans in pornographic wood block prints of the Edo period. Foreigners, and especially black men, have taken the place of prostitutes in the Japanese erotic imagination. A recent nonfiction best seller, entitled *Yellow Cab,* by Ieda Shoko, featured examples of wild sexual adventures enjoyed by Japanese women visiting New York. This is not the love that Tanizaki talked about. But at least it is women doing all the talking.

Sex with foreigners, in fantasy or in fact, is a long way from the pink dreams of innocent gender-bending. And yet there is a connection. Just as the licensed quarters were a traditional escape for men from the duties of family life, sexual adventurism overseas has become a modern escape for many independent women. Marriage for most Japanese women is still a social trap, commonly known as "the graveyard of life." It means the end of a career, of economic independence. And since heterosexual love in Japan usually means marriage, an increasing number of career women are stuck with celibacy, with or without trips abroad.

The alternative is of course the sexless intimacy of the fag hag and her chosen friends. The heroines of Yoshimoto's fiction are not exactly fag hags, nor are they innocent. Mikage and Satsuki are young women. But grown-up sexual relationships are still beyond their grasp. Instead, in the security of their private kitchens, they dream nostalgic dreams, and shed melancholy tears about the passing of time. This is the stuff of great Japanese poetry, and absolute kitsch. Yoshimoto Banana is not yet a mistress of poetry, but she is a past master of kitsch.

Publishers Weekly (review date 13 December 1993)

SOURCE: A review of *NP* in *Publishers Weekly,* Vol. 240, No. 50, December 13, 1993, p. 61.

[*In the following review, the critic describes* NP *as "ultimately unsatisfying."*]

Japanese novelist Yoshimoto follows her well-received *Kitchen* with [*NP,*] an off-beat, intriguing, but ultimately unsatisfying tale about incest, suicide and broken relationships. *NP* (after an old, sad song titled "North Point") is the name of a short-story collection published in America by celebrated émigré writer Sarao Takase. The book

seems, as one character says, to be cursed: Takase committed suicide, as did three would-be Japanese translators. Four years after the death of her boyfriend, who was the last of these translators, narrator Kazami Kano becomes involved with Takase's children, the twins Saki and Otohiko, and Otohiko's girlfriend, the willowy, messed up Sui Minowa. All three of them are obsessed with *NP* and particularly one story about a man's affair with a young girl whom he later discovers is his daughter—a thinly veiled description of Takase's affair with Minowa. With the ghostly figure of Takase, the four young people make for a messy stew of incest, lust and obsession that is eventually brought to a head by Minowa's shattering discovery that she is pregnant by Otohiko. Yoshimoto weaves some lyrical writing and philosophical intimations of the hand of fate into her minimalist prose, but on balance this story and its narcissistic characters fail to evoke much sympathy.

Donna Seaman (review date 1 February 1994)

SOURCE: A review of *NP,* in *Booklist,* Vol. 90, No. 11, February 1, 1994, p. 996.

[*In the following review, Seaman provides a positive assessment of* NP.]

Kitchen was a surprise hit last year for young Tokyo author Yoshimoto, so expectations will be high for this taut little melodrama. Yoshimoto has a distinctively pop, bemused, and telegraphic writing style. Her new novel's enigmatic title, ***NP,*** stands for "North Point," a sad old song that was a favorite of a writer named Sarao Takase, who used it as the title of a collection of 97 stories. After his suicide, a 98th story surfaces and becomes, or at least is rumored to be, the catalyst for two more suicides. Those deaths, and the 98th story's incestuous theme, set the fateful tone for several tense little romances. The narrator, a pretty young woman named Kazami, is amusing, sensitive, and high-strung. She becomes fascinated with Sarao Takase's children: the twins, Saki and Otohiko, and Sui, their half sister and, problematically, Otohiko's lover. Kazami finds herself attracted both to Sui, which surprises her, since she has never been in love with a woman before, and to Otohiko. Moments of telepathy and extravagant behavior lend a kooky air of mysticism and spontaneity to the proceedings and deepen our wonder at the dangers and idiosyncrasies of love. Yoshimoto's fans won't be disappointed.

Despite Yoshimoto's simple yet effective style and the challenging themes of incest, religion, and lesbianism, the youthful characters seem too wooden to allow [*NP*] to develop successfully.

—*David A. Beronä, in a review of* NP, *in* Library Journal, *January, 1994.*

David Galef   (review date 27 February 1994)

SOURCE: "Jinxed," in *The New York Times Book Review,* February 27, 1994, p. 23.

[In the following review, Galef argues that NP *suffers from superficiality and poor writing.]*

Like comic books for businessmen and green-tea ice cream, Banana Yoshimoto is a Japanese phenomenon that Americans may find difficult to understand. Though her previous novel, **Kitchen,** got mixed reviews in the United States, it was a best seller in Tokyo, and she is particularly attractive to the teen-age and young-adult set. Her protagonists tend to be young women adrift, sliding away from family into sensuous romance. The loosely constructed episodes are meant to evoke a mood of what the Japanese call "aware," a contemplative sadness akin to the original meaning of melancholy. In between are pregnant conversations, strange coincidences, erotic interludes and lyrical passages on the weather.

N.P., described as a novel, is actually a series of stories. A Japanese writer named Sarao Takase has completed a collection of 97 stories, also called *N.P.,* before committing suicide. But a 98th story is discovered after his death, and whoever translates it seems as doomed as Takase. The protagonist and narrator, a young woman named Kazami Kano, had a boyfriend, Shoji, who died in the attempt.

Drawn into Takase's world, Kazami is haunted by Takase's twin children, Otohiko and Saki. Also involved is Sui Minowa, an illegitimate daughter of Takase who embodies an odd mixture of mysticism and eros. The characters and incidents are light constructs meant to support a yearning for a return to some primal innocence; unfortunately they more often evoke childish wistfulness, a much shallower emotion.

Ms. Yoshimoto updates what is actually a traditional evocation of "aware" with a hip sensibility. In **Kitchen,** the twist was that the mother figure was really a father after a sex-change operation. In *N.P.* the underlying dynamic is incest, which also is the subject of Takase's 98th story. Takase turns out to have slept with his daughter Sui, who eventually gets pregnant by her half-brother, Otohiko. Kazami herself is also more than a little in love with Sui, a feeling eventually reciprocated—and the source of even more wistfulness, as Kazami recounts the strange events of this one summer.

Complicating the plot, and adding another metafictional layer, is the existence of a 99th story by Takase. This sketch concerns a man who cannot communicate with the wife and children he has abandoned. Kazami's father, it emerges, ran off with another woman, one reason that Kazami feels such an odd affinity with the Takase ménage. The desertions are in a sense balanced by new unions, though, ultimately, a sense of longing remains.

The problem with these otherwise serious matters is the lack of depth in the narrative. Repeatedly, Kazami will describe a simple coffee-shop scene or a brief conversation and exclaim over the sadness or strangeness of it. For instance, after Kazami and Saki agree to meet again, Kazami encircles the exchange with an air of pseudo-mystery:

"What had just happened, mental telepathy?" Glances always spell volumes. Too often, the mood seems prepackaged.

A more serious flaw is the prose itself. There are too many banalities like "a chill ran down my spine" and "some cruel, twisted fate." The translation by Ann Sherif is not entirely at fault in finding English equivalents for this Japanese mass-market version of melancholy. As for the origin of the title, we are told only that "N.P." stands for "North Point," the name of an old song, "a very sad one." Giving it pop lyrics is no improvement.

Meg Cohen   (review date March 1994)

SOURCE: "Top Banana," in *Harper's Bazaar,* No. 3388, March, 1994, p. 170.

[In the following review, Cohen offers praise for NP.]

When Banana Yoshimoto's novella **Kitchen** arrived on the American literary scene last year, many readers discovered a new soul mate. First published in Japan in 1987, it was praised for its artful simplicity and whimsical style; Yoshimoto proved to be a master storyteller with a lot of heart. And with the publication of her new book, *NP,* she has ventured out of the familiar confines of the kitchen and into a more restless, but no less magical, world.

Set in Japan, *NP* takes its title from a collection of 97 stories penned—in English—by a celebrated Japanese writer living in Boston. When a 98th story surfaces after the author's death, so does a distressing pattern: Anyone who tries to translate it into Japanese dies inexplicably. Kazami Kano, the novel's central character, is one of two people in possession of this cursed chapter (it was left to her when her boyfriend committed suicide while attempting the translation). "When I'm reading it," she confesses, "I always get this feeling of a thick, hot liquid brewing in my heart. A new universe enters my body, and takes on a life of its own within me."

Through the writings Kazami befriends the dead author's two children and his tragic young lover. As their lives become irrevocably intertwined, their friendship is challenged by powerful emotions: love, grief, need, dependence, fear, and passion. These four friends are bound to a common destiny through their shared knowledge of *NP.*

The novel's strength lies in Yoshimoto's insightful prose; her ability to make everyday events seem romantic is a rare gift. Her characters possess a discerning maturity for people in their early 20s, which lends a fantastical, almost timeless quality to the narration. Since **Kitchen** put America in such a state of Bananamania, it's not surprising that Yoshimoto has chosen to infuse *NP* with numerous American elements. However, it's ironic that the book centers around the danger involved in translating English into Japanese, when, in fact, Yoshimoto herself writes *only* in Japanese. But *NP,* with its eccentric plot twists and charming superstition, proves not only that Yoshimoto has broken the language barrier but also that there's plenty more where this came from.

Additional coverage of Yoshimoto's life and career is contained in the following source published by Gale Research: *Contemporary Authors*, Vol. 144.

☐ Contemporary Literary Criticism

Indexes

Literary Criticism Series
Cumulative Author Index
Cumulative Topic Index
Cumulative Nationality Index
Title Index, Volume 84

How to Use This Index

The main references

Calvino, Italo
1923-1985.....CLC 5, 8, 11, 22, 33, 39,
73; SSC 3

list all author entries in the following Gale Literary Criticism series:

BLC = *Black Literature Criticism*
CLC = *Contemporary Literary Criticism*
CLR = *Children's Literature Review*
CMLC = *Classical and Medieval Literature Criticism*
DA = *DISCovering Authors*
DC = *Drama Criticism*
HLC = *Hispanic Literature Criticism*
LC = *Literature Criticism from 1400 to 1800*
NCLC = *Nineteenth-Century Literature Criticism*
PC = *Poetry Criticism*
SSC = *Short Story Criticism*
TCLC = *Twentieth-Century Literary Criticism*
WLC = *World Literature Criticism, 1500 to the Present*

The cross-references

See also CANR 23; CA 85-88;
obituary CA 116

list all author entries in the following Gale biographical and literary sources:

AAYA = *Authors & Artists for Young Adults*
AITN = *Authors in the News*
BEST = *Bestsellers*
BW = *Black Writers*
CA = *Contemporary Authors*
CAAS = *Contemporary Authors Autobiography Series*
CABS = *Contemporary Authors Bibliographical Series*
CANR = *Contemporary Authors New Revision Series*
CAP = *Contemporary Authors Permanent Series*
CDALB = *Concise Dictionary of American Literary Biography*
CDBLB = *Concise Dictionary of British Literary Biography*
DLB = *Dictionary of Literary Biography*
DLBD = *Dictionary of Literary Biography Documentary Series*
DLBY = *Dictionary of Literary Biography Yearbook*
HW = *Hispanic Writers*
JRDA = *Junior DISCovering Authors*
MAICYA = *Major Authors and Illustrators for Children and Young Adults*
MTCW = *Major 20th-Century Writers*
NNAL = *Native North American Literature*
SAAS = *Something about the Author Autobiography Series*
SATA = *Something about the Author*
YABC = *Yesterday's Authors of Books for Children*

Literary Criticism Series
Cumulative Author Index

Barker, Harley Granville
See Granville-Barker, Harley
See also DLB 10

Barker, Howard 1946- . . . . **CLC 37**
See also CA 102; DLB 13

Barker, Pat 1943- . . . . **CLC 32**
See also CA 117; 122

Barlow, Joel 1754-1812 . . . . **NCLC 23**
See also DLB 37

Barnard, Mary (Ethel) 1909- . . . . . . **CLC 48**
See also CA 21-22; CAP 2

Barnes, Djuna
1892-1982 . . . **CLC 3, 4, 8, 11, 29; SSC 3**
See also CA 9-12R; 107; CANR 16; DLB 4,
9, 45; MTCW

Barnes, Julian 1946- . . . . **CLC 42**
See also CA 102; CANR 19; DLBY 93

Barnes, Peter 1931- . . . . **CLC 5, 56**
See also CA 65-68; CAAS 12; CANR 33,
34; DLB 13; MTCW

Baroja (y Nessi), Pio
1872-1956 . . . . **TCLC 8; HLC**
See also CA 104

Baron, David
See Pinter, Harold

Baron Corvo
See Rolfe, Frederick (William Serafino
Austin Lewis Mary)

Barondess, Sue K(aufman)
1926-1977 . . . . **CLC 8**
See also Kaufman, Sue
See also CA 1-4R; 69-72; CANR 1

Baron de Teive
See Pessoa, Fernando (Antonio Nogueira)

Barres, Maurice 1862-1923 . . . . . . **TCLC 47**
See also DLB 123

Barreto, Afonso Henrique de Lima
See Lima Barreto, Afonso Henrique de

Barrett, (Roger) Syd 1946- . . . . **CLC 35**
See also Pink Floyd

Barrett, William (Christopher)
1913-1992 . . . . **CLC 27**
See also CA 13-16R; 139; CANR 11

Barrie, J(ames) M(atthew)
1860-1937 . . . . **TCLC 2**
See also CA 104; 136; CDBLB 1890-1914;
CLR 16; DLB 10, 141; MAICYA;
YABC 1

Barrington, Michael
See Moorcock, Michael (John)

Barrol, Grady
See Bograd, Larry

Barry, Mike
See Malzberg, Barry N(athaniel)

Barry, Philip 1896-1949 . . . . **TCLC 11**
See also CA 109; DLB 7

Bart, Andre Schwarz
See Schwarz-Bart, Andre

Barth, John (Simmons)
1930- . . . . . . **CLC 1, 2, 3, 5, 7, 9, 10, 14,
27, 51; SSC 10**
See also AITN 1, 2; CA 1-4R; CABS 1;
CANR 5, 23; DLB 2; MTCW

Barthelme, Donald
1931-1989 . . . . . . **CLC 1, 2, 3, 5, 6, 8, 13,
23, 46, 59; SSC 2**
See also CA 21-24R; 129; CANR 20;
DLB 2; DLBY 80, 89; MTCW; SATA 7,
62

Barthelme, Frederick 1943- . . . . **CLC 36**
See also CA 114; 122; DLBY 85

Barthes, Roland (Gerard)
1915-1980 . . . . **CLC 24, 83**
See also CA 130; 97-100; MTCW

Barzun, Jacques (Martin) 1907- . . . . **CLC 51**
See also CA 61-64; CANR 22

Bashevis, Isaac
See Singer, Isaac Bashevis

Bashkirtseff, Marie 1859-1884 . . . **NCLC 27**

Basho
See Matsuo Basho

Bass, Kingsley B., Jr.
See Bullins, Ed

Bass, Rick 1958- . . . . **CLC 79**
See also CA 126

Bassani, Giorgio 1916- . . . . **CLC 9**
See also CA 65-68; CANR 33; DLB 128;
MTCW

Bastos, Augusto (Antonio) Roa
See Roa Bastos, Augusto (Antonio)

Bataille, Georges 1897-1962 . . . . **CLC 29**
See also CA 101; 89-92

Bates, H(erbert) E(rnest)
1905-1974 . . . . **CLC 46; SSC 10**
See also CA 93-96; 45-48; CANR 34;
MTCW

Bauchart
See Camus, Albert

Baudelaire, Charles
1821-1867 . . . . . **NCLC 6, 29; DA; PC 1;
WLC**

Baudrillard, Jean 1929- . . . . **CLC 60**

Baum, L(yman) Frank 1856-1919 . . . **TCLC 7**
See also CA 108; 133; CLR 15; DLB 22;
JRDA; MAICYA; MTCW; SATA 18

Baum, Louis F.
See Baum, L(yman) Frank

Baumbach, Jonathan 1933- . . . . . . **CLC 6, 23**
See also CA 13-16R; CAAS 5; CANR 12;
DLBY 80; MTCW

Bausch, Richard (Carl) 1945- . . . . . . **CLC 51**
See also CA 101; CAAS 14; CANR 43;
DLB 130

Baxter, Charles 1947- . . . . **CLC 45, 78**
See also CA 57-60; CANR 40; DLB 130

Baxter, George Owen
See Faust, Frederick (Schiller)

Baxter, James K(eir) 1926-1972 . . . . **CLC 14**
See also CA 77-80

Baxter, John
See Hunt, E(verette) Howard, Jr.

Bayer, Sylvia
See Glassco, John

Beagle, Peter S(oyer) 1939- . . . . **CLC 7**
See also CA 9-12R; CANR 4; DLBY 80;
SATA 60

Bean, Normal
See Burroughs, Edgar Rice

Beard, Charles A(ustin)
1874-1948 . . . . **TCLC 15**
See also CA 115; DLB 17; SATA 18

Beardsley, Aubrey 1872-1898 . . . . . **NCLC 6**

Beattie, Ann
1947- . . . . **CLC 8, 13, 18, 40, 63; SSC 11**
See also BEST 90:2; CA 81-84; DLBY 82;
MTCW

Beattie, James 1735-1803 . . . . **NCLC 25**
See also DLB 109

Beauchamp, Kathleen Mansfield 1888-1923
See Mansfield, Katherine
See also CA 104; 134; DA

Beaumarchais, Pierre-Augustin Caron de
1732-1799 . . . . **DC 4**

**Beauvoir, Simone (Lucie Ernestine Marie
Bertrand) de**
1908-1986 . . . . **CLC 1, 2, 4, 8, 14, 31, 44,
50, 71; DA; WLC**
See also CA 9-12R; 118; CANR 28;
DLB 72; DLBY 86; MTCW

Becker, Jurek 1937- . . . . **CLC 7, 19**
See also CA 85-88; DLB 75

Becker, Walter 1950- . . . . **CLC 26**

Beckett, Samuel (Barclay)
1906-1989 . . . . . . **CLC 1, 2, 3, 4, 6, 9, 10,
11, 14, 18, 29, 57, 59, 83; DA; SSC 16;
WLC**
See also CA 5-8R; 130; CANR 33;
CDBLB 1945-1960; DLB 13, 15;
DLBY 90; MTCW

Beckford, William 1760-1844 . . . . **NCLC 16**
See also DLB 39

Beckman, Gunnel 1910- . . . . **CLC 26**
See also CA 33-36R; CANR 15; CLR 25;
MAICYA; SAAS 9; SATA 6

Becque, Henri 1837-1899 . . . . **NCLC 3**

Beddoes, Thomas Lovell
1803-1849 . . . . **NCLC 3**
See also DLB 96

Bedford, Donald F.
See Fearing, Kenneth (Flexner)

Beecher, Catharine Esther
1800-1878 . . . . **NCLC 30**
See also DLB 1

Beecher, John 1904-1980 . . . . **CLC 6**
See also AITN 1; CA 5-8R; 105; CANR 8

Beer, Johann 1655-1700 . . . . **LC 5**

Beer, Patricia 1924- . . . . **CLC 58**
See also CA 61-64; CANR 13; DLB 40

Beerbohm, Henry Maximilian
1872-1956 . . . . **TCLC 1, 24**
See also CA 104; DLB 34, 100

Begiebing, Robert J(ohn) 1946- . . . . . **CLC 70**
See also CA 122; CANR 40

Behan, Brendan
1923-1964 . . . . **CLC 1, 8, 11, 15, 79**
See also CA 73-76; CANR 33;
CDBLB 1945-1960; DLB 13; MTCW

Behn, Aphra
1640(?)-1689 . . . . **LC 1; DA; DC 4; WLC**
See also DLB 39, 80, 131

Behrman, S(amuel) N(athaniel)
1893-1973 . . . . **CLC 40**
See also CA 13-16; 45-48; CAP 1; DLB 7,
44

Belasco, David 1853-1931 . . . . **TCLC 3**
See also CA 104; DLB 7

Belcheva, Elisaveta 1893- . . . . **CLC 10**

Beldone, Phil "Cheech"
See Ellison, Harlan

Beleno
See Azuela, Mariano

Belinski, Vissarion Grigoryevich
1811-1848 . . . . **NCLC 5**

Belitt, Ben 1911- . . . . **CLC 22**
See also CA 13-16R; CAAS 4; CANR 7;
DLB 5

Bell, James Madison
1826-1902 . . . . **TCLC 43; BLC**
See also BW 1; CA 122; 124; DLB 50

Bell, Madison (Smartt) 1957- . . . . . . **CLC 41**
See also CA 111; CANR 28

Bell, Marvin (Hartley) 1937- . . . . . **CLC 8, 31**
See also CA 21-24R; CAAS 14; DLB 5;
MTCW

Bell, W. L. D.
See Mencken, H(enry) L(ouis)

Bellamy, Atwood C.
See Mencken, H(enry) L(ouis)

Bellamy, Edward 1850-1898 . . . . . . **NCLC 4**
See also DLB 12

Bellin, Edward J.
See Kuttner, Henry

Belloc, (Joseph) Hilaire (Pierre)
1870-1953 . . . . **TCLC 7, 18**
See also CA 106; DLB 19, 100, 141;
YABC 1

Belloc, Joseph Peter Rene Hilaire
See Belloc, (Joseph) Hilaire (Pierre)

Belloc, Joseph Pierre Hilaire
See Belloc, (Joseph) Hilaire (Pierre)

Belloc, M. A.
See Lowndes, Marie Adelaide (Belloc)

Bellow, Saul
1915- . . . . . . **CLC 1, 2, 3, 6, 8, 10, 13, 15,
25, 33, 34, 63, 79; DA; SSC 14; WLC**
See also AITN 2; BEST 89:3; CA 5-8R;
CABS 1; CANR 29; CDALB 1941-1968;
DLB 2, 28; DLBD 3; DLBY 82; MTCW

Belser, Reimond Karel Maria de
1929- . . . . **CLC 14**

Bely, Andrey . . . . **TCLC 7**
See also Bugayev, Boris Nikolayevich

Benary, Margot
See Benary-Isbert, Margot

Benary-Isbert, Margot 1889-1979 . . . **CLC 12**
See also CA 5-8R; 89-92; CANR 4;
CLR 12; MAICYA; SATA 2, 21

Benavente (y Martinez), Jacinto
1866-1954 . . . . **TCLC 3**
See also CA 106; 131; HW; MTCW

Benchley, Peter (Bradford)
1940- . . . . **CLC 4, 8**
See also AITN 2; CA 17-20R; CANR 12,
35; MTCW; SATA 3

Benchley, Robert (Charles)
1889-1945 . . . . **TCLC 1, 55**
See also CA 105; DLB 11

Benedikt, Michael 1935- . . . . **CLC 4, 14**
See also CA 13-16R; CANR 7; DLB 5

Benet, Juan 1927- . . . . **CLC 28**
See also CA 143

Benet, Stephen Vincent
1898-1943 . . . . **TCLC 7; SSC 10**
See also CA 104; DLB 4, 48, 102; YABC 1

Benet, William Rose 1886-1950 . . . **TCLC 28**
See also CA 118; DLB 45

Benford, Gregory (Albert) 1941- . . . . **CLC 52**
See also CA 69-72; CANR 12, 24;
DLBY 82

Bengtsson, Frans (Gunnar)
1894-1954 . . . . **TCLC 48**

Benjamin, David
See Slavitt, David R(ytman)

Benjamin, Lois
See Gould, Lois

Benjamin, Walter 1892-1940 . . . . . **TCLC 39**

Benn, Gottfried 1886-1956 . . . . **TCLC 3**
See also CA 106; DLB 56

Bennett, Alan 1934- . . . . **CLC 45, 77**
See also CA 103; CANR 35; MTCW

Bennett, (Enoch) Arnold
1867-1931 . . . . **TCLC 5, 20**
See also CA 106; CDBLB 1890-1914;
DLB 10, 34, 98

Bennett, Elizabeth
See Mitchell, Margaret (Munnerlyn)

Bennett, George Harold 1930-
See Bennett, Hal
See also BW 1; CA 97-100

Bennett, Hal . . . . **CLC 5**
See also Bennett, George Harold
See also DLB 33

Bennett, Jay 1912- . . . . **CLC 35**
See also AAYA 10; CA 69-72; CANR 11,
42; JRDA; SAAS 4; SATA 27, 41

Bennett, Louise (Simone)
1919- . . . . **CLC 28; BLC**
See also BW 2; DLB 117

Benson, E(dward) F(rederic)
1867-1940 . . . . **TCLC 27**
See also CA 114; DLB 135

Benson, Jackson J. 1930- . . . . **CLC 34**
See also CA 25-28R; DLB 111

Benson, Sally 1900-1972 . . . . **CLC 17**
See also CA 19-20; 37-40R; CAP 1;
SATA 1, 27, 35

Benson, Stella 1892-1933 . . . . **TCLC 17**
See also CA 117; DLB 36

Bentham, Jeremy 1748-1832 . . . . . **NCLC 38**
See also DLB 107

Bentley, E(dmund) C(lerihew)
1875-1956 . . . . **TCLC 12**
See also CA 108; DLB 70

Bentley, Eric (Russell) 1916- . . . . . . **CLC 24**
See also CA 5-8R; CANR 6

Beranger, Pierre Jean de
1780-1857 . . . . **NCLC 34**

Berger, Colonel
See Malraux, (Georges-)Andre

Berger, John (Peter) 1926- . . . . . . **CLC 2, 19**
See also CA 81-84; DLB 14

Berger, Melvin H. 1927- . . . . **CLC 12**
See also CA 5-8R; CANR 4; CLR 32;
SAAS 2; SATA 5

Berger, Thomas (Louis)
1924- . . . . **CLC 3, 5, 8, 11, 18, 38**
See also CA 1-4R; CANR 5, 28; DLB 2;
DLBY 80; MTCW

Bergman, (Ernst) Ingmar
1918- . . . . **CLC 16, 72**
See also CA 81-84; CANR 33

Bergson, Henri 1859-1941 . . . . **TCLC 32**

Bergstein, Eleanor 1938- . . . . **CLC 4**
See also CA 53-56; CANR 5

Berkoff, Steven 1937- . . . . **CLC 56**
See also CA 104

Bermant, Chaim (Icyk) 1929- . . . . . . **CLC 40**
See also CA 57-60; CANR 6, 31

Bern, Victoria
See Fisher, M(ary) F(rances) K(ennedy)

Bernanos, (Paul Louis) Georges
1888-1948 . . . . **TCLC 3**
See also CA 104; 130; DLB 72

Bernard, April 1956- . . . . **CLC 59**
See also CA 131

Berne, Victoria
See Fisher, M(ary) F(rances) K(ennedy)

Bernhard, Thomas
1931-1989 . . . . **CLC 3, 32, 61**
See also CA 85-88; 127; CANR 32;
DLB 85, 124; MTCW

Berrigan, Daniel 1921- . . . . **CLC 4**
See also CA 33-36R; CAAS 1; CANR 11,
43; DLB 5

Berrigan, Edmund Joseph Michael, Jr.
1934-1983
See Berrigan, Ted
See also CA 61-64; 110; CANR 14

Berrigan, Ted . . . . **CLC 37**
See also Berrigan, Edmund Joseph Michael,
Jr.
See also DLB 5

Berry, Charles Edward Anderson 1931-
See Berry, Chuck
See also CA 115

Berry, Chuck . . . . **CLC 17**
See also Berry, Charles Edward Anderson

Berry, Jonas
See Ashbery, John (Lawrence)

Berry, Wendell (Erdman)
1934- . . . . **CLC 4, 6, 8, 27, 46**
See also AITN 1; CA 73-76; DLB 5, 6

Berryman, John
1914-1972 . . . . . . **CLC 1, 2, 3, 4, 6, 8, 10,
13, 25, 62**
See also CA 13-16; 33-36R; CABS 2;
CANR 35; CAP 1; CDALB 1941-1968;
DLB 48; MTCW

Bertolucci, Bernardo 1940- . . . . **CLC 16**
See also CA 106

Bertrand, Aloysius 1807-1841 . . . . **NCLC 31**

Bertran de Born c. 1140-1215 . . . . . **CMLC 5**

Besant, Annie (Wood) 1847-1933 . . . **TCLC 9**
See also CA 105

Bessie, Alvah 1904-1985 . . . . **CLC 23**
See also CA 5-8R; 116; CANR 2; DLB 26

Bethlen, T. D.
See Silverberg, Robert

Beti, Mongo . . . . **CLC 27; BLC**
See also Biyidi, Alexandre

Betjeman, John
1906-1984 . . . . **CLC 2, 6, 10, 34, 43**
See also CA 9-12R; 112; CANR 33;
CDBLB 1945-1960; DLB 20; DLBY 84;
MTCW

Bettelheim, Bruno 1903-1990 . . . . . . **CLC 79**
See also CA 81-84; 131; CANR 23; MTCW

Betti, Ugo 1892-1953 . . . . **TCLC 5**
See also CA 104

Betts, Doris (Waugh) 1932- . . . . **CLC 3, 6, 28**
See also CA 13-16R; CANR 9; DLBY 82

Bevan, Alistair
See Roberts, Keith (John Kingston)

Beynon, John
See Harris, John (Wyndham Parkes Lucas)
Beynon

Bialik, Chaim Nachman
1873-1934 . . . . **TCLC 25**

Bickerstaff, Isaac
See Swift, Jonathan

Bidart, Frank 1939- . . . . **CLC 33**
See also CA 140

Bienek, Horst 1930- . . . . **CLC 7, 11**
See also CA 73-76; DLB 75

Bierce, Ambrose (Gwinett)
1842-1914(?) . . . . **TCLC 1, 7, 44; DA;
SSC 9; WLC**
See also CA 104; 139; CDALB 1865-1917;
DLB 11, 12, 23, 71, 74

Billings, Josh
See Shaw, Henry Wheeler

Billington, (Lady) Rachel (Mary)
1942- . . . . **CLC 43**
See also AITN 2; CA 33-36R; CANR 44

Binyon, T(imothy) J(ohn) 1936- . . . . **CLC 34**
See also CA 111; CANR 28

Bioy Casares, Adolfo
1914- . . . . **CLC 4, 8, 13; HLC**
See also CA 29-32R; CANR 19, 43;
DLB 113; HW; MTCW

Bird, C.
See Ellison, Harlan

Bird, Cordwainer
See Ellison, Harlan

Bird, Robert Montgomery
1806-1854 . . . . **NCLC 1**

Birney, (Alfred) Earle
1904- . . . . **CLC 1, 4, 6, 11**
See also CA 1-4R; CANR 5, 20; DLB 88;
MTCW

Bishop, Elizabeth
1911-1979 . . . . . . **CLC 1, 4, 9, 13, 15, 32;
DA; PC 3**
See also CA 5-8R; 89-92; CABS 2;
CANR 26; CDALB 1968-1988; DLB 5;
MTCW; SATA 24

Bishop, John 1935- . . . . **CLC 10**
See also CA 105

Bissett, Bill 1939- . . . . **CLC 18**
See also CA 69-72; CAAS 19; CANR 15;
DLB 53; MTCW

Bitov, Andrei (Georgievich) 1937- . . . **CLC 57**
See also CA 142

Biyidi, Alexandre 1932-
See Beti, Mongo
See also BW 1; CA 114; 124; MTCW

Bjarme, Brynjolf
See Ibsen, Henrik (Johan)

Bjornson, Bjornstjerne (Martinius)
1832-1910 . . . . **TCLC 7, 37**
See also CA 104

Black, Robert
See Holdstock, Robert P.

Blackburn, Paul 1926-1971 . . . . . . **CLC 9, 43**
See also CA 81-84; 33-36R; CANR 34;
DLB 16; DLBY 81

Black Elk 1863-1950 . . . . **TCLC 33**
See also CA 144

Black Hobart
See Sanders, (James) Ed(ward)

Blacklin, Malcolm
See Chambers, Aidan

Blackmore, R(ichard) D(oddridge)
1825-1900 . . . . **TCLC 27**
See also CA 120; DLB 18

Blackmur, R(ichard) P(almer)
1904-1965 . . . . **CLC 2, 24**
See also CA 11-12; 25-28R; CAP 1; DLB 63

Black Tarantula, The
See Acker, Kathy

Blackwood, Algernon (Henry)
1869-1951 . . . . **TCLC 5**
See also CA 105

Blackwood, Caroline 1931- . . . . **CLC 6, 9**
See also CA 85-88; CANR 32; DLB 14;
MTCW

Blade, Alexander
See Hamilton, Edmond; Silverberg, Robert

Blaga, Lucian 1895-1961 . . . . **CLC 75**

Blair, Eric (Arthur) 1903-1950
See Orwell, George
See also CA 104; 132; DA; MTCW;
SATA 29

Blais, Marie-Claire
1939- . . . . **CLC 2, 4, 6, 13, 22**
See also CA 21-24R; CAAS 4; CANR 38;
DLB 53; MTCW

Blaise, Clark 1940- . . . . **CLC 29**
See also AITN 2; CA 53-56; CAAS 3;
CANR 5; DLB 53

Blake, Nicholas
See Day Lewis, C(ecil)
See also DLB 77

Blake, William
1757-1827 . . . . . **NCLC 13, 37; DA; WLC**
See also CDBLB 1789-1832; DLB 93;
MAICYA; SATA 30

Blasco Ibanez, Vicente
1867-1928 . . . . **TCLC 12**
See also CA 110; 131; HW; MTCW

Blatty, William Peter 1928- . . . . **CLC 2**
See also CA 5-8R; CANR 9

Bleeck, Oliver
See Thomas, Ross (Elmore)

Blessing, Lee 1949- . . . . **CLC 54**

Blish, James (Benjamin)
1921-1975 . . . . **CLC 14**
See also CA 1-4R; 57-60; CANR 3; DLB 8;
MTCW; SATA 66

Bliss, Reginald
See Wells, H(erbert) G(eorge)

Blixen, Karen (Christentze Dinesen)
1885-1962
See Dinesen, Isak
See also CA 25-28; CANR 22; CAP 2;
MTCW; SATA 44

Bloch, Robert (Albert) 1917- . . . . **CLC 33**
See also CA 5-8R; CANR 5; DLB 44;
SATA 12

Blok, Alexander (Alexandrovich)
1880-1921 . . . . **TCLC 5**
See also CA 104

Blom, Jan
See Breytenbach, Breyten

Bloom, Harold 1930- . . . . **CLC 24**
See also CA 13-16R; CANR 39; DLB 67

Bloomfield, Aurelius
See Bourne, Randolph S(illiman)

Blount, Roy (Alton), Jr. 1941- . . . . . **CLC 38**
See also CA 53-56; CANR 10, 28; MTCW

Bloy, Leon 1846-1917 . . . . **TCLC 22**
See also CA 121; DLB 123

Blume, Judy (Sussman) 1938- . . . **CLC 12, 30**
See also AAYA 3; CA 29-32R; CANR 13,
37; CLR 2, 15; DLB 52; JRDA;
MAICYA; MTCW; SATA 2, 31

Blunden, Edmund (Charles)
1896-1974 . . . . **CLC 2, 56**
See also CA 17-18; 45-48; CAP 2; DLB 20,
100; MTCW

Bly, Robert (Elwood)
1926- . . . . **CLC 1, 2, 5, 10, 15, 38**
See also CA 5-8R; CANR 41; DLB 5;
MTCW

Boas, Franz 1858-1942 . . . . **TCLC 56**
See also CA 115

Bobette
See Simenon, Georges (Jacques Christian)

Boccaccio, Giovanni
1313-1375 . . . . **CMLC 13; SSC 10**

Bochco, Steven 1943- . . . . **CLC 35**
See also AAYA 11; CA 124; 138

Bodenheim, Maxwell 1892-1954 . . . **TCLC 44**
See also CA 110; DLB 9, 45

Bodker, Cecil 1927- . . . . **CLC 21**
See also CA 73-76; CANR 13, 44; CLR 23;
MAICYA; SATA 14

Boell, Heinrich (Theodor) 1917-1985
See Boll, Heinrich (Theodor)
See also CA 21-24R; 116; CANR 24; DA;
DLB 69; DLBY 85; MTCW

Boerne, Alfred
See Doeblin, Alfred

Bogan, Louise 1897-1970..... **CLC 4, 39, 46**
See also CA 73-76; 25-28R; CANR 33;
DLB 45; MTCW

Bogarde, Dirk .... **CLC 19**
See also Van Den Bogarde, Derek Jules
Gaspard Ulric Niven
See also DLB 14

Bogosian, Eric 1953- .... **CLC 45**
See also CA 138

Bograd, Larry 1953-............. **CLC 35**
See also CA 93-96; SATA 33

Boiardo, Matteo Maria 1441-1494 .... **LC 6**

Boileau-Despreaux, Nicolas
1636-1711 .... **LC 3**

Boland, Eavan (Aisling) 1944-... **CLC 40, 67**
See also CA 143; DLB 40

Boll, Heinrich (Theodor)
1917-1985 .... **CLC 2, 3, 6, 9, 11, 15, 27,
39, 72; WLC**
See also Boell, Heinrich (Theodor)
See also DLB 69; DLBY 85

Bolt, Lee
See Faust, Frederick (Schiller)

Bolt, Robert (Oxton) 1924- .... **CLC 14**
See also CA 17-20R; CANR 35; DLB 13;
MTCW

Bombet, Louis-Alexandre-Cesar
See Stendhal

Bomkauf
See Kaufman, Bob (Garnell)

Bonaventura................... **NCLC 35**
See also DLB 90

Bond, Edward 1934-...... **CLC 4, 6, 13, 23**
See also CA 25-28R; CANR 38; DLB 13;
MTCW

Bonham, Frank 1914-1989........ **CLC 12**
See also AAYA 1; CA 9-12R; CANR 4, 36;
JRDA; MAICYA; SAAS 3; SATA 1, 49,
62

Bonnefoy, Yves 1923-........ **CLC 9, 15, 58**
See also CA 85-88; CANR 33; MTCW

Bontemps, Arna(ud Wendell)
1902-1973 .... **CLC 1, 18; BLC**
See also BW 1; CA 1-4R; 41-44R; CANR 4,
35; CLR 6; DLB 48, 51; JRDA;
MAICYA; MTCW; SATA 2, 24, 44

Booth, Martin 1944-............. **CLC 13**
See also CA 93-96; CAAS 2

Booth, Philip 1925-............. **CLC 23**
See also CA 5-8R; CANR 5; DLBY 82

Booth, Wayne C(layson) 1921- ..... **CLC 24**
See also CA 1-4R; CAAS 5; CANR 3, 43;
DLB 67

Borchert, Wolfgang 1921-1947 ..... **TCLC 5**
See also CA 104; DLB 69, 124

Borel, Petrus 1809-1859........ **NCLC 41**

Borges, Jorge Luis
1899-1986 ... **CLC 1, 2, 3, 4, 6, 8, 9, 10,
13, 19, 44, 48, 83; DA; HLC; SSC 4;
WLC**
See also CA 21-24R; CANR 19, 33;
DLB 113; DLBY 86; HW; MTCW

Borowski, Tadeusz 1922-1951...... **TCLC 9**
See also CA 106

Borrow, George (Henry)
1803-1881 .... **NCLC 9**
See also DLB 21, 55

Bosman, Herman Charles
1905-1951 .... **TCLC 49**

Bosschere, Jean de 1878(?)-1953... **TCLC 19**
See also CA 115

Boswell, James
1740-1795 .... **LC 4; DA; WLC**
See also CDBLB 1660-1789; DLB 104, 142

Bottoms, David 1949-............. **CLC 53**
See also CA 105; CANR 22; DLB 120;
DLBY 83

Boucicault, Dion 1820-1890...... **NCLC 41**

Boucolon, Maryse 1937-
See Conde, Maryse
See also CA 110; CANR 30

Bourget, Paul (Charles Joseph)
1852-1935 .... **TCLC 12**
See also CA 107; DLB 123

Bourjaily, Vance (Nye) 1922- .... **CLC 8, 62**
See also CA 1-4R; CAAS 1; CANR 2;
DLB 2, 143

Bourne, Randolph S(illiman)
1886-1918 .... **TCLC 16**
See also CA 117; DLB 63

Bova, Ben(jamin William) 1932-.... **CLC 45**
See also CA 5-8R; CAAS 18; CANR 11;
CLR 3; DLBY 81; MAICYA; MTCW;
SATA 6, 68

Bowen, Elizabeth (Dorothea Cole)
1899-1973 ...... **CLC 1, 3, 6, 11, 15, 22;
SSC 3**
See also CA 17-18; 41-44R; CANR 35;
CAP 2; CDBLB 1945-1960; DLB 15;
MTCW

Bowering, George 1935-........ **CLC 15, 47**
See also CA 21-24R; CAAS 16; CANR 10;
DLB 53

Bowering, Marilyn R(uthe) 1949-... **CLC 32**
See also CA 101

Bowers, Edgar 1924- .... **CLC 9**
See also CA 5-8R; CANR 24; DLB 5

Bowie, David................... **CLC 17**
See also Jones, David Robert

Bowles, Jane (Sydney)
1917-1973 .... **CLC 3, 68**
See also CA 19-20; 41-44R; CAP 2

Bowles, Paul (Frederick)
1910- .... **CLC 1, 2, 19, 53; SSC 3**
See also CA 1-4R; CAAS 1; CANR 1, 19;
DLB 5, 6; MTCW

Box, Edgar
See Vidal, Gore

Boyd, Nancy
See Millay, Edna St. Vincent

Boyd, William 1952-........ **CLC 28, 53, 70**
See also CA 114; 120

Boyle, Kay
1902-1992 ..... **CLC 1, 5, 19, 58; SSC 5**
See also CA 13-16R; 140; CAAS 1;
CANR 29; DLB 4, 9, 48, 86; DLBY 93;
MTCW

Boyle, Mark
See Kienzle, William X(avier)

Boyle, Patrick 1905-1982.......... **CLC 19**
See also CA 127

Boyle, T. C.
See Boyle, T(homas) Coraghessan

Boyle, T(homas) Coraghessan
1948- .... **CLC 36, 55; SSC 16**
See also BEST 90:4; CA 120; CANR 44;
DLBY 86

Boz
See Dickens, Charles (John Huffam)

Brackenridge, Hugh Henry
1748-1816 .... **NCLC 7**
See also DLB 11, 37

Bradbury, Edward P.
See Moorcock, Michael (John)

Bradbury, Malcolm (Stanley)
1932- .... **CLC 32, 61**
See also CA 1-4R; CANR 1, 33; DLB 14;
MTCW

Bradbury, Ray (Douglas)
1920- ... **CLC 1, 3, 10, 15, 42; DA; WLC**
See also AITN 1, 2; CA 1-4R; CANR 2, 30;
CDALB 1968-1988; DLB 2, 8; MTCW;
SATA 11, 64

Bradford, Gamaliel 1863-1932..... **TCLC 36**
See also DLB 17

Bradley, David (Henry, Jr.)
1950- .... **CLC 23; BLC**
See also BW 1; CA 104; CANR 26; DLB 33

Bradley, John Ed(mund, Jr.)
1958- .... **CLC 55**
See also CA 139

Bradley, Marion Zimmer 1930-..... **CLC 30**
See also AAYA 9; CA 57-60; CAAS 10;
CANR 7, 31; DLB 8; MTCW

Bradstreet, Anne
1612(?)-1672 .... **LC 4; DA; PC 10**
See also CDALB 1640-1865; DLB 24

Bragg, Melvyn 1939- .... **CLC 10**
See also BEST 89:3; CA 57-60; CANR 10;
DLB 14

Braine, John (Gerard)
1922-1986 .... **CLC 1, 3, 41**
See also CA 1-4R; 120; CANR 1, 33;
CDBLB 1945-1960; DLB 15; DLBY 86;
MTCW

Brammer, William 1930(?)-1978 .... **CLC 31**
See also CA 77-80

Brancati, Vitaliano 1907-1954..... **TCLC 12**
See also CA 109

Brancato, Robin F(idler) 1936- ..... **CLC 35**
See also AAYA 9; CA 69-72; CANR 11,
45; CLR 32; JRDA; SAAS 9; SATA 23

Brand, Max
See Faust, Frederick (Schiller)

Byron, George Gordon (Noel)
1788-1824 ..... NCLC **2, 12; DA; WLC**
See also CDBLB 1789-1832; DLB 96, 110

C.3.3.
See Wilde, Oscar (Fingal O'Flahertie Wills)

Caballero, Fernan 1796-1877..... **NCLC 10**

Cabell, James Branch 1879-1958 ... **TCLC 6**
See also CA 105; DLB 9, 78

Cable, George Washington
1844-1925 .... **TCLC 4; SSC 4**
See also CA 104; DLB 12, 74

Cabral de Melo Neto, Joao 1920-... **CLC 76**

Cabrera Infante, G(uillermo)
1929- .... **CLC 5, 25, 45; HLC**
See also CA 85-88; CANR 29; DLB 113;
HW; MTCW

Cade, Toni
See Bambara, Toni Cade

Cadmus
See Buchan, John

Caedmon fl. 658-680............ **CMLC 7**

Caeiro, Alberto
See Pessoa, Fernando (Antonio Nogueira)

Cage, John (Milton, Jr.) 1912-..... **CLC 41**
See also CA 13-16R; CANR 9

Cain, G.
See Cabrera Infante, G(uillermo)

Cain, Guillermo
See Cabrera Infante, G(uillermo)

Cain, James M(allahan)
1892-1977 .... **CLC 3, 11, 28**
See also AITN 1; CA 17-20R; 73-76;
CANR 8, 34; MTCW

Caine, Mark
See Raphael, Frederic (Michael)

Calasso, Roberto 1941- .... **CLC 81**
See also CA 143

Calderon de la Barca, Pedro
1600-1681 .... **LC 23; DC 3**

Caldwell, Erskine (Preston)
1903-1987 .... **CLC 1, 8, 14, 50, 60**
See also AITN 1; CA 1-4R; 121; CAAS 1;
CANR 2, 33; DLB 9, 86; MTCW

Caldwell, (Janet Miriam) Taylor (Holland)
1900-1985 .... **CLC 2, 28, 39**
See also CA 5-8R; 116; CANR 5

Calhoun, John Caldwell
1782-1850 .... **NCLC 15**
See also DLB 3

Calisher, Hortense
1911- .... **CLC 2, 4, 8, 38; SSC 15**
See also CA 1-4R; CANR 1, 22; DLB 2;
MTCW

Callaghan, Morley Edward
1903-1990 .... **CLC 3, 14, 41, 65**
See also CA 9-12R; 132; CANR 33;
DLB 68; MTCW

Calvino, Italo
1923-1985 ..... **CLC 5, 8, 11, 22, 33, 39,
73; SSC 3**
See also CA 85-88; 116; CANR 23; MTCW

Cameron, Carey 1952- .... **CLC 59**
See also CA 135

Cameron, Peter 1959-............. **CLC 44**
See also CA 125

Campana, Dino 1885-1932....... **TCLC 20**
See also CA 117; DLB 114

Campbell, John W(ood, Jr.)
1910-1971 .... **CLC 32**
See also CA 21-22; 29-32R; CANR 34;
CAP 2; DLB 8; MTCW

Campbell, Joseph 1904-1987 .... **CLC 69**
See also AAYA 3; BEST 89:2; CA 1-4R;
124; CANR 3, 28; MTCW

Campbell, (John) Ramsey 1946- .... **CLC 42**
See also CA 57-60; CANR 7

Campbell, (Ignatius) Roy (Dunnachie)
1901-1957 .... **TCLC 5**
See also CA 104; DLB 20

Campbell, Thomas 1777-1844 .... **NCLC 19**
See also DLB 93; 144

Campbell, Wilfred................ TCLC 9
See also Campbell, William

Campbell, William 1858(?)-1918
See Campbell, Wilfred
See also CA 106; DLB 92

Campos, Alvaro de
See Pessoa, Fernando (Antonio Nogueira)

Camus, Albert
1913-1960 .... **CLC 1, 2, 4, 9, 11, 14, 32,
63, 69; DA; DC 2; SSC 9; WLC**
See also CA 89-92; DLB 72; MTCW

Canby, Vincent 1924-............. **CLC 13**
See also CA 81-84

Cancale
See Desnos, Robert

Canetti, Elias 1905- ...... **CLC 3, 14, 25, 75**
See also CA 21-24R; CANR 23; DLB 85,
124; MTCW

Canin, Ethan 1960-............... **CLC 55**
See also CA 131; 135

Cannon, Curt
See Hunter, Evan

Cape, Judith
See Page, P(atricia) K(athleen)

Capek, Karel
1890-1938 ..... **TCLC 6, 37; DA; DC 1;
WLC**
See also CA 104; 140

Capote, Truman
1924-1984 ...... **CLC 1, 3, 8, 13, 19, 34,
38, 58; DA; SSC 2; WLC**
See also CA 5-8R; 113; CANR 18;
CDALB 1941-1968; DLB 2; DLBY 80,
84; MTCW

Capra, Frank 1897-1991.......... **CLC 16**
See also CA 61-64; 135

Caputo, Philip 1941-............. **CLC 32**
See also CA 73-76; CANR 40

Card, Orson Scott 1951- .... **CLC 44, 47, 50**
See also AAYA 11; CA 102; CANR 27;
MTCW

Cardenal (Martinez), Ernesto
1925- .... **CLC 31; HLC**
See also CA 49-52; CANR 2, 32; HW;
MTCW

Carducci, Giosue 1835-1907...... **TCLC 32**

Carew, Thomas 1595(?)-1640....... **LC 13**
See also DLB 126

Carey, Ernestine Gilbreth 1908-.... **CLC 17**
See also CA 5-8R; SATA 2

Carey, Peter 1943-............ **CLC 40, 55**
See also CA 123; 127; MTCW

Carleton, William 1794-1869...... **NCLC 3**

Carlisle, Henry (Coffin) 1926-...... **CLC 33**
See also CA 13-16R; CANR 15

Carlsen, Chris
See Holdstock, Robert P.

Carlson, Ron(ald F.) 1947-......... **CLC 54**
See also CA 105; CANR 27

Carlyle, Thomas 1795-1881 .. **NCLC 22; DA**
See also CDBLB 1789-1832; DLB 55; 144

Carman, (William) Bliss
1861-1929 .... **TCLC 7**
See also CA 104; DLB 92

Carnegie, Dale 1888-1955 .... **TCLC 53**

Carossa, Hans 1878-1956........ **TCLC 48**
See also DLB 66

Carpenter, Don(ald Richard)
1931- .... **CLC 41**
See also CA 45-48; CANR 1

Carpentier (y Valmont), Alejo
1904-1980 .... **CLC 8, 11, 38; HLC**
See also CA 65-68; 97-100; CANR 11;
DLB 113; HW

Carr, Emily 1871-1945........... **TCLC 32**
See also DLB 68

Carr, John Dickson 1906-1977 ...... **CLC 3**
See also CA 49-52; 69-72; CANR 3, 33;
MTCW

Carr, Philippa
See Hibbert, Eleanor Alice Burford

Carr, Virginia Spencer 1929-....... **CLC 34**
See also CA 61-64; DLB 111

Carrier, Roch 1937-........... **CLC 13, 78**
See also CA 130; DLB 53

Carroll, James P. 1943(?)-......... **CLC 38**
See also CA 81-84

Carroll, Jim 1951- .... **CLC 35**
See also CA 45-48; CANR 42

Carroll, Lewis .... NCLC 2; WLC
See also Dodgson, Charles Lutwidge
See also CDBLB 1832-1890; CLR 2, 18;
DLB 18; JRDA

Carroll, Paul Vincent 1900-1968.... **CLC 10**
See also CA 9-12R; 25-28R; DLB 10

Carruth, Hayden
1921- ...... **CLC 4, 7, 10, 18, 84; PC 10**
See also CA 9-12R; CANR 4, 38; DLB 5;
MTCW; SATA 47

Carson, Rachel Louise 1907-1964... **CLC 71**
See also CA 77-80; CANR 35; MTCW;
SATA 23

Carter, Angela (Olive)
1940-1992 ...... **CLC 5, 41, 76; SSC 13**
See also CA 53-56; 136; CANR 12, 36;
DLB 14; MTCW; SATA 66;
SATA-Obit 70

Carter, Nick
See Smith, Martin Cruz

Chaucer, Daniel
  See Ford, Ford Madox

Chaucer, Geoffrey
  1340(?)-1400 .... **LC 17; DA**
  See also CDBLB Before 1660

Chaviaras, Strates 1935-
  See Haviaras, Stratis
  See also CA 105

Chayefsky, Paddy .... **CLC 23**
  See also Chayefsky, Sidney
  See also DLB 7, 44; DLBY 81

Chayefsky, Sidney 1923-1981
  See Chayefsky, Paddy
  See also CA 9-12R; 104; CANR 18

Chedid, Andree 1920-............ **CLC 47**

Cheever, John
  1912-1982 ...... **CLC 3, 7, 8, 11, 15, 25,**
  64; DA; SSC 1; WLC
  See also CA 5-8R; 106; CABS 1; CANR 5,
  27; CDALB 1941-1968; DLB 2, 102;
  DLBY 80, 82; MTCW

Cheever, Susan 1943-.......... **CLC 18, 48**
  See also CA 103; CANR 27; DLBY 82

Chekhonte, Antosha
  See Chekhov, Anton (Pavlovich)

Chekhov, Anton (Pavlovich)
  1860-1904 ..... **TCLC 3, 10, 31, 55; DA;**
  SSC 2; WLC
  See also CA 104; 124

Chernyshevsky, Nikolay Gavrilovich
  1828-1889 .... **NCLC 1**

Cherry, Carolyn Janice 1942-
  See Cherryh, C. J.
  See also CA 65-68; CANR 10

Cherryh, C. J. .... **CLC 35**
  See also Cherry, Carolyn Janice
  See also DLBY 80

Chesnutt, Charles W(addell)
  1858-1932 .... **TCLC 5, 39; BLC; SSC 7**
  See also BW 1; CA 106; 125; DLB 12, 50,
  78; MTCW

Chester, Alfred 1929(?)-1971....... **CLC 49**
  See also CA 33-36R; DLB 130

Chesterton, G(ilbert) K(eith)
  1874-1936 .... **TCLC 1, 6; SSC 1**
  See also CA 104; 132; CDBLB 1914-1945;
  DLB 10, 19, 34, 70, 98; MTCW;
  SATA 27

Chiang Pin-chin 1904-1986
  See Ding Ling
  See also CA 118

Ch'ien Chung-shu 1910-........... **CLC 22**
  See also CA 130; MTCW

Child, L. Maria
  See Child, Lydia Maria

Child, Lydia Maria 1802-1880 .... **NCLC 6**
  See also DLB 1, 74; SATA 67

Child, Mrs.
  See Child, Lydia Maria

Child, Philip 1898-1978 .... **CLC 19, 68**
  See also CA 13-14; CAP 1; SATA 47

Childress, Alice
  1920- .... **CLC 12, 15; BLC; DC 4**
  See also AAYA 8; BW 2; CA 45-48;
  CANR 3, 27; CLR 14; DLB 7, 38; JRDA;
  MAICYA; MTCW; SATA 7, 48

Chislett, (Margaret) Anne 1943-.... **CLC 34**

Chitty, Thomas Willes 1926-....... **CLC 11**
  See also Hinde, Thomas
  See also CA 5-8R

Chomette, Rene Lucien 1898-1981 .. **CLC 20**
  See also Clair, Rene
  See also CA 103

Chopin, Kate .... **TCLC 5, 14; DA; SSC 8**
  See also Chopin, Katherine
  See also CDALB 1865-1917; DLB 12, 78

Chopin, Katherine 1851-1904
  See Chopin, Kate
  See also CA 104; 122

Chretien de Troyes
  c. 12th cent. - .... **CMLC 10**

Christie
  See Ichikawa, Kon

Christie, Agatha (Mary Clarissa)
  1890-1976 ...... **CLC 1, 6, 8, 12, 39, 48**
  See also AAYA 9; AITN 1, 2; CA 17-20R;
  61-64; CANR 10, 37; CDBLB 1914-1945;
  DLB 13, 77; MTCW; SATA 36

Christie, (Ann) Philippa
  See Pearce, Philippa
  See also CA 5-8R; CANR 4

Christine de Pizan 1365(?)-1431(?) .... **LC 9**

Chubb, Elmer
  See Masters, Edgar Lee

Chulkov, Mikhail Dmitrievich
  1743-1792 .... **LC 2**

Churchill, Caryl 1938-......... **CLC 31, 55**
  See also CA 102; CANR 22; DLB 13;
  MTCW

Churchill, Charles 1731-1764........ **LC 3**
  See also DLB 109

Chute, Carolyn 1947-............. **CLC 39**
  See also CA 123

Ciardi, John (Anthony)
  1916-1986 .... **CLC 10, 40, 44**
  See also CA 5-8R; 118; CAAS 2; CANR 5,
  33; CLR 19; DLB 5; DLBY 86;
  MAICYA; MTCW; SATA 1, 46, 65

Cicero, Marcus Tullius
  106B.C.-43B.C. .... **CMLC 3**

Cimino, Michael 1943-............ **CLC 16**
  See also CA 105

Cioran, E(mil) M. 1911-........... **CLC 64**
  See also CA 25-28R

Cisneros, Sandra 1954-...... **CLC 69; HLC**
  See also AAYA 9; CA 131; DLB 122; HW

Clair, Rene..................... **CLC 20**
  See also Chomette, Rene Lucien

Clampitt, Amy 1920- .... **CLC 32**
  See also CA 110; CANR 29; DLB 105

Clancy, Thomas L., Jr. 1947-
  See Clancy, Tom
  See also CA 125; 131; MTCW

Clancy, Tom..................... **CLC 45**
  See also Clancy, Thomas L., Jr.
  See also AAYA 9; BEST 89:1, 90:1

Clare, John 1793-1864 .... **NCLC 9**
  See also DLB 55, 96

Clarin
  See Alas (y Urena), Leopoldo (Enrique
  Garcia)

Clark, Al C.
  See Goines, Donald

Clark, (Robert) Brian 1932-........ **CLC 29**
  See also CA 41-44R

Clark, Curt
  See Westlake, Donald E(dwin)

Clark, Eleanor 1913- .... **CLC 5, 19**
  See also CA 9-12R; CANR 41; DLB 6

Clark, J. P.
  See Clark, John Pepper
  See also DLB 117

Clark, John Pepper 1935- .... **CLC 38; BLC**
  See also Clark, J. P.
  See also BW 1; CA 65-68; CANR 16

Clark, M. R.
  See Clark, Mavis Thorpe

Clark, Mavis Thorpe 1909-........ **CLC 12**
  See also CA 57-60; CANR 8, 37; CLR 30;
  MAICYA; SAAS 5; SATA 8, 74

Clark, Walter Van Tilburg
  1909-1971 .... **CLC 28**
  See also CA 9-12R; 33-36R; DLB 9;
  SATA 8

Clarke, Arthur C(harles)
  1917- ...... **CLC 1, 4, 13, 18, 35; SSC 3**
  See also AAYA 4; CA 1-4R; CANR 2, 28;
  JRDA; MAICYA; MTCW; SATA 13, 70

Clarke, Austin 1896-1974......... **CLC 6, 9**
  See also CA 29-32; 49-52; CAP 2; DLB 10,
  20

Clarke, Austin C(hesterfield)
  1934- .... **CLC 8, 53; BLC**
  See also BW 1; CA 25-28R; CAAS 16;
  CANR 14, 32; DLB 53, 125

Clarke, Gillian 1937- .... **CLC 61**
  See also CA 106; DLB 40

Clarke, Marcus (Andrew Hislop)
  1846-1881 .... **NCLC 19**

Clarke, Shirley 1925-............. **CLC 16**

Clash, The .... **CLC 30**
  See also Headon, (Nicky) Topper; Jones,
  Mick; Simonon, Paul; Strummer, Joe

Claudel, Paul (Louis Charles Marie)
  1868-1955 .... **TCLC 2, 10**
  See also CA 104

Clavell, James (duMaresq)
  1925-...................... **CLC 6, 25**
  See also CA 25-28R; CANR 26; MTCW

Cleaver, (Leroy) Eldridge
  1935- .... **CLC 30; BLC**
  See also BW 1; CA 21-24R; CANR 16

Cleese, John (Marwood) 1939- ..... **CLC 21**
  See also Monty Python
  See also CA 112; 116; CANR 35; MTCW

Cleishbotham, Jebediah
  See Scott, Walter

Cleland, John 1710-1789 .... LC 2
See also DLB 39

Clemens, Samuel Langhorne 1835-1910
See Twain, Mark
See also CA 104; 135; CDALB 1865-1917;
DA; DLB 11, 12, 23, 64, 74; JRDA;
MAICYA; YABC 2

Cleophil
See Congreve, William

Clerihew, E.
See Bentley, E(dmund) C(lerihew)

Clerk, N. W.
See Lewis, C(live) S(taples)

Cliff, Jimmy. .... CLC 21
See also Chambers, James

Clifton, (Thelma) Lucille
1936- .... CLC 19, 66; BLC
See also BW 2; CA 49-52; CANR 2, 24, 42;
CLR 5; DLB 5, 41; MAICYA; MTCW;
SATA 20, 69

Clinton, Dirk
See Silverberg, Robert

Clough, Arthur Hugh 1819-1861. . NCLC 27
See also DLB 32

Clutha, Janet Paterson Frame 1924-
See Frame, Janet
See also CA 1-4R; CANR 2, 36; MTCW

Clyne, Terence
See Blatty, William Peter

Cobalt, Martin
See Mayne, William (James Carter)

Coburn, D(onald) L(ee) 1938- ...... CLC 10
See also CA 89-92

Cocteau, Jean (Maurice Eugene Clement)
1889-1963 .... CLC 1, 8, 15, 16, 43; DA;
WLC
See also CA 25-28; CANR 40; CAP 2;
DLB 65; MTCW

Codrescu, Andrei 1946- .... CLC 46
See also CA 33-36R; CAAS 19; CANR 13,
34

Coe, Max
See Bourne, Randolph S(illiman)

Coe, Tucker
See Westlake, Donald E(dwin)

Coetzee, J(ohn) M(ichael)
1940- .... CLC 23, 33, 66
See also CA 77-80; CANR 41; MTCW

Coffey, Brian
See Koontz, Dean R(ay)

Cohen, Arthur A(llen)
1928-1986 .... CLC 7, 31
See also CA 1-4R; 120; CANR 1, 17, 42;
DLB 28

Cohen, Leonard (Norman)
1934- .... CLC 3, 38
See also CA 21-24R; CANR 14; DLB 53;
MTCW

Cohen, Matt 1942- .... CLC 19
See also CA 61-64; CAAS 18; CANR 40;
DLB 53

Cohen-Solal, Annie 19(?)- .... CLC 50

Colegate, Isabel 1931- .... CLC 36
See also CA 17-20R; CANR 8, 22; DLB 14;
MTCW

Coleman, Emmett
See Reed, Ishmael

Coleridge, Samuel Taylor
1772-1834 .... NCLC 9; DA; WLC
See also CDBLB 1789-1832; DLB 93, 107

Coleridge, Sara 1802-1852 .... NCLC 31

Coles, Don 1928- .... CLC 46
See also CA 115; CANR 38

Colette, (Sidonie-Gabrielle)
1873-1954 ...... TCLC 1, 5, 16; SSC 10
See also CA 104; 131; DLB 65; MTCW

Collett, (Jacobine) Camilla (Wergeland)
1813-1895 .... NCLC 22

Collier, Christopher 1930- .... CLC 30
See also CA 33-36R; CANR 13, 33; JRDA;
MAICYA; SATA 16, 70

Collier, James L(incoln) 1928- ..... CLC 30
See also CA 9-12R; CANR 4, 33; JRDA;
MAICYA; SATA 8, 70

Collier, Jeremy 1650-1726 .... LC 6

Collins, Hunt
See Hunter, Evan

Collins, Linda 1931- .... CLC 44
See also CA 125

Collins, (William) Wilkie
1824-1889 .... NCLC 1, 18
See also CDBLB 1832-1890; DLB 18, 70

Collins, William 1721-1759 .... LC 4
See also DLB 109

Colman, George
See Glassco, John

Colt, Winchester Remington
See Hubbard, L(afayette) Ron(ald)

Colter, Cyrus 1910- .... CLC 58
See also BW 1; CA 65-68; CANR 10;
DLB 33

Colton, James
See Hansen, Joseph

Colum, Padraic 1881-1972........ CLC 28
See also CA 73-76; 33-36R; CANR 35;
MAICYA; MTCW; SATA 15

Colvin, James
See Moorcock, Michael (John)

Colwin, Laurie (E.)
1944-1992 .... CLC 5, 13, 23, 84
See also CA 89-92; 139; CANR 20;
DLBY 80; MTCW

Comfort, Alex(ander) 1920-........ CLC 7
See also CA 1-4R; CANR 1, 45

Comfort, Montgomery
See Campbell, (John) Ramsey

Compton-Burnett, I(vy)
1884(?)-1969 ...... CLC 1, 3, 10, 15, 34
See also CA 1-4R; 25-28R; CANR 4;
DLB 36; MTCW

Comstock, Anthony 1844-1915 .... TCLC 13
See also CA 110

Conan Doyle, Arthur
See Doyle, Arthur Conan

Conde, Maryse 1937- .... CLC 52
See also Boucolon, Maryse
See also BW 2

Condillac, Etienne Bonnot de
1714-1780 .... LC 26

Condon, Richard (Thomas)
1915- .... CLC 4, 6, 8, 10, 45
See also BEST 90:3; CA 1-4R; CAAS 1;
CANR 2, 23; MTCW

Congreve, William
1670-1729 ... LC 5, 21; DA; DC 2; WLC
See also CDBLB 1660-1789; DLB 39, 84

Connell, Evan S(helby), Jr.
1924- .... CLC 4, 6, 45
See also AAYA 7; CA 1-4R; CAAS 2;
CANR 2, 39; DLB 2; DLBY 81; MTCW

Connelly, Marc(us Cook)
1890-1980 .... CLC 7
See also CA 85-88; 102; CANR 30; DLB 7;
DLBY 80; SATA 25

Connor, Ralph .... TCLC 31
See also Gordon, Charles William
See also DLB 92

Conrad, Joseph
1857-1924 .... TCLC 1, 6, 13, 25, 43;
DA; SSC 9; WLC
See also CA 104; 131; CDBLB 1890-1914;
DLB 10, 34, 98; MTCW; SATA 27

Conrad, Robert Arnold
See Hart, Moss

Conroy, Pat 1945-............. CLC 30, 74
See also AAYA 8; CA 85-88;
CANR 24; DLB 6; MTCW

Constant (de Rebecque), (Henri) Benjamin
1767-1830 .... NCLC 6
See also DLB 119

Conybeare, Charles Augustus
See Eliot, T(homas) S(tearns)

Cook, Michael 1933- .... CLC 58
See also CA 93-96; DLB 53

Cook, Robin 1940- .... CLC 14
See also BEST 90:2; CA 108; 111;
CANR 41

Cook, Roy
See Silverberg, Robert

Cooke, Elizabeth 1948- .... CLC 55
See also CA 129

Cooke, John Esten 1830-1886 ..... NCLC 5
See also DLB 3

Cooke, John Estes
See Baum, L(yman) Frank

Cooke, M. E.
See Creasey, John

Cooke, Margaret
See Creasey, John

Cooney, Ray .... CLC 62

Cooper, Henry St. John
See Creasey, John

Cooper, J. California. .... CLC 56
See also AAYA 12; BW 1; CA 125

Cooper, James Fenimore
1789-1851 .... NCLC 1, 27
See also CDALB 1640-1865; DLB 3;
SATA 19

Coover, Robert (Lowell)
1932- ..... CLC 3, 7, 15, 32, 46; SSC 15
See also CA 45-48; CANR 3, 37; DLB 2;
DLBY 81; MTCW

Copeland, Stewart (Armstrong)
1952- . . . . **CLC 26**
See also Police, The

Coppard, A(lfred) E(dgar)
1878-1957 . . . . **TCLC 5**
See also CA 114; YABC 1

Coppee, Francois 1842-1908 . . . . . . **TCLC 25**

Coppola, Francis Ford 1939- . . . . **CLC 16**
See also CA 77-80; CANR 40; DLB 44

Corbiere, Tristan 1845-1875 . . . . . **NCLC 43**

Corcoran, Barbara 1911- . . . . **CLC 17**
See also CA 21-24R; CAAS 2; CANR 11,
28; DLB 52; JRDA; SATA 3, 77

Cordelier, Maurice
See Giraudoux, (Hippolyte) Jean

Corelli, Marie 1855-1924 . . . . **TCLC 51**
See also Mackay, Mary
See also DLB 34

Corman, Cid . . . . **CLC 9**
See also Corman, Sidney
See also CAAS 2; DLB 5

Corman, Sidney 1924-
See Corman, Cid
See also CA 85-88; CANR 44

Cormier, Robert (Edmund)
1925- . . . . **CLC 12, 30; DA**
See also AAYA 3; CA 1-4R; CANR 5, 23;
CDALB 1968-1988; CLR 12; DLB 52;
JRDA; MAICYA; MTCW; SATA 10, 45

Corn, Alfred (DeWitt III) 1943- . . . . **CLC 33**
See also CA 104; CANR 44; DLB 120;
DLBY 80

Cornwell, David (John Moore)
1931- . . . . **CLC 9, 15**
See also le Carre, John
See also CA 5-8R; CANR 13, 33; MTCW

Corrigan, Kevin . . . . **CLC 55**

Corso, (Nunzio) Gregory 1930- . . . **CLC 1, 11**
See also CA 5-8R; CANR 41; DLB 5, 16;
MTCW

Cortazar, Julio
1914-1984 . . . . . . **CLC 2, 3, 5, 10, 13, 15,**
33, 34; HLC; SSC 7
See also CA 21-24R; CANR 12, 32;
DLB 113; HW; MTCW

Corwin, Cecil
See Kornbluth, C(yril) M.

Cosic, Dobrica 1921- . . . . **CLC 14**
See also CA 122; 138

Costain, Thomas B(ertram)
1885-1965 . . . . **CLC 30**
See also CA 5-8R; 25-28R; DLB 9

Costantini, Humberto
1924(?)-1987 . . . . **CLC 49**
See also CA 131; 122; HW

Costello, Elvis 1955- . . . . **CLC 21**

Cotter, Joseph Seamon Sr.
1861-1949 . . . . **TCLC 28; BLC**
See also BW 1; CA 124; DLB 50

Couch, Arthur Thomas Quiller
See Quiller-Couch, Arthur Thomas

Coulton, James
See Hansen, Joseph

Couperus, Louis (Marie Anne)
1863-1923 . . . . **TCLC 15**
See also CA 115

Court, Wesli
See Turco, Lewis (Putnam)

Courtenay, Bryce 1933- . . . . **CLC 59**
See also CA 138

Courtney, Robert
See Ellison, Harlan

Cousteau, Jacques-Yves 1910- . . . . . . **CLC 30**
See also CA 65-68; CANR 15; MTCW;
SATA 38

Coward, Noel (Peirce)
1899-1973 . . . . **CLC 1, 9, 29, 51**
See also AITN 1; CA 17-18; 41-44R;
CANR 35; CAP 2; CDBLB 1914-1945;
DLB 10; MTCW

Cowley, Malcolm 1898-1989 . . . . **CLC 39**
See also CA 5-8R; 128; CANR 3; DLB 4,
48; DLBY 81, 89; MTCW

Cowper, William 1731-1800 . . . . **NCLC 8**
See also DLB 104, 109

Cox, William Trevor 1928- . . . **CLC 9, 14, 71**
See also Trevor, William
See also CA 9-12R; CANR 4, 37; DLB 14;
MTCW

Cozzens, James Gould
1903-1978 . . . . **CLC 1, 4, 11**
See also CA 9-12R; 81-84; CANR 19;
CDALB 1941-1968; DLB 9; DLBD 2;
DLBY 84; MTCW

Crabbe, George 1754-1832 . . . . . . **NCLC 26**
See also DLB 93

Craig, A. A.
See Anderson, Poul (William)

Craik, Dinah Maria (Mulock)
1826-1887 . . . . **NCLC 38**
See also DLB 35; MAICYA; SATA 34

Cram, Ralph Adams 1863-1942 . . . . **TCLC 45**

Crane, (Harold) Hart
1899-1932 . . . . **TCLC 2, 5; DA; PC 3;**
WLC
See also CA 104; 127; CDALB 1917-1929;
DLB 4, 48; MTCW

Crane, R(onald) S(almon)
1886-1967 . . . . **CLC 27**
See also CA 85-88; DLB 63

Crane, Stephen (Townley)
1871-1900 . . . . **TCLC 11, 17, 32; DA;**
SSC 7; WLC
See also CA 109; 140; CDALB 1865-1917;
DLB 12, 54, 78; YABC 2

Crase, Douglas 1944- . . . . **CLC 58**
See also CA 106

Crashaw, Richard 1612(?)-1649 . . . . . . **LC 24**
See also DLB 126

Craven, Margaret 1901-1980 . . . . **CLC 17**
See also CA 103

Crawford, F(rancis) Marion
1854-1909 . . . . **TCLC 10**
See also CA 107; DLB 71

Crawford, Isabella Valancy
1850-1887 . . . . **NCLC 12**
See also DLB 92

Crayon, Geoffrey
See Irving, Washington

Creasey, John 1908-1973 . . . . **CLC 11**
See also CA 5-8R; 41-44R; CANR 8;
DLB 77; MTCW

Crebillon, Claude Prosper Jolyot de (fils)
1707-1777 . . . . **LC 1**

Credo
See Creasey, John

Creeley, Robert (White)
1926- . . . . **CLC 1, 2, 4, 8, 11, 15, 36, 78**
See also CA 1-4R; CAAS 10; CANR 23, 43;
DLB 5, 16; MTCW

Crews, Harry (Eugene)
1935- . . . . **CLC 6, 23, 49**
See also AITN 1; CA 25-28R; CANR 20;
DLB 6, 143; MTCW

Crichton, (John) Michael
1942- . . . . **CLC 2, 6, 54**
See also AAYA 10; AITN 2; CA 25-28R;
CANR 13, 40; DLBY 81; JRDA;
MTCW; SATA 9

Crispin, Edmund . . . . **CLC 22**
See also Montgomery, (Robert) Bruce
See also DLB 87

Cristofer, Michael 1945(?)- . . . . **CLC 28**
See also CA 110; DLB 7

Croce, Benedetto 1866-1952 . . . . . . **TCLC 37**
See also CA 120

Crockett, David 1786-1836 . . . . **NCLC 8**
See also DLB 3, 11

Crockett, Davy
See Crockett, David

Crofts, Freeman Wills
1879-1957 . . . . **TCLC 55**
See also CA 115; DLB 77

Croker, John Wilson 1780-1857 . . **NCLC 10**
See also DLB 110

Crommelynck, Fernand 1885-1970 . . **CLC 75**
See also CA 89-92

Cronin, A(rchibald) J(oseph)
1896-1981 . . . . **CLC 32**
See also CA 1-4R; 102; CANR 5; SATA 25,
47

Cross, Amanda
See Heilbrun, Carolyn G(old)

Crothers, Rachel 1878(?)-1958 . . . . . **TCLC 19**
See also CA 113; DLB 7

Croves, Hal
See Traven, B.

Crowfield, Christopher
See Stowe, Harriet (Elizabeth) Beecher

Crowley, Aleister . . . . **TCLC 7**
See also Crowley, Edward Alexander

Crowley, Edward Alexander 1875-1947
See Crowley, Aleister
See also CA 104

Crowley, John 1942- . . . . **CLC 57**
See also CA 61-64; CANR 43; DLBY 82;
SATA 65

Crud
See Crumb, R(obert)

Crumarums
See Crumb, R(obert)

Crumb, R(obert) 1943-. . . . . CLC 17
See also CA 106

Crumbum
See Crumb, R(obert)

Crumski
See Crumb, R(obert)

Crum the Bum
See Crumb, R(obert)

Crunk
See Crumb, R(obert)

Crustt
See Crumb, R(obert)

Cryer, Gretchen (Kiger) 1935-. . . . . . CLC 21
See also CA 114; 123

Csath, Geza 1887-1919. . . . . TCLC 13
See also CA 111

Cudlip, David 1933-. . . . . CLC 34

Cullen, Countee
1903-1946 . . . . . . TCLC 4, 37; BLC; DA
See also BW 1; CA 108; 124;
CDALB 1917-1929; DLB 4, 48, 51;
MTCW; SATA 18

Cum, R.
See Crumb, R(obert)

Cummings, Bruce F(rederick) 1889-1919
See Barbellion, W. N. P.
See also CA 123

Cummings, E(dward) E(stlin)
1894-1962 . . . . . . CLC 1, 3, 8, 12, 15, 68;
                                    DA; PC 5; WLC 2
See also CA 73-76; CANR 31;
CDALB 1929-1941; DLB 4, 48; MTCW

Cunha, Euclides (Rodrigues Pimenta) da
1866-1909 . . . . TCLC 24
See also CA 123

Cunningham, E. V.
See Fast, Howard (Melvin)

Cunningham, J(ames) V(incent)
1911-1985 . . . . CLC 3, 31
See also CA 1-4R; 115; CANR 1; DLB 5

Cunningham, Julia (Woolfolk)
1916- . . . . CLC 12
See also CA 9-12R; CANR 4, 19, 36;
JRDA; MAICYA; SAAS 2; SATA 1, 26

Cunningham, Michael 1952- . . . . CLC 34
See also CA 136

Cunninghame Graham, R(obert) B(ontine)
1852-1936 . . . . TCLC 19
See also Graham, R(obert) B(ontine)
Cunninghame
See also CA 119; DLB 98

Currie, Ellen 19(?)-. . . . . CLC 44

Curtin, Philip
See Lowndes, Marie Adelaide (Belloc)

Curtis, Price
See Ellison, Harlan

Cutrate, Joe
See Spiegelman, Art

Czaczkes, Shmuel Yosef
See Agnon, S(hmuel) Y(osef Halevi)

D. P.
See Wells, H(erbert) G(eorge)

Dabrowska, Maria (Szumska)
1889-1965 . . . . CLC 15
See also CA 106

Dabydeen, David 1955-. . . . . CLC 34
See also BW 1; CA 125

Dacey, Philip 1939-. . . . . CLC 51
See also CA 37-40R; CAAS 17; CANR 14,
32; DLB 105

Dagerman, Stig (Halvard)
1923-1954 . . . . TCLC 17
See also CA 117

Dahl, Roald 1916-1990. . . . . CLC 1, 6, 18, 79
See also CA 1-4R; 133; CANR 6, 32, 37;
CLR 1, 7; DLB 139; JRDA; MAICYA;
MTCW; SATA 1, 26, 73; SATA-Obit 65

Dahlberg, Edward 1900-1977. . . CLC 1, 7, 14
See also CA 9-12R; 69-72; CANR 31;
DLB 48; MTCW

Dale, Colin. . . . . TCLC 18
See also Lawrence, T(homas) E(dward)

Dale, George E.
See Asimov, Isaac

Daly, Elizabeth 1878-1967. . . . . CLC 52
See also CA 23-24; 25-28R; CAP 2

Daly, Maureen 1921-. . . . . CLC 17
See also AAYA 5; CANR 37; JRDA;
MAICYA; SAAS 1; SATA 2

Damas, Leon-Gontran 1912-1978 . . . CLC 84
See also BW 1; CA 125; 73-76

Daniel, Samuel 1562(?)-1619. . . . . . . LC 24
See also DLB 62

Daniels, Brett
See Adler, Renata

Dannay, Frederic 1905-1982 . . . . CLC 11
See also Queen, Ellery
See also CA 1-4R; 107; CANR 1, 39;
DLB 137; MTCW

D'Annunzio, Gabriele
1863-1938 . . . . TCLC 6, 40
See also CA 104

d'Antibes, Germain
See Simenon, Georges (Jacques Christian)

Danvers, Dennis 1947-. . . . . CLC 70

Danziger, Paula 1944- . . . . CLC 21
See also AAYA 4; CA 112; 115; CANR 37;
CLR 20; JRDA; MAICYA; SATA 30,
36, 63

Dario, Ruben 1867-1916 . . . . TCLC 4; HLC
See also CA 131; HW; MTCW

Darley, George 1795-1846. . . . . NCLC 2
See also DLB 96

Daryush, Elizabeth 1887-1977. . . . CLC 6, 19
See also CA 49-52; CANR 3; DLB 20

Daudet, (Louis Marie) Alphonse
1840-1897 . . . . NCLC 1
See also DLB 123

Daumal, Rene 1908-1944. . . . . TCLC 14
See also CA 114

Davenport, Guy (Mattison, Jr.)
1927- . . . . CLC 6, 14, 38; SSC 16
See also CA 33-36R; CANR 23; DLB 130

Davidson, Avram 1923-
See Queen, Ellery
See also CA 101; CANR 26; DLB 8

Davidson, Donald (Grady)
1893-1968 . . . . CLC 2, 13, 19
See also CA 5-8R; 25-28R; CANR 4;
DLB 45

Davidson, Hugh
See Hamilton, Edmond

Davidson, John 1857-1909. . . . . . . TCLC 24
See also CA 118; DLB 19

Davidson, Sara 1943-. . . . . CLC 9
See also CA 81-84; CANR 44

Davie, Donald (Alfred)
1922-. . . . . CLC 5, 8, 10, 31
See also CA 1-4R; CAAS 3; CANR 1, 44;
DLB 27; MTCW

Davies, Ray(mond Douglas) 1944- . . CLC 21
See also CA 116

Davies, Rhys 1903-1978. . . . . CLC 23
See also CA 9-12R; 81-84; CANR 4;
DLB 139

Davies, (William) Robertson
1913- . . . . . CLC 2, 7, 13, 25, 42, 75; DA;
                                                          WLC
See also BEST 89:2; CA 33-36R; CANR 17,
42; DLB 68; MTCW

Davies, W(illiam) H(enry)
1871-1940 . . . . TCLC 5
See also CA 104; DLB 19

Davies, Walter C.
See Kornbluth, C(yril) M.

Davis, Angela (Yvonne) 1944-. . . . . . CLC 77
See also BW 2; CA 57-60; CANR 10

Davis, B. Lynch
See Bioy Casares, Adolfo; Borges, Jorge
Luis

Davis, Gordon
See Hunt, E(verette) Howard, Jr.

Davis, Harold Lenoir 1896-1960. . . . CLC 49
See also CA 89-92; DLB 9

Davis, Rebecca (Blaine) Harding
1831-1910 . . . . TCLC 6
See also CA 104; DLB 74

Davis, Richard Harding
1864-1916 . . . . TCLC 24
See also CA 114; DLB 12, 23, 78, 79

Davison, Frank Dalby 1893-1970 . . . CLC 15
See also CA 116

Davison, Lawrence H.
See Lawrence, D(avid) H(erbert Richards)

Davison, Peter (Hubert) 1928- . . . . . CLC 28
See also CA 9-12R; CAAS 4; CANR 3, 43;
DLB 5

Davys, Mary 1674-1732. . . . . LC 1
See also DLB 39

Dawson, Fielding 1930-. . . . . CLC 6
See also CA 85-88; DLB 130

Dawson, Peter
See Faust, Frederick (Schiller)

Day, Clarence (Shepard, Jr.)
1874-1935 . . . . TCLC 25
See also CA 108; DLB 11

Day, Thomas 1748-1789. . . . . LC 1
See also DLB 39; YABC 1

Day Lewis, C(ecil)
1904-1972 . . . . **CLC 1, 6, 10**
See also Blake, Nicholas
See also CA 13-16; 33-36R; CANR 34;
CAP 1; DLB 15, 20; MTCW

Dazai, Osamu . . . . **TCLC 11**
See also Tsushima, Shuji

de Andrade, Carlos Drummond
See Drummond de Andrade, Carlos

Deane, Norman
See Creasey, John

de Beauvoir, Simone (Lucie Ernestine Marie Bertrand)
See Beauvoir, Simone (Lucie Ernestine Marie Bertrand) de

de Brissac, Malcolm
See Dickinson, Peter (Malcolm)

de Chardin, Pierre Teilhard
See Teilhard de Chardin, (Marie Joseph) Pierre

Dee, John 1527-1608 . . . . **LC 20**

Deer, Sandra 1940- . . . . **CLC 45**

De Ferrari, Gabriella . . . . **CLC 65**

Defoe, Daniel
1660(?)-1731 . . . . **LC 1; DA; WLC**
See also CDBLB 1660-1789; DLB 39, 95,
101; JRDA; MAICYA; SATA 22

de Gourmont, Remy
See Gourmont, Remy de

de Hartog, Jan 1914- . . . . **CLC 19**
See also CA 1-4R; CANR 1

de Hostos, E. M.
See Hostos (y Bonilla), Eugenio Maria de

de Hostos, Eugenio M.
See Hostos (y Bonilla), Eugenio Maria de

Deighton, Len . . . . **CLC 4, 7, 22, 46**
See also Deighton, Leonard Cyril
See also AAYA 6; BEST 89:2;
CDBLB 1960 to Present; DLB 87

Deighton, Leonard Cyril 1929-
See Deighton, Len
See also CA 9-12R; CANR 19, 33; MTCW

Dekker, Thomas 1572(?)-1632 . . . . **LC 22**
See also CDBLB Before 1660; DLB 62

de la Mare, Walter (John)
1873-1956 . . **TCLC 4, 53; SSC 14; WLC**
See also CDBLB 1914-1945; CLR 23;
DLB 19; SATA 16

Delaney, Franey
See O'Hara, John (Henry)

Delaney, Shelagh 1939- . . . . **CLC 29**
See also CA 17-20R; CANR 30;
CDBLB 1960 to Present; DLB 13;
MTCW

Delany, Mary (Granville Pendarves)
1700-1788 . . . . **LC 12**

Delany, Samuel R(ay, Jr.)
1942- . . . . **CLC 8, 14, 38; BLC**
See also BW 2; CA 81-84; CANR 27, 43;
DLB 8, 33; MTCW

De La Ramee, (Marie) Louise 1839-1908
See Ouida
See also SATA 20

de la Roche, Mazo 1879-1961 . . . . . . **CLC 14**
See also CA 85-88; CANR 30; DLB 68;
SATA 64

Delbanco, Nicholas (Franklin)
1942- . . . . **CLC 6, 13**
See also CA 17-20R; CAAS 2; CANR 29;
DLB 6

del Castillo, Michel 1933- . . . . **CLC 38**
See also CA 109

Deledda, Grazia (Cosima)
1875(?)-1936 . . . . **TCLC 23**
See also CA 123

Delibes, Miguel . . . . **CLC 8, 18**
See also Delibes Setien, Miguel

Delibes Setien, Miguel 1920-
See Delibes, Miguel
See also CA 45-48; CANR 1, 32; HW;
MTCW

DeLillo, Don
1936- . . . . . **CLC 8, 10, 13, 27, 39, 54, 76**
See also BEST 89:1; CA 81-84; CANR 21;
DLB 6; MTCW

de Lisser, H. G.
See De Lisser, Herbert George
See also DLB 117

De Lisser, Herbert George
1878-1944 . . . . **TCLC 12**
See also de Lisser, H. G.
See also BW 2; CA 109

Deloria, Vine (Victor), Jr. 1933- . . . **CLC 21**
See also CA 53-56; CANR 5, 20; MTCW;
SATA 21

Del Vecchio, John M(ichael)
1947- . . . . **CLC 29**
See also CA 110; DLBD 9

de Man, Paul (Adolph Michel)
1919-1983 . . . . **CLC 55**
See also CA 128; 111; DLB 67; MTCW

De Marinis, Rick 1934- . . . . **CLC 54**
See also CA 57-60; CANR 9, 25

Demby, William 1922- . . . . **CLC 53; BLC**
See also BW 1; CA 81-84; DLB 33

Demijohn, Thom
See Disch, Thomas M(ichael)

de Montherlant, Henry (Milon)
See Montherlant, Henry (Milon) de

Demosthenes 384B.C.-322B.C. . . . . **CMLC 13**

de Natale, Francine
See Malzberg, Barry N(athaniel)

Denby, Edwin (Orr) 1903-1983 . . . . . **CLC 48**
See also CA 138; 110

Denis, Julio
See Cortazar, Julio

Denmark, Harrison
See Zelazny, Roger (Joseph)

Dennis, John 1658-1734 . . . . **LC 11**
See also DLB 101

Dennis, Nigel (Forbes) 1912-1989 . . . . **CLC 8**
See also CA 25-28R; 129; DLB 13, 15;
MTCW

De Palma, Brian (Russell) 1940- . . . . **CLC 20**
See also CA 109

De Quincey, Thomas 1785-1859 . . . **NCLC 4**
See also CDBLB 1789-1832; DLB 110; 144

Deren, Eleanora 1908(?)-1961
See Deren, Maya
See also CA 111

Deren, Maya . . . . **CLC 16**
See also Deren, Eleanora

Derleth, August (William)
1909-1971 . . . . **CLC 31**
See also CA 1-4R; 29-32R; CANR 4;
DLB 9; SATA 5

Der Nister . . . . **TCLC 56**

de Routisie, Albert
See Aragon, Louis

Derrida, Jacques 1930- . . . . **CLC 24**
See also CA 124; 127

Derry Down Derry
See Lear, Edward

Dersonnes, Jacques
See Simenon, Georges (Jacques Christian)

Desai, Anita 1937- . . . . **CLC 19, 37**
See also CA 81-84; CANR 33; MTCW;
SATA 63

de Saint-Luc, Jean
See Glassco, John

de Saint Roman, Arnaud
See Aragon, Louis

Descartes, Rene 1596-1650 . . . . **LC 20**

De Sica, Vittorio 1901(?)-1974 . . . . . **CLC 20**
See also CA 117

Desnos, Robert 1900-1945 . . . . **TCLC 22**
See also CA 121

Destouches, Louis-Ferdinand
1894-1961 . . . . **CLC 9, 15**
See also Celine, Louis-Ferdinand
See also CA 85-88; CANR 28; MTCW

Deutsch, Babette 1895-1982 . . . . **CLC 18**
See also CA 1-4R; 108; CANR 4; DLB 45;
SATA 1, 33

Devenant, William 1606-1649 . . . . **LC 13**

Devkota, Laxmiprasad
1909-1959 . . . . **TCLC 23**
See also CA 123

De Voto, Bernard (Augustine)
1897-1955 . . . . **TCLC 29**
See also CA 113; DLB 9

De Vries, Peter
1910-1993 . . . . **CLC 1, 2, 3, 7, 10, 28, 46**
See also CA 17-20R; 142; CANR 41;
DLB 6; DLBY 82; MTCW

Dexter, Martin
See Faust, Frederick (Schiller)

Dexter, Pete 1943- . . . . **CLC 34, 55**
See also BEST 89:2; CA 127; 131; MTCW

Diamano, Silmang
See Senghor, Leopold Sedar

Diamond, Neil 1941- . . . . **CLC 30**
See also CA 108

di Bassetto, Corno
See Shaw, George Bernard

Dick, Philip K(indred)
1928-1982 . . . . **CLC 10, 30, 72**
See also CA 49-52; 106; CANR 2, 16;
DLB 8; MTCW

Dickens, Charles (John Huffam)
1812-1870 . . . . . **NCLC 3, 8, 18, 26; DA; WLC**
See also CDBLB 1832-1890; DLB 21, 55, 70; JRDA; MAICYA; SATA 15

Dickey, James (Lafayette)
1923- . . . . **CLC 1, 2, 4, 7, 10, 15, 47**
See also AITN 1, 2; CA 9-12R; CABS 2; CANR 10; CDALB 1968-1988; DLB 5; DLBD 7; DLBY 82, 93; MTCW

Dickey, William 1928- . . . . **CLC 3, 28**
See also CA 9-12R; CANR 24; DLB 5

Dickinson, Charles 1951- . . . . **CLC 49**
See also CA 128

Dickinson, Emily (Elizabeth)
1830-1886 . . **NCLC 21; DA; PC 1; WLC**
See also CDALB 1865-1917; DLB 1; SATA 29

Dickinson, Peter (Malcolm)
1927- . . . . **CLC 12, 35**
See also AAYA 9; CA 41-44R; CANR 31; CLR 29; DLB 87; JRDA; MAICYA; SATA 5, 62

Dickson, Carr
See Carr, John Dickson

Dickson, Carter
See Carr, John Dickson

Diderot, Denis 1713-1784 . . . . **LC 26**

Didion, Joan 1934- . . . . . **CLC 1, 3, 8, 14, 32**
See also AITN 1; CA 5-8R; CANR 14; CDALB 1968-1988; DLB 2; DLBY 81, 86; MTCW

Dietrich, Robert
See Hunt, E(verette) Howard, Jr.

Dillard, Annie 1945- . . . . **CLC 9, 60**
See also AAYA 6; CA 49-52; CANR 3, 43; DLBY 80; MTCW; SATA 10

Dillard, R(ichard) H(enry) W(ilde)
1937- . . . . **CLC 5**
See also CA 21-24R; CAAS 7; CANR 10; DLB 5

Dillon, Eilis 1920- . . . . **CLC 17**
See also CA 9-12R; CAAS 3; CANR 4, 38; CLR 26; MAICYA; SATA 2, 74

Dimont, Penelope
See Mortimer, Penelope (Ruth)

Dinesen, Isak . . . . **CLC 10, 29; SSC 7**
See also Blixen, Karen (Christentze Dinesen)

Ding Ling . . . . **CLC 68**
See also Chiang Pin-chin

Disch, Thomas M(ichael) 1940- . . . **CLC 7, 36**
See also CA 21-24R; CAAS 4; CANR 17, 36; CLR 18; DLB 8; MAICYA; MTCW; SAAS 15; SATA 54

Disch, Tom
See Disch, Thomas M(ichael)

d'Isly, Georges
See Simenon, Georges (Jacques Christian)

Disraeli, Benjamin 1804-1881 . . **NCLC 2, 39**
See also DLB 21, 55

Ditcum, Steve
See Crumb, R(obert)

Dixon, Paige
See Corcoran, Barbara

Dixon, Stephen 1936- . . . . . **CLC 52; SSC 16**
See also CA 89-92; CANR 17, 40; DLB 130

Dobell, Sydney Thompson
1824-1874 . . . . **NCLC 43**
See also DLB 32

Doblin, Alfred . . . . **TCLC 13**
See also Doeblin, Alfred

Dobrolyubov, Nikolai Alexandrovich
1836-1861 . . . . **NCLC 5**

Dobyns, Stephen 1941- . . . . **CLC 37**
See also CA 45-48; CANR 2, 18

Doctorow, E(dgar) L(aurence)
1931- . . . . . **CLC 6, 11, 15, 18, 37, 44, 65**
See also AITN 2; BEST 89:3; CA 45-48; CANR 2, 33; CDALB 1968-1988; DLB 2, 28; DLBY 80; MTCW

Dodgson, Charles Lutwidge 1832-1898
See Carroll, Lewis
See also CLR 2; DA; MAICYA; YABC 2

Dodson, Owen (Vincent)
1914-1983 . . . . **CLC 79; BLC**
See also BW 1; CA 65-68; 110; CANR 24; DLB 76

Doeblin, Alfred 1878-1957 . . . . **TCLC 13**
See also Doblin, Alfred
See also CA 110; 141; DLB 66

Doerr, Harriet 1910- . . . . **CLC 34**
See also CA 117; 122

Domecq, H(onorio) Bustos
See Bioy Casares, Adolfo; Borges, Jorge Luis

Domini, Rey
See Lorde, Audre (Geraldine)

Dominique
See Proust, (Valentin-Louis-George-Eugene-) Marcel

Don, A
See Stephen, Leslie

Donaldson, Stephen R. 1947- . . . . **CLC 46**
See also CA 89-92; CANR 13

Donleavy, J(ames) P(atrick)
1926- . . . . **CLC 1, 4, 6, 10, 45**
See also AITN 2; CA 9-12R; CANR 24; DLB 6; MTCW

Donne, John
1572-1631 . . . . **LC 10, 24; DA; PC 1**
See also CDBLB Before 1660; DLB 121

Donnell, David 1939(?)- . . . . **CLC 34**

Donoso (Yanez), Jose
1924- . . . . **CLC 4, 8, 11, 32; HLC**
See also CA 81-84; CANR 32; DLB 113; HW; MTCW

Donovan, John 1928-1992 . . . . **CLC 35**
See also CA 97-100; 137; CLR 3; MAICYA; SATA 29

Don Roberto
See Cunninghame Graham, R(obert) B(ontine)

Doolittle, Hilda
1886-1961 . . . . . **CLC 3, 8, 14, 31, 34, 73; DA; PC 5; WLC**
See also H. D.
See also CA 97-100; CANR 35; DLB 4, 45; MTCW

Dorfman, Ariel 1942- . . . . **CLC 48, 77; HLC**
See also CA 124; 130; HW

Dorn, Edward (Merton) 1929-. . . **CLC 10, 18**
See also CA 93-96; CANR 42; DLB 5

Dorsan, Luc
See Simenon, Georges (Jacques Christian)

Dorsange, Jean
See Simenon, Georges (Jacques Christian)

Dos Passos, John (Roderigo)
1896-1970 . . . . . . **CLC 1, 4, 8, 11, 15, 25, 34, 82; DA; WLC**
See also CA 1-4R; 29-32R; CANR 3; CDALB 1929-1941; DLB 4, 9; DLBD 1; MTCW

Dossage, Jean
See Simenon, Georges (Jacques Christian)

Dostoevsky, Fedor Mikhailovich
1821-1881 . . . . . . **NCLC 2, 7, 21, 33, 43; DA; SSC 2; WLC**

Doughty, Charles M(ontagu)
1843-1926 . . . . **TCLC 27**
See also CA 115; DLB 19, 57

Douglas, Ellen
See Haxton, Josephine Ayres

Douglas, Gavin 1475(?)-1522 . . . . **LC 20**

Douglas, Keith 1920-1944 . . . . **TCLC 40**
See also DLB 27

Douglas, Leonard
See Bradbury, Ray (Douglas)

Douglas, Michael
See Crichton, (John) Michael

Douglass, Frederick
1817(?)-1895 . . . . **NCLC 7; BLC; DA; WLC**
See also CDALB 1640-1865; DLB 1, 43, 50, 79; SATA 29

Dourado, (Waldomiro Freitas) Autran
1926- . . . . **CLC 23, 60**
See also CA 25-28R; CANR 34

Dourado, Waldomiro Autran
See Dourado, (Waldomiro Freitas) Autran

Dove, Rita (Frances)
1952- . . . . **CLC 50, 81; PC 6**
See also BW 2; CA 109; CAAS 19; CANR 27, 42; DLB 120

Dowell, Coleman 1925-1985 . . . . **CLC 60**
See also CA 25-28R; 117; CANR 10; DLB 130

Dowson, Ernest Christopher
1867-1900 . . . . **TCLC 4**
See also CA 105; DLB 19, 135

Doyle, A. Conan
See Doyle, Arthur Conan

Doyle, Arthur Conan
1859-1930 . . . . **TCLC 7; DA; SSC 12; WLC**
See also CA 104; 122; CDBLB 1890-1914; DLB 18, 70; MTCW; SATA 24

Doyle, Conan 1859-1930
See Doyle, Arthur Conan

Doyle, John
See Graves, Robert (von Ranke)

Doyle, Roddy 1958(?)- . . . . **CLC 81**
See also CA 143

Doyle, Sir A. Conan
See Doyle, Arthur Conan

Doyle, Sir Arthur Conan
See Doyle, Arthur Conan

Dr. A
See Asimov, Isaac; Silverstein, Alvin

Drabble, Margaret
1939- . . . . CLC 2, 3, 5, 8, 10, 22, 53
See also CA 13-16R; CANR 18, 35;
CDBLB 1960 to Present; DLB 14;
MTCW; SATA 48

Drapier, M. B.
See Swift, Jonathan

Drayham, James
See Mencken, H(enry) L(ouis)

Drayton, Michael 1563-1631 . . . . LC 8

Dreadstone, Carl
See Campbell, (John) Ramsey

Dreiser, Theodore (Herman Albert)
1871-1945 . . . . TCLC 10, 18, 35; DA;
WLC
See also CA 106; 132; CDALB 1865-1917;
DLB 9, 12, 102, 137; DLBD 1; MTCW

Drexler, Rosalyn 1926- . . . . CLC 2, 6
See also CA 81-84

Dreyer, Carl Theodor 1889-1968. . . . CLC 16
See also CA 116

Drieu la Rochelle, Pierre(-Eugene)
1893-1945 . . . . TCLC 21
See also CA 117; DLB 72

Drop Shot
See Cable, George Washington

Droste-Hulshoff, Annette Freiin von
1797-1848 . . . . NCLC 3
See also DLB 133

Drummond, Walter
See Silverberg, Robert

Drummond, William Henry
1854-1907 . . . . TCLC 25
See also DLB 92

Drummond de Andrade, Carlos
1902-1987 . . . . CLC 18
See also Andrade, Carlos Drummond de
See also CA 132; 123

Drury, Allen (Stuart) 1918- . . . . CLC 37
See also CA 57-60; CANR 18

Dryden, John
1631-1700 . . . LC 3, 21; DA; DC 3; WLC
See also CDBLB 1660-1789; DLB 80, 101,
131

Duberman, Martin 1930- . . . . CLC 8
See also CA 1-4R; CANR 2

Dubie, Norman (Evans) 1945- . . . . . . CLC 36
See also CA 69-72; CANR 12; DLB 120

Du Bois, W(illiam) E(dward) B(urghardt)
1868-1963 . . . . . . CLC 1, 2, 13, 64; BLC;
DA; WLC
See also BW 1; CA 85-88; CANR 34;
CDALB 1865-1917; DLB 47, 50, 91;
MTCW; SATA 42

Dubus, Andre 1936- . . . CLC 13, 36; SSC 15
See also CA 21-24R; CANR 17; DLB 130

Duca Minimo
See D'Annunzio, Gabriele

Ducharme, Rejean 1941- . . . . CLC 74
See also DLB 60

Duclos, Charles Pinot 1704-1772 . . . . . LC 1

Dudek, Louis 1918- . . . . CLC 11, 19
See also CA 45-48; CAAS 14; CANR 1;
DLB 88

Duerrenmatt, Friedrich
. . . . CLC 1, 4, 8, 11, 15, 43
See also Duerrenmatt, Friedrich
See also DLB 69, 124

Duerrenmatt, Friedrich
1921-1990 . . . . . . CLC 1, 4, 8, 11, 15, 43
See also Duerrenmatt, Friedrich
See also CA 17-20R; CANR 33; DLB 69,
124; MTCW

Duffy, Bruce (?)- . . . . CLC 50

Duffy, Maureen 1933- . . . . CLC 37
See also CA 25-28R; CANR 33; DLB 14;
MTCW

Dugan, Alan 1923- . . . . CLC 2, 6
See also CA 81-84; DLB 5

du Gard, Roger Martin
See Martin du Gard, Roger

Duhamel, Georges 1884-1966 . . . . CLC 8
See also CA 81-84; 25-28R; CANR 35;
DLB 65; MTCW

Dujardin, Edouard (Emile Louis)
1861-1949 . . . . TCLC 13
See also CA 109; DLB 123

Dumas, Alexandre (Davy de la Pailleterie)
1802-1870 . . . . NCLC 11; DA; WLC
See also DLB 119; SATA 18

Dumas, Alexandre
1824-1895 . . . . NCLC 9; DC 1

Dumas, Claudine
See Malzberg, Barry N(athaniel)

Dumas, Henry L. 1934-1968 . . . . . CLC 6, 62
See also BW 1; CA 85-88; DLB 41

du Maurier, Daphne
1907-1989 . . . . CLC 6, 11, 59
See also CA 5-8R; 128; CANR 6; MTCW;
SATA 27, 60

Dunbar, Paul Laurence
1872-1906 . . . . . . TCLC 2, 12; BLC; DA;
PC 5; SSC 8; WLC
See also BW 1; CA 104; 124;
CDALB 1865-1917; DLB 50, 54, 78;
SATA 34

Dunbar, William 1460(?)-1530(?) . . . . LC 20

Duncan, Lois 1934- . . . . CLC 26
See also AAYA 4; CA 1-4R; CANR 2, 23,
36; CLR 29; JRDA; MAICYA; SAAS 2;
SATA 1, 36, 75

Duncan, Robert (Edward)
1919-1988 . . . . CLC 1, 2, 4, 7, 15, 41, 55;
PC 2
See also CA 9-12R; 124; CANR 28; DLB 5,
16; MTCW

Dunlap, William 1766-1839 . . . . NCLC 2
See also DLB 30, 37, 59

Dunn, Douglas (Eaglesham)
1942- . . . . CLC 6, 40
See also CA 45-48; CANR 2, 33; DLB 40;
MTCW

Dunn, Katherine (Karen) 1945- . . . . . CLC 71
See also CA 33-36R

Dunn, Stephen 1939- . . . . CLC 36
See also CA 33-36R; CANR 12; DLB 105

Dunne, Finley Peter 1867-1936. . . . TCLC 28
See also CA 108; DLB 11, 23

Dunne, John Gregory 1932- . . . . CLC 28
See also CA 25-28R; CANR 14; DLBY 80

Dunsany, Edward John Moreton Drax
Plunkett 1878-1957
See Dunsany, Lord
See also CA 104; DLB 10

Dunsany, Lord . . . . TCLC 2
See also Dunsany, Edward John Moreton
Drax Plunkett
See also DLB 77

du Perry, Jean
See Simenon, Georges (Jacques Christian)

Durang, Christopher (Ferdinand)
1949- . . . . CLC 27, 38
See also CA 105

Duras, Marguerite
1914- . . . . . CLC 3, 6, 11, 20, 34, 40, 68
See also CA 25-28R; DLB 83; MTCW

Durban, (Rosa) Pam 1947- . . . . CLC 39
See also CA 123

Durcan, Paul 1944- . . . . CLC 43, 70
See also CA 134

Durkheim, Emile 1858-1917 . . . . . TCLC 55

Durrell, Lawrence (George)
1912-1990 . . . . CLC 1, 4, 6, 8, 13, 27, 41
See also CA 9-12R; 132; CANR 40;
CDBLB 1945-1960; DLB 15, 27;
DLBY 90; MTCW

Dutt, Toru 1856-1877 . . . . NCLC 29

Dwight, Timothy 1752-1817 . . . . . . NCLC 13
See also DLB 37

Dworkin, Andrea 1946- . . . . CLC 43
See also CA 77-80; CANR 16, 39; MTCW

Dwyer, Deanna
See Koontz, Dean R(ay)

Dwyer, K. R.
See Koontz, Dean R(ay)

Dylan, Bob 1941- . . . . . . CLC 3, 4, 6, 12, 77
See also CA 41-44R; DLB 16

Eagleton, Terence (Francis) 1943-
See Eagleton, Terry
See also CA 57-60; CANR 7, 23; MTCW

Eagleton, Terry . . . . CLC 63
See also Eagleton, Terence (Francis)

Early, Jack
See Scoppettone, Sandra

East, Michael
See West, Morris L(anglo)

Eastaway, Edward
See Thomas, (Philip) Edward

Eastlake, William (Derry) 1917- . . . . . CLC 8
See also CA 5-8R; CAAS 1; CANR 5;
DLB 6

Eastman, Charles A(lexander)
1858-1939 . . . . TCLC 55
See also YABC 1

Author Index

Ford, Elbur
See Hibbert, Eleanor Alice Burford

Ford, Ford Madox
1873-1939 .... **TCLC 1, 15, 39**
See also CA 104; 132; CDBLB 1914-1945;
DLB 34, 98; MTCW

Ford, John 1895-1973............ **CLC 16**
See also CA 45-48

Ford, Richard 1944-.............. **CLC 46**
See also CA 69-72; CANR 11

Ford, Webster
See Masters, Edgar Lee

Foreman, Richard 1937-.......... **CLC 50**
See also CA 65-68; CANR 32

Forester, C(ecil) S(cott)
1899-1966 .... **CLC 35**
See also CA 73-76; 25-28R; SATA 13

Forez
See Mauriac, Francois (Charles)

Forman, James Douglas 1932-...... **CLC 21**
See also CA 9-12R; CANR 4, 19, 42;
JRDA; MAICYA; SATA 8, 70

Fornes, Maria Irene 1930-...... **CLC 39, 61**
See also CA 25-28R; CANR 28; DLB 7;
HW; MTCW

Forrest, Leon 1937- .... **CLC 4**
See also BW 2; CA 89-92; CAAS 7;
CANR 25; DLB 33

Forster, E(dward) M(organ)
1879-1970 ..... **CLC 1, 2, 3, 4, 9, 10, 13,
15, 22, 45, 77; DA; WLC**
See also AAYA 2; CA 13-14; 25-28R;
CANR 45; CAP 1; CDBLB 1914-1945;
DLB 34, 98; DLBD 10; MTCW;
SATA 57

Forster, John 1812-1876 .... **NCLC 11**
See also DLB 144

Forsyth, Frederick 1938-...... **CLC 2, 5, 36**
See also BEST 89:4; CA 85-88; CANR 38;
DLB 87; MTCW

Forten, Charlotte L. .... **TCLC 16; BLC**
See also Grimke, Charlotte L(ottie) Forten
See also DLB 50

Foscolo, Ugo 1778-1827......... **NCLC 8**

Fosse, Bob .... **CLC 20**
See also Fosse, Robert Louis

Fosse, Robert Louis 1927-1987
See Fosse, Bob
See also CA 110; 123

Foster, Stephen Collins
1826-1864 .... **NCLC 26**

Foucault, Michel
1926-1984 .... **CLC 31, 34, 69**
See also CA 105; 113; CANR 34; MTCW

Fouque, Friedrich (Heinrich Karl) de la Motte
1777-1843 .... **NCLC 2**
See also DLB 90

Fournier, Henri Alban 1886-1914
See Alain-Fournier
See also CA 104

Fournier, Pierre 1916-............ **CLC 11**
See also Gascar, Pierre
See also CA 89-92; CANR 16, 40

Fowles, John
1926- .... **CLC 1, 2, 3, 4, 6, 9, 10, 15, 33**
See also CA 5-8R; CANR 25; CDBLB 1960
to Present; DLB 14, 139; MTCW;
SATA 22

Fox, Paula 1923-................ **CLC 2, 8**
See also AAYA 3; CA 73-76; CANR 20,
36; CLR 1; DLB 52; JRDA; MAICYA;
MTCW; SATA 17, 60

Fox, William Price (Jr.) 1926- ..... **CLC 22**
See also CA 17-20R; CAAS 19; CANR 11;
DLB 2; DLBY 81

Foxe, John 1516(?)-1587 .... **LC 14**

Frame, Janet .... **CLC 2, 3, 6, 22, 66**
See also Clutha, Janet Paterson Frame

France, Anatole................... **TCLC 9**
See also Thibault, Jacques Anatole Francois
See also DLB 123

Francis, Claude 19(?)- .... **CLC 50**

Francis, Dick 1920- .... **CLC 2, 22, 42**
See also AAYA 5; BEST 89:3; CA 5-8R;
CANR 9, 42; CDBLB 1960 to Present;
DLB 87; MTCW

Francis, Robert (Churchill)
1901-1987 .... **CLC 15**
See also CA 1-4R; 123; CANR 1

Frank, Anne(lies Marie)
1929-1945 .... **TCLC 17; DA; WLC**
See also AAYA 12; CA 113; 133; MTCW;
SATA 42

Frank, Elizabeth 1945-........... **CLC 39**
See also CA 121; 126

Franklin, Benjamin
See Hasek, Jaroslav (Matej Frantisek)

Franklin, Benjamin 1706-1790... **LC 25; DA**
See also CDALB 1640-1865; DLB 24, 43,
73

Franklin, (Stella Maraia Sarah) Miles
1879-1954 .... **TCLC 7**
See also CA 104

Fraser, (Lady) Antonia (Pakenham)
1932- .... **CLC 32**
See also CA 85-88; CANR 44; MTCW;
SATA 32

Fraser, George MacDonald 1925-.... **CLC 7**
See also CA 45-48; CANR 2

Fraser, Sylvia 1935-.............. **CLC 64**
See also CA 45-48; CANR 1, 16

Frayn, Michael 1933-...... **CLC 3, 7, 31, 47**
See also CA 5-8R; CANR 30; DLB 13, 14;
MTCW

Fraze, Candida (Merrill) 1945-..... **CLC 50**
See also CA 126

Frazer, J(ames) G(eorge)
1854-1941 .... **TCLC 32**
See also CA 118

Frazer, Robert Caine
See Creasey, John

Frazer, Sir James George
See Frazer, J(ames) G(eorge)

Frazier, Ian 1951-................ **CLC 46**
See also CA 130

Frederic, Harold 1856-1898...... **NCLC 10**
See also DLB 12, 23

Frederick, John
See Faust, Frederick (Schiller)

Frederick the Great 1712-1786 ...... **LC 14**

Fredro, Aleksander 1793-1876..... **NCLC 8**

Freeling, Nicolas 1927- .... **CLC 38**
See also CA 49-52; CAAS 12; CANR 1, 17;
DLB 87

Freeman, Douglas Southall
1886-1953 .... **TCLC 11**
See also CA 109; DLB 17

Freeman, Judith 1946-........... **CLC 55**

Freeman, Mary Eleanor Wilkins
1852-1930 .... **TCLC 9; SSC 1**
See also CA 106; DLB 12, 78

Freeman, R(ichard) Austin
1862-1943 .... **TCLC 21**
See also CA 113; DLB 70

French, Marilyn 1929-...... **CLC 10, 18, 60**
See also CA 69-72; CANR 3, 31; MTCW

French, Paul
See Asimov, Isaac

Freneau, Philip Morin 1752-1832.. **NCLC 1**
See also DLB 37, 43

Freud, Sigmund 1856-1939 .... **TCLC 52**
See also CA 115; 133; MTCW

Friedan, Betty (Naomi) 1921-...... **CLC 74**
See also CA 65-68; CANR 18, 45; MTCW

Friedman, B(ernard) H(arper)
1926-........................ **CLC 7**
See also CA 1-4R; CANR 3

Friedman, Bruce Jay 1930-.... **CLC 3, 5, 56**
See also CA 9-12R; CANR 25; DLB 2, 28

Friel, Brian 1929-........... **CLC 5, 42, 59**
See also CA 21-24R; CANR 33; DLB 13;
MTCW

Friis-Baastad, Babbis Ellinor
1921-1970 .... **CLC 12**
See also CA 17-20R; 134; SATA 7

Frisch, Max (Rudolf)
1911-1991 ..... **CLC 3, 9, 14, 18, 32, 44**
See also CA 85-88; 134; CANR 32;
DLB 69, 124; MTCW

Fromentin, Eugene (Samuel Auguste)
1820-1876 .... **NCLC 10**
See also DLB 123

Frost, Frederick
See Faust, Frederick (Schiller)

Frost, Robert (Lee)
1874-1963 .... **CLC 1, 3, 4, 9, 10, 13, 15,
26, 34, 44; DA; PC 1; WLC**
See also CA 89-92; CANR 33;
CDALB 1917-1929; DLB 54; DLBD 7;
MTCW; SATA 14

Froude, James Anthony
1818-1894 .... **NCLC 43**
See also DLB 18, 57, 144

Froy, Herald
See Waterhouse, Keith (Spencer)

Fry, Christopher 1907-........ **CLC 2, 10, 14**
See also CA 17-20R; CANR 9, 30; DLB 13;
MTCW; SATA 66

Grayson, Richard (A.) 1951- . . . . **CLC 38**
See also CA 85-88; CANR 14, 31

Greeley, Andrew M(oran) 1928- . . . . **CLC 28**
See also CA 5-8R; CAAS 7; CANR 7, 43;
MTCW

Green, Brian
See Card, Orson Scott

Green, Hannah . . . . **CLC 3**
See also CA 73-76

Green, Hannah
See Greenberg, Joanne (Goldenberg)

Green, Henry . . . . **CLC 2, 13**
See also Yorke, Henry Vincent
See also DLB 15

Green, Julian (Hartridge) 1900-
See Green, Julien
See also CA 21-24R; CANR 33; DLB 4, 72;
MTCW

Green, Julien . . . . **CLC 3, 11, 77**
See also Green, Julian (Hartridge)

Green, Paul (Eliot) 1894-1981 . . . . . . **CLC 25**
See also AITN 1; CA 5-8R; 103; CANR 3;
DLB 7, 9; DLBY 81

Greenberg, Ivan 1908-1973
See Rahv, Philip
See also CA 85-88

Greenberg, Joanne (Goldenberg)
1932- . . . . **CLC 7, 30**
See also AAYA 12; CA 5-8R; CANR 14,
32; SATA 25

Greenberg, Richard 1959(?)- . . . . **CLC 57**
See also CA 138

Greene, Bette 1934- . . . . **CLC 30**
See also AAYA 7; CA 53-56; CANR 4;
CLR 2; JRDA; MAICYA; SAAS 16;
SATA 8

Greene, Gael . . . . **CLC 8**
See also CA 13-16R; CANR 10

Greene, Graham
1904-1991 . . . . **CLC 1, 3, 6, 9, 14, 18, 27,**
37, 70, 72; DA; WLC
See also AITN 2; CA 13-16R; 133;
CANR 35; CDBLB 1945-1960; DLB 13,
15, 77, 100; DLBY 91; MTCW; SATA 20

Greer, Richard
See Silverberg, Robert

Greer, Richard
See Silverberg, Robert

Gregor, Arthur 1923- . . . . **CLC 9**
See also CA 25-28R; CAAS 10; CANR 11;
SATA 36

Gregor, Lee
See Pohl, Frederik

Gregory, Isabella Augusta (Persse)
1852-1932 . . . . **TCLC 1**
See also CA 104; DLB 10

Gregory, J. Dennis
See Williams, John A(lfred)

Grendon, Stephen
See Derleth, August (William)

Grenville, Kate 1950- . . . . **CLC 61**
See also CA 118

Grenville, Pelham
See Wodehouse, P(elham) G(renville)

Greve, Felix Paul (Berthold Friedrich)
1879-1948
See Grove, Frederick Philip
See also CA 104; 141

Grey, Zane 1872-1939 . . . . **TCLC 6**
See also CA 104; 132; DLB 9; MTCW

Grieg, (Johan) Nordahl (Brun)
1902-1943 . . . . **TCLC 10**
See also CA 107

Grieve, C(hristopher) M(urray)
1892-1978 . . . . **CLC 11, 19**
See also MacDiarmid, Hugh
See also CA 5-8R; 85-88; CANR 33;
MTCW

Griffin, Gerald 1803-1840 . . . . **NCLC 7**

Griffin, John Howard 1920-1980 . . . . **CLC 68**
See also AITN 1; CA 1-4R; 101; CANR 2

Griffin, Peter . . . . **CLC 39**

Griffiths, Trevor 1935- . . . . **CLC 13, 52**
See also CA 97-100; CANR 45; DLB 13

Grigson, Geoffrey (Edward Harvey)
1905-1985 . . . . **CLC 7, 39**
See also CA 25-28R; 118; CANR 20, 33;
DLB 27; MTCW

Grillparzer, Franz 1791-1872 . . . . . . **NCLC 1**
See also DLB 133

Grimble, Reverend Charles James
See Eliot, T(homas) S(tearns)

Grimke, Charlotte L(ottie) Forten
1837(?)-1914
See Forten, Charlotte L.
See also BW 1; CA 117; 124

Grimm, Jacob Ludwig Karl
1785-1863 . . . . **NCLC 3**
See also DLB 90; MAICYA; SATA 22

Grimm, Wilhelm Karl 1786-1859 . . **NCLC 3**
See also DLB 90; MAICYA; SATA 22

Grimmelshausen, Johann Jakob Christoffel
von 1621-1676 . . . . **LC 6**

Grindel, Eugene 1895-1952
See Eluard, Paul
See also CA 104

Grisham, John 1955(?)- . . . . **CLC 84**
See also CA 138

Grossman, David 1954- . . . . **CLC 67**
See also CA 138

Grossman, Vasily (Semenovich)
1905-1964 . . . . **CLC 41**
See also CA 124; 130; MTCW

Grove, Frederick Philip . . . . **TCLC 4**
See also Greve, Felix Paul (Berthold
Friedrich)
See also DLB 92

Grubb
See Crumb, R(obert)

Grumbach, Doris (Isaac)
1918- . . . . **CLC 13, 22, 64**
See also CA 5-8R; CAAS 2; CANR 9, 42

Grundtvig, Nicolai Frederik Severin
1783-1872 . . . . **NCLC 1**

Grunge
See Crumb, R(obert)

Grunwald, Lisa 1959- . . . . **CLC 44**
See also CA 120

Guare, John 1938- . . . . **CLC 8, 14, 29, 67**
See also CA 73-76; CANR 21; DLB 7;
MTCW

Gudjonsson, Halldor Kiljan 1902-
See Laxness, Halldor
See also CA 103

Guenter, Erich
See Eich, Guenter

Guest, Barbara 1920- . . . . **CLC 34**
See also CA 25-28R; CANR 11, 44; DLB 5

Guest, Judith (Ann) 1936- . . . . **CLC 8, 30**
See also AAYA 7; CA 77-80; CANR 15;
MTCW

Guild, Nicholas M. 1944- . . . . **CLC 33**
See also CA 93-96

Guillemin, Jacques
See Sartre, Jean-Paul

Guillen, Jorge 1893-1984 . . . . **CLC 11**
See also CA 89-92; 112; DLB 108; HW

Guillen (y Batista), Nicolas (Cristobal)
1902-1989 . . . . . **CLC 48, 79; BLC; HLC**
See also BW 2; CA 116; 125; 129; HW

Guillevic, (Eugene) 1907- . . . . **CLC 33**
See also CA 93-96

Guillois
See Desnos, Robert

Guiney, Louise Imogen
1861-1920 . . . . **TCLC 41**
See also DLB 54

Guiraldes, Ricardo (Guillermo)
1886-1927 . . . . **TCLC 39**
See also CA 131; HW; MTCW

Gunn, Bill . . . . **CLC 5**
See also Gunn, William Harrison
See also DLB 38

Gunn, Thom(son William)
1929- . . . . **CLC 3, 6, 18, 32, 81**
See also CA 17-20R; CANR 9, 33;
CDBLB 1960 to Present; DLB 27;
MTCW

Gunn, William Harrison 1934(?)-1989
See Gunn, Bill
See also AITN 1; BW 1; CA 13-16R; 128;
CANR 12, 25

Gunnars, Kristjana 1948- . . . . **CLC 69**
See also CA 113; DLB 60

Gurganus, Allan 1947- . . . . **CLC 70**
See also BEST 90:1; CA 135

Gurney, A(lbert) R(amsdell), Jr.
1930- . . . . **CLC 32, 50, 54**
See also CA 77-80; CANR 32

Gurney, Ivor (Bertie) 1890-1937 . . . **TCLC 33**

Gurney, Peter
See Gurney, A(lbert) R(amsdell), Jr.

Guro, Elena . . . . **TCLC 56**

Gustafson, Ralph (Barker) 1909- . . . . **CLC 36**
See also CA 21-24R; CANR 8, 45; DLB 88

Gut, Gom
See Simenon, Georges (Jacques Christian)

Guthrie, A(lfred) B(ertram), Jr.
1901-1991 . . . . **CLC 23**
See also CA 57-60; 134; CANR 24; DLB 6;
SATA 62; SATA-Obit 67

Harrison, Elizabeth Cavanna 1909-
See Cavanna, Betty
See also CA 9-12R; CANR 6, 27

Harrison, Harry (Max) 1925-...... **CLC 42**
See also CA 1-4R; CANR 5, 21; DLB 8;
SATA 4

Harrison, James (Thomas)
1937-............. **CLC 6, 14, 33, 66**
See also CA 13-16R; CANR 8; DLBY 82

Harrison, Kathryn 1961-.......... **CLC 70**
See also CA 144

Harrison, Tony 1937-............. **CLC 43**
See also CA 65-68; CANR 44; DLB 40;
MTCW

Harriss, Will(ard Irvin) 1922-...... **CLC 34**
See also CA 111

Harson, Sley
See Ellison, Harlan

Hart, Ellis
See Ellison, Harlan

Hart, Josephine 1942(?)-.......... **CLC 70**
See also CA 138

Hart, Moss 1904-1961............. **CLC 66**
See also CA 109; 89-92; DLB 7

Harte, (Francis) Bret(t)
1836(?)-1902........ **TCLC 1, 25; DA;
SSC 8; WLC**
See also CA 104; 140; CDALB 1865-1917;
DLB 12, 64, 74, 79; SATA 26

Hartley, L(eslie) P(oles)
1895-1972.................. **CLC 2, 22**
See also CA 45-48; 37-40R; CANR 33;
DLB 15, 139; MTCW

Hartman, Geoffrey H. 1929-...... **CLC 27**
See also CA 117; 125; DLB 67

Haruf, Kent 19(?)-................ **CLC 34**

Harwood, Ronald 1934-.......... **CLC 32**
See also CA 1-4R; CANR 4; DLB 13

Hasek, Jaroslav (Matej Frantisek)
1883-1923................... **TCLC 4**
See also CA 104; 129; MTCW

Hass, Robert 1941-............. **CLC 18, 39**
See also CA 111; CANR 30; DLB 105

Hastings, Hudson
See Kuttner, Henry

Hastings, Selina.................. CLC 44

Hatteras, Amelia
See Mencken, H(enry) L(ouis)

Hatteras, Owen.................. TCLC 18
See also Mencken, H(enry) L(ouis); Nathan,
George Jean

Hauptmann, Gerhart (Johann Robert)
1862-1946................... **TCLC 4**
See also CA 104; DLB 66, 118

Havel, Vaclav 1936-........ **CLC 25, 58, 65**
See also CA 104; CANR 36; MTCW

Haviaras, Stratis................ CLC 33
See also Chaviaras, Strates

Hawes, Stephen 1475(?)-1523(?) ..... **LC 17**

Hawkes, John (Clendennin Burne, Jr.)
1925-...... **CLC 1, 2, 3, 4, 7, 9, 14, 15,
27, 49**
See also CA 1-4R; CANR 2; DLB 2, 7;
DLBY 80; MTCW

Hawking, S. W.
See Hawking, Stephen W(illiam)

Hawking, Stephen W(illiam)
1942-........................ **CLC 63**
See also BEST 89:1; CA 126; 129

Hawthorne, Julian 1846-1934 ..... **TCLC 25**

Hawthorne, Nathaniel
1804-1864 ...... **NCLC 39; DA; SSC 3;
WLC**
See also CDALB 1640-1865; DLB 1, 74;
YABC 2

Haxton, Josephine Ayres 1921- .... **CLC 73**
See also CA 115; CANR 41

Hayaseca y Eizaguirre, Jorge
See Echegaray (y Eizaguirre), Jose (Maria
Waldo)

Hayashi Fumiko 1904-1951...... **TCLC 27**

Haycraft, Anna
See Ellis, Alice Thomas
See also CA 122

Hayden, Robert E(arl)
1913-1980 ..... **CLC 5, 9, 14, 37; BLC;
DA; PC 6**
See also BW 1; CA 69-72; 97-100; CABS 2;
CANR 24; CDALB 1941-1968; DLB 5,
76; MTCW; SATA 19, 26

Hayford, J(oseph) E(phraim) Casely
See Casely-Hayford, J(oseph) E(phraim)

Hayman, Ronald 1932-............ **CLC 44**
See also CA 25-28R; CANR 18

Haywood, Eliza (Fowler)
1693(?)-1756 .... **LC 1**

Hazlitt, William 1778-1830 ...... **NCLC 29**
See also DLB 110

Hazzard, Shirley 1931- .... **CLC 18**
See also CA 9-12R; CANR 4; DLBY 82;
MTCW

Head, Bessie 1937-1986... **CLC 25, 67; BLC**
See also BW 2; CA 29-32R; 119; CANR 25;
DLB 117; MTCW

Headon, (Nicky) Topper 1956(?)- ... **CLC 30**
See also Clash, The

Heaney, Seamus (Justin)
1939-......... **CLC 5, 7, 14, 25, 37, 74**
See also CA 85-88; CANR 25;
CDBLB 1960 to Present; DLB 40;
MTCW

Hearn, (Patricio) Lafcadio (Tessima Carlos)
1850-1904 .... **TCLC 9**
See also CA 105; DLB 12, 78

Hearne, Vicki 1946-.............. **CLC 56**
See also CA 139

Hearon, Shelby 1931-............. **CLC 63**
See also AITN 2; CA 25-28R; CANR 18

Heat-Moon, William Least......... CLC 29
See also Trogdon, William (Lewis)
See also AAYA 9

Hebbel, Friedrich 1813-1863 ..... **NCLC 43**
See also DLB 129

Hebert, Anne 1916- .... **CLC 4, 13, 29**
See also CA 85-88; DLB 68; MTCW

Hecht, Anthony (Evan)
1923-.................. **CLC 8, 13, 19**
See also CA 9-12R; CANR 6; DLB 5

Hecht, Ben 1894-1964 .... **CLC 8**
See also CA 85-88; DLB 7, 9, 25, 26, 28, 86

Hedayat, Sadeq 1903-1951....... **TCLC 21**
See also CA 120

Hegel, Georg Wilhelm Friedrich
1770-1831 .... **NCLC 46**
See also DLB 90

Heidegger, Martin 1889-1976 ...... **CLC 24**
See also CA 81-84; 65-68; CANR 34;
MTCW

Heidenstam, (Carl Gustaf) Verner von
1859-1940 .... **TCLC 5**
See also CA 104

Heifner, Jack 1946-.............. **CLC 11**
See also CA 105

Heijermans, Herman 1864-1924 ... **TCLC 24**
See also CA 123

Heilbrun, Carolyn G(old) 1926-..... **CLC 25**
See also CA 45-48; CANR 1, 28

Heine, Heinrich 1797-1856 .... **NCLC 4**
See also DLB 90

Heinemann, Larry (Curtiss) 1944- .. **CLC 50**
See also CA 110; CANR 31; DLBD 9

Heiney, Donald (William)
1921-1993 .... **CLC 9**
See also CA 1-4R; 142; CANR 3

Heinlein, Robert A(nson)
1907-1988 ..... **CLC 1, 3, 8, 14, 26, 55**
See also CA 1-4R; 125; CANR 1, 20;
DLB 8; JRDA; MAICYA; MTCW;
SATA 9, 56, 69

Helforth, John
See Doolittle, Hilda

Hellenhofferu, Vojtech Kapristian z
See Hasek, Jaroslav (Matej Frantisek)

Heller, Joseph
1923- .... **CLC 1, 3, 5, 8, 11, 36, 63; DA;
WLC**
See also AITN 1; CA 5-8R; CABS 1;
CANR 8, 42; DLB 2, 28; DLBY 80;
MTCW

Hellman, Lillian (Florence)
1906-1984 ...... **CLC 2, 4, 8, 14, 18, 34,
44, 52; DC 1**
See also AITN 1, 2; CA 13-16R; 112;
CANR 33; DLB 7; DLBY 84; MTCW

Helprin, Mark 1947- ..... **CLC 7, 10, 22, 32**
See also CA 81-84; DLBY 85; MTCW

Helvetius, Claude-Adrien
1715-1771 .... **LC 26**

Helyar, Jane Penelope Josephine 1933-
See Poole, Josephine
See also CA 21-24R; CANR 10, 26

Hemans, Felicia 1793-1835 ...... **NCLC 29**
See also DLB 96

Hemingway, Ernest (Miller)
1899-1961 .... **CLC 1, 3, 6, 8, 10, 13, 19,
30, 34, 39, 41, 44, 50, 61, 80; DA; SSC 1;
WLC**
See also CA 77-80; CANR 34;
CDALB 1917-1929; DLB 4, 9, 102;
DLBD 1; DLBY 81, 87; MTCW

Hempel, Amy 1951-.............. **CLC 39**
See also CA 118; 137

Henderson, F. C.
See Mencken, H(enry) L(ouis)

Henderson, Sylvia
See Ashton-Warner, Sylvia (Constance)

Henley, Beth .... CLC 23
See also Henley, Elizabeth Becker
See also CABS 3; DLBY 86

Henley, Elizabeth Becker 1952-
See Henley, Beth
See also CA 107; CANR 32; MTCW

Henley, William Ernest
1849-1903 .... TCLC 8
See also CA 105; DLB 19

Hennissart, Martha
See Lathen, Emma
See also CA 85-88

Henry, O. .... TCLC 1, 19; SSC 5; WLC
See also Porter, William Sydney

Henry, Patrick 1736-1799 .... LC 25

Henryson, Robert 1430(?)-1506(?).... LC 20

Henry VIII 1491-1547 .... LC 10

Henschke, Alfred
See Klabund

Hentoff, Nat(han Irving) 1925- ..... CLC 26
See also AAYA 4; CA 1-4R; CAAS 6;
CANR 5, 25; CLR 1; JRDA; MAICYA;
SATA 27, 42, 69

Heppenstall, (John) Rayner
1911-1981 .... CLC 10
See also CA 1-4R; 103; CANR 29

Herbert, Frank (Patrick)
1920-1986 .... CLC 12, 23, 35, 44
See also CA 53-56; 118; CANR 5, 43;
DLB 8; MTCW; SATA 9, 37, 47

Herbert, George 1593-1633 .... LC 24; PC 4
See also CDBLB Before 1660; DLB 126

Herbert, Zbigniew 1924- .... CLC 9, 43
See also CA 89-92; CANR 36; MTCW

Herbst, Josephine (Frey)
1897-1969 .... CLC 34
See also CA 5-8R; 25-28R; DLB 9

Hergesheimer, Joseph
1880-1954 .... TCLC 11
See also CA 109; DLB 102, 9

Herlihy, James Leo 1927-1993 ...... CLC 6
See also CA 1-4R; 143; CANR 2

Hermogenes fl. c. 175- .... CMLC 6

Hernandez, Jose 1834-1886 ...... NCLC 17

Herrick, Robert
1591-1674 .... LC 13; DA; PC 9
See also DLB 126

Herring, Guilles
See Somerville, Edith

Herriot, James 1916- .... CLC 12
See also Wight, James Alfred
See also AAYA 1; CANR 40

Herrmann, Dorothy 1941- .... CLC 44
See also CA 107

Herrmann, Taffy
See Herrmann, Dorothy

Hersey, John (Richard)
1914-1993 ...... CLC 1, 2, 7, 9, 40, 81
See also CA 17-20R; 140; CANR 33;
DLB 6; MTCW; SATA 25;
SATA-Obit 76

Herzen, Aleksandr Ivanovich
1812-1870 .... NCLC 10

Herzl, Theodor 1860-1904 .... TCLC 36

Herzog, Werner 1942- .... CLC 16
See also CA 89-92

Hesiod c. 8th cent. B.C.- .... CMLC 5

Hesse, Hermann
1877-1962 .... CLC 1, 2, 3, 6, 11, 17, 25,
69; DA; SSC 9; WLC
See also CA 17-18; CAP 2; DLB 66;
MTCW; SATA 50

Hewes, Cady
See De Voto, Bernard (Augustine)

Heyen, William 1940- .... CLC 13, 18
See also CA 33-36R; CAAS 9; DLB 5

Heyerdahl, Thor 1914- .... CLC 26
See also CA 5-8R; CANR 5, 22; MTCW;
SATA 2, 52

Heym, Georg (Theodor Franz Arthur)
1887-1912 .... TCLC 9
See also CA 106

Heym, Stefan 1913- .... CLC 41
See also CA 9-12R; CANR 4; DLB 69

Heyse, Paul (Johann Ludwig von)
1830-1914 .... TCLC 8
See also CA 104; DLB 129

Hibbert, Eleanor Alice Burford
1906-1993 .... CLC 7
See also BEST 90:4; CA 17-20R; 140;
CANR 9, 28; SATA 2; SATA-Obit 74

Higgins, George V(incent)
1939- .... CLC 4, 7, 10, 18
See also CA 77-80; CAAS 5; CANR 17;
DLB 2; DLBY 81; MTCW

Higginson, Thomas Wentworth
1823-1911 .... TCLC 36
See also DLB 1, 64

Highet, Helen
See MacInnes, Helen (Clark)

Highsmith, (Mary) Patricia
1921- .... CLC 2, 4, 14, 42
See also CA 1-4R; CANR 1, 20; MTCW

Highwater, Jamake (Mamake)
1942(?)- .... CLC 12
See also AAYA 7; CA 65-68; CAAS 7;
CANR 10, 34; CLR 17; DLB 52;
DLBY 85; JRDA; MAICYA; SATA 30,
32, 69

Hijuelos, Oscar 1951- ...... CLC 65; HLC
See also BEST 90:1; CA 123; HW

Hikmet, Nazim 1902(?)-1963 ...... CLC 40
See also CA 141; 93-96

Hildesheimer, Wolfgang
1916-1991 .... CLC 49
See also CA 101; 135; DLB 69, 124

Hill, Geoffrey (William)
1932- .... CLC 5, 8, 18, 45
See also CA 81-84; CANR 21;
CDBLB 1960 to Present; DLB 40;
MTCW

Hill, George Roy 1921- .... CLC 26
See also CA 110; 122

Hill, John
See Koontz, Dean R(ay)

Hill, Susan (Elizabeth) 1942- .... CLC 4
See also CA 33-36R; CANR 29; DLB 14,
139; MTCW

Hillerman, Tony 1925- .... CLC 62
See also AAYA 6; BEST 89:1; CA 29-32R;
CANR 21, 42; SATA 6

Hillesum, Etty 1914-1943 .... TCLC 49
See also CA 137

Hilliard, Noel (Harvey) 1929- ...... CLC 15
See also CA 9-12R; CANR 7

Hillis, Rick 1956- .... CLC 66
See also CA 134

Hilton, James 1900-1954 .... TCLC 21
See also CA 108; DLB 34, 77; SATA 34

Himes, Chester (Bomar)
1909-1984 .... CLC 2, 4, 7, 18, 58; BLC
See also BW 2; CA 25-28R; 114; CANR 22;
DLB 2, 76, 143; MTCW

Hinde, Thomas .... CLC 6, 11
See also Chitty, Thomas Willes

Hindin, Nathan
See Bloch, Robert (Albert)

Hine, (William) Daryl 1936- .... CLC 15
See also CA 1-4R; CAAS 15; CANR 1, 20;
DLB 60

Hinkson, Katharine Tynan
See Tynan, Katharine

Hinton, S(usan) E(loise)
1950- .... CLC 30; DA
See also AAYA 2; CA 81-84; CANR 32;
CLR 3, 23; JRDA; MAICYA; MTCW;
SATA 19, 58

Hippius, Zinaida .... TCLC 9
See also Gippius, Zinaida (Nikolayevna)

Hiraoka, Kimitake 1925-1970
See Mishima, Yukio
See also CA 97-100; 29-32R; MTCW

Hirsch, E(ric) D(onald), Jr. 1928- ... CLC 79
See also CA 25-28R; CANR 27; DLB 67;
MTCW

Hirsch, Edward 1950- .... CLC 31, 50
See also CA 104; CANR 20, 42; DLB 120

Hitchcock, Alfred (Joseph)
1899-1980 .... CLC 16
See also CA 97-100; SATA 24, 27

Hitler, Adolf 1889-1945 .... TCLC 53
See also CA 117

Hoagland, Edward 1932- .... CLC 28
See also CA 1-4R; CANR 2, 31; DLB 6;
SATA 51

Hoban, Russell (Conwell) 1925- .. CLC 7, 25
See also CA 5-8R; CANR 23, 37; CLR 3;
DLB 52; MAICYA; MTCW; SATA 1,
40, 78

Hobbs, Perry
See Blackmur, R(ichard) P(almer)

Hobson, Laura Z(ametkin)
1900-1986 .... CLC 7, 25
See also CA 17-20R; 118; DLB 28;
SATA 52

Isaacs, Susan 1943- . . . . **CLC 32**
See also BEST 89:1; CA 89-92; CANR 20, 41; MTCW

Isherwood, Christopher (William Bradshaw)
1904-1986 . . . . **CLC 1, 9, 11, 14, 44**
See also CA 13-16R; 117; CANR 35; DLB 15; DLBY 86; MTCW

Ishiguro, Kazuo 1954- . . . . . . **CLC 27, 56, 59**
See also BEST 90:2; CA 120; MTCW

Ishikawa Takuboku
1886(?)-1912 . . . . **TCLC 15; PC 10**
See also CA 113

Iskander, Fazil 1929- . . . . **CLC 47**
See also CA 102

Ivan IV 1530-1584 . . . . **LC 17**

Ivanov, Vyacheslav Ivanovich
1866-1949 . . . . **TCLC 33**
See also CA 122

Ivask, Ivar Vidrik 1927-1992 . . . . **CLC 14**
See also CA 37-40R; 139; CANR 24

Jackson, Daniel
See Wingrove, David (John)

Jackson, Jesse 1908-1983 . . . . **CLC 12**
See also BW 1; CA 25-28R; 109; CANR 27; CLR 28; MAICYA; SATA 2, 29, 48

Jackson, Laura (Riding) 1901-1991
See Riding, Laura
See also CA 65-68; 135; CANR 28; DLB 48

Jackson, Sam
See Trumbo, Dalton

Jackson, Sara
See Wingrove, David (John)

Jackson, Shirley
1919-1965 . . . . . **CLC 11, 60; DA; SSC 9; WLC**
See also AAYA 9; CA 1-4R; 25-28R; CANR 4; CDALB 1941-1968; DLB 6; SATA 2

Jacob, (Cyprien-)Max 1876-1944 . . . **TCLC 6**
See also CA 104

Jacobs, Jim 1942- . . . . **CLC 12**
See also CA 97-100

Jacobs, W(illiam) W(ymark)
1863-1943 . . . . **TCLC 22**
See also CA 121; DLB 135

Jacobsen, Jens Peter 1847-1885 . . **NCLC 34**

Jacobsen, Josephine 1908- . . . . **CLC 48**
See also CA 33-36R; CAAS 18; CANR 23

Jacobson, Dan 1929- . . . . **CLC 4, 14**
See also CA 1-4R; CANR 2, 25; DLB 14; MTCW

Jacqueline
See Carpentier (y Valmont), Alejo

Jagger, Mick 1944- . . . . **CLC 17**

Jakes, John (William) 1932- . . . . **CLC 29**
See also BEST 89:4; CA 57-60; CANR 10, 43; DLBY 83; MTCW; SATA 62

James, Andrew
See Kirkup, James

James, C(yril) L(ionel) R(obert)
1901-1989 . . . . **CLC 33**
See also BW 2; CA 117; 125; 128; DLB 125; MTCW

James, Daniel (Lewis) 1911-1988
See Santiago, Danny
See also CA 125

James, Dynely
See Mayne, William (James Carter)

James, Henry
1843-1916 . . . . . . **TCLC 2, 11, 24, 40, 47; DA; SSC 8; WLC**
See also CA 104; 132; CDALB 1865-1917; DLB 12, 71, 74; MTCW

James, M. R.
See James, Montague (Rhodes)

James, Montague (Rhodes)
1862-1936 . . . . **TCLC 6; SSC 16**
See also CA 104

James, P. D. . . . . **CLC 18, 46**
See also White, Phyllis Dorothy James
See also BEST 90:2; CDBLB 1960 to Present; DLB 87

James, Philip
See Moorcock, Michael (John)

James, William 1842-1910 . . . . . **TCLC 15, 32**
See also CA 109

James I 1394-1437 . . . . **LC 20**

Jameson, Anna 1794-1860 . . . . **NCLC 43**
See also DLB 99

Jami, Nur al-Din 'Abd al-Rahman
1414-1492 . . . . **LC 9**

Jandl, Ernst 1925- . . . . **CLC 34**

Janowitz, Tama 1957- . . . . **CLC 43**
See also CA 106

Jarrell, Randall
1914-1965 . . . . **CLC 1, 2, 6, 9, 13, 49**
See also CA 5-8R; 25-28R; CABS 2; CANR 6, 34; CDALB 1941-1968; CLR 6; DLB 48, 52; MAICYA; MTCW; SATA 7

Jarry, Alfred 1873-1907 . . . . **TCLC 2, 14**
See also CA 104

Jarvis, E. K.
See Bloch, Robert (Albert); Ellison, Harlan; Silverberg, Robert

Jeake, Samuel, Jr.
See Aiken, Conrad (Potter)

Jean Paul 1763-1825 . . . . **NCLC 7**

Jeffers, (John) Robinson
1887-1962 . . . . **CLC 2, 3, 11, 15, 54; DA; WLC**
See also CA 85-88; CANR 35; CDALB 1917-1929; DLB 45; MTCW

Jefferson, Janet
See Mencken, H(enry) L(ouis)

Jefferson, Thomas 1743-1826 . . . . **NCLC 11**
See also CDALB 1640-1865; DLB 31

Jeffrey, Francis 1773-1850 . . . . **NCLC 33**
See also DLB 107

Jelakowitch, Ivan
See Heijermans, Herman

Jellicoe, (Patricia) Ann 1927- . . . . . . **CLC 27**
See also CA 85-88; DLB 13

Jen, Gish . . . . **CLC 70**
See also Jen, Lillian

Jen, Lillian 1956(?)-
See Jen, Gish
See also CA 135

Jenkins, (John) Robin 1912- . . . . **CLC 52**
See also CA 1-4R; CANR 1; DLB 14

Jennings, Elizabeth (Joan)
1926- . . . . **CLC 5, 14**
See also CA 61-64; CAAS 5; CANR 8, 39; DLB 27; MTCW; SATA 66

Jennings, Waylon 1937- . . . . **CLC 21**

Jensen, Johannes V. 1873-1950 . . . . **TCLC 41**

Jensen, Laura (Linnea) 1948- . . . . . . **CLC 37**
See also CA 103

Jerome, Jerome K(lapka)
1859-1927 . . . . **TCLC 23**
See also CA 119; DLB 10, 34, 135

Jerrold, Douglas William
1803-1857 . . . . **NCLC 2**

Jewett, (Theodora) Sarah Orne
1849-1909 . . . . **TCLC 1, 22; SSC 6**
See also CA 108; 127; DLB 12, 74; SATA 15

Jewsbury, Geraldine (Endsor)
1812-1880 . . . . **NCLC 22**
See also DLB 21

Jhabvala, Ruth Prawer
1927- . . . . **CLC 4, 8, 29**
See also CA 1-4R; CANR 2, 29; DLB 139; MTCW

Jiles, Paulette 1943- . . . . **CLC 13, 58**
See also CA 101

Jimenez (Mantecon), Juan Ramon
1881-1958 . . . . **TCLC 4; HLC; PC 7**
See also CA 104; 131; DLB 134; HW; MTCW

Jimenez, Juan Ramon 1881-1958
See Jimenez (Mantecon), Juan Ramon

Jimenez, Ramon
See Jimenez (Mantecon), Juan Ramon

Jimenez Mantecon, Juan
See Jimenez (Mantecon), Juan Ramon

Joel, Billy . . . . **CLC 26**
See also Joel, William Martin

Joel, William Martin 1949-
See Joel, Billy
See also CA 108

John of the Cross, St. 1542-1591 . . . . **LC 18**

Johnson, B(ryan) S(tanley William)
1933-1973 . . . . **CLC 6, 9**
See also CA 9-12R; 53-56; CANR 9; DLB 14, 40

Johnson, Benj. F. of Boo
See Riley, James Whitcomb

Johnson, Benjamin F. of Boo
See Riley, James Whitcomb

Johnson, Charles (Richard)
1948- . . . . **CLC 7, 51, 65; BLC**
See also BW 2; CA 116; CAAS 18; CANR 42; DLB 33

Johnson, Denis 1949- . . . . **CLC 52**
See also CA 117; 121; DLB 120

Johnson, Diane 1934- . . . . **CLC 5, 13, 48**
See also CA 41-44R; CANR 17, 40; DLBY 80; MTCW

Johnson, Eyvind (Olof Verner)
1900-1976 . . . . **CLC 14**
See also CA 73-76; 69-72; CANR 34

Johnson, J. R.
See James, C(yril) L(ionel) R(obert)

Johnson, James Weldon
1871-1938 . . . . **TCLC 3, 19; BLC**
See also BW 1; CA 104; 125;
CDALB 1917-1929; CLR 32; DLB 51;
MTCW; SATA 31

Johnson, Joyce 1935- . . . . **CLC 58**
See also CA 125; 129

Johnson, Lionel (Pigot)
1867-1902 . . . . **TCLC 19**
See also CA 117; DLB 19

Johnson, Mel
See Malzberg, Barry N(athaniel)

Johnson, Pamela Hansford
1912-1981 . . . . **CLC 1, 7, 27**
See also CA 1-4R; 104; CANR 2, 28;
DLB 15; MTCW

Johnson, Samuel
1709-1784 . . . . **LC 15; DA; WLC**
See also CDBLB 1660-1789; DLB 39, 95,
104, 142

Johnson, Uwe
1934-1984 . . . . **CLC 5, 10, 15, 40**
See also CA 1-4R; 112; CANR 1, 39;
DLB 75; MTCW

Johnston, George (Benson) 1913- . . . **CLC 51**
See also CA 1-4R; CANR 5, 20; DLB 88

Johnston, Jennifer 1930- . . . . **CLC 7**
See also CA 85-88; DLB 14

Jolley, (Monica) Elizabeth 1923- . . . **CLC 46**
See also CA 127; CAAS 13

Jones, Arthur Llewellyn 1863-1947
See Machen, Arthur
See also CA 104

Jones, D(ouglas) G(ordon) 1929- . . . . **CLC 10**
See also CA 29-32R; CANR 13; DLB 53

Jones, David (Michael)
1895-1974 . . . . **CLC 2, 4, 7, 13, 42**
See also CA 9-12R; 53-56; CANR 28;
CDBLB 1945-1960; DLB 20, 100; MTCW

Jones, David Robert 1947-
See Bowie, David
See also CA 103

Jones, Diana Wynne 1934- . . . . **CLC 26**
See also AAYA 12; CA 49-52; CANR 4,
26; CLR 23; JRDA; MAICYA; SAAS 7;
SATA 9, 70

Jones, Edward P. 1950- . . . . **CLC 76**
See also BW 2; CA 142

Jones, Gayl 1949- . . . . **CLC 6, 9; BLC**
See also BW 2; CA 77-80; CANR 27;
DLB 33; MTCW

Jones, James 1921-1977 . . . . **CLC 1, 3, 10, 39**
See also AITN 1, 2; CA 1-4R; 69-72;
CANR 6; DLB 2, 143; MTCW

Jones, John J.
See Lovecraft, H(oward) P(hillips)

Jones, LeRoi . . . . **CLC 1, 2, 3, 5, 10, 14**
See also Baraka, Amiri

Jones, Louis B. . . . . **CLC 65**
See also CA 141

Jones, Madison (Percy, Jr.) 1925- . . . **CLC 4**
See also CA 13-16R; CAAS 11; CANR 7

Jones, Mervyn 1922- . . . . **CLC 10, 52**
See also CA 45-48; CAAS 5; CANR 1;
MTCW

Jones, Mick 1956(?)- . . . . **CLC 30**
See also Clash, The

Jones, Nettie (Pearl) 1941- . . . . **CLC 34**
See also BW 2; CA 137

Jones, Preston 1936-1979 . . . . **CLC 10**
See also CA 73-76; 89-92; DLB 7

Jones, Robert F(rancis) 1934- . . . . . . **CLC 7**
See also CA 49-52; CANR 2

Jones, Rod 1953- . . . . **CLC 50**
See also CA 128

Jones, Terence Graham Parry
1942- . . . . **CLC 21**
See also Jones, Terry; Monty Python
See also CA 112; 116; CANR 35; SATA 51

Jones, Terry
See Jones, Terence Graham Parry
See also SATA 67

Jones, Thom 1945(?)- . . . . **CLC 81**

Jong, Erica 1942- . . . . . . **CLC 4, 6, 8, 18, 83**
See also AITN 1; BEST 90:2; CA 73-76;
CANR 26; DLB 2, 5, 28; MTCW

Jonson, Ben(jamin)
1572(?)-1637 . . . . **LC 6; DA; DC 4; WLC**
See also CDBLB Before 1660; DLB 62, 121

Jordan, June 1936- . . . . **CLC 5, 11, 23**
See also AAYA 2; BW 2; CA 33-36R;
CANR 25; CLR 10; DLB 38; MAICYA;
MTCW; SATA 4

Jordan, Pat(rick M.) 1941- . . . . **CLC 37**
See also CA 33-36R

Jorgensen, Ivar
See Ellison, Harlan

Jorgenson, Ivar
See Silverberg, Robert

Josephus, Flavius c. 37-100 . . . . . . **CMLC 13**

Josipovici, Gabriel 1940- . . . . **CLC 6, 43**
See also CA 37-40R; CAAS 8; DLB 14

Joubert, Joseph 1754-1824 . . . . **NCLC 9**

Jouve, Pierre Jean 1887-1976 . . . . . . **CLC 47**
See also CA 65-68

Joyce, James (Augustine Aloysius)
1882-1941 . . . . . . **TCLC 3, 8, 16, 35; DA;**
SSC 3; WLC
See also CA 104; 126; CDBLB 1914-1945;
DLB 10, 19, 36; MTCW

Jozsef, Attila 1905-1937 . . . . **TCLC 22**
See also CA 116

Juana Ines de la Cruz 1651(?)-1695 . . . **LC 5**

Judd, Cyril
See Kornbluth, C(yril) M.; Pohl, Frederik

Julian of Norwich 1342(?)-1416(?) . . . . **LC 6**

Just, Ward (Swift) 1935- . . . . **CLC 4, 27**
See also CA 25-28R; CANR 32

Justice, Donald (Rodney) 1925- . . **CLC 6, 19**
See also CA 5-8R; CANR 26; DLBY 83

Juvenal c. 55-c. 127 . . . . **CMLC 8**

Juvenis
See Bourne, Randolph S(illiman)

Kacew, Romain 1914-1980
See Gary, Romain
See also CA 108; 102

Kadare, Ismail 1936- . . . . **CLC 52**

Kadohata, Cynthia . . . . **CLC 59**
See also CA 140

Kafka, Franz
1883-1924 . . . . **TCLC 2, 6, 13, 29, 47, 53;**
DA; SSC 5; WLC
See also CA 105; 126; DLB 81; MTCW

Kahanovitsch, Pinkhes 1884-1950
See Der Nister

Kahn, Roger 1927- . . . . **CLC 30**
See also CA 25-28R; CANR 44; SATA 37

Kain, Saul
See Sassoon, Siegfried (Lorraine)

Kaiser, Georg 1878-1945 . . . . **TCLC 9**
See also CA 106; DLB 124

Kaletski, Alexander 1946- . . . . **CLC 39**
See also CA 118; 143

Kalidasa fl. c. 400- . . . . **CMLC 9**

Kallman, Chester (Simon)
1921-1975 . . . . **CLC 2**
See also CA 45-48; 53-56; CANR 3

Kaminsky, Melvin 1926-
See Brooks, Mel
See also CA 65-68; CANR 16

Kaminsky, Stuart M(elvin) 1934- . . . **CLC 59**
See also CA 73-76; CANR 29

Kane, Paul
See Simon, Paul

Kane, Wilson
See Bloch, Robert (Albert)

Kanin, Garson 1912- . . . . **CLC 22**
See also AITN 1; CA 5-8R; CANR 7;
DLB 7

Kaniuk, Yoram 1930- . . . . **CLC 19**
See also CA 134

Kant, Immanuel 1724-1804 . . . . . . **NCLC 27**
See also DLB 94

Kantor, MacKinlay 1904-1977 . . . . . . **CLC 7**
See also CA 61-64; 73-76; DLB 9, 102

Kaplan, David Michael 1946- . . . . . . **CLC 50**

Kaplan, James 1951- . . . . **CLC 59**
See also CA 135

Karageorge, Michael
See Anderson, Poul (William)

Karamzin, Nikolai Mikhailovich
1766-1826 . . . . **NCLC 3**

Karapanou, Margarita 1946- . . . . **CLC 13**
See also CA 101

Karinthy, Frigyes 1887-1938 . . . . . . **TCLC 47**

Karl, Frederick R(obert) 1927- . . . . . **CLC 34**
See also CA 5-8R; CANR 3, 44

Kastel, Warren
See Silverberg, Robert

Kataev, Evgeny Petrovich 1903-1942
See Petrov, Evgeny
See also CA 120

Kataphusin
See Ruskin, John

Katz, Steve 1935- . . . . CLC 47
See also CA 25-28R; CAAS 14; CANR 12;
DLBY 83

Kauffman, Janet 1945- . . . . CLC 42
See also CA 117; CANR 43; DLBY 86

Kaufman, Bob (Garnell)
1925-1986 . . . . CLC 49
See also BW 1; CA 41-44R; 118; CANR 22;
DLB 16, 41

Kaufman, George S. 1889-1961. . . . . CLC 38
See also CA 108; 93-96; DLB 7

Kaufman, Sue . . . . CLC 3, 8
See also Barondess, Sue K(aufman)

Kavafis, Konstantinos Petrou 1863-1933
See Cavafy, C(onstantine) P(eter)
See also CA 104

Kavan, Anna 1901-1968 . . . . . . CLC 5, 13, 82
See also CA 5-8R; CANR 6; MTCW

Kavanagh, Dan
See Barnes, Julian

Kavanagh, Patrick (Joseph)
1904-1967 . . . . CLC 22
See also CA 123; 25-28R; DLB 15, 20;
MTCW

Kawabata, Yasunari
1899-1972 . . . . CLC 2, 5, 9, 18
See also CA 93-96; 33-36R

Kaye, M(ary) M(argaret) 1909-. . . . . CLC 28
See also CA 89-92; CANR 24; MTCW;
SATA 62

Kaye, Mollie
See Kaye, M(ary) M(argaret)

Kaye-Smith, Sheila 1887-1956. . . . . TCLC 20
See also CA 118; DLB 36

Kaymor, Patrice Maguilene
See Senghor, Leopold Sedar

Kazan, Elia 1909-. . . . . CLC 6, 16, 63
See also CA 21-24R; CANR 32

Kazantzakis, Nikos
1883(?)-1957 . . . . TCLC 2, 5, 33
See also CA 105; 132; MTCW

Kazin, Alfred 1915- . . . . CLC 34, 38
See also CA 1-4R; CAAS 7; CANR 1, 45;
DLB 67

Keane, Mary Nesta (Skrine) 1904-
See Keane, Molly
See also CA 108; 114

Keane, Molly. . . . . CLC 31
See also Keane, Mary Nesta (Skrine)

Keates, Jonathan 19(?)- . . . . CLC 34

Keaton, Buster 1895-1966 . . . . CLC 20

Keats, John
1795-1821 . . . NCLC 8; DA; PC 1; WLC
See also CDBLB 1789-1832; DLB 96, 110

Keene, Donald 1922- . . . . CLC 34
See also CA 1-4R; CANR 5

Keillor, Garrison . . . . CLC 40
See also Keillor, Gary (Edward)
See also AAYA 2; BEST 89:3; DLBY 87;
SATA 58

Keillor, Gary (Edward) 1942-
See Keillor, Garrison
See also CA 111; 117; CANR 36; MTCW

Keith, Michael
See Hubbard, L(afayette) Ron(ald)

Keller, Gottfried 1819-1890. . . . . . NCLC 2
See also DLB 129

Kellerman, Jonathan 1949- . . . . CLC 44
See also BEST 90:1; CA 106; CANR 29

Kelley, William Melvin 1937-. . . . . . CLC 22
See also BW 1; CA 77-80; CANR 27;
DLB 33

Kellogg, Marjorie 1922-. . . . . CLC 2
See also CA 81-84

Kellow, Kathleen
See Hibbert, Eleanor Alice Burford

Kelly, M(ilton) T(erry) 1947-. . . . . . . CLC 55
See also CA 97-100; CANR 19, 43

Kelman, James 1946-. . . . . CLC 58

Kemal, Yashar 1923- . . . . CLC 14, 29
See also CA 89-92; CANR 44

Kemble, Fanny 1809-1893 . . . . NCLC 18
See also DLB 32

Kemelman, Harry 1908-. . . . . CLC 2
See also AITN 1; CA 9-12R; CANR 6;
DLB 28

Kempe, Margery 1373(?)-1440(?) . . . . . LC 6

Kempis, Thomas a 1380-1471 . . . . . . LC 11

Kendall, Henry 1839-1882. . . . . . . NCLC 12

Keneally, Thomas (Michael)
1935- . . . . . . CLC 5, 8, 10, 14, 19, 27, 43
See also CA 85-88; CANR 10; MTCW

Kennedy, Adrienne (Lita)
1931- . . . . CLC 66; BLC
See also BW 2; CA 103; CABS 3;
CANR 26; DLB 38

Kennedy, John Pendleton
1795-1870 . . . . NCLC 2
See also DLB 3

Kennedy, Joseph Charles 1929-. . . . . CLC 8
See also Kennedy, X. J.
See also CA 1-4R; CANR 4, 30, 40;
SATA 14

Kennedy, William 1928-. . . CLC 6, 28, 34, 53
See also AAYA 1; CA 85-88; CANR 14,
31; DLB 143; DLBY 85; MTCW;
SATA 57

Kennedy, X. J.. . . . . CLC 42
See also Kennedy, Joseph Charles
See also CAAS 9; CLR 27; DLB 5

Kent, Kelvin
See Kuttner, Henry

Kenton, Maxwell
See Southern, Terry

Kenyon, Robert O.
See Kuttner, Henry

Kerouac, Jack . . . . . CLC 1, 2, 3, 5, 14, 29, 61
See also Kerouac, Jean-Louis Lebris de
See also CDALB 1941-1968; DLB 2, 16;
DLBD 3

Kerouac, Jean-Louis Lebris de 1922-1969
See Kerouac, Jack
See also AITN 1; CA 5-8R; 25-28R;
CANR 26; DA; MTCW; WLC

Kerr, Jean 1923-. . . . . CLC 22
See also CA 5-8R; CANR 7

Kerr, M. E. . . . . CLC 12, 35
See also Meaker, Marijane (Agnes)
See also AAYA 2; CLR 29; SAAS 1

Kerr, Robert . . . . CLC 55

Kerrigan, (Thomas) Anthony
1918- . . . . CLC 4, 6
See also CA 49-52; CAAS 11; CANR 4

Kerry, Lois
See Duncan, Lois

Kesey, Ken (Elton)
1935- . . . . . . CLC 1, 3, 6, 11, 46, 64; DA;
WLC
See also CA 1-4R; CANR 22, 38;
CDALB 1968-1988; DLB 2, 16; MTCW;
SATA 66

Kesselring, Joseph (Otto)
1902-1967 . . . . CLC 45

Kessler, Jascha (Frederick) 1929-. . . . CLC 4
See also CA 17-20R; CANR 8

Kettelkamp, Larry (Dale) 1933- . . . . CLC 12
See also CA 29-32R; CANR 16; SAAS 3;
SATA 2

Keyber, Conny
See Fielding, Henry

Keyes, Daniel 1927-. . . . . CLC 80; DA
See also CA 17-20R; CANR 10, 26;
SATA 37

Khayyam, Omar
1048-1131 . . . . CMLC 11; PC 8

Kherdian, David 1931-. . . . . CLC 6, 9
See also CA 21-24R; CAAS 2; CANR 39;
CLR 24; JRDA; MAICYA; SATA 16, 74

Khlebnikov, Velimir . . . . TCLC 20
See also Khlebnikov, Viktor Vladimirovich

Khlebnikov, Viktor Vladimirovich 1885-1922
See Khlebnikov, Velimir
See also CA 117

Khodasevich, Vladislav (Felitsianovich)
1886-1939 . . . . TCLC 15
See also CA 115

Kielland, Alexander Lange
1849-1906 . . . . TCLC 5
See also CA 104

Kiely, Benedict 1919-. . . . . CLC 23, 43
See also CA 1-4R; CANR 2; DLB 15

Kienzle, William X(avier) 1928- . . . . CLC 25
See also CA 93-96; CAAS 1; CANR 9, 31;
MTCW

Kierkegaard, Soren 1813-1855. . . . NCLC 34

Killens, John Oliver 1916-1987. . . . . CLC 10
See also BW 2; CA 77-80; 123; CAAS 2;
CANR 26; DLB 33

Killigrew, Anne 1660-1685. . . . . LC 4
See also DLB 131

Kim
See Simenon, Georges (Jacques Christian)

Kincaid, Jamaica 1949- . . . CLC 43, 68; BLC
See also BW 2; CA 125

King, Francis (Henry) 1923-. . . . . CLC 8, 53
See also CA 1-4R; CANR 1, 33; DLB 15,
139; MTCW

Author Index

Linton, Eliza Lynn 1822-1898 . . . . **NCLC 41**
See also DLB 18

Li Po 701-763 . . . . **CMLC 2**

Lipsius, Justus 1547-1606 . . . . **LC 16**

Lipsyte, Robert (Michael)
 1938- . . . . **CLC 21; DA**
See also AAYA 7; CA 17-20R; CANR 8;
 CLR 23; JRDA; MAICYA; SATA 5, 68

Lish, Gordon (Jay) 1934- . . . . **CLC 45**
See also CA 113; 117; DLB 130

Lispector, Clarice 1925-1977 . . . . . . **CLC 43**
See also CA 139; 116; DLB 113

Littell, Robert 1935(?)- . . . . **CLC 42**
See also CA 109; 112

Little, Malcolm 1925-1965
See Malcolm X
See also BW 1; CA 125; 111; DA; MTCW

Littlewit, Humphrey Gent.
See Lovecraft, H(oward) P(hillips)

Litwos
See Sienkiewicz, Henryk (Adam Alexander
 Pius)

Liu E 1857-1909 . . . . **TCLC 15**
See also CA 115

Lively, Penelope (Margaret)
 1933- . . . . **CLC 32, 50**
See also CA 41-44R; CANR 29; CLR 7;
 DLB 14; JRDA; MAICYA; MTCW;
 SATA 7, 60

Livesay, Dorothy (Kathleen)
 1909- . . . . **CLC 4, 15, 79**
See also AITN 2; CA 25-28R; CAAS 8;
 CANR 36; DLB 68; MTCW

Livy c. 59B.C.-c. 17 . . . . **CMLC 11**

Lizardi, Jose Joaquin Fernandez de
 1776-1827 . . . . **NCLC 30**

Llewellyn, Richard . . . . **CLC 7**
See also Llewellyn Lloyd, Richard Dafydd
 Vivian
See also DLB 15

Llewellyn Lloyd, Richard Dafydd Vivian
 1906-1983 . . . . **CLC 80**
See also Llewellyn, Richard
See also CA 53-56; 111; CANR 7;
 SATA 11, 37

Llosa, (Jorge) Mario (Pedro) Vargas
See Vargas Llosa, (Jorge) Mario (Pedro)

Lloyd Webber, Andrew 1948-
See Webber, Andrew Lloyd
See also AAYA 1; CA 116; SATA 56

Llull, Ramon c. 1235-c. 1316 . . . . . **CMLC 12**

Locke, Alain (Le Roy)
 1886-1954 . . . . **TCLC 43**
See also BW 1; CA 106; 124; DLB 51

Locke, John 1632-1704 . . . . **LC 7**
See also DLB 101

Locke-Elliott, Sumner
See Elliott, Sumner Locke

Lockhart, John Gibson
 1794-1854 . . . . **NCLC 6**
See also DLB 110, 116, 144

Lodge, David (John) 1935- . . . . **CLC 36**
See also BEST 90:1; CA 17-20R; CANR 19;
 DLB 14; MTCW

Loennbohm, Armas Eino Leopold 1878-1926
See Leino, Eino
See also CA 123

Loewinsohn, Ron(ald William)
 1937- . . . . **CLC 52**
See also CA 25-28R

Logan, Jake
See Smith, Martin Cruz

Logan, John (Burton) 1923-1987 . . . . . **CLC 5**
See also CA 77-80; 124; CANR 45; DLB 5

Lo Kuan-chung 1330(?)-1400(?) . . . . . . **LC 12**

Lombard, Nap
See Johnson, Pamela Hansford

London, Jack . . **TCLC 9, 15, 39; SSC 4; WLC**
See also London, John Griffith
See also AITN 2; CDALB 1865-1917;
 DLB 8, 12, 78; SATA 18

London, John Griffith 1876-1916
See London, Jack
See also CA 110; 119; DA; JRDA;
 MAICYA; MTCW

Long, Emmett
See Leonard, Elmore (John, Jr.)

Longbaugh, Harry
See Goldman, William (W.)

Longfellow, Henry Wadsworth
 1807-1882 . . . . **NCLC 2, 45; DA**
See also CDALB 1640-1865; DLB 1, 59;
 SATA 19

Longley, Michael 1939- . . . . **CLC 29**
See also CA 102; DLB 40

Longus fl. c. 2nd cent. - . . . . **CMLC 7**

Longway, A. Hugh
See Lang, Andrew

Lopate, Phillip 1943- . . . . **CLC 29**
See also CA 97-100; DLBY 80

Lopez Portillo (y Pacheco), Jose
 1920- . . . . **CLC 46**
See also CA 129; HW

Lopez y Fuentes, Gregorio
 1897(?)-1966 . . . . **CLC 32**
See also CA 131; HW

Lorca, Federico Garcia
See Garcia Lorca, Federico

Lord, Bette Bao 1938- . . . . **CLC 23**
See also BEST 90:3; CA 107; CANR 41;
 SATA 58

Lord Auch
See Bataille, Georges

Lord Byron
See Byron, George Gordon (Noel)

Lorde, Audre (Geraldine)
 1934-1992 . . . . **CLC 18, 71; BLC**
See also BW 1; CA 25-28R; 142; CANR 16,
 26; DLB 41; MTCW

Lord Jeffrey
See Jeffrey, Francis

Lorenzo, Heberto Padilla
See Padilla (Lorenzo), Heberto

Loris
See Hofmannsthal, Hugo von

Loti, Pierre . . . . **TCLC 11**
See also Viaud, (Louis Marie) Julien
See also DLB 123

Louie, David Wong 1954- . . . . **CLC 70**
See also CA 139

Louis, Father M.
See Merton, Thomas

Lovecraft, H(oward) P(hillips)
 1890-1937 . . . . **TCLC 4, 22; SSC 3**
See also CA 104; 133; MTCW

Lovelace, Earl 1935- . . . . **CLC 51**
See also BW 2; CA 77-80; CANR 41;
 DLB 125; MTCW

Lovelace, Richard 1618-1657 . . . . **LC 24**
See also DLB 131

Lowell, Amy 1874-1925 . . . . **TCLC 1, 8**
See also CA 104; DLB 54, 140

Lowell, James Russell 1819-1891 . . **NCLC 2**
See also CDALB 1640-1865; DLB 1, 11, 64,
 79

Lowell, Robert (Traill Spence, Jr.)
 1917-1977 . . . **CLC 1, 2, 3, 4, 5, 8, 9, 11,
  15, 37; DA; PC 3; WLC**
See also CA 9-12R; 73-76; CABS 2;
 CANR 26; DLB 5; MTCW

Lowndes, Marie Adelaide (Belloc)
 1868-1947 . . . . **TCLC 12**
See also CA 107; DLB 70

Lowry, (Clarence) Malcolm
 1909-1957 . . . . **TCLC 6, 40**
See also CA 105; 131; CDBLB 1945-1960;
 DLB 15; MTCW

Lowry, Mina Gertrude 1882-1966
See Loy, Mina
See also CA 113

Loxsmith, John
See Brunner, John (Kilian Houston)

Loy, Mina . . . . **CLC 28**
See also Lowry, Mina Gertrude
See also DLB 4, 54

Loyson-Bridet
See Schwob, (Mayer Andre) Marcel

Lucas, Craig 1951- . . . . **CLC 64**
See also CA 137

Lucas, George 1944- . . . . **CLC 16**
See also AAYA 1; CA 77-80; CANR 30;
 SATA 56

Lucas, Hans
See Godard, Jean-Luc

Lucas, Victoria
See Plath, Sylvia

Ludlam, Charles 1943-1987 . . . . . **CLC 46, 50**
See also CA 85-88; 122

Ludlum, Robert 1927- . . . . **CLC 22, 43**
See also AAYA 10; BEST 89:1, 90:3;
 CA 33-36R; CANR 25, 41; DLBY 82;
 MTCW

Ludwig, Ken . . . . **CLC 60**

Ludwig, Otto 1813-1865 . . . . **NCLC 4**
See also DLB 129

Lugones, Leopoldo 1874-1938 . . . . . **TCLC 15**
See also CA 116; 131; HW

Lu Hsun 1881-1936 . . . . **TCLC 3**

Lukacs, George . . . . **CLC 24**
See also Lukacs, Gyorgy (Szegeny von)

Lukacs, Gyorgy (Szegeny von) 1885-1971
See Lukacs, George
See also CA 101; 29-32R

Luke, Peter (Ambrose Cyprian)
1919- .... **CLC 38**
See also CA 81-84; DLB 13

Lunar, Dennis
See Mungo, Raymond

Lurie, Alison 1926-........ **CLC 4, 5, 18, 39**
See also CA 1-4R; CANR 2, 17; DLB 2;
MTCW; SATA 46

Lustig, Arnost 1926-............. **CLC 56**
See also AAYA 3; CA 69-72; SATA 56

Luther, Martin 1483-1546 .... **LC 9**

Luzi, Mario 1914-................ **CLC 13**
See also CA 61-64; CANR 9; DLB 128

Lynch, B. Suarez
See Bioy Casares, Adolfo; Borges, Jorge
Luis

Lynch, David (K.) 1946-......... **CLC 66**
See also CA 124; 129

Lynch, James
See Andreyev, Leonid (Nikolaevich)

Lynch Davis, B.
See Bioy Casares, Adolfo; Borges, Jorge
Luis

Lyndsay, Sir David 1490-1555 ...... **LC 20**

Lynn, Kenneth S(chuyler) 1923-.... **CLC 50**
See also CA 1-4R; CANR 3, 27

Lynx
See West, Rebecca

Lyons, Marcus
See Blish, James (Benjamin)

Lyre, Pinchbeck
See Sassoon, Siegfried (Lorraine)

Lytle, Andrew (Nelson) 1902-...... **CLC 22**
See also CA 9-12R; DLB 6

Lyttelton, George 1709-1773........ **LC 10**

Maas, Peter 1929- .... **CLC 29**
See also CA 93-96

Macaulay, Rose 1881-1958 ..... **TCLC 7, 44**
See also CA 104; DLB 36

Macaulay, Thomas Babington
1800-1859 .... **NCLC 42**
See also CDBLB 1832-1890; DLB 32, 55

MacBeth, George (Mann)
1932-1992 .... **CLC 2, 5, 9**
See also CA 25-28R; 136; DLB 40; MTCW;
SATA 4; SATA-Obit 70

MacCaig, Norman (Alexander)
1910- .... **CLC 36**
See also CA 9-12R; CANR 3, 34; DLB 27

MacCarthy, (Sir Charles Otto) Desmond
1877-1952 .... **TCLC 36**

MacDiarmid, Hugh
.... **CLC 2, 4, 11, 19, 63; PC 9**
See also Grieve, C(hristopher) M(urray)
See also CDBLB 1945-1960; DLB 20

MacDonald, Anson
See Heinlein, Robert A(nson)

Macdonald, Cynthia 1928-...... **CLC 13, 19**
See also CA 49-52; CANR 4, 44; DLB 105

MacDonald, George 1824-1905 ..... **TCLC 9**
See also CA 106; 137; DLB 18; MAICYA;
SATA 33

Macdonald, John
See Millar, Kenneth

MacDonald, John D(ann)
1916-1986 .... **CLC 3, 27, 44**
See also CA 1-4R; 121; CANR 1, 19;
DLB 8; DLBY 86; MTCW

Macdonald, John Ross
See Millar, Kenneth

Macdonald, Ross ..... **CLC 1, 2, 3, 14, 34, 41**
See also Millar, Kenneth
See also DLBD 6

MacDougal, John
See Blish, James (Benjamin)

MacEwen, Gwendolyn (Margaret)
1941-1987 .... **CLC 13, 55**
See also CA 9-12R; 124; CANR 7, 22;
DLB 53; SATA 50, 55

Macha, Karen Hynek
1810-1846 .... **NCLC 46**

Machado (y Ruiz), Antonio
1875-1939 .... **TCLC 3**
See also CA 104; DLB 108

Machado de Assis, Joaquim Maria
1839-1908 .... **TCLC 10; BLC**
See also CA 107

Machen, Arthur.................. **TCLC 4**
See also Jones, Arthur Llewellyn
See also DLB 36

Machiavelli, Niccolo 1469-1527 .. **LC 8; DA**

MacInnes, Colin 1914-1976...... **CLC 4, 23**
See also CA 69-72; 65-68; CANR 21;
DLB 14; MTCW

MacInnes, Helen (Clark)
1907-1985 .... **CLC 27, 39**
See also CA 1-4R; 117; CANR 1, 28;
DLB 87; MTCW; SATA 22, 44

Mackay, Mary 1855-1924
See Corelli, Marie
See also CA 118

Mackenzie, Compton (Edward Montague)
1883-1972 .... **CLC 18**
See also CA 21-22; 37-40R; CAP 2;
DLB 34, 100

Mackenzie, Henry 1745-1831 .... **NCLC 41**
See also DLB 39

Mackintosh, Elizabeth 1896(?)-1952
See Tey, Josephine
See also CA 110

MacLaren, James
See Grieve, C(hristopher) M(urray)

Mac Laverty, Bernard 1942-....... **CLC 31**
See also CA 116; 118; CANR 43

MacLean, Alistair (Stuart)
1922-1987 .... **CLC 3, 13, 50, 63**
See also CA 57-60; 121; CANR 28; MTCW;
SATA 23, 50

Maclean, Norman (Fitzroy)
1902-1990 .... **CLC 78; SSC 13**
See also CA 102; 132

MacLeish, Archibald
1892-1982 .... **CLC 3, 8, 14, 68**
See also CA 9-12R; 106; CANR 33; DLB 4,
7, 45; DLBY 82; MTCW

MacLennan, (John) Hugh
1907-1990 .... **CLC 2, 14**
See also CA 5-8R; 142; CANR 33; DLB 68;
MTCW

MacLeod, Alistair 1936- .... **CLC 56**
See also CA 123; DLB 60

MacNeice, (Frederick) Louis
1907-1963 .... **CLC 1, 4, 10, 53**
See also CA 85-88; DLB 10, 20; MTCW

MacNeill, Dand
See Fraser, George MacDonald

Macpherson, (Jean) Jay 1931-...... **CLC 14**
See also CA 5-8R; DLB 53

MacShane, Frank 1927-........... **CLC 39**
See also CA 9-12R; CANR 3, 33; DLB 111

Macumber, Mari
See Sandoz, Mari(e Susette)

Madach, Imre 1823-1864........ **NCLC 19**

Madden, (Jerry) David 1933- .... **CLC 5, 15**
See also CA 1-4R; CAAS 3; CANR 4, 45;
DLB 6; MTCW

Maddern, Al(an)
See Ellison, Harlan

Madhubuti, Haki R.
1942- .... **CLC 6, 73; BLC; PC 5**
See also Lee, Don L.
See also BW 2; CA 73-76; CANR 24;
DLB 5, 41; DLBD 8

Madow, Pauline (Reichberg) .... **CLC 1**
See also CA 9-12R

Maepenn, Hugh
See Kuttner, Henry

Maepenn, K. H.
See Kuttner, Henry

Maeterlinck, Maurice 1862-1949 ... **TCLC 3**
See also CA 104; 136; SATA 66

Maginn, William 1794-1842....... **NCLC 8**
See also DLB 110

Mahapatra, Jayanta 1928-......... **CLC 33**
See also CA 73-76; CAAS 9; CANR 15, 33

Mahfouz, Naguib (Abdel Aziz Al-Sabilgi)
1911(?)-
See Mahfuz, Najib
See also BEST 89:2; CA 128; MTCW

Mahfuz, Najib.................. **CLC 52, 55**
See also Mahfouz, Naguib (Abdel Aziz
Al-Sabilgi)
See also DLBY 88

Mahon, Derek 1941-.............. **CLC 27**
See also CA 113; 128; DLB 40

Mailer, Norman
1923- ...... **CLC 1, 2, 3, 4, 5, 8, 11, 14,
28, 39, 74; DA**
See also AITN 2; CA 9-12R; CABS 1;
CANR 28; CDALB 1968-1988; DLB 2,
16, 28; DLBD 3; DLBY 80, 83; MTCW

Maillet, Antonine 1929-........... **CLC 54**
See also CA 115; 120; DLB 60

Mais, Roger 1905-1955 .... **TCLC 8**
See also BW 1; CA 105; 124; DLB 125;
MTCW

Maistre, Joseph de 1753-1821.... **NCLC 37**

Maitland, Sara (Louise) 1950-...... **CLC 49**
See also CA 69-72; CANR 13

Major, Clarence
1936- .... **CLC 3, 19, 48; BLC**
See also BW 2; CA 21-24R; CAAS 6;
CANR 13, 25; DLB 33

Major, Kevin (Gerald) 1949-....... **CLC 26**
See also CA 97-100; CANR 21, 38;
CLR 11; DLB 60; JRDA; MAICYA;
SATA 32

Maki, James
See Ozu, Yasujiro

Malabaila, Damiano
See Levi, Primo

Malamud, Bernard
1914-1986 ..... **CLC 1, 2, 3, 5, 8, 9, 11,
18, 27, 44, 78; DA; SSC 15; WLC**
See also CA 5-8R; 118; CABS 1; CANR 28;
CDALB 1941-1968; DLB 2, 28;
DLBY 80, 86; MTCW

Malaparte, Curzio 1898-1957 ..... **TCLC 52**

Malcolm, Dan
See Silverberg, Robert

Malcolm X .... **CLC 82; BLC**
See also Little, Malcolm

Malherbe, Francois de 1555-1628..... **LC 5**

Mallarme, Stephane
1842-1898 .... **NCLC 4, 41; PC 4**

Mallet-Joris, Francoise 1930-...... **CLC 11**
See also CA 65-68; CANR 17; DLB 83

Malley, Ern
See McAuley, James Phillip

Mallowan, Agatha Christie
See Christie, Agatha (Mary Clarissa)

Maloff, Saul 1922- .... **CLC 5**
See also CA 33-36R

Malone, Louis
See MacNeice, (Frederick) Louis

Malone, Michael (Christopher)
1942- .... **CLC 43**
See also CA 77-80; CANR 14, 32

Malory, (Sir) Thomas
1410(?)-1471(?) .... **LC 11; DA**
See also CDBLB Before 1660; SATA 33, 59

Malouf, (George Joseph) David
1934- .... **CLC 28**
See also CA 124

Malraux, (Georges-)Andre
1901-1976 ..... **CLC 1, 4, 9, 13, 15, 57**
See also CA 21-22; 69-72; CANR 34;
CAP 2; DLB 72; MTCW

Malzberg, Barry N(athaniel) 1939-... **CLC 7**
See also CA 61-64; CAAS 4; CANR 16;
DLB 8

Mamet, David (Alan)
1947- .... **CLC 9, 15, 34, 46; DC 4**
See also AAYA 3; CA 81-84; CABS 3;
CANR 15, 41; DLB 7; MTCW

Mamoulian, Rouben (Zachary)
1897-1987 .... **CLC 16**
See also CA 25-28R; 124

Mandelstam, Osip (Emilievich)
1891(?)-1938(?) .... **TCLC 2, 6**
See also CA 104

Mander, (Mary) Jane 1877-1949... **TCLC 31**

Mandiargues, Andre Pieyre de...... **CLC 41**
See also Pieyre de Mandiargues, Andre
See also DLB 83

Mandrake, Ethel Belle
See Thurman, Wallace (Henry)

Mangan, James Clarence
1803-1849 .... **NCLC 27**

Maniere, J.-E.
See Giraudoux, (Hippolyte) Jean

Manley, (Mary) Delariviere
1672(?)-1724 .... **LC 1**
See also DLB 39, 80

Mann, Abel
See Creasey, John

Mann, (Luiz) Heinrich 1871-1950... **TCLC 9**
See also CA 106; DLB 66

Mann, (Paul) Thomas
1875-1955 .... **TCLC 2, 8, 14, 21, 35, 44;
DA; SSC 5; WLC**
See also CA 104; 128; DLB 66; MTCW

Manning, David
See Faust, Frederick (Schiller)

Manning, Frederic 1887(?)-1935... **TCLC 25**
See also CA 124

Manning, Olivia 1915-1980...... **CLC 5, 19**
See also CA 5-8R; 101; CANR 29; MTCW

Mano, D. Keith 1942- .... **CLC 2, 10**
See also CA 25-28R; CAAS 6; CANR 26;
DLB 6

Mansfield, Katherine
.... **TCLC 2, 8, 39; SSC 9; WLC**
See also Beauchamp, Kathleen Mansfield

Manso, Peter 1940- .... **CLC 39**
See also CA 29-32R; CANR 44

Mantecon, Juan Jimenez
See Jimenez (Mantecon), Juan Ramon

Manton, Peter
See Creasey, John

Man Without a Spleen, A
See Chekhov, Anton (Pavlovich)

Manzoni, Alessandro 1785-1873.. **NCLC 29**

Mapu, Abraham (ben Jekutiel)
1808-1867 .... **NCLC 18**

Mara, Sally
See Queneau, Raymond

Marat, Jean Paul 1743-1793....... **LC 10**

Marcel, Gabriel Honore
1889-1973 .... **CLC 15**
See also CA 102; 45-48; MTCW

Marchbanks, Samuel
See Davies, (William) Robertson

Marchi, Giacomo
See Bassani, Giorgio

Margulies, Donald .... **CLC 76**

Marie de France c. 12th cent. -.... **CMLC 8**

Marie de l'Incarnation 1599-1672.... **LC 10**

Mariner, Scott
See Pohl, Frederik

Marinetti, Filippo Tommaso
1876-1944 .... **TCLC 10**
See also CA 107; DLB 114

Marivaux, Pierre Carlet de Chamblain de
1688-1763 .... **LC 4**

Markandaya, Kamala .... **CLC 8, 38**
See also Taylor, Kamala (Purnaiya)

Markfield, Wallace 1926-.......... **CLC 8**
See also CA 69-72; CAAS 3; DLB 2, 28

Markham, Edwin 1852-1940 ..... **TCLC 47**
See also DLB 54

Markham, Robert
See Amis, Kingsley (William)

Marks, J
See Highwater, Jamake (Mamake)

Marks-Highwater, J
See Highwater, Jamake (Mamake)

Markson, David M(errill) 1927-.... **CLC 67**
See also CA 49-52; CANR 1

Marley, Bob .... **CLC 17**
See also Marley, Robert Nesta

Marley, Robert Nesta 1945-1981
See Marley, Bob
See also CA 107; 103

Marlowe, Christopher
1564-1593 ..... **LC 22; DA; DC 1; WLC**
See also CDBLB Before 1660; DLB 62

Marmontel, Jean-Francois
1723-1799 .... **LC 2**

Marquand, John P(hillips)
1893-1960 .... **CLC 2, 10**
See also CA 85-88; DLB 9, 102

Marquez, Gabriel (Jose) Garcia...... **CLC 68**
See also Garcia Marquez, Gabriel (Jose)

Marquis, Don(ald Robert Perry)
1878-1937 .... **TCLC 7**
See also CA 104; DLB 11, 25

Marric, J. J.
See Creasey, John

Marrow, Bernard
See Moore, Brian

Marryat, Frederick 1792-1848 .... **NCLC 3**
See also DLB 21

Marsden, James
See Creasey, John

Marsh, (Edith) Ngaio
1899-1982 .... **CLC 7, 53**
See also CA 9-12R; CANR 6; DLB 77;
MTCW

Marshall, Garry 1934-............ **CLC 17**
See also AAYA 3; CA 111; SATA 60

Marshall, Paule
1929- .... **CLC 27, 72; BLC; SSC 3**
See also BW 2; CA 77-80; CANR 25;
DLB 33; MTCW

Marsten, Richard
See Hunter, Evan

Martha, Henry
See Harris, Mark

Martial 40-103 .... **PC 10**

Martin, Ken
See Hubbard, L(afayette) Ron(ald)

Martin, Richard
See Creasey, John

Martin, Steve 1945- . . . . CLC 30
See also CA 97-100; CANR 30; MTCW

Martin, Violet Florence
1862-1915 . . . . TCLC 51

Martin, Webber
See Silverberg, Robert

Martindale, Patrick Victor
See White, Patrick (Victor Martindale)

Martin du Gard, Roger
1881-1958 . . . . TCLC 24
See also CA 118; DLB 65

Martineau, Harriet 1802-1876. . . . NCLC 26
See also DLB 21, 55; YABC 2

Martines, Julia
See O'Faolain, Julia

Martinez, Jacinto Benavente y
See Benavente (y Martinez), Jacinto

Martinez Ruiz, Jose 1873-1967
See Azorin; Ruiz, Jose Martinez
See also CA 93-96; HW

Martinez Sierra, Gregorio
1881-1947 . . . . TCLC 6
See also CA 115

Martinez Sierra, Maria (de la O'LeJarraga)
1874-1974 . . . . TCLC 6
See also CA 115

Martinsen, Martin
See Follett, Ken(neth Martin)

Martinson, Harry (Edmund)
1904-1978 . . . . CLC 14
See also CA 77-80; CANR 34

Marut, Ret
See Traven, B.

Marut, Robert
See Traven, B.

Marvell, Andrew
1621-1678 . . . . . LC 4; DA; PC 10; WLC
See also CDBLB 1660-1789; DLB 131

Marx, Karl (Heinrich)
1818-1883 . . . . NCLC 17
See also DLB 129

Masaoka Shiki. . . . . TCLC 18
See also Masaoka Tsunenori

Masaoka Tsunenori 1867-1902
See Masaoka Shiki
See also CA 117

Masefield, John (Edward)
1878-1967 . . . . CLC 11, 47
See also CA 19-20; 25-28R; CANR 33;
CAP 2; CDBLB 1890-1914; DLB 10;
MTCW; SATA 19

Maso, Carole 19(?)- . . . . CLC 44

Mason, Bobbie Ann
1940- . . . . CLC 28, 43, 82; SSC 4
See also AAYA 5; CA 53-56; CANR 11,
31; DLBY 87; MTCW

Mason, Ernst
See Pohl, Frederik

Mason, Lee W.
See Malzberg, Barry N(athaniel)

Mason, Nick 1945- . . . . CLC 35
See also Pink Floyd

Mason, Tally
See Derleth, August (William)

Mass, William
See Gibson, William

Masters, Edgar Lee
1868-1950 . . . . . . TCLC 2, 25; DA; PC 1
See also CA 104; 133; CDALB 1865-1917;
DLB 54; MTCW

Masters, Hilary 1928- . . . . CLC 48
See also CA 25-28R; CANR 13

Mastrosimone, William 19(?)- . . . . . . CLC 36

Mathe, Albert
See Camus, Albert

Matheson, Richard Burton 1926- . . . CLC 37
See also CA 97-100; DLB 8, 44

Mathews, Harry 1930- . . . . CLC 6, 52
See also CA 21-24R; CAAS 6; CANR 18,
40

Mathews, John Joseph 1894-1979. . . CLC 84
See also CA 19-20; 142; CANR 45; CAP 2

Mathias, Roland (Glyn) 1915- . . . . . . CLC 45
See also CA 97-100; CANR 19, 41; DLB 27

Matsuo Basho 1644-1694. . . . . PC 3

Mattheson, Rodney
See Creasey, John

Matthews, Greg 1949- . . . . CLC 45
See also CA 135

Matthews, William 1942- . . . . CLC 40
See also CA 29-32R; CAAS 18; CANR 12;
DLB 5

Matthias, John (Edward) 1941- . . . . . . CLC 9
See also CA 33-36R

Matthiessen, Peter
1927- . . . . CLC 5, 7, 11, 32, 64
See also AAYA 6; BEST 90:4; CA 9-12R;
CANR 21; DLB 6; MTCW; SATA 27

Maturin, Charles Robert
1780(?)-1824 . . . . NCLC 6

Matute (Ausejo), Ana Maria
1925- . . . . CLC 11
See also CA 89-92; MTCW

Maugham, W. S.
See Maugham, W(illiam) Somerset

Maugham, W(illiam) Somerset
1874-1965 . . . . . . CLC 1, 11, 15, 67; DA;
SSC 8; WLC
See also CA 5-8R; 25-28R; CANR 40;
CDBLB 1914-1945; DLB 10, 36, 77, 100;
MTCW; SATA 54

Maugham, William Somerset
See Maugham, W(illiam) Somerset

Maupassant, (Henri Rene Albert) Guy de
1850-1893 . . . . NCLC 1, 42; DA; SSC 1;
WLC
See also DLB 123

Maurhut, Richard
See Traven, B.

Mauriac, Claude 1914- . . . . CLC 9
See also CA 89-92; DLB 83

Mauriac, Francois (Charles)
1885-1970 . . . . CLC 4, 9, 56
See also CA 25-28; CAP 2; DLB 65;
MTCW

Mavor, Osborne Henry 1888-1951
See Bridie, James
See also CA 104

Maxwell, William (Keepers, Jr.)
1908- . . . . CLC 19
See also CA 93-96; DLBY 80

May, Elaine 1932- . . . . CLC 16
See also CA 124; 142; DLB 44

Mayakovski, Vladimir (Vladimirovich)
1893-1930 . . . . TCLC 4, 18
See also CA 104

Mayhew, Henry 1812-1887 . . . . . . NCLC 31
See also DLB 18, 55

Maynard, Joyce 1953- . . . . CLC 23
See also CA 111; 129

Mayne, William (James Carter)
1928- . . . . CLC 12
See also CA 9-12R; CANR 37; CLR 25;
JRDA; MAICYA; SAAS 11; SATA 6, 68

Mayo, Jim
See L'Amour, Louis (Dearborn)

Maysles, Albert 1926- . . . . CLC 16
See also CA 29-32R

Maysles, David 1932- . . . . CLC 16

Mazer, Norma Fox 1931- . . . . CLC 26
See also AAYA 5; CA 69-72; CANR 12,
32; CLR 23; JRDA; MAICYA; SAAS 1;
SATA 24, 67

Mazzini, Guiseppe 1805-1872 . . . . NCLC 34

McAuley, James Phillip
1917-1976 . . . . CLC 45
See also CA 97-100

McBain, Ed
See Hunter, Evan

McBrien, William Augustine
1930- . . . . CLC 44
See also CA 107

McCaffrey, Anne (Inez) 1926- . . . . . . CLC 17
See also AAYA 6; AITN 2; BEST 89:2;
CA 25-28R; CANR 15, 35; DLB 8;
JRDA; MAICYA; MTCW; SAAS 11;
SATA 8, 70

McCann, Arthur
See Campbell, John W(ood, Jr.)

McCann, Edson
See Pohl, Frederik

McCarthy, Charles, Jr. 1933-
See McCarthy, Cormac
See also CANR 42

McCarthy, Cormac 1933- . . . . CLC 4, 57
See also McCarthy, Charles, Jr.
See also DLB 6, 143

McCarthy, Mary (Therese)
1912-1989 . . . CLC 1, 3, 5, 14, 24, 39, 59
See also CA 5-8R; 129; CANR 16; DLB 2;
DLBY 81; MTCW

McCartney, (James) Paul
1942- . . . . CLC 12, 35

McCauley, Stephen (D.) 1955- . . . . . CLC 50
See also CA 141

McClure, Michael (Thomas)
1932- . . . . CLC 6, 10
See also CA 21-24R; CANR 17; DLB 16

McCorkle, Jill (Collins) 1958-...... **CLC 51**
See also CA 121; DLBY 87

McCourt, James 1941-............ **CLC 5**
See also CA 57-60

McCoy, Horace (Stanley)
1897-1955 .... **TCLC 28**
See also CA 108; DLB 9

McCrae, John 1872-1918........ **TCLC 12**
See also CA 109; DLB 92

McCreigh, James
See Pohl, Frederik

McCullers, (Lula) Carson (Smith)
1917-1967 .... **CLC 1, 4, 10, 12, 48; DA;**
SSC 9; WLC
See also CA 5-8R; 25-28R; CABS 1, 3;
CANR 18; CDALB 1941-1968; DLB 2, 7;
MTCW; SATA 27

McCulloch, John Tyler
See Burroughs, Edgar Rice

McCullough, Colleen 1938(?)-...... **CLC 27**
See also CA 81-84; CANR 17; MTCW

McElroy, Joseph 1930- .... **CLC 5, 47**
See also CA 17-20R

McEwan, Ian (Russell) 1948- ... **CLC 13, 66**
See also BEST 90:4; CA 61-64; CANR 14,
41; DLB 14; MTCW

McFadden, David 1940-.......... **CLC 48**
See also CA 104; DLB 60

McFarland, Dennis 1950- .... **CLC 65**

McGahern, John 1934-........ **CLC 5, 9, 48**
See also CA 17-20R; CANR 29; DLB 14;
MTCW

McGinley, Patrick (Anthony)
1937-...................... **CLC 41**
See also CA 120; 127

McGinley, Phyllis 1905-1978 ...... **CLC 14**
See also CA 9-12R; 77-80; CANR 19;
DLB 11, 48; SATA 2, 24, 44

McGinniss, Joe 1942-............ **CLC 32**
See also AITN 2; BEST 89:2; CA 25-28R;
CANR 26

McGivern, Maureen Daly
See Daly, Maureen

McGrath, Patrick 1950-.......... **CLC 55**
See also CA 136

McGrath, Thomas (Matthew)
1916-1990 .... **CLC 28, 59**
See also CA 9-12R; 132; CANR 6, 33;
MTCW; SATA 41; SATA-Obit 66

McGuane, Thomas (Francis III)
1939-............... **CLC 3, 7, 18, 45**
See also AITN 2; CA 49-52; CANR 5, 24;
DLB 2; DLBY 80; MTCW

McGuckian, Medbh 1950-........ **CLC 48**
See also CA 143; DLB 40

McHale, Tom 1942(?)-1982....... **CLC 3, 5**
See also AITN 1; CA 77-80; 106

McIlvanney, William 1936-....... **CLC 42**
See also CA 25-28R; DLB 14

McIlwraith, Maureen Mollie Hunter
See Hunter, Mollie
See also SATA 2

McInerney, Jay 1955-............ **CLC 34**
See also CA 116; 123

McIntyre, Vonda N(eel) 1948- ..... **CLC 18**
See also CA 81-84; CANR 17, 34; MTCW

McKay, Claude ..... **TCLC 7, 41; BLC; PC 2**
See also McKay, Festus Claudius
See also DLB 4, 45, 51, 117

McKay, Festus Claudius 1889-1948
See McKay, Claude
See also BW 1; CA 104; 124; DA; MTCW;
WLC

McKuen, Rod 1933-............. **CLC 1, 3**
See also AITN 1; CA 41-44R; CANR 40

McLoughlin, R. B.
See Mencken, H(enry) L(ouis)

McLuhan, (Herbert) Marshall
1911-1980 .... **CLC 37, 83**
See also CA 9-12R; 102; CANR 12, 34;
DLB 88; MTCW

McMillan, Terry (L.) 1951-..... **CLC 50, 61**
See also BW 2; CA 140

McMurtry, Larry (Jeff)
1936- .... **CLC 2, 3, 7, 11, 27, 44**
See also AITN 2; BEST 89:2; CA 5-8R;
CANR 19, 43; CDALB 1968-1988;
DLB 2, 143; DLBY 80, 87; MTCW

McNally, T. M. 1961- .... **CLC 82**

McNally, Terrence 1939-...... **CLC 4, 7, 41**
See also CA 45-48; CANR 2; DLB 7

McNamer, Deirdre 1950-.......... **CLC 70**

McNeile, Herman Cyril 1888-1937
See Sapper
See also DLB 77

McPhee, John (Angus) 1931- ...... **CLC 36**
See also BEST 90:1; CA 65-68; CANR 20;
MTCW

McPherson, James Alan
1943-.................. **CLC 19, 77**
See also BW 1; CA 25-28R; CAAS 17;
CANR 24; DLB 38; MTCW

McPherson, William (Alexander)
1933-...................... **CLC 34**
See also CA 69-72; CANR 28

McSweeney, Kerry .... **CLC 34**

Mead, Margaret 1901-1978........ **CLC 37**
See also AITN 1; CA 1-4R; 81-84;
CANR 4; MTCW; SATA 20

Meaker, Marijane (Agnes) 1927-
See Kerr, M. E.
See also CA 107; CANR 37; JRDA;
MAICYA; MTCW; SATA 20, 61

Medoff, Mark (Howard) 1940-... **CLC 6, 23**
See also AITN 1; CA 53-56; CANR 5;
DLB 7

Medvedev, P. N.
See Bakhtin, Mikhail Mikhailovich

Meged, Aharon
See Megged, Aharon

Meged, Aron
See Megged, Aharon

Megged, Aharon 1920-............ **CLC 9**
See also CA 49-52; CAAS 13; CANR 1

Mehta, Ved (Parkash) 1934-....... **CLC 37**
See also CA 1-4R; CANR 2, 23; MTCW

Melanter
See Blackmore, R(ichard) D(oddridge)

Melikow, Loris
See Hofmannsthal, Hugo von

Melmoth, Sebastian
See Wilde, Oscar (Fingal O'Flahertie Wills)

Meltzer, Milton 1915-............ **CLC 26**
See also AAYA 8; CA 13-16R; CANR 38;
CLR 13; DLB 61; JRDA; MAICYA;
SAAS 1; SATA 1, 50

Melville, Herman
1819-1891 .... **NCLC 3, 12, 29, 45; DA;**
SSC 1; WLC
See also CDALB 1640-1865; DLB 3, 74;
SATA 59

Menander
c. 342B.C.-c. 292B.C.... **CMLC 9; DC 3**

Mencken, H(enry) L(ouis)
1880-1956 .... **TCLC 13**
See also CA 105; 125; CDALB 1917-1929;
DLB 11, 29, 63, 137; MTCW

Mercer, David 1928-1980.......... **CLC 5**
See also CA 9-12R; 102; CANR 23;
DLB 13; MTCW

Merchant, Paul
See Ellison, Harlan

Meredith, George 1828-1909... **TCLC 17, 43**
See also CA 117; CDBLB 1832-1890;
DLB 18, 35, 57

Meredith, William (Morris)
1919-............... **CLC 4, 13, 22, 55**
See also CA 9-12R; CAAS 14; CANR 6, 40;
DLB 5

Merezhkovsky, Dmitry Sergeyevich
1865-1941 .... **TCLC 29**

Merimee, Prosper
1803-1870 .... **NCLC 6; SSC 7**
See also DLB 119

Merkin, Daphne 1954-........... **CLC 44**
See also CA 123

Merlin, Arthur
See Blish, James (Benjamin)

Merrill, James (Ingram)
1926- .... **CLC 2, 3, 6, 8, 13, 18, 34**
See also CA 13-16R; CANR 10; DLB 5;
DLBY 85; MTCW

Merriman, Alex
See Silverberg, Robert

Merritt, E. B.
See Waddington, Miriam

Merton, Thomas
1915-1968 .. **CLC 1, 3, 11, 34, 83; PC 10**
See also CA 5-8R; 25-28R; CANR 22;
DLB 48; DLBY 81; MTCW

Merwin, W(illiam) S(tanley)
1927-..... **CLC 1, 2, 3, 5, 8, 13, 18, 45**
See also CA 13-16R; CANR 15; DLB 5;
MTCW

Metcalf, John 1938-............. **CLC 37**
See also CA 113; DLB 60

Metcalf, Suzanne
See Baum, L(yman) Frank

Mew, Charlotte (Mary)
1870-1928 .... **TCLC 8**
See also CA 105; DLB 19, 135

Mewshaw, Michael 1943-.......... **CLC 9**
See also CA 53-56; CANR 7; DLBY 80

Meyer, June
See Jordan, June

Meyer, Lynn
See Slavitt, David R(ytman)

Meyer-Meyrink, Gustav   1868-1932
See Meyrink, Gustav
See also CA 117

Meyers, Jeffrey   1939- . . . . **CLC 39**
See also CA 73-76; DLB 111

Meynell, Alice (Christina Gertrude Thompson)
1847-1922 . . . . **TCLC 6**
See also CA 104; DLB 19, 98

Meyrink, Gustav . . . . **TCLC 21**
See also Meyer-Meyrink, Gustav
See also DLB 81

Michaels, Leonard
1933- . . . . **CLC 6, 25; SSC 16**
See also CA 61-64; CANR 21; DLB 130;
MTCW

Michaux, Henri   1899-1984 . . . . . . **CLC 8, 19**
See also CA 85-88; 114

Michelangelo   1475-1564. . . . . **LC 12**

Michelet, Jules   1798-1874 . . . . **NCLC 31**

Michener, James A(lbert)
1907(?)- . . . . **CLC 1, 5, 11, 29, 60**
See also AITN 1; BEST 90:1; CA 5-8R;
CANR 21, 45; DLB 6; MTCW

Mickiewicz, Adam   1798-1855 . . . . . **NCLC 3**

Middleton, Christopher   1926- . . . . . . **CLC 13**
See also CA 13-16R; CANR 29; DLB 40

Middleton, Richard (Barham)
1882-1911 . . . . **TCLC 56**

Middleton, Stanley   1919- . . . . **CLC 7, 38**
See also CA 25-28R; CANR 21; DLB 14

Migueis, Jose Rodrigues   1901- . . . . . **CLC 10**

Mikszath, Kalman   1847-1910 . . . . . **TCLC 31**

Miles, Josephine
1911-1985 . . . . **CLC 1, 2, 14, 34, 39**
See also CA 1-4R; 116; CANR 2; DLB 48

Militant
See Sandburg, Carl (August)

Mill, John Stuart   1806-1873 . . . . . **NCLC 11**
See also CDBLB 1832-1890; DLB 55

Millar, Kenneth   1915-1983 . . . . **CLC 14**
See also Macdonald, Ross
See also CA 9-12R; 110; CANR 16; DLB 2;
DLBD 6; DLBY 83; MTCW

Millay, E. Vincent
See Millay, Edna St. Vincent

Millay, Edna St. Vincent
1892-1950 . . . . . . **TCLC 4, 49; DA; PC 6**
See also CA 104; 130; CDALB 1917-1929;
DLB 45; MTCW

Miller, Arthur
1915- . . . . **CLC 1, 2, 6, 10, 15, 26, 47, 78;**
DA; DC 1; WLC
See also AITN 1; CA 1-4R; CABS 3;
CANR 2, 30; CDALB 1941-1968; DLB 7;
MTCW

Miller, Henry (Valentine)
1891-1980 . . . . **CLC 1, 2, 4, 9, 14, 43, 84;**
DA; WLC
See also CA 9-12R; 97-100; CANR 33;
CDALB 1929-1941; DLB 4, 9; DLBY 80;
MTCW

Miller, Jason   1939(?)- . . . . **CLC 2**
See also AITN 1; CA 73-76; DLB 7

Miller, Sue   1943- . . . . **CLC 44**
See also BEST 90:3; CA 139; DLB 143

Miller, Walter M(ichael, Jr.)
1923- . . . . **CLC 4, 30**
See also CA 85-88; DLB 8

Millett, Kate   1934- . . . . **CLC 67**
See also AITN 1; CA 73-76; CANR 32;
MTCW

Millhauser, Steven   1943- . . . . **CLC 21, 54**
See also CA 110; 111; DLB 2

Millin, Sarah Gertrude   1889-1968 . . **CLC 49**
See also CA 102; 93-96

Milne, A(lan) A(lexander)
1882-1956 . . . . **TCLC 6**
See also CA 104; 133; CLR 1, 26; DLB 10,
77, 100; MAICYA; MTCW; YABC 1

Milner, Ron(ald)   1938- . . . . **CLC 56; BLC**
See also AITN 1; BW 1; CA 73-76;
CANR 24; DLB 38; MTCW

Milosz, Czeslaw
1911- . . **CLC 5, 11, 22, 31, 56, 82; PC 8**
See also CA 81-84; CANR 23; MTCW

Milton, John   1608-1674 . . . **LC 9; DA; WLC**
See also CDBLB 1660-1789; DLB 131

Minehaha, Cornelius
See Wedekind, (Benjamin) Frank(lin)

Miner, Valerie   1947- . . . . **CLC 40**
See also CA 97-100

Minimo, Duca
See D'Annunzio, Gabriele

Minot, Susan   1956- . . . . **CLC 44**
See also CA 134

Minus, Ed   1938- . . . . **CLC 39**

Miranda, Javier
See Bioy Casares, Adolfo

Mirbeau, Octave   1848-1917 . . . . . . **TCLC 55**
See also DLB 123

Miro (Ferrer), Gabriel (Francisco Victor)
1879-1930 . . . . **TCLC 5**
See also CA 104

Mishima, Yukio
. . . . . . **CLC 2, 4, 6, 9, 27; DC 1; SSC 4**
See also Hiraoka, Kimitake

Mistral, Frederic   1830-1914 . . . . . **TCLC 51**
See also CA 122

Mistral, Gabriela . . . . **TCLC 2; HLC**
See also Godoy Alcayaga, Lucila

Mistry, Rohinton   1952- . . . . **CLC 71**
See also CA 141

Mitchell, Clyde
See Ellison, Harlan; Silverberg, Robert

Mitchell, James Leslie   1901-1935
See Gibbon, Lewis Grassic
See also CA 104; DLB 15

Mitchell, Joni   1943- . . . . **CLC 12**
See also CA 112

Mitchell, Margaret (Munnerlyn)
1900-1949 . . . . **TCLC 11**
See also CA 109; 125; DLB 9; MTCW

Mitchell, Peggy
See Mitchell, Margaret (Munnerlyn)

Mitchell, S(ilas) Weir   1829-1914 . . **TCLC 36**

Mitchell, W(illiam) O(rmond)
1914- . . . . **CLC 25**
See also CA 77-80; CANR 15, 43; DLB 88

Mitford, Mary Russell   1787-1855 . . **NCLC 4**
See also DLB 110, 116

Mitford, Nancy   1904-1973 . . . . **CLC 44**
See also CA 9-12R

Miyamoto, Yuriko   1899-1951 . . . . . **TCLC 37**

Mo, Timothy (Peter)   1950(?)- . . . . . . **CLC 46**
See also CA 117; MTCW

Modarressi, Taghi (M.)   1931- . . . . . . **CLC 44**
See also CA 121; 134

Modiano, Patrick (Jean)   1945- . . . . . **CLC 18**
See also CA 85-88; CANR 17, 40; DLB 83

Moerck, Paal
See Roelvaag, O(le) E(dvart)

Mofolo, Thomas (Mokopu)
1875(?)-1948 . . . . **TCLC 22; BLC**
See also CA 121

Mohr, Nicholasa   1935- . . . . . . **CLC 12; HLC**
See also AAYA 8; CA 49-52; CANR 1, 32;
CLR 22; HW; JRDA; SAAS 8; SATA 8

Mojtabai, A(nn) G(race)
1938- . . . . **CLC 5, 9, 15, 29**
See also CA 85-88

Moliere   1622-1673 . . . . **LC 10; DA; WLC**

Molin, Charles
See Mayne, William (James Carter)

Molnar, Ferenc   1878-1952 . . . . **TCLC 20**
See also CA 109

Momaday, N(avarre) Scott
1934- . . . . **CLC 2, 19; DA**
See also AAYA 11; CA 25-28R; CANR 14,
34; DLB 143; MTCW; NNAL; SATA 30,
48

Monette, Paul   1945- . . . . **CLC 82**
See also CA 139

Monroe, Harriet   1860-1936 . . . . **TCLC 12**
See also CA 109; DLB 54, 91

Monroe, Lyle
See Heinlein, Robert A(nson)

Montagu, Elizabeth   1917- . . . . **NCLC 7**
See also CA 9-12R

Montagu, Mary (Pierrepont) Wortley
1689-1762 . . . . **LC 9**
See also DLB 95, 101

Montagu, W. H.
See Coleridge, Samuel Taylor

Montague, John (Patrick)
1929- . . . . **CLC 13, 46**
See also CA 9-12R; CANR 9; DLB 40;
MTCW

Montaigne, Michel (Eyquem) de
1533-1592 . . . . **LC 8; DA; WLC**

Montale, Eugenio   1896-1981 . . . **CLC 7, 9, 18**
See also CA 17-20R; 104; CANR 30;
DLB 114; MTCW

Montesquieu, Charles-Louis de Secondat
1689-1755 . . . . LC 7

Montgomery, (Robert) Bruce   1921-1978
See Crispin, Edmund
See also CA 104

Montgomery, L(ucy) M(aud)
1874-1942 . . . . TCLC 51
See also AAYA 12; CA 108; 137; CLR 8;
DLB 92; JRDA; MAICYA; YABC 1

Montgomery, Marion H., Jr.   1925- . . CLC 7
See also AITN 1; CA 1-4R; CANR 3;
DLB 6

Montgomery, Max
See Davenport, Guy (Mattison, Jr.)

Montherlant, Henry (Milon) de
1896-1972 . . . . CLC 8, 19
See also CA 85-88; 37-40R; DLB 72;
MTCW

Monty Python . . . . CLC 21
See also Chapman, Graham; Cleese, John
(Marwood); Gilliam, Terry (Vance); Idle,
Eric; Jones, Terence Graham Parry; Palin,
Michael (Edward)
See also AAYA 7

Moodie, Susanna (Strickland)
1803-1885 . . . . NCLC 14
See also DLB 99

Mooney, Edward   1951- . . . . CLC 25
See also CA 130

Mooney, Ted
See Mooney, Edward

Moorcock, Michael (John)
1939- . . . . CLC 5, 27, 58
See also CA 45-48; CAAS 5; CANR 2, 17,
38; DLB 14; MTCW

Moore, Brian
1921- . . . . CLC 1, 3, 5, 7, 8, 19, 32
See also CA 1-4R; CANR 1, 25, 42; MTCW

Moore, Edward
See Muir, Edwin

Moore, George Augustus
1852-1933 . . . . TCLC 7
See also CA 104; DLB 10, 18, 57, 135

Moore, Lorrie . . . . CLC 39, 45, 68
See also Moore, Marie Lorena

Moore, Marianne (Craig)
1887-1972 . . . . CLC 1, 2, 4, 8, 10, 13, 19,
47; DA; PC 4
See also CA 1-4R; 33-36R; CANR 3;
CDALB 1929-1941; DLB 45; DLBD 7;
MTCW; SATA 20

Moore, Marie Lorena   1957-
See Moore, Lorrie
See also CA 116; CANR 39

Moore, Thomas   1779-1852 . . . . NCLC 6
See also DLB 96, 144

Morand, Paul   1888-1976 . . . . CLC 41
See also CA 69-72; DLB 65

Morante, Elsa   1918-1985 . . . . CLC 8, 47
See also CA 85-88; 117; CANR 35; MTCW

Moravia, Alberto . . . . . . CLC 2, 7, 11, 27, 46
See also Pincherle, Alberto

More, Hannah   1745-1833 . . . . NCLC 27
See also DLB 107, 109, 116

More, Henry   1614-1687 . . . . LC 9
See also DLB 126

More, Sir Thomas   1478-1535 . . . . . . LC 10

Moreas, Jean . . . . TCLC 18
See also Papadiamantopoulos, Johannes

Morgan, Berry   1919- . . . . CLC 6
See also CA 49-52; DLB 6

Morgan, Claire
See Highsmith, (Mary) Patricia

Morgan, Edwin (George)   1920- . . . . . CLC 31
See also CA 5-8R; CANR 3, 43; DLB 27

Morgan, (George) Frederick
1922- . . . . CLC 23
See also CA 17-20R; CANR 21

Morgan, Harriet
See Mencken, H(enry) L(ouis)

Morgan, Jane
See Cooper, James Fenimore

Morgan, Janet   1945- . . . . CLC 39
See also CA 65-68

Morgan, Lady   1776(?)-1859 . . . . . . NCLC 29
See also DLB 116

Morgan, Robin   1941- . . . . CLC 2
See also CA 69-72; CANR 29; MTCW

Morgan, Scott
See Kuttner, Henry

Morgan, Seth   1949(?)-1990 . . . . CLC 65
See also CA 132

Morgenstern, Christian
1871-1914 . . . . TCLC 8
See also CA 105

Morgenstern, S.
See Goldman, William (W.)

Moricz, Zsigmond   1879-1942 . . . . . TCLC 33

Morike, Eduard (Friedrich)
1804-1875 . . . . NCLC 10
See also DLB 133

Mori Ogai . . . . TCLC 14
See also Mori Rintaro

Mori Rintaro   1862-1922
See Mori Ogai
See also CA 110

Moritz, Karl Philipp   1756-1793 . . . . . . LC 2
See also DLB 94

Morland, Peter Henry
See Faust, Frederick (Schiller)

Morren, Theophil
See Hofmannsthal, Hugo von

Morris, Bill   1952- . . . . CLC 76

Morris, Julian
See West, Morris L(anglo)

Morris, Steveland Judkins   1950(?)-
See Wonder, Stevie
See also CA 111

Morris, William   1834-1896 . . . . NCLC 4
See also CDBLB 1832-1890; DLB 18, 35, 57

Morris, Wright   1910- . . CLC 1, 3, 7, 18, 37
See also CA 9-12R; CANR 21; DLB 2;
DLBY 81; MTCW

Morrison, Chloe Anthony Wofford
See Morrison, Toni

Morrison, James Douglas   1943-1971
See Morrison, Jim
See also CA 73-76; CANR 40

Morrison, Jim . . . . CLC 17
See also Morrison, James Douglas

Morrison, Toni
1931- . . CLC 4, 10, 22, 55, 81; BLC; DA
See also AAYA 1; BW 2; CA 29-32R;
CANR 27, 42; CDALB 1968-1988;
DLB 6, 33, 143; DLBY 81; MTCW;
SATA 57

Morrison, Van   1945- . . . . CLC 21
See also CA 116

Mortimer, John (Clifford)
1923- . . . . CLC 28, 43
See also CA 13-16R; CANR 21;
CDBLB 1960 to Present; DLB 13;
MTCW

Mortimer, Penelope (Ruth)   1918- . . . . CLC 5
See also CA 57-60; CANR 45

Morton, Anthony
See Creasey, John

Mosher, Howard Frank   1943- . . . . . . CLC 62
See also CA 139

Mosley, Nicholas   1923- . . . . CLC 43, 70
See also CA 69-72; CANR 41; DLB 14

Moss, Howard
1922-1987 . . . . CLC 7, 14, 45, 50
See also CA 1-4R; 123; CANR 1, 44;
DLB 5

Mossgiel, Rab
See Burns, Robert

Motion, Andrew   1952- . . . . CLC 47
See also DLB 40

Motley, Willard (Francis)
1909-1965 . . . . CLC 18
See also BW 1; CA 117; 106; DLB 76, 143

Motoori, Norinaga   1730-1801 . . . . NCLC 45

Mott, Michael (Charles Alston)
1930- . . . . CLC 15, 34
See also CA 5-8R; CAAS 7; CANR 7, 29

Mowat, Farley (McGill)   1921- . . . . . CLC 26
See also AAYA 1; CA 1-4R; CANR 4, 24,
42; CLR 20; DLB 68; JRDA; MAICYA;
MTCW; SATA 3, 55

Moyers, Bill   1934- . . . . CLC 74
See also AITN 2; CA 61-64; CANR 31

Mphahlele, Es'kia
See Mphahlele, Ezekiel
See also DLB 125

Mphahlele, Ezekiel   1919- . . . . . CLC 25; BLC
See also Mphahlele, Es'kia
See also BW 2; CA 81-84; CANR 26

Mqhayi, S(amuel) E(dward) K(rune Loliwe)
1875-1945 . . . . TCLC 25; BLC

Mr. Martin
See Burroughs, William S(eward)

Mrozek, Slawomir   1930- . . . . CLC 3, 13
See also CA 13-16R; CAAS 10; CANR 29;
MTCW

Mrs. Belloc-Lowndes
See Lowndes, Marie Adelaide (Belloc)

Mtwa, Percy   (?)- . . . . CLC 47

Mueller, Lisel 1924-. . . . . **CLC 13, 51**
See also CA 93-96; DLB 105

Muir, Edwin 1887-1959 . . . . **TCLC 2**
See also CA 104; DLB 20, 100

Muir, John 1838-1914 . . . . **TCLC 28**

Mujica Lainez, Manuel
1910-1984 . . . . **CLC 31**
See also Lainez, Manuel Mujica
See also CA 81-84; 112; CANR 32; HW

Mukherjee, Bharati 1940- . . . . **CLC 53**
See also BEST 89:2; CA 107; CANR 45;
DLB 60; MTCW

Muldoon, Paul 1951- . . . . **CLC 32, 72**
See also CA 113; 129; DLB 40

Mulisch, Harry 1927-. . . . . **CLC 42**
See also CA 9-12R; CANR 6, 26

Mull, Martin 1943-. . . . . **CLC 17**
See also CA 105

Mulock, Dinah Maria
See Craik, Dinah Maria (Mulock)

Munford, Robert 1737(?)-1783 . . . . **LC 5**
See also DLB 31

Mungo, Raymond 1946-. . . . . **CLC 72**
See also CA 49-52; CANR 2

Munro, Alice
1931- . . . . **CLC 6, 10, 19, 50; SSC 3**
See also AITN 2; CA 33-36R; CANR 33;
DLB 53; MTCW; SATA 29

Munro, H(ector) H(ugh) 1870-1916
See Saki
See also CA 104; 130; CDBLB 1890-1914;
DA; DLB 34; MTCW; WLC

Murasaki, Lady. . . . . **CMLC 1**

Murdoch, (Jean) Iris
1919- . . . . . . **CLC 1, 2, 3, 4, 6, 8, 11, 15,
22, 31, 51**
See also CA 13-16R; CANR 8, 43;
CDBLB 1960 to Present; DLB 14;
MTCW

Murnau, Friedrich Wilhelm
See Plumpe, Friedrich Wilhelm

Murphy, Richard 1927-. . . . . **CLC 41**
See also CA 29-32R; DLB 40

Murphy, Sylvia 1937-. . . . . **CLC 34**
See also CA 121

Murphy, Thomas (Bernard) 1935-. . . **CLC 51**
See also CA 101

Murray, Albert L. 1916- . . . . **CLC 73**
See also BW 2; CA 49-52; CANR 26;
DLB 38

Murray, Les(lie) A(llan) 1938- . . . . . **CLC 40**
See also CA 21-24R; CANR 11, 27

Murry, J. Middleton
See Murry, John Middleton

Murry, John Middleton
1889-1957 . . . . **TCLC 16**
See also CA 118

Musgrave, Susan 1951- . . . . **CLC 13, 54**
See also CA 69-72; CANR 45

Musil, Robert (Edler von)
1880-1942 . . . . **TCLC 12**
See also CA 109; DLB 81, 124

Musset, (Louis Charles) Alfred de
1810-1857 . . . . **NCLC 7**

My Brother's Brother
See Chekhov, Anton (Pavlovich)

Myers, Walter Dean 1937- . . . **CLC 35; BLC**
See also AAYA 4; BW 2; CA 33-36R;
CANR 20, 42; CLR 4, 16; DLB 33;
JRDA; MAICYA; SAAS 2; SATA 27, 41,
71

Myers, Walter M.
See Myers, Walter Dean

Myles, Symon
See Follett, Ken(neth Martin)

Nabokov, Vladimir (Vladimirovich)
1899-1977 . . . . . **CLC 1, 2, 3, 6, 8, 11, 15,
23, 44, 46, 64; DA; SSC 11; WLC**
See also CA 5-8R; 69-72; CANR 20;
CDALB 1941-1968; DLB 2; DLBD 3;
DLBY 80, 91; MTCW

Nagai Kafu. . . . . **TCLC 51**
See also Nagai Sokichi

Nagai Sokichi 1879-1959
See Nagai Kafu
See also CA 117

Nagy, Laszlo 1925-1978. . . . . **CLC 7**
See also CA 129; 112

Naipaul, Shiva(dhar Srinivasa)
1945-1985 . . . . **CLC 32, 39**
See also CA 110; 112; 116; CANR 33;
DLBY 85; MTCW

Naipaul, V(idiadhar) S(urajprasad)
1932- . . . . **CLC 4, 7, 9, 13, 18, 37**
See also CA 1-4R; CANR 1, 33;
CDBLB 1960 to Present; DLB 125;
DLBY 85; MTCW

Nakos, Lilika 1899(?)- . . . . **CLC 29**

Narayan, R(asipuram) K(rishnaswami)
1906- . . . . **CLC 7, 28, 47**
See also CA 81-84; CANR 33; MTCW;
SATA 62

Nash, (Frediric) Ogden 1902-1971 . . **CLC 23**
See also CA 13-14; 29-32R; CANR 34;
CAP 1; DLB 11; MAICYA; MTCW;
SATA 2, 46

Nathan, Daniel
See Dannay, Frederic

Nathan, George Jean 1882-1958 . . . **TCLC 18**
See also Hatteras, Owen
See also CA 114; DLB 137

Natsume, Kinnosuke 1867-1916
See Natsume, Soseki
See also CA 104

Natsume, Soseki . . . . **TCLC 2, 10**
See also Natsume, Kinnosuke

Natti, (Mary) Lee 1919-
See Kingman, Lee
See also CA 5-8R; CANR 2

Naylor, Gloria
1950- . . . . **CLC 28, 52; BLC; DA**
See also AAYA 6; BW 2; CA 107;
CANR 27; MTCW

Neihardt, John Gneisenau
1881-1973 . . . . **CLC 32**
See also CA 13-14; CAP 1; DLB 9, 54

Nekrasov, Nikolai Alekseevich
1821-1878 . . . . **NCLC 11**

Nelligan, Emile 1879-1941 . . . . **TCLC 14**
See also CA 114; DLB 92

Nelson, Willie 1933-. . . . . **CLC 17**
See also CA 107

Nemerov, Howard (Stanley)
1920-1991 . . . . **CLC 2, 6, 9, 36**
See also CA 1-4R; 134; CABS 2; CANR 1,
27; DLB 6; DLBY 83; MTCW

Neruda, Pablo
1904-1973 . . . . . **CLC 1, 2, 5, 7, 9, 28, 62;
DA; HLC; PC 4; WLC**
See also CA 19-20; 45-48; CAP 2; HW;
MTCW

Nerval, Gerard de 1808-1855. . . . . . . **NCLC 1**

Nervo, (Jose) Amado (Ruiz de)
1870-1919 . . . . **TCLC 11**
See also CA 109; 131; HW

Nessi, Pio Baroja y
See Baroja (y Nessi), Pio

Nestroy, Johann 1801-1862 . . . . . . **NCLC 42**
See also DLB 133

Neufeld, John (Arthur) 1938- . . . . . . **CLC 17**
See also AAYA 11; CA 25-28R; CANR 11,
37; MAICYA; SAAS 3; SATA 6

Neville, Emily Cheney 1919-. . . . . . . **CLC 12**
See also CA 5-8R; CANR 3, 37; JRDA;
MAICYA; SAAS 2; SATA 1

Newbound, Bernard Slade 1930-
See Slade, Bernard
See also CA 81-84

Newby, P(ercy) H(oward)
1918- . . . . **CLC 2, 13**
See also CA 5-8R; CANR 32; DLB 15;
MTCW

Newlove, Donald 1928- . . . . **CLC 6**
See also CA 29-32R; CANR 25

Newlove, John (Herbert) 1938-. . . . . **CLC 14**
See also CA 21-24R; CANR 9, 25

Newman, Charles 1938-. . . . . **CLC 2, 8**
See also CA 21-24R

Newman, Edwin (Harold) 1919- . . . . **CLC 14**
See also AITN 1; CA 69-72; CANR 5

Newman, John Henry
1801-1890 . . . . **NCLC 38**
See also DLB 18, 32, 55

Newton, Suzanne 1936-. . . . . **CLC 35**
See also CA 41-44R; CANR 14; JRDA;
SATA 5, 77

Nexo, Martin Andersen
1869-1954 . . . . **TCLC 43**

Nezval, Vitezslav 1900-1958 . . . . . . **TCLC 44**
See also CA 123

Ng, Fae Myenne 1957(?)-. . . . . **CLC 81**

Ngema, Mbongeni 1955- . . . . **CLC 57**
See also BW 2; CA 143

Ngugi, James T(hiong'o). . . . . **CLC 3, 7, 13**
See also Ngugi wa Thiong'o

Ngugi wa Thiong'o 1938-. . . . . **CLC 36; BLC**
See also Ngugi, James T(hiong'o)
See also BW 2; CA 81-84; CANR 27;
DLB 125; MTCW

Nichol, B(arrie) P(hillip)
1944-1988 . . . . **CLC 18**
See also CA 53-56; DLB 53; SATA 66

Parasol, Peter
  See Stevens, Wallace

Parfenie, Maria
  See Codrescu, Andrei

Parini, Jay (Lee) 1948- . . . . CLC 54
  See also CA 97-100; CAAS 16; CANR 32

Park, Jordan
  See Kornbluth, C(yril) M.; Pohl, Frederik

Parker, Bert
  See Ellison, Harlan

Parker, Dorothy (Rothschild)
  1893-1967 . . . . CLC 15, 68; SSC 2
  See also CA 19-20; 25-28R; CAP 2;
  DLB 11, 45, 86; MTCW

Parker, Robert B(rown) 1932- . . . . . . CLC 27
  See also BEST 89:4; CA 49-52; CANR 1,
  26; MTCW

Parkes, Lucas
  See Harris, John (Wyndham Parkes Lucas)
  Beynon

Parkin, Frank 1940- . . . . CLC 43

Parkman, Francis, Jr.
  1823-1893 . . . . NCLC 12
  See also DLB 1, 30

Parks, Gordon (Alexander Buchanan)
  1912- . . . . CLC 1, 16; BLC
  See also AITN 2; BW 2; CA 41-44R;
  CANR 26; DLB 33; SATA 8

Parnell, Thomas 1679-1718 . . . . LC 3
  See also DLB 94

Parra, Nicanor 1914- . . . . CLC 2; HLC
  See also CA 85-88; CANR 32; HW; MTCW

Parrish, Mary Frances
  See Fisher, M(ary) F(rances) K(ennedy)

Parson
  See Coleridge, Samuel Taylor

Parson Lot
  See Kingsley, Charles

Partridge, Anthony
  See Oppenheim, E(dward) Phillips

Pascoli, Giovanni 1855-1912 . . . . . . TCLC 45

Pasolini, Pier Paolo
  1922-1975 . . . . CLC 20, 37
  See also CA 93-96; 61-64; DLB 128;
  MTCW

Pasquini
  See Silone, Ignazio

Pastan, Linda (Olenik) 1932- . . . . . . CLC 27
  See also CA 61-64; CANR 18, 40; DLB 5

Pasternak, Boris (Leonidovich)
  1890-1960 . . . . . . CLC 7, 10, 18, 63; DA;
  PC 6; WLC
  See also CA 127; 116; MTCW

Patchen, Kenneth 1911-1972 . . . CLC 1, 2, 18
  See also CA 1-4R; 33-36R; CANR 3, 35;
  DLB 16, 48; MTCW

Pater, Walter (Horatio)
  1839-1894 . . . . NCLC 7
  See also CDBLB 1832-1890; DLB 57

Paterson, A(ndrew) B(arton)
  1864-1941 . . . . TCLC 32

Paterson, Katherine (Womeldorf)
  1932- . . . . CLC 12, 30
  See also AAYA 1; CA 21-24R; CANR 28;
  CLR 7; DLB 52; JRDA; MAICYA;
  MTCW; SATA 13, 53

Patmore, Coventry Kersey Dighton
  1823-1896 . . . . NCLC 9
  See also DLB 35, 98

Paton, Alan (Stewart)
  1903-1988 . . . . . . CLC 4, 10, 25, 55; DA;
  WLC
  See also CA 13-16; 125; CANR 22; CAP 1;
  MTCW; SATA 11, 56

Paton Walsh, Gillian 1937-
  See Walsh, Jill Paton
  See also CANR 38; JRDA; MAICYA;
  SAAS 3; SATA 4, 72

Paulding, James Kirke 1778-1860 . . NCLC 2
  See also DLB 3, 59, 74

Paulin, Thomas Neilson 1949-
  See Paulin, Tom
  See also CA 123; 128

Paulin, Tom . . . . CLC 37
  See also Paulin, Thomas Neilson
  See also DLB 40

Paustovsky, Konstantin (Georgievich)
  1892-1968 . . . . CLC 40
  See also CA 93-96; 25-28R

Pavese, Cesare 1908-1950 . . . . TCLC 3
  See also CA 104; DLB 128

Pavic, Milorad 1929- . . . . CLC 60
  See also CA 136

Payne, Alan
  See Jakes, John (William)

Paz, Gil
  See Lugones, Leopoldo

Paz, Octavio
  1914- . . . . CLC 3, 4, 6, 10, 19, 51, 65;
  DA; HLC; PC 1; WLC
  See also CA 73-76; CANR 32; DLBY 90;
  HW; MTCW

Peacock, Molly 1947- . . . . CLC 60
  See also CA 103; DLB 120

Peacock, Thomas Love
  1785-1866 . . . . NCLC 22
  See also DLB 96, 116

Peake, Mervyn 1911-1968 . . . . . . CLC 7, 54
  See also CA 5-8R; 25-28R; CANR 3;
  DLB 15; MTCW; SATA 23

Pearce, Philippa . . . . CLC 21
  See also Christie, (Ann) Philippa
  See also CLR 9; MAICYA; SATA 1, 67

Pearl, Eric
  See Elman, Richard

Pearson, T(homas) R(eid) 1956- . . . . CLC 39
  See also CA 120; 130

Peck, Dale 1968(?)- . . . . CLC 81

Peck, John 1941- . . . . CLC 3
  See also CA 49-52; CANR 3

Peck, Richard (Wayne) 1934- . . . . . . CLC 21
  See also AAYA 1; CA 85-88; CANR 19,
  38; JRDA; MAICYA; SAAS 2; SATA 18,
  55

Peck, Robert Newton 1928- . . . . CLC 17; DA
  See also AAYA 3; CA 81-84; CANR 31;
  JRDA; MAICYA; SAAS 1; SATA 21, 62

Peckinpah, (David) Sam(uel)
  1925-1984 . . . . CLC 20
  See also CA 109; 114

Pedersen, Knut 1859-1952
  See Hamsun, Knut
  See also CA 104; 119; MTCW

Peeslake, Gaffer
  See Durrell, Lawrence (George)

Peguy, Charles Pierre
  1873-1914 . . . . TCLC 10
  See also CA 107

Pena, Ramon del Valle y
  See Valle-Inclan, Ramon (Maria) del

Pendennis, Arthur Esquir
  See Thackeray, William Makepeace

Penn, William 1644-1718 . . . . LC 25
  See also DLB 24

Pepys, Samuel
  1633-1703 . . . . LC 11; DA; WLC
  See also CDBLB 1660-1789; DLB 101

Percy, Walker
  1916-1990 . . . . CLC 2, 3, 6, 8, 14, 18, 47,
  65
  See also CA 1-4R; 131; CANR 1, 23;
  DLB 2; DLBY 80, 90; MTCW

Perec, Georges 1936-1982 . . . . CLC 56
  See also CA 141; DLB 83

Pereda (y Sanchez de Porrua), Jose Maria de
  1833-1906 . . . . TCLC 16
  See also CA 117

Pereda y Porrua, Jose Maria de
  See Pereda (y Sanchez de Porrua), Jose
  Maria de

Peregoy, George Weems
  See Mencken, H(enry) L(ouis)

Perelman, S(idney) J(oseph)
  1904-1979 . . . CLC 3, 5, 9, 15, 23, 44, 49
  See also AITN 1, 2; CA 73-76; 89-92;
  CANR 18; DLB 11, 44; MTCW

Peret, Benjamin 1899-1959 . . . . TCLC 20
  See also CA 117

Peretz, Isaac Loeb 1851(?)-1915 . . . TCLC 16
  See also CA 109

Peretz, Yitzhok Leibush
  See Peretz, Isaac Loeb

Perez Galdos, Benito 1843-1920 . . . TCLC 27
  See also CA 125; HW

Perrault, Charles 1628-1703 . . . . LC 2
  See also MAICYA; SATA 25

Perry, Brighton
  See Sherwood, Robert E(mmet)

Perse, St.-John . . . . CLC 4, 11, 46
  See also Leger, (Marie-Rene Auguste) Alexis
  Saint-Leger

Peseenz, Tulio F.
  See Lopez y Fuentes, Gregorio

Pesetsky, Bette 1932- . . . . CLC 28
  See also CA 133; DLB 130

Peshkov, Alexei Maximovich 1868-1936
  See Gorky, Maxim
  See also CA 105; 141; DA

Pessoa, Fernando (Antonio Nogueira)
1888-1935 . . . . **TCLC 27; HLC**
See also CA 125

Peterkin, Julia Mood 1880-1961. . . . **CLC 31**
See also CA 102; DLB 9

Peters, Joan K. 1945- . . . . **CLC 39**

Peters, Robert L(ouis) 1924- . . . . **CLC 7**
See also CA 13-16R; CAAS 8; DLB 105

Petofi, Sandor 1823-1849 . . . . **NCLC 21**

Petrakis, Harry Mark 1923- . . . . **CLC 3**
See also CA 9-12R; CANR 4, 30

Petrarch 1304-1374. . . . . **PC 8**

Petrov, Evgeny . . . . **TCLC 21**
See also Kataev, Evgeny Petrovich

Petry, Ann (Lane) 1908- . . . . . . **CLC 1, 7, 18**
See also BW 1; CA 5-8R; CAAS 6;
CANR 4; CLR 12; DLB 76; JRDA;
MAICYA; MTCW; SATA 5

Petursson, Halligrimur 1614-1674 . . . . **LC 8**

Philipson, Morris H. 1926- . . . . **CLC 53**
See also CA 1-4R; CANR 4

Phillips, David Graham
1867-1911 . . . . **TCLC 44**
See also CA 108; DLB 9, 12

Phillips, Jack
See Sandburg, Carl (August)

Phillips, Jayne Anne
1952- . . . . **CLC 15, 33; SSC 16**
See also CA 101; CANR 24; DLBY 80;
MTCW

Phillips, Richard
See Dick, Philip K(indred)

Phillips, Robert (Schaeffer) 1938-. . . **CLC 28**
See also CA 17-20R; CAAS 13; CANR 8;
DLB 105

Phillips, Ward
See Lovecraft, H(oward) P(hillips)

Piccolo, Lucio 1901-1969. . . . . **CLC 13**
See also CA 97-100; DLB 114

Pickthall, Marjorie L(owry) C(hristie)
1883-1922 . . . . **TCLC 21**
See also CA 107; DLB 92

Pico della Mirandola, Giovanni
1463-1494 . . . . **LC 15**

Piercy, Marge
1936- . . . . **CLC 3, 6, 14, 18, 27, 62**
See also CA 21-24R; CAAS 1; CANR 13,
43; DLB 120; MTCW

Piers, Robert
See Anthony, Piers

Pieyre de Mandiargues, Andre 1909-1991
See Mandiargues, Andre Pieyre de
See also CA 103; 136; CANR 22

Pilnyak, Boris . . . . **TCLC 23**
See also Vogau, Boris Andreyevich

Pincherle, Alberto 1907-1990 . . . **CLC 11, 18**
See also Moravia, Alberto
See also CA 25-28R; 132; CANR 33;
MTCW

Pinckney, Darryl 1953- . . . . **CLC 76**
See also BW 2; CA 143

Pindar 518B.C.-446B.C. . . . . **CMLC 12**

Pineda, Cecile 1942- . . . . **CLC 39**
See also CA 118

Pinero, Arthur Wing 1855-1934 . . . **TCLC 32**
See also CA 110; DLB 10

Pinero, Miguel (Antonio Gomez)
1946-1988 . . . . **CLC 4, 55**
See also CA 61-64; 125; CANR 29; HW

Pinget, Robert 1919- . . . . **CLC 7, 13, 37**
See also CA 85-88; DLB 83

Pink Floyd . . . . **CLC 35**
See also Barrett, (Roger) Syd; Gilmour,
David; Mason, Nick; Waters, Roger;
Wright, Rick

Pinkney, Edward 1802-1828 . . . . . **NCLC 31**

Pinkwater, Daniel Manus 1941- . . . . **CLC 35**
See also Pinkwater, Manus
See also AAYA 1; CA 29-32R; CANR 12,
38; CLR 4; JRDA; MAICYA; SAAS 3;
SATA 46, 76

Pinkwater, Manus
See Pinkwater, Daniel Manus
See also SATA 8

Pinsky, Robert 1940- . . . . **CLC 9, 19, 38**
See also CA 29-32R; CAAS 4; DLBY 82

Pinta, Harold
See Pinter, Harold

Pinter, Harold
1930- . . . . . **CLC 1, 3, 6, 9, 11, 15, 27, 58,
73; DA; WLC**
See also CA 5-8R; CANR 33; CDBLB 1960
to Present; DLB 13; MTCW

Pirandello, Luigi
1867-1936 . . . . . . **TCLC 4, 29; DA; WLC**
See also CA 104

Pirsig, Robert M(aynard)
1928- . . . . **CLC 4, 6, 73**
See also CA 53-56; CANR 42; MTCW;
SATA 39

Pisarev, Dmitry Ivanovich
1840-1868 . . . . **NCLC 25**

Pix, Mary (Griffith) 1666-1709 . . . . **LC 8**
See also DLB 80

Pixerecourt, Guilbert de
1773-1844 . . . . **NCLC 39**

Plaidy, Jean
See Hibbert, Eleanor Alice Burford

Planche, James Robinson
1796-1880 . . . . **NCLC 42**

Plant, Robert 1948- . . . . **CLC 12**

Plante, David (Robert)
1940- . . . . **CLC 7, 23, 38**
See also CA 37-40R; CANR 12, 36;
DLBY 83; MTCW

Plath, Sylvia
1932-1963 . . . . . **CLC 1, 2, 3, 5, 9, 11, 14,
17, 50, 51, 62; DA; PC 1; WLC**
See also CA 19-20; CANR 34; CAP 2;
CDALB 1941-1968; DLB 5, 6; MTCW

Plato 428(?)B.C.-348(?)B.C. . . . . **CMLC 8; DA**

Platonov, Andrei . . . . **TCLC 14**
See also Klimentov, Andrei Platonovich

Platt, Kin 1911- . . . . **CLC 26**
See also AAYA 11; CA 17-20R; CANR 11;
JRDA; SAAS 17; SATA 21

Plick et Plock
See Simenon, Georges (Jacques Christian)

Plimpton, George (Ames) 1927- . . . . . **CLC 36**
See also AITN 1; CA 21-24R; CANR 32;
MTCW; SATA 10

Plomer, William Charles Franklin
1903-1973 . . . . **CLC 4, 8**
See also CA 21-22; CANR 34; CAP 2;
DLB 20; MTCW; SATA 24

Plowman, Piers
See Kavanagh, Patrick (Joseph)

Plum, J.
See Wodehouse, P(elham) G(renville)

Plumly, Stanley (Ross) 1939- . . . . . . **CLC 33**
See also CA 108; 110; DLB 5

Plumpe, Friedrich Wilhelm
1888-1931 . . . . **TCLC 53**
See also CA 112

Poe, Edgar Allan
1809-1849 . . . . . **NCLC 1, 16; DA; PC 1;
SSC 1; WLC**
See also CDALB 1640-1865; DLB 3, 59, 73,
74; SATA 23

Poet of Titchfield Street, The
See Pound, Ezra (Weston Loomis)

Pohl, Frederik 1919- . . . . **CLC 18**
See also CA 61-64; CAAS 1; CANR 11, 37;
DLB 8; MTCW; SATA 24

Poirier, Louis 1910-
See Gracq, Julien
See also CA 122; 126

Poitier, Sidney 1927- . . . . **CLC 26**
See also BW 1; CA 117

Polanski, Roman 1933- . . . . **CLC 16**
See also CA 77-80

Poliakoff, Stephen 1952- . . . . **CLC 38**
See also CA 106; DLB 13

Police, The . . . . **CLC 26**
See also Copeland, Stewart (Armstrong);
Summers, Andrew James; Sumner,
Gordon Matthew

Pollitt, Katha 1949- . . . . **CLC 28**
See also CA 120; 122; MTCW

Pollock, (Mary) Sharon 1936- . . . . . . **CLC 50**
See also CA 141; DLB 60

Pomerance, Bernard 1940- . . . . **CLC 13**
See also CA 101

Ponge, Francis (Jean Gaston Alfred)
1899-1988 . . . . **CLC 6, 18**
See also CA 85-88; 126; CANR 40

Pontoppidan, Henrik 1857-1943 . . . **TCLC 29**

Poole, Josephine . . . . **CLC 17**
See also Helyar, Jane Penelope Josephine
See also SAAS 2; SATA 5

Popa, Vasko 1922- . . . . **CLC 19**
See also CA 112

Pope, Alexander
1688-1744 . . . . **LC 3; DA; WLC**
See also CDBLB 1660-1789; DLB 95, 101

Porter, Connie (Rose) 1959(?)- . . . . . **CLC 70**
See also BW 2; CA 142

Porter, Gene(va Grace) Stratton
1863(?)-1924 . . . . **TCLC 21**
See also CA 112

Quiller-Couch, Arthur Thomas
    1863-1944 .... **TCLC 53**
    See also CA 118; DLB 135

Quin, Ann (Marie) 1936-1973 ...... **CLC 6**
    See also CA 9-12R; 45-48; DLB 14

Quinn, Martin
    See Smith, Martin Cruz

Quinn, Simon
    See Smith, Martin Cruz

Quiroga, Horacio (Sylvestre)
    1878-1937 .... **TCLC 20; HLC**
    See also CA 117; 131; HW; MTCW

Quoirez, Francoise 1935- .... **CLC 9**
    See also Sagan, Francoise
    See also CA 49-52; CANR 6, 39; MTCW

Raabe, Wilhelm 1831-1910 .... **TCLC 45**
    See also DLB 129

Rabe, David (William) 1940-... **CLC 4, 8, 33**
    See also CA 85-88; CABS 3; DLB 7

Rabelais, Francois
    1483-1553 .... **LC 5; DA; WLC**

Rabinovitch, Sholem 1859-1916
    See Aleichem, Sholom
    See also CA 104

Radcliffe, Ann (Ward) 1764-1823 .. **NCLC 6**
    See also DLB 39

Radiguet, Raymond 1903-1923 .... **TCLC 29**
    See also DLB 65

Radnoti, Miklos 1909-1944 .... **TCLC 16**
    See also CA 118

Rado, James 1939- .... **CLC 17**
    See also CA 105

Radvanyi, Netty 1900-1983
    See Seghers, Anna
    See also CA 85-88; 110

Rae, Ben
    See Griffiths, Trevor

Raeburn, John (Hay) 1941-........ **CLC 34**
    See also CA 57-60

Ragni, Gerome 1942-1991 .... **CLC 17**
    See also CA 105; 134

Rahv, Philip 1908-1973 .... **CLC 24**
    See also Greenberg, Ivan
    See also DLB 137

Raine, Craig 1944- .... **CLC 32**
    See also CA 108; CANR 29; DLB 40

Raine, Kathleen (Jessie) 1908- ... **CLC 7, 45**
    See also CA 85-88; DLB 20; MTCW

Rainis, Janis 1865-1929 .... **TCLC 29**

Rakosi, Carl.................... **CLC 47**
    See also Rawley, Callman
    See also CAAS 5

Raleigh, Richard
    See Lovecraft, H(oward) P(hillips)

Rallentando, H. P.
    See Sayers, Dorothy L(eigh)

Ramal, Walter
    See de la Mare, Walter (John)

Ramon, Juan
    See Jimenez (Mantecon), Juan Ramon

Ramos, Graciliano 1892-1953 ..... **TCLC 32**

Rampersad, Arnold 1941-......... **CLC 44**
    See also BW 2; CA 127; 133; DLB 111

Rampling, Anne
    See Rice, Anne

Ramuz, Charles-Ferdinand
    1878-1947 .... **TCLC 33**

Rand, Ayn
    1905-1982 ...... **CLC 3, 30, 44, 79; DA;
                                                        WLC**
    See also AAYA 10; CA 13-16R; 105;
        CANR 27; MTCW

Randall, Dudley (Felker)
    1914- .... **CLC 1; BLC**
    See also BW 1; CA 25-28R; CANR 23;
        DLB 41

Randall, Robert
    See Silverberg, Robert

Ranger, Ken
    See Creasey, John

Ransom, John Crowe
    1888-1974 .... **CLC 2, 4, 5, 11, 24**
    See also CA 5-8R; 49-52; CANR 6, 34;
        DLB 45, 63; MTCW

Rao, Raja 1909- .... **CLC 25, 56**
    See also CA 73-76; MTCW

Raphael, Frederic (Michael)
    1931- .... **CLC 2, 14**
    See also CA 1-4R; CANR 1; DLB 14

Ratcliffe, James P.
    See Mencken, H(enry) L(ouis)

Rathbone, Julian 1935- .... **CLC 41**
    See also CA 101; CANR 34

Rattigan, Terence (Mervyn)
    1911-1977 .... **CLC 7**
    See also CA 85-88; 73-76;
        CDBLB 1945-1960; DLB 13; MTCW

Ratushinskaya, Irina 1954- .... **CLC 54**
    See also CA 129

Raven, Simon (Arthur Noel)
    1927- .... **CLC 14**
    See also CA 81-84

Rawley, Callman 1903-
    See Rakosi, Carl
    See also CA 21-24R; CANR 12, 32

Rawlings, Marjorie Kinnan
    1896-1953 .... **TCLC 4**
    See also CA 104; 137; DLB 9, 22, 102;
        JRDA; MAICYA; YABC 1

Ray, Satyajit 1921-1992........ **CLC 16, 76**
    See also CA 114; 137

Read, Herbert Edward 1893-1968.... **CLC 4**
    See also CA 85-88; 25-28R; DLB 20

Read, Piers Paul 1941- ...... **CLC 4, 10, 25**
    See also CA 21-24R; CANR 38; DLB 14;
        SATA 21

Reade, Charles 1814-1884 .... **NCLC 2**
    See also DLB 21

Reade, Hamish
    See Gray, Simon (James Holliday)

Reading, Peter 1946- .... **CLC 47**
    See also CA 103; DLB 40

Reaney, James 1926- .... **CLC 13**
    See also CA 41-44R; CAAS 15; CANR 42;
        DLB 68; SATA 43

Rebreanu, Liviu 1885-1944 .... **TCLC 28**

Rechy, John (Francisco)
    1934- .... **CLC 1, 7, 14, 18; HLC**
    See also CA 5-8R; CAAS 4; CANR 6, 32;
        DLB 122; DLBY 82; HW

Redcam, Tom 1870-1933 .... **TCLC 25**

Reddin, Keith.................... **CLC 67**

Redgrove, Peter (William)
    1932-................... **CLC 6, 41**
    See also CA 1-4R; CANR 3, 39; DLB 40

Redmon, Anne.................... **CLC 22**
    See also Nightingale, Anne Redmon
    See also DLBY 86

Reed, Eliot
    See Ambler, Eric

Reed, Ishmael
    1938-... **CLC 2, 3, 5, 6, 13, 32, 60; BLC**
    See also BW 2; CA 21-24R; CANR 25;
        DLB 2, 5, 33; DLBD 8; MTCW

Reed, John (Silas) 1887-1920 ...... **TCLC 9**
    See also CA 106

Reed, Lou........................ **CLC 21**
    See also Firbank, Louis

Reeve, Clara 1729-1807 .... **NCLC 19**
    See also DLB 39

Reid, Christopher (John) 1949-..... **CLC 33**
    See also CA 140; DLB 40

Reid, Desmond
    See Moorcock, Michael (John)

Reid Banks, Lynne 1929-
    See Banks, Lynne Reid
    See also CA 1-4R; CANR 6, 22, 38;
        CLR 24; JRDA; MAICYA; SATA 22, 75

Reilly, William K.
    See Creasey, John

Reiner, Max
    See Caldwell, (Janet Miriam) Taylor
        (Holland)

Reis, Ricardo
    See Pessoa, Fernando (Antonio Nogueira)

Remarque, Erich Maria
    1898-1970 .... **CLC 21; DA**
    See also CA 77-80; 29-32R; DLB 56;
        MTCW

Remizov, A.
    See Remizov, Aleksei (Mikhailovich)

Remizov, A. M.
    See Remizov, Aleksei (Mikhailovich)

Remizov, Aleksei (Mikhailovich)
    1877-1957 .... **TCLC 27**
    See also CA 125; 133

Renan, Joseph Ernest
    1823-1892 .... **NCLC 26**

Renard, Jules 1864-1910 .... **TCLC 17**
    See also CA 117

Renault, Mary.............. **CLC 3, 11, 17**
    See also Challans, Mary
    See also DLBY 83

Rendell, Ruth (Barbara) 1930- .. **CLC 28, 48**
    See also Vine, Barbara
    See also CA 109; CANR 32; DLB 87;
        MTCW

Renoir, Jean 1894-1979 .... **CLC 20**
    See also CA 129; 85-88

Resnais, Alain 1922-.............. **CLC 16**

Robinson, William, Jr.   1940-
See Robinson, Smokey
See also CA 116

Robison, Mary   1949- . . . . **CLC 42**
See also CA 113; 116; DLB 130

Rod, Edouard   1857-1910 . . . . **TCLC 52**

Roddenberry, Eugene Wesley   1921-1991
See Roddenberry, Gene
See also CA 110; 135; CANR 37; SATA 45

Roddenberry, Gene . . . . **CLC 17**
See also Roddenberry, Eugene Wesley
See also AAYA 5; SATA-Obit 69

Rodgers, Mary   1931- . . . . **CLC 12**
See also CA 49-52; CANR 8; CLR 20;
JRDA; MAICYA; SATA 8

Rodgers, W(illiam) R(obert)
1909-1969 . . . . **CLC 7**
See also CA 85-88; DLB 20

Rodman, Eric
See Silverberg, Robert

Rodman, Howard   1920(?)-1985 . . . . . **CLC 65**
See also CA 118

Rodman, Maia
See Wojciechowska, Maia (Teresa)

Rodriguez, Claudio   1934- . . . . **CLC 10**
See also DLB 134

Roelvaag, O(le) E(dvart)
1876-1931 . . . . **TCLC 17**
See also CA 117; DLB 9

Roethke, Theodore (Huebner)
1908-1963 . . . . . . **CLC 1, 3, 8, 11, 19, 46**
See also CA 81-84; CABS 2;
CDALB 1941-1968; DLB 5; MTCW

Rogers, Thomas Hunton   1927- . . . . . **CLC 57**
See also CA 89-92

Rogers, Will(iam Penn Adair)
1879-1935 . . . . **TCLC 8**
See also CA 105; 144; DLB 11

Rogin, Gilbert   1929- . . . . **CLC 18**
See also CA 65-68; CANR 15

Rohan, Koda . . . . **TCLC 22**
See also Koda Shigeyuki

Rohmer, Eric . . . . **CLC 16**
See also Scherer, Jean-Marie Maurice

Rohmer, Sax . . . . **TCLC 28**
See also Ward, Arthur Henry Sarsfield
See also DLB 70

Roiphe, Anne (Richardson)
1935- . . . . **CLC 3, 9**
See also CA 89-92; CANR 45; DLBY 80

Rojas, Fernando de   1465-1541 . . . . . **LC 23**

**Rolfe, Frederick (William Serafino Austin
Lewis Mary)**   1860-1913 . . . . . . **TCLC 12**
See also CA 107; DLB 34

Rolland, Romain   1866-1944 . . . . **TCLC 23**
See also CA 118; DLB 65

Rolvaag, O(le) E(dvart)
See Roelvaag, O(le) E(dvart)

Romain Arnaud, Saint
See Aragon, Louis

Romains, Jules   1885-1972 . . . . **CLC 7**
See also CA 85-88; CANR 34; DLB 65;
MTCW

Romero, Jose Ruben   1890-1952 . . . **TCLC 14**
See also CA 114; 131; HW

Ronsard, Pierre de   1524-1585 . . . . **LC 6**

Rooke, Leon   1934- . . . . **CLC 25, 34**
See also CA 25-28R; CANR 23

Roper, William   1498-1578 . . . . **LC 10**

Roquelaure, A. N.
See Rice, Anne

Rosa, Joao Guimaraes   1908-1967 . . . **CLC 23**
See also CA 89-92; DLB 113

Rosen, Richard (Dean)   1949- . . . . **CLC 39**
See also CA 77-80

Rosenberg, Isaac   1890-1918 . . . . . . **TCLC 12**
See also CA 107; DLB 20

Rosenblatt, Joe . . . . **CLC 15**
See also Rosenblatt, Joseph

Rosenblatt, Joseph   1933-
See Rosenblatt, Joe
See also CA 89-92

Rosenfeld, Samuel   1896-1963
See Tzara, Tristan
See also CA 89-92

Rosenthal, M(acha) L(ouis)   1917- . . . **CLC 28**
See also CA 1-4R; CAAS 6; CANR 4;
DLB 5; SATA 59

Ross, Barnaby
See Dannay, Frederic

Ross, Bernard L.
See Follett, Ken(neth Martin)

Ross, J. H.
See Lawrence, T(homas) E(dward)

Ross, Martin
See Martin, Violet Florence
See also DLB 135

Ross, (James) Sinclair   1908- . . . . **CLC 13**
See also CA 73-76; DLB 88

Rossetti, Christina (Georgina)
1830-1894 . . . **NCLC 2; DA; PC 7; WLC**
See also DLB 35; MAICYA; SATA 20

Rossetti, Dante Gabriel
1828-1882 . . . . **NCLC 4; DA; WLC**
See also CDBLB 1832-1890; DLB 35

Rossner, Judith (Perelman)
1935- . . . . **CLC 6, 9, 29**
See also AITN 2; BEST 90:3; CA 17-20R;
CANR 18; DLB 6; MTCW

Rostand, Edmond (Eugene Alexis)
1868-1918 . . . . **TCLC 6, 37; DA**
See also CA 104; 126; MTCW

Roth, Henry   1906- . . . . **CLC 2, 6, 11**
See also CA 11-12; CANR 38; CAP 1;
DLB 28; MTCW

Roth, Joseph   1894-1939 . . . . **TCLC 33**
See also DLB 85

Roth, Philip (Milton)
1933- . . . . . . **CLC 1, 2, 3, 4, 6, 9, 15, 22,
31, 47, 66; DA; WLC**
See also BEST 90:3; CA 1-4R; CANR 1, 22,
36; CDALB 1968-1988; DLB 2, 28;
DLBY 82; MTCW

Rothenberg, Jerome   1931- . . . . **CLC 6, 57**
See also CA 45-48; CANR 1; DLB 5

Roumain, Jacques (Jean Baptiste)
1907-1944 . . . . **TCLC 19; BLC**
See also BW 1; CA 117; 125

Rourke, Constance (Mayfield)
1885-1941 . . . . **TCLC 12**
See also CA 107; YABC 1

Rousseau, Jean-Baptiste   1671-1741 . . . **LC 9**

Rousseau, Jean-Jacques
1712-1778 . . . . **LC 14; DA; WLC**

Roussel, Raymond   1877-1933 . . . . . **TCLC 20**
See also CA 117

Rovit, Earl (Herbert)   1927- . . . . **CLC 7**
See also CA 5-8R; CANR 12

Rowe, Nicholas   1674-1718 . . . . **LC 8**
See also DLB 84

Rowley, Ames Dorrance
See Lovecraft, H(oward) P(hillips)

Rowson, Susanna Haswell
1762(?)-1824 . . . . **NCLC 5**
See also DLB 37

Roy, Gabrielle   1909-1983 . . . . **CLC 10, 14**
See also CA 53-56; 110; CANR 5; DLB 68;
MTCW

Rozewicz, Tadeusz   1921- . . . . **CLC 9, 23**
See also CA 108; CANR 36; MTCW

Ruark, Gibbons   1941- . . . . **CLC 3**
See also CA 33-36R; CANR 14, 31;
DLB 120

Rubens, Bernice (Ruth)   1923- . . . **CLC 19, 31**
See also CA 25-28R; CANR 33; DLB 14;
MTCW

Rudkin, (James) David   1936- . . . . . . **CLC 14**
See also CA 89-92; DLB 13

Rudnik, Raphael   1933- . . . . **CLC 7**
See also CA 29-32R

Ruffian, M.
See Hasek, Jaroslav (Matej Frantisek)

Ruiz, Jose Martinez . . . . **CLC 11**
See also Martinez Ruiz, Jose

Rukeyser, Muriel
1913-1980 . . . . **CLC 6, 10, 15, 27**
See also CA 5-8R; 93-96; CANR 26;
DLB 48; MTCW; SATA 22

Rule, Jane (Vance)   1931- . . . . **CLC 27**
See also CA 25-28R; CAAS 18; CANR 12;
DLB 60

Rulfo, Juan   1918-1986 . . . . **CLC 8, 80; HLC**
See also CA 85-88; 118; CANR 26;
DLB 113; HW; MTCW

Runeberg, Johan   1804-1877 . . . . . . **NCLC 41**

Runyon, (Alfred) Damon
1884(?)-1946 . . . . **TCLC 10**
See also CA 107; DLB 11, 86

Rush, Norman   1933- . . . . **CLC 44**
See also CA 121; 126

Rushdie, (Ahmed) Salman
1947- . . . . **CLC 23, 31, 55**
See also BEST 89:3; CA 108; 111;
CANR 33; MTCW

Rushforth, Peter (Scott)   1945- . . . . . **CLC 19**
See also CA 101

Ruskin, John   1819-1900 . . . . **TCLC 20**
See also CA 114; 129; CDBLB 1832-1890;
DLB 55; SATA 24

Secundus, H. Scriblerus
See Fielding, Henry

Sedges, John
See Buck, Pearl S(ydenstricker)

Sedgwick, Catharine Maria
1789-1867 .... **NCLC 19**
See also DLB 1, 74

Seelye, John 1931- .... **CLC 7**

Seferiades, Giorgos Stylianou 1900-1971
See Seferis, George
See also CA 5-8R; 33-36R; CANR 5, 36;
MTCW

Seferis, George .... **CLC 5, 11**
See also Seferiades, Giorgos Stylianou

Segal, Erich (Wolf) 1937- .... **CLC 3, 10**
See also BEST 89:1; CA 25-28R; CANR 20,
36; DLBY 86; MTCW

Seger, Bob 1945-................ **CLC 35**

Seghers, Anna .... **CLC 7**
See also Radvanyi, Netty
See also DLB 69

Seidel, Frederick (Lewis) 1936-..... **CLC 18**
See also CA 13-16R; CANR 8; DLBY 84

Seifert, Jaroslav 1901-1986..... **CLC 34, 44**
See also CA 127; MTCW

Sei Shonagon c. 966-1017(?) ...... **CMLC 6**

Selby, Hubert, Jr. 1928- ..... **CLC 1, 2, 4, 8**
See also CA 13-16R; CANR 33; DLB 2

Selzer, Richard 1928-............. **CLC 74**
See also CA 65-68; CANR 14

Sembene, Ousmane
See Ousmane, Sembene

Senancour, Etienne Pivert de
1770-1846 .... **NCLC 16**
See also DLB 119

Sender, Ramon (Jose)
1902-1982 .... **CLC 8; HLC**
See also CA 5-8R; 105; CANR 8; HW;
MTCW

Seneca, Lucius Annaeus
4B.C.-65................... **CMLC 6**

Senghor, Leopold Sedar
1906- .... **CLC 54; BLC**
See also BW 2; CA 116; 125; MTCW

Serling, (Edward) Rod(man)
1924-1975 .... **CLC 30**
See also AITN 1; CA 65-68; 57-60; DLB 26

Serna, Ramon Gomez de la
See Gomez de la Serna, Ramon

Serpieres
See Guillevic, (Eugene)

Service, Robert
See Service, Robert W(illiam)
See also DLB 92

Service, Robert W(illiam)
1874(?)-1958 ...... **TCLC 15; DA; WLC**
See also Service, Robert
See also CA 115; 140; SATA 20

Seth, Vikram 1952-................ **CLC 43**
See also CA 121; 127; DLB 120

Seton, Cynthia Propper
1926-1982 .... **CLC 27**
See also CA 5-8R; 108; CANR 7

Seton, Ernest (Evan) Thompson
1860-1946 .... **TCLC 31**
See also CA 109; DLB 92; JRDA; SATA 18

Seton-Thompson, Ernest
See Seton, Ernest (Evan) Thompson

Settle, Mary Lee 1918- .... **CLC 19, 61**
See also CA 89-92; CAAS 1; CANR 44;
DLB 6

Seuphor, Michel
See Arp, Jean

Sevigne, Marie (de Rabutin-Chantal) Marquise
de 1626-1696 .... **LC 11**

Sexton, Anne (Harvey)
1928-1974 .... **CLC 2, 4, 6, 8, 10, 15, 53;**
DA; PC 2; WLC
See also CA 1-4R; 53-56; CABS 2;
CANR 3, 36; CDALB 1941-1968; DLB 5;
MTCW; SATA 10

Shaara, Michael (Joseph Jr.)
1929-1988 .... **CLC 15**
See also AITN 1; CA 102; DLBY 83

Shackleton, C. C.
See Aldiss, Brian W(ilson)

Shacochis, Bob .... **CLC 39**
See also Shacochis, Robert G.

Shacochis, Robert G. 1951-
See Shacochis, Bob
See also CA 119; 124

Shaffer, Anthony (Joshua) 1926-.... **CLC 19**
See also CA 110; 116; DLB 13

Shaffer, Peter (Levin)
1926- .... **CLC 5, 14, 18, 37, 60**
See also CA 25-28R; CANR 25;
CDBLB 1960 to Present; DLB 13;
MTCW

Shakey, Bernard
See Young, Neil

Shalamov, Varlam (Tikhonovich)
1907(?)-1982 .... **CLC 18**
See also CA 129; 105

Shamlu, Ahmad 1925- .... **CLC 10**

Shammas, Anton 1951-............ **CLC 55**

Shange, Ntozake
1948- .... **CLC 8, 25, 38, 74; BLC; DC 3**
See also AAYA 9; BW 2; CA 85-88;
CABS 3; CANR 27; DLB 38; MTCW

Shanley, John Patrick 1950-....... **CLC 75**
See also CA 128; 133

Shapcott, Thomas William 1935- ... **CLC 38**
See also CA 69-72

Shapiro, Jane.................... **CLC 76**

Shapiro, Karl (Jay) 1913- .. **CLC 4, 8, 15, 53**
See also CA 1-4R; CAAS 6; CANR 1, 36;
DLB 48; MTCW

Sharp, William 1855-1905 .... **TCLC 39**

Sharpe, Thomas Ridley 1928-
See Sharpe, Tom
See also CA 114; 122

Sharpe, Tom.................... **CLC 36**
See also Sharpe, Thomas Ridley
See also DLB 14

Shaw, Bernard.................... **TCLC 45**
See also Shaw, George Bernard
See also BW 1

Shaw, G. Bernard
See Shaw, George Bernard

Shaw, George Bernard
1856-1950 .... **TCLC 3, 9, 21; DA; WLC**
See also Shaw, Bernard
See also CA 104; 128; CDBLB 1914-1945;
DLB 10, 57; MTCW

Shaw, Henry Wheeler
1818-1885 .... **NCLC 15**
See also DLB 11

Shaw, Irwin 1913-1984....... **CLC 7, 23, 34**
See also AITN 1; CA 13-16R; 112;
CANR 21; CDALB 1941-1968; DLB 6,
102; DLBY 84; MTCW

Shaw, Robert 1927-1978 .... **CLC 5**
See also AITN 1; CA 1-4R; 81-84;
CANR 4; DLB 13, 14

Shaw, T. E.
See Lawrence, T(homas) E(dward)

Shawn, Wallace 1943- .... **CLC 41**
See also CA 112

Sheed, Wilfrid (John Joseph)
1930- .... **CLC 2, 4, 10, 53**
See also CA 65-68; CANR 30; DLB 6;
MTCW

Sheldon, Alice Hastings Bradley
1915(?)-1987
See Tiptree, James, Jr.
See also CA 108; 122; CANR 34; MTCW

Sheldon, John
See Bloch, Robert (Albert)

Shelley, Mary Wollstonecraft (Godwin)
1797-1851 .... **NCLC 14; DA; WLC**
See also CDBLB 1789-1832; DLB 110, 116;
SATA 29

Shelley, Percy Bysshe
1792-1822 .... **NCLC 18; DA; WLC**
See also CDBLB 1789-1832; DLB 96, 110

Shepard, Jim 1956-............... **CLC 36**
See also CA 137

Shepard, Lucius 1947-............ **CLC 34**
See also CA 128; 141

Shepard, Sam
1943- .... **CLC 4, 6, 17, 34, 41, 44**
See also AAYA 1; CA 69-72; CABS 3;
CANR 22; DLB 7; MTCW

Shepherd, Michael
See Ludlum, Robert

Sherburne, Zoa (Morin) 1912-...... **CLC 30**
See also CA 1-4R; CANR 3, 37; MAICYA;
SAAS 18; SATA 3

Sheridan, Frances 1724-1766........ **LC 7**
See also DLB 39, 84

Sheridan, Richard Brinsley
1751-1816 ... **NCLC 5; DA; DC 1; WLC**
See also CDBLB 1660-1789; DLB 89

Sherman, Jonathan Marc.......... **CLC 55**

Sherman, Martin 1941(?)-......... **CLC 19**
See also CA 116; 123

Sherwin, Judith Johnson 1936-... **CLC 7, 15**
See also CA 25-28R; CANR 34

Sherwood, Frances 1940-.......... **CLC 81**

Sherwood, Robert E(mmet)
1896-1955 .... **TCLC 3**
See also CA 104; DLB 7, 26

Shestov, Lev 1866-1938 . . . . TCLC 56

Shiel, M(atthew) P(hipps)
   1865-1947 . . . . TCLC 8
   See also CA 106

Shiga, Naoya 1883-1971 . . . . CLC 33
   See also CA 101; 33-36R

Shimazaki Haruki 1872-1943
   See Shimazaki Toson
   See also CA 105; 134

Shimazaki Toson . . . . TCLC 5
   See also Shimazaki Haruki

Sholokhov, Mikhail (Aleksandrovich)
   1905-1984 . . . . CLC 7, 15
   See also CA 101; 112; MTCW; SATA 36

Shone, Patric
   See Hanley, James

Shreve, Susan Richards 1939- . . . . . . CLC 23
   See also CA 49-52; CAAS 5; CANR 5, 38;
   MAICYA; SATA 41, 46

Shue, Larry 1946-1985 . . . . CLC 52
   See also CA 117

Shu-Jen, Chou 1881-1936
   See Hsun, Lu
   See also CA 104

Shulman, Alix Kates 1932- . . . . . . CLC 2, 10
   See also CA 29-32R; CANR 43; SATA 7

Shuster, Joe 1914- . . . . CLC 21

Shute, Nevil . . . . CLC 30
   See also Norway, Nevil Shute

Shuttle, Penelope (Diane) 1947- . . . . . CLC 7
   See also CA 93-96; CANR 39; DLB 14, 40

Sidney, Mary 1561-1621 . . . . LC 19

Sidney, Sir Philip 1554-1586 . . . . LC 19; DA
   See also CDBLB Before 1660

Siegel, Jerome 1914- . . . . CLC 21
   See also CA 116

Siegel, Jerry
   See Siegel, Jerome

Sienkiewicz, Henryk (Adam Alexander Pius)
   1846-1916 . . . . TCLC 3
   See also CA 104; 134

Sierra, Gregorio Martinez
   See Martinez Sierra, Gregorio

Sierra, Maria (de la O'LeJarraga) Martinez
   See Martinez Sierra, Maria (de la
   O'LeJarraga)

Sigal, Clancy 1926- . . . . CLC 7
   See also CA 1-4R

Sigourney, Lydia Howard (Huntley)
   1791-1865 . . . . NCLC 21
   See also DLB 1, 42, 73

Siguenza y Gongora, Carlos de
   1645-1700 . . . . LC 8

Sigurjonsson, Johann 1880-1919 . . . TCLC 27

Sikelianos, Angelos 1884-1951 . . . . TCLC 39

Silkin, Jon 1930- . . . . CLC 2, 6, 43
   See also CA 5-8R; CAAS 5; DLB 27

Silko, Leslie (Marmon)
   1948- . . . . CLC 23, 74; DA
   See also CA 115; 122; CANR 45; DLB 143

Sillanpaa, Frans Eemil 1888-1964 . . . CLC 19
   See also CA 129; 93-96; MTCW

Sillitoe, Alan
   1928- . . . . CLC 1, 3, 6, 10, 19, 57
   See also AITN 1; CA 9-12R; CAAS 2;
   CANR 8, 26; CDBLB 1960 to Present;
   DLB 14, 139; MTCW; SATA 61

Silone, Ignazio 1900-1978 . . . . CLC 4
   See also CA 25-28; 81-84; CANR 34;
   CAP 2; MTCW

Silver, Joan Micklin 1935- . . . . CLC 20
   See also CA 114; 121

Silver, Nicholas
   See Faust, Frederick (Schiller)

Silverberg, Robert 1935- . . . . CLC 7
   See also CA 1-4R; CAAS 3; CANR 1, 20,
   36; DLB 8; MAICYA; MTCW; SATA 13

Silverstein, Alvin 1933- . . . . CLC 17
   See also CA 49-52; CANR 2; CLR 25;
   JRDA; MAICYA; SATA 8, 69

Silverstein, Virginia B(arbara Opshelor)
   1937- . . . . CLC 17
   See also CA 49-52; CANR 2; CLR 25;
   JRDA; MAICYA; SATA 8, 69

Sim, Georges
   See Simenon, Georges (Jacques Christian)

Simak, Clifford D(onald)
   1904-1988 . . . . CLC 1, 55
   See also CA 1-4R; 125; CANR 1, 35;
   DLB 8; MTCW; SATA 56

Simenon, Georges (Jacques Christian)
   1903-1989 . . . . CLC 1, 2, 3, 8, 18, 47
   See also CA 85-88; 129; CANR 35;
   DLB 72; DLBY 89; MTCW

Simic, Charles 1938- . . . CLC 6, 9, 22, 49, 68
   See also CA 29-32R; CAAS 4; CANR 12,
   33; DLB 105

Simmons, Charles (Paul) 1924- . . . . . CLC 57
   See also CA 89-92

Simmons, Dan 1948- . . . . CLC 44
   See also CA 138

Simmons, James (Stewart Alexander)
   1933- . . . . CLC 43
   See also CA 105; DLB 40

Simms, William Gilmore
   1806-1870 . . . . NCLC 3
   See also DLB 3, 30, 59, 73

Simon, Carly 1945- . . . . CLC 26
   See also CA 105

Simon, Claude 1913- . . . . . . CLC 4, 9, 15, 39
   See also CA 89-92; CANR 33; DLB 83;
   MTCW

Simon, (Marvin) Neil
   1927- . . . . CLC 6, 11, 31, 39, 70
   See also AITN 1; CA 21-24R; CANR 26;
   DLB 7; MTCW

Simon, Paul 1942(?)- . . . . CLC 17
   See also CA 116

Simonon, Paul 1956(?)- . . . . CLC 30
   See also Clash, The

Simpson, Harriette
   See Arnow, Harriette (Louisa) Simpson

Simpson, Louis (Aston Marantz)
   1923- . . . . CLC 4, 7, 9, 32
   See also CA 1-4R; CAAS 4; CANR 1;
   DLB 5; MTCW

Simpson, Mona (Elizabeth) 1957- . . . CLC 44
   See also CA 122; 135

Simpson, N(orman) F(rederick)
   1919- . . . . CLC 29
   See also CA 13-16R; DLB 13

Sinclair, Andrew (Annandale)
   1935- . . . . CLC 2, 14
   See also CA 9-12R; CAAS 5; CANR 14, 38;
   DLB 14; MTCW

Sinclair, Emil
   See Hesse, Hermann

Sinclair, Iain 1943- . . . . CLC 76
   See also CA 132

Sinclair, Iain MacGregor
   See Sinclair, Iain

Sinclair, Mary Amelia St. Clair 1865(?)-1946
   See Sinclair, May
   See also CA 104

Sinclair, May . . . . TCLC 3, 11
   See also Sinclair, Mary Amelia St. Clair
   See also DLB 36, 135

Sinclair, Upton (Beall)
   1878-1968 . . . . . . CLC 1, 11, 15, 63; DA;
                                                   WLC
   See also CA 5-8R; 25-28R; CANR 7;
   CDALB 1929-1941; DLB 9; MTCW;
   SATA 9

Singer, Isaac
   See Singer, Isaac Bashevis

Singer, Isaac Bashevis
   1904-1991 . . . . CLC 1, 3, 6, 9, 11, 15, 23,
                       38, 69; DA; SSC 3; WLC
   See also AITN 1, 2; CA 1-4R; 134;
   CANR 1, 39; CDALB 1941-1968; CLR 1;
   DLB 6, 28, 52; DLBY 91; JRDA;
   MAICYA; MTCW; SATA 3, 27;
   SATA-Obit 68

Singer, Israel Joshua 1893-1944 . . . TCLC 33

Singh, Khushwant 1915- . . . . CLC 11
   See also CA 9-12R; CAAS 9; CANR 6

Sinjohn, John
   See Galsworthy, John

Sinyavsky, Andrei (Donatevich)
   1925- . . . . CLC 8
   See also CA 85-88

Sirin, V.
   See Nabokov, Vladimir (Vladimirovich)

Sissman, L(ouis) E(dward)
   1928-1976 . . . . CLC 9, 18
   See also CA 21-24R; 65-68; CANR 13;
   DLB 5

Sisson, C(harles) H(ubert) 1914- . . . . . CLC 8
   See also CA 1-4R; CAAS 3; CANR 3;
   DLB 27

Sitwell, Dame Edith
   1887-1964 . . . . CLC 2, 9, 67; PC 3
   See also CA 9-12R; CANR 35;
   CDBLB 1945-1960; DLB 20; MTCW

Sjoewall, Maj 1935- . . . . CLC 7
   See also CA 65-68

Sjowall, Maj
   See Sjoewall, Maj

Skelton, Robin 1925- . . . . CLC 13
   See also AITN 2; CA 5-8R; CAAS 5;
   CANR 28; DLB 27, 53

Spaulding, Douglas
 See Bradbury, Ray (Douglas)

Spaulding, Leonard
 See Bradbury, Ray (Douglas)

Spence, J. A. D.
 See Eliot, T(homas) S(tearns)

Spencer, Elizabeth 1921- . . . . **CLC 22**
 See also CA 13-16R; CANR 32; DLB 6;
 MTCW; SATA 14

Spencer, Leonard G.
 See Silverberg, Robert

Spencer, Scott 1945- . . . . **CLC 30**
 See also CA 113; DLBY 86

Spender, Stephen (Harold)
 1909- . . . . **CLC 1, 2, 5, 10, 41**
 See also CA 9-12R; CANR 31;
 CDBLB 1945-1960; DLB 20; MTCW

Spengler, Oswald (Arnold Gottfried)
 1880-1936 . . . . **TCLC 25**
 See also CA 118

Spenser, Edmund
 1552(?)-1599 . . . . **LC 5; DA; PC 8; WLC**
 See also CDBLB Before 1660

Spicer, Jack 1925-1965 . . . . . . **CLC 8, 18, 72**
 See also CA 85-88; DLB 5, 16

Spiegelman, Art 1948- . . . . **CLC 76**
 See also AAYA 10; CA 125; CANR 41

Spielberg, Peter 1929- . . . . **CLC 6**
 See also CA 5-8R; CANR 4; DLBY 81

Spielberg, Steven 1947- . . . . **CLC 20**
 See also AAYA 8; CA 77-80; CANR 32;
 SATA 32

Spillane, Frank Morrison 1918-
 See Spillane, Mickey
 See also CA 25-28R; CANR 28; MTCW;
 SATA 66

Spillane, Mickey . . . . **CLC 3, 13**
 See also Spillane, Frank Morrison

Spinoza, Benedictus de 1632-1677 . . . . **LC 9**

Spinrad, Norman (Richard) 1940- . . . **CLC 46**
 See also CA 37-40R; CAAS 19; CANR 20;
 DLB 8

Spitteler, Carl (Friedrich Georg)
 1845-1924 . . . . **TCLC 12**
 See also CA 109; DLB 129

Spivack, Kathleen (Romola Drucker)
 1938- . . . . **CLC 6**
 See also CA 49-52

Spoto, Donald 1941- . . . . **CLC 39**
 See also CA 65-68; CANR 11

Springsteen, Bruce (F.) 1949- . . . . . . **CLC 17**
 See also CA 111

Spurling, Hilary 1940- . . . . **CLC 34**
 See also CA 104; CANR 25

Squires, (James) Radcliffe
 1917-1993 . . . . **CLC 51**
 See also CA 1-4R; 140; CANR 6, 21

Srivastava, Dhanpat Rai 1880(?)-1936
 See Premchand
 See also CA 118

Stacy, Donald
 See Pohl, Frederik

Stael, Germaine de
 See Stael-Holstein, Anne Louise Germaine
 Necker Baronn
 See also DLB 119

Stael-Holstein, Anne Louise Germaine Necker
 Baronn 1766-1817 . . . . **NCLC 3**
 See also Stael, Germaine de

Stafford, Jean 1915-1979 . . . **CLC 4, 7, 19, 68**
 See also CA 1-4R; 85-88; CANR 3; DLB 2;
 MTCW; SATA 22

Stafford, William (Edgar)
 1914-1993 . . . . **CLC 4, 7, 29**
 See also CA 5-8R; 142; CAAS 3; CANR 5,
 22; DLB 5

Staines, Trevor
 See Brunner, John (Kilian Houston)

Stairs, Gordon
 See Austin, Mary (Hunter)

Stannard, Martin 1947- . . . . **CLC 44**
 See also CA 142

Stanton, Maura 1946- . . . . **CLC 9**
 See also CA 89-92; CANR 15; DLB 120

Stanton, Schuyler
 See Baum, L(yman) Frank

Stapledon, (William) Olaf
 1886-1950 . . . . **TCLC 22**
 See also CA 111; DLB 15

Starbuck, George (Edwin) 1931- . . . . **CLC 53**
 See also CA 21-24R; CANR 23

Stark, Richard
 See Westlake, Donald E(dwin)

Staunton, Schuyler
 See Baum, L(yman) Frank

Stead, Christina (Ellen)
 1902-1983 . . . . **CLC 2, 5, 8, 32, 80**
 See also CA 13-16R; 109; CANR 33, 40;
 MTCW

Stead, William Thomas
 1849-1912 . . . . **TCLC 48**

Steele, Richard 1672-1729 . . . . **LC 18**
 See also CDBLB 1660-1789; DLB 84, 101

Steele, Timothy (Reid) 1948- . . . . . . **CLC 45**
 See also CA 93-96; CANR 16; DLB 120

Steffens, (Joseph) Lincoln
 1866-1936 . . . . **TCLC 20**
 See also CA 117

Stegner, Wallace (Earle)
 1909-1993 . . . . **CLC 9, 49, 81**
 See also AITN 1; BEST 90:3; CA 1-4R;
 141; CAAS 9; CANR 1, 21; DLB 9;
 DLBY 93; MTCW

Stein, Gertrude
 1874-1946 . . . . . . **TCLC 1, 6, 28, 48; DA;**
 WLC
 See also CA 104; 132; CDALB 1917-1929;
 DLB 4, 54, 86; MTCW

Steinbeck, John (Ernst)
 1902-1968 . . . . . . **CLC 1, 5, 9, 13, 21, 34,**
 45, 75; DA; SSC 11; WLC
 See also AAYA 12; CA 1-4R; 25-28R;
 CANR 1, 35; CDALB 1929-1941; DLB 7,
 9; DLBD 2; MTCW; SATA 9

Steinem, Gloria 1934- . . . . **CLC 63**
 See also CA 53-56; CANR 28; MTCW

Steiner, George 1929- . . . . **CLC 24**
 See also CA 73-76; CANR 31; DLB 67;
 MTCW; SATA 62

Steiner, K. Leslie
 See Delany, Samuel R(ay, Jr.)

Steiner, Rudolf 1861-1925 . . . . **TCLC 13**
 See also CA 107

Stendhal
 1783-1842 . . . . . **NCLC 23, 46; DA; WLC**
 See also DLB 119

Stephen, Leslie 1832-1904 . . . . **TCLC 23**
 See also CA 123; DLB 57, 144

Stephen, Sir Leslie
 See Stephen, Leslie

Stephen, Virginia
 See Woolf, (Adeline) Virginia

Stephens, James 1882(?)-1950 . . . . . . **TCLC 4**
 See also CA 104; DLB 19

Stephens, Reed
 See Donaldson, Stephen R.

Steptoe, Lydia
 See Barnes, Djuna

Sterchi, Beat 1949- . . . . **CLC 65**

Sterling, Brett
 See Bradbury, Ray (Douglas); Hamilton,
 Edmond

Sterling, Bruce 1954- . . . . **CLC 72**
 See also CA 119; CANR 44

Sterling, George 1869-1926 . . . . **TCLC 20**
 See also CA 117; DLB 54

Stern, Gerald 1925- . . . . **CLC 40**
 See also CA 81-84; CANR 28; DLB 105

Stern, Richard (Gustave) 1928- . . . **CLC 4, 39**
 See also CA 1-4R; CANR 1, 25; DLBY 87

Sternberg, Josef von 1894-1969 . . . . . **CLC 20**
 See also CA 81-84

Sterne, Laurence
 1713-1768 . . . . **LC 2; DA; WLC**
 See also CDBLB 1660-1789; DLB 39

Sternheim, (William Adolf) Carl
 1878-1942 . . . . **TCLC 8**
 See also CA 105; DLB 56, 118

Stevens, Mark 1951- . . . . **CLC 34**
 See also CA 122

Stevens, Wallace
 1879-1955 . . . . **TCLC 3, 12, 45; DA;**
 PC 6; WLC
 See also CA 104; 124; CDALB 1929-1941;
 DLB 54; MTCW

Stevenson, Anne (Katharine)
 1933- . . . . **CLC 7, 33**
 See also CA 17-20R; CAAS 9; CANR 9, 33;
 DLB 40; MTCW

Stevenson, Robert Louis (Balfour)
 1850-1894 . . . . **NCLC 5, 14; DA;**
 SSC 11; WLC
 See also CDBLB 1890-1914; CLR 10, 11;
 DLB 18, 57, 141; JRDA; MAICYA;
 YABC 2

Stewart, J(ohn) I(nnes) M(ackintosh)
 1906- . . . . **CLC 7, 14, 32**
 See also CA 85-88; CAAS 3; MTCW

Swenson, May
1919-1989 . . . . CLC **4, 14, 61; DA**
See also CA 5-8R; 130; CANR 36; DLB 5;
MTCW; SATA 15

Swift, Augustus
See Lovecraft, H(oward) P(hillips)

Swift, Graham 1949- . . . . CLC **41**
See also CA 117; 122

Swift, Jonathan
1667-1745 . . . . . . LC **1; DA; PC 9; WLC**
See also CDBLB 1660-1789; DLB 39, 95,
101; SATA 19

Swinburne, Algernon Charles
1837-1909 . . . . . . TCLC **8, 36; DA; WLC**
See also CA 105; 140; CDBLB 1832-1890;
DLB 35, 57

Swinfen, Ann . . . . CLC **34**

Swinnerton, Frank Arthur
1884-1982 . . . . CLC **31**
See also CA 108; DLB 34

Swithen, John
See King, Stephen (Edwin)

Sylvia
See Ashton-Warner, Sylvia (Constance)

Symmes, Robert Edward
See Duncan, Robert (Edward)

Symonds, John Addington
1840-1893 . . . . NCLC **34**
See also DLB 57, 144

Symons, Arthur 1865-1945 . . . . TCLC **11**
See also CA 107; DLB 19, 57

Symons, Julian (Gustave)
1912- . . . . CLC **2, 14, 32**
See also CA 49-52; CAAS 3; CANR 3, 33;
DLB 87; DLBY 92; MTCW

Synge, (Edmund) J(ohn) M(illington)
1871-1909 . . . . TCLC **6, 37; DC 2**
See also CA 104; 141; CDBLB 1890-1914;
DLB 10, 19

Syruc, J.
See Milosz, Czeslaw

Szirtes, George 1948- . . . . CLC **46**
See also CA 109; CANR 27

Tabori, George 1914- . . . . CLC **19**
See also CA 49-52; CANR 4

Tagore, Rabindranath
1861-1941 . . . . TCLC **3, 53; PC 8**
See also CA 104; 120; MTCW

Taine, Hippolyte Adolphe
1828-1893 . . . . NCLC **15**

Talese, Gay 1932- . . . . CLC **37**
See also AITN 1; CA 1-4R; CANR 9;
MTCW

Tallent, Elizabeth (Ann) 1954- . . . . . CLC **45**
See also CA 117; DLB 130

Tally, Ted 1952- . . . . CLC **42**
See also CA 120; 124

Tamayo y Baus, Manuel
1829-1898 . . . . NCLC **1**

Tammsaare, A(nton) H(ansen)
1878-1940 . . . . TCLC **27**

Tan, Amy 1952- . . . . CLC **59**
See also AAYA 9; BEST 89:3; CA 136;
SATA 75

Tandem, Felix
See Spitteler, Carl (Friedrich Georg)

Tanizaki, Jun'ichiro
1886-1965 . . . . CLC **8, 14, 28**
See also CA 93-96; 25-28R

Tanner, William
See Amis, Kingsley (William)

Tao Lao
See Storni, Alfonsina

Tarassoff, Lev
See Troyat, Henri

Tarbell, Ida M(inerva)
1857-1944 . . . . TCLC **40**
See also CA 122; DLB 47

Tarkington, (Newton) Booth
1869-1946 . . . . TCLC **9**
See also CA 110; 143; DLB 9, 102;
SATA 17

Tarkovsky, Andrei (Arsenyevich)
1932-1986 . . . . CLC **75**
See also CA 127

Tartt, Donna 1964(?)- . . . . CLC **76**
See also CA 142

Tasso, Torquato 1544-1595 . . . . LC **5**

Tate, (John Orley) Allen
1899-1979 . . . . CLC **2, 4, 6, 9, 11, 14, 24**
See also CA 5-8R; 85-88; CANR 32;
DLB 4, 45, 63; MTCW

Tate, Ellalice
See Hibbert, Eleanor Alice Burford

Tate, James (Vincent) 1943- . . . CLC **2, 6, 25**
See also CA 21-24R; CANR 29; DLB 5

Tavel, Ronald 1940- . . . . CLC **6**
See also CA 21-24R; CANR 33

Taylor, Cecil Philip 1929-1981 . . . . . CLC **27**
See also CA 25-28R; 105

Taylor, Edward 1642(?)-1729 . . . . LC **11; DA**
See also DLB 24

Taylor, Eleanor Ross 1920- . . . . CLC **5**
See also CA 81-84

Taylor, Elizabeth 1912-1975 . . . CLC **2, 4, 29**
See also CA 13-16R; CANR 9; DLB 139;
MTCW; SATA 13

Taylor, Henry (Splawn) 1942- . . . . . . CLC **44**
See also CA 33-36R; CAAS 7; CANR 31;
DLB 5

Taylor, Kamala (Purnaiya) 1924-
See Markandaya, Kamala
See also CA 77-80

Taylor, Mildred D. . . . . CLC **21**
See also AAYA 10; BW 1; CA 85-88;
CANR 25; CLR 9; DLB 52; JRDA;
MAICYA; SAAS 5; SATA 15, 70

Taylor, Peter (Hillsman)
1917- . . . . . . CLC **1, 4, 18, 37, 44, 50, 71;
SSC 10**
See also CA 13-16R; CANR 9; DLBY 81;
MTCW

Taylor, Robert Lewis 1912- . . . . CLC **14**
See also CA 1-4R; CANR 3; SATA 10

Tchekhov, Anton
See Chekhov, Anton (Pavlovich)

Teasdale, Sara 1884-1933 . . . . TCLC **4**
See also CA 104; DLB 45; SATA 32

Tegner, Esaias 1782-1846 . . . . NCLC **2**

Teilhard de Chardin, (Marie Joseph) Pierre
1881-1955 . . . . TCLC **9**
See also CA 105

Temple, Ann
See Mortimer, Penelope (Ruth)

Tennant, Emma (Christina)
1937- . . . . CLC **13, 52**
See also CA 65-68; CAAS 9; CANR 10, 38;
DLB 14

Tenneshaw, S. M.
See Silverberg, Robert

Tennyson, Alfred
1809-1892 . . NCLC **30; DA; PC 6; WLC**
See also CDBLB 1832-1890; DLB 32

Teran, Lisa St. Aubin de . . . . CLC **36**
See also St. Aubin de Teran, Lisa

Teresa de Jesus, St. 1515-1582 . . . . . . LC **18**

Terkel, Louis 1912-
See Terkel, Studs
See also CA 57-60; CANR 18, 45; MTCW

Terkel, Studs . . . . CLC **38**
See also Terkel, Louis
See also AITN 1

Terry, C. V.
See Slaughter, Frank G(ill)

Terry, Megan 1932- . . . . CLC **19**
See also CA 77-80; CABS 3; CANR 43;
DLB 7

Tertz, Abram
See Sinyavsky, Andrei (Donatevich)

Tesich, Steve 1943(?)- . . . . CLC **40, 69**
See also CA 105; DLBY 83

Teternikov, Fyodor Kuzmich 1863-1927
See Sologub, Fyodor
See also CA 104

Tevis, Walter 1928-1984 . . . . CLC **42**
See also CA 113

Tey, Josephine . . . . TCLC **14**
See also Mackintosh, Elizabeth
See also DLB 77

Thackeray, William Makepeace
1811-1863 . . . . NCLC **5, 14, 22, 43; DA;
WLC**
See also CDBLB 1832-1890; DLB 21, 55;
SATA 23

Thakura, Ravindranatha
See Tagore, Rabindranath

Tharoor, Shashi 1956- . . . . CLC **70**
See also CA 141

Thelwell, Michael Miles 1939- . . . . . CLC **22**
See also BW 2; CA 101

Theobald, Lewis, Jr.
See Lovecraft, H(oward) P(hillips)

Theodorescu, Ion N. 1880-1967
See Arghezi, Tudor
See also CA 116

Theriault, Yves 1915-1983 . . . . CLC **79**
See also CA 102; DLB 88

Theroux, Alexander (Louis)
1939- . . . . CLC **2, 25**
See also CA 85-88; CANR 20

Transtromer, Tomas Gosta
　See Transtroemer, Tomas (Goesta)

Traven, B. (?)-1969 . . . . **CLC 8, 11**
　See also CA 19-20; 25-28R; CAP 2; DLB 9,
　56; MTCW

Treitel, Jonathan 1959- . . . . **CLC 70**

Tremain, Rose 1943- . . . . **CLC 42**
　See also CA 97-100; CANR 44; DLB 14

Tremblay, Michel 1942- . . . . **CLC 29**
　See also CA 116; 128; DLB 60; MTCW

Trevor, Glen
　See Hilton, James

Trevor, William
　1928- . . . . **CLC 7, 9, 14, 25, 71**
　See also Cox, William Trevor
　See also DLB 14, 139

Trifonov, Yuri (Valentinovich)
　1925-1981 . . . . **CLC 45**
　See also CA 126; 103; MTCW

Trilling, Lionel 1905-1975 . . . . **CLC 9, 11, 24**
　See also CA 9-12R; 61-64; CANR 10;
　DLB 28, 63; MTCW

Trimball, W. H.
　See Mencken, H(enry) L(ouis)

Tristan
　See Gomez de la Serna, Ramon

Tristram
　See Housman, A(lfred) E(dward)

Trogdon, William (Lewis) 1939-
　See Heat-Moon, William Least
　See also CA 115; 119

Trollope, Anthony
　1815-1882 . . . . . . **NCLC 6, 33; DA; WLC**
　See also CDBLB 1832-1890; DLB 21, 57;
　SATA 22

Trollope, Frances 1779-1863 . . . . . **NCLC 30**
　See also DLB 21

Trotsky, Leon 1879-1940 . . . . **TCLC 22**
　See also CA 118

Trotter (Cockburn), Catharine
　1679-1749 . . . . **LC 8**
　See also DLB 84

Trout, Kilgore
　See Farmer, Philip Jose

Trow, George W. S. 1943- . . . . **CLC 52**
　See also CA 126

Troyat, Henri 1911- . . . . **CLC 23**
　See also CA 45-48; CANR 2, 33; MTCW

Trudeau, G(arretson) B(eekman) 1948-
　See Trudeau, Garry B.
　See also CA 81-84; CANR 31; SATA 35

Trudeau, Garry B. . . . . **CLC 12**
　See also Trudeau, G(arretson) B(eekman)
　See also AAYA 10; AITN 2

Truffaut, Francois 1932-1984 . . . . . . **CLC 20**
　See also CA 81-84; 113; CANR 34

Trumbo, Dalton 1905-1976 . . . . **CLC 19**
　See also CA 21-24R; 69-72; CANR 10;
　DLB 26

Trumbull, John 1750-1831 . . . . . . **NCLC 30**
　See also DLB 31

Trundlett, Helen B.
　See Eliot, T(homas) S(tearns)

Tryon, Thomas 1926-1991 . . . . . . **CLC 3, 11**
　See also AITN 1; CA 29-32R; 135;
　CANR 32; MTCW

Tryon, Tom
　See Tryon, Thomas

Ts'ao Hsueh-ch'in 1715(?)-1763 . . . . . . **LC 1**

Tsushima, Shuji 1909-1948
　See Dazai, Osamu
　See also CA 107

Tsvetaeva (Efron), Marina (Ivanovna)
　1892-1941 . . . . **TCLC 7, 35**
　See also CA 104; 128; MTCW

Tuck, Lily 1938- . . . . **CLC 70**
　See also CA 139

Tu Fu 712-770 . . . . **PC 9**

Tunis, John R(oberts) 1889-1975 . . . **CLC 12**
　See also CA 61-64; DLB 22; JRDA;
　MAICYA; SATA 30, 37

Tuohy, Frank . . . . **CLC 37**
　See also Tuohy, John Francis
　See also DLB 14, 139

Tuohy, John Francis 1925-
　See Tuohy, Frank
　See also CA 5-8R; CANR 3

Turco, Lewis (Putnam) 1934- . . . **CLC 11, 63**
　See also CA 13-16R; CANR 24; DLBY 84

Turgenev, Ivan
　1818-1883 . . . . . . **NCLC 21; DA; SSC 7;
　　　　　　　　　　　　　　　　　　WLC**

Turgot, Anne-Robert-Jacques
　1727-1781 . . . . **LC 26**

Turner, Frederick 1943- . . . . **CLC 48**
　See also CA 73-76; CAAS 10; CANR 12,
　30; DLB 40

Tusan, Stan 1936- . . . . **CLC 22**
　See also CA 105

Tutu, Desmond M(pilo)
　1931- . . . . **CLC 80; BLC**
　See also BW 1; CA 125

Tutuola, Amos 1920- . . . **CLC 5, 14, 29; BLC**
　See also BW 2; CA 9-12R; CANR 27;
　DLB 125; MTCW

Twain, Mark
　. . . **TCLC 6, 12, 19, 36, 48; SSC 6; WLC**
　See also Clemens, Samuel Langhorne
　See also DLB 11, 12, 23, 64, 74

Tyler, Anne
　1941- . . . . **CLC 7, 11, 18, 28, 44, 59**
　See also BEST 89:1; CA 9-12R; CANR 11,
　33; DLB 6, 143; DLBY 82; MTCW;
　SATA 7

Tyler, Royall 1757-1826 . . . . **NCLC 3**
　See also DLB 37

Tynan, Katharine 1861-1931 . . . . . . **TCLC 3**
　See also CA 104

Tytell, John 1939- . . . . **CLC 50**
　See also CA 29-32R

Tyutchev, Fyodor 1803-1873 . . . . . **NCLC 34**

Tzara, Tristan . . . . **CLC 47**
　See also Rosenfeld, Samuel

Uhry, Alfred 1936- . . . . **CLC 55**
　See also CA 127; 133

Ulf, Haerved
　See Strindberg, (Johan) August

Ulf, Harved
　See Strindberg, (Johan) August

Ulibarri, Sabine R(eyes) 1919- . . . . . **CLC 83**
　See also CA 131; DLB 82; HW

Unamuno (y Jugo), Miguel de
　1864-1936 . . . . **TCLC 2, 9; HLC; SSC 11**
　See also CA 104; 131; DLB 108; HW;
　MTCW

Undercliffe, Errol
　See Campbell, (John) Ramsey

Underwood, Miles
　See Glassco, John

Undset, Sigrid
　1882-1949 . . . . **TCLC 3; DA; WLC**
　See also CA 104; 129; MTCW

Ungaretti, Giuseppe
　1888-1970 . . . . **CLC 7, 11, 15**
　See also CA 19-20; 25-28R; CAP 2;
　DLB 114

Unger, Douglas 1952- . . . . **CLC 34**
　See also CA 130

Unsworth, Barry (Forster) 1930- . . . . **CLC 76**
　See also CA 25-28R; CANR 30

Updike, John (Hoyer)
　1932- . . . . . . **CLC 1, 2, 3, 5, 7, 9, 13, 15,
　　　　　　　23, 34, 43, 70; DA; SSC 13; WLC**
　See also CA 1-4R; CABS 1; CANR 4, 33;
　CDALB 1968-1988; DLB 2, 5, 143;
　DLBD 3; DLBY 80, 82; MTCW

Upshaw, Margaret Mitchell
　See Mitchell, Margaret (Munnerlyn)

Upton, Mark
　See Sanders, Lawrence

Urdang, Constance (Henriette)
　1922- . . . . **CLC 47**
　See also CA 21-24R; CANR 9, 24

Uriel, Henry
　See Faust, Frederick (Schiller)

Uris, Leon (Marcus) 1924- . . . . **CLC 7, 32**
　See also AITN 1, 2; BEST 89:2; CA 1-4R;
　CANR 1, 40; MTCW; SATA 49

Urmuz
　See Codrescu, Andrei

Ustinov, Peter (Alexander) 1921- . . . . **CLC 1**
　See also AITN 1; CA 13-16R; CANR 25;
　DLB 13

v
　See Chekhov, Anton (Pavlovich)

Vaculik, Ludvik 1926- . . . . **CLC 7**
　See also CA 53-56

Valdez, Luis (Miguel)
　1940- . . . . **CLC 84; HLC**
　See also CA 101; CANR 32; DLB 122; HW

Valenzuela, Luisa 1938- . . . **CLC 31; SSC 14**
　See also CA 101; CANR 32; DLB 113; HW

Valera y Alcala-Galiano, Juan
　1824-1905 . . . . **TCLC 10**
　See also CA 106

Valery, (Ambroise) Paul (Toussaint Jules)
　1871-1945 . . . . **TCLC 4, 15; PC 9**
　See also CA 104; 122; MTCW

Valle-Inclan, Ramon (Maria) del
　1866-1936 . . . . **TCLC 5; HLC**
　See also CA 106; DLB 134

Vonnegut, Kurt, Jr.
1922- . . . . . . **CLC 1, 2, 3, 4, 5, 8, 12, 22, 40, 60; DA; SSC 8; WLC**
See also AAYA 6; AITN 1; BEST 90:4; CA 1-4R; CANR 1, 25; CDALB 1968-1988; DLB 2, 8; DLBD 3; DLBY 80; MTCW

Von Rachen, Kurt
See Hubbard, L(afayette) Ron(ald)

von Rezzori (d'Arezzo), Gregor
See Rezzori (d'Arezzo), Gregor von

von Sternberg, Josef
See Sternberg, Josef von

Vorster, Gordon 1924- . . . . **CLC 34**
See also CA 133

Vosce, Trudie
See Ozick, Cynthia

Voznesensky, Andrei (Andreievich)
1933- . . . . **CLC 1, 15, 57**
See also CA 89-92; CANR 37; MTCW

Waddington, Miriam 1917- . . . . **CLC 28**
See also CA 21-24R; CANR 12, 30; DLB 68

Wagman, Fredrica 1937- . . . . **CLC 7**
See also CA 97-100

Wagner, Richard 1813-1883. . . . . . . **NCLC 9**
See also DLB 129

Wagner-Martin, Linda 1936- . . . . **CLC 50**

Wagoner, David (Russell)
1926- . . . . **CLC 3, 5, 15**
See also CA 1-4R; CAAS 3; CANR 2; DLB 5; SATA 14

Wah, Fred(erick James) 1939- . . . . . . **CLC 44**
See also CA 107; 141; DLB 60

Wahloo, Per 1926-1975 . . . . **CLC 7**
See also CA 61-64

Wahloo, Peter
See Wahloo, Per

Wain, John (Barrington)
1925- . . . . **CLC 2, 11, 15, 46**
See also CA 5-8R; CAAS 4; CANR 23; CDBLB 1960 to Present; DLB 15, 27, 139; MTCW

Wajda, Andrzej 1926- . . . . **CLC 16**
See also CA 102

Wakefield, Dan 1932- . . . . **CLC 7**
See also CA 21-24R; CAAS 7

Wakoski, Diane
1937- . . . . **CLC 2, 4, 7, 9, 11, 40**
See also CA 13-16R; CAAS 1; CANR 9; DLB 5

Wakoski-Sherbell, Diane
See Wakoski, Diane

Walcott, Derek (Alton)
1930- . . . . **CLC 2, 4, 9, 14, 25, 42, 67, 76; BLC**
See also BW 2; CA 89-92; CANR 26; DLB 117; DLBY 81; MTCW

Waldman, Anne 1945- . . . . **CLC 7**
See also CA 37-40R; CAAS 17; CANR 34; DLB 16

Waldo, E. Hunter
See Sturgeon, Theodore (Hamilton)

Waldo, Edward Hamilton
See Sturgeon, Theodore (Hamilton)

Walker, Alice (Malsenior)
1944- . . . . . . **CLC 5, 6, 9, 19, 27, 46, 58; BLC; DA; SSC 5**
See also AAYA 3; BEST 89:4; BW 2; CA 37-40R; CANR 9, 27; CDALB 1968-1988; DLB 6, 33, 143; MTCW; SATA 31

Walker, David Harry 1911-1992 . . . . **CLC 14**
See also CA 1-4R; 137; CANR 1; SATA 8; SATA-Obit 71

Walker, Edward Joseph 1934-
See Walker, Ted
See also CA 21-24R; CANR 12, 28

Walker, George F. 1947- . . . . **CLC 44, 61**
See also CA 103; CANR 21, 43; DLB 60

Walker, Joseph A. 1935- . . . . **CLC 19**
See also BW 1; CA 89-92; CANR 26; DLB 38

Walker, Margaret (Abigail)
1915- . . . . **CLC 1, 6; BLC**
See also BW 2; CA 73-76; CANR 26; DLB 76; MTCW

Walker, Ted . . . . **CLC 13**
See also Walker, Edward Joseph
See also DLB 40

Wallace, David Foster 1962- . . . . **CLC 50**
See also CA 132

Wallace, Dexter
See Masters, Edgar Lee

Wallace, Irving 1916-1990 . . . . **CLC 7, 13**
See also AITN 1; CA 1-4R; 132; CAAS 1; CANR 1, 27; MTCW

Wallant, Edward Lewis
1926-1962 . . . . **CLC 5, 10**
See also CA 1-4R; CANR 22; DLB 2, 28, 143; MTCW

Walpole, Horace 1717-1797 . . . . **LC 2**
See also DLB 39, 104

Walpole, Hugh (Seymour)
1884-1941 . . . . **TCLC 5**
See also CA 104; DLB 34

Walser, Martin 1927- . . . . **CLC 27**
See also CA 57-60; CANR 8; DLB 75, 124

Walser, Robert 1878-1956 . . . . **TCLC 18**
See also CA 118; DLB 66

Walsh, Jill Paton . . . . **CLC 35**
See also Paton Walsh, Gillian
See also AAYA 11; CLR 2; SAAS 3

Walter, Villiam Christian
See Andersen, Hans Christian

Wambaugh, Joseph (Aloysius, Jr.)
1937- . . . . **CLC 3, 18**
See also AITN 1; BEST 89:3; CA 33-36R; CANR 42; DLB 6; DLBY 83; MTCW

Ward, Arthur Henry Sarsfield 1883-1959
See Rohmer, Sax
See also CA 108

Ward, Douglas Turner 1930- . . . . **CLC 19**
See also BW 1; CA 81-84; CANR 27; DLB 7, 38

Ward, Mary Augusta
See Ward, Mrs. Humphry

Ward, Mrs. Humphry
1851-1920 . . . . **TCLC 55**
See also DLB 18

Ward, Peter
See Faust, Frederick (Schiller)

Warhol, Andy 1928(?)-1987 . . . . **CLC 20**
See also AAYA 12; BEST 89:4; CA 89-92; 121; CANR 34

Warner, Francis (Robert le Plastrier)
1937- . . . . **CLC 14**
See also CA 53-56; CANR 11

Warner, Marina 1946- . . . . **CLC 59**
See also CA 65-68; CANR 21

Warner, Rex (Ernest) 1905-1986 . . . . **CLC 45**
See also CA 89-92; 119; DLB 15

Warner, Susan (Bogert)
1819-1885 . . . . **NCLC 31**
See also DLB 3, 42

Warner, Sylvia (Constance) Ashton
See Ashton-Warner, Sylvia (Constance)

Warner, Sylvia Townsend
1893-1978 . . . . **CLC 7, 19**
See also CA 61-64; 77-80; CANR 16; DLB 34, 139; MTCW

Warren, Mercy Otis 1728-1814 . . . **NCLC 13**
See also DLB 31

Warren, Robert Penn
1905-1989 . . . . **CLC 1, 4, 6, 8, 10, 13, 18, 39, 53, 59; DA; SSC 4; WLC**
See also AITN 1; CA 13-16R; 129; CANR 10; CDALB 1968-1988; DLB 2, 48; DLBY 80, 89; MTCW; SATA 46, 63

Warshofsky, Isaac
See Singer, Isaac Bashevis

Warton, Thomas 1728-1790 . . . . **LC 15**
See also DLB 104, 109

Waruk, Kona
See Harris, (Theodore) Wilson

Warung, Price 1855-1911 . . . . **TCLC 45**

Warwick, Jarvis
See Garner, Hugh

Washington, Alex
See Harris, Mark

Washington, Booker T(aliaferro)
1856-1915 . . . . **TCLC 10; BLC**
See also BW 1; CA 114; 125; SATA 28

Washington, George 1732-1799 . . . . . . **LC 25**
See also DLB 31

Wassermann, (Karl) Jakob
1873-1934 . . . . **TCLC 6**
See also CA 104; DLB 66

Wasserstein, Wendy
1950- . . . . **CLC 32, 59; DC 4**
See also CA 121; 129; CABS 3

Waterhouse, Keith (Spencer)
1929- . . . . **CLC 47**
See also CA 5-8R; CANR 38; DLB 13, 15; MTCW

Waters, Roger 1944- . . . . **CLC 35**
See also Pink Floyd

Watkins, Frances Ellen
See Harper, Frances Ellen Watkins

Watkins, Gerrold
See Malzberg, Barry N(athaniel)

Watkins, Paul 1964- . . . . **CLC 55**
See also CA 132

Watkins, Vernon Phillips
1906-1967 . . . . CLC 43
See also CA 9-10; 25-28R; CAP 1; DLB 20

Watson, Irving S.
See Mencken, H(enry) L(ouis)

Watson, John H.
See Farmer, Philip Jose

Watson, Richard F.
See Silverberg, Robert

Waugh, Auberon (Alexander) 1939- . . CLC 7
See also CA 45-48; CANR 6, 22; DLB 14

Waugh, Evelyn (Arthur St. John)
1903-1966 . . . . . . CLC 1, 3, 8, 13, 19, 27,
44; DA; WLC
See also CA 85-88; 25-28R; CANR 22;
CDBLB 1914-1945; DLB 15; MTCW

Waugh, Harriet 1944- . . . . CLC 6
See also CA 85-88; CANR 22

Ways, C. R.
See Blount, Roy (Alton), Jr.

Waystaff, Simon
See Swift, Jonathan

Webb, (Martha) Beatrice (Potter)
1858-1943 . . . . TCLC 22
See also Potter, Beatrice
See also CA 117

Webb, Charles (Richard) 1939- . . . . . . CLC 7
See also CA 25-28R

Webb, James H(enry), Jr. 1946- . . . . CLC 22
See also CA 81-84

Webb, Mary (Gladys Meredith)
1881-1927 . . . . TCLC 24
See also CA 123; DLB 34

Webb, Mrs. Sidney
See Webb, (Martha) Beatrice (Potter)

Webb, Phyllis 1927- . . . . CLC 18
See also CA 104; CANR 23; DLB 53

Webb, Sidney (James)
1859-1947 . . . . TCLC 22
See also CA 117

Webber, Andrew Lloyd . . . . CLC 21
See also Lloyd Webber, Andrew

Weber, Lenora Mattingly
1895-1971 . . . . CLC 12
See also CA 19-20; 29-32R; CAP 1;
SATA 2, 26

Webster, John 1579(?)-1634(?) . . . . DC 2
See also CDBLB Before 1660; DA; DLB 58;
WLC

Webster, Noah 1758-1843 . . . . NCLC 30

Wedekind, (Benjamin) Frank(lin)
1864-1918 . . . . TCLC 7
See also CA 104; DLB 118

Weidman, Jerome 1913- . . . . CLC 7
See also AITN 2; CA 1-4R; CANR 1;
DLB 28

Weil, Simone (Adolphine)
1909-1943 . . . . TCLC 23
See also CA 117

Weinstein, Nathan
See West, Nathanael

Weinstein, Nathan von Wallenstein
See West, Nathanael

Weir, Peter (Lindsay) 1944- . . . . CLC 20
See also CA 113; 123

Weiss, Peter (Ulrich)
1916-1982 . . . . CLC 3, 15, 51
See also CA 45-48; 106; CANR 3; DLB 69,
124

Weiss, Theodore (Russell)
1916- . . . . CLC 3, 8, 14
See also CA 9-12R; CAAS 2; DLB 5

Welch, (Maurice) Denton
1915-1948 . . . . TCLC 22
See also CA 121

Welch, James 1940- . . . . CLC 6, 14, 52
See also CA 85-88; CANR 42

Weldon, Fay
1933(?)- . . . . CLC 6, 9, 11, 19, 36, 59
See also CA 21-24R; CANR 16;
CDBLB 1960 to Present; DLB 14;
MTCW

Wellek, Rene 1903- . . . . CLC 28
See also CA 5-8R; CAAS 7; CANR 8;
DLB 63

Weller, Michael 1942- . . . . CLC 10, 53
See also CA 85-88

Weller, Paul 1958- . . . . CLC 26

Wellershoff, Dieter 1925- . . . . CLC 46
See also CA 89-92; CANR 16, 37

Welles, (George) Orson
1915-1985 . . . . CLC 20, 80
See also CA 93-96; 117

Wellman, Mac 1945- . . . . CLC 65

Wellman, Manly Wade 1903-1986 . . CLC 49
See also CA 1-4R; 118; CANR 6, 16, 44;
SATA 6, 47

Wells, Carolyn 1869(?)-1942 . . . . . . TCLC 35
See also CA 113; DLB 11

Wells, H(erbert) G(eorge)
1866-1946 . . . . TCLC 6, 12, 19; DA;
SSC 6; WLC
See also CA 110; 121; CDBLB 1914-1945;
DLB 34, 70; MTCW; SATA 20

Wells, Rosemary 1943- . . . . CLC 12
See also CA 85-88; CLR 16; MAICYA;
SAAS 1; SATA 18, 69

Welty, Eudora
1909- . . . . . . CLC 1, 2, 5, 14, 22, 33; DA;
SSC 1; WLC
See also CA 9-12R; CABS 1; CANR 32;
CDALB 1941-1968; DLB 2, 102, 143;
DLBY 87; MTCW

Wen I-to 1899-1946 . . . . TCLC 28

Wentworth, Robert
See Hamilton, Edmond

Werfel, Franz (V.) 1890-1945 . . . . . . TCLC 8
See also CA 104; DLB 81, 124

Wergeland, Henrik Arnold
1808-1845 . . . . NCLC 5

Wersba, Barbara 1932- . . . . CLC 30
See also AAYA 2; CA 29-32R; CANR 16,
38; CLR 3; DLB 52; JRDA; MAICYA;
SAAS 2; SATA 1, 58

Wertmueller, Lina 1928- . . . . CLC 16
See also CA 97-100; CANR 39

Wescott, Glenway 1901-1987 . . . . CLC 13
See also CA 13-16R; 121; CANR 23;
DLB 4, 9, 102

Wesker, Arnold 1932- . . . . CLC 3, 5, 42
See also CA 1-4R; CAAS 7; CANR 1, 33;
CDBLB 1960 to Present; DLB 13;
MTCW

Wesley, Richard (Errol) 1945- . . . . CLC 7
See also BW 1; CA 57-60; CANR 27;
DLB 38

Wessel, Johan Herman 1742-1785 . . . . LC 7

West, Anthony (Panther)
1914-1987 . . . . CLC 50
See also CA 45-48; 124; CANR 3, 19;
DLB 15

West, C. P.
See Wodehouse, P(elham) G(renville)

West, (Mary) Jessamyn
1902-1984 . . . . CLC 7, 17
See also CA 9-12R; 112; CANR 27; DLB 6;
DLBY 84; MTCW; SATA 37

West, Morris L(anglo) 1916- . . . . . CLC 6, 33
See also CA 5-8R; CANR 24; MTCW

West, Nathanael
1903-1940 . . . . . TCLC 1, 14, 44; SSC 16
See also CA 104; 125; CDALB 1929-1941;
DLB 4, 9, 28; MTCW

West, Owen
See Koontz, Dean R(ay)

West, Paul 1930- . . . . CLC 7, 14
See also CA 13-16R; CAAS 7; CANR 22;
DLB 14

West, Rebecca 1892-1983 . . CLC 7, 9, 31, 50
See also CA 5-8R; 109; CANR 19; DLB 36;
DLBY 83; MTCW

Westall, Robert (Atkinson)
1929-1993 . . . . CLC 17
See also AAYA 12; CA 69-72; 141;
CANR 18; CLR 13; JRDA; MAICYA;
SAAS 2; SATA 23, 69; SATA-Obit 75

Westlake, Donald E(dwin)
1933- . . . . CLC 7, 33
See also CA 17-20R; CAAS 13; CANR 16,
44

Westmacott, Mary
See Christie, Agatha (Mary Clarissa)

Weston, Allen
See Norton, Andre

Wetcheek, J. L.
See Feuchtwanger, Lion

Wetering, Janwillem van de
See van de Wetering, Janwillem

Wetherell, Elizabeth
See Warner, Susan (Bogert)

Whalen, Philip 1923- . . . . CLC 6, 29
See also CA 9-12R; CANR 5, 39; DLB 16

Wharton, Edith (Newbold Jones)
1862-1937 . . . . . . TCLC 3, 9, 27, 53; DA;
SSC 6; WLC
See also CA 104; 132; CDALB 1865-1917;
DLB 4, 9, 12, 78; MTCW

Wharton, James
See Mencken, H(enry) L(ouis)

Wharton, William (a pseudonym)
.... CLC 18, 37
See also CA 93-96; DLBY 80

Wheatley (Peters), Phillis
1754(?)-1784 .... LC 3; BLC; DA; PC 3;
WLC
See also CDALB 1640-1865; DLB 31, 50

Wheelock, John Hall 1886-1978 .... CLC 14
See also CA 13-16R; 77-80; CANR 14;
DLB 45

White, E(lwyn) B(rooks)
1899-1985 .... CLC 10, 34, 39
See also AITN 2; CA 13-16R; 116;
CANR 16, 37; CLR 1, 21; DLB 11, 22;
MAICYA; MTCW; SATA 2, 29, 44

White, Edmund (Valentine III)
1940- .... CLC 27
See also AAYA 7; CA 45-48; CANR 3, 19,
36; MTCW

White, Patrick (Victor Martindale)
1912-1990 .. CLC 3, 4, 5, 7, 9, 18, 65, 69
See also CA 81-84; 132; CANR 43; MTCW

White, Phyllis Dorothy James 1920-
See James, P. D.
See also CA 21-24R; CANR 17, 43; MTCW

White, T(erence) H(anbury)
1906-1964 .... CLC 30
See also CA 73-76; CANR 37; JRDA;
MAICYA; SATA 12

White, Terence de Vere 1912- ...... CLC 49
See also CA 49-52; CANR 3

White, Walter F(rancis)
1893-1955 .... TCLC 15
See also White, Walter
See also BW 1; CA 115; 124; DLB 51

White, William Hale 1831-1913
See Rutherford, Mark
See also CA 121

Whitehead, E(dward) A(nthony)
1933- .... CLC 5
See also CA 65-68

Whitemore, Hugh (John) 1936- ..... CLC 37
See also CA 132

Whitman, Sarah Helen (Power)
1803-1878 .... NCLC 19
See also DLB 1

Whitman, Walt(er)
1819-1892 ..... NCLC 4, 31; DA; PC 3;
WLC
See also CDALB 1640-1865; DLB 3, 64;
SATA 20

Whitney, Phyllis A(yame) 1903- .... CLC 42
See also AITN 2; BEST 90:3; CA 1-4R;
CANR 3, 25, 38; JRDA; MAICYA;
SATA 1, 30

Whittemore, (Edward) Reed (Jr.)
1919- .... CLC 4
See also CA 9-12R; CAAS 8; CANR 4;
DLB 5

Whittier, John Greenleaf
1807-1892 .... NCLC 8
See also CDALB 1640-1865; DLB 1

Whittlebot, Hernia
See Coward, Noel (Peirce)

Wicker, Thomas Grey 1926-
See Wicker, Tom
See also CA 65-68; CANR 21

Wicker, Tom .... CLC 7
See also Wicker, Thomas Grey

Wideman, John Edgar
1941- .... CLC 5, 34, 36, 67; BLC
See also BW 2; CA 85-88; CANR 14, 42;
DLB 33, 143

Wiebe, Rudy (Henry) 1934-... CLC 6, 11, 14
See also CA 37-40R; CANR 42; DLB 60

Wieland, Christoph Martin
1733-1813 .... NCLC 17
See also DLB 97

Wiene, Robert 1881-1938........ TCLC 56

Wieners, John 1934-.............. CLC 7
See also CA 13-16R; DLB 16

Wiesel, Elie(zer)
1928- .... CLC 3, 5, 11, 37; DA
See also AAYA 7; AITN 1; CA 5-8R;
CAAS 4; CANR 8, 40; DLB 83;
DLBY 87; MTCW; SATA 56

Wiggins, Marianne 1947-.......... CLC 57
See also BEST 89:3; CA 130

Wight, James Alfred 1916-
See Herriot, James
See also CA 77-80; SATA 44, 55

Wilbur, Richard (Purdy)
1921- .... CLC 3, 6, 9, 14, 53; DA
See also CA 1-4R; CABS 2; CANR 2, 29;
DLB 5; MTCW; SATA 9

Wild, Peter 1940-............... CLC 14
See also CA 37-40R; DLB 5

Wilde, Oscar (Fingal O'Flahertie Wills)
1854(?)-1900 .... TCLC 1, 8, 23, 41; DA;
SSC 11; WLC
See also CA 104; 119; CDBLB 1890-1914;
DLB 10, 19, 34, 57, 141; SATA 24

Wilder, Billy .... CLC 20
See also Wilder, Samuel
See also DLB 26

Wilder, Samuel 1906-
See Wilder, Billy
See also CA 89-92

Wilder, Thornton (Niven)
1897-1975 ...... CLC 1, 5, 6, 10, 15, 35,
82; DA; DC 1; WLC
See also AITN 2; CA 13-16R; 61-64;
CANR 40; DLB 4, 7, 9; MTCW

Wilding, Michael 1942- .... CLC 73
See also CA 104; CANR 24

Wiley, Richard 1944-............. CLC 44
See also CA 121; 129

Wilhelm, Kate .... CLC 7
See also Wilhelm, Katie Gertrude
See also CAAS 5; DLB 8

Wilhelm, Katie Gertrude 1928-
See Wilhelm, Kate
See also CA 37-40R; CANR 17, 36; MTCW

Wilkins, Mary
See Freeman, Mary Eleanor Wilkins

Willard, Nancy 1936-........... CLC 7, 37
See also CA 89-92; CANR 10, 39; CLR 5;
DLB 5, 52; MAICYA; MTCW;
SATA 30, 37, 71

Williams, C(harles) K(enneth)
1936- .... CLC 33, 56
See also CA 37-40R; DLB 5

Williams, Charles
See Collier, James L(incoln)

Williams, Charles (Walter Stansby)
1886-1945 ....TCLC 1, 11
See also CA 104; DLB 100

Williams, (George) Emlyn
1905-1987 .... CLC 15
See also CA 104; 123; CANR 36; DLB 10,
77; MTCW

Williams, Hugo 1942-............ CLC 42
See also CA 17-20R; CANR 45; DLB 40

Williams, J. Walker
See Wodehouse, P(elham) G(renville)

Williams, John A(lfred)
1925- .... CLC 5, 13; BLC
See also BW 2; CA 53-56; CAAS 3;
CANR 6, 26; DLB 2, 33

Williams, Jonathan (Chamberlain)
1929- .... CLC 13
See also CA 9-12R; CAAS 12; CANR 8;
DLB 5

Williams, Joy 1944-............. CLC 31
See also CA 41-44R; CANR 22

Williams, Norman 1952- .... CLC 39
See also CA 118

Williams, Tennessee
1911-1983 ..... CLC 1, 2, 5, 7, 8, 11, 15,
19, 30, 39, 45, 71; DA; DC 4; WLC
See also AITN 1, 2; CA 5-8R; 108;
CABS 3; CANR 31; CDALB 1941-1968;
DLB 7; DLBD 4; DLBY 83; MTCW

Williams, Thomas (Alonzo)
1926-1990 .... CLC 14
See also CA 1-4R; 132; CANR 2

Williams, William C.
See Williams, William Carlos

Williams, William Carlos
1883-1963 .... CLC 1, 2, 5, 9, 13, 22, 42,
67; DA; PC 7
See also CA 89-92; CANR 34;
CDALB 1917-1929; DLB 4, 16, 54, 86;
MTCW

Williamson, David (Keith) 1942-.... CLC 56
See also CA 103; CANR 41

Williamson, Jack.................. CLC 29
See also Williamson, John Stewart
See also CAAS 8; DLB 8

Williamson, John Stewart 1908-
See Williamson, Jack
See also CA 17-20R; CANR 23

Willie, Frederick
See Lovecraft, H(oward) P(hillips)

Willingham, Calder (Baynard, Jr.)
1922- .... CLC 5, 51
See also CA 5-8R; CANR 3; DLB 2, 44;
MTCW

Willis, Charles
See Clarke, Arthur C(harles)

Willy
See Colette, (Sidonie-Gabrielle)

Willy, Colette
See Colette, (Sidonie-Gabrielle)

Wilson, A(ndrew) N(orman) 1950- . . **CLC 33**
See also CA 112; 122; DLB 14

Wilson, Angus (Frank Johnstone)
1913-1991 . . . . **CLC 2, 3, 5, 25, 34**
See also CA 5-8R; 134; CANR 21; DLB 15,
139; MTCW

Wilson, August
1945- . . **CLC 39, 50, 63; BLC; DA; DC 2**
See also BW 2; CA 115; 122; CANR 42;
MTCW

Wilson, Brian 1942- . . . . **CLC 12**

Wilson, Colin 1931- . . . . **CLC 3, 14**
See also CA 1-4R; CAAS 5; CANR 1, 22,
33; DLB 14; MTCW

Wilson, Dirk
See Pohl, Frederik

Wilson, Edmund
1895-1972 . . . . **CLC 1, 2, 3, 8, 24**
See also CA 1-4R; 37-40R; CANR 1;
DLB 63; MTCW

Wilson, Ethel Davis (Bryant)
1888(?)-1980 . . . . **CLC 13**
See also CA 102; DLB 68; MTCW

Wilson, John 1785-1854 . . . . **NCLC 5**

Wilson, John (Anthony) Burgess 1917-1993
See Burgess, Anthony
See also CA 1-4R; 143; CANR 2; MTCW

Wilson, Lanford 1937- . . . . **CLC 7, 14, 36**
See also CA 17-20R; CABS 3; CANR 45;
DLB 7

Wilson, Robert M. 1944- . . . . **CLC 7, 9**
See also CA 49-52; CANR 2, 41; MTCW

Wilson, Robert McLiam 1964- . . . . . **CLC 59**
See also CA 132

Wilson, Sloan 1920- . . . . **CLC 32**
See also CA 1-4R; CANR 1, 44

Wilson, Snoo 1948- . . . . **CLC 33**
See also CA 69-72

Wilson, William S(mith) 1932- . . . . . **CLC 49**
See also CA 81-84

Winchilsea, Anne (Kingsmill) Finch Counte
1661-1720 . . . . **LC 3**

Windham, Basil
See Wodehouse, P(elham) G(renville)

Wingrove, David (John) 1954- . . . . . . **CLC 68**
See also CA 133

Winters, Janet Lewis . . . . **CLC 41**
See also Lewis, Janet
See also DLBY 87

Winters, (Arthur) Yvor
1900-1968 . . . . **CLC 4, 8, 32**
See also CA 11-12; 25-28R; CAP 1;
DLB 48; MTCW

Winterson, Jeanette 1959- . . . . **CLC 64**
See also CA 136

Wiseman, Frederick 1930- . . . . **CLC 20**

Wister, Owen 1860-1938 . . . . **TCLC 21**
See also CA 108; DLB 9, 78; SATA 62

Witkacy
See Witkiewicz, Stanislaw Ignacy

Witkiewicz, Stanislaw Ignacy
1885-1939 . . . . **TCLC 8**
See also CA 105

Wittig, Monique 1935(?)- . . . . **CLC 22**
See also CA 116; 135; DLB 83

Wittlin, Jozef 1896-1976 . . . . **CLC 25**
See also CA 49-52; 65-68; CANR 3

Wodehouse, P(elham) G(renville)
1881-1975 . . . **CLC 1, 2, 5, 10, 22; SSC 2**
See also AITN 2; CA 45-48; 57-60;
CANR 3, 33; CDBLB 1914-1945;
DLB 34; MTCW; SATA 22

Woiwode, L.
See Woiwode, Larry (Alfred)

Woiwode, Larry (Alfred) 1941- . . . **CLC 6, 10**
See also CA 73-76; CANR 16; DLB 6

Wojciechowska, Maia (Teresa)
1927- . . . . **CLC 26**
See also AAYA 8; CA 9-12R; CANR 4, 41;
CLR 1; JRDA; MAICYA; SAAS 1;
SATA 1, 28

Wolf, Christa 1929- . . . . **CLC 14, 29, 58**
See also CA 85-88; CANR 45; DLB 75;
MTCW

Wolfe, Gene (Rodman) 1931- . . . . **CLC 25**
See also CA 57-60; CAAS 9; CANR 6, 32;
DLB 8

Wolfe, George C. 1954- . . . . **CLC 49**

Wolfe, Thomas (Clayton)
1900-1938 . . . **TCLC 4, 13, 29; DA; WLC**
See also CA 104; 132; CDALB 1929-1941;
DLB 9, 102; DLBD 2; DLBY 85; MTCW

Wolfe, Thomas Kennerly, Jr. 1931-
See Wolfe, Tom
See also CA 13-16R; CANR 9, 33; MTCW

Wolfe, Tom . . . . **CLC 1, 2, 9, 15, 35, 51**
See also Wolfe, Thomas Kennerly, Jr.
See also AAYA 8; AITN 2; BEST 89:1

Wolff, Geoffrey (Ansell) 1937- . . . . . **CLC 41**
See also CA 29-32R; CANR 29, 43

Wolff, Sonia
See Levitin, Sonia (Wolff)

Wolff, Tobias (Jonathan Ansell)
1945- . . . . **CLC 39, 64**
See also BEST 90:2; CA 114; 117; DLB 130

Wolfram von Eschenbach
c. 1170-c. 1220 . . . . **CMLC 5**
See also DLB 138

Wolitzer, Hilma 1930- . . . . **CLC 17**
See also CA 65-68; CANR 18, 40; SATA 31

Wollstonecraft, Mary 1759-1797 . . . . . . **LC 5**
See also CDBLB 1789-1832; DLB 39, 104

Wonder, Stevie . . . . **CLC 12**
See also Morris, Steveland Judkins

Wong, Jade Snow 1922- . . . . **CLC 17**
See also CA 109

Woodcott, Keith
See Brunner, John (Kilian Houston)

Woodruff, Robert W.
See Mencken, H(enry) L(ouis)

Woolf, (Adeline) Virginia
1882-1941 . . . . **TCLC 1, 5, 20, 43, 56;
DA; SSC 7; WLC**
See also CA 104; 130; CDBLB 1914-1945;
DLB 36, 100; DLBD 10; MTCW

Woollcott, Alexander (Humphreys)
1887-1943 . . . . **TCLC 5**
See also CA 105; DLB 29

Woolrich, Cornell 1903-1968 . . . . **CLC 77**
See also Hopley-Woolrich, Cornell George

Wordsworth, Dorothy
1771-1855 . . . . **NCLC 25**
See also DLB 107

Wordsworth, William
1770-1850 . . . . **NCLC 12, 38; DA; PC 4;
WLC**
See also CDBLB 1789-1832; DLB 93, 107

Wouk, Herman 1915- . . . . **CLC 1, 9, 38**
See also CA 5-8R; CANR 6, 33; DLBY 82;
MTCW

Wright, Charles (Penzel, Jr.)
1935- . . . . **CLC 6, 13, 28**
See also CA 29-32R; CAAS 7; CANR 23,
36; DLBY 82; MTCW

Wright, Charles Stevenson
1932- . . . . **CLC 49; BLC 3**
See also BW 1; CA 9-12R; CANR 26;
DLB 33

Wright, Jack R.
See Harris, Mark

Wright, James (Arlington)
1927-1980 . . . . **CLC 3, 5, 10, 28**
See also AITN 2; CA 49-52; 97-100;
CANR 4, 34; DLB 5; MTCW

Wright, Judith (Arandell)
1915- . . . . **CLC 11, 53**
See also CA 13-16R; CANR 31; MTCW;
SATA 14

Wright, L(auralai) R. 1939- . . . . **CLC 44**
See also CA 138

Wright, Richard (Nathaniel)
1908-1960 . . . . **CLC 1, 3, 4, 9, 14, 21, 48,
74; BLC; DA; SSC 2; WLC**
See also AAYA 5; BW 1; CA 108;
CDALB 1929-1941; DLB 76, 102;
DLBD 2; MTCW

Wright, Richard B(ruce) 1937- . . . . . . **CLC 6**
See also CA 85-88; DLB 53

Wright, Rick 1945- . . . . **CLC 35**
See also Pink Floyd

Wright, Rowland
See Wells, Carolyn

Wright, Stephen Caldwell 1946- . . . . **CLC 33**
See also BW 2

Wright, Willard Huntington 1888-1939
See Van Dine, S. S.
See also CA 115

Wright, William 1930- . . . . **CLC 44**
See also CA 53-56; CANR 7, 23

Wu Ch'eng-en 1500(?)-1582(?) . . . . **LC 7**

Wu Ching-tzu 1701-1754 . . . . **LC 2**

Wurlitzer, Rudolph 1938(?)- . . . **CLC 2, 4, 15**
See also CA 85-88

Wycherley, William 1641-1715 . . . . **LC 8, 21**
See also CDBLB 1660-1789; DLB 80

Wylie, Elinor (Morton Hoyt)
1885-1928 . . . . **TCLC 8**
See also CA 105; DLB 9, 45

Wylie, Philip (Gordon) 1902-1971 . . . **CLC 43**
See also CA 21-22; 33-36R; CAP 2; DLB 9

Wyndham, John
See Harris, John (Wyndham Parkes Lucas
Beynon)

Wyss, Johann David Von
1743-1818 . . . . **NCLC 10**
See also JRDA; MAICYA; SATA 27, 29

Yakumo Koizumi
See Hearn, (Patricio) Lafcadio (Tessima Carlos)

Yanez, Jose Donoso
See Donoso (Yanez), Jose

Yanovsky, Basile S.
See Yanovsky, V(assily) S(emenovich)

Yanovsky, V(assily) S(emenovich)
1906-1989 . . . . **CLC 2, 18**
See also CA 97-100; 129

Yates, Richard 1926-1992 . . . . . **CLC 7, 8, 23**
See also CA 5-8R; 139; CANR 10, 43;
DLB 2; DLBY 81, 92

Yeats, W. B.
See Yeats, William Butler

Yeats, William Butler
1865-1939 . . . . . **TCLC 1, 11, 18, 31; DA;**
WLC
See also CA 104; 127; CANR 45;
CDBLB 1890-1914; DLB 10, 19, 98;
MTCW

Yehoshua, A(braham) B.
1936- . . . . **CLC 13, 31**
See also CA 33-36R; CANR 43

Yep, Laurence Michael 1948- . . . . . . **CLC 35**
See also AAYA 5; CA 49-52; CANR 1;
CLR 3, 17; DLB 52; JRDA; MAICYA;
SATA 7, 69

Yerby, Frank G(arvin)
1916-1991 . . . . **CLC 1, 7, 22; BLC**
See also BW 1; CA 9-12R; 136; CANR 16;
DLB 76; MTCW

Yesenin, Sergei Alexandrovich
See Esenin, Sergei (Alexandrovich)

Yevtushenko, Yevgeny (Alexandrovich)
1933- . . . . **CLC 1, 3, 13, 26, 51**
See also CA 81-84; CANR 33; MTCW

Yezierska, Anzia 1885(?)-1970 . . . . . **CLC 46**
See also CA 126; 89-92; DLB 28; MTCW

Yglesias, Helen 1915- . . . . **CLC 7, 22**
See also CA 37-40R; CANR 15; MTCW

Yokomitsu Riichi 1898-1947 . . . . . . **TCLC 47**

Yonge, Charlotte (Mary)
1823-1901 . . . . **TCLC 48**
See also CA 109; DLB 18; SATA 17

York, Jeremy
See Creasey, John

York, Simon
See Heinlein, Robert A(nson)

Yorke, Henry Vincent 1905-1974 . . . **CLC 13**
See also Green, Henry
See also CA 85-88; 49-52

Yoshimoto, Banana . . . . **CLC 84**
See also Yoshimoto, Mahoko

Yoshimoto, Mahoko 1964-
See Yoshimoto, Banana
See also CA 144

Young, Al(bert James)
1939- . . . . **CLC 19; BLC**
See also BW 2; CA 29-32R; CANR 26;
DLB 33

Young, Andrew (John) 1885-1971 . . . . **CLC 5**
See also CA 5-8R; CANR 7, 29

Young, Collier
See Bloch, Robert (Albert)

Young, Edward 1683-1765 . . . . **LC 3**
See also DLB 95

Young, Marguerite 1909- . . . . **CLC 82**
See also CA 13-16; CAP 1

Young, Neil 1945- . . . . **CLC 17**
See also CA 110

Yourcenar, Marguerite
1903-1987 . . . . **CLC 19, 38, 50**
See also CA 69-72; CANR 23; DLB 72;
DLBY 88; MTCW

Yurick, Sol 1925- . . . . **CLC 6**
See also CA 13-16R; CANR 25

Zabolotskii, Nikolai Alekseevich
1903-1958 . . . . **TCLC 52**
See also CA 116

Zamiatin, Yevgenii
See Zamyatin, Evgeny Ivanovich

Zamyatin, Evgeny Ivanovich
1884-1937 . . . . **TCLC 8, 37**
See also CA 105

Zangwill, Israel 1864-1926 . . . . **TCLC 16**
See also CA 109; DLB 10, 135

Zappa, Francis Vincent, Jr. 1940-1993
See Zappa, Frank
See also CA 108; 143

Zappa, Frank . . . . **CLC 17**
See also Zappa, Francis Vincent, Jr.

Zaturenska, Marya 1902-1982 . . . . **CLC 6, 11**
See also CA 13-16R; 105; CANR 22

Zelazny, Roger (Joseph) 1937- . . . . . **CLC 21**
See also AAYA 7; CA 21-24R; CANR 26;
DLB 8; MTCW; SATA 39, 57

Zhdanov, Andrei A(lexandrovich)
1896-1948 . . . . **TCLC 18**
See also CA 117

Zhukovsky, Vasily 1783-1852 . . . . **NCLC 35**

Ziegenhagen, Eric . . . . **CLC 55**

Zimmer, Jill Schary
See Robinson, Jill

Zimmerman, Robert
See Dylan, Bob

Zindel, Paul 1936- . . . . **CLC 6, 26; DA**
See also AAYA 2; CA 73-76; CANR 31;
CLR 3; DLB 7, 52; JRDA; MAICYA;
MTCW; SATA 16, 58

Zinov'Ev, A. A.
See Zinoviev, Alexander (Aleksandrovich)

Zinoviev, Alexander (Aleksandrovich)
1922- . . . . **CLC 19**
See also CA 116; 133; CAAS 10

Zoilus
See Lovecraft, H(oward) P(hillips)

Zola, Emile (Edouard Charles Antoine)
1840-1902 . . . . . . **TCLC 1, 6, 21, 41; DA;**
WLC
See also CA 104; 138; DLB 123

Zoline, Pamela 1941- . . . . **CLC 62**

Zorrilla y Moral, Jose 1817-1893 . . **NCLC 6**

Zoshchenko, Mikhail (Mikhailovich)
1895-1958 . . . . **TCLC 15; SSC 15**
See also CA 115

Zuckmayer, Carl 1896-1977 . . . . **CLC 18**
See also CA 69-72; DLB 56, 124

Zuk, Georges
See Skelton, Robin

Zukofsky, Louis
1904-1978 . . . . **CLC 1, 2, 4, 7, 11, 18**
See also CA 9-12R; 77-80; CANR 39;
DLB 5; MTCW

Zweig, Paul 1935-1984 . . . . **CLC 34, 42**
See also CA 85-88; 113

Zweig, Stefan 1881-1942 . . . . **TCLC 17**
See also CA 112; DLB 81, 118

Literary Criticism Series
Cumulative Topic Index

This index lists all topic entries in the Gale's *Classical and Medieval Literature Criticism, Contemporary Literary Criticism, Literature Criticism from 1400 to 1800, Nineteenth-Century Literature Criticism,* and *Twentieth-Century Literary Criticism.*

Age of Johnson LC 15: 1-87
Johnson's London, 3-15
aesthetics of neoclassicism, 15-36
"age of prose and reason," 36-45
clubmen and bluestockings, 45-56
printing technology, 56-62
periodicals: "a map of busy life," 62-74
transition, 74-86

AIDS in Literature CLC 81: 365-416

American Abolitionism NCLC 44: 1-73
overviews, 2-26
abolitionist ideals, 26-46
the literature of abolitionism, 46-72

American Black Humor Fiction TCLC 54: 1-85
characteristics of black humor, 2-13
origins and development, 13-38
black humor distinguished from related literary trends, 38-60
black humor and society, 60-75
black humor reconsidered, 75-83

American Civil War in Literature NCLC 32: 1-109
overviews, 2-20
regional perspectives, 20-54
fiction popular during the war, 54-79
the historical novel, 79-108

American Frontier in Literature NCLC 28: 1-103
definitions, 2-12
development, 12-17
nonfiction writing about the frontier, 17-30
frontier fiction, 30-45
frontier protagonists, 45-66
portrayals of Native Americans, 66-86
feminist readings, 86-98
twentieth-century reaction against frontier literature, 98-100

American Popular Song, Golden Age of TCLC 42: 1-49
background and major figures, 2-34

the lyrics of popular songs, 34-47

American Proletarian Literature TCLC 54: 86-175
overviews, 87-95
American proletarian literature and the American Communist Party, 95-111
ideology and literary merit, 111-17
novels, 117-36
Gastonia, 136-48
drama, 148-54
journalism, 154-59
proletarian literature in the United States, 159-74

American Romanticism NCLC 44: 74-138
overviews, 74-84
sociopolitical influences, 84-104
Romanticism and the American frontier, 104-15
thematic concerns, 115-37

American Western Literature TCLC 46: 1-100
definition and development of American Western literature, 2-7
characteristics of the Western novel, 8-23
Westerns as history and fiction, 23-34
critical reception of American Western literature, 34-41
the Western hero, 41-73
women in Western fiction, 73-91
later Western fiction, 91-9

Art and Literature TCLC 54: 176-248
overviews, 176-193
definitions, 193-219
influence of visual arts on literature, 219-31
spatial form in literature, 231-47

Arthurian Literature CMLC 10: 1-127
historical context and literary beginnings, 2-27
development of the legend through

Malory, 27-64
development of the legend from Malory to the Victorian Age, 65-81
themes and motifs, 81-95
principal characters, 95-125

Arthurian Revival NCLC 36: 1-77
overviews, 2-12
Tennyson and his influence, 12-43
other leading figures, 43-73
the Arthurian legend in the visual arts, 73-6

Australian Literature TCLC 50: 1-94
origins and development, 2-21
characteristics of Australian literature, 21-33
historical and critical perspectives, 33-41
poetry, 41-58
fiction, 58-76
drama, 76-82
Aboriginal literature, 82-91

Beat Generation, Literature of the TCLC 42: 50-102
overviews, 51-9
the Beat generation as a social phenomenon, 59-62
development, 62-5
Beat literature, 66-96
influence, 97-100

***Bildungsroman* in Nineteenth-Century Literature** NCLC 20: 92-168
surveys, 93-113
in Germany, 113-40
in England, 140-56
female *Bildungsroman*, 156-67

Bloomsbury Group TCLC 34: 1-73
history and major figures, 2-13
definitions, 13-17
influences, 17-27
thought, 27-40
prose, 40-52
and literary criticism, 52-4

Topic Index

CLC Cumulative Nationality Index

ALBANIAN
Kadare, Ismail **52**

ALGERIAN
Camus, Albert **1, 2, 4, 9, 11, 14, 32, 63, 69**
Cohen-Solal, Annie **50**

AMERICAN
Abbey, Edward **36, 59**
Abbott, Lee K., Jr. **48**
Abish, Walter **22**
Abrahams, Peter **4**
Abrams, M. H. **24**
Acker, Kathy **45**
Adams, Alice **6, 13, 46**
Addams, Charles **30**
Adler, C. S. **35**
Adler, Renata **8, 31**
Ai **4, 14, 69**
Aiken, Conrad **1, 3, 5, 10, 52**
Albee, Edward **1, 2, 3, 5, 9, 11, 13, 25, 53**
Alexander, Lloyd **35**
Algren, Nelson **4, 10, 33**
Allard, Janet **59**
Allen, Edward **59**
Allen, Paula Gunn **84**
Allen, Woody **16, 52**
Alleyne, Carla D. **65**
Allison, Dorothy **78**
Alta **19**
Alter, Robert B. **34**
Alther, Lisa **7, 41**
Altman, Robert **16**
Ammons, A. R. **2, 3, 5, 8, 9, 25, 57**
Anaya, Rudolfo A. **23**
Anderson, Jon **9**
Anderson, Poul **15**
Anderson, Robert **23**
Angell, Roger **26**

Angelou, Maya **12, 35, 64, 77**
Anthony, Piers **35**
Apple, Max **9, 33**
Appleman, Philip **51**
Archer, Jules **12**
Arendt, Hannah **66**
Arnow, Harriette **2, 7, 18**
Arrick, Fran **30**
Ashbery, John **2, 3, 4, 6, 9, 13, 15, 25, 41, 77**
Asimov, Isaac **1, 3, 9, 19, 26, 76**
Auchincloss, Louis **4, 6, 9, 18, 45**
Auden, W. H. **1, 2, 3, 4, 6, 9, 11, 14, 43**
Auel, Jean M. **31**
Auster, Paul **47**
Bach, Richard **14**
Baker, Elliott **8**
Baker, Nicholson **61**
Baker, Russell **31**
Bakshi, Ralph **26**
Baldwin, James **1, 2, 3, 4, 5, 8, 13, 15, 17, 42, 50, 67**
Bambara, Toni Cade **19**
Bandanes, Jerome **59**
Banks, Russell **37, 72**
Baraka, Imamu Amiri **1, 2, 3, 5, 10, 14, 33**
Barbera, Jack **44**
Barnard, Mary **48**
Barnes, Djuna **3, 4, 8, 11, 29**
Barrett, William **27**
Barth, John **1, 2, 3, 5, 7, 9, 10, 14, 27, 51**
Barthelme, Donald **1, 2, 3, 5, 6, 8, 13, 23, 46, 59**
Barthelme, Frederick **36**
Barzun, Jacques **51**
Bass, Rick **79**
Baumbach, Jonathan **6, 23**
Bausch, Richard **51**
Baxter, Charles **45, 78**

Beagle, Peter S. **7**
Beattie, Ann **8, 13, 18, 40, 63**
Becker, Walter **26**
Beecher, John **6**
Begiebing, Robert J. **70**
Behrman, S. N. **40**
Belitt, Ben **22**
Bell, Madison Smartt **41**
Bell, Marvin **8, 31**
Bellow, Saul **1, 2, 3, 6, 8, 10, 13, 15, 25, 33, 34, 63, 79**
Benary-Isbert, Margot **12**
Benchley, Peter **4, 8**
Benedikt, Michael **4, 14**
Benford, Gregory **52**
Bennett, Hal **5**
Bennett, Jay **35**
Benson, Jackson J. **34**
Benson, Sally **17**
Bentley, Eric **24**
Berger, Melvin **12**
Berger, Thomas **3, 5, 8, 11, 18, 38**
Bergstein, Eleanor **4**
Bernard, April **59**
Berriault, Gina **54**
Berrigan, Daniel J. **4**
Berrigan, Ted **37**
Berry, Chuck **17**
Berry, Wendell **4, 6, 8, 27, 46**
Berryman, John **1, 2, 3, 4, 6, 8, 10, 13, 25, 62**
Bessie, Alvah **23**
Bettelheim, Bruno **79**
Betts, Doris **3, 6, 28**
Bidart, Frank **33**
Birch, Allison **65**
Bishop, Elizabeth **1, 4, 9, 13, 15, 32**
Bishop, John **10**
Blackburn, Paul **9, 43**

513

Nationality Index

Nationality Index

ISBN 0-8103-4993-0

9 780810 349933